Lecture Notes in Computer Science 11748

Founding Editors

Gerhard Goos
Karlsruhe Institute of Technology, Karlsruhe, Germany
Juris Hartmanis
Cornell University, Ithaca, NY, USA

Editorial Board Members

Elisa Bertino
Purdue University, West Lafayette, IN, USA
Wen Gao
Peking University, Beijing, China
Bernhard Steffen
TU Dortmund University, Dortmund, Germany
Gerhard Woeginger
RWTH Aachen, Aachen, Germany
Moti Yung
Columbia University, New York, NY, USA

More information about this series at http://www.springer.com/series/7409

David Lamas · Fernando Loizides ·
Lennart Nacke · Helen Petrie ·
Marco Winckler · Panayiotis Zaphiris (Eds.)

Human-Computer Interaction – INTERACT 2019

17th IFIP TC 13 International Conference
Paphos, Cyprus, September 2–6, 2019
Proceedings, Part III

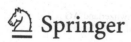 Springer

Editors
David Lamas (iD)
Tallinn University
Tartu, Estonia

Lennart Nacke (iD)
University of Waterloo
Waterloo, ON, Canada

Marco Winckler (iD)
Nice Sophia Antipolis University
Sophia Antipolis, France

Fernando Loizides (iD)
Cardiff University
Cardiff, UK

Helen Petrie (iD)
University of York
York, UK

Panayiotis Zaphiris (iD)
Cyprus University of Technology
Limassol, Cyprus

ISSN 0302-9743   ISSN 1611-3349   (electronic)
Lecture Notes in Computer Science
ISBN 978-3-030-29386-4   ISBN 978-3-030-29387-1   (eBook)
https://doi.org/10.1007/978-3-030-29387-1

LNCS Sublibrary. SL3 – Information Systems and Applications, incl. Internet/Web, and HCI

© IFIP International Federation for Information Processing 2019
This work is subject to copyright. All rights are reserved by the Publisher, whether the whole or part of the material is concerned, specifically the rights of translation, reprinting, reuse of illustrations, recitation, broadcasting, reproduction on microfilms or in any other physical way, and transmission or information storage and retrieval, electronic adaptation, computer software, or by similar or dissimilar methodology now known or hereafter developed.
The use of general descriptive names, registered names, trademarks, service marks, etc. in this publication does not imply, even in the absence of a specific statement, that such names are exempt from the relevant protective laws and regulations and therefore free for general use.
The publisher, the authors and the editors are safe to assume that the advice and information in this book are believed to be true and accurate at the date of publication. Neither the publisher nor the authors or the editors give a warranty, expressed or implied, with respect to the material contained herein or for any errors or omissions that may have been made. The publisher remains neutral with regard to jurisdictional claims in published maps and institutional affiliations.

This Springer imprint is published by the registered company Springer Nature Switzerland AG
The registered company address is: Gewerbestrasse 11, 6330 Cham, Switzerland

Foreword

The 17th IFIP TC13 International Conference on Human-Computer Interaction, INTERACT 2019, took place during September 2–6, 2019, in Paphos, Cyprus. This conference was held at the Coral Beach Hotel & Resort. The conference was co-sponsored by the Cyprus University of Technology and Tallinn University, in cooperation with ACM and ACM SIGCHI.

The International Federation for Information Processing (IFIP) was created in 1960 under the auspices of UNESCO. The Technical Committee 13 (TC13) of the IFIP aims at developing the science and technology of human-computer interaction (HCI). TC13 has representatives from 32 countries, 2 international organizations, apart from 14 expert members and observers. TC13 started the series of INTERACT conferences in 1984. These conferences have been an important showcase for researchers and practitioners in the field of HCI. Situated under the open, inclusive umbrella of the IFIP, INTERACT has been a truly international in its spirit and has attracted researchers from several countries and cultures. The venues of the INTERACT conferences over the years bear a testimony to this inclusiveness.

INTERACT 2019 continued the INTERACT conscious efforts to lower barriers that prevent people from developing countries to participate in conferences. Thinkers and optimists believe that all regions of the world can achieve human development goals. Information and communication technologies (ICTs) can support this process and empower people to achieve their full potential. Today ICT products have many new users and many new uses, but also present new challenges and provide new opportunities. It is no surprise that HCI researchers are showing great interest in these emergent users. INTERACT 2019 provided a platform to explore these challenges and opportunities, but also made it easier for people from developing countries to participate.

Furthermore, hosting INTERACT 2019 in a small country with a small HCI community presented an opportunity to expose the local industry and academia to the concepts of HCI and user-centered design. The rich history and culture of the island of Cyprus provided a strong networking atmosphere and collaboration opportunities.

Students represent the future of our community. They bring in new energy, enthusiasm, and fresh ideas. However, it is often hard for students to participate in international conferences. INTERACT 2019 made special efforts to bring students to the conference. The conference had low registration costs, and thanks to our sponsors, we could provide several travel grants.

Finally, great research is the heart of a good conference. Like its predecessors, INTERACT 2019 aimed to bring together high-quality research. As a multidisciplinary field, HCI requires interaction and discussion among diverse people with different interests and backgrounds. The beginners and the experienced, theoreticians and practitioners, and people from diverse disciplines and different countries gathered together in Paphos to learn from each other and to contribute to each other's growth.

We thank all the authors who chose INTERACT 2019 as the venue to publish their research.

We received a total of 669 submissions distributed in 2 peer reviewed tracks, 4 curated tracks, and 4 juried tracks. Of these, the following contributions were accepted:

- 111 Full Papers (peer reviewed)
- 55 Short Papers (peer reviewed)
- 7 Industry Case Studies (curated)
- 3 Courses (curated)
- 9 Demonstrations (curated)
- 18 Interactive Posters (juried)
- 2 Panels (curated)
- 9 Workshops (juried)
- 1 Field Trips (juried)
- 17 Doctoral Consortium (juried)

The acceptance rate for contributions received in the peer-reviewed tracks was 29% for full papers and 28% for short papers. In addition to full papers and short papers, the present proceedings feature contributions accepted in the form of industry case studies, courses, demonstrations, interactive posters, panels, and description of accepted workshops. The contributions submitted to workshops were published in adjunct proceedings.

INTERACT 2019 innovated the reviewing process with the introduction of sub-committees. Each subcommittee had a chair and set of associated chairs who were in charge of coordinating the reviewing process with the help of expert reviewers. Hereafter we list the ten subcommittees of INTERACT 2019:

- Accessibility and Assistive Technologies
- Design for Business and Safety/Critical Interactive Systems
- Design of Interactive Entertainment Systems
- HCI Education and Curriculum
- Information Visualization
- Interaction Design for Culture and Development
- Interactive Systems Technologies and Engineering
- Methodologies for User-Centred Design
- Social Interaction and Mobile HCI
- Understanding Human Aspects of HCI

The final decision on acceptance or rejection of full papers was taken in a Program Committee meeting held in London, United Kingdom in March 2019. The full papers chairs, the subcommittee chairs, and the associate chairs participated in this meeting. The meeting discussed a consistent set of criteria to deal with inevitable differences among the large number of reviewers. The final decisions on other tracks were made by the corresponding track chairs and reviewers, often after electronic meetings and discussions.

INTERACT 2019 was made possible by the persistent efforts across several months by 10 subcommittees chairs, 62 associated chairs, 28 track chairs, and 510 reviewers. We thank them all.

September 2019   Panayiotis Zaphiris
                                                                    David Lamas

INTERACT 2019 was made possible by the persistent efforts across several months by 10 subcommittees chairs, 62 associated chairs, 28 track chairs, and 510 reviewers. We thank them all.

September 2019

Panayiotis Zaphiris
David Lamas

IFIP TC13 (http://ifip-tc13.org/)

Established in 1989, the International Federation for Information Processing Technical Committee on Human–Computer Interaction (IFIP TC 13) is an international committee of 32 member national societies and 10 Working Groups, representing specialists of the various disciplines contributing to the field of human-computer interaction. This includes (among others) human factors, ergonomics, cognitive science, computer science, and design. INTERACT is its flagship conference of IFIP TC 13, staged biennially in different countries around the world. The first INTERACT conference was held in 1984 running triennially and became a biennial event in 1993.

IFIP TC 13 aims to develop the science, technology, and societal aspects of HCI by encouraging empirical research; promoting the use of knowledge and methods from the human sciences in design and evaluation of computer systems; promoting a better understanding of the relation between formal design methods and system usability and acceptability; developing guidelines, models, and methods by which designers may provide better human-oriented computer systems; and, cooperating with other groups, inside and outside IFIP, to promote user-orientation and humanization in systems design. Thus, TC 13 seeks to improve interactions between people and computers, to encourage the growth of HCI research and its practice in industry and to disseminate these benefits worldwide.

The main orientation is to place the users at the center of the development process. Areas of study include: the problems people face when interacting with computers; the impact of technology deployment on people in individual and organizational contexts; the determinants of utility, usability, acceptability, learnability, and user experience; the appropriate allocation of tasks between computers and users especially in the case of automation; modeling the user, their tasks, and the interactive system to aid better system design; and harmonizing the computer to user characteristics and needs.

While the scope is thus set wide, with a tendency toward general principles rather than particular systems, it is recognized that progress will only be achieved through both general studies to advance theoretical understanding and specific studies on practical issues (e.g., interface design standards, software system resilience, documentation, training material, appropriateness of alternative interaction technologies, design guidelines, the problems of integrating interactive systems to match system needs, and organizational practices, etc.).

In 2015, TC13 approved the creation of a Steering Committee (SC) for the INTERACT conference. The SC is now in place, chaired by Anirudha Joshi and is responsible for:

- Promoting and maintaining the INTERACT conference as the premiere venue for researchers and practitioners interested in the topics of the conference (this requires a refinement of the topics above)
- Ensuring the highest quality for the contents of the event

- Setting up the bidding process to handle the future INTERACT conferences (decision is made up at TC 13 level)
- Providing advice to the current and future chairs and organizers of the INTERACT conference
- Providing data, tools, and documents about previous conferences to the future conference organizers
- Selecting the reviewing system to be used throughout the conference (as this impacts the entire set of reviewers)
- Resolving general issues involved with the INTERACT conference
- Capitalizing history (good and bad practices)

In 1999, TC 13 initiated a special IFIP Award, the Brian Shackel Award, for the most outstanding contribution in the form of a refereed paper submitted to and delivered at each INTERACT. The award draws attention to the need for a comprehensive human-centered approach in the design and use of information technology in which the human and social implications have been taken into account. In 2007, IFIP TC 13 launched an Accessibility Award to recognize an outstanding contribution in HCI with international impact dedicated to the field of accessibility for disabled users. In 2013, IFIP TC 13 launched the Interaction Design for International Development (IDID) Award that recognizes the most outstanding contribution to the application of interactive systems for social and economic development of people in developing countries. Since the process to decide the award takes place after papers are sent to the publisher for publication, the awards are not identified in the proceedings.

This year a special agreement has been made with the *International Journal of Behaviour and Information Technology* (published by Taylor and Francis) with Panos Markopoulos as editor in chief. In this agreement, authors of BIT whose papers are within the field of HCI are offered the opportunity to present their work at the INTERACT conference. Reciprocally, a selection of papers submitted and accepted for presentation at INTERACT are offered the opportunity to extend their contribution to be published in BIT.

IFIP TC 13 also recognizes pioneers in the area of HCI. An IFIP TC 13 pioneer is one who, through active participation in IFIP Technical Committees or related IFIP groups, has made outstanding contributions to the educational, theoretical, technical, commercial, or professional aspects of analysis, design, construction, evaluation, and use of interactive systems. IFIP TC 13 pioneers are appointed annually and awards are handed over at the INTERACT conference.

IFIP TC 13 stimulates working events and activities through its Working Groups (WGs). Working Groups consist of HCI experts from many countries, who seek to expand knowledge and find solutions to HCI issues and concerns within their domains. The list of Working Groups and their area of interest is given below.

WG13.1 (Education in HCI and HCI Curricula) aims to improve HCI education at all levels of higher education, coordinate and unite efforts to develop HCI curricula, and promote HCI teaching.

WG13.2 (Methodology for User-Centered System Design) aims to foster research, dissemination of information and good practice in the methodical application of HCI to software engineering.

WG13.3 (HCI and Disability) aims to make HCI designers aware of the needs of people with disabilities and encourage the development of information systems and tools permitting adaptation of interfaces to specific users.

WG13.4 (also WG2.7) (User Interface Engineering) investigates the nature, concepts, and construction of user interfaces for software systems, using a framework for reasoning about interactive systems and an engineering model for developing user interfaces.

WG 13.5 (Human Error, Resilience, Reliability, Safety and System Development) seeks a framework for studying human factors relating to systems failure, develops leading-edge techniques in hazard analysis and safety engineering of computer-based systems, and guides international accreditation activities for safety-critical systems.

WG13.6 (Human-Work Interaction Design) aims at establishing relationships between extensive empirical work-domain studies and HCI design. It will promote the use of knowledge, concepts, methods, and techniques that enable user studies to procure a better apprehension of the complex interplay between individual, social, and organizational contexts and thereby a better understanding of how and why people work in the ways that they do.

WG13.7 (Human–Computer Interaction and Visualization) aims to establish a study and research program that will combine both scientific work and practical applications in the fields of HCI and Visualization. It integrates several additional aspects of further research areas, such as scientific visualization, data mining, information design, computer graphics, cognition sciences, perception theory, or psychology, into this approach.

WG13.8 (Interaction Design and International Development) is currently working to reformulate its aims and scope.

WG13.9 (Interaction Design and Children) aims to support practitioners, regulators, and researchers to develop the study of interaction design and children across international contexts.

WG13.10 (Human-Centered Technology for Sustainability) aims to promote research, design, development, evaluation, and deployment of human-centered technology to encourage sustainable use of resources in various domains.

New Working Groups are formed as areas of significance in HCI arise. Further information is available on the IFIP TC13 website: http://ifip-tc13.org/.

WG13.3 (HCI and Disability) aims to make HCI designers aware of the needs of people with disabilities and encourage the development of information systems and tools permitting adaptation of interfaces to specific users.

WG13.4 (also WG2.7) (User Interface Engineering) investigates the nature, concepts, and construction of user interfaces for software systems, using a framework for reasoning about interactive systems and an engineering model for developing user interfaces.

WG13.5 (Human Error, Resilience, Reliability, Safety and System Development) seeks a framework for studying human factors relating to systems failure, develops leading-edge techniques in hazard analysis and safety engineering of computer-based systems, and guides international accreditation activities for safety-critical systems.

WG13.6 (Human-Work Interaction Design) aims at establishing relationships between extensive empirical work-domain studies and HCI design. It will promote the use of knowledge, concepts, methods, and techniques that enable user studies to procure a better apprehension of the complex interplay between individual, social, and organizational contexts and thereby a better understanding of how and why people work in the ways that they do.

WG13.7 (Human-Computer Interaction and Visualization) aims to establish a study and research program that will combine both scientific work and practical application in the field, of HCI and Visualization. It integrates several additional aspects of further research areas, such as scientific visualization, data mining, information design, computer graphics, cognition science, perception theory, or psychology, into this approach.

WG13.8 (Interaction Design and International Development) is currently working to reformulate its aims and scope.

WG13.9 (Interaction Design and Children) aims to support practitioners, regulators, and researchers, to develop the study of interaction design and children across international contexts.

WG13.10 (Human-Centered Technology for Sustainability) aims to promote research, design, development, evaluation, and deployment of human-centered technology to encourage sustainable use of resources in various domains.

New Working Groups are formed as areas of significance in HCI arise. Further information is available on the IFIP TC13 website: http://ifip-tc13.org/.

IFIP TC13 Members

Officers

Chair

Philippe Palanque, France

Vice-chair for Awards

Paula Kotze, South Africa

Vice-chair for Communications

Helen Petrie, UK

Vice-chair for Growth and Reach Out INTERACT Steering Committee Chair

Jan Gulliksen, Sweden

Vice-chair for Working Groups

Simone D. J. Barbosa, Brazil

Treasurer

Virpi Roto, Finland

Secretary

Marco Winckler, France

INTERACT Steering Committee Chair

Anirudha Joshi

Country Representatives

Australia
Henry B. L. Duh
Australian Computer Society

Austria
Geraldine Fitzpatrick
Austrian Computer Society

Belgium
Bruno Dumas
Interuniversity Micro-Electronics Center (IMEC)

Brazil
Milene Selbach Silveira
Brazilian Computer Society (SBC)

Bulgaria
Stoyan Georgiev Dentchev
Bulgarian Academy of Sciences

Canada
Lu Xiao
Canadian Information Processing Society

Croatia
Andrina Granic
Croatian Information Technology Association (CITA)

Cyprus
Panayiotis Zaphiris
Cyprus Computer Society

Czech Republic
Zdeněk Míkovec
Czech Society for Cybernetics and Informatics

Finland
Virpi Roto
Finnish Information Processing
  Association

France
Philippe Palanque
Société informatique de France (SIF)

Germany
Tom Gross
Gesellschaft fur Informatik e.V.

Hungary
Cecilia Sik Lanyi
John V. Neumann Computer Society

India
Anirudha Joshi
Computer Society of India (CSI)

Ireland
Liam J. Bannon
Irish Computer Society

Italy
Fabio Paternò
Italian Computer Society

Japan
Yoshifumi Kitamura
Information Processing Society of Japan

The Netherlands
Regina Bernhaupt
Nederlands Genootschap voor
  Informatica

New Zealand
Mark Apperley
New Zealand Computer Society

Norway
Frode Eika Sandnes
Norwegian Computer Society

Poland
Marcin Sikorski
Poland Academy of Sciences

Portugal
Pedro Campos
Associacão Portuguesa para o
  Desenvolvimento da Sociedade da
  Informação (APDSI)

Serbia
Aleksandar Jevremovic
Informatics Association of Serbia

Singapore
Shengdong Zhao
Singapore Computer Society

Slovakia
Wanda Benešová
The Slovak Society for Computer
  Science

Slovenia
Matjaž Debevc
The Slovenian Computer Society
  Informatika

South Africa
Janet L. Wesson and Paula Kotze
The Computer Society of South Africa

Sweden
Jan Gulliksen
Swedish Interdisciplinary Society for
  Human-Computer Interaction
Swedish Computer Society

Switzerland
Denis Lalanne
Swiss Federation for Information
  Processing

Tunisia
Mona Laroussi
Ecole Supérieure des Communications
  De Tunis (SUP'COM)

UK
José Abdelnour Nocera
British Computer Society (BCS)

UAE
Ghassan Al-Qaimari
UAE Computer Society

International Association Members

ACM
Gerrit van der Veer
Association for Computing Machinery
(ACM)

CLEI
Jaime Sánchez
Centro Latinoamericano de Estudios en
Informatica

Expert Members

Carmelo Ardito, Italy
Orwa, Kenya
David Lamas, Estonia
Dorian Gorgan, Romania
Eunice Sari, Australia/Indonesia
Fernando Loizides, UK/Cyprus
Ivan Burmistrov, Russia

Julio Abascal, Spain
Kaveh Bazargan, Iran
Marta Kristin Larusdottir, Iceland
Nikolaos Avouris, Greece
Peter Forbrig, Germany
Torkil Clemmensen, Denmark
Zhengjie Liu, China

Working Group Chairpersons

WG 13.1 (Education in HCI and HCI Curricula)

Konrad Baumann, Austria

WG 13.2 (Methodologies for User-Centered System Design)

Regina Bernhaupt, The Netherlands

WG 13.3 (HCI and Disability)

Helen Petrie, UK

WG 13.4/2.7 (User Interface Engineering)

José Creissac Campos, Portugal

WG 13.5 (Human Error, Resilience, Reliability, Safety and System Development)

Chris Johnson, UK

WG13.6 (Human-Work Interaction Design)

Barbara Rita Barricelli, Italy

WG13.7 (HCI and Visualization)

Peter Dannenmann, Germany

WG 13.8 (Interaction Design and International Development)

José Adbelnour Nocera, UK

WG 13.9 (Interaction Design and Children)

Janet Read, UK

WG 13.10 (Human-Centred Technology for Sustainability)

Masood Masoodian, Finland

International Association Members

ACM
Gerrit van der Veer
Association for Computing Machinery
(ACM)

CLEI
Jaime Sánchez
Centro Latinoamericano de Estudios en
Informática

Expert Members

Carmelo Ardito, Italy
O'wa, Kenya
David Lamas, Estonia
Dorian Gorgan, Romania
Eunice Sari, Australia/Indonesia
Fernando Loizides, UK/Cyprus
Ivan Burmistrov, Russia

Julio Abascal, Spain
Kaveh Bazargan, Iran
Maria Kristin Lárusdóttir, Iceland
Nikolaos Avouris, Greece
Peter Forbrig, Germany
Torkil Clemmensen, Denmark
Zhengjie Liu, China

Working Group Chairpersons

WG 13.1 (Education in HCI and HCI Curricula)
Konrad Baumann, Austria

WG 13.6 (Human-Work Interaction Design)
Barbara Rita Barricelli, Italy

WG 13.2 (Methodologies for User-Centered System Design)
Regina Bernhaupt, The Netherlands

WG 13.7 (HCI and Visualization)
Peter Dannenmann, Germany

WG 13.3 (HCI and Disability)
Helen Petrie, UK

WG 13.8 (Interaction Design and International Development)
José Abdelnour Nocera, UK

WG 13.4/WG 2.7 (User Interface Engineering)
José Creissac Campos, Portugal

WG 13.9 (Interaction Design and Children)
Janet Read, UK

WG 13.5 (Human Error, Resilience, Reliability, Safety and System Development)
Chris Johnson, UK

WG 13.10 (Human-Centred Technology for Sustainability)
Masood Masoodian, Finland

Conference Organizing Committee

General Conference Chairs

David Lamas, Estonia
Panayiotis Zaphiris, Cyprus

Technical Program Chairs

Fernando Loizides, UK
Marco Winckler, France

Full Papers Co-chairs

Helen Petrie, UK
Lennart Nacke, Canada

Short Papers Co-chairs

Evangelos Karapanos, Cyprus
Jim CS Ang, UK

Interactive Posters Co-chairs

Carmelo Ardito, Italy
Zhengjie Liu, China

Panels Co-chairs

Darelle van Greunen, South Africa
Jahna Otterbacher, Cyprus

**Demonstrations and Installations
Co-chairs**

Giuseppe Desolda, Italy
Vaso Constantinou, Cyprus

Courses Co-chairs

Parisa Eslambolchilar, UK
Regina Bernhaupt, The Netherlands

Workshops Co-chairs

Antigoni Parmaxi, Cyprus
Jose Abdelnour Nocera, UK

Doctoral Consortium Co-chairs

Andri Ioannou, Cyprus
Nikolaos Avouris, Greece

Student Design Consortium Co-chairs

Andreas Papallas, Cyprus
Eva Korae, Cyprus

Field Trips Chairs

Andreas Papallas, Cyprus
Anirudha Joshi, India
Panayiotis Zaphiris, Cyprus

Industry Case Studies Co-chairs

Aimilia Tzanavari, USA
Panagiotis Germanakos, Germany

Proceedings Chairs

Fernando Loizides, UK
Marco Winckler, France

Sponsorship Chair

Andreas Papallas, Cyprus

Student Volunteers Chair

Vaso Constantinou, Cyprus

Web and Social Media Chair

Aekaterini Mavri, Cyprus

Program Committee

Sub-committee Chairs

Elisa Mekler, Switzerland
Fabio Paterno, Italy
Gerhard Weber, Germany
Jan Gulliksen, Sweden
Jo Lumsden, UK

Laurence Nigay, France
Nikolaos Avouris, Greece
Philippe Palanque, France
Regina Bernhaupt, The Netherlands
Torkil Clemmensen, Denmark

Associated Chairs

Adrian Bussone, UK
Anirudha Joshi, India
Antonio Piccinno, Italy
Bridget Kane, Sweden
Bruno Dumas, Belgium
Carla Maria Dal Sasso Freitas, Brazil
Célia Martinie, France
Chi Vi, UK
Christine Bauer, Austria
Daniel Buzzo, UK
Daniela Trevisan, Brazil
Davide Spano, Italy
Denis Lalanne, Switzerland
Dhaval Vyas, Australia
Dorian Gorgan, Romania
Effie Law, UK
Elisa Mekler, Switzerland
Fabio Paterno, Italy
Frank Steinicke, Germany
Frode Eika Sandnes, Norway
Gavin Sim, UK
Gerhard Weber, Germany
Giuseppe Desolda, Italy
Jan Gulliksen, Sweden
Jan Stage, Denmark
Jan Van den Bergh, Belgium
Janet Wesson, South Africa
Jenny Darzentas, Greece
Jo Lumsden, UK
Jolanta Mizera-Pietraszko, Poland
Jose Abdelnour Nocera, UK

José Creissac Campos, Portugal
Katrina Attwood, UK
Kaveh Bazargan, Iran
Kibum Kim, South Korea
Laurence Nigay, France
Luis Teixeira, Portugal
Lynne Coventry, UK
Marcin Sikorski, Poland
Margarita Anastassova, France
Marta Laursdottir, Iceland
Matistella Matera, Italy
Nervo Verdezoto, UK
Nikolaos Avouris, Greece
Özge Subasi, Austria
Patrick Langdon, UK
Paula Kotze, South Africa
Pedro Campos, Portugal
Peter Forbrig, Germany
Peter Johnson, UK
Philippe Palanque, France
Regina Bernhaupt, The Netherlands
Sayan Sarcar, Japan
Simone Barbosa, Brazil
Simone Stumpf, UK
Stefania Castellani, France
Tom Gross, Germany
Torkil Clemmensen, Denmark
Valentin Schwind, Germany
Virpi Roto, Finland
Yoshifumi Kitamura, Japan
Zdenek Mikovec, Czech Republic

Reviewers

Adalberto Simeone, Belgium
Aditya Nittala, Germany
Adriana Vivacqua, Brazil
Aekaterini Mavri, Cyprus
Agneta Eriksson, Finland
Aidan Slingsby, UK
Aku Visuri, Finland
Alaa Alkhafaji, UK
Alasdair King, UK
Alberto Boem, Japan
Alberto Raposo, Brazil
Albrecht Schmidt, Germany
Aleksander Bai, Norway
Alessio Malizia, UK
Alexander Wachtel, Germany
Alexandra Covaci, UK
Alexandra Mendes, Portugal
Alexandre Canny, France
Ali Rizvi, Canada
Ali Soyoof, Iran
Alisa Burova, Finland
Alistair Edwards, UK
Alla Vovk, UK
Amina Bouraoui, Tunisia
Ana Cristina Garcia, Brazil
Ana Paula Afonso, Portugal
Ana Serrano, Spain
Anders Lundström, Sweden
Anderson Maciel, Brazil
Andre Suslik Spritzer, Brazil
André Zenner, Germany
Andrea Marrella, Italy
Andreas Sonderegger, Switzerland
Andrew Jian-lan Cen, Canada
Andrew MacQuarrie, UK
Andrew McNeill, UK
Andrey Krekhov, Germany
Andrii Matviienko, Germany
Andy Dearden, UK
Angus Forbes, USA
Anind Dey, USA
Anja Exler, Germany
Anke Dittmar, Germany

Anna Bramwell-Dicks, UK
Anna Feit, Switzerland
Anna-Lena Mueller, Germany
Annette Lamb, USA
Anthony Giannoumis, Norway
Antigoni Parmaxi, Cyprus
Antonio Gonzalez-Torres, Costa Rica
Antonio Piccinno, Italy
Arash Mahnan, USA
Arindam Dey, Australia
Aristides Mairena, Canada
Arjun Srinivasan, USA
Arminda Lopes, Portugal
Asam Almohamed, Australia
Ashkan Pourkand, USA
Asim Evren Yantac, Turkey
Aurélien Tabard, France
Aykut Coşkun, Turkey
Barbara Barricelli, Italy
Bastian Dewitz, Germany
Beiyu Lin, USA
Ben Morrison, UK
Benedict Gaster, UK
Benedikt Loepp, Germany
Benjamin Gorman, UK
Benjamin Weyers, Germany
Bernd Ploderer, Australia
Bineeth Kuriakose, Norway
Bosetti Bosetti, France
Brady Redfearn, USA
Brendan Cassidy, UK
Brendan Spillane, Ireland
Brian Freiter, Canada
Brianna Tomlinson, USA
Bruno Dumas, Belgium
Burak Merdenyan, UK
Cagatay Goncu, Australia
Cagri Tanriover, USA
Carlos Silva, Portugal
Carmen Santoro, Italy
Cecile Boulard, France
Célia Martinie, France
Chaolun Xia, USA

Charlotte Magnusson, Sweden
Chee Siang Ang, UK
Chelsea Kelling, Finland
Chloe Eghtebas, Germany
Christian Sturm, Germany
Christina Schneegass, Germany
Christina Vasiliou, UK
Christophe Kolski, France
Christopher Johnson, UK
Christopher Lueg, Switzerland
Christopher Power, UK
Christos Mousas, USA
Cinzia Cappiello, Italy
Clarisse Sieckenius de Souza, Brazil
Claudio Jung, Brazil
Clauirton Siebra, Brazil
Cléber Corrêa, Brazil
Clodis Boscarioli, Brazil
Cornelia Murko, Austria
CRI Putjorn, Thailand
Cristina Gena, Italy
Cynara Justine, India
Daisuke Sato, Japan
Damien Mac Namara, Ireland
Dan Fitton, UK
Daniel Lopes, Portugal
Daniel Mallinson, USA
Daniel Orwa Ochieng, Kenya
Daniel Ziegler, Germany
Daniela Fogli, Italy
Danula Hettiachchi, Australia
Dario Bertero, Japan
David Navarre, France
David Zendle, UK
Davy Vanacken, Belgium
Debaleena Chattopadhyay, USA
Deepak Akkil, Finland
Dejin Zhao, USA
Demetrios Lambropoulos, USA
Denis Berdjag, France
Dennis Wolf, Germany
Deqing Sun, USA
Dhaval Vyas, Australia
Dimitra Anastasiou, Luxembourg
Diogo Cabral, Portugal
Dmitrijs Dmitrenko, UK

Donal Rice, Ireland
Dorian Gorgan, Romania
Dorothé Smit, Austria
Dragan Ahmetovic, Italy
Ebtisam Alabdulqader, UK
Ee Xion Tan, Malaysia
Elena Not, Italy
Elizabeth Buie, UK
Elizabeth Shaw, Australia
Emad Aghayi, USA
Emma Nicol, UK
Emmanuel Pietriga, France
Englye Lim, Malaysia
Eric Barboni, France
Éric Céret, France
Erica Halverson, USA
Eva Cerezo, Spain
Evangelos Karapanos, Cyprus
Fabien Ringeval, France
Fabio Morreale, New Zealand
Fausto Medola, Brazil
Federico Botella, Spain
Felipe Soares da Costa, Denmark
Filippo Sanfilippo, Norway
Florence Lehnert, Luxembourg
Florian Daniel, Italy
Florian Güldenpfennig, Austria
Florian Heller, Belgium
Florian Weidner, Germany
Francesca Pulina, Italy
Francesco Ferrise, Italy
Francisco Nunes, Portugal
François Bérard, France
Frank Nack, The Netherlands
Frederica Gonçalves, Portugal
Frode Eika Sandnes, Norway
Gabriel Turcu, Romania
Ganesh Bhutkar, India
George Raptis, Greece
Gerd Berget, Norway
Gerhard Weber, Germany
Gerrit Meixner, Germany
Gianfranco Modoni, Italy
Giulio Mori, Italy
Giuseppe Desolda, Italy
Giuseppe Santucci, Italy

Goh Wei, Malaysia
Guilherme Bertolaccini, Brazil
Guilherme Guerino, Brazil
Günter Wallner, Austria
Gustavo Tondello, Canada
Hatice Kose, Turkey
Heidi Hartikainen, Finland
Heike Winschiers-Theophilus, Namibia
Heiko Müller, Finland
Hsin-Jou Lin, USA
Hua Guo, USA
Hugo Paredes, Portugal
Huy Viet Le, Germany
Hyunyoung Kim, France
Ian Brooks, UK
Ilaria Renna, France
Ilya Makarov, Russia
Ilya Musabirov, Russia
Ilyena Hirskyj-Douglas, Finland
Ioanna Iacovides, UK
Ioannis Doumanis, UK
Isabel Manssour, Brazil
Isabel Siqueira da Silva, Brazil
Isabela Gasparini, Brazil
Isidoros Perikos, Greece
Iyubanit Rodríguez, Costa Rica
Jaakko Hakulinen, Finland
James Eagan, France
James Nicholson, UK
Jan Derboven, Belgium
Jan Plötner, Germany
Jana Jost, Germany
Janet Read, UK
Janki Dodiya, Germany
Jason Shuo Zhang, USA
Jayden Khakurel, Denmark
Jayesh Doolani, USA
Ji-hye Lee, Finland
Jingjie Zheng, Canada
Jo Herstad, Norway
João Guerreiro, USA
Joe Cutting, UK
Johanna Hall, UK
Johanna Renny Octavia, Belgium
Johannes Kunkel, Germany
John Mundoz, USA

John Rooksby, UK
Jolanta Mizera-Pietraszko, Poland
Jonas Oppenlaender, Finland
Jonggi Hong, USA
Jonna Häkkilä, Finland
Jörg Cassens, Germany
Jorge Cardoso, Portugal
Jorge Goncalves, Australia
José Coelho, Portugal
Joseph O'Hagan, UK
Judith Borghouts, UK
Judy Bowen, New Zealand
Juliana Jansen Ferreira, Brazil
Julie Doyle, Ireland
Julie Williamson, UK
Juliette Rambourg, USA
Jürgen Ziegler, Germany
Karen Renaud, UK
Karin Coninx, Belgium
Karina Arrambide, Canada
Kasper Rodil, Denmark
Katelynn Kapalo, USA
Katharina Werner, Austria
Kati Alha, Finland
Katrin Wolf, Germany
Katta Spiel, Austria
Kellie Vella, Australia
Kening Zhu, China
Kent Lyons, USA
Kevin Cheng, China
Kevin El Haddad, Belgium
Kiemute Oyibo, Canada
Kirsi Halttu, Finland
Kirsten Ellis, Australia
Kirsten Ribu, Norway
Konstanti Chrysanthi, Cyprus
Kris Luyten, Belgium
Kurtis Danyluk, Canada
Kyle Johnsen, USA
Lachlan Mackinnon, UK
Lara Piccolo, UK
Lars Lischke, The Netherlands
Lars Rune Christensen, Denmark
Leigh Clark, Ireland
Lene Nielsen, Denmark
Lilian Motti Ader, Ireland

Liliane Machado, Brazil
Lilit Hakobyan, UK
Lisandro Granville, Brazil
Lonni Besançon, Sweden
Loredana Verardi, Italy
Lorisa Dubuc, UK
Lorna McKnight, UK
Loukas Konstantinou, Cyprus
Luciana Cardoso de Castro Salgado,
  Brazil
Luciana Nedel, Brazil
Lucio Davide Spano, Italy
Ludmila Musalova, UK
Ludvig Eblaus, Sweden
Luigi De Russis, Italy
Luis Leiva, Finland
Lynette Gerido, USA
Mads Andersen, Denmark
Mads Bødker, Denmark
Maher Abujelala, USA
Maliheh Ghajargar, Sweden
Malin Wik, Sweden
Malte Ressin, UK
Mandy Korzetz, Germany
Manjiri Joshi, India
Manuel J. Fonseca, Portugal
Marc Kurz, Austria
Marcelo Penha, Brazil
Marcelo Pimenta, Brazil
Márcio Pinho, Brazil
Marco Gillies, UK
Marco Manca, Italy
Marcos Baez, Italy
Marcos Serrano, France
Margarita Anastassova, France
María Laura Ramírez Galleguillos,
  Turkey
Maria Rosa Lorini, South Africa
Marian Cristian Mihaescu, Romania
Marianela Ciolfi Felice, France
Marion Koelle, Germany
Marios Constantinides, UK
Maristella Matera, Italy
Marius Koller, Germany
Mark Billinghurst, Australia
Mark Carman, Italy

Marko Tkalcic, Italy
Martin Feick, Germany
Martin Tomitsch, Australia
Mary Barreto, Portugal
Massimo Zancanaro, Italy
Matthew Horton, UK
Matthias Heintz, UK
Mauricio Pamplona Segundo, Brazil
Max Bernhagen, Germany
Max Birk, The Netherlands
Mehdi Ammi, France
Mehdi Boukallel, France
Meinald Thielsch, Germany
Melissa Densmore, South Africa
Meraj Ahmed Khan, USA
Michael Burch, The Netherlands
Michael Craven, UK
Michael McGuffin, Canada
Michael Nees, USA
Michael Rohs, Germany
Michela Assale, Italy
Michelle Annett, Canada
Mike Just, UK
Mikko Rajanen, Finland
Milene Silveira, Brazil
Miriam Begnum, Norway
Mirjam Augstein, Austria
Mirko Gelsomini, Italy
Muhammad Haziq Lim Abdullah,
  Malaysia
Muhammad Shoaib, Pakistan
Nadine Vigouroux, France
Natasa Rebernik, Spain
Naveed Ahmed, UAE
Netta Iivari, Finland
Nick Chozos, UK
Nico Herbig, Germany
Niels Henze, Germany
Niels van Berkel, UK
Nikola Banovic, USA
Nikolaos Avouris, Greece
Nimesha Ranasinghe, USA
Nis Bornoe, Denmark
Nitish Devadiga, USA
Obed Brew, UK
Ofir Sadka, Canada

Oscar Mayora, Italy
Panayiotis Koutsabasis, Greece
Panos Markopoulos, The Netherlands
Panote Siriaraya, Japan
Paola Risso, Italy
Paolo Buono, Italy
Parinya Punpongsanon, Japan
Pascal Knierim, Germany
Pascal Lessel, Germany
Patrick Langdon, UK
Paul Curzon, UK
PD Lamb, UK
Pedro Campos, Portugal
Peter Forbrig, Germany
Peter Ryan, Luxembourg
Philip Schaefer, Germany
Philipp Wacker, Germany
Philippe Palanque, France
Philippe Renevier Gonin, France
Pierre Dragicevic, France
Pierre-Henri Orefice, France
Pietro Murano, Norway
Piyush Madan, USA
Pradeep Yammiyavar, India
Praminda Caleb-Solly, UK
Priyanka Srivastava, India
Pui Voon Lim, Malaysia
Qiqi Jiang, Denmark
Radhika Garg, USA
Radu Jianu, UK
Rafael Henkin, UK
Rafał Michalski, Poland
Raian Ali, UK
Rajkumar Darbar, France
Raquel Hervas, Spain
Raquel Robinson, Canada
Rashmi Singla, Denmark
Raymundo Cornejo, Mexico
Reem Talhouk, UK
Renaud Blanch, France
Rina Wehbe, Canada
Roberto Montano-Murillo, UK
Rocio von Jungenfeld, UK
Romina Kühn, Germany
Romina Poguntke, Germany
Ronnie Taib, Australia

Rosa Lanzilotti, Italy
Rüdiger Heimgärtner, Germany
Rufat Rzayev, Germany
Rui José, Portugal
Rui Madeira, Portugal
Samir Aknine, France
Sana Maqsood, Canada
Sanjit Samaddar, UK
Santosh Vijaykumar, UK
Sarah Völkel, Germany
Sari Kujala, Finland
Sayan Sarcar, Japan
Scott Trent, Japan
Sean Butler, UK
Sebastian Günther, Germany
Selina Schepers, Belgium
Seokwoo Song, South Korea
Sergio Firmenich, Argentina
Shah Rukh Humayoun, USA
Shaimaa Lazem, Egypt
Sharon Lynn Chu, USA
Shichao Zhao, UK
Shiroq Al-Megren, USA
Silvia Gabrielli, Italy
Simone Kriglstein, Austria
Sirpa Riihiaho, Finland
Snigdha Petluru, India
Songchun Fan, USA
Sónia Rafael, Portugal
Sonja Schimmler, Germany
Sophie Lepreux, France
Srishti Gupta, USA
SRM Dilrukshi Gamage, Sri Lanka
SRM_Daniela Girardi, Italy
Stefan Carmien, UK
Stefano Valtolina, Italy
Stéphane Conversy, France
Stephanie Wilson, UK
Stephen Snow, UK
Stephen Uzor, UK
Steve Reeves, New Zealand
Steven Jeuris, Denmark
Steven Vos, The Netherlands
Subrata Tikadar, India
Sven Mayer, Germany
Taehyun Rhee, New Zealand

Takuji Narumi, Japan
Tanja Walsh, UK
Ted Selker, USA
Terje Gjøsæter, Norway
Tetsuya Watanabe, Japan
Thierry Dutoit, Belgium
Thilina Halloluwa, Australia
Thomas Kirks, Germany
Thomas Neumayr, Austria
Thomas Olsson, Finland
Thomas Prinz, Germany
Thorsten Strufe, Germany
Tifanie Bouchara, France
Tilman Dingler, Australia
Tim Claudius Stratmann, Germany
Timo Partala, Finland
Toan Nguyen, USA
Tomi Heimonen, USA
Tommaso Turchi, UK
Tommy Dang, USA
Troy Nachtigall, The Netherlands
Uran Oh, South Korea
Val Mitchell, UK
Vanessa Cesário, Portugal
Vanessa Wan Sze Cheng, Australia
Venkatesh Rajamanickam, India
Verena Fuchsberger, Austria
Verity McIntosh, UK
Victor Adriel de Jesus Oliveira, Austria

Victor Kaptelinin, Sweden
Vincenzo Deufemia, Italy
Vinoth Pandian Sermuga Pandian,
  Germany
Vishal Sharma, USA
Vit Rusnak, Czech Republic
Vita Santa Barletta, Italy
Vito Gentile, Italy
Vung Pham, USA
Walter Correia, Brazil
Weiqin Chen, Norway
William Delamare, Japan
Xiaoyi Zhang, USA
Xiying Wang, USA
Yann Laurillau, France
Yann Savoye, UK
Yannis Dimitriadis, Spain
Yiannis Georgiou, Cyprus
Yichen Lu, Finland
Ying Zhu, USA
Yong Ming Kow, SAR China
Young-Ho Kim, South Korea
Yue Jiang, USA
Yu-Tzu Lin, Denmark
Z Toups, USA
Zdeněk Míkovec, Czech Republic
Zhanna Sarsenbayeva, Australia
Zhihang Dong, USA
Zhisheng Yan, USA

Sponsors and Partners

Sponsors

 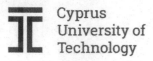 **Research** Centre on **Interactive** Media
Smart Systems and **Emerging** Technologies

 Springer

Partners

 ifip

International Federation for Information Processing

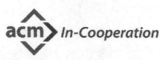 Cyprus
University of
Technology

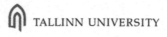 TALLINN UNIVERSITY

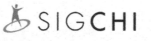 In-Cooperation

In-cooperation with ACM

SIGCHI

In-cooperation with SIGCHI

Sponsors and Partners

Sponsors

Research Centre on Interactive Media, Smart Systems, and Emerging Technologies

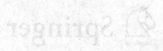

Springer

Partners

ifip

International Federation for Information Processing

Cyprus University of Technology

In-Cooperation

In-cooperation with ACM

SIGCHI

In-cooperation with SIGCHI

Contents – Part III

Methods for User Studies

Mobile HCI

Personalization and Recommender Systems

Pointing, Touch, Gesture and Speech-Based Interaction Techniques

Social Networks and Social Media Interaction

Interaction Design for Culture and Development II

Interaction Design for Culture and
Development II

A Contrastive Study of Pre- and Post-legislation Interaction Design for Communication and Action About Personal Data Protection in e-Commerce Websites

Clarisse Sieckenius de Souza[✉] [iD]

Departamento de Informática, PUC-Rio, Rio de Janeiro, RJ 22451-900, Brazil
clarisse@inf.puc-rio.br

Abstract. The European General Data Protection Regulation (GDPR) has had a major impact on data collection and processing practices. It has also challenged interaction design aiming to support the effectiveness of data owners' rights, their informed decisions, and their actions regarding how personal information is used by companies, governments, and others. Similar legislation has been issued in various non-European countries, which means that, in this respect, the HCI community has an important role to play for users all over the world. This paper presents the conclusions of a contrastive study with four major e-commerce websites in Portugal, where data protection law has been effective since 2018, and four analogs in Brazil, where the national Data Protection Law (DPL) has been sanctioned but will only be effective in 2020. The purpose of the study is to examine the pre-legislation to post-legislation evolution in the design of interaction for communication and action about personal data protection matters, so as to anticipate some of the threats and opportunities ahead of us. Using concepts and elements of Semiotic Engineering methods and techniques, we found that, within the scope of this study, GDPR seems to have had little impact on what European users can do and experience online, compared to pre-DPL Brazilian users. We discuss some of the possible reasons for this and conclude with thoughts on the role of interaction design in empowering data owners for this new regulation era.

Keywords: General Data Protection Regulation (GDPR) · Interaction design · Semiotic Engineering

1 Introduction

The European General Data Protection Regulation (GDPR) [1] has had a major impact on data collection and processing practices. It has also challenged the design of interaction aiming to support the effectiveness of data owners' rights, their informed decisions, and action regarding how personal information is used by companies, governments, and others [2]. Similar legislation has been issued in various non-European countries, such as Brazil [3], for example, where part of this research takes place. The HCI community has thus an important role to play in helping users from all

© IFIP International Federation for Information Processing 2019
Published by Springer Nature Switzerland AG 2019
D. Lamas et al. (Eds.): INTERACT 2019, LNCS 11748, pp. 3–23, 2019.
https://doi.org/10.1007/978-3-030-29387-1_1

over the world to access and exert their rights in this new era of data protection legislation.

E-businesses constitute an interesting domain to evaluate what interaction design currently allows users to do or not do with respect to personal data management. Years ago, when e-commerce started to flourish, one of the major technical challenges was to secure sensitive user data like name and identity, home address, and credit card numbers. Moreover, legislation protecting consumers, sellers, and service providers had to be enforced by online processes. These factors gave rise to important advancements in data security and privacy, as well as to legislation-compliant business process modeling and implementation techniques.

Personal data protection (PDP) legislation does involve security, privacy and legislation-compliant business processes, for which we have decades of successful research and development efforts. But it also involves new complex elements, such as informed consent and the interpretation or justification of algorithmic decision making, about which there is much less available knowledge to support urgently needed solutions.

This paper presents the conclusions of a contrastive study with four major e-commerce websites in Portugal and four analogs in Brazil. As a European country, Portugal must enforce GDPR requirements for all online businesses that collect and process their clients' data. Brazil, however, is at a different stage. The Brazilian Data Protection Law (DPL) has been issued in August 2018, and will become effective only in 2020. We are specifically interested in how interaction design may have changed (or needs to change) in order to ensure the users' ability to know and exert their rights *online*.

Portugal and Brazil are used in the study because both countries speak the same language and share much of their culture. The focus of the contrast is PDP-related interaction communication and action for first-time website visitors. These visitors are the ones who must take the most important step in personal data collection and pro-cessing matters, they must give the data collectors and processors their *informed consent*. As a requirement for such consent, they must be able to understand and anticipate their rights, what kinds of decisions they can make, and actions they can take regarding their data. Appropriately informed consent should allow users to infer (even if in very general terms) *how* to act and what kind of response to expect in key situations, such as when exercising the right to be forgotten, or to retrieve their personal data from one provider and transfer it to another.

We used concepts and elements of Semiotic Engineering [4] methods and tech-niques to capture the content and style of *metacommunication* in the selected websites. Metacommunication, as proposed by Semiotic Engineering, is an especially productive concept for this kind of analysis. Very briefly, according to this semiotic theory of HCI, user interfaces are *communication proxies* that *speak for* interaction designers in dia-logs with users, which take place at interaction time. Through their structure and behavior, systems interfaces *tell users* about the modes, the means, the possibilities, and the effects of the kinds of *communication* that they may have with software systems and applications. By so doing, they also communicate one party's *intent* to the other. Hence, human-computer interaction, in Semiotic Engineering terms, is a case of social *metacommunication* between humans, expressing the designers' communication

about how, when, where, why, and for what purposes users can, in turn, communicate back with the designed technology.

Compared to user-centered HCI alternatives [5–7], for instance, the analysis of metacommunication has the advantage of bringing software designers and users *together* at interaction time [8], that is, of investigating how senders' and receivers' communicative goals are expressed and enabled, how different communicative strategies support interface-mediated meaning negotiations, how artificial interface languages and protocols occasionally create asymmetries of power, and so on, and so forth.

Our findings show that metacommunication design in this particular context is surprisingly poor, both in Portuguese and Brazilian websites. In other words, so far, GDPR seems to have had little impact on what users can do **while interacting** with the analyzed European websites, in comparison with the non-European, pre-legislation ones. Based on our findings, we argue that if nothing changes with respect to *supporting interaction for personal data management and decision making*, we may, against our will, end up contributing to the ineffectiveness of GDPR and similar legislation around the world. Hence the role of interaction designers in this context is critical, as Bus and Nguyen had already concluded following a different line of reasoning [9].

This paper is organized in five sections, starting with the present introduction. Section 2 is a commentary on related work. Section 3 describes our contrastive study, with special attention to the theory and the methodology that was used. Section 4 presents our findings. Finally, Sect. 5 discusses our conclusions and contribution, the limitations of this study, and some directions for future research.

2 Related Work

Although GDPR is not just about privacy, this is a central notion in the European regulation. Privacy studies go a long way in HCI [10]. Legally, however, the role of the user after GDPR has changed in important ways. For example, European users are now *legally entitled* to specific privacy management rights, like giving and revoking consent for the collection and processing of their data. To be sure, GDPR is, to a considerable extent, the result of cultural change regarding privacy and information abuse online. But it also raises new questions, like the users' right to monetize their personal data in profitable ways, and the consequences of controlling intelligent agents by learning how they predict user behavior, and then playing the reverse game to evade control [2].

Users have been long known to agree with terms of services (ToS) and privacy policies (PP), having little understanding (or no understanding at all) of what such terms and policies are saying [11–16]. The problem is often traced back to the fact that ToS and PP are contracts, and contracts are typically written by lawyers and for lawyers, even though they regulate the mutual interest and relations of lawyers' clients [17–19].

In a comprehensive analysis of privacy-related empirical research, Acquisti and colleagues [14] have identified three recurring *themes*. First, users are uncertain about what privacy trade-offs entail. Second, privacy decisions and behavior are always

dependent on context. The same person can manifest widely different preferences in slightly different situations. Third, people or groups with more insight into the factors that determine privacy decisions can influence the behavior of others (and thus change one's individually manifest decisions). This perspective sheds light on previous research results suggesting that people neglect privacy issues [20–22], or that they control privacy threats by such strategies as falsification, passive reaction, and identity modification [23].

Earlier GDPR-related research underlines the importance of personal data management tools for users to take actual control of their data [9]. More recent research work discusses the available kinds of solutions, paradigms or technical support for this. In a survey of current technological solutions for processing personal data, Carvalho and co-authors [24] study the ways how consent is affirmatively expressed. These include consent by electronic signature, consent sent by email or SMS, consent by access code, consent by confirmation buttons, and several others. All of them have risks, some more than others. Another study by Politou and co-authors [25], analyzes two high-impact rights defined by GDPR: consent revocation and the right to be forgotten. The authors underline software implementation challenges associated with both, and conclude that one of the main reasons for the fact that very few companies are now capable of complying to GDPR is that GDPR provides "little if any technical guidance for entities that are obliged to implement it" [p. 15]. One possible solution, they think, is to develop low-level implementation guidelines and business-wide requirements modelling.

Regarding usability and interaction design in the PDP domain, earlier work by Pettersson and co-authors [26] reports on an extensive study with different user interface paradigms for privacy-enhanced identity management. One paradigm differentiates users' roles (what they are doing), and typically assigns pseudonyms to each role. Users can then choose which role they want to play when privacy decisions must be taken. Another paradigm differentiates users' context relations (with whom they are interacting), which allows for *bookmarking* privacy decisions along with website addresses, for example. Finally, the third paradigm associates privacy preferences with physical locations (it *maps* privacy options). Every paradigm opens up different interaction design solutions and has specific usability testing determinants that researchers must keep in mind while investigating user behavior.

Regarding usability research specifically or more closely related to GDPR, Renaud and Shepherd [27] have compiled a list of previously proposed guidelines that can respond to GDPR compliance requirements. The authors have included some of their own to the list. Moreover, interdisciplinary work taking HCI and legal factors into consideration address the use of contract visualizations and icons [18, 19] to simplify the *legalese* and the complexity of concepts and terms in ToS and PP statements. We should finally note that machine learning and AI techniques have also been explored to face the challenges of usable GDPR compliance. For example, some studies propose to automate the evaluation of published terms and policies [28, 29]. Others propose to summarize ToS and PP content, and use it to support question answering dialogs with users [30].

3 The Contrastive Study

The goal of our contrastive study was to examine the spectrum of evolution in interaction design for PDP communication and action, in actual and comparable online applications. There are different approaches to covering the change from *before* to *after* data protection regulations. One of them is temporal (historical, diachronic). Another is spatial (structural, synchronic). The former analyzes the *same* set of objects as they evolve over time, while the latter analyzes *different* sets of objects, which are at different evolutionary stages, at the same physical point in time. For convenience, we chose the structural, synchronic approach. In addition to avoiding the costs of longitudinal studies with evidence being traced back to two or more years past, this alternative also allowed us to discount the change of cultural attitude toward personal data protection during the historical period comprised by a longitudinal approach. In our synchronic perspective, we used the current cultural context of the two sets of analyzed objects, namely the post-legislation interaction design of European websites, and the pre-legislation design of comparable non-European websites.

3.1 The Objects of the Study

The objects of our study were four supermarket websites in Portugal – Continente (www.continente.pt), Froiz (www.froiz.pt), Pingo Doce (www.pingodoce.pt), and Jumbo (www.jumbo.pt) – and four equivalent ones in Brazil – Zona Sul (www.zonasul.com.br), Extra (www.deliveryextra.com.br), Super Prix (www.superprix.com.br), and Pão de Açúcar (www.paodeacucar.com). Together they constitute two mutually exclusive subsets of objects. The Portuguese websites were inspected in January 2019, when GDPR had been effective for more than seven months. The Brazilian websites, inspected on the same dates, demonstrate the state of affairs seventeen months before Brazilian businesses had to comply to the national data protection legislation.

The comparability of objects in both subsets was established by the following criteria. First, all objects belong to the same business sector. Second, in all of the websites we could run the same inspection scenario. Third, both countries have current legislation about how businesses collect, control and process their citizens' personal data online. Brazil, however, is not at the same stage of legal enforcement as Portugal. Finally, both countries speak the same language and share much of their cultural characteristics (Brazil has been colonized by Portugal, and has also been the seat of the Portuguese empire from 1808 to 1821).

3.2 Semiotic Engineering

The entire study was informed by Semiotic Engineering [4, 31, 32]. By looking at social communication mediated by computer programs that *express*, on behalf of participating humans, these participants' communicative intent and content to each other, Semiotic Engineering has the advantage of connecting many points and findings that have been addressed separately by previous research.

Our use of Semiotic Engineering concentrated on the concept of **metacommunication**, (introduced in Sect. 1) and the three classes of computer-mediated social interaction signs that the theory investigates, namely: **static signs**, **dynamic signs**, and **metalinguistic signs**. They can be used to define different communication strategies, depending on the communication purposes, the context, the means and the modes of interaction made available to the engaged parties.

Before we define each one of the metacommunication sign classes, it is useful to note that in typical communication settings participants alternate between two roles: the role of *senders* and that of *receivers*. The *meaning* of signs that they exchange is rarely (if ever) the *same*. Yet, communication is possible mainly because of two factors. First, participants typically share a considerable volume of world knowledge, socio-cultural practices and values, linguistic competence, and so on. Second, inevitable misunderstanding can frequently be prevented, detected, and corrected during communication, by means of strategies that are vastly employed on a daily basis, by virtually every human being. Therefore, when we talk about *the meaning of signs* in metacommunication, we should bear in mind that there are always two human parties involved – the system's designers and the users – in addition to a computational mediator, the system's interface. In the following definitions, when talking about *the* meaning of signs, we refer to the meaning that *humans* (designers or users) assign to them, which may or may not coincide, but still share substantial elements with one another.

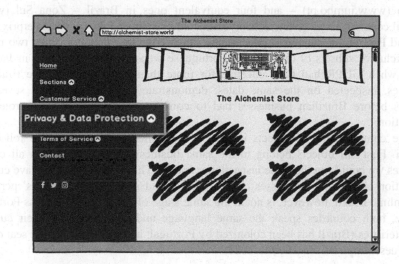

Fig. 1. Illustration of a static sign (a side bar menu item magnified for readability)

Static signs are those expressed and interpreted *instantly*. For example, look at Fig. 1, depicting a snapshot of the interface mockup for an imaginary e-commerce web application called *The Alchemist Store*. The side bar menu item named "Privacy & Data Protection" (see the magnified portion of the image) probably means different things for interaction designers and application users. When they see the phrase "Privacy & Data Protection" followed by the upward arrow, designers know exactly what they

mean by it. Users, however, may look at this sign and have only an incomplete (or even an incorrect) interpretation of what it means. For example, users may interpret this menu item sign as the equivalent of "the access point to knowing more about or taking action with respect to Privacy & Data Protection." Although this interpretation is correct, it remains incomplete if the users cannot anticipate which actions can be taken, under which circumstances, for which purposes, and so on.

When users assign incomplete or incorrect interpretations to static signs, another class of metacommunication signs is typically used to complete and correct such meanings. **Dynamic signs** are (shorter or longer) sequences of static signs that span over time, most often as the result of user-system interaction. The meaning of the entire sequence cannot be assigned instantly by any static sign present in its initial state. For example, in Fig. 2 we sketch the expression of an extremely short dynamic sign that a first-time user of *The Alchemist Store* will typically encounter. Its duration spans from the pre-click to the post-click state of the system.

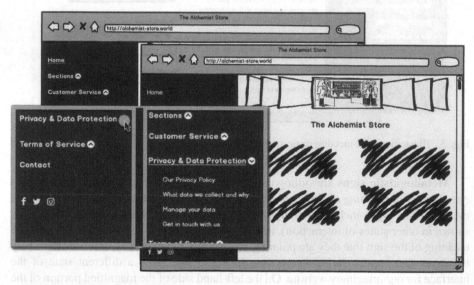

Fig. 2. Illustration of a dynamic sign (side bar menu items magnified for readability)

As already mentioned, the static sign shown in Fig. 1 gives a first-time user an imprecise (and potentially wrong) idea of what this website's designers mean by "Privacy and Data Protection". However, her *interaction* shown in Fig. 2 communicates to her new meanings that this system's designers have assigned to the static menu item "Privacy and Data Protection". On the background screen, whose menu entries are seen on the left-hand side of the magnified area of the image, the user *gets the message* that she can click on the arrowhead to learn more about what she can do regarding privacy and data protection, and she does it. Then, comes the foreground screen, whose menu entries are seen on the right-hand side of the magnified area of the image. The system's response to the user's clicking on "Privacy & Data Protection" communicates

additional messages intended by the designers, namely: that she can learn about "[The service provider's] Privacy Policy"; "What data [the service] collects and why"; how she can "Manage [her] data"; and finally, how she can "Get in touch with [them]". Thus, at the end of this tiny sequence of interaction – which constitutes the dynamic sign – the user has new shared meanings with her indirect and asynchronous interlocutors, the system's designers.

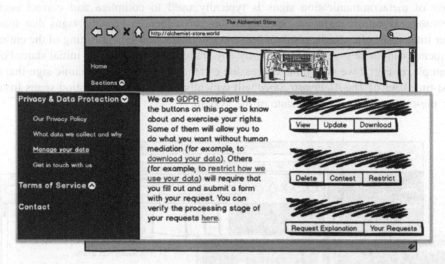

Fig. 3. Illustration of a metalinguistic sign (side bar and page content magnified for readability)

Metalinguistic signs are orthogonal to other signs. Their distinctive feature is to *communicate something about other signs* in the interface language. Typical examples of metalinguistic signs include warnings (with signs that refer to dynamic or static signs shown in other states of interaction), tool tips (with signs that help users understand the meaning of the sign that they are pointing at), and other explanatory or informative help messages that appear during interaction. In Fig. 3, we show a different state of the interface for our imaginary website. On the left-hand side of the magnified portion of the image, we see once again the submenu items for the "Privacy & Data Protection" option. The "Manage your data" option is active. On the right-hand side of the magnified portion, we see the sketch of page content accompanied by push buttons, communicating instantly what users can do in order to "Manage [their] data": to View, to Update, to Download, to Delete, to Contest (the use of), to Restrict (the use of), to Request [an] Explanation (about the use or effect of computations upon) their personal data, and to access [their] Requests. The center portion of the image, however, contains text that *communicates about the meaning of interface signs* on the left- and right-hand side of the image. These are **metalinguistic signs**. For example, the text informs that "[some] of [the buttons] will allow you to do what you want without human mediation (for example, to download your data)." This is a sign that *explains* other interface signs. The same occurs with another

portion of the text, saying that "[others] (for example, to restrict how we use your data) will require that you fill out and submit a form with your request."

Interaction designers combine static, dynamic and metalinguistic signs to compose several metacommunication strategies with which to get their message across to users. The effect of such strategies can be investigated in depth with specific Semiotic Engineering methods, like the Communicability Evaluation Method [31]. In this paper, however, we are not going to investigate empirically how users receive and interpret the designers' communication. We will only characterize, based on empirical semiotic evidence, how metacommunication is expressed by the designers, then discuss the range of potential effects that can be analytically expected to follow from such expressions. As an example of what we mean by analytical effects, compare the metacommunication message communicated through the mockup in Fig. 4 with that communicated through the mockup in Fig. 1. Regardless of other merits or flaws in each design (which will not be discussed in this paper), even without asking the users, it is analytically evident, by the mere presence and arrangement of static interface signs, as well as their conventional meaning, that data protection is more salient in the communication expressed by the designers of the interface in Fig. 1 than in meta-communication expressed by the designers of the interface in Fig. 4. In particular, regarding the latter, because the design uses static signs that have been long seen on website interfaces prior to GDPR (cf. "Terms of Use" and "Privacy Policy" at the very bottom of the page), the message conveyed by this specific portion of design suggests that there is nothing new in post-GDPR design in this website.

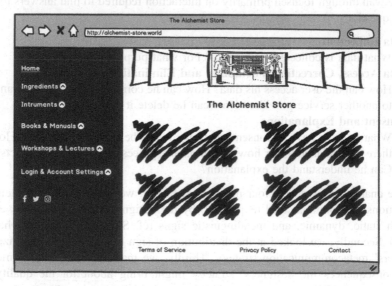

Fig. 4. Alternative entry page design of *The Alchemist Store*

3.3   Method

Semiotic Engineering methods are *interpretive* (qualitative), and explore the meaning of interface and interaction signs for both the producers (designers) and consumers (users) of digital technology [31, 32]. The contrast between intended and perceived meanings in metacommunication is one of the richest results that Semiotic Engineering methods can yield. Yet, studies focused solely on the *emission* or the *reception* of metacommunication can also reveal the effects of certain semiotic features of algorithmically-mediated social communication between humans.

In this study we focused on the **emission** of metacommunication, that is, on the designers' **expression** of their message to users. The evidence for semiotic engineering analysis was collected by means of an interactive **walkthrough** of the interface, where the analyst played the role of a first-time visitor to the website, guided by the content of the following inspection scenario:

> *Antonio, a business administrator in his early fifties, is spending vacations with friends and family in a nice region of his native country that he has never been to in his entire life. Tomorrow, the group will have a barbecue in the front garden of the house they are renting, and Antonio is in charge of buying snacks and drinks for ten people. He decides to buy them online, but immediately realizes that the food chain where he usually shops when at home does not provide services in the place where he is now. He must then use a new online supermarket service.*
>
> *Antonio is extremely careful with personal data protection when shopping. So, before he starts, he wants to learn what data the company collects, for what purposes, how they handle it, and finally what rights he has as the owner of the data.*

The walkthrough focused primarily on interaction required to find answers to three sets of questions:

- **Data Collection**
  - What data is collected? By whom? For what purposes?
- **Data Access, Correction, Portability and Elimination**
  - How can the user access his data? How can he correct it? How can he transfer it to another service provider? How can he delete it (be forgotten)?
- **Consent and Explanations**
  - What does he have to consent to? Can consent be partial or revoked? How? Is there an explanation for how the automatic processing of his data affects him? Can he understand the explanation?

The analysis consisted of four main steps. Firstly, we looked at how content *and* interactions are communicated (expressed) by the designers of the analyzed websites through static, dynamic, and metalinguistic signs (cf. Subsect. 3.2 to see what this means). Secondly, we looked at the distribution of sign classes and characterized the designers' metacommunication strategy. Thirdly, we made an overall assessment of what consequences the designers' strategy might bring about for the quality and effectiveness of GDPR-related communication and action.

The final step of the analysis was to contrast the findings of post-GDPR Portuguese websites and pre-DPL Brazilian websites. Differences and similarities regarding communication strategies and their consequences for users should allow us to appreciate the evolution of interaction design to support users' decisions and actions for

personal data protection. The walkthroughs were carried out using Firefox 64.0.2, with the recommended (default) configurations for cookies and security. The browser's interface language was set to Portuguese, which is also the language of the eight inspected websites.

4 Findings

We begin this presentation of findings by noting that evidence of GDPR-related metacommunication collected during the walkthroughs of all websites is almost entirely made up of **metalinguistic signs** explaining the properties, behavior, policies, and terms of use of *other* interaction signs, namely the website's interface for online shoppers. Figure 5 presents one example of massively textual communication from designers to users about the users' personal data protection rights, and what they should do to exert them. Although this might not come as a surprise, given the novelty of the law and data governance practices, the upshot of the virtual *absence* of metacommunication achieved with static and dynamic signs (like, for example, the mockups shown in Sect. 3.2) is that users can do little more than read and navigate through long spans of text, rather than directly access and download collected personal data, request the deletion, limitation, or specific restrictions of personal data usage *online*, as suggested in Fig. 3.

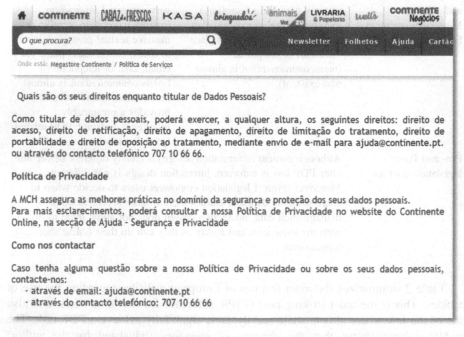

Fig. 5. A typical interface to exert personal data protection rights

Moreover, as can also be seen on Fig. 5, for a first-time visitor, metacommunication is thoroughly opaque regarding *how* the users' rights are handled by the businesses analyzed in our study. All of the European ones, tell users to <u>send email</u> (Fig. 5 "<u>mediante envio de e-mail</u>") or <u>call a telephone</u> number (Fig. 5 "<u>através de contacto telefónico</u>") to make their requests. In other words, most of the GDPR-related tasks cannot be carried out online, through interaction *with the website*. As previous research has shown [33], since the early days of e-commerce and e-businesses, users seem to perceive the broader social context (especially the 'people') behind interfaces. This has been evident, for example, with the alternate use of "it" (the interface) and "they" (website owners) when verbalizing interaction with websites. The absence of interaction to achieve GDPR-related tasks is, thus, likely to motivate perceptions that although *a website* or *a system* may collect and process users' personal data and online behavior, *it* has nothing to do with the obligations of data controllers and processors obligations (*their* obligations). Websites may then be seen (and possibly used) as a protective shield for legally responsible parties. Table 1 summarizes our top-level findings.

Table 1. Overview of findings.

Dimensions of analysis	Portuguese websites	Brazilian websites
Users' Rights to Know, Decide, and Act	All four websites addressed the users' rights	Two of the websites partially addressed the users' *new* rights
Interaction Design and Metacommunication Strategies	Very restricted *interaction* (mainly navigation, scrolling); massive textual *communication* to users; most action takes place via email or telephone (*metacommunication* is almost non-existent)	Three of the websites support very restricted *interaction* (mainly navigation, scrolling); massive textual *communication* to users; action takes place via email, chat or telephone (*metacommunication* is almost non-existent). One website provides a presumably *intelligent assistant*. PDP-related Q&A is, however, very poor
Pre- and Post-legislation contrast	Although content (information design) is clearly different before and after PDP law is enforced, interaction design is not different. Moreover, even if legislation empowers users to decide when to share personal data and entitles them to take several actions to manage such data, interaction design does not allow them to do so with the same ease and agility as they can do their online shopping transactions	

Table 2 summarizes the main features of European websites regarding the use of cookies. This is the most striking post-GDPR difference for first-time users, and also one of the few where simple static and dynamic signs fully achieve a PDP task. The middle column shows that the phrasing of messages (translated by the author) underlines the advantages of using cookies, and in some cases suggests that users can

not accept to use cookies. Although they can technically do it, if they care to read lengthy textual instructions and follow links to web browsers' documentation on how to block cookies, once they load the current website home page, cookies are *immediately* in use with default browser configurations. Moreover, most cookie notifications are placed at the bottom of a browser's screen laden with animations advertising products and discounts. These will most likely distract the user's attention away from relevant PDP information.

Table 2. Overview of freely translated communication about cookies in Portuguese websites.

Website	Metacommunication message and location on screen	Further information/dialog
Continente (PT)	*"Our website uses cookies to enhance and personalize your navigation experience. As you continue navigation you consent to the use of cookies. Learn more"* **Location:** BOTTOM OF BROWSER'S WINDOW	If the user clicks on "Learn more", a pop-up window is opened with fixed questions about cookies. The answers appear as the user clicks on the arrow control (see Fig. 6)
Froiz (PT)	*"This website uses cookies to enhance your experience. As you continue to navigate you agree with such use. If you want to know more, see our Cookies Policy. I understand. More information"* **Location:** BOTTOM OF BROWSER'S WINDOW	If the user clicks on "More information", a new tab is opened, showing a web page with plain textual explanations about cookies. The text contains no active links
Pingo Doce (PT)	*"This website uses cookies and other tracking technologies to help navigation and [enhance] our ability to provide feedback, analyze the use of our website, [...] present promotional information about our services and products, and provide content for third parties. Check our Cookies Policy. I accept"* **Location:** BOTTOM OF BROWSER'S WINDOW	If the user decides to check the Cookies Policy, a new tab is opened, showing a web page with typographically designed information about cookies. It even includes a link to an independent legal consultancy group's website, where abundant information about cookies is provided
Jumbo (PT)	*"We use cookies, of our own and third parties, to enhance your navigation experience and to show you publicity oriented to your preferences and navigation habits Click on 'Accept' to confirm that you have read this and that you accept our Cookies Policy. Accept"* **Location:** POP-UP HOVERING ON THE RIGHT-SIDE OF THE BROWSER'S WINDOW	If the user clicks on the "Cookies Policy" link, he navigates to a webpage with typographically organized information about cookies. The problem is that the pop-up can only be closed by clicking on 'Accept'. The pop-up stays in front of the content which should help the user decide (see Fig. 7). The practical effect is that of a *nagging splash screen* to persuade users to act as the website owners expect

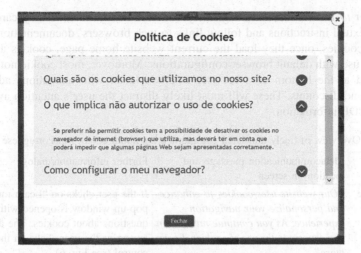

Fig. 6. Pop-up window with information about cookies in Continente's website

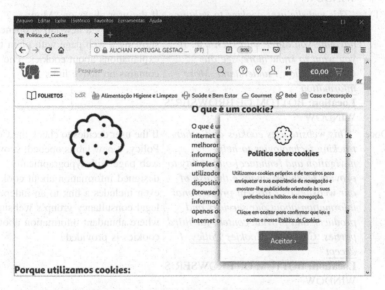

Fig. 7. Encumbered communication about cookies in Jumbo's website

Brazilian websites do not warn the users about the use of cookies (which they all use). The irony is that, even though European websites warn their users about it, users have no option to say "no", at least to the first load of cookies placed when they hit the home page of the analyzed websites. This communication problem has more to it than meets the eye. In these websites, cookie control is the result of interactions with *web browsers*, not *web servers*. Therefore, although metacommunication is carried out in one channel, one context, and with two fairly defined interlocutors (the user and the e-commerce 'website'), a silent third party who is mediating the entire process – a web

browser – is the only one that can effectively do something if users do not agree with the website's terms of cookie use. The consequence for communication and user experience may is that, if users want to communicate with the online shopping website on different terms, they cannot *tell it to the website*. They have to tell it to *a silent mediator*, who suddenly steps into the scene. This situation is very similar to the one presented in Table 1, where communication needed to turn the users' rights into full effect is systematically directed to *mediators* that can only be reached by email and telephone.

Further relevant PDP-related evidence comes from a Brazilian website, Super Prix, which uses a different pattern of metacommunication. Instead of the plain navigation-scrolling option to 'learn more' about ToS and PP, Super Prix initially offers interaction with an 'intelligent assistant'. At first, if the user clicks on an ostensive "May I help?" button floating on the side of the page, a pop-up window is shown encouraging users to just *ask* ("Perguntar") what they want to know. The added arrow on the right side of the screenshot image in Fig. 8 indicates the location and design of the pop-up dialog.

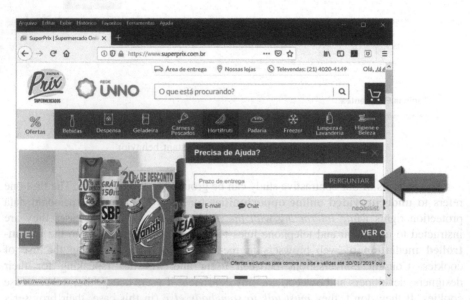

Fig. 8. Brazilian website "free text" interaction when users need help

Intelligent assistance is more explicitly invoked when users follow the link to this website's Privacy Policy. In Fig. 9, however, we show an example of the assistant's behavior when asked: "What do you have to offer re: Personal Data Protection" (author's translation from Portuguese). The user gets two links to information: "What happens with my credit card data?" and "What must I do to change my registered data?". These links are the *answer* to several other questions like: "May I erase my data?", "May I see what data you collect?", and so on. Beneath the brittle chatbot cover, Fig. 9 also demonstrates the tendency to direct conversation to non-algorithmic

interaction. The other tabs to the right of "Atendimento Inteligente" (Intelligent Assistance) are: "Fale Conosco" (Contact, via email) and "Atendimento via Chat" (Online Chat), with human intervention.

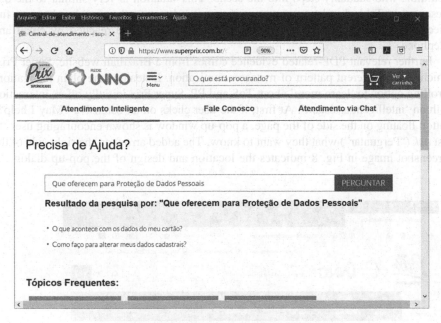

Fig. 9. Super Prix intelligent assistant behavior

The findings of our contrastive study can be grouped in three clusters. The first one refers to **underprovided online opportunities** for users to exert their personal data protection rights *while interacting with the analyzed websites*. In all cases they are instructed to use email and telephone lines to do it. The second refers to the **uncontrolled mediation** of web browsers in metacommunications regarding the use of cookies. Consent conversations between users and websites (speaking for their designers, developers and owners) are only consistent if users *accept* that websites use cookies. If they don't, they *must talk to somebody else* (in this case, their browser's configuration interface). Finally, we also found evidence that **intelligent conversational agents are not yet an option** to inform and guide users in their attempts to know how businesses handle their GDPR obligations. All relevant information, steps and decisions relative to enforcing data protection rights are explicitly directed to human-to-human communication channels like email and telephone lines. Algorithmic mediation, which has long been in place for e-commerce – a comparable data-sensitive and legally ruled application area – is clearly not used. In the next section we will discuss these findings and present our conclusions about the significance of this study.

5 Concluding Remarks

The qualitative study presented in this paper has not been designed to answer questions like "how has interaction design changed after GDPR?", or "how do e-businesses handle their clients' data protection rights online?" in a generalizing sense. The validity of this study is limited by the analysis of only a small set of websites, the contingency of walkthroughs guided by a specific scenario, and the researcher's inevitable interpretation biases. However, as qualitative methodology requires, the researcher has strived to discount such limitations. The adopted strategy has been to use an explicit orienting theory throughout the process. Semiotic Engineering has provided not only the initial categories of analysis (with the concept of metacommunication and the three classes of signs that are used to compose designer-to-user metacommunication messages), but also a framework to organize sociotechnical relations among parties involved in PDP-related interactions and transaction online. The following paragraphs should show that this study's main contribution is to support the elaboration of *qualified hypotheses* for subsequent predictive (or non-predictive) more general inquiries with larger samples of interactive systems that collect, store, and process their users' personal data.

The findings reported in Sect. 4 are *themselves* part of the meanings that might be inferred from metacommunication by more reflective users. For instance, users might ask what the owners and producers of the analyzed websites mean by declining to engage in PDP-related interactions in the same way as they engage in buying and selling interactions. The just as interesting reverse question could be asked by reflective interaction designers: What might users take this strategy to mean?

The Semiotic Engineering perspective used in the study can also add significant elements to the current debate on privacy by design [34, 35] and usability aspects of GDPR-related interactions online. Because it takes *metacommunication* as its object of investigation, and metacommunication involves software producers, software users, and software itself, this theory can shed light on certain aspects of current scientific discussions that are not necessarily framed in connection with one another.

The three classes of signs investigated by the theory (see Subsect. 3.2) establish different conditions of meaning making in HCI. Static signs support instant meaning making, often associated with intuitiveness and ease of use. Metalinguistic signs, in turn, support indefinitely many levels of referential meaning making, which can augment or correct previous meanings assigned to the interaction objects in reference. It is the class of dynamic signs, however, that creates the most complex and intriguing conditions for meaning making. We will refer to this as *algorithmically-negotiated meaning making*. On the one hand, the expression underlines the fact that dynamic signs are controlled by *algorithms* (computing rules), and are thus inherently akin to what Peircean semioticians refer to as *legi signs*, or signs that are established by some kind of law [36]. On the other, the expression also underlines the fact that human meanings are always *negotiated* in social communication. A communication sender (S) can never be sure that the communication receiver (R) has captured what she (S) means by a single piece of communication. Likewise, a receiver (R) can never be sure that what he (R) takes the sender's (S) communication to mean is actually what

she means. As a result, social communication is full of interpretation checkpoints and verifications, adjustments, corrections, redundancy, explanations, and other meaning-negotiation procedures that cannot, unfortunately, ultimately guarantee that senders and receivers share the *same* meanings. Certain semiotic theories actually suggest that they never do [36].

Computer-mediation, however, creates and enforces meaning stability (or *algorithmic meaning*) that governs metacommunication between human parties. The algorithm that captures a user's click on the "Accept" ('Aceitar') button on Jumbo's cookie use notification interface (Fig. 7) defines the necessary and sufficient technological conditions for a user's explicit consent to having cookies placed on her device. The same will be true of other algorithms defining the necessary and sufficient technological conditions for users to access, modify, delete or transport their personal data. The problem, as Fig. 7 conveniently demonstrates, is **how interaction design communicates to users the meaning of algorithms**. The rhetorical effect of a pop-up window that will not disappear unless the user clicks on the "Accept" ('Aceitar') button is to rush users into accepting the terms of service. In other words, interaction design may *add* meanings to the algorithmic rule that establishes the technological protocol for consent. On the other hand, the walkthrough has shown that the pop-up window is actually preventing users from reading this website's cookie policy (some portions of it are occluded behind the nagging window). If interaction designers did not mean it to happen, it is now the algorithms that are adding (undesired) meanings to the designers' and possibly the owners' intended message, inducing users to accept personal data usage terms without reading them. The challenge indicated by this piece of evidence is that interaction designers and software engineers do not always negotiate models and implementation meanings with one another [32]. Thus, if algorithms are to be taken as an expression of the law, not only interaction design, but also software development processes may need new meaning-negotiation tools for design and development teams to compose and express their message in unison and accordance with the owners' intent.

Furthermore, dynamic signs may well be the reason why GDPR and DPL matters in the Portuguese and Brazilian websites we analyzed are channeled to and processed by humans, rather than algorithms. This view connects with Politou and colleagues' research [25], as well as with studies coming from other domains. For example, Katsh's analysis [37] of the state of the art in online dispute resolutions (ODR) says that in "the earliest forms of [ODR] [...] email seemed an appropriate tool for communication between disputants and between disputants and third parties." [p. 7] Now, however, "the role of software has been recognized in discussions of legal doctrine by the expression *code is the law*." [p. 8] Algorithms, as of now, are not ready to *stand for* GDPR or DPL.

Our future work with Semiotic Engineering is to explore the merits of alternative metacommunication strategies for PDP communication, decision-making, and action. GDPR is only a trigger for research that aims to contribute for greater transparency in the digital world [38], striving to enable ethics and fairness in power relations established by algorithmically-mediated metacommunication among humans. This is the call we want to make with this work, that as members of the interaction design community,

we *tell* users what is ethically and otherwise important for them to know about their rights, and *help* developers and owners express what they mean to say more effectively.

Acknowledgments. The author thanks the Brazilian National Council for Scientific and Technological Development (CNPq) for partially funding this research, with grant #304224/2017-0. She also thanks anonymous Interact 2019 reviewers, her students, and colleagues for insightful comments and suggestions that improved the original version of this paper.

References

1. The European Parliament and Council General Data Protection Regulation. https://eur-lex. europa.eu/legal-content/EN/TXT/PDF/?uri=CELEX:32016R0679. Accessed Jan 2019
2. Hildebrandt, M.: Slaves to big data. Or are we? IDP. Revista de Internet, Derecho y Política **17**, 7–44 (2013)
3. Governo Brasileiro LEI 13.709/2018 (LEI ORDINÁRIA), 14 August 2018. http://legislacao. planalto.gov.br/legisla/legislacao.nsf/Viw_Identificacao/lei%2013.709-2018. Accessed Jan 2019
4. de Souza, C.S.: The Semiotic Engineering of Human-Computer Interaction. MIT Press, Cambridge (2005)
5. Norman, D.A., Draper, S.W.: User Centered System Design: New Perspectives on Human-Computer Interaction. Lawrence Erlbaum Associates, Hillsdale (1986)
6. Holtzblatt, K., Wendell, J.B., Wood, S.: Rapid Contextual Design: A How-to Guide to Key Techniques for User-Centered Design. Elsevier, Amsterdam (2004)
7. Ritter, F.E., Baxter, G.D., Churchill, E.F.: User-centered systems design: a brief history. In: Ritter, F.E., Baxter, G.D., Churchill, E.F. (eds.) Foundations for Designing User-Centered Systems, pp. 33–54. Springer, London (2014). https://doi.org/10.1007/978-1-4471-5134-0_2
8. de Souza, C.S.: Semiotic engineering: bringing designers and users together at interaction time. Interact. Comput. **17**(3), 317–341 (2005)
9. Bus, J., Nguyen, M.-H.C.: Personal data management – a structured discussion. In: Hildebrandt, M., O'Hara, K., Waidner, M. (eds.) Digital Enlightenment Yearbook 2013: The Value of Personal Data, vol. 270, pp. 270–287. IOS Press, Amsterdam (2013)
10. Iachello, G., Hong, J.: End-user privacy in human-computer interaction. Found. Trends Hum.-Comput. Interact. **1**(1), 1–137 (2007)
11. Obar, J.A., Oeldorf-Hirsch, A.: The biggest lie on the Internet: ignoring the privacy policies and terms of service policies of social networking services. Inf. Commun. Soc. 1–20 (2018). https://doi.org/10.1080/1369118X.2018.1486870
12. Carolan, E.: The continuing problems with online consent under the EU's emerging data protection principles. Comput. Law Secur. Rev. **32**(3), 462–473 (2016)
13. Nguyen, J.H., Vu, K.-P.L.: Does privacy information influence users' online purchasing behavior? In: Smith, M.J., Salvendy, G. (eds.) Human Interface 2011. LNCS, vol. 6771, pp. 349–358. Springer, Heidelberg (2011). https://doi.org/10.1007/978-3-642-21793-7_39
14. Acquisti, A., Brandimarte, L., Loewenstein, G.: Privacy and human behavior in the age of information. Science **347**(6221), 509–514 (2015)
15. Angulo, J., Ortlieb, M.: "WTH..!?!" Experiences, reactions, and expectations related to online privacy panic situations. In: Cranor, L.F., Biddle, R., Consolvo, S. (eds.) SOUPS 2015 Proceedings of the Eleventh USENIX Conference on Usable Privacy and Security, pp. 19–38. USENIX Association (2015)

16. Tsai, J.Y., Egelman, S., Cranor, L., Acquisti, A.: The effect of online privacy information on purchasing behavior: an experimental study. Inf. Syst. Res. **22**(2), 254–268 (2011)
17. Berger-Walliser, G., Bird, R.C., Haapio, H.: Promoting business success through contract visualization. J. Law Bus. Ethics **17**, 55 (2011)
18. Rossi, A., Palmirani, M.: From words to images through legal visualization. In: Pagallo, U., Palmirani, M., Casanovas, P., Sartor, G., Villata, S. (eds.) AICOL 2015-2017. LNCS (LNAI), vol. 10791, pp. 72–85. Springer, Cham (2018). https://doi.org/10.1007/978-3-030-00178-0_5
19. Rossi, A., Palmirani, M.: A visualization approach for adaptive consent in the European data protection framework. In: Parycek, P., Edelman, N. (eds.) Proceedings of the 2017 Conference for E-Democracy and Open Government (CeDEM), pp. 159–170. IEEE Computer Society, Piscataway (2017)
20. Zhao, J., Binns, R., van Kleek, M., Shadbolt, N.: Privacy languages: are we there yet to enable user controls? In: Proceedings of the 20th International Conference Companion on World Wide Web, pp. 799–806. International World Wide Web Conferences Steering Committee (2016)
21. Schaub, F., Balebako, R., Durity, A.L., Cranor, L.F.: A design space for effective privacy notices. In: Cranor, L.F., Biddle, R., Consolvo, S. (eds.) SOUPS 2015 Proceedings of the Eleventh USENIX Conference on Usable Privacy and Security, pp. 1–17. USENIX Association (2015)
22. Cranor, L.F., Guduru, P., Arjula, M.: User interfaces for privacy agents. ACM Trans. Comput.-Hum. Interact. **13**(2), 135–178 (2006)
23. Chen, K., Rea Jr., A.I.: Protecting personal information online: a survey of user privacy concerns and control techniques. J. Comput. Inf. Syst. **44**(4), 85–92 (2004)
24. Carvalho, A.C., Martins, R., Antunes, L.: How to express explicit and auditable consent. In: McLaughlin, K., et al. (eds.) Proceedings of the 16th Annual Conference on Privacy, Security and Trust (PST), pp. 1–5. IEEE Computer Society, Piscataway (2018)
25. Politou, E., Alepis, E., Patsakis, C.: Forgetting personal data and revoking consent under the GDPR: challenges and proposed solutions. J. Cybersecur. **1**, 1–20 (2018)
26. Pettersson, J.S., et al.: Making PRIME usable. In: Proceedings of SOUPS 2005 Proceedings of the 2005 Symposium on Usable Privacy and Security, pp. 53–64. ACM, New York (2005)
27. Renaud, K., Shepherd, L.A.: How to make privacy policies both GDPR-compliant and usable. In: Creese, S., Renaud, R., Pedersen, J.M., Keane, E. (eds.) Proceedings of the 2018 International Conference on Cyber Situational Awareness, Data Analytics and Assessment (Cyber SA), pp. 1–8. IEEE Computer Society, Piscataway (2018)
28. Contissa, G., et al.: Claudette meets GDPR: automating the evaluation of privacy policies using artificial intelligence, pp. 1–59 (2018). SSRN: https://ssrn.com/abstract=3208596 or http://dx.doi.org/10.2139/ssrn.3208596
29. Tesfay, W.B., Hofmann, P., Nakamura, T., Kiyomoto, S., Serna, J.: PrivacyGuide: towards an implementation of the EU GDPR on internet privacy policy evaluation. In: Proceedings of the Fourth ACM International Workshop on Security and Privacy Analytics, pp. 15–21. ACM, New York (2018)
30. Zaeem, R.N., German, R.L., Barber, K.S.: PrivacyCheck: automatic summarization of privacy policies using data mining. ACM Trans. Internet Technol. **18**(4), 53:1–53:18 (2018)
31. de Souza, C.S., Leitão, C.F.: Semiotic Engineering Methods for Scientific Research in HCI. Synthesis Lectures on Human-Centered Informatics. Morgan & Claypool, San Rafael (2009)
32. de Souza, C.S., Cerqueira, R., Afonso, L.M., Brandão, R.R.M., Ferreira, J.S.J.: Software Developers as Users: Semiotic Investigations in Human-Centered Software Development. Springer, Cham (2016). https://doi.org/10.1007/978-3-319-42831-4

33. Light, A., Wakeman, I.: Beyond the interface: users' perceptions of interaction and audience on websites. Interact. Comput. **13**(3), 325–351 (2001)
34. Colesky, M., Hoepman, J., Hillen, C.: A critical analysis of privacy design strategies. In: 2016 IEEE Security and Privacy Workshops (SPW), pp. 33–40. IEEE Computer Society, Los Alamitos (2016)
35. Cavoukian, A.: Privacy by design: the definitive workshop. A foreword by Ann Cavoukian, Ph.D. Identity Inf. Soc. **3**(2), 247–251 (2010)
36. Merrell, F.: Peirce, Signs, and Meaning. University of Toronto Press, Toronto (1997)
37. Katsh, E.: Online dispute resolution: some implications for the emergence of law in cyberspace. Int. Rev. Law Comput. Technol. **21**(2), 97–107 (2007)
38. Edwards, L., Veale, E.: Slave to the algorithm: why a right to an explanation is probably not the remedy you are looking for. Duke Law Technol. Rev. **16**, 18–84 (2017)

A Study of Outbound Automated Call Preferences for DOTS Adherence in Rural India

Arpit Mathur[(✉)], Shimmila Bhowmick[(✉)], and Keyur Sorathia[(✉)]

Embedded Interaction Lab, Indian Institute of Technology (IIT) Guwahati, Guwahati, India
arpitmathur19@gmail.com, shimmila.bhowmick@gmail.com, keyurbsorathia@gmail.com

Abstract. Outbound automated calls present an excellent opportunity to deliver messages among low-technology literate users from a resource-constrained environment, such as rural India. While automated calls have been used for various purposes in rural settings, sufficient research has not been done to understand the motivation for attending the calls, preferred contents, call duration, time, preferred gender of voice, content learnability and preference of automated call over SMS for information delivery. In this paper, we present a study conducted among 40 early-stage Tuberculosis (TB) positive patients to investigate content learnability and preferences of outbound automated calls aimed to increase DOTS adherence. The results indicate the demand for easily actionable contents, evenings as preferred time and less than 5 min as ideal call duration for automated calls. We found the preference of automated calls over SMS for information delivery. We also observed a significant increase in learnability among participants who listened to the complete call as compared to participants who did not. We present these findings in detail and suitable recommendations.

Keywords: Automated calls · IVR · ICTD · HCI4D · Health education

1 Introduction

Outbound automated calls have shown potential in delivering voice-based messages at scale, hence presenting itself as a key alternative for easy information delivery services such as reminders [3, 8] and adherence [2, 13]. It offers advantages of cost savings [11], convenience, simplicity, and privacy [13]. Moreover, it demands low prerequisites such as basic feature phones, no dedicated training, and education [17].

The adoption of outbound automated calls has increased [15] due to increased mobile phone penetration in rural India [5]. Prior research indicates the need for appropriate call timing [17], duration [10, 17], suitable contents and familiar voice persona to increase the effectiveness of automated calls [16]. Although sufficient research is conducted in developed regions and urban settings [12, 16], limited research is done in studying these factors and its influence in rural settings, especially among users with low-resource settings.

© IFIP International Federation for Information Processing 2019
Published by Springer Nature Switzerland AG 2019
D. Lamas et al. (Eds.): INTERACT 2019, LNCS 11748, pp. 24–33, 2019.
https://doi.org/10.1007/978-3-030-29387-1_2

In this paper, we present results of a user study conducted among 40 early-stage (in their first month of treatment) TB positive patients who are undergoing Directly Observed Treatment Short course (DOTS) treatment. These patients come from remote regions of 2 districts of the northeastern state of India, Assam. We sent one outbound automated call to each patient to increase awareness on various early-stage TB care topics. The automated calls were followed by a telephonic interview and post-call questionnaire to study the preferred (i) contents (ii) time of the call (iii) call duration and (iv) preference of gender of voice. We also studied learnability among the participants after one week of the automated call. This study is a part of ongoing field trials of "*Swasthyaa*" [4], which is an end-to-end ICT ecosystem aimed to reduce initial and retreatment TB defaulters through real-time tracking and monitoring of patients' health progress.

2   Related Work

Numerous studies [13, 17, 22, 23] utilizing advantages of outbound automated calls have been conceptualized and studied in developing regions. Automated calls have been used to support HIV treatment, mainly for adherence reminders and have been used to collect adherence data [21]. Joshi et al. [17] used automated calls to support the treatment of HIV/AIDS patients in India. The study found that patients preferred receiving daily calls of shorter duration as opposed to a long call at a preferred time. Helzer et al. [10] used outbound automated calls consumption and randomized the duration of phone calls received by participants. During the study over 3 months, the duration of the phone call was reduced to reach a mean of approximately 2 min due to the diminishing motivations of participants. Other studies have used automated calls for motivation and improved quality of life for asthma [18], physical activity [19], coronary syndrome [20], however, limited studies have been conducted to explore best practices in terms of duration, content, gender of voice, and time of an outbound automated call, especially among users of low-resource settings.

3   Introduction to Swasthyaa

Swasthyaa [4] is an Information Communication Technology (ICT) based solution aimed to reduce initial and retreatment TB defaulters. It complements the TB care efforts initiated by the Government of Assam (a northeastern state in India) via real-time tracking and monitoring the health progress of each presumptive and positive TB patient enrolled in local health centers. It consists of mobile & a web application, Interactive Voice Response (IVR) and a newly designed TB blister packet. The web and mobile application are designed for health administrators to track health progress of each patient, whereas IVR and blister packets allow patients to register DOTS intake regularly. In addition to tracking and monitoring health progress, it sends periodic automated calls explaining TB care methods, government initiatives, food habits, family care and motivational messages to increase adherence among the patients.

4   Outbound Automated Call Description

A simulated, 3 min and 48 s outbound automated voice call was recorded in the Assamese language. The call was sent with a hypothetical female persona Dr. Heena Saikia. The choice of a female persona as a health professional was to increase the confidence and acceptance of the shared contents. Heena Saikia is a commonly found Assamese name and was chosen to increase familiarity among the users. The call presented information on the government initiatives such as free DOTS & Nikshay Poshan Yojana (monthly Rs. 500 to buy healthy food), the importance of TB adherence and DOTS course completion, possible side effects of medications, nutrition, home hygiene, methods of cough and sputum disposal, and the poor effects of tobacco and alcohol. The message did not require input from the user to listen to the call. Government health professionals developed and approved the health contents before delivering to patients.

5   Study Objectives

The objective of this study was to learn about the preferences of automated calls among users of low-resource settings. We believe that incorporating these preferences will increase the acceptance, adoption, and effectiveness of the automated calls aimed to increase adherence in rural areas. We studied the following preferences: (i) the duration of the automated call (ii) the preferred time of a day where the automated calls should be made (iii) preference of male or female voice for an automated call and (iv) preferred platform of information delivery, i.e., preference of a voice call or SMS. We also studied the learnability of the contents to understand the effectiveness of an automated call as a suitable platform for information awareness.

6   Methodology

6.1   Participants

We selected 40 participants (M = 32, F = 8) from *Swasthyaa's* database who were in their first month of the DOTS treatment. They belonged to 5 rural blocks from Darrang and Kamrup district of the Assam state. The monthly income of the participants ranged from Rs. 500–10,000 (US\$7–US\$143) (Mean = US\$49, SD = US\$45). 11 participants' monthly income was below Rs. 1,000 (US\$14), whereas 22 and 7 participants earned Rs. 1,000–5,000 (US\$14–72) and Rs. 5,000–10,000 (US\$72–144) each month respectively. Of the 40 participants, 14 were daily wage workers (i.e., farm laborers, rag pickers, etc.) 3 were retired, 5 were students, 2 were homemakers, 5 small business owners, and 11 with regular incomes. The age of the participants ranged from 18–60 years (mean = 34.15, SD = 13.08). The age, monthly income, location and occupation of participants were already available in *Swasthyaa's* database. We collected this information during patient registration process. 30 participants owned feature phones, out of which 17 shared it among family members. They used the mobile phone for

making & receiving calls. No other advance usage (including the use of SMS) was observed among them. 10 participants owned low-cost smartphones which were used to make-receive calls and sent messages on WhatsApp. Participants had limited knowledge and understanding of TB as a disease and were only aware of the free DOTS program. No other information such as food habits, side effects or other government benefits were known to the participants. The existing knowledge of participants was obtained from Senior Treatment Supervisor (STS), a government official who directly interacts with patients and is responsible for DOTS adherence and completion.

6.2   Procedure

We recorded the calls using a Philips DVT6010 audio recorder for this study. We manually called the participants between 1900 to 2100 h. The time of the call was guided by the hypothesis that participants would be at leisure and unengaged during this period. Moreover, the chosen timing also served the purpose of acting as a reminder at the end of the day for patients who may have missed the dosage. Once the participant picked up the call, the recording was played out loud on a speaker and placed next to the mobile phone's microphone to mimic the effect of an automated call. If a patient did not pick up the call, they were called again up to three times on consecutive days. No patients were called more than once a day. Following the automated call, we called the patients within an hour. A structured telephonic interview was conducted to learn about the preferred time of the call, duration, voice preference and platform for information delivery (i.e., SMS or automated call). Participants were asked to provide their choices without any specific option given by the moderator. However, they were probed further in case they provided vague answers. For example, if the participants answered morning as the preferred time for an automated call, we asked them to provide a specific time (e.g., 0800, 0900 h, etc.). We also conducted unstructured interviews to identify qualitative findings such as motivations behind preferred choices, listening to the automated call and the preferred contents on TB care. The interviews lasted 20–25 min per person. A female moderator conducted the interviews in Hindi or Assamese language depending upon participants' preference. All of their responses were noted and recorded for further analysis. Each participant was called again after one week to study the content learnability. A telephonic questionnaire consisting of 6 questions was used to study the learnability. The 6 questions were - (i) how long does the DOTS course take to cure TB? (ii) when should you stop taking TB medication? (iii) what are the consequences of not taking medicine for complete DOTS course? (iv) what should you buy with the money provided via the Nikshay Poshan Yojna? (v) if you face side-effects such as nausea or vomiting due to the medication, what should you do? (vi) which of the following options is an incorrect way of disposing of sputum during TB? We provided 3 options verbally to each participant for all questions. We took prior consent from each participant before recording the call.

6.3   Data Collection Methods

We collected the data by noting down the answers in a notebook while conducting telephonic interviews. We also recorded the call to revisit the findings. The data to measure learnability was collected by writing down the correct choice given by the participants. We further gave scores (1 - correct answer, 0 - incorrect answer) to analyze the content learnability.

7   Results

7.1   Motivation to Listen to Automated Calls

Out of 40 participants, 27 participants listened to the complete duration of the call (3 min 48 s) whereas 13 did not listen to the complete call. Out of 13 participants, 3 listened between 90 s to 180 s, and 10 listened to it for less than 90 s. The participants' ability to listen to the call was hindered by the poor network connectivity, as 9 participants cited it as a reason to disconnect the call. One participant stated, "*I wanted to listen to the entire message, but I could hear only pieces of information, so I disconnected the call.*" 2 participants each mentioned boredom and irrelevant contents to disconnect the call. Figure 1(a) shows the reasons for disconnecting the call before completion.

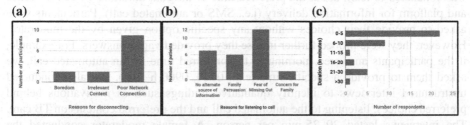

Fig. 1. (a) Reasons for disconnecting the call before completion (b) Reasons to listen to complete call duration and (c) Duration preference for the automated call

Qualitative findings revealed 4 major factors responsible for listening to the complete duration of the call. The foremost being the fear of missing out any health information that may improve their deteriorating health, as reported by 12 out of 27 participants. For instance, a participant stated, "*I want to recover as soon as possible. I don't want to lose on any new information that will worsen my health. Hence, I listened to ensure I consume each information that helps me recover quickly*".

No other means to find relevant information was also one of the foremost reasons for listening to the complete call. As revealed by 7 participants, they did not know any other source to collect information regarding TB treatment. No health administrators provided any information on TB care during DOTS, and they were not aware of any technological means (e.g., internet browsing) to find new information by themselves.

One participant remarked, *"This is the first time anyone in my family has been found TB positive, and we are unaware what to do and what to expect. We do not know where to look for information, or whom to ask."*

6 participants who used a shared mobile phone revealed that a family member persuaded them to listen to the call. A participant, who is a young adult and first TB positive patient in his family said, *"I did not feel like listening to the call, but my father insisted that it will be helpful for me, and instructed me to listen to the complete call."* Another participant reported, *"I was resting in bed when my wife handed me the phone and asked me to listen to the call."* Similarly, 2 participants stated concern for family members' future as a primary motivation to listen to the call. Another participant said, *"I liked the part when the doctor said that the disease would not spread to others if I follow my DOTS regime regularly. I do not want any of my family members to have TB as it is very painful."* These findings are similar to findings presented by Cauldbeck et al. [22] indicating a positive correlation between family support and adherence. Figure 1(b) shows the 4 major motivations to listen to the complete call.

7.2   Preferred Time for Automated Call

Out of 40 participants, 32 preferred receiving automated calls in the evening between 1800–2200 h. Out of the 32 participants, 25 preferred a call between 1900–2100 h, whereas 5 and 2 participants preferred between 1800–1900 h and 2100–2200 h respectively. It is mainly due to its easy availability and convenience to attend a call post working hours. A participant stated, *"I generally come home by 1900 h from work, so I prefer an evening call after it (1900 h)."* A teenage participant stated, *"I don't have a mobile phone myself. My father has a mobile phone who comes around 2000 h. Hence, I can only listen to the call only after 2000 h."*

4 participants preferred the call during a lunch break between 1200–1400 h. A participant explained, *"I get free from work between 1300 to 1400 h for lunch, and generally have nothing else to do. I do not mind listening to a phone call at this time."* Similarly, 4 participants preferred a call in the morning between 0900–1100 h. These participants were retired and preferred receiving a call when other family members had left for work.

7.3   Preferred Gender of Voice for Automated Call

26 participants said that they had no preference for the gender of the voice of the automated call. 10 participants said that a female voice was more appropriate, stating that it reflects compassion. A participant responded, *"A female voice shows more concern and gives you the relief that you will become healthy."* 4 participants said that a male voice was more appropriate, stating it will communicate in poor network connectivity. One participant remarked, *"I could not hear the female voice due to the faulty network, but maybe I would have been able to hear a man. His voice would have been clearer."*

7.4   Preferred Duration of Automated Call

9 of the 40 participants said that they preferred the duration of the call to be less than 5 min. 22 participants said that they preferred the duration of the call to be less than 10 min, stating that they would lose interest in a longer automated call. A participant said, *"If the call comes while I am busy working, I will not listen to it if it is long. So I want the call to be shorter than 5 min."* The remaining participants said that they did not mind listening to a long call, as long as it provided new and relevant information. A participant stated, *"I have the disease and want to get cured quickly. Hence, I don't mind listening to a long call if it provides relevant TB information."* Figure 1(c) shows the participants' preferred duration for an automated call.

7.5   Preference Between Automated Call and SMS

14 participants preferred an SMS over an automated call due to its ability to review it later at convenience. A participant said, *"I prefer to receive the information through text message so that I can access it at another time, in case I'm busy."* 26 participants stated discomfort in reading messages due to smaller screen display and the inability to view and read messages as primary reasons to prefer an automated call over SMS. This finding is similar to the finding proposed by Joshi et al. [17] which suggests a minimal use of SMS-based systems in developing countries because of low-literacy. A participant said, *"I have many unread messages on my phone, so I might miss out on the messages that have information about my TB."*

Participants also emphasized the need to preserve and access the contents of an automated call. One participant mentioned, *"I would have liked the option to record the call. I would have recorded the call and listened to it again whenever I wanted to."*

The data showed a moderate positive correlation ($R = +0.583$) between education and the preference between SMS and automated call. Participants with a higher number of education years preferred receiving information through SMS.

Only 1 participant preferred receiving a message instead of a voice call despite having received no schooling. She claimed, *"Even though I cannot read, I can show the message to my daughter-in-law, and she can interpret it for me. The message can also be forwarded to others."*

7.6   Content Learnability

We calculated the learnability score based on the number of correct answers out of 6 questions (correct answer = 1, incorrect answer = 0). The overall mean learnability was 4.52 (SD = 1.36). The mean learnability score for participants who listened to the complete call and who did not was 4.77 (SD = 1.39) and 4 (SD = 1.15) respectively. We conducted an unpaired sample t-test to determine the learnability differences in both groups. The results indicated a significant increase in learnability ($p = 0.036$) for participants who listened to the complete call as compared to who did not.

We also studied the correlation of learnability scores to age and education years. The results indicate a moderate negative correlation between learnability scores and age ($R = -0.671$). Older participants showed lower learnability as compared to younger

participants. We also observed a moderate positive correlation (R = +0.598) of learnability scores to education years. Participants with higher education years showed increased learnability scores.

7.7 Content Preferences

Majority of the participants preferred information that was immediate and easy to implement, i.e., nutrition, effects of tobacco and alcohol, and government schemes. A participant stated, *"I liked the fact that I was informed to consume specific food items which I could immediately add to my diet."* A few participants also demanded additional information on government schemes as they found it inadequate. For instance, one participant said, *"It should also explain the step through which I can avail the benefits of the government scheme (not limiting to benefits of government schemes)."* 3 participants could not recall the contents, hence could not give their preferences. 10 participants did not provide any preference as all the information was new and equally important for these participants.

8 Conclusion

We conducted a study with 40 participants to understand the content learnability, preferred time of the call, duration, gender of voice and preference of automated call over SMS for an outbound automated call. We identified 4 major motivational factors (i) fear of missing out important information (ii) no alternate source of information (iii) family members' persuasion and (iv) concern for family members for listening to the complete call. We also found poor network connectivity as a prominent reason to disconnect the calls. Thus, an adaptive call strategy is recommended for users residing in poor connectivity areas where repeated attempts should be made for calls that are disconnected in between the conversation. We recommend maximum upto 5 min of calls disseminated between 1900–2100 h for increased adoption due to the availability of the mobile phone and convenience. The call duration can be extended upto 10 min if delivered at a convenient time with new and relevant contents. We also recommend the use of automated calls among users of resource-constrained environment as compared to SMS. The system should allow content preservation through easy recording of an automated call or a call-back feature to later refer the information. Actionable contents immediately and easily applied in their daily routine is recommended to increase adoption of the disseminated contents. Although it is yet to be proven through scientific studies, we believe that our findings can also be applied to other contexts as preferences of call timing, call duration, gender of voice and time of call are often independent to the chosen context of study.

The study had certain limitations. It includes reliance on self-reporting data and the remote interviews conducted via telephone. In the future, we plan to overcome the limitations and further conduct a longitudinal study to statistically prove the findings presented in this paper.

References

1. Amankwaa, I., Boateng, D., Quansah, D.Y., Akuoko, C.P., Evans, C.: Effectiveness of short message services and voice call interventions for antiretroviral therapy adherence and other outcomes: a systematic review and meta-analysis. PLoS ONE 13(9), e0204091 (2018)
2. Cizmic, A.D., Heilmann, R.M., Milchak, J.L., et al.: Impact of interactive voice response technology on primary adherence to bisphosphonate therapy: a randomized controlled trial. Osteoporos. Int. 26, 2131–2136 (2015)
3. Cutrona, S.L., et al.: Improving rates of outpatient influenza vaccination through EHR portal messages and interactive automated calls: a randomized controlled trial. J. Gen. Internal Med. 33(5), 659–667 (2018)
4. Sorathia, K.: Swasthyaa - Strengthening TB Care (2018). http://www.embeddedinteractions. com/Files/Swasthyaa_Introduction.pdf
5. Mishra, S.K.: Telecom Regulatory Authority of India. Press Release No. 22/2019 (2019). https://main.trai.gov.in/sites/default/files/PR_No.22of2019_0.pdf
6. Andersson, C.: Comparison of WEB and Interactive Voice Response (IVR) methods for delivering brief alcohol interventions to hazardous-drinking university students: a randomized controlled trial. Eur. Addict. Res. 21, 240–252 (2015)
7. Derose, S.F., Green, K., Marrett, E., et al.: Automated outreach to increase primary adherence to cholesterol-lowering medications. JAMA Intern. Med. 173, 38 (2013). http://www.embeddedinteractions.com/Files/Swasthyaa_Introduction.pdf
8. Rodrigues, R., et al.: Supporting adherence to anti-retroviral therapy with mobile phone reminders: results from a cohort in South India. PloS One 7(8), e40723 (2012)
9. Stacy, J.N., Schwartz, S.M., Ershoff, D., et al.: Incorporating tailored interactive patient solutions using interactive voice response technology to improve statin adherence: results of a randomized clinical trial in a managed care setting. Popul Health Manag. 12, 241–254 (2009)
10. Helzer, J.E., Rose, G.L., Badger, G.J., et al.: Using interactive voice response to enhance brief alcohol intervention in primary care settings. J. Stud. Alcohol Drugs 69, 251–258 (2008)
11. Ndwe, T.J., Barnard, E., Foko, T.: Correlation between rapid learnability and user preference in IVR systems for developing regions. In: 2013 IST-Africa Conference & Exhibition, pp. 1–9. IEEE, May 2013
12. Tsoli, S., Sutton, S., Kassavou, A.: Interactive voice response interventions targeting behaviour change: a systematic literature review with meta-analysis and meta-regression. BMJ Open 8(2), e018974 (2018)
13. Swendeman, D., Jana, S., Ray, P., Mindry, D., Das, M., Bhakta, B.: Development and pilot testing of daily interactive voice response (IVR) calls to support antiretroviral adherence in India: a mixed-methods pilot study. AIDS Behav. 19(2), 142–155 (2015)
14. Piette, J.D.: Interactive voice response systems in the diagnosis and management of chronic disease. Am. J. Managed Care 6(7), 817–827 (2000)
15. Telecom Regulatory Authority of India. Annual Report 2018 (2019). https://main.trai.gov.in/sites/default/files/Annual_Report_21022019.pdf
16. Suhm, B.: IVR usability engineering using guidelines and analyses of end-to-end calls. In: Gardner-Bonneau, D., Blanchard, H.E. (eds.) Human Factors and Voice Interactive Systems, pp. 1–41. Springer, Boston (2008). https://doi.org/10.1007/978-0-387-68439-0_1
17. Joshi, A., et al.: Supporting treatment of people living with HIV/AIDS in resource limited settings with IVRs. In: Proceedings of the SIGCHI Conference on Human Factors in Computing Systems, pp. 1595–1604. ACM, April 2014

18. Vollmer, W.M., Feldstein, A., Smith, D.H., et al.: Use of health information technology to improve medication adherence. Am. J. Manag. Care **17**, SP79–SP87 (2011)
19. Migneault, J.P., Dedier, J.J., Wright, J.A., et al.: A culturally adapted telecommunication system to improve physical activity, diet quality, and medication adherence among hypertensive African-Americans: a randomized controlled trial. Ann. Behav. Med. **43**, 62–73 (2012)
20. Sherrard, H., Duchesne, L., Wells, G., et al.: Using interactive voice response to improve disease management and compliance with acute coronary syndrome best practice guidelines: a randomized controlled trial. Can. J. Cardiovasc. Nurs. **25**, 10–15 (2015)
21. Haberer, J., Kiwanuka, J., Nansera, D., Wilson, I., Bangsberg, D.: Challenges in using mobile phones for collection of antiretroviral therapy adherence data in a resource-limited setting. AIDS and Behav. **14**, 1294–1301 (2010)
22. Cauldbeck, M., et al.: Adherence to anti-retroviral therapy among HIV patients in Bangalore, India. AIDS Res. Ther. **6**, 7 (2009)
23. Pai, N., et al.: Using automated voice calls to improve adherence to iron supplements during pregnancy: a pilot study. In: ICTD (2013)

Investigating Mobile Banking in Mali: HCI Experience of 'Man in the Street'

Fatoumata G. Camara[1]([✉]), Daouda Traoré[2], Gaëlle Calvary[1], and Amal Kali[3]

[1] Univ. Grenoble Alpes, CNRS, Grenoble INP, LIG, 38000 Grenoble, France
fatoumatag.camara@gmail.com, gaelle.calvary@univ-grenoble-alpes.fr
[2] University of Ségou, Ségou, Mali
daoudatr2008@gmail.com
[3] Orange Labs, 2 Avenue Pierre Marzin, 22300 Lannion, France
amal.kali@orange.com

Abstract. Many studies investigating the use of mobile banking in developing countries focus on specific user groups (i.e., illiterates, low- and semi-literates, the unbanked, and/or poor, rural and underserved communities). Therefore, existing literature fails to provide understandings about mobile banking use in the developing world from a general perspective.

In this paper, we report on a study conducted in Mali to understand the use of a mobile banking service. In total, 77 people coming from different neighborhoods of Bamako and exercising a large spectrum of jobs participated in the study. The paper sheds light on the use of mobile phone and mobile banking in Mali; suggests additional features, particularly related to communication, for the mobile banking service; and discusses findings that are of relevance for Human-Computer Interaction for Development (HCI4D) in general.

Keywords: HCI4D · User studies · Mobile banking · Mali

1 Introduction

The use of mobile banking services in developing countries has been investigated in many studies [11–15,18]. One common point is the focus on specific user groups as highlighted in Table 1. Table 1 shows that previous studies addressing the use of mobile banking services in the developing world have mostly targeted people without literacy or with a low- or semi-literary and/or with low income. If the aforementioned user groups can be assumed to take much advantage from mobile banking, there are not representative of an entire population. By focusing on specific user groups, previous studies addressed specific problems. For instance, Medhi et al. reported that hierarchical navigation and scroll bars hinder the use of money-transfer for non- and semi-literate [12].

Grenoble INP—Institute of Engineering Univ. Grenoble Alpes.

© IFIP International Federation for Information Processing 2019
Published by Springer Nature Switzerland AG 2019
D. Lamas et al. (Eds.): INTERACT 2019, LNCS 11748, pp. 34–42, 2019.
https://doi.org/10.1007/978-3-030-29387-1_3

Table 1. Studies related to mobile banking in the developing world.

Reference	Targeted user group(s)	Location(s)
[11]	Low-income	South Africa
[12]	Non-literate, semi-literate	India, Kenya, the Philippines, South Africa
[13]	Novice, low-literate	India, Kenya, the Philippines, South Africa
[14]	Low-income, low-literate	India, Kenya, the Philippines, South Africa
[15]	Poor people	Kiberia (a slum in Naorobi), Bukura (a village in Western Kenya)
[18]	Low-income, low-literate	Kenya

Investigating the use of mobile banking in the developing world with larger audiences is of great importance in order to get more general understandings and their implications for future services design and development. In this work, we report on a questionnaire study conducted to understand the use of a mobile banking service in Mali. The study was mainly carried out in Bamako, the capital city, but involved a sample of participants selected independently from gender, degree of education and literacy, profession, income, and residential area. In addition to shedding light on usage around the mobile banking service and suggesting new features for the mobile banking service, we report interesting findings that are of relevance for Human-Computer Interaction for Development (HCI4D) [10].

2   Context of the Research

Mali is located in West Africa with an area of 1.241.238 square kilometers and a population of 18.542.000 inhabitants [2]. French is the official language in Mali, but remains mainly the administrative one. Indeed, the majority of Malians mostly communicates with each other in Bambara in the everyday life: Bambara is the national language. According to statistics from the United Nations Educational, Scientific and Cultural Organization (UNESCO), the literacy rate among the population aged from 15 years has been increasing in Mali and reached 33.07% in 2015 [1].

The mobile banking service under investigation offers the primary functionalities of such a system: money transfer as well as cash deposit and withdraw. The service also provides additional functionalities, which are purchase of communication credit and tickets for events (e.g., concerts), bills payment (e.g., TV subscriptions, electricity, insurance), cash delivery, remittance transfers to partnered merchants (e.g., restaurants, gas stations, pharmacies), and access to different types of information (e.g., account balance, transactions fees).

The service users can complete transactions using own phones (through USSD or the mobile application) and/or at dedicated kiosks (Fig. 1) or partnered corner shops widely spread across cities.

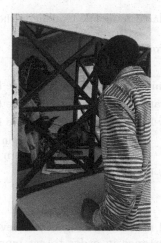

Fig. 1. A customer completing a transaction at a dedicated kiosk in Ségou.

It is important to mention that the mobile application is only available for Android devices. It is also important to mention that the mobile application of the service under investigation is not a user-friendly one. An expert evaluation revealed that the app suffers from major usability problems, particularly in terms of consistency.

3   The Study and Participants

We investigated the use of the mobile banking service through a questionnaire study, which consisted of two phases: the pre-questionnaire and the actual questionnaire. In both phases, the questionnaire was paper-based and administrated as a face-to-face structured interview. The researcher was in charge of asking questions and filling the paper-based material with the respondent's answers. All participants were compensated with a communication credit card.

3.1   The Pre-questionnaire

The pre-questionnaire was aimed to assess the pertinence of identified topics to be addressed; assess the appropriateness of questions formulation and, possibly, identify, other relevant topics to be considered. The pre-questionnaire was composed of closed, but also open questions in order to get a better understanding of spectrum of answers for some topics.

The pre-questionnaire was tested with 26 people in total. Even though the whole study was mainly carried out in Bamako, the pre-questionnaire phase involved 9 people from Ségou (a region of Mali laying in the south-center part of the country). Respondents were 17 men and 7 women, aged from 19 to 74 (mean: 37) and exercising different jobs: 1 human resources manager, 1 jeweler,

2 chauffeurs, 1 sales representative, 1 accountant, 1 program director, 1 agent of the mobile banking service, 4 teachers, 5 students, 1 official, 1 guard, 2 administrators, 1 military man, 3 retirees, and 1 domestic worker. With such a wide range of professions, the pre-questionnaire phase involved people with different levels of education, literacy, and income. The 26 respondents were also from different neighborhoods of Bamako and Ségou and, some of them, had close ties with rural areas. For instance, the domestic worker has received no formal education at all; the chauffeur lives in Bamako while his family (his wife and two children) stays in the village.

Prequestionnaire sessions were audio-recorded and lasted 25 min in average. Recordings were subsequently analyzed using content analysis.

3.2   The Questionnaire

The pre-questionnaire phase allowed to identify possible answers for the open questions as well as additional relevant topics. On the basis of these outcomes, we elaborated a second version of the questionnaire (i.e., the actual questionnaire) with only closed questions and organized around the following topics: (a) demographic information (age, gender, marital status); (b) use of the mobile phone (number of phones and SIMs, communication means, Internet usage); (c) usage of the mobile banking service (types and purposes of transactions, means for completing transactions, frequency of use, communication around transactions, satisfaction with the mobile banking service); (d) relationship with traditional banking institutions and mobile banking-bank accounts association; (e) questionnaire administration conditions (language, social tie between the enumerator and the respondent, location, compensation acceptance, photo taking).

77 people responded to the questionnaire: 53% male and 47% female aged from 19 to 59 (mean age: 30). As respondents were randomly selected, we encountered them everywhere: in homes, at work places but, also and mainly, on the street. In the overall, respondents were from over 20 neighborhoods of Bamako and exercised more than 30 different jobs at the time of the study. The neighborhoods involved in the study included both areas labeled as 'advantaged' and areas labeled as 'disadvantaged'. Participants' jobs also included professions requiring a high degree of literacy and with high income (e.g., engineer) as well as professions requiring only a low degree (or no) literacy and with lower income (e.g., taxi driver, tailor).

4   Findings

The findings reported in following sections are based on only data from the actual questionnaire phase.

4.1   Current Usage of Mobile Phone

Mobile phone use in Africa has been previously investigated (e.g., in [19,20]). The aim here is not to compare our results with the ones reported elsewhere but, rather, to get a good understanding of the respondents profiles.

All respondents were mobile phone users. Data highlighted a widespread use of dual SIM phones since 59% of the participants declared to own only one phone while 73% declared to use two SIMs with the same phone (mostly from different Mobile Network Operators).

Smartphones appeared to be the predominant type of phone among our respondents' mobile phones. 81% of mobile phones owned by questionnaire respondents were Smartphones. This high percentage of Smartphone ownership is not surprising and can be explained by the high penetration of low-cost Smartphones in the Malian market.

The majority of respondents declared to have Internet connection on their phone through data (83%) and appeared to be heavy mobile apps users. For instance, 75% of them declared to use WhatsApp for voice calls and 62% for messaging; 66% of them declared to use YouTube.

4.2   Current Usage of the Mobile Banking Service

In [16], Ndiwalana et al. present a survey, that did not focus on people without bank account or with low-literacy or low-income, to study mobile banking use in Uganda. Indeed, in [16], respondents included people with no formal schooling as well as people with degree (or above); people with no personal account as well as people with an account. Additionally, if the survey was only carried out it Kampala (the capital of Uganda), according to the authors, many parts of the city were involved in the study. Considering the aforementioned, the work presented in [16] is particularly relevant to our work.

In this section, we report our findings and discuss them in relation to the ones of Ndiwalana et al.

Users. All our respondents were users of the mobile banking service. Yet, the study involved illiterate as well as literate and high-income as well as low-income individuals. In addition, among respondents, 49% had at least one bank account and 32% several bank accounts. Only 18% of respondents did not own a bank account at the time of the study. Therefore, as in Uganda, not only the user groups predominantly addressed in the literature are mobile banking users in Mali. Indeed, in [16], 94% of the survey respondents reported a high level of literacy in own language and 73% declared having access to other financial services through a personal account in a formal institution.

Purposes of Transactions. Data highlighted that respondents use the mobile banking service to complete mostly the following transactions: money deposit into their own account (99%), money transfer to someone else's account (97%), withdrawal of money sent by another person (100%), communication credit purchase (93%), and bills payment (54%). Only 5% of respondents declared to use the service for other purposes.

We further investigated purposes of money transfers between individuals. Unsurprisingly, social mutual aid appeared as one of the main purposes for transactions within our respondents (Fig. 2). We analyzed the social circles involved in such transactions and data highlighted that: 87% of respondents send to and

receive money from the immediate family, 64% to and from the extended family, 22% to and from friends, 12% to and from acquittances, 9% to and from colleagues.

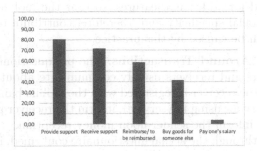

Fig. 2. Purposes of money transfers between individuals.

These findings are globally aligned with the ones reported by Ndiwalana and colleagues: providing and receiving financial support from people is the main purpose for money transfers; mobile banking is also used for other diverse purposes. However, it is important to highlight that the percentage of respondents sending and receiving money from the immediate family is higher within our sample (in comparison to the sample investigated by Ndiwalana et al.) and that the percentage respondents sending and receiving money from the extended family is even significantly higher within our respondents sample. This finding likely highlights differences in relationships between social circles in Mali and in Uganda.

Frequency of Use. Within respondents, 35% declared to use the service several times a week, 23% several times a month, 22% up to several times a day, 9% once a week, 7% once a month, and 4% several times a year. These results suggest that our participants are heavier mobile banking users compared to participants in the survey conducted by Ndiwalana et al. in which the majority declared using mobile money at least one a month.

The findings discussed above highlight that a large percentage of participants are intensive and frequent users of the mobile banking service. Therefore, the user groups predominantly addressed in the literature are not the only ones to take benefit from mobile banking in Mali.

Means for Completing Transactions. USSD, dedicated kiosks, and corner shops represent the different means for accessing to the mobile banking service. All respondents declared to use the service using the phone through USSD and dedicated kiosks/corner shops. Despite 81% of respondents possessing Smartphones, only 13% declared to use the mobile app for the mobile banking service.

Interestingly, we discovered that the sender, the receiver and, eventually, the operator at the dedicated kiosk or the corner shop are not the only ones involved in money transfers between individuals. Indeed, 39% participants declared to charge other people to send or receive money on their behalf and 15% reported to

have sent or received money on the behalf of other people. Further, we discovered that relationships between the ones and the others reflect social hierarchies in the Malian society: parents, older people, and employers charge respectively children, younger people, employees to complete transactions on their behalf. This finding highlights the need for additional features, so that the mobile banking service can support this social specificity and, therefore, contribute to reducing errors and scams that can be caused by this practice.

Communication Around Transactions. The pre-questionnaire phase highlighted that senders and receivers usually communicate about money transfers to: check whether the receiver is registered with the mobile banking service (registration is necessary for using the service), inform the receiver prior and/or after sending money, or inform the sender upon money reception.

Data collected through the actual questionnaire confirmed, indeed, that: 92% of participants communicate with the receiver before and after they send money; 83% of participants communicate with the sender before and after they receive money. However, since the mobile banking service does not include any communication features, respondents declared to rely on other means in order to communicate around money transfers: standard calls for all of them (100%) and SMS for 30%. Mobile apps such as WhatsApp and Viber appeared to be only a little involved in such communications.

On the basis of this finding, we suggest that the mobile banking service integrates a feature allowing the user to check if a given phone number or contact is registered with the service. Additionally, we suggest that the mobile banking service proposes to initiate a call or send a text (that can be automatically generated using the transaction information) after sending or receiving money. Considering that money transfers can involve several people, the user could be provided with the possibility to send a text to one more recipients.

Satisfaction with the Mobile Banking Service. We recorded a high rate of satisfaction from questionnaire respondents with the mobile banking service. More than half of respondents (60%) are satisfied; 39% are fairly satisfied; only 1% declared to be poorly satisfied.

5 Discussion and Future Work

This paper reports on a study conducted in Mali to investigate the use of a mobile banking service. To the best of our knowledge, our work is the first of the kind to address this country. Unlike most previous studies related to mobile banking use in the developing world, we did not focus on specific user groups (illiterates, low- and semi-literates, the unbanked, and/or poor, rural and underserved communities). As a result, we shed light on usage around the mobile phone and mobile banking in Mali from a more global perspective. We highlighted countries specificities. We also discussed differences between Mali and Uganda.

Despite our respondents being, for many, Smartphones owners and mobile apps users, only 13% declared using the mobile banking service through the

mobile app. Indeed, our expert evaluation of the service mobile app highlighted major usability issues. Therefore, in our opinion, poor usability explains the low adoption of the service mobile application. Nevertheless, data showed a high rate of satisfaction among respondents. This suggests that utility clearly takes precedence here over usability since the mobile banking service does serve a purpose. Furthermore, it is important to remember that our study participants included people who should not be not able to use the mobile banking service mobile app because of literacy. So, with our aim to address the 'man in the street' (instead of focusing on literacy, for instance), we also highlight that good usability matters for every user and identified different additional features to improve the mobile banking service. As a consequence, future studies should shift the focus beyond literacy to focus on utility and consider usability for all. This recommendation should be considered for HCI4D projects in general since a broader review of the literature highlighted that many different studies focus on specific users groups [4–9,17,20]. To do so, we propose that future work investigates adaptation to the context of use as a means to address literacy. If there is no consensus on the definition of the context of use, adaptation generally takes the user into account. We propose considering degree of literacy through the user dimension of the context of use. As such, research on adaptation can take advantage of knowledge from HCI4D (and other relevant ones) to tackle illiteracy. Literacy issues, of all kinds, would be then addressed in less stereotypical manner particularly considering that not only developing countries face such issues [3].

In future work, we plan to investigate further in order to understand the extent to which cultural values influence technology use and adoption in Mali. In particular, we would like to investigate whether some cultural values held by Malians could explain people's satisfaction with the mobile banking service studied in this work.

References

1. UNESCO Institute for Statistics. http://uis.unesco.org/en/country/ML
2. World population prospects: the 2017 revision (2017). https://population.un.org/wpp/
3. Chaudry, B.M., Connelly, K.H., Siek, K.A., Welch, J.L.: Mobile interface design for low-literacy populations. In: Proceedings of the 2nd ACM SIGHIT International Health Informatics Symposium, IHI 2012, pp. 91–100. ACM, New York (2012)
4. Chetty, M., Tucker, W., Blake, E.: Developing locally relevant software applications for rural areas: a South African example. In: Proceedings of the 2004 Annual Research Conference of the South African Institute of Computer Scientists and Information Technologists on IT Research in Developing Countries, SAICSIT 2004, pp. 239–243. South African Institute for Computer Scientists and Information Technologists, Republic of South Africa (2004)
5. DeRenzi, B., et al.: E-IMCI: improving pediatric health care in low-income countries. In: Proceedings of the SIGCHI Conference on Human Factors in Computing Systems, CHI 2008, pp. 753–762. ACM, New York (2008)
6. Dodson, L.L., Sterling, S.R., Bennett, J.K.: Minding the gaps: cultural, technical and gender-based barriers to mobile use in oral-language Berber communities in

Morocco. In: Proceedings of the Sixth International Conference on Information and Communication Technologies and Development: Full Papers, ICTD 2013, vol. 1, pp. 79–88. ACM, New York (2013). https://doi.org/10.1145/2516604.2516626

7. Gandhi, R., Veeraraghavan, R., Toyama, K., Ramprasad, V.: Digital green: participatory video for agricultural extension. In: International Conference on Information and Communication Technologies and Development, pp. 1–10. IEEE (2007)

8. Ghosh, K., Parikh, T.S., Chavan, A.L.: Design considerations for a financial management system for rural, semi-literate users. In: CHI 2003 Extended Abstracts on Human Factors in Computing Systems, CHI EA 2003, pp. 824–825. ACM, New York (2003)

9. Grisedale, S., Graves, M., Grünsteidl, A.: Designing a graphical user interface for healthcare workers in rural India. In: Proceedings of the ACM SIGCHI Conference on Human Factors in Computing Systems, CHI 1997, pp. 471–478. ACM, New York (1997)

10. Ho, M., Smyth, T., Kam, M., Dearden, A.: Human computer interaction for international development: the past, present and future. Inf. Technol. Int. Dev. 5(4), 1–18 (2009)

11. Ivatury, G., Pickens, M.: Mobile-phone banking and low-income customers: evidence from South Africa. CGAP, United Nations Foundation, Vodafone Group Foundation (2006)

12. Medhi, I., Gautama, S.N., Toyama, K.: A comparison of mobile money-transfer UIs for non-literate and semi-literate users. In: Proceedings of the SIGCHI Conference on Human Factors in Computing Systems, CHI 2009, pp. 1741–1750. ACM, New York (2009)

13. Medhi, I., Patnaik, S., Brunskill, E., Gautama, S.N., Thies, W., Toyama, K.: Designing mobile interfaces for novice and low-literacy users. ACM Trans. Comput.-Hum. Interact. 18(1) (2011)

14. Medhi, I., Ratan, A., Toyama, K.: Mobile-banking adoption and usage by low-literate, low-income users in the developing world. In: Aykin, N. (ed.) IDGD 2009. LNCS, vol. 5623, pp. 485–494. Springer, Heidelberg (2009). https://doi.org/10.1007/978-3-642-02767-3_54

15. Morawczynski, O., Pickens, M.: Poor people using mobile financial services: observations on customer usage and impact from M-PESA. CGAP Brief (2009)

16. Ndiwalana, A., Morawczynski, O., Popov, O.: Mobile money use in Uganda: a preliminary study 2010, January 2010

17. Parmar, V., Groeneveld, G., Jalote-Parmar, A., Keyson, D.: Tangible user interface for increasing social interaction among rural women. In: Proceedings of the 3rd International Conference on Tangible and Embedded Interaction, TEI 2009, pp. 139–145. ACM, New York (2009)

18. Ratan, A.: Using technology to deliver financial services to low-income households: a preliminary study of Equity Bank and M-PESA customers in Kenya. Technical report, Microsoft Research (01 2008)

19. Watson, M., Atuick, E.A.: Cell phones and alienation among Bulsa of Ghana's upper east region: "the call calls you away". Afr. Stud. Rev. 58, 113–132 (2015)

20. Wyche, S., Simiyu, N., Othieno, M.E.: Understanding women's mobile phone use in rural Kenya: an affordance-based approach. Mob. Media Commun. 7, 94–110 (2018). https://doi.org/10.1177/2050157918776684

Towards Safe Spaces Online:
A Study of Indian Matrimonial Websites

Vishal Sharma(✉), Bonnie Nardi(✉), Juliet Norton(✉), and A. M. Tsaasan(✉)

UC Irvine, Irvine, CA, USA
{vishals1,nardi,jnnorton,tsaasan}@uci.edu

Abstract. We studied Indian matrimonial websites that facilitate arranged marriages, focusing on how they are designed to foster safety and inclusivity. We conducted 20 interviews with marriage seekers and parents to understand how they use the sites. We examined government policy, technical affordances, human services, and the presence of the social network. We contrast matrimonial sites to dating websites in the Indian context. Matrimonial websites' affordances suggest ways we might make other kinds of sites safer.

Keywords: Matrimonial sites · Safe spaces · Arranged marriage ·
Safety · Inclusion · Marginalized communities ·
Computer-mediated communication · India

1 Introduction

90% of all Indian marriages are arranged marriages [59,83]. Indian matrimonial websites offer what we refer to as a "safe space" by helping family members *stay involved in and watching over the matrimonial process*. They promote inclusivity by *facilitating spousal search for persons from marginalized groups including the disabled, widowed, divorced, and HIV positive*.

Meeting someone online in any context is fraught with dangers—from physical safety to fraudulent financial dealings to deceptions of greater and lesser magnitude [26,58]. The perils of dating websites are well known (see [14,22,86]). Vulnerable individuals operating more or less solo are often taken advantage of [45].

Such vulnerability has not historically been a problem In India, where people have lived in co-located joint families of three to four generations taking part in shared activities [16,69]. These activities include arranging marriages; the extended family and friends participate in all stages of the matrimonial process, from spousal search to the wedding, and even beyond as the couple adjusts to a new life. However, urbanization and influences from other cultures have transformed Indian family structure, with a decreasing number of joint families and an increasing number of nuclear families [69]. As families engage in less daily interaction, there are fewer opportunities for the extended family to take part in

© IFIP International Federation for Information Processing 2019
Published by Springer Nature Switzerland AG 2019
D. Lamas et al. (Eds.): INTERACT 2019, LNCS 11748, pp. 43–66, 2019.
https://doi.org/10.1007/978-3-030-29387-1_4

the matrimonial process [4,69]. Matrimonial websites open the pool of potential spouses to those beyond the family's immediate social network, a network that shrinks as the Indian diaspora grows.

We use the concept of safe space from the work of Scheuerman et al. [67] who studied safe spaces for transgender people. They defined a safe space as a "conceptual space ... to denote safety from any emotional harm and othering (being treated as abnormal or alien)". We use the work of Karusala and Kumar [38] who studied women's safety in India. They emphasized the role of the *social network* in providing safety by observing that women felt safe when *family or friends were present and concerned about their safety* [38]. These broad concepts of safety go beyond the specific populations these authors studied.

Safety and inclusivity are related: if a person is excluded from a social space, online or offline, the absence of like-minded others reduces the chances of finding help in unsafe situations and in preventing unsafe situations from arising in the first place. The presence of social support creates an inclusive space, providing safety to form relationships. For example, the internet affords a safe space for queer people to explore their sexuality in the presence of sympathetic others [11, 67]. We define a safe space as an environment where the presence of a social network has the capacity to create safety, both social and psychological.

A key motivation for our study is to respond to Al-Dawood et al.'s [5] point that "[The] HCI literature has chiefly focused on how technology is used in cultures where premarital relationships ... such as dating, flirting, and mixed-gender gatherings are the norms and accepted." Indian matrimonial websites were introduced in the 1990s, and have been used extensively [53], yet they have not been studied very much. For example, since 2006, over 26 million people made use of Matrimony.com [81], but HCI research scarcely touches on these websites. To the best of our knowledge, this paper is the first HCI study to explore the features and services of matrimonial sites and how they operate as a safe space. We ask the following research questions:

RQ1: How do matrimonial websites foster safety and inclusivity?
RQ2: How to foster safety and inclusivity on social networking and dating sites?

We discuss how Indian matrimonial websites build on traditional cultural values of Indian arranged marriages rather than disrupting them. We explore how tradition and history can be values in design. Blevis et al. [12] note that, "As designers we are up against a culture of planned obsolescence...that [fails to] recall and sustain history–sometimes very ancient history." We investigate safety and inclusivity through an empirical examination of matrimonial sites and analysis of interviews with users. This paper has multiple contributions: (a) to understand how digital technology supports a widely practiced form of marriage; (b) to understand how matrimonial websites have carefully designed technical affordances and social supports for promoting safety that may be useful in other contexts; and, (c) to promote reflective HCI that critiques the way we conduct and approach research impacting people globally (see [21,78]).

2 Related Work

We discuss research related to safe spaces in three topical areas: children's use of the internet, online queer communities, and online dating.

2.1 Online Platforms for Children

The increase in children's use of the internet has raised questions regarding safety, and the literature has provided foundational work that informs our own. The HCI community has studied parents' concerns and involvement in sharing their children's information online [7,19,29,48,87]. Online safety measures for children include regular communication between parents and children [27], direct parental participation in children's internet use [32], blocking software and filters [19], and community education [77]. Ammari et al. [7] note that parents follow *preventive strategies* such as telling family members their preferences for sharing their children's content, and creating separate profiles for the children. Parents use *corrective strategies* such as insisting others remove content related to their children [7] and *parental disclosure management* such as deciding with their partner what child-related content to share online [7]. However, parents may post about their children's behavior, development, and appearance [48]. It is not always clear when parents freely share and when they attempt to limit their children's online exposure.

2.2 Online Queer Communities

Members of the queer community face challenges offline including social exclusion [64], bullying [57], harassment [57,90], threats [57], verbal taunts [90], and mental distress [64]. They may be subjected to disapproval and derogation [41]. Thus, many turn to the internet for a measure of safety. Sometimes anonymity allows them to explore and discuss their sexuality [55]. The self-selected nature of online communities allows queer people to find others who will be accepting [67]. Woodland [88] observes the formation of virtual queer spaces to "provide safe(r) spaces for queer folk to gather." Fraser [28] notes that "Websites designed by or for queer youth ... [provide a] safe space devoid of homophobia ... [to] explore sexuality, find information, and make friends."

Roy [65] observes that the internet has become an essential part of the Indian queer movement, noting that in the 1990s, the internet provided a safe space when offline contact among members was impossible [47]. Bhattacharjya and Ganesh [11] argue that the internet helps the Indian queer community by buttressing transnational queer rights movements [11], noting that "the need for [a] safe space is probably the single most important factor that underlies the formation of digital queer spaces" [11]. The presence of peer support in queer communities is a crucial part of safety, and we build on this observation in our formulation of space spaces with respect to arranged marriage.

2.3   Online Dating

The most obvious comparison to matrimonial sites is dating websites, so we review the literature on this topic. Dating websites enable people to meet without implying that marriage will be of interest [6]. Philips and Morrissey [58] wryly observe: "[T]he online world is not [entirely] a safe place and the internet is not necessarily a superhighway to love." Anonymity allows people to behave differently than they would in real life [25,34]. They may create an "ideal self" which is not authentic [24,30]. They may misrepresent information about physical appearance, age, criminal history, and marital status [25,34,84]. Serious misrepresentations reduce safety, giving rise to harassment [45], romance scams [14], and identity fraud [86]. Online dating may result in financial loss, blackmailing, and exploitation of a participant's vulnerable emotional state [22].

Masden and Edwards [45] note that harassment is a common issue. Smith and Duggan [73] report that 42% of female participants and 17% of male participants experienced harassment on dating websites. Witty [86] highlights identity fraud including creating profiles with stolen pictures, declaring love at a very early stage, and requesting to move the relationship offline in order to financially deceive. Safety in online dating is a complex and evolving concern [60]. Daters are aware of at least some of the pitfalls. They may try to overcome them by reading signals and deconstructing cues [82] such as email addresses [20], personal homepage links [40], and the messages' timing [85]. Ellison et al. [24] underline the importance of even small cues in assessing a potential date, such as spelling and the way messages are presented.

3   Background

To understand the context of this paper, basic information about practices of Indian arranged marriage and the working of matrimonial sites is needed. Much of this information may be unfamiliar to many of our readers and will be useful in interpreting our findings.

3.1   Arranged Marriage in India

Historically, the process of finding a spouse in India involved long discussions between family members that eventuated in unanimous agreement [17]. This pattern still holds and has not changed despite many other changes in Indian society [59]. Marriage is not merely the union of two individuals [69], but an alliance between two families [8]. Marriage thus has a huge impact on families' everyday lives, and its arrangement requires meticulous attention [63]. Marriage seekers' relatives and neighbors discreetly (even secretly), perform background checks on potential spouses and the potential spouse's family, examining matters such as infidelity and criminal activity.

If both families find a potential match desirable, they move ahead with the next stage in which the marriage seekers meet, talk, and exchange life histories,

goals, and desires [69]. These meetings take place in a formal setting, in the families' presence [59]. If the potential spouses like each other, they confirm their consent to marry. An exchange of gifts between the families then marks the commencement of the new relationship, followed by the marriage ceremony [59].

Xiaohe and Whyte [89] note that arranged marriages may be misconceived as forced marriages. However, arranged marriage typically requires the informed consent of the future spouses [79]. In South Asian countries including India, Pakistan, Indonesia, and Bangladesh [50,56,59], as well as most Middle Eastern countries [5,56], arranged marriages are the most common means of finding a spouse. Penn [56] remarks that arranged marriages, "[practiced by] half of the world's population ... will become more pervasive in the future since they predominate in countries with high rates of population growth."

3.2 Indian Matrimonial Websites

Most users of matrimonial websites in India utilize three websites: Shaadi.com, Bharatmatrimony.com, and Jeevansathi.com [83]. Business has grown dramatically as the sites provide efficient spousal search when conventional methods of locating a spouse are not working [37]. They allow users to create profiles within regional, religious, community-specific, and linguistic sub-sites [83]. For instance, a marriage seeker can create a profile on Shaadi.com's regional sub-site, Tamilmatrimony.com.

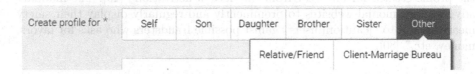

Fig. 1. Profile creation on Shaadi.com

Matrimonial websites allow the marriage seeker and friends and family to create and contribute to an extensive online profile with rich information about the potential spouse (Fig. 1). Such information is consistent with typical Indian practices of thoroughly evaluating potential spouses. For example, the mother of a marriage seeker might begin a search by setting up an online profile for her son. She specifies his personal information such as age, weight, and marital status, as well as his preferences for food, alcohol, and smoking. Profiles specify caste, geographic location, native language, the number of siblings, parents' occupations, and time and place of the marriage seeker's birth for horoscope matching [76]. Profiles include education and career-related information such as the marriage seeker's salary and employer, hobbies and photos [76]. The profile shows the profile creator and the marriage seeker's relationship (Fig. 2). The profile creator examines the profiles of potential spouses and shortlists them based

on compatibility with the marriage seeker. Everyone involved, including the marriage seeker, discusses the profiles to further narrow down the selection. Once everyone approves the profiles, the profile creator sends connection requests to potential spouses. A connection request is similar to a friend request on Facebook, with a brief personal note including a greeting and contact information. Although there are a few Indian-produced dating websites for casual dating, people use only matrimonial websites when there is a serious intent of marrying.

Here is a typical marriage seeking scenario taken from the "Marriage Success Stories" section of Jeevansathi.com. Vasudha, a 31-year-old woman, describes her matrimonial experience:

> When [my family and I were searching for a potential spouse] I received a request from [a] Delhi guy named Gaurav ... [Our] parents spoke to each other and found it fine to take [the relationship] forward ... We spoke on calls for around two months and then we met ... After around 6 months our parents met, everybody was fine to take it forward ... We got engaged on 26th Nov 2017 and finally married on 11th Dec 2017.

In June 2016, the Ministry of Communication and Information Technology mandated that matrimonial websites authenticate users with proof of identity and address [80]. It is compulsory that "Service providers should make a declaration that the website is strictly for matrimonial purposes and not a dating website and should not be used for posting obscene material" [49]. The government requires records of IP addresses: "Matrimonial websites should store the IP address of the profile creator for one year from the date of activation" [49]. The mandate advised matrimonial websites to prominently and regularly display their safety measures and to "[caution] users against possible fraudsters who asks for favors, money, etc." [80].

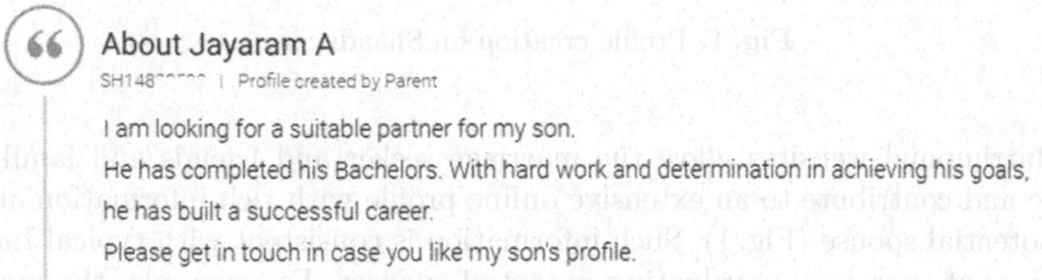

About Jayaram A
SH148°°°°° | Profile created by Parent

I am looking for a suitable partner for my son.
He has completed his Bachelors. With hard work and determination in achieving his goals, he has built a successful career.
Please get in touch in case you like my son's profile.

Fig. 2. Profile creator and marriage seeker's relationship shown on Shaadi.com

The government requires that matrimonial websites not allow login until the company has verified the phone number and email address of the profile creator. Verification is performed through One-Time Password, valid for one login. Then the website staff screens the profile before it goes live. After an initial screening, every time the user updates the profile, the staff screens again. The websites explicitly state on their homepages that they provide services only to marriage

seekers. For example, Jeevansathi.com says: "Jeevansathi is only meant for users with a bonafide [sic] intent to enter into a matrimonial alliance and is not meant for users interested in dating only." Once documents are uploaded and verified, the websites provide trust badges. For example, Bharatmatrimony.com provides five trust badges: an identity badge that requires uploading a government-issued ID, a professional badge to upload certificates of education, a social badge to link Facebook or LinkedIn profiles, a reference badge to add personal or professional references, and an employment badge to upload a pay slip or proof of employment.

Matrimonial websites take verification very seriously. Staff verify the marriage seeker's identity and address by checking public documents such as the driver's license and passport. Because the websites are supervised by a government agency, the Cyber Crime Investigation Cell, the sites have access to official records. Jeevansathi.com checks the credibility of a profile by an in-person visit to the marriage seeker's address. A "relationship executive" phones within 48 h of profile creation and schedules a visit, collecting copies of the official documents to confirm the date of birth, address, highest educational qualification, occupation, income, and marital status. In case of a discrepancy between the information on the profile and the documents, the websites suspend the profile until clarifications can be obtained.

The websites also provide easy reporting of threats to the security team. For example, here are few threats that a marriage seeker can report on Shaadi.com:

1. "Fake/Misleading profile: incorrect profile information, the phone number is incorrect/unreachable, more than one profile, photo belongs to someone else."
2. "Member is already married/engaged: I know this person, told by a member over chat/phone, found through social media/acquaintance."

Some matrimonial websites are responsive to diverse life circumstances as people seek suitable marriage prospects. For example, they provide services to the divorced and widowed, and people whose marriages have been annulled. The marriage seeker selects the marital statuses acceptable to him or her while creating a profile. For example, Jeevansathi.com has these statuses: "Never Married", "Awaiting Divorce", "Divorced", "Widowed", and "Annulled". Once the marriage seeker creates the profile, the website does not allow a change in the marital status in order to protect the integrity of the information. Other sites have branched out to other demographics, e.g., 40plusmatrimony.com caters to those over 40. Matrimonial websites reach out to people who are not English literate, who do not have access to digital services, or who may not be digitally literate enough to use such services. The websites have "matrimony bureaus", which are local agencies with human mediators to assist in the online process [54]. A relationship executive meets with the marriage seeker and helps set up a profile. The executive navigates through potential spouses' profiles and describes the profile information to the marriage seeker who notes the details of profiles they like. Later the marriage seeker shares the information with the family for shortlisting. The executive continues to be available until the last stage of marriage.

4   Methods

We interviewed 20 people including eight men and 12 women. Participants ranged in age from 25 to 60. We interviewed two parents, three siblings, a married couple, 11 prospective spouses, and two matrimony bureau personnel. 15 participants were living in India, one in Canada, and four in the United States at the time of the interviews. The families of those in the U.S. and Canada and their potential spouses were living in India. Participants were from the Hindu religious community which comprises 80% of India's population [36]. We recruited participants using personal contacts, snowball sampling, and by posting recruiting messages on social media. Recruiting and interviewing took place from February–April 2018.

The first author interviewed people over the phone in English, one of the official languages of India and spoken widely [9]. We chose telephone interviews because participants were living in various locations. Each interview took between 45–60 min and was audio-recorded. All participants were anonymized in transcripts. We have included grammatical errors in interview segments quoted in the Findings. We asked participants about their online matrimony process, for reflections on their experiences, and what they think of the safety measures that matrimonial websites provide.

We studied Shaadi.com, Bharatmatrimony.com, and Jeevansathi.com, analyzing their affordances and some user posts. We created dummy profiles because profiles were not accessible without registration. We did not personally contact anyone on the sites. Names used in the paper are pseudonyms. We followed a grounded theory approach [18] to analyze interviews. The authors met weekly for five months, first reading through the data and performing coding at the sentence level, iterating multiple times. We used codes such as "social network presence", "government involvement", "policy implementation", and "technical affordances". Then we grouped the codes into higher level categories such as "inclusivity", "safety", "trust", "empowerment", and "credibility". Out of these, we formed higher-level themes. We then found quotes in which participants' thoughts clearly expressed their ideas and feelings on the topics we present in Findings. The different stakeholders' perspectives–marriage seekers, parents, siblings, and matrimony bureau personnel–were all considered to provide validity to our work.

5   Findings

We discuss how matrimonial websites provide safety to marriage seekers. Our participants compared dating websites to their use of matrimonial websites. We discovered that matrimonial websites not only provide measures of safety to all who use them but also open new marital possibilities of inclusion for people with disabilities and for inter-caste marriages.

5.1   Alternatives to Dating Websites

We found three principal features of Indian matrimonial sites that foster safety: (1) They support the involvement of family and friends in the search for a spouse; (2) They provide detailed information for selecting a spouse, integral to the process of finding a spouse in an arranged marriage; and, (3) They perform careful profile verification to protect users from deception and shady practices. These three features stand in contrast to dating websites which do not provide detailed information, do not support the family's participation, and do not provide information verification.

Our interview participants reported that on dating websites a person cannot be sure about another person's intentions. For example, Aarti, a 27-year-old woman working as a software engineer in Bangalore, said:

"I have been on Tinder, but my motive to be on Tinder was definitely not to find a life partner. I used Tinder because I moved to a new city where I did not know anyone. So, I thought that it would be a good way to connect with new people and to get to know the city a little better. But I personally have never thought about these dating websites as an avenue for exploring [and searching] life partner. I think it is the general perception around these dating websites. Obviously, people also have very different motives on these dating websites. Due to such things, one does not consider them [for searching spouse] ... [A matrimonial website] I think is a formal platform and you know that there will be high chances that only people who are interested to get married would be present on the platform ... [because it is] only dedicated to the·purpose where guys and girls meet so that they can get married."

Aarti told us that on matrimonial websites if she feels unsafe or if someone threatens her *"I can at least ... contact the website administrators. I can report the issue [or threat]."* She mentioned that on dating websites *"[Y]ou cannot do this ... you have nowhere [and no one] to reach out [in case of a threat]."*

Interviewees stressed that matrimonial sites facilitate the involvement of family and friends unlike the complete lack of such involvement on dating sites. Simran, a 29-year-old with a business degree, worked in human resources at Fidelity Investments in Bangalore. Her parents lived near New Delhi. She told us that *"[My] parents created [my] profile on Jeevansathi.com, Shaadi.com, and Bharatmatrimony.com ... [My parents and I] were active on these websites. If someone has shown interest in [my] profile, I would go and check the profile. If I like it ... I will discuss it with my parents. Similarly, if my parents like a profile, they will tell me about it and I would go through [the profile]."* She mentioned that *"I started using [matrimonial websites] around 2013 ... It took [me] two and a half year to find [a] spouse ... So, everything was finalized in 2015 ... Before that, I met at least 20–25 [prospective spouses]."* She ended up meeting her husband on Jeevansathi.com. After the marriage, Simran moved to Connecticut with her husband who works at Infosys as a software engineer. Simran compared dating sites and matrimonial sites:

"[W]hen your family is out of the scene, deep down you know it is a bit dicey and you cannot rely on [a dating website] ... if I meet someone through Tinder, I don't know whether to trust that person. In matrimonial websites, generally, my parents would contact a prospective mate's parents. So, they would have spoken to each other. We have the parents' number and the potential mate's number. So, if something does not go well, we know where to contact the parents."

Simran further added that dating websites do not provide crucial details required for arranging a marriage: *"In India, there is a lot of emotions around marriage ... [Through dating websites] I might know just one side of [the person]. It is not possible that I would know about his parents, siblings, background, how [he] behaves at home, with [his] parents or with the extended family members."*

Yashika, a 25-year-old studying for a Ph.D. in Economics in New Zealand, explained how her sister had found her husband through a family member, emphasizing the importance of the social network. She said *"We knew my brother-in-law's uncle. He was a close family friend ... [M]y brother-in-law's mom is a relative of my Aunt ... [M]y mom and dad went to my brother-in-law's house [and] they liked the family. They liked him. After a few meetings, they said the family is cultured and educated and then we went ahead with the proposal."* She noted the presence and involvement of her parents and family when her sister was seeking a spouse. At the time of the interview, Yashika's family was searching for a spouse for her on matrimonial websites as she had not similarly met anyone in her family's social network. She told us that in India, *"Marriage is between two families not between two individuals."* Therefore, the family's presence and involvement throughout the process is essential. She added:

"I am seeking for seriousness in the relationship, rather than just dating or being in a relationship ... I feel that dating websites are more or less for a time pass [because your family is not involved]. It's like no strings attached kind of policy on dating websites."

Typically, in arranged marriage, the marriage seeker's family employs multiple methods for assessing the credibility of a potential spouse's information. Though marriage seekers may now use matrimonial websites, they still cross-verify the information offline. Matrimonial websites have eased the cross-checking. For example, Aarti said:

"On matrimonial websites, you have information about the family, ... the educational, professional background of the family and the potential spouse, ... the place where the [potential spouse] works or the field in which this person works, how much he earns, and where he lives. So, it's much more credible because you want to run an [offline] background check which becomes...easier."

Sheila, a 52-year-old mother in Chennai, found her daughter-in-law through a website. Her son worked as a civil engineer in a construction firm in Los Angles. The daughter-in-law was employed at a software firm in Bangalore. After the

marriage, she moved with her husband to California and found a job as a software engineer. Sheila explained how the process of verifying the potential spouse's information worked:

> "[For my son,] after we selected the [potential spouse's] profile, we told our relatives who were living in the same area to check [her] background. If everything is fine, then only we [will proceed] ... [We found that] her father [was] related to my nephew. We contacted [my nephew], and he said it is a very good family and everything is fine. Then we moved ahead [with] the process."

Abhishek, a 32-year-old managing an IT firm in Hyderabad, met his wife through Jeevansathi.com. He used the website for two and a half years. He told us:

> "[When] things got serious, I tried to do some background verification through my own links. Someone I know in that particular city. It is not difficult to find someone who can probably help you to figure out if a person is the same as what the person claims to be."

Abhishek himself searched for his spouse. He told us he did not involve his parents until he conducted a background check and was sure the profile was authentic. He emphasized that the detailed information on matrimonial websites is very important because "[M]arriage is about whether another person can fit into your family." The information helps in assessing the spouses' compatibility compared to, as he said, "a dating website where a person is writing about hobbies, life's motto."

Sheila and Abhishek's accounts indicate the importance of human verification for assessing the credibility of the potential spouse's information. Building on this understanding, matrimonial websites provide an in-person verification service through the relationship executive. Raghav, a 31-year-old with an MBA working in human resources in an IT firm in New Delhi, explained:

> "[The officials from a matrimonial website] will visit your house ... [and] check whether you are a real person who has registered with that website. Once they visit and check then they put an authentication badge that this profile has been verified by us."

Sheila told us:

> "In my brother's case, actually he appointed some person [for profile verification] ... He told me [that] if you want, that service can be provided by the matrimony website itself. He used this service and he got all the information [verified]."

Matrimonial websites perform thorough verification technically and through human mediators. The detailed information generated, and involvement of family, create a safe space to marriage seekers as they perform a matrimonial search.

5.2   Safe Spaces for People with Disabilities

Matrimonial websites offer a socially and psychologically safe space for people with disabilities. This safety is a social breakthrough in India because people with disabilities face antipathy and social rejection offline [2,3]. A person with a disability is often shunned from social gatherings [3,72]. People fear that a disabled person might become a burden on the family [2,3] if they cannot perform household chores and because they often seek practical and/or financial assistance [2]. Disabled persons are often perceived as asexual [46], sexually deviant [2], infertile [3], incompetent to raise children [3], and unsuitable for marriage [74]. Such stereotypes reduce marital prospects [2]. Sivanandan [72] comments that parents feel pressure about their disabled child's future settlement, security, and care.

Ashok, a 37-year-old man with a physical disability and a singer by profession, whom we interviewed, told us:

> "[D]isability reduces your market value to a drastic extent [offline]. If I did not have a disability I would be, probably, worth more ... You think a guy walking with a crutch, living a low life can approach a girl and say hi? ... There is no freaking way I would ever stand a chance to go approach some random girl or her parents and say I am interested in your daughter. That would have never worked out at all. People consciously avoid [me] in the social gatherings."

For disabilities that are not immediately visible, such as infertility, the family tries to hide the marriage seeker's condition to the extent possible [2,72]. Though the Hindu Marriage Act permits the annulment of a marriage when a spouse's disability is concealed before marriage, such concealment still occurs [2,72]. Even though these marriages usually result in annulment [72], parents may still act out of desperation and hope that in their child's case, the marriage will succeed. For visible disabilities such as impaired mobility, a woman may marry a much older or divorced man [2], while a man usually marries a woman from a poorer community or from a lower caste [2].

The affordances of matrimonial websites improve the situation a great deal. Disabled persons do not have to conceal impairments. When a potential spouse accepts a connection request, the disability has already been made known because it is part of the information in the profile. For instance, Ashok told us:

> "[Matrimonial websites] have opened up that minuscule window of opportunity that a man or a woman who has created his own profile can now connect to [profiles across] the country and maybe they meet someone there, who knows."

Ashok began by creating matrimonial profiles for his cousin, which then encouraged him to create his own profile. He explained:

> "A couple of years ago I reached out to one girl through the matrimonial website. She was working in IT. Her parents were unbelievably good. They responded to my request. I mentioned that I have a disability and they said

they know [because it was mentioned on the matrimonial profile] but they don't want to judge me on that basis. They gave me the email address of their daughter and said talk to her and if you guys get along with each other we will talk further."

Although Ashok and the young woman did not end up together, the matrimonial site provided an opportunity to find a desirable potential spouse and facilitated connection.

Ramesh, a 55-year-old man with a disabled daughter, shared his experience of finding his daughter a spouse on Abilitymatrimony.com, a sub-site of Bharatmatrimony.com. Here is the fragment of what Ramesh wrote on Abilitymatrimony.com:

"One fine evening I was having my tea, a surprise call came from Delhi and the person asked [whether he could marry my daughter]. I said yes but who are you and [what do you do?] He detailed [that] he was [disabled] like my daughter and they [the marriage seeker and his family] were from Bihar and the same caste [as ours]. I asked when they can come to their village [as they were living somewhere else because] I would like to meet [them]. Within a month they came. I visited their home, met with [the] boy and we agreed about marriage ... Now both [my daughter and son-in-law] are [living happily]."

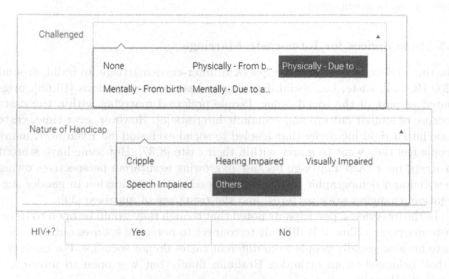

Fig. 3. Representation of marriage seeker's disability on Jeevansathi.com

Ashok, born with cerebral palsy, lived in Chennai. He used Tinder and OkCupid for more than two years. He compared dating to matrimonial websites and discussed the drawbacks of Tinder and OkCupid:

"In my opinion ... dating sites such as Tinder or OkCupid ... have [not] worked out to be great [for me] ... Tinder kind of works, but it does not work for ordinary [and disabled] people. It only works for highly attractive male and female [persons]... [On dating websites] there were a lot of people that have reached out to me and were surprised when I met them in person. So, after all of these years of having unpleasant surprises I have made this explicitly clear to mention in the very first sentence of my description on the profile that I have a physical disability ... I make sure that they know that they are talking to a person with a disability."

While dating websites provide free form text boxes for personal information, they have not yet normalized the ability spectrum with fields to mention and categorize disability. It thus becomes a somewhat awkward burden and marginalizing experience for the disabled person to explain.

While parents may try to hide a marriage seeker's disability, the matrimonial websites normalize disability through the affordances of the user interface. Figure 3 shows a typical example. Jeevansathi.com has five options to categorize disability: "Physically-From birth", "Physically-Due to accident", "Mentally-From birth", "Mentally-Due to accident", and "None". A marriage seeker can select the nature of disability: "Cripple", "Speech Impaired", "Hearing Impaired", "Visually Impaired", and "Others". The website also provides options to represent HIV status (Fig. 3). These categories bring disability into the open, indicating that it is merely part of a profile like education, personal preferences, or occupation.

5.3   Safe Spaces for Inter-caste Marriage

Matrimonial websites foster safe spaces for inter-caste marriage. In India, around 1200 BC [23], caste, i.e., social distinctions based on occupations [10,66], originated as part of the social order. People preferred marrying within the caste because of similar culture and economic interests [8]. However, over time, caste grew into a rigid hierarchy that has led to social exclusion [8]. Even now, many people feel they want to marry within their caste [8,37]. But some have started to accept inter-caste marriage because of growing egalitarian perspectives owing to social and demographic changes such as education, reduction in gender segregation, changing work patterns, and the rising age of marriage [39].

In the interviews, participants noted that though they would be open to inter-caste marriage, offline it is difficult to connect to potential spouses outside one's caste because usually people from different castes do not socialize. For example, Ashok belonged to an orthodox Brahmin family but was open to inter-caste marriage. He said:

"[I]f you reach out to people [offline] outside your caste, the response rate from not belonging to your caste, regardless of [whether] they are from the higher or lower class, seems to be poor. Even if there is a response, culturally [and] lifestyle-wise you [both] don't seem to kind of get along

or go along that well ... I have engaged with people outside of my caste [offline] ... [and] things have never worked out."

However, Ashok noted that the potential spouses he contacted offline were still seeking intra-caste marriages. The matrimonial sites open up a bigger, different pool of potential spouses by including those who are open to inter-caste marriage. Raghav, who met his wife through a matrimonial website, emphasized the importance of the wider pool:

"I frankly wanted to register to these websites because I wanted to keep my options open. I was not inclined to selecting only a girl [from my caste]. So, finally, I married a girl [from outside my caste] ... So, it has been an inter-caste arranged marriage for me. So, I never wanted to focus on a specific [caste] which happens [in an offline search]. I wanted to be open and meet a person whom I like not [necessarily in] the [caste] ... [These websites] have [provided] a very helpful platform in terms of formalizing the process [and] giving you more options."

Aarti, Raghav's wife, told us that both the families were open to inter-caste marriage. Her mother saw Raghav's profile and sent a connection request. Raghav liked Aarti's profile and accepted the request. Raghav lived with his parents in Delhi. Aarti's parents lived in Delhi, but she lived in Bangalore. Both sets of parents first talked over the phone. The families met and liked each other. Raghav then visited Aarti. They liked each other. Then they got married. Both well-educated families were unconcerned about a potential spouse's caste. Aarti said:

"We did not have any filter based on the [caste] as such. In fact, my husband is not from my own [caste] and it is an arranged marriage through [a matrimonial website] ... Both, my husband and I were not fixated on the [caste] part. I am sure there are people who think this way that they can find [a potential mate] from their own [caste]. But we did not have any such filter."

Raghav and Aarti told us that they liked each other because they shared common interests and each had the attributes the other was looking for. Raghav said that for him to select a spouse the *"very important factor was that [I have] ... a basic level of liking,...[and] basic level of chemistry [with her] ... I was looking for someone who is well-educated and comes from a decent family background ... I wanted to marry someone who is a little bit creative. So, [by] looking at the description of the profile I could judge that the person is creative."* He mentioned that he liked Aarti because *"Her [profile] description was a little bit different. So, that piqued my interest. So, then I contacted her."* Matrimonial websites provide a place of inclusion to marriage seekers like Raghav and Aarti seeking marital horizons beyond caste.

Rahul, a 30-year-old with an MBA, worked at Oracle in Canada. His parents lived in India. His family conducted an extensive spousal search offline within their caste. They wanted to find a spouse whose education was on par with

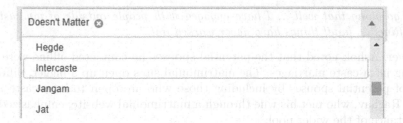

Fig. 4. Drop-down menu showing castes that the marriage seeker can select

Rahul's but they could not find a suitable match. The family belonged to the Barber caste which tends to have a lower level of education. Rahul said:

> *"I come from a Barber [caste] which is a low caste in India ... there are not too many girls [in this caste] who are that much educated. At least in our vicinity. My relatives could not help me find a suitable match since three-four years"*

Rahul's family shifted to matrimonial websites for a bigger pool of spouses. At the time of the interview, Rahul and his family were still searching. Rahul told us that through matrimonial websites he was getting a bigger and better pool of potential spouses.

Figure 4 shows the attribute to select acceptable castes. Marriage seekers can select specific castes from the drop-down menu or select "Intercaste". The default is "Does not matter". When a marriage seeker selects "Intercaste", the search result shows potential spouses from castes other than that of the marriage seeker. For "Does not matter" the search shows potential spouses within and outside the marriage seeker's caste.

6   Discussion

We discuss design implications to foster online safety and inclusivity broadly.

6.1   Designing for Online Safety

Dating websites, often rife with deception [25], would be more useful if they provided a measure of safety. Obada-Obieh and Somayaji [52] emphasize that "[D]ating websites, are not adequately served by standard security practices." Our study found that, by contrast, security practices are a key part of Indian matrimonial websites, with their detailed information about prospective spouses, profile screening, easy reporting of threats, links to social and professional media profiles, and human services of in-person verification. Some of these services could be useful on dating websites. Obada-Obieh and Somayaji [52] argue that dating websites such as Tinder, Match.com, and Plenty of Fish should "verify the users they recommend" through means similar to credit card verification

or security clearances. They should conduct background checks of the users to ensure profiles' credibility [52].

An important means of ensuring safety on Indian matrimonial websites is the involvement of the national government. This involvement was very important to our participants. Shivam, a 29-year-old man who worked as an IT engineer told us:

> *"The rule that government imposed on matrimonial websites shows that the government is interested in the citizens' online safety and will take proper actions if our safety is breached. This makes the matrimonial websites safer because we know if anything wrong happens, we can easily report to the police without any second thought."*

Gray [31], an attorney, points out that American dating websites are subject to no laws whatsoever to protect users from fraud and misrepresentation. If there is a problem, a user must search on their own for the perpetrator, a difficult and often futile task [31]. We agree with Gray that a policy along the lines of what the Indian government implemented could foster online safety. The government's interest could help avoid the problems that plague dating websites today.

Safety is one of the few truly universal values we can point to. The creation and maintenance of safety (online and offline) require social and financial investments. If we do not make such investments, how serious are we about safety? The HCI community is slowly paying more attention to policy [33]. Shneiderman et al. [70] say that "[HCI] can influence education, commerce, healthcare, and government." We emphasize that we can also influence policies regarding online safety. As the virtual world expands, what policies should be implemented to foster safety? This is a big question and one we hope the HCI community will continue to study.

We might reasonably ask how much of the safety of matrimonial websites is attributable to Indian cultural values and how much to the design of the websites. Clearly, it is some of both. Indian culture embeds safety in the matrimonial process through the involvement of family and the social network. But the design of matrimonial websites has also played a role through a carefully considered set of affordances and practices such as verification.

While the sites build on the traditional safety of family involvement in the matrimonial process, at the same time, matrimonial websites have challenged other traditional Indian values through designs that foster safety for marginalized groups: the disabled, divorced, widowed, HIV-positive. The government has gone even further than traditional culture in mandating safety as a value by making it legally actionable. This development is especially important in the context of changing residential patterns where nuclear families have less ready access to the resources of the extended family. If Indian matrimonial websites can provide effective technical affordances and human services to foster online safety, it seems likely that we can learn from them, and do a better job at online safety in other venues.

6.2   Designing for Online Inclusion

Designing for inclusion consists of designing, building, and managing a common space where people from varying communities participate [13]. Hourcade and Bullock-Rest [35] note that "When designing [for diverse populations] there is a need to connect to people's needs, abilities, context, and daily realities." This kind of design is not easy. How can we cater to the needs and capabilities of certain communities, and in doing so not exclude other communities? Ulrich and Eppinger [51] argue that inclusive design "[Is] very difficult [as]...providing access to [a certain group of users]...can make the [design] significantly more difficult to use by [general users]." Al-Dawood et al. [5] faced this issue in designing a Saudi Arabian matrimonial website. They observe that their design may not be applicable to all communities, and may favor certain value systems. They ask, "How do we avoid marginalizing a group of users with design?"

Indian matrimonial websites address the question by providing services for as many groups as possible, serving people with disabilities, the divorced or widowed, those with annulled marriages, older adults, HIV positive persons, and those seeking inter-caste marriages. The design fosters safety for various groups by reaching out to them in the context of emerging values (and markets for matrimonial products) in Indian society. It is no accident that the websites have made significant investments in understanding safety, designing for inclusion, and taking some risks by including those who are often excluded in traditional Indian society.

But matrimonial websites also leverage the shared traditional cultural value of Indian arranged marriage. In the West it is received wisdom that digital technology must be "disruptive" [68], encouraging people to discard what they have and replace it with something new. Industry manufactures products with the intent of having customers replace what they have just bought, and uses advertising to persuade consumers that their current products are obsolete and outdated [15]. Blevis et al. [12] argue that "To serve its own interests, our economic system produces incessant moments of disorder and disruption rather than graceful performative luxury, and tells us this is a good thing." In Indian society, however, this pattern of consumption does not hold. People prefer and know the value of repair and renewal [43]. Indian matrimonial websites have taken care not to disrupt the whole culture. As we design technology, we should question the idea that disruption is always the better outcome.

Matrimonial websites have been financially successful by honoring traditional cultural values and disrupting only certain values. The sites' annual growth is 130% compared to 88% for dating websites [1]. Over 12 million Indians use matrimonial websites each year to search for and connect to potential spouses [1]. Noticing the success of the sites, major U.S. firms have invested in them, e.g., Yahoo and Venture Capital invested $8.5 million in Bharatmatrimony.com [69]. The HCI community can take a cue from these websites, building technologies that reinforce positive cultural values, and making some calculated risks in replacing certain values with better counterparts, just as the matrimonial websites have.

Indian matrimonial websites take inclusion seriously by providing in-person assistance through human mediators. Such mediation is important in many places where people have trouble using digital services for various reasons. In African and Asian countries, with a combined population of 4.8 billion people, only 1 in 5 have access to digital services [62]. In India, out of 1.3 billion people, only 50 million are English literate [61], though most digital services are in the English language [44]. Matrimonial websites overcome problems of access and language through human mediation, setting a good example for all of us who want to take inclusion seriously.

Although arranged marriage may sound exotic or even backward to many in the West, half of the world practices arranged marriage [56]. The many studies of dating websites we have are interesting and useful, but they are not especially relevant to half the world. We have a tendency in the HCI community to consider research in the West as applicable to or representative of the global population. Kou et al. [42] argue that "[The HCI community] favors the idea that studies conducted in Western countries such as the U.S. and the U.K. are more likely to produce 'normal' and putatively universally applicable knowledge ... [Whereas] studies of non-Western countries ... are expected to produce exotic, highly contextualized knowledge that does not travel beyond their borders." Arranged marriage is not an exotic practice, and it is certain to become even more prevalent because of the higher rates of population growth in the countries where it is practiced [56].

Rastogi et al. [62] note that the next billion users of digital technology will come from the Global South, especially from India and China. Srinivasan [75] highlights that "[W]eb technologies [are usually] produced, designed, and built for Western audiences." He argues that "The digital world need not solely be conceived in Western, elite terms, but instead can and should be re-envisioned as a space that empowers the values, priorities, and ontologies held by global users from the 'margins', within the developing world [because these] users ... hold the potential to dramatically influence research on digital cultures, particularly around the question of whose voices drive the architectures, algorithms, and languages of new media" [75]. We argue, with Al-Dawood et al. [5], that HCI should normalize and encourage research in societies with different cultural values and practices. Shneiderman and Hochheiser [71] note that "[D]iversity promotes quality. The challenge of designing for experts and novices, English and non-English speakers, low-motivated users, users with disabilities, elderly users or children promotes creative thinking that leads to better solutions for all users." We propose to shift from how we better design for inclusion to how we approach research in a way that honors inclusion more broadly. We hope to see more research that is itself inclusive of varying cultures and societies.

7 Conclusion and Future Work

We presented a qualitative study of how Indian matrimonial websites foster online safety and inclusivity. We argued the importance of the presence of the

social network, government involvement, technical affordances, and human services in promoting online safety and inclusivity. We found that matrimonial websites have opened marital possibilities for people in marginalized communities of India, and for inter-caste marriages. Safety and inclusivity are broad and subjective values. Designing to foster these values for a particular group, considering its needs and capabilities, may exclude other groups. In our future work, we would like to explore contradictions that arise when the needs of different groups are in play, and how we can manage them for fairness and social good. We hope this study inspires prosocial work, creating and promoting safe spaces for diverse communities that cater to positive cultural values.

Acknowledgements. We would like to thank the reviewers for their constructive feedback. We thank Stacy Branham, Kevin Storer, and Meena Devii Muralikumar for their valuable feedback and encouragement.

References

1. Future trend of online matrimony industry in India - medium (2017). https://medium.com/@solutionswebomania/future-trend-of-online-matrimony-industry-in-india-b0a2c34fd417. Accessed 07 Jan 2019
2. Addlakha, R.: How young people with disabilities conceptualize the body, sex and marriage in urban India: four case studies. Sex. Disabil. **25**(3), 111–123 (2007)
3. Adhikari, A.: Perception of general public towards sexuality of persons with disabilities. Paripex-Indian J. Res. **7**(4) (2018)
4. Agrawal, A.: Cyber-matchmaking among Indians: re-arranging marriage and doing 'kin work'. South Asian Popular Cult. **13**(1), 15–30 (2015)
5. Al-Dawood, A., Abokhodair, N., El Mimouni, H., Yarosh, S.: Against marrying a stranger: marital matchmaking technologies in Saudi Arabia. In: Proceedings of DIS 2017, pp. 1013–1024. ACM (2017)
6. Al-Saggaf, Y.: Males' trust and mistrust of females in muslim matrimonial sites. J. Inf. Commun. Ethics Soc. **11**(3), 174–192 (2013)
7. Ammari, T., Kumar, P., Lampe, C., Schoenebeck, S.: Managing children's online identities: how parents decide what to disclose about their children online. In: Proceedings of CHI 2015, pp. 1895–1904. ACM (2015)
8. Ansari, A.: Inter religion marriages and its challenges: an introspection. Res. J. Soc. Sci. **9**(7) (2018)
9. Azam, M., Chin, A., Prakash, N.: The returns to English-language skills in India. Econ. Dev. Cult. Change **61**(2), 335–367 (2013)
10. Berreman, G.D.: Race, caste, and other invidious distinctions in social stratification. Race **13**(4), 385–414 (1972)
11. Bhattacharjya, M., Ganesh, M.I.: Negotiating intimacy and harm: female internet users in Mumbai. EROTICS: Sex, Rights Internet 66 (2011)
12. Blevis, S.A., Blevis, E., Nardi, B.: All the tea in China interaction design inspiration. In: Proceedings of C&C 2019. ACM (2019)
13. Britain, G.: Inclusion by Design: Equality, Diversity and the Built Environment. Commission for Architecture and the Built Environment (2008)
14. Buchanan, T., Whitty, M.T.: The online dating romance scam: causes and consequences of victimhood. Psychol. Crime Law **20**(3), 261–283 (2014)

15. Bulow, J.: An economic theory of planned obsolescence. Q. J. Econ. **101**(4), 729–749 (1986)
16. Chadda, R.K., Deb, K.S.: Indian family systems, collectivistic society and psychotherapy. Indian J. Psychiatry **55**(Suppl. 2), S299 (2013)
17. Chowdhury, F.I., Trovato, F.: The role and status of women and the timing of marriage in five Asian countries. J. Comp. Family Stud. **25**, 143–157 (1994)
18. Corbin, J., Strauss, A.: Basics of qualitative research: techniques and procedures for developing grounded theory (2008)
19. Dombrowski, S.C., LeMasney, J.W., Ahia, C.E., Dickson, S.A.: Protecting children from online sexual predators: technological, psychoeducational, and legal considerations. Prof. Psychol.: Res. Pract. **35**(1), 65 (2004)
20. Donath, J.S.: Identity and deception in the virtual community. In: Communities in Cyberspace, pp. 37–68. Routledge (2002)
21. Dourish, P., Finlay, J., Sengers, P., Wright, P.: Reflective HCI: towards a critical technical practice. In: Proceedings of Alt-CHI 2004, vol. 24, pp. 1727–1728. Citeseer (2004)
22. Edmunds, S.: Scammers & Online Dating Fraud: 2015 Trends and Tactics. Global Dating Insights, New York (2015)
23. Elliott, A.: Caste system in India - postcolonial studies (2017). https://scholarblogs.emory.edu/postcolonialstudies/2014/06/20/caste-system-in-india/. Accessed 08 May 2019
24. Ellison, N., Heino, R., Gibbs, J.: Managing impressions online: self-presentation processes in the online dating environment. J. CMC **11**(2), 415–441 (2006)
25. Ellison, N.B., Hancock, J.T., Toma, C.L.: Profile as promise: a framework for conceptualizing veracity in online dating self-presentations. New Media Soc. **14**(1), 45–62 (2012)
26. Fiore, A.T., Donath, J.S.: Homophily in online dating: when do you like someone like yourself? In: Alt-CHI 2005, pp. 1371–1374. ACM (2005)
27. Fleming, M., Rickwood, D., et al.: Teens in cyberspace: do they encounter friend or foe? Youth Stud. Aust. **23**(3), 46 (2004)
28. Fraser, V.: Queer closets and rainbow hyperlinks: the construction and constraint of queer subjectivities online. Sex. Res. Soc. Policy **7**(1), 30–36 (2010)
29. Ghosh, A.K., Badillo-Urquiola, K., Guha, S., LaViola Jr., J.J., Wisniewski, P.J.: Safety vs. surveillance: what children have to say about mobile apps for parental control. In: Proceedings of CHI 2018, p. 124. ACM (2018)
30. Gibbs, J.L., Ellison, N.B., Heino, R.D.: Self-presentation in online personals: the role of anticipated future interaction, self-disclosure, and perceived success in internet dating. Commun. Res. **33**(2), 152–177 (2006)
31. Gray, T.E.: Internet dating websites: a refuge for internet fraud. Fla. Coast. L. Rev. **12**, 389 (2010)
32. Greenfield, P.M.: Inadvertent exposure to pornography on the internet: implications of peer-to-peer file-sharing networks for child development and families. J. Appl. Dev. Psychol. **25**(6), 741–750 (2004)
33. Grimpe, B., Hartswood, M., Jirotka, M.: Towards a closer dialogue between policy and practice: responsible design in HCI. In: Proceedings of CHI 2014, pp. 2965–2974. ACM (2014)
34. Hancock, J.T., Toma, C., Ellison, N.: The truth about lying in online dating profiles. In: Proceedings of CHI 2007, pp. 449–452. ACM (2007)
35. Hourcade, J.P., Bullock-Rest, N.E.: Universal interactions: challenges and opportunities. Interactions **18**(2), 76–79 (2011)

36. Jaiswal, T.: Indian Arranged Marriages: A Social Psychological Perspective, vol. 79. Routledge, Abingdon (2014)
37. Joshi, K., Kumar, S.: Matchmaking using fuzzy analytical hierarchy process, compatibility measure and stable matching for online matrimony in India. J. Multi-Criteria Decis. Anal. **19**(1–2), 57–66 (2012)
38. Karusala, N., Kumar, N.: Women's safety in public spaces: examining the efficacy of panic buttons in New Delhi. In: Proceedings of CHI 2017, pp. 3340–3351. ACM (2017)
39. Kaur, R.: Across-region marriages: poverty, female migration and the sex ratio. Econ. Polit. Weekly 2595–2603 (2004)
40. Kibby, M.: Sex, identity and the home page. Media Int. Aust. **84**(1), 39–45 (1997)
41. Kosciw, J.G., Greytak, E.A., Giga, N.M., Villenas, C., Danischewski, D.J.: The 2015 national school climate survey: the experiences of lesbian, gay, bisexual, transgender, and queer youth in our nation's schools. GLSEN (2016)
42. Kou, Y., Gray, C.M., Toombs, A., Nardi, B.: The politics of titling: the representation of countries in chi papers. In: Alt-CHI 2018, p. alt16. ACM (2018)
43. Kumar, H., Bhaduri, S.: Jugaad to grassroot innovations: understanding the landscape of the informal sector innovations in India. Afr. J. Sci. Technol. Innov. Dev. **6**(1), 13–22 (2014)
44. Kumar, N.: Facebook for self-empowerment? A study of Facebook adoption in urban India. New Media Soc. **16**(7), 1122–1137 (2014)
45. Masden, C., Edwards, W.K.: Understanding the role of community in online dating. In: Proceedings of CHI 2015, pp. 535–544. ACM (2015)
46. Milligan, M.S., Neufeldt, A.H.: The myth of asexuality: a survey of social and empirical evidence. Sex. Disabil. **19**(2), 91–109 (2001)
47. Mitra, R., Gajjala, R.: Queer blogging in Indian digital diasporas: a dialogic encounter. J. Commun. Inq. **32**(4), 400–423 (2008)
48. Morris, M.R.: Social networking site use by mothers of young children. In: Proceedings of CSCW 2014, pp. 1272–1282. ACM (2014)
49. Mukherjee, R.: Govt to matrimonial sites: Check id proof & store IP addresses - medianama, June 2016. https://www.medianama.com/2016/06/223-government-matrimonial-sites-id-proof/. Accessed 14 Mar 2018
50. Myers, J.E., Madathil, J., Tingle, L.R.: Marriage satisfaction and wellness in India and the United States: a preliminary comparison of arranged marriages and marriages of choice. J. Couns. Dev. **83**(2), 183–190 (2005)
51. Newell, A.F., Gregor, P.: "User sensitive inclusive design"–in search of a new paradigm. In: Proceedings on the 2000 Conference on Universal Usability, pp. 39–44. ACM (2000)
52. Obada-Obieh, B., Somayaji, A.: Can i believe you?: establishing trust in computer mediated introductions. In: Proceedings of the 2017 New Security Paradigms Workshop on ZZZ, pp. 94–106. ACM (2017)
53. Pal, J.K.: Social networks enabling matrimonial information services in India. Int. J. LIS **2**(4), 54–64 (2010)
54. Pal, J.K.: Review on matrimonial information systems and services-an Indian perspective. Int. Res. J. LIAS **1**(4), 126–135 (2011)
55. Pascoe, C.J.: Resource and risk: youth sexuality and new media use. Sex. Res. Soc. Policy **8**(1), 5–17 (2011)
56. Penn, R.: Arranged marriages in Western Europe: media representations and social reality. J. Comp. Family Stud. **42**, 637–650 (2011)

57. Pereira, G.C., Baranauskas, M.C.C.: Supporting people on fighting lesbian, gay, bisexual, and transgender (LGBT) prejudice: a critical codesign process. In: Proceedings of the IHC-XVI, p. 46. ACM (2017)
58. Philips, F., Morrissey, G.: Cyberstalking and cyberpredators: a threat to safe sexuality on the internet. Convergence **10**(1), 66–79 (2004)
59. Polzenhagen, F., Frey, S.: Are marriages made in heaven? A cultural-linguistic case study on Indian-English matrimonials. In: Sharifian, F. (ed.) Advances in Cultural Linguistics. CL, pp. 573–605. Springer, Singapore (2017). https://doi.org/10.1007/978-981-10-4056-6_26
60. Ramirez, A., Walther, J.B., Burgoon, J.K., Sunnafrank, M.: Information-seeking strategies, uncertainty, and computer-mediated communication. Hum. Commun. Res. **28**(2), 213–228 (2002)
61. Rao, S.S.: Bridging digital divide: efforts in India. Telematics Inform. **22**(4), 361–375 (2005)
62. Rastogi, R., Cutrell, E., Gupta, M., Jhunjhunwala, A., Narayan, R., Sanghal, R.: Connecting the next billion web users. In: Proceedings of WWW 2011 Companion, pp. 329–330. ACM (2011)
63. Regan, P.C., Lakhanpal, S., Anguiano, C.: Relationship outcomes in Indian-American love-based and arranged marriages. Psychol. Rep. **110**(3), 915–924 (2012)
64. Robinson, K.H., Bansel, P., Denson, N., Ovenden, G., Davies, C.: Growing up queer: issues facing young Australians who are gender variant and sexuality diverse. Young and Well Cooperative Research Centre (2014)
65. Roy, S.: From Khush List to Gay Bombay. Mobile Cultures: New Media in Queer Asia, p. 180 (2003)
66. Sana, A.: The caste system in India and its consequences. Int. J. Sociol. Soc. Policy **13**(3/4), 1–76 (1993)
67. Scheuerman, M.K., Branham, S.M., Hamidi, F.: Safe spaces and safe places: unpacking technology-mediated experiences of safety and harm with transgender people. In: Proceedings of CSCW 2018, vol. 2, p. 155 (2018)
68. Schumpeter, J.A.: Capitalism, Socialism and Democracy. Routledge, Abingdon (2010)
69. Seth, N.: Online matrimonial sites and the transformation of arranged marriage in India. In: Virtual Communities: Concepts, Methodologies, Tools and Applications. IGI Global (2011)
70. Shneiderman, B., Card, S., Norman, D.A., Tremaine, M., Waldrop, M.M.: Chi@ 20: fighting our way from marginality to power. In: Alt-CHI 2002, pp. 688–691. ACM (2002)
71. Shneiderman, B., Hochheiser, H.: Universal usability as a stimulus to advanced interface design. Behav. Inf. Technol. **20**(5), 367–376 (2001)
72. Sivanandan, V.: Marital status of persons with disabilities in India-an analysis. J. Disabil. Manag. Spec. Educ. **1**(2), 25 (2018)
73. Smith, A., Duggan, M.: Online Dating & Relationships. Pew Research Center's Internet & American Life Project (2013)
74. Spratt, J.M.: A deeper silence: the unheard experiences of women with disabilities and their sexual and reproductive health experiences: Kiribati, the Solomon Islands and Tonga Fiji. United Nations Population Fund Pacific Sub-Regional Office, Suva, Fiji (2013)
75. Srinivasan, R.: Re-thinking the cultural codes of new media: the question concerning ontology. New Media Soc. **15**(2), 203–223 (2013)

76. Stanco, M.: Indiascapes. Images and words from globalised India. Rivista di letterature moderne e comparate **64**(1), 90–93 (2011)
77. Stanley, J., et al.: Child abuse and the internet. J. Home Econ. Inst. Aust. **9**(1), 5 (2002)
78. Stolterman, E., Croon Fors, A.: Critical HCI research: a research position proposal. Des. Philos. Pap. **1** (2008)
79. Stopes-Roe, M., Cochrane, R.: Citizens of This Country: The Asian-British, vol. 68. Multilingual Matters (1990)
80. Sudhanshu, R.K.: Matrimony.pdf. http://wcd.nic.in/sites/default/files/Matrimony. pdf. Accessed 16 May 2018
81. Sushma: Matrimony.com is raking in big profits despite the popularity of dating apps like tinder and woo – quartz India, May 2018. https://qz.com/india/1269345/ matrimony-com-is-raking-in-big-profits-despite-the-popularity-of-dating-apps- like-tinder-and-woo/. Accessed 23 Apr 2019
82. Tidwell, L.C., Walther, J.B.: Computer-mediated communication effects on disclosure, impressions, and interpersonal evaluations: getting to know one another a bit at a time. Hum. Commun. Res. **28**(3), 317–348 (2002)
83. Titzmann, F.M.: Changing patterns of matchmaking: the Indian online matrimonial market. Asian J. Women's Stud. **19**(4), 64–94 (2013)
84. Toma, C.L., Hancock, J.T.: Reading between the lines: linguistic cues to deception in online dating profiles. In: Proceedings of CSCW 2010, pp. 5–8. ACM (2010)
85. Walther, J.B., Tidwell, L.C.: Nonverbal cues in computer-mediated communication, and the effect of chronemics on relational communication. J. Organ. Comput. Electron. Commer. **5**(4), 355–378 (1995)
86. Whitty, M.T.: The scammers persuasive techniques model: development of a stage model to explain the online dating romance scam. J. Criminol. **53**, 665–684 (2013)
87. Wisniewski, P., Ghosh, A.K., Xu, H., Rosson, M.B., Carroll, J.M.: Parental control vs. teen self-regulation: is there a middle ground for mobile online safety? In: Proceedings of CSCW 2017, pp. 51–69. ACM (2017)
88. Woodland, R.: Pagan statues gay/lesbian identity and the construction of. The cybercultures reader, p. 416 (2000)
89. Xiaohe, X., Whyte, M.K.: Love matches and arranged marriages: a Chinese replication. J. Marriage Family 709–722 (1990)
90. Ybarra, M.L., Mitchell, K.J., Palmer, N.A., Reisner, S.L.: Online social support as a buffer against online and offline peer and sexual victimization among US LGBT and non-LGBT youth. Child Abuse Negl. **39**, 123–136 (2015)

What About My Privacy, Habibi?
Understanding Privacy Concerns and Perceptions of Users from Different Socioeconomic Groups in the Arab World

Mennatallah Saleh[1,2]([✉]), Mohamed Khamis[3], and Christian Sturm[1]

[1] Hamm-Lippstadt University of Applied Science, Hamm, Germany
Menna.eSaleh@gmail.com, Christian.Sturm@hshl.de
[2] Technical University of Berlin, Berlin, Germany
[3] University of Glasgow, Glasgow, UK
Mohamed.Khamis@glasgow.ac.uk

Abstract. This paper contributes an in-depth understanding of privacy concerns and perceptions of Arab users. We report on the first comparison of privacy perceptions among (1) users from high socioeconomic groups in Arab countries (HSA), (2) users from medium to low socioeconomic groups in Arab countries (LSA), and (3) as a baseline, users from high socioeconomic groups in Germany (HSG). Our work is motivated by the fact that most research in privacy focused on Western, Educated, Industrialized, Rich, and Democratic (WEIRD) societies. This excludes a segment of the population whose cultural norms and socioeconomic status influence privacy perception and needs. We report on multiple novel findings and unexpected similarities and differences across the user groups. For example, shoulder surfing is more common across LSA and HSG, and defamation is a major threat in LSA. We discuss the implications of our findings on the design of privacy protection measures for investigated groups.

Keywords: Emerging users · Privacy · Culture · WEIRD · Arabs

1 Introduction

The ubiquity of technology around us has brought users a myriad of benefits. On the downside, the ability to access private information almost anywhere and at anytime comes with implications on user privacy. Acknowledging this issue, a plethora of research investigated the privacy perceptions and concerns of users [18,21,34,35,39,54]. While these works significantly extended our understanding of user privacy, it remains unclear if these findings generalize to the wider populations of the world. In particular, there is a gap in the knowledge of privacy perceptions and concerns of Arab users and the societies within the Arab world.

Electronic supplementary material The online version of this chapter (https://doi.org/10.1007/978-3-030-29387-1_5) contains supplementary material, which is available to authorized users.

© IFIP International Federation for Information Processing 2019
Published by Springer Nature Switzerland AG 2019

D. Lamas et al. (Eds.): INTERACT 2019, LNCS 11748, pp. 67–87, 2019.
https://doi.org/10.1007/978-3-030-29387-1_5

This problem is amplified by the fact that the vast majority of previous studies in this area were conducted with participants from Western, Industrialized, Rich, and Democratic (WEIRD) societies [36,37]. The term WEIRD was coined by Henrich et al. [37] in 2010, and since then researchers in behavioral psychology have acknowledged that participants from WEIRD societies can often be psychological outliers [36,37] because they represent less than 15% of the world population. The Human-Computer Interaction community has recently acknowledged this issue in HCI research too [60]. Furthermore, there has been a recent increasing interest within the Usable Security and Privacy community to move away from "one-size fits all" approach [66]. Since socioeconomic groups and cultures are known to influence users' perceptions of technology and its implications [15,42,44], it is important to consider the potential impact of the socioeconomic profile on the individual's privacy perceptions. For example, would sharing of a mobile device be perceived to out-weigh privacy concerns for low-income individuals? Do Arabs' emphasis on reputation influence their protective measures against privacy invasion? These reasons underline the necessity to expand our understanding of privacy needs and concerns of different user groups, including users from different cultures, as well as users from different socioeconomic groups. To contribute in this direction, we focus on different socioeconomic groups within the Arab world, and compare results to participants from WEIRD societies.

We chose the context of Arabs since their privacy needs and concerns are relatively under-investigated in the literature. We expect to find novel concerns and perceptions among this user group due to the unique cultures and values that are shared among Arab countries. Preliminary investigations have already suggested that there may be significant differences in privacy invasion experiences between Arabs and non-Arabs [54]. To name a few relevant examples: Arabs adhere to cultural values that could influence privacy perceptions. This, in turn, could have an impact on the perceived implications of privacy violations. For example, Arab women who wear a headscarf, aka Hijab, are likely to be more careful in protecting their private pictures from men who are not part of the woman's family. They could, in turn, perceive the leak of private pictures to be more dangerous compared to women in other societies. Another example is the significance of dignity and reputation in the Arab world [59,61]; an ill-reputation caused by acts of defamation could influence an Arab's relationships, as well as social and economic opportunities. These differences encouraged the CHI, DIS and CSCW communities to investigate needs and concerns of Arab users in the respective fields [5,8,41,51,62].

In this work, we report on the first in-depth investigation of privacy concerns and perceptions of users from high and medium to low socioeconomic groups in two Arab countries. We refer to them hereafter as **HSA** and **LSA** for short. We limited our pool of participants to those who are residing in said countries to reduce the influence of external factors. As a baseline for comparison, we compare results to participants from high socioeconomic groups in Germany (**HSG**). In particular, we report on a survey (N = 156) that was distributed among participants who are from and reside in Egypt, Saudi Arabia, and Germany. We reached out for HSA and HSG participants through a questionnaire distributed

online, and LSA participants by distributing a printed Arabic translation of the questionnaire to workers of a hospital. Among the findings, we found that consequences of privacy invasion could be particularly severe for LSA users, and that shoulder surfing occurs more often among LSA and HSG participants. We discuss the implications on designing privacy protection for said communities.

2 Related Work

In 1986, Shwartz discussed the phenomenon of withdrawal into privacy. He showed how increasing the secrecy and boundaries between people causes more intrigue and hence makes these boundaries more likely to be broken by others [58]. However, with the widespread use of social networks, some argue that social norms evolved and users are now comfortable sharing information openly with others [67]. We investigate the current state of privacy concerns and perceptions in low and high socioeconomic Arab groups.

2.1 Studying Privacy Perceptions

Privacy invasion has been studied in multiple situations. Types of privacy invasion attacks that were investigated include identity theft, impersonation, spying, profile harvesting, defamation, impersonation, credit card theft and shoulder surfing [23,40]. Shoulder surfing is defined as the act of observing other people's information without their consent [23].

Every society values and expresses privacy differently than others [65]. The concept of the "average user" is now being abolished by many researchers. Egelman and Peer introduced psychographic targeting of privacy and security mitigations that relied on user profile understanding [22]. They found that decision making styles were better predictors for privacy attitudes than the Big Five personality traits. Wisniewskia et al. also categorized users into six profiles depending on their sharing and privacy attitudes on Online Social Networks (OSNs) and offered design implications for each user group [68]. Yoo et al. investigated the effect of the hacking of a popular online Korean market on the privacy perceptions of its users [70]. Findings show that mild previous experiences reduce the perceptions of loss and that privacy concerns increase loss perceptions.

This suggests that privacy perception is influenced by one's background. Next, we discuss how cultural backgrounds influence privacy perceptions.

2.2 Cultures and Privacy Interplay

Sambasivan et al. emphasized the importance of understanding the role culture plays in technology use and hence its influence on design [56].

Cultures also play a central role in shaping privacy concerns and perceptions. Privacy researchers also noticed this gap and attempted to investigate influences of national culture on privacy perception. Dinev et al. compared privacy perception about government surveillance in USA and Italy [18]. Results show

that Italian participants had lower privacy concerns. Habrach et al. conducted a survey on eight countries concluding that Japanese and German participants had higher privacy concerns on their smartphones than those from Australia, Canada, Italy, Netherlands, UK and USA. A survey on 325 Arab participants showed that females are more concerned than males about their online privacy and that Egyptians are more comfortable with privacy on social networks than Emiratis [48]. Li et al. have predicted privacy based on the cultural dimensions of an individual, emphasizing the importance of the difference culture makes in privacy decision making [44]. Harbach et al. compared risk perceptions across USA and Germany [34]. They found that participants from USA were more concerned about identity theft, while Germans were more concerned about hidden costs in services, frauds and scams. Eiband et al. collected real shoulder surfing stories from participants from different countries including Germany, Egypt, USA, Bulgaria, India, Italy, Romania, Russia and South Korea [23]. However their aim was not to compare cultures, bur rather to find evidence for shoulder surfing in the real world; they did confirm that it is a real threat that indeed occurs and has negative consequences on the user. Bellman et al. investigated how the Hofstede cultural dimensions affect the perception and found that individualism, masculinity and power distance all affected privacy attitude [13].

While national culture is a very important predictor of privacy perceptions and attitudes, it is not sufficient. Wang et al. show the important role education plays in privacy and how the participants with higher education have higher privacy concerns [63]. Schwartz labels privacy as a luxury that not all users can afford [58], and some users seem to agree [55]. Other researchers noticed phenomena such as phone sharing and designed solutions that increase security for these setups [53]. These works suggest that socioeconomic factors, such as education and income, also influence privacy perceptions. There is a need to revisit the claim of privacy affordability due to the myriad of sensitive information that is at risk of privacy invasion, and due to its potential serious consequences particularly in underdeveloped and conservative cultures. Acknowledging this, some researchers investigated ways of improving security for emergent users [38]. For example, previous work looked into increasing security in phone sharing scenarios among emergent users [3,53]. Ahmed et al. studied privacy invasions by local repair shops in Bangladesh [2]. They found that repairers often look at private contents on customers' phones. In another study, Ahmed et al. studied how government-imposed mandatory biometric registration for each mobile phone results in concerns and suspicions within the Bangladeshi population [4]. Sambasivan et al. studied how women in south Asia navigate privacy within complicated gender power balance [55].

These works underline the importance of understanding the influence of both geographic and socioeconomic distributions on privacy perceptions.

3   Target Groups

Previous work in privacy and security reveals that there is a gap in understanding the privacy concerns and perceptions of users from the Arab world. Furthermore,

there has been a steadily increasing adoption of technology among more users of low socioeconomic groups, This user group shows a set of under-investigated design needs and concerns that are influenced by their unique privacy perception.

Preliminary work in this area has shown that there might be significant differences in privacy invasion experiences in Arab communities compared to non-Arab ones [54]. It has also been established that a person's level of income could influence their privacy concerns [58]. This led us to add two target groups in our work: Users from High Socioeconomic groups in Arab countries (HSA), and users from Low Socioeconomic groups in Arab countries (LSA). We chose to study two Arab countries: Egypt and Saudi Arabia. Egypt is the Arab country in Africa with the most internet users (over 37 million users), Saudi Arabia the Arab country in the Middle East with the most internet users (24 million out of a 32 million population) [31]. Egypt and Saudi Arabia are Arab countries that share many cultural dimensions due to common traditions and religion [26,30].

Second, we chose users from High Socioeconomic groups in Germany (HSG) as a baseline because (1) it is a typical Western, Educated, Industrialized, Rich and Democratic society, (2) this user group has been extensively studied in previous work [23,33–35]. We focused our work on women because previous work has shown that women have more privacy concerns in the Arab world, so we recruited more female participants [1,12].

4 Questionnaire Development

The questionnaire[1] was distributed online to high socioeconomic participants (HSA and HSG) and offline for medium to low socioeconomic participants (LSA). The questionnaire was developed in English and translated to Arabic for LSA participants. Its translation was validated in terms of language and cultural appropriateness by native speakers. A challenge in cultural studies in HCI is ensuring that questions are tapping into the same constructs when the questionnaire is administered in different cultures [16]. Thus, to ensure cultural appropriateness, we conducted a pre-study where participants were asked to answer the questionnaire then explain any difficulties or comments. Participants had some issues with the questionnaire structure which we edited, but there were no cultural issues reported. In addition, we are also familiar with the cultural backgrounds of all our user groups by being integrated in their communities. We used non-biased wordings and provided more space for participants to use their own words through critical incident recall and open ended questions.

4.1 Questionnaire Design

National culture was determined by asking participants where they are from and where they reside. Socioeconomic status was determined through anonymous questions about the participant's occupation, income, education, and residence type, which are the most widely recognized measures for determining socioeconomic statuses [25,28]. The questionnaire was designed to collect very sensitive

---

[1] Questionnaire can be found in the supplementary material section on Springer.

data, so the anonymity of the results and its separation from the demographic data was emphasized throughout the questionnaire. This has been shown to ensure high level of honesty when answering questions [45].

We used the critical incident technique [9]. Participants were asked to freely recall a privacy violation incident using critical incidents that they have experienced or have witnessed. This facilitates the narration of the experiences and makes the reflection on the questions more reliable as it relates to own life events. To reduce social desirability bias, no negative connotations were used to describe the attacker or the incidents [20]. Instead, the terms victim and attacker were replaced by gender neutral personas. We used "Vic" and "Cas" in the English version, and "Nour" and "Ehsan" in the Arabic version. We conducted two prestudies with 10 participants in which we iteratively improved the clarity of the questionnaire and its organization by incorporating their feedback. All data was anonymous and that the participants gave an informed consent that we can store and use their anonymous responses for research non-commercial purposes. Participants who filled the online questionnaire and wished to be considered for the shopping voucher provided their emails; we separated emails before analysis and discarded them after compensations were issued. No contact details were collected from those who filled the printed version.

4.2   Questionnaire Structure

The questionnaire was divided into five sections:

Experience with Privacy Invasion. The first section collected information about participant's experience with privacy invasion. Several types of privacy invasions were listed and participants were asked to report if they experienced them, and were asked to rank their perceived severity from 1 (Extremely Severe) to 5 (Not Severe at all). Next, participants were asked to report a privacy violation incident they experienced or observed in the form of an open question. This was followed by questions on why participants perceived the situation to involve privacy invasion, and the participant's role in the incident, i.e., whether the participant was Cas, Vic, or a third-party observer.

Details About the Incident. In the second section, more information about the privacy invasion incident was collected. We asked for the relationship between the victim and the attacker, the consequences of the attack, the content that was violated, the feelings of the participant towards the incident and the locations and genders of those involved.

Relationships and Privacy Dynamics. In the following section, participants were asked to answer when and whom they believe can access their private information without them considering it a privacy violation. Our aim from this question was to understand if participants from the investigated user groups perceive privacy invasions by certain individuals to be acceptable. This was motivated by preliminary indicators that some Arabs perceive the invasion of children privacy to be justified [54].

Applied Preventative Measures. After that, participants were asked to report who they constantly try to protect their information from (e.g., colleagues, family, etc.) and reasons behind that. This was done to investigate if relationships play different roles depending on nationality and/or socioeconomic group.

Demographics and Socioeconomic Group. Finally, participants were asked to report their demographics to identify their socioeconomic status, including their occupation, academic degree, residence and monthly income, as well as their country of origin and residence [25, 28]. Inspired by prior work to exclude invalid data [23], we asked participants to rate the honesty of their response on a five-point Likert scale.

4.3   Distribution and Recruitment

In HSA and HSG, due to their educational background they were used to surveys and hence it was easy to introduce ourselves and our survey objectives through mailing lists and social media. For LSA, participants were at first hesitant. We established rapport by visiting the community personally, talking to the participants generally about social media and privacy, and showing them that we are "on their side". The questionnaire was distributed through social networks and through Egyptian, Saudi and German university mailing lists. To include more LSA participants who might not be reachable online, the questionnaire was printed and administered to nurses in 3 hospitals in Egypt. The nurses' educational degrees were either Diplomas or university education with an average salary of less than 3000 EGP per month. Based on their education, occupation and income, they are considered from a medium to low socioeconomic group according to prior work on socioeconomic status scale in Egypt [25]. Participants were compensated with shopping vouchers or credit points for their studies.

4.4   Limitations

Self-report bias is a significant shortcoming of questionnaires [19], and ours it not an exception; participants answer what they thought or believed the situation to be, not what actually happened. We attempted to counteract this by providing neutral connotations for attacker and victim to avoid strong positive or negative associations that would increase the bias. Still, only 12% of participants reported themselves as attackers or "Cas", most likely due to the social desirability bias [20]. Another issue is that to reach out for LSA participants, we administered a paper-based version of the questionnaire. This may have led to bias as online participants are self-selected, i.e., a participant might decide not to fill in the questionnaire if they do not want to. To balance this potential bias, offline questionnaires that included many empty response fields were excluded completely, and the addition of the honesty question was considered where if participants responded that they were not honest when answering the survey, their result was also excluded. While there are limitations to questionnaires, this tool has

74   M. Saleh et al.

given us the ability to reach a wide variety of participants. In addition, using the critical incident recall and allowing participants to use their own words and ideas generated interesting results. We even got feedback from the participants that the questionnaire was intriguing and fun.

5 Results

Table 1 shows a summary of the major results reported by the participants.

The survey was filled by 166 participants. We excluded 8 participants for not answering the majority of questions. Furthermore, we excluded 2 participants who responded "disagree" or "strongly disagree" when asked about the honesty of their responses. Out of the remaining 156 participants, 58 participants were males and 98 were females. The gender bias is due to the LSA group who were mostly female nurses. Out of all participants, there were 39 LSA participants from Egypt, 58 HSA participants (36 from Egypt and 22 from Saudi Arabia) and 61 HSG participants from Germany. Participants' ages ranged from 18 to 57 with a mean age of 31 (SD = 10.9).

Responses were coded by one researcher then revised by another to ensure consistency and avoid bias. Open-ended questions were labeled and thematic analysis, loosely based on the work of Guest et al. and Miles et al., was used to extract the following themes [32, 46].

5.1 Theme 1: Experienced Types of Privacy Invasions

In the first section, we asked participants about the types of privacy invasions they experienced. We provided a list of the following privacy invasion attacks, and asked them to choose the ones they have experienced as an attacker, victim or third-party observer. These included identity theft, impersonation, profile harvesting, spying, shoulder surfing, hacking, credit card theft, involuntary attacks. These types of attacks were extracted from [17]; we then added shoulder surfing [23] and credit card theft [40]. Figure 1 shows the type of privacy invasions experienced by all groups.

Results show that while shoulder surfing is the most experienced form of attacks, participants from the HSA do not report it as often. A possible reason is that shoulder surfing occurs mostly in public transport [23] which is commonly used by HSG and LSA, public transport is not commonly used by individuals who belong to high socioeconomic subgroups in the middle east (i.e., HSA participants) [27].

Hacking, identity theft and defamation are generally common, and relatively more common in the LSA group. This is fueled by acts of defamation as a form of vengeance, and the importance of reputation in this culture [29,52].

According to the Central Bank of Egypt, only 33% of Egyptian adults have bank accounts [49]. Our results show that credit card theft is not experienced often (6 out of 39) among LSA participants since individuals with low income in Arab countries usually do not own credit cards or even bank accounts. On the

Table 1. Based on the results of a survey (N = 156), we report on differences and similarities between users from: Low Socioeconomic Arab societies (LSA), High Socioeconomic Arab Societies (HSA) and High Socioeconomic German Socities (HSG).

Aspect	LSA	HSA	HSG
Hacking	Black Hat	Grey Hat	Grey Hat
Shoulder Surfing	Frequent	Infrequent	Frequent
Perceived Intentions	Malicious and targeted	Random	Random
Consequences of Attack	Serious consequences	Some consequences	No consequences
Acceptability of privacy invasion situations	Not accepted	Accepted in case of parents invading child privacy	In case of death or individual safety
Acceptability of personal information access from individuals	Sometimes by spouses	Sometimes by spouses	Not accepted
Change of privacy perception after an attack	Yes	Yes	No
Most Commonly invaded platforms	Smartphones (58.97%)	Smartphones (30.19%) and laptops (28.3%)	Smartphones (51.79%)

other hand, it is experienced more often among HSA participants (17 out of 58). It is not often experienced often among HSG (6 out of 61). A possible reason is that Germans tend to prefer cash transactions [11,34].

Finally, device sharing attacks were only experienced in the LSA group (23 times). This is expected since phone sharing is more common in low socioeconomic societies [69].

In addition to selecting the types of privacy invasions they experienced in the last section, we further asked participants to report a particular privacy invasion incident that they recall in an open-ended question. We clarified that they can report incidents in which they were attackers, victims, or third-party observers. The following section describes the attack that participants deemed most relevant to report then describe in detail. In addition to the privacy invasions types reported in Sect. 5.1, a new type of privacy invasion emerged from the data, that we labeled "physical breach". We use this term to refer to attacks where the attacker gains access to the victim's device by being physically present in the same place, for example accessing their phone by borrowing it, participants forgetting to logout and attackers using their accounts, or observing the victim's credentials and using them later. We also added a category: "application privacy invasion" as participants complained that applications on their phones invaded

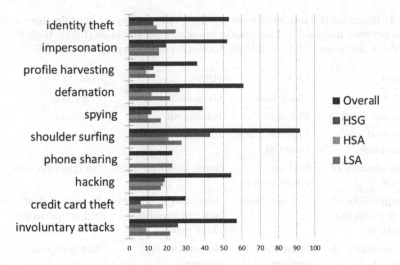

Fig. 1. Number of attacks experienced across the 3 participant groups. The results show that shoulder surfing is one of the most common privacy invasion types experienced across all groups. However, HSG and LSA groups experience it more often than HSA. Credit card theft is less common in HSG and LSA. Identity theft is most common in LSA, while attacks related to device sharing are exclusive to LSAs.

their privacy. Most of the LSA (34 out of 39) participants reported forms of hacking as their privacy invasion incidents. This was not matched in HSA (17 out of 58) and HSG (18 out of 61) participants, whose leading form of invasions were physical breach (61 out of 119) and shoulder surfing (45 out of 119).

In addition, LSA participants also reported more "black-hat hacking" cases, i.e., incidents where the hacker has a malicious intent and causes personal damage with actions such as identity theft and defamation. Over 50% (19 out of 34) of the hacking incidents reported by LSA participants involved attackers spreading private information about the victim, in particular personal photos. Personal information was spread to the victim's acquaintances, which often resulted in severe damage to the victim's relationships. One participant walked us through how her relationship with her fiancee was affected after her Facebook profile was hacked. Over 70% (26 out of 34) of the hacking incidents reported were also directed towards the victim specifically with an intent to personally hurt them and were preempted rather than being random events. Around half (21 out of 34) of these attacks were by strangers, while the other half was by attackers that the victim knew personally, such as colleagues, friends, or sometimes even spouses. This can be due to the revengeful nature of this particular user group [7], this will be discussed in further details in Sect. 5. In addition, most of the hacking events included female victims (20 out of 37). Many of them included male hackers to female victims (13 out of 37).

On the other hand, most of the attacks experienced by HSA (12 out of 17) and HSG (10 out of 14) were "grey-hat hacking" where the hacker wanted to enjoy the

process of hacking and gaining access to the participants account over actually harming them in their personal lives or relationships. Participants from both HSA and HSG groups had their email or Facebook accounts hacked. According to their responses, no real damage occurred with the exception of when hackers requested money from the victim's friends or from the victim himself to recover the account.

5.2   Theme 2: Perceived Intentions of Attackers

Participants were asked about the perceived reasons for the privacy invasion and the intentions of the attacker. In HSA and HSG, responses included coincidence (5), curiosity (14), and boredom (5) which mostly showed mild negative connotation or perception of the attacker. This is also inline with previous findings about certain types of attacks such as shoulder surfing [23]. Some HSA and HSG participants (24 out of 119) reported that the attacker sought money, which showed negative connotation but was not directly related to this particular victim. Participants stated that the attackers who stole the victim's identity asked them or their friends for in return for the account. On the other hand, participants from LSA reported reasons such as revenge, defamation, immoral attacker and spying. This shows that LSA individuals perceive attackers to have a higher negative association than HSA and HSG victims. In addition, LSA individuals reported that they believe these attacks to be directed at that particular victim and not casual attacks that could have affected anyone. For example P129 mentioned "my colleagues did this [attack] because they are jealous of me" and P142 mentioned "revenge" as a reason for the attack. This phenomenon can be explained in two ways: it could be that the LSA participants are more anxious, suspicious or mistrustful of attackers, or it could be that indeed acts of defamation and revenge are more common within LSA societies.

5.3   Theme 3: Consequences and Reactions to the Attack

The reported consequences of the attacks varied according to the participants' groups. HSA usually reported "no serious consequences". For example, P08 stated "Cas knew private things about Vic, but there were no severe consequences". On a few occasions (5 out of 58), the consequences included reporting the incident to social network administrators, bank management or even to the police. Around 70% (39 out of 58) of HSA participants also reported that the relationships between the attacker and the victim were affected by the attack. For example, P05 reported that Cas and Vic's relationship after the attack featured "uncomfortableness with Vic keeping more distance".

On the other hand, HSG participants mostly reported "no consequences" (48 out of 61) except in the case of shoulder surfing where they often changed their behavior and became more careful about using their devices in public. For example P70 said that the consequence of these attacks is "Rarely texting in public places" and P85 highlighted "Extra awareness from other possible Cas in the future" as a consequence. They also reported that the relationships were

mostly (40 out of 61) unaffected by the attack. For example, when asked about how the relationship was affected P106 replied "not much, since Vic knows that Cas will never stop doing those things, no matter how mad they make Vic".

On the other hand, LSA (39 out of 39) reported the consequences to be more serious and used terms like "loss of trust" (7), "ruined relationships" (12), "defamation" (11) and even "divorce" (1). For example P132 reported that "Vic faced a lot of upsetting encounters from her friends because of the information spread about them". LSA participants (39 out of 39) reported that relationships were strongly affected by attacks with more long term consequences than HSA.

These attacks also influenced the privacy perception of LSA participants more than HSG and HSA participants. HSG participants' majority (40 out of 61) were not influenced by the attacks and their privacy perception did not change. For example, when asked if the situation affected their privacy perception P117 replied saying "No, because I am already cautious". However, around 65% (37 out of 58) of HSA participants had their privacy perception changed after the reported incidents while all LSA participants reported a change of perception. Hacking and physical breach attacks caused the most influence on privacy perception change over other types of attacks.

Finally, when reporting on whether or not the participants viewed the situation as resolved, all attacks involving spouses as the attackers (total of 8 attacks) were perceived as not resolved across the three groups. HSA participants viewed attacks by strangers as mostly resolved, while LSA participants had higher expectations before they can consider an incident to be resolved. For example, they do not consider a situation in which "account access was regained" to be resolved, since this does not undo the implications of the attack. This is likely due to the perceived strong consequences of the attacks. Finally, HSG participants showed no tendency in reporting whether or not attacks were resolved, with almost 50% reporting resolved and 50% unresolved.

5.4   Theme 4: Acceptability of Privacy Invasion

Participants were asked about situations in which they believe privacy invasion is acceptable, e.g., certain individuals whom they would allow to access personal information without considering it a privacy invasion. HSG (22 out of 61) mostly reported that they believe privacy invasion to be justified only in case the safety of an individual is at stake, or after a person's death. For example P116 mentioned that if "[a] person gone missing, accessing private info might help finding them; law enforcement" it would be acceptable to invade their privacy. On the other hand, HSA were almost equally divided between the acceptance of privacy invasion by parents (11 out of 58) to their children or not accepting privacy invasion at all (13 out of 58). For example, P52 replied "Parent checking on the kids (viewing history of searches and views)". LSA (37 out of 39) mostly did not report any situation where privacy invasion was justified.

Results show that majority of participants (128 out of 156) from the three user groups did not accept personal information access from anyone. Although a few mentioned acceptability from friends, spouses and close family members,

the majority believed it to be unjustified. However, around 20% (19 out of 100) of LSA and HSA accepted personal information access from spouses, opposed to 7% among HSG.

5.5 Theme 5: Privacy Invasion Platforms

Participants reported multiple platforms on which privacy invasion incidents took place. Most prominently, privacy invasions occurred on desktop computers (26), laptops (31), tablets (2) and smartphones (71). Most of the privacy invasions in incidents reported by HSG and LSA participants involved smartphones: 51.8% (29 out of 56) of incidents reported by HSGs and 59% (23 out of 39) of those reported by LSAs. On the other hand, HSA participants reported that only 16 incidents out of 53 involved smartphones (30.2%). This difference can be again attributed to the relative less use of public transport by HSA participants, in which the majority of smartphone shoulder surfing takes place [23]. Another possible reason is that LSA users are more likely to have smartphones opposed to other more expensive devices such as tablets, desktops or laptop computers.

6   Discussion

This study investigated privacy invasion experiences and attitudes of 156 participants in Germany, Egypt and Saudi Arabia. Participants in Egypt are divided to those with high socioeconomic status and medium-low socioeconomic status. Findings show differences and similarities among the three groups in all areas of investigation. Table 1 summarizes the results by comparing the differences and similarities experienced across all three participant groups. The first obvious insight is that users from LSA, HSA and HSG have different privacy-related experiences and perceptions, privacy concerns, and privacy requirements.

In this section we discuss the findings in light of prior work, and conclude each subsection with implications for future work in this area.

6.1   LSAs Need Usable Privacy Filters

Western cultures are relatively less conservative, and hence implications of photos leaks could be less severe. On the other hand, the Arab culture is governed by religion and traditions [6,48]. Revealing personal information is very sensitive and care must be taken to whom it is revealed to. For example, photos especially of women tend to be kept private. Women who send their photos to strangers are frowned upon and their reputation is highly affected. Hence, attackers accessing someone's social network accounts, and taking their photos then claiming that the women have sent them or posting them publicly is very dangerous to a woman's reputation. Also, women who wear headscarfs might exchange photos without their headscarfs with female friends online. If these photos are leaked or retrieved maliciously by an attacker, the victim might be subject to embarrassment, and harassment by friends and family [29,43].

Implication: Future systems can auto detect private photos using computer vision and machine learning (e.g., detecting the absence of headscarf or intimate moments) and classify them as private ones.

The Arab culture is a collectivist one [29], certain information must be shared with relatives and friends, otherwise the person will be perceived as hiding information, a sign of mistrust in the Arab world. This is the reason why sensitive information might be shared in private messages in the first place.

Implication: This highlights the need for specialized systems that (1) can support these sharing patterns with trusted individuals, while at the same time (2) protect its users from unintended privacy leaks especially those that could have negative implications due to the user's culture, and (3) are usable to accommodate LSA users who could be less tech-savvy than other user groups. These systems need to be accessible for low-literate users. One of the reported problems by LSA users is not knowing how data can be accessed and used against them, or how their privacy can be violated. This prompts for solutions that raise awareness of users. A simple solution that can be applied is providing periodic pop-up notifications for privacy filters that users can apply. This can help users understand the threat associated with this data and how it can be avoided.

6.2 Malicious Privacy Invasions Are More Common in LSA Societies

One of the most popular concerns by participants is privacy invasion in online social networks. Participants reported being hacked or leaking sensitive information to attackers. These findings are consistent with previous work which found that 7.1% of Arab respondents to a survey believed that "online social networks might cause troubles" [48]. To combat these effects, Cutillo et al. created Safebook [17]. Safebook is a social network that has an extra layer of safety which stops the creation of fake accounts hence reducing the incidences of impersonation. Safebook also does not allow revealing information about someone by another person unless their consent is received. Another effort to increase safety in social networks is Persona by Baden et al. [10]. Persona emphasizes the role of user in their own privacy by displaying only the information that users explicitly give consent to share.

Black Hat Hacking Among LSA. LSA experienced more "black hat hacking" than HSA and HSG. This could be due to the fact that the lower socioeconomic groups hold more to the Arabic traditions than HSA which tends to be more westernized due to exposure to Western education systems and frequent travel [57]. Hence, the reveal of personal information can be very threatening to LSA. Hackers are also more often acquaintances or even family members which shows that these hacks are targeted with the malicious intent of defamation and harm and often motivated by vengeance.

Implication: There should be more emphasis on the insider threat when designing solutions for LSA users [50]. This begs the question of how to balance protection against insider threats while allowing sharing to trusted individuals.

This topic requires further research. One potentially interesting direction is having systems communicate to users the potential misuses of their information, or giving users control over the content even when shared beyond the user's first contact (e.g., tell the user if their photo was forwarded, downloaded, or posted somewhere on the web).

Shoulder Surfing Is More Common in LSA and HSG. Results also show that shoulder surfing is experienced more in LSA and HSG. This could be due to the fact that the most common location for shoulder surfing is public transportation [23] and individuals in HSA societies do not use public transportation often, but rather use personal cars and taxis [27].

Implication: Since privacy invasions have serious consequences in LSA, our results confirm the need for privacy protection mechanisms. Many works proposed effective approaches for security and privacy protection yet they are not employed in today's every day technologies. For example, von Zezschwitz et al. [72] proposed mechanisms to protect the visual privacy of photos from shoulder surfing while users browse images on their phones. Eiband et al. [24] proposed protecting text content on mobile devices from shoulder surfing by displaying it in the user's handwriting, which is easy for the legitimate user to understand, but difficult for observers to read. There are many works that protect illegitimate access to social networks [10], and mobile devices (i.e. secure authentication) [71]. Our results confirm that these additional measures for protecting privacy are very important, since they can reduce the potentially severe threats that certain user groups could be subject to.

6.3   Trust Is Fragile Among Arab Users

LSA viewed the attacks to have more serious consequences, this concurs with the belief that defamation can cause serious damage to this user group [29]. It also shows that preventative measures are very important to accommodate this group. The common preventative technique used offline is trust recommendation. Offline, reputation is held through actions and word of mouth which is maintained in a circle of acquaintances often within a neighbourhood or workplace. This system can be implemented online by building trust recommendation social networks. Other groups show less serious consequences due to the more open minded nature of the relationships and the less malicious nature of the attacks. The Arab cultures are also more collectivist cultures, that is why they tend to have a more trusting attitude [29]. However, the privacy attacks they experience and the damage caused by these attacks can cause them to lose trust. This loss of trust is conveyed by the change in privacy perception observed in HSA and LSA after the attacks compared to HSG. Attacks from spouses are never perceived as resolved. While attacks from strangers are viewed as resolved in HSA and HSG because once the accounts are regained or the information is dealt with, participants do not expect anything further due to the mild nature of the consequences. On the other hand, LSA do not perceive issues to be resolved since the consequences are very strong.

6.4   Exaggerated Fears

Participants from lower socioeconomic status in Arab countries are usually paranoid about their own safety [47]. They believe that they are constantly being monitored or attacked. This can be due to their limited resources and their fear of not being secure enough, or due to the limited understanding of the security features of technological devices. Therefore, they can easily believe that any attack is directed to them even if it were a mere coincidence. LSA users often think that others are participating in acts of defamation or revenge against them, as suggested by P129 (LSA), who thought others are after her privacy due to jealousy.

While lots of efforts are now directed towards customization for marginalized groups. Some of the techniques and methodologies used may have hidden consequences. For example, participatory design methods are used to tailor designs such as the work done by Weber et al. [64]. However, care must be taken as personalization can make users, and particularly LSA ones, worry or lose trust of the system if it is perceived to be requesting more data than it needs [14]. This can also be counteracted by providing culture-appropriate awareness raising techniques such as privacy filters mentioned above.

6.5   Privacy Invasion Acceptance

In terms of privacy invasion acceptance, participants from LSA did not accept privacy invasion at all. This could be due to the strong consequences that the previous privacy invasion encounters caused. On the other hand, many HSA participants believed that parents can invade children privacy. This is deeply routed in the Arab culture, where parents are perceived as having control and being responsible over all nature of child safety and well-being. This is not reflected in the HSG participants who see only personal safety, national threats and death as acceptable reasons for privacy invasion. The implication of this phenomenon on device access and access modes should be studied.

7   Conclusion and Future Work

In this study, we investigated the privacy invasion perceptions of 156 participants. A survey was conducted online and offline with participants from Germany, Egypt and Saudi Arabia. Egyptian participants were divided between high and medium-low socioeconomic groups. Participants were asked to report privacy invasion incidents they experienced, their feelings and attitudes towards them and how it changed their privacy perception. They were also asked about their acceptability of privacy invasions in special circumstances or by special people. Finally, they were asked about who they protect their privacy from. Participants from LSA experienced more harmful attacks that resulted in stronger consequences on their relationships and reputations. Participants from HSG were more forgiving and experienced milder consequences. However, they showed a

change of attitude when it came to attacks of shoulder surfing. Participants from HSA were in the middle of both extremes. They showed some concern about the attacks they faced. In addition, HSA participants believed privacy invasion to be accepted by parents to monitor children, while HSG sometimes believed it to be acceptable in case of safety or death and LSA never believed it to be acceptable. Designs must therefore be customized to each user group to assist them in respecting their privacy and protecting their data.

These results underline that privacy-related experiences, perceptions, concerns and requirements are different between LSA, HSA and HSG societies. This implies that privacy protection mechanisms should be designed with differences between different socioeconomic groups in mind, rather than following a one-size-fits all approach with WEIRD societies in the forefront. Furthermore, we confirm that privacy invasions are more common in LSA societies, and that trust among Arab users is fragile. This emphasizes the importance of trust and privacy protection when designing systems.

Our results highlight the need for usable privacy protection systems that are tailored for each user group. For future work, we plan to study privacy in more Arab cultures, and also investigate similar and different perceptions among the studied groups and users from low socioeconomic groups in WEIRD countries.

References

1. Abokhodair, N., Vieweg, S.: Privacy & social media in the context of the Arab Gulf. In: Proceedings of the DIS 2016, pp. 672–683. ACM (2016)
2. Ahmed, S.I., Guha, S., Rifat, M.R., Shezan, F.H., Dell, N.: Privacy in repair: an analysis of the privacy challenges surrounding broken digital artifacts in Bangladesh. In: Proceedings of the ICTD 2016, pp. 11:1–11:10. ACM (2016). https://doi.org/10.1145/2909609.2909661
3. Ahmed, S.I., Haque, M.R., Chen, J., Dell, N.: Digital privacy challenges with shared mobile phone use in Bangladesh. Proc. ACM Hum.-Comput. Interact. 1(CSCW), 17:1–17:20 (2017). https://doi.org/10.1145/3134652
4. Ahmed, S.I., Haque, M.R., Guha, S., Rifat, M.R., Dell, N.: Privacy, security, and surveillance in the Global South: a study of biometric mobile sim registration in Bangladesh. In: Proceedings of the CHI 2017, pp. 906–918. ACM (2017). https://doi.org/10.1145/3025453.3025961
5. Al-Dawood, A., Abokhodair, N., El mimouni, H., Yarosh, S.: "Against marrying a stranger": marital matchmaking technologies in Saudi Arabia. In: Proceedings of the DIS 2017, pp. 1013–1024. ACM (2017). https://doi.org/10.1145/3064663.3064683
6. Alabdulqader, E., Lazem, S., Khamis, M., Dray, S.: Exploring participatory design methods to engage with Arab communities (2018). https://doi.org/10.1145/3170427.3170623
7. Almaney, A.J., Alwan, A.: Communicating with the Arabs: A Handbook for the Business Executive. Waveland Press, Long Grove (1982)
8. Alsheikh, T., Rode, J.A., Lindley, S.E.: (Whose) value-sensitive design: a study of long-distance relationships in an Arabic cultural context. In: Proceedings of the CSCW 2011, pp. 75–84. ACM (2011). https://doi.org/10.1145/1958824.1958836

9. Anderson, L., Wilson, S.: Critical incident technique (1997)
10. Baden, R., Bender, A., Spring, N., Bhattacharjee, B., Starin, D.: Persona: an online social network with user-defined privacy. In: ACM SIGCOMM Computer Communication Review, vol. 39, pp. 135–146. ACM (2009)
11. Bagnall, J., et al.: Consumer cash usage: a cross-country comparison with payment diary survey data (2014). https://ssrn.com/abstract=2796990
12. Belk, R., Sobh, R.: Gender and privacy in Arab Gulf states: implications for consumption and marketing. In: Handbook of Islamic Marketing, pp. 71–96 (2011)
13. Bellman, S., Johnson, E.J., Kobrin, S.J., Lohse, G.L.: International differences in information privacy concerns: a global survey of consumers. Inf. Soc. **20**(5), 313–324 (2004)
14. Briggs, P., Simpson, B., De Angeli, A.: Personalisation and trust: a reciprocal relationship? In: Karat, C.M., Blom, J.O., Karat, J. (eds.) Designing Personalized User Experiences in eCommerce. HCIS, vol. 5, pp. 39–55. Springer, Dordrecht (2004). https://doi.org/10.1007/1-4020-2148-8_4
15. Ching, C.C., Basham, J.D., Jang, E.: The legacy of the digital divide: gender, socioeconomic status, and early exposure as predictors of full-spectrum technology use among young adults. Urban Educ. **40**(4), 394–411 (2005)
16. Clemmensen, T., Roese, K.: An overview of a decade of journal publications about culture and human-computer interaction (HCI). In: Katre, D., Orngreen, R., Yammiyavar, P., Clemmensen, T. (eds.) HWID 2009. IAICT, vol. 316, pp. 98–112. Springer, Heidelberg (2010). https://doi.org/10.1007/978-3-642-11762-6_9
17. Cutillo, L.A., Molva, R., Strufe, T.: Safebook: a privacy-preserving online social network leveraging on real-life trust. IEEE Commun. Mag. **47**(12), 94–101 (2009)
18. Dinev, T., Bellotto, M., Hart, P., Russo, V., Serra, I.: Internet users privacy concerns and beliefs about government surveillance. J. Glob. Inf. Manag. **14**(4), 57–93 (2006). https://doi.org/10.4018/jgim.2006100103
19. Dunning, D., Heath, C., Suls, J.M.: Flawed self-assessment: implications for health, education, and the workplace. Psychol. Sci. Public Interest **5**(3), 69–106 (2004)
20. Edwards, A.L.: The social desirability variable in personality assessment and research (1957)
21. Egelman, S., Jain, S., Portnoff, R.S., Liao, K., Consolvo, S., Wagner, D.: Are you ready to lock? In: Proceedings of the CCS 2014, pp. 750–761. ACM (2014). https://doi.org/10.1145/2660267.2660273
22. Egelman, S., Peer, E.: The myth of the average user: improving privacy and security systems through individualization. In: Proceedings of the NSPW 2015, pp. 16–28. ACM (2015). https://doi.org/10.1145/2841113.2841115
23. Eiband, M., Khamis, M., von Zezschwitz, E., Hussmann, H., Alt, F.: Understanding shoulder surfing in the wild: stories from users and observers. In: Proceedings of the CHI 2017, pp. 4254–4265. ACM (2017). https://doi.org/10.1145/3025453.3025636
24. Eiband, M., von Zezschwitz, E., Buschek, D., Hussmann, H.: My scrawl hides it all: protecting text messages against shoulder surfing with handwritten fonts. In: Proceedings of the CHI EA 2016, pp. 2041–2048. ACM (2016). https://doi.org/10.1145/2851581.2892511
25. El-Gilany, A., El-Wehady, A., El-Wasify, M.: Updating and validation of the socioeconomic status scale for health research in Egypt/mise à jour et validation d'une échelle du statut socioéconomique pour la recherche en santé en égypte. East. Mediterr. Health J. **18**(9), 962 (2012)
26. El-Gilany, A.H., Amr, M., Hammad, S.: Perceived stress among male medical students in Egypt and Saudi Arabia: effect of sociodemographic factors. Ann. Saudi Med. **28**(6), 442–448 (2008)

27. Elias, W., Shiftan, Y.: The influence of individual's risk perception and attitudes on travel behavior. Transp. Res. Part A: Policy Pract. **46**(8), 1241–1251 (2012). http://www.sciencedirect.com/science/article/pii/S0965856412000882
28. Fahmy, S.: Determining simple parameters for social classifications for health research. Bull. High Inst. Public Health **13**, 95–108 (1983)
29. Feghali, E.: Arab cultural communication patterns. Int. J. Intercult. Relat. **21**(3), 345–378 (1997)
30. Finardi, U., Buratti, A.: Scientific collaboration framework of BRICS countries: an analysis of international coauthorship. Scientometrics **109**(1), 433–446 (2016). https://doi.org/10.1007/s11192-016-1927-0
31. Miniwatts Marketing Group: Internet world stats. https://www.internetworldstats.com/stats.htm. Accessed 18 Sept 2018
32. Guest, G., MacQueen, K.M., Namey, E.E.: Applied Thematic Analysis. Sage Publications, Thousand Oaks (2011)
33. Harbach, M., De Luca, A., Malkin, N., Egelman, S.: Keep on lockin' in the free world: a multi-national comparison of smartphone locking. In: Proceedings of the CHI 2016, pp. 4823–4827. ACM (2016). https://doi.org/10.1145/2858036.2858273
34. Harbach, M., Fahl, S., Smith, M.: Who's afraid of which bad wolf? A survey of IT security risk awareness. In: Proceedings of the IEEE CSF 2014, pp. 97–110, July 2014. https://doi.org/10.1109/CSF.2014.15
35. Harbach, M., von Zezschwitz, E., Fichtner, A., Luca, A.D., Smith, M.: It's a hard lock life: a field study of smartphone (un)locking behavior and risk perception. In: Proceedings of the SOUPS 2014, pp. 213–230. USENIX Association (2014). https://www.usenix.org/conference/soups2014/proceedings/presentation/harbach
36. Henrich, J., Heine, S.J., Norenzayan, A.: Most people are not weird. Nature **466**(7302), 29 (2010)
37. Henrich, J., Heine, S.J., Norenzayan, A.: The weirdest people in the world? Behav. Brain Sci. **33**(2–3), 61–83 (2010). https://www.ncbi.nlm.nih.gov/pubmed/20550733
38. Jones, M., et al.: Beyond "yesterday's tomorrow": future-focused mobile interaction design by and for emergent users. Pers. Ubiquitous Comput. **21**(1), 157–171 (2017). https://doi.org/10.1007/s00779-016-0982-0
39. Karlson, A.K., Brush, A., Schechter, S.: Can i borrow your phone?: understanding concerns when sharing mobile phones. In: Proceedings of the CHI 2009, pp. 1647–1650. ACM (2009)
40. Kelley, E.E., Motika, F., Motika, P.V., Motika, E.M.: Secure credit card, US Patent 6,641,050, 4 Nov 2003
41. Lazem, S., Jad, H.A.: We play we learn: exploring the value of digital educational games in rural Egypt. In: Proceedings of the CHI 2017, pp. 2782–2791. ACM (2017). https://doi.org/10.1145/3025453.3025593
42. Lee, I., Choi, B., Kim, J., Hong, S.J.: Culture-technology fit: effects of cultural characteristics on the post-adoption beliefs of mobile internet users. Int. J. Electron. Commer. **11**(4), 11–51 (2007)
43. Levmore, S., Nussbaum, M.C.: The Offensive Internet. Harvard University Press, Cambridge (2010)
44. Li, Y., Kobsa, A., Knijnenburg, B.P., Nguyen, M.C.: Cross-cultural privacy prediction. Proc. Priv. Enhancing Technol. **2017**(2), 113–132 (2017)
45. Marques, D., Guerreiro, T., Carriço, L.: Measuring snooping behavior with surveys: it's how you ask it. In: Proceedings of the CHI EA 2014, pp. 2479–2484. ACM (2014)

46. Miles, M.B., Huberman, A.M., Huberman, M.A., Huberman, M.: Qualitative Data Analysis: An Expanded Sourcebook. Sage, Thousand Oaks (1994)
47. Mirowsky, J., Ross, C.E.: Paranoia and the structure of powerlessness. Am. Sociol. Rev. **48**, 228–239 (1983)
48. Mohamed, A.A.A.: Online privacy concerns among social networks' users/question concernant les affaires personnelles des utilisateurs de réseaux sociaux en ligne. Cross-Cult. Commun. **6**(4), 74 (2010)
49. Mounir, H.: Only 33% of Egyptian adults own bank accounts: deputy CBE governor (2017). https://dailynewsegypt.com/2017/10/24/33-egyptian-adults-bank-accounts-deputy-cbe-governor/. Accessed 18 Sept 2018
50. Muslukhov, I., Boshmaf, Y., Kuo, C., Lester, J., Beznosov, K.: Know your enemy: the risk of unauthorized access in smartphones by insiders. In: Proceedings of the MobileHCI 2013, pp. 271–280. ACM (2013). https://doi.org/10.1145/2493190.2493223
51. Nassir, S., Leong, T.W.: Traversing boundaries: understanding the experiences of ageing Saudis. In: Proceedings of the CHI 2017, pp. 6386–6397. ACM (2017). https://doi.org/10.1145/3025453.3025618
52. Nobles, A.Y., Sciarra, D.T.: Cultural determinants in the treatment of Arab Americans: a primer for mainstream therapists. Am. J. Orthopsychiatry **70**(2), 182 (2000)
53. Robinson, S., Pearson, J., Reitmaier, T., Ahire, S., Jones, M.: Make yourself at phone: reimagining mobile interaction architectures with emergent users. In: Proceedings of the CHI 2018, pp. 407:1–407:12. ACM (2018). https://doi.org/10.1145/3173574.3173981
54. Saleh, M., Khamis, M., Sturm, C.: Privacy invasion experiences and perceptions: a comparison between Germany and the Arab world. In: Proceedings of the CHI EA 2018. ACM (2018). https://doi.org/10.1145/3170427.3188671
55. Sambasivan, N., et al.: "Privacy is not for me, it's for those rich women": performative privacy practices on mobile phones by women in South Asia. In: Proceedings of the SOUPS 2018, pp. 127–142. USENIX Association (2018). https://www.usenix.org/conference/soups2018/presentation/sambasivan
56. Sambasivan, N., Jain, N., Checkley, G., Baki, A., Herr, T.: A framework for technology design for emerging markets. Interactions **24**(3), 70–73 (2017). https://doi.org/10.1145/3058496
57. Sayed, F.H.: Transforming Education in Egypt: Western Influence and Domestic Policy Reform. American University in Cairo Press, Cairo (2006)
58. Schwartz, B.: The social psychology of privacy. Am. J. Sociol. **73**(6), 741–752 (1968)
59. Solove, D.J.: Speech, privacy, and reputation on the internet. In: Lovmore, S., Nussbaum, M. (eds.) The Offensive Internet (2010)
60. Sturm, C., Oh, A., Linxen, S., Abdelnour Nocera, J., Dray, S., Reinecke, K.: How WEIRD is HCI?: extending HCI principles to other countries and cultures. In: Proceedings of the CHI EA 2015, pp. 2425–2428. ACM (2015). https://doi.org/10.1145/2702613.2702656
61. Sunstein, C.: Believing false rumors. The (2010)
62. Talhouk, R., et al.: Syrian refugees and digital health in Lebanon: opportunities for improving antenatal health. In: Proceedings of the CHI 2016, pp. 331–342. ACM (2016). https://doi.org/10.1145/2858036.2858331
63. Wang, P., Petrison, L.A.: Direct marketing activities and personal privacy: a consumer survey. J. Direct Mark. **7**(1), 7–19 (1993)

64. Weber, S., Harbach, M., Smith, M.: Participatory design for security-related user interfaces. In: Proceedings of the USEC 2015 (2015)
65. Westin, A.F., Ruebhausen, O.M.: Privacy and Freedom. Ig Publishing, New York (2015)
66. Wilkinson, D., et al.: Moving beyond a "one-size fits all" approach: exploring individual differences in privacy (2018). https://doi.org/10.1145/3170427.3170617
67. Wisniewski, P., Islam, A.N., Knijnenburg, B.P., Patil, S.: Give social network users the privacy they want. In: Proceedings of the CSCW 2015, pp. 1427–1441. ACM (2015). https://doi.org/10.1145/2675133.2675256
68. Wisniewski, P.J., Knijnenburg, B.P., Lipford, H.R.: Making privacy personal: profiling social network users to inform privacy education and nudging. Int. J. Hum.-Comput. Stud. **98**, 95–108 (2017). http://www.sciencedirect.com/science/article/pii/S1071581916301185
69. Yardi, S., Bruckman, A.: Income, race, and class: exploring socioeconomic differences in family technology use. In: Proceedings of the CHI 2012, pp. 3041–3050. ACM (2012). https://doi.org/10.1145/2207676.2208716
70. Yoo, C.W., Ahn, H.J., Rao, H.R.: An exploration of the impact of information privacy invasion (2012)
71. von Zezschwitz, E., De Luca, A., Brunkow, B., Hussmann, H.: SwiPIN: fast and secure pin-entry on smartphones. In: Proceedings of the CHI 2015, pp. 1403–1406. ACM (2015). https://doi.org/10.1145/2702123.2702212
72. von Zezschwitz, E., Ebbinghaus, S., Hussmann, H., De Luca, A.: You can't watch this!: privacy-respectful photo browsing on smartphones. In: Proceedings of the CHI 2016, pp. 4320–4324. ACM (2016). https://doi.org/10.1145/2858036.2858120

Interaction Design for Culture and Development III

Interaction Design for Culture and
Development III

An HCI Perspective on Distributed Ledger Technologies for Peer-to-Peer Energy Trading

Sabrina Scuri[1]([⊠]) [iD], Gergana Tasheva[2], Luísa Barros[2],
and Nuno Jardim Nunes[3] [iD]

[1] ITI/LARSYS, Madeira-ITI, 9020-105 Funchal, Portugal
`sabrina.scuri@m-iti.org`
[2] Madeira-ITI, 9020-105 Funchal, Portugal
[3] ITI/LARSYS, IST - U. Lisbon, 1049-001 Lisbon, Portugal
`nunojnunes@tecnico.ulisboa.pt`

Abstract. Distributed Ledger Technologies (DLT), such as blockchain, are gaining increasing attention in the energy sector, where they can be used to support Peer-to-Peer (P2P) energy trading. Several proof-of-concept and pilot projects are running all over the world to test this specific use case. However, despite much work addressing the technical and regulatory aspects related to DLT for P2P energy trading, our understanding of the human aspects affecting the adoption of these systems and technologies is still minimal.

The development of a decentralized energy market poses interesting challenges to the HCI community and raises important questions that need to be answered: do people trust a system which is, by definition, trust-free? How do they perceive P2P energy trading? What are their needs and motivations for engaging in energy trading? Moreover, are people willing to use cryptocurrencies as a medium of exchange for energy? And, to what extent is full-automation desirable?

To shed light on these and related questions, we developed and tested *PowerShare*, a decentralized, P2P energy trading platform. In this paper, we report on our findings from interviews with nine families that have used *PowerShare* for a month. Motivated by our empirical findings we conclude by highlighting guidelines for designing P2P energy trading platforms and elaborate directions for further research.

Keywords: Human Computer Interaction · Peer-to-Peer Networks · Sustainable HCI · Distributed Ledger Technologies · Energy trading

1 Introduction

Energy has become established as an essential topic of interest for Human-Computer Interaction (HCI) research, particularly concerning the area of sustainable HCI [1, 2]. While most of the research focuses on Eco-feedback technologies (i.e. the technology providing feedback on behaviors with a goal of reducing environmental impact), others have also looked at how energy is an intricate design concept (i.e., both an immaterial concept but also a commodified and usable resource) [3]. However, little HCI research focused on changing energy infrastructures, which represents an increasingly relevant

© IFIP International Federation for Information Processing 2019
Published by Springer Nature Switzerland AG 2019
D. Lamas et al. (Eds.): INTERACT 2019, LNCS 11748, pp. 91–111, 2019.
https://doi.org/10.1007/978-3-030-29387-1_6

topic in the face of climate action. Modern energy production and distribution infrastructures are facing exceptional challenges: from the limited ability to accommodate low carbon generation (intrinsically invariable and hard to predict) to the electrification of important heat and transport sectors (leading to energy peaks that are disproportionately higher than the existing trends).

In this paper, we build on the state of the art by looking at changes in energy at the infrastructure level. We do this by looking at how new Peer-to-Peer (P2P) and microgrid technologies are radically changing the days when energy was centrally produced in large power plants and then distributed to our homes as a commodity. People are increasingly installing solar photovoltaic (PV) panels – i.e. panel modules composed of photovoltaic cells, made from various semi-conductor materials, which convert solar radiation into electricity [4] - on their rooftops or investing in other renewable energy devices. These smaller grid systems link localized power sources, often referred to as "distributed generation" sources. This scenario is challenging energy management systems because the supply of electricity on the grid has to equal demand to cope with the changes in renewables. However, more importantly, people can now choose to power their homes via a range of local renewable energy sources, and store or sell excess energy in their electric vehicles, home battery systems or to their neighbors. This is made possible by participating in a P2P energy trading network, which consists of a community of energy users composed of both consumers and prosumers - i.e. users equipped with small-scale energy generation units (like rooftop solar PV panels), which function as both energy producer and consumer [5]. Within a microgrid energy market, prosumers can store their energy surplus within a storage device, if there is any, or use it to supply peers in energy need [6]. Two are the main components enabling the energy exchange within such network [7]: (1) a virtual energy trading platform, i.e. the technical infrastructure which manages generation, demand and consumption data - collected through the smart meters installed within the house of each participant in the network - and performs payments; and (2) the physical energy network, i.e. a distribution grid where the energy exchange among peers takes place. To ensure accurate records of these transactions, microgrids are looking at blockchain technology. With the vanishing hype of cryptocurrencies distributed energy trading emerges as one of the most promising areas of application for blockchain technology. In fact, blockchain is one viable way to decentralize and share the microgrid accounting both in developed countries (facing the pressures of reducing their environmental impact), but also in developing countries (where segments of the population don't have access to national grids and centralized energy production).

The contribution of this paper is threefold. First, we position the challenges of blockchain technology for HCI research with a particular emphasis on issues of technology adoption and trust. Second, we illustrate through the design and real-world deployment of a neighborhood P2P energy trading system how these technologies challenge people's perceptions of energy and its trading and sharing. Third, we summarize our findings in terms of relevant design concepts such as economic rationality, rewarding, community, transparency and trust. We then conclude summarizing these findings as lessons learned on deployment of Distributed Ledger Technologies (DLT) for decentralized energy systems and design guidance for further HCI research in the domain of energy infrastructure and sustainable HCI in general.

2 Related Work

While much research addresses the technical shortcomings of DLT, not much investigation was conducted on the HCI front. Elsden et al. [8] argue that the field of HCI has evolved, spreading beyond the traditional domain of user interfaces into more profound questions surrounding the impact of new technologies on people. In their work, the authors outline the main groups of blockchain applications currently on the market by examining over 200 blockchain startups and their distinctive features. By doing so, they have set out a 'blueprint' for HCI researchers into the challenges and opportunities of blockchain technologies for the field.

Recent work by Sas and Khairuddin [9] focuses on the earliest blockchain application, Bitcoin, and explores the trust issues surrounding the use of bitcoins and cryptocurrencies alike. The authors argue that blockchain offers a unique case study for the exploration of trust since previous work undertaken in the field has focused on e-commerce and e-payment systems which are traditionally centralized, heavily regulated and non-anonymous. In addition, it must be pointed out that despite the extensive body of literature on trust in business-to-consumer (B2C) e-commerce [10–14], the role of trust in consumer-to-consumer (C2C) markets has received little attention, with few significant contributions to date [15–17]. Within this context, it is particularly worth mentioning the model proposed by Hawlitschek et al. [18]. In this work, the authors regard trust as a complex construct with multiple targets (peers, platform and product) and dimensions (ability, integrity, and benevolence), which are addressed from two different perspectives: the one of the buyer and the one of the supplier. Their findings highlight the pivotal role of the platform – which "primarily acts as a mediator between the peers" – in establishing trust among users, concluding that "trust towards the platform significantly increase users' sharing intentions–both for the supply and the demand side" [18]. This conceptual model provides an important contribution towards understanding trust in P2P markets, nevertheless, one can argue about its applicability to a blockchain-based system where there is no such trusted intermediary [19]. As blockchain technologies are decentralized, unregulated and anonymous, Sas and Khairuddin [9] claim that the applicability of previous HCI models on trust to the emerging domain of blockchain is questionable and new frameworks need to be established. The study builds upon a previous work by the same authors [20] on trust in bitcoin technology which aimed to establish one such framework for HCI research. In this early paper, the authors classify three different types of trust – technological, social and institutional. The users' trust in the technology can be divided into the perceived advantages of the technology, its usability and the perceived skills of the user to work with it. The social trust can be described as the level of trust between the different stakeholders engaged with the technology. Finally, the institutional trust applies to the rules and regulations surrounding each activity attributed to the technology.

The present paper explores all the above aspects regarding the technological, social and institutional trust behind new energy infrastructures based on P2P energy trading and combines them with a set of novel features unique to energy trading in distributed energy infrastructures. Parallel to the work by Sas and Khairuddin [9] who conducted 20 semi-structured interviews of bitcoin users in an attempt to identify trust

characteristics not yet known to HCI researchers and the wider public, here we strive to detect further trust implications specific to P2P energy trading applications. Although blockchain applications vary in their purpose, the underlying technology is inherently identical. Therefore, it is pertinent to shed light on several challenges and opportunities discussed in the HCI community.

2.1   Challenges to Blockchain Technology Adoption

Arguably the most common challenge mentioned in the scientific community related to adoption of blockchain concerns the required level of trust among actors. Whereas in a centralized and regulated system trust is handed to either a third party or a government entity, in blockchain applications trust is diffused among the individual participants. Elsden et al. [8] state that blockchain facilitates transactions, consensus and shared history between otherwise 'trustless' actors. Trustless refers to the lack of a centralized body in blockchain applications. The concept of a 'trustless trust' states that certain activities are made trustworthy by not needing to trust anyone in particular. Elseden and colleagues base their work on the hypothesis that the trust among new actors is sealed by the trust in the robust technical protocols behind blockchain, thus eliminating the human factor. In such a model, paradoxically, the lack of human involvement in the governance of technology leads to a higher level of trust among the stakeholders. Sas and Khairuddin [9] argue that despite the robustness of the technology, one cannot simply eliminate or disregard the human factor. In their research ([9] and [20]), the authors emphasize the considerable risk brought by 'dishonest partners of transaction'. In the later study [9], they report on the distrust some users have towards the community, several of whom have been cheated, demonstrating the need to have more information about the users one is engaging with and more importantly, their integrity and moral code. The authors also underline the lack of verification procedures surrounding blockchain applications. They identify four different types of insecure transactions, the majority of which are related to human factors. Namely, the insecurity can arise due to users themselves, the other user engaged in the transaction, a person or an entity not engaged in the transaction and the inability of the technology to address all of the above.

The lack of information and understanding is a further aspect which needs to be investigated by the HCI community. Sas and Khairuddin [20] claim that merchants, i.e. sellers, feel challenged by their limited knowledge about the buyer and worry if they will receive their payment from them. The same can be said about the buyers who might not be confident in the quality of the service they will receive. The authors report that this mutual distrust arises from the limited information both sides have on how the technology works and on the identities of the actors involved. The lack of information and/or understanding of the technology is also mentioned by Elseden et al. [8], which further hint at the perplexity of tokenization and question whether a token can correctly represent the true value of a service. In addition, Sas and Khairuddin [9] brings the issue of reputation surrounding blockchain, which has often been linked with online black-market activities.

Finally, Sas and Khairuddin [9] shed light into a new aspect previously not studied – data privacy. The authors question whether users are aware of the consequences of

sharing their data and preferences via smart contracts and whether the 'right to be forgotten' will have any standing in blockchain applications. This is a question of governance and rules and it has been classified as institutional trust. Though, how can users exercise institutional trust in blockchain technologies which are inherently built upon a *laissez faire* principle? All of those are important questions for the HCI community.

Besides the challenges described in the academic literature, which also apply to our energy infrastructure case study, after an extensive analysis of existing P2P energy trading platforms, we have identified automations as an additional aspect deserving further investigation. P2P energy trading applications are built out of the strive for more efficient and intelligent energy systems which give greater control to users. However, the lack of literacy on the subject matter and the possible enigma which such new technologies can represent to users can be a challenge. Even though some platforms offer their users the ability to trade manually and set different preferences for each trade, most existing businesses operate under the 'install and forget' principle. That is, after the initial installation and set-up of preferred parameters, users are no longer required to participate in the market actively. The system executes the trades automatically given the preferred time of day, amount of energy required and/or offered and more. Such automation is envisioned to reduce the perception of complexity users might have about blockchain technologies and improve the ease of use. Yet, one overarching research question we ask in this paper is to what extent does automation facilitate the increase in blockchain technology adoption for distributed energy infrastructures.

2.2 Adoption Drivers

The majority of HCI research done on DLT has focused predominantly on the challenges rather than the drivers behind their adoption. It is Sas and Khairuddin [9] who have paved the way by identifying several favorable aspects of blockchain which could strengthen users' motivation to adopt the technology. The decentralized nature of the technology is the first main driver. According to the semi-structured interviews conducted by the authors, users appreciate the lack of a third-party financial institution when executing transactions. Moreover, third parties have often been perceived as untrustworthy and rather deceitful. If a token is viewed in the same way as an asset, then in blockchain applications the user is the sole owner of that asset, an element strongly welcomed by interviewees. This is closely connected to the second major motivation Sas and Khairuddin have pinpointed - blockchain is unregulated. As a result of the perception of 'regaining control' over one's business, most participants in the study have claimed to feel more empowered and privileged. Blockchain represents not only a revolution in technology, but also a grassroots movement. Carrying a bitter-sweet anarchist sentiment, or rather 'militant' [9], this view is strongly connected to the negative notion of governments and central power who in users' perspective have become the enemies of the people. The lack of absolute power in blockchain applications means that the probability of abuse of this power over users' assets is highly minimized. In such a model, the decrease in risk contributes to the increase of trust. Users also acknowledge the simplified authorization process involved in making

transactions in comparison to the overcomplicated central system. This in turn leads to faster, almost instant transactions. Finally, the ease of use has also been highlighted as a major contributor to the increase in trust. Besides the technology-related motivations, blockchain is also described as a tool to boost democracy [8]. It is claimed that blockchain applications encourage the establishment of flatter and more decentralized democratic organizations on the local level. Elseden et al. [8] call this the ability of blockchain to 'harness crowds and publics' in order to challenge central authority. Nonetheless, one can have a different interpretation of such a development and argue that whereas it is an opportunity for users, it represents a considerable challenge to governments. This is also valid for P2P energy trading applications which have the ability to create local communities and challenge large electricity retailers.

P2P energy trading is revolutionary not only in its use of blockchain systems, but also in the further boost of decentralized energy generation and sourcing of local power. Previous HCI research in those domains is highly limited, thus further investigation is needed. In their study, Meeuw et al. [21] examine the importance of locally sourced power for users in Switzerland. Through their work, the authors determine that the demand for renewable energy is equally high to the demand for locally sourced energy. They claim that in our traditional energy system, the services offered by utility companies lack transparency, do not offer any sort of control to their customers and no information on where their energy has been produced or consumed. P2P energy trading applications can change that. Meeuw et al. believe that if the consumers have a greater understanding of how the electrical system works and are given more customized information regarding their own production or consumption, wider technology adoption will be secured. However, the authors also claim that transactions on the blockchain can also be perceived as insecure which, in the authors' view, severely limits the acceptance of the technology. Furthermore, they report on the reluctance of rooftop-photovoltaic (PV) owners to share data, particularly the location of their systems. This is an important aspect which needs to be further investigated with participants in P2P energy trading activities.

3   PowerShare

To better understand people's perceptions of novel energy infrastructures we developed and deployed an energy monitoring and sharing system called *PowerShare*. The *PowerShare* application is connected with an Energy Trading Management System (ETMS) that is responsible for managing users' accounts, energy demand and offer, and providing data about the users' overall energy consumption and production acquired from smart-meters. The overall system was part of a larger pilot developed in the context of the H2020 SMILE (SMart IsLand Energy systems) project - www.h2020smile.eu.

3.1   System Architecture

PowerShare comprises a mobile application developed for Android devices (running Android 4.4.2 or higher with API level $\geq$ 19), through which users are given the

opportunity to set criteria for energy trading (e.g. price per kWh), access their cryptocurrency wallet (in this case IOTA - www.iota.org), keep track of the transactions performed, and get feedback on their energy consumption and production patterns. For the purpose of our study, we provided participants with an initial IOTA balance corresponding to around 10 €. The application connects to an Energy Trading Management System (ETMS), which receives production and consumption data from the smart meters installed in each household and manages the energy exchanges thus simulating a future distributed P2P energy infrastructure. In addition, since none of the participants in the study has an energy storage system, production and consumption data collected through the smart meters were used to simulate a 3000 W battery (one for each household), which was "virtually" charged and discharged by the ETMS.

3.2 Mobile Application Design

The *PowerShare* mobile application was designed based on the analysis of existing platforms for P2P energy trading and the review of previous studies on energy feedback [22–27]. A first low-fi prototype of the app was subjected to heuristic evaluation, and then pilot tested with a small group of researchers and students from the Interactive Technologies Institute in Madeira. Based on results from the pilot test, we identified and removed the main bottlenecks concerning both the UI layout and the navigation flow. A revised low-fi prototype was then developed and tested with different subjects (similar to the previous sample in terms of demographic characteristics, but with no experience of the first prototype).

The app consists of six main sections and is structured as follows:

Home. The "home" provides real-time feedback (i.e. current production and consumption) and displays information about (a) amount of energy available for trading, (b) current day's transactions, and (c) share of renewable energy consumption on the user's overall weekly energy consumption. As shown in Fig. 1a, real-time feedback is always displayed on the screen, while the other information is accessible through a tab menu. This choice is due to the fact that real-time feedback has been found to be particularly effective in raising people awareness on their energy use patterns [22–24] and, since it provides an overview of the user's current production and consumption, can be extremely useful to quickly react to variations in the user energy demand - e.g. increase energy offer in case the battery is full and consumption unusually low.

Historical Feedback. As shown in Fig. 1b, this section provides an overview of consumption and production data over time, with three different levels of temporal granularity (daily, weekly and monthly). Historical feedback was found to be one of the most important features of an energy feedback system [25, 26] and, at the same time, provides a set of information that could support users in better understanding their energy behaviors and thus, identifying the best criteria for purchasing and/or selling energy surplus accordingly. For this reason, the information is presented in a great deal of detail, providing the breakdown of both production and consumption (e.g. consumption is divided in energy purchased from the traditional supplier, supplied by peers, and self-consumption).

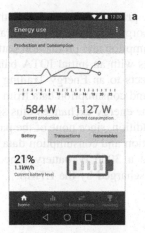 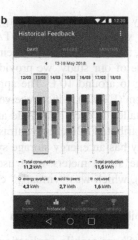

Fig. 1. "Home" (a) and "Historical feedback" (b).

Transactions. This section comprises the definition of criteria for purchasing and/or selling energy surplus - e.g. price per kWh - (see Fig. 2a), and a list of all transactions made by the user (see Fig. 2b). As shown in Fig. 2a, the price per kWh is the only mandatory field, with two options between which one is to choose: (1) a fixed price ("minimum" in case of selling and "maximum" in case of purchasing), or (2) a price tied to the one contracted with the electricity company. The latter option is specifically targeted to consumers that are subjected to dynamic pricing - i.e. the cost for energy purchased varies throughout the day based on market demands. Optional trading criteria are: (1) definition of specific time slots for trading; (2) limit trading to a list of selected buyers and/or suppliers; and (3) set a portion of the overall battery capacity to keep for self-consumption only. While registering the account, users are provided with the opportunity to choose between two trading modes - i.e. "automatic" and "manual". By selecting the automatic mode, users can start trading immediately, while if choosing manual mode, they have to access the "Transactions" section and set purchasing and selling criteria. A dialog window informs users about the possibility to modify this choice at any time through their profile settings.

Ranking. Since social comparison was proven to be effective in fostering sustainable behaviors [27], this section was designed to show the comparison between renewable energy consumption shares of all users (see Fig. 2c). Each week, the list of top ten most 'green' users is released. While registering the account, users are asked for permission to share this information with the community - i.e. user name and his/her renewable energy consumption share - and informed that they can modify this choice at any time by accessing their profile settings.

Wallet. The IOTA cryptocurrency wallet is accessible from an overflow menu. It provides users with the opportunity to check their mIOTA balance and manage payments.

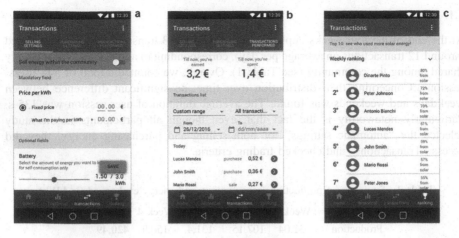

Fig. 2. "Transactions" (a–b) and "Ranking" (c).

Settings. This section, accessible from the overflow menu, simply serves to access and modify the account settings.

4 Methods

In order to investigate the human aspects affecting users' engagement with P2P energy trading systems, a small empirical study was designed and conducted in Funchal (Madeira Island). Ten residential prosumers living within the same neighborhood community were recruited through snowball sampling and asked to use *PowerShare* for a month. Nine out of the ten participants recruited took part in the study (one decided to withdraw). The households have from 1 to 6 family members, with an average of three people per household. Five families out of nine have children with ages ranging from 4 to 22 years. Age ranges of participants and family members vary between 4 years old and 81 (average age is 35.55 years old). Professional occupation and educational background are very diverse among the sample. All participants in the study are prosumers and own solar PV panels. At the beginning of the study, participants had an average of 6 months experience as energy prosumers. Informed consent was provided to all participants. The research team verified the existing communication infrastructure (internet connection) and, together with local technicians, installed the required equipment (smart meters and gateways) to collect production and consumption data. Baseline data was collected for a period of two months.

The system deployment started at the beginning of September and lasted four weeks. An Android tablet was provided to those participants that did not have a mobile device matching the minimum requirements for running the app. In addition, all participants received a weekly email providing a summary of their energy consumption, production and exchange. Interactions with the mobile application have been electronically monitored throughout the study.

4.1 Quantitative Data

At the end of the four-weeks deployment, a total of 333 transactions were performed (around 12 transactions on average per day), corresponding to about 7.5 kWh of energy shared among the community (see Table 1). Overall, we counted a total of 548 users' sessions. Concerning their distribution over time, no significant difference between weekdays and weekends was found. The average duration of user session was 135 s. Particularly noteworthy is the fact that, even though all participants in the study selected the "automatic settings" for both selling and purchasing energy, they did access "Transactions" and checked trading criteria.

Table 1. Summary of production, consumption, and energy exchanged (in kWh).

	Week 1	Week 2	Week 3	Week 4	Total
Production	31,04	107,15	131,4	150,9	**420,49**
Consumption	202,85	431,36	450,37	476,62	**1561,2**
Exchanged	0	1,39	3,33	2,64	**7,36**

4.2 Qualitative Data

At the end of the one-month deployment, semi-structured individual interviews were conducted with participants to explore their understanding, concerns, and motivations for engaging in P2P energy trading. Interviews started with a warm-up discussion about perceived advantages/disadvantages of engaging in P2P energy trading. Other questions targeted the way participants used the application (e.g. when and how often, most and less used features, usability issues faced, etc.), as well as their needs and motivations as users for engaging with the system. In addition, questions related to privacy, blockchain and cryptocurrency were included. Interviews took place in the respondents' home, lasted an average of 30 min, and were fully recorded and transcribed.

A general inductive approach was adopted for thematic data analysis [28]. All individual statements were printed on separate cards. Affinity diagrams were used to identify main themes and develop categories. To ensure reliability of the analysis, two researchers analyzed and coded each interview independently. Resulting themes and categories were compared and discussed. The researchers deliberated on coding discrepancies and disagreements, until consensus was reached.

5 Results

In this section we start by outlining users' motivation for engaging in P2P energy trading. We then describe the main characteristics of DLT and how they affect adoption of a P2P energy trading platform, and finally dive into the way people used the system.

5.1   Motivations to Engage in P2P Energy Trading

Economic Rationale. In line with previous work [29], we observed the emergence of the rational-economic model as of the main reasons for becoming a prosumer. This model assumes that people are willing to engage in behaviors that are economically advantageous: *"I have high consumption, compared to the average, because all my appliances are electric...we don't use gas. For this reason, I'd like to further increase my production capacity to cover my energy needs"* (Participant 4). However, our results suggest that economic factors are not the main motivation for engaging in energy trading. Despite the rational of several P2P energy trading platforms presented to prosumers as a way to further monetize their generation assets, results from our findings show that energy trading is not perceived as a business opportunity: *"I saw my transactions history on the app, but...it is very little, around 2 €...something really little.* (He opened the app) *See, I've spent 2,40 € and gained just 0,28 €. It is very little. I was expecting to get more. [...] Personally, I'd like to install more panels and increase my production...but in my case it would be only for self-consumption purpose. Of course, if in ten years my consumption would decrease, leading me to have surplus energy, then, in that case, I'm fine with selling it!"* (Participant 2); *"I don't bother with earning money with the app. I was more interested in understanding how the system could work and how well solar panels work in this context."* (Participant 5).

Sense of Community. While the economic rationale seems not to be a strong motivation for engaging in P2P energy trading, several participants mentioned the sense of community as an important aspect: *"I like the idea of trading with neighbors. That is true! We live close, we know each other, we are friends"* (Participant 3). Interestingly, one of the people interviewed said that he would be also willing to share his surplus energy with neighbors for free, further suggesting that the sense of being part of and act as a community is more valuable than any economic incentive: *"The electricity company is an anonymous entity, while my neighbors are people I know. [...] Trading with neighbors, to me, is more like an excuse to start a conversation...to have a chat with them, like 'look, I've sold you energy today'. [...] If I'm giving my surplus to a neighbor I don't care being paid for it, because there is a neighborhood's relationship between us"* (Participant 2).

Individual Intrinsic Reward. We found that engaging in P2P energy trading could also provide some kind of individual intrinsic reward in the form of personal gratification. On the one hand, the system is perceived as something that requires some expertise, which consequently identifies the user as an expert: *"Some people may have difficulties engaging with this kind of system. I'd be willing to use it but other people... it depends on your knowledge and background. It's not an easy thing; it is not for everyone"* (Participant 7). On the other hand, we noticed that engaging in P2P energy trading seems to have an effect on pro-environmental personal norm activation [29], by positively affecting people's moral and emotional beliefs: *"[about P2P energy trading] as a concept...I mean, we know it is renewable energy. It has a different impact. It makes me feel better, as a person, because I'm exploiting natural resources"* (Participant 2).

Transparent, Secure and Fair Billing. Interviewees also mentioned the opportunity to access real-time data, based on actual meter readings, as a valuable aspect of using this system: "*A big advantage of this system relates to metering and billing. The current billing system is based on consumption estimation. Actual meter readings are not carried out so frequently. With this system we have access to real-time data. It is automatic and based on actual data. This is important!*" (Participant 1).

5.2   Characteristics of Distributed Ledger Technologies and Their Impact on Users' Adoption of P2P Energy Trading Systems

As suggested in the related work, several of the main characteristics of DLT could turn into barriers towards their adoption. Building from our findings, in the following sections we describe some of those characteristics and their impact on users' intention to engage in P2P energy trading.

Trust in a Trustless System. DLT, like blockchain technology, are often defined as "trustless" [9]. Indeed, due to their decentralized consensus mechanism, they do not require a third-party trusted central authority to validate transactions. Decentralization is one of the cornerstones of DLT, which allows for fast transactions at low costs. Nevertheless, several researchers seem to agree that this may also raise serious trust issues among users [8, 20, 30]. Among our interviewees, only one mentioned some concerns about the lack of a central authority (institutional trust): "*I'd prefer having a central entity managing the system. Some kind of institution I can trust*" (Participant 9). It should be also pointed out that Participant 9 is new in the neighborhood and still doesn't know many people there. We believe this aspect may have a big impact on trust, since all other interviewees, when asked about possible trust issues, did not express any concern about this aspect, stressing the fact that they are members of the same community and know each other (trust between users): "*They are my neighbors. I know them. I trust them*" (Participant 3). In addition, our findings suggest that transparency of the system (trust in the technology), which is another core feature of DLS, would further mitigate concerns due to the lack of a trusted central entity: "*I think the system is trustworthy. I'd feel comfortable using it because…I mean, I can go check all transactions I've performed*" (Participant 1); "*I don't see any security issue…I'd feel comfortable using it. The platform is clear. I can see the amount of energy I consumed, energy I could have consumed from neighbors or sold to them. I think, yes. It is transparent from this perspective*" (Participant 4).

Data Sharing and Privacy Concerns. Another aspect representing a potential barrier in using DLT is the pseudo-anonymity of traders [9]. To work around this issue in *PowerShare* users are de-anonymized, so that every trader can see the list of all community members and with whom he/she has traded. In addition, in order to test the effectiveness of social comparison in keeping users engaged with the application, (with permission from the user) the share of RES in his/her overall energy consumption is displayed in the weekly ranking. We believed that this workaround could strongly increase transparency and trust in the system but, contemporarily, may also raise some privacy issues. Surprisingly, only one respondent reported little concern with sharing the above-mentioned information: "*I don't think this kind of data could be of any*

harm...energy usage is not like personal health information...in a way, it's kind of neutral. [...] But, probably, I'd prefer to not share that information with the others since I'm living by myself and I'm a woman" (Participant 9). Two other participants mentioned a possible risk linked to the information provided through the weekly ranking, even though they both specified it is not a concern for them: *"There might be people who don't want to share their percentage of renewable energy consumption, since a change in their weekly consumption may reveal that they are not at home. This is the only issue I can think about, but it is not a concern to me"* (Participant 7); *"Perhaps, knowing people consumption details could be used for commercial purposes or could disclose personal information, like when you're at home or not...but...no, I am not overly concerned with privacy of my energy data"* (Participant 6). All the other participants clearly stated that sharing such information was not an issue.

Technology's Embedded Complexity. Results from our study show that DLT are perceived as extremely technical and not easy to understand for non-specialists. In line with what was hypothesized by [8], this aspect appeared to be a possible barrier towards the adoption of the system: *"it's extremely technical. There are a lot of codes... it's very engineeristic. I mean, if you are a geek it's ok, otherwise...no, it's too much"* (Participant 9). In general terms, we observe a lack of literacy on DLT and, especially, on cryptocurrencies, which leads people to be suspicious about them: *"I don't trust these things. I prefer to keep my feet rooted on the ground. To me they do not exist! I don't understand how cryptocurrencies work...who issues them?"* (Participant 7). Even though almost half of the interviewees claimed to be open to use cryptocurrencies as a medium of exchange for energy, several concerns have been raised: *"I don't know cryptocurrencies very well, but I'm open to them. The only cryptocurrency I use is PayPal, which, I think, is a kind of crypto...even if it is a prepaid account, since first I have to transfer money to my PayPal balance...it is a kind of crypto, isn't it?!...but it is not bitcoin. [...] cryptocurrencies are less stable than fiat currencies. Also, they are not enough regulated and there is a lot of market speculation...especially with bitcoins. So, I guess there are some risks associated with cryptocurrencies. [...] As a concept it seems fine to me, but it could be risky since the market is not very regulated"* (Participant 2), and *"I'd prefer to use fiat currencies. Mainly for security reason, in the sense that you always lose money when exchanging cryptocurrencies to fiat currencies...it is not worth it"* (Participant 3). Finally, in accordance with Elsden et al. [8], respondents questioned whether cryptocurrencies can represent the actual value of energy: *"I think that euros are more meaningful. A currency that is used in everyday life helps people understanding the value of what they are consuming, or trading, or sharing"* (Participant 9).

5.3   Usage Patterns and Information Needs

Effectiveness of Social-Comparison. In line with previous work [31, 32], our findings suggest that social-comparison is an effective strategy to keep users engaged with the system and influence energy-related behavior in households. The weekly ranking provided by *PowerShare* was indeed one of the most popular features among

participants in the study: "*I used to check the ranking. [...] some days I was in the top positions. It is cool.* [the ranking] *is an interesting idea*" (Participant 3). Competing with other users appeared to be a silent motivation for improving participants' individual performance, pushing them to increase the share of RES in their overall energy consumption, and thus leading users to be more willing to engage in P2P energy trading: "*I must confess! The feature I used the most was the Ranking. You know, to see how I was doing in terms of green energy consumption. [...] My main concern relates to using more green energy...so, I'd be willing to improve my installation and engage in energy trading*" (Participant 1).

Social Inaccessibility. We noticed that it was almost always the householder the only one taking over the task of using the system: "*I was the only one using the app. My wife doesn't care about it* (laugh)...*she doesn't care if she is consuming a lot of energy. My kids...I've tried to show them the app but, it didn't catch their attention...they don't care...they don't pay the bill* (laugh)" (Participant 2). Lack of interest for energy-related behavior in those family members that are not responsible for managing households' expenses has been widely observed in previous studies [31]. Despite several studies on user engagement with eco-feedback applications have been conducted to explore different strategies for designing more engaging systems [29, 33–35], a lot of work still needs to be done in this area, which represents an interesting challenge for HCI research.

Learning-Before-Doing. An interesting aspect that emerged from the interviews was that some users started exploring the transactions settings later on during the study. In fact, after going through a learning period to better understand their energy usage patterns, they reported: "*I've set parameters two days ago* (he explained parameters selected). *It took me a while to fully explore the app. At the very beginning I used the app only from my perspective: how much energy I am producing or consuming...this, to manage my consumption differently. For example, taking advantage of high production to use the washing machine. Then, I've explored it a bit more and defined some trading criteria*" (Participant 2). During the interviews, users have also asked questions and suggested further improvements to the application in terms of information provided, thus demonstrating interest and willingness to become more proficient with the system: "*I have a doubt...here, in the historical feedback. Now, there is no battery, it's simulated. Ok?! So, is the 'self-consumption from battery' included in my 'overall consumption'? [...] Are batteries expensive? What could it be the price for a, let's say, 3 kWh battery? [...] I'd like to have more control over my consumption. Like knowing the actual consumption of different appliances and which one consumes the most*" (Participant 7); and "*Can I still modify the settings? Can I play with it? Transactions aren't real, I know, but...it's just to get an idea of the potential of such system*" (Participant 4).

In addition, the quantitative usage patterns collected support this conclusion. Several participants reported to use the application daily (even more than once per day), to check their performance: "*I used it almost every day. Especially at the end of the day, to check my overall daily consumption, and around midday to get an idea of peak production*" (Participant 7), as well as to make far-reaching inferences about their consumption and production patterns, and adapt their behaviors based on the feedback

received: "*I use the app to check and control our production...to understand which are the hours of peak production, and take advantage of them [...]. I look at it mainly at the end of the day, or whenever I am at home, to make comparisons and control consumption as well. For example, when the production is high, I turn on the dishwasher*" (Participant 8).

Different Ways for Providing Feedback Data. An interesting aspect that emerged from the interviews was that people seem to prefer accessing eco-feedback data through different channels. When asked about the weekly summary received via email, almost all interviewees reported to consider it as useful as the information provided through the app: "*I'm satisfied with the information provided through the application, but also the weekly summary was useful. I think they complement each other. I mean, on the app I can see my daily performance, while, through the summary, I can also get an idea of how my performance is evolving*" (Participant 1). In addition, we noticed that the weekly summary has been found particularly useful to keep track of participants' performance when their interaction with the system was affected by lack of time: "*I used to check both the app and the weekly summary, depending on my schedule. When I was particularly busy, I only looked at the summary, but when I had more free time, and especially at the beginning of the study, I mostly used the app*" (Participant 4). Several users also mentioned the possibility of accessing feedback data through a web-page as a valuable improvement to the system: "*I'd prefer to access the system on the web. Like, through a website or a web-page where I can see my data. I think it would have been great to have that opportunity*" (Participant 4).

One last aspect that should be taken into account, is the way data are presented. All interviewees appreciated having data about production, consumption and energy exchanges represented in a visual form. One of them, clearly explained his preference for this form of presentation by comparing the app with the monthly bill: "*The bill is not easy to read. I guess it provides a lot of information, but it is confusing. It has a lot of numbers and text...and everything is too small*" (Participant 1).

6   Discussion

Based on our findings deploying DLT for energy systems, we elaborate guidelines to inform the design of P2P energy trading platforms. These findings sustain the need for further HCI research in the domain of energy infrastructure and sustainable HCI in general since they ultimately depend on end-user adoption. In order for these new infrastructures to evolve they need to move beyond addressing economic rationality to address issues of trust, control, transparency, learning and the family/community context.

6.1   Supporting Transparency and Control

As reported by [8, 9], limited understanding of DLT could strongly impact users trust in the technology. Transparency of the system is fundamental to mitigate this potential barrier; thus, a P2P platform should provide easy access to accurate and detailed

real-time production, consumption and transaction data. For the same reason, users need to feel they have control over the system. Despite all participants in our study selected the automatic mode, several of them reported to feel reassured by having the opportunity to manually define criteria for trading. This suggests that full-automation - i.e. the 'install and forget' principle -, which is part of the value proposition of several existing P2P energy trading platforms, may not be as effective as expected. Another design implication, related to transparency and control, deals with data sharing. Although none of the interviewees reported concerns about sharing data within the community, they seem to be aware of the possible consequences this could bring. Therefore, a P2P energy trading platform should always provide users with high control over their data and personal information.

6.2   Designing Around People, Not the Technology

Findings indicate that DLT are perceived as extremely technical and not easy to understand for non-specialists. While designing a P2P energy trading platform a major effort should be devoted to 'translating' the technology behind the system. Cryptocurrencies should be presented as an asset, while all monetary values reported in conventional currencies (€ or $). Processes should be simplified, data entry made as easy as possible, and all confusing, abstract or useless information should be removed (e.g. 'wallet password' instead of 'IOTA seed password'). For the same reason, data should preferably be provided in a visual form.

6.3   Supporting Learning

Before actively engaging in energy trading, people need to go through a learning period to get a better understanding of their energy usage patterns. Providing detailed information (e.g. both real-time and historical feedback, multiple levels of temporal granularity, production and consumption breakdown) is an effective strategy for fostering the adoption of such system. Contemporarily, in order to avoid information overload, as well as to meet different routines and schedules, the information should be spread across multiple channels. A mobile application, for example, may serves the purpose of providing glanccable information - e.g. real-time feedback - users can quickly act (and react) upon. While a website would be more suitable for providing data with a great deal of detail, allowing users to make comparisons, inferences, and finally come to understand their habits.

6.4   Leveraging Sense of Community to Mitigate Lack of Institutional Trust

Findings suggest that developing a P2P energy trading community at neighborhood scale, where people are close and know each other, may be an effective strategy to mitigate the lack of institutional trust. In fact, in order to reduce the impact of not having a third-party central authority, we need to increase trust in peers. Nevertheless, things change when envisioning a wider application, for instance at the city level. Scaling up the system means creating a community where people might not know each

other, which in turns is likely to negatively impact both trust and privacy concerns. In such scenario, fostering the sense of 'being part of a community' is even more crucial. A P2P energy trading community, especially a large-scale one, should be a 'space' where people sharing the same values are encouraged to act towards a common goal. Priority should be given to the result of a collective effort instead of individual achievements. Some interesting works in the field of social psychology [36–38] suggest indeed that collective efficacy – "the belief that groups of people are efficacious in solving tasks" [38] - is a strong driver for engaging in community pro-environmental behaviors. This leads us to hypothesize that a group contingency approach [39] could be an effective strategy for designing large-scale distributed energy infrastructures. Nonetheless, it has also been argued that trust remains a potential barrier towards cooperation [40]. Thus, the value of collective efficacy as a workaround for the scalability issue of P2P energy trading is still mere speculation and requires investigation.

6.5 Involving All Family Members

A further design implication that emerged from our study concerns the need of designing a system able to engage all family members. Based on our findings, we have identified two possible strategies to reach this goal. On the one hand, we can leverage social-comparison and motivational strategies, like rewards and competition, which could be particularly effective in engaging pre-teenage children. On the other hand, a design based on the norm-activation model, which shows the environmental impact of our behaviors and fosters a critical reflection on them, may induce feelings of accountability on those family members that are more concerned about issues related to parenting and family well-being.

7 Conclusion

In the last years efforts to decarbonize the electric grid have led to important changes in the energy infrastructure. For instance, the lower manufacturing costs of PV systems provides a cost-effective alternative to conventional power plants enabling end-users to reduce their energy bills and carbon footprints. In a scenario where a considerable portion of the energy is provided by local renewable sources the management of spinning resources is much more complex and unpredictable. There is a lot of buzz and deception around DLT at the moment, but their use in the energy sector could provide an ideal solution to a genuine problem. That is, the shared nature of energy resources and the difficulty of tracking the large volume of transactions – from energy supply and demand, to actual exchanges at the edge of the grid.

Despite several pilot projects currently running all over the world and much work being done to address the technical and regulatory aspects related to the application of DLT in the energy sector, our understanding of the human aspects affecting the adoption of P2P energy trading is still minimal. This paper attempts to fill this gap. Through the real-world deployment of *PowerShare*, a neighborhood P2P energy trading system, we explored how DLT challenge people's perceptions of energy and identified some relevant design implications for the development of these systems.

Besides the concepts described in HCI literature (i.e. trust, control and transparency), study findings have identified further drivers and challenges to DLT adoption not mentioned in previous studies (namely, learning and social context), which represent interesting directions for further HCI research. In particular, we argue the need of exploring the effectiveness of different design strategies - namely social pressure, norm activation, and group contingency - in improving users' engagement and accessibility of the system to all family members. Another aspect that deserve to be further investigated regards the way energy and its new infrastructure is represented. To increase transparency, and consequently support learning, the complex dynamics behind energy consumption, production and exchange should become clearly visible. How to do so, is a matter of further investigation. Most importantly, we encourage the HCI community to address the lack of understanding about P2P energy trading and DLT. Findings from the real-world deployment of *PowerShare* indicate that people are interested, open and willing to engage with such system. However, the embedded complexity of DLT, could make this a daunting challenge and thus become a barrier towards the successful implementation of distributed energy infrastructures. This is not a trivial issue, since it requires a deep understanding of how technologies shape and are shaped by social and cultural factors. The development of decentralized energy systems entails a paradigm shift which goes beyond technological change, thus implying the need of designing DLT applications around and together with users. It is precisely in this regard that HCI research could provide a major contribution, informing the development of a new and more sustainable energy system.

Acknowledgments. This work was funded by the European Union Horizon 2020 research and innovation programme under grant agreement number 731249.

References

1. Dourish, P.: HCI and environmental sustainability: the politics of design and the design of politics. In: Proceedings of the 8th ACM Conference on Designing Interactive Systems, pp. 1–10. ACM, New York (2010). https://doi.org/10.1145/1858171.1858173
2. Blevis, E.: Sustainable interaction design: invention & disposal, renewal & reuse. In: Proceedings of the SIGCHI Conference on Human Factors in Computing Systems, pp. 503–512. ACM, New York (2007). https://doi.org/10.1145/1240624.1240705
3. Pierce, J., Paulos, E.: Materializing energy. In: Proceedings of the 8th ACM Conference on Designing Interactive Systems, pp. 113–122. ACM, New York (2010). https://doi.org/10.1145/1858171.1858193
4. Tyagi, V.V., Rahim, N.A., Rahim, N.A., Jeyraj, A., Selvaraj, L.: Progress in solar PV technology: research and achievement. Renew. Sustain. Energy Rev. **20**, 443–461 (2013). https://doi.org/10.1016/j.rser.2012.09.028
5. Park, C., Yong, T.: Comparative review and discussion on P2P electricity trading. Energy Procedia **128**, 3–9 (2017). https://doi.org/10.1016/j.egypro.2017.09.003
6. Morstyn, T., Farrell, N., Darby, S.J., McCulloch, M.D.: Using peer-to-peer energy-trading platforms to incentivize prosumers to form federated power plants. Nat. Energy **3**(2), 94–101 (2018). https://doi.org/10.1038/s41560-017-0075-y

7. Tushar, W., Yuen, C., Mohsenian-Rad, H., Saha, T., Poor, H.V., Wood, K.L.: Transforming energy networks via peer to peer energy trading: potential of game theoretic approaches. IEEE Signal Process. Mag. **35**(4), 90–111 (2018). https://doi.org/10.1109/MSP.2018. 2818327

8. Elsden, C., Manohar, A., Briggs, J., Harding, M., Speed, C., Vines, J.: Making sense of blockchain applications: a typology for HCI. In: Proceedings of the 2018 CHI Conference on Human Factors in Computing Systems, p. 458. ACM, New York (2018). https://doi.org/10. 1145/3173574.3174032

9. Sas, C., Khairuddin, I.E.: Design for trust: an exploration of the challenges and opportunities of bitcoin users. In: Proceedings of the 2017 CHI Conference on Human Factors in Computing Systems, pp. 6499–6510. ACM, New York (2017). https://doi.org/10.1145/ 3025453.3025886

10. Lee, M.K., Turban, E.: A trust model for consumer internet shopping. Int. J. Electron. Commer. **6**(1), 75–91 (2001). https://doi.org/10.1080/10864415.2001.11044227

11. McKnight, D.H., Chervany, N.L.: What trust means in e-commerce customer relationships: an interdisciplinary conceptual typology. Int. J. Electron. Commer. **6**(2), 35–59 (2001). https://doi.org/10.1080/10864415.2001.11044235

12. McKnight, D.H., Choudhury, V., Kacmar, C.: Developing and vali-dating trust measures for e-commerce: an integrative typology. Inf. Syst. Res. **13**(3), 334–359 (2002). https://doi.org/ 10.1287/isre.13.3.334.81

13. Gefen, D., Straub, D.W.: Consumer trust in B2C e-Commerce and the importance of social presence: experiments in e-products and e-services. Omega **32**(6), 407–424 (2004). https:// doi.org/10.1016/j.omega.2004.01.006

14. Tan, F.B., Sutherland, P.: Online consumer trust: a multi-dimensional model. J. Electron. Commer. Organ. **2**(3), 40–58 (2004). https://doi.org/10.4018/jeco.2004070103

15. Jones, K., Leonard, L.N.: Trust in consumer-to-consumer electronic commerce. Inf. Manag. **45**(2), 88–95 (2008). https://doi.org/10.1016/j.im.2007.12.002

16. Leonard, L.N.: Attitude influencers in C2C e-commerce: buying and selling. J. Comput. Inf. Syst. **52**(3), 11–17 (2012)

17. Yoon, H.S., Occeña, L.G.: Influencing factors of trust in consumer-to-consumer electronic commerce with gender and age. Int. J. Inf. Manag. **35**(3), 352–363 (2015). https://doi.org/10. 1016/j.ijinfomgt.2015.02.003

18. Hawlitschek, F., Teubner, T., Weinhardt, C.: Trust in the sharing economy. Die Unternehmung **70**(1), 26–44 (2016). https://doi.org/10.5771/0042-059X-2016-1-26

19. Hawlitschek, F., Notheisen, B., Teubner, T.: The limits of trust-free systems: a literature review on blockchain technology and trust in the sharing economy. Electron. Commer. Res. Appl. **29**, 50–63 (2018). https://doi.org/10.1016/j.elerap.2018.03.005

20. Sas, C., Khairuddin, I.E.: Exploring trust in Bitcoin technology: a framework for HCI research. In: Proceedings of the Annual Meeting of the Australian Special Interest Group for Computer Human Interaction, pp. 338–342. ACM, New York (2015). https://doi.org/10. 1145/2838739.2838821

21. Meeuw, A., Schopfer, S., Ryder, B., Wortmann, F.: LokalPower: enabling local energy markets with user-driven engagement. In: Extended Abstracts of the 2018 CHI Conference on Human Factors in Computing Systems. ACM (2018). https://doi.org/10.1145/3170427. 3188610

22. Darby, S.: The effectiveness of feedback on energy consumption: a review for DEFRA of the literature on metering, billing and direct displays. Technical report, University of Oxford (2006)

23. Allen, D., Janda, K.: The effects of household characteristics and energy use consciousness on the effectiveness of real-time energy use feedback: a pilot study. In: Proceedings of the ACEEE Summer Study on Energy Efficiency in Buildings, pp. 1–12 (2006)
24. Barreto, M., Karapanos, E., Nunes, N.: Why don't families get along with eco-feedback technologies?: a longitudinal inquiry. In: Proceedings of the Biannual Conference of the Italian Chapter of SIGCHI. ACM, New York (2013). https://doi.org/10.1145/2499149. 2499164
25. Fitzpatrick, G., Smith, G.: Technology-enabled feedback on domestic energy consumption: articulating a set of design concerns. IEEE Pervasive Comput. 8(1), 37–44 (2009). https:// doi.org/10.1109/MPRV.2009.17
26. Petkov, P., Köbler, F., Foth, M., Krcmar, H.: Motivating domestic energy conservation through comparative, community-based feedback in mobile and social media. In: Proceedings of the 5th International Conference on Communities & Technologies, pp. 21–30. ACM, New York (2011). https://doi.org/10.1145/2103354.2103358
27. Siero, F.W., Bakker, A.B., Dekker, G.B., Van Den Burg, M.T.: Changing organizational energy consumption behaviour through comparative feedback. J. Environ. Psychol. 16(3), 235–246 (1996). https://doi.org/10.1006/jevp.1996.0019
28. Thomas, D.R.: A general inductive approach for analyzing qualitative evaluation data. Am. J. Eval. 27(2), 237–246 (2006). https://doi.org/10.1177/1098214005283748
29. Froehlich, J., Findlater, L., Landay, J.: The design of eco-feedback technology. In: Proceedings of the SIGCHI Conference on Human Factors in Computing Systems, pp. 1999–2008. ACM, New York (2010). https://doi.org/10.1145/1753326.1753629
30. Hawlitschek, F., Notheisen, B., Mertens, C., Teubner, T., Weinhardt, C.: Trust-free systems in the trust age? A review on blockchain and trust in the sharing economy. In: Hohenheim Discussion Papers in Business, Economics and Social Sciences, University of Hohenheim (2017)
31. Johnson, D., Horton, E., Mulcahy, R., Foth, M.: Gamification and serious games within the domain of domestic energy consumption: a systematic review. Renew. Sustain. Energy Rev. 73, 249–264 (2017). https://doi.org/10.1016/j.rser.2017.01.134
32. Foster, D., Lawson, S., Blythe, M., Cairns, P.: Wattsup?: motivating reductions in domestic energy consumption using social networks. In: Proceedings of the 6th Nordic Conference on Human-Computer Interaction: Extending Boundaries, pp. 178–187. ACM, New York (2010). https://doi.org/10.1145/1868914.1868938
33. Quintal, F., Barreto, M., Nunes, N., Nisi, V., Pereira, L.: WattsBurning on my mailbox: a tangible art inspired eco-feedback visualization for sharing energy consumption. In: Kotzé, P., Marsden, G., Lindgaard, G., Wesson, J., Winckler, M. (eds.) INTERACT 2013. LNCS, vol. 8120, pp. 133–140. Springer, Heidelberg (2013). https://doi.org/10.1007/978-3-642-40498-6_10
34. Rodgers, J., Bartram, L.: Exploring ambient and artistic visualization for residential energy use feedback. IEEE Trans. Visual Comput. Graphics 17(12), 2489–2497 (2011). https://doi. org/10.1109/TVCG.2011.196
35. Nisi, V., Nunes, N.J., Quintal, F., Barreto, M.: SINAIS from Fanal: design and evaluation of an art-inspired eco-feedback system. In: Proceedings of the Biannual Conference of the Italian Chapter of SIGCHI. ACM, New York (2013). https://doi.org/10.1145/2499149. 2499151
36. Koletsou, A., Mancy, R.: Which efficacy constructs for large-scale social dilemma problems? Individual and collective forms of efficacy and outcome expectancies in the context of climate change mitigation. Risk Manag. 13(4), 184–208 (2011). https://doi.org/ 10.1057/rm.2011.12

37. Chen, M.F.: Self-efficacy or collective efficacy within the cognitive theory of stress model: which more effectively explains people's self-reported proenvironmental behavior? J. Environ. Psychol. **42**, 66–75 (2015). https://doi.org/10.1016/j.jenvp.2015.02.002
38. Barth, M., Jugert, P., Fritsche, I.: Still underdetected–social norms and collective efficacy predict the acceptance of electric vehicles in Germany. Transp. Res. Part F: Traffic Psychol. Behav. **37**, 64–77 (2016). https://doi.org/10.1016/j.trf.2015.11.011
39. Slavin, R.E., Wodarski, J.S., Blackburn, B.L.: A group contingency for electricity conservation in master-metered apartments. J. Appl. Behav. Anal. **14**(3), 357–363 (1981). https://doi.org/10.1901/jaba.1981.14-357
40. Lubell, M.: Environmental activism as collective action. Environ. Behav. **34**(4), 431–454 (2002). https://doi.org/10.1177/00116502034004002

Child-Generated Personas to Aid Design Across Cultures

Gavin Sim[1]([⊠]) [iD], Abhishek Shrivastava[2], Matthew Horton[1],
Simran Agarwal[2], Pampana Sai Haasini[2], Chandini Sushma Kondeti[2],
and Lorna McKnight[1]

[1] University of Central Lancashire, Preston PR1 2HE, UK
grsim@uclan.ac.uk
[2] Indian Institute of Technology Guwahati, Guwahati 781039, Assam, India

Abstract. Designers frequently use personas to model potential users, but these personas need to be accurate portrayals of people. With personas needed to facilitate a cross-cultural participatory design project, it was recognized that the personas needed to not only describe children appropriately, but also capture differences in behaviours between cultures. 56 children aged 7–10 in the UK and India participated in the creation of personas of elementary school children, describing aspects such as school life, family life and technology use. A tool developed to evaluate personas demonstrated that both sets of children could individually create plausible personas, while content analysis of the personas demonstrated that children focused on behavioural and activity-based narratives that were similar between the two groups, with only limited cultural differences identified. The findings suggest that child-generated personas can be a viable method in the design process, and may offer insights that aid cross-cultural design.

Keywords: Personas · Children · Culture · Child-generated personas

1 Introduction

The participation of end users in the design of technologies has long been an important principle in Human–Computer Interaction (HCI) and Child–Computer Interaction (CCI). The use of children as participants in HCI research is not a new concept [1, 2] with their roles ranging from design partners to testers, though more recent research has shown that participatory design and co-design practices tend to be favoured by the CCI community. Sessions are generally used to capture design ideas in situations where the participants doing the design are the very same people who will ultimately use the product or service, for example, children designing interactive games for museums that they were likely to visit [3]. However, participatory design sessions with children are often also used to gain design ideas from children for products that they may not use themselves, with the assumption that they will be similar to the target users. Challenges can therefore arise when children are contributing to the design of products for children who are far removed from their own culture and values.

© IFIP International Federation for Information Processing 2019
Published by Springer Nature Switzerland AG 2019
D. Lamas et al. (Eds.): INTERACT 2019, LNCS 11748, pp. 112–131, 2019.
https://doi.org/10.1007/978-3-030-29387-1_7

Within the context of this study, designers in India were tasked with developing a product for children in India and the UK to reduce plastic consumption. The designers would have access to children in India that could help inform the design of the product but they would have no direct access to children in the UK. Thus, participatory design methods could only incorporate the values of the Indian children, which may differ from those in the UK. This scenario is not uncommon when developing products or technological solutions for a global audience [4, 5]. It may be that children in India can act as surrogates for the UK children or that alternative techniques may be required.

Children as designers of products for other children is a theme that has been well studied by the community [6–8]. Mazzone et al. [6] 'informed' teenagers that they were designing for other teenagers when they were actually designing for themselves. In the study by Read et al. [7], young children were introduced to a large toy hippo that neither spoke their language nor was able to manage finger-based interaction. Given these limitations, the children explored ways to understand the hippo by asking questions about his likes and dislikes and by talking with one another to better understand his needs, thus the collaborative aspect of participatory design was seen to be valuable in this context.

Designing for 'different' users raises new questions about the use of participatory design methods. Some of these questions have been raised by researchers working with adults, for example, Okamoto et al. [9] proposed new methods for looking at lifestyles and cultural backgrounds when doing participatory design with adults. A defence of moving participatory design away from design for self is given by Irani et al. [10] who discuss how design research and practice is always culturally located. Sim et al. [8] used sensitizing techniques with children who attempted to design a serious game for children of another culture, but despite the children being immersed into the other culture the end results showed the children were largely just designing games for themselves. Thus, when designers only have access to children from their own culture yet the product or service is intended for a different set of users, other techniques may be required.

One technique that may aid designers to understand children from different cultures is through the use of personas. Personas represent fictitious archetypical users that depict their needs and goals [11]. Within HCI it is a method to communicate information about the user(s) to designers, developers and other stakeholders [12]. Despite the vast amount of research on the creation and use of personas there is very little research on their use in cross-cultural design, especially with children and for products designed for children. Therefore, this research aimed to investigate whether child-generated personas could aid designers in a project to develop a technological solution that can be used by children in the UK and India to reduce plastic consumption. The primary objective was to determine whether children could generate useful personas. If so, these personas could then be evaluated by the project team to foster a shared understanding of the differences and similarities between the children in the UK and India. From the corpus of personas, a small subset could then be synthesized to be used in the design phase to help shape the specification and requirements. The capacity for children to generate personas has been examined briefly by other researchers [13] and this paper aims to contribute to this body of knowledge along with a critical reflection of the value of these as a design aid.

The main objective of this work therefore was to determine whether children could generate useful personas that could be examined by the project team to foster a shared understanding of the differences and similarities between the children in the UK and India. Based upon this objective two research questions were created:

- Can child-generated personas be produced that are realistic and potentially useful to designers?
- Can differences be identified through the analysis of personas that may aid designers and developers?

The first question aimed to determine whether children in the UK and India could create personas that provide useful information that could help the project team understand children's behaviors, likes, dislikes and routines. The second question aimed to understand the differences between the children to help shape the design requirements as no product had been specified at this stage.

2   Related Work

Within the literature three different perspectives on personas have been proposed over the years: goal-directed [14], role-based [15] and engaging and fiction-based [16]. Two main research topics related to personas have been identified by Moser et al. [17], the first being making them more memorable for those who need them and finally the study of how to develop and create personas. The second research area will be the focus of the work presented in this study.

2.1   Personas

Within HCI, personas have been created using various techniques and methods, mainly using real data. In essence, designers gather information about the users' needs, preferences, and behaviours to consolidate these into a number of fictional individuals [15]. There are many challenges for designers in determining how to segment the users to ensure a sufficient representation of the target audience is obtained [18]. Thus designers need to be able to create realistic personas that sufficiently represent the users. It is suggested that by using narrative, pictures and names this helps practitioners imagine they are designing for a real person [19]. It has been argued that one of the key desirable objectives of the persona set is for them to generate empathy within the design team [20]. Creating empathy can enable designers to understand and identify with the needs of the users.

Within the context of CCI, personas have been used in a range of product developments. Child personas were critiqued by Antle [21, 22], who identified and expanded upon three dimensions that are required: childhood needs, developmental abilities, and experiential goals. For example, 'childhood needs' discussed the importance of positive social relationships, whilst 'developmental needs' did not explicitly state rules but touched on aspects of theory such as Piaget's age-dependent stages [23]. Child personas offer the designers the opportunity to deflect from their own childhood experiences and memories which may bias their decision making.

Personas have since been incorporated into methods for designing for and with children. In one study, personas in the form of a comic board presentation were created in a series of facilitated workshops with children [24]. In the first workshop each child worked with an adult facilitator to create the cartoon personas, then had two subsequent workshops where storyboards were produced and finally a prototype of the system was created. Child-generated personas were also created in [13], where 15 children worked in 4 groups to create personas based upon their educational ability. This was based upon the assumption that children would find it easier to create personas that shared similar traits to them, but it is unclear from their study whether children could feasibly create personas independently or for children of a different age or ability. In another study, cultural probes were used to capture and document children's experiences and these were analysed by the researchers to synthesise persona sets for games design [25], but unlike the previous studies children were not used in the direct creation of the personas. A three-phased approach for creating child personas was reported in research by [26] to develop a survey tool to create personas. In this study children were initially interviewed, followed by the creation of a survey tool, and using data from the first two phases the survey tool was validated. The work of [26] did not create personas but provided designers with the means to generate personas from survey data. Therefore, although children can and do contribute to the creation of personas it has not clearly been established how to do this effectively; at present there appear to be a number of options, and the cost benefit of these for practitioners is yet to be established.

2.2 Persona Validation

There has been criticism over the use of personas, as it has been argued that they cannot be falsified or disproved due to their fictitious nature, thus their scientific validity can be drawn into question [27]. Other concerns focus on the development process and the fact that they can be biased by the creator [28], contain personal bias and prejudices [29] and if they are only generated from a small set of user data they may not adequately represent the user group [30]. However, despite these criticisms the HCI community has continued to embrace personas within a user-centred design methodology.

In the work by Faily and Flechais [31] the emphasis was on grounding the personas in empirical data, thus enabling characteristics within each persona to be traced to the original source. This may be judged as a means of validating the persona through a grounded theory approach. The approach to validating personas based on real data is common within HCI [32, 33], yet other techniques have been applied. For example, heuristics have been used when validating personas in an e-Commerce context [34]. In a recent study by Salminen et al., a survey tool was created for understanding the perception of designers towards a persona based on psychology and market research techniques [35]. Their survey tool consisted of 44 questions covering 11 constructs identified from the literature, and would enable designers or practitioners to validate the quality of personas. This approach may be useful when designers are creating technology for a population similar to themselves but in cross-cultural design it may not be appropriate or may need modifying. For example, it would be hard to rate constructs such as familiarity and similarity for populations that are not similar to the rater.

2.3 Designing for Other Cultures

Culture is a complex phenomenon, with many theoretical perspectives and definitions. There appears to be agreement that culture is something relatively stable, accounting for durable differences between societies [30]. Culture refers to the cumulative deposit of knowledge, experience, beliefs, values, attitudes, meanings, hierarchies, religion, notions of time, roles, spatial relations, concepts of the universe, and material objects and possessions acquired by a group of people in the course of generations through individual and group striving [36]. There is evidence to suggest that people from Western and Asian cultures may use different cultural theories to construct and reconstruct their life experiences [37]. Thus culture is an important consideration in the design of technology for a global population and there has been research by the HCI community into cultural aspects of design [38] and evaluation [39].

In evaluation studies of automotive interfaces [40], the UK and India were selected as they were judged to be sufficiently different based upon cultural dimensions proposed by Hofstede [41, 42]. These dimensions were used to frame the evaluation of the interface, with the results highlighting differences based upon power distance and collectivism, but not all the differences identified by Hofstede were revealed. Hofstede's dimensions have also been used to evaluate the interfaces of e-commerce sites across different European countries [43]. However, it is worth noting that Hofstede's approach has come under criticism over the years, as it has been suggested that defining national characters can cause stereotypes to emerge, and a theory that defines culture based upon social structures might be more appropriate [12]. For example, Sahay and Walsham [44] proposed a framework that describes the possible influences that social structures have on the shaping of managerial attitudes in India, and how the structures themselves could be influenced through the role of human agency. Alternatively, a theory such as Schein's Organizational Culture Model [45] may offer further insights, but the 3 categories within this model do not so clearly map onto personas. Any models such as these will have their limitations, yet due to the prevalence of Hofstede's approach in the HCI literature, it is suggested that Hofstede's dimensions may be an appropriate lens to help understand how culture is expressed within personas.

Personas have been used to aid the development of technology and products across cultures (e.g. [46]), but despite this there can be practical issues in the data gathering process to facilitate their creation. For example, to produce a waste management system for a rural village in India researchers used ethnographic techniques by immersing themselves within the village for 3 months [46]. This data gathering process may not be feasible for all designs, thus alternative methods may be desirable. In research by [38], personas were created for entire families rather than individuals to aid the design of a water service for a village in India. This adaptation to the method is rather rare, as personas tend to represent a single user of the system rather than portraying a collection of users. There has also been some criticism of the persona process when used across culture due to its implicit colonial tendency in depicting 'the other' [47]. Thus it is important to ensure there is minimal power distribution when creating personas of different cultures. This highlights the importance of understanding the human, their values and culture when designing technology.

3 Method

3.1 Participants

School children from the UK and India participated in this research study. Ethical approval was sought at both universities involved in the study, and children were informed about the nature of the study prior to the research and at the end, in line with ethical practices outlined in [48]. Within the UK, the participants were a class of 32 children aged 7–9 years old, from one primary (elementary) school in the North West of England. As part of the ethical approval process the head teacher examined the study and agreed that the proposed activity would be appropriate for the age group. The school analysed the study material and sought consent from parents, whilst consent was also sought from the children on the day. The children within this school are predominantly white middle-class children and it was anticipated that this might be reflected within the personas.

The participants from India were from a large school in the North East of India consisting of classes spanning Kindergarten to Higher Secondary. 24 children aged 8–10 participated in the study. Researchers first met school authorities to explain the objectives of their study, and inform them of the nature of the activities that the researchers planned to undertake and of the data collection methods. The researchers took sufficient care to mention confidentiality in data collection. The school authorities were concerned about the careful use of time and of maintaining a conducive child-friendly environment during all the interactions, and so they gave researchers access to the intended group of children for limited durations, which was typically of 40 min. Similar to the children from the UK school, all the children were judged to be predominantly middle-class. Two researchers who were experienced at designing with children facilitated the persona creation session within the UK, whilst three designers with limited experience of working with children facilitated the Indian session.

3.2 Apparatus

A persona template for the children to complete was designed in collaboration with their teacher. The focus of the discussion was about the amount of writing that would be realistic for them to complete within the timeframe and the amount of space required for them. The persona template was divided into 5 sections to reflect the activities within the children's lives, see Fig. 1 for completed examples from the UK and India.

The first section required children to provide generic demographic data (name, age, family members, pets, likes and dislikes) and select 1 of 50 child images to represent their persona. The next two sections were chosen to aid the understanding of life in school and within their home (labelled 'school life' and 'family life'), whilst the final two sections were selected to reflect the activities the children participate in during their spare time (labelled 'hobbies' and 'technology use'). These sections were identified as being important aspects of children's lives in which they interact with people and technology and have been the focus of child personas in other research [13, 49].

118   G. Sim et al.

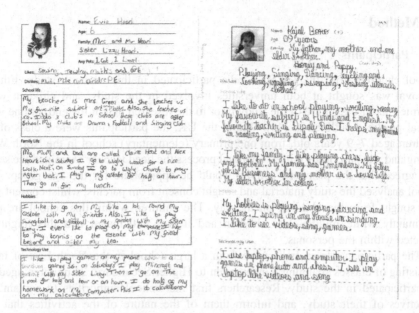

Fig. 1. Example of completed persona template from the UK (left) and India (right).

However, the template was not designed to catch interaction or user goals for a specific scenario, which does mean that empathy within a design scenario may be difficult to measure.

A survey tool was developed based on work conducted by Salminen et al. [35] to evaluate the persona. In Salminen et al.'s work, they note that there is limited research on evaluating personas, but propose a survey tool to measure perceptions of personas based on criteria derived from literature. Our survey consisted of the first four criteria used in Salminen et al.'s study: credibility, consistency, completeness and usefulness or willingness to use. Only four constructs were used as some of the other factors were judged to be inappropriate within the context of this work: for example, it was not felt to be appropriate for adults to rate their interpersonal attraction to a child's persona, or to judge how similar they felt they were to the children. Each of Salminen et al.'s constructs was evaluated through scaled responses to four questions; only example questions for each construct were accessible at the time of this study, so these were used along with the synthesis of an additional three questions, to produce 4 questions for each construct in line with the original survey tool. These questions were answered using a 5-point rating scale, from strongly disagree to strongly agree. The reliability and validity of the tool was re-established using the same techniques as the original study [35] with the alpha reliabilities for each construct shown in the analysis section below.

3.3 Procedure

UK School. The study took place in the children's classroom and was scheduled to last one hour. Two researchers who both had considerable experience of working with children and two teachers were present to assist the children. Prior to the children completing the personas, they were given a 10 min briefing via a PowerPoint presentation consisting of 3 slides. The first slide described what personas are, the second slide introduced the research aims and ethics, and finally a completed persona for a teacher within a fictitious school was shown to enable the children to understand the activity. At the end of this briefing the children were then informed about the ground rules for creating the personas:

- They cannot use real names of children in their school or parents etc.
- They cannot use personal details such as real street names, and therefore the children were asked to base the information on a fictitious village called 'Wiggly Wells' with the children attending Wiggly Wells Primary School.

The children were divided into 4 groups of between 7–8 children based on the seating arrangements within the classroom. Each group would create personas for different ages of children within Wiggly Wells Primary School, so that at the end of the study personas would have been created to represent all the children within a primary school. The first group would create personas for the Reception class and Year 1 (ages 5–6), the second group would be for Year 2 (ages 7–8), the third group Year 3 (ages 9–10) and the final group Year 4 (aged 11). Each child was given a blank template and 50 pictures of children were placed on each of the tables so that the children could select one picture to illustrate their persona. The activity was split into 3 stages, the first requiring the children to complete the first part of the template (select a picture and demographic data). During this stage the researchers and teachers assisted any child who was struggling with any aspect of the process. The biggest challenge during this stage appeared to be the creation of names for either family members or pets, for example one child was struggling to think of a name for a pet rabbit. At the end of stage one, the children were then reintroduced to the types of information that may be included in the school life and family life sections and were given approximately 15 min to complete this, and the same process was applied in stage 3 for the hobbies and technology use. During the final two stages the researchers assisted and encouraged the children to complete the personas, as some of the children need encouragement and prompts to expand the information they were writing. For example, some of the children were stating they played a sport but not how often or the position they played and they were encouraged to enhance their personas. To avoid repetition in the final two sections, the children were encouraged not to talk about computer games within the hobbies section and to focus on non-technology based activities such as sporting clubs.

At the end of the session the children were thanked and consent was again discussed with the children to ensure that they did not mind us keeping the personas. The personas the children had created were photocopied by the teachers to give to the children.

Indian School. The same study was replicated within the primary school in India but due to differences in class times the sessions needed to be altered. Three researchers carried out the activity and they worked with 6 children at a time to complete the personas over two 40 min sessions as it was not feasible to complete the personas in a single class interval of 40 min. The decision was also made not to create personas for the younger age range as the teachers felt that they may struggle to complete this task, therefore personas were generated for children in the age range of 8 to 11 years old.

3.4   Analysis

The personas were analysed in three stages. In the first stage, three of the researchers read each persona and rated them based on the survey tool to determine if the individual child could create a realistic persona. In line with the study by [35], Cronbach's alpha reliability test was calculated for each of the 4 constructs. This was to establish whether the survey tool enabled researchers to accurately rate the usefulness of the personas, in order for the first research question to be answered. Without a high consistency score then it would not be possible to infer that the child-generated personas are perceived to be useful.

A high level of reliability was demonstrated for each of the four constructs as shown in Table 1. The decision was made to remove one of the items, 'The picture of the persona matches other information' for the consistency category, as this resulted in an alpha value of <.70 and this may have been attributed to the fact that children had access to a limited selection of pictures.

Table 1. Alpha reliability scores for each construct on the persona evaluation survey tool.

Construct	Items	Alpha
Credibility	1. This persona seems like a real person 2. This sounds like a made-up person to me 3. I could believe this describes a real child 4. The information provided seems realistic	.944
Consistency	1. The picture of the persona matches other information 2. The family information is in line with the other information provided 3. The likes and dislikes do not fit with the rest of the persona 4. The sections seem to connect into a consistent persona	.789
Completeness	1. There is plenty of information about the persona 2. There is enough information here for me to learn what this person is like 3. This persona seems to be missing useful information 4. The information seems very general and could apply to many people	.972
Usefulness and willingness to use	1. I would make use of this persona in my work 2. I found this persona helpful for understanding a child like this 3. Designers could use this to help them understand children 4. I don't feel I need this information to help me understand a child like this	.977

The next stage of analysis involved two researchers re-examining the personas using conventional content analysis [50]. For each of the sections in the personas, starting with 'school life', each persona was analysed by reading through the comments and generating themes and subthemes. Researchers identified topics that they felt were similar to each other, and themes were created from these. For example, in 'school life' children often commented about their friends; this generated the theme of 'friends', and subthemes emerged within this based on the narratives within the personas. In this example, the subthemes related to 'best friends', 'lots of friends', and 'playing with friends'. During this process the wording of themes was altered in some instances to reflect the inclusion of additional subthemes. An example of this was within the 'hobbies' category, where the theme of 'play' was amended to represent 'outside play' and 'playing indoors'. This approach was continued until the two researchers were satisfied that the themes adequately reflected the persona data for both the Indian and UK child generated personas. After the initial themes were identified, an independent researcher re-examined the data for consistency and one theme was reclassified to better represent the data.

The final stage was to explore representations of culture. Two researchers examined all the personas to identify if any section provided cultural references that could be mapped to Hofstede's dimensions [41, 42] and coded them using the following codes:

1. Individualism (a) vs Collectivism (b)
2. Small Power Distance (a) vs Large Power Distance (b)
3. Masculinity (a) vs Femininity (b)
4. Uncertainty Avoidance (a) vs Uncertainty Tolerance (b)
5. Long Term Orientation (a) vs Short Term Orientation (b)
6. Indulgence (a) vs Restraint (b)

The two researchers examined each of the personas, and if they felt any narrative provided a cultural reference based on Hofstede's dimensions then this was coded to the relevant dimension – for example a code of 3b would relate to Femininity. A frequency count was then performed, to identify how many of the personas incorporated some narrative that matched each dimension.

4   Results

All 56 children managed to complete a persona, with only 1 of the UK personas having a blank section as they ran out of time to complete it.

The results are presented in two sections: the results from the survey tool, followed by the results of the content analysis and cultural analysis.

4.1   Survey Results

In order to answer the question of whether children can produce realistic personas, the survey data was analysed based on the four constructs represented in the survey tool, and the results are shown in Table 2.

Table 2. Means and standard deviations for the four constructs for the UK and Indian personas

	Credibility	Consistency	Completeness	Usefulness
UK	3.75 (.95)	4.05 (.85)	3.06 (1.17)	3.27 (.92)
India	4.27 (.45)	4.04 (.57)	3.61 (.84)	3.5 (.88)

The personas all score above 3, indicating a perceived level of realism in the personas, but the completeness and usefulness and willingness to use scores are lower compared to the credibility and consistency. This could be attributed to the fact that a number of children in the hobbies and technology section purely listed items rather than elaborating on them, which brought these scores down. It may have also been attributed to methodological issues with the template and procedure.

4.2   Content Analysis Results

To explore the differences, the personas were analysed based on conventional content analysis. For the UK personas 11 themes emerged in the 'school life' section, whilst for India there were 14 themes. The second section of 'family life' had 8 themes for the UK personas and 9 for India, whilst for 'hobbies' there were 6 themes for the UK and 5 for India. The final section of 'technology use' had 9 themes in the UK personas compared to 5 in the Indian set. The key results are summarised in Table 3 below. Only the subthemes that appeared in more than 40% of the personas are detailed here, to reflect the dominant narrative within the personas. For example, in 'school life' a total of 11 subthemes emerged but only 4 of these are presented in Table 3 below. Other subthemes including 'class' are not represented in the table, where children were just stating the school class they were in, but all the data was used for comparisons.

Table 3. Key themes identified in the content analysis

Persona section	UK themes	% of personas	India themes	% of personas
School life	Favourite subject	84	Getting to school	100
	Getting to school	44	Favourite subject	95
	Personal traits	44	Break	50
	Club(s)	41	Teacher	50
			Play after school	42
Home life	Activities	63	Parents	100
	Siblings	41	Family activities	83
	Playing outside	40		
Hobbies	Sport	91	Indoor play	83
			sport	58
Technology	Phone	56	Computer	87
	Tablet	50	Phone	83
	Console	50	Games	62
	Computer	47	Apps	50
	Games	46		

In the section on 'school life' within the UK, personal traits such as loving school and good behaviour were reflected in the child-generated personas whilst these attributes were not evident in the Indian personas. In addition, 41% of the child personas from the UK attended some form of club before or after school and this was not the case in India with children appearing to go home for lunch. Within the Indian personas there was more discussion of activities they did during break which are culturally different to the UK, for example 'eating tiffin' and 'playing Kabaddi'.

Within the 'home life' section all the child-generated personas from India discussed their parents with a strong emphasis on family activities including 'grandparents telling them stories', 'studies with mother' and 'playing Ludo with grandparents'; these activities were not evident in the UK personas, which tended to focus on going to church and walking pets. Siblings and in particular 'playing with' them was a theme that emerged within the UK personas, whilst there was little mention of siblings in the Indian sets.

In the 'hobbies' section, sports dominated the UK sets and also featured heavily in the Indian personas. Football and cycling were mentioned the most in India, whilst football and swimming were most common in the UK. Despite some similarities, the way the children in the UK portrayed themselves was different, with the focus being on being successful. For example, one child stated 'he plays as a midfielder and he is a goal scoring machine' and another stated 'they scored 72 goals for wiggly wells'. Indoor play features in the majority of the personas created by Indian children with activities such as drawing, singing and dancing being incorporated into half the personas.

In the final section of 'technology use', the biggest difference was with regards to the access to technology. No children in India had access to games consoles or tablets in any of the generated personas. In the UK personas children tended to focus on the make of the phones rather than the behaviour of the child with the device, which came across more in the India personas. For example, in the Indian personas there was lots of discussion about watching videos on the phones and playing games. The type of games differed between the two groups with Fortnite and Fifa being dominant in the UK, and games such as Chess, Clash of Clans and GTA being mentioned many times within the India set. The use of apps such as Whatsapp featured in 50% of the Indian personas, but there was no mention in the UK of specific apps being used.

4.3   Cultural Analysis Results

Table 4 below shows the percentage of children in the UK and India whose personas contained aspects relating to Hofstede's dimensions of culture. The columns represent the sections in the personas and the numbers align to Hofstede's dimensions as reported in Sect. 3.4 above. There were no instances in any of the personas of narrative relating to the following categories: Large Power Distance, Uncertainty Tolerance and Long or Short Term Orientation. Examining each persona there was evidence of cultural differences surrounding the dimension of Indulgence in some sections. In the personas generated by the children in the UK, 31% stated in the demographic information that they liked to play games but hated homework, and this was not evident in any of the Indian personas. In 20% of the Indian personas children were portrayed as hard

working in the 'family life' section through doing extra studies in the evening, and this did not come across in any of the UK personas. In the Indian personas 95% of the children explicitly stated that they used technology to play games, notably on a computer. This was higher than the UK but this could have been attributed to the way it was coded, as consoles have multiple functionality but it was only coded as Indulgence if the persona mentioned playing games. There were very little cultural differences identified in the 'school life' section of the personas, with activities related to Indulgence (e.g. having fun and playing with friends) being evident in both sets.

Differences were also identified in the dimension of Masculinity. 75% of personas in India demonstrated a Masculine role within the family environment based on gender roles: in these personas the father usually went to work whilst the mother was portrayed as a housewife.

Table 4. Percentage of personas that are mapped to Hofstede's dimensions

Hofstede's dimensions	UK					India				
	Dem.	Sch.	Fam.	Hob.	Techn.	Dem.	Sch.	Fam.	Hob.	Techn.
1a		9	9					4		
1b		9	37	12	6	4	4	42		
2a			9					4		
3a	9	12	12	31	19	4	8	75	4	
3b		12				4	4	8		17
4a			16	6				4		
6a	31	50	31	6	44	4	29	8	8	95
6b				6				20		

For the Hobbies section, aspects of Masculinity appeared in the UK personas, especially the notion of competition, winning and being the best. For example, one persona stated 'Tennis team has won 4 tournaments' and another stated 'Plays for Wiggly Wells Primary School FC and was top scorer in club history and league history'. In the final section of 'technology use' again there was instances of Masculinity that were not evident in the Indian personas. The UK personas tended to be rather boastful in their ownership of technology, for example one child claimed to have 'Xbox, Xbox1, iPhone 7, iPhone 6 s, PS3, PS4, PS4 Pro, and a TV in his bedroom' whist this was not evident in the Indian personas as there was no mention of specific devices by names (e.g. iPhone) and there was no game console ownership.

5   Discussion

The first research question aimed to identify whether children could generate realistic personas. A tool was developed based upon research from Salminen et al. [35] and the results indicated that the personas were realistic. Despite this, there were certain aspects in some of the personas that may not have been complete or especially useful based on

the ratings from the Likert scale. However, comparing the personas to examples provided within the literature indicated that the detail is comparable to personas generated by children in other studies [13]. Previous work had demonstrated that children in groups could generate a persona [13] and their rationale for using groups was that they might find it easier to create personas with traits similar to their own. In the study presented in this paper, children generated personas individually rather than in a group context and as such a diverse array of personas were generated. This demonstrates that it is possible to use individual children in a facilitated session to generate personas that are perceived to be realistic.

In order to examine the personas a survey-based approach was taken based upon previous research [35]. Although this approach enables a judgement to be made on a number of constructs relating to the quality of the personas it does not offer any ecological validity of their usefulness in the design process. It may be that the information provided in the persona is realistic, but offers very little insight beyond the designers' existing knowledge of children to help inform design decisions. Therefore, it is questionable whether the approach taken in [35] is completely appropriate for validating personas. The survey tool presented may be most useful in conjunction with other techniques and insights from the designers.

In total, 56 personas were created by the children in the UK and India, and for designers this number is impractical to work with in the design process whereby a small number of personas is usually required to represent the target audience [16]. The analysis of the personas did enable the designers involved in this project to gain insights that could aid the design. Reflecting on the process it was conjectured that through observing the children creating the personas and analyzing the data a greater understanding of children within the UK and India would be obtained. It was also felt that by having access to the persona sets, these could be amalgamated into a small number of personas using affinity mapping [51] or correspondence analysis [18] to form a small number of personas that could represent the users. For inexperienced designers creating products for children the data provided by the children offers awareness of behaviours and routines that may be difficult to obtain from conventional persona creation techniques such as observations [15].

The second research question aimed to ascertain whether differences could be identified between the two sets of personas. This research highlights that child-generated personas may indeed be useful for designers or developers to understand different populations that they may not necessarily be familiar with. There were clear differences relating to the family, gender roles and the way children in the UK focussed on success and winning in sport. An example of these differences can be found in the Indian personas where children tended to present a list of hobbies without expanding on the details such as '*My favourite hobbies is swimming, dancing, singing and I like to craft.*' compared to the UK children who elaborated on the facts '*Plays for the tennis team in Wiggly Wells. The tennis team has won 4 tournaments.*'.

The use of content analysis was a useful way of capturing and analysing the behavioural differences. For example, within the child-generated personas in India there were games specific to the Asian culture being mentioned such as Kabaddi, and routines around school and family life that were different from the UK children. The parents and family activities played an important role in the Indian personas, for

example '*I play cricket with my father. I study with my mother. I ask my uncle when I need something. I do story competition with my grandmother. I say some random stories in the competition. I play "Luka chupi" with my grandfather. My father is a doctor. My mother is a housewife. During holidays, we travel. We also go to my uncle's house. At my uncle's house, I play with my cousins.*' This type of narrative was not present in the personas from the UK. In particular, for the HCI community there were clear differences in the use and access to technology that would influence the design decisions. This has been examined in a range of technology contexts such as security [52] and education [53] but little focus has been paid to design with and for children. The UK personas had a strong emphasis on Apple products, in particular phones and tablets. From the current and previous projects working with middle class families in India, observations suggest that tablets have not become mainstream and games consoles are rare. These are important factors that would need to be considered and identified if developing for both cultures.

Although the content analysis method enabled similarities and differences to be identified, this approach alone may result in an incomplete picture of the differences being documented. When examining the persona sets, other subtle differences were observed that did not fall into the categories. One such observation was the fact that children in the UK tended to specify the timings of events and activities, for example '*Trains 2 days a week, Mondays and Thursdays. Does Spanish on Thursday at 5 pm–7 pm.*' and from another persona '*After that, I play on my estate for half an hour. Then go in for my lunch*'. Timings were not evident in the personas created by Indian children. It may be that this is a cultural difference as India is perceived to be a past orientated society and as such are rather relaxed about timings [54]. Culture is an important consideration and there are different theoretical perspectives relating to culture and within the personas it is an important factor to consider if personas were to be aggregated or used to aid design decisions. Although Hofstede's dimensions have been criticised [55], within the context of the work presented in this research it highlights that child-generated personas may indeed be useful for designers or developers to understand cultures that they may not necessarily be familiar with. For example, Masculinity differed between the two groups especially around family life. In India the women were often portrayed as staying at home whilst this was not the case in the UK. However care needs to be taken to ensure that the personas do not stereotype a population [29, 56], as it may be that this portrayal of family life is not reflected in other parts of India or the UK.

When comparing results and interpreting the data it is important to consider the methodological limitations and differences to determine how these may have impacted on the results. First, there were clearly time differences between the duration of the study in India and the UK that could have affected the detail provided by the children in the personas. Due to the different time requirements of classes, the UK children completed the personas in a 1 h session, whilst the children in India completed them in two 40 min sessions. The facilitators in India also worked with two children at a time so could more easily prompt the children, whereas in the UK the whole class was creating the personas simultaneously. Although no analysis was performed on the number of words generated, both sets of personas tended to provide a similar level of detail on the last two sections of 'hobbies' and 'technology use'. The children may

have struggled to expand on these sections without additional support but it is unlikely to be related to fatigue as the children in India completed these sections in the second session after a break. It was observed that some of the children in India struggled to write and expand on points, as they were concerned with inaccurate spelling of words. This factor was not shown in the UK, where the children instead spent considerable time worrying about what name to give to pets and family members and this slowed the process down. In the analysis of the personas using the survey tool, one of the constructs related to completeness, with a question on whether enough detail was provided. It is worth noting that the template used may have had an impact on the amount of detail provided. Although this was designed in consultation with the teacher, it had limited space for writing, and the size of the children's handwriting may have affected the level of detail. Some of the children in the UK drew lines in the boxes and wrote several lines whilst others would fill the box with one or two sentences, whereas in contrast the children in India asked for a separate piece of paper if they filled the box and this was not the case in the UK.

6 Conclusions

This study aimed to investigate two research questions, the first of which was whether children in the UK and India could generate realistic personas. In total 56 personas were created by children. The personas were analysed through a survey tool that demonstrated a high level of perceived realism based on four constructs: Credibility, Consistency, Completeness, and Usefulness or Willingness to Use. For designers this method may be useful, as the children could create detailed personas that could aid the decision making process or be used to synthesize a small number of personas. The advantage of this is that it mitigates some aspects of the data collection process that have been traditionally used in persona creation, such as interviews, which may be time consuming.

The second research question aimed to determine whether differences could be identified within the narratives in the personas. Using content analysis the 56 personas were analysed. The results highlighted a number of differences related to aspects such as gender roles, competition and expectations around study. To analyse differences it is important to examine the data through multiple lenses, as a single method may not be able to distinguish some important differences such as culture.

To conclude, child-generated personas can be a viable method to aid designers and developers understand children within the context of design. When the project is across cultures, child-generated personas can offer insights that may aid the decision making process.

Further research will aim to refine the methodology for creating the personas by examining the impact the template has on the level of detail the children provide as well as exploring additional methods for eliciting responses from children. The personas will also be re-examined to identify segmentation techniques that will enable a useful number of personas to be selected. The designers in India and the UK will create a subset of personas for their country and these will be evaluated for consistency across the project team. This subset of personas will then ultimately be used to inform the

design of the technological solution to reduce plastic consumption. Finally, future work will also then be able to reflect on the use of these personas in the design.

Acknowledgements. We would like to thank the staff and pupils at Heskin Pemberton's Primary School in the UK and Central School, IIT Guwahati in India for their participation and involvement in the study.

References

1. Druin, A., Stewart, J., Proft, D., Bedersen, B.B., Hollan, J.D.: KidPad: a design collboration between children, technologists, and educators. In: CHI 1997. ACM Press, Atlanta (1997)
2. Scaife, M., Rogers, Y., Aldrich, F., Davies, M.: Designing for or designing with? Informant design for interactive learning environments. In: CHI 1997. ACM Press, Atlanta (1997)
3. Dindler, C., Iversen, O.S., Smith, R., Veersawmy, R.: Participatory design at the museum: inquiring into children's everyday engagement in cultural heritage. In: OZCHI 2010, pp. 72–79. ACM, Brisbane (2010)
4. Downes, L., Mui, C.: Unleashing the Killer App: Digital Strategies for Market. Harvard Business School Press, Cambridge (1998)
5. Roellig, L.: Designing global brands: critical lessons. Des. Manag. J. (Former Ser.) **12**(4), 40–45 (2001)
6. Mazzone, E., Read, J.C., Beale, R.: Design with and for disaffected teenagers. In: 5th Nordic Conference on Human-Computer Interaction: Building Bridges, pp. 290–297. ACM, Lund (2008)
7. Read, J.C., Horton, M., Mazzone, E., Cassidy, B., McKnight, L.: Designing for Mr Hippo - introducing concepts of marginalisation to children designers. In: Interaction Design and Children, Italy. ACM (2009)
8. Sim, G., Horton, M., Read, J.C.: Sensitizing: helping children design serious games for a surrogate population. In: Vaz de Carvalho, C., Escudeiro, P., Coelho, A. (eds.) Serious Games, Interaction, and Simulation. LNICST, vol. 161, pp. 58–65. Springer, Cham (2016). https://doi.org/10.1007/978-3-319-29060-7_10
9. Okamoto, M., Komatsu, H., Gyobu, I., Ito, K.: Participatory design using scenarios in different cultures. In: Jacko, J.A. (ed.) HCI 2007. LNCS, vol. 4550, pp. 223–231. Springer, Heidelberg (2007). https://doi.org/10.1007/978-3-540-73105-4_25
10. Irani, L., Vertesi, J., Dourish, P., Kkavita, P., Grinter, R.E.: Postcolonial computing: a lens on design and development. In: CHI 2010. ACM, Atlanta (2010)
11. Cooper, A., Reimann, R., Cronin, D.: Modeling users: personas and goals. In: About Face 2.0: The Essentials of Interaction Design, chap. 5, pp. 55–74. Wiley Publishing, Indianapolis (2003)
12. Pruitt, J., Grudin, J.: Personas: practice and theory. In: Proceedings of DUX 2003: The 2003 Conference on Designing for User Experiences. ACM (2003)
13. Itenge-Wheeler, H., Winschiers-Theophilus, H., Soro, A., Breeton, M.: Child designers creating personas to diversify design perspectives and concepts for their own technology enhanced library. In: Proceedings of the 17th ACM Conference on Interaction Design and Children. ACM (2018)
14. Cooper, A.: The inmates are running the asylum: why high-tech products drive us crazy and how to restore the sanity. Sams, Indianapolis (2004)

15. Grudin, J., Pruitt, J.: Personas, participatory design and product development: an infrastructure for engagement. In: Proceedings of Participation and Design Conference (PDC2002), Sweden (2002)
16. Nielsen, L.: Personas. In: The Encyclopedia of Human-Computer Interaction, 2nd edn. Interaction Design Foundation (2016)
17. Moser, C., Fuchsberger, V., Neureiter, K., Sellner, W., Tscheligi, M.: Revisiting personas: the making-of for special user groups. In: CHI 2012 Extended Abstracts on Human Factors in Computing Systems. ACM (2012)
18. Laporte, L., Slegers, K., De Grooff, D.: Using correspondence analysis to monitor the persona segmentation process. In: Proceedings of the 7th Nordic Conference on Human-Computer Interaction: Making Sense Through Design. ACM (2012)
19. Miaskiewicz, T., Sumner, T., Kozar, K.A.: A latent semantic analysis methodology for the identification and creation of personas. In: Proceedings of the SIGCHI Conference on Human Factors in Computing Systems. ACM (2008)
20. Maness, J.M., Miaskiewicz, T., Sumner, T.: Using personas to understand the needs and goals of institutional repository users. D-Lib Mag. 14(9/10), 1082–9873 (2016)
21. Antle, A.N.: Child-based personas: need, ability and experience. Cogn. Technol. Work 10 (2), 155–166 (2008)
22. Antle, A.N.: Child-personas: fact or fiction? In: Proceedings of the 6th Conference on Designing Interactive Systems. ACM (2006)
23. Piaget, J.: Piaget's theory. In: Mussen, P. (ed.) Carmichael's Manual of Child Psychology, vol. 1, pp. 703–832. Wiley, New York (1970)
24. Wärnestål, P., Svedberg, P., Nygren, J.: Co-constructing child personas for health-promoting services with vulnerable children. In: Proceedings of the SIGCHI Conference on Human Factors in Computing Systems. ACM (2014)
25. Moser, M., Fuchsberger, V., Tscheligi, M.: Using probes to create child personas for games. In: Proceedings of the 8th International Conference on Advances in Computer Entertainment Technology. ACM (2011)
26. da Costa, A.C., Rebelo, F., Teles, J., Noriege, P.: Child-persona: how to bring them to reality? Procedia Manuf. 3(1), 6520–6527 (2015)
27. Chapman, C.N., Milham, R.P.: The personas' new clothes: methodological and practical arguments against a popular method. In: Proceedings of the Human Factors and Ergonomics Society Annual Meeting. SAGE Publications, Los Angeles (2006)
28. Ronkko, K.: An empirical study demonstrating how different design constraints, project organization and contexts limited the utility of personas. In: Proceedings of the 38th Annual Hawaii International Conference on System Sciences, HICSS 2005. IEEE (2005)
29. Hill, C.G., et al.: Gender-inclusiveness personas vs. stereotyping: can we have it both ways? In: Proceedings of the 2017 CHI Conference on Human Factors in Computing Systems. ACM (2017)
30. Minkov, M., Blagoev, V., Hofstede, G.: The boundaries of culture: do questions about societal norms reveal cultural differences? J. Cross Cult. Psychol. 44(7), 1094–1106 (2013)
31. Faily, S., Flechais, I.: Persona cases: a technique for grounding personas. In: Proceedings of the SIGCHI Conference on Human Factors in Computing Systems. ACM (2011)
32. Chapman, C.N., Love, E., Milham, R.P., Elrif, P., Alford, J.L.: Quantitative evaluation of personas as information. In: Proceedings of the Human Factors and Ergonomics Society Annual Meeting. SAGE Publications, Los Angeles (2008)
33. Salminen, J., et al.: Generating cultural personas from social data: a perspective of Middle Eastern users. In: 5th International Conference on Future Internet of Things and Cloud Workshops (FiCloudW). IEEE (2017)

34. Thoma, V., Williams, B.: Developing and validating personas in e-commerce: a heuristic approach. In: Gross, T., et al. (eds.) INTERACT 2009. LNCS, vol. 5727, pp. 524–527. Springer, Heidelberg (2009). https://doi.org/10.1007/978-3-642-03658-3_56
35. Salminen, J., Kwak, H., Santos, J.M., Jung, S.G., An, J., Jansen, B.J.: Persona perception scale: developing and validating an instrument for human-like representations of data. In: Extended Abstracts of the 2018 CHI Conference on Human Factors in Computing Systems. ACM (2018)
36. Porter, R.E., Samovar, L.A.: An introduction to intercultural communication. In: Samovar, L.A., Porter, R.E. (eds.) Intercultural Communication: A Reader, 7th edn, pp. 4–26. Wadsworth, Belmont (1994)
37. Wirtz, D., Chiu, C.Y., Diener, E., Oishi, S.: What constitutes a good life? Cultural differences in the role of positive and negative. J. Pers. **77**(4), 1167–1196 (2009)
38. Putnam, C., Kolko, B., Wood, S.: Communicating about users in ICTD: leveraging HCI personas. In: Proceedings of the Fifth International Conference on Information and Communication Technologies and Development. ACM (2012)
39. Sim, G., Horton, M., Danino, N.: Evaluating game preference using the Fun Toolkit across cultures. In: Proceedings of the 26th Annual BCS Interaction Specialist Group Conference on People and Computers. British Computer Society (2012)
40. Khan, T., Pitts, M., Williams, M.A.: Cross-cultural differences in automotive HMI design: a comparative study between UK and Indian users' design preferences. J. Usability Stud. **11** (2), 45–65 (2016)
41. Hofstede, G., Hofstede, G.J., Minkov, M.: Cultures and Organizations. McGraw Hill, New York (1997)
42. Hofstede, G., Hofstede, G.J., Minkov, M.: Cultures and Organizations: Software of the Mind, 3rd edn. McGraw-Hill Education, New York (2010)
43. De Angeli, A., Kyriakoullis, L.: Globalisation vs. localisation in e-commerce: cultural-aware interaction design. In: Conference on Advanced Visual Interfaces, pp. 250–253. ACM, Venezia (2006)
44. Sahay, S., Walsham, G.: Social structure and managerial agency in India. Organ. Stud. **18**(3), 415–444 (1997)
45. Schein, E.H.: Coming to a new awareness of organizational culture. Sloan Manag. Rev. **25** (2), 3–16 (1984)
46. Vestergaard, L., Hauge, B., Hansen, C.T.: Almost like being there; the power of personas when designing for foreign cultures. CoDesign **12**(4), 257–274 (2016)
47. Cabrero, D.G., Winschiers-Theophilus, H., Abdelnour-Nocera, J.: A critique of personas as representations of the other in cross-cultural technology design. In: Proceedings of the First African Conference on Human Computer Interaction. ACM (2016)
48. Read, J.C., Horton, M., Fitton, D., Sim, G.: Empowered and informed: participation of children in HCI. In: Bernhaupt, R., Dalvi, G., Joshi, A., Balkrishan, D.K., O'Neill, J., Winckler, M. (eds.) INTERACT 2017. LNCS, vol. 10514, pp. 431–446. Springer, Cham (2017). https://doi.org/10.1007/978-3-319-67684-5_27
49. Horton, M., Read, J.C., Fitton, D., Little, L., Toth, N.: Too cool at school: understanding cool teenagers. Psychnol. J. **10**(2), 73–91 (2012)
50. Hsieh, H.F., Shannon, S.E.: Three approaches to qualitative content analysis. Qual. Health Res. **15**(9), 1277–1288 (2005)
51. Sundt, A., Davis, E.: User personas as a shared lens for library UX. Weave: J. Libr. User Exp. **1**(6) (2017)
52. Dinev, T., Goo, J., Hu, Q., Nam, K.: User behaviour towards protective information technologies: the role of national cultural differences. Inf. Syst. J. **19**(4), 391–412 (2009)

53. Rogers, P.C., Graham, C.R., Mayes, C.T.: Cultural competence and instructional design: exploration research into the delivery of online instruction cross-culturally. Educ. Tech. Res. Dev. **55**(2), 197–217 (2007)
54. Vaught, B.C., Abraham, Y.T.: Cultural diversity and interpersonal communication skills: a study of Indian managers. Leadersh. Organ. Dev. J. **13**(7), 26–31 (1992)
55. McSweeney, B.: Hofstede's model of national cultural differences and their consequences: a triumph of faith – a failure of analysis. Hum. Relat. **55**(1), 89–118 (2002)
56. Marsden, N., Haag, M.: Stereotypes and politics: reflections on personas. In: Proceedings of the 2016 CHI Conference on Human Factors in Computing Systems. ACM, San Jose (2016)

How Do They Use Their Smartphones: A Study on Smartphone Usage by Indian Students

Subrata Tikadar[✉] and Samit Bhattacharya

Indian Institute of Technology Guwahati, Guwahati, India
subratatikadar@gmail.com, samit3k@gmail.com

Abstract. It is very important to know users' behavior to design and build effective interactive systems, tools, or applications. The behavioral study not only helps to assure the success of any design or product but also helps other researchers from various related areas. In this study, we have systematically collected and analyzed the behavioral data for smartphone usage by 1711 students of 188 academic institutions throughout India. We have observed students' behavior on smartphone usages both inside and outside the classroom. We conducted the study focusing on two aspects: to find the behavioral differences on the smartphone usage based on the gender, and academic level; and to identify the most frequently performed smartphone activities by the students inside and outside the classroom. Although there are few similarities with the existing related studies, we have found many dissimilarities as well. It is expected that the findings of the study will help many researchers from various fields including HCI, Mobile HCI, Behavioral Science, Psychology, and Education.

Keywords: Academic class · Classroom activities · Indian students · Smartphone usage · Students' behavior

1 Introduction

With the increasing adoption of new technologies and gradual decreasing cost of Internet connectivity, smartphone ownership among students has become very common in developed as well as in developing countries. Today we rarely find a college student who does not have a smartphone. Nowadays, many school students also use smartphones beyond the school hours, and sometimes in the classroom without the knowledge of teacher and administration. Present day smartphones are so advanced that we cannot but term them as 'pocket-computer.' Students use their smartphones for various academic and non-academic purposes. Academic purposes include taking class-note, participating in real-time online poll, accessing online course material, surfing educational sites and so on. Non-academic purposes include playing games, accessing instant messaging services and social networking websites, listening to music, watching movies, monitoring health, booking tickets (air, railway, bus, movie etc.) and hotels, online shopping, performing financial transactions, and other daily-life activities (booking cab, using location access service and so on) [1, 20, 28, 29].

© IFIP International Federation for Information Processing 2019
Published by Springer Nature Switzerland AG 2019
D. Lamas et al. (Eds.): INTERACT 2019, LNCS 11748, pp. 132–151, 2019.
https://doi.org/10.1007/978-3-030-29387-1_8

Many researchers and academicians have tried and are trying to identify the effect (and probable reason of it) of using smartphones inside and outside the classroom. For instance, it has been observed that using digital devices in the classroom may cause distraction and exhaustion, especially when those are used for non-academic purposes [12]. These distractions and exhaustions are in addition to the common classroom distractions and fatigues [11, 21]. Common distractions include conversation among students, and other noises in and outside the classroom. Ragan et al. [26] found that students have a tendency to use digital devices largely for non-academic purposes, even when they are in the classroom. When the students are addicted to some non-academic applications, their academic performances hampers [14]. Classroom learning can be affected due to multitasking activities, even if the tasks are classroom related [29]. Other harms of smartphone overuse among students are insomnia, lack of attention, social anxiety, impulsive behavior, depression and stress [19, 33]. These may affect the classroom learning and performance of the students, directly and/or indirectly.

These are the instances of possible downsides of using smartphones by students, particularly when they are in the classroom. However, there are many evidences where researchers have clearly reported that there is no negative impact of using smartphones by students, even when they are in the classroom [10, 15]. In fact, there are many direct and indirect advantages of using smartphone in and outside the classroom [5]. Sometimes the advantages are more than disadvantages [16]. For instance, findings of Wang et al. [34] depicts that interactions through smartphone while learning helps students to learn better and score higher grades. Cacho [5] also mentioned that smartphones are useful tools for education. Roberts and Rees [28] also reported that mobile devices help university students a lot to learn things in a better way. Now a days, learning through mobile devices like smartphone is so popular and beneficial that a new term called 'm-learning' has been fostered [7, 9, 13]. Recently, a new kind of learning environment called 'blended learning environment' has also been popularized. In this kind of learning environment, Information and Communication Technology (ICT) is blended into traditional face-to-face classrooms to achieve the benefits of both [2, 8, 25, 32]. For instance, Tikadar et al. [32] have shown that teaching-learning through mobile devices like smartphones in traditional face-to-face classrooms is more beneficial and effective.

Although there are both advantages and disadvantages of using smartphones by students, it is clear that proper monitoring and restriction in the use of non-academic applications are very important [1, 12, 19]. For instance, Lee et al. [19], in their study observed that one group of students scored higher grades than other group because of different frequency and duration of academic and non-academic 'apps' (smartphone applications) usages. This was in spite of the fact that every student of the two groups used same number and similar types of apps over the period of the study.

A survey about smartphone usage behavior of students, therefore, is required on regular basis. This helps us not only to be aware of the habits and preferences of the students for using smartphone but also to know the probable reasons of such preferences. For example, most of the time students use non-academic apps in the classroom when they are bored by uninteresting lectures [21]. The survey also helps the academicians and policymakers to allow and/or restrict particular applications to specific groups of students. Groups may depend on age, gender, level of education, ethnicity,

socio-economic status, and so on. Academicians as well as app developers can also decide to build appropriate tools and apps for specific groups.

Although the existing studies regarding smartphone usage (e.g., [4, 19–21, 23]) are rich and informative, they are either not up-to-date or not done on the Indian students. This is in spite of the fact that India has the largest student population (as per Census 2011, India has 315 million students, which is the largest number of students) in the world[1]. Moreover, the behavior may change based on the ethnicity of the students (details are described in related work section). It might not be a right decision to be taken for Indian students, if required, based on the behavior of some non-Indian students. In this article, we, therefore, present an up-to-date survey on smartphone usage by Indian students.

The explicit research questions we wanted to address by the behavioral study are: (i) Which smartphone activities are generally performed by the Indian students? (ii) Which of the activities are performed most frequently and least frequently both inside and outside the classroom for academic and non-academic purposes? and (iii) Is there any difference in behavior on performing smartphone activities based on gender and academic level (school, UG and PG) of the students?

Here, the 'behavior' indicates habits and preferences for performing smartphone activities. The 'smartphone' refers to a mobile phone that performs many of the functions of a computer, typically having a touchscreen interface, Internet access, and an operating system capable of running downloaded apps. The term 'Indian students' represents all the students who are born and studying in India. Note that in India, generally 'school students' refers to students of (I-XII) standards; whereas 'college students' indicates undergraduate (UG), and 'university students' means postgraduate (PG) which includes research scholars (doctoral students) as well.

2 Related Survey Works

Just few years back (until 2013–2014); laptops were the most used digital device in the classroom. Students used laptops for various academic and non-academic purposes. Therefore, researchers and academicians used to observe the students' behavior on using such devices and the effect of the same [1, 11, 12, 26, 29].

Recently, Smartphones have replaced laptops [5, 19, 28]. Reasons of the replacement include high computing power and huge memory support to run every types of apps and software in spite of the smaller size of the devices; inclusion of many important functionalities (e.g., 'qwerty' keyboard, camera, audio recorder, high-resolution display) and sensors to support gesture based inputs; millions[2] of free or low-cost apps in app-stores to support almost every necessities (e.g., programming, office productivity, media production, web browsing, location based interactions, social media, communication and entertainment); and most importantly the affordability of the devices [15, 35]. The low-cost high-speed Internet connectivity acts as a positive

---

[1] https://timesofindia.indiatimes.com/india/At-315-million-India-has-the-most-students-in-world/articleshow/37669667.cms.

[2] https://www.statista.com/statistics/276623/number-of-apps-available-in-leading-app-stores/.

catalyst to its widespread popularity. The portability and ubiquitous nature of the devices is another reasons for them being popular.

Researchers' interests now, therefore, have shifted to observe the students' behavior on smartphone usages instead of laptops. For instance, Bowen and Pistilli [4] conducted a survey to know the students' preference for using mobile apps. In September – October 2011, they asked 1566 students of Purdue University about their device, activities, duration and purpose of use, and preferences for 'native mobile app' and 'mobile web browser' for executing the activities. They found that majority of the students had preferred mobile native apps rather than mobile web browsers, both for academic and non-academic activities. Today, we can realize the importance of their preference – there are now more than seven millions apps[1] in app-stores. McCoy conducted a survey in 2013 and again in 2015 to know the smartphone usage behavior and perception of American students [20, 21]. He wanted to observe the frequency and duration of smartphone usage by the students for non-academic purpose in the classroom. In 2014, Lee et al. [19] conducted a survey on smartphone overuse among the undergraduate students of a Korean university. They observed that duration of app usage is more crucial than the type of app the students use. In the same year, Robert and Rees [28] conducted a survey on using mobile devices in the classroom. They wanted to know students' preference for using two different devices (smartphone and laptop) for various activities, and the duration of individual activities. In the survey at Bond University (on 99 students), they noticed that students use their mobile phones mainly for non-academic purposes whereas laptops for academic purposes. Park [23], again in 2014, conducted a survey to know the smartphone addiction among Korean students and the effect of the same. They found that females are more addictive towards apps related to social bonding. In 2015, Müller et al. [22] conducted a survey on 176 US students to observe and compare the use of smartphones and tablets for various activities. They observed that smartphones are used more than tablets. Their survey results also depict that the students use both their smartphones and tablets mainly for non-academic purposes. In 2016, Rahman and Shahibi [27] noticed that students prefer to use smartphones rather than laptops, even for the academic activities. In the same year, Cacho [5] also observed that students are very much positive to use their smartphone for academic purposes, particularly for 'm-learning'.

All these works have found various important facts about smartphone usage and its effect among the student community. At the same time, these works hint us to conduct an up-to-date survey. This is because of the changes of students' behavior regarding the smartphone usages with time. There are several reasons for such changes. Technological progress is one of the major reasons for such type of behavioral changes. For instance, consider the usage of SMS (Short Message Service) over time. In 2005, the average number of SMS usage in UK and Denmark was 21–36 per day [3]. In 2011, students used to send 15 SMS per day on average (the number is 39, in case of a girl) [31]. However, in 2014 only 41% of UK students used to send more than five[3] SMS per day. Now-a-days we use SMS only for official purposes, to get OTPs, and in case of emergency. Various stakeholders use SMS for advertisement and promotions, but those

---

[3] https://www.statista.com/statistics/466675/frequency-of-using-main-mobile-phone-for-sms-texting-uk/.

are non-personal use. This is probably because people are now habituated with other advanced texting services like IMS (Instant Messaging Services). Other reasons of changes on students' preferences and behavior include their age group, gender, class of study, financial status, and ethnicity. For instance, study of Park and Lee [23, 24] has shown that students' behavior on smartphone usage may change based on their gender. Study of Schroeder et al. [30] has shown that students' behavior changes based on age group and class of study. As per their study, frequency of texting by college students is more than that of school students. However, interestingly, this frequency gradually decreases with the time, as the students get older.

Bowen and Pistilli [4] reported that 40% of the students used iPhone in US in 2012, whereas iPhone share in India is only 2–3% to date[4] (in 2018). This is the proof how statistics differ based on ethnicity as well as financial background of the students. Therefore, an up-to-date survey of smartphone usage, particularly on Indian students is important. This is because the related existing surveys are either old or based on a particular group of students (e.g., students of a particular class of a particular institute of a particular geographical location [19, 23, 30]). Most importantly, we did not find any recent survey where Indian students' behavior on smartphone usage were observed. We, therefore, decided to conduct a contemporary survey throughout India (covering all the states and union territories), among each level of students of every discipline. The survey methodology and findings are reported in the subsequent sections.

3 Methodology

We performed a descriptive type quantitative survey with semi ordered categorical close ended questions [6, 18]. The questions in the survey form are 'semi ordered categorical' because the options are in between nominal and ordinal. We followed the guideline from [18] to conduct the survey. The details are as follows.

3.1 Preparation of Survey Questionnaire

In this survey, we wanted to know students' habits and frequency of using smartphones both for academic and non-academic purposes. Our special focus was to know the types of activities performed on smartphone by Indian students when they are in the classroom. For preparing the survey questionnaire, we had to know all the possible activities generally performed by the students, both inside and outside the classroom. We conducted an initial pilot study for this. Total 121 UG and PG students, of a national academic institute, participated in the pilot study. We chose the particular institute to conduct the pilot study because there is always a high probability of having students from almost every regions of the country in such an institute of national repute (the same has been affirmed by our study).

In the pilot study, we asked the students to anonymously report all the activities done by them with their smartphone. From their reports, we found that they perform 29 possible activities (Fig. 8) with their smartphone.

---

[4] https://9to5mac.com/2018/07/24/apple-marketshare-in-india-falls/.

We prepared the survey questionnaire based on this study. The link of the survey form has been given in the footnote[5]. In the survey, we asked each student about the frequency of doing the 29 activities. We kept seven options for the participants (they had to choose one out of those options). In the second part of each question, we asked them whether they perform that when they are in the classroom. Figure 1 shows an example question used in the questionnaire. We kept a 30th question to know whether the students perform any other activities, except the specified 29 activities.

Additionally, in the beginning of the survey form, there was a portion to collect demographic data. The data include participants' 'gender', 'age', 'academic-class', 'name of the institute', 'native place', and 'annual family income'.

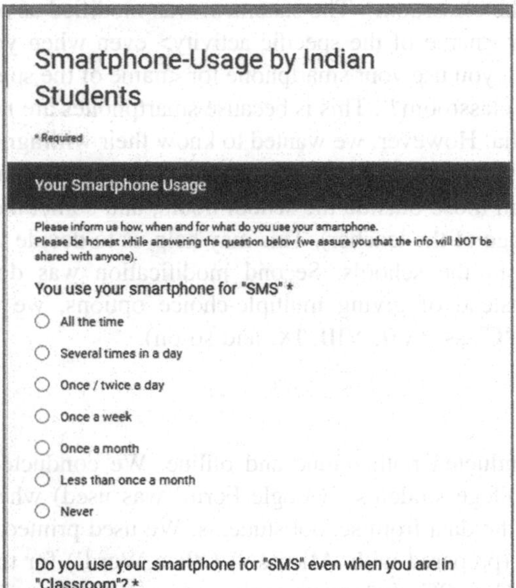
Smartphone-Usage by Indian Students

* Required

Your Smartphone Usage

Please inform us how, when and for what do you use your smartphone.
Please be honest while answering the question below (we assure you that the info will NOT be shared with anyone).

You use your smartphone for "SMS" *

- All the time
- Several times in a day
- Once / twice a day
- Once a week
- Once a month
- Less than once a month
- Never

Do you use your smartphone for "SMS" even when you are in "Classroom"? *

- Yes
- No

BACK NEXT

Never submit passwords through Google Forms.

Fig. 1. Example question used in online survey questionnaire

All the questions in the survey form were mandatory, except the question regarding annual family income. The survey was anonymous; nowhere had we asked the name of the students. We did the survey anonymously to get more number of responses as well as to get honest responses from the participants. Some students might hesitate to

[5] https://docs.google.com/forms/d/e/1FAIpQLSdL9jS3dy3QOFjgZeHAhFYMA7JRcsntMUp6T5nxLQAjiMZzgA/viewform?usp=sf_link.

provide correct information if the form was not anonymous. The questions were written in simple English (and explained wherever required) to make it understandable by every student, keeping the fact in mind that students from India are from diverse backgrounds in the context of medium of instruction. Note that logging the usage detail instead of self-report throughout India may be cumbersome and unethical as the students may have a lot of privacy sensitive data. We took special care while preparing the survey questionnaire to get the accuracy in data and to minimize the latent issues as we targeted a large number of heterogeneous participants [18].

We prepared another version of the survey form (to collect data from school students) with exactly the same questionnaire with two minor modifications. First modification was done in the second part of each of the questions (whether they do a specific activity in the classroom). The statement was modified as 'do you want to use your smartphone for <name of the specific activity> even when you are in the classroom?' instead of 'do you use your smartphone for <name of the specific activity> even when you are in the classroom?'. This is because smartphones are not allowed in many of the schools in India. However, we wanted to know their willingness and preferences for the various smartphone activities in the classroom, if they were allowed (as they are habituated to perform those outside the school-hours, and sometimes in the classroom without the knowledge of the teacher). This may help us to decide whether the devices should be allowed in the schools. Second modification was done for asking the 'academic-class'. Instead of giving multiple-choice options, we simply provided a space to write their 'Class' (VII, VIII, IX, and so on).

3.2 Approach

The survey was conducted both online and offline. We conducted online survey to collect data from college students ('Google Form' was used) whereas offline survey was done to collect the data from school students. We used printed copies of the other version of the form (prepared with 'Microsoft Office Word') for this.

We requested UG & PG students to participate in the survey by writing a formal mail mentioning the purpose of the survey and providing the link of the survey form, wherever the email addresses were available. We also collected the e-mail addresses of the HODs, Principals, Deans, Directors and other administrators of various institutions allover India and requested them to circulate the online survey form among their students. We also requested them to ask their students to participate in the survey. For this, we targeted all IITs (Indian Institute of Technology), all NITs (National Institute of Technology), all IIITs (Indian Institute of Information Technology), other reputed AICTE (All India Council for Technical Education) approved government and private engineering colleges, almost all reputed general degree colleges and universities of central and state government, and all reputed medical colleges. We got positive response and appreciation for conducting the survey from everywhere we approached. Table 1 presents the number of institutions we approached with their categories as well as number of institutes from where students have participated in the survey. Figure 2 represents the location distribution of the Institutes.

We also approached six schools through the Principals of the schools (sometimes called 'Headmaster/Headmistress') to collect data from school students. All of them

Table 1. Description of approached and participating institutions

Type of institution	Specification	Approached	Participated
Engineering and technology	IIT	23	14
	NIT	31	17
	IIIT	23	19
	Others	56	46
General	General Degree (Science, Arts, Commerce) Colleges and Universities	88	74
Medical	AIIMS and Others	29	12
School	Secondary and Higher Secondary Schools	06	06

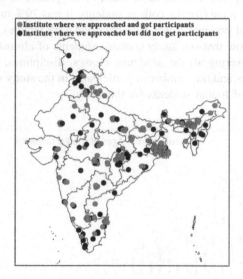

● Institute where we approached and got participants
● Institute where we approached but did not get participants

Fig. 2. Distribution of institutions we approached and collected data throughout India

helped us to conduct the survey in their schools. Among these six schools, two were KVs ('Kendriya Vidyalaya' Sanskrit phrase meaning central school), three were state government's schools and one was a private school running central government's curriculum. Two schools were situated in Guwahati (Assam) and four were in Kolkata (West Bengal). Medium of instructions for all these schools is English. We distributed the printed copy of the offline version of the form among the school students and collected the filled-up form with the help of the class teachers. Although the data collection procedure was completely anonymous, we assured them of not sharing their responses with anyone, not even with their teachers or guardians.

3.3   Participants

We have reported 1711 students' behavioral data on smartphone usages from 188 academic institutions throughout India. Among those, 1469 students (belonging to 182 institutes) responded to the online survey. Remaining 242 students' data were collected offline from the six schools. The data were collected in the period from December 2017 to July 2018. Figure 3, 4, 5, 6 and 7 represent the demographic information of the participants. Distribution of the age-frequency of the participants is presented in Fig. 3. Figure 4 represents participants' category based on their discipline of studies and institutes. Academic classes of the participants are depicted in Fig. 5. Distribution of the native places of the participants is presented in Fig. 6 ('Others' here mean they did not mention the name of the states or UT properly, e.g., they reported the native place as 'India', 'states', 'Union Territory' and so on). Figure 7 shows the financial backgrounds of the participants. Overall distribution of the gender of the participants were 76% male and 24% female (for the college students, it was 79% male and 21% female whereas for the school students, it was 52% male and 48% female). The statistics of the demographic data show that our study contains students of almost all ages from each location of India, covering all the academic classes, disciplines, and financial backgrounds. The statistics and the number of participants in the study show that we have a good representation of Indian students for the study.

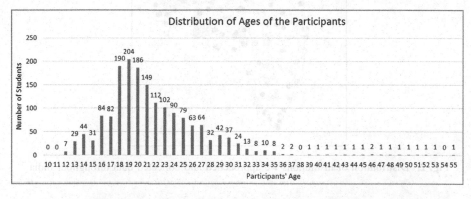

Fig. 3. Distribution of age frequencies of the participants

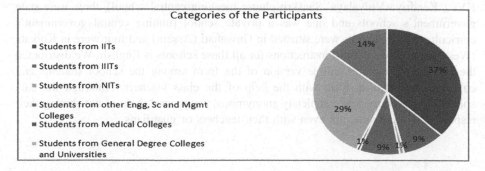

Fig. 4. Distribution of participants' categories based on their discipline of studies and institutes

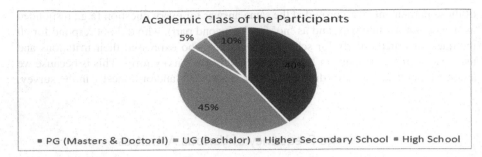

Fig. 5. Distribution of participants' academic class

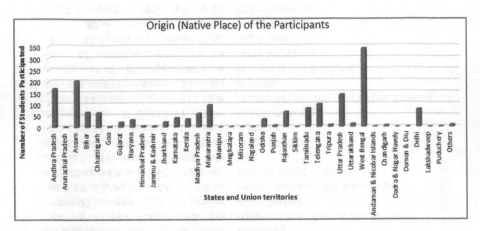

Fig. 6. Number of participants from different regions of the country

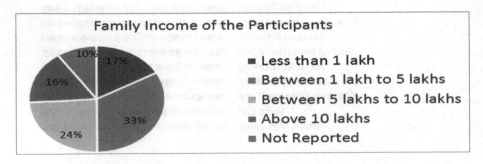

Fig. 7. Participants' financial background

Overview of Outliers. The actual number of students participated were 1784 (1522 from online and 262 from offline survey), out of which 73 (53 from online and 20 from offline survey) students were rejected as outliers. We therefore considered the rest of the participants (1711) for our analysis and discussion. For selecting outliers, we manually scrutinized the responses of all the participants. We did not consider the data

of those participants who provided the same answer for every question (e.g., responded as 'never' for the first part, and as 'no' for the second part), who did not respond for all the questions (particularly for school students), or who expressed their irritations and used bad words and slangs in 'comments' field of the survey form. This is because we assumed that these students did not participate seriously and/or honestly in the survey.

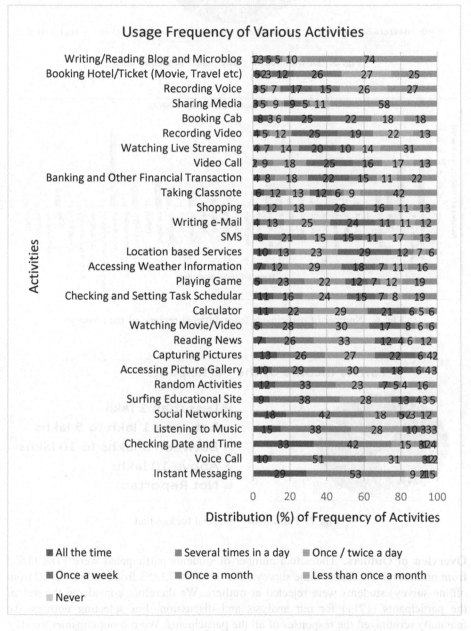

Fig. 8. Overall statistics of smartphone usages by Indian students

4 Results and Findings

Figure 8 represents the overall survey statistics. For instances, the blue colored portion (labelled 29) of the bottom most bar of the figure (bar chart) means that 29% of the students use their smartphones all the time for instant messaging; brown colored portion (labelled 53) of the same bar means that 53% of the students use their smartphones several times in a day for instant messaging; and so on.

Survey result depicts that the following activities are done by the students most frequently: Instant messaging (91% at least once/twice a day[6], and 82% at least several times a day); voice call (92% at least once/twice a day, and 61% at least several times a day); checking date and time (90% at least once/twice a day, and 75% at least several times a day); listening to music (81% at least once/twice a day, and 53% at least several times a day); social networking (78% at least once/twice a day, and 60% at least several times a day); and surfing educational site (75% at least once/twice a day, and 47% at least several times a day).

Second most frequent activities done by the students are random activities, accessing picture gallery, capturing pictures, reading news, watching movie/video, using calculator, checking and setting task scheduler, and playing game. Accessing weather information, accessing location based services, reading and writing SMS, writing emails, shopping, taking class-note, and financial transactions are found as third most frequently done activities. Rest of the activities are rarely done by the students.

Figure 9 represents the overall statistics of the students' activities on their smartphone inside the classroom. For example, the blue colored portion of the bottommost bar (labelled 66) means that 66% students use their smartphone for checking date and time, even when they are in the classroom. The most frequently done activities inside the classroom are checking date and time (66%), running calculator app (60%), instant messaging (56%), surfing educational site (49%), and social networking (40%). The activities with next level of frequency in the classroom are random activities (34%), SMS (32%), task scheduling (31%), reading news (29%), accessing picture gallery (29%), playing games (27%), capturing pictures (25%), and writing emails (20%). Rest of the activities are rarely performed by the students inside the classroom.

We also asked the students whether they use their smartphone for any other purposes excluding the specified 29 activities. 75% students have reported that they do nothing other than the specified activities. Rest of the 25% students have mentioned various other activities. Few of the other activities are as follows. 47 (3%) students reported that they read e-books (half of them read academic e-books, others read non-academic e-books like novel and magazine). 30 (2%) students have reported that they watch porn. 26 students (1.5%) have reported that they use their smartphone as alarm clock. Four groups of students (1% each) have reported that they use their smartphone for monitoring health, editing photo and video, participating in 'Quora', and flashing torch. Few students (0.5%) have reported that they develop apps in their smartphone.

---

[6] The term 'at least once/twice a day' means either they use it 'all the time' or 'several times a day' or 'once/twice a day'; similarly, 'at least several times' means either they use it 'all the time' or 'several times a day'; and so on.

144   S. Tikadar and S. Bhattacharya

Many other groups of very few students (2–5 students in each group) have reported about various other activities including writing diary, running dating app, playing digital musical instruments, checking stock market, paying bills and maintaining digital wallet, running stopwatch, searching job, and running dictionary app. However, frequency of doing these other activities are rare, as reported by the students. Moreover, none of the students has reported that these other activities are performed in the classroom.

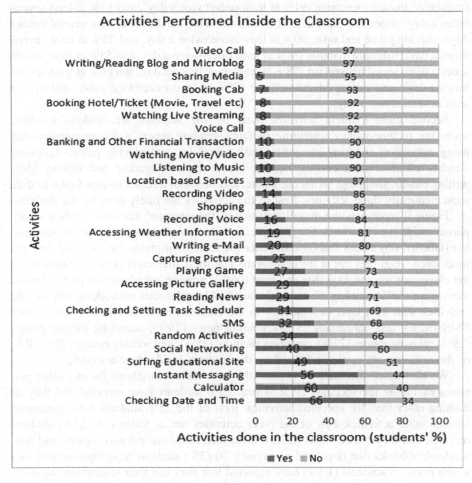

Fig. 9. Smartphone usages statistics inside the classroom

Overall survey results prove that most of the time students have a tendency to perform those activities in the classroom, which are performed most frequently by them in general (except the voice call). Other than these overall statistics of the smartphone usages, we have also observed the behavioral differences of smartphone usage based on students' gender, and academic level.

4.1 Usage Differences Based on Gender

We found that the male students play games, perform social networking, write e-mails, read news, surf educational sites, perform financial transactions, check date and time, and perform random activities more than female students. On the other hand, the female students use mobile camera to take pictures, access picture galleries, and send SMSs more than the male students. While testing the significance of the differences statistically, we have found that the differences are significant only for playing games ($p = 0.04$), and reading news ($p = 0.02$). Note that we have used t-test for all the statistical tests mentioned in the paper. We considered $\alpha = 0.05$. This means that the difference is significant with 95% confidence, if and only if the p value is found to be <0.05.

Similar gender based differences on performing smartphone activities have been observed inside the classroom as well, except listening to music and writing e-mail (female students listen to music more than the male students, whereas male students writes more e-mails than the female students inside the classroom). However the gender based differences for these two activities inside the classroom are found insignificant. Inside the classroom, significant differences have been found for playing games ($p = 0.02$), and reading news ($p = 0.02$). These two activities are performed by the male students significantly more than the female students in general as well. This observation indicates that the smartphone usage differences based on gender are similar, both inside and outside the classroom.

4.2 Usage Differences Based on Academic Level

Our survey result depicts few dissimilarities in students' behavior on smartphone usage depending upon the level of academic class.

School vs College and University. We have observed that the school students perform video calls, send SMSs, play games, take pictures, watch live streaming, share multimedia data, and record videos as well as voices more frequently than the college and university students. On the other hand, the college and university students perform voice calls, perform instant messaging, do social networking, surf educational sites, read news, access picture galleries, perform financial transactions, check date and time, check and set task scheduler, and perform random activities more frequently than the school students. However, among these, significant differences have been found for SMS ($p = 0.002$), watching live streaming ($p = 0.04$), sharing media ($p = 0.03$), social networking ($p = 0.04$), and random activities ($p = 0.03$).

Inside the classroom, majorly following activities are done more frequently by the UG and PG students compared to the school students (for school students, we asked their willingness to do the various activities in the classroom as sometimes they are not allowed to use smartphones in the classroom): Playing game, instant messaging, social networking, surfing educational site, writing e-mail, reading news, accessing picture gallery, checking date and time, scheduling tasks, calculator, and different random activities. When we performed statistical test, it has been found that the differences are significant for performing all these activities ($p \leq 0.04$). Possible reasons may include underage, and the restriction of using such device in the school (although the school students have reported their willingness of using those activities inside the classroom, that may not be exactly the same when they will be allowed to use).

UG vs PG. We also have observed the differences of the usage behavior among the UG and PG students. It has been observed that the UG students play games, listen to music, watch live streaming, record videos and voices, use calculator, and take class notes more frequently compared to the PG students. On the other hand, the PG students perform instant messaging, surf educational sites, write e-mails, read news, do shopping, and perform banking and other financial transactions more frequently than the UG students. In this case, we found significant differences for watching live streaming (p = 0.03), recording voice (p = 0.03), writing e-mail (p = 0.03), and shopping (p = 0.01).

Inside the classroom, the UG students play games, listen to music, watch movies and videos, do social networking, surf educational sites, read news, capture pictures, access picture galleries, watch live streaming, record videos and voices, and perform random activities more frequently compared to the PG students. Nevertheless, these differences were found insignificant while tested statistically. We have not found any activity, which is performed by the PG students more frequently than the UG students inside the classroom.

We summarize the findings of the study in Table 2.

Table 2. Summary of the findings

SN	Observational aspect	Findings and/or lesson learned
1	Number of activities generally performed by the students	29 (see Figs. 8 and 9 to for the name of the activities)
2	Five most frequently performed activities (in general)	Instant messaging, voice calls, checking date and time, listening to music, and accessing social networking sites (presented in descending order)
3	Five least frequently performed activities (in general)	Writing/reading blogs, booking hotels/tickets, recording voices, sharing media, and booking cabs (presented in ascending order)
4	Five most frequently performed activities (inside the classroom)	Checking date and time, calculator, instant messaging, surfing educational sites, and social networking (presented in descending order)
5	Five least frequently performed activities (inside the classroom)	Video calls, writing/reading blogs/microblogs, sharing media, booking cabs, and booking tickets and hotels (presented in ascending order)
6	General Observation	In the classroom, students have a tendency to perform all the activities frequently which are performed most frequently by them in general (except the 'voice call')
7	Behavioral differences based on gender	Male students read news and play games more than female students both inside and outside the classrooms
8	Behavioral difference based on academic level	(i) school students watch live streaming and share media significantly more than college students (ii) college students perform social networking, and random activities significantly more than school students (iii) UG students watch live streaming, and record voice significantly more than the PG students (iv) PG students write e-mails and do shopping significantly more than the UG students

5 Discussions

The research questions that we wanted to address by the behavioral study were: (i) which smartphone activities are generally performed by the Indian students? Our answer to that question is that there are 29 activities including instant messaging, voice call, listening to music and so on; (ii) which of the activities are performed most frequently and least frequently both inside and outside the classroom for academic and non-academic purposes? We have observed that the activities like instant messaging, voice call are performed most frequently and the activities like writing/reading blogs, booking hotels/tickets are performed least frequently in general (none of these are related to academic); inside the classroom, activities like checking date and time, calculator are performed most frequently (majority of those are non-academic) and the activities like video calls, writing/reading blogs/microblogs are performed least frequently; (iii) Is there any difference in behavior on performing smartphone activities based on gender and academic level (school, UG and PG) of the students? The answer is yes. We have found significant differences on performing smartphone activities based on the gender and academic level (e.g., PG students write e-mails and do shopping significantly more than the UG students, male students read news and play games more than female students and so on).

Significant gender differences have been found in case of playing games and reading news. Male students perform these activities more than female students. Research may be conducted to identify the probable reasons for the lack of interest of the female students in these activities, and their fascination for spending more time in some other activities like taking picture, and accessing picture gallery. For instance, one reason for playing less games by the female students may be the lack of interesting elements for many of them in most of the existing games. Game designers may rethink about this while design a game for targeting more number of players. While observing the differences of usage between college and school students, we have noticed that the school students send SMS, watch live streaming, and share media significantly more than college students. On the other hand, the college students perform social networking and random activities considerably more than the school students. Reasons for these may include less usage of the devices (parents' monitoring for restricted use of smartphones), lack of openness and less connection with the outer world for school students. The college students may habituated with using instant messaging service instead of SMS for communicating with their relatively larger number of contacts. While comparing the UG and PG students we have found that the PG students write numerous e-mail and do shopping more than the UG students. Reasons for writing more mail may include requirement for staying in touch and formal interactions with a large number of people for their job applications, teaching assistantships, and research guidance as well as collaborations. Students tend to become less dependent on their parents as they grow older. Sometimes they start earning or getting fellowships while they are in PG courses. These may be the probable reasons for more shopping by PG students compared to a UG students. If we compare among the school, UG, and PG students, it is noticeable that the school students perform media related activities (e.g., sharing media, live streaming) more than the UG students whereas the UG students

perform those more than the PG students. The probable reasons may include the lack of interests because of the age differences [30].

Our survey results contradict many aspects of the earlier findings. Kukulska-Hulme et al. [17] reported that SMS is the most frequently performed activity among all the activities performed on the smartphone. As per their findings, three top most usages (in Australia, Hong Kong, Portugal, Sweden, and UK) were SMS, browsing website, and listening to music (in descending order). However, we have found instant messaging as most frequently performed activity and the three top most usages are instant messaging, voice call, and checking date and time (in descending order). The reasons might be the availability of advanced messaging service, lower cost for Internet connection, and ethnicity. We found dissimilarities in one of the least frequently used activities as well. As per our survey result, booking hotel/ticket (movie, travel) is the second least frequently activity which was not found in their list of 'least performed activities'. The possible reason may be the ethnicity; may be India and Indian students are still not technologically advanced in that extend. Another reasons for this may be their consideration of only mature students in their study.

Our survey results also contradict the finding of Jena [15]. He reported that the use of smartphones for academic purposes is more than that of the non-academic purposes. However, our survey results portray the opposite scenario; students use their smartphones mainly for non-academic purposes, rather than academic purposes. The reasons for such difference might be their limited and specific participants for study; they collected data from 310 postgraduate students of business management.

There is partial contradiction between our findings and the findings of Park [23]. Although his findings about gender differences on smartphone is similar in many aspects, our result mainly contradicts two such aspects. Firstly, for SMS, they found that the males are more addicted than females; whereas we have found that females are more addicted to SMS than males. However, the differences are not statistically significant (p = 0.19). Secondly, they found that males are more addicted to listen to music than females; whereas we found that addiction of listening to music on smartphone is similar ($\sim$80% at least once/twice a day, and $\sim$54% at least several times in a day) for both the male and female students. In fact, sometimes (e.g., in the classroom) the female students listen to music more than the male students. Ethnicity, technological growth and changes in society may be few of the probable reasons for these kind of contradictory statistics.

We expect that this updated knowledge will be useful in many ways, both for the researchers of HCI/Mobile-HCI as well of other multidisciplinary domains. For instance, in a blended learning platform, if we want to systematically identify whether a student is performing some study related activities or using the device for some unexpected activities (e.g., playing game, watching movies and so on), we first require to know all possible activities performed by the student. Academicians and policy-makers can decide whether the devices should be allowed or not in the Institute, based on the level of academic-class (e.g., for school students). Even if allowed, they can make policy for the controlled use of smartphones inside and outside the classroom for maximizing the benefits and minimizing the harms from it. Students should also restrict the use of their devices for academic purpose only especially when they are in the classroom. Based on the students' interest, academicians and researchers can build

effective tools and systems having interesting features. For instance, inclusion of features of social networking apps in a blended learning classroom system may increase the rate of acceptance of the same and consequently the learning outcomes. Consideration of users' interests while designing and developing new systems and applications increases the rate of acceptance of the product. Therefore, smartphone makers as well as app developers can utilize the knowledge for designing and developing new phones and its apps. The knowledge may be useful for the researchers of behavioral science as well. They can analyze the results to explore the cognitive processes among students of different groups. Sociologists and psychologists may treat a student (of a particular group) or make effective guidelines for them keeping in mind their interests and habits. This is equally applicable for parents and teachers.

6 Conclusion

We conducted a behavioral study to find out the smartphone activities performed by the Indian students and the frequencies of those activities both inside and outside the classroom. The study is important since the literature reveals that ethnicity plays important role in the student behavior and there is no up-to-date survey on the smartphone usage behavior of the Indian students. We also studied the differences in the behavior of the students based on their gender and academic level. We have found that twenty nine activities are generally performed by the Indian students. Most of the frequently performed activities are also performed frequently inside the classroom. Majority of the frequently performed activities are non-academic, both inside and outside the classroom. We have found significant differences in the behavior based on the gender and academic level of the students. Findings including gender based difference in playing games, and academic level based difference in performing media related activities corroborate the findings of the related studies. At the same time, findings including gender based difference in listening to music, and the tendency of using the smartphone for non-academic purposes contradict the earlier findings in the related studies. We hope that the survey and its findings will help many multidisciplinary researchers.

Acknowledgements. We sincerely acknowledge the contribution of Mr. Shashank Kotyan and all the survey participants (both students and the faculty members). We also thank all the reviewers and the shepherd for their constructive suggestions to improve the quality of the manuscript.

References

1. Awwad, F., Ayesh, A., Awwad, S.: Are laptops distracting educational tools in classrooms. Procedia-Soc. Behav. Sci. **103**(1), 154–160 (2013)
2. Bär, H., Tews, E., Rößling, G.: Improving feedback and classroom interaction using mobile phones. In: Proceedings of Mobile Learning, Qwara, Malta, pp. 55–62 (2005)

3. Barkhuus, L.: Why everyone loves to text message: social management with SMS. In: Proceedings of the 2005 International ACM SIGGROUP Conference on Supporting Group Work, pp. 324–325. ACM, Sanibel Island (2005)
4. Bowen, K., Pistilli, M.D.: Student preferences for mobile app usage. Research Bulletin. EDUCAUSE Center for Applied Research, Louisville (2012, forthcoming). http://www.educause.edu/ecar
5. Cacho, R.M.: Student teachers' smartphone academic uses and preferences: perspectives for mobile-aided pedagogy. In: 2016 14th International Conference on ICT and Knowledge Engineering (ICT&KE), pp. 57–61. IEEE, Bangkok (2016)
6. Cairns, P., Cox, A.L. (eds.): Research Methods for Human-Computer Interaction. Cambridge University Press, Cambridge (2011)
7. Chen, C.M., et al.: Personalized intelligent m-learning system for supporting effective English learning. In: IEEE International Conference on Systems, Man and Cybernetics (SMC 2006), vol. 6, pp. 4898–4903. IEEE, Taipei (2006)
8. Du, H., Rosson, M.B., Carroll, J.M.: Augmenting classroom participation through public digital backchannels. In: Proceedings of the 17th ACM International Conference on Supporting Group Work, pp. 155–164. ACM, Sanibel Island (2012)
9. Evans, C.: The effectiveness of m-learning in the form of podcast revision lectures in higher education. Comput. Educ. 50(2), 491–498 (2008)
10. Ezemenaka, E.: The usage and impact of internet enabled phones on academic concentration among students of tertiary institutions: a study of University of Ibadan, Nigeria. Int. J. Educ. Dev. ICT 9(3), 162–173 (2013)
11. Fried, C.B.: In-class laptop use and its effects on student learning. Comput. Educ. 50(3), 906–914 (2008)
12. Gaudreau, P., Miranda, D., Gareau, A.: Canadian university students in wireless classrooms: what do they do on their laptops and does it really matter? Comput. Educ. 70(1), 245–255 (2014)
13. Georgiev, T., Georgieva, E., Smrikarov, A.: M-learning-a new stage of e-learning. In: International Conference on Computer Systems and Technologies, (CompSysTech 2004), vol. 4, no. 28, Rousse, Bulgaria, pp. 1–4 (2004)
14. Giunchiglia, F., Zeni, M., Gobbi, E., Bignotti, E., Bison, I.: Mobile social media and academic performance. In: Ciampaglia, G.L., Mashhadi, A., Yasseri, T. (eds.) SocInfo 2017. LNCS, vol. 10540, pp. 3–13. Springer, Cham (2017). https://doi.org/10.1007/978-3-319-67256-4_1
15. Jena, R.K.: The impact and penetration of smartphone usage in student's life. Glob. J. Bus. Manag. 8(1), 29–35 (2014)
16. Kay, R., Lauricella, S.: Exploring the benefits and challenges of using laptop computers in higher education classrooms: a formative analysis. Can. J. Learn. Technol./La revue canadienne de l'apprentissage et de la technologie 37(1), 1–18 (2011)
17. Kukulska-Hulme, A., et al.: Mature students using mobile devices in life and learning. Int. J. Mob. Blended Learn. (IJMBL) 3(1), 18–52 (2011)
18. Lazar, J., Feng, J.H., Hochheiser, H.: Research Methods in Human-Computer Interaction. Wiley, Hoboken (2010)
19. Lee, U., et al.: Hooked on smartphones: an exploratory study on smartphone overuse among college students. In: Proceedings of the 32nd Annual ACM Conference on Human Factors in Computing Systems, CHI 2014, pp. 2327–2336. ACM, Toronto (2014)
20. McCoy, B.: Digital distractions in the classroom: student classroom use of digital devices for non-class related purposes. J. Media Educ. 4(4), 5–14 (2013)
21. McCoy, B.R.: Digital distractions in the classroom phase II: student classroom use of digital devices for non-class related purposes. J. Media Educ. 4(4), 5–14 (2016)

22. Müller, H., et al.: Understanding and comparing smartphone and tablet use: Insights from a large-scale diary study. In: Proceedings of the Annual Meeting of the Australian Special Interest Group for Computer Human Interaction, OzCHI 2015, pp. 427–436. ACM, Parkville (2015)

23. Park, N.: Gender difference in social networking on smartphones: a case study of Korean college student smartphone users. 정보통신정책연구 (Int. Telecommun. Policy Rev. Res.) 21(2), 1–18 (2014)

24. Park, N., Lee, H.: Nature of youth smartphone addiction in Korea. 언론정보연구 (Media Inf. Res.) 51(1), 100–132 (2014)

25. Pohl, A., Gehlen-Baum, V., Bry, F.: Introducing Backstage–a digital backchannel for large class lectures. Interact. Technol. Smart Educ. 8(3), 186–200 (2011)

26. Ragan, E.D., et al.: Unregulated use of laptops over time in large lecture classes. Comput. Educ. 78(1), 78–86 (2014)

27. Rahman, N.F.A., Shahibi, M.S.: The growth of smartphone usage among students. Res. Hub 2(1), 64–68 (2016)

28. Roberts, N., Rees, M.: Student use of mobile devices in university lectures. Australas. J. Educ. Technol. 30(4), 415–426 (2014)

29. Sana, F., Weston, T., Cepeda, N.J.: Laptop multitasking hinders classroom learning for both users and nearby peers. Comput. Educ. 62(1), 24–31 (2013)

30. Schroeder, B.L., et al.: Individual differences in middle school and college students' texting. In: Proceedings of the Human Factors and Ergonomics Society Annual Meeting, vol. 60, no. 1, pp. 1215–1219. Sage, Los Angeles (2016)

31. Shahyad, S., et al.: A Comparison of motivation, frequency and content of SMS messages sent in boys and girls high school student. Procedia-Soc. Behav. Sci. 15(1), 895–898 (2011)

32. Tikadar, S., Bhattacharya, S., Tamarapalli, V.: A blended learning platform to improve teaching-learning experience. In: 2018 IEEE 18th International Conference on Advanced Learning Technologies (ICALT), pp. 87–89. IEEE, Mumbai (2018)

33. Van den Eijnden, R.J., et al.: Online communication, compulsive Internet use, and psychosocial well-being among adolescents: a longitudinal study. Dev. Psychol. 44(3), 655–665 (2008)

34. Wang, R., et al.: StudentLife: assessing mental health, academic performance and behavioral trends of college students using smartphones. In: Proceedings of the 2014 ACM International Joint Conference on Pervasive and Ubiquitous Computing (UbiComp 2014), pp. 3–14. ACM, Seattle (2014)

35. Woodcock, B., Middleton, A., Nortcliffe, A.: Considering the smartphone learner: an investigation into student interest in the use of personal technology to enhance their learning. Student Engagem. Exp. J. 1(1), 1–15 (2012)

ICT Acceptance for Information Seeking Amongst Pre- and Postnatal Women in Urban Slums

Anirudha Joshi[1(✉)], Debjani Roy[2(✉)], Aakash Ganju[3(✉)],
Manjiri Joshi[1(✉)], and Susmita Sharma[1(✉)]

[1] Indian Institute of Technology, Bombay, Mumbai, India
{anirudha,manjirij}@iitb.ac.in,
sharma.susmita@gmail.com
[2] Srishti Institute of Art, Design and Technology, Bangalore, India
debjani.r@gmail.com
[3] Saath Health, Mumbai, India
aakash@saathealth.com

Abstract. This paper reports findings from a study aimed to understand how urban poor pre- and postnatal women in India use ICT tools like mobile phones for information seeking. The study was divided in 2 phases. In phase 1, we conducted semi-structured interviews with 66 pre- and postnatal women from urban poor slums located in 4 cities in India. In phase 2, we conducted a survey with 102 pre- and postnatal women from urban poor slum located in 9 cities in India. The aim was to understand care giving during and after pregnancy, nutrition, terminology used during pregnancy, and interpretation of visual material. This paper summarizes the findings, which include the importance of the use of appropriate terminology to design content in a multilingual country, identifying triggers for information seeking behaviour, and approaches to technology acceptance for information seeking. Based on these findings, we make suggestions for design of future ICT-based interventions in resource constraint settings.

Keywords: Digital health · Maternal heath · ICTD · Developing regions · mHealth · Healthcare

1 Introduction

Pre- and postnatal health is an important phase for every woman going through motherhood. Over the years there has been a decrease in maternal mortality, however every day approximately 830 women die during pregnancy and childbirth, of which 99% deaths occur in developing countries, including India [1]. Interventions related to safe motherhood have been a prime concern of most health agencies in India. However, due to geographical vastness and sociocultural diversity, maternal mortality varies across states of India, making uniform implementation of health-sector reforms difficult [2]. Poor literacy and lack of awareness continue to be barriers. This leads to low

© IFIP International Federation for Information Processing 2019
Published by Springer Nature Switzerland AG 2019
D. Lamas et al. (Eds.): INTERACT 2019, LNCS 11748, pp. 152–160, 2019.
https://doi.org/10.1007/978-3-030-29387-1_9

utilization of maternal and reproductive healthcare services, jeopardizes women's health, and leads to poor postnatal development of children [3–5].

A significant development in the past decade has been the explosive growth of mobile phones. This has further impacted the use of ICTs in the health care sector [6]. In developing countries, adoption of mobile phones has surpassed many of structural barriers like low income, low education, and lack of social power. While basic and feature phones are popular among the poor, the popularity of smartphones is on the rise.

Mobile phones can be and are being used to provide people with timely, accurate, and specialized health information. Researchers are interested in the potential of ICTs to enable positive change in developing regions and communities in the areas of health, education, and economic status of the poor [4]. Studies include analysis of mHealth in maternal and new-born health programs [7], designing models for adapting ICT for healthcare workers [8], and understanding implications of ICT in public health [9]. In India, other studies have focused on mobile phones in the rural healthcare [10], enhancing pregnancy care [11], and understanding the role of ICT in accelerating the adoption of healthy behaviours [12]. However, healthcare and health promotions are complex human endeavours. Intille suggests four components to an effective strategy to motivate behaviour change using just-in-time information: (1) present a simple, tailored message that is easy to understand, (2) at an appropriate time, (3) at an appropriate place, and (4) using a non-irritating strategy [13].

In spite of such literature, do we understand how new ICT solutions are used and how we can design them to improve health outcomes of mothers and their children in developing countries? In this paper, we present findings on information seeking behaviour and acceptance of technology as a medium to gather information, amongst pre- and postnatal women in the urban slums of India. The aim is to provide guidelines to support researchers involved in designing of ICT based healthcare interventions.

2 The Study

The primary objective of the study was to evaluate how pre- and postnatal women use ICT tools like mobile phones for information access. The study was part of a programme called mMitra. In this programme, urban poor women are given automated voice calls twice a week from the third month of their pregnancy till the child becomes one year old. Each call lasts 2–3 min and gives information about pre- and postnatal health and nutrition that is relevant to the woman or the child at that time. The programme was initiated in 2014. When we conducted the study in 2016, mMitra had been deployed with over 100,000 women.

The study was conducted in 2 phases. Phase 1 was a qualitative study that used semi-structured interviews with poor women in urban slums. The purpose of this phase was to contextualize a woman's journey through the pre- and postnatal phases and understand their information needs related to health, nutrition, terminologies related to pregnancy, effect of visually communicating information, information seeking behaviour, and use of technology. It also aimed to understand the women's journey through pregnancy and the first year of the child. The study was conducted in 2 languages –

Hindi and Marathi. The participants were recruited with help of NGOs, hospitals, and local references. The data gathered was analysed using an affinity diagram.

Phase 2 of the study focused on a broader validation of the insights gained from the qualitative findings of phase 1. As we describe below, three main themes stood out in the findings of phase 1 – use of terminologies associated with maternal and child health, correlating these with visual representation, and technology use and acceptance. We designed a structured questionnaire focussing on these themes. There was no overlap between phases 1 and 2.

3   Phase 1 Findings

In the first phase, we interviewed 66 participants in 4 cities (Mumbai, Delhi, Bhopal, and Nashik). Among these, 36 were enrolled in the mMitra programme, while 30 were not enrolled. There were 41 pregnant women and 25 new mothers. Their age ranged from 18 to 38. Their education ranged from none to under-graduate level. Among these, 5 participants had no education, while 3 were had a bachelor's degree. 36 participants reported that they owned a phone of their own, of which 18 were basic phones, 1 feature phone, and 17 smart phones. Other participants relied on a shared device with the husband or other family members. 21 participants described their occupation as "housewives". Other occupations included helping husband in shop, working as a housekeeping staff in an office, police, doing embroidery, cooking, and as saleswomen in an automobile showroom. Two participants were taking courses in tailoring and nursing.

We found that terminology plays a very important role when designing audio-based information. This is especially so for a population that is diverse, multilingual, multicultural, less educated, and when the users are unfamiliar with the content. We found that users of mMitra often found it difficult to follow the formal terms used in the phone calls. Further, several people in urban India tend to be multi-lingual. This implies that their comprehension in the language they choose to receive communication in may not be very high. Many people did not understand the formal terms used in mMitra such as terms for breastfeeding (स्तनपान stanpan), periods (माहवारी mahwari), delivery (प्रसव prasav/प्रसूति prasuti), and sex (संभोग sambhog). Users suggested alternative, more colloquial terms, which might be better suited. A related problem was that in the same language a thing may be known by a different name in a different place. For example, finger millet is referred as *nachni* in Maharashtra and *ragi* in Northern India. Participants in Bhopal, Mumbai and Nashik used the term "*sonography*", while in Delhi participants called it "*ultrasound*". It may be possible to use multiple terminologies to cover regional diversity. However, in voice messages, this would make the messages lengthier. An alternative would be to use visual representations to complement audio messages.

By and large, users of mMitra were comfortable to receive voice calls, especially as they could listen to the content privately. Several women only had access to a shared phone used by multiple users, including children in the household. A phone call enabled them to attend to the information privately.

However, we found that certain kinds of information are best communicated visually. To stimulate conversations during the interviews, we used visuals from existing pregnancy and child-care books. Participants found the visuals engaging as it made the information more relatable to their own experiences. Visuals and illustrated books are "browsable" allowing users to pay attention only to those bits that catch their attention. In contrast, audio must be heard completely from start to finish. It is difficult to browse audio information in a similar way. This causes attention to drift while listening to long messages in audio alone. In particular, we found that procedural information works best with visuals, animations or videos. For example, a message in mMitra turned out to be particularly confusing. It advised pregnant women to sleep on the side with a pillow "between their legs". Several women did not understand what this exactly meant until they saw the image in Fig. 1. Other examples of such procedural information were how to hold a baby, or how to breastfeed.

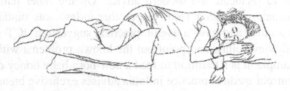

Fig. 1. Correct posture for sleeping was best demonstrated with the help of a visual. Such procedural information is difficult to communicate through audio alone.

Thirdly, visuals help users understand things that are not normally visible. For example, how a baby turns in the womb, or how the umbilical cord is cut are not common sights. *"If a book like this is there, one can understand. I have never seen like that. One gets to know how baby stays in stomach. The conceptual idea of how the baby grows with the other abdominal organs intact in a mother's body helps us understand how systems work independently"*, explained one participant. Visuals also help give references when terminologies are unfamiliar. The terminologies that users were not familiar with, but could be easily understood with the help of visuals, include terms for food items from a different region, sex, private parts, and medical procedures.

Visuals trigger curiosity and encourage users to ask questions. There were instances when the women, while flipping through the books, paused on pages referring to sex during pregnancy. This made them curious to ask questions such as *"if one has sex during pregnancy, will it harm the baby?"*. They find it difficult to discuss such topics openly otherwise.

Visuals also have some drawbacks. Sometimes standalone visuals could be misleading and need verbal explanation. For example, a demonstration of how a pregnant woman should lift a baby (or any other weight) was interpreted as "playing with a baby". Secondly, visuals need to be localised. Some of our images were from an international book. One such image showed a woman with short hair, and some users misunderstood it as a picture of a man.

While broadcasting information helps mMitra reach out to women easily, it can help more if the women could also choose information of their interest. The information that

is communicated to the women through traditional means (such as brochures or leaflets) can be scrutinized by family members. This takes away women's privacy. Many times women hide such issues or wait for a long time before asking for help. Examples where women postponed seeking help included white discharge, spotting, nipple cracks, or inverted nipples. ICTs can offer the women the opportunity to choose a topic and access the information discretely. We observed that women were more interested in understanding the well-being of their baby than caring about themselves. They were motivated towards understanding food and nutrition for the new-born.

We also found that there is tension between "modern" and "traditional" information. A common conflict that a pregnant woman experiences is related to the difference between the information she gets from family members and that given by doctors, NGOs, peer group, or through a technology-mediated intervention. Where some participants confessed to getting confused between the two, others tried to balance seemingly contradictory information. If someone disagreed with the traditional information, she tried to inculcate the modern advice. On the other hand, a participant thought that information coming from her mother-in-law was outdated though the mother-in-law is a nurse and gave a useful, practical suggestion. ICT systems need to acknowledge both viewpoints, and point out the known problems with the traditional practices. For example, it is a tradition to feed a new-born baby honey or goat's milk at birth, while the current medical practice in India advises exclusive breastfeeding till the baby becomes 6 months old [14]. A system needs to acknowledge that such traditions exist in society, but instead of merely saying "don't do it", should also elaborate how it could harm the baby. We must remember that the pregnant woman is not the only person in the household engaged with the pregnancy. We found that it will be particularly useful to engage the husband and the mother-in-law in the communication.

We found that the users had mixed opinions about accepting technology for seeking information about pregnancy or neonatal care. This was often dependant on the level of privacy the woman had while using the phone. As noted above, 38 out of 66 women had phones of their own, while the rest used a phone shared either with their husband, or with other members of the family. Shared phone use put additional constraints on when women could access the phone calls, especially in "joint" families, where the couple resided with parents and siblings of the husband. Often, users were not comfortable listening to the messages when family members (other than the husband) were around and would disconnect the calls.

On the other hand, the attitude towards technology adoption was quite different in "nuclear" families (wherein the couple lived by themselves or with their children), even if phones were shared. Getting calls on the husband's device was fine for most women as it provided the husband an opportunity to understand what is going on in their life and be empathetic. Here, the technology delivered authenticated information in privacy. In fact, users found that technology was more approachable for certain information that one couldn't perhaps ask the doctor easily, such as methods of contraception, if it is it okay to have sex during pregnancy, and when is it OK to start having sex after delivery. Once technology was acceptable, people were happy to go beyond one-way automated calls. They wanted to ask questions rather than just get broadcasted information, and some had follow-up questions after getting some information.

The feature appreciated the most in mMitra was delivery of the right message at the right time. Hence people could find a context for the messages and could relate it to their current situation. mMitra messages were considered important, but at times they were long, and included multiple levels of information. Sometimes messages were not clear on the first go and the users wanted to hear them again. In several instances, participants remembered the concepts and actions, but forgot the terms used for those concepts or actions. They tried to remember things about which they are convinced and found actionable. Messages related to nutrition and baby care had the maximum recall. We repeated some messages for some users during the interview. Repetition of the messages helped them recall and reinforce the information. Some mMitra users told us that they recorded information to use later, or to share with peers.

4 Phase 2 Findings

From the insights generated from the phase 1, we developed a structured questionnaire focusing on terminology and technology usage. The objective of this phase was to inform the design of future interventions and to base the findings in a broader geographical area of India. We conducted the survey with 102 pre- and postnatal women from urban slums located in 9 cities (Allahabad, Bhopal, Delhi, Indore, Mumbai, Nanded, Nashik, Pune, and Ranchi). Among these, 36 were enrolled in the mMitra programme, while 66 were not enrolled. Their age ranged from 18 to 35. At the time of the survey, 42 women were pregnant and 60 were new mothers who had delivered less than a year ago. Education ranged from none to undergraduate. 11 participants had no education and 11 participants had a bachelor's degree. In terms of occupations, 83 reported themselves as housewives (of which 12 were working till they got married), 3 had a temporary job, 9 were self-employed, and 7 women had a permanent job.

As part of the technology test, we tried to find out the kind of devices used by the participants and their attitudes towards technology use. 58/102 women had their own phones while the rest shared their devices with their husband (most commonly) or with other family members. 36/102 women had a basic phone, 41 women had a feature phone and 24 women had a smartphone. Marriage seems play an important role in device usage both ways. Some participants said that they had a phone, but it was taken away from them after they got married. On the other hand, some women reported that they were gifted a phone at the time of their wedding.

We asked participants to perform some common tasks on their own devices. While 101/102 participants could make a call by dialling the number, only 48 could save a contact. Some said that they would delegate the task of saving contacts to members of their family. Among other tasks, 58 participants could listen to music (including FM radio or music stored on the phone), 50 participants could take pictures or browse pictures, 30 participants could watch videos (including YouTube videos), and 24 participants could use the internet for searching or Whatsapp. One issue was that while most participants were not fluent with English, most phones were set in English. Only 4/102 participants used the phone in Hindi or Marathi, and only 2 participants could switch languages in their phones. Usage of technology varied geographically. People

living in the large cities of Mumbai and Delhi could use phones more deftly, while people in smaller cities were not so familiar with them.

For the terminology test, we identified 11 commonly used mMitra terms in Hindi and Marathi. We first asked the user the meaning of the standalone term. If the participant did not understand the standalone term, we gave them three hints. First, we placed the term in a meaningful sentence to provide context. If the term was still not understood, we provided a longer second sentence with even more context than the first. Finally, we showed the participant a visual related to some of the terms. Table 1 summarises our findings of the terminology test. We can see that while more women could recognise a term when used in a meaningful sentence than just the standalone term, providing visuals helped even more. The two cases where visuals did not help were "contraception" (an abstract term) and bladder (an unrecognisable part of the body). We can see that visuals help in comprehension, but the users must be familiar with the visual. Further, we cannot use visuals every time. It was difficult for us to give appropriate visual references for terms such as menstruation, colostrum, and discharge.

Table 1. Results of the terminology tests for Hindi (N = 62) and Marathi (N = 40). The numbers indicate the percentage of people who understood the term after getting more information.

English	Hindi	% understood by 62 Hindi speakers			
		As a term	In context 1	In context 2	With visuals
Breastfeeding	स्तनपान	32%	45%	53%	98%
Menstruation	महावारी	44%	53%	68%	-
Contraception	गर्भ-निरोध	31%	39%	50%	63%
Uterus	गर्भाशय	16%	19%	29%	44%
Delivery	प्रसूति	16%	35%	45%	-
Sex	संभोग	19%	56%	60%	84%
Colostrum	खीस	0%	8%	55%	-
Bladder	मूत्राशय	15%	29%	39%	39%
Discharge	रिसाव	56%	60%	-	-
Vagina	योनि	13%	42%	45%	-

English	Marathi	% understood by 40 Marathi speakers			
		As a term	In context 1	In context 2	With visuals
Breastfeeding	स्तनपान	60%	73%	80%	100%
Menstruation	पाळी	100%	-	-	-
Contraception	संततिनियमन	13%	30%	58%	75%
Uterus	गर्भाशय	35%	38%	45%	55%
Delivery	बाळंतपण	95%	98%	98%	-
Sex	लैंगिक संबंध	53%	68%	80%	88%
Colostrum	चीक	65%	78%	88%	-
Bladder	मूत्राशय	23%	33%	38%	40%
Discharge	साव	20%	78%	-	-
Vagina	योनि	38%	45%	60%	63%

Hindi and Marathi are "near" languages and share many words. Even then, carrying a term that is understood in one language to the other may not work. The terms for breastfeeding, uterus, bladder and vagina are common between Marathi and Hindi. They were understood by a higher proportion of Marathi speakers without context, while they did not do so well among Hindi speakers. Hindi is also a much more widespread language than Marathi geographically. This probably explains why Marathi speaking users generally understood more terms than Hindi speakers.

5 Discussion and Conclusions

We conducted qualitative interviews with 66 urban poor pre- and postnatal women in several cities in India followed by structured surveys with 102 similar participants. 36 participants in each group were enrolled with mMitra, a service that provides information related to pregnancy and child care through automated calls. On the whole, the users of mMitra found the provided information useful and they believe it will be good for themselves and their baby. Without such services, women have a limited access to authentic information on these topics. Further, users prefer to access some kinds of information (e.g. sex during pregnancy) from the privacy of their phones rather than asking a doctor at a clinic.

While mobile phones are permeating in the society, many women still struggle to use several available features. The fact that phones are often shared mean that some women don't have exclusive access to a device. In the context of a service related to maternal health, this leads to privacy concerns, especially if the phones are shared with family members other than the husband. On the other hand, our study also identifies the need to engage with the broader ecosystem of the pre- and postnatal woman, especially the husband and the mother-in-law. At times information received from mMitra is inconsistent with traditional information received from the family members or others in the society. Future efforts are needed to help the users resolve such contradictions and make practical choices confidently.

Content should be formulated using multiple commonly used terminologies to cover regional diversity. Users could not understand some "formal" Hindi or Marathi words used in mMitra. This includes terms related to parts of the body, sex, breastfeeding, contraception, and terms used for food items. Users suggested several colloquial alternatives. In a communication that is predominantly based on audio, using multiple colloquial terms might increase the length of the audio making it harder to follow. One option is to do more extensive localisation (beyond just language). Another option is using visuals. Visuals (photographs, illustrations, animations or videos) could help clarify some of these terms, and especially procedural content such as breastfeeding, sleeping with a pillow, or lifting weights. Visuals should be familiar to the users and many will still need to be localised. We should also be mindful that visuals could cause more privacy concerns.

Our study identifies the need and the opportunity to go beyond only broadcasting information. Users cannot absorb all audio information in the first go. They need options to repeat information and to share it with peers or family members. Users would also like to ask questions of their own, or questions arising after listening to the

provided information. Such interactivity needs to be added without introducing complexity and keeping in mind the technology abilities of the users.

Acknowledgement. This research was conducted in partnership with Johnson & Johnson and BabyCenter, as part of a long-standing effort to harness the power of mobile technology to educate and empower new and expectant mothers and their families.

References

1. WHO - Maternal Health. www.who.int/maternal-health/en. Accessed 04 June 2019
2. Vora, K.S., et al.: Maternal health situation in India: a case study. J. Health Popul. Nutr. **27** (2), 184 (2009)
3. Mberu, B.U., Haregu, T.N., Kyobutungi, C., Ezeh, A.C.: Health and health-related indicators in slum, rural, and urban communities: a comparative analysis. Glob. Health Action **9**(1), 33163 (2016)
4. Ramachandran, D., Canny, J., Das, P.D., Cutrell, E.: Mobile-izing health workers in rural India. In: Proceedings of the SIGCHI Conference on Human Factors in Computing Systems, pp. 1889–1898. ACM, April 2010
5. Singh, P.K., Rai, R.K., Alagarajan, M., Singh, L.: Determinants of maternity care services utilization among married adolescents in rural India. PLoS ONE **7**(2), e31666 (2012)
6. Hilbert, M.: Digital gender divide or technologically empowered women in developing countries? A typical case of lies, damned lies, and statistics. In: Women's Studies International Forum, Pergamon, vol. 34, no. 6, pp. 479–489, November 2011
7. Tamrat, T., Kachnowski, S.: Special delivery: an analysis of mHealth in maternal and newborn health programs and their outcomes around the world. Matern. Child Health J. **16** (5), 1092–1101 (2012)
8. Jimoh, L., Pate, M.A., Lin, L., Schulman, K.A.: A model for the adoption of ICT by health workers in Africa. Int. J. Med. Inform. **81**(11), 773–781 (2012)
9. Sahay, S.: Are we building a better world with ICTs? Empirically examining this question in the domain of public health in India. Inf. Technol. Dev. **22**(1), 168–176 (2016)
10. Chib, A., Cheong, Y.J., Lee, L.C.L., Ng, C.H.C., Tan, C.K., Kameswari, V.L.V.: The hope of mobile phones in Indian rural healthcare. J. Health Inform. Dev. Countries **6**(1), 406–421 (2012)
11. Bagalkot, N., et al.: Towards enhancing everyday pregnancy care: reflections from community stakeholders in South India. In: Proceedings of the 9th Indian Conference on Human Computer Interaction, pp. 71–74. ACM, December 2018
12. Garai, A., Ganesan, R.: Role of information and communication technologies in accelerating the adoption of healthy behaviors. J. Fam. Welfare Spec. Issue **56**, 109–118 (2010)
13. Intille, S.S.: A new research challenge: persuasive technology to motivate healthy aging. IEEE Trans. Inf. Technol. Biomed. **8**(3), 235–237 (2004)
14. Robinson, H., Buccini, G., Curry, L., Perez-Escamilla, R.: The World Health Organization Code and exclusive breastfeeding in China, India, and Vietnam. Matern. Child Nutr. **15**(1), e12685 (2019)

Sugar Ka Saathi – A Case Study Designing Digital Self-management Tools for People Living with Diabetes in Pakistan

Kehkashan Zeb[1(✉)], Stephen Lindsay[1], Suleman Shahid[2],
Waleed Riaz[2], and Matt Jones[1]

[1] FIT Lab, Swansea University, Swansea, UK
806259@swansea.ac.uk
[2] CS Department, Lahore University of Management Sciences, Lahore, Pakistan

Abstract. This paper presents the results of an iterative participatory process to design a smart self-management tool for less-literate people living with diabetes in Pakistan. Initially, interviews and focus groups with sixty-nine people living with diabetes identified issues that they face when self-managing including uncontrollable factors, lack of diabetes awareness, low-tech mobile phones, and poor internet availability. We developed personas grounded in the scoping results and adjusted our PD approach to focus on more tangible design artefacts before running narrative scoping PD sessions. Working from older, illiterate persona, we designed a phone-line delivered Interactive Voice Response (IVR) system.

We developed a functional IVR Prototype "Sugar ka Saathi" (Diabetes Companion) with input from a group of 4 Pakistan-based healthcare professionals, to act as a design probe in the PD process. We tested the IVR probe with fifty-seven of the original scoping participants which validated the knowledge transferred by the IVR and its acceptability. Invisible design videos were shown to elaborate the IVR and community concept to thirteen participants through two filmed videos using our existing persona characters from the scoping studies, these videos helped to engage older people with diabetes in PD sessions.

Keywords: Human computer interaction · Participatory design ·
Interactive Voice Response

1 Diabetes in Pakistan: Challenge and Digital Potential

People engaging in diabetes management require continuous support, however, in rural Punjab, Pakistan illiteracy and poverty prevent many people from receiving it. Sixty percent of the population lives in rural areas [41] where healthcare facilities are not readily accessible and the prevalence of diabetes both in rural and urban areas is high with, in 2017, over seven million cases recorded amongst a population of 208 million people [21]. People do not have access to important self-management tools for diabetes such as glucose monitoring, exercise tracking, and dietary planning [9, 22, 32]. These barriers discourage people from trying to take the necessary, routine steps needed to manage their condition and this further aggravates them.

© IFIP International Federation for Information Processing 2019
Published by Springer Nature Switzerland AG 2019
D. Lamas et al. (Eds.): INTERACT 2019, LNCS 11748, pp. 161–181, 2019.
https://doi.org/10.1007/978-3-030-29387-1_10

Fortunately, mobile phones are widespread with 3% of people owning smartphone and 50% owning feature phones [20]. Previous research shows that these mobile phones have the potential to act as a platform for healthcare interventions [6, 18]. Even without smart features, mobile devices can deliver information such as help in identification of early diabetes symptoms [3] and management strategies such as diet plans.

However, our scoping work revealed that the mostly older patients living with diabetes are not inclined towards using electronic devices such as smartphones, computers, and laptops [8]. Consequently, in this work, we explored how a technology intervention could help them to improve their lifestyle while working within the constraints of their resistance towards using most electronic devices. The process to do this required us to address two questions: firstly, what techniques could we use to work alongside older people living with diabetes and understand what would and would not be acceptable? Second, what form could an intervention take that would we be possible to deploy given the constraints on literacy and technology?

2 Literature Review

Previous work has examined the role of digital tools in the self-management of healthcare conditions in a range of developing contexts addressing a wide range of different diseases. The work highlights a wide range of different barriers that are context dependent and disease dependent.

One of the most comprehensive breakdowns of barriers to treatment in developing contexts looked at treatment of breast cancer in Bangladesh [40]. The work broke down the challenges that people encounter along the lines of: prevent treatment obtainment issues successfully including communication problems in rural areas, scarcity of doctors, gender discrimination, transportation hazards; harmful common beliefs and practices such as herbal medicine reliance; treatment monitoring issues such as long term monitoring abandonment, lack of consistency and fading out behaviors and a range of environmental issues like load shedding, network connectivity and mobile theft [40].

The need to motivate people to engage is widely observed in work local to Pakistan that looks at diabetes management [42] and in culturally related contexts such as India [19]. The studies find that many patients are resigned to their condition and do not believe in the efficacy of self-management approaches so are reluctant to start to engage with them. In this challenge, the family and broader care network are accorded considerable importance as a pathway to help people move beyond their biases and engage in effective self-management [43]. In South Asian countries such as India and Pakistan, households often go beyond the immediate nuclear family such as grandparents and adult siblings and their children, so the family makeup is rich and complex.

With regards to specific self-management approaches, critically reflecting on and analyzing one's experiences is highlighted as vital for diabetes management [43] but criticality can be a difficult skill to impart.

2.1 Design

In healthcare, participation in the design process empowers patients and leads to the design of more successful, useful systems [11] as the end-users needs become prioritized in the design process. Participatory Design (PD) techniques have shown their worth when designing healthcare interventions in developing countries [4, 38], however, projects in economically developing regions show that there are many challenges. For example, the correct identification of stakeholders is not clear at the outset of many of these processes [4, 37]. Even after identification, composing PD groups in ways that encourage engagement from all stakeholders can be difficult [4] because more traditional or rigid social structures inhibit participants. This has led researchers to observe that members of their PD groups do not respect the goal of democratization of the process. In addition, most studies focus on the PD of health systems [36] rather than designing novel or bespoke technology.

Language barriers can also pose a significant challenge as a more diverse collection of languages are often spoken [34]. PD techniques that focus on systems design frequently assume participants literacy, but this is not always (or even often) the case especially in developing countries [35].

2.2 Interactive Voice-Response

Our work brought us to consider Interactive Voice Response (IVR) delivered over phone lines. A range of projects have used IVR to address the healthcare needs of illiterate people living in developing contexts. For example, [9] supports people living with HIV or AIDS in India by sending reminders and logging personal wellbeing. [29] uses IVR to provide medication reminders, descriptions of symptoms and tips on self-management for Syrian people living with diabetes. [43] supports community health workers over IVR allowing them to coordinate with one another.

Across these systems we see the capacity for IVR to work with illiterate populations as it requires no reading ability and minimal numeracy to select options on a keypad. The systems work for people who live with low levels of technology access as they can be delivered on mobile or home phones and the technology is low cost. IVR can be used to keep a record of patient's health condition, and the content saving on server side has the potential to make IVRs more secure.

Beyond direct support, an IVR system can keep people with diabetes motivated by interacting with them more frequently than a healthcare professional. Previous community-based radio systems that used IVR to conduct radio sessions, like "Avaaj Otalo" [30] and "Sehat ki Vanni" [29] proved successful in their respective settings and helped community members by delivering information. Because IVR phone lines require no formal tech-literacy beyond making a phone call, they can overcome the barriers identified in technology adoption.

Although IVR systems are marginally more expensive than conventional webhosting, they can be made sustainable by including advertisements to minimize the financial burden on a host organization [24]. These IVR systems can assist illiterate people with diabetes by providing medication reminders, descriptions of symptoms,

and tips for self-management to help them with the issues they describe around Monitoring.

IVR is based on content which is usually maintained on server-side and moderators [31] can help to manage this content. Consider the example of community radios where moderators can rate and sort content for IVR radio forums CGNet Swara [27] and Gram Vaani [28] are examples of Community Self-Management tools delivered over IVR systems using health care professionals as moderators.

3 Scoping Work: Understanding Solution Pathways

We initially set out to understand the needs and attitudes of people who live with diabetes in rural Pakistan by speaking with a range of people directly. We selected PICTIVE - a technique that relies on involving participants in design activities (using pen and paper) and recording them [23] – because of its similarity to techniques used in some other work [39]. However, the PICTIVE technique did not work with study participants, as we found that demographic factors such as age, literacy level and technical exposure of participants allowed some to express themselves on paper with confidence but most not.

In addition, in this initial work, older, less-literate, females with diabetes were hesitant to show their views on paper, therefore, we interviewed participants so they could be more comfortable sharing their life experiences. As a consequence, we decided to move away from the approach instead conduct semi-structured interviews to understand the challenges they faced mirroring approaches seen in other research [4].

3.1 Method

A total of sixty-nine people with diabetes, two diabetes educators, and two doctors who specialize in diabetes treatment participated in the newly organized semi-structured interviews and focus groups. Out of sixty-nine participants, twenty were male and forty-nine were female, broadly reflecting the male-female demographic ratio.

We performed one-to-one interviews (typically lasting twenty minutes) with fourteen people with diabetes and sixteen focus groups (typically lasting thirty minutes) with forty-one people with diabetes. Each focus group featured two to four participants and was conducted in home settings.

After getting formal permission from National Hospital of Faisalabad [14] and The Diabetes Institute Pakistan (DIP) of Lahore [13] one-to-one interviews were performed with fourteen people with diabetes and four healthcare professionals (20–30 min each).

Most study participants were over fifty years old, had little awareness of technology and had lived with diabetes for between two and eight years with some exceptions including a male participant who had lived with diabetes for thirty years and a female with four months diabetic history.

Language was an issue in these sessions - Urdu is the national language of Pakistan but Punjabi is the local language of Pakistan's province, Punjab. The use of Urdu is common amongst mostly literate people however Punjabi is favored amongst illiterate

people. In this study, most of the interviews with participants were conducted in Punjabi but interviews with healthcare professionals were conducted in Urdu.

We sought ethics approval from Swansea University College of Science and paid particular attention to how we would obtain informed consent from illiterate participants. Researchers explained the purpose of the study to participants and in the many cases where the participants could not read study information and consent forms, and their consent was recorded along with their signatures.

3.2   Analysis

During the analysis stage, we transcribed the recorded videos from scoping activities and translated them from Punjabi or Urdu into English. The process of transcription helped in data familiarization. The transcripts were then analyzed using the Thematic Analysis approach outlined by Braune and Clarke [17] to identify themes within the data. These themes are discussed below with sample quotes from participants (Fig. 1).

Uncontrollable Factors Driving Resignation

The attitudes of our participants toward their healthcare were resigned due to uncontrollable factors. This set a context for our discussion which the research team had not expected. For example, people with diabetes lived with external stresses beyond their means to control and they criticized both the diabetes educators' way of imparting information and how realistic it was to implement their suggestions. A fifty-seven years old literate female study participant said:

> *"They told us strategies like do not get stressed and do not think about things that worry you, but how is it possible to not think?"*

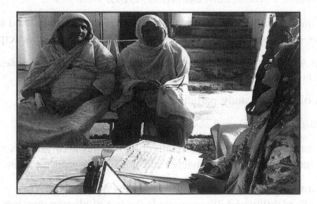

Fig. 1. Participatory design session in Malikpur in home settings

Stress was a detrimental factor in the lives of the people living with diabetes involved in this study. This was particularly the case for women since not only were they responsible for family matters as well as their diabetes; but also, usually lacked a good forum to voice their anxieties. A forty-five years old illiterate female study participant said:

"Stress affects my glucose level, which is because of several family matters, which are not in my control".

A healthcare professional from DIP, Lahore told that:

"Although there is no cure-all solution for diabetes, one can still keep it under control by remaining motivated and keen to self-manage".

However, people with diabetes often struggled with motivation and felt that their diabetic condition was beyond their control. For example, a fifty-five years old literate female study participant, living with diabetes for six years, typified the resignation many participants expressed when she said:

"It's God's will that a person is suffering from a disease and only God can cure it, I cannot spend the rest of my life keeping track of my glucose readings".

Adherence to Self-management Regimes

Diabetic patients need to adhere to an altered dietary plan where they eat many smaller meals that can be difficult to maintain, especially given many participants expressing their resignation to living with the condition. For example, a fifty-five years old female participant, enrolled in a Diabetes Education program, stated:

"Diabetes Educators recommended us to take small meals at regular intervals rather than taking heavy meals at a single go, in that way we will feel fuller. But how can you teach the elderly like that? They can use this method for kids but not for the elderly people!"

As diabetes is a lifetime condition, the behavior of the patient towards self-management can change over time as a sixty years old illiterate female participant said:

"When diagnosed with diabetes, the first two years I cared not to eat sugary things. But since last the 6–7 months, I walk regularly and become careless about food".

Desi medicine (herbal medicine) - plant-based medicine usually used to maintain or improve health - was popular in rural areas, one illiterate female participant said:

"I ate ground Jambolan (fruit), which assisted me in reducing my diabetes medicine from two tablets a day to one tablet a day".

A 60 years old female study participant told us that:

"I had hepatitis; local herbal medicine was effective to cure it".

However – in Guru-Nanak Pura, a relatively wealthier area – ladies explained that they only use medicines from pharmacies and not local herbal medicines.

Glucometers and Bodily Awareness for Diabetes Monitoring

Issues such as affordability and illiteracy made the use of glucometers less common and instead most study participants relied on perception of their body symptoms to gauge their glucose level as a fifty-five years old illiterate female participant said:

"My body condition and changes tell me about the level of sugar in the body, when it trembles sugar is high, and I experience fatigue and related symptoms when my sugar level is low".

While discussing the regular logging of information, another fifty-two years old literate female participant said:

"To record these glucose readings using mobile application is a lengthy process, and I do not want to spend the rest of my life using these lengthy processes!"

People with diabetes often complained that monitoring and entering glucose levels was hard and time-consuming. A literate female participant talked about undue stress caused by taking diabetes readings all the time:

"For the last 5–6 years, I've been suffering from diabetes. At the start, I was taking regular readings but then I stopped taking regular readings as this problem is for a lifetime, so what is the use of having this stress all the time? However, at times when I do not feel well, I take the glucose reading to know the cause".

This approach, though palatable to many participants, undermines the medically correct monitoring process with a glucometer. However, the motivation to take readings did vary from person to person, for example, another male patient reported:

"I check glucose reading 2 times daily fasting and during the day for 11–12 years since the problem began."

A sixty-two years old female study participant told us she monitors her condition and if she feels her glucose level is high then she takes two tablets instead of one which shows the general tendency of PWLD towards self-medication.

Awareness and Disregard of Self-management Techniques
Diet management is the key to keep glucose levels under control as a diabetes doctor in the DIP mentioned: *"Diabetes management education is more important than medicine"*. A Diabetes educator told us that:

"The role of diabetes educators rises from the fact that for a diabetes patient, regular self-management of disease is crucial".

Another diabetes educator in the National Hospital of Faisalabad emphasized that:

"A patient rarely understands their condition and so they rely on doctor's medicine only, although the use of medicine is only one factor for controlling the condition".

However, when questioned about their knowledge of diabetes, 55 years old literate female participant said:

"A person suffering from disease knows how to take care of his condition within a few days of having that condition."

On the question of eating habits 60 years old illiterate female study participant said:

"Rich people can answer such questions as what you eat. We just eat chapatti and drink water and do not afford to eat fruit".

These contrasting views highlighted a gulf in understanding between the healthcare professionals' treatment approaches and the routines patients were willing to undertake. Lack of information about diabetes and its associated symptoms was a hurdle for people with diabetes especially at the time of onset and early period of the condition as many participants told us about being diagnosed after experiencing worst symptoms:

"My diabetes started with the frequent need to urinate, even I was unconscious for three days with the glucose level as high as 600".

This reinforces the need for the Pakistani illiterate population to have information about what diabetes is, how it starts, what the preventive measures are to avoid the elevated glucose levels even before diabetes is diagnosed to avoid complications.

Technology Adoption in Rural and Urban Groups

Use of technology to help self-manage diabetes was varied. Amongst less literate study participants who typically lived in less well-resourced settings it was lower, however, literate middle-class participants used computers, laptops, and smartphones, especially the younger one. However, the majority of participants were older, less inclined towards technology and had limited resources, a female participant who came to DIP Lahore from a rural area for a check-up said:

"I do not use a mobile phone; do not even know how to receive the call".

Another study participant from 75 Chak told us that:

"I do not use the phone often and only listen to the received phone call".

In particular, the interviews highlighted that less literate people with diabetes living in rural areas do not use mobile phones with internet access. However, in DIP, doctors and people with diabetes showed an interest in using mobile applications as they were using the WhatsApp messaging service to communicate with each other. A few patients had access to mobile phones with the internet as a 35 years old literate female patient commented:

"I use a mobile phone often with internet availability, I can use different applications like WhatsApp, I am in contact with the doctor on the mobile phone about my current condition and I seek advice from him and will definitely use mobile phone applications to track my condition."

Co-morbidity

Many of the study participants have different coexisting conditions, such as diabetes, hepatitis, muscular pains, stroke, heart issues as a study participant told:

"Due to high sugar and blood pressure I had stoke".

Many people with diabetes reported eyesight issues which affect their seeing ability, due to high glucose level. Some of them get their eyesight checked while others do not get it checked due to affordability. Other issues highlighted in interviews were, hearing issue thus required us to speak loudly. Hepatitis is found widespread especially in villages, 75 Chak, 76 Chak, and 80 Chak.

3.3   User-Centered Study: Extracting Personas from Scoping Study

The scoping study uncovered different user groups, and this led us to develop personas to illustrate them. These personas give us greater insight into needs and wants of our study participants, which differ due to education levels, age, and gender.

4   Participatory Design

Because we found our participants significantly better in communicating verbally than through reading or writing, we selected a range of techniques to fit into what we thought of as a verbal design approach – one which generated design artefacts and feedback that was primarily verbal. This meant using a set of approaches that emphasize verbal communication as opposed to emphasizing written notes.

When the research team discussed the first stage of our work, our reflections suggested that many of our study participants' beliefs about their own self-efficacy affected the degree of engagement we could get when working with them. PD depends upon genuine interaction between researchers and the participants and our belief entering this process was that patients' stories about their lived experiences should inform and inspire our work as researchers as we need access to the insights that only they hold. Our semi-structured interviews gained useful insights and presenting PD based IVR probes also garnered engagement but the follow-up activities we planned were less successful.

Our interviews also showed us that the people with diabetes were eager to share their personal experiences and tell us stories so narrative scoping techniques were selected. While stories can be defined as informal and subjective accounts of personal experience, narrative accounts are more formal and structured [1]. To exploit this, we used 'Persona character development' as the basis for collecting these accounts of personal experiences of our study participants and formulating new ideas in relation to the persona created based on our initial scoping (see Table 1). Therefore, in place of tangible, co-created artefacts of the design process, personas were used to capture the results of the storytelling [15] in the Narrative Scoping work.

We also encountered issues stemming from a lack of willingness by some participants to speak up about their problems. This echoes findings from previous work [4] and, in this case, we believed that these issues arose from social norms that typically expect younger or female members of a group to show deference by remaining quiet. We addressed this by conducting PD exercises in one-to-one settings or with small groups of similar participants comfortable with each other already, either being friends where we could recruit them in groups or at least drawing groups from similar demographics such as a group of all older women. This decision emphasized the importance of the verbal elements of the design process and tried to ensure that everyone in a group could speak more freely.

4.1   PD Session Using Narrative Scoping

Four PD sessions were conducted with seventeen people with diabetes from Ashraf town, Malikpur. The participants were recruited through snowballing using local connections; 9 people with diabetes had already been involved in initial scoping. Four participants were male, and rest were female.

The narrative scoping sessions were divided into two parts: (1) Narrative interview session acting as an icebreaker; and (2) Personas of "Liaquat Hussain" and "Mukhtaraan Bibi" used for 'Persona Character Development'. While discussing the capability of using technology, participants agreed that an older female persona would

Table 1. Personas based on scoping study.

PERSONA	DETAILS	GOALS
Liaquat Hussain	Diabetes Patient for 12 years Age: 57 Literate Profession: Manager Marital Status: Married Residence: Faisalabad	He often uses Internet-based applications on the computer but less often on the mobile phone. He tries to maintain his diabetes well with food and exercise as recommended by the doctor, but adherence is an issue.
Anees Khan	Diabetes Educator Age: 25 Literate Profession: Diabetes Educator Marital Status: Single Residence: Faisalabad	He is usually in contact with illiterate people with diabetes having limited resources. He educates them to create diabetes awareness. He is available through NGO only in few hospitals and clinics. Mostly people with diabetes do not have direct access to him.
Saeeda Begum	Diabetes Patient for 5 years Age: 55 Literate Profession: Teacher Marital Status: Married Residence: Lahore	She is less interested in the use of mobile phone and often use it for listening to calls. She is knowledgeable about diabetes care.
Mukhtraan Bibi	Diabetes Patient for 17 years. Age: 70 years Illiterate Profession: House Keeper Marital Status: Widowed Faisalabad	She is struggling financially. She does not have direct access to diabetes related knowledge other than doctor. She is willing to listen to a helpline. She uses the phone for receiving a call.

benefit from the use of IVR technology; however, a middle-aged male Persona has access to a smartphone and will be happy to use smart-phone based solution for diabetes management.

We initially chose the "Mukhtaraan Bibi" persona due to its greater number in this study. Overall in persona-based narrative scoping sessions participants agreed that: "If she receives a call, she can listen to it, but it's difficult that she calls by herself". The

psychological help and reassurance "Mukhtaraan Bibi" will get from this helpline will help her in keeping her better motivated for managing her diabetic condition.

5 Exploring the Potential of Interactive Voice Response

The user scoping study showed in rural areas most participants had not used IVR. Therefore, "Sugar ka Saathi" was built to study use cases, usability, and act as a design prompt. A functional IVR Prototype was designed and developed with input from a group of 4 Pakistan-based healthcare professionals. Table 2 shows how themes from the initial scoping were responded to in the design of the system. This prototype acted as an IVR Design Probe and was deployed with 57 of the original scoping participants after creating their user profile on the IVR system. This validated the acceptability of IVR technology and also revealed people living with diabetes's reliance upon their wider community.

Table 2. Ideas for IVR based on different themes taken from the initial scoping.

Themes	Potential IVR based responses
Awareness of diabetes	Persona Mapped to the IVR System present diabetes Information verified by diabetes doctors
Adherence	Medicine reminders; Encouraging feedback if the recorded glucose level seems appropriate; Constructive feedback if the recorded glucose level is higher than normal
Monitoring	Daily reminders from the system to enter your glucose reading if it is not being entered for a user that day; If a glucose reading has not been entered in seven days motivational messages from the system
Co morbidity	Present information on different diseases; User profiling and recommender algorithm to present this information according to user's customized needs
Struggle with diabetes	IVR System can incorporate a community Radio Program to help people by listening to problems and allowing responses by experts; Questions and answer forum for offline use; Social Network where people with diabetes interact with peers

5.1 IVR Probe Design and Development

The prototype of Sugar ka Saathi was designed to create an awareness of diabetes management amongst less literate study participants. The persona of diabetes educator "Anees Khan" was used to deliver information on the IVR system. The information to be presented on the IVR system was based on existing websites validated by healthcare professionals in National Hospital Faisalabad (see feedback in Fig. 2).

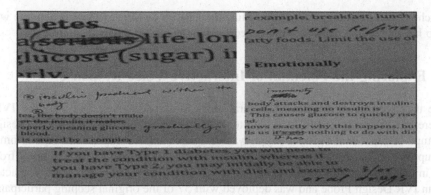

Fig. 2. Doctor's feedback on "Sugar Ka Saathi" content.

The next stage is to convert the information into a branching flowchart to base the IVR calls off (an overview is shown below in Fig. 3). All audio prompts were translated and recorded into both Punjabi and Urdu languages using good voice quality to ensure system comprehensibility.

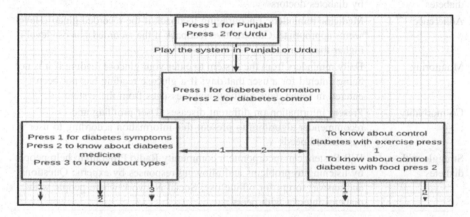

Fig. 3. Flowchart for "Sugar Ka Saathi" development.

"Sugar Ka Saathi" was built on Asterisk VOIP (Voice over Internet Protocol) platform and was developed using PERL Asterisk Gateway Interface (AGI). A MySQL server stores a system log. The telephone communication between the asterisk server and user was done over SIP (Session Initiation Protocol).

The maximum depth among all the submenus in "Sugar Ka Saathi" is four levels and the maximum width is three for the main menu while most of the other sub-menus have a maximum width of two in line with previous work [33]. There are two types of audio response in "Sugar Ka Saathi": navigational prompts at nodes and informational prompts at leaves. On average, the prompt length is 15 s and the maximum length is

25 s. At any sub-menu, the user has the option to navigate back to the previous menu or to end the call. If the user doesn't enter input against a prompt, "Sugar Ka Saathi" waits for a few seconds and repeats that prompt. It also notifies the user of a wrong input at any stage and repeats the prompt.

5.2 "Sugar Ka Saathi" User Testing

We worked with a user group ranging from 35 to 70 years old. All users spoke Punjabi and understood numerals, but only 3 of the users could read written Urdu. After the creation of the user profile in the system, all study participants were given a briefing that explains the "Sugar Ka Saathi" functions and how to use them. After that users completed tasks:

1. Retrieve basic information about diabetes.
2. Navigate back to the main menu from a sub-menu.
3. Find out how they can manage or control diabetes.

Study Participants gave feedback and suggestions and later informal discussion help to get more in-depth feedback about the "Sugar Ka Saathi" clarifying the design (Fig. 4).

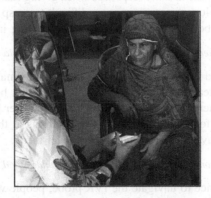

Fig. 4. Researcher showing demo of IVR in participatory design sessions in Faisalabad.

Users were interested in the system because it provided useful and relevant information regarding diabetes management. Existing mobile owners were confident using the IVR on their own and were relatively successful in interpreting and using the system. However, infrequent mobile users required help to adapt to the system and those with good levels of literacy were more confident in using the system. Some participants inquired about the "Sugar Ka Saathi" (helpline) number so they could call from their own mobile phones which further supported IVR's potential to become a viable solution to serve illiterate or semi-literate people.

Initially, the participants were hesitant in using the system but, after a short briefing on the use and information that was disseminated through it, they gained confidence

and found it useful. Each study participant was given a set of tasks during the evaluation. Twenty out of fifty-seven participants could comfortably complete their tasks with no prompt repetitions. Ten participants had better information retrieval times than the rest because of prior experience with the telephone helpline experience. The rest of the participants completed their tasks with a single prompt repetition except for seven users who needed three repetitions of the prompt.

Users were successful in comprehending both navigational and informational responses although only five users had prior experience with an IVR system. Users waited for responses to repeat for their selection if they could not understand it for the first time which showed a quick grasp of the IVR system after the initial explanation about the repetition functionality. Some users would wait for the prompt to the end before pressing the button while others would press immediately after hearing the option of their choice. Some infrequent mobile users did not understand the prompt during their first call. Something confused them about the functioning of the IVR System and therefore required repetition to understand the navigational responses. Ten users could not complete their tasks.

The semi-structured interviews after the tasks revealed despite understanding the navigational responses the first time, some participants were allowing them to repeat because of a lack of confidence in their own ability to use the system and most of the participants could quickly press the correct selection before the responses completed. In contrast, they repeated informational responses when giving relatively longer (20–25 s) ones showing that these longer responses were difficult to grasp in one listening. Upon asking one participant about listening twice to healthy eating information, she said:

"The information was interesting and for remembering this information I listened to it twice".

In the semi-structured interviews, users suggested that the navigational responses in the IVR system were clear, but each repetition helped them become more confident they had understood. There were two instances where the user had pressed the wrong option, unintentionally, for example, pressing two buttons at the same time. On both occasions, they could navigate back to the upper-level menu.

"Voice quality of IVR prompts is good, and I could easily understand them".

When given the chance to navigate the IVR probe, people with diabetes wished to inquire about topics of particular interest, for example, diet management was one of the favorite topics as most of the participants reported that they faced difficulties in managing the glucose levels. The knowledge acquired from other information sources such as doctors was insufficient in the effective management of diabetes. IVR probe users found the exercises and healthy eating tips useful.

During feedback interviews, some participants showed the desire to get information for their personal problems.

"What if I can get customized information regarding my problem".

Research shows that an IVR system can have many functions such as medicine reminder, glucose reading reminder and motivating feedback from the system based on the weekly reading.

Affordability of IVR was an issue as study participants were not ready to bear the cost and mentioned:

"I want the system to be free (Mufat), as I am hardly meeting both ends and cannot afford IVR call".

Since the system was unaffordable by many study participants, advertisements by system is proposed to make IVR sustainable [24]. Most participants have agreed to use this system and provided their phone numbers showing the willingness to receive the call from the IVR System. The desire to use helpline again, confirmed us that users like it as this saying:

"I will love to listen to IVR system call again".

Therefore, a more generalized IVR system that considers different diseases and provides information for them simultaneously has a greater likelihood to benefit the patient. Some of our users want to seek knowledge from the system, one semi-literate user said:

"The information provided by this helpline is basic, this system will be beneficial if it has more information."

Another illiterate 60 years old IVR design probe user gives the suggestion:

"What if I can ask questions of my choice and get answers for them?"

One issue found during the use of the IVR probe was the inability of the users to dial numbers, due to eyesight issue, related to their high glucose level. This inability to dial numbers would lead users to seek the help of peers such as the family, for making phone calls and a few people with diabetes mentioned in the study the need to be able to delegate their work:

"Please explain the system to my son or daughter".

5.3 Developing Our View Point

Looking at user engagement with IVR and desire to get more and customized information from the system, we choose the recommender algorithm [33] and user profiling [7] as potential technologies. Our study participants repeatedly mention the desire to get more information from the system. However, navigating a large amount of information in IVR is not possible with conventional information hierarchy. Therefore, a user profile maintained in the system based on user preferences will later help the intelligent system to give appropriate knowledge to people with diabetes. This intelligent system can address the varied information needs of our study participants such as comorbidity, by keeping track of information, which is already presented and by tracking the new information, users are presented with, based on their profile.

6 Understanding the Potential for Community IVR in Diabetes Management

The community element is very important for the use of any technology platform with our illiterate and older participants as, in IVR probe testing, many participants reported that they will seek the help of their children while interacting with an IVR system, because of eyesight or literacy issues. Reliance on peers apart from the close-knit family system is also clear from the user study, as in 75 Chak, participants relied on each other's knowledge and ability to manage the disease, it becomes clear when 40 years old illiterate female participant told:

"I will seek the help of Baji (elder peer participant) to seek information from the IVR".

This shows not only participants hesitation to use technology but also reliance on peers. People with diabetes often require external motivation and support to help them self-manage their activities and diet [32] and community can play an important role in teaching and motivating them [5]. Community-based healthcare systems like 'Patients Like Me' [16] encourage better self-management. However, these approaches are not accessible to illiterate study participants because of their requirement to know how to read and write.

There is an opportunity for the community model to help motivate people with diabetes to adapt to a healthy lifestyle [29]. Changing a person's attitude towards diabetes management is not possible with technology alone, but it requires a holistic role played by the community, technology, and a person's motivation together to take better care of their diabetic condition. The community can act as a stimulating agent, to serve that purpose and technology can play a vital role by connecting the community to increase diabetes awareness.

Broadly, community self-management, whether realized through the medium of digital technologies or social approaches, can be divided into "Peer Self-Management" and "Community Self-Management". In Community Self-Management, all stakeholders collaborate and share information to address an issue, an example would be an IVR question-answer forum. In Peer self-management, 2–3 patients work as a group to help each other to keep their glucose level on track, the approach is already seen when people managing their own cases of diabetes take the time to help newly diagnosed people with diabetes to manage their condition [14].

The use of a moderator is vital as a health care professional acting as a moderator to guide discussions can make the system more trustworthy. Community Self-Management (sometimes called community moderation) is another option which reduces the need to use a moderator such as the Sangeet Swara project in which community rates every post which helps in moderation [26]. Although less resource intensive to run, the validity of healthcare information shared in peer-self management moderated forums can be questionable as the healthcare professional opinion is crucial when developing a large-scale system.

6.1 PD Workshop Using Invisible Design

Invisible Design [25] is a technique for generating ideas with study participants using ambiguous films in which characters discuss technology use without directly showing technology. There were total 13 people with diabetes who took part in 1-1 PD sessions, out of 13 participants, 2 were male and 11 were female. These 1-1 PD sessions were conducted in locations of "75 Chak", and "Ashraf town Malikpur". After participants used the IVR based design probe for 15–20 min navigating through various features such as basic information about how to manage diabetes, they saw two videos based on the Invisible Design approach which helped to generate ideas with PD workshop participants focusing on community-based IVR. We showed the filmed scenario using the personas of 'Diabetes Doctor' and 'Diabetes Patient' as shown below, where they discussed the use of Community IVR System in three minutes long movie. Participants were quick in grasping the concept behind Community based IVR. They showed enthusiasm using a communal application where they could listen to other people's ideas and share their own insights. We saw that our less-literate participants responded to Invisible Design technique as they know the IVR concept using design Probe. This makes IVR system discussion in invisible design video easy to imagine. Overall it can be concluded that PD techniques based on verbal communication, either verbal discussion or showing video has the potential to engage illiterate participants (Fig. 5).

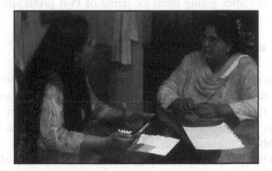

Fig. 5. Invisible design video with a doctor telling patient about the use of IVR technology.

7 Discussion

7.1 Methodological Challenges

Since a majority of our participants were reluctant to use conventional PD techniques to design the system itself, we switched over to Narrative Scoping work and used Invisible Design in our workshops. While PD techniques that showed different visual options to our semi-literate participants resulted in greater degrees of engagement and enthusiasm as compared to more free-form ideation; they also restricted the design space and did not reflect the original aspirations of PD. Although some issues we encountered have been reported in other work conducted in other contexts, the specific set of issues we encountered were unique to the Pakistani context we were working at.

7.2   Pragmatic Challenges

The role of government in the healthcare sector is minimal and expenses are borne solely by the patients in Pakistan. The quality of healthcare facilities in the private and public sector are not comparable. As a result, those who cannot afford the best facilities are left with inadequate resources. Since decent facilities are a by-product of urbanization, they are usually relegated to cities, leaving the rural citizens deprived.

Creating a platform-independent solution that is compatible with all the different types of mobile phone models present in Pakistan is difficult. People in rural areas often rely on older Nokia mobile phones due to their affordability and suitability for their use while smartphones are usually more popular in urban areas though still not widespread.

7.3   Attitudes and Beliefs

The PD process has many needs such as participants should be able to convey their viewpoint as their literacy level influences the process. Illiterate PD participants who cannot understand the textual interface may find it difficult to accept the technology introduced with a smartphone. However, research [41] showed the less literate participants can understand the pictures with voice-overs in smartphone applications. In this research when we produced more concrete IVR prototypes and showed them to people with diabetes it resulted in increased engagement levels in the concept of invisible design video after giving them the demo of IVR prototype.

8   Conclusion and Future Directions

Our initial thinking revolved around a user-driven approach because of the realization that people with diabetes requirements are important and accounting them. The research uncovers the behavior towards technological intervention amongst the less literate people with diabetes through an IVR system design probe that disseminates information for diabetes management.

We plan to extend this project by doing full scale deployment of this IVR system using server so that people with diabetes can use in their home settings. We will incorporate new features based on the user study analysis such as to design and develop a scalable system to give information dynamically, including the option for co-morbid diseases in this system, developing a healthcare Social Network system over IVR to address community support for people with diabetes in managing diabetes. Diabetes based IVR could be a good starting point to empower people with diabetes in Pakistan and this has potential to serve as a stepping stone towards the design of a powerful tool that can educate the rural community about healthcare strategies.

Acknowledgement. Cherish-De support for this project helped to make this study a reality, we hope to deploy a fully functional helpline after participatory contribution from users.

References

1. East, L., Jackson, D., O'Brien, L., Peters, K.: Storytelling: an approach that can help to develop resilience. Nurse Res. **17**(3), 17–25 (2010)
2. Joshi, A.: Supporting treatment of people living with HIV/AIDS in resource limited settings with IVRs. In: Proceedings of the SIGCHI Conference on Human Factors in Computing Systems, 26 April 2014, pp. 1595–1604. ACM (2014)
3. Agency for Healthcare Research and Quality (AHRQ). Improving Care for Diabetes Patients Through Intensive Therapy and a Team Approach, November 2001. https://archive.ahrq.gov/research/findings/factsheets/diabetes/diabria/diabria.pdf. Accessed 5 Jan 2018
4. Hussain, S., Sanders, E.B., Steinert, M.: Participatory design with marginalized people in developing countries: challenges and opportunities experienced in a field study in Cambodia. Int. J. Des. **6**(2), 91–109 (2012)
5. Kumar, N.: Projecting health: community-led video education for maternal health. In: Proceedings of the Seventh International Conference on Information and Communication Technologies and Development, 15 May 2015, p. 17. ACM (2015)
6. Mamykina, L., Miller, A.D., Mynatt, E.D., Greenblatt, D.: Constructing identities through storytelling in diabetes management. In: Proceedings of the SIGCHI Conference on Human Factors in Computing Systems, 10 April 2010, pp. 1203–1212. ACM (2010)
7. Middleton, S.E., Shadbolt, N.R., De Roure, D.C.: Ontological user profiling in recommender systems. ACM Trans. Inf. Syst. (TOIS) **22**(1), 54–88 (2004)
8. Vaportzis, E., Giatsi Clausen, M., Gow, A.J.: Older adults perceptions of technology and barriers to interacting with tablet computers: a focus group study. Front. Psychol. **4**(8), 1687 (2017)
9. Mamykina, L., Mynatt, E.D., Kaufman, D.R.: Investigating health management practices of individuals with diabetes. In: Proceedings of the SIGCHI Conference on Human Factors in Computing Systems, 22 April 2006, pp. 927–936. ACM (2006)
10. Triantafyllakos, G., Palaigeorgiou, G., Tsoukalas, I.A.: Fictional characters in participatory design sessions: Introducing the "design alter egos" technique. Interact. Comput. **22**(3), 165–175 (2010)
11. Chapman, L.: Design for chronic illness: exploring service systems & new technologies for patients with type 2 diabetes
12. Simonsen, J., Robertson, T. (eds.): Routledge International Handbook of Participatory Design. Routledge, Abingdon (2012)
13. Diabetic's Institute Pakistan Website. http://www.diabetespakistan.com/lahoremain.php. Accessed 29 Aug 2017
14. National Hospital Faisalabad Website. http://www.nationalhospital.enic.pk/. Accessed 30 Aug 2017
15. Bidwell, N.J., Reitmaier, T., Marsden, G., Hansen, S.: Designing with mobile digital storytelling in rural Africa. In: Proceedings of the SIGCHI Conference on Human Factors in Computing Systems, 10 April 2010, pp. 1593–1602. ACM (2010)
16. Patients Like Me. https://www.patientslikeme.com/. Accessed 17 Sept 2017
17. Braun, V., Clarke, V.: Using thematic analysis in psychology. Qual. Res. Psychol. **3**(2), 77–101 (2006)
18. Muller, M.J.: Participatory design: the third space in HCI. Hum.-Comput. Interact.: Dev. Process. **4235**, 165–185 (2003)
19. Rafique, G., Shaikh, F.: Identifying needs and barriers to diabetes education in patients with diabetes. J.-Pak. Med. Assoc. **56**(8), 347 (2006)

20. The rise of mobile and social media in Pakistan. http://www.dawn.com/news/1142701. Accessed 22 Jan 2019
21. Demographics of Pakistan. https://en.wikipedia.org/wiki/Demographics_of_Pakistan. Accessed 17 Jan 2019
22. Hinder, S., Greenhalgh, T.: "This does my head in". Ethnographic study of self-management by people with diabetes. BMC Health Serv. Res. **12**(1), 83 (2012)
23. Muller, M.J.: PICTIVE—an exploration in participatory design. In: Proceedings of the SIGCHI Conference on Human Factors in Computing Systems, 27 April 1991, pp. 225–231. ACM (1991)
24. Kharal, A., Naseem, M., Ahmad, S.S., Raza, A.A.: Sustainable IVR-based social media for the developing world
25. Briggs, P., et al.: Invisible design: exploring insights and ideas through ambiguous film scenarios. In: Proceedings of the Designing Interactive Systems Conference, 11 June 2012, pp. 534–543. ACM (2012)
26. Vashistha, A., Cutrell, E., Borriello, G., Thies, W.: Sangeet swara: a community-moderated voice forum in rural India. In: Proceedings of the 33rd Annual ACM Conference on Human Factors in Computing Systems, 18 April 2015, pp. 417–426. ACM (2015)
27. Mudliar, P., Donner, J., Thies, W.: Emergent practices around CGNet Swara: a voice forum for citizen journalism in rural India. Inf. Technol. Int. Dev. **9**(2), 65–79 (2013)
28. Gram Vaani. http://gramvaani.org/. Accessed 18 Sept 2018
29. Kazakos, K.: A real-time IVR platform for community radio. In: Proceedings of the 2016 CHI Conference on Human Factors in Computing Systems, 7 May 2016, pp. 343–354. ACM (2016)
30. Patel, N., Chittamuru, D., Jain, A., Dave, P., Parikh, T.S.: Avaaj Otalo: a field study of an interactive voice forum for small farmers in rural India. In: Proceedings of the SIGCHI Conference on Human Factors in Computing Systems, 10 April 2010, pp. 733–742. ACM (2010)
31. Grover, A.S., Plauché, M., Barnard, E., Kuun, C.: HIV health information access using spoken dialogue systems: touchtone vs. speech. In: 2009 International Conference on Information and Communication Technologies and Development (ICTD), 17 April 2009, pp. 95–107. IEEE (2009)
32. Mamykina, L., Mynatt, E., Davidson, P., Greenblatt, D.: MAHI: investigation of social scaffolding for reflective thinking in diabetes management. In: Proceedings of the SIGCHI Conference on Human Factors in Computing Systems, 6 April 2008, pp. 477–486. ACM (2008)
33. Yang, Y., Liu, C., Li, C., Hu, Y., Niu, Y., Li, L.: The recommendation systems for smart TV. In: 2014 International Conference on Computing, Communication and Networking Technologies (ICCCNT), 11 July 2014, pp. 1–6. IEEE (2014)
34. Gardner-Bonneau, D.: Guidelines for speech-enabled IVR application design. In: Gardner-Bonneau, D. (ed.) Human Factors and Voice Interactive Systems. SECS, vol. 498, pp. 147–162. Springer, Boston (1999). https://doi.org/10.1007/978-1-4757-2980-1_7
35. Sherwani, J., et al.: Healthline: speech-based access to health information by low-literate users. In: 2007 International Conference on Information and Communication Technologies and Development, ICTD 2007, 15 December 2007, pp. 1–9. IEEE (2007)
36. Korpela, M., Soriyan, H.A., Olufokunbi, K.C.: Activity analysis as a method for information systems development. Scand. J. Inf. Syst. **12**(1–2), 191–210 (2001)
37. Chib, A.: Research on the impact of the information society in the global South: an introduction to SIRCA. In: Chib, A., May, J., Barrantes, R. (eds.) Impact of Information Society Research in the Global South, pp. 1–17. Springer, Singapore (2015). https://doi.org/10.1007/978-981-287-381-1_1

38. Bowen, S., Dearden, A., Wright, P., Wolstenholme, D., Cobb, M.: Participatory healthcare service design and innovation. In: Proceedings of the 11th Biennial Participatory Design Conference, 29 November 2010, pp. 155–158. ACM (2010)
39. Jones, M., et al.: Beyond yesterday's tomorrow: future-focused mobile interaction design by and for emergent users. Pers. Ubiquitous Comput. 21(1), 157–171 (2017)
40. Haque, M.M., et al.: e-ESAS: evolution of a participatory design-based solution for breast cancer (BC) patients in rural Bangladesh. Pers. Ubiquitous Comput. 19(2), 395–413 (2015)
41. Medhi-Thies, I., Ferreira, P., Gupta, N., O'Neill, J., Cutrell, E.: KrishiPustak: a social networking system for low-literate farmers. In: Proceedings of the 18th ACM Conference on Computer Supported Cooperative Work & Social Computing, pp. 1670–1681. ACM, February 2015
42. Ahmed, F., Asim-Bin-Zafar, M.R., Ghafoor, E., Rehman, R.A., Uddin, Q.: Impact of 24-hour helpline service for people with diabetes. Pak. J. Med. Sci. 33(3), 747 (2017)
43. Yadav, D., et al.: Sangoshthi: empowering community health workers through peer learning in rural India. In: Proceedings of the 26th International Conference on World Wide Web, pp. 499–508. International World Wide Web Conferences Steering Committee, April 2017

38. Bowen, S., Dearden, A., Wright, P., Wolstenholme, D., Cobb, M.: Participatory healthcare service design and innovation. In: Proceedings of the 11th Biennial Participatory Design Conference, 29 November 2010, pp. 155–158. ACM (2010)

39. Jensen, M., et al.: Beyond yesterday's tomorrow: future-focused mobile interaction design by and for emergent users. Pers. Ubiquitous Comput. 21(1), 157–171 (2017)

40. Haque, M.M., et al.: e-ESAS: evolution of a participatory design-based solution for breast cancer (BC) patients in rural Bangladesh. Pers. Ubiquitous Comput. 19(2), 395–413 (2015)

41. Medhi-Thies, I., Ferreira, P., Gupta, N., O'Neill, J., Cutrell, E.: KrishiPustak: a social networking system for low-literate farmers. In: Proceedings of the 18th ACM Conference on Computer Supported Cooperative Work & Social Computing, pp. 1670–1681. ACM, February 2015

42. Ahmed, I., Asim Bin Zafar, M.R., Obaton, T., Rehman, R.A., Uddin, O.: Impact of 24 hour helpline service for people with diabetes. Pak. J. Med. Sci. 33(4), 742 (2017)

43. Yadav, D., et al.: Sangoshthi: empowering community health workers through e-learning in rural India. In: Proceedings of the 26th International Conference on World Wide Web, pp. 499–508. International World Wide Web Conferences Steering Committee, April 2017

Interaction in Public Spaces

Interaction in Public Spaces

Design Challenges for Mobile and Wearable Systems to Support Learning on-the-move at Outdoor Cultural Heritage Sites

Alaa Alkhafaji[1,2]($\boxtimes$) (iD), Sanaz Fallahkhair[3], and Mihaela Cocea[1] (iD)

[1] School of Computing, University of Portsmouth, Portsmouth, UK
{Alaa.alkhafaji,Mihaela.cocea}@port.ac.uk,
Alaa.alkhafaja@gmail.com
[2] Department of Computer Science, College of Science,
Mustansiriyah University, Baghdad, Iraq
[3] School of Computing, University of Brighton, Brighton, UK
S.fallahkhair@brighton.ac.uk

Abstract. This paper presents a novel set of design challenges for the development of mobile and wearable applications to be used at cultural heritage sites. These challenges were drawn out based on a user study that was carried out to evaluate a mobile application prototype, SmartC. SmartC was designed for supporting people in taking learning opportunities at sites whenever they need informally while they are on the move. Augmented reality and wearable computing, i.e. smart eye glasses, were used in this research with the aim of bringing the past to life, as well as enhancing visitors' engagement. SmartC was evaluated by 26 participants, potential end-users, in the field. The evaluation study mainly focused on the interaction and usability aspects, which contribute to the field of HCI. The paper outlines several issues and challenges that were identified based on the evaluation study, summarised as: (1) interaction design related; (2) wearable computing related; (3) surroundings and environment related; (4) learner related; (5) context of use; and (6) technical issues. This paper also identifies aspects that relate to methods to be used and applied to such cases for evaluation studies.

Keywords: Ubiquitous learning · Mobile location-based services ·
Outdoors cultural heritage · Augmented reality · Wearable computing

1 Introduction

Cultural heritage sites carry the historical values of society [1]. Cultural heritage, therefore, reflects the identity of societies [2] and it is considered the gateway people use to discover history. Thus, it is not surprising that researchers are constantly seeking a better way to enhance the interpretation of sites [3–6], which consequently enhance the experience and learning from them. Interpretation is not only about presenting factual information, but more importantly about evoking the emotional and intellectual connection between visitors and attractions [7], that would promote the sense of loyalty and belonging to the community, as well as increase awareness of cultural heritage

© IFIP International Federation for Information Processing 2019
Published by Springer Nature Switzerland AG 2019
D. Lamas et al. (Eds.): INTERACT 2019, LNCS 11748, pp. 185–207, 2019.
https://doi.org/10.1007/978-3-030-29387-1_11

places. To achieve this, the objective of sites' authorities [8] is to enhance sites' interpretation, as well as visitors' engagement, which will lead to increase attendance; this, in turn, would improve learning from sites. This is challenging nowadays due to few reasons, which include: (a) a lack of interest in visiting sites as often, which makes it challenging to derive people to visit sites [9]; (b) people do not see visiting sites as a learning trip but rather as entertainment; (c) the rapid pace of life does not leave much time for people to visit sites and explore them. As experiencing sites usually involves moving from one attraction to another and changing of contexts to acquire information, enabling learning while moving, which we refer to learning on-the-move, for this purpose it would be an excellent choice. Visitors, often visit sites with friends and family to socialise and at the same time experience the site and feel the place [10]. This might cause visitors to spend a limited amount of time to explore sites and learn about them, as they would prefer to stay with the group most of the time. Thus, it could be essential to have a tool that enables them to stay with the group most of the time, while simultaneously learning about the attractions [11]. Additionally, visitors often have a limited amount of time they are willing to spend at sites, as they need to return to other activities after the visit. Additionally, it would be more challenging if there are kids within a group of visitors, as they are usually not as patient as adults. Technology would be an excellent tool for this, which could be achieved by utilising location-based notification to deliver information regarding the history of and the available services at nearby sites. This has not been given a great attention in the literature as shown in the next section.

Although, technologies have been introduced to enhance visitors' experience, most of them are introduced with respect to indoors cultural heritage [12–14]. Emerging technologies, such as immersive and ubiquitous technologies have a great potential to enhance engagement at sites as well as visitors' experience [15]. They would bring the past closer and help visitors experience life back in time [16], but so far, they have been dedicated mainly for indoor settings, such as museums and galleries. However, outdoors cultural heritage is as important as indoors, and they might need extra attention, as usually attractions are distributed around cities with no members of staff available, but with labels and sometimes limited audio devices [17]. Additionally, the context of outdoors sites is different than indoors where variables such as weather and level of brightness (i.e. sun light), are easy to control. Based on the literature review in the next section, few studies were dedicated for outdoor settings. Also, augmented reality (AR) technology has been introduced to enhance interaction at cultural heritage sites but, again, mainly for indoor settings, as explained in the next section. However, using it in outdoor contexts has different challenges, which have not been explored greatly in the literature, as few studies have been conducted outdoors. Consequently, there is a need to explore further and deeper to better understand how variables of outdoor settings would affect the experience, and how visitors will deal with them; this would help researchers address challenges that might arise.

Based on the review outlined in the next section, there is a lack of technologies that help visitors of outdoor sits to learn-on-the-move and provide them with the right information at the right time based on location, automatically without any intervention from users. Such technology would be very helpful for visitors who are in a new place and do not know what points of interest may be nearby; it would also help visitors to

smartly invest the time of the visit by receiving information while moving around individually or with a group. Furthermore, few studies introduced features to show how attractions appeared in the past using AR, which could be a very interesting feature for enhancing visitors' engagement according to previous studies [9, 17], that would also enhance the sites' interpretation, which is very important as culture heritage reflects the identity of society [18]. Consequently, it would enhance attendance, which is always the objective of cultural heritage authorities [8]. Therefore, in the long-term, that would have a great impact on conserving sites as the visitors' attendance is a key aspect that contributes to sites maintenance [8], which in turn contributes to a better economy. Another important aspect of showing attractions how they looked in the past, is that it brings the past to life, which would reinforce the link between the present and the past, which, in turn, would help stimulate the perpetuation of culture [19].

This paper presents a user-study in the field for the evaluation of a mobile app that adopts smart and ubiquitous learning technology, SmartC. SmartC was designed to provide a learning tool to be used at outdoor cultural heritage sites informally. The study provided an insight into how visitors react to using an AR app in outdoor settings of cultural heritage. The results of the study helped outline a set of design challenges for designing such services, which would assist researchers who work in this area to overcome challenges that might arise. SmartC was designed to assist visitors of cultural heritage take learning opportunities whenever they need regardless of time and place utilising mobile and wearable computing, i.e. smart eyeglasses. The smart eyeglasses would help free visitors' hands and enjoy the experience while at the same time acquiring information. Additionally, they would help them look at the actual artefact while acquiring information, which would support the association of the given information with the corresponding artefact [17]. SmartC was designed to help visitors learn informally whilst on-the-move by delivering instant information automatically based on location regarding cultural attractions and artefacts when passing by. Additionally, SmartC provides a service to show how attractions appeared back in time using AR technology. SmartC was developed based on a framework for developing such services that was introduced in previous research [11, 17], which was formulated based on three empirical studies to gather user requirements; the user study presented in this paper was conducted to evaluate SmartC in the field with 26 potential end-users. The focus of the evaluation study was mainly on the interaction between users and the app, as it is considered a key factor of user satisfaction that would significantly enhance their engagement [20, 21]. Design challenges were identified during the study for designers to keep in mind when designing such services, which are outlined in this paper. Additionally, the limitations of the study setting are discussed, which would be helpful information in guiding researchers in setting such studies. A scenario-based design method was used to depict the context of use to guide the design. The adopted scenario was developed based on general requirements for designing such services that were identified in a previous study [22]. The next section provides an overview of similar technologies and highlights their limitations.

2 Related Work

Ubiquitous computing offers technology that interweaves into our lives and the surrounding environment in an unobtrusive way [23, 24]. It offers features that allow people to be freed from the restriction of time and place, which would be an excellent choice for enhancing the experience at cultural heritage sites, as the experience at sites involves a lot of changing in contexts, and it happens at different times. It is context-aware computing which allows visitors to receive information based on the context while they are moving. This section provides an overview regarding similar technologies and highlights their limitations.

Mobile technology has been increasingly utilised to support people experiencing cultural heritage sites. Studies such as in [25–28] have introduced mobile guides particularly for enhancing the experience at cultural heritage sites. However, none of them was introduced to provide visitors with information regarding the surrounding attractions based on location automatically while moving. Geo-focussed services have recently drawn a great attention especially for activities at outdoor settings. These services use mobile devices and the Global Position System (GPS) for doing activities based on location. It is considered as a good tool for encouraging people to socialise while doing physical activities (e.g. geo-caching) [29] and were mainly introduced for outdoor settings such as in [30–36]. However, none of them was dedicated for enhancing visitors' experience at outdoor cultural heritage sites for learning, nor were they utilised to understand visitors'/learners' behaviour and attitude while using such services in outdoor settings, with the aim to identifying design challenges.

AR technology has been recently utilised in cultural heritage contexts to enhance visitors' experience. Some projects have been designed for indoor cultural heritage sites such as in [7, 37–41]. Some others were introduced for outdoor settings such as in [42–45]. Nonetheless, they have not introduced notifications on-the-move based on location and at the same time show how attractions looked in the past, which would be an essential feature for enhancing visitors' engagements, as well as sites' interpretation. Utilising wearable computing such as smart eye glasses to learn from cultural heritage sites is yet immature in the literature; a few technologies were introduced in this respect such as [12, 46–49]. Although these technologies utilised wearable computing, but they were not aimed at supporting visitors' learning on-the-move, where they receive right information at the right time based on location and at the same time helping them experience life back in time.

Several mobile apps were designed for indoor cultural heritage settings to be used at museums. For example as in [13, 14, 50, 51]. Nevertheless, these technologies were not introduced to meet the particular need of outdoor setting, as a few things need to be considered in outdoors such as: the weather, the noise, and the daytime, which do not matter in indoor.

More research was carried out with respect to outdoors cultural heritage in terms of field studies to evaluate similar technologies, such as in [6, 52, 53], but none of them explored how visitors react to challenges that might arise at outdoor setting, nor

observed how they perform in different learning modes to experience sites (i.e. individual and group). Additionally, none of them outlined design challenges for designing such services, nor provide guidance for researchers in setting such studies, that would assist researchers when conducting similar studies.

Despite the growing literature of ubiquitous learning technologies, there is still a lack of systems that support visitors intelligently to learn informally based on location at outdoors cultural heritage while moving without the need of intervention from users. Learning on-the-move would enhance learners/visitors' experience at cultural heritage sites as it saves the time and effort visitors spend looking for information regarding sites. In addition, none of the aforementioned systems provides the right information at the right time in a form of notifications based on location when learners pass nearby sites or attractions. This could be a very helpful feature for learners who are in new places where they do not know what is interesting surrounding them, which help them invest their visit's time effectively. SmartC is designed to help visitors of outdoor sites take learning opportunities on-the-move regardless of time and place, which is presented in this paper. SmartC utilises AR to enable visitors experience life back in time by providing a feature to show how sites looked back in time. This feature would be a good choice in helping people feel heritage places and experience life back in time; that would help them understand the local history [8, 54]. Additionally, it utilises smart eye glasses to free visitors' hands and let them enjoy the experience without the need of carrying a mobile device all the time, while at the same time acquiring information. This would enhance the interaction between visitors and artefacts. SmartC was evaluated in the field with potential end-users. Deeper insights were obtained regarding how visitors/learners deal with challenges at sites. Consequently, design challenges for developing such services were identified to assist designers of such services, as a considerable amount of time and effort would be saved if they are considered. Such challenges have not been given a great attention in the aforementioned studies. Furthermore, limitations related to study settings that were identified during the study are outlined, which would guide researchers in setting such studies. Next section presents the scenario-based method design.

3 Scenario-Based Design

A scenario-based design method was used to visualise the context of use in order to implement the prototype [22, 55], which was developed based on a subset of general requirements for designing such services. It is important to note, the general requirements were extracted from a framework for designing such services [17]. The adopted general requirements (GRs) are:

1. The service should maintain a content object
2. The service should support learning on the move
3. The service should support learners interact with context easily and efficiently
4. The service should consider the challenges that might arise in using mobile devices in outdoor settings.

One scenario depicted the context of using augmented reality via smart eyeglasses, which is illustrated below.

Scenario: Mary is the mum of 16-year-old Amy. Mary is very passionate about cultural heritage and wants to get her daughter to learn about her culture. Amy does not find visiting cultural heritage sites very interesting as she sees sites as ruined abandoned places like a dead habitation. Mary found a mobile app that has an interesting service that enables visitors to experience life back in time, which helps visitors to be closer to the past. The service could be delivered through the mobile phone's camera or smart eyeglasses. Mary thought that might help changes Amy's perspective about historical places. This service enables visitors to travel inside history and watch people's life back in time. She took Amy to a historical place that used to be a battlefield back at a particular period of time and encouraged her to use this service. Amy chose to use the smart eye glasses with a headset as she thought that would enable her to immerse in the atmosphere. The service displayed a real situation of the life back in time. Amy imagined herself walking down a street watching and listening to events surrounding her. Amy enjoyed the experience a lot, which gave her a real picture of how life back in time used to be and she understood stories behind events that happened back in time. That experience helped her appreciate history and made her feel proud about her culture. It helped change her opinion about visiting cultural heritage sites; Amy now sees that place differently, as the site is brought to life and not only a bunch of abandoned bricks.

The scenario was further analysed to pull out more detailed requirements (low-level requirements - LRs), which then led to develop features and services that better serve this context, which are illustrated in the Table 1.

These features and services were implemented in a working system with the aim of evaluating them with potential end-users to extract their perspective regarding using it in context. The next section presents the architecture and the main interfaces of SmartC.

Table 1. LRs with the adopted features and GRs they are belong to

GRs	LRs	Features
2	Delivering instant information regarding historical places when passing by	Receiving notifications on-the-move
1 & 3	Provide different information format to deliver historical information	Multi-mode information format (i.e. text, audio, video & images)
3	Adopt a feature that enables learners to immerse themselves in the experience and use their senses to experience the life back in time	Use augmented reality to show how sites appeared in the past
3	Allow learners to use wearable and immersive technologies at sites	Harnessing smart eye glasses
4	Handling the potential errors	Error and process messages

4   SmartC – Architecture and Interfaces

A smart and ubiquitous learning application prototype was developed, which is called SmartC. The aforementioned scenario guided the design of SmartC, which helped in developing features and services; this section presents the design and implementation of SmartC. SmartC is a native android app, which was designed for smartphones and to be used in outdoor cultural heritage settings. A Sony XPERIA android device was used throughout the design and implementation stage. Sony android smart eyeglasses were used in this research, which helped investigate how learners react to them in the field.

SmartC adopted context-aware technology with the use of location-based services (LBS) to provide historical information on-the-move, harnessing mobile and wearable technologies. The implemented version of SmartC was designed around a set of general requirements that were set out based on a framework for such services [17]. It is an informal learning environment which delivers contextual historical information to enhance learning from outdoor cultural heritage sites, also to support people to learn about sites while they are doing their daily routines. The contextual information is delivered through the mobile device's screen and smart eye glasses based on location in the form of notifications. The notification comes up when learners pass close to an attraction to draw their attention that there is an attraction nearby, which could interest them. Learners have an opportunity to access more information regarding that attraction when viewing the notification message. The smart eyeglasses help learners to engage their sight with the attractions and artefacts simultaneously with receiving information.

This app uses geo-fence technology, which is placing a virtual boundary around a geographical area. It works when a user enters or leaves the area, which is identified by latitude and longitude of the area [56]. For this app, a circle shape of a radius of 100 m was used to identify the geographical area of each involved attraction.

The mobile device gets triggered when a learner enters that virtual zone, which it is tracked using the GPS of the device. The device pushes a notification to alert the learner when he/she gets close to an attraction. Notifications are pushed via the app through the mobile-based interface and the glasses-based interface simultaneously when the mobile device gets triggered (see Fig. 1). It provides multimode information format to deliver the information. In addition, it utilises AR to show how attractions appeared in the past (see Figs. 2 and 3).

SmartC was evaluated in the field by potential end-users to capture users' perspective regarding using the app in the context. The evaluation study is presented in the next section.

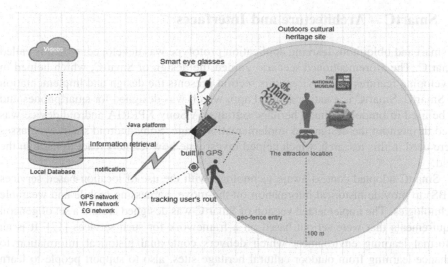

Fig. 1. Architecture of SmartC

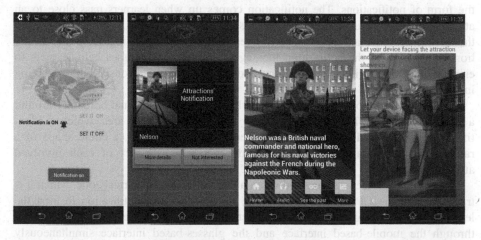

Fig. 2. Main screens of SmartC

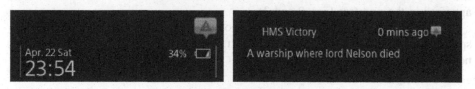

Fig. 3. Smart eye glasses interfaces

5   The User Study

A user study was conducted to evaluate the SmartC app that was designed to be used at outdoor cultural heritage sites. This study was carried out to obtain users' feedback regarding their experience in using the app, which, in turn, helps to capture usability issues. Consequently, it helps setting out design challenges for designing similar technologies.

5.1   Methods

Three research techniques were combined in this study, which are: questionnaire, observation and a brief group interview. Emails and social media were used to target participants who were recruited using the convenience sampling method. Permission to use the Historic Dockyard in Portsmouth, UK, as a proof-of-concept was obtained from the authorities of the site. Participants were asked to use the app while walking around. The app was given to them in Android devices alongside a sheet to describe how it works. A simple statistical analysis using SPSS was used to obtain the mean for the data.

5.2   Study Design

Four sessions were carried out at the Historic Dockyard between 10th and 12th October 2016 to conduct this study; each session lasted around 2 h; the tour and the discussion took around one hour each. This study used a combination of three techniques as it was mentioned: questionnaire, observation and group interview. The questionnaire technique involves different types of questions: scale of five, closed questions of two choices (yes/no) and open-ended questions. The questionnaire has three sections: usability evaluation, features rating, and overall acceptance.

Six categories, which were adopted from the ISO metric questionnaire, were involved in the usability section [57]. The categories include: suitability for learning, self-descriptiveness, controllability, conformity with user expectations, error tolerance, and learnability [58]. The category "suitability of individualisation" was omitted, as the related features to this category were not included in this version of the app for pragmatic reasons such as personalising the app is required users to create their own account to personalise it based on their preferences. Additionally, to have a better experience of such features, users would be required to use it for a few days, which was not feasible in this evaluation study, where a few sessions of two hours were dedicated. Each included category involves a set of statements that participants were asked to state to what extent they agree or disagree with. A Likert scale of five was used, where 1 = predominantly disagree and 5 = predominantly agree.

This study also gathered users' feedback regarding the usefulness of features. Features include: (1) The audio explanations; (2) The attraction's image within the notification's dialogue; (3) Receiving notifications based on the location; (4) The text explanations; (5) The attraction's image within the attraction's page; (6) The attraction's image within the audio page; (7) The historical/documentary videos; (8) Seeing how attractions looked in the past; (9) Take a photo; (10) Short messages giving

feedback about tasks process; (11) Error messages; (12) Receiving notifications on the glasses.

Participants were asked to rate these features on a scale of five, where 1 = useless and 5 = useful. Furthermore, participants were asked regarding their overall attitude towards this app.

To obtain more in-depth opinions regarding the experience in using the app, a brief group interview was held with participants after filling the questionnaire. Participants were asked about their experience using the app and to point out any challenges that they experienced, if any. In addition, they were asked if they have any suggestions for improving the app. Notes were taken by the researcher to document participants' answers.

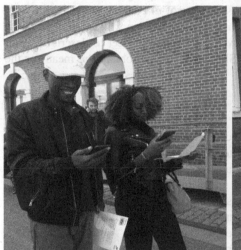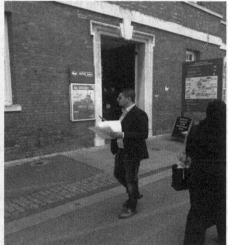

Fig. 4. Participants while using the SmartC app in the field

An observational technique was used to capture any problems or difficulties users might experience when using the app at outdoor settings. Although, filming was not allowed at the site due to the naval-base security issues, notes were taking during the tour (Fig. 4).

5.3 Participants

26 participants took part in this study; all of them were residents in the UK/Portsmouth; their age ranged between 20 and 71. Participants were 8 females and 18 males from different nationalities: Iraq, Britain, Germany, Iran, Sweden, Libya, Nigeria, Senegal, Jordan and Colombia. Their occupations were: 19 students, one engineer, one project manager, one unemployed, one teaching fellow and three retired.

5.4   Results

The usability evaluation study with users was carried out to highlight the weak and strong points of the app from the users' perspective. Due to the nature of the informal learning as there is no standard scheme for the assessment of informal learning [59], it could be difficult to measure the effectiveness of learning and to assess how much information users take back from the visit. However, suitability for learning was assessed within the usability section. The main scope for this evaluation study was to assess the interaction design, which contributes to the field of mobile human-computer interaction (HCI). The results of the three techniques are given below.

The results of the usability questionnaire reveal positive attitudes from participants regarding the usability aspects of the app. The average of each category ranged between 3.06 and 4.25, which indicates participants found it usable and easy to use (see Table 2).

Table 2. The usability results

The category	The average	The category	The average
Suitability for learning	3.94	Conformity with user expectations	3.84
Self-descriptiveness	4.05	Error tolerance	3.06
Controllability	3.71	Learnability	4.25

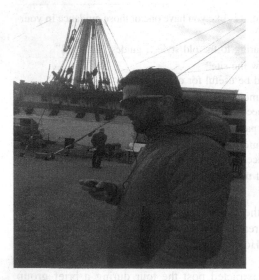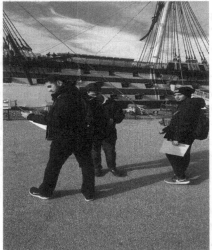

Fig. 5. Participants while using SmartC via smart eye glasses and mobile phones in the field

Alongside the evaluation of the interaction design, there was an assessment of how suitable the app was for learning. The results suggest the average of this category is 3.94 (see Table 2). This indicates SmartC is suitable for learning, which would

facilitate acquiring information at outdoor cultural heritage sites effectively. In this light, although the evaluation from a learning perspective was relatively in a small scale, SmartC would be considered as a useful tool for learning (Fig. 5).

Regarding the usefulness of the app, the results indicate that all features provided by the app are useful, as the mean ranges between 3.75 and 4.77. Participants liked receiving notifications based on location. Moreover, the results suggest that the audio explanation is the most popular information format amongst participants. Participants claimed that seeing attractions how they appeared in the past is very interesting and has a lot of potential. Three participants out of four reacted positively towards receiving notifications through the glasses and found it useful as it kept their hands free during the tour. One participant preferred to see the attractions with her own eyes instead of using the glasses; however, the device could be disabled when it is not needed. Participants highlighted some weaknesses in relation to the features of SmartC; some of these comments are given below:

"Lack of map, lack of direction, lack of [map] with direction of the attractions in historical time sequence"

"Hard to receive notification, simple design", "Volume of audios not high enough, little bit fiddly to see photo in past, not able to see the video after [leaving] attraction"

With respect to the overall acceptance, the vast majority of participants liked the app and stated they are happy to use it and recommend it to friends. Participants made some comments to illustrate their choice of why they would like to use the app. Some of these comments are given below:

"It provides flexibility of spreading knowledge, it is like you have one of those guidance in your pocket all the time"
"It is helpful, easier and lighter to use comparing to the old style… guides for [sites]"
It is a good idea especially if you don't know the site"
"Idea of the app is quite interesting. It would be useful for open area like dockyard"
"Having an app for android on my phone is more feasible when visiting such sites rather than using devices provided by the sites, which need a bit of time for learning how to use it"
"Because of the content and seeing it in the past gives a good [idea] to how it was"
"It is very user friendly, you get interesting information that you would not get it just walking around, save spending on tourist' audio devices"
"I find it very useful and useful save a bit of time if you are in heritage"

One comment suggested to not use the app as one participant put: "No, because usually I walk around the attractions and read about the detailed information given and take my time to understand the writing". However, he stated that he would recommend it to friends.

The participants' perspectives were extracted post the tour during a brief group interview, which helped to obtain in-depth insight regarding their experience in using the app in the field. Participants were very positive towards it and found it interesting and easy to use. However, they pointed out some challenges that they experienced during the tour, which include:

(1) keep receiving the same notification for the same attraction for a couple of times when passing nearby.
(2) Losing the current notification (i.e. when viewing a notification for a certain attraction and then move to another one, could not go back to the previous one).
(3) The old image in the "see it in the past" feature does not appear constantly as it is based on the location and it disappears once the device moves slightly.
(4) An internet connection was needed to play the video which was not very good at the Historic Dockyard.
(5) The audio did not stop when the participants used the back button of the device.

Several suggestions were given by participants to improve the app such as:

(1) Add directions to the attractions.
(2) Provide the distance to the attraction that users get notified about from their current location.
(3) Make it easier to see what is nearby through a map with all attractions.
(4) Provide alternatives to watch the video easily such as downloading.
(5) Facilitate accessing the information of the attractions they passed by whenever they want.
(6) Include public services in the notification service (e.g. cafes or toilets).
(7) Take the daytime (day or night) into consideration when designing an app as the sun spells make it harder to see the screen sometimes.
(8) Make the audio loud enough to be easily listened to within a group.
(9) Provide a list of the nearby attractions instead of receiving notifications based on the location as one participant put. The perspective behind this suggestion was users need to get close enough to an attraction to get notified which may lead to missing an attraction if not. However, support people to learn on-the-move while they are doing their daily activities is the main point of providing notifications based on location.

The observational technique was used to observe how participants interact with the app during the tour and they deal with challenges that might arise. Fortunately, the weather was nice most days, with only one session on a cold day, which was not expected and consequently participants were not well clothed. That affected the tour slightly as they were not very comfortable walking around in outdoor settings. Participants divided themselves spontaneously into groups. Some participants walked around individually listening to an audio explanation and finding out more about attractions on their own. Some others used the app in a group using one device, and there were some participants who walked around as a group but using the app individually. All the groups were walking around, having conversations regarding the attractions, helping each other with using the app and discussing some weaknesses and strengths of the app.

Participants interacted with SmartC using mobile devices and smart eye glasses. Two narrative scenarios are given below to show how it was used. The scenarios are based on the real experiences that two participants had while using the app – the used names are not the participants' real names. In these scenarios, two examples of the involved attractions are used to depict the context.

(a) Scenario I: Jane used mobile phone only:

Jane put the notification on and walked around with her mobile phone in her pocket. While walking, she sensed and heard a notification on her phone; she got the phone out of her pocket to find a notification regarding the lord Nelson's statue as shown in Fig. 2. She had two options, which are: ignoring the notification or accessing more details. Jane chose to access more details as she knew a little about this famous figure in Portsmouth and was interested to know more; then she was taken to the corresponding attraction's page. She pressed on the "Audio" button and listened to the explanation while walking. When the audio has finished, Jane seemed amazed about the information she was given. So, she got excited to see how the lord looked back in time and what he used to wear; she pressed on the "See in the past" button and followed the instruction on the screen until she was able to see the old picture of the figure. Although it was not very easy to obtain this picture, she kept trying until it appeared, which indicates she has a great interest to experience life back in time. Then she moved to see the video, which she found interesting and added more information to what she listened to. This stimulated a short discussion between her and a group of participants who were close; the discussion was regarding: (i) events they watched in the video; (ii) the feature itself (i.e. the video format). Also, they mentioned the other features as well (details are given later in this section).

(b) Scenario II: Hani used mobile phone and smart eyeglasses:

Hani initiated the app on the phone to start the journey. He put his phone in his pocket and the glasses on. At the beginning, Hani could not see the glasses' interface as it needed to be in a specific position to be able to see the interface. Eventually, he managed to see the main interface, but the text was not very clear as the sunlight affected the visibility. Hani walked around with the smart glasses. While walking, he noticed a notification on the top right side of the glasses' interface as shown in Fig. 3. Then he used the control pad to navigate through until he found the notification; however, Hani could not figure out how to use it easily. The notification was telling that the warship HMS Victory was close. He tapped on the control pad to access more details regarding the ship. The details were brief and just enough to draw his attention to the significance of the artefact, which he found interesting. He seemed satisfied as he was able to see the actual artifact through the glasses while reading the text on the glasses' screen. As he wanted to know more about it, Hani picked his mobile phone out to access more details (i.e. audio, video and see it in the past). Hani listened to the audio and used the "see it in the past" feature using his mobile phone as these are not available through the glasses in this version of SmartC. Nonetheless, he kept the glasses on while listening to the audio, which helped him associate the given information via the audio with the text on the glasses while looking at the ship. Whilst listening to the audio with the glasses on went smoothly, it seemed he had difficulty seeing the old picture of the ship; he needed take the glasses off to see the picture clearly as the transition between the two devices was not as smooth as he expected. He though the transition between the devices will be done automatically based on which device is active at that time, which was not the case. After Hani had enough information regarding the artefact, he had the glasses on again and placed his mobile phone

back in his pocket; he enjoyed walking around and receiving notifications for the other attractions and artefacts via the glasses and only picked his mobile phone out when he needed to access more details.

The aforementioned scenarios show that SmartC is controlled mainly by the mobile phone. The role of smart eyeglasses in this version of SmartC is as a second screen to show visitors notifications and brief details regarding attractions and artifacts. This would help visitors have preliminary ideas regarding the attractions nearby, which would be enough to help them make a decision to access more details or not, before taking their mobile phone out. The two devices support each other to provide an easy and useful experience. The received notification is available in both devices simultaneously, but the glasses support the visitors' experience of sites without carrying their phones all the time; they do not need to take their mobile phone out their pocket if the received information is not very interesting for them. Hence, we could conclude that the devices support each other in terms of the usefulness and comfort of using the app, as the mobile phone provides more information (useful), and the glasses free visitors' hands while walking (comfort). However, this version of the glasses has a control pad that visitors needed to carry in their hands to control the glasses' interface. A newer version of smart glasses would free their hand completely.

It was noticed that participants were comfortable in using the app and navigating through and managed to use almost all the features easily. It is also true that participants who were walking in groups collaborated to find attractions and helped each other use the app and overcome challenges and interacted with their surroundings more often than those who walked alone. Interestingly, it was noticed that some participants walked away from the group when they discovered something interesting, to focus on the experience and find out more about a particular aspect of the attraction, and they rejoin the group to have a conversation regarding what they found interesting. Additionally, participants showed more tolerance to error and challenges while with groups than those who walked individually. It was also noticed that participants who were always in a group, spent more time to finish the tour than those who experienced it individually. This may be due to the participants in the group setting enjoying socialising at the same time as experiencing the cultural heritage attractions; they took advantage of the 'take picture' feature to mark their experience, whereas those who were most of the time experiencing the site individually seemed to mostly enjoy being outdoors alongside feeling the place and constructing their own experience.

Most participants liked receiving notifications based on their current location; also, they liked the content especially in an audio format, which they found very useful. The service of "see it in the past" drew participants' attention and helped participants to engage with the attractions and to find out more information about them. Participants did not spend a considerable amount of time reading the texts on the screen, instead they played the audio to listen and walk. It was noticed that participants did not manage to find some attractions easily, for instance, they received a notification regarding HMS M.33 while they were near Nelson's statue, which they could not see, as HMS victory was blocking the sight. However, they emphasised that the provided picture on the app that illustrates how the attraction looks like helped them to find it. It was also noticed that the app did not work properly through some participants' own devices, which was because some required resources on the device were not enabled, such as

camera and location-based services. In addition, several challenges were noticed during the tour:

(1) Wi-Fi, GPS and 3G did not work properly which affected the performance of the app slightly and that was due to many radars around, as it is a naval-base site. Consequently, the notifications were sometimes hard to receive which needed to re-start the notification (switch it off and switch it on again).

(2) Video did not play for a couple of times at some points, for the same previous reason, which needed participants to move their location slightly to be able to obtain a good signal to play the video.

(3) The surrounding environment included challenges such as: daytime (day or night), weather (sunny or rainy), and noise. All these matters could also affect the users' experience, which are needed to be considered in designing such services.

(4) Visitors' level of familiarity with technology could affect the experience. Some participants were less familiar in using mobile devices in general, which made the use of the app slightly harder.

(5) The technical differences in operating systems of the android devices, as some devices show a good quality in picking locations more than the others. In addition, some explanation messages did not appear on some devices which made it challenging for some participants to figure out how some services work.

Overall, the results of both techniques, the interview and the observation, are consistent which gives a level of confirmation of the findings.

6 Design Challenges – Discussion

The user study presented in this paper helped in identifying issues and challenges in designing such services, which would help designers who are working in this field.

Participants, in general, found the app useful and easy to use and with a lot of potential for facilitating acquiring historical information on-the-move. In addition, the results indicate the app is suitable for learning. The results suggest that learners/visitors of cultural heritage sites enjoy the visit and the learning experience in groups as they can have a conversation regarding attractions and enjoy being outdoor with friends and family that clearly support social and collaborative learning. Additionally, the results show that participants were able to switch between different types of learning (individually and collaboratively) easily whenever they needed. They enjoyed being able to walk away from the group to further explore interesting aspects and return to the group to share the experience. This shows that technology would support both learning types and facilitate switching between them seamlessly.

Although the results suggest that SmartC is easy to use, some challenges and issues were identified in the study, which could be categorised into: (a) interaction design related, (b) wearable computing related, (c) surrounding environment related, (d) user related, and (e) technical issues related; details are given below.

6.1   Interaction Design Related

Some issues within the interaction design need to be considered to make the experience better using the mobile device.

(a) The messages (error and feedback) need to be more obvious (e.g. keep it for longer, make it brighter, or make it in the middle of the screen);
(b) The audio should stop when leaving the page using any means (the app standard button or the device standard button);
(c) The volume of the audio and video need to be loud enough to be heard within a group; however, a headset splitter could be used to overcome this issue;
(d) The augmented reality view (i.e. the image that illustrates how an attraction appeared in the past) in the "see it in the past" feature needs to be less faded and should be displayed for longer, even when changing the direction of the device slightly, to be easily seen.

6.2   Wearable Computing Related

Some issues were captured in using the wearable computing i.e. the smart eyeglasses, should be considered, which are limited in this version to:

(a) The transition between the glasses and the mobile devices, which is needed to be done smoothly.
(b) The usability aspect in terms of switching it off when it is not needed as it was challenging during the study.
(c) The visibility of the text on the wearable devices' screen is challenging on a bright day, which needs to consider the adopted shades or colours.
(d) The version and the brand of the utilised device (e.g. Sony smart glasses) needs to be chosen carefully to better serve the design of such services.

6.3   Surrounding Environment Related

The issues related to the surroundings include: daytime (day or night), weather (sunny, rainy or windy), the level of noise and the level of busyness of the heritage site. All these matters could also affect the experience, which could be addressed by providing different themes (i.e. colours) for day and night, and different modes for busy and quiet time.

6.4   Learner Related

User related issues include visitors' level of familiarity with technology and preferences, which could obstruct the experience. The results revealed that the level of familiarity with the mobile devices could be an issue in this context as it might make the use of the app challenging. In addition, users' preferences might cause them to not use the provided services if they do not meet their needs.

6.5   Context of Use

The results suggest that learners would like to use mobile devices to learn at sites in different context, which include:

(a) Individually and in-group: this study showed that participants like to learn in-group as it helped them to socialise and at the same time to share knowledge with others. In addition, they like being on their own as this helped in spending as much time as they wanted to explore sites. In short, learning in groups promotes a sense of community, but learning individually allows the learner to craft his/her own experience, both types of learning were seen in the evaluation study.
(b) On-site and off-site: results indicate visitors of sites enjoy walking around at sites and acquiring information in the context. Additionally, the results revealed that visitors of cultural heritage sites would like to have access to the acquired information not only in-site but off-site too, which would enable them to review the experience they had.

6.6   Technical Issues

Some technical issues came up during the study, as it was mentioned earlier, which include: (a) receiving the same notification more than once, (b) poor network signal which makes it hard to play a video or even receiving a notification, (c) android devices differences in terms of operating system, as some devices showed good quality in receiving notifications, and others showed poor quality in displaying some messages.

7   Implications Related to Study Settings

The setting of this empirical evaluation study involved several aspects that needed to be considered to make the contexts of use (the context in which the service will be evaluated) as ideal as possible in terms of setting the venue of the study.

In setting the venue, several aspects needed to be considered, such as: the weather as it is for outdoor settings; the size of the site in terms of the area and the number of attractions included, as it should have several attractions which are needed to be relatively close to each other to make it easier for participants to have the tour, but not too close that might affect the experience, i.e. receiving notifications. Additionally, in terms of the area, it needed to not be too large, just big enough for participants of all ages to have a proper tour at the site to visit all involved attractions comfortably in a short period of time. The Historic Dockyard was chosen, which has several attractions in outdoor settings that are relatively close to each other but not too close to affect receiving notifications. This choice also served the type of participation the evaluation studies adopted, which were organised groups and individuals.

Conducting a field study in the outdoor setting experienced some challenges such as the weather – as mentioned earlier, as there was a slight disruption due to unexpected weather conditions in one session, it was relatively cold, and participants were not prepared for such weather as it was not meant to be as cold in October in Portsmouth. However, the tour was enough to draw a conclusion regarding using the app. This

limitation was addressed by taking advantage of cafes and seating areas with shelters to take refuge and discuss the experience amongst participants for a while.

Based on the discussion so far, choosing a site that is suitable for such empirical studies in the field is relatively subjective to a number of aspects such as: (a) the type of participants targeted, as if the targeted sample is elderly or children the criteria is different than adults who are willing to walk around a big site in a short period of time; (b) the duration dedicated for the study as dedicating two hours for a session is different than a day per session; (c) the type of participation, having an organised tour with a group of participants led by the researcher is different than individual session with the researcher, and this also is different than participants having a tour independently on their own based on their convenience. The first type is constrained by the time participants are willing to dedicate to the study as a whole, as they need to be all at the venue at a certain time and finish at a certain time; a group interview post-visit with all participants took part in each session to collect feedback. The second type is conducting individual sessions, which is slightly different from the first one, as it needs only to be convenient to one participant whilst the first one should be convenient to all participants taking part. In relation to the third one, where participation is not constrained to a number of hours but instead it is open to their time and preferences, this type is not necessarily to be in groups as often, and allows individuals to break from the group as needed; in this case, the venue could be in a spread area and the participants could choose a convenient time and which part of the tour they want to have based on their preferences. This type could be an excellent option for evaluating aspects such as personalisation as participants could create their own account and use the service for a few days to have the full experience to give useful feedback. The first type of participation was adopted in the study reported in this paper.

8 Conclusions

We have presented an evaluation study of SmartC, a mobile and wearable system for learning at outdoor cultural heritage sites. A scenario-based design method was used to depict the context of use to offer a useful insight for guiding the design of SmartC. SmartC was evaluated by end-users, in the field, which was conducted with 26 participants with the aim of capturing issues, and challenges that might occur when using a mobile application prototype at outdoor cultural heritage sites.

SmartC is a smart and ubiquitous learning prototype utilising mobile and wearable computing. It was designed to contribute to enhance the informal learning experience at outdoor cultural heritage sites. Smart eyeglasses were used to capture the users' perspective regarding using wearable computing, smart eyeglasses in particular. The results reveal that users liked the app and emphasised it was user-friendly and easy to use. In addition, the results indicate that there is a potential for using smart eyeglasses at sites as they are unobtrusive devices, which could be worn and taken off very easily.

Several issues were identified, which could be categorised as: (1) interaction design related; (2) wearable computing related; (3) surroundings and environment related; (4) learner related; (5) context of use; and (6) technical issues.

Several aspects were identified that need to be considered in setting such empirical studies, which would help researchers in setting a venue for such field studies.

There is an area that we envision to carry out further work, which is developing design recommendations for helping designers in designing such services.

References

1. Nuryanti, W.: Heritage and postmodern tourism. Ann. Tour. Res. **23**(2), 249–260 (1996)
2. González, M.V.: Intangible heritage tourism and identity. Tour. Manag. **29**(4), 807–810 (2008)
3. Angelaccio, M., et al.: Smart and mobile access to cultural heritage resources: a case study on ancient italian renaissance villas. In: 2012 IEEE 21st International Workshop on Enabling Technologies: Infrastructure for Collaborative Enterprises (WETICE). IEEE (2012)
4. Bellotti, F., et al.: Designing cultural heritage contents for serious virtual worlds. In: 2009 15th International Conference on Virtual Systems and Multimedia, VSMM 2009. IEEE (2009)
5. Berndt, E., Carlos, J.: Cultural heritage in the mature era of computer graphics. IEEE Comput. Graph. Appl. **20**(1), 36–37 (2000)
6. McGookin, D., et al.: Exploring seasonality in mobile cultural heritage. In: Proceedings of the 2017 CHI Conference on Human Factors in Computing Systems. ACM (2017)
7. Casella, G., Coelho, M.: Augmented heritage: situating augmented reality mobile apps in cultural heritage communication. In: Proceedings of the 2013 International Conference on Information Systems and Design of Communication. ACM (2013)
8. Silberberg, T.: Cultural tourism and business opportunities for museums and heritage sites. Tour. Manag. **16**(5), 361–365 (1995)
9. Alkhafaji, A., Fallahkhair, S., Cocea, M., Crellin, J.: A survey study to gather requirements for designing a mobile service to enhance learning from cultural heritage. In: Verbert, K., Sharples, M., Klobučar, T. (eds.) EC-TEL 2016. LNCS, vol. 9891, pp. 547–550. Springer, Cham (2016). https://doi.org/10.1007/978-3-319-45153-4_60
10. Prentice, R.: Experiential cultural tourism: museums & the marketing of the new romanticism of evoked authenticity. Mus. Manag. Curatorship **19**(1), 5–26 (2001)
11. Alkhafaji, A., Fallahkhair, S., Cocea, M.: Towards gathering initial requirements of developing a mobile service to support informal learning at cultural heritage sites. In: Cognition and Exploratory Learning in the Digital Age (CELDA 2015), p. 51 (2015)
12. Koren, I., Klamma, R.: Smart ambient learning with physical artifacts using wearable technologies. In: Intelligent Environments (Workshops) (2015)
13. Suriyakul, W., Vavoula, G.: Mobile family learning in the science museum. In: mLearn 2017, Lamaca, Cyprus (2017)
14. Vavoula, G., et al.: Myartspace: design and evaluation of support for learning with multimedia phones between classrooms and museums. Comput. Educ. **53**(2), 286–299 (2009)
15. Weiser, M.: The computer for the 21st century. Sci. Am. **265**(3), 94–104 (1991)
16. BBC. British Museum offers virtual reality tour of Bronze Age, 4 August 2015. http://www.bbc.co.uk/news/technology-33772694
17. Alkhafaji, A.: The development of a theoretical framework for designing smart and ubiquitous learning environments for outdoor cultural heritage. School of Computing, Portsmouth (2018)

18. UNESCO, Managing Cultural Wold Heritage. The United Nations Educational, Scientific and Cultural Organization (UNESCO), Paris (2013)
19. Du Cros, H.: A new model to assist in planning for sustainable cultural heritage tourism. Int. J. Tour. Res. **3**(2), 165–170 (2001)
20. Soloway, E., Guzdial, M., Hay, K.E.: Learner-centered design: the challenge for HCI in the 21st century. Interactions **1**(2), 36–48 (1994)
21. Winters, N., Price, S.: Mobile HCI and the learning context: an exploration. In: Proceedings of Context in Mobile HCI Workshop at MobileHCI 2005 (2005)
22. Carroll, J.M.: Making Use: Scenario-Based Design of Human-Computer Interactions. MIT Press, Cambridge (2000)
23. Dourish, P.: What we talk about when we talk about context. Pers. Ubiquit. Comput. **8**(1), 19–30 (2004)
24. Dingler, T., Bagg, T., Grau, Y., Henze, N., Schmidt, A.: *uCanvas*: a web framework for spontaneous smartphone interaction with ubiquitous displays. In: Abascal, J., Barbosa, S., Fetter, M., Gross, T., Palanque, P., Winckler, M. (eds.) INTERACT 2015. LNCS, vol. 9298, pp. 402–409. Springer, Cham (2015). https://doi.org/10.1007/978-3-319-22698-9_27
25. Candello, H.: Multimedia information delivery on mobile cultural applications. In: Stephanidis, C., Antona, M. (eds.) UAHCI 2013. LNCS, vol. 8011, pp. 583–592. Springer, Heidelberg (2013). https://doi.org/10.1007/978-3-642-39194-1_67
26. Suh, Y., Shin, C., Woo, W.: A mobile phone guide: spatial, personal, and social experience for cultural heritage. IEEE Trans. Consum. Electron. **55**(4), 2356–2364 (2009)
27. van Aart, C., Wielinga, B., van Hage, W.R.: Mobile cultural heritage guide: location-aware semantic search. In: Cimiano, P., Pinto, H.Sofia (eds.) EKAW 2010. LNCS (LNAI), vol. 6317, pp. 257–271. Springer, Heidelberg (2010). https://doi.org/10.1007/978-3-642-16438-5_18
28. Chianese, A., Piccialli, F., Valente, I.: Smart environments and cultural heritage: a novel approach to create intelligent cultural spaces. J. Locat. Serv. **9**(3), 209–234 (2015)
29. Schlatter, B.E., Hurd, A.R.: Geocaching: 21st-century hide-and-seek. J. Phys. Educ. Recreat. Dance **76**(7), 28–32 (2005)
30. Gray, H.R.: Geo-caching: place-based discovery of virginia state parks and museums. J. Mus. Educ. **32**(3), 285–291 (2007)
31. Tussyadiah, I.P., Zach, F.J.: The role of geo-based technology in place experiences. Ann. Tour. Res. **39**(2), 780–800 (2012)
32. Pongpaichet, S., et al.: Situation fencing: making geo-fencing personal and dynamic (2013)
33. Clough, G.: Geolearners: location-based informal learning with mobile and social technologies. IEEE Trans. Learn. Technol. **3**(1), 33–44 (2010)
34. Mendes, R.N., Rodrigues, T., Rodrigues, A.: Urban geo-caching. What happened in Lisbon during the last decade. In: International Archives of the Photogrammetry, Remote Sensing and Spatial Information Sciences, pp. 29–31 (2013)
35. Benford, S., et al.: Can you see me now? ACM Trans. Comput.-Hum. Interact. (TOCHI) **13**(1), 100–133 (2006)
36. O'Hara, K.: Understanding geocaching practices and motivations. In: Proceedings of the SIGCHI Conference on Human Factors in Computing Systems. ACM (2008)
37. Damala, A., et al.: Bridging the gap between the digital and the physical: design and evaluation of a mobile augmented reality guide for the museum visit. In: Proceedings of the 3rd International Conference on Digital Interactive Media in Entertainment and Arts. ACM (2008)
38. Fritz, F., Susperregui, A., Linaza, M.: Enhancing cultural tourism experiences with augmented reality technologies. In: The 6th International Symposium on Virtual Reality, Archaeology and Cultural Heritage VAST (2005)

39. Chang, Y.-L., et al.: Apply an augmented reality in a mobile guidance to increase sense of place for heritage places. J. Educ. Technol. Soc. **18**(2), 166–178 (2015)
40. Zoellner, M., et al.: An augmented reality presentation system for remote cultural heritage sites. In: Proceedings of the 10th International Symposium on Virtual Reality, Archaeology and Cultural Heritage VAST. Citeseer (2009)
41. Haugstvedt, A.-C., Krogstie, J.: Mobile augmented reality for cultural heritage: a technology acceptance study. In: 2012 IEEE International Symposium on Mixed and Augmented Reality (ISMAR). IEEE (2012)
42. Vlahakis, V., et al.: Archeoguide: first results of an augmented reality, mobile computing system in cultural heritage sites. In: Virtual Reality, Archaeology, and Cultural Heritage (2001)
43. Liarokapis, F., Mountain, D.: A mobile framework for tourist guides. In: Workshop on Virtual Museums, Proceedings of the 8th International Symposium on Virtual Reality, Archaeology and Cultural Heritage (VAST 2007), Eurographics, Brighton, UK (2007)
44. Takacs, G., et al.: Outdoors augmented reality on mobile phone using loxel-based visual feature organization. In: Proceedings of the 1st ACM International Conference on Multimedia Information Retrieval. ACM (2008)
45. Caggianese, G., Neroni, P., Gallo, L.: Natural interaction and wearable augmented reality for the enjoyment of the cultural heritage in outdoor conditions. In: De Paolis, L.T., Mongelli, A. (eds.) AVR 2014. LNCS, vol. 8853, pp. 267–282. Springer, Cham (2014). https://doi.org/10.1007/978-3-319-13969-2_20
46. Feiner, S., et al.: A touring machine: prototyping 3D mobile augmented reality systems for exploring the urban environment. Pers. Technol. **1**(4), 208–217 (1997)
47. Sparacino, F.: The museum wearable: real-time sensor-driven understanding of visitors' interests for personalized visually-augmented museum experiences (2002)
48. Leue, M.C., Jung, T., tom Dieck, D.: Google glass augmented reality: generic learning outcomes for art galleries. In: Tussyadiah, I., Inversini, A. (eds.) Information and Communication Technologies in Tourism 2015, pp. 463–476. Springer, Cham (2015). https://doi.org/10.1007/978-3-319-14343-9_34
49. Höllerer, T., et al.: Exploring MARS: developing indoor and outdoor user interfaces to a mobile augmented reality system. Comput. Graph. **23**(6), 779–785 (1999)
50. Hall, T., Bannon, L.: Designing ubiquitous computing to enhance children's learning in museums. J. Comput. Assist. Learn. **22**(4), 231–243 (2006)
51. Sung, Y.T., et al.: Mobile guide system using problem-solving strategy for museum learning: a sequential learning behavioural pattern analysis. J. Comput. Assist. Learn. **26**(2), 106–115 (2010)
52. Betsworth, L., et al.: Performative technologies for heritage site regeneration. Pers. Ubiquit. Comput. **18**(7), 1631–1650 (2014)
53. Andreoli, R., et al.: A framework to design, develop, and evaluate immersive and collaborative serious games in cultural heritage. J. Comput. Cult. Herit. (JOCCH) **11**(1), 4 (2017)
54. Poria, Y., Butler, R., Airey, D.: Links between tourists, heritage, and reasons for visiting heritage sites. J. Travel Res. **43**(1), 19–28 (2004)
55. Carroll, J.M., et al.: Requirements development in scenario-based design. IEEE Trans. Softw. Eng. **24**(12), 1156–1170 (1998)
56. Rodriguez Garzon, S., Deva, B.: Geofencing 2.0: taking location-based notifications to the next level. In: Proceedings of the 2014 ACM International Joint Conference on Pervasive and Ubiquitous Computing. ACM (2014)

57. Gediga, G., Hamborg, K.-C., Düntsch, I.: The IsoMetrics usability inventory: an operationalization of ISO 9241-10 supporting summative and formative evaluation of software systems. Behav. Inf. Technol. **18**(3), 151–164 (1999)
58. Fallahkhair, S.: Development of a cross platform support system or language learners via interactive television and mobile phone, Brighton (2009)
59. Skule, S.: Learning conditions at work: a framework to understand and assess informal learning in the workplace. Int. J. Train. Dev. **8**(1), 8–20 (2004)

Instant Rephotography

Juliano Franz(✉), Anderson Maciel, and Luciana Nedel

Institute of Informatics, Federal University of Rio Grande do Sul (UFRGS),
Porto Alegre, Brazil
{jmfranz,amaciel,nedel}@inf.ufrgs.br

Abstract. When traveling, a very common issue is to ask for the help of a stranger to take a photo on a touristic spot. Indeed, often the results of this short collaboration are not as previously imagined. In this paper, we introduce the concept of *instant rephotography*, a technique based on a simple and intuitive user interface, and in an efficient and low cost algorithm that finds the matching between two images. The user interface guides the photographer to position the camera in the right place that was once imagined by the camera owner, automatically taking the new photo. To correctly choose the new photo, we propose an algorithm based on ORB (Oriented FAST and Rotated BRIEF) feature points acquired from the reference and current photos, and on inertial sensors embedded in the photo device, a smartphone. To validate the concepts introduced, we implemented an Android App called Smart-Tourist Camera, conceived to help tourists to take good pictures during travels. Three different user studies involving 124 volunteers were conducted and results have shown that the photographs taken with the application are perceived as better than otherwise, and that users would use the App during their travels.

Keywords: Computer photography · Sensors fusion · Rephotography

1 Introduction

Rephotography is the act of recreating a photograph in the same site with a time span between the two images [2]. Images created in that matter are usually taken from the same point of view and with the same framing as a reference image made in the past. Examples include a series of "Then & Now" books that show two views of the same sites in a big city around a century apart [13] and are being used for historical purposes.

In this paper, we contribute in computational photography with the introduction of a novel rephotography approach. We motivate our work around the travel photography problem, a scenario where a typical tourist needs help from a stranger to take a picture of him/herself. Using the conventional approach, the outcome is rarely as good as expected. There are several reasons for that. Most people are in a hurry and, when someone asks them for this favor, they

© IFIP International Federation for Information Processing 2019
Published by Springer Nature Switzerland AG 2019
D. Lamas et al. (Eds.): INTERACT 2019, LNCS 11748, pp. 208–227, 2019.
https://doi.org/10.1007/978-3-030-29387-1_12

often try to do it as quickly as possible. Others have time but might not have the skills to correctly frame a photo. Those that know what they are doing are uncommon, and still, that does not mean the result will be satisfying because people just think differently. Furthermore, even the ones that find a stranger with time and skill to help them, might not be able to explain what he or she wants due to language barriers. In this context, however, our assumption is that if the vantage point, lens coverage and composition could be fixed in some way, all the stranger would have to do is to press the shutter button.

More specifically the approach proposed in this work focus on trying to solve a common scenario in travel photography: *a person (tourist) wants its photo taken at a touristic place according to a specific framing, i.e. camera's yaw angle, point of origin and orientation, however, s/he needs to rely on another person (stranger) to operate the camera thus relinquishing control over the camera parameters.* STC focus on bringing back the control over the framing of the camera back to the camera owner by allowing s/he to set a frame of reference (or picture of reference) which will be used by the application to guide the stranger before capturing the photograph. STC enables the tourist to pre-frame the picture that s/he wants to be part of without the need to explain it to the stranger. By doing this, it minimizes, if not discards, external interference on how the image should look. STC also makes it easier for the stranger to participate in the transaction because s/he does not need to think about picture quality as all the stranger has to do is follow simple on-screen instructions of translation and rotation which are guiding the camera towards the pre-set reference.

Having in mind that rephotography techniques are used to illustrate such "then and now" situations, in this paper we introduce the concept of *instant rephotography*, and present a fast method to help users to recreate an image made just a few seconds earlier. Differently from the common uses of rephotography, in this case, the focus application is casual and the techniques used should provide a transparent and easy to use user interface. This implies, as well, in providing a very fast algorithm to detect the correct camera position and orientation. Figure 1 illustrates the ideas behind *instant rephotography*.

The main contributions of this work are:

- An efficient and power-friendly algorithm to measure the distance between two photos and to guide the photographer to correctly position the camera
- A clear and intuitive user interface that can be operated by anyone without any instruction
- The Smart-Tourist Camera (STC), an Android App that allows instant rephotography using a smartphone

The remainder of this paper is organized as follows. The next section presents previous related work. Section 3 introduces the instant rephotography technique and gives details about its implementation. Section 4 describes the three user experiments we conducted to verify the system effectiveness and acceptability, and discusses the results achieved. Finally, we discuss our findings an implications in Sect. 5 and Sect. 6 concludes this work and presents directions for future work.

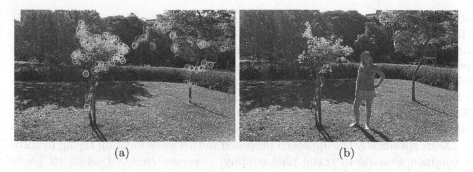

(a)   (b)

Fig. 1. The tourist makes a photo with the tree (a) exactly as she wants. Then, she hands the camera to somebody else, asking the other person to take a picture of himself in the same landscape. The algorithm detects keypoints (red circles) in the original picture (a); the user interface guides the photographer to place and point the camera in the suitable position and orientation; and a new photo is automatically taken when the desired pose is reached (b). (Color figure online)

2   Related Work and Background

Authors have discussed that rephotography techniques are important due to the fact that they can be used to study the evolution of locations, buildings and architectural proprieties over time. However, as discussed by Lee et al. [10], recreating a photograph is a challenging task because in order to recreate a viewpoint one needs to fix six degrees of freedom. Lee et al. propose that, because of such challenge, rephotography should be done off-site in post processing. In their work they combine a series of new images from different angles with a 3D point cloud and depth map of the location. The data is then paired with the reference photograph in order to recreate the photograph by combining the new images to be as similar as possible to the reference.

Shingu et al. [19] propose another technique to help users recreating a previous viewpoint. In their work, they make use of an augmented reality system to properly repeat a photography. ARToolkit markers are placed in the scene to extract information of the camera position and orientation in the real world. With that information they render a visual marker on the camera screen indicating to the user where he should place the camera in order to recreate the previous viewpoint.

Real time rephotography algorithms have also been explored before [2]. Bae et al. introduced a solution to recreate photographs from the past using a reference photograph and image processing techniques *in loco*. In their work, they have shown that it is not possible to recreate a photograph relying only on naive composition, i.e. trying to recompose an image just by looking at the old one. According to them, there is a need for computational assistance. Their approach, however, required a time costly calibration phase, as well as the use of a computer attached to the camera to handle the image processing. The entire process limits the user freedom and requires around thirty minutes to recreate a

single photograph which is unacceptable in many situations, such as the travel photography scenario.

Similar techniques that are used for rephotography were used by Vazquez and Steinfeld [20] to help vision impaired persons to take better street photographs to document issues in the city. They suggest a technique for smartphones that tries to help the user to fix camera roll and extracts region of interest areas from the image, in real time, helping the user to move the camera to keep them properly framed. On the same topic, Balata et al. [3] also proposed a smartphone based guidance tool to assist vision impaired people to take better composed photos. In their work, they introduce two photographic guiding techniques (central and golden-ratio) and two methods for guiding users: voice and vibration. They found no statistical difference between the performance of blind folded participants however self-reported comfort with voice guide was higher than with vibration.

Wang et al. [21] proposes a technique analogous to ours: a smart camera application used to suggest where the tourist should stay in the picture for a better composed final image. They use image segmentation and photographic rules to analyse a reference photo. The result from segmentation is used to render a shadow in the camera live-view which then indicates where is the ideal standing position for the person who wants to appear in the photo to stand at. The photographer uses the shadow to guide the subject to its location. Rawat et al. [16] also discuss a smart camera application to aid users in taking better composed using machine learning feedback. They use a collection of geo-tagged photos from public sources to train the guidance algorithm. Users of their method can then use their assistance method based on their current location in the world. The system calculates a score regarding the aesthetics of the image and guides the user to maximize the score.

HCI researchers also explored how camera applications in modern smart-phones can create the opportunity for collaborative photo-taking. Jarusriboon-chai et al. [8] designed and evaluated a camera application that is shared across two mobile devices. They explore two collaborative ways of taking photographs: first using one device and sharing it between two participants and second, using two devices with different functions one as the trigger and the other one as the viewfinder. They found that both techniques increased collaboration when compared to a baseline with no sharing (two separate independent devices) while the second method proved to further increase interaction between participants. James and Ünlüer [22] also explored collaborative photography but in a manner closer to what our work proposes: bringing strangers together to create an image. One stranger is the subject—or the person who ask for help—and the other one is the photographer—or the person who is willing to help. They developed an application that can notify nearby users with the app installed, using embedded geo-location, that someone needs help to have their photo taken.

One challenge that researchers had until a few years ago to properly develop real time rephotography solutions was the fact that was almost impossible to deploy algorithms into cameras available in the market. This problem was broadly discussed by Levoy [11]. With a smarphone's camera and processor

improvement in the past few years it became easier to test new techniques outside laboratory environment. An alternative to smartphones is the Frankencamera proposed by Adams et al. [1] which can be assembled using off-the-shelf components found in electronics stores.

The implementation of instant rephotography requires the identification of feature points and then, the re-orientation of the camera to match the desired frame. While the identification of feature points is based on computer vision algorithms, the re-orientation of the camera can be achieved by tracking the movements of the camera.

Feature detectors and extractors are used since the beginning of computer vision. In the context of rephotography, detectors can be used to analyze a reference photo and to detect features to be used as cues to frame a new image. Scale-Invariant Feature Transform (SIFT) [12] is an algorithm to detect and describe local features in images which is largely used mainly because it is capable of finding keypoints that are invariant to location, scale and rotation. Mikolajczyk and Schmid [14] tested SIFT against other descriptor methods including the author's method. SIFT outperformed most of the algorithms tested.

Another common feature descriptor is the Speeded Up Robust Features (SURF) [4], which is partially based on SIFT. SURF is several times faster and more accurate then SIFT. However, both SIFT and SURF are not intended for use in mobile applications because of their high computational cost [18,24].

A better algorithm for mobile devices is the Oriented FAST and Rotated BRIEF (ORB) introduced by Rublee et al. [18]. ORB is a fusion of FAST (Features from Accelerated Segment Test) keypoint detector [17] and BRIEF (Binary Robust Independent Elementary Features) descriptor [5] with many modifications to enhance the performance, and is an interesting alternative for both SIFT and SURF. Because ORB is more adapted to the limited capability of mobile devices it was chosen as the base algorithm for our work.

3   Smart-Tourist Camera

Our approach for instantaneous rephotography can be better understood when described in the scenario of tourist photography. In this section we illustrate our technique and its materialization into the Smart-Tourist Camera (STC) application for Android smartphones. As mentioned before, STC aims to solve the problem that occurs when someone needs the assistance of a third party to take photographs for them, a very common situation when the tourist wants to be part of the photography (see Fig. 1). Nevertheless, the approach can be generalized for a diversity of applications, such as crime-scene reconstruction, augmented reality systems, analysis of construction sites, etc. The software was designed based on three guiding principles:

1. It has be simple to use
2. It should have a easy to learn interface
3. It has to complete the task in a short period of time

3.1   System Overview

The STC main objective is to avoid the need for the stranger to think on how the photography should be framed thus minimizing mistakes. By doing so the software take most of the responsibility away from the stranger.

STC consists of an application that can be deployed on any smartphone or even embedded in modern compact cameras. The minimum requirement is that they have an inertial measurement unit (IMU) with at least 6 degrees of freedom (DOF) and computational power to run computer vision algorithms. The prototype developed in this work was implemented on an Android mobile phone.

The software works by using a reference photo and a frame of reference that was set by the camera owner. Once the owner sets the reference frame, the phone can be delivered to anyone in the crowd and all this person has to do is to follow the on-screen instructions.

The application works as follows: first the tourist goes where s/he wants the camera to be, and takes a reference photo from the scene. Then, s/he delivers the camera to the third-party, here called a user. The user then points the camera towards the scene and follows the on-screen instructions. Once the camera detects that it is close enough to the reference photo it automatically takes a series of photos. The application cycle is represented in Fig. 2.

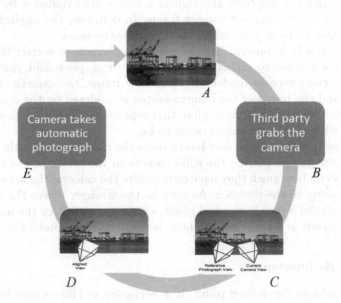

Fig. 2. Application pipeline: User takes a reference photograph (A); stranger assumes control of the application (B); stranger follows the on-screen instructions (C); application detects that the current view is similar to the reference photo (D); instant rephotography is created (E).

3.2 User Interface

A successful, and thus fast, interaction with the application is only possible if the UI is simple enough to be used by someone with no previous training. This work differs from the one proposed by Bae et al. [2] specially on the interface. Their work presented a complex interface that required time to use and learn, while our own has a simple interface that requires no more then 30 s to learn.

The user interface was designed to be as simple as possible and is divided in two different screens: the owner's and the stranger's interface.

The owner's interface is used to set the reference photo and has only two interface elements: the current camera view, and a button to take the photo, as regularly seen in other smartphone camera apps (see Fig. 3a). To set the reference image, the owner has only to point the lens to the desired target and hit the button. This interaction is the same of any point-and-shoot camera.

The stranger's interface (see Fig. 3b, c and d) is more critical. It has to be easy enough for someone to understand it within a few seconds. Have in mind that probably most users will use this interface only once thus, it should be simple. The interface has no buttons, but gives two kinds of instructions for the user: how much and in which sense the camera should be rotated and translated to capture the correct photo.

The interface minimizes external distraction – i.e. any details that could distract the user coming from the camera's image are avoided – by adding a strong vignette to the current camera frame. In doing so, the application tries to help the user to focus only on the on-screen instructions.

The first step in reconstructing the reference photo is to correct the camera rotation. This is done by changing the camera's roll, pitch and yaw to set it according to the reference model. At every new frame, the camera orientation is updated and the image of the camera status is rendered on the center of the screen. All the user has to do is to align that representation with a ghost camera that shows where the real camera needs to be.

Regarding translation, the user has to move the camera towards the direction that the arrow points, placing the solid camera in the center of the screen. To help the users on how much they have to translate the camera, the arrow changes its size according to the distance. As soon as the stranger places the camera in the middle, all the screen is dimmed black, a message asking for the user to hold the camera steady is shown, a new photo is taken and the interaction ends.

3.3 Pose Estimation

In order to achieve the desired result, it is necessary to know where the camera is pointing at and compare it to where it should be.

Inertial measurement units (IMU) today are tiny and almost every wearable electronic or mobile device, such as cellphones and cameras, have them embedded. They provide at least 6 degrees of freedom (DOF), but most of the devices today are designed with 9 DOF units (3-axis accelerometer, 3-axis gyroscope,

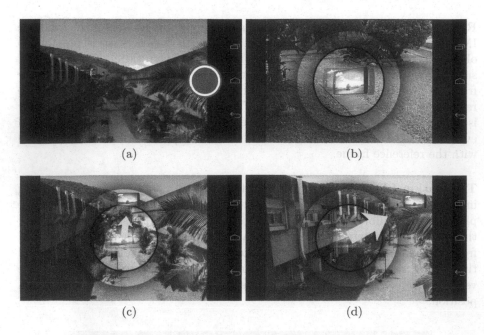

Fig. 3. UI used for instant rephotography. Owner's UI used to set the reference photo (a). Stranger UI: stranger rotates and translates the device to superimpose the two cameras in the interface (b). The solid camera orientation suggests the amount of rotation needed, while the blue arrow indicates the movement direction (c). The size of the arrow changes according to the amount of translation required (d). (Color figure online)

and 3-axis magnetometer). Woodman [23] goes through the different types of devices, explaining how they can be used together to track movements.

This combined use of sensors is known as sensor fusion and is widely used in mobile devices. Sensor fusion is mostly used to track head movements in modern head-mounted displays as used by Ercan and Erdem [6] and in some cases it is used to help estimating camera position in the real world. Current state of the art IMU units have their fusion algorithms embedded in a dedicated hardware thus freeing CPU usage for that task.

In our instant rephotography technique, sensor fusion is used to estimate the current camera orientation relative to a reference frame. This connection between both has already been used in several applications involving mobile devices, augmented and virtual reality environments [7].

In our technique, both rotation and translation axis ought to be evaluated to replicate the reference photograph properly. In the following sections we discuss how our technique handles translation and rotation during the rephotography process.

Rotation Sensing. With a sensor fusion technique that uses all of the available IMU sensors (accelerometer, gyroscope, and magnetometer), it is possible to obtain the quaternion (a 4 dimension representation of a rotation which does not suffer from gimbal locks) data that represents the camera orientation for every frame. Using that information it is possible to calculate the difference from the reference rotation to the current one. This rotation difference is calculated by isolating each axis and subtracting the reference angle from the current one. If every axis difference is less than a set threshold, the phone orientation is aligned with the reference frame.

Translation Identification. To identify the camera translation, we are using image processing algorithms. At the moment that the camera takes the reference photograph, the library extracts keypoints from the image, as seen in Fig. 4. After the keypoints are extracted, they are saved with the reference frame obtained from the rotation sensors. We use the keypoints from the reference image and the ones extracted from the current frame on the camera to create a distance vector, in screen space, which will guide the user towards the original camera position.

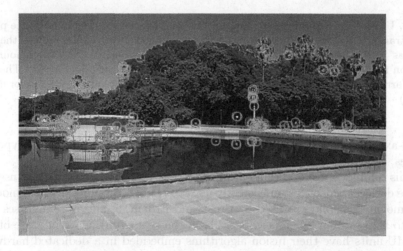

Fig. 4. Image showing the detected keypoints from a reference photograph.

The UI uses this distance vector to render the information for the user (the blue arrow) pointing out to where he or she should move the camera. When the magnitude of the distance vector is smaller then a defined threshold, than the correspondence between them in the rephotography process is made.

During the trials, the average number of extracted keypoints was 83 while the average of good matches was 42. This difference occurs because not every keypoint found in the reference image is present in the final image. For instance, if a moving object (a person walking) was captured when the reference image was created.

3.4   Shake Avoidance

Sometimes the image produced by cameras, especially in low light situations, suffers from blur originated from camera shaking. This problem can also affect our algorithm because the photographer is always moving the camera towards the correct placement. In order to reduce or avoid camera blur, once the camera is in the correct position, the application takes a sequence of photographs instead of a single one.

The intent to capture more than one image is an attempt to minimize the occurrence of image blur. However, we noticed that blur can still occur.

3.5   Implementation Details

The application was partially implemented in Java (Android API, and UI) and in C++ (Computer vision algorithms) using JNI as a gate between programming languages. OpenCV was used as the image processing core.

The chosen feature extractor and descriptor is the ORB which is currently the state of the art for this type of task in mobile devices. Aside from having a good resistance to noise on the images, it is also processor friendly. ORB also runs faster then traditional extractors on mobile devices [18].

The keypoints are matched using an exhaustive algorithm that takes the descriptor of one feature in the reference image and matches with all other features in the current image. The match with the smallest distance is then chosen. From each individual match we calculate a vector from the current keypoint to the reference one and extracted its angle and magnitude. Once all the individual vectors are processed, the final distance vector is created. Its magnitude (Eq. 1) and angle (Eq. 2) are calculated by averaging all the individual vectors from each match.

$$\|DistVector\| = \frac{\sum_{n=1}^{GoodMatches} \|n\|}{GoodMatches} \tag{1}$$

$$\Theta_{DistVector} = \frac{\sum_{n=1}^{GoodMatches} \arctan(\Theta_{GoodMatches})}{GoodMatches} \tag{2}$$

A wrapper around the Android Sensor Manager API was created to implement the Sensor Event Listener calls. The API provides a special virtual sensor called Rotation Vector. This sensor is a combination of all available motion sensors present on the phone and it represents the angular orientation of the device around an axis (x, y, or z). The refresh value of the sensors was preset to the default value of $1,000 \, \mu s$.

The main advantage of using the Rotation Vector present in the Android API is that it will always try to use the best fusion method in different mobile devices. In Algorithm 1 we present the implementation of the algorithm in pseudo-code.

Algorithm 1. STC pseudo-code

```
takeReferencePhotograph(referenceImage, referenceFrame);
extractKeypoints(referenceImage,referenceKeypoints);
while newFrame do
    fixRotation(referenceFrame);
    if rotationIsCorrect then
        extractKeypoints(newFrame, currentKeypoints);
        matchKeypoints(referenceKeypoints, currentKeypoints);
        calculateDistanceVector();
        if vectorMagnitude < threshold then
            takeFinalPhotograph(newFrame)
```

---

4   Experimental Evaluation

In order to assess our instant rephotography technique using the Smart-Tourist Camera application we proposed three experimental studies. The objective of the first study was to test the effectiveness of the technique and the usability of the interface, without any commitment with the quality of the photos taken. In the second user study, we evaluated the instant rephotography technique in a simulated travel situation. Participants asked a stranger to take a photo using a conventional camera application and then rated the photo qualitatively. The goal of this user study was to evaluate how satisfied the user is with a photo taken by someone else. Finally, in the third user study, we compared the quality of photos taken using STC with that of conventional photos taken without the help of our instant rephotography technique. The goal of this third user study was to verify if STC can improve the perceived quality of tourist photos.

We conducted the three studies in three different locations in the city of *Miliways, End of the Universe*. We did not recycled participants from one study in the others to ensure that there was no training effect with the application. There was no compensation for participating in our study.

The proposed studies are based on probability sampling, where the target population are men and women from the age of 15 to 55 years old. The participants were selected through stratified sampling in parks around town and at the University campus.

4.1   Study A: User Interface Evaluation

In this first study the objective was to test if the technique and the application worked properly, disregarding the quality of the final image. To be considered functional we assumed that it would have to fulfil three requirements: it should be easy, fast, and the final photo should be similar to the reference one disregarding the composition or quality of the reference image.

To assess how easy and fast it is to use the proposed interface, we evaluated if participants were able to use the application in the role of the stranger and

registered the time span between the instant they started interacting and the moment the photograph was taken.

To assess similarity with the reference photo, participants were invited to imagine and take a reference photograph where the only constraint was that it had to be in landscape orientation (to minimize the number of variables). Then, the final and the reference photos were shown and the participant was asked to answer, in a 5-points Likert scale, how similar they judge the final photo is compared with the reference one.

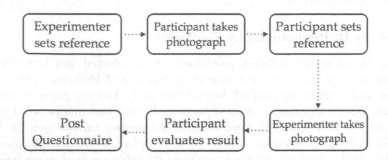

Fig. 5. Diagram demonstrating the protocol used in the user study A.

During the trials, participants first received the camera with a reference preset by the experimenter and were only asked to follow the on-screen instructions without any further instructions. Later the participant was invited to set him/herself a new arbitrary reference image – playing the role of the tourist – and the experimenter followed the instructions. Then, they were informed about how the application worked and what was its purpose. Finally, the participant was invited to answer the post questionnaire form. Figure 5 illustrates the protocol used in this study.

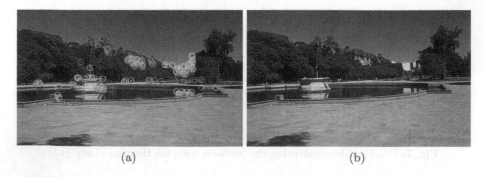

(a)   (b)

Fig. 6. Example of a reference photograph (red circles highlight the extracted keypoints) (a), and a rephotography automatically taken by a participant using STC (b). (Color figure online)

For the user study A, we had 40 participants (55% women and 45% men) with a mean age of 26.1 and $\sigma \pm 7.86$ years.

Results. Participants averaged 8.62 s ($\sigma = 4.79$) before STC took the automatic picture. All the users from study A were able to complete the study.

In the post task questionnaire, 90% of the participants answered that the reference and the final photographs where similar (ratings 4 and 5 of the scale), while 87.5% said that they would use the application (ratings 4 and 5) during one of their travels if the application was available. Figure 6 presents an example of a result from study A.

4.2   Study B: Rephotography Similarity

For this second study, different participants were selected and introduced to the following scenario: *You are a tourist visiting this of Milliways. Lets assume that you wish a photo of yourself here at this park. You are going to need the assistance from a stranger to shoot it for you. Assume that this person (another participant) is that stranger. First imagine the picture without you on it and take this photo as a reference. Then, go to the place where you imagined you would be and the stranger will try to replicate the reference photograph using the application.*

After the image was taken, the first participant was asked to evaluate – using a 5-point Likert scale – how similar the final photograph was to the one they have previously done. Figure 7 illustrates the protocol for this user study.

The primary goal of this study was to evaluate our instant rephotography technique in a scenario similar to a travel situation. We achieved that by pairing participants with people that they did not know, hence strangers. The only information that was given to them was that they should follow the on-screen instructions.

In this study, we collected 40 participants (45% women and 55% men), with an average age of 29.05 and $\sigma \pm 9.54$ years.

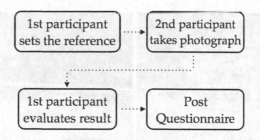

Fig. 7. Diagram demonstrating the protocol used for the user study B.

Results. The results of this study are similar to the ones from study A. The major difference between the two studies was the use of two participants in this

one – in the first user study the reference photo was taken by the experimenter
–, and the fact that now the first participant must to appear in the automatic
picture taken by the application.

All participants answered that the final photograph was similar to the one
they had imagined (ratings 4 and 5), while 80% of the participants also answered
that they would use the application during their travels if it was available (Fig. 8).
Figure 9 depicts a pair of images taken during this study.

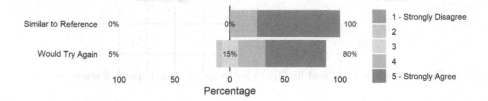

Fig. 8. Likert responses from the second study.

4.3   Study C: To Use STC or Not to Use It?

We selected a new set of participants for the last user study. The scenario was
similar to the one used in the user study B. However, this time the stranger
was first asked by the tourist subject to take a picture of him/her, without
any assistance from the software, similarly to how it works when we travel and
ask for a stranger to take a photo of us. Later, he/she was invited to take
the picture again, this time using the Smart-Tourist Camera with a reference
image set by the *tourist* participant. Once the stranger completed the task,
the two resulting images, manual and assisted, were scrambled and shown in
the smartphone screen. Then, the experimenter asked the tourist participant
to choose the image that they thought was the best. Figure 10 illustrates the
protocol used for this study.

Later, after all the participants finished the trials, we thought it could be
interesting to have a third opinion. All the images were then combined in pairs
(without and with assistance) and were randomly shown to a third set of evaluators. The evaluators were unaware of the existence of the application. For each
person in this last group, a sequence of image pairs was displayed and they were
asked to select the best image on each pair.

We had 20 participants (75% women and 25% men) with an average age of
32.05 and $\sigma \pm 10.92$ years for the first part of the experiment, and 24 participants
(17% women and 83% men) with an average age of 29.29 and $\sigma \pm 5.64$ years for
the second part.

Results. Twenty volunteers participated in the first part of this study, 10 as
tourists and 10 as photographers. In the blind test, 9 out of the 10 tourists

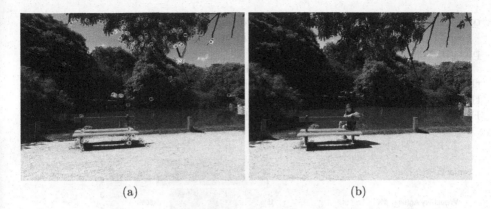

(a)   (b)

Fig. 9. Reference (a) and final (b) photos for one participant of study B.

participants indicated they preferred the image taken using the rephotography assistance.

For the second part of the study, 24 people volunteered to select the image they prefer in each of the 10 pairs of photographs. Remember that those people did not know about the existence of the instant rephotography technique and only analyzed the images. Results are: 146 selections (60.8%) indicated preference for the assisted photographs, 94 (39.2%) preferred the manual photos. Analyzing from the perspective of the 10 pairs of photos, only 2 pairs received more selections for the photograph taken manually than the automatic counterpart. These 2 were exactly those that presented low focus or motion blur issues on the automatic photo.

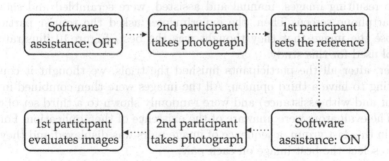

Fig. 10. Diagram demonstrating the protocol of the user study C.

5   Discussion

Findings from the three users studies indicate that our instant rephotography technique was successful in assisting our participants to take (or re-take) similar

photos with very little effort and time. We believe that all the three initial design conditions conditions— simple to use, easy to learn, fast interaction— were met as we observed no difficulties for the participants to follow the on screen instructions while keeping the interaction time short (average of 8.62 s) without any instruction on how to use the application.

During the tests, most of the 124 participants involved were surprised by the possibility of such application and were very receptive to its concept. Participants were also surprised by how simple it was to make it work. With that in mind, it is possible to assume that there is a lack for such application or another type of solution for such problem, i.e. helping tourists. We also observed this positive behavior in the first two studies where the majority of our participants were interested in installing the application in their own phone to try to use it when they were traveling.

One possible reason for such positive feedback, could be that when asked to comment about their experience with photos taken from strangers, all of them shared the same memories of quite a few frustrating photos. The major complain was that even if they did not liked the photograph they usually felt uncomfortable to ask for that stranger to shoot it again. The ones that actually did ask, also commented that sometimes even with a couple of different shots they could not get the final result that they were expecting.

Interestingly results from both the *tourist* participant and third party evaluators indicated that photos taken using our method were preferred over the ones without, however, our method focus is not on composition or image quality but rather on enforcing the desired vantage point created by the users. We posit that STC is complementary to other methods proposed in the HCI community that aim to help users better compose their travel photos. We posit that it could be paired particularly well with composition helpers [15,16] since our method makes no assumption about the composition knowledge of the *tourist* user when s/he is setting the reference image. Computer assisted framing tools could then help the *tourist* to create a high quality reference frame (or a more visually appealing one) thus enhancing the final photograph while ensuring the desired vantage point.

In order to reduce interaction time we opted to use thresholds when matching the translation and rotation references of the mobile device as a 6DOF match would be particularly hard to achieve thus time consuming. Participants rated the reference and final photograph similar which indicates that a one-to-one match is indeed not needed. However, this can lead to small differences, or problems, in the final photograph. The difference is more prominent when the camera is not completely aligned with the horizon (as observed in the before and after depicted in Fig. 6) than with the thresholds in the translation. Future refinement in the algorithm should prioritize the horizon's line over the other two rotation axis.

After the user trials we observed that although most of the photos were taken in a large active public park, the scenes were not necessarily overly crowded, a common situation in some touristic sites. We informally tested the stability of

our technique in a busy open street market and observed no problems in re-creating the image although interaction time increased but was still under 20 s. Figure 11 shows two before and after photos from our informal tests.

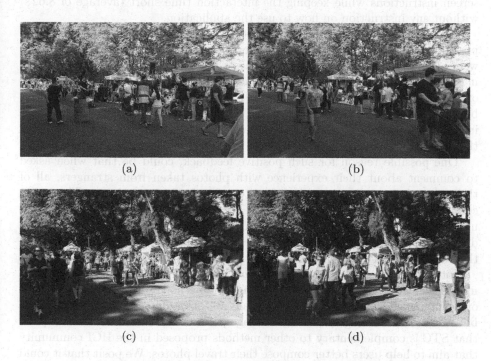

(a)   (b)

(c)   (d)

Fig. 11. Reference (a, c) and final (b, d) photos for the tests in crowded spaces.

5.1 Limitations

The proposed technique has some limitations similar to other photography tech-niques that are based on computer vision techniques. Because it is in part video based it needs at least a partially lit scene in order to find the keypoints. We also do not address different focal lenses *i.e.* different zoom levels. Although zoom could be taken into account in the keypoint matching we assumed a fixed lens and locked the digital zoom feature in our application.

We opted to use global exposure measurement during our user trials because it is the default exposure method of point-and-shoot cameras. The problem with this method is that it can create dark, back-lit or unbalanced images when the light conditions are challenging. Although this problem is not related to our algorithm, exposure problems were present in two images taken by participant where one was part of the A-B testing by the external evaluators.

6   Conclusions and Future Work

In this paper, we introduced the concept of instant rephotography based on: existing techniques for rephotography, in the inertial sensors embedded in smartphones and automatic cameras, and in a specific need for suitable photos when one wants to take part of it and shall ask for the help of somebody else. With our technique it is possible to make use of rephotography with a lightweight and fast framework, and as a consequence, to deploy such techniques in mobile devices hence enabling a simpler and fast use.

Our method fits great to the tourist's problem with their photographs. However, it is also suitable for many other applications, e.g. group and family photos. Our user experiments demonstrated that one reason for it to have worked so well in the travel photography scenario is the short interaction time and the UI intuitiveness and ease of use. Experiments also revealed that the assisted photographs are considered better then manual photos with statistical significance.

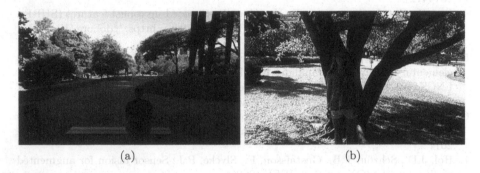

(a)   (b)

Fig. 12. Problematic images captured by STC: final image (a) of user #16 where it is possible to see exposure problems and final image (b) of user #9 that shows exposure problems with back-lightning.

Currently, the minimal amount of matched keypoints is set to one. Nonetheless, when a small number of matches is found, the system becomes confused leading to a greater time span before the automatic photography to be concluded. Further studies should access a minimum threshold, however we have not had problems during the user study regarding this matter.

As future work, we wish to create a method for the camera owner to set an area of interest so the camera can measure light correctly. The reason for that feature is to avoid problems with back-lightning where the subject is not correctly exposed. Such a problem can be seen in Fig. 12.

Also, it is interesting to create an advanced shake avoidance system. We plan to add a post-processing stage that tries to minimize or remove image blur. As STC already has the IMU data at the time of the shot, it could save this information and use it in a deblurring stage, e.g. the one used by Joshi et al. [9].

Acknowledgments. This study was partly funded by the Coordenação de Aperfeiçoamento de Pessoal de Nível Superior - Brasil (CAPES) - Finance Code 001, and partly by CNPq. We also acknowledge FAPERGS (project 17/2551-0001192-9) and CNPq-Brazil (project 311353/2017-7) for their financial support. Thanks to all individuals that volunteered for the user tests.

References

1. Adams, A., et al.: The frankencamera: an experimental platform for computational photography. In: ACM SIGGRAPH 2010 Papers, SIGGRAPH 2010, pp. 29:1–29:12. ACM, New York (2010). http://doi.acm.org/10.1145/1833349.1778766
2. Bae, S., Agarwala, A., Durand, F.: Computational rephotography. ACM Trans. Graph. **29**(3), 24:1–24:15 (2010). https://doi.org/10.1145/1805964.1805968
3. Balata, J., Mikovec, Z., Neoproud, L.: BlindCamera: central and golden-ratio composition for blind photographers. In: Proceedings of the Multimedia, Interaction, Design and Innovation, pp. 8:1–8:8 (2015). http://doi.acm.org/10.1145/2814464.2814472
4. Bay, H., Ess, A., Tuytelaars, T., Van Gool, L.: Speeded-up robust features (SURF). Comput. Vis. Image Underst. **110**(3), 346–359 (2008). https://doi.org/10.1016/j.cviu.2007.09.014
5. Calonder, M., Lepetit, V., Strecha, C., Fua, P.: BRIEF: binary robust independent elementary features. In: Daniilidis, K., Maragos, P., Paragios, N. (eds.) ECCV 2010. LNCS, vol. 6314, pp. 778–792. Springer, Heidelberg (2010). https://doi.org/10.1007/978-3-642-15561-1_56. http://dl.acm.org/citation.cfm?id=1888089.1888148
6. Ercan, A., Erdem, A.: On sensor fusion for head tracking in augmented reality applications. In: American Control Conference (ACC) 2011, pp. 1286–1291, June 2011
7. Hol, J.D., Schzön, T.B., Gustafsson, F., Slycke, P.J.: Sensor fusion for augmented reality. In: FUSION, pp. 1–6. IEEE (2006)
8. Jarusriboonchai, P., Olsson, T., Lyckvi, S.L., Väänänen, K.: Let's take photos together: exploring asymmetrical interaction abilities on mobile camera phones. In: Proceedings of the 18th International Conference on Human-Computer Interaction with Mobile Devices and Services - MobileHCI 2016, pp. 529–540 (2016). http://dl.acm.org/citation.cfm?doid=2935334.2935385
9. Joshi, N., Kang, S.B., Zitnick, C.L., Szeliski, R.: Image deblurring using inertial measurement sensors. In: ACM SIGGRAPH 2010 Papers, SIGGRAPH 10, pp. 30:1–30:9. ACM, New York (2010). http://doi.acm.org/10.1145/1833349.1778767
10. Lee, K.T., Luo, S.J., Chen, B.Y.: Rephotography using image collections. Comput. Graph. Forum (2011). https://doi.org/10.1111/j.1467-8659.2011.02042.x
11. Levoy, M.: Experimental platforms for computational photography. IEEE Comput. Graph. Appl. **30**(5), 81–87 (2010)
12. Lowe, D.G.: Object recognition from local scale-invariant features. In: Proceedings of the International Conference on Computer Vision, ICCV 1999, vol. 2, p. 1150. IEEE Computer Society, Washington (1999). http://dl.acm.org/citation.cfm?id=850924.851523
13. McNulty, E.: Boston Then and Now. Thunder Bay Press, San Diego (2002)
14. Mikolajczyk, K., Schmid, C.: A performance evaluation of local descriptors. IEEE Trans. Pattern Anal. Mach. Intell. **27**(10), 1615–1630 (2005). https://doi.org/10.1109/TPAMI.2005.188

15. Ni, B., Xu, M., Cheng, B., Wang, M., Yan, S., Tian, Q.: Learning to photograph: a compositional perspective. IEEE Trans. Multimed. **15**(5), 1138–1151 (2013). https://doi.org/10.1109/TMM.2013.2241042

16. Rawat, Y.S., Kankanhalli, M.S.: Context-aware photography learning for smart mobile devices. ACM Trans. Multimed. Comput. Commun. Appl. **12**(1s), 1–24 (2015). https://doi.org/10.1145/2808199

17. Rosten, E., Drummond, T.: Machine learning for high-speed corner detection. In: Leonardis, A., Bischof, H., Pinz, A. (eds.) ECCV 2006. LNCS, vol. 3951, pp. 430–443. Springer, Heidelberg (2006). https://doi.org/10.1007/11744023_34

18. Rublee, E., Rabaud, V., Konolige, K., Bradski, G.: ORB: an efficient alternative to SIFT or SURF. In: Proceedings of the 2011 International Conference on Computer Vision, ICCV 2011, pp. 2564–2571. IEEE Computer Society, Washington (2011). https://doi.org/10.1109/ICCV.2011.6126544

19. Shingu, J., Rieffel, E., Kimber, D., Vaughan, J., Qvarfordt, P., Tuite, K.: Camera pose navigation using augmented reality. In: 2010 9th IEEE International Symposium on Mixed and Augmented Reality (ISMAR), pp. 271–272. IEEE (2010)

20. Vazquez, M., Steinfeld, A.: An assisted photography method for street scenes. In: Proceedings of the 2011 IEEE Workshop on Applications of Computer Vision (WACV), WACV 2011, pp. 89–94. IEEE Computer Society, Washington (2011). https://doi.org/10.1109/WACV.2011.5711488

21. Wang, Y., et al.: Where2Stand. ACM Trans. Intell. Syst. Technol. **7**(1), 1–22 (2015). https://doi.org/10.1145/2770879

22. Wen, J., Ünlüer, A.: Redefining the fundamentals of photography with cooperative photography (Mum), pp. 37–47 (2015). https://doi.org/10.1145/2836041.2836045

23. Woodman, O.J.: An introduction to inertial navigation. Technical report UCAM-CL-TR-696, University of Cambridge, Computer Laboratory, August 2007. http://www.cl.cam.ac.uk/techreports/UCAM-CL-TR-696.pdf

24. Yang, X., Cheng, K.T.T.: Accelerating SURF detector on mobile devices. In: Proceedings of the 20th ACM International Conference on Multimedia, MM 2012, pp. 569–578. ACM, New York (2012). http://doi.acm.org/10.1145/2393347.2393427

Personal Digital Signage for Shared Spaces

Kimmo Tarkkanen[✉], Tommi Tuomola, Mira Pohjola,
and Jarkko Paavola

Turku University of Applied Sciences, Joukahaisenkatu 3, 20520 Turku, Finland
kimmo.tarkkanen@turkuamk.fi

Abstract. A wayfinding is an everyday activity where the interaction design has traditionally based on landmarks, visual maps, signs, and social collaboration. In the mobile computing era, we have witnessed more techno-centric development of wayfinding and navigation where people turn to their mobile navigation applications rather than to cues in the surrounding environment. However, in many wayfinding situations, using mobile devices is not very applicable due to safety reasons, indoor limitations or practical needs. To overcome the identified challenges, this paper introduces a personal digital signage, which combines the benefits of traditional directional signs and an underlying mobile technology for wayfinding purposes. The paper begins with formulating the design problem and introducing the premises of the solution. We evaluate and refine the solution with usability studies in a mass event (N = 24) and in a hurry situation in a campus building (N = 48). Test results show that the proposed solution was highly acceptable and rated good in usability among participants. The effectiveness as reaching the target destination was excellent and the efficiency measured as time increased only moderately compared with the optimal performance. We conclude that the solution performs well in indoor spaces where the navigational accuracy depends on the amount and positioning of screens installed as is the case with traditional signs. The study calls for re-thinking the interaction design of navigation and wayfinding without use of mobile devices.

Keywords: Wayfinding · Personal sign · Interaction design · Usability

1 Introduction

Wayfinding refers to the actions of people navigating from place to another in their environment. It is a common activity in shared spaces and surroundings, for example in office buildings and mass events, which are not previously familiar to us. In addition to navigational aids provided in the location, the effectiveness and efficiency of wayfinding depends on the route complexity, the disabilities of people, aging and their level of experience [1–4]. For example, if the route is very complex, it will cause less effective walking to the destination [2].

Fundamentals of wayfinding have remained the same since the Polynesian supernal navigation methods where plans and situated collaborative actions are our resources towards the target destination (cf. [5]). Today, wayfinding with mobile devices in outdoor environments is popular and efficient due to online maps and satellite

© IFIP International Federation for Information Processing 2019
Published by Springer Nature Switzerland AG 2019
D. Lamas et al. (Eds.): INTERACT 2019, LNCS 11748, pp. 228–236, 2019.
https://doi.org/10.1007/978-3-030-29387-1_13

positioning. On the other hand, technology-aided indoor navigation has not yet reached the same level of popularity, whilst many urban, shared spaces (e.g. sights in city centers, office buildings and airports) would benefit from indoor positioning and technology-supported wayfinding. These locations are usually designed for masses of people, local citizens, casual business visitors, and tourists alike. Indoor wayfinding even in a large shopping mall can be difficult[1]. Imagine a situation where you, as a first-time visitor, arrive at the main entrance of the university campus building. You are already late from an important meeting and fairly recall the name or the number of the meeting room (or the correct building in the campus area). Presumably, you look for navigation aid from physical signs, indoor maps, digital kiosks, apps or personal face-to-face communication (e.g. going to an information desk or asking people passing by), while, you are running in the hallway of the complex building, which contains hundreds of rooms and thousands of square meters.

The problem is that current technical and traditional navigation solutions are rather weak to support the above situation of hurry. First, indoor positioning technology and navigation applications are still coming to markets, although some products exist[2], which allow browsing, searching and getting directions to target locations in a digital map of the building. Second, even if the products were available for the wayfinding in the building, there are navigation situations when people are not able to use their mobile phones (e.g. when carrying a baggage in an airport) nor it would be very practical. Paying attention to the small screen on the mobile phone while walking and hurrying in traffic is a safety issue as well, as popular augmented reality games have demonstrated. Therefore, we turn our focus on traditional wayfinding aids, which do not require constant mobile phone interaction.

The efficient and effective use of digital kiosks in an urgent need of navigation help is deteriorated by that each type of kiosk has its own design, varying content and interaction pattern. Therefore, the kiosk suits better for peaceful and unhurried navigation situations. Orientation signs like maps in the wall and in the kiosk require the users to memorize the information and confirm the destination shown on them [6]. The memorizing problem exists with maps of the mobile apps as well, unless the device is continuously at hand and in sight. Oral directions and visual maps acquired in the situation can be misunderstood and get forgotten before reaching the destination. Digital kiosks can become entirely useless without adequate perceptual cues to right direction or relative distances [7]. Furthermore, using maps, kiosks and information desk services inevitably involve some delay in the hurrying situation as the person needs to stop, queue, interact, interpret and memorize the information content. The problem of physical signposts, and signage in general, are that those are less likely to exist for every destination. In our example above, unless the destination is one of the main places in the location (e.g. a frequently visited lecture hall), but just a meeting room among many other similar destinations, you rarely find a sign. Signs are static and

---

[1] One of the largest shopping malls in Finland, which opened on September 2018, has not attracted enough visitors. The visitors have claimed the mall about its navigational complexity, which has also been assumed as a one reason to poor volumes.

[2] Apple's Indoor Survey utility app combines WiFi and sensor data to enable indoor positioning, and applications like www.mapspeople.com, www.mazemap.com and https://proximi.io/.

are designed to serve the general needs of crowds rather than specific and situated needs of individuals. Nevertheless, in hurried navigation situations, the benefits of signage are evident. For example, metro stations, airports, and traffic in general all over the world, use signage, which is quickly observable, internationally interpretable and can release your hands from using the mobile phone to carrying a baby and a baggage or driving a car. Directional signs are used to help the users to follow instructions and to direct people to move straight ahead [6]. If signage is used, it must be consistently available, legible, and systematic [8]. The general-purpose signs, such as directional arrows are easier to comprehend than special or tailored signs. For example, healthcare related symbols in the hospital environment are not as understandable as the general signs [9]. In the mass events and very crowded places, signs at strategic positions provide helpful information both when approaching the site and inside the venue. Yet, the experiences of the event visitors can deteriorate if the signs are unclear, with too small font sizes, overcomplicated that are difficult to understand, absent or inappropriately positioned [10].

The question is how to design wayfinding interactions and navigational aid for hurrying situations in our shared spaces that would overcome the drawbacks yet preserve the benefits of physical signs? In the above described example situation, if you don't observe any physical signs to your final destination, what you may see, are the aforementioned kiosks, larger digital displays or projections on the walls. Probably, these on-site TV screens welcome you to the current events of the campus or inform you the lunch menu of the student restaurant. Screens can have many kinds of digital content, but rarely those are navigational or serve and improve the experience of first-time visitors. However, the benefit of digital content in navigation is that the content is changeable and thus possible to personalize unlike static, physical signposts. Accompanied with digital image projections, every flat surface could be a potential place for a navigation sign.

Our answer and approach in this paper is to utilize on-site screens for personalized navigation help in shared urban spaces. Therefore, we created a solution called personal digital signage (PDS). To our knowledge, there are not existing solutions like PDS, which personalize signs and allow navigation without mobile device use. The study follows a constructive research tradition and the research process of a design science where the design and proofing its usefulness is central [11]. In this introduction part, we have formulated a research problem, which we aim to solve with the PDS. We empirically evaluate how useful and usable PDS is for navigation in a hurry situation in a university building (N = 48) and in a mass event (N = 24). Next, we introduce our solution and the evaluation results. Lastly, we conclude benefits and limits of our approach and ponder the future research and development questions.

2 Personal Digital Signage (PDS) Solution

The fundamental idea of the PDS solution is to exploit the benefits of a physical signpost, yet extend its ability to serve multiple destinations and users. The multiplicity requirement means that the content must be digital and implement rules, which could notify personal destinations even in a mass event. To preserve the other benefits of

physical signs, the solution must implement true mobility i.e. users should focus on the signs and not on their digital devices. Third, using digital signs should not risk users' privacy in anyway, but work as similar as other physical signposts without digital content.

The proposed system[3] constitutes of a server, a SQL database, screens installed in the building with Bluetooth beacons (2–4 pieces per screen), and a mobile application for the user. For the testing purposes, the physical signs are large TVs/screens connected to Raspberry Pi computers with WLAN connection to the server. The Android-based mobile application works as a user interface for choosing a final destination from a given set of possible destinations loaded from the server/database (Fig. 1). After choosing the final destination, the application communicates with the server by sending beacon group RSSI status changes and the user does not need to use the mobile application in the location. With the Bluetooth service turned on in the mobile device, the user can access the location/building where the screens with Bluetooth beacons communicate to users the direction to the next screen and the final destination. The mobile application has given the user an avatar, which is visible in the screen with the name of the final destination and the directional arrow. Arrows are represent directions towards cardinal and half-cardinal points and are implemented as 2D or 3D symbols. Screens are positioned at crucial guidance points in the building. Multiple users and directions can be served at the same time. The closest user of the screen appears in the top of the list (based on RSSI signal strength) and the fixed time of visibility (first in, first out – principle) guarantees that everybody gets served. The maximum amount of users visible at the same time depends mainly on the screen size.

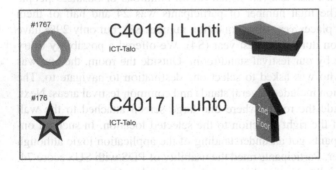
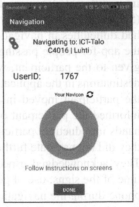

Fig. 1. On the right: The user interface of the mobile application with the avatar (waterdrop) and the destination information. On the left: An example of a screen showing the direction to two different destinations with 3D arrows (2nd floor and behind on the right).

---

[3] The video of the PDS system is available here: https://kutt.it/SCN4Jc.

3 Evaluation Results

We evaluated the PDS in two different settings: In a mass event (business festival) and in an office building (university campus). In the latter context, we organized two separate evaluation rounds and after each round we improved the system following the principles of design science. Evaluations aimed at confirming usability and usefulness of the PDS in these settings as well as guiding the subsequent development. In order to quantify users' satisfaction, perceived efficiency and effectiveness, we applied System Usability Scale (SUS) questionnaire [12], which is a brief and highly reliable usability scale [13], which shows also correlation to market success [14, 15]. In addition to SUS, the questionnaire included background information, such as age, job title and visitor profile, and subjective ratings on statements about PDS efficiency and effectiveness: (S1) I think that with this product I would find different rooms and places quickly (S2) I think that this product would improve my navigation performance in the locations I am not familiar with (S3) I visit rooms and buildings unfamiliar to me very often (S4) I have had difficulties finding rooms and buildings unfamiliar to me during the past year. These were answered similarly to SUS with 5-point Likert scale from strongly disagree (1) to strongly agree (5). Open answers were collected with the question: What were the most important elements that made your navigation task easy/difficult? In addition, participants measured themselves the actual navigation time and reported the completion success in the campus tests.

3.1 Business People in the Mass Event

The test took place in a business festival, which draws hundreds of business people from different domains. The total number of participants was 24 and half of them (50%) agreed visiting new places very often (question number S3), but only 29% have had difficulties in navigation during the past year (S4). We offered a possibility to try the app for people passing by our festival stand/room. Outside the room, the app was given to the participant, who was asked to select one destination to navigate to. The destinations in the application included several stands and common festival areas. Next, the participant moved inside the room, where one large screen attached to the wall informed the participant of the right direction to the selected location. In such an on-hands introduction, participants got an understanding of the application logic although they did not navigate further. Participants rated the usability of PDS with SUS score 74. They acknowledged especially the simplicity of the application logic, fast response time of the signs, use of personal user icons in the signs and the absence of the mobile phone during the navigation task. The interpretation of the SUS score is that the users consider the system highly acceptable, and as an adjective, the score means good usability [16]. In the open answers, participants thought that the amount and positioning of screens would be the main problem in practice. However, the participants evaluated the efficiency (S1) and effectiveness (S2) of PDS very high: 88% of the participants agreed or strongly agreed that the system would help them finding locations quickly, and 83% of the participants agreed that the system would improve their performance. This encouraged us to continue the development.

3.2 Student Visitors in the Campus Building

The test took place in the ICT building located in the university campus area. The building contains offices, meeting rooms and lecture halls on six floors (Fig. 2). The building has an information desk near the main entrance, which employees handle about 30 requests in a day related to indoor navigation. On a day of a mass event (conferences, student events), the amount of requests is much higher.

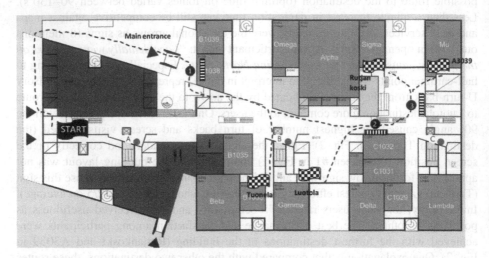

Fig. 2. The map of the ICT building including optimal paths (dashed lines from start) and four screens (numbered) on the way to target locations (goal flags).

The application was tested with engineering and business students on June 2018 (N = 28) and the second time on February 2019 (N = 10), same time with visitors from a primary school (N = 10). Of these participants, only 29% visit unfamiliar places very often (S3). However, during the past year, 47% of participants have experienced difficulties in navigation (S4).

In the first test, we had four different target destinations in the first floor of the building and three large screens for the wayfinding interaction towards these destinations (Fig. 2). Based on the insights of business festival, the positioning of three screens was planned to support the minimum amount of screens needed for navigation, yet we did not use any stationary screens but installed new ones into the most appropriate positions concerning finding the destinations. With the specific positions, we could also study the different types of directional arrow symbols showed in the screens and their effect on the PDS usability. We implemented 2D arrows (Fig. 3), which directed to (half-)cardinal points (e.g. south-east) and could include a 90° angle (around the corner - arrow) as well. Participants were orally instructed to hurry, because they were already late from the meeting time mentioned in the scenario (an email invitation). Participants were sent in one minute intervals to different destinations, in order to avoid participants directly following each other in the building, yet allowing multiple directions to appear in the same screen.

Participants in the first test of the ICT building rated the usability of PDS with SUS score 74. The result is good despite that half of the participants in the study suffered from poor WiFi network connection in one Raspberry Pi device, which meant the users had to wait their avatar appearing on the screen, if at all. The subjective efficiency decreased (71%) compared to business festival, although PDS was considered a bit more useful (89%) in the complex building. The problem increased their navigation times as well. On average, the navigation times were 55 s more (+45%) than the fastest possible route to the destination (optimal time on routes varied between 90–130 s). Less than a minute increase in navigation time can still be competitive against maps and desk services. Another difficulty were the directional arrows as signs (8 mentions out of 42 in open questions). As one participant puts it: *"I accidentally went upstairs on the first try, cause the arrow was pointing North-East"*. Especially, arrows pointing to half-cardinal points were difficult to interpret in flat 2D representation. The compulsory U-turn back from the screen 2 indicated by the arrow to the south-east made the route to Luotola destination more complex to the users. On the other hand, the arrow with the 90° angle caused the highest number of turn backs and screen visits needed (the destination Tuonela in Fig. 2). Either the angle was not understood correctly or the screen position (the screen #1 in Fig. 1) combined with the building layout was not appropriate for the arrow sign with angle. The participants who required to use this sign (Tuonela) gave the poorest efficiency ratings for the whole system (3.42/5 on average). Interestingly, the same users rated SUS scores (85) and the perceived usefulness as positively as others. The best performance and satisfaction among participants were achieved with the furthest destinations in the building (Rutjankoski and A3039 in Fig. 2). One explanation is that compared with the other two destinations, these routes continue straight from the main entrance and include more screens near the destinations (screens numbered 2 and 3 in Fig. 2). The actual effectiveness of the system was high, because only one participant out of 28 did not find the destination before giving up the task.

For the second test in the same building, we made few improvements and changes to the system. First of all, we redesigned the arrows to 3D format (Fig. 1) due to earlier misinterpretations related to directions. Second, we expanded the available destinations to three different floors instead of guiding the users in the ground floor only. Third, instead of installing only new screens, we used three stationary installed screens of the building (Fig. 3). Participants were instructed as in the first test. They rated the usability of PDS with SUS score 82, which is better than in the earlier tests in the business festival and in the ICT building. Both the perceived efficiency (90%) and the perceived effectiveness (90%) improved slightly from the first tests. Every participant found the target destination, and on average the navigation time was 29% (52 s) more than the fastest possible time to reach the target, which was an improvement as well. In open answers, participants considered the 3D arrows as clear and informative about the right path, whereas the amount and positioning of screens got negative feedback. Thus, the accuracy of navigation and user experience would improve if the screen positions are planned for the navigation purpose. Currently, the stationary screens of the ICT building fit for approximate navigation only.

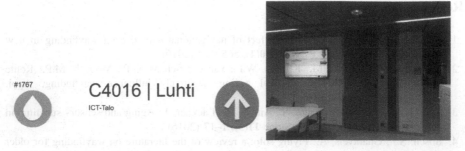

Fig. 3. Left: 2D arrows used in the first test were vague (up or forward?). Right: Stationary installed screens in the lobby were used in the second test.

4 Conclusions

In the mobile computing era, the development of wayfinding and navigation has been fast, yet rather techno-centric. As its materialization, numerous of different mobile navigation applications require that people concentrate on their smart phones rather than on navigational cues in the real surroundings. A theoretical contribution of this study is that it calls for re-thinking the interaction design of indoor wayfinding with the modern technology from more human, socio-technical and practice-based perspective than just as a technological advancement to come. More traditional wayfinding techniques and elements, such as directional signs, are still appropriate in many navigation situations where the (constant) use of mobile devices is not. Probably, this notion and our study results encourage others to exploit the most recent technology for getting people to non-interact with the technology (i.e. requiring less concentration on your technology in everyday life).

Our approach is ubiquitously simplistic and embedded: It leaves the mobile on the background and exploits navigation aids that are personalized and familiar to everybody. Our evaluation cases with PDS show that people find such personalized and digitalized navigation guidance based on traditional signs both usable and useful. Most challenging is the amount and positioning of screens, which set the limits for the navigation accuracy and user experience in practical implementations. Another challenge is to find a proper model for user visibility in the screen i.e. when and how long one should appear on the screen in a mass event or in a building with hundreds of navigators in a minute. This is also an implementation site specific question. Yet, even with few existing screens in the tested location, the proposed system is able to effectively and efficiently guide the visitor and improve their visiting experience. Therefore, the practical implication of the study lies in this proof-of-concept and its usefulness, which invite HCI community to design future wayfinding interactions more socially sustainable than technical.

Acknowledgements. This work has been supported by 6Aika project called Smart City Guidance funded by the European Regional Development Fund (ERDF).

References

1. Woollett, K., Maguire, E.A.: The effect of navigational expertise on wayfinding in new environments. J. Environ. Psychol. **30**(4), 565–573 (2010)
2. Zijlstra, E., Hagedoorn, M., Krijnen, W.P., van der Schans, C.P., Mobach, M.P.: Route complexity and simulated physical ageing negatively influence wayfinding. Appl. Ergonomics **56**, 62–67 (2016)
3. Levy-Tzedek, S., Maidenbaum, S., Amedi, A., Lackner, J.: Aging and sensory substitution in a virtual navigation task. PloS one **11**(3), 1–17 (2016)
4. Bosch, S.J., Gharaveis, A.: Flying solo: a review of the literature on wayfinding for older adults experiencing visual or cognitive decline. Appl. Ergonomics **58**, 327–333 (2017)
5. Suchman, L.: Plans and Situated Actions. The Problem of Human-Machine Communication. Cambridge University Press, Cambridge (1987)
6. Zheng, M.C.: Time constraints in emergencies affecting the use of information signs in wayfinding behavior. Procedia-Soc. Behav. Sci. **35**, 440–448 (2012)
7. Boumenir, Y., Georges, F., Rebillard, G., Valentin, J., Dresp-Langley, B.: Wayfinding through an unfamiliar environment. Percept. Mot. Skills **111**(3), 829–847 (2010)
8. Marquez, D.X., Hunter, R.H., Griffith, M.H., Bryant, L.L., Janicek, S.J., Atherly, A.J.: Older adult strategies for community wayfinding. J. Appl. Gerontol. **36**(2), 213–233 (2015)
9. Hashim, M.J., Alkaabi, M.S.K.M., Bharwani, S.: Interpretation of way-finding healthcare symbols by a multicultural population: navigation signage design for global health. Appl. Ergonomics **45**(3), 503–509 (2014)
10. Filingeri, V., Eason, K., Waterson, P., Haslam, R.: Factors influencing experience in crowds–the participant perspective. Appl. Ergonomics **59**, 431–441 (2017)
11. Peffers, K., Tuunanen, T., Rothenberger, M.A., Chatterjee, S.: A design science research methodology for information systems research. J. Manag. Inf. Syst. **24**(3), 45–77 (2007)
12. Brooke, J.: SUS-A quick and dirty usability scale. In: Thomas, B.W., Weerdmeester, B., McClelland, I.L. (eds.) Usability Evaluation in Industry, pp. 189–194. Taylor & Francis, London (1996)
13. Sauro, J., Lewis, J.R.: Correlations among prototypical usability metrics: evidence for the construct of usability. In: Proceedings of the SIGCHI Conference on Human Factors in Computing Systems, pp. 1609–1618. ACM (2009)
14. Brooke, J.: SUS: a retrospective. J. Usability Stud. **8**(2), 29–40 (2013)
15. Bangor, A., Joseph, K., Sweeney-Dillon, W., Stettler, G., Pratt, J.: Using the SUS to help demonstrate usability's value to business goals. In: Proceedings of the Human Factors and Ergonomics Society Annual Meeting, vol. 57, no. 1, pp. 202–205 (2013)
16. Bangor, A., Kortum, P., Miller, J.: Determining what individual SUS scores mean: Adding an adjective rating scale. J. Usability Stud. **4**(3), 114–123 (2009)

SeaMote - Interactive Remotely Operated Apparatus for Aquatic Expeditions

Marko Radeta[1]([⊠]), Miguel Ribeiro[2], Dinarte Vasconcelos[2], Jorge Lopes[1], Michael Sousa[1], João Monteiro[3], and Nuno Jardim Nunes[2]

[1] ITI/LARSyS, Universidade da Madeira, Tigerwhale, Funchal, Portugal
{marko.radeta,jorge.lopes,michael.sousa}@m-iti.org
[2] ITI/LARSyS, Instituto Superior Técnico, Lisbon, Portugal
{jose.miguel.ribeiro,dinarte.vasconcelos,nunojnunes}@tecnico.ulisboa.pt
[3] MARE – Marine and Environmental Sciences Centre, Caniçal, Portugal
jmonteiro@mare-centre.pt
https://iti.larsys.pt, https://tecnico.ulisboa.pt/,
http://www.mare-centre.pt

Abstract. IoT has been widely adopted by HCI communities and citizen scientists to sense and control the surrounding environments. While their applications are mostly reported in urban settings, they remain scarce in aquatic settings. Oceans are undergoing an immense increase of human generated pollution ranging from noise to marine litter, where current USV solutions to detect its impact on environment remain at high cost. In our study, we design a first low-cost, long-range, radio controlled USV, based on IoT and LoRa, intended to be used for aquatic expeditions collecting environmental telemetry. We gather temperature, humidity, GPS position, footage and provide a mobile interface for remote controlling the USV. With this pilot study, we provide an initial study of the suitable simplistic GUI for long-range remote sensing in aquatic setting. We discuss the findings and propose future applications and Internet of Water Things as future research direction.

Keywords: LoRa · Internet of Water Things (IoWT) ·
Unmanned Surface Vehicles (USVs) · Ubiquitous computing ·
Ocean conservation · Environmental telemetry

1 Introduction

In this paper, we report on a first exploratory study using IoT devices and related long-range (LoRa) wireless communication devices used in a marine setting, in collaboration with marine biologists. To the best of our knowledge, this

Electronic supplementary material The online version of this chapter (https://doi.org/10.1007/978-3-030-29387-1_14) contains supplementary material, which is available to authorized users.

© IFIP International Federation for Information Processing 2019
Published by Springer Nature Switzerland AG 2019
D. Lamas et al. (Eds.): INTERACT 2019, LNCS 11748, pp. 237–248, 2019.
https://doi.org/10.1007/978-3-030-29387-1_14

is the first attempt to develop interactive systems that operate in the previously described setting, i.e., using low-cost IoT and LoRa technologies while providing marine biologists with a unique interface to explore coastal areas using remotely operated unmanned vehicles. A second contribution is the design of a modular platform (named, Seamote), which serves to allow remote real-time control and environmental telemetry of other IoT devices to be used in marine environments. Seamote acts as a data mule, capable of communicating with a wide range of control devices (e.g. mobile applications, remote controllers, artificial intelligence automated inputs, etc.), converting its' payloads to control the end-devices used in marine setting (e.g. IoT devices for environmental telemetry, biota active telemetry and tracking, USVs - Unmanned Surface Vehicles, etc). In this study, Seamote is designed to be used by marine biologists and other stakeholders (i.e. tourists and citizen scientists), with the ultimate goal to obtain higher spatial-temporal resolution data (e.g. marine mammal footage, acoustic recordings and environmental data). An overarching contribution of this paper is to raise aware-ness in the design and HCI communities for the opportunities which lie outside of urban environments. We achieve this through a systematic review of the litera-ture and challenges for marine science and oceanography. Then we relate to these challenges and technological opportunities for the design and HCI communities. Seamote depicts three major key research questions:

- **[RQ1]**. How to design a low-cost LoRa-based Internet of Water Things (IoWT)?
- **[RQ2]**. Which interaction challenges emerge from remotely operated devices?
- **[RQ3]**. How to leverage environmental telemetry using LoRa?

2   Related Work

2.1   State of the Art in Aquatic Setting

Current research in oceanography greatly depends on satellite imagery, sensors and deployment platforms (e.g. Acoustic Doppler Current Profilers, Conductiv-ity, Temperature and Depth profilers, Autonomous Underwater Vehicles, oceano-graphic buoys) to collect crucial information, such as Sea Surface Temperature [16,32], variations in salinity and temperature over depth [15,17,29] and cur-rents direction and intensity [4,6], for their studies. Similarly, scientists focusing in the biology and ecology of marine organisms and habitats, also rely on multiple tools, instruments and sensors to collect data and better understand the links between abiotic and biotic factors and variables. Technological advances over the last decades have allowed deep-sea researchers to survey habitats, conduct experiments and collect samples remotely (e.g. with Remote Operated Vehicles - ROVs, drop-cameras, multi-beam sonar) and/or from the safety of custom designed submarines with comprehensive payloads designed for scientific pur-poses [12,26,30,31,33].

2.2   IoT in Aquatic Setting

Several studies have been reported to use UAV's for environmental telemetry [4,24,28]. Other recent works are also reported to use IoT and provide low-cost solutions for water monitoring [1,9,13,19] as well as tackling the problem of marine litter [8]. ROVs and USVs can be used for surveillance applications in the ocean, not only on the surface, but also underwater. These types of vehicles can be operated remotely be wired or wireless communication systems. Mahfuzh and colleges developed an ROV [10,21] to make maneuvers underwater and on the surface. Their vehicle has 6 motor actuators on two motor controllers, commanded by a microcontroller. It is remotely controlled by a joystick and the radio commands are sent via a 2.4 GHz wireless communication, which has a very limited range [25]. Various aquatic technologies have been used for oceanographic data collection, offshore exploration, surveillance, surface water quality and navigation [2,3,14,20]. While IoT provides an enormous potential allowing remote technical diagnostics and improved safety, including management of the energy distribution, monitoring equipment, improving passenger experience, enhancing navigation and tracking cargo [11,18], IoT remains scarce in aquatic applications.

2.3   HCI in Aquatic Setting

Instead, when focusing on HCI applications, several studies have been reported to already use ROV's. For instance, a work explored the usage of GUI for the control of UAV's [7] providing the usability studies of persons in charge. Similarly, another work explored the similar approach used for ground control station staff [34]. Also, HCI applications have been reported to use gestural inputs to control remote operated vehicles [5,23]. However, these all reported studies either rely on desktop applications, providing complex GUI applications and or these studies are not seen in aquatic settings. When dealing with marine environment, a recent study provided the interface and system for gathering and classifying cetacean acoustics using Wi-Fi. This study used whale watching tourists as citizen scientists to obtain these data [27]. In our study, we designed a system that goes one step further, allowing citizen scientists and marine biologists to collect larger corpora of cetaceans. Although interactive applications in HCI communities have been also reported to be tested within the water, such as the multimedia sensory table based on total internal reflection [22]. Conversely, no previous studies explored the potential of combining the HCI with LoRa, IoT, and embedding it into aquatic setting. In our study, we design the remote operating system and modular platform for allowing such interactions.

3   Methodology

This section describes the system apparatus, architecture and an overview of the designed Internet of Water Things (IoWT) system. The location chosen for the

pilot tests was the local marina with an entrance to the sea. Subjects of the study were 3 participants (with age range between 24–34) who were approached on the spot. They were 2 males, including a sailor and computer engineer, and 1 female with linguistic background. All participants reported to have previous experience with the usage of smart phone applications. For the pilot test, all participants were using Think-aloud protocol and were asked to express their opinion about the effectiveness, efficiency and satisfaction when using the Seamote apparatus. They were given the Seamote App coupled with Seamote Bridge to perform initial usability tests. The given task was to operate the USV to a specific boat, explore the nearby waters, and to return, avoiding the obstacles found on the sea surface. Before each test run, to each participant a demo run was provided, depicting the maneuverability of the Seamote. Seamote apparatus is designed from three main components: (i) Seamote App, a mobile application for remote control of the device; (ii) Seamote Bridge, a designed case with microcontroller serving to receive signals from the Seamote App and communicate with the device using LoRa; and (iii) Semote USV, an IoWT remotely operated device for collecting the data.

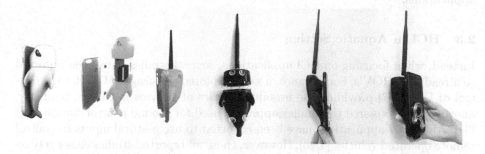

Fig. 1. Seamote Bridge. An evolution of special design case with the embedded micro-controller and LoRa antenna, capable to be mounted to the smartphone using suction cups.

Seamote Bridge. Being a custom designed case, it serves to contain basic microcontroller hardware. It is comprised of a single LoPy4 with an antenna and battery, shown in Fig. 1. Acting as a network integrator, Seamote Bridge runs a HTTP server, which receives commands from the control devices, in the form of POST requests, and forwards them in further via LoRa payloads to the USV end devices. Algorithm is designed to stop sending motor commands with included lag (between 1–2 s) should the participant stop using the Seamote App. In this setup, LoRa is not being used with the LoRaWAN network, and is used instead as a point-to-point communication, thus not requiring a gateway with an internet connection. The access to the HTTP server is done via an Access Point (AP) running on the Seamote Bridge, which also features a captive portal,

popping-up on a Seamote App as a dialog upon connecting to the AP. Also, we designed an encasing of the Seamote Bridge which resembles a marine creature, in this case a tiger shark. It serves to contain the electronics inside, being coupled with the smartphone via suction cups, and being supported by the tail and fins, as depicted in Fig. 1.

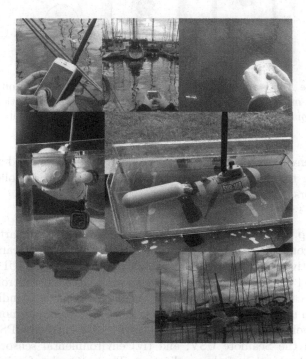

Fig. 2. Seamote USV - deployed in-situ, used for the preliminary tests with participants. Top: Seamote App, used from the marina standpoint. Middle: Seamote USV buoyancy and stability tests. Bottom: Underwater imagery collected by the participants and Seamote USV against other marine vessels found in local marina.

Seamote USV. In this study, device is a surface vehicle with enabled LoRa communication capable of reaching the remote land locations. This device is based on an existing *Nikko Sub-168*, a narrow range ROV toy, with dimensions of $17 \times 7 \times 11$ cm. Rationale for using this device was the low-cost, out-of-the-box solution which contains two propellers of two blades each. Existing radio antenna and batteries have been replaced with new hardware based on a Pycom LoPy4 microcontroller. The purpose of using this microcontroller was due to it being a low-cost LoRa enabled chip which can support the testing controls of motors using LoRa. It is in further equipped with a PySense board, which includes an accelerometer, temperature, light, humidity and battery voltage sensors. Aim of

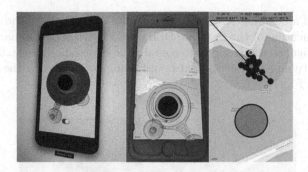

Fig. 3. Seamote App - an evolution of a mobile application GUI. From left to right: using a joystick mounted with a tangible analog stick using silicon suction cups. Image to the right: a map depicting the latitude and longitude of the Seamote USV.

the collected environmental telemetry is to be in future compared with external data, verifying to which extent does the casing and microcontroller biases the PySense sensors.

Seamote App. This study proposed the usage of simplistic smartphone application to be connected to the Seamote Bridge, allowing the Seamote USV to be fully operative from single screen. Mobile application and GUI are designed to encompass 4 core functionalities: (i) a joystick, used for controlling the end device, in this case the Seamote USV; (ii) ongoing battery level indicator, allowing the user to understand the battery level for both logic and motor batteries; (iii) a map, pointing out the past trajectories and current GPS coordinates obtained from the Seamote USV; and (iv) environmental sensor data, being displayed on the header of the application. The rationale of using the digital joystick was to simplify the usual four stock buttons, allowing the user to more easier maneuver the Seamote USV with a single hand while having the location indicator on map. Seamote App is in further connected via Wi-Fi to the access point located on our Seamote Bridge (Fig. 3).

4 Results

4.1 IoWT LoRa Deployment [RQ1]

Design of the Seamote system provided to be robust enough to withstand the Beaufort scale 1, as well as to successfully pass the buoyancy and water-tightness tests. In Fig. 2, it is possible to observe the Seamote system deployed in-situ. Understanding the collected images, Seamote system successfully managed to sustain the deployment, collection of data, environmental telemetry and retrieval to the surface, and all by the remote control from the remote marina location

using LoRa. SD cards were also used, allowing the long-term collection of parameters capable for later retrieval, such as the environmental sensor data, application commands and board meta-data (battery levels and LoRa parameters). In Fig. 4, we depict the paths taken by the three participants performed from the origin to the goal points denoted in colors. The points shown in the figure were captured by the GPS (with its associated error) aboard the Seamote USV and recorded in the Seamote Bridge, while also being forwarded to the Seamote App. The distance from the start to each goal was on average 19.8 meters and the tests took approximately 5 min each, where participants were exploring additional circling and maneuverability of the Seamote USV.

4.2   User Interaction Observations [RQ2]

Using Think-aloud protocol, all three participants reported the Seamote apparatus to be effective (having the data in real-time). Regarding the efficiency, they stated that more instantaneous responsiveness should be added to the Seamote USV. Moreover, they expressed high satisfaction (enjoying in overall the remote control). In further, subjects suggested the option for autopilot mode with predefined routes in the Seamote App, pointing that this way Seamote USV could perform a more efficient long-range survey. Interestingly, all three participants expressed the need to have a button to stop the Seamote USV, even if our system already stops the engines if not being used for 2 s. Also, there were additional concerns with the suction cups used as a tangible joystick was not calibrated to run the Seamote USV with full throttle, where 2 participants removed the suction cup and used the joystick on the GUI.

4.3   Environmental Telemetry [RQ3]

In Fig. 5 we portray the temperature and humidity, obtained from the Seamote USV during the tests. Data shows temperature changes with peaks when taken out of the water between tests, as well as the influence of heat by the motors. Also, we observe nuances in humidity readings indicating the time spent in water. In Fig. 6, we plot the RSSI against the SNR. Although the short distance did not allow for the RSSI to be weak, this shows that the noise was kept consistent in the aquatic environment. The SNR showed values ranging from 5 to 7, indicating a good ratio that allows the radio to capture the signal against the environment noise - RSSI ($M = -44.8$, $SD = 7.9$) and SNR ($M = 6.3$, $SD = 0.5$) with $n = 265$. Figure 7 depicts the most used commands issued from the application, having forwards at full speed more used. Figure 8 depicts the pitch and roll recorded during the tests, showing a clear tendency of the Seamote USV to lean backwards. This is consistent with control commands from Seamote App, lifting the nose and dipping the back of the USV. Roll parameter proves to be stable in aquatic settings, as observed in the tests, only being tilted by abrupt corners, and always remaining in the correct position, due to the underwater camera stabilizing the center of mass.

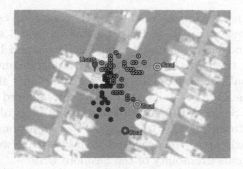

Fig. 4. Seamote In-situ test - 3 GPS trips denoted in colors from one point of the harbour to the other and back.

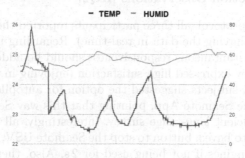

Fig. 5. Environmental telemetry sensor data obtained from the Seamote USV.

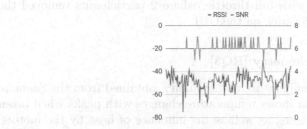

Fig. 6. Signal to Noise Ratio (SNR) consistent across different Received Signal Strength Indicator (RSSI) in water environments.

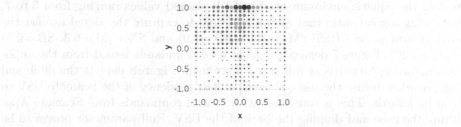

Fig. 7. X and Y map of the commands sent from the mobile application. Color and size denote the usage frequency of those positions (green indicating more). (Color figure online)

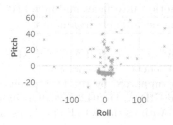

Fig. 8. USV pitch and roll indicating a tendency to lean backwards, as the primary motion in the tests was a forwards motion.

5   Discussion

In this study we present Seamote, an integrative LoRa-based IoWT apparatus for aquatic deployment, consisted from 3 designed modules: a mobile application (Seamote App), casing for the phone (Seamote Bridge), and an Internet of Water Things (IoWT) low-cost device, used for aquatic surveys (Seamote USV). While observing the results of our research questions, we find that it is possible to design and deploy IoWT applications [RQ1]. Moreover, LoRa proved to be adequate for the remote control of the USV, as reported by the participants [RQ2]. Conversely, obtained environmental telemetry shows the feasibility of collecting such data [RQ3]. More studies, and usability tests need to be performed to provide a more clear insight to the best tangible user interface and feedback. Currently, there are several limitations of Seamote apparatus such as the USV size and speed, as the design of circuits has been reappropriated to match into the existing toy casing. This hinders the Seamote to travel the larger distances which is allowed by LoRa. Also, such device can withstand solely Beaufort scale 1, avoiding the risk of permanent device dislocation. Future controller should support stronger casings while Seamote App needs to be tailored to allow multiple devices. Additional optimization should be performed to allow constant exchange of payloads among the devices. Future work will focus on integration of active tracking of acoustic tags, providing a flexible network of receivers capable of transmitting data in real-time. Seamote apparatus will be scaled up to support sun/wind power generation for long-term deployment and remote monitoring of environmental conditions. With Seamote apparatus, it is possible to sense and react to captured data, used in survey missions in marine biology. Also, Seamote can control multiple USVs and UAVs. Drones can be used to capture aerial images of the ocean, using real-time image vision algorithms to detect marine litter. Other versatile sensory input can also be mounted to the current microcontroller, e.g. dissolved oxygen, hydrophone, sonar, salinity, turbidity, plankton collectors, etc. Finally, Seamote apparatus provided in this pilot study has a threefold impact on aforementioned related work: (i) it provides a low-cost solution for the state of the art sensors found on market, as sensing the oceans remains still expensive; (ii) it challenges the IoT applications to be design for aquatic environment, allowing the new research direction in Internet of Water Things (IoWT); and finally (iii) it opens

the door for the new interaction interfaces and novel HCI applications which are to be applied in challenging oceanic environments.

Acknowledgements. Study is part of LARGESCALE project with grant no. 32474 by Fundação para a Ciência e a Tecnologia (FCT) and Portuguese National Funds (PIDDAC). It is also supported by the FCT grants SFRH/BD/135854/2018, SFRH/DB/136005/2018, and UID/MAR/04292/2019 including Fundo Social Europeu M1420-09-5369-FSE-000001. Authors thank to Filipe Alves and Ventura—Nature emotions for access to sea vessel.

References

1. Ahmad, D., Kumar, A.: IoT based smart river monitoring system. Int. J. Adv. Res. Ideas Innov. Technol. **4**(2), 60–64 (2018)
2. Ahmedi, F., et al.: InWaterSense: an intelligent wireless sensor network for monitoring surface water quality to a river in Kosovo. Int. J. Agric. Environ. Inf. Syst. (IJAEIS) **9**(1), 39–61 (2018)
3. Akyildiz, I.F., Pompili, D., Melodia, T.: Underwater acoustic sensor networks: research challenges. Ad Hoc Netw. **3**(3), 257–279 (2005)
4. Bandini, F., et al.: Bathymetry observations of Inland water bodies using a tethered single-beam sonar controlled by an unmanned aerial vehicle. Hydrol. Earth Syst. Sci. **22**(8), 4165–4181 (2018)
5. Bolin, J., Crawford, C., Macke, W., Hoffman, J., Beckmann, S., Sen, S.: Gesture-based control of autonomous UAVs. In: Proceedings of the 16th Conference on Autonomous Agents and MultiAgent Systems, pp. 1484–1486. International Foundation for Autonomous Agents and Multiagent Systems (2017)
6. Bourles, B., Molinari, R., Johns, E., Wilson, W., Leaman, K.: Upper layer currents in the western tropical North Atlantic (1989–1991). J. Geophys. Res. Oceans **104**(C1), 1361–1375 (1999)
7. Cavett, D., Coker, M., Jiménez, R., Yaacoubi, B.: Human-computer interface for control of unmanned aerial vehicles. In: 2007 IEEE Systems and Information Engineering Design Symposium, pp. 1–6 (2007)
8. Chaczko, Z., Kale, A., Santana-Rodríguez, J.J., Suárez-Araujo, C.P.: Towards an IoT based system for detection and monitoring of microplastics in aquatic environments. In: 2018 IEEE 22nd International Conference on Intelligent Engineering Systems (INES), pp. 000057–000062. IEEE (2018)
9. Chavan, M., Patil, M.V.P., Chavan, S., Sana, S., Shinde, C.: Design and implementation of IoT based real time monitoring system for aquaculture using Raspberry Pi. Int. J. Recent Innov. Trends Comput. Commun. **6**(3), 159–161 (2018)
10. Christ, R.D., Wernli Sr., R.L.: The ROV Manual: A User Guide for Remotely Operated Vehicles. Butterworth-Heinemann, Oxford (2013)
11. Corredor, J.E.: Signal conditioning, data telemetry, command signaling and platform positioning in ocean observing. Coastal Ocean Observing, pp. 101–111. Springer, Cham (2018). https://doi.org/10.1007/978-3-319-78352-9_5
12. Desbruyères, D., et al.: Variations in deep-sea hydrothermal vent communities on the Mid-Atlantic Ridge near the Azores plateau. Deep Sea Res. Part I **48**(5), 1325–1346 (2001)
13. Encinas, C., Ruiz, E., Cortez, J., Espinoza, A.: Design and implementation of a distributed IoT system for the monitoring of water quality in aquaculture. In: Wireless Telecommunications Symposium (WTS 2017), pp. 1–7. IEEE (2017)

14. Gkikopouli, A., Nikolakopoulos, G., Manesis, S.: A survey on underwater wireless sensor networks and applications. In: 2012 20th Mediterranean Conference on Control & Automation (MED), pp. 1147–1154. IEEE (2012)
15. Hansson, L., Agis, M., Maier, C., Weinbauer, M.G.: Community composition of bacteria associated with cold-water coral Madrepora oculata: within and between colony variability. Mar. Ecol. Prog. Ser. **397**, 89–102 (2009)
16. Hayes, R., Goreau, T.: Satellite-derived sea surface temperature from Caribbean and Atlantic coral reef sites, 1984–2003. Rev. de Biología Trop. **56**(1), 97–118 (2008)
17. Inniss, L., et al.: The first global integrated marine assessment: world ocean assessment (2017)
18. Jakovlev, S., Voznak, M., Andziulis, A., Kurmis, M.: Communication technologies for the improvement of marine transportation operations. IFAC Proc. Vol. **46**(15), 469–474 (2013)
19. Jianjun, W.: The design and development of the aquatic resources and water environment monitoring and control system based on IoT. Adv. J. Food Sci. Technol. **12**(12), 673–678 (2016)
20. Kamruzzaman, J., Wang, G., Karmakar, G., Ahmad, I., Bhuiyan, M.Z.A.: Acoustic sensor networks in the internet of things applications (2018)
21. Lyu, B., et al.: Combined small-sized USV and ROV observation system for long-term, large-scale, spatially explicit aquatic monitoring. In: 2018 OCEANS-MTS/IEEE Kobe Techno-Oceans (OTO), pp. 1–6. IEEE (2018)
22. Mann, S., Janzen, R., Huang, J.: WaterTouch: an aquatic interactive multimedia sensory table based on total internal reflection in water. In: Proceedings of the 19th ACM International Conference on Multimedia, pp. 925–928. ACM (2011)
23. Mashood, A., Noura, H., Jawhar, I., Mohamed, N.: A gesture based kinect for quadrotor control. In: 2015 International Conference on Information and Communication Technology Research (ICTRC), pp. 298–301. IEEE (2015)
24. Matos, J., Postolache, O.: IoT enabled aquatic drone for environmental monitoring. In: 2016 International Conference and Exposition on Electrical and Power Engineering (EPE), pp. 598–603. IEEE (2016)
25. Mustari, M.S., Amri, A., Samman, F.A., Tola, M.: Remotely operated vehicle for surveilance applications on and under water surface (2017)
26. Pham, C.K., et al.: Marine litter distribution and density in European seas, from the shelves to deep basins. PLoS ONE **9**(4), e95839 (2014)
27. Radeta, M., Nunes, N.J., Vasconcelos, D., Nisi, V.: Poseidon-passive-acoustic ocean sensor for entertainment and interactive data-gathering in opportunistic nautical-activities. In: Proceedings of the 2018 on Designing Interactive Systems Conference, pp. 999–1011. ACM (2018)
28. Raju, K.R.S.R., Varma, G.H.K.: Knowledge based real time monitoring system for aquaculture using IoT. In: 2017 IEEE 7th International Advance Computing Conference (IACC), pp. 318–321. IEEE (2017)
29. Risk, M.J., Hall-Spencer, J., Williams, B.: Climate records from the Faroe-Shetland channel using Lophelia Pertusa (Linnaeus, 1758). In: Freiwald, A., Roberts, J.M. (eds.) Cold-Water Corals and Ecosystems. ERLANGEN, pp. 1097–1108. Springer, Heidelberg (2005). https://doi.org/10.1007/3-540-27673-4_55
30. Robinson, L.F., Adkins, J.F., Scheirer, D.S., Fernandez, D.P., Gagnon, A., Waller, R.G.: Deep-sea scleractinian coral age and depth distributions in the Northwest Atlantic for the last 225,000 years. Bull. Mar. Sci. **81**(3), 371–391 (2007)
31. Rodríguez, Y., Pham, C.K.: Marine litter on the seafloor of the Faial-Pico passage, Azores Archipelago. Mar. Pollut. Bull. **116**(1–2), 448–453 (2017)

32. Smale, D.A., Wernberg, T.: Satellite-derived SST data as a proxy for water temperature in nearshore benthic ecology. Mar. Ecol. Prog. Ser. **387**, 27–37 (2009)
33. Trenkel, V.M., Francis, R.C., Lorance, P., Mahévas, S., Rochet, M.J., Tracey, D.M.: Availability of deep-water fish to trawling and visual observation from a remotely operated vehicle (ROV). Mar. Ecol. Prog. Ser. **284**, 293–303 (2004)
34. Won, J.Y., Lee, H.J.: UAV ground control station GUI guidelines: for the designer, developer and operator's needs. In: Proceedings of HCI Korea, HCIK 2015, pp. 44–50. Hanbit Media Inc. (2014). http://dl.acm.org/citation.cfm?id=2729485.2729493

TouchGlass: Raycasting from a Glass Surface to Point at Physical Objects in Public Exhibits

Florent Cabric[1](✉), Emmanuel Dubois[1], Pourang Irani[1,2], and Marcos Serrano[1]

[1] University of Toulouse, Toulouse, France
{florent.cabric,emmanuel.dubois,pourang.irani, marcos.serrano}@irit.fr
[2] HCI Lab, University of Manitoba, Winnipeg, Canada
irani@cs.umanitoba.ca

Abstract. Physical objects such as natural items or fine art pieces are often placed behind glass cases to protect them from dust and damage. Generally, interacting with such objects is indirect, based for example on an adjacent touch interface detracting users' attention from the object. In this paper, we explore whether the glass case could be used as an input surface to point and select distant physical objects. With such an approach, the glass case offers a physical delimiter for interaction to avoid unintended activations. We explore this innovative approach through a two steps approach. First, we carry an informative study with 46 participants to validate the most appropriate "walk-up and use" technique. Our results show that using a ray orthogonal to the glass surface is the most natural approach in a public setting. Next, we further explore this orthogonal raycasting technique and conduct a target acquisition experiment to evaluate the impact on target selection performance of the target size, target distance, presence of spatial references and user's head position with regards to the glass case. Results reveal that using the glass as touch surface allows to easily select targets as small as 3 cm up to 35 cm away from the glass. From these results, we provide a set of guidelines to design interactive exhibits using a touch glass case.

Keywords: Touch input · Distant pointing · Transparent touch surface · Absolute pointing · Evaluation · Physical objects

1 Introduction

Physical objects such as natural history items or fine art pieces are often placed behind a glass case in public exhibits to protect them from dust or damage. Most of these exhibits are not interactive, hence the level of information that can be displayed is usually limited to small physical notes. The few interactions in this context are often

---

Electronic supplementary material The online version of this chapter (https://doi.org/10.1007/978-3-030-29387-1_15) contains supplementary material, which is available to authorized users.

© IFIP International Federation for Information Processing 2019
Published by Springer Nature Switzerland AG 2019
D. Lamas et al. (Eds.): INTERACT 2019, LNCS 11748, pp. 249–269, 2019.
https://doi.org/10.1007/978-3-030-29387-1_15

based on a touch input on a separated display [1], which detracts the user from the exhibit artifact.

While these objects are placed behind a glass, few projects have explored how to use such glass cases to interact with objects inside the case. Previous solutions include the use of augmented reality through smartphones or tablets [2]. Those solutions require the user to install a dedicated application. Alternative proposals include the use of mid-air gestures [3], which suffer from discoverability and delimiter problems. Interacting on the glass case instead has several advantages: (1) it offers a physical delimiter for interaction (touching the glass) avoiding unintended activations; (2) it does not visually deviate the user from the physical content displayed inside the glass case; (3) finally, it is technically robust, low-cost and easy to implement on existing glass cases thanks to current touch technologies (e.g. infrared panels).

In this paper, we explore how to select a physical object behind a glass by using 2D touch input on the glass itself (cf. Fig. 1). We first analyze the different "walk-up and use" approaches that users would employ when faced with a tactile glass. To this end, we ran a study aimed at exploring the users' spontaneous way of pointing at an object behind a glass. The results reveal that the most frequent interaction is similar to the way objects are selected on touch screens (i.e. through raycasting using a 2D ray perpendicular to the glass surface). However, unlike classical direct interaction on touch-screens, this setup introduces a spatial gap between the object to select (showcased in the glass case) and the touch surface (i.e. the glass). This gap may affect the ability of the user to touch the surface on a place that is associated with the target behind the glass.

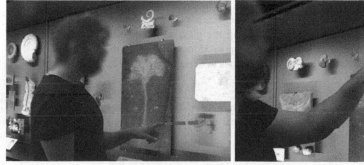
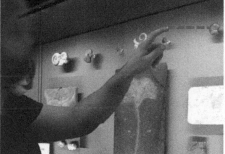

Fig. 1. A user selecting different physical objects through a glass case

In a second step, we evaluate the impact of the target size, the target distance, the presence of spatial references and the user's head position with regards to the glass case, on target selection using an orthogonal ray. This experiment reveals that using the glass to point at objects is a viable approach, as it allows to easily select targets as small as 3 cm up to 35 cm away from the glass.

Our contributions are (1) a first study revealing the best "walk-up-and-use" approach to interact with augmented glass cases; (2) a target acquisition controlled

study assessing the performance of pointing on a glass case using an orthogonal ray, and (3) guidelines for designing pointing systems in interactive exhibits using a glass as touch input.

2 Related Work

Our work focuses on the use of an interactive glass case to point at a distant object, i.e. an object out of user's arms reach. Direct and indirect touch input has been widely studied in different contexts (large surfaces [4], single-pointer interaction [5], pen-based input [6], etc.). The originality of our approach is that the object to select is not just behind the tactile surface, but physically distant from it. In such a context, raycasting is the most widely used technique for direct pointing, while using a separated touch surface is the most frequent technique for indirect pointing. We synthesize works related to these two aspects (*direct vs. indirect*) in the following sections and describe concrete examples of distant pointing techniques in public situations.

2.1 Raycasting as a Direct Technique for Pointing at Distant Objects

Most techniques to select objects in space are related to raycasting, which is the standard technique to point and select objects in virtual environments [7–9]. To control the ray direction in the real world, most approaches used either the finger [10, 11] or a handheld object [12–14]. These techniques have been used in volumetric displays [15, 16] and AR systems [17–19], which can display the entire ray. However, using such raycasting techniques in the real world raises two major problems: the parallax effect and the lack of feedback to render either the ray in midair or the resulting pointer/cursor.

Parallax Effect. In the context of touch surfaces, the parallax effect has been defined as "a difference between the perceived location at a particular UI element and users' actual touch location on the surface" [20]: it is related to the inability for the user's eye to focus simultaneously at two different depths (called binocular parallax), e.g. the tip of the finger and the distant object. Errors due to this parallax are designated as "parallax errors" by Migge et Kunz [21]. An example of such effect can be found on public interactive displays protected by a thick tactile glass (e.g. ATM): in this context, Khamis et al. [20] studied the gap between the touch and the pointer. They explored the effect of several correcting methods to increase the accuracy of touch, which improved significantly the accuracy of pointing tasks. In a different context, Lee et al. [22] designed a binocular cursor to increase pointing performance. In both cases, the pro-posed solutions require to display visual feedback to alleviate the parallax effect. However, in our context, the glass case has no display capabilities.

Lack of Feedback. Concerning the difficulty to provide a feedback when using a raycasting technique for pointing at a distant object, previous works applied projection mapping, which draws the ray projection (i.e. the cursor) on the physical surface. For instance, Bandyopadhyay et al. [23] used a lamp as a pointing device to select physical objects. Some researchers applied laser pointers to represent the ray projection [24].

Even though these approaches usually work well with one large object, they can be limited when dealing with small objects, such as insects in a museum, or when there is no projection surface in between two items, i.e. when they are hanging.

Recently, Freeman et al. [25] investigated pointing at levitating small spherical objects with mid-air movement of the index finger. The technique consisted of a 3D raycast, without any visual feedback of the ray (except for the target shaking when pointed at). However, since they investigated a very small distance between finger and target (from 5 cm to 8 cm), their results are difficult to extend to our usage context (i.e. public exhibit), where objects are usually further away from the glass.

2.2 Indirect Touch-Techniques for Pointing at a Distant Object

There are two types of indirect touch pointing techniques: absolute (i.e. the input device sends its position (x, y)) or relative (i.e. the input device sends its movement (Δx, Δy)) [26]. Relative solutions require to permanently visualize the current position of the pointer. In our context displaying a pointer is not viable (as explained in the previous section), so this section focuses on absolute indirect pointing solutions only.

Previous works explored the main factors influencing absolute indirect pointing. A first important factor is the presence of a tactile spatial reference. For instance, landmarks placed on the back-of-device contribute to increasing accuracy [27]. A second factor is the relative size and aspect ratios between the input and the display, which may negatively influence success rate of target selection [28]. Finally, a third important factor is the type of feedback. Previous studies on touch input for large projected displays revealed that, even without feedback, users can select 90% of targets [29]. This means that absolute pointing is still a good candidate when no feedback is provided. However, these three studies focused on interaction with 2D touchscreens while in our case we investigate the use of a transparent glass surface with a large physical gap between the glass and the target.

2.3 Pointing at Items Behind Glass in Public Exhibits

Previous research proposed a variety of approaches to promote a more engaging experience with exhibit items. For instance, [30] proposed using mid-air gestures, detected with a Kinect, to point at an object behind a glass. Plasencia et al. [3] implemented a similar approach, augmenting the glass case with AR capabilities. The system detected the hand position using a Leap Motion and the augmented glass showed the hand reflection to facilitate the object selection. The flashlight metaphor was investigated in public exhibits [31, 32] through a system that augments physical museum pieces using video projection. Pointing requires using a 6 DOF controller or a Leap Motion. The main limitation of these approaches is that they require to augment the glass cases with some projection mapping. Moreover, mid-air gestures suffer from a lack of delimiter, which can lead to false positives. Finally, the need to spatially track hand and fingers can usually only be performed on a reduced volume.

2.4   Synthesis

On the one hand, raycasting is a popular direct pointing technique for reaching distant objects, but can introduce a parallax effect and will suffer from the lack of feedback in the real world. On the other hand, indirect techniques appear to be very effective even without feedback but tend to break the interaction flow as they split the user's attention between different input and output spaces.

In our work, we explore how to combine these two approaches to take advantage of their respective benefits, which results in the concept of *ray casting from a glass surface*. In a public exhibit context, the use of a ray casting technique should make the interaction easy to discover and learn. The glass can be considered as an indirect input surface, which offers the advantage of providing a physical delimiter and should facilitate pointing without feedback.

To our knowledge, this concept of ray casting from a glass surface has not been studied before and constitutes a different interaction setup than those previously cited: the touch surface is transparent and the object to select is at a distance behind it. Therefore, we carried a two steps approach to explore this new environment: first, we led an informative study to find the most natural interaction in a public context; then, we further explored the most used approach in a controlled experiment to assess its performance.

3   Informative Study

While using a glass to select a physical object placed behind it presents several advantages as mentioned earlier, casting a ray only requires to define an origin and a direction or a target. Hence there are different possible ways of casting a ray from the glass surface: by using the finger orientation [10, 15, 25] (i.e. finger oriented raycasting cf. Fig. 2A), by using an eye-finger raycasting [33–35] (also known as image-plane technique cf. Fig. 2B) or by placing the finger in front of the object and using the glass surface as a touchscreen (i.e. raycasting orthogonal to the glass cf. Fig. 2C). However, an appropriate interaction technique for a public context needs to be as self-explanatory [36] as possible, so that passers-by interact with the glass with a minimum of instructions.

To find out the most appropriate interaction, we conducted an informative study in a public environment with passers-by. The goal of this study was to explore how participants would intuitively make use of the glass to point at an object behind it.

3.1   Experimental Protocol

Task and Instructions. Five white physical spheres with a diameter of 2 cm were positioned on cardboard, placed 55 cm behind the glass. Four of them defined the corners of a 33 × 26 cm side rectangle, while the fifth one was positioned in the middle of the rectangle. Participants received the following instruction: *"Please point at each of the five white spheres, using the glass case in front of you as a support for the interaction"*. Before pointing at a target, participants were requested to orally

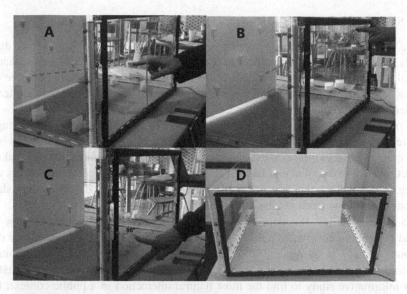

Fig. 2. Three types of raycasting performed by participants: (A) Oriented, (B) Eye-Finger, and (C) Orthogonal. Detailed view of the glass and targets (D).

precise which target they were planning to select. Participants had to select all of them in a free order. Participants were not aware of these three categories when taking part into the experiment.

Participants. We recruited 46 participants (39 males and 7 females) aged between 19 and 62 (M = 33). All participants were recruited in the hall of the local university as they passed-by: 13 were university members, 26 were computer science students, five were engineers and two were administrative employees.

Apparatus. The glass case was installed during 10 h in a hall of our local university. The glass panel (78.5 × 44 cm) was placed on a 90 cm height table. Users had to position themselves in the middle of the glass panel and at a distance where all targets were visible and the glass case easily reachable with their arm (cf. Fig. 2).

Collected Data. All the experiment was video-recorded. After all trials were completed, we asked the participants to provide a graphical representation of how their finger was positioned and oriented to perform each selection task. Based on the video recording and the representations provided by the participants, experimenters clustered the results into three categories, corresponding to the possible approaches presented for casting a ray from the glass: (1) oriented raycasting, i.e. using their finger orientation; (2) eye-finger raycasting, i.e. aiming at the object with the finger; and (3) orthogonal raycasting, i.e. casting a ray perpendicular to the glass. The experimenter cross-checked the video and the graphical representation to ensure there were no inconsistencies between the method used and the one reported by the participants.

3.2   Results

Among the 46 participants, 40 of them used some sort of raycasting to select targets as expected, while 4 participants used gestural input and 2 participants misunderstood the instructions (i.e. they tried to reach the objects by avoiding the glass case). Therefore, our analysis of the type of raycasting focuses on the 40 participants who employed some sort of raycasting to point at the objects behind the glass.

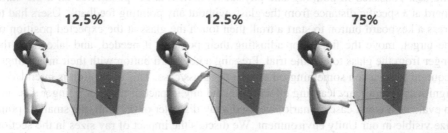

Fig. 3. Percentage of participants that employed each type of raycasting: oriented raycasting (left), eye-finger raycasting (center) and orthogonal raycasting (right).

Our results reveal that among those 40 participants, 5 participants (12,5%) cast an oriented ray (i.e. using their finger orientation) to select targets; 5 participants (12,5%) cast an eye-finger ray (i.e. aligning eye, finger, and object); while 30 participants (75%) cast a ray orthogonal to the glass surface, as illustrated in Fig. 3.

3.3   Conclusion

75% of the participants that used a raycasting, adopted an orthogonal ray as the most "walk-up and use" technique in a public context. One possible explanation for this is that this approach eliminates the parallax effect since the finger, eye, and object do not need to be aligned. Therefore, in our subsequent work, we consider such interaction and do not try to compensate for the parallax effect. Incidentally, this interaction only requires to track the user's finger position on the glass, making its implementation quite simple using an infrared touch panel. The main challenge then is to assess whether such form of interaction is efficient in terms of precision. To tack this question, we conduct a controlled pointing study.

4   Pointing Study: Design

The goal of this study is to investigate the impact of four factors on pointing at objects behind a glass-case when using a ray cast perpendicular to the glass. These factors are (1) target size, (2) target distance from the glass, (3) presence of spatial references and (4) users' head position. Additionally, since interaction in public spaces needs to be easy and quick to use, we also investigated how well users perform the first contact with the touch glass, i.e. before any adjustment, in terms of deviation from the target:

this could provide valuable information for interaction designers about targets shape and size (we discuss its implications in the Discussion section). Finally, since our main goal is to explore the performance of such an interactive technique, we did not compare it to any baseline technique.

4.1 Task and Instructions

The task consisted in pointing one physical spherical target positioned on a 2D cardboard at a specific distance from the glass, without any pointing feedback. Users had to press a keyboard button to start a trial, then touch the glass at the expected position of the target, move the finger for adjusting their pointing if needed, and take back the finger from the glass to end the trial. Pressing a keyboard button with their index finger required to focus on something other than the glass case. This disruption is intended to significantly limit any learning effect. To avoid any impact of the user's finger size and to evaluate a worst case scenario, we used a ray diameter of 0.2 mm, the smallest point size visible in our Unity environment. We discuss the impact of ray sizes in the section Discussion.

We asked participants to select the target at land-on as precisely as possible, and, if they did not reach the target, to move the finger as fast as possible to adjust their pointing. They had to use the index finger of their dominant hand. As mentioned earlier, projection, and therefore dynamic feedback, may not be possible in museum glass cases. Hence, the only interaction feedback used in our study is a white dot to indicate the next target to select (displayed next to the target). The dot became green or red to indicate selection success or failure at land-on. This interaction feedback allowed the user to stay focused on the target throughout the experiment. All these steps are summed up in the Fig. 4 and several trials are presented in the adjunct video.

Of course, in a public context, the pointing would result in displaying some domain related information to the visitor (e.g. in a museum context, the name of the creator, the composition of a rock, etc.): this museographic feedback is generally displayed on a separate display but could also be presented in a more direct manner using spatialized sound or an inside glass projection. Anyway, exploring how to render this museographic information is out of the scope of our work.

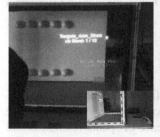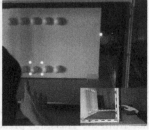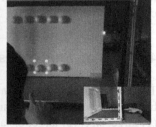

Fig. 4. The three steps of a trial: (left) the starting press on the keyboard, (center) the land-on pointing on the glass-case and (right) the adjustment gesture on the glass-case. (Color figure online)

4.2   Target Conditions

We evaluated different target sizes, target distances to the glass, target closeness to a spatial reference and the user's head position with regards to the glass case (and hence to the targets). We defined four target sizes, from 1 to 4 cm in diameter, to cover the spectrum of smallest targets found in a museum. Similar sizes have also been examined in earlier work on targets for touch [37–39], deemed reachable from 10.5 mm to 26 mm.

Our targets were positioned at three different distances to the glass (15, 35 and 55 cm) as a proxy for close, medium and long distances.

For each setting, we positioned 10 spherical targets (cf. Fig. 5) on a 2D cardboard. The targets were aligned on 2 horizontal lines, i.e. 5 targets per line, to explore the impact of a spatial reference on pointing. This condition required to fix the targets in the same locations. The top line was approx. in the middle of the glass case (i.e. without any spatial reference), while the bottom line was close to the bottom of the case (acting as a spatial reference).

Finally, the user could be sitting, i.e. with the head in front of the targets, or standing up, i.e. with the head above the targets. We ensured that all participants positioned their head and body at the same height by using a footstool.

4.3   Participants

We recruited 12 participants aged between 21 and 48 (M = 29.5, SD = 8.26). 11 participants were recruited at the university and were undergraduate students (4), Ph.D. students (4), research assistants (3) or engineer (1). Ten participants were right-handed and two left-handed.

4.4   Design and Procedure

The experiment followed a 4 × 3 × 2 × 2 within-participant design with target Size (1, 2, 3 or 4 cm diameter sphere), Distance to the glass (15, 35 and 55 cm), Spatial reference (with or without) and User's head position (in front or above). The User's head position was counterbalanced over participants, and Distance and Size were randomly ordered so that two consecutive trials with the same Distance or Size could not appear. The rest of the trials were ordered randomly. The whole experiment lasted between 70 and 110 min.

We created a specific set of 10 targets (containing the different sizes) for training. The training session consisted in selecting every target on this set for every distance and height (i.e. 10 × 3 × 2 = 60 trials). This training lasted approx. 10 min and represents 7,6% of the whole experiment.

In total, we collected 4 Sizes × 3 Distances × 2 Spatial reference × 2 User's head position × 5 targets × 3 repetitions = 720 trials per participant and 8640 trials in total.

4.5   Apparatus

We built a glass case using four plexiglass sheets of 78.5 cm × 44 cm × 0.5 cm (L × H × T). For finger tracking, we used an infrared panel (ZaagTech X series v7, 70 cm × 40 cm, with 40 touch points, resolution of 32 768 * 32 768, touch response time of 7 ms–13 ms), USB connected to the computer running the study. The available touch interaction surface was 70 cm × 40 cm. The panel was attached to one side of the glass case. We also reinforced the plexiglass sheet by adding a metal structure all around it to avoid any deformation or movement of the sheet during the interaction. We used two video projectors (to avoid the possible occlusion caused by the participant's arm) connected through a DisplayPort hub – HDMI, to ensure that the visual inter-action feedback was displayed even if the user obstructed one of them. We ensured that there was no light reflection on the glass that could hinder interaction. Between each participant, the glass case was cleaned to remove all finger marks. In public context, anti-fingerprint spray can be used to limit any dirt from touches.

We implemented the whole setup on an HP EliteBook laptop running Microsoft Windows 10. Our experiment software was implemented in C# and Unity (version 2018 1.5). Touch events were sent to the application using the TUIO protocol. We modeled the physical environment in Unity to ensure that the interaction feedback was displayed around the target.

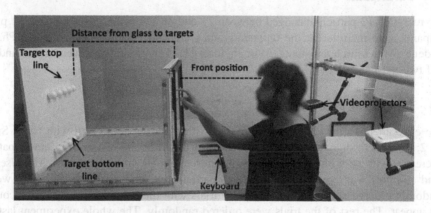

Fig. 5. Experimental setup.

4.6   Collected Data and Data Processing

We logged all touch events from keyboard press until finger land-off (from the glass case). As we were interested in understanding how well users perform the first contact (land-on) with the glass case, we logged for each trial the land-on and land-off finger positions and times (i.e. first and last contact with the glass).

We refined the land-on points analysis with two metrics (cf. Fig. 6) already used in [40, 41]: offset and spread. Both metrics rely on the computation of the centroid, i.e. the average land-on position for each target and condition.

The offset is defined as the Euclidean distance (i.e. absolute value) between the center of the target and the centroid, for each condition. In this paper, we also compute the offsetX and offsetY, which represents the relative distance in x and y between the centroid and the center of the target (i.e. a signed value).

Spread represents the distribution of the land-on points around the centroid, computed as the diameter of the smallest circle containing 95% of all land-on points.

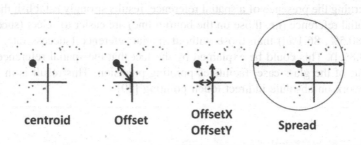

centroid   Offset   OffsetX   Spread
                                  OffsetY

Fig. 6. Illustration of metrics used to analyze land-on points.

Regarding the data analysis, we chose to rely on estimation techniques with 95% Confidence Intervals (CIs) as recommended by the APA [42]. All CIs are 95% BCa bootstrap confidence intervals. Scripts used to compute the geometric average and confidence intervals were used in [43] and are available online [44].

5   Pointing Study Results

We split the analysis into two parts. First, we present the results regarding the target selection task in terms of success rate and time. Then, we analyze the land-on gesture in terms of offset and spread, as explained earlier.

5.1   Target Selection Success Rate

We started by analyzing the results for each target size, independently of the target distance, the user's head position or the spatial reference. Unsurprisingly, the 1 cm targets were the hardest to reach with only 55.8% (CI[48.7%, 65.1%]) of successful trials (cf. Fig. 7). The 2 cm targets were easier to acquire but remain generally difficult, with a success rate of 78.1% (CI[75.8%, 80.6]). The 3 cm and 4 cm targets have a success rate over 90% (3 cm targets: 90.8%, CI[89.5%, 92.4%]; 4 cm targets: 93.2%, CI [90.3%, 95.3%]). For these two larger target sizes, we observed during the experiment that after some successful trials, some users performed the task too fast, i.e. removing the finger before the feedback appeared, leading to some erroneous selections.

Concerning the distance between the glass case and the targets, independently of the other factors, it appears that targets placed 15 cm away were always easier to select (success rate: 82.5% CI[80.1%, 85.4%]) than those placed at 55 cm (success rate: 76.6% CI[73.1%, 80.4%]). However no clear conclusion are revealed when comparing the 15 cm condition to the 35 cm condition (79.3% CI[75.7%, 83%]). This result holds true for all target sizes except for the 1 cm target, which is equally difficult to select for the three distances (i.e. all CIs overlap, cf. Fig. 7).

Concerning the presence of a spatial reference, results strongly establish that targets with a spatial reference (i.e. those on the bottom line) are easier to select (success rate: 83%, CI[80.5%, 86.1%]) than those without spatial reference (success rate: 76%, CI [73.%, 79.8%]). This could be explained by the fact that the spatial reference, i.e. the bottom part of the glass case, facilitates pointing precision. This result is in line with previous work on absolute indirect touch pointing [29].

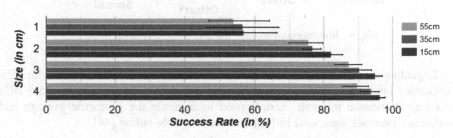

Fig. 7. Average success rate in % (with 95% CIs) according to target size and distance to the glass.

According to the collected data, the user's head position does not seem to influence the success rate (above: 79.2%, CI[75.9%, 82.7%]; front: 79.8% CI[76.9%, 83.3%]). This result is quite surprising, as we expected the front condition to favor target selection.

5.2 Trial Completion Time

Regarding trial completion time for the different target sizes, results underline the difficulty of selecting the 1 cm targets: in this case, it took users almost 10 s to complete the task (9.4 s, CI[8.1, 10.4]). For the other target sizes (cf. Fig. 8), completion time clearly decreases when the target size increases (2 cm targets: 4.6 s, CI [4.0, 5.1]; 3 cm targets: 3 s, CI[2.6, 3.3]; 4 cm targets: 2.3 s; CI[2.1, 2.6]).

For target distance, we observed the same effect. Although the success rate is very similar for 35 and 55 cm, results strongly establish that on average completion time is smaller when targets are closer to the user (15 cm: 4 s, CI[3.5, 4.6]; 35 cm: 5 s, CI[4.5, 5.4]; 55 cm: 5.33 s, CI[4.6, 6.19], cf. Fig. 8).

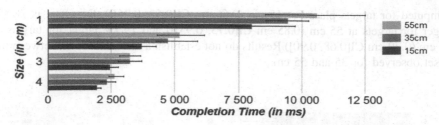

Fig. 8. Average time completion in ms (with 95% CIs) according to target size and distance to the glass.

Results did not reveal any effect of spatial reference or user's head position on completion time.

5.3 Land-on Pointing: Centroid, Offset and Spread

We analyzed land-on pointing results in terms of pointing centroids, offset and spread. In this part, we use 95% confidence interval without bootstrapping.

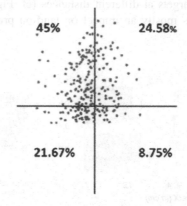

Fig. 9. Distribution of all land-on pointing centroids around the targets. Most of them occur in the top-left area.

Centroid Analysis. Plotting all centroid positions on the same referential gives an overview of pointing at land-on. More than 65% of all centroids are situated on the left of the targets. Almost 70% are situated on the top with 45% on the upper left part (cf. Fig. 9). This result indicates that users had a general tendency to point too high and too far on the left of the physical targets. We further refine this overview by looking at offset, offsetX, and offsetY for our different conditions.

Offset, OffsetX and OffsetY. We found no difference on offset values regarding target size, hence we analysed the results for all target sizes included. Concerning target distance, offset grows with increasing distance (cf. Fig. 10): in comparison to the offset

computed for targets placed at 15 cm (0.66 cm CI[0.55, 0.76])), the offset is 28.8% larger for targets at 55 cm (0.85 cm CI[0.75, 0.95])) and 19.7% larger for targets at 35 cm (0.79 cm CI[0.68, 0.90]) Results do not establish a clear difference between the offset observed for 35 and 55 cm.

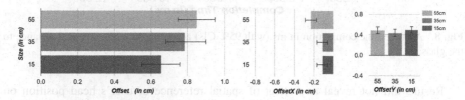

Fig. 10. Average offset (left), offsetX (center) and offsetY (right) in cm (with 95% CIs) according to target distance to the glass.

We refine this analysis by looking at offsetX and offsetY. Interestingly, while we can find the same trend for offsetX (i.e. offsetX average is 29.8% larger for targets at 55 cm and 16.4% larger for targets at 35 cm than for those at 15 cm), results reveal no difference in offsetY for targets at different distances (cf. Fig. 10). We can conclude that the distance factor has mostly an impact on land-on precision on the horizontal axis.

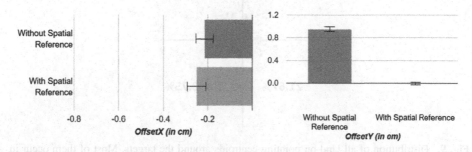

Fig. 11. Average offsetX (left) and offsetY (right) in cm (with 95% CIs) according to spatial reference condition.

Regarding the effect of the spatial reference on the offset value, we observed that the average offset is 125% larger for the targets without spatial reference than those with a spatial reference: offset is 1.06 cm (CI[1.02, 1.10]) without spatial reference vs. 0.47 cm (CI[0.44, 0.49]) with a spatial reference. When looking at the impact of target position on offsetX and offsetY, results do not reveal any difference on offsetX. However, offsetY is larger for the targets without spatial reference (0.95 cm CI[0.87, 1.04]) than those with a spatial reference (0.01 cm CI[0.05, 0.04]), as illustrated in Fig. 11.

This analysis can be reinforced when we plot all centroids (cf. Fig. 12) according to both target positions. We can see the large vertical distribution for targets without spatial reference compared to targets with reference.

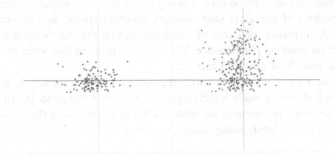

Fig. 12. Distribution of centroids according to the spatial reference: with (left) or without (right).

Finally, we analyzed the offset according to the User's head position, we found that offset is almost 60% larger when the user's head is in front of the targets (0.65 cm CI [0.61, 0.68]) than above them (0.88 cm CI[0.82, 0.95]). This result holds true for both offsetX and offsetY. This result is surprising since we could expect targets in the front condition to be easier to point, as the user's gaze is aligned with the finger and the target.

Spread. The spread represents the distribution of land-on points around the centroid. Results are in line with our previous findings. Target distance has an impact on spread, which is clearly higher when the distance increases (15 cm: 2.95 cm, CI[2.81, 3.10]; 35 cm: 3.91 cm, CI[3.76, 4.06]; 55 cm: 4.23 cm, CI[4.10, 4.36] cf. Fig. 13).

Furthermore, targets with a spatial reference strongly reduce (cf. Fig. 13) the spread with 3.24 cm (CI[3.15, 3.33]) compared to target without spatial reference (4.16 cm CI [4.02, 4.30]).

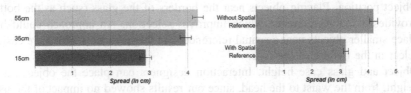

Fig. 13. Average spread in cm (with 95% CIs) by target distance (left) and by spatial reference (right).

The target size and user's head position conditions do not seem to have an impact on spread.

5.4   Summary

Our study revealed that both target size and distance to the glass have a strong impact on pointing performance. Very small targets (1 cm) are very hard to point and take a long time to reach. Using larger targets and placing them closer to the glass increases both success rate and completion time. Placing the targets near a spatial reference, such as near the bottom of the glass case, reduces pointing spread and favours pointing performance. A surprising outcome of this study is that the user's point of view has limited impact on pointing performance. We actually observed that when the targets are in front of the user, land-on offset increases.

Overall, our results show that using the glass as touch surface is a promising approach, which allows to easily select targets as small as 3 cm up to 35 cm away from the glass. In the following section, we analyzed the implications of these results for the design of interactive exhibits using touch on a glass.

6   Discussion

Overall, our results show that using the glass as touch surface is a promising approach, which allows to easily select targets as small as 3 cm up to 35 cm away from the glass. In the following section, we analyzed the implications of these results for the design of interactive exhibits using touch on a glass.

6.1   Design Guidelines

Our guidelines can help interaction designers to select the appropriate target size, distance, position and height in the context of absolute indirect pointing on a glass case surrounding a physical object:

- Object size. Designers should favour using orthogonal raycasting from the glass-case for pointing at physical objects placed behind the glass that are larger than 2 cm.
- Object distance to the glass. Objects should be placed at less than 35 cm from the glass. Only objects of 4 cm in size or more, should be placed further away since they still have an average success rate above 90%.
- Object position. Placing objects near the borders of the glass (such as the bottom) provides a spatial reference which improves selection. An approach could be to place smaller objects near a spatial reference, and larger objects which are easier to select in the middle of the case.
- Object and glass case height. Interaction designers can place the objects at any height, from the waist to the head, since our results showed no impact of the user's head position relatively to the object on selection accuracy.

6.2   Improving Target Selection

Our results underline that using a glass as a touch surface to interact with exhibit items is a promising approach, which can be used with relatively small targets placed up to

35 cm away from the glass. Here we present different ways to improve target selection, which could be helpful to facilitate interaction with even smaller and further targets.

Ray Diameter. We chose to study pointing on a physical object by casting a ray with a diameter of 0.2 mm. Since the average offset to the target at land-on ranges from 0.6 to 0.8 cm on average, using a larger diameter will improve target reaching for all conditions. We reran the analysis of our experimental data with two different ray diameters of 1 cm and 2 cm: we found that targets reach on first land-on increases from 42% with a 0.2 mm ray, to 60% with a 1 cm ray and to 73% with a 2 cm ray.

Increase Target Virtual Size. Increasing the virtual size (i.e. the area that can be selected) of targets is a well-known approach [45, 46] to improve pointing performance when the target real size cannot be changed. Our analysis on the spread and the offset shows that land-on points tend to be located above the target. Expanding the virtual size of targets with a vertical rectangular bounding box could facilitate pointing.

6.3 Perspectives

Beyond studying the impact of a different ray diameter or target virtual size, as detailed earlier, a first perspective is to carry a longitudinal in-situ study to analyze the visitors' behavior with such system in a public exhibit. This study would also permit to assess how and where to present the information requested through the direct pointing action on the glass case. As said earlier, the museographic feedback is generally displayed on a separate display but could also be presented in a more direct manner using spatialized sound or an inside glass projection. A second perspective would be to extend our approach to enable selecting volumetric targets. This could be of interest to interact with physical architectural models, which are usually placed behind a glass case. For instance, a model of an airport terminal can be useful for passengers to visualize their way to reach the appropriate terminal. To this end, we need to propose and study solutions for extending our current 2D selection to 3D. One solution will be to adapt existing raycasting disambiguation techniques [16, 47, 48].

7 Conclusion

In this work, we presented a study of *ray casting from a glass surface* for pointing on physical objects behind a glass. This study was motivated by an informative experiment which allowed us to identify the best "walk-up and use" approach for raycasting using an interactive glass case: a raycasting orthogonal to the glass surface. We further studied this particular type of raycasting in a target acquisition experiment. The goal was to evaluate the use of a glass as touch input to point at physical targets placed behind the glass, according to target size, target distance, the presence of spatial references and user's head position with regards to the glass case. Our experimental results reveal that using a glass as touch surface to point at exhibit items behind it is a promising approach, which can be used with relatively small targets placed up to 35 cm away from the glass. Using these results, we proposed several design guidelines for interaction with a physical object behind a glass.

Acknowledgments. This work is partially funded by the French region Occitanie, the neOCampus project (University Toulouse 3) and the AP2 project (ANR grant: AP2 ANR-15-CE23-0001).

References

1. Roberts, J., Banerjee, A., Hong, A., McGee, S., Horn, M., Matcuk, M.: Digital exhibit labels in museums: promoting visitor engagement with cultural artifacts. In: Proceedings of the 2018 CHI Conference on Human Factors in Computing Systems, CHI 2018, pp. 1–12 (2018). https://doi.org/10.1145/3173574.3174197
2. Spindler, M., Dachselt, R.: PaperLens: advanced magic lens interaction above the tabletop. In: Proceedings of the ACM International Conference on Interactive Tabletops and Surfaces, ITS 2009, p. 1 (2009). https://doi.org/10.1145/1731903.1731948
3. Martinez Plasencia, D., Berthaut, F., Karnik, A., Subramanian, S.: Through the combining glass. In: Proceedings of the 27th Annual ACM Symposium on User Interface Software and Technology, UIST 2014, pp. 341–350 (2014). https://doi.org/10.1145/2642918.2647351
4. Schmidt, D., Block, F., Gellersen, H.: A comparison of direct and indirect multi-touch input for large surfaces. In: Gross, T., et al. (eds.) INTERACT 2009. LNCS, vol. 5726, pp. 582–594. Springer, Heidelberg (2009). https://doi.org/10.1007/978-3-642-03655-2_65
5. Sears, A., Shneiderman, B.: High precision touchscreens: design strategies and comparisons with a mouse. Int. J. Man-Mach. Stud. **34**, 593–613 (1991). https://doi.org/10.1016/0020-7373(91)90037-8
6. Forlines, C., Balakrishnan, R.: Evaluating tactile feedback and direct vs. indirect stylus input in pointing and crossing selection tasks. In: Proceedings of ACM CHI 2008 Conference on Human Factors in Computing Systems, vol. 1, pp. 1563–1572 (2008). https://doi.org/10.1145/1357054.1357299
7. Argelaguet, F., Andujar, C.: A survey of 3D object selection techniques for virtual environments. Comput. Graph. (Pergamon). **37**, 121–136 (2013). https://doi.org/10.1016/j.cag.2012.12.003
8. Mine, M.: Virtual Environment Interaction Techniques (1995)
9. Debarba, H.G., Grandi, J.G., Maciel, A., Nedel, L., Boulic, R.: Disambiguation canvas: a precise selection technique for virtual environments. In: Kotzé, P., Marsden, G., Lindgaard, G., Wesson, J., Winckler, M. (eds.) INTERACT 2013. LNCS, vol. 8119, pp. 388–405. Springer, Heidelberg (2013). https://doi.org/10.1007/978-3-642-40477-1_24
10. Matulic, F., Vogel, D.: Multiray: multi-finger raycasting for large displays. In: Proceedings of the 2018 CHI Conference on Human Factors in Computing Systems, CHI 2018, pp. 1–13 (2018). https://doi.org/10.1145/3173574.3173819
11. Song, C.G., Kwak, N., Jeong, H.: Developing an efficient technique of Selection and Manipulation in Immersive VE. In: VRST, pp. 142–146 (2000). https://doi.org/10.1145/502390.502417
12. Gallo, L., De Pietro, G., Marra, I.: 3D interaction with volumetric medical data: experiencing the Wiimote. In: Proceedings of the 1st international Conference on Ambient Media and Systems, pp. 1–6 (2008). https://doi.org/10.4108/icst.ambisys2008.2880
13. Hincapié-Ramos, J.D., Guo, X., Irani, P.: Designing interactive transparent exhibition cases. In: 7th International Workshop on Personalized Access to Cultural Heritage: The Future of Experiencing Cultural Heritage, pp. 16–19 (2014)

14. Teather, R.J., Stuerzlinger, W.: Pointing at 3D targets in a stereo head-tracked virtual environment. In: Proceedings of the IEEE Symposium on 3D User Interfaces, 3DUI 2011, pp. 87–94 (2011). https://doi.org/10.1109/3dui.2011.5759222
15. Grossman, T., Wigdor, D., Balakrishnan, R.: Multi-finger gestural interaction with 3D volumetric displays. ACM Trans. Graph. **24**, 931 (2005). https://doi.org/10.1145/1073204. 1073287
16. Grossman, T., Balakrishnan, R.: The design and evaluation of selection techniques for 3D volumetric displays. In: Proceedings of the 19th Annual ACM Symposium on User Interface Software and Technology, UIST 2006, p. 3 (2006). https://doi.org/10.1145/1166253. 1166257
17. Benko, H., Feiner, S.: Balloon selection: a multi-finger technique for accurate low-fatigue 3D selection. In: Proceedings of the IEEE Symposium on 3D User Interfaces, 3DUI 2007, pp. 79–86 (2007). https://doi.org/10.1109/3dui.2007.340778
18. Lee, M., Green, R., Billinghurst, M.: 3D natural hand interaction for AR applications. In: 2008 23rd International Conference Image and Vision Computing New Zealand, IVCNZ (2008). https://doi.org/10.1109/ivcnz.2008.4762125
19. Lee, S., Lim, Y., Chun, J.: 3D interaction in Augmented Reality with stereo-vision technique. In: 2013 15th International Conference on Advanced Communication Technology (ICACT), pp. 401–405 (2013)
20. Khamis, M., Buschek, D., Thieron, T., Alt, F., Bulling, A.: EyePACT: eye-based parallax correction on touch-enabled interactive displays. In: Proceedings of the ACM on Interactive, Mobile, Wearable and Ubiquitous Technologies, vol. 1, pp. 146:1–146:18 (2018). https://doi.org/10.1145/3161168
21. Migge, B., Kunz, A.: User model for predictive calibration control on interactive screens. In: Proceedings of the 2010 International Conference on Cyberworlds, CW 2010, pp. 32–37 (2010). https://doi.org/10.1109/cw.2010.18
22. Lee, J.H., Bae, S.: Binocular cursor: enabling selection on transparent displays troubled by binocular parallax. In: Proceedings of the SIGCHI Conference on Human Factors in Computing Systems (CHI), pp. 3169–3172 (2013). https://doi.org/10.1145/2470654. 2466433
23. Bandyopadhyay, D., Raskar, R., Fuchs, H.: Dynamic shader lamps: painting on movable objects. In: Proceedings of the IEEE and ACM International Symposium on Augmented Reality, ISAR 2001, pp. 207–216 (2001). https://doi.org/10.1109/isar.2001.970539
24. Myers, B.A., et al.: Interacting at a distance: measuring the performance of laser pointers and other devices. In: Proceedings of the SIGCHI Conference on Human Factors in Computing Systems Changing Our World, Changing Ourselves, CHI 2002, p. 33 (2002). https://doi.org/10.1145/503376.503383
25. Freeman, E., Williamson, J., Subramanian, S., Brewster, S.: Point-and-shake: selecting from levitating object displays. In: Proceedings of CHI, pp. 1–10 (2018). https://doi.org/10.1145/3173574.3173592
26. Hinckley, K., Wigdor, D.: Input technologies and techniques. In: The Human-Computer Interaction Handbook: Fundamentals, Evolving Technologies and Emerging Applications, pp. 151–168 (2002)
27. Corsten, C., Cherek, C., Karrer, T., Borchers, J.: HaptiCase: back-of-device tactile landmarks for eyes-free absolute indirect touch. In: Proceedings of the ACM CHI 2015 Conference on Human Factors in Computing Systems, vol. 1, pp. 2171–2180 (2015). https://doi.org/10.1145/2702123.2702277

28. Gilliot, J., Casiez, G., Roussel, N.: Impact of form factors and input conditions on absolute indirect-touch pointing tasks. In: Proceedings of the 32nd Annual ACM Conference on Human Factors in Computing Systems, CHI 2014, pp. 723–732 (2014). https://doi.org/10.1145/2556288.2556997
29. Pietroszek, K., Lank, E.: Clicking blindly: using spatial correspondence to select targets in multi-device environments. In: Proceedings of the 14th International Conference on Human Computer Interaction with Mobile Devices and Services, MobileHCI 2012, pp. 331–334 (2012). https://doi.org/10.1145/2371574.2371625
30. Gehring, S., Löchtefeld, M., Daiber, F., Böhmer, M., Krüger, A.: Using intelligent natural user interfaces to support sales conversations. In: Proceedings of the 2012 ACM International Conference on Intelligent User Interfaces, IUI 2012, p. 97 (2012). https://doi.org/10.1145/2166966.2166985
31. Green, J., Pridmore, T., Benford, S.: Exploring attractions and exhibits with interactive flashlights. Pers. Ubiquit. Comput. 18, 239–251 (2014). https://doi.org/10.1007/s00779-013-0661-3
32. Ridel, B., Reuter, P., Laviole, J.: The Revealing Flashlight: interactive spatial augmented reality for detail exploration of cultural heritage artifacts. J. Comput. Cult. Heritage 7, 1–18 (2014). https://doi.org/10.1145/0000000.0000000
33. Pierce, J.S., Forsberg, A.S., Conway, M.J., Hong, S., Zeleznik, R.C., Mine, M.R.: Image plane interaction techniques in 3D immersive environments. In: Proceedings of the 1997 Symposium on Interactive 3D Graphics, SI3D 1997, p. 39 (1997). https://doi.org/10.1145/253284.253303
34. Pierce, J.S., Steams, B.C., Pausch, R.: Voodoo dolls: seamless interaction at multiple scales in virtual environments, pp. 141–145 (1999)
35. Hoang, T.N., Porter, S.R., Thomas, B.H.: Augmenting image plane AR 3D interactions for wearable computers. In: Conferences in Research and Practice in Information Technology Series, pp. 9–16 (2009)
36. Marquardt, N., Greenberg, S.: Informing the design of proxemic interactions. IEEE Pervasive Comput. 11, 14–23 (2012). https://doi.org/10.1109/MPRV.2012.15
37. Hall, A.D., Cunningham, J.B., Roache, R.P., Cox, J.W.: Factors affecting performance using touch-entry systems: tactual recognition fields and system accuracy. J. Appl. Psychol. 4, 711–720 (1988)
38. Vogel, D., Baudisch, P.: Shift: a technique for operating pen-based interfaces using touch. In: Proceedings of the SIGCHI Conference on Human Factors in Computing Systems, CHI 2007, p. 657 (2007). https://doi.org/10.1145/1240624.1240727
39. Wang, F., Ren, X.: Empirical evaluation for finger input properties in multi-touch interaction. In: Proceedings of the 27th International Conference on Human Factors in Computing Systems, CHI 2009, p. 1063 (2009). https://doi.org/10.1145/1518701.1518864
40. Holz, C., Baudisch, P.: The generalized perceived input point model and how to double touch accuracy by extracting fingerprints. In: Proceedings of the 28th International Conference on Human Factors in Computing Systems, CHI 2010, p. 581 (2010). https://doi.org/10.1145/1753326.1753413
41. Roudaut, A., Pohl, H., Baudisch, P.: Touch input on curved surfaces. In: Proceedings of the International Conference on Human Factors in Computing Systems, CHI 2011, pp. 1011–1020 (2011). https://doi.org/10.1145/1978942.1979094
42. VandenBos, G.R.: Publication Manual of the American Psychological Association, 6th edn. American Psychological Association, Washington, D.C. (2009)
43. Dubois, E., Serrano, M., Raynal, M.: Rolling-menu: rapid command selection in toolbars using roll gestures with a multi-DoF Mouse. In: Proceedings of the Conference on Human Factors in Computing Systems, April 2018. https://doi.org/10.1145/3173574.3173941

44. AVIZ Group: R Macros for Data Analysis. www.aviz.fr/reliefshearing
45. McGuffin, M., Balakrishnan, R.: Acquisition of expanding targets. In: Proceedings of the SIGCHI Conference on Human Factors in Computing Systems: Changing our World, Changing Ourselves, CHI 2002, pp. 57–64 (2002). https://doi.org/10.1145/503376.503388
46. McGuffin, M.J., Balakrishnan, R.: Fitts' law and expanding targets. ACM Trans. Comput.-Hum. Interact. **12**, 388–422 (2005). https://doi.org/10.1145/1121112.1121115
47. Kopper, R., Bacim, F., Bowman, D.A.: Rapid and accurate 3D selection by progressive refinement. In: Proceedings of the IEEE Symposium on 3D User Interfaces, 3DUI 2011, pp. 67–74 (2011). https://doi.org/10.1109/3dui.2011.5759219
48. Vanacken, L., Grossman, T., Coninx, K.: Exploring the effects of environment density and target visibility on object selection in 3D virtual environments. In: Proceedings of the IEEE Symposium on 3D User Interfaces 2007, 3DUI 2007, pp. 115–122 (2007). https://doi.org/10.1109/3dui.2007.340783

44. AVIZ Group. R. Matrix for Data Analysis. www.aviz.fr/wiki/matrix.org
45. McGuffin, M.J., Balakrishnan, R.: Acquisition of expanding targets. In: Proceedings of the SIGCHI Conference on Human Factors in Computing Systems. Changing our World, Changing Ourselves. CHI 2002, pp. 57–64 (2002). https://doi.org/10.1145/503376.503388
46. McGuffin, M.J., Balakrishnan, R.: Fitts' law and expanding targets. ACM Trans. Comput.-Hum. Interact. 12, 388–422 (2005). https://doi.org/10.1145/1121112.1121115
47. Stoppel, S., Bruckner, S.: Brewmaster: rapid and accurate 3D selection by progressive refinement. In: Proceedings of the IEEE Symposium on 3D User Interface. 3DUI 2011, pp. 67–74 (2011). https://doi.org/10.1109/3dui.2011.5759210
48. Vanacken, L., Grossman, T., Coninx, K.: Exploring the effects of environment density and target visibility on object selection in 3D virtual environments. In: Proceedings of the IEEE Symposium on 3D User Interfaces 2007, 3DUI 2007, pp. 115–122 (2007). https://doi.org/10.1109/3dui.2007.340783

Interaction Techniques for Writing and Drawing

Additive Voronoi Cursor:
Dynamic Effective Areas Using Additively
Weighted Voronoi Diagrams

Jacky Kit Cheung[✉], Oscar Kin-Chung Au[✉], and Kening Zhu[✉]

School of Creative Media, City University of Hong Kong, Kowloon, Hong Kong
ckitsa@gmail.com, {kincau,keninzhu}@cityu.edu.hk

Abstract. We present Additive Voronoi Cursor (AVC) – a new cursor technique for target selection by dynamically resizing the area cursor based on the analysis of the two different phases of mouse movement: the ballistic and the correction phases during target selection. On-screen Targets can be divided into respective areas dynamically based on both target distribution and cursor velocity. We assumed that to select a target, a user will first perform ballistic/fast cursor movement aiming to the target roughly, then correct the cursor position with slower movement towards the desired target. Therefore, after the ballistic movement, the desired target would locate within the local region closed to the cursor. We defined Additive Weighted Voronoi Diagrams with selectable targets by assigning larger weights to the nearby objects right after the ballistic cursor movement. Therefore, the effective areas of the nearby objects are enlarged, and they can be selected more easily and quickly. We had compared our cursor technique with recent developed area-cursor methods. The results showed that our method performed significantly better on certain configurations.

Keywords: Area cursor · Additively weighted Voronoi diagram ·
Movement-phase-aware cursor · Fitts' law

1 Introduction

Target selection is a fundamental task for acquiring graphical-user-interface (GUI) components such as buttons, icons and menu options. Most screen-based applications, such as gaming and information visualization, still require frequent use of mouse selection. While manipulation tasks in design applications increase the frequency of using shortcuts, they still need to cooperate with mouse operations. With the increment in both size and resolution of computer displays, it becomes less efficient for a user to acquire small on-screen elements on the large display with the traditional cursor technique. In recent years, several techniques have been proposed to address this problem and to improve selection performance. One of the approaches is to reduce the

Electronic supplementary material The online version of this chapter (https://doi.org/10.1007/978-3-030-29387-1_16) contains supplementary material, which is available to authorized users.

© IFIP International Federation for Information Processing 2019
Published by Springer Nature Switzerland AG 2019
D. Lamas et al. (Eds.): INTERACT 2019, LNCS 11748, pp. 273–292, 2019.
https://doi.org/10.1007/978-3-030-29387-1_16

cursor movement by directly changing the locations of the cursor or targets [1, 2, 12, 19, 21]. These techniques performed better than the traditional cursor technique in a sparse desktop environment. However, they are sensitive to the density and layout of the on-screen selectable components, and their performance would degrade if the target to be captured was surrounded by multiple nearby objects. As it is common to have non-uniform target distributions and clusters of small targets in GUIs, these techniques may not always improve the target-selection performance over the traditional technique.

Some techniques for dense target environments have been proposed in recent researches, such as expanding the targets' size [9, 10, 23], dynamically controlling the display ratio [5], and applying multiple cursors [6, 18]. One promising technique developed from the area cursor [17, 29] is the Bubble cursor [11] and its variations [14]. The Bubble cursor dynamically adjusted the cursor's activation area such that only the closest target would be captured. This is equivalent to expanding the boundary of each target to the Voronoi region with the target center being the region center, so that the Voronoi diagram defined by all targets fills the whole screen space. The definition of targets' selectable regions in most of these area-cursor techniques only relies on Standard Voronoi diagram, and ignores the cursor motion. We believe that there is a potential design space for designing a new area cursor technique by considering targets' effective areas as dynamic Voronoi diagram which is defined by both target distribution and cursor motion.

In this paper, we present the Additive Voronoi Cursor (AVC), a new target-selection technique by dynamically resizing on-screen targets' effective areas based on the analysis of the two different phases of mouse movement: the Ballistic and the Correction phases. During the process of target selection, we assume the user will perform a ballistic movement with a fast speed to bring the cursor to the desired target roughly, then adjust the cursor position with a slower correction movement towards the desired target. With AVC, the screen space was treated as an Additively Weighted Voronoi Diagrams (AWVD), and divided into respective areas dynamically, according to the target distribution and the cursor location at the time of entering the correction phase. In general, we assumed that the desired target should be located within the local region near to the cursor during the correction phase. We defined AWVD with selectable targets as Voronoi sites by assigning larger weights to the targets closer to the cursor in the correction phase, such that the effective area of the nearby targets would be enlarged as shown in Fig. 3, allowing easier and faster selection than ordinary Bubble-cursor-like methods. In this paper, we focus on the selection task in desktop computer setting. We believe our pointing techniques could be also applicable to VR/AR domains, as target selection by pointing operations is the common UI in VR/AR systems, and the bubble-like area cursor techniques are commonly used in these systems.

The rest of the paper is organized as follows: after reviewing the related work, we will present the design and implementation of two types of AVC - Additive Voronoi Cursor (AVC) and Additive Voronoi Cursor with Manhattan distance (AVC+M), and evaluate their performance with existing area cursor methods. Experiment results showed that our method performed significantly better among the tested area cursor methods. Finally, we will report that the performance of the AVC and AVC+M can be modeled with the Fitts' law.

2   Related Work

The Fitts' law is typically used to study target selection in GUIs [22, 27]. It is a model for predicting the movement time MT in target selection tasks as:

$$MT = a + b \cdot \log 2(AW + 1) \tag{1}$$

where A is the distance (or amplitude) between the cursor and the target. W is the target width. a and b are two empirically determined constants, depending on selection technique, hardware configuration and user behavior. The equation indicates that the efficiency of selection tasks can be improved either by reducing the movement amplitude A, increasing the target width W, or a combination of both.

In early work, selection techniques based on jumping cursors/objects [1, 2, 12, 19] or multiple cursors [6, 18] were proposed to reduce the movement amplitude of target-selection tasks. However, these techniques are sensitive to the target layout and density. In addition, the jumpy interface and increased visual elements would lead to visual distraction, thus degrade user performance.

Area-Cursor techniques used an area cursor with a large activation region [17], instead of a single-pixel hotspot in the traditional point cursor to increase the efficiency of target selection. This is equivalent to enlarging the effective target size. They made selection easier, but may capture multiple objects at the same time, leading to ambiguities. This problem can be solved by integrating a point cursor into the area cursor [29], or by interactively adjusting the cursor area on multi-touch input [25]. The Bubble cursor [11] tackled this problem by dynamically resizing the activation area of a particular target based on the proximity of surrounding targets, by which only one target would be captured at a time. This is equivalent to partitioning the screen space into a Voronoi diagram which is defined by all targets, thus maximizing the overall activation area of all targets. Starburst [3] used a different partitioning method, which adapted to clustered targets with non-uniform distributions. Several variations of the Bubble cursor have been proposed [16, 20]. Recently, speed-dependent area-cursor techniques [8, 28] were proposed. Chapuis et al. [8] developed DynaSpot, in which the cursor behaved as a point cursor at low speed and an area cursor at high speed, and thus allowed pointing anywhere in the empty space without requiring an explicit mode switching. Note that in all these area-cursor techniques the targets' potential effective areas were defined by standard Voronoi diagram with Euclidean distance function. In this paper we consider to explore the design space of area cursor techniques by define the effective areas as dynamic Voronoi diagram with a different distance function.

More recently, an area-cursor technique with dynamic target effective areas, named IFC, was proposed [28]. IFC adopted a dynamic fan-shape area cursor which was based on both the speed and moving direction of the cursor movement, such that only the targets in front of the moving direction of the cursor would be selectable, potentially allowing larger targets' effective widths and shorter cursor moving distance. However, the response of target capturing of IFC is different from Bubble-like cursor techniques, and it may be difficult for users to control the cursor orientation smoothly without sufficient practice.

Guillon et al. [14] studied the impact of display styles on the performance with Bubble-like area cursors. The experiment results showed that showing the effective areas of all targets led to the best performance. However, the study only focused on static effective areas, thus the results may not apply to area cursors with dynamic effective areas such as IFC and our proposed technique. Another interesting finding by Guillon et al. [14] is that the area cursor with Manhattan distance metric has a similar performance as the original Euclidean-distance-based area cursor. Therefore, we also considered the Manhattan distance metric in our area cursor design, and studied the performance difference between our Manhattan distance-based and Euclidean distance-based cursor techniques.

Several target selection techniques were based on dynamically adjusting the control-display ratio, thus changing the underlying movement amplitude as well as target width. Sticky icons [29] and Semantic pointing [5] slowed down the cursor when approaching a selectable target, thus increasing the underlying target width for easier acquisition. However, both techniques were sensitive to the layout and density of the targets. While they may work well in a sparse desktop environment, problems may arise when targets are clustered, as some targets located along the path to the intended target may slow down the cursor movement. The Vacuum [4] dynamically brought prospective targets closed to the cursor. This method significantly reduced the moving distance of the cursor for selecting distant targets, but it required additional visual aids and complex cursor operations to control the scanning region.

3 Additive Voronoi Cursor

The Additive Voronoi Cursor is based on the area-cursor technique and is designed to support faster and easier target selection during the correction phase. We assumed that in a general selection task, the user will first perform the fast ballistic cursor movement to bring the cursor close to the desired target, followed by the slow correction movement to precisely select the desired target. We repartitioned the screen space immediately after the cursor movement changing from the ballistic phase to the correction phase, so that targets closer to the cursor will have relative bigger effective areas than those further away from the cursor. Different from the standard Voronoi partition used in the ordinary Bubble area cursor, we hypothesized that the dynamic partition of the additively weighted Voronoi diagram (AWVD) in AVC would improve the efficiency of the correction cursor movement.

Note that other literature [15, 24] considered that the whole target-selection task involves extra phases besides the ballistic and correction phases, such as the searching phase before the starting of mouse movement, and the verifying phase after the correction movement and before the mouse clicking occurs. However, in this work, we do not focus on these extra phases, as the time spending on them would not significantly affect by area cursor techniques. Therefore, we designed AVC to mainly determine the ballistic and the correction phases based on the cursor moving speed, and repartition the effective areas as an AWVD immediately after the change from the ballistic phase to the correction phase.

We defined the cursor movement enters the ballistic phase once the cursor speed is faster than a speed threshold s_B, and the cursor movement enters the correction phase once its speed is slower than another speed threshold s_B, such that $s_B > s_C$. An example of such phase switching is demonstrated in Fig. 1. We have conducted a preliminary study to optimize the thresholds values for AVC, which is described in the next section.

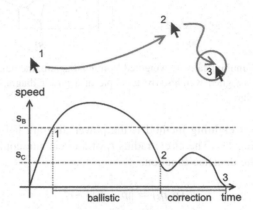

Fig. 1. Target selection example and phase detection. A fast ballistic movement is performed first to roughly bring the cursor close to the desired target (1 -> 2), followed by the slow correction step to exactly select the desired target (2 -> 3).

3.1 Selecting Distance Functions for Voronoi Diagrams

We have considered different methods of 2D partition for better partitioning the screen space with the centers of selectable targets as the set of sites. In particular, we focused on the definition of the distance function $d(p, q)$ that used in the computation of Voronoi Diagram, where p is a 2D point on the screen and q is the center of one of the selectable targets. The distance function mainly controlling the sizes of the partitioned regions which would be the effective area of the corresponding target. Standard Voronoi diagram directly uses the Euclidean distance function, by altering this we could control the target effective width to a certain extent. One possible way to alter the original Euclidean distance function used in standard Voronoi diagram computation is to apply weights to each site multiplicatively:

$$d_m(p, q_i) = \frac{\|p - q_i\|}{w_i} \qquad (2)$$

where w_i is the weight assigned to the target q_i. In general, a bigger weight will result in a bigger corresponding Voronoi region. However, a multiplicatively weighted Voronoi diagram (MWVD) [7] often contains non-convex regions, as well as enclave and exclave regions (Fig. 2a). Therefore, using MWVD for the effective areas in target selection might make the selection process unpredictable and unintuitive, because the enclave and exclave shapes might introduce unexpectable switching of captured targets during the selection process.

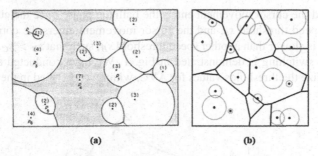

(a)   **(b)**

Fig. 2. (a) Example of multiplicatively weighted Voronoi diagram, the numbers next to the sites are the corresponding assigned weights. (b) Example of a power diagram, the circle sites are displayed in grayed color.

Another possible weighting method is the power diagram [7] which replaces the point sites with circle sites. The circle radius r_i of a circle site could be considered as the site weight for the distance function.

$$d_p(p, q_i) = \|p - q_i\|^2 - r_i^2 \tag{3}$$

While the power diagrams could ensure straight region boundaries and convex Voronoi regions, one main drawback is that the site center could be outside the corresponding Voronoi regions (Fig. 2b). This could result in unselectable targets even when the cursor is close to them, particularly when the targets locations or the circle radius r_i are unevenly distributed. Therefore, we abandoned this weighting method.

Instead we decided to use the AWVD, to define the effective areas of the targets. The AWVD uses the weighted distance function given by

$$d_a(p, q_i) = \|p - q_i\| - w_i \tag{4}$$

Even some regions could be non-convex in the AWVD, every non-convex region is star-shaped with respect to its site (target center). This means that from the center q_i we can draw a line to any point in the region, and the line will be contained entirely within the region, ensuring the selectability of the target [7]. Also, since AWVD only contains connected convex and star-shaped regions, there will be no undesired enclave and exclave regions.

We adopted a gradient weighting function centered at the cursor to define the weight values. Therefore, the targets close to the cursor will receive relatively larger weights than distant ones, so their corresponding regions will be elongated radiationally from the cursor position (Fig. 3), allowing a larger effective width along with the possible moving directions from the cursor to the nearby targets. Specifically, we used a linear gradient function (Fig. 4), centered at the cursor position when the cursor movement just enters the correction phase, to define the additive weights for repartitioning the screen space. Figure 3 shows the different effective areas defined by the unweighted Voronoi diagram and the AWVD, notice that in the latter case how longer effective areas are defined in the directions from the cursor to nearby targets. This enlarged effective area allows users to select nearby targets easier and faster.

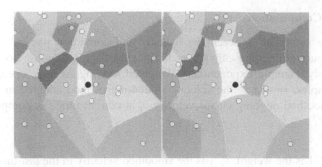

Fig. 3. Different effective areas defined by the unweighted Voronoi diagram (**left**) and the additive weighted Voronoi diagram (**right**).

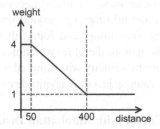

Fig. 4. The weighting function used for our cursor technique. The x-axis is the distance from the cursor position to the target center (in pixels), and the y-axis is the weight values assigned to the target.

To provide the best performance, the parameters of this linear gradient function should be selected based on the screen resolution and other hardware configurations, as well as the user preferences. The weight assignment would affect the shape changes of the effective regions of selectable targets. If the scaling factor is too large, then two nearby targets have large differences in their weights, the target effective area with larger weight would dominance the nearby region and the region of the other target will disappear. Therefore, we select a scaling factor as shown in Fig. 4 that would never cause such undesired effects and produce enough elongation of effective areas of targets near to the cursor position when the cursor entering the correction phase. We adopted these settings in our empirical experiment, resulting in the desired Voronoi-diagram partition with enlarged effective areas for nearby targets. Therefore we used these empirical settings in our controlled user study.

It may be possible that the user's desired target is not located close to the cursor right after switching to the correction phase. The user can use another ballistic movement to move the cursor to another screen region roughly, or slowly move the cursor and search the desired targets at another region. In either case, the previous "repartitioned" effective areas will not affect the next selection operation, as only the local region near to the old cursor position (at the time switching to correction phase) was repartitioned by the additively weighted Voronoi diagram.

3.2   Speed Computation

To detect the switching between the ballistic and correction phases, one needs to compute the current ongoing cursor speed. Since the captured mouse positions can be noisy, we apply a simple Exponentially Weighted Moving Average operation to filter the noisy samples, similar to the velocity smoothing method adopted in [28]. Specifically, the smoothed ongoing cursor velocity $\tilde{v}_t$ at current time t is computed as

$$\tilde{v}_t = (1 - \lambda)\tilde{v}_{t-1} + \lambda\tilde{v}_t \qquad (5)$$

where $0 \le \lambda \le 1$ is the weight, $\tilde{v}_{t-1}$ is the smoothed velocity in the last time step, while $\tilde{v}_t$ is the current unsmoothed velocity value. We need a smoothed cursor speed computation to remove noisy speed samples that caused by the raw mouse input (particularly the zero speed values produced when two successive cursor samples have the same position), therefore cursor speed smoothing is necessary for our cursor technique. We have tested with both 30 and 60 times per second settings for cursor speed computation with moving average smoothing, and found that both settings can produce satisfied and smooth speed estimation, therefore we choice 30 fps for our experiments. The weight λ is set to 0.95 and the velocity was sampled 30 times per second. With the smoothed velocity, the speed value is just the magnitude of the velocity vector $s_t = |\tilde{v}_t|$.

3.3   Additional Voronoi Cursor with Manhattan Distance Metric (AVC+M)

As reported in [14] that the area cursor technique with the Manhattan distance-based Voronoi diagram (MTE) gives comparable performance than the Euclidean distance-based area cursor (VTE), it is interesting that what would the performance of AVC be if adopting the MTE. Therefore, in our experiment, we also involved AVC with the Manhattan distance metric (AVC+M). The distance function of AVC+M is given as

$$d_a(p, q_i) = \|p - q_i\|_M - w_i \qquad (6)$$

where $\|\cdot\|_M$ is the Manhattan distance metric. Notice that different from AVC, AVC+M always generates straight line region boundaries in vertical, horizontal and 45°-oriented directions (Fig. 5), which may result in different performance when comparing with AVC.

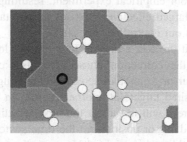

Fig. 5. AVC+M always generates straight line region boundaries in vertical, horizontal and 45°-oriented directions.

3.4 Implicit Display Style

The results in [14] showed that explicitly showing the all static target effective areas gives better performance than other displaying styles. However, this does not apply to AVC since the target effective areas are dynamically updated according to the user's interaction. Moreover, displaying effective areas of all targets would overwhelm selectable targets and other UI elements, thus would not be appropriate for many applications. According to the findings of recent pieces of literature [15, 28], an area cursor with dynamic target effective areas should hide the effective areas for better performance, as displaying the effective areas would distract users' attention and degrade target selection speed. Therefore, we adopted the implicit display style and hid the dynamic target effective areas, so that users will not aware of the update of the underlying Voronoi diagram when the cursor movement is switched from ballistic phase to correction phase. Also, for a fairer comparison, we hide the target effective areas for all cursor techniques being tested in our experiment. The Voronoi regions displayed in the figures and the accompanying video were only for visualization purposes only.

4 Experiment

4.1 Preliminary Study: Ballistic and Correction Movement Speed

Since AVC dynamically resizes the effective areas of the on-screen objects right after the Ballistic phase, it is important to robustly detect the phase change without affecting the user performance. We have conducted a preliminary study to optimize the threshold values of the mouse speed for detecting Ballistic and Correction phases in our proposed AVC technique. Note that the speed thresholds found in this preliminary study were only optimized for the specified screen resolution and mouse configuration. For other screen/mouse configurations, the optimized threshold values may be different.

Apparatus. This study was conducted on a PC Notebook with a Quad-Core 2.7 GHz CPU, a 17″ display screen of resolution 1920 × 1080 and a Logitech optical mouse (DPI = 1000). It was installed with MS Windows 10 and the default mouse speed setting. The "Enhance Pointer Precision" function is turned off, thus no cursor acceleration was used in the experiment.

Participants. We recruited 9 participants (6 males and 3 females) of 21 to 30 (Mean = 27.2, SD = 2.86) within the university. All participants are right-handed frequent computer users, and they use their dominant hand to control the mouse.

Procedure and Design. Previous research [7] has proved that the distractors along the start and goal target would not affect the performance of a task selection task, but only the distractors close to the goal targets would affect. Therefore this study followed the settings from [8, 28], with the aim of studying how different threshold speeds for classifying the Ballistic and Correction movements would affect user performance of target selection using AVC under various configurations of the moving distance/amplitude and the crowdedness. Sixteen circular candidate targets of 8 pixels in

radius were evenly distributed on a large circle with the possible diameter of 256, 512, and 768 pixels which defined the movement amplitude. The large circle was placed at the screen center, and the centers of the candidate targets lied on the circumference of the large circle, as shown in Fig. 6a. At the start of every selection task, the software randomly marked a pair of opposite targets as start and goal targets, and drew the start target in yellow, and the goal target in green color, respectively. When a target was captured by the cursor, it was surrounded by a blue stroke. Participants were instructed to click the start target first and then select the goal targets as quickly and as accurately as possible using AVC. In order to mimic a more realistic target-selection scenario, another four targets of the same size were placed around the goal target as distractors. Two of them were placed along the direction of movement (one before and one after the goal target), and the other two distractors were placed perpendicular to the direction of movement (one on the left and one on the right). The distractors were all equally away from the goal targets with a distance of three times the target's diameter (48 pixels).

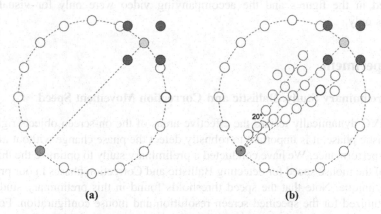

(a)   (b)

Fig. 6. (a) The screen layout for the preliminary study. The yellow circle is the start target while the green circle is the goal target. The target being captured would be surrounded by a blue stroke. The four grey circles are the main distractors to control the effective width of the goal target. Note that the color and the dashed line shown above is for illustration purpose only. Except for the start target, goal target and the selected target as shown above, other targets are 1-pixel black outlined circles in white color without any lines. (b) The study interface of the main experiment, in addition to (a). The second group distractors are distributed a 20° slice beginning from start target to the nearest main distractor. (Color figure online)

We designed our experiment as a $3 \times 3 \times 3$ within-participant study with the following factors: (1) three amplitudes (in pixels), A: 256, 512, 768; (2) three speed thresholds for identifying the ballistic phase (in pixels/s), s_B: 80, 100, 120; and (3) three speed thresholds for identifying the correction phase (in pixels/s), s_C: 30, 50, 70. Based on the screen resolution and mouse configuration, we achieved the weighting function (Fig. 4) and $\{s_B, s_C\}$ as $\{100, 50\}$. We offset a positive and negative value to the $\{s_B, s_C\}$ to provide those factors with 3 different values, to form the predefined factor values of the experiment. The experiment was divided into groups of different

combinations of the s_B and s_C, which were ordered with a Latin-square-based counterbalance. In each group, participants performed the selection tasks in different values of **A**. Each **A** value repeated 16 times with the 16 pairs of opposite start and goal targets appearing in a randomized order. The whole experiment lasted for approximately 30 min for each participant. While we noted that the movement distance/amplitude might potentially affect the selection performance, in this study we mainly focused on how different speed thresholds would affect the user performance of target selection.

The time duration between clicking the start target and selecting the goal target was measured as task-completion time, and the overall error rate of each participant (i.e. the percentage of failed tasks) was recorded. A task would be marked as failed if the participant selected an incorrect goal target before selecting the correct one. If a participant selected an incorrect target, he/she still needed to select the correct target to complete the task. Before starting the selection tasks, the participants were given a 5-min training session to get familiar with the user interface. A total of 3,888 selecting tasks were performed, with each of the users performing a total of 432 tasks.

Results and Discussion. With the **A**, s_B, and s_C as the independent factors, we statistically analyzed their effects on the task completion time and the error rate. Table 1 shows the variant result of mean movement time and error rate for each configuration. We have performed Bonferroni correction for multiple pairwise comparisons and checked the normality of the data for the experiments in this paper.

Table 1. Mean task completion times and error rates for different s_B and s_C.

(s_B, s_C)	Mean task completion time				Error rate			
	A256	A512	A768	Avg	A256	A512	A768	Avg
(80, 30)	725	847	1028	867	12.5%	6.9%	14.6%	11.3%
(80, 50)	740	845	1031	872	7.0%	6.4%	20.4%	11.3%
(80, 70)	741	903	1029	891	9.7%	9.7%	15.3%	11.6%
(100, 30)	738	860	985	861	6.9%	4.9%	9.7%	7.2%
(100, 50)	739	879	991	869	5.6%	6.3%	9.8%	7.2%
(100, 70)	761	874	1007	881	9.7%	9.0%	9.0%	9.3%
(120, 30)	777	857	990	875	13.9%	7.0%	7.0%	9.3%
(120, 50)	748	880	1021	882	9.0%	5.6%	11.3%	8.6%
(120, 70)	769	902	1037	903	5.6%	9.9%	9.0%	8.2%

Task-Completion Time. Three-way ANOVA showed that the **A** ($F_{(2,3861)} = 327.2$, $p < 0.0005$) and s_C ($F_{(2,3861)} = 3.72$, $p < 0.05$) had a significant effect on the task-completion time, while there was a marginal effect of s_B on the task-completion time ($F_{(2,3861)} = 2.85$, $p = 0.058$). There was no significant interaction effect of these three factors on the task completion time. It was obvious that the task-completion time should increase as the amplitude increases, so we mainly focused on optimizing the combination of the s_B and s_C.

Post-hoc pairwise comparison showed that across all three different amplitudes, $s_C = 30$ yielded significantly shorter task-completion time than $s_C = 50$ ($p < 0.05$) and was marginally faster than $s_C = 70$ ($p = 0.052$). Configurations with $s_B = 100$ was marginally faster than 120 ($p = 0.052$), and slightly faster than 80.

Error Rate. Three-way ANOVA showed that s_B ($F_{(2,3861)} = 2.85$, $p < 0.005$) and A ($F_{(2,3861)} = 4.47$, $p < 0.05$) had a significant effect on the error rate, while there was no significant or marginal effect of the Correction Speed Threshold s_C on the error rate. There was no significant interaction effect of these three factors on the error rate.

Post-hoc pairwise comparison showed that condition $s_B = 100$ yielded significantly less error than $s_B = 80$ ($p < 0.05$), and slightly but not significantly less error than $s_B = 120$. The higher error rate occurred when $s_B = 80$ is mainly due to the incorrect movement mode switching during the correction phase, as the threshold is too low to trigger, thus the effective areas of targets were updated unexpectedly, and the selection tasks became more difficult to complete.

Considering the effect of both thresholds on the task-completion time and the error rate, we finally chose $s_B = 100$ and $s_C = 30$ for the main experiment.

4.2 Main Experiment: Performance Comparison

After determining the speed thresholds for the ballistic and correction phases, we conducted the main experiment to evaluate the performance of the proposed AVC and AVC+M with comparing to other area cursor methods, including Bubble Cursor [11], Manhattan Target Expansion (MTE) [14] and Implicit Fan Cursor (IFC) [28].

Apparatus. Same as those in the preliminary study.

Participants. 10 participants (7 males and 3 females) of age 19 to 38 (Mean = 27.6, SD = 5.27) were recruited within the university. All participants are right-handed frequent computer users, and they use their dominant hand to control the mouse. These participants did not participate in the preliminary study.

Task and Procedure. Similar to the preliminary study, we followed the general procedure adopted in Bubble [11] and IFC [28] for comparing cursor techniques. The study interface was similar to the one that we used in the preliminary study, but with different sets of testing factors. Participants are instructed to select the start and goal targets alternatively in each trial, which was drawn in yellow and green color respectively. The target would be highlighted by a blue surrounding stroke when the target is being captured. Participants were instructed to first click the start target and then select the goal target as fast as and as accurate as possible. When an incorrect target was selected (after the start target is clicked) in an individual task, the task would be marked as failed and participants needed to re-select the correct goal target (without re-clicking the start target).

We observed that some participants in the preliminary study would perform multiple clicks after an incorrect selection, trying to complete the task with random clicking positions near the correct goal target. This usually causes unnecessary long task completion time that we would like to avoid. Therefore, we instructed the participants

not to perform random clicks in the trial, and we observed no such random clicking behavior among all participants.

In this experiment, we included two sets of distractors of the same size as the goal target. Four main distractors were placed around the goal target as introduced in the previous study to control the maximum effective width of the goal target. Another set of distractors were placed along the path from the start target to the goal target. The number of these distractors was determined by the Amplitude. They were distributed in a 20° slice beginning from the start target to the nearest main distractor (Fig. 6b).

Design. Our study was a $5 \times 3 \times 3 \times 3$ within-participant design with the following factors: (1) five area-cursor techniques **TECH** for comparison: AVC, AVC+M, Bubble Cursor, IFC, MTE; (2) three target radius **R**: 8, 16, 32 pixels; (3) three amplitudes **A**: 256, 512, 768 pixels; (4) three distractor ratio **DRATIO**: 1.5, 3 and 5 (the ratio of the distance between the goal target and each main distractor to the target width).

For AVC and AVC+M, we adopted the s_B (100 pixels/s) and the s_C (30 pixels/s) we selected in the preliminary study. IFC introduced additional factors such as "RotaAngle" and "DistractorDensities" to study the task performance of different cursor techniques. These factors would mainly affect the target selection if the cursor technique is velocity dependent (i.e. depends on both cursor speed and moving direction). Since our proposed technique is speed dependent only, these factors would not affect the size of target effective areas much, and therefore we abandoned these factors. We also followed the concern proposed in IFC [28], that different pointing methods may have different defined target effective width, to examine directly how the **DRATIO** would affect the performance of each area cursor techniques instead of using a constant density factor.

Each participant performed the study in a single session consisting of 5 groups of area cursor techniques in a counterbalanced order by Latin Square. In each group, the participants needed to perform 384 trials of selection tasks, with each trial to click the start target and then select the goal target with the assigned area cursor technique. The task completion time, and the overall error rate were recorded. In each group, participants performed the tasks under different combinations of **R** $\times$ **A** $\times$ **DRATIO**. Each combination repeated 16 times with the 16 pairs of opposite start and goal targets appearing in a randomized order. We have dropped the trials with **R** = 32 and **A** = 256 as the targets are too close among each other. Thus, a total of 19,200 selection tasks were conducted in the experiment. In this analysis, **R**, **A**, and **DRATIO** were given in random order. Participants were informed about the type of **TECH** that was going to be used, and were educated about the technique before the trails of the **TECH** group is started. A 5-min warm-up session was given to allow participants to get familiar with the techniques and tasks. They were given a 10-min break between each **TECH** group. Each participant took approximately 1.5 h to complete the whole experiment.

Results and Discussion. *Task Completion Time.* Table 2 shows the results of the four-way ANOVA analysis of variance on task completion time. We only show factors with significant effects and skip those insignificant ones. We can observe that **TECH** ($F_{(4,1080)} = 61.6$, p < 0.0005), **A** ($F_{(2,1080)} = 74.9$, p < 0.0005), **R** ($F_{(2,1080)} = 147.4$, p < 0.0005) and **DRATIO** ($F_{(2,1080)} = 17.4$, p < 0.0005) have significant effects on the

task-completion time. A significant interaction effect can also be observed in
TECH × R and **R × DRATIO**. These results show that different **TECHs** were
affected differently by the factors.

Table 2. The significant ANOVA results for the task completion time of **TECH × A × R ×
DRATIO**. (DF is the degree of freedom.)

Factors	DF	F	p
TECH	4	61.608	<0.0005
A	2	74.945	<0.0005
R	2	147.405	<0.0005
DRATIO	2	17.415	<0.0005
TECH × R	8	2.810	<0.005
R × DRATIO	4	3.963	<0.005

Post-hoc test showed that the AVC and AVC+M were significantly faster than
Bubble (AVC vs Bubble: p < 0.0005; AVC+M vs Bubble: p < 0.05) and IFC (AVC vs
IFC & AVC+M vs IFC: p < 0.0005). The average mean task completion time was
730.2 ms for AVC, 752.1 ms for AVC+M, 815.3 ms for Bubble, 994.9 ms for IFC,
769.8 ms for MTE as shown in Fig. 7a. In general, AVC gives 5.1% improvement in
term of the task-completion time over MTE, which was the best cursor method with
implicit display style in Guillon et al.'s research [14]; while both Manhattan distance-
based methods (AVC+M and MTE) provided the similar performance. The significant
difference between AVC and Manhattan distance-based methods suggested that our
new dynamic Voronoi diagrams can better utilize the local screen region for faster
target selection than the original bubble and Manhattan distance-based methods.

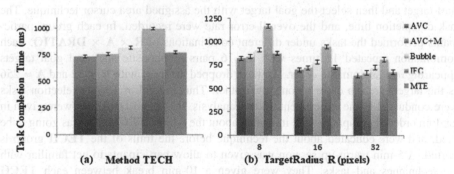

Fig. 7. (a) The mean task completion time of different cursor techniques **TECH** (b) and that
grouped by target radius **R**. In this and all later charts, error bars represent standard error.

There was a significant interaction effect of **R** and **TECH** ($F_{(8,1080)} = 2.810$,
p < 0.005). Figure 7b shows the mean task completion time of different techniques
TECH grouped by **R**. Post-hoc pairwise comparison (Table 3) showed that AVC (with
all **R**), and AVC+M (with **R** = 8, 16) are significantly faster than Bubble and IFC,

while AVC+M was only significantly faster than IFC with **R** = 32. The results showed that AVC (and even AVC+M) were efficient in acquiring smaller targets. On the other hand, both AVC and AVC+M did not have a significant difference to MTE with all **R**.

Table 3. Significant differences for mean task completion time among **TECH** grouped by target radius **R**, where a < b means **TECH** b was significantly faster than **TECH** a. (A = AVC, Am = AVC+M, B = Bubble, I = IFC, M = MTE)

R	Comparison
8, 16	I < B < A, Am I < M
32	I < B < A I < Am, M

Error Rate. Four-way ANOVA showed that both **TECH** ($F_{(4,1080)} = 11.4$, p < 0.0005), **A** ($F_{(2,1080)} = 27.4$, p < 0.0005), **R** ($F_{(2,1080)} = 14.4$, p < 0.0005) and **DRATIO** ($F_{(2,1080)} = 13.0$, p < 0.0005) placed a significant effect on the error rate, as shown in Table 4. Figure 8a shows the mean error rate of different TECH. Post-hoc pairwise comparison revealed that AVC yielded significantly less error than the IFC cursor (p < 0.0005) and the AVC+M method (p < 0.05), and there was no significant difference among the AVC, MTE, and Bubble cursor, in terms of the error rate. In addition, the AVC+M yielded significantly more error than the MTE did in general (p < 0.005). IFC had a significantly higher error rate than other techniques, this may due to the orientation-based control style of IFC, which is different from other tested cursor techniques and could have a steeper learning curve and require longer training to master.

Table 4. The significant ANOVA results for the error rate of **TECH** × **A** × **R** × **DRATIO**. (DF is the degree of freedom.)

Factors	DF	F	p
TECH	4	11.365	<0.0005
A	2	27.382	<0.0005
R	2	14.411	<0.0005
DRATIO	2	13.016	<0.0005
TECH × A	8	2.272	<0.05
TECH × DRATIO	8	2.056	<0.05

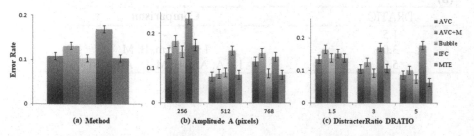

Fig. 8. (a) The mean error rate of different cursor techniques **TECHs**, and that of grouped by (b) Amplitude **A**, (c) DistractorRatio **DRATIO**

TECH and **A** had a significant interaction effect on the error rate ($F_{(8,1080)} = 2.27$, $p < 0.05$). Post-hoc pairwise comparison (Table 5a) showed that the AVC and AVC+M were significantly more accurate than the IFC with $A = 256$ (AVC vs IFC: $p < 0.0005$; AVC+M vs IFC: $p < 0.005$) and $A = 512$ (AVC vs IFC & AVC+M vs IFC: $p < 0.0005$). However, both AVC ($p < 0.05$) and AVC+M ($p < 0.0005$) were significantly less accurate than the MTE, and AVC+M was significantly less accurate than Bubble while $A = 768$ ($p < 0.05$). AVC+M and MTE produced straight line region boundaries as shown in Fig. 5, which caused the selection process became unpredictable. While selecting a target along with a long enough amplitude, the immediate change of the target area might confuse the users, and hence the error rate was increased for larger amplitude. Figure 8b shows the mean error rate of different techniques **TECH** grouped by **A**. All techniques had a higher error rate with $A = 256$, comparative to higher amplitude. This might due to the fact that the participants had shorter overall cursor-moving time when the goal target was closer, and hence they would be easier to perform incorrect selections due to short response time. While Bubble, IFC, and MTE each had similar error rates with $A = 512$ and $A = 768$, AVC and AVC+M captured a relatively higher error rate with $A = 768$ than those when $A = 512$. A possible explanation is that the accuracy of ballistic motion dropped when the amplitude increased. This increased the distances between the cursor and the goal target when entering the correction phase, causing the goal target received a relatively smaller weight and a smaller effective area, thus increased the overall error rate. As the higher-speed or consecutive ballistic motions were usually used for selecting targets with larger amplitudes, a sophisticated speed-based weighting scheme, other than a fixed weighting function, could be used to define the AWVD, in order to improve the performance and error rates in large amplitude selection tasks.

Table 5. Significant differences for mean error rate among **TECHs** grouped by (a) amplitude **A**, (b) DistractorRatio **DRATIO**, where a < b means **TECH** b had less error rate than **TECH** a. (A = AVC, Am = AVC+M, B = Bubble, I = IFC, M = MTE)

(a)

A	Comparison
256	I < A, Am, B, M
512	I < A, Am, B, M
768	Am, I < B, M A < M

(b)

DRATIO	Comparison
1.5	-
3.0	I < A, Am, B, M
5.0	I < A, Am, B, M Am < M

TECH and **DRATIO** also had a significant interaction effect on the error rate ($F_{(8,1080)} = 2.06$, p < 0.05). Post-hoc pairwise comparison (Table 5b) showed that the five methods did not have significant error rate differences among others while the **DRATIO** was small enough (**DRATIO** = 1.5). Figure 8c had explained that the error rate of both methods was high due to the smaller effective width. AVC and AVC+M were both significantly more accurate than the IFC cursor with **DRATIO** = 3.0 (AVC: p < 0.005; AVC+M: p < 0.05) and **DRATIO** = 5.0 (p < 0.0005). Figure 8c shows the mean error rate of different **TECH** grouped by **DRATIO**. We observed that **DRATIO** had less effect for IFC on error rate. Except for IFC, the error rate of other **TECH** was gradually decreased as the distractor ratio increases, mainly owing to the effective area become larger.

Lastly, we could also observed that the method of IFC was significantly slower than the other four methods (p < 0.0005), and in general IFC had significantly higher error rate than the other four methods except for the cases of **A** = 768 and **DRATIO** = 1.5. IFC had a better performance than other tested area cursor techniques in their paper, this might be owing to IFC was the only technique that used implicit display style in their experiment, while in our paper, all tested area cursor techniques used implicit display style and the effect of different display styles on performance, as reported in [15, 28], could be minimized.

5 Fitts' Law Index of Difficulty

Figure 9 illustrates the index of performance of the five **TECHs** by plotting the relationship between task completion time and index of difficulty (ID). We define the ID for each selection trials using the effective target width (EW) of the goal target.

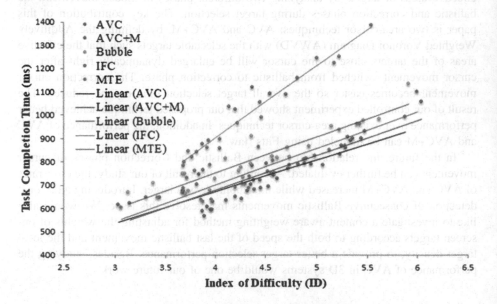

Fig. 9. Linear regression of different TECH.

Since AVC, AVC+M and IFC define effective areas non-statically, the effective widths of targets are unknown before the selection is performed when using these techniques. Therefore, for a fair comparison, we consider the EW as clicking distance (the distance between goal target and the clicking position) for all techniques. Specifically, we take the average clicking distance for each combination of amplitude, target radius and distractor ratio for all tested cursor techniques, compute the IDs and linearly fit 24 points for each technique as shown in Fig. 9. Table 6 lists the intercept, slope and r^2 values for each technique. We can see that all techniques fit the linear model with reasonable r^2 values, thus the performance of the AVC and AVC+M can be modeled using Fitts' law. AVC had the smallest slope among all TECHs. indicating AVC is easier to master than other tested cursor techniques.

Table 6. Linear fit: intercept, slope and r^2 values for different TECH. ($t = a + b \times ID$)

TECH	Intercept a	Slope b	r^2
AVC	130	136	0.764
AVC+M	86.5	148	0.814
Bubble	139	153	0.855
IFC	−339	310	0.938
MTE	76.6	156	0.820

6 Conclusion and Future Work

This paper introduced a new target-selection technique that dynamically resizes the effective areas of targets by analyzing two different phases of mouse movement: the ballistic and correction phases during target selection. The key contribution of this paper is two area-cursor techniques: AVC and AVC+M, by defining the Additively Weighted Voronoi Diagram (AWVD) with the selectable targets such that the effective areas of the targets close to the cursor will be enlarged dynamically right after the cursor movement switched from ballistic to correction phase. The correction cursor movement becomes easier so the overall target selection time can be reduced. The result of our controlled experiment showed that our proposed technique achieved better performance over existing area-cursor techniques. In addition, the performance of AVC and AVC+M can be modeled using Fitts' law.

In the future, the relationship between Ballistic and Correction phases of cursor movement can be further evaluated. According to the result of our study, the error rates of AVC and AVC+M increased while the amplitude was larger. Introducing additional detection of consecutive Ballistic movements may resolve this issue. We would also like to investigate a content-aware weighting method for adjusting the weights of on-screen targets according to both the speed of the last ballistic movement and the local target density, to provide a better target selection performance. Besides, studying the performance of AVC in 3D systems would be one of our future work.

References

1. Asano, T., Sharlin, E., Kitamura, Y., Takashima, K., Kishino, F.: Predictive interaction using the delphian desktop. In: Proceedings of the 18th Annual ACM Symposium on User Interface Software and Technology, pp. 133–141. ACM, October 2005
2. Baudisch, P., et al.: Drag-and-pop and drag-and-pick: techniques for accessing remote screen content on touch-and pen-operated systems. In: Proceedings of INTERACT, vol. 3, pp. 57–64, August 2003
3. Baudisch, P., Zotov, A., Cutrell, E., Hinckley, K.: Starburst: a target expansion algorithm for non-uniform target distributions. In: Proceedings of the Working Conference on Advanced Visual Interfaces, pp. 129–137. ACM, May 2008
4. Bezerianos, A., Balakrishnan, R.: The vacuum: facilitating the manipulation of distant objects. In: Proceedings of the SIGCHI Conference on Human Factors in Computing Systems, pp. 361–370. ACM, April 2005
5. Blanch, R., Guiard, Y., Beaudouin-Lafon, M.: Semantic pointing: improving target acquisition with control-display ratio adaptation. In: Proceedings of the SIGCHI Conference on Human Factors in Computing Systems, pp. 519–526. ACM, April 2004
6. Blanch, R., Ortega, M.: Rake cursor: improving pointing performance with concurrent input channels. In: Proceedings of the SIGCHI Conference on Human Factors in Computing Systems, pp. 1415–1418. ACM, April 2009
7. Boots, B.N., Chiu, S.N., Okabe, A., Sugihara, K.: Spatial Tessellations: Concepts and Applications of Voronoi Diagrams, 2nd edn (2000)
8. Chapuis, O., Labrune, J.B., Pietriga, E.: DynaSpot: speed-dependent area cursor. In: Proceedings of the SIGCHI Conference on Human Factors in Computing Systems, pp. 1391–1400. ACM, April 2009
9. Cockburn, A., Brock, P.: Human on-line response to visual and motor target expansion. In: Proceedings of Graphics Interface 2006, pp. 81–87. Canadian Information Processing Society, June 2006
10. Cockburn, A., Firth, A.: Improving the acquisition of small targets. In: O'Neill, E., Palanque, P., Johnson, P. (eds.) People and Computers XVII—Designing for Society, pp. 181–196. Springer, London (2004). https://doi.org/10.1007/978-1-4471-3754-2_11
11. Grossman, T., Balakrishnan, R.: The bubble cursor: enhancing target acquisition by dynamic resizing of the cursor's activation area. In: Proceedings of the SIGCHI Conference on Human Factors in Computing Systems, pp. 281–290. ACM, April 2005
12. Guiard, Y., Blanch, R., Beaudouin-Lafon, M.: Object pointing: a complement to bitmap pointing in GUIs. In: Proceedings of Graphics Interface 2004, pp. 9–16. Canadian Human-Computer Communications Society, May 2004
13. Gutwin, C.: Improving focus targeting in interactive fisheye views. In: Proceedings of the SIGCHI Conference on Human Factors in Computing Systems, pp. 267–274. ACM, April 2002
14. Guillon, M., Leitner, F., Nigay, L.: Investigating visual feedforward for target expansion techniques. In: Proceedings of the 33rd Annual ACM Conference on Human Factors in Computing Systems, pp. 2777–2786. ACM, April 2015
15. Guillon, M., Leitner, F., Nigay, L.: Target expansion lens: it is not the more visual feedback the better!. In: Proceedings of the International Working Conference on Advanced Visual Interfaces, pp. 52–59. ACM, June 2016
16. Hertzum, M., Hornbæk, K.: Input techniques that dynamically change their cursor activation area: a comparison of bubble and cell cursors. Int. J. Hum.-Comput. Stud. 65(10), 833–851 (2007)

17. Kabbash, P., Buxton, W.A.: The "prince" technique: Fitts' law and selection using area cursors. In: Proceedings of the SIGCHI Conference on Human Factors in Computing Systems, pp. 273–279. ACM Press/Addison-Wesley Publishing Co., May 1995
18. Kobayashi, M., Igarashi, T.: Ninja cursors: using multiple cursors to assist target acquisition on large screens. In: Proceedings of the SIGCHI Conference on Human Factors in Computing Systems, pp. 949–958. ACM, April 2008
19. Lank, E., Cheng, Y.C.N., Ruiz, J.: Endpoint prediction using motion kinematics. In: Proceedings of the SIGCHI Conference on Human Factors in Computing Systems, pp. 637–646. ACM, April 2007
20. Laukkanen, J., Isokoski, P., Räihä, K.J.: The cone and the lazy bubble: two efficient alternatives between the point cursor and the bubble cursor. In: Proceedings of the SIGCHI Conference on Human Factors in Computing Systems, pp. 309–312. ACM, April 2008
21. Li, W.H.A., Fu, H., Zhu, K.: BezelCursor: Bezel-initiated cursor for one-handed target acquisition on mobile touch screens. Int. J. Mob. Hum. Comput. Interact. (IJMHCI) 8(1), 1–22 (2016)
22. MacKenzie, I.S.: Fitts' law as a research and design tool in human-computer interaction. Hum.-Comput. Interact. 7(1), 91–139 (1992)
23. McGuffin, M.J., Balakrishnan, R.: Fitts' law and expanding targets: experimental studies and designs for user interfaces. ACM Trans. Comput.-Hum. Interact. (TOCHI) 12(4), 388–422 (2005)
24. Meyer, D.E., Abrams, R.A., Kornblum, S., Wright, C.E., Keith Smith, J.E.: Optimality in human motor performance: ideal control of rapid aimed movements. Psychol. Rev. 95(3), 340 (1988)
25. Moscovich, T., Hughes, J.F.: Multi-finger cursor techniques. In: Proceedings of Graphics Interface 2006, pp. 1–7. Canadian Information Processing Society, June 2006
26. Pietriga, E., Appert, C.: Sigma lenses: focus-context transitions combining space, time and translucence. In: Proceedings of the SIGCHI Conference on Human Factors in Computing Systems, pp. 1343–1352. ACM, April 2008
27. Soukoreff, R.W., MacKenzie, I.S.: Towards a standard for pointing device evaluation, perspectives on 27 years of Fitts' law research in HCI. Int. J. Hum.-Comput. Stud. 61(6), 751–789 (2004)
28. Su, X., Au, O.K.C., Lau, R.W.: The implicit fan cursor: a velocity dependent area cursor. In: Proceedings of the SIGCHI Conference on Human Factors in Computing Systems, pp. 753–762. ACM, April 2014
29. Worden, A., Walker, N., Bharat, K., Hudson, S.: Making computers easier for older adults to use: area cursors and sticky icons. In: Proceedings of the ACM SIGCHI Conference on Human Factors in Computing Systems, pp. 266–271. ACM, March 1997

Investigating the Potential of EEG for Implicit Detection of Unknown Words for Foreign Language Learning

Christina Schneegass[✉], Thomas Kosch, Albrecht Schmidt,
and Heinrich Hussmann

LMU Munich, 80337 Munich, Germany
{christina.schneegass,thomas.kosch,albrecht.schmidt,
heinrich.hussmann}@ifi.lmu.de

Abstract. Ubiquitous technologies change the way we learn new languages. They provide easy access to multilingual media content within everyday scenarios to enhance language skills or improve vocabulary. The detection of learners' vocabulary deficiencies is an integral part of effective language learning. However, retrieving translations during everyday media consumption causes inattention and hinders fluent learning. In this paper, we investigate Electroencephalography (EEG) to assess single-word incomprehension within non-native learning contents. In a user study (N = 10), we employed Rapid Serial Visual Presentation (RSVP) to display text while recording Event-Related Potentials (ERPs) for different word difficulties. Our results show that incomprehension of words can be detected in participants' neural responses, as is confirmed by post hoc ratings. We conclude with use case scenarios in which our approach can facilitate seamless vocabulary deficiency detection in everyday life.

Keywords: EEG · Language proficiency detection ·
Implicit interaction

1 Introduction

We often encounter foreign media contents in our daily lives: when we read international news articles on social media, when we do not want to wait for dubbed versions of movies, or when we are on holiday and business trips in foreign countries. Although we can rely on today's technology to provide us with instant translations [17], learning and speaking another language is still important for our communication skills [20,48].

However, language learning is time-consuming and highly individual. To provide efficient learning support, we need to adapt the content to target each person's specific knowledge gaps [54]. One way to discover these gaps is by continuously monitoring the users' understanding when engaging with second language content [5]. When a problem occurs, we can ensure thorough comprehension

© IFIP International Federation for Information Processing 2019
Published by Springer Nature Switzerland AG 2019
D. Lamas et al. (Eds.): INTERACT 2019, LNCS 11748, pp. 293–313, 2019.
https://doi.org/10.1007/978-3-030-29387-1_17

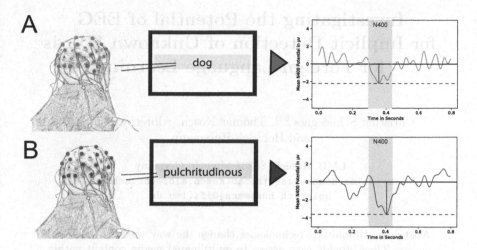

Fig. 1. Our concept entails the recording of EEG data while the user is reading texts including known words as opposed to unknown words on a screen. Encountering (A) known words results in a weaker N400 amplitude compared to (B) unknown words.

by interventions with either explicit or implicit user input. Explicit input, for example looking up a word in the dictionary, requires time and causes distraction. By using implicit data to detect problems in understanding, we can create interfaces, which support the user without interrupting the learning process.

In this paper, we investigate the potential of Electroencephalography (EEG) for the implicit detection of gaps in users' vocabulary knowledge for learning foreign language contents. In particular, we evaluate Event-Related Potentials (ERPs) [7] to differentiate between known and unknown words in English second language reading (see Fig. 1) along with a native language baseline. In our experiment, we presented the texts as a Rapid Serial Visual Presentation (RSVP) approach, which displays text as one word at a time [46].

In a within-subject user study (N = 10), we specifically looked into N400 ERPs, which are known to be indicators for syntactic processing, during the reading of native and second language text [50]. We included words, which are known and unknown to the participants and verified the participants' understanding via post hoc ratings. Based on these results, we conclude our work with the presentation of three use case perspectives for EEG based assessment of foreign language proficiency and learning support.

By being able to continuously assess language proficiency during media consumption, we are able to build language-aware interfaces to customize and optimize language learning support. Keeping in mind the rapid development of consumer-grade EEG devices, such interfaces will soon be able to provide a method for constant and unobtrusive assessment of language skills in everyday scenarios. Although we focused on the application of text reading in language learning, this method is not limited to this domain and might be suitable in other contexts.

The contributions of this paper are threefold:

1. We show the feasibility of EEG as a method to continuously monitor comprehension during second-language text reading.
2. Based on our results, we discuss recommendations on how to facilitate this implicit input mechanism to support language learning in everyday scenarios.
3. We present potential future personalized and optimized language learning applications.

2   Related Work

Our work is based on previous research in the following two areas: (1) applications for language learning with media in everyday environments and (2) the cognitive processes behind EEG readings as well as their evaluation in terms of language processing and learning.

2.1   Language Learning in Everyday Scenarios

Learning through media and encountering foreign languages on a daily basis can have advantages that exceed those of classical classroom learning. This is mainly due to the presentation of contents in context [62]. But having context is not necessarily sufficient for comprehension. Thanks to ubiquitous computing devices, we can engage with contents and more importantly, request translations anytime and anywhere [17].

However, interrupting everyday tasks (e.g., learning vocabulary by watching a Spanish TV show) to receive a translation for a specific word via our smartphone, can be distracting from the content itself. This phenomenon, named media multitasking, can have a negative effect on recall and comprehension due to higher cognitive load in this situation [65].

Besides active user interventions, certain applications gather implicit user data to assess language comprehension and support learning. For example, language proficiency is reflected in users' gaze features. Karolus et al. [35] evaluated language proficiency for texts shown on public displays by analyzing fixations and blink duration of users. This novel approach shows the potential of eye tracking as assessment for language proficiency and experienced workload of users [40,41]. For the assessment of advanced learners, Berzak, Katz and Levy [5] go one step further and prove the feasibility of gaze information to assess the degree of language comprehension. In a setup where English-second-language learners were presented with one-liners, the system could accurately predict participants' comprehension scores when compared to standardized tests [5]. However, the eyes respond with similar movements to various linguistic events and do not provide insights into more specific language processes of the brain [53].

Another promising method to implicitly estimate users' understanding during learning is Electroencephalography. The analysis of EEG data can reflect users' engagement, workload, attention, vigilance, fatigue, error recognition, emotions, flow, and immersion [23]. The following section will give a detailed description of this technique and its facets that are relevant to language processing.

2.2   Electroencephalography

Electroencephalography (EEG) is a noninvasive technique to measure electric potential from the brain by placing conductive electrodes on a person's scalp [3]. In contrast to other imaging techniques such as functional magnetic resonance imaging (fMRI), EEG hardware is comparably cheap and accessible for non-medical researchers and has a high temporal resolution [69]. EEG can detect brain responses within milliseconds of the stimulus presentation, thus, making it a feasible tool to monitor implicit reactions to learning contents [3]. The electrodes can measure potentials from $1\,\mu v$ up to $100\,\mu v$ (microvolts) in relation to a reference point, which is an additional electrode attached to the scalp or earlobe [21]. The two main features of EEG data that are frequently evaluated are (1) changes in frequency bands and (2) Event-Related Potentials (ERPs). ERPs are waveforms, representing positive and negative voltage fluctuations of the brain (an example ERP is shown in Fig. 1). ERPs are responses to a given stimulus [70] originating in either sensory, motor, or cognitive events [43] (e.g., moving a hand or hearing a sound). The evaluation of ERPs can, besides others, infer the amount of processing resources [37] or cognitive load [58] in a given moment. Due to the high temporal resolution of EEG in general, this measurement allows for the differentiation of responses to individual words or speech sounds. Therefore, EEG can be applied as a method to examine differences in real-time first and second language processing [12]. Unfortunately, movements of the eyes and head, as well as muscle contractions, can cause noise in EEG data. Therefore, these measurements require additional effort to reduce extraneous influences and eliminate noise artifacts [11].

Research has shown that EEG can be applied for various purposes, exceeding its original application in medical research [19]. Due to advancements in both data classification software and EEG hardware quality [51], current technologies are becoming an increasingly robust tool for brain response evaluations even in real-world scenarios [39]. Within the last decade, research achieved important improvements in building small, wireless, and low-cost EEG devices [15]. Debener et al. [14] even built a portable EEG with printed electrodes using a smartphone for signal delivery and acquisition, and proved its feasibility for comfortable EEG signal capturing over many hours [14]. To support natural communication, Bleichner et al. [6] explored a nearly invisible EEG setup through the integration of electrodes into a baseball cap while reliably recording P300 ERPs [6]. These advancements show the potential of EEG to be applied in everyday scenarios.

2.3   Event-Related Potentials

ERPs can be used to evaluate brain activity during second language processing. These potentials are averaged responses from a group of trials as a reaction to a given experimental stimulus. The assumption is that a certain electrical potential occurs at a consistent time after the presentation of a stimulus to the participant [12,25] (e.g., a non-word or a word out of context).

Due to the high temporal resolution, ERPs can reflect responses occurring within a few hundred milliseconds after the stimulus is presented. Thus, ERPs can provide insights about the processing of individual words within sentences. Since the potentials of consecutive words can overlap, serial presentation of words can foster effective detection of ERPs. Either slow rate serial presentation or artificial separation of the words can maintain the correct mapping of stimulus and response [12]. Experiments showed that semantic relationships within sentences are shown in N400 potentials: negative-going brain potential between 250–500 ms after the presentation of any potentially meaningful stimulus, peaking at around 400 ms [45]. However, the exact onset of the response is depending on the reading speed and can occur earlier if the speed is close to normal [42]. N400s can reveal the strength of the semantic relationship of words in context, as Kutas and Federmeier [44] highlight in their review, and the difficulty of semantic integration [50]. In addition, N400s show that there is an influence on semantic processing mechanisms when comparing first and second language processing [2,26]. A study by Holcomb and Neville [32] found that N400s increase immediately after the processing of non-words. N400s also represent the plausibility of verb-object combinations and appear with larger amplitudes when a word is unknown, used inappropriately, or is a pseudoword [4,45]. In addition, the amplitudes of N400 potentials reflect how expected a word is within a sentence [44,45]. Since related work performed studies on the processing of non words [32], unexpected words [44], or words out of context [45] sentences are often incoherent, or words sound unnatural. We adapted the study setup so that it would approximate our use cases by using coherent texts from a validated source and included real English words unknown to the participants. In our case, *unknown* words are those the participants were not able to translate to their native language.

In summary, related work showed the importance and potential of implicit measures to assess language proficiency for real-world applications. The use of EEG data is gaining popularity due to reduced acquisition costs and technical research proving the applicability in everyday settings. In particular, the analysis of N400 ERPs shows potential to assess the language proficiency of individuals.

3   Methodology

Based on related work, the main goal of this work is to answer the following research question:

RQ: Can we detect gaps in users' second language vocabulary knowledge during text reading by analyzing the amplitudes of the resulting N400 potentials?

To answer the research question, we conducted a lab study in which participants were required to read texts on a computer screen while recording their EEG signals.

Table 1. Overview of the Lexile measures [47] for E1 and E2 in both their original and revised versions utilized for the study.

	E1$_{orig}$	E1$_{rev}$	E2$_{orig}$	E2$_{rev}$
Total sentence length	29	29	24	24
Lexile measure	600L–700L	900L–1000L	1000L–1100L	1000L–1100L
Mean number of words per sentence length	14.96	15.34	17.36	17.36
Total word count	419	445	434	434

3.1 Text Difficulty Selection

For this study, we included texts from the corpus of the *Asian and Pacific Speed Readings for ESL Learner* [56]. These texts include predefined English language texts on topics related to Asia and the Pacific with a supplementary set of ten single-choice comprehension questions per topic. The texts was specifically chosen because it features frequent words and easy grammar [57] to be easily understandable. We chose to include excerpts from three texts ("Life in the South Pacific Islands", "Buddhism", and "Hong Kong") and translated the first one (further termed *N1*) into the participants' native language to serve as a baseline. N1 included 30 sentences and in total 452 words, which we split into two texts of 15 sentences each. The presentation of either subset was randomized among participants to avoid effects caused by the content.

The second and third text, named *E1* and *E2*, were in English, the participants' second language. E1 contained 29 and E2 24 sentences (∼450 words per text, for more details see Table 1) to generate a sufficient set of trials while not straining the user. The two texts E1 and E2 were randomly assigned to the participants for a within-subject design. We revised each text to contain ten sentences with one uncommon word (e.g., "adscititious"), selected with the help of a thesaurus and a list of unfamiliar words[1]. Including just one difficult word per sentence creates a realistic scenario and prevents the overlapping of ERPs. In regards to the changes performed in the texts, we adapted the comprehension questionnaires for E1 and E2. Each question is meant to check the understanding of one sentences containing a potentially unknown word.

To confirm the difficulty level of the texts, we used the *Lexile Analyzer*[2]. This tool analyzes texts and provides an approximate reading level for it based on the metrics (1) word commonness, which is reported to correlate highly with text difficulty, and (2) complexity of syntax [47]. The Lexile score can range between 200L (L for Lexile) for beginner reading, up to 1700L for advanced texts [47]. Table 1 specifies the Lexile Measures for E1 and E2 in the original version and a revised version that includes unknown words. It can be seen that the effect

---

[1] www.en.oxforddictionaries.com/explore/weird-and-wonderful-words - last access 2019-06-03.
[2] www.lexile.com - last access 2019-06-03.

of difficult words on the Lexile score is only noticeable in E1, since E2 already includes many proper names and consists of longer sentences. Since the Lexile Analyzer only supports English texts, we further confirm the understandability of our texts through subjective post-hoc ratings. Participants had to answer comprehension questions as well as specify every word which they could not translate.

3.2   Text Presentation

We presented the texts in a Rapid Serial Visual Presentation (RSVP) mode, showing each one word at a time on the screen to reduce saccadic eye movements during normal reading behavior [59] (see Fig. 2). A decrease of eye movements will lead to reduced noise in the data generated by the muscles around the eye. Furthermore, since RSVP only displays one word, the matching of the EEG signal to the dedicated stimulus can be easily performed. The word presentation rate was set to 170 words per minute (WPM) based on the findings of [8], who showed that participants' reading comprehension is best at speeds ranging from 171 to 350WPM. We decided to set the speed to the lower end of this spectrum since our participants are non-native speakers and to minimize overlaps in the signals due to the processing of consecutive words (cf. Sect. 2.3).

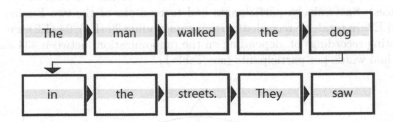

Fig. 2. In the RSVP approach, text is displayed each one word at a time. The words are centered to minimize eye movements.

3.3   Apparatus

Our setup consisted of a display (Dell U2715H; 27 in.; 60 Hz refresh rate) and a Brainvision Liveamp[3] EEG device comprising a sampling rate of 500 Hz. The EEG device provides a bandpass filter ranging from 0.1 to 1000 Hz and does not include a notch filter. Electrodes were placed in accordance to the International 10–20 layout (ground electrode: *Fpz*, reference electrode: *FCz*; see Fig. 3).

---

[3] www.brainproducts.com - last access 2019-06-03.

3.4   Procedure

At the beginning of the study, we welcomed the participants and handed them a detailed study description. The description contained the study motivation and goal as well as its process. Every participant signed a consent form and randomly picked and crossed out an ID from a prepared sheet of possible IDs to assure adequate anonymity. Then they filled in a short demographic questionnaire asking for age, gender, highest educational degree, vision impairment, and neuronal diseases or disorders. Furthermore, they were asked to set all electronic devices into flight mode so as not to influence the data recording.

We carefully explained the EEG system, measured participants' head circumference to select between four different actiCAP sizes (54 cm, 56 cm, 58 cm and 60 cm), and instructed them to put on the cap. Afterward, we attached 32 electrodes (plus 2 reference electrodes) to the participants' scalp using the actiCAPs' designated 10/20 positioning system [33] (the electrode layout can furthermore be seen in Fig. 3). We increased the conductivity of all 34 electrodes with high viscosity electrolyte gel and examined their impedance for reliable performance. The experiment started when the impedance of all electrodes reached the threshold of 10 kΩ. The signals were recorded in a quiet, dimly lit experimental room equipped with a desk and a comfortable chair, around 80 cm away from the screen.

At first, participants had to read one subset of the N1 baseline text (15 sentences). Successively, participants had to read one of the two English texts E1 and E2. In total, we recorded participants reading 29 (E1)/24 (E2) sentences, generating recordings of, depending on the randomization, between 434 and 445 individual words per participants (see Table 1).

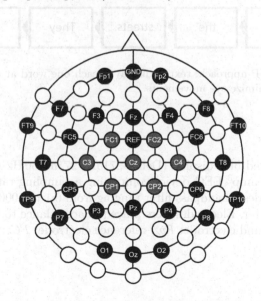

Fig. 3. The red electrodes located around the parietal lobe were used for analysis.

To evaluate how much additional perceived workload was induced by the second language texts, we presented each participant with two NASA Task Load Index (NASA-TLX) questionnaires [27,28], one after the baseline and one after the foreign text. Both texts were followed by a comprehension test consisting of ten questions designed to target the understanding of the sentences that included unknown words. Furthermore, to confirm that participants could not translate the words that were meant to be unknown, we presented them with a print-out version of the text. We asked them to highlight all the words, which they cannot translate to their native language. In summary, for both texts the following procedure was applied:

1. Read text as RSVP
2. Answer NASA-TLX for this text
3. Fill in ten item comprehension questionnaire
4. Post hoc rating of unknown words in printed text
5. Short rest phase.

3.5 Sample

We recruited twelve participants via a university mailing list and an internal social media channel. As a requirement, we asked for our German and English proficiency. A minimum English proficiency of B1 according to the Common European Framework of Reference for Languages (CEFR)[4] was given due to the standards of the german high school diploma. Furthermore, we did not include participants with severe vision problems and neurological disorders. Every study participant was rewarded with an Amazon voucher. We removed two participants from our evaluation due to technical difficulties.

Within our adjusted sample size of $N = 10$ (5 female, 5 male), the participants' age ranged from 18–60 ($M = 31.6$, $SD = 14.41$). They held at least a high school degree (6), some even a master degree (3), or a doctoral degree (1). Due to high school being the lowest minimal educational level of our sample, we can assume a minimum English proficiency level of B2 [18] or more for every participant.

3.6 Data Processing

We use Python with the library MNE to process the recorded EEG data[5]. EEG data were bandpass filtered [55] (0.5–40 Hz) to attenuate the influence of artifacts (e.g., blinks, eye, and head movement) as well as the 50 Hz remote power line noise. We consider the electrodes *Cz*, *C3*, *C4*, *CP1*, *CP2*, *FC1*, and *FC2* as the parietal lobe is linked to the processing of spoken and written language [68]. We identified eye blinks using Python MNE and removed them manually. We did not perform an independent component analysis as we employed 32 electrodes

---

[4] www.coe.int/en/web/common-european-framework-reference-languages/level-descriptions - last access 2019-06-03.

[5] www.martinos.org/mne/stable/index.html - last access 2019-06-03.

and we did not intend to remove the contribution of cortical components that might have been resolved into the summed activity of non-cortical dipoles. To analyze ERPs independently from known and unknown words, we slice the data set into triggers for known and unknown words. We look at the first second of neural responses for each word as we are interested in investigating the N400 ERPs that occur between 300 ms and 600 ms after displaying the stimuli.

4   Results

We statistically analyzed the collected data for differences in ERP magnitudes. We submitted the magnitudes of the averaged N400s for known and unknown words to an analysis of variances (ANOVA). Furthermore, we investigated the subjectively perceived workload and reading comprehension. Our results contain the EEG responses to 4390 words, of which 100 are classified as likely to be unknown to the users.

4.1   Event-Related Potentials

We divided the measured data into each epoch for known and unknown words. Each epoch has the same duration as a single word is displayed on the screen. We averaged each epoch for every participant and normalized the magnitude of the data to enable person-independent comparisons for native, known, and unknown words. Mauchly's test did not show a violation of sphericity. A repeated measures ANOVA was performed including the three conditions native, known, and unknown words as independent variables and the N400 amplitudes as depending variable. The analysis revealed a significant main effect ($F(2, 18) = 13.33$, $p < .001$). A post hoc test using a Bonferroni correction revealed a significant effect in N400 potentials between known and unknown words ($p < .001$, $d = 2.648$) as well as unknown and native words ($p = .031$, $d = -1.024$). We found no significant effect between the amplitudes of native and known English words. Figure 4 shows the averaged N400 across all participants for known and unknown words. The mean amplitude for known words was higher ($M = -1.201$, $SD = 0.662$) compared to the mean amplitude of unknown words ($M = -2.885$, $SD = 0.057$). Figure 5 illustrates the difference of the N400 magnitudes for known and unknown words.

4.2   Perceived Workload

The workload during the reading of native text was perceived as lower as during English texts. The NASA-TLX is subdivided into six facets of workload: mental, physical, temporal, performance, effort, and frustration [28]. The NASA-TLX was presented as a detailed scale ranging from one (very low demand) to 20 (very high demand). For a general analysis, we added up the individual facets of the NASA-TLX to create one overall score, which therefore had a range from 1 to 120 (6×20, the max value of one facet). This score was lower for native

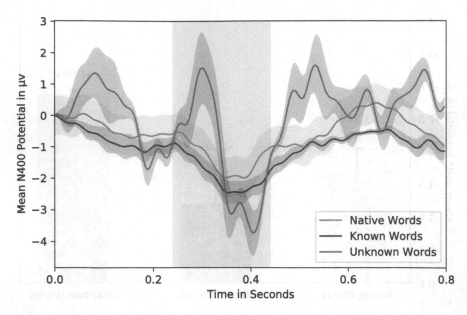

Fig. 4. N400 measured for known and unknown words. A larger mean amplitude is measured for unknown words compared to known words.

language text ($M = 40.4$, $SD = 19.08$) as opposed to the foreign text ($M = 53$, $SD = 18.66$). We performed a paired samples t-test comparing the overall perceived workload of the two languages (native vs. English). The results revealed a significant difference between the languages ($p < .05$, $t(9) = 2.842$, $d = -0.899$), showing a large effect in the direction of a lower mean workload in the native language texts. A Shapiro-Wilk test showed no indication for a deviation of normality ($p = .915$).

Moreover, paired samples t-tests within the individual facets showed significant differences between the two languages in terms of perceived mental workload ($t(9) = -3.452$, $p < .05$, $d = -0.506$), perceived temporal demand (i.e., feeling rushed; $t(9) = -2.339$, $p < .05$, $d = -0.740$), and perceived performance (i.e., reading and understanding the texts; $t(9) = -2.872$, $p < .05$, $d = -0.899$). All of these results showed negative values for Cohen's d, indicating higher loads for the English texts. Figure 6 shows the mean raw NASA-TLX score between both languages.

4.3 Text Comprehension

There was each one questionnaire to test the comprehension of the N1, E1, and E2 texts. On average, the participants achieved the best scores in the N1 questionnaire with around 7 correct answers (correct answers out of ten, $M = 6.9$, $SD = 2.13$), followed by E2 ($M = 6.6$, $SD = 1.82$). The text with the least amount of correct answers was E1 ($M = 5.4$, $SD = 2.19$).

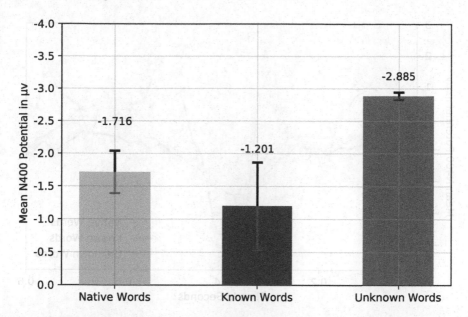

Fig. 5. Mean N400 amplitudes for known and unknown words. Unknown words elicit a statistical significant effect in amplitudes compared to known words. The bars depict the standard error.

4.4 Post Hoc Word Review

Participants performed a post hoc rating of all words, highlighting each word for which they can not come up with a translation. No participant highlighted any word of the N1 text. We can furthermore confirm the low difficulty of the E1 and E2 due to the fact that not a single word of all three texts was perceived as difficult besides our artificial modifications. When looking at the 10 modified words of E1 in detail, the results show a high consensus among the participants who read the text. Out of the 10 potentially unknown words, 7 are confirmed as unknown by all five participants ($M = 4.6$, $SD = 0.7$). In the text E2, the confirmation of the unknown words turned out to be less distinct. Only three out of the 10 words were highlighted by all participants. On average, the potentially unknown words are highlighted by 4.2 participants ($SD = 0.63$).

5   Discussion

We conducted a user study to investigate the feasibility of ERPs to detect vocabulary gaps. Our results show a statistically significant main effect in N400 amplitudes between known and unknown words as well as between native and unknown words. In the following, we discuss the implications of our results.

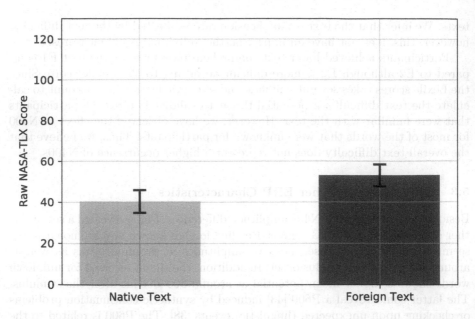

Fig. 6. Mean raw NASA-TLX scores for both languages. Reading native languages resulted in less workload compared to foreign languages. The bars depict the standard error.

5.1 Detecting Vocabulary Gaps

The results from our study show that we can use EEG data, N400 ERPs in particular, to assess the word-based language proficiency by measuring a significant effect between the amplitudes caused by known and unknown words. This confirms EEG as a valid tool for vocabulary gap detection. Although the descriptive ERP data showed minor differences between the N400 amplitudes of reading native words and reading known second-language words, the statistical analysis did not result in a significant difference. We conclude that N400s, independent from the presented language, have common properties [66]. Going beyond the results of the conducted study, our results encourage further investigations on neural activity of second language processing.

5.2 Subjective Workload and Comprehension

When comparing the results of the raw NASA-TLX questionnaires we recognize a significant difference in perceived workload when reading native as opposed to English words. This shows that subjectively perceived workload was manipulated in conjunction with our finding in N400 amplitude. The comprehension tests show that there is a difference of complexity when comparing the two English texts. However, when marking the unknown words in the print-outs, the participants reached a 70% consensus. Therefore, we assume that the participants perceived the unknown words as equally difficult to translate in both English

texts. We infer that the text comprehension rate is affected by the text difficulty, however, this does not have an impact on the individual N400 measures.

Participants achieved lower text comprehension scores for the text E1 compared to E2 although E2 is more difficult according to the Lexile score. Since the Lexile scores takes several syntactic and semantic factors into account to calculate the text difficulty, a potential threat to validity is posed by participants that were familiar with the text. However, we have observed the effect of N400 for most of the words that were unknown for participants. Thus, we believe that the overall text difficulty does not represent a higher occurrence of N400s.

5.3   Differences in Other ERP Characteristics

Besides the characteristic N400 amplitude differences, Fig. 4 revealed a set of further differences in the EEG signals. Reading foreign known and unknown words seems to reflect in increased positive amplitudes at around 100 ms as well as around 300 ms after stimulus onset. In addition, the signal received for unknown words shows a higher mean potential at around 500–600 ms after the stimulus. The latter could reveal a P600 [43] induced by syntactic continuation problems or checking upon unexpected (linguistic) events [38]. The P600 is related to the P300 [10], which can be a result of the 'oddball' effect. The oddball effect is a phenomenon of inattention blindness and can occur if an unexpected stimulus appears [64]. In our case, the unknown words suddenly interrupted the fluent reading behaviour. It is common, that a P300 occurs simultaneously with an N200 [10]. Further statistical analysis need to evaluate the differences of other ERP components in the recorded signals.

5.4   Limitations

A major challenge of this approach is the sum of influencing factors, which would reflect in the EEG data when applied in a real-world setting. We minimized these effects by conducting a study in a laboratory setting and were able to control people's attention and task load. Therefore, we do not know to what extent our results are generalizable to other situations. Including additional measurements such as gaze tracking could help to compensate for other influences in the application of EEG data in everyday settings. Furthermore, we have to examine in small steps the potential of this approach when faced with further stimuli (e.g., by adding video or auditory material). The applicability for other text presentation modes, for example including a sentence-based text presentation mode as an approximation of subtitles used in videos, needs to be evaluated. Furthermore, we acknowledge that our study employed a low sample size. However, we replicated the methodology from other HCI studies that have successfully employed similar sample sizes [29,63] and therefore, believe that this study can highlight the potential of EEG for implicit language proficiency detection. We see our work as a first proof of concept and as to be following the path of other EEG research publishing novel ideas for real-world scenarios [30,60].

6   Use Cases for EEG as Ubiquitous Language Learning Support

In the following, we present potential use case perspectives to show the application of EEG data on vocabulary comprehension to support language learning in everyday environments.

Use Case 1 - RSVP Reading on Small Screen Devices

Designing efficient reading interfaces on devices with limited screen space, such as a smartwatch, is challenging within mobile contexts [16]. The usage of RSVP, where the whole screen presents a single word, is one interface design option that has been evaluated [24]. It has the advantage of presenting text in a reasonably large font and allows reading with little eye movement. However, this interface has one inherent limitation: Being presented with just one word at the time, a user cannot take a step back when encountering problems of understanding due to unknown words. With the insights from analyzing the EEG data, we would be able to detect in real-time when the user encounters unknown words or potentially troublesome concepts during reading as illustrated in Fig. 7a. By combining a smartwatch and a mobile EEG device we could use an algorithm to dynamically adapt the content and interface. For example, offer real-time support by showing words for a longer time, provide translations, or by show unknown words more frequently in other media contents. The realization of this scenario is, however, depending on the development of portable and pervasive EEG devices, which have the potential to become affordable [15], unobtrusive [14], nearly invisible [6], and feasible for applications including natural actions and cognition [13].

Use Case 2 - Media Consumption on Screen

Using media content in foreign languages has been often reported to be a useful tool to improve language skills [31]. One area, where our approach can be beneficial, is the presentation of subtitles in videos. Including subtitles in audiovisual content can support the acquisition and the improvement of language skills [52,67]. There are already tools exploring the potential of subtitle translations (GliFlix [61]), or second screen application to present important concepts of TV shows (*Flickstuff* [36]). By using our EEG based approach in monitoring users' comprehension during media usage as shown in Fig. 7b, we can provide an effective tool for real-time and post hoc vocabulary learning support, such as personalized vocabulary lists. To implement this, one would couple the EEG monitoring and analysis with gaze tracking to detect the current focus of the users and thus, to identify the word in question.

Use Case 3 - Media Content in Ubiquitous Environments with Smart Glasses

What we envision for subtitles on a screen could also be transferred into real-world environments. In our everyday life, we encounter signs and texts as they are ubiquitous in our surroundings. With a setup consisting of smart glasses that include a camera, we can link gaze tracking to a mobile EEG. Thus, it will become feasible to also detect signs and texts not understood by the user on

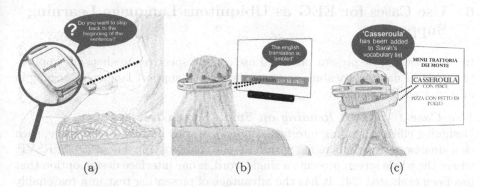

Fig. 7. Possible use case scenarios for EEG based language comprehension (a): Reading on small screen devices. (b): Media consumption on a screen with subtitle reading enhanced with gaze-tracking. (c): Reading media content in a real-world environment with supplementary smart glasses.

many digital and analogue devices such as advertisements or public screens. The general approach to apply comprehension analysis in the physical surrounding is to detect what the user is perceiving and assess their brain's reaction. Figure 7c illustrates our vision that this can be realized by smart glasses and a front-facing camera. With the help of optical character recognition [49], it is feasible to monitor text in the users' surroundings [22] and provide individual support.

7   Conclusion and Future Work

The findings from our work provide evidence for the potential of Electroen-cephalography (EEG) data to support language learning. In particular, Event-related Potentials (ERPs) are a feasible measurement for the detection of incom-prehension on a one-word basis. Having an approach to support the continu-ous assessment of second-language text comprehension brings us one step closer towards the design of ubiquitous learning support. We tested the approach in the context of text reading and aimed to recognize vocabulary incomprehension to support language learning. Still, this method is not limited to this applica-tion scenario and is of particular interest to many areas of ubiquitous technol-ogy. Three possible use case scenarios were outlined in this work, highlighting the additional value an EEG based word comprehension system would offer. Additionally to the use case of foreign language reading, future work should investigate the transfer of this approach to evaluate spoken language compre-hension. Thereby, this technique could support real life communication, which is, in particular, important in conversations where the two involved parties show different levels of language proficiency. Furthermore, different foreign languages may elicit different magnitudes in the measured N400 amplitudes. Investigating the difference of N400 amplitudes within different languages is subject for future work.

Although this work supports the assumption that ERPs have a high potential for vocabulary learning support, further evaluation needs to clarify the feasibility for real-time support. In general, ERPs are noisy and, therefore, need to be averaged over many trials. However, requiring the user to take a training phase and applying deep learning can be beneficial, as priorly applied for emotion classification [34,71] or the evaluation of motor imagery signals [1,9]. The result could be the establishment of an individual baseline. This baseline could function as a classifier to distinguish known and unknown words based on the ERP signals in real-time settings. Moreover, the RSVP approach introduces certain degrees of freedom, e.g., text presentation speed. Providing maximum speed while still being able to measure ERPs needs to be evaluated in future work. We believe that this work provides a first step on a path towards a new generation of personal assistance system based on the usage of EEG technology.

References

1. An, X., Kuang, D., Guo, X., Zhao, Y., He, L.: A deep learning method for classification of EEG data based on motor imagery. In: Huang, D.-S., Han, K., Gromiha, M. (eds.) ICIC 2014. LNCS, vol. 8590, pp. 203–210. Springer, Cham (2014). https://doi.org/10.1007/978-3-319-09330-7_25
2. Ardal, S., Donald, M.W., Meuter, R., Muldrew, S., Luce, M.: Brain responses to semantic incongruity in bilinguals. Brain Lang. **39**(2), 187–205 (1990)
3. Baillet, S., Mosher, J.C., Leahy, R.M.: Electromagnetic brain mapping. IEEE Signal Process. Mag. **18**(6), 14–30 (2001)
4. Bentin, S., McCarthy, G., Wood, C.C.: Event-related potentials, lexical decision and semantic priming. Electroencephalogr. Clin. Neurophysiol. **60**(4), 343–355 (1985)
5. Berzak, Y., Katz, B., Levy, R.: Assessing language proficiency from eye movements in reading. arXiv preprint arXiv:1804.07329 (2018)
6. Bleichner, M.G., et al.: Exploring miniaturized EEG electrodes for brain-computer interfaces. An EEG you do not see? Physiol. Rep. **3**(4), 1–9 (2015)
7. Borovsky, A., Kutas, M., Elman, J.: Learning to use words: event-related potentials index single-shot contextual word learning. Cognition **116**(2), 289–296 (2010)
8. Chen, C.H., Chien, Y.H.: Effects of RSVP display design on visual performance in accomplishing dual tasks with small screens. Int. J. Des. **1**(1), 27–35 (2007)
9. Cheng, P., Autthasan, P., Pijarana, B., Chuangsuwanich, E., Wilaiprasitporn, T.: Towards asynchronous motor imagery-based brain-computer interfaces: a joint training scheme using deep learning. arXiv preprint arXiv:1808.10852 (2018)
10. Coulson, S., King, J.W., Kutas, M.: Expect the unexpected: event-related brain response to morphosyntactic violations. Lang. Cogn. Process. **13**(1), 21–58 (1998)
11. Cutmore, T.R., James, D.A.: Identifying and reducing noise in psychophysiological recordings. Int. J. Psychophysiol. **32**(2), 129–150 (1999)
12. Davidson, D.: Brain activity during second language processing (ERP). In: The Encyclopedia of Applied Linguistics (2012)
13. De, M.V., Debener, S.: Mobile EEG: towards brain activity monitoring during natural action and cognition. Int. J. Psychol. **91**(1), 1–2 (2014)
14. Debener, S., Emkes, R., De Vos, M., Bleichner, M.: Unobtrusive ambulatory EEG using a smartphone and flexible printed electrodes around the ear. Sci. Rep. **5**, 16743 (2015)

15. Debener, S., Minow, F., Emkes, R., Gandras, K., De Vos, M.: How about taking a low-cost, small, and wireless EEG for a walk? Psychophysiology **49**(11), 1617–1621 (2012)

16. Dingler, T., Rzayev, R., Schwind, V., Henze, N.: RSVP on the go: implicit reading support on smart watches through eye tracking. In: Proceedings of the 2016 ACM International Symposium on Wearable Computers, pp. 116–119. ACM (2016)

17. Doherty, S.: Translations—the impact of translation technologies on the process and product of translation. Int. J. Commun. **10**, 23 (2016)

18. Council of Europe, Council for Cultural Co-operation. Education Committee. Modern Languages Division: Common European Framework of Reference for Languages: Learning, Teaching, Assessment. Cambridge University Press, Cambridge (2001)

19. van Erp, J., Lotte, F., Tangermann, M.: Brain-computer interfaces: beyond medical applications. Computer **45**(4), 26–34 (2012)

20. Fan, S.P., Liberman, Z., Keysar, B., Kinzler, K.D.: The exposure advantage: early exposure to a multilingual environment promotes effective communication. Psychol. Sci. **26**(7), 1090–1097 (2015)

21. Fisch, B.: Fisch and Spehlmann's EEG Primer: Basic Principles of Digital and Analog EEG, 3rd edn. Elsevier, Amsterdam (1999)

22. Fragoso, V., Gauglitz, S., Zamora, S., Kleban, J., Turk, M.: Translatar: a mobile augmented reality translator. In: 2011 IEEE Workshop on Applications of Computer Vision (WACV), pp. 497–502. IEEE (2011)

23. Frey, J., Mühl, C., Lotte, F., Hachet, M.: Review of the use of electroencephalography as an evaluation method for human-computer interaction. arXiv preprint arXiv:1311.2222 (2013)

24. Gannon, E., He, J., Gao, X., Chaparro, B.: RSVP reading on a smart watch. In: Proceedings of the Human Factors and Ergonomics Society Annual Meeting, vol. 60, pp. 1130–1134. SAGE Publications, Los Angeles (2016)

25. Hagoort, P., Hald, L., Bastiaansen, M., Petersson, K.M.: Integration of word meaning and world knowledge in language comprehension. Science **304**(5669), 438–441 (2004)

26. Hahne, A.: What's different in second-language processing? Evidence from event-related brain potentials. J. Psycholinguist. Res. **30**(3), 251–266 (2001)

27. Hart, S.G.: NASA-task load index (NASA-TLX); 20 years later. In: Proceedings of the Human Factors and Ergonomics Society Annual Meeting, vol. 50, pp. 904–908. Sage Publications, Los Angeles (2006)

28. Hart, S.G., Staveland, L.E.: Development of NASA-TLX (task load index): results of empirical and theoretical research. In: Advances in Psychology, vol. 52, pp. 139–183. Elsevier (1988)

29. Hassib, M., Pfeiffer, M., Schneegass, S., Rohs, M., Alt, F.: Emotion actuator: embodied emotional feedback through electroencephalography and electrical muscle stimulation. In: Proceedings of the 2017 CHI Conference on Human Factors in Computing Systems, pp. 6133–6146. ACM (2017)

30. Hassib, M., Schneegass, S., Eiglsperger, P., Henze, N., Schmidt, A., Alt, F.: EngageMeter: a system for implicit audience engagement sensing using electroencephalography. In: Proceedings of the 2017 CHI Conference on Human Factors in Computing Systems, pp. 5114–5119. ACM (2017)

31. Herron, C., Morris, M., Secules, T., Curtis, L.: A comparison study of the effects of video-based versus text-based instruction in the foreign language classroom. Fr. Rev. **68**, 775–795 (1995)

32. Holcomb, P.J., Neville, H.J.: Auditory and visual semantic priming in lexical decision: a comparison using event-related brain potentials. Lang. Cogn. Process. 5(4), 281–312 (1990)
33. Jasper, H.H.: The ten-twenty electrode system of the international federation. Electroencephalogr. Clin. Neurophysiol. 10, 370–375 (1958)
34. Jirayucharoensak, S., Pan-Ngum, S., Israsena, P.: EEG-based emotion recognition using deep learning network with principal component based covariate shift adaptation. Sci. World J. 2014, 10 p. (2014)
35. Karolus, J., Wozniak, P.W., Chuang, L.L., Schmidt, A.: Robust gaze features for enabling language proficiency awareness. In: Proceedings of the 2017 CHI Conference on Human Factors in Computing Systems, pp. 2998–3010. ACM (2017)
36. Knittel, J., Dingler, T.: Mining subtitles for real-time content generation for second-screen applications. In: Proceedings of the ACM International Conference on Interactive Experiences for TV and Online Video, pp. 93–103. ACM (2016)
37. Kok, A.: Event-related-potential (ERP) reflections of mental resources: a review and synthesis. Biol. Psychol. 45(1–3), 19–56 (1997)
38. Kolk, H.H., Chwilla, D.J., Van Herten, M., Oor, P.J.: Structure and limited capacity in verbal working memory: a study with event-related potentials. Brain Lang. 85(1), 1–36 (2003)
39. Kosch, T., Funk, M., Schmidt, A., Chuang, L.: Identifying cognitive assistance with mobile electroencephalography: a case study with in-situ projections for manual assembly. In: Proceedings of the 10th ACM SIGCHI Symposium on Engineering Interactive Computing Systems. ACM (2018). https://doi.org/10.1145/3229093
40. Kosch, T., Hassib, M., Buschek, D., Schmidt, A.: Look into my eyes: using pupil dilation to estimate mental workload for task complexity adaptation. In: Proceedings of the 2018 CHI Conference Extended Abstracts on Human Factors in Computing Systems, CHI EA 2018. ACM, New York (2018). https://doi.org/10.1145/3170427.3188643
41. Kosch, T., Hassib, M., Wozniak, P., Buschek, D., Alt, F.: Your eyes tell: leveraging smooth pursuit for assessing cognitive workload. In: Proceedings of the 2018 CHI Conference on Human Factors in Computing Systems, CHI 2018. ACM, New York (2018). https://doi.org/10.1145/3173574.3174010
42. Kutas, M.: Event-related brain potentials (ERPs) elicited during rapid serial visual presentation of congruous and incongruous sentences. Electroencephalogr. Clin. Neurophysiol. 40(Suppl.), 406–411 (1987)
43. Kutas, M., Dale, A.: Electrical and magnetic readings of mental functions. Cogn. Neurosci. 53, 197–242 (1997)
44. Kutas, M., Federmeier, K.D.: Electrophysiology reveals semantic memory use in language comprehension. Trends Cogn. Sci. 4(12), 463–470 (2000)
45. Kutas, M., Hillyard, S.A.: Reading senseless sentences: brain potentials reflect semantic incongruity. Science 207(4427), 203–205 (1980)
46. Legge, G.E., Mansfield, J.S., Chung, S.T.: Psychophysics of reading: XX. Linking letter recognition to reading speed in central and peripheral vision. Vis. Res. 41(6), 725–743 (2001)
47. Lennon, C., Burdick, H.: The Lexile framework as an approach for reading measurement and success (2004). Electronic publication on www.lexile.com
48. Liberman, Z., Woodward, A.L., Keysar, B., Kinzler, K.D.: Exposure to multiple languages enhances communication skills in infancy. Dev. Sci. 20(1), e12420 (2017)
49. Mori, S., Nishida, H., Yamada, H.: Optical Character Recognition. Wiley, New York (1999)

50. Mueller, J.L.: Electrophysiological correlates of second language processing. Second Lang. Res. **21**(2), 152–174 (2005)
51. Mullen, T.R., et al.: Real-time neuroimaging and cognitive monitoring using wearable dry EEG. IEEE Trans. Biomed. Eng. **62**(11), 2553–2567 (2015)
52. Neuman, S.B., Koskinen, P.: Captioned television as comprehensible input: effects of incidental word learning from context for language minority students. Read. Res. Q. **27**, 95–106 (1992)
53. Osterhout, L., McLaughlin, J., Kim, A., Greenwald, R., Inoue, K.: Sentences in the brain: event-related potentials as real-time reflections of sentence comprehension and language learning. In: The On-Line Study of Sentence Comprehension: Eyetracking, ERP, and Beyond, pp. 271–308 (2004)
54. Pearson, P.D., Hiebert, E.H., Kamil, M.L.: Vocabulary assessment: what we know and what we need to learn. Read. Res. Q. **42**(2), 282–296 (2007)
55. Proakis, J.G.: Digital Signal Processing: Principles Algorithms and Applications. Pearson Education, New Delhi (2001)
56. Quinn, E., Nation, I.S.P.: Speed Reading: A Course For Learners of English. Oxford University Press, Oxford (1974)
57. Quinn, E., Nation, I.S.P., Millett, S.: Asian and Pacific Speed Readings for ESL Learners. English Language Institute Occasional Publication, p. 24 (2007)
58. Roy, R.N., Charbonnier, S., Campagne, A., Bonnet, S.: Efficient mental workload estimation using task-independent EEG features. J. Neural Eng. **13**(2), 026019 (2016)
59. Rubin, G.S., Turano, K.: Reading without saccadic eye movements. Vis. Res. **32**(5), 895–902 (1992)
60. Sahami Shirazi, A., Funk, M., Pfleiderer, F., Glück, H., Schmidt, A.: MediaBrain: annotating videos based on brain-computer interaction. In: Mensch & Computer 2012: interaktiv informiert-allgegenwärtig und allumfassend!? (2012)
61. Sakunkoo, N., Sakunkoo, P.: GliFlix: using movie subtitles for language learning. In: Proceedings of the 26th Symposium on User Interface Software and Technology. ACM (2013)
62. Secules, T., Herron, C., Tomasello, M.: The effect of video context on foreign language learning. Mod. Lang. J. **76**(4), 480–490 (1992)
63. Shirazi, A.S., Hassib, M., Henze, N., Schmidt, A., Kunze, K.: What's on your mind?: mental task awareness using single electrode brain computer interfaces. In: Proceedings of the 5th Augmented Human International Conference, p. 45. ACM (2014)
64. Stokes, T.A., Welk, A.K., Zielinska, O.A., Gillan, D.J.: The oddball effect and inattentional blindness: How unexpected events influence our perceptions of time. In: Proceedings of the Human Factors and Ergonomics Society Annual Meeting, vol. 61, pp. 1753–1757. SAGE Publications, Los Angeles (2017)
65. Van Cauwenberge, A., Schaap, G., Van Roy, R.: "TV no longer commands our full attention": effects of second-screen viewing and task relevance on cognitive load and learning from news. Comput. Hum. Behav. **38**, 100–109 (2014)
66. Van Hell, J.G., Tokowicz, N.: Event-related brain potentials and second language learning: syntactic processing in late L2 learners at different L2 proficiency levels. Second Lang. Res. **26**(1), 43–74 (2010)
67. Vanderplank, R.: Resolving inherent conflicts: autonomous language learning from popular broadcast television. In: Barriers and Bridges: Media Technology in Language Learning, pp. 119–133 (1994)
68. Wise, R.J.S., Brownsett, S.L.E.: The contribution of the parietal lobes to speaking and writing. Cereb. Cortex **20**(3), 517–523 (2009)

69. Wolpaw, J.R., Birbaumer, N., McFarland, D.J., Pfurtscheller, G., Vaughan, T.M.: Brain-computer interfaces for communication and control. Clin. Neurophysiol. **113**(6), 767–791 (2002)
70. Zani, A., Proverbio, A.M.: Cognitive electrophysiology of mind and brain. In: The Cognitive Electrophysiology of Mind and Brain, pp. 3–12. Elsevier (2003)
71. Zheng, W.L., Zhu, J.Y., Peng, Y., Lu, B.L.: EEG-based emotion classification using deep belief networks. In: 2014 IEEE International Conference on Multimedia and Expo (ICME), pp. 1–6. IEEE (2014)

Search Support for Exploratory Writing

Jonas Oppenlaender[1](✉), Elina Kuosmanen[1], Jorge Goncalves[2],
and Simo Hosio[1]

[1] University of Oulu, Oulu, Finland
{jonas.oppenlaender,elina.kuosmanen,simo.hosio}@oulu.fi
[2] University of Melbourne, Melbourne, Australia
jorge.goncalves@unimelb.edu.au

Abstract. Writing articles involves searching, exploring, evaluating and reflecting upon different perspectives. To this end, online search engines are commonly used tools to support writing. However, online search engines, such as Google, fall short in supporting complex queries that satisfy multiple criteria simultaneously. In this paper, we present our studies with *GAS*, a crowd-powered tool that allows writers to discover viewpoints, solutions and ideas that best fulfil multiple criteria simultaneously. Our user studies validate GAS as a beneficial companion to online search engines in supporting writing. We found that GAS helps people come up with ideas and write with more confidence, resulting in a higher self-reported article quality and accuracy when compared to only using an online search engine. Through our experiments, we also develop an understanding of the distinct process that people employ when searching for and exploring open-ended, subjective information to support exploratory writing.

Keywords: Exploratory writing · Crowdsourcing ·
Exploratory search · Complex search · Creativity support ·
Qualitative insights

1 Introduction

Writing an article typically requires creative thinking and foraging for further information [37]. *Exploratory writing* [6,29] has been used in the literature to describe the cognitive exploration of information with the aim of gathering information for a writing piece, primarily in the context of fictional writing or teaching. While this term has no clear and widely agreed upon definition in academic literature, in this paper we define exploratory writing as writing aimed at exploring, understanding and reflecting upon different perspectives of a specific topic. To this end, writers can reach vast amounts of information effortlessly through online search engines (OSE). These search engines are engineered to support the most frequently occurring search queries with one search dimension at a time (*e.g.*, cheap, best, fastest) [12,34]. However, online search engines fall short

© IFIP International Federation for Information Processing 2019
Published by Springer Nature Switzerland AG 2019
D. Lamas et al. (Eds.): INTERACT 2019, LNCS 11748, pp. 314–336, 2019.
https://doi.org/10.1007/978-3-030-29387-1_18

in supporting *complex* search queries which reflect a personal multidimensional information need [1,7].

As an example, consider the task of writing an article about movies that simultaneously have the *worst* actors and the *greatest* visual effects. You will, most likely, discover search results about one of those subjective criteria at a time, but not results that best fulfil both requirements. This is the case for two main reasons. First, webmasters typically optimise the content of their websites for the most popular information needs, a practice called Search Engine Optimisation (SEO). Second, online search engines also optimise their operations to support the most popular search queries. Yet, there is an identified need for supporting multidimensional search and discovery of unpopular information [35]. For instance, people suffering from back pain may want to discover *fast, cheap and long-lasting ways of treating back pain* – a real-world information need for which online search engines are not well-equipped [21].

In this paper, we present our studies with *GAS*, an adapted version of the decision support concept presented by Hosio et al. in [19]. GAS allows authors to explore and draw inspiration from a knowledge base of open-ended, subjective data on a specific topic. Thus, it aims to support exploratory writers in both searching and exploring information. In our primarily qualitative inquiry, we investigate GAS in supporting exploratory writing. More specifically, we evaluate how it supports complex search tasks when writing a short article. The results from our studies validate GAS as a useful companion to major online search engines in discovering information. GAS helps writers in developing an idea for an article more quickly than online search engines. GAS also reduces the time required to explore the space of possible solutions. Finally, according to self-reported assessment, GAS helps people write articles of higher quality and with higher confidence. Through participant observation and qualitative insights, we also contribute a writer-oriented understanding [22] of the distinct strategies and composing processes that people adopt when searching for open-ended, subjective information in supporting exploratory writing. Finally, we discuss our results in light of related work and focus on the challenges that people encounter when researching a topic online for exploratory writing.

2   Related Work

Our work is situated at the intersection of online tools for supporting writing, information discovery, and creativity. Before delving into these topics, we elaborate on exploratory writing to provide context for our work.

2.1   Exploratory Writing and Complex Search

Exploratory writing is a term with no widely agreed upon academic definition. Lee et al. articulated exploratory writing as "the act of pre-writing for a final writing piece to examine a writer's own thoughts and beliefs and discover more about his/her inner mind and connect to the outside world" [29]. Pre-writing is a

"stage of discovery in the writing process when a person assimilates his 'subject' to himself" [39]. Exploratory writing, from this perspective, is "thinking-on-paper [...] to discover, develop and clarify our own ideas" [6]. It is a preparatory activity that is conducted to gather topical and non-topical material in support of the topical progression of a final writing piece [28]. Murray referred to this activity as "unfinished writing" [31].

Exploratory writing is motivated by a gap in the knowledge of the writer. Exploratory writing may be used to focus ideas and investigate questions [6]. Exploratory writing thus involves and develops critical thinking and reflection [29]. Consequently, one domain in which mentions of the term exploratory writing can be found in the literature is teaching of writing and active learning, e.g. in [6,17,29]. Bean, for instance, recommends exploratory writing as an informal writing assignment for use in classrooms to promote critical thinking and learning in students [6]. Haushalter used exploratory, informal writing as a teaching method in an introductory Biochemistry class to engage students in critical thinking and as a mechanism for students to engage with domain-specific knowledge [17]. In this context, exploratory writing may be regarded as exploring and discovering through language [31].

Writers engaged in exploratory writing strive to get an overview over a topic by understanding different perspectives. The task of exploratory writing is an ill-structured problem [44] that requires accessing a large amount of potentially relevant information. Exploratory writing therefore, by definition, involves searching for new information. As such, exploratory writing is a knowledge-crystallisation activity [37] and documents the outcome of an *exploratory search*, with the piece of writing as its final output. Exploratory search refers to the use of "a combination of searching and browsing behaviours to navigate through (and to) information" [49]. Exploratory writers engage in this exploratory search [49] in the context of an information-seeking problem that is open-ended and multifaceted. More specifically, exploratory writers engage in *complex search* tasks. A complex search involves complex information [1] and decisions on how to assess the obtained search results [7]. Such complex search tasks require a disproportionate amount of attention [16], because complex information needs are different from simple information needs, where users search for single information elements [1]. As exploratory writing requires reasoning over multiple pieces of evidence [47] and integrating multiple elements of information, the involved complex search tasks incur a high cognitive load on the writer [46].

Contrary to the literature, we see exploratory writing as *final* writing aimed at exploring, understanding and reflecting upon different perspectives on a non-fictional topic. This type of writing is conducted to stimulate discourse about a topic, investigate questions, eliminate alternatives, or contrast different concepts in written form [6]. In this writing activity, exploratory writers must consider a trade-off between two competing aspects in their search strategy. First, the aim of the writer is to search and find the required information quickly to support the ongoing writing effort. Second, the writer may want to browse and explore the information space to either find the optimal answer or to contrast answers.

To this end, *exploratory search systems* "provide guidance in exploring unfamiliar information landscapes" [49], and therefore support exploratory writing.

The design space for exploratory activities is clearly emerging [3,16,26,27]. For instance, Kittur et al. investigated the costs and benefits of structuring information during the sensemaking process [26]. In this paper, we provide the first systematic investigation of exploratory writing from the perspective of exploratory search systems and complex search for online information. We contribute to shaping the space of exploratory writing in the extracurricular context of non-fictional writing. In the following section, we review key online tools and resources that support exploratory writing and that are most closely related to our work.

Table 1. Online websites and their affordances in supporting exploratory writing.

Website type	Example	Exemplary affordance
Online search engines	Google	Information on any topic, primarily in unstructured form
Open knowledge bases	Wikipedia	Basic information in unstructured form (with exception of tables)
Structured knowledge bases	Wikidata	Structured data, primarily created for consumption by machines
Social media	Twitter	Short information about trending topics and events
Question & answer websites	Quora	Asynchronous answers on any topic
Crowdsourcing platforms	Mechanical Turk	Scalable information from anonymous contributors
Personal social networks	Facebook	Personalised opinions and recommendations

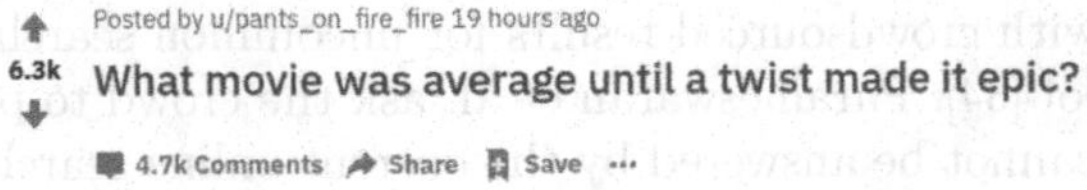

↑
6.3k **What movie was average until a twist made it epic?**
↓

💬 4.7k Comments   ↗ Share   🔖 Save   ⋯

Posted by u/pants_on_fire_fire 19 hours ago

Fig. 1. Example of a complex search task as posted on the AskReddit community.

2.2   Online Support for Writing

Online search engines, such as *Google* and *Bing*, are common tools for discovering, exploring, understanding and reflecting upon different perspectives related

to a given topic. Prior work has highlighted the need to support finding unpopular information [48]. The lookup-based information retrieval model of online search engines is, however, best suited for fact-finding and question-answering with focus on one key search criterion [34,49] and it is not feasible for online search engines to cover the "long tail" of information needs [10]. Instead, online search engines are aligned with their users' search behaviour which follows a power law distribution [35].

Searching for information on the Web is not limited to online search engines. Table 1 gives an overview of the affordances of a selected, but not exhaustive, list of websites that writers may consult in support of their exploratory writing. For instance, open knowledge bases, such as Wikipedia, provide information on a broad spectrum of subject matters. The extended social network of the exploratory writer may further offer support in the exploration of a topic [36].

Relating to the example given in the introduction, Fig. 1 depicts an AskReddit[1] post in which a Reddit user inquires about *movies that are average until a twist made them epic*. The high number of replies in this discussion (over 4,700 comments in less than 19 h) demonstrates the difficulties of getting a comprehensive overview of the answers provided in online communities. While the rich discussion answers the question, such information requests support the *planning* of a writing piece, but not the immediate *writing*. While social computing and social media websites, such as Reddit, Twitter and Quora, can provide answers to complex queries, results are provided asynchronously and not in a timely fashion, therefore thwarting the writing effort.

Ultimately, organising and curating user-created content is a challenging task, and the need for case-specific approaches for acquiring and organising information is clear. Crowdsourcing is one contemporary approach to collect vast amounts of information cost-effectively and accurately.

2.3   Crowd-Powered Search and Writing Tools

The potential of crowdsourcing in supporting writing has been established in the literature [9]. Crowdsourcing has further been applied to searching for information – a key activity in supporting writing. For instance, Bernstein et al. augment a search engine with crowdsourced results for uncommon search queries [10]. In their DataSift tool [34], Parameswaran et al. ask the crowd to provide solutions for queries that cannot be answered by the current online search engines. These queries include multiple dimensions, human judgement calls, and ambiguity. CrowdDB [15] is another example of a tool addressing queries that search engines fail to answer. The authors discuss the difficulty of processing crowd-contributed data that does not follow the closed-world assumption of traditional database systems. CrowdQ [13] uses the crowd to decompose complex queries into query patterns that facilitate answering all instances of future complex queries. In their CrowdSearcher platform [11], Brambilla et al. take a community-based crowdsourcing approach, thus leveraging the diversity of communities with different

---

[1] www.reddit.com/r/AskReddit/.

characteristics and capabilities. With Aardvark [18], a web-based social search engine, users were able to ask subject matter experts in their extended social network for information. Witkeys in China are another example of knowledge market systems in which users can pose questions that cannot be answered easily by online search engines [50].

While the above crowdsourcing systems are able to quickly produce an answer to a complex search task, they do not inherently support the exploration of a multidimensional information space. Questions posed in these systems are one-off queries, and the results may arrive much later. Exploring a topic from multiple perspectives requires multiple queries, possibly in a cascaded fashion [13], which makes the search expensive and time-intensive. Furthermore, the space of possible solutions cannot be explored after the information was retrieved without the user expending cognitive effort on analysing and comparing the search results. There is a need for supporting the exploration of the multidimensional information space in a more swift and effortless way.

To this end, Hosio et al. created a crowd-powered personal decision support system that can be used to collect a knowledge base on arbitrary topics [19,20]. Such knowledge bases can be used to discover best-matching solutions, defined by a set of optimal criteria values, to an arbitrary problem. In this paper, we adopt the approach of Hosio et al. for information discovery. We investigate our tool's ability for supporting exploratory writing instead of decision-making.

3 System Description

To support exploratory writing, we obtained and used *AnswerBot*, the crowd-sourced decision support system presented in by Hosio et al. in [19]. The system provides decision support in form of short textual ideas that can be sorted according to different criteria (see Fig. 2). A crucial consideration in this system, and by extension in GAS, is the data model that facilitates the information discovery. The data model structures a problem space into (1) a set of *ideas* to address the problem, (2) a set of *criteria* (search dimensions) to consider in evaluating the ideas, and (3) the assessment of how each of the ideas fulfil the criteria. Both the ideas, the criteria, and the rating of each idea across all criteria are provided by the crowd.

The content of the knowledge base can be collected from any source that involves the crowd, *e.g.* online labour markets, such as Amazon Mechanical Turk, or any online platforms by posting a link to the data collection mechanism. In discovering the best-matching ideas, the system calculates the closest-matching ideas based on the Euclidean distance of crowdsourced ground-truth values to the desired criteria configuration. In doing so, the system applies *wisdom of the crowd* [45]. We direct the reader to the original article on the system and the newer account for a detailed overview [19,21].

We made minor modifications to AnswerBot's visual query interface by removing the branding and the links to the homepage. We named our system *GAS* – a lightweight, web-based tool for structured exploration of crowdsourced

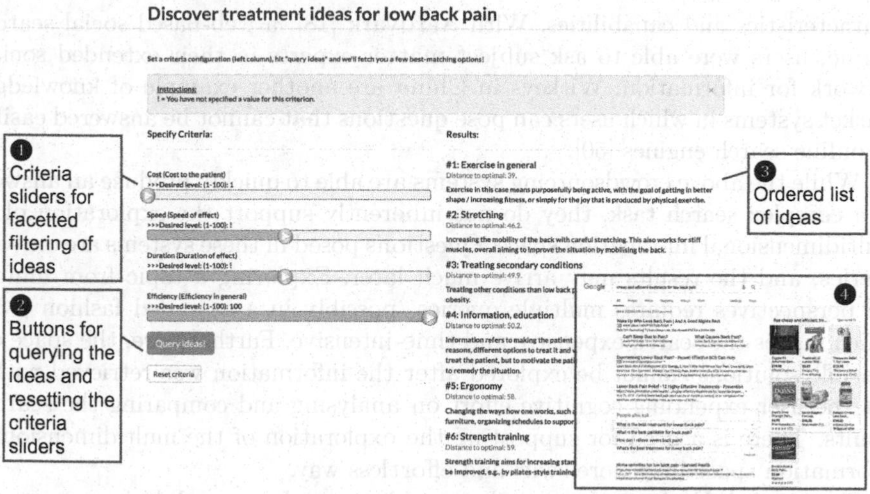

Fig. 2. Main image: searching for *cheap* and *efficient* treatments for low back pain with GAS. Bottom right (❹): results for the same query in Google (search location in this example: Washington, D.C.).

knowledge, to support writing. By design, the system is intended for querying and discovering crowdsourced, open-ended ideas. GAS is not a replacement for Web search engines, but aimed at helping writers in exploring the information space as a complementary tool.

Users of the GAS system set the desired criteria combination by using sliders in the left column of the GAS look-up interface (see ❶ in Fig. 2). Corresponding results are retrieved (with a click on a button ❷) and displayed in the right column (❸ in Fig. 2). Figure 2 compares a search on GAS and Google for *cheap but efficient treatments for low back pain*, as an example. This exact case with the original system was discussed in-depth in [21].

4   Evaluation

To investigate to what extent GAS can support exploratory writing, we set up two distinct studies. Next, we provide details of the knowledge bases used in the studies.

4.1   Crowdsourced Knowledge Bases

The knowledge bases in AnswerBot are collected dynamically over time to answer topic-specific information needs: they are not transferable between different problem domains. For this paper, we obtained and reused three knowledge bases collected by the AnswerBot platform and documented in [8, 21]. The three data collection campaigns are summarised in Table 2. Data for T1 and T2 was collected "organically" in a several months long campaign promoted on social media

Table 2. Overview of the data collection campaigns.

	T1. RACISM	T2. LBP	T3. DIETS
	What are good means to prevent everyday racism?	What are good ways to treat low back pain?	What are good weight-loss diets?
Contributors	1,515	353	70
Ideas	84	108	21
Criteria	5	4	6
Assessments	13,654	9,001	8,607
Collection	Organic	Organic	Prolific
Criteria source	Sociologists	MDs, physiotherapists	Website visitors

outlets, forums and mailing lists. T3 was collected via Prolific[2], a crowdsourcing platform.

4.2 Study 1: Writing with and Without GAS

We conducted a within-subject study with 24 participants (15 male, 9 female, age range 21 to 38 years, $Mean = 27.2$ years, $SD = 4.36$ years, $Mdn = 25$ years). Participants were recruited through a mailing list and posters on our campus. Participants included 3 recently graduated Master students, 1 Associate Professor, 1 MBA, 2 bachelor students, 3 PhD students and 14 Master students. Given the participants' academic background, we consider them as knowledgeable in exploring topics and writing essays. Master students at our institution are regularly engaged as research assistants, which includes researching information and writing. All participants reported being familiar with researching information online, but not having experience with complex searches. Only two participants reported using logical keywords and operators in their daily searches. Participation in the study required approximately 30 min and was rewarded with a cinema ticket voucher worth US $12.

The participants conducted the study independently on a computer provided by us, situated in a semi-controlled work environment. First, a guided tutorial consisting of written instructions and oral explanations provided by a researcher familiarised the participant with the interface of GAS, using topic T3. The writing part of the study consisted of two preset writing tasks (T1 and T2), an online survey, and a follow-up interview. Similar preset essay tasks have been used earlier, e.g. in investigating computer-aided creative writing [41].

In the writing part, each participant was asked to write two short articles. Participants were intentionally given a tight time limit of only 5 min for each writing task to test the participants' ability of finding and exploring information quickly. The available criteria in the "mitigating racism" task (T1) were

---

[2] www.prolific.ac.

as follows: (1) ability to influence, (2) speed of solution, (3) cost for society, (4) efficiency, and (5) legality of solution. For the "curing low back pain" task (T2), the criteria were: (1) cost to the patient, (2) speed of effect, (3) duration of effect, and (4) efficiency. Each of the writing tasks consisted of one topic (T1 or T2) and a randomly selected combination of two criteria values (see Fig. 3). The tasks were completed under one of two conditions:

- OSE: supported only by a major online search engine, such as Google, and
- GAS+OSE: supported by the combination of GAS and a major online search engine, such as Google, i.e., participants were allowed to use both the search engine and GAS, on their own volition.

Our study design, on purpose, did not include a choice of using only GAS, as this would force the users to use a non-realistic and somehow enforced setup and thus decrease the ecological validity of the results. Instead, the participants had a choice of using the tools as they saw fit. The order of the conditions and topics was counterbalanced to avoid carry-over and learning effects. Each task was completed in an instance of Etherpad[3], pre-filled with task instructions.

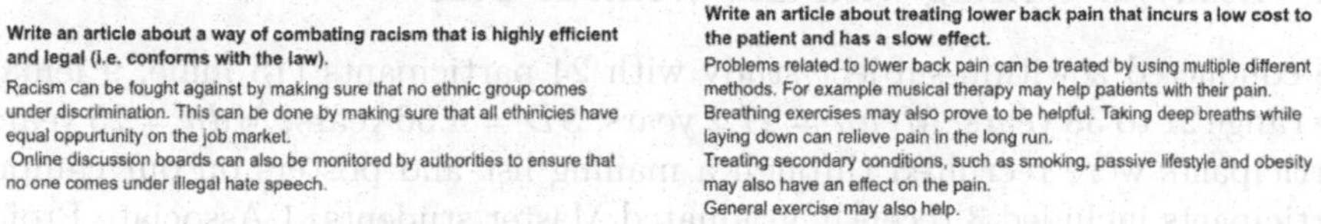

Write an article about a way of combating racism that is highly efficient and legal (i.e. conforms with the law).

Racism can be fought against by making sure that no ethnic group comes under discrimination. This can be done by making sure that all ethinicies have equal oppurtunity on the job market.
  Online discussion boards can also be monitored by authorities to ensure that no one comes under illegal hate speech.

(a) OSE condition

Write an article about treating lower back pain that incurs a low cost to the patient and has a slow effect.

Problems related to lower back pain can be treated by using multiple different methods. For example musical therapy may help patients with their pain.
Breathing exercises may also prove to be helpful. Taking deep breaths while laying down can relieve pain in the long run.
Treating secondary conditions, such as smoking, passive lifestyle and obesity may also have an effect on the pain.
General exercise may also help.

(b) GAS+OSE condition

Fig. 3. Participant P1's tasks and articles.

After completing the writing tasks, we collected subjective responses, reported on a 7-point Likert scale, to questions relating to five aspects of the writing task:

- mental effort (e.g., for searching, remembering, thinking, and deciding) from 1 (Low) to 7 (High),
- difficulty of finding the initial idea for the article, from 1 (Very Difficult) to 7 (Very Easy),
- difficulty of finding content for the article, from 1 (Very Difficult) to 7 (Very Easy),
- task difficulty, from 1 (Very Easy) to 7 (Very Difficult),
- perception of usefulness of the information provided by each tool, from 1 (Not At All Useful) to 7 (Extremely Useful),
- how well the tools supported the writing, from 1 (Not At All Helpful) to 7 (Extremely Helpful),

---

[3] www.etherpad.org.

- self-assessed adherence to the task criteria, from 1 (Not At All) to 7 (To A Great Extent),
- self-assessed quality of the written articles, from 1 (Very Poor) to 7 (Excellent),

and the overall preference (OSE versus GAS+OSE). For a lightweight evaluation of mental effort and task difficulty, we adopted the questions from Siangliulue et al. [43].

Finally, we conducted one-on-one interviews with each participant immediately after the questionnaire was completed. The interviews were semi-structured in nature and focused on further exploring the choices of the participant and the observed behaviour. After the study ended, we analysed the interview data using thematic coding [38]. Thematic coding is an approach to identify themes in qualitative data. We applied this approach to construct a framework that guided our investigation.

4.3   Study 2: Writers' Workshop

To gain more insights into the writing and search strategies, as well as to validate the strategies that we derived from the interview data, we conducted a concluding workshop with six participants (W1-W6, Bachelor and Master level students, two of which had participated in the main study), recruited from the same University campus. The workshop was led by two researchers, one of which acted as scribe. In the workshop, one participant volunteered to think-aloud and give verbal instructions to one of the researchers who operated the GAS system. After 15 min of searching and exploring for information concerning both topics T1 and T2, the other workshop participants were allowed to join the process and discuss freely around GAS and its functionalities. We include findings from the workshop in the qualitative data analysis and in the discussion.

5   Results

While our investigation is primarily of qualitative nature, we also report quantitative insights in this section.

5.1   Quantitative Data Analysis

In the following, we report statistics from the analysis of the Likert-scale questionnaire responses (see Fig. 4). We compare the two writing conditions (OSE and GAS+OSE) using Wilcoxon's signed rank test with continuity correction. We used an alpha level of .05 for all statistical tests.

Finding an initial idea for the article was rated significantly easier when using GAS as a complementary tool, $Mdn = 5$, compared to using OSE, $Mdn = 4$, $V = 40.5$, $p = .008$. Participants also responded that finding content for the article was easier when using GAS, $Mdn = 6$, compared to the OSE condition,

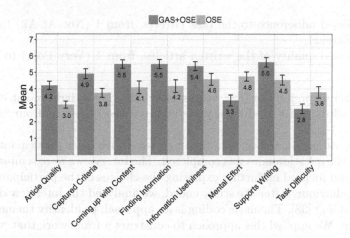

Fig. 4. Mean Likert-scale responses as reported by the participants.

$Mdn = 4, V = 64.5, p = .013$. Overall, participants thought that GAS supported their writing better, $Mdn = 6$, than the information provided by the online search engine alone, $Mdn = 5, V = 30.5, p = .005$). Using GAS also significantly reduced the participants' mental effort, $Mdn = 3$, compared to OSE, $Mdn = 5$, $V = 254, p = .001$. However, the data afforded by GAS was not deemed to be significantly more useful in solving the complex search task, $Mdn = 6$, as compared to the OSE condition, $Mdn = 5, V = 36, p = .015$). Nevertheless, the task was perceived to be less difficult under condition GAS+OSE, $Mdn = 2$, compared to condition OSE, $Mdn = 3.5, V = 178.5, p = .046$. An overwhelmingly high percentage of the participants (87.5%) preferred to solve the task with a combination of GAS and the search engine, 12.5% preferred to only work with Google. None of the participants preferred using the data solely provided by GAS.

The number of words in the articles did not significantly differ between the OSE ($Min = 12, Max = 185, Mean = 82.2, Mdn = 80$) and GAS+OSE ($Min = 26, Max = 665, Mean = 102.8, Mdn = 74.5$) conditions ($V = 137.5$, $p = .5$), even though the texts written with GAS had on average a higher number of words. Figure 3 depicts the two articles written by participant P1. Both articles address the criteria of the complex task to some extent. We note, however, that the article written under condition GAS+OSE is more nuanced. This intuition is confirmed by the self-reported ratings of the participants. Overall, the participants thought that their own articles written with support of the information provided by GAS, $Mdn = 5$, were better matching the task criteria than with the support of the search engine, $Mdn = 3.5, V = 50.5, p = .003$. The participants rated the quality of their own article written with support of GAS significantly higher, $Mdn = 4.5$, than the one written with help of the online search engine, $Mdn = 3, V = 17, p < .001$. When asked to compare both articles, 14 participants (58.33%) said that the article written with both GAS and

the online search engine was better. Five participants rated the article written with support of the online search engine as better, and another five participants said the two articles were about the same quality.

5.2 Qualitative Insights into Search and Exploration Strategies for Exploratory Writing

Based on the thematic grouping of the coded interview data, we developed a framework that is indicative of how participants engaging in exploratory writing in our study addressed their information needs (see Fig. 5). While our framework follows a stage-process model of writing, as defined for instance by Rohman [39], we acknowledge that writing is an iterative cognitive activity [14] and that there may be iterations between searching, idea generation, refining and writing. Given how we derived the model, the stages of our framework are reflected in the headings of our following qualitative analysis.

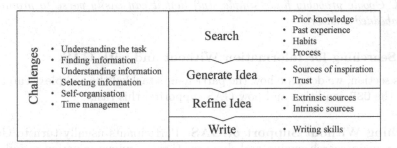

Fig. 5. The main activities and influencing factors observed in exploratory writing

Our framework relates to many existing models for information discovery and writing. For instance, Kerne and Smith's information discovery framework "examines interactions of human cognition with digital information in tasks that draw upon information resources while developing ideas" [25]. This framework is concerned with inner knowledge states and knowledge transformations, whereas our framework is more focused on the immediate writing process and the external factors that influence the exploratory search. Compared to Marchionini's exploratory search activities [30], our model is concerned with search, idea generation and writing. Lastly, Flower and Hayes's writing model [14] is a detailed model of the writing process, but was written before the inception of the Internet. For an overview of related models from the context of information retrieval and exploratory search, we direct the reader to White and Roth's synthesis lecture on exploratory search [49].

5.3   Challenges in Writing with Google Alone

The topics were perceived as challenging and the combination of the criteria seemed contradicting at first (P13). It does not come as a surprise that combining the two criteria in an article was perceived as *"most difficult"* (P4).

> *"The challenge was writing something useful. All I wrote was pieces and bits from topics. It's not a good article."* (P24)

The time limit was considered a major challenge by several participants. During the study, we noticed that participants had to click away cookie consent overlays, and several participants ended up in dead ends due to being mislead about the contents of websites or information being locked behind paywalls. Integrating information from disparate sources (P14) and finding reliable information (P11) were further reported as challenges. Advertisements on the search engine (*c.f.* Fig. 2), in particular, were not considered trustworthy by the participants. For some participants, this distrust for advertisement extended to the embedded answers provided by Google. As W5 noted, *"embedded answers oversimplify what I need. Google probably finds simple stuff that it can easily parse to promote as the embedded answer."*

5.4   Searching for Information Without and with GAS

In this section, we describe how the participants tackled the complex search task under the OSE condition and how GAS supported this task.

Searching Without Support of GAS. Participants usually turn to Google as their main search engine and draw on their previous experience and prior knowledge.

> *"Usually before writing, I try to think what knowledge I already have about the topic, and based on that I start searching the information, usually using Google."* (P1)

If no prior knowledge about a topic exists, the participants turn to Wikipedia for basic information or consult peers and domain experts.

We observed that some participants followed a two-stage query strategy in solving the complex search task. In this *criteria-driven* approach, participants used the criteria to drive results, first searching for one criterion on the search engine, then filtering among the results for the second criterion.

> *"First, I searched for one criteria. Then from those results, I figured out the other criteria."* (P4)

P3 reported that he *"read at least five articles on Google, found similarities among the results, and wrote based on that."* This approach was however limited by the insufficient quality of the results provided by the search engine, which lead P21 to comment: *"What I found was too broad. I could not match the criteria."* Some participants perceived the online search engine not useful in solving the complex search task.

"I doubted that the search engine would be able to produce results, so I did not even try." (P1)

The search engine results were described as *"soup of information"* (P5), providing *"results optimised for only the most searched things"* (P14), *"links to general articles"* (P19), and a *"confusing amount of information"* (P3). *"Some of the search engine results were hard to read,"* noted participant P1 who skimmed through legal texts. Some participants expected to see embedded answers (*e.g.* P5), but did not receive such information in the search engine results.

Searching, Supported by GAS. GAS was conversely perceived as *"specific and goal-oriented"* (P15) and *"straight forward"* (P18) in retrieving information for a specific topic. GAS allows to *"focus your search instead of browsing"* (P23). The *"condensed and easily readable data format"* (P1) of GAS was perceived as useful in solving the task. GAS was reported as making the task *"easier"* (*e.g.* P13). Since the results provided by GAS are organised around a topic, the tool *"provides a headstart into the article"* (P24), affording a *"kind of intuitiveness"* (P23).

"On Google, you need to think about the search phrase. [GAS] simplifies finding answers based on several criteria." (P5)

Participants were able to find information with GAS faster than with the online search engine. P1, for instance, noted that she *"did not have to make several searches."*

"While the search engine provides results for only one criteria, [GAS] weighs in all criteria." (P13)

GAS directly provides relevant content, without having to go through links, like on the online search engine. This allowed the participants to compare findings of GAS and the online search engine, if time permitted. Participants used GAS for getting an overview of the information space and helping to *"understand answers in a larger context"* (P5). The structured data afforded by GAS enables the writer to compare results, explore different viewpoints, and systematically consider the trade-offs between answers to a question. GAS affords a ludic exploration of the information space spanned by the available ideas and criteria.

Status Quo Bias. We noticed a status quo bias [40] among certain participants. Google was reported by these participants as being the *"easiest way"* (P20) of retrieving information. The participants from this group did not try GAS and simply completed the tasks using Google.

"If you have a tool and it's very useful, and you already use it before, you go directly to use it instead of the new thing." (P20)

Another participant from this group said that he would *"need to practice [GAS] before using it"* (P16). This answer surprised us, given that we made sure to give each participant an exhaustive interactive introduction to GAS.

In the group of users who preferred the search engine, interacting with the search engine was perceived as being more natural than interacting with the sliders in the user interface of GAS.

> *"I had to read through all the criteria descriptions in [GAS]. When using Google, the question is entered and answers are given."* (P22)

Overall, a clear majority of 21 out of 24 participants preferred to use the combination of GAS and Google in solving the complex writing tasks. As P5 remarked, *"the combined approach would produce best results."*

5.5   Inception of the Initial Idea

We observed four different approaches relating to how the information afforded by GAS informed the participants' search strategies [5] and search tactics [4] for finding the fundamental idea of the article. We call these approaches source-of-inspiration, knowledge-driven, structure-driven and hybrid.

Source-of-Inspiration Approach. The information provided by GAS was deemed insufficient for longer articles, but good for inspiration. The majority of our participants used GAS as the sole source of inspiration for finding the main idea for their article. Some of the participants used the answers provided by GAS as-is, copying and pasting the answers *"without thinking"* (P17). GAS is *"for getting started,"* noted P18. For more inquisitive users, GAS *"provided a list of actionable keywords to search for in the search engine"* (P13). Another approach under this theme was to summarise existing answers from GAS.

Knowledge-Driven Approach. Participants who used this approach used their intuition and prior knowledge for coming up with an idea for the article and then *"continued that direction"* (P2), with or without support of GAS or the search engine. This approach was particularly prevalent in the group of participants affected by the status quo bias. P4 noted that she *"could not find anything matching on Google, only a general idea"* and that she *"used [her] general knowledge to solve the task."* Past research has shown that emerging candidate solutions may guide the user interaction behaviour [49]. For some participants, this internal guidance was so strong that they did not make use of the search engine or GAS to their full extent (or even at all). Digging deeper into this behaviour, these participants said they knew the search engine would not have been able to solve their information need. Instead, they decided to formulate their initial intuition, informed by prior knowledge, into written form.

Structure-Driven Approach. In this approach – a subset of the knowledge-driven approach – participants first came up with an idea and structure for the article on their own, and then turned to GAS and the search engine. P5 discussed his writing process in detail, which consisted of first understanding

the requirements, writing headings for each section, and finally finding pieces of information that support each heading. P14 also first sketched out a rough idea before turning to the search engine. The search engine was used to fill in the blanks in the structure. GAS conversely was perceived helpful in coming up with the initial structure for the article.

Hybrid Approach. Many participants combined GAS and the search engine, using GAS to get a *"rough idea about a question and possible directions to look at"* (P14). P5 reported that he *"started with GAS, choosing criteria. From there, [he] expanded to understand more on Google about these answers and to develop a broader understanding."*

5.6 Idea Refinement

A clear majority of the participants turned to the search engine as an external source for refining the article, primarily with the intention of finding more information. We noticed a *berrypicking approach* [5] for integrating information. Participants skimmed through the snippets provided by the search engine and GAS, and harvested elements to integrate into the writing. P2 reported that he *"searched for articles [on the search engine], read through the information, and integrated relevant pieces into the article."* With support of GAS, this approach was more profound and all-consuming. According to our observations, significantly more information was copied and pasted when using GAS.

Another way of refining the article was through self-reflection, *i.e.*, not using external sources, to bring the article into one's "personal context" [39]. As P1 reported, he had to rewrite the text to *"sound more like me."* P21 describes his experience in refining the initial idea for the article: *"I tried to improvise and add more. I tried to make it more related to the criteria."* Further activities included reading through the whole article for coherence, and pruning of gathered information. We noticed a change in the writing behaviour when using GAS, compared to the OSE condition. With support of the search engine, participants reported that the idea refinement was largely *"writing, trying to find support, then edit and improve"* (P17). With GAS, refinement shifted towards editing, rephrasing, and *"skimming through, making it more legible"* (P17). We noticed significantly less own development in the texts of the participants when using GAS.

5.7 Trusting the Answers Provided by GAS

The crowdsourced knowledge base was accepted by the participants as being trustworthy. One participant compared the knowledge base to Wikipedia, stating that he *"completely trusted GAS. It felt trustworthy"* (P17). When asked why, the participant said *"for some reason I took it for granted. I don't know why".* Participants considered the content of the crowdsourced knowledge base to be a mix of specialist and non-specialist opinions. This mix was perceived as more trustworthy than the search engine results.

However, several participants brought up the issue of the provenance of the crowdsourced information, due to not being able to confirm the source of the provided information. An interesting outlier to this behaviour was one workshop participant who wished to verify all ideas suggested by GAS by finding articles on diets from *e.g.* the National Health Service (NHS) and Google Scholar. This particular participant (P18) had a background in nutritional sciences, which may partially explain this behaviour given their expertise in the matter: *"In order to use it, I would personally want to check the validity of the data."* While P18 wished to see references, he acknowledged that it is difficult to provide references for people's opinion. In the end, users trusted their common sense when it came to integrating information from the crowd-powered knowledge base into the article.

6   Discussion

The pervasive access to a seemingly unlimited amount of information online has transformed the process of writing. Insights, debate, and argumentation with varying degrees of reliability from a plethora of different sources and on practically any imaginable topic are always just a few Google searches away [5]. Several online tools exist to help navigate this *information overload* for different purposes, some of which we list in Table 1. The major search engines are doing a wonderful job in enabling discovery among all the user-generated content out there, but they are – understandably – far from perfect in supporting a specific application area such as writing. While the results that most strongly speak for this from our studies are overall more qualitative than quantitative in nature, the response to the Likert-scale (as depicted in Fig. 4) also suggests that tools like ours warrant consideration. On the other hand, it is important to note that any new tools competing for attention have a long struggle ahead: The status quo bias we observed among our participants suggests that many potential users will not give new tools even a chance.

In these studies, we set to explore the perceived value of the tool for its users. While it is certainly important to evaluate the quality of the writing in future studies, we scope our investigation solely on the writing process and the users' experience as something that we can confidently provide results and reflections on. We point to similar publications [23,32] that also evaluated their respective system in this manner.

6.1   GAS as a Tool for Supporting Writing and Information Discovery

In this paper, we emphasise exploratory writing as an activity that involves searching and exploring the information space of the topic [49]. To support such writing, we modified the AnswerBot system by Hosio et al. [19]. Our solution, GAS, ranks open-ended content across multiple criteria simultaneously – an approach versatile for provisioning decision support for real-world problems [21]

but also for discovering ideas that best fulfil a set of search criteria. Thus, it affords a straightforward approach to solving *complex search tasks* [1] that the online search engines have been shown to struggle with [34].

The participants of our studies demonstrated clear stages in their exploratory writing processes (see Fig. 5). Turning our eyes to the challenges encountered when using an online search engine in these stages, we are able to isolate the characteristics of GAS that warrant further exploration and provide useful pointers for designers of similar solutions.

In the *Search Stage*, participants expressed issues with non-relevant information and content motivated by commercial interests on Google. As expected, the clutter of advertisements (see Fig. 2) was often mentioned, but also the embedded answers by Google itself were found as troublesome and to provide too simple solutions for sophisticated information needs. GAS, on the other hand, helps to focus on only the relevant subset of information, a characteristic of high quality Human-Information Interaction [1]. While GAS provides a clutter-free view to relevant information, it does not generalise well: one knowledge base only caters for one problem with a set of criteria and answers at a time.

GAS excels in simultaneously providing multiple relevant "seed ideas" to work with in the *Idea Generation Stage*. This was true when exploring only two simultaneous criteria, and the verdict was even more clear when experimenting with three, four or even five criteria simultaneously in the Writers' Workshop. The opinion on GAS was rather unanimous in the Writers' Workshop, with GAS being dubbed as "far superior" to Google in brainstorming for an initial batch of ideas. However, the crowdsourced knowledge bases clearly failed to provide comprehensive enough content on the ideas, and the participants, not only in the workshop but throughout our study, opted to switch to Google to expand and seek validation for the ideas discovered with GAS.

In the *Idea Refinement Phase*, Google was expressed to be a more compelling option than our tool. This is particularly due to the lack of perceived trust in the source of the provided information. Indeed, the origin of information is one of the greatest factors that influence perceived trust, regardless of the content itself [33]. In this regard, GAS may be perceived as a rather ambiguous source of information: what is a crowd, and how can we communicate the provenance of the crowd-powered information to the end-users? People have an intuitive understanding of what is trustworthy, as also exemplified by the workshop participant wishing to find validation for ideas by GAS from NHS or Google Scholar. But eliciting knowledge from a crowd is far more complicated than processing webpages for inclusion in a search engine's index. Reaching to a large pool of verifiable and trustworthy experts is not an easy feat. In retrospect, in our study we could have investigated such trust aspects as well, since the knowledge base we used on low back pain includes data harvested from clinical professionals only [21]. We leave examining these issues for future work.

6.2 Supporting Creativity with the Crowds

Computer-aided programs have been used to teach and support creative writing (*e.g.* [41]), long before the convenience of the now-ubiquitous Internet. In HCI, creativity support has been positioned as one of the grand challenges for scientists to look into [42]. We argue that crowdsourced support for creativity might play an interesting role in this challenge.

GAS, for instance, allows for an intuitive means to tap into the ideas, viewpoints and personal opinions that a crowd has accumulated over time. Therefore, the usefulness of tools like GAS for creativity grows as a function of the number of diverse, knowledgeable and independent individuals participating in the data collection stage [45]. The trade-off to strike lies between costs and utility: collecting a crowdsourced knowledge base to sufficiently cover a specific topic requires a lot of effort, time, and, in most cases, money.

It is not just the access to diverse ideas that matters in creative writing. The authors should optimally be intrinsically motivated in their writing task [2]. In our studies, we did not specifically measure aspects of creativity, but in the Writers' Workshop it was brought up that GAS might be helpful in shedding light on information that a writer might fail to consider if using *e.g.* Google only. It is the criteria, not the given solutions and ideas, that opened up the investigator's mind to consider *unknown unknowns*: the criteria constitute the proverbial lens that a given problem can be examined through. For instance, we might not discover too many surprising diets from a crowd, but when asking what type of criteria people value in diets, we might get a diverse range of aspects that one might fail to otherwise consider in their thought processes.

Finally, creativity is not something that is reserved for the selected few. Gifted novices are almost as good at judging the level of creativity as seasoned expert authors [24]. Thus, a crowdsourced solution like ours could be useful for a wide range of people in exploring how to expand their ideas and enhance their writing results. But, as implied earlier, we do not suggest crowdsourced approaches as competitors to the established online search engines. Search engines organise everyone's content, whereas GAS organises content harvested with a specific topic in mind. This also highlights the importance of correctly choosing the criteria in the beginning. GAS will not provide any clues for missing criteria, potentially severely limiting its usefulness in creativity support. Of course, online search engines are equally limited to the user-generated content online and further optimised for the most popular, relatively simple search tasks [10].

6.3 Limitations of the Study

We acknowledge several limitations in our study. First, while we made every effort to simulate a realistic work environment, the participants' awareness of being studied most likely affected their work quality. Self-reported introspective analysis of the writing quality may further lead to inaccurate reportings [14,22]. However, the positive findings in the self-reports were supported by the consensus

in the qualitative analysis on how our tool complements online search in the various stages of the exploratory writing process.

Further, the study design may have imposed minor carry-over effects. We addressed this in our study by assigning the participants unrelated topics consisting of randomised criteria. Participants were also required to go through the interactive tutorial before starting the study.

Finally, it is not unfair to question the motives of the participants. The information-seeking problem was extrinsically motivated with a cinema ticket as reward. If the problem was intrinsically motivated, the search strategies and tactics may have differed from what we observed. This needs to be explored in future studies.

7 Conclusion

In this paper, we investigated supporting the search for and exploration of information for exploratory writing. While online search engines excel in supporting single criterion look-up of information, they fall short in providing answers to complex queries consisting of combinations of multiple criteria. Our user studies of search behaviours with GAS, a crowd-powered knowledge base of a specific topic, validate GAS as a useful companion to major online search engines, such as Google, especially in supporting idea generation. Further, the study participants self-assessed the articles written with GAS as being of higher quality and better matching the given writing tasks. Overall, both our quantitative and qualitative data constitute compelling evidence of the potential of crowd-powered tools in supporting writing and creativity.

Acknowledgement. This work is partially funded by the Academy of Finland (grants 313224-STOP, 316253-SENSATE and 318927-6Genesis Flagship).

References

1. Albers, M.J.: Human-information interaction with complex information for decision-making. Informatics **2**(2), 4–19 (2015)
2. Amabile, T.M.: Motivation and creativity: effects of motivational orientation on creative writers. J. Pers. Soc. Psychol. **48**(2), 393 (1985)
3. Andolina, S., Klouche, K., Cabral, D., Ruotsalo, T., Jacucci, G.: InspirationWall: supporting idea generation through automatic information exploration. In: Proceedings of the 2015 ACM SIGCHI Conference on Creativity and Cognition (C&C 2015), pp. 103–106. ACM, New York (2015)
4. Bates, M.J.: Information search tactics. J. Am. Soc. Inf. Sci. **30**(4), 205–214 (1979)
5. Bates, M.J.: The design of browsing and berrypicking techniques for the online search interface. Online Rev. **13**(5), 407–424 (1989)
6. Bean, J.C.: Engaging Ideas: The Professor's Guide to Integrating Writing, Critical Thinking, and Active Learning in the Classroom. Jossey-Bass, San Francisco (2001)
7. Bell, D.J., Ruthven, I.: Searcher's assessments of task complexity for web searching. In: McDonald, S., Tait, J. (eds.) ECIR 2004. LNCS, vol. 2997, pp. 57–71. Springer, Heidelberg (2004). https://doi.org/10.1007/978-3-540-24752-4_5

8. van Berkel, N., Hosio, S., Goncalves, J., Kostakos, V.: Informed diet selection: increasing food literacy through crowdsourcing. In: Proceedings of the Designing Recipes for Digital Food Futures CHI 2018 Workshop (2018)
9. Bernstein, M.S., et al.: Soylent: a word processor with a crowd inside. In: Proceedings of the 23nd Annual ACM Symposium on User Interface Software and Technology (UIST 2010), pp. 313–322. ACM, New York (2010)
10. Bernstein, M.S., Teevan, J., Dumais, S., Liebling, D., Horvitz, E.: Direct answers for search queries in the long tail. In: Proceedings of the SIGCHI Conference on Human Factors in Computing Systems (CHI 2012), pp. 237–246. ACM, New York (2012)
11. Bozzon, A., Brambilla, M., Ceri, S.: Answering search queries with crowdsearcher. In: Proceedings of the 21st International Conference on World Wide Web (WWW 2012), pp. 1009–1018. ACM, New York (2012)
12. Collins-Thompson, K., Hansen, P., Hauff, C.: Search as learning (dagstuhl seminar 17092). Dagstuhl Rep. 7(2), 135–162 (2017). http://drops.dagstuhl.de/opus/volltexte/2017/7357
13. Demartini, G., Trushkowsky, B., Kraska, T., Franklin, M.J.: CrowdQ: crowdsourced query understanding. In: Conference on Innovative Data Systems Research (CIDR 2013) (2013)
14. Flower, L., Hayes, J.R.: A cognitive process theory of writing. Coll. Compos. Commun. 32(4), 365–387 (1981)
15. Franklin, M.J., Kossmann, D., Kraska, T., Ramesh, S., Xin, R.: CrowdDB: answering queries with crowdsourcing. In: Proceedings of the 2011 ACM SIGMOD International Conference on Management of Data (SIGMOD 2011), pp. 61–72. ACM, New York (2011)
16. Hahn, N., Chang, J.C., Kittur, A.: Bento browser: complex mobile search without tabs. In: Proceedings of the 2018 CHI Conference on Human Factors in Computing Systems (CHI 2018), pp. 251:1–251:12. ACM, New York (2018)
17. Haushalter, K.A.: Developing critical thinking in introductory biochemistry through exploratory writing in an electronic collaborative learning environment. FASEB J. 21(5), A297 (2007)
18. Horowitz, D., Kamvar, S.D.: The anatomy of a large-scale social search engine. In: Proceedings of the 19th International Conference on World Wide Web (WWW 2010), pp. 431–440. ACM, New York (2010)
19. Hosio, S., Goncalves, J., Anagnostopoulos, T., Kostakos, V.: Leveraging wisdom of the crowd for decision support. In: Proceedings of the 30th International BCS Human Computer Interaction Conference: Fusion! (HCI 2016). BCS Learning & Development Ltd., Swindon (2016)
20. Hosio, S., Goncalves, J., van Berkel, N., Klakegg, S.: Crowdsourcing situated & subjective knowledge for decision support. In: Proceedings of the 2016 ACM International Joint Conference on Pervasive and Ubiquitous Computing: Adjunct (UbiComp 2016), pp. 1478–1483. ACM, New York (2016)
21. Hosio, S., et al.: Crowdsourcing treatments for low back pain. In: Proceedings of the 2018 CHI Conference on Human Factors in Computing Systems (CHI 2018). ACM, New York (2018)
22. Hyland, K.: Teaching and Researching Writing, 3rd edn. Routledge, New York (2016)
23. Iqbal, S.T., Teevan, J., Liebling, D., Thompson, A.L.: Multitasking with play write, a mobile microproductivity writing tool. In: Proceedings of the 31st Annual ACM Symposium on User Interface Software and Technology, UIST 2018, pp. 411–422. ACM, New York (2018)

24. Kaufman, J.C., Gentile, C.A., Baer, J.: Do gifted student writers and creative writing experts rate creativity the same way? Gifted Child Q. **49**(3), 260–265 (2005)

25. Kerne, A., Smith, S.M.: The information discovery framework. In: Proceedings of the 5th Conference on Designing Interactive Systems: Processes, Practices, Methods, and Techniques (DIS 2004), pp. 357–360. ACM, New York (2004)

26. Kittur, A., Peters, A.M., Diriye, A., Telang, T., Bove, M.R.: Costs and benefits of structured information foraging. In: Proceedings of the SIGCHI Conference on Human Factors in Computing Systems (CHI 2013), pp. 2989–2998. ACM, New York (2013)

27. Klouche, K., Ruotsalo, T., Cabral, D., Andolina, S., Bellucci, A., Jacucci, G.: Designing for exploratory search on touch devices. In: Proceedings of the 33rd Annual ACM Conference on Human Factors in Computing Systems (CHI 2015), pp. 4189–4198. ACM, New York (2015)

28. Lautamatti, L.: Observations on the development of the topic in simplified discourse. AFinLAn Vuosikirja **8**(22), 71–104 (1978)

29. Lee, J., Son, J., Settle, Q.: Exploratory writing in student learning. Int. J. Fashion Des. Technol. Educ. **9**(1), 9–15 (2016)

30. Marchionini, G.: Exploratory search: from finding to understanding. Commun. ACM **49**(4), 41–46 (2006)

31. Murray, D.M.: Teach writing as process not product. Leaflet **71**, 11–14 (1972)

32. Nebeling, M., et al.: WearWrite: crowd-assisted writing from smartwatches. In: Proceedings of the 2016 CHI Conference on Human Factors in Computing Systems, CHI 2016, pp. 3834–3846. ACM, New York (2016)

33. Nurse, J.R., Rahman, S.S., Creese, S., Goldsmith, M., Lamberts, K.: Information quality and trustworthiness: a topical state-of-the-art review. In: The International Conference on Computer Applications and Network Security (ICCANS 2011), pp. 492–500. IEEE (2011)

34. Parameswaran, A., Teh, M.H., Garcia-Molina, H., Widom, J.: DataSift: a crowd-powered search toolkit. In: Proceedings of the 2014 ACM SIGMOD International Conference on Management of Data (SIGMOD 2014), pp. 885–888. ACM, New York (2014)

35. Petersen, C., Simonsen, J.G., Lioma, C.: Power law distributions in information retrieval. ACM Trans. Inf. Syst. **34**(2), 1–37 (2016)

36. Pirolli, P.: Powers of 10: modeling complex information-seeking systems at multiple scales. Computer **42**(3), 33–40 (2009)

37. Pirolli, P., Card, S.: Information foraging. Psychol. Rev. **106**(4), 643–675 (1999)

38. Robson, C., McCartan, K.: Real World Research, 4th edn. Wiley, Chichester (2016)

39. Rohman, D.G.: Pre-writing the stage of discovery in the writing process. Coll. Compos. Commun. **16**(2), 106–112 (1965)

40. Samuelson, W., Zeckhauser, R.: Status quo bias in decision making. J. Risk Uncertain. **1**(1), 7–59 (1988)

41. Sharples, M.: Cognition, computers and creative writing. The University of Edinburgh, Edinburgh, UK (1984)

42. Shneiderman, B.: Creativity support tools: a grand challenge for HCI researchers. In: Redondo, M., Bravo, C., Ortega, M. (eds.) Engineering the User Interface: From Research to Practice, pp. 1–9. Springer, London (2009). https://doi.org/10.1007/978-1-84800-136-7_1

43. Siangliulue, P., Chan, J., Dow, S.P., Gajos, K.Z.: IdeaHound: improving large-scale collaborative ideation with crowd-powered real-time semantic modeling. In: Proceedings of the 29th Annual Symposium on User Interface Software and Technology (UIST 2016), pp. 609–624. ACM, New York (2016)

44. Simon, H.A.: The structure of Ill structured problems. Artif. Intell. 4(3), 181–201 (1973)

45. Surowiecki, J.: The wisdom of crowds. Anchor (2005)

46. Sweller, J.: Cognitive load during problem solving: effects on learning. Cogn. Sci. 12(2), 257–285 (1988)

47. Talmor, A., Berant, J.: The web as a knowledge-base for answering complex questions. In: Proceedings of the 2018 Conference of the North American Chapter of the Association for Computational Linguistics: Human Language Technologies, pp. 641–651. Association for Computational Linguistics (2018)

48. White, R.W., Bilenko, M., Cucerzan, S.: Studying the use of popular destinations to enhance web search interaction. In: Proceedings of the 30th Annual International ACM SIGIR Conference on Research and Development in Information Retrieval (SIGIR 2007), pp. 159–166. ACM, New York (2007)

49. White, R.W., Roth, R.A.: Exploratory search: beyond the query-response paradigm. In: Marchionini, G. (ed.) Synthesis Lectures on Information Concepts, Retrieval, and Services #3. Morgan & Claypool, New York (2009)

50. Yang, J., Adamic, L.A., Ackerman, M.S.: Crowdsourcing and knowledge sharing: strategic user behavior on Taskcn. In: Proceedings of the 9th ACM Conference on Electronic Commerce (EC 2008), pp. 246–255. ACM, New York (2008)

Visual Methods for the Design of Shape-Changing Interfaces

Miriam Sturdee[✉] [iD], Aluna Everitt[iD], Joseph Lindley[iD], Paul Coulton[iD],
and Jason Alexander[iD]

Lancaster University, Bailrigg, Lancaster LA1 4YW, UK
{m.sturdee,a.everitt,j.lindley,p.coulton,j.alexander}@lancaster.ac.uk
http://www.lancaster.ac.uk

Abstract. Shape-changing interfaces use physical change in shape as input and/or output. As the field matures, it will move from technology-driven design toward more formal processes. However, this is challenging: end-users are not aware of the capabilities of shape-change, devices are difficult to demonstrate, and presenting single systems can 'trap' user-thinking into particular forms. It is crucial to ensure this technology is developed with requirements in mind to ensure successful end-user experiences. To address this challenge, we developed and tested (n = 50) an approach that combines low-fidelity white-box prototypes and high-fidelity video footage with end-user diagram and scenario sketching to design context dependent devices. We analysed the outputs of our test process and identified themes in device design requirements, and from this constructed a shape-change stack model to support practitioners in developing, classifying, and synthesising end-user requirements for this novel technology.

Keywords: Shape-changing interfaces · Sketching · Visual methods

1 Introduction

Shape-changing interfaces are complex, tangible interactive objects, surfaces and spaces allowing rich computational experiences and physicalization of information. Examples include mobile phones that bend at the corners to alert you to a call or a text [39], table top surfaces that raise up to pass you your tablet [9], and the organic, liquid metal art installations that move in ever increasing complexity [24]. Shape-changing interfaces allow dynamic shape as physical input and output, as well as supporting other sensory interaction, and herald the next stage in computing hardware. At present the field is largely technology driven, with end-user applications emerging from the affordances of the available platform. Despite the diverse range of prototypes researchers have developed [55], there are no formal methods, guidelines, or tool-kits specifically developed for

© IFIP International Federation for Information Processing 2019
Published by Springer Nature Switzerland AG 2019
D. Lamas et al. (Eds.): INTERACT 2019, LNCS 11748, pp. 337–358, 2019.
https://doi.org/10.1007/978-3-030-29387-1_19

shape-changing interface development – with the exception of rapid prototyping, often using modular devices [20].

For existing systems, User-Centered Design ensures that the tasks, needs, and context of end-users drive and reflect upon the development of a new system, but we cannot presently apply this to shape-changing interfaces. This is because current shape-changing interface design is not targeted at solving a particular problem, or trying to design specific hardware or interaction – we are purely striving for innovation. In addition to this, possible end users are not aware of shape-change as a technology, what it can do, and the range of available hardware is difficult to demonstrate due to issues of location, portability or safety. In the cases where users are given the opportunity to interact with a shape-changing interface prototype, they may also become "trapped" into thinking about shape-change as being of one particular form (e.g. actuated pins [6]). Much of the work on shape-change appears to pick from different areas of existing design processes, but does not seek to employ them as a specific methodology during the research process: for example, building hardware is often the first step in exploring shape-changing interfaces, and is then followed by a short usability study for whichever application best suits the platform [54,58]; or studies might focus on user-ideation or co-design for non-specific products [5,56]. The reason behind this may be that, traditional, sequential processes (e.g. planning, user research, user evaluation, information architecture) may not fit exactly with emergent hardware which does not already have a predefined role.

At this early stage, we hope to utilise readily available methods to provide a baseline of requirements for shape-changing interfaces. By focusing on a practical start-point – requirements generation – we believe we can begin to adapt and build formal design process for this exciting technology from the ground up. Following the generation of requirements, we can model these to form an overview of the field and its possibilities. This paper therefore contributes: (1) A practical, readily available approach for requirements generation for shape-changing interfaces; (2) A 50 participant study that demonstrates the validity of this approach to generate requirements for this novel technology; (3) A thematic analysis of the generated user requirements; (4) A shape-change stack model to support practitioners in design requirements-gathering activities for shape-changing interfaces, intended to provide a cohesive resource for those building and testing shape-changing interfaces with the view to their eventual adoption.

2   Related Work

Generating requirements for devices that do not yet exist is an exciting challenge. To address this, we suggest utilising accessible techniques in order to inform and engage potential end-users about shape-changing interfaces. Understanding current applications and approaches to shape-change – alongside these already validated techniques – can assist in beginning to design and develop formal processes for these novel devices.

2.1 Shape-Changing Interfaces

Shape-changing interfaces are an exciting subset of tangible computing hardware, with the potential to not only use 3D form in input/output, but to also allow for this form to be manipulated by the user, and sometimes, self actuated. Examples include (but are not limited to): interactive tabletop surfaces such as *InFORM* [9] or the elastic-pin hybrid *Tablehop* [49]; rapid prototyping devices like *ShapeClip* [20]; mobile phones like *WhammyPhone* which explores bendable audio interaction [14] or *Reflex* which uses the bend action to enhance reading on small displays [54]; furniture such as the unexpectedly actuating *CoMotion* bench [17]; or even public installations like *Aegis Hyposurface* [16] and *Protrude/Flow* [24]. Although a large number of works focus on hardware development, there also exist examples which periodically review, critique and ponder the state of the field of shape-change, notably Rasmussen et al. [44], Coelho and Zigelbaum [3], and recently, Sturdee and Alexander [55] but these offer general overviews of interactive capabilities or material properties rather than advice on building these novel devices (although the latter suggests material properties may be a helpful starting point for a design framework). Additionally, research touches upon particular aspects of design for these devices such as emotional or anthropometric content [27], vocabularies for design [45] or constructing form language for shape-change [61], but there still exists a gap in the literature for a consolidated framework or process for the building and development of shape-changing interfaces.

2.2 Requirements for Shape-Change

Requirements are the things a system should have in order to function and fulfil the needs of the user [26]. They can be gathered in a systematic (as with software requirements engineering) [52] or informal manner, with a preference for the former. However requirements engineering has not yet been directly applied to shape-change, and there are no existing parameters. Stakeholders (in this case potential users) have no existing schema for shape-change, so first the concept and structures must be communicated and the solution space expanded. For shape-change, the easiest way is to demonstrate and allow interaction with existing hardware, but this is not practical given constraints such as geographical location and accessing multiple devices from different research labs. The second challenge is how to capture the stakeholder responses as you cannot simply interview the user about their experiences with a product that does not exist, and that they have not used. To overcome these barriers, we might explore the possibility of using creative methods [38] to elicit early stage requirements in three ways: by employing an efficient method of *communication* [62] to describe the state-of-the-art of shape-change; by creating opportunities for *interaction* [41]; and by using an accessible method of information *production* [2].

2.3 Accessible Techniques for Design Requirements Generation

The techniques described below enable us to address the challenge of generating design requirements for shape-change.

Video. High-quality video is often produced alongside published work in order provide quick explanations of a hardware or system concept, without reading the accompanying text. It can also be used to inform, communicate or explore concepts [62]. To a large percentage of users, receiving information in this way is a normal, accessible part of smart (and other) device interaction (such as *YouTube* or *Vimeo*) [10]. For actuated prototypes, a realistic rendering style was found to be the optimal way of communicating a concept to users in a study of shape-changing phones [40], whereas Gong et al. [15] suggest that high quality videos depicting novel hardware allow users to "suspend their disbelief" and make judgements about how useful a prospective technology might be. Videos have also been used within studies in combination with low-fidelity prototypes to generate high-level comments [34] which suggests that combining this media with other techniques may yield useful results. In context, video also enables us to present work that we do not have access to, due to geographical, or other constraints, and is an apt method to communicate high-level concepts.

Low Fidelity Prototypes. Low-fidelity prototypes are quick mock-ups of designs or devices allowing concept testing without committing to an expensive or lengthy build, making them ideal in the requirements-gathering stage of the design process [48]. In HCI, concepts such as *paper-prototyping* [51] and *rapid-prototyping* [20] are often used, examined and critiqued for their role in research. For shape-change, the difficulty in creating low-fidelity prototypes is mirrored by the range of technically complex hardware and interactive capabilities of the high-fidelity, working prototypes. By thinking about the *materiality* of shape-change however, we can emphasise its tangible nature in a simple, easy-to-build manner. Schmid et al. suggests and tests a form-first approach using glass objects to generate ideas for tangible interfaces [50]. The reasoning behind using low-fidelity, *white box*, prototypes to explore shape-change are twofold: (1) Existing prototypes are often bulky, heavy, expensive and situated in laboratories across the globe; (2) White box prototypes allow for the presentation of matter in a consistent way (i.e. all the same size, colour) so that participants are unbiased by incidental details. Examples include: Kwak's *Repertory Grid Study* [27] where a variety of actuated white box prototypes were created to explore the expressive and emotional qualities in shape-change; Petrelli's work on tangible interfaces which looked at the psychological affect inherent with concepts of shape and haptic interaction [41]; and, Winther et al. who generated white box prototypes following an exploration of form language for shape-changing interfaces [61]. The recent shift in HCI toward the importance of *materials* [11] also suggests there are benefits in considering our most simple, tactile interactions, (e.g. Atkinson et al.'s consideration of natural, gestural interaction with soft materials [1]). White

box prototypes are helpful, as humans may require material *anchors* to be, by their nature, "sketchy" in order to facilitate cognitive processes [35].

Sketching and Storyboards. Sketches are often seen as low-fidelity – they are rough ideas that welcome opinion and modification [7], and also explain concepts that are hard to suggest with words [12]. Sketching has long been part of the user-centred design process, and Buxton's book *Sketching User Experiences* has actively encouraged and enhanced researcher engagement with this format [2]. Sketches are also cheap to produce, and are an inclusive way of generating output as they require only access to a pen and paper – and have additional cognitive benefits [13]. Sketching also has an established place in the design of user interfaces (UI), giving rise to computer-based UI design programs which either utilise, or appear to be sketches and storyboards [18,28] and can be annotated or embedded with metadata [19]. Storyboards used in the design process can also lead to more effective design [60] or help communicate research findings [22]. There is already a precedence for using storyboards to generate requirements, whether via sketched, computationally enhanced outputs [19] or the traditional, hand drawn versions [57], and participatory sketching has also been shown to help generate requirements for real-world interaction (e.g. elevators) [59]. Storyboards and comics are also already used in HCI within areas such as software engineering [60] and cyber-security [30,63], and are accessible, quick-to-produce medium for proposing future scenarios. Finally, sketching in direct application to shape-change has already been employed in the user ideation process [56], as a way of exploring the design of interactions for shape-changing devices [45] and even to examine a futuristic material [23].

3   Method

To generate requirements for shape-changing interfaces, we asked participants to experience the materiality of shape-change [55] with white-box prototypes (Fig. 1), and then sketch ideas, diagrams and scenarios. We took inspiration from the described techniques, and Read et al.'s approach to exploring organic user interfaces (comics and material prototyping used in combination to communicate ideas about materiality and change [46]) – for shape-change we can blend parts of the analytic and design stages where feasible. Shape-change is diverse in its materiality and potential interaction range, so to attempt to represent and explain this technology in a simple, single step would be prohibitive. We used a combination of videos to inform and educate, low-fidelity, white-box prototypes to enable exploration and basic interaction, and sketched output in the form of diagrams and storyboards to both assist in explanation and later, interpretation (the diagrams play the role of *annotation* or *metadata* for the storyboards [18]). The desired outcome of this process is to "reduce the distance" between the researcher and the end user [37] and create a meaningful collaboration.

3.1 Study Overview

The study was a five-stage process lasting between 40 min to 1 h, including explanation, questions and feedback: (1) Introduction to shape-change using video material from existing research; (2) Exploration and interaction with white box prototypes; (3) Idea generation; (4) Idea elaboration and diagram creation; (5) Storyboarding and scenario generation. The participant output was collected for coding and analysis.

3.2 Participants

Fifty participants (24 male/26 female) were recruited using social media, email, or from volunteering after observing the study set-up directly in shared social/study spaces. For example, 8 participants responded to a pre-organised workshop call hosted internally within the university, another 12 participated after approaching the study team voluntarily in a shared postgraduate student study and social space, and 8 were invited via email and snowball sampling to participate whilst the study was set up in a general-use study-hub meeting room on the university campus. Participants with diverse social and professional backgrounds took part (of the 50, 22 were not involved in academic research or study, and 28 were either students or university staff). Those participants who were not affiliated with the university were recruited via email and word of mouth from existing social and professional relationships of the study team, and encompassed backgrounds as diverse as call-centre worker, marketing manager and retiree. The age range of participants was 21–69, (mean 49).

3.3 Video Material

Participants were shown 7 videos relating to existing research, chosen for quality, specific actuation type and related to the material properties of white box prototypes. The videos served to inform those taking part about the state-of-the-art in shape-change research, and introduce the concepts of materiality in prototyping. The chosen works were: *Physical Telepresence* [29] (actuated interface); *Protrude, Flow* [24] (liquid interface); *Lightcloth* [21] (paper/cloth interface); *ReFlex* [54] (bendable interface); *Paddle* [43] (foldable interface); *Claytric Surface* [36] (malleable interface); *Obake* [4] (elastic/inflatable interface).

3.4 White Box Prototypes

We created 7 white box prototypes reflecting the materiality of a range of existing shape-changing interfaces representative of current functional prototypes within the field [55], one of which also demonstrated the ability of these interfaces to change state via jamming [8] – see Fig. 1 for categories and images. By utilising white-box prototypes spanning a range of materials, we can communicate the intended interaction of shape-changing interfaces in a simple, portable manner.

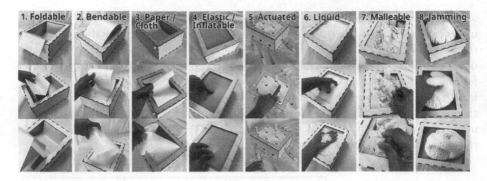

Fig. 1. White-box prototypes based on shape-change categories from [55], with examples of how interaction occurs for each: 1. Foldable; 2. Bendable; 3. Paper/cloth; 4. Elastic/inflatable; 5. Actuated; 6. Liquid; 7. Malleable; 8. Jamming.

3.5 Ideation, Elaboration and Storyboarding

Participants were asked to explore the white box prototypes through touch and comparison, then write down ideas for applications, hardware, surfaces or spaces that would benefit or enhance their own lives in some way (e.g. in work, hobbies, social contexts). This was based on the process employed in Sturdee et al.'s public ideation study [56]. Following this, they were asked to choose their favourite idea and expand on it via sketching a diagram and writing notes about – for example – how it works, the user base, interaction, and so on. Finally, the chosen idea was put into context within a storyboarded scenario of use (see Fig. 3).

4 Analysis

Fifty participants generated 255 ideas and corresponding sketches for shape-changing interfaces, applications, surfaces and spaces (mean 5.1). They then selected one idea to elaborate upon (n = 50). The majority of chosen ideas were indicative of shape-changing hardware (43/50) rather than specific applications for a generic device, although most would allow for multiple applications. Two of the chosen ideas did not specifically address shape-changing technology so were not used in the analysis.

4.1 Generating Design Requirements

To elicit requirements from the data, four HCI researchers (to limit bias: one independent from the study, one uninvolved in data collection) coded the data using open coding [53] and affinity diagramming with post-its [33]. Initially, one data set was chosen at random and examined by all researchers, who then generated post-it notes suggesting requirements, interactive properties, context and possible implications for the technology. The group then split into pairs and

worked on the data, and these pairs were rotated. Requirements were extracted in several ways (see Figs. 2 and 3 for an example of participant data): *directly* through notation on the diagrams and storyboards (e.g. device is 20 × 20 cm, device is portable); from examining the *interaction* (device has furry texture, folding and closure must be possible); from the proposed *output* (mimics organic form); and from *context* (device has therapeutic purpose). The *implications* of the technology then arose from the idea of having access to a lifelike, adaptable non-organic representation of a pet – e.g. decline in pet ownership. A guide to the coding and requirements generation is overlaid on Fig. 2.

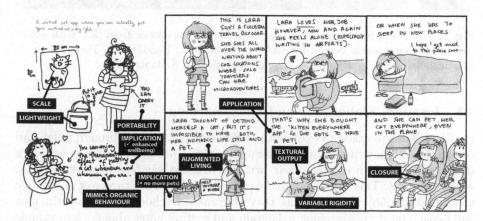

Fig. 2. Diagram & scenario for *Kitten Everywhere* app, annotated to show how requirements were generated. For example, bottom right – the kitten's paw is overlapping the person's hand and reconnecting with the interface surface – *closure* [47].

Mid-way through the process we examined emergent themes and categories, and it became clear that there was more than simple hardware/software requirements and basic human factors. The post-it notes were then recategorised under specific titles (for example) scale, interaction, portability, multi-sensory, device dependent properties, context of use and so on. The remainder of the initial data analysis was then completed (with further categories emerging) before the next stage, where the clear hardware/software requirements and interaction types (based on [44]), the *physical properties* were temporarily separated off, and the complex, *operational properties* were recoded entirely by the group. Finally, all the categorisations and themes were cross-referenced with the original data and recoded where necessary to create multiple categorical levels, then proofed and the entire dataset digitised and checked for errors. The complete user-generated data set can be downloaded as an appendix.

4.2 Results

Analysis of the 255 participant idea sketches produced 506 coded items across three categories – *Requirements (333), Applications (104)* and *Implications (69)*

– with multiple sub-categories. An item refers to all text-based outputs from the coding process. Items from *Requirements* and *Applications* were synthesised to produce the stack model in Fig. 4 by using top level categories for each and ordering them logically for a prototype build process. From those items falling under the *Requirements* category, we provide those most frequently occurring so as to give an overview of how people appear to think about shape-change (Sect. 5), and show a categorisation of the top level themes which enables a stacked requirements model (Sect. 6). Finally, we analyse individual findings and current works to demonstrate the validity of the stack model (Sect. 7).

5   Frequently Occurring Requirements

In total, 333 requirements were generated, across 5 top level categories (Input, Output, Construction & Assembly, Control Systems, and Interactions & Behaviour) which directly relate to the top level headings for the stack model in Fig. 4. The following text contains the highest frequency sub-themes emerging from the analysis (in order of highest frequency), suggesting specific, perhaps essential, requirements for the design of shape-changing interfaces. Examples of sections of original data relating to the categories below are shown in Fig. 3.

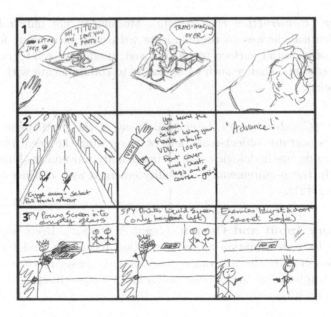

Fig. 3. Examples of shape-changing interface relating to frequently occurring requirements: (1) Photo album for blind; (2) Battle armour; (3) Drinkable tablet.

Between Device Communication (*Interactions & Behaviour*). This finding suggests that our current devices will co-exist with their newer, physically dynamic counterparts. Concepts such as *up-scaling* of film or image from 2D to physical 3D are explored. Shape-change is also expected to communicate *between* devices (e.g. Photo album for the blind – Fig. 3(1)).

Rigidity (*Construction & Assembly*). Varying the material qualities of a device was communicated by the *jamming* box, and was used in conjunction with other material categories to create behaviours in which a device or application moves between states depending on context of use. This variation is especially important in generic devices where multiple uses are anticipated (e.g. interface which becomes a playable guitar).

Strength (*Construction & Assembly*). Shape-change is not only expected to display data, provide comfort or simulate environments, it is expected to be load-bearing in architecture, move boulders with the tap of an application and support multiple bodies as a sofa, car, or podium. To this end, the materials and construction used to create shape-change must be physically robust (e.g. flooring) for the intended application.

Modularity (*Construction & Assembly*). Modularity not only refers to the ability of identical devices to communicate with each other, but for parts of other types of material surface to be removed, used, and reintegrated, or for components of shape-change such as actuators to communicate with each other (e.g. toy blocks).

Portability (*Construction & Assembly*). Many of the participant ideas were categorised as portable object-scale devices, suggesting the need for novel batteries or charging methodologies such as using body movement (kinetic), solar, or wireless. In the requirements, portability emerged as a distinct theme (e.g. armour – Fig. 3(2)).

Multi-sensory Input and Output (*Input & Output*). Users are expecting interfaces to have deformation as an interaction technique, and for this technology to also employ the full range other human senses in their application and design, emphasising the organic potential of shape-change (e.g. drinkable computer – Fig. 3(3)).

Organic Movement (*Interactions & Behaviour*). By attributing natural and humanistic qualities to range of movement, shape-change crosses into the territory of Artificial Intelligence, or the mimicking of life. Organic movement in shape-change links to *comfort* and *sensitivity*, reflecting a positive behaviour (e.g. prosthetics).

Device Personalisation (*Interactions & Behaviour*). For planar, screen based devices, personalisation usually takes the form of a physical accessory such as a screen protector, or amendments to the display or applications. These amendments can also be attributed to shape-changing devices, but additionally we might control the shape, texture and even how it connects with our bodies (e.g. adaptive training shoes).

6 Toward a Design Requirements Model

Our synthesis of requirements of shape-changing interfaces revealed five over-arching categories, each at a different level of abstraction. Together, they logically fit into a stacked layer model (Fig. 4) describing levels of requirement and implementation in shape-changing interfaces, and differentiating between physical/operational characteristics. Under the top-level categories, we also identified eight sub-categories of requirements. The top-level categories are outlined below alongside the *Implications* category which was major theme arising from the data not directly connected to design requirements.

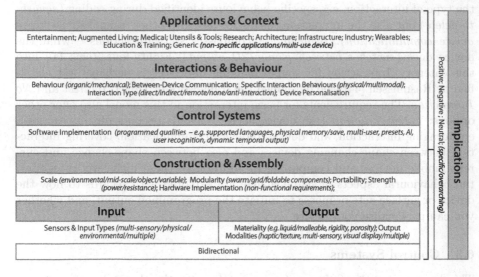

Fig. 4. The stacked model of implementation, based on the requirements generated during the study – see Sect. 5 for frequently occurring requirements.

6.1 Applications and Context

Applications are defined as the specific use envisaged for the device (e.g. battle armour in Fig. 3(3)), and "apps" (such as *Kitten Everywhere* in Fig. 2). *Context* applies to where, when, what and why of using the application (e.g. at home, working hours, provide remote massage, travel less for work). Just over a

fifth of the items produced during coding were application and context related. Often the context also dictates the application, and this is especially the case for generic, catch-all devices. Poupyrev et al. [42] reviewed potential uses for actuated, tangible interfaces ten years ago and suggested applications and areas based on the literature at that time, creating five categories: *Aesthetics; Information Communication; Mechanical Work; Controls – Data Consistency;* and, *People to People Communication*. In the intervening 10 years however, the range of devices and applications has grown and the five categories remain relevant, but can be blended into the overarching contextual categories generated from more recent work [56]. The application areas generated in this work can be mapped directly onto those found in Sturdee et al. [56] (with the exception of the *infrastructure* category), with some exact application ideas being repeated such as responsive computational flowers, remote massage, or actuated storybooks for children. However we also propose here a wider *generic* category where the properties of the device or surface are used for multiple use-cases.

6.2   Interactions and Behaviour

Interaction refers to the relationship the user has with the device and includes the type of interaction, e.g. specific behaviours identified during coding (*squash-to-delete*) but also the interaction the device has with other technology (*between device communication*). *Behaviour* encompasses software actions – what the device does (*switches between planar/3D output*). Eighty-four items fall into this category. Interaction for shape-changing interfaces is perhaps best classified by Rasmussen [44] who developed the framework of *Direct, Indirect* and *No Interaction*. The requirements for basic interaction in this model also offer other options: *anti-interaction* (the device actively avoids or puts off, interaction), encouraging interaction, and device-to-device communication, covering interaction between shape-changing devices and also between shape-change and current mobile devices and computers. In addition to these high level categories, the behavioural aspects of shape-change are explored with regards to how the device or surface acts or moves to initiate the programmed output, and whether you can personalise your device.

6.3   Control Systems

This layer covers the *Software Implementation* for the shape-changing device, outlining *how* the device puts the hardware features into use in programmed, pre-set features and attributes. This is the least dense layer with 20 items, and includes requirements such as *physical shape-memory* and *must have user recognition software*. This can be thought of as the interface operating system.

6.4   Construction and Assembly

The physical requirements that are unrelated to sensory input and output are contained in this layer, it contains specific information on hardware and

appearance of the device (such as size and portability) as well as non-functional requirements (*washable, lightweight*). It also contains the *Hardware Implementation* which includes information such as *integral camera* or *low latency over internet*. This layer contains over a third of the requirements and over a fifth of the total items.

6.5   Input and Output

This layer describes input and output sensors for shape-change, incorporating multi-sensory information in addition to visual and shape output, and specific information such as GPS, speed, texture, temperature and air pressure. Despite a tendency toward two-way multi-sensory interaction for generic shape-changing devices, bi-directionality was not seen as an essential quality for application specific shape-change, which contradicts previous work which suggests this is an overarching feature of tangible interfaces [3].

6.6   Implications

Sixty-nine *implications* were generated from the context and use cases implied by the applications. An implication, in this format is a possible direct result or reaction deriving from the adoption and use of a shape-changing technology. The *Implications* were realised both from the application ideas that were generated, but also from specifics within the scenarios and diagrams that the participants created. They are categorised into: *Positive* (of benefit to the majority of the population, such as faster recovery from debilitating injury, improved well-being, and sustainability); *Neutral* (not clearly mapped onto a specific target group or are cannot be categorised, such as "more money for cinemas" or "consequences of shape-changing AI left to own decisions") and *Negative* (of negative benefit to the majority of the population, such as removing the need for labouring work, or reducing human contact). The possibility of AI taking jobs from people is already a hot topic, and shape-change could enable a far greater obsolescence.

7   Using the Requirements Model

We envision that the stack model can be of use for researchers, to be used as a reference list showing the relationship between different parts of the stack, to ensure users consider requirements at all levels (important because the decisions at one layer effect the layers above and below). It could also help categorise and synthesise many requirements together, and function as a tool to direct users to think about certain types/areas of requirements during early design phases. Designers could also use it to ensure they have considered input at all levels (as incorrect assumptions at one level can propagate), and technologists can use it to understand the impact of their technology decisions (bottom layers) on the upper layers. Within the existing framework of shape-change, it could also be used to assist researchers to better understand existing prototypes – however, we envisage further development before it can be fully adopted by the community.

7.1 Applying the Requirements Model to the Dataset

The overarching requirements and subcategories are distributed across the stack, with a slight bias toward the multi-sensory, bottom layer of the stack (input/output). Software implementation (*Control Systems*) is the most under-represented layer, perhaps due to the participant sample we used (non-computer background), but this omission could be addressed by asking users to specifically think within the stack system. Looking at the participant data in relation to the stack model, we could re-analyse the diagrammatical and storyboard data and identify extra requirements that the user may not have explicitly thought about during the study. In the case of the *drinkable tablet* (Fig. 3(3)) which we know has *variable rigidity* and is *safe to ingest* we might now return to the under-represented *software implementation* and extract the information that if it is a tablet then it also runs apps, and we can see from the sketch that it also supports a 2D planar screen, meaning it should be backward-compatible. The demonstrates that the stack model therefore can support directed thinking for the researchers by identifying specific areas and therefore eliciting further requirements. Observation of the participants during the study suggests that a mixture of top-down and bottom-up approach is used to create the data: either where an application idea was realised via consideration of what hardware would be required to achieve that goal, or beginning with an idea relating to a specific hardware type based on the white box prototypes, and moving up the stack for application and contextual design. For example, the *drinkable tablet* idea (Fig. 3(3)) came directly from the liquid interface prototype (Fig. 1(6)), blended with the idea of variable rigidity (Fig. 1(8)), and although in context of a science fiction story, the practical information remains relatable. Following the ideation and diagram creation, the context in which a drinkable tablet would be helpful was then realised – in this case the spy conceals their data by ingesting it – and a scenario based on this idea was drawn.

7.2 Application to Existing Prototypes

We applied a retrospective analysis of the stack model to two existing, contrasting, prototypes to confirm the layers fit with current research, and to get an idea of where build focus was. The choice of prototype was made by examining the methodological processes of existing works, focusing on: *Decision-making* – what was the initial inspiration or background to the work?; *Technology used* – was it existing, based upon other prototypes, or a novel implementation; *Context* – what need does the work fulfil?; *Behaviour* – what form of shape-change does the prototype exhibit?; and, *Inputs/Outputs* – how is the prototype controlled and what display mechanism does it have? By querying existing research using the stack model as a basis it is possible to retrospectively apply its principles.

Kodama's ferrofluid works [24] are born of the desire to emulate organic movement and create art, therefore the focus in the stack is on application, and the interactive/behavioural qualities: a top-down perspective (Table 1, left). Conversely, for *ShapeClip* [20] the focus was on the hardware: building a bidirectional

Table 1. The stack model for shape-change applied retrospectively to *Morpho-Tower* [24] and *Shape-Clip* [20].

Applications & Context		Applications & Context	
Artistic installation		Rapid-prototyping	
Interactions & Behaviour		**Interactions & Behaviour**	
Dynamic reaction to changes in magnetic field, trembling/rotating, defying gravity, increase/decrease in size, organic movement, forms spikes along magnetic field lines		Variable topology, height changes in response to input, reconfigurable	
Control systems		**Control systems**	
Variable magnetic fluid		Javascript API, RGB value sampling, supports HTML5, WebSocket-to-Serial bridge, awareness of clip-position	
Construction & Assembly		**Construction & Assembly**	
Ferrofluid contained in plate, helical iron tower		Stepper motor, LDRs, RGB LED, ATmega328p, arduino, 3D printed base, circuit board, modular, portable,	
Physical Input	**Materiality/Output**	**Physical Input**	**Materiality/Output**
Magnetic field, electromagnet	Liquid, dynamic shape, texture	Light sensor, gesture, force, data	Actuated pins, form, colour, light

actuation device that was low cost, modular and easy to use (Table 1, right). This suggests a focus on the lower two layers of the stack (bottom-up), with omissions in detailing interaction behaviours. Both papers refer to future hardware improvements, applications or use-cases (e.g. *advertising, sound equaliser*; *third skin*) but do not consider the longer-term implications for their projects (this loosely supports the notion that this research is very technology driven, and not focused on long term adoption [25]). This is not a criticism of existing research, but identifies the requirements focus for different types of shape-change, and where researchers have concentrated their efforts. It also demonstrates the difference between *application* (*Morpho Tower*) and *utility* (*ShapeClip*).

7.3 Limitations and Additions

During the coding, it became clear that the aesthetic and emotional aspects of shape-change were largely overlooked, relegated to resulting from – or being incidental to – the device or application itself. Participants tended to focus on the practical aspects of shape-change, which usually started with an application idea (top of the stack) rather than a hardware type, although some items (e.g. shape-changing, responsive flowers) were built with aesthetics in mind, and the non-functional and functional requirements were built around that notion. The lack of focus on aesthetics may suggest two things: That design for aesthetically pleasing objects is a given; or that the desire and design for aesthetics occurs further down the stack – for example, comfort and beauty may be built into the construction phases of implementation (which makes sense if the purpose of the device is as a furniture provider). In terms of emotional content or outputs, these are more likely be an implication of, or bound up in, the type of application (such as a virtual physical pet to provide company). However, Kwak et al. [27] noted that the *behaviour* of his prototypes was implied by their actuation, and gave rise to emotional content e.g. *stubbornness* or feeling *hopeful*. This links to the *Interactions & Behaviour* category within the stack, within which a number of the behavioural themes related to organic movement, meaning emotions would

be built in after the software implementation cycle. The stack model could thus be adapted to add a subcategory of *emotional content*, bound up in the design of organic movement (one of the minor themes from the coding process), whereas aesthetics would become a category within *Construction & Assembly*.

8   Discussion

The stack model and analysis suggests that the methodology has the potential to expand our understanding of how these devices will be built, and applies an organisational structure to the development process; whereas the implications generated can stimulate discussion about future adoption of physically dynamic interfaces. Our methods fulfil their intended purpose: we communicated complex, novel technology to non-expert end-users who were able to generate detailed outputs from which researchers could elicit requirements. The commonly occurring sub-themes also threw up some novel requirements for shape-change that (to our knowledge) have not been documented. Between device communication *within* shape-change is not a new concept, but these requirements also consider integration of shape-changing interfaces into existing technological structure – e.g. having an integrated USB port, or sending planar data to be up-scaled. Device personalisation has been addressed in shape-change, but only in attribution of types of actuation to different mobile phone notifications [39], when personalisation could potentially also involve texture, form, complex organic movement and multi-sensory experiences – that shape-change should be multi-sensory is another under-explored facet, especially given that the only essential output is change in form. Finally, although many of the requirements are pre-existing in other technology development processes, the way the stack model addresses these requirements, and how the extra dimensions of movement, organic behaviours (and so on) are integrated makes the result specific to the application of shape-changing technology. The fact that we are producing similarities with other work also means that we are in a good place to begin formalising process and practice for shape-change design requirements needed to be approached in a tailored way to shape-change, and we have appropriately managed this process.

8.1   Methodological Reflection

Due to the range of materials, interaction and applications possible, we did not use a specific scenario or hardware type (e.g. shape-change for mobile gaming/a music app for a malleable device). Given the nature of our approach, we felt that choosing one application or problem would ask the researcher to arbitrarily define that issue, and bias the process toward one kind of shape-change. By asking users to define their own problem and solution, we explored the nature of the process in way that still provided focus. During introduction and ideation, participants found the videos helpful, though two found it difficult to relate what they had seen to the boxes which did not self-actuate. Others became quite excited by the boxes, choosing to have one next to them so they could return to

a concept, or taking part of the material (malleable) with them to work through interactions. The *jamming* prototype box was seen as the most engaging, as the material concept was novel and the transition between states illustrated how a shape-changing interface might move between material properties, but also because it was in context of the other boxes. Another observation was one of the *hedonic* qualities of material interaction [44], some participants enjoyed touching the materials, and focused upon how the pleasant sensations could be utilised. Removal of either of the stages would be detrimental, as establishing technological context sets the scene and explains *what*, but providing tangible, low-fidelity examples encourages participants to ask questions and suggest improvements about *how* without focusing on single use-cases.

The sketching and storyboarding process allowed the contextualisation of ideas in an easily understandable, visual output. Some participants expressed anxiety during the task, but were reassured by focusing on the ideas rather than producing high quality artwork. Sketching even had a positive effect: "*I haven't drawn in years, I had forgotten how much fun it was*". Given the success engaging with end-users for shape-change, we envisage this process being used in the early stages of new research. In future work, the technique could be applied using a single white box prototype, and specific application, and to explore the next stages of developing shape-changing interfaces – functional prototype development/interface design), and the stack model evaluated in the early development of shape-changing interfaces.

8.2   Implications for Adoption?

As well as approaching user-centred design from the standpoint of shape-changing interfaces, we are also attempting to consolidate research in this area, and encourage the organised advancement of specific interfaces. HCI as a field has been accused of an unfocused attitude toward research, rarely developing topics so that they enter the mainstream [25], or criticised for focusing on short-term utility [32], so by offering up a methodology to engage with possible end users and suggest constructive avenues to pursue we attempt to counteract this view. As an extension to this, some researchers suggest reaching even further into the future to explore not only the adoption of technology, but the implications of that adoption [31] – how might domesticating technology affect people in both positive and negative ways? An unexpected but welcome side effect of the requirements-gathering process was the generation of implications surrounding the adoption of shape-change. This allows researchers to focus on potentially interesting build-concepts but to also ask *should we*?

9   Conclusion

We investigated both the application of visual methods to explore complex technology, and also the value of providing structure to the design and development phase of shape-changing interfaces. Novel requirement themes emerged

such as the need for integration into existing technology, device personalisation and between device communication, alongside those already existing in technology. The process used has provided a helpful means of accessing thoughts on pre-existing technology in novice users, and may assist others in researching along these lines by using sketching and lo-fidelity prototyping – capitalising on the engaging and hedonic qualities of shape-change. Not only this, but the formal guidelines for design and development of shape-change could help researchers at the beginning of their work in prototype development. We also imagine that the technique of image generation and analysis requires further work to consolidate it as a viable technique in HCI research, perhaps in the context of other types of prototype or interface design.

Despite the focus of participants on the practical and not aesthetic aspects, aesthetics can be built in by designers and developers once the practicalities of the build are concrete – and the same can apply to *emotionality*. These particular elements of shape-change are evident in other work in the field, e.g. Kwak et al. [27] and Rasmussen et al. [44], so by integrating our work with that of others in future research, we can formulate a 'world-view' of shape-change – made stronger still by examining existing processes in commercial design and engineering. This may help the field towards adoption rather than becoming trapped in a cycle of rapid development without fixed end-goals. The overall implications of this work relate not only to the eventual adoption of shape-change technology, but how this might change the way in which we consume technology in the future.

To summarise – shape-changing interfaces are complex, emergent technologies for which it is difficult to apply pre-existing processes – to address this, we used non-expert users to generate design requirements for these devices by sketching and diagramming their thoughts after working with video and white-box prototypes. The process produced multiple levels of design requirements which were discerned from open coding of the resulting images. These were categorised and analysed to form a stack model for shape-changing interfaces, which can be applied to future work in platform development. The findings demonstrate new ways of approaching the design of shape-changing interfaces and the continuing development of these highly complex computational experiences. Finally, we also considered the practicalities of adoption, and the long term implications of shape-change.

References

1. Atkinson, D., et al.: Tactile perceptions of digital textiles: a design research approach. In: Proceedings of the SIGCHI Conference on Human Factors in Computing Systems, pp. 1669–1678. ACM (2013)
2. Buxton, B.: Sketching User Experiences: Getting the Design Right and the Right Design. Morgan Kaufmann, Burlington (2010)
3. Coelho, M., Zigelbaum, J.: Shape-changing interfaces. Pers. Ubiquit. Comput. 15(2), 161–173 (2011). https://doi.org/10.1007/s00779-010-0311-y

4. Dand, D., Hemsley, R.: Obake: interactions on a 2.5D elastic display. In: Proceedings of the Adjunct Publication of the 26th Annual ACM Symposium on User Interface Software and Technology, pp. 109–110. ACM (2013). https://doi.org/10.1145/2508468.2514734

5. Everitt, A., Alexander, J.: PolySurface: a design approach for rapid prototyping of shape-changing displays using semi-solid surfaces. In: Proceedings of the 2017 Conference on Designing Interactive Systems, pp. 1283–1294. ACM (2017). https://doi.org/10.1145/3064663.3064677

6. Everitt, A., Taher, F., Alexander, J.: ShapeCanvas: an exploration of shape-changing content generation by members of the public. In: Proceedings of the 2016 CHI Conference on Human Factors in Computing Systems, pp. 2778–2782. ACM (2016). https://doi.org/10.1145/2858036.2858316

7. Fish, J., Scrivener, S.: Amplifying the mind's eye: sketching and visual cognition. Leonardo **23**(1), 117–126 (1990)

8. Follmer, S., Leithinger, D., Olwal, A., Cheng, N., Ishii, H.: Jamming user interfaces: programmable particle stiffness and sensing for malleable and shape-changing devices. In: Proceedings of the 25th Annual ACM Symposium on User Interface Software and Technology, pp. 519–528. ACM (2012)

9. Follmer, S., Leithinger, D., Olwal, A., Hogge, A., Ishii, H.: inFORM: dynamic physical affordances and constraints through shape and object actuation. In: Uist, vol. 13, pp. 417–426 (2013). https://doi.org/10.1145/2501988.2502032

10. Frommer, D.: These are the 10 most popular mobile apps in America. Blog, August 2017. http://www.recode.net/2017/8/24/16197218/top-10-mobile-apps-2017-comscore-chart-facebook-google. Accessed 28 Aug 2017

11. Giaccardi, E., Karana, E.: Foundations of materials experience: an approach for HCI. In: Proceedings of the 33rd Annual ACM Conference on Human Factors in Computing Systems, pp. 2447–2456. ACM (2015). https://doi.org/10.1145/2702123.2702337

12. Goldschmidt, G.: The dialectics of sketching. Creat. Res. J. **4**(2), 123–143 (1991). https://doi.org/10.1080/10400419109534381

13. Goldschmidt, G.: Manual sketching: why is it still relevant? In: Ammon, S., Capdevila-Werning, R. (eds.) The Active Image. PET, vol. 28, pp. 77–97. Springer, Cham (2017). https://doi.org/10.1007/978-3-319-56466-1_4

14. Gomes, A., Priyadarshana, L., Carrascal, J.P., Vertegaal, R.: WhammyPhone: exploring tangible audio manipulation using bend input on a flexible smartphone. In: Proceedings of the 29th Annual Symposium on User Interface Software and Technology, pp. 159–161. ACM (2016). https://doi.org/10.1145/2984751.2985742

15. Gong, J., Li, L., Vogel, D., Yang, X.D.: Cito: an actuated smartwatch for extended interactions. In: Proceedings of the 2017 CHI Conference on Human Factors in Computing Systems, pp. 5331–5345. ACM (2017)

16. Goulthorpe, M., Burry, M., Dunlop, G.: Aegis hyposurface: the bordering of university and practice. In: Proceedings of ACADIA, pp. 344–349. Association for Computer-Aided Design in Architecture (2001)

17. Grönvall, E., Kinch, S., Petersen, M.G., Rasmussen, M.K.: Causing commotion with a shape-changing bench: experiencing shape-changing interfaces in use. In: Proceedings of the 32nd Annual ACM Conference on Human Factors in Computing Systems, pp. 2559–2568. ACM (2014). https://doi.org/10.1145/2556288.2557360

18. Haesen, M., et al.: Using storyboards to integrate models and informal design knowledge. In: Hussmann, H., Meixner, G., Zuehlke, D. (eds.) Model-Driven Development of Advanced User Interfaces. SCI, vol. 340, pp. 87–106. Springer, Heidelberg (2011). https://doi.org/10.1007/978-3-642-14562-9_5

19. Haesen, M., Luyten, K., Coninx, K.: Get your requirements straight: storyboarding revisited. In: Gross, T., et al. (eds.) INTERACT 2009. LNCS, vol. 5727, pp. 546–549. Springer, Heidelberg (2009). https://doi.org/10.1007/978-3-642-03658-3_59

20. Hardy, J., Weichel, C., Taher, F., Vidler, J., Alexander, J.: ShapeClip: towards rapid prototyping with shape-changing displays for designers. In: Proceedings of the 33rd Annual ACM Conference on Human Factors in Computing Systems, pp. 19–28. ACM (2015). https://doi.org/10.1145/2702123.2702599

21. Hashimoto, S., Suzuki, R., Kamiyama, Y., Inami, M., Igarashi, T.: LightCloth: senseable illuminating optical fiber cloth for creating interactive surfaces. In: Proceedings of the SIGCHI Conference on Human Factors in Computing Systems, pp. 603–606. ACM (2013). https://doi.org/10.1145/2470654.2470739

22. Haughney, E.: Using comics to communicate qualitative user research findings. In: CHI 2008 Extended Abstracts on Human Factors in Computing Systems, pp. 2209–2212. ACM (2008). https://doi.org/10.1145/1358628.1358653

23. Ishii, H., Lakatos, D., Bonanni, L., Labrune, J.B.: Radical atoms: beyond tangible bits, toward transformable materials. Interactions 19(1), 38–51 (2012)

24. Kodama, S.: Dynamic ferrofluid sculpture: organic shape-changing art forms. Commun. ACM 51(6), 79–81 (2008)

25. Kostakos, V.: The big hole in HCI research. Interactions 22(2), 48–51 (2015)

26. Kotonya, G., Sommerville, I.: Requirements Engineering: Processes and Techniques. Wiley, Hoboken (1998)

27. Kwak, M., Hornbæk, K., Markopoulos, P., Bruns Alonso, M.: The design space of shape-changing interfaces: a repertory grid study. In: Proceedings of the 2014 Conference on Designing Interactive Systems, pp. 181–190. ACM (2014). https://doi.org/10.1145/2598510.2598573

28. Landay, J.A., Myers, B.A.: Sketching interfaces: toward more human interface design. Computer 34(3), 56–64 (2001). https://doi.org/10.1109/2.910894

29. Leithinger, D., Follmer, S., Olwal, A., Ishii, H.: Physical telepresence: shape capture and display for embodied, computer-mediated remote collaboration. In: Proceedings of the 27th Annual ACM Symposium on User Interface Software and Technology, pp. 461–470. ACM (2014). https://doi.org/10.1145/2642918.2647377

30. Lewis, M.M., Coles-Kemp, L.: Who says personas can't dance? The use of comic strips to design information security personas. In: CHI 2014 Extended Abstracts on Human Factors in Computing Systems, pp. 2485–2490. ACM (2014)

31. Lindley, J., Coulton, P., Sturdee, M.: Implications for adoption. In: Proceedings of the 2017 CHI Conference on Human Factors in Computing Systems, pp. 265–277. ACM (2017). https://doi.org/10.1145/3025453.3025742

32. Linehan, C., et al.: Alternate endings: using fiction to explore design futures. In: CHI 2014 Extended Abstracts on Human Factors in Computing Systems, pp. 45–48. ACM (2014). https://doi.org/10.1145/2559206.2560472

33. Lucero, A.: Using affinity diagrams to evaluate interactive prototypes. In: Abascal, J., Barbosa, S., Fetter, M., Gross, T., Palanque, P., Winckler, M. (eds.) INTERACT 2015. LNCS, vol. 9297, pp. 231–248. Springer, Cham (2015). https://doi.org/10.1007/978-3-319-22668-2_19

34. Mackay, W.E., Ratzer, A.V., Janecek, P.: Video artifacts for design: bridging the gap between abstraction and detail. In: Proceedings of the 3rd Conference on Designing Interactive Systems: Processes, Practices, Methods, and Techniques, pp. 72–82. ACM (2000). https://doi.org/10.1145/347642.347666

35. Malafouris, L.: The cognitive basis of material engagement: where brain, body and culture conflate. In: Rethinking Materiality: The Engagement of Mind with the Material World, pp. 53–61. McDonald Institute Monographs, Cambridge (2004)

36. Matoba, Y., Sato, T., Takahashi, N., Koike, H.: ClaytricSurface: an interactive surface with dynamic softness control capability. In: ACM SIGGRAPH 2012 Emerging Technologies, p. 6. ACM (2012). https://doi.org/10.1145/2343456.2343462
37. Muller, M.J.: Participatory design: the third space in HCI. In: Human-Computer Interaction: Development Process, vol. 4235, pp. 165–185 (2003)
38. Nelson, J., Buisine, S., Aoussat, A.: Anticipating the use of future things: towards a framework for prospective use analysis in innovation design projects. Appl. Ergon. 44(6), 948–956 (2013). https://doi.org/10.1016/j.apergo.2013.01.002
39. Park, Y.W., Park, J., Nam, T.J.: The trial of bendi in a coffeehouse: use of a shape-changing device for a tactile-visual phone conversation. In: Proceedings of the 33rd Annual ACM Conference on Human Factors in Computing Systems, pp. 2181–2190. ACM (2015). https://doi.org/10.1145/2702123.2702326
40. Pedersen, E.W., Subramanian, S., Hornbæk, K.: Is my phone alive? A large-scale study of shape change in handheld devices using videos. In: Proceedings of the 32nd Annual ACM Conference on Human Factors in Computing Systems, pp. 2579–2588. ACM (2014). https://doi.org/10.1145/2556288.2557018
41. Petrelli, D., Soranzo, A., Ciolfi, L., Reidy, J.: Exploring the aesthetics of tangible interaction: experiments on the perception of hybrid objects. In: Proceedings of the TEI 2016: Tenth International Conference on Tangible, Embedded, and Embodied Interaction, pp. 100–108. ACM (2016). https://doi.org/10.1145/2839462.2839478
42. Poupyrev, I., Nashida, T., Okabe, M.: Actuation and tangible user interfaces: the Vaucanson duck, robots, and shape displays. In: Proceedings of the 1st International Conference on Tangible and Embedded Interaction, pp. 205–212. ACM (2007)
43. Ramakers, R., Schöning, J., Luyten, K.: Paddle: highly deformable mobile devices with physical controls. In: Proceedings of the 32nd Annual ACM Conference on Human Factors in Computing Systems, pp. 2569–2578. ACM (2014)
44. Rasmussen, M.K., Pedersen, E.W., Petersen, M.G., Hornbæk, K.: Shape-changing interfaces: a review of the design space and open research questions. In: Proceedings of the SIGCHI Conference on Human Factors in Computing Systems, pp. 735–744. ACM (2012). https://doi.org/10.1145/2207676.2207781
45. Rasmussen, M.K., Troiano, G.M., Petersen, M.G., Simonsen, J.G., Hornbæk, K.: Sketching shape-changing interfaces: exploring vocabulary, metaphors, use, and affordances. In: CHI, pp. 2740–2751 (2016)
46. Read, J.C., Fitton, D., Horton, M.: Theatre, playdoh and comic strips: designing organic user interfaces with young adolescent and teenage participants. Interact. Comput. 25(2), 183–198 (2013). https://doi.org/10.1093/iwc/iws016
47. Roudaut, A., Karnik, A., Löchtefeld, M., Subramanian, S.: Morphees: toward high shape resolution in self-actuated flexible mobile devices. In: Proceedings of the SIGCHI Conference on Human Factors in Computing Systems, pp. 593–602. ACM (2013)
48. Rudd, J., Stern, K., Isensee, S.: Low vs. high-fidelity prototyping debate. Interactions 3(1), 76–85 (1996). https://doi.org/10.1145/223500.223514
49. Sahoo, D.R., Hornbæk, K., Subramanian, S.: TableHop: an actuated fabric display using transparent electrodes. In: Proceedings of the 2016 CHI Conference on Human Factors in Computing Systems, pp. 3767–3780. ACM (2016)
50. Schmid, M., Rümelin, S., Richter, H.: Empowering materiality: inspiring the design of tangible interactions. In: Proceedings of the 7th International Conference on Tangible, Embedded and Embodied Interaction, pp. 91–98. ACM (2013)

51. Sefelin, R., Tscheligi, M., Giller, V.: Paper prototyping-what is it good for? A comparison of paper-and computer-based low-fidelity prototyping. In: CHI 2003 Extended Abstracts on Human Factors in Computing Systems, pp. 778–779. ACM (2003). https://doi.org/10.1145/765891.765986
52. Sommerville, I., Sawyer, P.: Requirements Engineering: A Good Practice Guide. Wiley, New York (1997)
53. Strauss, A., Corbin, J.M.: Basics of Qualitative Research: Grounded Theory Procedures and Techniques. Sage Publications Inc., Thousand Oaks (1990)
54. Strohmeier, P., Burstyn, J., Carrascal, J.P., Levesque, V., Vertegaal, R.: ReFlex: a flexible smartphone with active haptic feedback for bend input. In: Proceedings of the TEI 2016: Tenth International Conference on Tangible, Embedded, and Embodied Interaction, pp. 185–192. ACM (2016)
55. Sturdee, M., Alexander, J.: Analysis and classification of shape-changing interfaces for design and application-based research. ACM Comput. Surv. (CSUR) 51(1), 2 (2018). https://doi.org/10.1145/3143559
56. Sturdee, M., Hardy, J., Dunn, N., Alexander, J.: A public ideation of shape-changing applications. In: Proceedings of the 2015 International Conference on Interactive Tabletops & Surfaces, pp. 219–228. ACM (2015). https://doi.org/10.1145/2817721.2817734
57. Sutherland, M., Maiden, N.: Storyboarding requirements. IEEE Softw. 27(6), 9–11 (2010). https://doi.org/10.1109/MS.2010.147
58. Taher, F., Jansen, Y., Woodruff, J., Hardy, J., Hornbæk, K., Alexander, J.: Investigating the use of a dynamic physical bar chart for data exploration and presentation. IEEE Trans. Vis. Comput. Graph. 23(1), 451–460 (2017). https://doi.org/10.1109/TVCG.2016.2598498
59. Wang, J.Y., Ramberg, R., Kuoppala, H.: User participatory sketching: a complementary approach to gather user requirements. In: Proceedings of APCHI 2012: The 10th Asia Pacific Conference on Computer Human Interaction, pp. 481–490 (2012)
60. Williams, A.M., Alspaugh, T.A.: Articulating software requirements comic book style. In: 2008 Third International Workshop on Multimedia and Enjoyable Requirements Engineering-Beyond Mere Descriptions and with More Fun and Games, MERE 2008, pp. 4–8. IEEE (2008). https://doi.org/10.1109/MERE.2008.3
61. Winther, M., Vallgårda, A.: A basic form language for shape-changing interfaces. In: Proceedings of the TEI 2016: Tenth International Conference on Tangible, Embedded, and Embodied Interaction, pp. 193–201. ACM (2016). https://doi.org/10.1145/2839462.2839496
62. Ylirisku, S.P., Buur, J.: Designing with Video: Focusing the User-Centred Design Process. Springer, London (2007). https://doi.org/10.1007/978-1-84628-961-3
63. Zhang Kennedy, L., Chiasson, S., Biddle, R.: The role of instructional design in persuasion: a comics approach for improving cybersecurity. Int. J. Hum. Comput. Interact. 32(3), 215–257 (2016). https://doi.org/10.1080/10447318.2016.1136177

Methods for User Studies

An Approach to Identifying What Has Gone Wrong in a User Interaction

Andrea Marrella[✉], Lauren Stacey Ferro, and Tiziana Catarci

DIAG, Sapienza Università di Roma, Rome, Italy
{marrella,lsferro,catarci}@diag.uniroma1.it

Abstract. Nowadays, there is an increasing number of software applications offering task-based interactions through mobile devices or (directly) via the surrounding technological environment. Such interactions, which are difficult to assess with traditional user evaluation techniques due to their volatility, are usually recorded in dedicated *interaction logs*, which are then sent back to the software developers who must make sense of them. To date, *log studies* are mainly used to extract user behaviours from interaction logs for profiling purposes, or to compare such behaviors across different system variants. In this paper, we present a novel approach based on a declarative specification of *interaction models* that exploits logs for identifying exactly *what has gone wrong during a user interaction*, detecting which user actions may have caused usability issues and suggesting reparative actions for solving them.

1 Introduction

The modern revolution in Information Technology (IT) has allowed us to interact in advanced ways with a plethora of mobile devices and technological artefacts embedded in the surrounding environment. This has led to new shapes of user interfaces (UIs) and styles of interaction. Today's UIs range from simple mobile input devices with touchscreens and clickable symbols to complex artifacts without there being any visible surface presenting controls or displays of any kind. While the general feeling is that such increased interactivity is a positive feature, associated with being flexible and in control [18], the volatility of modern interactions has made more complex their in-depth analysis.

In the Human-Computer Interaction (HCI) field, *usability* is the key feature to capture the *quality of an interaction* with a UI in terms of measurable parameters such as time taken to (and learn how to) perform relevant tasks and number of errors made [3]. To measure the usability of a UI, the literature proposes several *user evaluation* techniques (the work [13] identified 95 techniques in 2003), which belong to three categories: *lab studies*, *field studies* and *log studies*.

In *lab studies*, participants are brought into a laboratory and asked to perform certain tasks of interest. Analysts can learn a lot about how participants interact with a UI, but the observed behavior happens in a controlled and artificial setting and may not be representative of what would be observed "in the wild" [20].

© IFIP International Federation for Information Processing 2019
Published by Springer Nature Switzerland AG 2019
D. Lamas et al. (Eds.): INTERACT 2019, LNCS 11748, pp. 361–370, 2019.
https://doi.org/10.1007/978-3-030-29387-1_20

Alternatively, *field studies* collect data from participants conducting their own activities in their natural environments. Data collected in this way tends to be more authentic than in lab studies, but the presence of an evaluator observing what participants are doing may interfere with the natural flow of the interaction [16]. Both techniques are expensive in terms of the time that they require to collect the data. This can limit the number of user tests that can be performed.

To mitigate the above limitations, it became common practice to capture the interactions with a UI during daily use and save them into log files for later analysis employing dedicated *log studies* [11]. *Interaction logs* include the user actions (from low-level keystrokes to content shared via social media) recorded "in situ" as people interact with UIs of software applications, uninfluenced by external observers. Interaction logs have the benefit of being easy to capture at scale (they can include data from tens to hundreds of millions of people), enabling to observe even small differences that exist between populations, including unusual behaviour that is hard to capture with the other studies. For this reason, today major software companies employ expert analysts to reveal user insights from interaction logs. Log studies can have an *observational* nature [21,34], when they are targeted to profile the end users of an application for marketing purposes, or an *experimental* nature [2,22,35], which is oriented to enable comparisons between two or more UIs (e.g., A/B testing).

Under the umbrella of log studies, this paper presents a novel approach that exploits interaction logs for a different yet little-explored challenge, namely the *automated identification of what has gone wrong during a user interaction*. Our approach is based on the concept of *alignment*. It verifies whether the user's "observed" behavior, which is recorded in a specific interaction log and reflects the basic user actions performed during the interaction with a UI while executing a relevant task, matches the "intended" behavior represented as a model of the interaction itself. A perfect alignment between the log and the model is not always possible, thus making *deviations* be highlighted. The approach can identify which user actions are responsible to cause such deviations, thus detecting potential usability issues with respect to the interaction model, and suggests reparative actions for solving them. Despite in the HCI literature many notations have been proposed for describing human-computer dialogs as interaction models [28], to realize our approach we opted for the DECLARE language [29], which enjoys formal semantics grounded in Linear Temporal Logic (LTL) [30] that has been proven to be adequate for designing interaction models [10].

The rest of the paper is organized as follows. Section 2 introduces a running example that will be used to explain our approach. In Sect. 3, we provide the relevant background necessary to understand the paper. Then, Sect. 4 presents an overview of our approach, while Sect. 5 concludes the paper with a critical discussion about its general applicability and tracing future work.

2   Running Example

As a running example, let us consider a situation where Amazon wants to check if its shopping mobile app for iPhone has the potential for improvements with

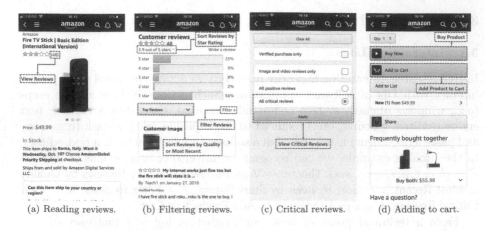

(a) Reading reviews.   (b) Filtering reviews.   (c) Critical reviews.   (d) Adding to cart.

Fig. 1. Some screenshots of the UI of Amazon shopping mobile app

regards to its UI design[1], with a specific focus on the feature that allows the users to *read the critical reviews* of a product before buying it. As shown in Fig. 1(a), to access the reviews of a product (in our case, a "Fire TV stick"), a user can select the link at the right of the review stars that shows how many reviews are associated to the product. Then, a new screen enables us to view reviews by stars rating, to sort them by their quality or by most recent, and to filter them, cf. the dedicated drop-down menu and links in Fig. 1(b), in particular the "Filter ≫" link. This third option takes users to a different screen, cf. Fig. 1(c), which allows to select only the critical reviews of the product, i.e., those reviews with 1, 2 or 3 stars. Finally, Fig. 1(d) shows two buttons that allow a user to add the product to the cart or to directly buy it, respectively.

Given the above scenario, we assume that the analysts of Amazon want to assess the usability of the UI of the mobile app with respect to the task: "*Read only the critical reviews associated to a Fire TV stick, and then buy it*". To this end, the common practice would be to employ a lab or a field study, which requires to involve several users that must be observed by external evaluators over an extended period of time during their interaction with the UI. The major obstacle is that the cost and time required to conduct lab and field testing against a stable release of a software application are often too high [14]. Consequently, in the "after-release" stage, companies tend to fix usability/learning issues only when such issues are reported by the end-users in form of complaints [11].

In this paper, we exploit the above scenario to present an approach that can identify potential usability issues in a UI by directly employing the "knowledge" stored into interaction logs. This knowledge, presented in the form of execution traces, reflects the concrete user interactions happened with a UI.

---

[1] The authors are not affiliated with Amazon in any way. The running example is just an exploration of some possible design issues of Amazon shopping mobile app.

3   Background

3.1   Interaction Logs

In HCI research, interaction logs arise from the user actions recorded when people interact with UIs of software applications. Such actions include all the steps (e.g., windows opened, system commands executed, check boxes clicked, text entered/edited, gestures, etc.) required to accomplish a relevant task (e.g., copy and paste a document) using the UI of a software application (e.g., a text editor). In the running example, we can recognize a universe of user actions of interest $Z = \{b, c, f, n, r, s, v\}$, such that: $v =$ View Reviews, $s =$ Sort Reviews by Quality or Most Recent, $r =$ Sort Reviews by Stars Rating, $f =$ Filter Reviews, $n =$ View Critical Reviews, $b =$ Buy Product, $c =$ Add Product to Cart.

From a technical point of view, an interaction log is a multi-set of *execution traces*. Each trace consists of a sequence of *user actions* related to the *single execution* of a specific relevant task. Multiple executions of the same task may consist of the same sequence of actions executed and, hence, result in the same trace. This motivates the definition of an interaction log as a multi-set. If we consider our running example, the following $L_1 = [\langle v, f, n, b \rangle, \langle v, c \rangle, \langle v, r, b \rangle, \langle v, s, f, n, b \rangle, \langle v, f, n, b \rangle, \langle v, s, r, b \rangle, \langle n, b \rangle]$ is an example of interaction log consisting of 7 traces.

The concept of time is usually explicitly modeled in a way that user actions in a trace are sorted according to the timestamp of their occurrence. Interaction logs can be collected on a client machine or on remote servers. Client-side logging can be included in operating systems, applications such as browsers or e-readers, or special purpose logging software or hardware. Server-side logging is commonly used by service providers such as web search engines or e-commerce sites.

In this paper, we assume that the user's actions associated to a relevant task are already clustered in execution traces that refer to single enactments of the task itself. In a nutshell, our approach leverages on interaction logs containing only such kinds of execution traces. The identification and the extraction of relevant tasks from raw log data is out of the scope of this paper. Interested readers can refer to [8,25,31] for an insightful discussion of this topic.

3.2   Modeling Human-Computer Dialogs as Declare Models

The HCI literature is rich of notations for expressing human-computer dialogs that allow to see at a glance the structure of a dialog [10,28]. Existing notations can be categorized in two main classes: *diagrammatic* and *textual*. Diagrammatic notations include (among the others) various forms of state transition networks (STNs) [37], Petri nets [33], Harel state charts [15], flow charts [10], JSD diagrams [32] and ConcurTaskTrees (CTT) [24]. Textual notations include regular expressions [36], LTL [30], Communicating Sequential Processes (CSPs) [9], GOMS [19], modal action logic [4], BNF and production rules [12].

While there are major differences in expressive power between different notations, an increased expressive power is not always desirable as it may suggest a

harder to understand description, i.e., the dialog of a UI can become unmanageable. To guarantee a good trade-off between expressive power and understandability of the models, we decided to use DECLARE [29] for their specification. DECLARE is a declarative modeling language that allows us to describe a set of (temporally extended) constraints that must be satisfied by a user interaction. In DECLARE, the orderings of user actions are implicitly specified by constraints and any interaction that does not violate them is considered legal. The semantics of DECLARE is grounded in LTL. Compared with procedural approaches (e.g., CTT or Petri Nets), where all allowed behaviours must be explicitly represented in interaction models, DECLARE constraints are more suitable to describe interactions including many possible behaviours. Being based on LTL, where *all what is not explicitly specified is allowed*, few DECLARE constraints can specify many possible behaviors at once. Notably, the adoption of DECLARE constraints makes the definition of interaction models independent of the formalization in LTL.

In the following, we summarize some of the most relevant DECLARE constraints (the reader can refer to [29] for a full description of the language). Constraints *existence(A)* and *absence(A)* require that A occurs at least once and never occurs in every execution trace, respectively. The *response(A, B)* constraint specifies that when A occurs, then B should eventually occur after A. The *precedence(A, B)* constraint indicates that B can occur only if A has occurred before. The *succession(A, B)* constraint states that both response and precedence relations hold between A and B. The *chain succession(A, B)* constraint states that A and B must occur one immediately after the other. DECLARE also includes some negative constraints to explicitly forbid the execution of actions. According to the *not succession(A, B)* constraint, any occurrence of A can not be eventually followed by B. Finally, the *not chain succession(A, B)* constraint states that A and B can not occur one immediately after the other.

If we consider our running example, we can specify the interaction model that describes the expected behaviour underlying the relevant task: *"Read only the critical reviews associated to a Fire TV stick, and then buy it"* as the set consisting of the following DECLARE constraints:

- *absence(s)* means that action s = Sort Reviews by Quality or Most Recent can not ever be performed.
- *existence(b)* means that action b = Buy Product must be executed at a certain point of the interaction.
- *precedence(n, b)* forces n = View Critical Reviews to precede b = Buy Product.

Formally speaking, a DECLARE model $D = (Z, \pi_D)$ consists of a universe of user actions Z involved in an interaction log and a set of DECLARE constraints π_D defined over such actions. With the above interaction model, an HCI designer may want to express that to correctly execute the task under observation a product must be eventually bought (i.e., *existence(b)*) after the user has read the critical reviews associated to it (i.e., *precedence(n, b)*). Sorting reviews by quality or by most recent is considered as a user mistake (i.e., *absence(s)*). The fact that some of the actions identified in Sect. 3.1 are not involved in any DECLARE constraint means that they are not considered as potential sources of

usability issues. For example, no matter if a user sorts reviews of a product by stars rating or adds the product to the cart before buying it, since such actions do not violate any constraint in the DECLARE model. To be more specific, given an execution trace belonging to an interaction log, the problem we want to address in this paper is to identify *all potential violations* of DECLARE constraints representing an interaction model in the trace. Such violations, which reflect potential usability issues, can be detected and repaired by our approach.

4 Approach

As shown in Fig. 2, our approach relies on 4 steps to be performed in sequence.

First, it is necessary to collect an interaction log L containing execution traces that describe concrete interactions performed by end users to achieve the objectives of a relevant task of interest. As already pointed out in Sect. 3.1, in this paper we do not focus on how such interaction logs are recorded. We assume that they can be generated through massive web-based user tests, which large companies often periodically conduct with thousands of end users.

Secondly, it is required to formalize the potential dialog between the user and the UI by employing a collection of DECLARE constraints (i.e., a DECLARE model) as interaction model. Using DECLARE, the model consists just of those constraints *that must not be violated* by a user interaction during the execution of a relevant task. Interestingly, an interaction model may allow different strategies to perform a relevant task. For example, if we consider the DECLARE model associated to the relevant task of the running example (see Sect. 3.2), the number of ways to properly achieve the objectives of the task are potentially unbounded. For instance, the execution traces $\tau_1 = \langle v, f, n, b \rangle$ and $\tau_2 = \langle n, b \rangle$ represent (both) good ways to execute the relevant task. This basically means that a same task can be completed through different traces of user actions in the UI with equivalent results, as may happen in real UIs.

Thirdly, given a DECLARE model of the relevant task of interest and an interaction log associated to it, we can construct the *alignment* between any of the traces extracted from the log and the model. The alignment activity consists of *replaying* any user action included in a trace over the interaction model. Sometimes, actions as recorded in the log cannot be matched to any of the actions allowed by the model. A *deviation* can manifest itself in *skipping* actions that have been executed in the log but are not allowed by the model (e.g., a user sorting the reviews by their quality or by most recent), or in *inserting* actions, namely, some actions that should have been executed (i.e., prescribed by the model) but are not observed in the log (e.g., reading the critical reviews of a product is needed before to buy it). If an alignment between a log trace and model contains at least a deviation, it means that the trace refers to a user interaction that is not compliant with the allowed behavior represented by the model. As a matter of fact, the alignment moves (i.e., skipping or inserting actions) indicate where the interaction is not conforming with the model by pinpointing the deviations that have caused this nonconformity. Pinpointing the actual reasons of nonconformity is crucial for identifying potential usability issues.

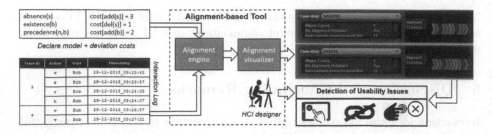

Fig. 2. An overview of the proposed approach

For example, given the trace $\tau_3 = \langle v, s, r, b \rangle$ taken by our running example and the interaction model described by the DECLARE constraints in Sect. 3.2, an alignment activity will identify that: *(i)* action s = Sort Reviews by Quality or Most Recent has been executed even if forbidden by the model, and *(ii)* action n = View Critical Reviews is required by the model (even if it does not appear in the trace), and must be executed before b = Buy Product. In a real interaction log, this same trace can appear hundreds of time. The alignment of trace τ_3 with the model will instruct to *skip* action s and *insert* action n before b, i.e., the aligned trace is $\hat{\tau}_3 = \langle v, del(s), r, add(n), b \rangle$. Recovery instructions are labeled with *add* and *del* to capture those wrong/missing actions that must be removed/inserted from/into the aligned trace to make it compliant with the model.

Our approach takes inspiration from conformance checking techniques in the Business Process Management field [5], where concrete tools exist [1,6,7] that allow us to *(i)* compute alignments between logs and declarative models, and to *(ii)* detect and visually locate deviations (in form of recovery instructions) on top of a trace, e.g., see the right part of Fig. 2. The analysis of the recovery instructions enables the last step of our approach, which is targeted to support an HCI designer to detect potential usability issues in the UI. For example, considering $\hat{\tau}_3 = \langle v, del(s), r, add(n), b \rangle$, it is possible to infer that the user was confused about how to filter critical reviews, probably due to the lack of visual cues in the UI of the mobile app, or could not find the feature. Based on this, a possible solution could be to update the UI by reducing the friction for sorting and filtering reviews. For example, both the "Filter By" and "Sort By" features can be organized as drop down menus and clearly labeled in the UI.

We finally notice that the alignment considers also the *severity* of a deviation, by assigning a non-zero cost for repairing a wrong/missing action. For instance, pushing the "Help" button to access to the help features of the UI should not be punished too hard: it might have been unnecessary but it does not imply any concrete violation of the interaction model. Using a dedicated severity function, for each trace we can derive the alignment with the lowest cost, i.e., the *optimal alignment*, which allows us to infer the *fitness value*. The fitness is a metric that reflects the extent to which the traces of a log can be associated with valid execution paths specified by the model. To be more specific, the fitness value can vary from 0 to 1 (*perfect fitness*), and quantifies the amount of deviations

between a trace and a model. This value is particularly useful when HCI designers want to quickly assess if the amount of deviations of a UI decreases over time, update after update.

5   Discussion and Concluding Remarks

Interaction logs and log studies represent an important tool to collect insightful data about how users interact with a UI, capturing actual user behavior and not recalled behaviors or subjective impressions. In this paper, we have presented an alignment-based approach that exploits interaction logs for identifying what has gone wrong during a user interaction with a UI to detect potential usability issues. To tackle this challenge, our approach leverages explicit interaction models defined as DECLARE constraints, which is a novelty in the HCI literature.

We found in the literature three similar approaches that analyze interaction logs with support of explicit interaction models to identify mistakes during a user interaction [23,26,27]. The main difference of our approach with respect to the previous ones relies in the definition of the models. In fact, previous works employ CTT (cf. [26,27]) and Petri Nets (cf. [23]) for the definition of the models, forcing the designer to define *all potential behaviours* of a user interaction, which is unrealistic when the UI allows several paths to complete a task. Conversely, in our approach, the use of DECLARE models enables an HCI designer to define *just the behaviour of interest*, making easier the definition of the models.

One major objective of our approach is to show that the use of automated mechanisms to interpret logs may offer a compromise solution and an interesting complement to pre-release lab and field testing, reducing at the same time the efforts required to perform user evaluations of UIs of already-released applications. In addition, understanding exactly what happened during such interactions is crucial for developing a culture of *transparency* and *explainability* of UIs [17].

A weakness of our approach is that the logs must be already organized in execution traces that refer to the specific task under evaluation. This activity, which is out of the scope of this paper, is not trivial, and requires the use of large web-based user tests that enable to generate and organize the content of such interaction logs. Consequently, a first future work is to devise a methodology to understand how to collect proper interaction logs to use as input for our approach. Then, to validate our approach, we are working on designing a longitudinal study to be performed with real users. Finally, we aim at identifying some "thresholds" in the amount of deviations found that may help to *(i)* automatically coupling deviations to usability issues and *(ii)* classifying them according to their severity (e.g., "critical", "important" or not "important" issues).

Acknowledgments. This research work has been partly supported by the "Dipartimento di Eccellenza" grant, the H2020 RISE project FIRST, the H2020 ERC project NOTAE, and the Sapienza grants IT-SHIRT, ROCKET and METRICS.

References

1. Adriansyah, A., van Dongen, B.F., van der Aalst, W.M.P.: Conformance checking using cost-based fitness analysis. In: EDOC 2011 (2011)
2. Balagtas-Fernandez, F., Hussmann, H.: A methodology and framework to simplify usability analysis of mobile applications. In: ASE 2009 (2009)
3. Benyon, D.: Designing interactive systems: a comprehensive guide to HCI, UX and interaction design, 3/E (2014)
4. Campos, J.C., Sousa, M., Alves, M.C.B., Harrison, M.D.: Formal verification of a space system's user interface with the IVY workbench. IEEE SMC 46(2), 303–316 (2016)
5. Carmona, J., van Dongen, B., Solti, A., Weidlich, M.: Conformance Checking: Relating Processes and Models. Springer, Heidelberg (2018). https://doi.org/10.1007/978-3-319-99414-7
6. De Giacomo, G., Maggi, F.M., Marrella, A., Patrizi, F.: On the disruptive effectiveness of automated planning for LTLf-based trace alignment. In: AAAI 2017 (2017)
7. De Giacomo, G., Maggi, F.M., Marrella, A., Sardiña, S.: Computing trace alignment against declarative process models through planning. In: ICAPS 2016 (2016)
8. Dev, H., Liu, Z.: Identifying frequent user tasks from application logs. In: IUI 2017. ACM (2017)
9. Dignum, M.: A model for organizational interaction: based on agents, founded in logic. SIKS (2004)
10. Dix, A., Finlay, J., Abowd, G., Beale, R.: Human-Computer Interaction. Pearson, London (2004)
11. Dumais, S., Jeffries, R., Russell, D.M., Tang, D., Teevan, J.: Understanding user behavior through log data and analysis. In: Olson, J.S., Kellogg, W.A. (eds.) Ways of Knowing in HCI, pp. 349–372. Springer, New York (2014). https://doi.org/10.1007/978-1-4939-0378-8_14
12. Feary, M.S.: A toolset for supporting iterative human automation: Interaction in design. NASA Ames Research Center (2010)
13. Ferre, X., Juristo, N., Moreno, A.M.: Improving software engineering practice with HCI aspects. In: Ramamoorthy, C.V., Lee, R., Lee, K.W. (eds.) SERA 2003. LNCS, vol. 3026, pp. 349–363. Springer, Heidelberg (2004). https://doi.org/10.1007/978-3-540-24675-6_27
14. Ferre, X., Villalba, E., Julio, H., Zhu, H.: Extending mobile app analytics for usability test logging. In: Bernhaupt, R., Dalvi, G., Joshi, A., K. Balkrishan, D., O'Neill, J., Winckler, M. (eds.) INTERACT 2017. LNCS, vol. 10515, pp. 114–131. Springer, Cham (2017). https://doi.org/10.1007/978-3-319-67687-6_9
15. Harel, D.: Statecharts: a visual formalism for complex systems. Sci. Comput. Program. 8(3), 231–274 (1987)
16. Hartson, H.R., Andre, T.S., Williges, R.C.: Criteria for evaluating usability evaluation methods. Int. J. Hum.-Comput. Interact. 13(4), 373–410 (2001)
17. Holzinger, A., Biemann, C., Pattichis, C.S., Kell, D.B.: What do we need to build explainable AI systems for the medical domain? arXiv:1712.09923 (2017)
18. Janlert, L.E., Stolterman, E.: Things That Keep Us Busy: The Elements of Interaction. MIT Press, Cambridge (2017)
19. John, B.E., Kieras, D.E.: The GOMS family of user interface analysis techniques: comparison and contrast. ACM TOCHI 3(4), 320–351 (1996)

20. Kjeldskov, J., Skov, M.B.: Was it worth the hassle?: Ten years of mobile HCI research discussions on lab and field evaluations. In: MobileHCI 2014. ACM (2014)

21. Lau, T., Horvitz, E.: Patterns of search: analyzing and modeling web query refinement. In: Kay, J. (ed.) UM99 User Modeling. CICMS, vol. 407, pp. 119–128. Springer, Vienna (1999). https://doi.org/10.1007/978-3-7091-2490-1_12

22. Lettner, F., Holzmann, C.: Automated and unsupervised user interaction logging as basis for usability evaluation of mobile applications. In: 10th International Conference on Advances in Mobile Computing & Multimedia, pp. 118–127. ACM (2012)

23. Marrella, A., Catarci, T.: Measuring the learnability of interactive systems using a Petri Net based approach. In: 2018 Designing Interactive Systems Conference (2018)

24. Mori, G., Paternò, F., Santoro, C.: CTTE: support for developing and analyzing task models for interactive system design. IEEE Trans. Softw. Eng. 28(8), 797–813 (2002)

25. Oliver, N., Smith, G., Thakkar, C., Surendran, A.C.: SWISH: semantic analysis of window titles and switching history. In: IUI 2006. ACM (2006)

26. Paganelli, L., Paternò, F.: Tools for remote usability evaluation of web applications through browser logs and task models. Behav. Res. Methods Instrum. Comput. 35(3), 369–378 (2003)

27. Parvin, P.: Real-time anomaly detection in elderly behavior. In: ACM SIGCHI Symposium on Engineering Interactive Computing Systems, EICS 2018. ACM (2018)

28. Paterno, F.: Model-Based Design and Evaluation of Interactive Applications, 1st edn. Springer, London (1999). https://doi.org/10.1007/978-1-4471-0445-2

29. Pesic, M., Schonenberg, H., van der Aalst, W.M.P.: DECLARE: full support for loosely-structured processes. In: EDOC, pp. 287–300 (2007)

30. Pnueli, A.: The temporal logic of programs. In: Foundations of Computer Science (1977)

31. Shen, J., et al.: Detecting and correcting user activity switches: algorithms and interfaces. In: IUI 2009. ACM (2009)

32. Sutcliffe, A.G., Wang, I.: Integrating human computer interaction with Jackson system development. Comput. J. 34(2), 132–142 (1991)

33. Sy, O., Bastide, R., Palanque, P., Le, D., Navarre, D.: PetShop: a CASE tool for the Petri Net based specification and prototyping of CORBA systems. In: Petri Nets, vol. 2000, p. 78 (2000)

34. Tyler, S.K., Teevan, J.: Large scale query log analysis of re-finding. In: Third ACM International Conference on Web Search and Data Mining, pp. 191–200. ACM (2010)

35. Valle, T., Prata, W., et al.: Automated usability tests for mobile devices through live emotions logging. In: 17th International Conference on Human-Computer Interaction with Mobile Devices and Services Adjunct, pp. 636–643. ACM (2015)

36. Van Den Bos, J., Plasmeijer, M.J., Hartel, P.H.: Input-output tools: a language facility for interactive and real-time systems. IEEE Trans. Softw. Eng. 9(3), 247–259 (1983)

37. Wasserman, A.I.: Extending state transition diagrams for the specification of human-computer interaction. IEEE Trans. Softw. Eng. 8, 699–713 (1985)

Analyzing Online Videos: A Complement to Field Studies in Remote Locations

Taufik Akbar Sitompul[1,2(✉)] and Markus Wallmyr[1,2]

[1] School of Innovation, Design and Engineering, Mälardalen University,
Västerås, Sweden
{taufik.akbar.sitompul,markus.wallmyr}@mdh.se
[2] Department of Product Management, CrossControl AB, Västerås, Sweden

Abstract. The paper presents a complementary method, called online video study, to conducting field studies in remote locations, by using available videos on YouTube. There are two driving factors for the online video study. Firstly, there are some occasions where conducting field studies are difficult, for example, due to the remoteness of the location where the research subject is located. Secondly, there is a growing interest among researchers to use available data on the internet as their research data source. To give a context, the study specifically investigates how operators of forest harvesters work in their natural settings. The online video study was started by collecting suitable videos on YouTube using certain criteria. We found 26 videos that meet our criteria, which also provide diverse samples of forest harvesters, operators, and working situations. We used five prior field studies, which investigated forest harvesters-related issues, to evaluate the feasibility of our approach. The results of the online video study method are promising, since we are able to find answers for research questions that we have predefined. The paper does not only contribute to the understanding of how operators of forest harvesters work in natural settings, but also the feasibility of conducting the online video study, which can be utilized when the research subject is located in remote locations.

Keywords: Field studies · Forest harvesters · YouTube · Online videos

1 Introduction

Modern forest harvesters are capable of performing multiple functions, such as monitoring the machine's status, measuring the tree's length and diameter, and recording the collected data [7]. In addition, the harvester head itself is also capable of felling and delimbing trees, cutting based on the defined length, color marking, and stump removal [20]. Despite various functionalities mentioned previously, a forest harvester can only perform as good as its operator, thus resulting in a high demand for skilled operators [27]. An extensive training is required to become an operator, since forest harvesters are complex machines [34]. Moreover, operating forest harvesters is also a mentally demanding task, since operators are required to perform multiple activities both simultaneously and repetitively, such as observing the ground's condition, identifying which trees that should be cut, detecting surrounding objects and obstacles, as well as

© IFIP International Federation for Information Processing 2019
Published by Springer Nature Switzerland AG 2019
D. Lamas et al. (Eds.): INTERACT 2019, LNCS 11748, pp. 371–389, 2019.
https://doi.org/10.1007/978-3-030-29387-1_21

supervising the machine's operations [15, 27]. A study shows that the cognitive workload in operating a forest harvester is comparably similar to operating a fighter plane [4].

Since operators are the crucial part in the productivity of forest harvesters, it is important to actually understand how operators work with forest harvesters in natural settings. Therefore, conducting field studies is methodologically suitable for this purpose. However, as the name implies, forest harvesters are used in the forest, thus there is a lack of accessibility for researchers to be there. In addition to access to locations, researchers also need access to research subjects and organizations. As an example, researchers can always go to the forest, but they cannot conduct field studies if they do not have access or permission to get inside forest harvesters, to observe and communicate with operators, or to be around forest harvesters. In addition, forest harvesters are also used during both days and nights, regardless of the season. Therefore, although not completely impossible, it is difficult for non-forestry workers to conduct field studies in this context. Therefore, there is a need for other methods that can be utilized, even though the researcher is not at the same location as the research subject.

Looking at some prior field studies that investigated forest harvesters-related issues, we found that most field studies were able to observe a limited number of operators and forest harvesters. Sirén [28], Häggström et al. [12], and Nurminen et al. [23] respectively observed four, six, and eight operators in their studies. Wallmyr [33] observed operators of several types of industrial vehicles, including one forest harvester. Spinelli and Visser [30] reported the largest number of samples in their study. They do not state the exact number of forest harvesters and operators, but their data were collected from 34 sites in six countries over an extended time period of 8 years.

The objective of this paper is to explore the feasibility of a complementary method, hereafter referred to as online video study, where observations can still be conducted even though it is difficult for the researcher to be physically present, due to the remoteness of the location. To give a context to the study, this paper specifically discusses about the feasibility of using online video study to observe operators of heavy vehicles when performing their work. In this case, we selected to observe operators of forest harvesters, since the machines are used in remote locations. The feasibility of the online video study was evaluated based on the results of analyzing available forest harvester videos on YouTube, as well as comparing our approach with some prior related field studies.

The rest of this paper is divided into five sections. Section 2 presents related work regarding the use of available online videos as research data. Sections 3 and 4 respectively describe the method used to conduct the study and the results of the study. Section 5 discusses advantages and disadvantages of the online video study, while Sect. 6 concludes this paper.

2 Related Work

We are living in an era where everyone can easily produce data and share them with others via the internet. The availability of user-generated data on the internet provides new opportunities for research, where researchers can use the available data to carry out

their research [19]. As an example of this phenomenon, the concept of online ethnography, also called as netnography, is emerging as an alternative method to the traditional ethnography for studying human-related phenomena through the internet [16, 17]. Instead of being physically present in the place where the research subject is located, the netnography researcher is observing in the virtual world where the research subject is present, such as in forums, blogs, or social media.

As the largest video-sharing website, YouTube stores an enormous amount of videos that has been generated by its users. In 2015, YouTube claimed that users uploaded 400 hours of videos to the website every minute [3]. The abundance of available user-generated videos on YouTube has also gained interest of researchers, who in the past decade have utilized those available videos as their research data [11, 29]. Although most researchers analyzed videos on YouTube to study the impact of those videos on users, there are also researchers who analyzed the videos as an alternative to traditional methods [29]. As an example, Fusaro et al. [9] analyzed 100 home videos of children on YouTube using Autism Diagnostic Observation Schedule (ADOS) scoring, to determine whether they have the potential of autism. The results show that the method is feasible for detecting symptoms of autism earlier than the traditional diagnosis process, where the observation was done within clinical environments.

Using the work of Fusaro et al. [9] as a source of inspiration, we explore the possibility of analyzing available videos on the internet as a complementary method to conducting field studies. Here, we treated the videos on YouTube as the recordings from an actual field study. This way, we can still observe operators of forest harvesters, without being physically present in situ and having to record the videos by ourselves.

3   Method

The study basically consists of two stages: collecting relevant videos on YouTube and analyzing the collected videos to encode specific information of interest and search for additional findings. This makes it similar to conducting traditional field studies, but the data are collected through online sources rather than doing it in the field.

3.1   Video Collection

The relevant videos were collected using the search feature on YouTube, using the search term "forest harvester cabin". The search results were then sorted based on relevancy. After that, we manually sorted the videos, based on the following criteria:

1. The video must be recorded from inside the cabin.
2. The video must have a resolution of at least 360 pixels.
3. The video must have at least 3 minutes of duration.

We continued the search until page 25 of the search results, which was also equal to 500 videos. Unfortunately, the current version of YouTube does not show the total number of search results anymore, but the amount of relevant videos decreased greatly after page 20. In total, we found 26 videos that matched our criteria with a total duration

of 4 hours, 9 minutes, and 25 seconds. Among these 26 videos there were two videos that showed the same operator, thus the collected videos represent 25 different operators.

Although the number of relevant videos was less than what we expected, the collected videos show more operators and have a much longer duration than Häggström et al. [12] (see Table 1). Although the duration of videos of Nurminen et al. [23] was much longer, with 12 hours and 30 minutes, it is quite understandable why they needed much longer duration, considering the objective of their study. Both Sirén [28] and Spinelli and Visser [30] did not record their data in the video form.

3.2 Video Analysis

The analysis was done by watching the videos while trying to find whether the videos contain answers to the predefined research questions. When we found something, we documented the specific event that occurred in a note. These notes served like a field note when conducting field studies, where the researcher makes a note for each finding while observing the research subject [32].

Following are the research questions that we wanted to see if the online field study could give answers to:

RQ1. How the operators actually operate the forest harvesters?
RQ2. How are the situations where the operators work?
RQ3. Where the operators are looking at when operating the forest harvesters?
RQ4. What are the problematic areas in operating the forest harvesters?

The analysis was done by both authors. Since the collected videos were produced and uploaded by other people, prior experience in the domain is required in order to understand the context of videos that will be analyzed, thus making the analysis more valid [19]. One author has about 15 years of experience in forest harvesting operations, including experience in conducting a field study in this context. At the same time, the different levels of experience in the domain are required to avoid "blind spots", since people with the same background tend to focus on the same things [2]. Another author has a year of experience in forest harvesting operations and no prior experience in conducting a field study in this context. The analysis was first made on an individual basis. This individual analysis was followed up together, where we compared our findings. Similar findings were accepted immediately. As for the different findings, the videos were referred again to determine whether they should be accepted or discarded.

4   Results

The collected videos show a diverse set of forest harvesters, such as various brands, type of cabins, and number of monitors installed in the cabin (see Table 1). The diversity also includes other characteristics, such as situations where forest harvesters were used, operators' skills, type of operation, country, type of ground, season, time, and type of trees that were cut. The brands of forest harvesters and the countries, where forest harvesters were used, were determined based on the titles or the captions of the videos. We defined the brand or the country as unknown, when such information was

Table 1. Samples' comparison between the online video study and the five prior field studies

Criteria	Häggström et al. [12]	Nurminen et al. [23]	Sirén [28]	Spinelli and Visser [30]	Wallmyr [33]	Online video study
Duration of recorded videos	1 h, 24 min, and 51 s	12 h and 30 min	No videos were recorded	No videos were recorded	Not reported	4 h, 9 min, and 25 s
Number of forest harvesters' operators	6	9	4	Not reported	1	25
Operator's gender	Male (6)	Not reported	Not reported	Not reported	Male (1)	Male (18) and unknown (8)
Operator's experience	Experienced (8)	Experienced (8)	Experienced (2) and less-experienced (2)	Not reported	Experienced (1)	Experienced (21) and less-experienced (5)
Type of operation	Thinning (4) and final felling (2)	Thinning (5) and final felling (9)	Thinning	Final felling	Thinning	Thinning (11), final felling (14), and not specified (1)
Manufacturers of forest harvesters	Ponsse (3), Komatsu (2), and EcoLog (1)	Timberjack (4), Ponsse (1), Valmet (1), Logman (1)	Valmet (1)	Not reported	Not reported	John Deere (8), Ponsse (8) Komatsu (4), Valmet (3), EcoLog (1), Log Set (1), and Rottne (1)
Type of cabins	Rotated cabin (3) and fixed cabins (3)	Not reported	Not reported	Not reported	Not reported	Rotated cabins (23) and fixed cabins (3)
Number of monitors in the cabin	Not reported	Not reported	Not reported	Not reported	1 monitor (1)	1 monitor (12), 2 monitors (3), 3 monitors (1), and unknown (10)
Country	Sweden	Finland	Finland	Italy (26), USA (3), Portugal (2), Spain (1), Austria (1), and Canada (1)	Sweden	Sweden (7), Finland (6), Austria (2), Poland (1), UK (1), USA (1), France (1), and unknown (5)
Season	Autumn	Summer and autumn	Autumn, winter, and spring	Not reported	Winter	Winter (8) and not winter (18)
Working time	Not reported	Not reported	Not reported	Not reported	Day	Day (22), night (3), and dusk (1)

(*continued*)

Table 1. (*continued*)

Criteria	Häggström et al. [12]	Nurminen et al. [23]	Sirén [28]	Spinelli and Visser [30]	Wallmyr [33]	Online video study
Ground	Not reported	Even ground	Even ground	Even ground (17) and uneven ground (17)	Not reported	Even ground (23) and uneven ground (3)
Type of tree	Not reported	Pine, spruce, birch, and aspen	Spruce	Not reported	Not reported	Spruce, pine, birch, and hemlock

Note: The parentheses in this table are used to state the quantity of specific information, whenever such information is available.

not available. Other types of information, such as operator's gender, experience, type of operation, etc., are determined based on the information collected when watching the videos. When the results of the observation do not provide clear information regarding a specific type of information, it was also written as unknown.

Table 1 also presents the characteristics of samples from the other five field studies mentioned in Sects. 1 and 2, which were used to demonstrate the diversity of samples in the online video study. When there is sample-characteristic information that was not specifically mentioned in the other five field studies, we put it as not reported. It is important to note that the comparison was done to evaluate if the online field study would have limitations and it was not intended to determine which approaches are better.

Although our approach generally provides broad results and a diverse set of samples, the prior field studies were able to provide specialized and in-depth results. Sirén [28] was able to investigate the damage on trees during thinning operations. Nurminen et al. [23] were able to estimate the time consumption of operators of both forest harvesters and forwarders in performing their tasks, while Spinelli and Visser [30] were able to calculate delays in harvester operations. Both Häggström et al. [12] and Wallmyr [33] were able to determine where operators were looking at when performing their tasks.

4.1 Research Questions-Related Findings

Four research questions were defined before the study. The first two questions were made to evaluate whether online videos could be used to gain basic understanding of harvesting operations, while the latter questions were made to find issues and problems when interacting with the machine and performing harvesting operations.

RQ1: How the Operators Actually Operate the Forest Harvesters?
25 out of 26 collected videos clearly show the order of harvesting operations, including the basic workflow and individual flavors of this work. The videos generally conclude that forest harvesters work in the following order:

1. Selecting which three that will be cut.
2. Driving the forest harvester to the place where the target tree is located.
3. Grabbing the tree.
4. Cutting the tree.
5. Felling the tree.
6. Pulling or lifting the fallen tree to a nearby pile, or starting a new pile.
7. Cutting the tree to shorter logs based on certain lengths.
8. Putting away the remaining parts of the tree that have low or no economic values.
9. Repeat the whole process.

The operation cycle above can be seen in all videos, regardless of external conditions and geographical locations. Moreover, each operation cycle can be performed within a short period, in general, less than 30 seconds. Therefore, several operation cycles can be observed, even though the duration of the videos is just 3 minutes. However, the required time to perform each operation cycle can also increase significantly due to several factors, such as less-skilled operators, working in slopes, trees with long length and wide diameter, dual trees in the harvester head, and the distance from one tree to another. As an example, we found one video where the operator took more than three minutes to completely process a single tree, since the diameter of the tree was quite large, thus the operator had to perform several cuts with the saw in order to fell the tree.

The videos also showcase the two major types of operations using forest harvesters: thinning and final felling. Thinning refers to the activity where operators are required to cut certain trees and keep other trees intact, while final felling refers to the activity where operators are required to cut all trees in the designated area. A thinning operation involves more driving of the forest harvester to the place where the target tree is located, while also avoiding hitting other trees in the area. Thus, making this type of operation tends to be longer for each operation cycle. On the contrary, in a final felling operation, the operator takes more trees from the same location before having to drive the forest harvester to the next location, thus each operation cycle tends to be both simpler and shorter.

From the videos, it was not possible to tell how the operators selected which trees that should be cut or kept in the thinning operations. From 11 videos that showed thinning operations, there was only one video where the trees that should be cut were clearly marked (see Fig. 1). In the remaining 10 videos, the operators were the ones who decided which trees that should be cut or kept. As such, these operators do not only have to operate forest harvesters, but also make judgement on the trees that should be kept or cut down to provide a good condition and prospective value for the remaining trees.

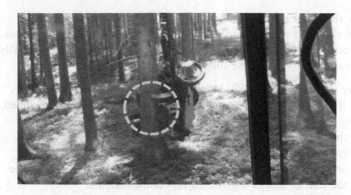

Fig. 1. Trees that should be cut were marked with red paint [21]. (Color figure online)

While deciding which trees that should be cut or kept, operators are also required to remove unwanted trees in the area. Unwanted trees are trees that are considered to have low or no economical values, which should be removed to give spaces for trees that have economical values to grow. Most operators removed unwanted trees by grabbing, and then cutting them. However, there were a few operators who removed unwanted trees by hitting them down. This was done using two techniques: hitting the unwanted tree down using the harvester head or hitting small unwanted trees while felling bigger trees.

RQ2: How are the Situations Where the Operators Work?

The collected videos mostly show operators working alone in the forest. 24 out of 26 videos showed that operators were working alone, since no ground personnel or other vehicles, such as forwarders, were seen nearby. There was one video that showed a forwarder around the forest harvester, but no interaction was seen between these two vehicles. The forest harvester was busy in cutting trees, while the forwarder was collecting logs on the ground. In addition, there was also a video that showed two ground workers around a forest harvester. The ground workers were also involved in felling trees. They brought the felled trees near the forest harvester, so that the harvester head could easily grab the trees, delimb them, and then cut them to shorter logs.

The collected videos also show that forest harvesters are used at any time of the day, during the entire year, and in diverse weather conditions. Although most of the operations were done during day time, four videos showed operations at dusk and night (see Table 1). The good lighting on forest harvesters gave a good visibility even at dusk and night. Additionally, eight videos showed operations that were done in winter, which can be observed by the presence of snow on the ground. The operations in winter and non-winter seasons are basically the same.

RQ3: Where the Operators are Looking at when Operating the Forest Harvesters?

Although we cannot have detailed analysis on areas of attention when operating forest harvesters like what Häggström et al. [12] and Wallmyr [33] have done using eye-tracking glasses (see Fig. 2), we are still able to determine where the operators were looking at when performing their tasks. There are five videos where the recording

cameras were attached on the operator's heads, thus we could estimate the direction of operators' attention (see Fig. 2).

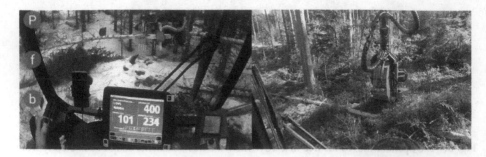

Fig. 2. The left figure shows the view taken using eye-tracking glasses, where the green dots represent the operator's gaze [33]. The right figure shows the view from a camera attached on the operator's head [26]. (Color figure online)

These videos show that the operators spend most of their time by looking through the front windscreen. This situation is understandable, since most of the operation occurred in front of the cabin. It is even more prevalent in the cabin that can be rotated automatically, following the direction of the harvester head. In this case, the front windscreen is always facing to the direction where the operation is happening. The operators sometimes looked through the left and right windscreens to get a better view when pulling or lifting a felled tree, as well as when driving the forest harvesters. The operators often looked up before and when felling a tree. This was done to ensure that the felling tree will have a clear path when it falls and it will not fall in the wrong direction, which might hit the forest harvester or other standing trees.

RQ4: What are the Problematic Areas in Operating Forest Harvesters?

Difficulties in Operating Forest Harvesters
From our perspective, 21 out of 26 operators in the collected videos seem to be quite skilled since they were able to perform each operation in one attempt and with a fluent and efficient working process. This makes it more difficult to determine the most difficult parts in operating forest harvesters. However, we can still find few occasions where even skilled operators seem to have some difficulties. There were two videos that showed situations where the operators had to measure the felled tree multiple times, before cutting it. They even had to move the felled tree in a way where the tree's diameter can be seen directly from the front windscreen (see Fig. 3). This problem probably appeared due to the harvester's measuring system was not showing the right measurement based on the operators' intuition. Therefore, they had to verify the tree's diameter using their own eyes. Additionally, there was one video that showed a situation where an operator had a difficulty in removing a tree's branches. However, this kind of difficulties is more related to the forest harvester's capability rather than the operator's skills.

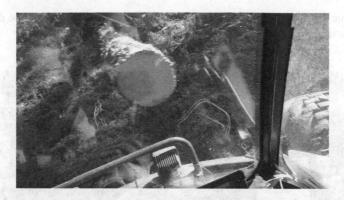

Fig. 3. The operator moved the tree in a way where the tree's diameter can be seen clearly from the front windscreen [26].

Looking at the videos where the operators are less skilled or not familiar with the machine, we can also observe difficult areas in operating forest harvesters. Firstly, moving the harvester head to the target tree is a quite difficult operation, since the harvester head is moved in a 3D space using a boom with several axes and joints. There were three operators who often had to perform several attempts just to grab a standing tree. Secondly, the controls of a forest harvester are complex and different among brands. One video showed this situation, where an operator who was trying a new forest harvester, often had to look at the buttons on the armrests before pressing them in order to avoid pressing wrong buttons (see Fig. 4). This implies that it is not easy to remember all functionalities of the instrumentation in forest harvesters.

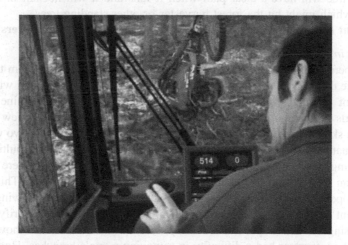

Fig. 4. The operator was looking at the buttons on the armrest before pressing them [8].

Ergonomic Issues in Operating Forest Harvesters
One issue in driving these big machines in the forest is the excessive rotation when looking behind the machine. Most modern forest harvesters are equipped with a rear camera and the video stream from the rear camera is displayed on the monitor inside the cabin. This feature enables operators to observe the environment behind the machine easily without having to turn their bodies. However, there were three forest harvesters, where such feature is missing. Consequently, the operators had to turn their bodies every time they were reversing the forest harvester (see Fig. 5).

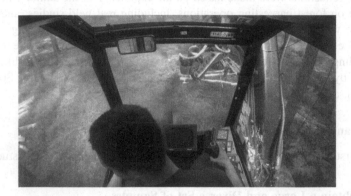

Fig. 5. The operator was turning his body when reversing the forest harvester [31].

From the results for RQ3, we know that the operators often looked up when felling a tree and they also looked through both left and right windscreens when moving the tree or the forest harvester. Those activities were done to get a better visibility, thus implying the current cabin designs do not provide a good visibility for the operators. When performed repetitively, those activities may cause neck injuries to the operators in the long term [24].

Half of the collected videos suggested that forest harvesters generate a lot of vibration. Broadly speaking, forest harvesters generate internal vibration, due to the working engine. The working engine does not only generate vibration, but also loud noise. However, the internal vibration is less prevalent than the vibration caused by external factors, such weight of the tree, uneven ground, and type of operation. Heavier trees cause more vibration than lighter trees. Similarly, working on slopes also causes more vibration than working on even grounds. Lastly, thinning operations tend to produce more vibration since operators are required to drive the forest harvester more frequently. The vibration may cause musculo-skeletal injuries to the operators' body [14].

In the videos, where the operators' hands were visible, we can also observe that operating a forest harvester involves excessive controls of the joysticks. This situation may cause muscular strains on the operator's hands in the long term if the design of the armrests, including the joysticks, does not match with the operator's physical needs [22].

5   Discussion

The results from the online video study seem promising, since it provided a method to efficiently obtain a lot of field samples and the results are comparable to the findings gained from traditional field studies. However, conducting an online video study using available videos on YouTube also has its own advantages and disadvantages that might affect the outcome of the study. We will here discuss about our approach in relation to traditional field studies. As designers, we were encouraged to reflect on our practices [25]. These reflections were made based on the experience of the author who has prior knowledge on forest harvesting operations, including real field studies, and the other author who was relatively new to both field studies and forest harvesting operations. Our purpose with the online video study was to evaluate whether we could gain understanding on how operators of forest harvesters work in the field, like the ones conducted by Häggström et al. [12], Nurminen et al. [23], Sirén [28], Spinelli and Visser [30], and Wallmyr [33].

5.1   Advantages of Alternative Field Study

We will first highlight the advantages of conducting the online video study in this context.

Easy to Obtain a Large and Diverse Set of Samples

The online video study provides a very efficient approach to obtain an overview of operations from different sources, operators, working situations, and environments. As shown in Table 1, the online video study has a much larger number of operators than what the other four prior studies had. At the same time, larger samples also bring more diversity in the types of forest harvesters used, working situations, and operators' background. The collected videos also showed the use of forest harvesters in several different locations and countries. This is in comparison to prior field studies of forest harvesters, where four out of five field studies were conducted in a single country. Additionally, Nurminen et al. [23] and Häggström et al. [12] specifically reported that their results are valid for the specific country, where their field studies were conducted.

Broad Results

Diverse samples also provide a broader set of results, while at the same time being able to provide comparable results to prior field studies that we have compared to. For example, Nurminen et al. [23] were able to provide highly-detailed analysis of the time consumption cycle, and this could also be estimated through an online video study. Both Häggström et al. [12] and Wallmyr [33] were able to provide highly-detailed analysis of operators' attention using eye-tracking glasses, while Sirén [28] and Spinelli and Visser [30] were able to respectively provide exhaustive analysis on tree damage and delays in harvesting operations. These kinds of details are not possible to gain through the online field study, since the data were collected using specific devices. Nonetheless, we can still generally estimate where operators were looking at by observing the videos that were taken using cameras on the operator's head.

Adaptability and Flexibility

The results in the online video study were obtained by analyzing the collected videos based on the defined search criteria. Expanding or changing the scope of the research can be easily done by changing the search criteria. As an example, the scope can be changed to a specific country by searching for keywords in the language of that country. In the case of traditional field studies, it is not so feasible to change the scope of the research, since the researcher needs to do everything from zero again.

Time Saving for Collecting the Videos

Conducting an online video study takes away the time needed to visit the place where the research subject is located, since the videos are stored on the internet and publicly available with no cost. Gaining the same kind of result through physical visits would require a substantially larger effort and investment. Wallmyr [33] specifically reported that it took him several hours to be present at the working site, where forest harvesters were used. In addition, the time needed is supposed to be even longer if the time spent for preparing the field study is also considered.

Safer Option for the Researcher

In traditional field studies, the researcher has to be physically present in situ. By doing that, researchers are vulnerable to any accident that may happen at the work site. Although accidents when conducting forest harvesters-related field studies are unheard, accidents that involved ground workers and operators are sometimes occurring [10]. Moreover, from the results for RQ2, we know that forest harvesters are used at any time during the entire year, regardless of the season. There is also a risk where the weather might hinder the study.

Less Ethical Issues

Using videos on YouTube as the research data provides less ethical issues than collecting the data through traditional field studies, especially in terms of privacy. In traditional field studies, the researcher needs to be careful and transparent in collecting, presenting, and storing information of the research subject [18]. On the other hand, videos on YouTube are considered as public data, thus privacy is no longer an issue [17].

Lack of Intrusiveness

The presence of the researcher in a field study may influence the research subject, thus making the collected data less representative of normal work conditions [19]. This phenomenon has also been observed in the context of forest harvesters, where operators tend to perform better during the study than normal working situations [23]. From 26 videos that we have collected, only four videos were recorded by someone else inside the cabin. The remaining 22 videos were recorded by the operators themselves. Although there is still a possibility that the operators might be pretending when the videos were recorded [1], the self-recorded videos do not provide intrusiveness like what traditional field studies do. Although this is not a guarantee for unbiased behaviors, however, as an example, there was an operator who put his left foot on the dashboard while operating the forest harvester (see Fig. 6). This unique behavior is unlikely to occur when there was someone else inside the cabin.

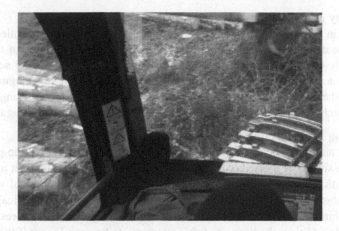

Fig. 6. The operator put his foot on the dashboard while operating the forest harvester [13]

5.2   Disadvantages of Alternative Field Study

There are several things that the online video study lacks to achieve with respect to traditional field studies.

Lack of Multi-sensory Experience of Being On-Site

Observing via videos limits what can be experienced in the real world to visual and audio information only. It also lacks the same degree of detailed information as within a real situation, for example, a sound might be heard, but it is much harder to assess the direction and its source. Other types of information, such as vibration, can be seen in the videos, but it is much harder to assess how it affects the interaction. The view is also locked to the direction of the camera, making it impossible to look around and asses how the interaction is affected by what is happening in the surroundings, or what kind of information that the operator might be missing. Moreover, the videos cannot convey the working conditions in the same way, such as the machine status that can be heard and felt through the engine's revolutions per minute (RPM), the hydraulics operation, and the machine's vibration when a tree falls to the ground. The videos can neither give the same understanding of the operators' situation, for example, when the machine is leaning on a slope, moving over a big rock in the ground, or hitting into a tree when driving through a small passage.

Prior Domain Knowledge is Recommended

Having prior knowledge in the domain is very valuable to understand what is really happening in the videos, thus enabling the researcher to gain valuable information [19]. However, although the researcher has no prior knowledge, conducting an online video study is still useful if the purpose is to increase the domain knowledge, which could help the researcher to prepare sufficiently before conducting an actual field study.

Limitations for Custom Setups

The position and the angle of the camera highly influence what kind of information that can be observed. From 26 videos, we identified four different positions of the camera:

attached on the dashboard, attached on the operator's head, attached behind the operator in the cabin, and held by another person inside the cabin. Each positioning provides different information. For example, videos that were recorded using a head-mounted camera provide information on where the operator was looking at. However, this kind of videos does not show the operator's body, thus limiting the possibility to observe ergonomic issues. The opposite situation appears using videos that were recorded from behind the operator, where the operator's body is visible, but we are unable to see where the operator was actually looking at. If we then add additional requirements, for example, the videos have to show the operator's hands, the number of relevant videos gets even smaller.

Lack of Interaction with the Operator

Another missing aspect is the interaction with the operator of the machine. In traditional field studies, a two-way communication can happen as the researcher meets and rides with the operator, where questions can be asked directly on what is happening during operations. Additionally, the researcher can also ask the operator to do a think aloud session [6] or discuss findings with the operator. On the contrary, having this kind of communication is not possible in an online video study [17, 19]. However, platforms, such as YouTube, allow its users to interact with each other, so the researcher can still post a question in the comment section. The problems with this approach are the disconnection between the times when the question is asked and when the videos were recorded, the delay in having follow-up questions, and the risk that it will take a long time to for a question to be answered, if it will be answered at all.

Difficulties to Dig into Details in Terms of Interaction

Due to the angles from where the videos were recorded, it is not really possible to see the interaction between operators, controlling instruments, and presented information inside the cabin. For example, since operators' hands were rarely visible, it is difficult to determine what kind of inputs given by the operator. In addition, even though monitors were visible in some of the videos, it was not possible to follow the flow of information or how the operator utilized the presented information. In traditional field studies, the researcher can observe these activities directly.

Reduced Situation Awareness

Another missing aspect in the videos is the coordination between the operator's attention to different areas and what is happening in the surroundings. In some videos, it is possible to see how the operator was rotating his head, but it was difficult to simultaneously see the area and then judge what the operator was looking at, as it could be outside of the visible range of the camera. Being present in the field, it is easier to develop an understanding of the situation and determine where the operator is looking at. Having said that, either of these approaches is really comparable to combined approaches, such as eye tracking, to find out where the operator is paying visual attention.

Lack of Information Regarding the Operator

To judge the experience of an operator might also be difficult in traditional field studies. However, when the researcher meets the operator, there is an opportunity to ask experience-related questions to the operator. This is even more difficult in this online

video study, since we judged their experience based on how well the operators perform their work. The result might also be biased to the type of interested operators that are interested in technology, to the degree that they also have the equipment and knowledge to produce and upload videos.

5.3   A Complementary or Alternative Approach?

Being able to understand the user "in the wild" is a necessity to provide good interaction design and user experience [5]. As shown in the previous sections, the online video study provides an efficient way to perform observation on real users in the wild. The approach also has some benefits and some drawbacks compared to traditional field studies. Can online video studies then be an alternative to traditional field studies? Well, in some cases, yes, and in some cases, no. To fully compare the level of the results, each method will require additional studies and comparisons. Online video studies do provide comparable results to traditional field studies in terms of understanding operators' processes and basic behaviors, thus the approach can be considered as an alternative when real field studies are difficult to perform. However, their different advantages and characteristics rather make them complements then alternatives. Online videos cannot replace the high fidelity and rich-information evaluations that could be achieved by taking part together with the operator in the real environment.

Using online videos is however a valuable complement, either as a main study or an initial study prior to conducting an actual field study. We can see this advantage since one of the authors, who observed the videos, is relatively new in the domain and has no experience in conducting a field study in this context. Here, the online video study became a base to learn about things like the process of operation, to make initial findings, and to get questions to ask. However, solid domain knowledge is less viable to obtain using this approach, since it is difficult to distinguish between planned behaviors and interactions in different situations based on particular details of interest. The online video study can also be a complement to field studies, as seen from one of the authors who have more experience in harvesting operations, since the videos could be used to align or provoke earlier findings and knowledge. The bigger set of samples also made it possible to see more occasions on identified and potential issues or problems.

6   Conclusion

The paper presents a complementary approach for conducting field studies in remote locations, using available online videos. There are two driving factors for this complementary approach: (1) conducting traditional field studies might be difficult to perform due to the remoteness of the location where the research subject is situated and (2) the increasing availability of publicly available videos on the internet as research data source.

To give a context for the study, we set out to perform a study of forest harvesters' operators in their natural settings. As the name implies, forest harvesters are used in the forests, thus there is a lack of accessibility to the working site. The online video study

was started by searching for suitable videos on YouTube. 26 videos matched the criteria that have been set, resulting in a diverse set of samples of forest harvesters, operators, and working situations. Each video was then viewed against a set of research questions, as well as to find qualitative results.

To further evaluate the feasibility of our approach, we compared it with five existing papers, where traditional field studies were used to study forest harvesters-related issues. Sirén [28] investigated the damage on trees during thinning operations. Nurminen et al. [23] studied the time consumption of operators of both forest harvesters and forwarders in performing their tasks, while Spinelli and Visser [30] specifically studied delays in harvesting operations. Both Häggström et al. [12] and Wallmyr [33] investigated where operators are looking at when performing their tasks using eye-tracking glasses.

The online video field study generates a lot of data and the diverse set of samples also brings broader results compared to the other five field studies. It is possible to generate similar information after analyzing the videos, but the results from the videos do not provide the same level of details as the other five field studies. Moreover, using videos on YouTube as a source of research data provides several advantages that traditional field studies struggle to offer, such as bigger and diverse samples, broader results, time saving, etc. At the same time, the online video study also has some disadvantages that traditional field studies do not have, such as the need for prior knowledge, the lack of multisensory information, reduced situation awareness, etc.

Finally, this paper does not only contribute to the understanding of how operators of forest harvesters work in natural settings, but also assess the feasibility of conducting an online video field study when the research subject is located in remote locations. The results are promising and imply that researchers can learn a lot from analyzing videos that have been produced by other people and made public through online media. It is up to the researcher to decide whether to conduct a traditional field study or an online video study depending on research needs and available resources.

Acknowledgements. This research has received funding from the European Union's Horizon 2020 research and innovation programme under the Marie Skłodowska-Curie grant agreement number 764951, CrossControl AB, and the Swedish Knowledge Foundation (KK-stiftelsen) through the ITS-EASY program.

References

1. Garcia, A.C., et al.: Ethnographic Approaches to the Internet. J. Contemp. Ethnogr. **38**(1), 52–84 (2010)
2. Barbour, R.S.: Quality of data analysis. In: Flick, U. (ed.) The SAGE Handbook of Qualitative Data Analysis, pp. 496–509. SAGE Publications Ltd., London (2013)
3. Brouwer, B.: YouTube now gets over 400 hours of content uploaded every minute. https://www.tubefilter.com/2015/07/26/youtube-400-hours-content-every-minute/. Accessed 4 Jan 2019
4. Burman, L., Löfgren, B.: Human-machine interaction improvements of forest machines. In: Forest Engineering Conference (2007)
5. Buxton, B.: Sketching User Experiences. Morgan Kaufman, Boston (2007)

6. Collins, A., et al.: Cognitive apprenticeship: making thinking visible. Am. Educ. **15**(3), 6–11, 38–46 (1991)
7. Farias, A.O.: Exploring opportunities for the integration of GNSS with forest harvester data to improve forest management. University of Canterbury (2016)
8. https://www.youtube.com/watch?v=uRZ9ST67UWY. Accesed 4 Jan 2019
9. Fusaro, V.A., et al.: The potential of accelerating early detection of autism through content analysis of YouTube videos. PLoS ONE **9**(4), 1–6 (2014)
10. Ghaffariyan, M.R.: Analysis of forestry work accidents in five Australian forest companies for the period 2004 to 2014. J. For. Sci. **62**(12), 545–552 (2016)
11. Giglietto, F., et al.: The open laboratory: limits and possibilities of using Facebook, Twitter, and YouTube as a research data source. J. Technol. Hum. Serv. **30**(3–4), 145–159 (2012)
12. Häggström, C., et al.: Examining the gaze behaviors of harvester operators: an eye-tracking study. Int. J. For. Eng. **26**(2), 96–113 (2015)
13. https://www.youtube.com/watch?v=9QAZxF-hxyI. Accesed 4 Jan 2019
14. Jack, R.J., Oliver, M.: A review of factors influencing whole-body vibration injuries in forestry mobile machine operators. Int. J. For. Eng. **19**(1), 51–65 (2008)
15. Jankovský, M., et al.: Objective and subjective assessment of selected factors of the work environment of forest harvesters and forwarders. J. For. Sci. **62**(1), 8–16 (2016)
16. Kozinets, R.: Netnography: Redefined. SAGE Publications Ltd., London (2015)
17. Kozinets, R.V., et al.: Netnographic analysis: understanding culture through social. In: Flick, U. (ed.) The SAGE Handbook of Qualitative Data Analysis, pp. 262–276. SAGE Publications Ltd., London (2013)
18. Mack, N., et al.: Qualitative Research Methods: A Data Collector's Field Guide. Family Health International, Durham (2005)
19. Marotzki, W., et al.: Analysing virtual data. In: Flick, U. (ed.) The SAGE Handbook of Qualitative Data Analysis, pp. 450–564. SAGE Publications Ltd., London (2013)
20. Miettinen, M., Kulovesi, J., Kalmari, J., Visala, A.: New measurement concept for forest harvester head. In: Howard, A., Iagnemma, K., Kelly, A. (eds.) Field and Service Robotics. STAR, vol. 62, pp. 35–44. Springer, Heidelberg (2010). https://doi.org/10.1007/978-3-642-13408-1_4
21. https://www.youtube.com/watch?v=irDxNnzM868. Accesed 4 Jan 2019
22. Murphy, T., Oliver, M.L.: Development and design of a dynamic armrest for hydraulic-actuation joystick controlled mobile machines. Appl. Ergon. **39**(3), 316–324 (2008)
23. Nurminen, T., et al.: Time consumption analysis of the mechanized cut-to-length harvesting system. Silva Fenn. **40**(2), 335–363 (2006)
24. Østensvik, T., et al.: Muscle Activity Patterns in the Neck and Upper Extremities Among Machine Operators in Different Forest Vehicles. Int. J. For. Eng. **19**(2), 11–20 (2008)
25. Schön, D.: The Reflective Practitioner: How Professionals Think in Action. Basic Books, New York (1983)
26. https://www.youtube.com/watch?v=H4NXA3rejyg. Accesed 4 Jan 2019
27. da Silva Lopes, E., Pagnussat, M.B.: Effect of the behavioral profile on operator performance in timber harvesting. Int. J. For. Eng. **28**(3), 134–139 (2017)
28. Sirén, M.: Tree damage in single-grip harvester thinning operations. Int. J. For. Eng. **12**(1), 29–38 (2001)
29. Snelson, C.: YouTube across the disciplines: a review of the literature. MERLOT J. Online Learn. Teach. **7**(1), 159–169 (2011)
30. Spinelli, R., Visser, R.: Analyzing and estimating delays in harvester operations. Int. J. For. Eng. **19**(1), 36–41 (2018)
31. https://www.youtube.com/watch?v=kH1p6rN9ve8. Accesed 4 Jan 2019

32. Walford, G.: The practice of writing ethnographic fieldnotes. Ethnogr. Educ. **4**(2), 117–130 (2009)
33. Wallmyr, M.: Seeing through the eyes of heavy vehicle operators. In: Bernhaupt, R., Dalvi, G., Joshi, A., Balkrishan, D.K., O'Neill, J., Winckler, M. (eds.) INTERACT 2017. LNCS, vol. 10514, pp. 263–282. Springer, Cham (2017). https://doi.org/10.1007/978-3-319-67684-5_16
34. Zöscher, J.: Education and work safety in forestry – situation in Austria. In: Proceedings of the 43rd International Symposium FORMEC, Padova (2010)

Evidence Humans Provide When Explaining Data-Labeling Decisions

Judah Newman[1], Bowen Wang[1], Valerie Zhao[1], Amy Zeng[1],
Michael L. Littman[2], and Blase Ur[1]($\boxtimes$)

[1] University of Chicago, Chicago, IL 60637, USA
{jgnewman,bowenwang1996,vzhao,amyzeng,blase}@uchicago.edu
[2] Brown University, Providence, RI 02912, USA
mlittman@cs.brown.edu

Abstract. Because machine learning would benefit from reduced data requirements, some prior work has proposed using humans not just to label data, but also to explain those labels. To characterize the evidence humans might want to provide, we conducted a user study and a data experiment. In the user study, 75 participants provided classification labels for 20 photos, justifying those labels with free-text explanations. Explanations frequently referenced concepts (objects and attributes) in the image, yet 26% of explanations invoked concepts *not* in the image. Boolean logic was common in implicit form, but was rarely explicit. In a follow-up experiment on the Visual Genome dataset, we found that some concepts could be partially defined through their relationship to frequently co-occurring concepts, rather than only through labeling.

Keywords: Machine teaching · ML · Explanations · Data labeling

1 Introduction

Supervised learning is the paradigm in which algorithms are trained with instances of data matched with carefully assigned labels. Based on these pairings of training instances and labels, a typical supervised-learning algorithm produces a classifier—a function that maps input examples (an image, a snippet of speech) to a binary label indicating whether the input is an instance of the target class. The ability to take such a dataset and produce an accurate classifier has improved dramatically over the years, finding success in domains including image classification [7], machine translation [21], and speech recognition [17].

Nonetheless, this technology is still limited to domains where labeled data is naturally plentiful or where there are strong incentives to make labeled data plentiful. To reduce the need for huge sets of training data, HCI work on machine

---

Electronic supplementary material The online version of this chapter (https://doi.org/10.1007/978-3-030-29387-1_22) contains supplementary material, which is available to authorized users.

© IFIP International Federation for Information Processing 2019
Published by Springer Nature Switzerland AG 2019
D. Lamas et al. (Eds.): INTERACT 2019, LNCS 11748, pp. 390–409, 2019.
https://doi.org/10.1007/978-3-030-29387-1_22

teaching has begun to consider how to enable richer interactions between humans and machines and how to better support data labeling. Many of these efforts aim to capture extra information from humans to improve the algorithms since humans learn new concepts with much less data than current algorithms [11], presumably because of the extra background information they possess.

Explanations for why a human applied a particular label to a data instance is a promising type of extra information humans could provide. Stumpf et al. [19] investigated rich explanations for classifying email, highlighting how user feedback has the potential to significantly improve machine learning (*ML*). If explanations can successfully reduce the number of instances that must be labeled, there are three main benefits for classifying whether images contain given objects or attributes, which we collectively term *concepts*. First, classifiers could be efficiently defined ex post facto for concepts overlooked in initial data labeling by relating the overlooked concept to concepts that had already been labeled. Second, new concepts could be defined with less effort from humans by relating new concepts to those existing algorithms can already recognize. Third, this approach could enable personalized ML in building classifiers to recognize subjective concepts like "my house," rather than only "a house" in general.

To characterize the types of evidence humans could provide when explaining and justifying data-labeling decisions, we performed a formative user study and a companion experiment on an existing dataset. While prior work has focused on text classification [3,10], we examine the more complicated domain of image classification. To cast a broad net in eliciting evidence humans might provide in their explanations, participants in our user study typed explanations in unconstrained natural language. In total, 75 participants labeled whether or not twenty images represented a given *target concept* (e.g., "crossroads," "old") and spent at least one minute for each explaining their classification in prose.

We centered our analysis on answering the following five research questions:

- **RQ 1:** What broad types of evidence do participants use to justify a label?
- **RQ 2:** How did participants structure explanations?
- **RQ 3:** How did the evidence and structure vary by person, task, and label?
- **RQ 4:** How often did explanations include ambiguous language, and how often did participants neglect to explicitly make logical connections?
- **RQ 5:** How did participants perceive their teaching and the overall process?

Explanations frequently referred to objects and attributes visible in the image. Surprisingly, 26% of explanations invoked objects and attributes *not* visible in the image. Participants often described spatial relationships (e.g., "next to") when explaining labels for an object ("nightstand") and functional relationships (e.g., X "uses" Y) when explaining labels for an action ("eating"). Many explanations also referred to abstract concepts (e.g., "style", "technology"), which existing object-recognition algorithms struggle to identify.

We observed a number of common structures in explanations. Overall, 26% of explanations included a generalized definition of the target concept before the participant explained why the image did or did not represent that target

concept. While only 15% of explanations contained explicit Boolean logic, many other responses implicitly relied on Boolean logic. We also observed a number of ambiguities in explanations that would impair their direct application.

Based on the types of connections between co-occurring concepts that participants referenced in their explanations, we further explored whether target concepts could be defined in terms of their relationship to other concepts through an experiment on the Visual Genome data set [8]. We used heuristics to automatically generate potential *definitions* for each of the 2,243 target concepts that appeared at least 100 times in Visual Genome. Each definition was a statement in Boolean logic containing up to five auxiliary concepts (e.g., "wetsuit" was defined as likely to occur in images containing "water" and a "surfboard" and the color "black"). We imagined that all images for which that logical statement was true could be classified as containing the target concept, and all images containing none of those auxiliary concepts would be classified as not containing the target concept. Doing so, which notably does not require any additional human labeling of images, we found that 4.9% of the 2,243 target concepts could already be classified with $F1 \geq 0.5$, while 29% could be classified with $F1 \geq 0.25$. While such accuracy is insufficient for training current algorithms, this experiment demonstrates that these co-occurring concepts can be used to partially define new concepts, bootstrapping future interactions.

We conclude by discussing how our characterization of the evidence participants provided when explaining image-classification labels suggests design directions for user interfaces that collect similar information in systematic and structured ways, enabling the information to be used directly by algorithms. We further discuss how the results of our Visual Genome experiment suggest new interactions for minimizing human image-labeling effort. To spur further research on explanatory machine learning, we are publicly releasing our anonymized dataset for the user study and the code from our experiment.[1]

2   Related Work

Crowdsourcing is a primary method of gathering labels for ML algorithms. However, incorporating human input can often introduce variability. For example, Kulesza et al. [9] identified how users' notions of the target concept evolves as they complete labeling tasks, resulting in inconsistent labels. New collaboration methods use crowdsourcing to address unclear label guidelines. For example, in the Revolt platform, Chang et al. [5] created a group workflow where users label items, discuss conflicts, and make revisions. Revolt presents the labels from these stages to a worker who makes the final decisions. Motivated by this work's findings around ambiguity in labeling, we included "unsure" as an option for labels. Uncertainty may also come from the task itself. Laput et al. [12] used crowdsourced answers to simple questions from sensor data (e.g. "how many drinks are on the table?") to train classifiers. Tasks that required personal judgment or additional context led to poor performance.

---

[1] Available at: https://github.com/UChicagoSUPERgroup/interact19.

The broad research area of machine teaching has focused on enabling richer interactions between humans and algorithms, allowing humans to teach machines concepts through mechanisms other than simply labeling data. Allowing users to provide explanations for labels in supervised learning builds on work around dividing problems into smaller parts [18]. By emphasizing concept decomposition, machine teaching can be useful for applications with abundant unlabeled data where contextual information is necessary. Prior work has identified best practices for helping humans train machines. Amershi et al. [2] noted three elements of effective machine teaching: (1) illustrating the current state of the learned concept; (2) helping users select higher-quality training examples; and (3) presenting multiple learning models. Data labeling and classification are the most popular ways for users to interact with ML systems, but people naturally want to provide more feedback than just labels [20]. Amershi et al. [1] found that richer user interactions and increased transparency can improve model accuracy.

A relatively small literature has investigated human-provided explanations in the context of training ML algorithms, our core aim. Stumpf et al. [19] proposed leveraging user feedback in the form of rich explanations to improve email classification. In subsequent work, Kulesza et al. [10] proposed explanations for improving debugging within end-user programming, again related to email classification. Brooks et al. [3] focused more broadly on using interactive feedback to improve text classifiers, finding particular benefits from visual summaries.

Rather than attempting to parse free-text explanations, Ratner et al. [15] let users define logical labeling functions based on arbitrary heuristics. In follow-up work, Hancock et al. [6] proposed applying techniques from natural-language processing to automatically translate free-text explanations into logical labeling functions. In contrast, we take a step back and examine broader types of explanatory information free-text explanations contain. Further, most prior work on explanatory ML was on text classification; we examine image classification.

While we focus on using explanations to improve ML training, a burgeoning literature has begun to explore the opposite problem of explaining existing algorithms. For example, Stumpf et al. [20] explored generating explanations for a naïve Bayes classifier. They found that the explanation paradigm influences user feedback. With the recent success of deep learning, there has been increasing concern about the interpretability of neural networks. Among the many recent attempts to explain deep learning, Park et al. [14] used an attention model pointing at features influencing classification.

3   User-Study Methodology

The goal for our user study was to identify the types of evidence humans provide in explaining and justifying data labels, as well as to characterize how they structured their presentation of this evidence. This understanding can inform the design of future interfaces that elicit the same types of information in a more structured and directly actionable form. This section describes our data sources, participant recruitment, and study protocol.

3.1 Terminology

We tasked participants with "teaching a computer" new concepts. We define a **concept** to be any noun, verb, adjective, or adverb that could plausibly appear in an image. We distinguish among the following concept types:

- **Object:** Noun (e.g., *crossroads* or *plane*),
- **Attribute:** Adjective or Adverb (e.g., *old* or *fast*),
- **Action:** Verb (e.g., *eating* or *smiling*).

We also divide concepts into abstract and concrete concepts. We defined abstract concepts as those that are not generalizable from viewing a single instance, such as "decor," "weather," and "technology."

Following a study introduction, we presented participants with a series of photos that either did or did not contain the concept. The participant was asked to *label* whether or not a concept was present in the image. We adopt the following terminology, in which an image a participant saw is termed an *instance*:

- **Positive instance:** A photo that *did* contain a concept.
- **Negative instance:** A photo that *did not* contain a concept.

We included both positive and negative instances to characterize how explanations differed based on whether the participant was identifying how they recognized a concept or noting which aspects essential to a concept were missing.

3.2 Source Data

Participants labeled the twenty images shown in Table 1. These images encompassed four target concepts, with five different instances (photos) for each concept. To disperse learning effects, we randomized the order of the four concepts. Within a concept, the order of the five instances was also randomized. The four target concepts included two objects (*nightstand* and *crossroad*), one action (*eating*), and one attribute (*old*). We chose these concepts to represent different levels of abstractness, ranging from the concrete (*nightstand*) to the abstract (*old*). These different target concepts also allow us to examine how explanations vary across slightly different tasks. Because we hypothesized that participants' explanations would differ for positive and negative instances, we selected three positive and two negative instances per concept.

The photos and metadata were taken from Visual Genome [8], which contains 108,077 images. On average, each image contains 35 objects and 26 attributes labeled by Mechanical Turk workers. We used Visual Genome because each photo includes labels for objects and attributes, providing us with a rich list of concepts. After selecting the four target concepts for the study, we chose positive instances by searching Visual Genome for that concept, randomly selecting three. We chose two negative instances for each by randomly selecting two photos from among those that contained related concepts, but not the target, according to the Visual Genome labels.

Table 1. The twenty images participants labeled (and explained) in our user study. Each concept includes three positive instances and two negative instances.

3.3 Procedure and Study Structure

We recruited participants on Amazon's Mechanical Turk for "a research study on teaching computers." Workers aged 18+ who lived in the United States and had completed 100+ HITs with a 95%+ approval rating were eligible. Through pilot studies, we adjusted the number of tasks so that the study would average 30 min to minimize fatigue [4]. We compensated participants $5 (USD).

The study began with an introduction emphasizing the importance of detailed explanations and that participants were teaching a computer, not a human. We then introduced the first target concept and presented the five instances of that target concept sequentially. For each instance, the participant selected "yes," "no," or "unsure" to "is there a *target concept* in the photo above?"

After the participant chose a label, we asked them to explain their classification decision in a multi-line text box. To encourage detailed explanations, participants could not proceed until one minute had elapsed.

After the participant labeled and explained all five instances for a target concept, we asked five *reflection questions* to evaluate their self-perceptions of their teaching. To gauge perceptions of generalizability, we asked about perceptions of

the thoroughness of their teaching for images similar to the five study instances and all future images. At the end of the study, we asked three *process-reflection questions* about how participants approached teaching a computer.

3.4   Analysis Methods and Metrics

To answer our research questions, we both quantitatively and qualitatively analyzed the explanation text. As a first step, members of the research team read all free-text explanations and informally noted types of evidence and structures they observed. Explanations that any member of the research team identified as especially representative or unique were discussed at a series of full-group research meetings. Following this exploratory process, the members of the research team formally developed a codebook based on these notes. A coder would read an explanation, identify all concepts the explanation referenced, and then answer eleven numerical or true/false questions about the explanation's semantics and structure pinpointed in our exploratory process. Some examples of the numerical or true/false questions are as follows: "How many spatial relationships does this explanation contain?" "How many objects did the explanation reference that are not in the photo?"

Four members of the research team were in charge of the coding process. To ensure consistent understanding of the codebook, all members of the coding team used the codebook to code 60 random explanations. The coding team then met to review those 60 explanations to ensure that their understanding of the codebook was aligned. After discussing differences in this set, two members of the research team were assigned to independently code each explanation. The results of the coding were our main data set for answering RQ 1 through RQ 4. The mean Cohen's κ across the characteristics the team coded was 0.681. We analyzed participants' responses to reflection questions (RQ 5) separately following an analogous process. The mean Cohen's κ for reflection questions was 0.824.

4   User Study Results

We had 75 participants in our user study. Each participant labeled and explained 20 instances. Thus, our data comprises 1,500 explanations. Participants mentioned 19,749 unique concepts across these 1,500 explanations. As shown in Table 2, each image had between two and nine concepts that were mentioned in at least 20 different participants' explanations for that image.

RQ 1 (Evidence in Explanations) Explanations Connect the Target Concept to Other Concepts. Participants' explanations of why they classified an image as containing a target concept or not often referred to other concepts present in the image. We refer to these other concepts as *auxiliary concepts*. Participants referenced an average of 3.65 auxiliary concepts per explanation. Our coding revealed that 60% of the concepts referenced were concrete concepts visible in the photo, 7% were concrete concepts *not* visible in the photo,

Table 2. A summary of the responses for the twenty images in our study, including the majority of participants' *consensus label* for whether the image depicted the concept. *Frequent concepts* are the number of distinct concepts mentioned by ≥20 participants each, and we note how many of these frequent concepts were visible in the image.

Image	Consensus label	# frequent concepts	% frequent concepts visible
Crossroads-1	Yes	6	100%
Crossroads-2	No	5	60%
Crossroads-3	Yes	6	100%
Crossroads-4	Yes	4	25%
Crossroads-5	Yes	7	100%
Eating-1	Yes	9	88%
Eating-2	Yes	9	88%
Eating-3	Yes	8	100%
Eating-4	No	5	60%
Eating-5	No	8	50%
Nightstand-1	Yes	7	72%
Nightstand-2	Yes	6	100%
Nightstand-3	Yes	7	85%
Nightstand-4	No	6	50%
Nightstand-5	No	5	40%
Old-1	Yes	7	57%
Old-2	Yes	5	60%
Old-3	Yes	8	75%
Old-4	No	6	67%
Old-5	Yes	2	50%

Table 3. Proportion of relationships that were *spatial* or *functional* by target concept.

and 33% were abstract concepts. These three categories impose different requirements for future interfaces and ML algorithms. While current computer-vision systems recognize concrete objects well [16], handling concepts not visible in a photo and abstract concepts requires new methods.

Explanations revealed it was not just the presence or absence of certain concepts, but rather the way they connect that influenced labeling decisions. For example, in the explanation below, the participant identifies specific relationships between concepts that define eating. The mere presence of concepts like food, a table, or people is insufficient.

"There are plates with food on a table with people sitting around it. There are utensils such as a knife and fork on the plates that people use to eat the food with."

Within participants' explanations, we frequently observed target-auxiliary relationships that can be characterized as either spatial or functional relationships. We defined spatial relationships to be those that can be identified by the relative position of pixels in an image, whereas a functional relationship requires a more complex understanding of interactions. As shown in Table 3, 81% of target-auxiliary relationships in participants' explanations were spatial, while the remaining 19% were functional.

We were also interested in how participants connected the concepts to which their explanations referred. Thus, we examined how often participants explicitly used Boolean logic, as well as how many steps their reasoning encoded.

We searched for the use of logical "and" and "or" connectors as evidence of explicit Boolean logic. The use of Boolean logic indicates more complicated reasoning than direct correlations, echoing the types of reasoning work in weakly supervised learning has begun to explore [15]. The following explanation is an example of using Boolean logic in an explanation because the classification decision depends on a logical combination:

"This is not eating. Eating involves someone actively putting food into their mouth and swallowing it."

Few Explanations Contained Explicit Boolean Logic. Roughly 15% of explanations contained explicit Boolean logic. Many explanations, however, appeared to contain Boolean logic implicitly, such as the following example:

"A nightstand is a small table placed beside a bed for people to place items on. So, the small table in the corner is a nightstand."

One might conclude that such an explanation implicitly requires both that there is a small table *and* that the table be located beside a bed *and* that the purpose of the table is for holding items. To accurately characterize our data, we chose not to code such implicit examples as exemplifying Boolean logic. However, implicit examples appeared commonly.

A Fraction of Explanations Employed Multi-step Reasoning. Another metric to characterize the complexity of reasoning is the number of logical jumps made in an explanation. The more steps, the harder it could be for a computer to learn from their explanation. The following explanation contains only one logical step:

"I based my decision on the fact that I saw a bed. Usually a bed has a night stand beside it."

In contrast, the following explanation instead exemplifies two-step reasoning:

"People are sitting at a table with plates of food in front of them. Some of them are holding a fork, indicating they are, or expect to be, eating the food on their plate."

The participant first identifies people at a table, augmenting this with the fact that they can use the forks they have to eat. It is difficult to communicate multi-step reasoning to a computer; relative to simple correlation, it requires greater understanding of entities and their relationships.

Multi-step reasoning was not common in participants' explanations. 53% of explanations used single-step reasoning, directly connecting all evidence (auxiliary concepts) to the target concept. 6% of explanations involved two logical steps, while the remaining 1% included at least three logical steps. Surprisingly, 40% of the explanations never explicitly connected the evidence provided to the target concept. We discuss such ambiguities further below as part of RQ4.

RQ 2 (Explanation Structure) Abstract, Generalized Definitions of Target Concepts Were Common. In addition to, or in place of, evidence from the photo itself, some explanations contained a generalized, abstract definition of the target concept. We termed these *definitional structures*. The following explanation is one such example because it defines the general class "nightstand," rather than commenting directly on specific evidence in a data instance:

"A nightstand is a small table placed beside a bed for people to place items on. So, the small table in the corner is a nightstand."

We found that 26% of explanations included such a definitional structure. The proportion of explanations that included a definitional structure varied across target concepts: 42% of "nightstand" explanations, 28% of "crossroad" explanations, 20% of "eating" explanations, and 11% of "old" explanations contained a definitional structure. This variation suggests that participants may have used definitional structures more frequently for more concrete concepts, such as "nightstand."

Explanations Used an Identify-Explain Structure. Explanations often consisted of two parts. First, participants would identify particular aspects of the photo. They would subsequently explain how those aspects connected to their classification decision. The following explanation is one of the many examples of this structure:

"There are roads in the image. The two roads meet and cross each other. There is a stop sign. There are usually stops signs or traffic lights at a crossroad."

We found that 58% of explanations followed this identify-explain structure. That the majority of explanations did so suggests that future interfaces for eliciting explanations may benefit from explicitly incorporating this two-step process.

Participants Occasionally Described Their Process. Finally, some participants explained the process they used to reach a decision. For example, they would talk about where they first looked or what drew their attention. In total, 18% of explanations, including the example below, did so:

> "Well, I looked to the right and saw a desk. Then I looked to the left and saw a lamp. That is a good sign of a nightstand. Then there were books on it. Definitely a nightstand."

RQ 3 (Inter-participant/Inter-task Variation). We observed differences in explanations across participants and tasks.

Participants Used More Functional Relationships to Explain Eating. Relationships were functional or spatial. As shown in Table 3, participants used a higher proportion of functional relationships when explaining eating classifications (35%) than when explaining classifications for the other three target concepts (9%–16%). We speculate this is because eating is an action, which functional relationships lend themselves to describing.

The Types of Auxiliary Concepts Referenced Varied Based on the Target Concept. As shown in Table 4, participants' explanations contained a comparatively higher proportion of abstract auxiliary concepts when explaining classifications for "old." Notably, "old" itself is an abstract concept. In contrast, "nightstand" is a fairly concrete concept.

We also found that participants referenced concepts not in the photo more frequently for negative instances than for positive instances, as shown in Table 5. This result may seem intuitive since, for negative instances, the target concept itself is not contained in the photo. However, for both positive and negative instances, participants sometimes referred to objects not visible in the photo, which has implications for designing user interfaces for explanatory labeling, which we elaborate on in Sect. 6. Note that we observed two main reasons explanations for negative instances (those not containing the target) nonetheless referenced auxiliary concepts visible in the image. First, participants sometimes pointed out concepts incongruous with the target concept, such as:

> "This is a dining room. There are no nightstands in dining rooms."

Second, participants would point out auxiliary concepts that, in isolation, might be suggestive of the presence of the target concept, and then highlight missing auxiliary concepts or incorrect relationships between concepts. The following is one such example (for a negative instance of "nightstand"):

Table 4. Proportion of *concrete* and *abstract* concepts by target concept.

Target	Type of Concepts
Crossroads	0 10 20 30 40 50 60 70 80 90 100
Eating	0 10 20 30 40 50 60 70 80 90 100
Nightstand	0 10 20 30 40 50 60 70 80 90 100
Old	0 10 20 30 40 50 60 70 80 90 100

■ Concrete Concepts ■ Abstract Concepts

Table 5. Proportion of concepts *visible* for positive ("yes")/negative ("no") instances.

Instance	Visibility of Concepts
Positive	0 10 20 30 40 50 60 70 80 90 100
Negative	0 10 20 30 40 50 60 70 80 90 100

■ Visible ■ Non-visible

"There are tables in the photo, but they are not beside a bed. There are no lamps on the tables. There are objects on the table, but they are kitchen objects."

The Usage of Parts of Speech Differed Across Target Concepts. While computer vision systems are particularly adept at recognizing objects in images [16], we observed many parts of speech in participants' explanations, as shown in Table 6. Summing across all explanations, 58% of unique concepts mentioned were objects (nouns), while 20% were actions (verbs). Attributes (adjectives and adverbs) were much less common than objects; only 14% of concepts were adjectives and only 8% were adverbs, though this may be an artifact of our task involving only static images. The non-negligible inclusion of concepts that were verbs or adjectives reinforces the need to account for other parts of speech when eliciting explanations from users. The usage of concepts of different parts of speech differed by target concept. Even though nouns were used the majority of the time, participants tended to use more words that were of the same part of speech as the target concept. For example, 24% of the auxiliary concepts used in the explanations for "old" were adjectives, while 7%–15% of auxiliary concepts were adjectives for the other three target concepts.

Explanations Varied in Length. The length of explanations ranged widely. While the mean length was 29 words, explanations ranged from a single word to 114 words long. Each participant used between 129 and 1,373 words in total (summed across the 20 instances), with a median of 528 words. Explanation length also varied slightly by target concept. Explanations for *crossroad* were

Table 6. Part-of-speech distribution by target concept.

Concept	Part of Speech
Crossroads	0 10 20 30 40 50 60 70 80 90 100
Eating	0 10 20 30 40 50 60 70 80 90 100
Nightstand	0 10 20 30 40 50 60 70 80 90 100
Old	0 10 20 30 40 50 60 70 80 90 100

Noun Verb Adjective Adverb

shorter than for the other three concepts. Furthermore, participants gave slightly longer explanations for positive instances than for negative instances.

RQ 4 (Ambiguities in Explanations). Explanations sometimes contained ambiguities that would impair algorithms from using them directly. We observed two key ambiguities: not explicitly connecting the explanation to the target concept and using undefined pronouns.

Some Evidence Did Not Connect to the Target Concept. As mentioned earlier, 40% of explanations never explicitly connected the evidence to the target concept. The example below contains potentially important information. However, because it does not explicitly connect to the target concept ("nightstand"), it would be difficult for a machine to use:

"Although this appears to be a hotel room, there is still a small table located between the beds with a lamp on it and a clock."

In contrast, the explanation below did not provide as much information as the one above, but likely would be easier for an algorithm to leverage because the evidence is explicitly connected to the target concept ("crossroad"):

"This is a crossroad. Two streets intersect or cross, making it a crossroad."

Ambiguous Pronouns Were Used Frequently. The other source of ambiguity comes from the use of ambiguous pronouns. About 10% of explanations, including the example below, used ambiguous pronouns. It is difficult to use an explanation when what "this" refers to is unspecified:

"While this is something that can be eaten, there is nobody doing the eating in this image."

RQ 5 (Reflection). Although participants had no objective basis on which to evaluate the quality of their teaching, we were curious how well they felt they did. If a participant feels they have sufficiently taught the computer how

Table 7. Participants' self-reported agreement with the following statement: "I feel I have thoroughly taught the computer to identify whether or not future images similar to the five examples in this study represent *CONCEPT*."

Target	Agreement
Crossroads	0 10 20 30 40 50 60 70 80 90 100
Eating	0 10 20 30 40 50 60 70 80 90 100
Nightstand	0 10 20 30 40 50 60 70 80 90 100
Old	0 10 20 30 40 50 60 70 80 90 100

Strongly agree Agree Neutral Disagree Strongly disagree

to complete a task, the motivation to continue teaching may decline. Across all four concepts, over 50% of participants agreed or strongly agreed that "I feel I have thoroughly taught the computer to identify whether or not future images similar to the five examples in this study represent the *target concept*." Given current and likely future ML data requirements, these judgments are almost certainly highly overconfident. As shown in Table 7, participants were even more confident about classifying photos similar to those in the study despite labeling and explaining only five instances. Participants felt more confident for concrete concepts (e.g., nightstand) than abstract ones.

In our process-reflection questions, 77% of participants reported they would have changed their explanation if justifying their classification to a human, rather than a computer. Notably, 19% of participants said they would check the human's understanding of the concept; P27 said, "I would be able to ask them if they had any questions about it. I could not do that with a computer." Further, 11% of participants wanted more physical input modalities, such as gestures.

5 Experiment on Automated Labeling

Participants in our user study often explained classification labels by relating the target concept to other concepts in the image. Buoyed by our findings, we conducted an experiment to estimate the degree to which inter-concept relationships can be used to automatically apply classification labels.

For instance, if a dataset already labeled by either humans or off-the-shelf object-recognition software does not contain a label for a concept (e.g., "wetsuit"), how helpful would it be if a human explained to the system that images containing "water," a "surfboard," and the color "black" likely contain a "wetsuit?" Currently, humans need to label whether every image in a huge training dataset contains a wetsuit. Using a human-provided explanation like the one above, could most images be automatically and very accurately classified as *not*

containing that concept? If only a few images remain, human labeling effort could be used far more productively.

5.1 Procedure

For each target concept, we automatically constructed a statement in Boolean logic defining that target concept in terms of up to five auxiliary concepts. We simulated automated labeling by applying that logical definition to predict the presence or absence of that target concept in all images in Visual Genome 1.4 [8]. We treated the presence or absence of the target concept's label in Visual Genome's label set for that image as the ground truth classification. To balance precision and recall, we used the F_1 score as our metric. F_1 is the harmonic mean between precision and recall. If our target concept is "wetsuit," the precision is the percentage of photos we label as containing a wetsuit that actually contain a wetsuit. Recall is the percentage of all photos that contain a wetsuit that we label as containing a wetsuit.

We first investigated this approach by defining the four target concepts from our user study based on the evidence participants provided. In particular, we used the five auxiliary concepts most frequently included in participants' explanations. However, this study only investigated a small number of concepts. To benchmark this conceptual approach more broadly, we also automatically constructed definitions for all 2,243 target concepts that appear at least 100 times in Visual Genome. For each, we selected the five concepts from among those that often co-occur with the target and that had the highest F_1 scores when individually defining the target concept.

We then constructed all possible logical combinations of the five auxiliary concepts, including those that exclude some of the five. We chose the definition with the highest F_1 score and used it in all further analyses. For example, the auxiliary concepts for "watch" were "wrist," "shirt," "wear," "play," and "man," leading to the following definition: *(play | wrist) & (wrist | man) & (shirt | man | wear)*. This definition alone had $F_1 = 0.34$ classifying "watch" in Visual Genome without any further human labeling. To simulate labeling negative instances (the bulk of any dataset), we labeled all images containing *none* of the auxiliary concepts as negative instances.

Synonyms can affect data accuracy by causing one to wrongly believe an image of a dog to not contain a dog because it contains the synonymous label "canine," but not "dog." To partially account for this, we treated co-occurrence in a WordNet [13] synset as a match. Nonetheless, we manually observed that we may *underestimate* labeling success, such as some nightstand images being labeled "table," but not "nightstand," despite the two not being synonyms.

5.2 Results

We first present results of applying our approach to "nightstand," "eating," "crossroads," and "old" using the explanatory data collected in our user study.

We then simulate this approach for all 2,243 target concepts that appeared frequently in Visual Genome.

Definitions Relating Target to Auxiliary Concepts Can, with Minimal Human Effort, Partially Label Images. Using the auxiliary concepts study participants most frequently referenced for "nightstand," the definition *lamp & bed* could be used to label nightstands in Visual Genome with $F_1 = 0.48$ (0.37 precision, 0.69 recall). While insufficient for immediate ML use, minimal human labeling could make it sufficient. Without this definition, a human would have needed to apply "nightstand" labels to all 108,077 Visual Genome images. In contrast, this simple definition suggested there were nightstands in 873 images, 322 of which actually contained a nightstand. Labeling all images that contained neither "lamp" nor "bed" as negative instances would result in 102,167 true negatives (those without a nightstand) and only 8 false negatives. This automated method left 5,902 images unlabeled, of which 142 contained a nightstand.

If humans manually corrected the labels of the 873 images the automated method classified as having a "nightstand," it would leave 322 true positives, 102,718 true negatives, and 8 false negatives ($F_1 = 0.99$ on 103,048 images). That said, it would exclude the 5,902 images that contain either a "lamp" or a "bed," and these images might represent particularly helpful training data as potential boundary cases.

"Nightstand" was the most concrete of the four concepts, and thus easiest to define. Study participants were more likely to write definitional structures for "nightstand" than the others. In line with this finding, automated labeling of the other three target concepts from the user study yielded worse results, yet still showed some promise. "Eat" (substituted for "eating," which Visual Genome synsets lacked) was automatically defined as *(person & food) | (plate & table) | (plate & mouth) | (food & mouth) | (table & mouth)*; $F_1 = 0.15$. "Intersection" (substituted for "crossroads") was defined as *(road & stop & street) | (road & direction & sign) | (road & sign & street) | (stop & sign & street)*; $F_1 = 0.15$. The definition for "old" was *look | boat | picture* ($F_1 = 0.08$), overfitting to an image of an old boat from the user study (see Table 1) (Table 8).

We then applied the same method to all 2,243 target concepts that appear at least 100 times in Visual Genome 1.4. This allowed us to simulate the technique more broadly.

This Approach Generalizes to Many Concepts. Overall, we found 29% of these 2,243 target concepts could be classified with $F_1 \geq 0.25$, while 4.9% could be classified with $F_1 \geq 0.5$. Figure 1 shows the full distribution of F_1 scores.

Many targets were defined in terms of auxiliary concepts that make intuitive sense, suggesting humans would likely have volunteered similar ones. For example, "bride" was defined as *groom | bridal gown* with $F_1 = 0.81$. "Melted" was defined as *cheese & (crust | burned)* with $F_1 = 0.47$.

Some of the most effective definitions were very succinct:

- *sofa | bed | headboard* ⇒ "pillow" ($F_1 = 0.64$)
- *beach* ⇒ "sand" ($F_1 = 0.61$)

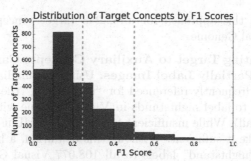

Fig. 1. Histogram of F_1 score ranges (e.g., the leftmost is 0.0–0.1) for the 2,243 target concepts that appeared in ≥ 100 Visual Genome images.

Table 8. Comparison of definitions for the four target concepts generated from the results of the user study and simulated labeling.

Concept	Source	Most accurate definition	F1 score
Nightstand	User study	lamp & bed	0.48
	Simulated	(quilt & bedroom) | (headboard & bed) | (bedspread & bedroom)	0.42
Eat	User study	(person & food) | (plate & table) | (plate & mouth) | (food & mouth) | (table & mouth)	0.15
	Simulated	giraffe | zebra | crop	0.29
Intersection	User study	(road & stop & street) | (road & direction & sign) | (road & sign & street) | (stop & sign & street)	0.11
	Simulated	(crossing | stopped) & (trafficlight | traffic | crossing) & (trafficlight | traffic | signal | stopped)	0.19
Old	User study	look | boat | picture	0.08
	Simulated	(rusty | building | brick) & (rusty | brick | wooden) & (rusty | building | window | wooden) & (building | brick | window | wooden)	0.16

– *cheese \| pepperoni \| crust* $\Rightarrow$ "pizza" ($F_1 = 0.60$)
– *feather \| beak* $\Rightarrow$ "bird" ($F_1 = 0.55$).

Many of the target concepts with low F_1 scores were relatively abstract. In particular, based on Visual Genome's categorization of labels, F_1 scores for objects were higher than those for attributes or relationships. In total, 37% of objects could be classified with $F_1 \geq 0.25$, and 6.5% with $F_1 \geq 0.50$.

Automatic Classifications of Negative Instances Were Highly Accurate. We labeled images to be negative instances if they contained *none* of the auxiliary concepts in the automatically generated definition. This heuristic proved ≥95% accurate for 98.8% of the 2,243 target concepts. Furthermore, it was ≥90% accurate for 99.6% of target concepts.

6   Conclusions and Discussion

In a user study, we elicited and characterized 75 humans' free-text explanations of data labels for the type of image-classification tasks used in supervised learning. Through a follow-up simulation experiment on the Visual Genome dataset, we showed how the types of explanatory information we observed can underpin semi-automated labeling of large datasets for hundreds of concepts. Our protocol, including publicly releasing our anonymized dataset, was approved by our IRB. Participants opted into this data release.

6.1   Design Implications and Future Work

Our simulation results showed the initial promise of semi-automated labeling based on relating a target to auxiliary concepts. Besides evaluating the performance of this method on more training sets, building and testing interfaces for eliciting such definitions is key future work. Many participants in the user study defined the target concept abstractly before referencing the image, which suggests that interfaces could empower users to do so without specific examples. Breaking down teaching into multiple steps is supported by prior work in machine teaching [18]. Specific data instances could then help communicate to users the system's current understanding of a concept, as in Revolt [5]. These interfaces could be compared against others grounded in specific instances, which sometimes overfit (e.g., the "old" boat).

Nonetheless, the tendency for participants' explanations to logically combine evidence implicitly, rather than explicitly, highlights the need for designing interactions or interfaces that elicit such logic explicitly. Inspired by visual programming, one could imagine an interface that lets users "wire" concepts together to indicate these connections.

Recent work has sought to improve classifiers by applying NLP techniques to free-text explanations of labels, finding some success even without an HCI focus [6]. That work focused on text classification, not image classification. Nevertheless, our findings suggest best practices for designing user interfaces to minimize ambiguities when capturing text-based explanations. Many of participants' explanations contained ambiguous pronouns. An interface could automatically detect them and guide the user in clarifying any pronouns they used. Participants also often neglected to directly connect the evidence they presented to the target concept, which a multi-step interaction may be able to correct.

Other work has proposed letting humans define computational functions to automatically label training data [15]. This approach might be unnecessary for

labeling concrete objects, given the lack of multi-step reasoning and Boolean logic observed in the user study, as well as the simple, succinct, and accurate definitions that emerged from our Visual Genome simulation experiment. Future work could investigate the usability of such an approach, which may enable definitions of abstract concepts (e.g., "old") our experiments struggled with.

We grounded our task in explanations to "a computer" as we felt that would best capture typical data labeling processes. While we asked participants to speculate and self-report how they would have changed their explanations if they had been teaching a human, we could also run a study where they actually taught a human. This future work could give insight into how particpants might unwittingly change their explanations when teaching a computer. It could also highlight techniques that are used when teaching another person that could be simulated by a dynamic interface.

Lastly, future work could investigate input modalities. Based on the identify-explain process, users could point at important parts of an image, then connect each to the target.

6.2 Limitations

Study participants were an unrepresentative convenience sample recruited on Amazon's Mechanical Turk, limiting generalizability. A timing minimum different from the 60 s we used may have elicited different explanations. Further, we collected rich human-subjects data in our user study, but only for a small number of target concepts. Due to the small number of target concepts and small number of instances tested per concept, our findings may not generalize to different concepts or instances. Explanations may have been different for different concepts. Exploring explanations for a different group of concepts could be an avenue for future work. We partially address this limited generalizability by conducting a simulated experiment on 2,243 Visual Genome concepts.

References

1. Amershi, S., Cakmak, M., Knox, W.B., Kulesza, T.: Power to the people: the role of humans in interactive machine learning. In: Proceedings of AAAI (2014)
2. Amershi, S., Fogarty, J., Kapoor, A., Tan, D.: Effective end-user interaction with machine learning. In: Proceedings of AAAI (2011)
3. Brooks, M., Amershi, S., Lee, B., Drucker, S.M., Kapoor, A., Simard, P.: FeatureInsight: visual support for error-driven feature ideation in text classification. In: Proceedings of VAST (2015)
4. Buhrmester, M., Kwang, T., Gosling, S.D.: Amazon's Mechanical Turk: a new source of inexpensive, yet high-quality, data? Perspect. Psychol. Sci. 6, 3–5 (2011)
5. Chang, J.C., Amershi, S., Kamar, E.: Revolt: collaborative crowdsourcing for labeling machine learning datasets. In: Proceedings of CHI (2017)
6. Hancock, B., Varma, P., Wang, S., Bringmann, M., Liang, P., Ré, C.: Training classifiers with natural language explanations. In: Proceedings of ACL (2018)
7. He, K., Zhang, X., Ren, S., Sun, J.: Deep residual learning for image recognition. In: Proceedings of CVPR (2016)

8. Krishna, R., et al.: Visual genome: connecting language and vision using crowd-sourced dense image annotations. Int. J. Comput. Vis. **123**, 32–73 (2016)
9. Kulesza, T., Amershi, S., Caruana, R., Fisher, D., Charles, D.: Structured labeling to facilitate concept evolution in machine learning. In: Proceedings of CHI (2014)
10. Kulesza, T., Burnett, M., Wong, W.K., Stumpf, S.: Principles of explanatory debugging to personalize interactive machine learning. In: Proceedings of IUI (2015)
11. Lake, B.M., Ullman, T.D., Tenenbaum, J.B., Gershman, S.J.: Building machines that learn and think like people. In: Proceedings of Behavioral and Brain Sciences (2016)
12. Laput, G., Lasecki, W.S., Wiese, J., Xiao, R., Bigham, J.P., Harrison, C.: Zensors: adaptive, rapidly deployable, human-intelligent sensor feeds. In: Proceedings of CHI (2015)
13. Miller, G.A.: WordNet: a lexical database for English. Commun. ACM **38**, 39–41 (1995)
14. Park, D.H., Hendricks, L.A., Akata, Z., Schiele, B., Darrell, T., Rohrbach, M.: Attentive explanations: justifying decisions and pointing to the evidence. arXiv:1612.04757 (2016)
15. Ratner, A., Bach, S.H., Ehrenberg, H., Fries, J., Wu, S., Ré, C.: Snorkel: rapid training data creation with weak supervision. Proc. VLDB **11**(3), 269–282 (2017)
16. Ren, S., He, K., Girshick, R., Sun, J.: Faster R-CNN: towards real-time object detection with region proposal networks. In: Proceedings of NIPS (2015)
17. Saon, G., Kuo, H.K.J., Rennie, S., Picheny, M.: The IBM 2015 English conversational telephone speech recognition system. arXiv:1505.05899 (2015)
18. Simard, P.Y., et al.: Machine teaching: a new paradigm for building machine learning systems. arXiv:1707.06742 (2017)
19. Stumpf, S., et al.: Toward harnessing user feedback for machine learning. In: Proceedings of IUI (2007)
20. Stumpf, S., et al.: Interacting meaningfully with machine learning systems: three experiments. Int. J. Hum.-Comput. Stud. **67**, 639–662 (2009)
21. Wang, M., Lu, Z., Zhou, J., Liu, Q.: Deep neural machine translation with linear associative unit. arXiv:1705.00861 (2017)

How Do Users Perceive a Design-in-Use Approach to Implementation? A Healthcare Case

Morten Hertzum[1](✉) ⓘ and Arnvør Torkilsheyggi[2]

[1] University of Copenhagen, Copenhagen, Denmark
hertzum@hum.ku.dk
[2] Roskilde University, Roskilde, Denmark

Abstract. The implementation of information systems in organizational settings is a protracted process that includes the mutual adaptation of system and organization to each other after the system has gone live. We investigate a design-in-use approach to this implementation process. Rather than a centrally run implementation process with preset goals, the management in the studied hospital tasked the individual departments with exploring and embracing the possibilities afforded by a network of interconnected electronic whiteboards. The responsibility for driving this process was assigned to local super users in the departments. On the basis of interviews with 17 clinicians we find that (a) they perceive the design-in-use approach in conflicting ways, (b) the super users are more positive about the approach than the end-users, (c) standardization across departments conflicts with design in use within departments, (d) intradepartmental change is perceived more positively, (e) the design-in-use process is inextricably sociotechnical, and (f) the clinicians' perception of design in use is more about implementing change than about preparing it or about training and support. The conflicting perceptions of the design-in-use approach, for example, include whether it gained momentum, met local needs, and made for an engaging process. We discuss the implications of our findings for a design-in-use approach to implementation.

Keywords: Design in use · Organizational implementation · Healthcare

1 Introduction

The implementation of a new information system in an organization temporarily disturbs work and normally leads to a productivity dip in the period following go-live [26, 35]. While a quick return to baseline productivity suggests a well-executed implementation process, it also incurs the risk that work practices with the new system congeal too quickly. If so, the organization will not reap the full benefit of the new system [44]. To reap the full benefit it is necessary for the organization to experiment with the possibilities afforded by the system and to seize the opportunities that emerge from this experimentation [38]. Such a process requires that the users are prepared to prolong the period in which work practices are fluid in order to spend time exploring

© IFIP International Federation for Information Processing 2019
Published by Springer Nature Switzerland AG 2019
D. Lamas et al. (Eds.): INTERACT 2019, LNCS 11748, pp. 410–430, 2019.
https://doi.org/10.1007/978-3-030-29387-1_23

what new ways of working the system affords. That is, it requires that the users are prepared to engage in a design-in-use process. We investigate this preparedness.

The empirical setting for our investigation is the organization-wide implementation of a network of interconnected electronic whiteboards for intra- and interdepartmental coordination at a hospital. Management in the studied hospital took a design-in-use approach to implementation. Rather than a centrally run implementation process that stipulated up front how to use the whiteboard, management tasked the individual departments with exploring and embracing the possibilities afforded by the whiteboard. This design-in-use approach to implementation signaled a commitment to reaping benefit from the whiteboard, even if it meant prolonging the implementation process. However, it also meant that successful implementation became dependent on the users' preparedness to design their use of the whiteboard rather than simply use it according to preset procedures. Specifically, the group of super users was assigned a key role as drivers of the local implementation process. We interviewed 17 clinicians about their thoughts on the implementation process. On that basis we seek to answer two research questions:

- *How do the users perceive the design-in-use approach to implementation?* To answer this question we make a content analysis of the interviewees' statements and catalog the opportunities and barriers they mention.
- *Do the users' perceptions vary across user groups?* The answer to this supplementary question consists of comparing the distribution of the content categories for super users and end-users and for physicians and nurses.

In the following we review related work, account for our method of data collection and analysis, present the results of the study, and discuss their implications.

2   Related Work

Research on design in use aims to capture "practices of interpretation, appropriation, assembly, tailoring and further development of computer support in what is normally regarded as deployment or use" [9, p. 125]. This definition suggests that design in use is a fairly informal and largely user-driven set of practices. However, the definition also implies a permeable boundary between design in use and the more planned and management-initiated activities of system implementation.

2.1   Design in Use

Orlikowski [28] shows that the implementation of information systems is only a partially planned process. While part of the process can, and should, be planned in advance and executed as planned, other parts emerge in unplanned ways during use and become visible only in retrospect. These emergent parts of implementation present and deny opportunities that may be pursued in additional, opportunity-based efforts to obtain benefit from a system or may call for revising plans to avoid adverse side effects

[14, 29]. As a result, the implementation process continues over an extended period of time; it is not restricted to the first few weeks after a system has gone live. Design-in-use research embraces this continuation by contending that go-live does not mark a shift from design to use [1, 5, 8, 10, 12, 16, 18, 19, 24, 41, 42]. Rather, design continues into use in the sense that users design, as opposed to merely adopt, their ways of working with a new system. The continued design activities are informed by the users' experiences from using the system for real work and may involve configuring the system as well as adjusting work practices.

The boundary between design in use and system implementation depends largely on the extent to which design in use proceeds as an informal process among peers or has become a more formalized process with organizationally defined roles and responsibilities. Organizational structures for deciding and coordinating which changes to pursue become increasingly needed with systems that are still more configurable and thereby make it possible to pursue a still wider range of changes [8]. With increasing managerial support design in use increasingly becomes an approach to systems implementation. We distinguish three broad classes of design-in-use processes with respect to managerial support.

First, multiple studies have investigated design in use as it unfolded in situations with no formal organizational support. For example, Mackay [20] studied how customizations were shared among the users of an application package. While most users made some customizations to adapt the package to their needs and desires, a small group of users spent considerable time making customizations and became adept at it. The members of this group became the go-to persons when their colleagues had questions about customization; furthermore, the group members started to share useful customizations. Although this sharing was widespread "few of the managers were aware that customization files were being exchanged and none were aware of the extent of sharing" [20, p. 219]. Thus, these design-in-use activities took place without organizational support. Relatedly, Park et al. [30] analyzed how doctors started making notes on pieces of paper when an electronic medication record required them to remember information they gathered at the bedside until they later visited the charting room to enter it in the electronic record. This apparently mundane example of design in use remained organizationally unrecognized until it was realized that the notes necessitated further design in use because they contained sensitive patient information and, therefore, had to be discarded in a secure manner.

Second, design in use has been studied in settings with organizational support for the users' tailoring activities. In several of these cases design in use started as an informal activity performed by technically minded individuals for personal purposes and only gradually received organizational recognition and support [e.g., 31, 39, 42]. While many of these design-in-use activities have produced valued extensions to base functionality, others have salvaged the base functionality by contributing "the work to make IT work" [7, p. 296]. Multiple studies find that the available organizational support for design-in-use activities tends to be inadequate. For example, Dittrich et al. [9] conclude that a better infrastructure for supporting design in use is necessary to achieve the vision declared for the studied municipal website. They base this conclusion on the uneven availability of developer support for design-in-use activities combined with the high organizational value of the templates developed by a user who had access to support. At

the same time, Spencer [39] documents user frustration with the organizational practices introduced to support design in use. The source of the frustration was that the practices were bureaucratic and prioritized long-term evolution over here-and-now changes. The kind of support emphasized by these authors is technical. In contrast, Hartswood et al. [11] point to a need for support in devising, or repairing, the work processes that surround new systems. In their study the evolving use of a speech-recognition system shifted additional workload to the secretaries, who had to handle speech-recognition errors left uncorrected by the clinicians. After the secretaries raised this problem, the ward instituted a work procedure where the secretaries returned letters with uncorrected errors to the clinicians. This procedure regulated the collaborative use of the opportunities afforded by the system and rebalanced the workload.

Third, design in use may be the planned approach to implementation. In their review of the factors critical to implementation success, Nah et al. [25] emphasize issues such as exploiting the best practices offered by the system, fitting work practices to the system to minimize the need for customizations, and championing the system to manage resistance. These issues are largely directed at realizing the benefits that were planned ahead of go-live. An exclusive focus on planned change has been criticized by Orlikowski and Hofman [29], who instead emphasize the importance of identifying and embracing emergent change. As a result, design in use is central to their approach to improvisational change management. Design in use serves the double purpose of responding to local circumstances in a manner that pursues planned ends and seizes the opportunities provided by emergent change [14]. To fulfill this purpose Markus [21] stresses the importance of troubleshooting and shakedown in the period immediately after go-live; Karasti et al. [16] show the need to sustain design-in-use processes for years or even decades; Yetim et al. [45] propose to extend systems with an embedded tool for collecting design-in-use ideas; and Hertzum and Simonsen [15] catalog the competences needed locally to be able to configure systems and work practices for each other.

2.2   Perceptions of Design in Use

Users expect that their systems can be tailored to their needs, but to exploit the possibilities afforded by a system local practices must also be adapted to the system [3, 4]. Both components of this mutual adaptation of system and practices to each other are candidates for design in use but they may be perceived differently. Users tend to appreciate design in use – by embracing it themselves or valuing their colleagues' design-in-use efforts – when systems are adapted to local needs and it is voluntary whether to adopt the adaptations [20, 42]. When design in use is integral to the planned approach to implementation and, thereby, at least partially mandatory then the perception of design in use becomes dependent on the available support [1, 34]. For example, Åsand and Mørch [46] find that end-users mostly prefer to receive support from super users with local and domain knowledge, rather than from technical IT staff. Other studies identify a need for support from allies with the organizational power to ensure that local design-in-use solutions are

spread and adopted in the organization [27, 41]. However, the main issue with respect to support is, probably, that the available support is often perceived as insufficient and, thereby, as constraining the possibilities for design in use [e.g., 8, 11, 24].

Several studies report tensions that affect the users' perception of design in use negatively. For example, Karasti et al. [16] report that the users struggled to maintain a focus on evolving the system in accordance with their long-term needs because the developers who supported design in use had a shorter temporal perspective. Torkil-sheyggi and Hertzum [41] report a tension between management's expectations to the design-in-use process and the goals pursued in the local design-in-use efforts. This tension was aggravated by simultaneous, but uncoordinated, evolution in management expectations and locally pursued goals. In contrast, other studies report from design-in-use processes that were positively perceived and led to recognized improvements in local practices. For example, the Norwegian rehabilitation hospital Sunnaas has implemented and evolved videoconferencing through a deliberate design-in-use pro-cess that has spanned two decades [1]. This process has, among other things, intro-duced follow-up consultations in which the patients participate from their home via videoconference. In Germany, the POLITeam project improved the process of vote preparation [32]. The improvement opportunity was, however, not planned ahead but realized "rather accidentally" [32, p. 207] after the system had been in use for several months and, then, led to a redesign of the workflow. At a Dutch hospital a new computerized physician order entry system succeeded because the nurses, unexpect-edly, adopted the system to document nursing care [2]. When it became apparent that the physicians – the originally intended users of the system – would not adopt it, the system was revised to accommodate its new users and the workflow was revised by allowing the physicians to authorize orders by signing printouts from the system.

Mehandjiev et al. [22] investigated how end-user development (EUD) was per-ceived by EUD researchers, IT managers, and end-users. EUD comprises the tools and activities that seek to "enable non-software specialists to develop nontrivial software artefacts to support their work" [22, p. 371]. It, thus, constitutes an approach to the technical component of design in use. In terms of advantages the participants perceived that EUD could speed up software development, make users more efficient in their main job tasks, make users' work more interesting, and increase the agility of orga-nizations in responding to external market pressures. The perceived risks included that the users might not be motivated, that the learning curve might be too steep, and that the developed software might be low quality. With respect to quality, it has been found that errors are prevalent in EUD software [33] and that end-users are often overcon-fident in the correctness of their software [17]. Mehandjiev et al. [22] propose that EUD software should be audited by professional developers to bolster quality, but they also recognize that auditing is somewhat at odds with EUD, which stimulates an informal process. Relatedly, Mørch and Andersen [24] present a process of mutual development, in which end-users and professional developers collaborate on making changes after go-live. Through this mutual process the development organization gets customer input for relevant changes and the end-users get more advanced changes than they would be able to develop on their own.

3   Method

This study was based on interviews. Prior to the interviews the study was approved by hospital management. The interviewees individually consented to take part.

3.1   Setting

The study setting was a hospital in Region Zealand, one of the five healthcare regions in Denmark. The hospital had 250 beds and about 35,000 annual admissions. We have been following the implementation and use of the network of electronic whiteboards at the hospital since the first whiteboards were introduced in the emergency department in 2009 [36]. Because the whiteboard was a success in the emergency department [13] it was introduced on all departments in the hospital in December 2012. The overall purpose of the whiteboard was to support coordination in and among the departments by sharing information about the status and flow of the patients and by providing at-a-glance access to selected information from the electronic patient record. However, management adopted a design-in-use approach in the hospital-wide implementation of the whiteboard [41]. That is, the individual department was tasked with exploring and embracing the specific possibilities afforded by the whiteboard in the department. To drive this process of configuring the whiteboard and the clinical work for each other, super users were appointed in each department. The whiteboard was accessible on all computers and permanently shown on large wall-mounted displays, see Fig. 1. It gave one row of information for each patient. This information might, for example, include time of arrival, name, room, responsible physician, status of laboratory tests, and a transfer checklist.

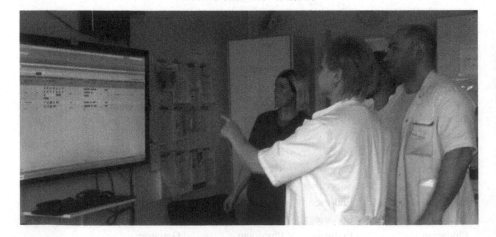

Fig. 1. Clinicians meeting by the whiteboard.

Configuring the whiteboard for a department involved defining views that showed different subsets of the patients, choosing the fields of information to appear in each

view, and facilitating the incorporation of the views in the clinicians' work practices. A prominent example of an outcome of the design-in-use process was the reorganization of the communication between the general wards and the team of physiotherapists. This interdepartmental change started by the physiotherapists' decision to require that physiotherapy was ordered on the whiteboard to improve their possibilities for planning their work. Physiotherapy had previously been ordered on the phone or face to face. The general-ward nurses were, instead, to write the orders in the notes field on the whiteboard in their department; the team of physiotherapists would monitor the corresponding field on their whiteboard. To enforce the change the physiotherapists subsequently stopped attending the morning meetings at the general wards because the general-ward nurses continued to make face-to-face orders during these meetings. Gradually, the physiotherapists also began to provide their conclusions from completed physiotherapy as notes on the whiteboard because these notes were noticed immediately on the general wards, whereas notes in the electronic patient record were often not.

3.2 Interviewees

Because we were interested in the clinicians' perception of the design-in-use process we chose interviews as our method of data collection. We interviewed 17 super users, end-users, and local managers, see Table 1. All interviewees were clinicians directly involved in the day-to-day performance of the work supported by the whiteboard. Thus, all of them had experienced the implementation process first hand. The interviewees represented eight of the hospital's ten clinical departments and mostly consisted of physicians and nurses, but other professional groups were also included.

Table 1. The interviewees.

Job title	Role	Professional group	Department
Healthcare assistant	Super user	Healthcare assistant	Geriatric
Deputy manager	Super user	Nurse	Gynecological and Obstetrical
Midwife	Super user	Midwife	Gynecological and Obstetrical
Physician	Super user	Physician	Medical
Nurse	Super user	Nurse	Medical
Head of department	Super user	Physician	Orthopedic Surgical
Nurse	Super user	Nurse	Pediatric
Secretary	Super user	Secretary	Pediatric
Physiotherapist	Super user	Therapist	Rheumatology
Occupational therapist	Super user	Therapist	Rheumatology
Chief physician	End-user	Physician	Emergency
Nurse	End-user	Nurse	Emergency
Physician	End-user	Physician	Geriatric
Deputy manager	End-user	Nurse	Orthopedic Surgical
Chief physician	End-user	Physician	Surgical
Head of department	Management	Physician	Gynecological and Obstetrical
Head nurse	Management	Nurse	Surgical

3.3   Procedure

The interviews were conducted in the fall of 2014, one and a half years after the whiteboard was introduced in all departments at the hospital. Thus, the interviewees' perceptions of the design-in-use approach to implementation were based on substantial experience. In addition, the design-in-use process was still ongoing and thereby present to mind for the interviewees. The interviewees were identified in collaboration with the system administrator for the whiteboard. He received a description of our study with a request to interview clinicians distributed across departments, staff groups, and roles in relation to the whiteboard.

After identifying the interviewees we initially contacted them by email. To give the interviewees a sense of the interview topics, the email included the guiding questions for the interview: (a) How do you, in your department, use the whiteboard, and for what? (b) How have you worked with configuring the whiteboard and incorporating it in your workflows? (c) What do you see as the biggest challenges in getting everybody in the department to use the whiteboard? (d) To what extent do you experience that the whiteboard, in its present configuration, supports intra- and interdepartmental coordination? (e) What would it take for the whiteboard to support intra- and interdepartmental coordination better? These questions covered the implementation process and the resulting use of the whiteboard from multiple angles, thereby adding nuance to the interviewees' thoughts on the design-in-use approach to implementation. The interviews lasted an average of 52 minutes.

3.4   Data Analysis

The data analysis involved four steps. First, we transcribed the 17 interviews verbatim from the audio recordings. Second, we read through the transcripts and identified all segments in which the interviewees made expressions about how they perceived the design-in-use approach to implementation. This step resulted in the identification of 433 segments. To maintain the context of the segments we marked them up in the transcripts rather than extracted them from the transcripts. Third, we coded the segments with respect to the six classifications in Table 2. For the classifications of valence, object, stage, and scope each segment was coded with one of the classification categories or with 'other' if none of the categories matched the content of the segment. For the classifications of opportunities and barriers we chose against preset categories and, instead, descriptively annotated the segments that expressed opportunities or barriers. This process produced 143 annotations about opportunities and 224 annotations about barriers. Fourth, we established categories of opportunities and barriers in a bottom-up manner by grouping annotations with similar content. The three last steps of the data analysis were completed by the first author alone. Thus, we cannot provide measures of inter-rater agreement.

We coded the valence of the segments to get a direct indication of the extent to which the interviewees were positive or negative toward the design-in-use approach to implementation. The balance between positive and negative valence is important to any assessment of how users perceive design in use. The rationale for the object classification was the sociotechnical nature of design-in-use processes. This classification

distinguished between information technology and work processes, while also allowing for their combined presence. The stage classification concerned how far the design-in-use process had progressed from preparing change, through implementing it, to training and support in a change that was already in place. At the studied hospital it was new that the super users became responsible for preparing and implementing change; they had long been tasked with training and supporting their colleagues. The scope classification distinguished between intra- and interdepartmental change. We included this classification because users might have the knowledge and network necessary to make them comfortable with devising change internal to their department but lack the knowledge, network or inclination to engage in the increased complexity of interdepartmental change. Finally, we included the classifications of opportunities and barriers to catalog the features that the users perceived as positive and negative, respectively, about the design-in-use approach.

Table 2. Classification categories.

Classification	Category	Description
Valence	Positive	In favor of a design-in-use approach to implementation
	Negative	Against a design-in-use approach to implementation
	Neutral	Neither for nor against a design-in-use approach
Object	Information technology	Technological aspects, such as system configuration
	Work process	Socio-organizational aspects, such as new procedures
	Both	Information system and work process combined
Stage	Preparing change	Analyzing situation, devising solution, planning change
	Implementing change	Configuring system, revising processes, motivating use
	Training and support	Scheduled learning sessions and in-situ consultation
Scope	Intradepartmental	Changes within a single department
	Interdepartmental	Changes in the collaboration among departments
	Both	Changes within and among departments
Opportunities		Positive features of a design-in-use approach
Barriers		Negative features of a design-in-use approach

4   Results

In the following we first analyze the valence, object, stage, and scope classifications, then the opportunities and barriers, and finally variations across user groups. Sections 4.1 and 4.2 address the first research question, Sect. 4.3 the second.

4.1 Perception of the Design-in-Use Approach to Implementation

Table 3 shows the distribution of the clinicians' 433 comments across the categories of the valence, object, stage, and scope classifications. With respect to *valence* the clinicians made a substantial number of positive comments about the design-in-use approach to implementation as well as a substantial number of negative comments. The positive comments included: *"I think it is wildly visionary to roll out [the whiteboard] across the entire hospital"*, *"It is super fast to configure the whiteboard"*, and *"It has changed our work processes ... In all sorts of ways."* In contrast, the negative comments included: *"We do not need to design an IT system, we need to get an IT system"*, *"It is cumbersome and slow to get anything done and approved"*, and *"There were all those possibilities for tailoring it yourself and every department was allowed to do that. It ended in a mess."* Overall, there were slightly more negative (48%) than positive (40%) comments, and few neutral (12%). The low number of neutral comments might, in part, reflect that several of our interview questions asked the clinicians about their views on the design-in-use process, rather than merely asked them to describe it. However, it also reflected that the clinicians had opinions about many aspects of the process and therefore mostly talked about it in non-neutral terms.

Table 3. Perception of the design-in-use approach to implementation, $N = 433$ comments.

Classification	Category	Valence			Total	Percent
		Pos.	Neg.	Neu.		
Valence	Positive	174	0	0	174	40
	Negative	0	209	0	209	48
	Neutral	0	0	50	50	12
Object	Information technology	61	99	15	175	40
	Work process	24	38	15	77	18
	Both	89	72	20	181	42
Stage	Preparing change	43	86	14	143	33
	Implementing change	111	99	19	229	53
	Training and support	19	20	17	56	13
	Other	1	4	0	5	1
Scope	Intradepartmental	82	59	26	167	39
	Interdepartmental	65	60	11	136	31
	Both	27	90	13	130	30

With respect to the *object* classification it was evident that the clinicians' perception of the design-in-use process revolved around the whiteboard technology: 40% of the comments concerned the technology and another 42% the combination of technology and work processes. Only 18% of the comments were exclusively about work processes. That is, the clinicians tended to think of the changes in terms of the whiteboard because it triggered the changes or made them possible. For example, the physiotherapists' improved possibilities for planning their work was thought of in terms of the

decision to use the whiteboard for ordering physiotherapy because the improved planning possibilities was contingent on this use of the whiteboard. Notably, the categories of the object classification contained different proportions of negative comments. While 57% of the comments about technology were negative, only 40% of the comments about the combination of technology and work processes were negative. Comments about the technology tended to concern its limitations, while comments about the combination of technology and work processes more often were about how the design-in-use process led to constructive use of the whiteboard.

The *stage* classification showed that the clinicians mostly perceived the design-in-use process as implementing change (53%). Implementing change was the stage at which the design-in-use process influenced the clinical work directly by requiring the clinicians to change their ways of working. That is, implementing change involved the super users, who were driving the change, as well as the end-users, who were to adopt it. In contrast, the stages of preparing change (33%) and training and support (13%) were somewhat removed from the clinical work. As much as 60% (86 of 143) of the comments about preparing change were negative. For example, one end-user stated that *"We do not need more information on the whiteboard"*, thereby indicating that preparing change was superfluous. The proportion of negative comments was lower for implementing change (43%) and for training and support (36%).

With respect to the *scope* classification the design-in-use process was fairly evenly distributed across intradepartmental (39%), interdepartmental (31%), and combined (30%) change. Intradepartmental changes involved fewer clinicians with better opportunities for informally discussing design-in-use ideas because they routinely met during their shifts. Conversely, interdepartmental changes were more organizationally complex to achieve but resulted in some of the most valued changes. For example, the coordination of when patients were ready for surgery became more transparent after the ready-for-surgery checklist was moved to the whiteboard. A super user explained:

> There are seven things that must be satisfied: Is the patient wearing a wristband [with a barcode]? Is the patient fasting? Has a surgeon been down to see the patient? You can follow the progress. And when they have seven out of seven [checklist items ticked off] then they can be picked up. I think it works well.

By moving the checklist from paper to the whiteboard the patients' progress toward satisfying all seven checklist items was no longer just available to the general ward that filled out the checklist but also to the surgical ward that was to receive the patient. This improved the possibilities for planning at the surgical ward. The relative simplicity of intradepartmental change was reflected in a high proportion of positive comments (49%), whereas the higher complexity of the changes that involved both intra- and interdepartmental change resulted in 69% negative comments.

4.2 Opportunities and Barriers

The clinicians experienced 15 different opportunities in the design-in-use process and 16 different barriers to it, see Tables 4 and 5. A key finding from the analysis of opportunities and barriers was that the clinicians disagreed substantially. For example, 18 comments described how the design-in-use process gained momentum from early

successes and external events (Opportunity 1, Table 4) but, at the same time, 20 comments stated that the design-in-use process lacked momentum (Barrier 4, Table 5). In total, 54% of the 143 opportunity comments (Opportunities 1, 2, 5, 7, 9, 11, 13, 15) were contradicted by 57% of the 224 barrier comments (Barriers 4, 11, 14, 8, 6, 1, 2, 7). That is, about half of the opportunities and barriers were contested by clinicians who held opposing views. This amount of disagreement about the pros and cons of the design-in-use process might constitute a meta-level barrier.

Table 4. Opportunities, $N = 143$.

Opportunity group	Count
1. Gaining momentum from early successes and external events	18
2. Design-in-use approach allows for meeting local needs	16
3. Gradual realization and incorporation of needs and possibilities	16
4. Opportunities for better coordination across departments, professional groups etc.	16
5. Whiteboard-mediated coordination is an improvement over phone calls	15
6. Super users serve as champions	13
7. Whiteboard is easy to use, so training and support have not taxed the super users	12
8. Opportunities for better overview	8
9. Opportunities for standardization	6
10. Good balance between benefit and data entry	6
11. Design-in-use approach makes for a proactive and engaging process	5
12. Exploiting benefits of printing the whiteboard	5
13. Exploiting benefits of integration with other systems	4
14. Works because nurses and secretaries perform data entry for physicians	2
15. Physicians see a point in being part	1

Four of the opportunities captured what might be considered generic design-in-use qualities: (a) design-in-use approach allowed for meeting local needs, (b) gradual realization and incorporation of needs and possibilities, (c) design-in-use approach made for a proactive and engaging process, and possibly (d) gaining momentum from early successes and external events. In addition, two opportunities emphasized the important facilitating conditions that the super users championed the design-in-use process and that the process achieved a good balance between benefit and data entry. The remaining opportunities were specific to the whiteboard and the local use context, including the opportunities for better coordination, overview, and standardization. Seizing such opportunities was central to the design-in-use process. For example, it was unanticipated that the clinicians began printing the whiteboard to have it at hand at all times and to obtain a copy for personal annotation. A nurse expressed the value of this seemingly unsophisticated change in the use of the whiteboard: *"It was at that point I said: Now we are approaching something useful."* In one department the accidental feature that the printout extended over two pages became a clear-cut way of assigning responsibility for the patients to the physicians on duty:

We do it in the way that one [physician] takes the first page of patients – because the printout is on two pages – and the other physician takes the patients on the second page. That helps a lot.

Table 5. Barriers, $N = 224$.

Barrier group	Count
1. A misunderstanding to believe that clinicians want to engage in design in use	23
2. Lack of system integrations limits whiteboard possibilities and duplicates work	22
3. Design-in-use process experienced as rushed, top-down, and administrative	21
4. Lack of momentum	20
5. Competing with other activities for resources and attention	17
6. Lack of standardization restricts the interdepartmental use of the whiteboard	15
7. Physicians have been peripheral to the design-in-use process	14
8. The need for training and support has been underestimated	14
9. Limitations inherent in the whiteboard technology and their physical location	13
10. Process has lacked direction, which should have been provided top-down	12
11. Little local need for the changes that can be made by design in use of whiteboard	12
12. Implementation of work processes lags behind implemented whiteboard facilities	12
13. Standardization across departments conflicts with design in use within departments	9
14. Replacing phone calls with whiteboard-mediated coordination is not non-loss	7
15. Design-in-use approach is dependent on the few committed people	7
16. Super users lack required knowledge	6

The most frequently mentioned barrier was that it was a misunderstanding to believe that the clinicians wanted to engage in design in use. A physician end-user explained that his interest was to treat patients, an interest he considered common to the physicians: *"We have our focus on the patients. The IT systems we use are those we have to use. It is not that IT interests us."* From this point of view the design-in-use process was an unwelcome distraction because it took time away from the patients. The second-most frequently mentioned barrier was specific to the whiteboard and the local context. This barrier emphasized the lack of integration between the whiteboard and other clinical systems. Thus, using the whiteboard for new purposes tended to involve duplication of work. The last of the top-three barriers was the experience that the design-in-use process had been rushed, top-down, and oriented toward administrative issues: *"They want to extract some numbers, to be able to see how often we tick off this or that, whether we have ticked it off, what we use."* That is, the design-in-use approach had not been presented and performed in a manner that had made this end-user feel part of the process; rather the process was perceived as driven by concerns for quality assessment rather than clinical utility. The remaining barriers included lack of momentum (which meant that too little happened or it happened too slowly), lack of time (because other activities demanded resources and attention), lack of direction (which created uncertainty about what kinds of changes to pursue), lack of knowledge

(among the super users who were to drive the design-in-use process), and lack of standardization (which restricted the possibilities for interdepartmental use of the whiteboard). A further barrier with respect to standardization was that the standards that were implemented to facilitate interdepartmental whiteboard use restricted the possibilities for tailoring the whiteboard to intradepartmental needs. These restrictions were extra frustrating because the need for standardization was only realized gradually; thus, some early intradepartmental changes had to be rolled back to comply with standards that were introduced later to facilitate interdepartmental use:

We end up doing everything twice. It was hugely frustrating that we had set it all up the way we wanted – we thought that now it is perfect for me – only to realize that this doesn't work [interdepartmentally]. That's a bummer. Then we had to change a lot of it. And that is worse than the initial sense of freedom.

4.3   Variation Across User Groups

To investigate variation across user groups we selected the roles and professional groups with at least three representatives among the interviewees. For roles this selection led to comparing the ten super users with the five end-users; for professional groups it led to comparing the six physicians with the six nurses. Table 6 shows the results. Overall, the comments were somewhat differently distributed for super users versus end-users and similarly distributed for physicians versus nurses.

Table 6.   Variation across user groups.

Classification	Category	Role		Professional group	
		Super user %	End-user %	Physician %	Nurse %
Valence	Positive	48	30	33	40
	Negative	38	56	57	48
	Neutral	14	13	10	12
Object	Information technology	39	36	39	47
	Work process	14	23	21	12
	Both	47	42	40	40
Stage	Preparing change	31	30	38	32
	Implementing change	54	54	47	52
	Training and support	14	13	11	15
	Other	1	3	4	0
Scope	Intradepartmental	39	25	34	41
	Interdepartmental	25	39	28	33
	Both	36	36	39	25

Two differences should be noted. First, the super users were more positive and less negative than the end-users (see Table 6). Either the clinicians who were more positive about the design-in-use approach became super users or the super users' larger

involvement in this process made them more positive. This difference underlined the barrier that the design-in-use process was dependent on the few clinicians who were committed to the process (Barrier 15, Table 5). These few committed clinicians were in the group of super users. Second, the super users focused more on intradepartmental change, whereas the end-users focused more on interdepartmental change (see Table 6). Intradepartmental change was the super users' immediate responsibility and it was, probably, easier for them to accomplish because they had their primary knowledge and network in their department. In contrast, interdepartmental change involved negotiation and alignment with other departments. While the super users as a group appeared somewhat reluctant to engage this increased complexity, the end-users focused on the interdepartmental changes because they were the most evident outcomes of the design-in-use process. Several end-users had some difficulty giving examples of outcomes other than the interdepartmental changes of using the whiteboard for ordering physiotherapy and for coordinating when patients were ready for surgery.

5 Discussion

Design in use will only happen if motivated users make it happen. Thus, the clinicians' perception of the design-in-use approach is both an outcome of the implementation process and a key input to it. If they perceive the approach negatively, it is unlikely to succeed. If it succeeds, they are likely to perceive it positively.

5.1 How Do Users Perceive a Design-in-Use Approach to Implementation?

At the studied hospital the clinicians have one and a half years of experience with the design-in-use approach to the implementation of the whiteboard. That is, their perception of the approach has had time to form and settle. In summary, we find that:

- The clinicians perceive the design-in-use approach to implementation in conflicting ways. In addition to many positive as well as many negative comments, the clinicians disagree about the associated opportunities and barriers.
- The super users are more positive about the approach than the end-users. As a consequence the super users serve as champions for the system, and the design-in-use approach is highly dependent on these few, committed people.
- Intradepartmental change is perceived more positively, probably because it is easier to achieve. The super users focus more on intradepartmental change, the end-users more on interdepartmental change, which is possibly more valuable.
- Standardization across departments conflicts with design in use within departments. While the clinicians acknowledge the need for standardization, the conflict affects their perception of the design-in-use approach negatively.
- The design-in-use approach is inextricably sociotechnical but the clinicians perceive the technology – the whiteboard – as more prominent than the work process. Less than one in five comments are exclusively about the work process.

- The clinicians' perception of design in use is more about implementing change than about preparing it or about training and support. That is, the approach becomes salient to the clinicians when its results start to influence their work.
- While the super users and end-users perceive the design-in-use approach somewhat differently, the physicians and nurses perceive it similarly. Thus, the clinicians' perception of the approach varies with their role in it, not with their primary task.

The clinicians' conflicting perceptions of the design-in-use approach have multiple and interrelated sources. One of these sources is the scope of the design-in-use activities. We propose that the clinicians probably perceive intradepartmental change more positively because it is easier to achieve and therefore proceeds more smoothly. In contrast, interdepartmental change is more organizationally complex, extends beyond the super users' immediate network, and requires the development and adoption of standards that reduce the clinicians' freedom in configuring the whiteboard for intradepartmental needs. This argument accords with Sanchez and Mahoney [37], who emphasize that changes internal to organizational components are much simpler than changes that cut across component boundaries because intra-component changes can be handled locally whereas inter-component changes require organization-wide learning and decisions. That said, the potential benefit of inter-component changes is larger because they may introduce structural improvements. The ordering of physiotherapy provides an example. However, the standardization involved in pursuing interdepartmental changes is a source of frustration and exemplifies the generally recognized friction between global and local concerns in the evolution of an infrastructure [40]. While this study shows that the clinicians' appreciation of design in use interrelates with the scope of the pursued changes, further work is needed to spell out these interrelations in detail.

Another source of the clinicians' perceptions of the design-in-use approach is its blending of technical and work-process change. The technology – the whiteboard – features prominently in the clinicians' perception of the design-in-use approach but in contrast to Mehandjiev et al. [22] without worrying about the technical quality of the configurations. The absence of this worry may suggest that the clinicians are over-confident in the quality of their configurations [17] or that it is simple to configure the whiteboard. In either case, the perceived simplicity of configuring the whiteboard is an important contextual factor because it means that the super users have more time available for revising the work processes associated with the whiteboard. The design-in-use process is at least as much about revising work processes as it is about technical configuration. This sociotechnical outlook probably reflects that the whiteboard as such is of negligible interest to the clinicians, who instead perceive the whiteboard as the driver of changes that improve their work processes or, in other clinicians' opinion, largely fail to improve them. It reinforces the sociotechnical outlook that the design-in-use activities occur during use; traditional design (i.e., design before use) may be more prone to a predominantly technical outlook. The qualities of design in use, as opposed to design before use, are also highlighted by the finding that the clinicians' perception of the design-in-use approach is more about implementing change than about preparing it or about training and support. Truex et al. [43] argue that it is when a design starts to affect users in their daily work that the design becomes salient to them and they become

parameterized

motivated to influence it. That is, the clinicians are more likely to realize the implications of the whiteboard after they have started to use it and they are more likely to be able and motivated to voice their needs and concerns after they have started to use it.

A further source of the clinicians' perceptions of the design-in-use approach is whether they expect to receive a finalized system or are prepared to engage in design in use. Many clinicians expect and prefer to receive a system that has already been configured for their needs and, thus, is ready for use. However, some clinicians are prepared to continue the design of the system and associated work practices on the basis of their experiences from starting to use the system. The latter group appears to engage in design in use because they like it, find it useful, and believe they will be good at it [6]. When previous design-in-use studies distinguish between different groups of people it has mostly been to investigate collaborations and tensions between users and developers [8], between users and management [41], and between super users and technical IT support [46]. It has not been to investigate how different user groups may disagree about whether design in use is an appealing process.

We find that the distinction between super users and end-users explains some of the difference in the clinicians' perception of the design-in-use process but that the distinction between physicians and nurses does not. The clinicians' conflicting perceptions of the design-in-use approach makes it a critical decision who are selected as super users to drive the process but it also adds to the super users' task by extending it with a role of championing the whiteboard. To champion the whiteboard the super users must be able to influence their colleagues' attitudes and behavior. They must also be prepared to employ an outgoing and advocating approach rather than merely to provide opportunities that their colleagues may adopt or bypass as they see fit. Management could have supported the super users in this championing role but, instead, adopted a rather hands-off approach, which made it easier for the disinclined clinicians to remain uncommitted to the design-in-use process.

5.2   Implications

We see four implications of the study for a design-in-use approach to implementation. First, a design-in-use approach to implementation is dependent on a limited number of positively inclined users. It is unadvisable to adopt a design-in-use approach unless such users can be identified ahead of the implementation process. These users cannot be presumed to have all the competences necessary to accomplish design in use. Targeted support is necessary. Second, design-in-use activities with a wide scope are perceived more negatively. Thus, a design-in-use approach may be best suited for intradepartmental change. While appreciated intradepartmental change can be accomplished through design-in-use processes that proceed bottom-up, interdepartmental change requires more coordination, more formality, and probably a collaboration more similar to mutual development [24]. Third, some users expect to receive a finalized system. These users will experience a design-in-use approach to implementation as unprofessional and they will be reluctant to take time away from their primary tasks to contribute to design-in-use activities. Organizations can work to change their attitude,

can task those who engage in design-in-use activities with the additional task of championing the system, or can risk underutilizing the system. Fourth, in order for design in use to happen the system must be used. Thus, to get the design-in-use approach going management must ensure system use. This requires clarity about the purposes for which the system must, as a minimum, be used.

5.3   Limitations

Three limitations should be remembered in interpreting the results of this study. First, the study is restricted to one hospital and one design-in-use process. The results cannot be presumed to generalize to all design-in-use approaches to implementation. On the contrary, design in use is a situated process through which a particular system and a particular use context are adapted to each other. Second, while the interviewees span six professional groups, we acknowledge that the majority of the interviewees are physicians or nurses. For example, there is only one secretary among the interviewees even though secretaries are involved in the clinical work [23] and in the use of the studied whiteboard. In addition, we interviewed more super users than end-users but at the hospital there are many more end-users than super users. The rationale for including many super users in the sample was their central role in the design-in-use activities. Third, our sample of interviewees is too small to enable statistical analyses of whether the users' perception of the design-in-use approach differs across professional groups or between super users and end-users. We would welcome a large-scale survey of how different user groups perceive design-in-use processes. The present study provides categories and findings for informing such a survey.

6   Conclusion

The clinicians at the studied hospital hold conflicting views about the design-in-use approach to the implementation of the network of interconnected electronic whiteboards. While some clinicians, especially the super users, welcome the approach and find that it allows for meeting gradually realized local needs, other clinicians expect new systems to be fully configured prior to go-live. The conflicting perceptions show that a design-in-use approach to implementation is not a panacea. Rather, it requires careful communication, targeted support, and may be better suited for intradepartmental than interdepartmental change.

Acknowledgements. This paper is dedicated to the memory of the second author, Arnvør Torkilsheyggi, who tragically died before the paper saw publication. The paper reports work conducted in the Clinical Communication project, which was a research and development collaboration between Region Zealand, Imatis, Roskilde University, and University of Copenhagen. The second author's participation in the project was co-funded by Region Zealand. We are grateful to Claus R. Mortensen for his support in identifying the interviewees. Special thanks are due to the interviewees.

References

1. Aanestad, M., Driveklepp, A.M., Sørli, H., Hertzum, M.: Participatory continuing design: "living with" videoconferencing in rehabilitation. In: Kanstrup, A.M., Bygholm, A., Bertelsen, P., Nøhr, C. (eds.) Participatory Design and Health Information Technology, pp. 45–59. IOS Press, Amsterdam (2017)
2. Aarts, J., Berg, M.: Same system, different outcomes: comparing the implementation of computerized physician order entry in two Dutch hospitals. Methods Inf. Med. **45**(1), 53–61 (2006)
3. Balka, E., Wagner, I.: Making things work: dimensions of configurability as appropriation work. In: Proceedings of the CSCW 2006 Conference on Computer Supported Cooperative Work, pp. 229–238. ACM Press, New York (2006)
4. Bikson, T.K., Eveland, J.D.: Sociotechnical reinvention: implementation dynamics and collaboration tools. Inf. Commun. Soc. **1**(3), 270–290 (1998)
5. Bjögvinsson, E., Ehn, P., Hillgren, P.-A.: Design things and design thinking: contemporary participatory design challenges. Des. Issues **28**(3), 101–116 (2012)
6. Blackwell, A.F.: End-user developers – what are they like? In: Paternò, F., Wulf, V. (eds.) New Perspectives in End-User Development, pp. 121–135. Springer, Cham (2017). https://doi.org/10.1007/978-3-319-60291-2_6
7. Bowers, J.: The work to make a network work: studying CSCW in action. In: Proceedings of the CSCW 1994 Conference on Computer Supported Cooperative Work, pp. 287–298. ACM Press, New York (1994)
8. Dittrich, Y., Bolmsten, J., Eriksson, J.: End user development and infrastructuring – sustaining organizational innovation capabilities. In: Paternò, F., Wulf, V. (eds.) New Perspectives in End-User Development, pp. 165–206. Springer, Cham (2017). https://doi.org/10.1007/978-3-319-60291-2_8
9. Dittrich, Y., Eriksén, S., Hansson, C.: PD in the wild: evolving practices of design in use. In: Binder, T., Gregory, J., Wagner, I. (eds.) Proceedings of the Seventh Conference on Participatory Design, PDC2002, pp. 124–134. CPSR, Palo Alto (2002)
10. Fischer, G.: End-user development and meta-design: foundations for cultures of participation. J. Organ. End User Comput. **22**(1), 52–82 (2010)
11. Hartswood, M., et al.: Co-realisation: towards a principled synthesis of ethnomethodology and participatory design. Scand. J. Inf. Syst. **14**(2), 9–30 (2002)
12. Henderson, A., Kyng, M.: There's no place like home: continuing design in use. In: Greenbaum, J., Kyng, M. (eds.) Design at Work: Cooperative Design of Computer Systems, pp. 219–240. Erlbaum, Hillsdale (1991)
13. Hertzum, M.: Electronic emergency-department whiteboards: a study of clinicians' expectations and experiences. Int. J. Med. Inform. **80**(9), 618–630 (2011)
14. Hertzum, M., Simonsen, J.: Effects-driven IT development: specifying, realizing, and assessing usage effects. Scand. J. Inf. Syst. **23**(1), 3–28 (2011)
15. Hertzum, M., Simonsen, J.: Configuring information systems and work practices for each other: what competences are needed locally? Int. J. Hum.-Comput. Stud. **122**, 242–255 (2019)
16. Karasti, H., Baker, K., Millerand, F.: Infrastructure time: long-term matters in collaborative development. Comput. Support. Coop. Work **19**(3&4), 377–415 (2010)
17. Ko, A.J., et al.: The state of the art in end-user software engineering. ACM Comput. Surv. **43**(3), article 21 (2011)

18. Ludwig, T., Dax, J., Pipek, V., Wulf, V.: A practice-oriented paradigm for end-user development. In: Paternò, F., Wulf, V. (eds.) New Perspectives in End-User Development, pp. 23–41. Springer, Cham (2017). https://doi.org/10.1007/978-3-319-60291-2_2

19. Maceli, M., Atwood, M.E.: "Human crafters" once again: supporting users as designers in continuous co-design. In: Dittrich, Y., Burnett, M., Mørch, A., Redmiles, D. (eds.) IS-EUD 2013. LNCS, vol. 7897, pp. 9–24. Springer, Heidelberg (2013). https://doi.org/10.1007/978-3-642-38706-7_3

20. Mackay, W.E.: Patterns of sharing customizable software. In: Proceedings of the CSCW 1990 Conference on Computer Supported Cooperative Work, pp. 209–221. ACM Press, New York (1990)

21. Markus, M.L.: Technochange management: using IT to drive organizational change. J. Inf. Technol. 19(1), 4–20 (2004)

22. Mehandjiev, N., Sutcliffe, A., Lee, D.: Organizational view of end-user development. In: Lieberman, H., Paternó, F., Wulf, V. (eds.) End User Development. HCIS, vol. 9, pp. 371–399. Springer, Dordrecht (2006). https://doi.org/10.1007/1-4020-5386-X_17

23. Møller, N.L.H., Vikkelsø, S.: The clinical work of secretaries: Exploring the intersection of administrative and clinical work in the diagnosing process. In: Dugdale, J., Masclet, C., Grasso, M., Boujut, J.F., Hassanaly, P. (eds.) From Research to Practice in the Design of Cooperative Systems: Results and Open Challenges, pp. 33–47. Springer, London (2012). https://doi.org/10.1007/978-1-4471-4093-1_3

24. Mørch, A.I., Andersen, R.: Mutual development: the software engineering context of end-user development. J. Organ. End User Comput. 22(2), 36–57 (2010)

25. Nah, F.F.-H., Zuckweiler, K.M., Lau, J.L.-S.: ERP implementation: chief information officers' perceptions of critical success factors. Int. J. Hum.-Comput. Interact. 16(1), 5–22 (2003)

26. Nicolaou, A.I.: Firm performance effects in relation to the implementation and use of enterprise resource planning systems. J. Inf. Syst. 18(2), 79–105 (2004)

27. Okamura, K., Fujimoto, M., Orlikowski, W.J., Yates, J.: Helping CSCW applications succeed: The role of mediators in the context of use. Inf. Soc. 11(3), 157–172 (1995)

28. Orlikowski, W.J.: Improvising organizational transformation over time: a situated change perspective. Inf. Syst. Res. 7(1), 63–92 (1996)

29. Orlikowski, W.J., Hofman, J.D.: An improvisational model for change management: the case of groupware technologies. Sloan Manag. Rev. 38(2), 11–22 (1997)

30. Park, S.Y., Chen, Y., Rudkin, S.: Technological and organizational adaptation of EMR implementation in an emergency department. ACM Trans. Comput.-Hum. Interact. 22(1), 1:01–1:24 (2015)

31. Pipek, V., Kahler, H.: Supporting collaborative tailoring. In: Lieberman, H., Paternó, F., Wulf, V. (eds.) End User Development. HCIS, vol. 9, pp. 315–345. Springer, Dordrecht (2006). https://doi.org/10.1007/1-4020-5386-X_15

32. Pipek, V., Wulf, V.: A groupware's life. In: Bødker, S., Kyng, M., Schmidt, K. (eds.) Proceedings of the Sixth European Conference on Computer-Supported Cooperative Work, ECSCW 1999, pp. 199–218. Kluwer, Amsterdam (1999)

33. Powell, S.G., Baker, K.R., Lawson, B.: A critical review of the literature on spreadsheet errors. Decis. Support Syst. 46(1), 128–138 (2008)

34. Pries-Heje, L., Dittrich, Y.: ERP implementation as design: looking at participatory design for means to facilitate knowledge integration. Scand. J. Inf. Syst. 21(2), 27–58 (2009)

35. Priestman, W., Sridharan, S., Vigne, H., Collins, R., Seamer, L., Sebire, N.J.: What to expect from electronic patient record system implementation: lessons learned from published evidence. J. Innov. Health Inform. 25(2), 92–104 (2018)

36. Rasmussen, R., Fleron, B., Hertzum, M., Simonsen, J.: Balancing tradition and transcendence in the implementation of emergency-department electronic whiteboards. In: Molka-Danielsen, J., Nicolaisen, H.W., Persson, J.S. (eds.) Selected Papers of the Information Systems Research Seminar in Scandinavia 2010, pp. 73–87. Tapir Academic Press, Trondheim (2010)

37. Sanchez, R., Mahoney, J.T.: Modularity, flexibility, and knowledge management in product and organization design. Strateg. Manag. J. 17(Winter Special Issue), 63–76 (1996)

38. Simonsen, J., Hertzum, M.: Sustained participatory design: extending the iterative approach. Des. Issues 28(3), 10–21 (2012)

39. Spencer, M.: Brittleness and bureaucracy: software as a material for science. Perspect. Sci. 23(4), 466–484 (2015)

40. Star, S.L., Ruhleder, K.: Steps toward an ecology of infrastructure: design and access for large information spaces. Inf. Syst. Res. 7(1), 111–134 (1996)

41. Torkilsheyggi, A., Hertzum, M.: Incomplete by design: a study of a design-in-use approach to systems implementation. Scand. J. Inf. Syst. 29(2), article 2 (2017)

42. Trigg, R.H., Bødker, S.: From implementation to design: tailoring and the emergence of systematization in CSCW. In: Proceedings of the CSCW 1994 Conference on Computer Supported Cooperative Work, pp. 45–54. ACM Press, New York (1994)

43. Truex, D.P., Baskerville, R., Klein, H.: Growing systems in emergent organizations. Commun. ACM 42(8), 117–123 (1999)

44. Tyre, M.J., Orlikowski, W.J.: Windows of opportunity: temporal patterns of technological adaptation in organizations. Organ. Sci. 5(1), 98–118 (1994)

45. Yetim, F., Draxler, S., Stevens, G., Wulf, V.: Fostering continuous user participation by embedding a communication support tool in user interfaces. AIS Trans. Hum.-Comput. Interact. 4(2), 153–168 (2012)

46. Åsand, H.-R.H., Mørch, A.I.: Super users and local developers: the organization of end user development in an accounting company. J. Organ. End User Comput. 18(4), 1–21 (2008)

Lifelogging in the Wild: Participant Experiences of Using Lifelogging as a Research Tool

Anders Bruun$^{(\boxtimes)}$ and Martin Lynge Stentoft

Aalborg University, Selma Lagerlöfs Vej 300, 9920 Aalborg East, Denmark
bruun@cs.aau.dk, martinstentoft@gmail.com

Abstract. Research in the wild has emerged in HCI as a way of studying participant experiences in natural environments. Also, lifelogging tools such as physiological sensors have become more feasible for gathering data continuously in the wild. This could complement traditional in-waves approaches such as observations and interviews. Given the emerging nature of sensors, few studies have employed these in the wild. We extend previous work by exploring the use of a physiological sensor and camera to examine how participants appropriate and experience wearing these. Participants were engaged in viewing the photos taken during the day and used the sensor and camera data to recall details about their daily experiences and reflect on these. However, participants also went through some efforts in making the camera blend into the environment in order not to break social norms.

Keywords: Research in the wild · Lifelogging · Physiological sensor · GSR · Narrative clip camera · Provocative design

1 Introduction

Studying user experiences in the wild has seen an increase in popularity within the field of Human-Computer Interaction (HCI) [34]. Research in the wild is aimed at understanding behavior and technology use in people's everyday lives outside the confinements of the laboratory [34]. Using data collection methods from the domain of lifelogging complements classical ethnographic approaches typically used to study in the wild phenomena [34]. Lifelogging research emphasizes the use of technology to make participants reflect on and report events from their everyday lives. Such technology could involve mobile contextual sensors, e.g. GPS location data to track where participants have been over the course of a day. However, wearable cameras, particularly the SenseCam seems to be the most emphasized technology to support data collection in Lifelogging studies, see e.g. [2, 5, 20, 23, 25, 32, 36]. SenseCam is worn around participants' neck and captures an image every 30 s or when the user chooses to take a photo manually. Images taken through a wearable camera have proven to be very effective cues for study participants in recalling and describing past events [36]. This makes such technology useful in complementing traditional in-situ observations or interviews [34].

© IFIP International Federation for Information Processing 2019
Published by Springer Nature Switzerland AG 2019
D. Lamas et al. (Eds.): INTERACT 2019, LNCS 11748, pp. 431–451, 2019.
https://doi.org/10.1007/978-3-030-29387-1_24

Lifelogging technology enable researchers to continuously collect data within natural settings [27], and this have become more feasible with the availability, price and pervasiveness of new wearable sensor technologies [34]. As a result, studies using wearable physiological sensors to measure e.g. galvanic skin response and heart rate have emerged within the HCI research community, although still to a much lesser extent than the SenseCam, cf. [2, 8–10, 31, 37]. Furthermore, such physiological sensors enable researchers to measure the key user experience dimension of emotions [4, 17]. Given the current level of wearability, such physiological sensors seem well suited to study user experiences in the wild. However, we have not been able to find any HCI studies combining the use of a wearable camera and physiological sensors to capture images at emotionally charged events.

This study extends previous work by exploring how study participants appropriate and experience wearing a lifelogging tool that uses a physiological sensor to automatically activate image capture from a wearable camera. We describe the design of our tool and study its usage in the wild. To emphasize the emotional dimension of daily experiences and to engage participants in daily reflections, we employed a provocative design approach in developing the tool. We designed the tool such that the camera can only be curated through emotional reactions, i.e. users cannot control when to the camera takes a photo. Rather, photos are taken when the physiological sensor detects an increase in excitement.

The strength of provocative design is that of challenging existing norms, e.g. by triggering dilemmas through interaction design, or designing something well-known in a very different way. Recent studies used provocative design to motivate people into reflecting on their behavior, see e.g. [33, 34]. However, it is crucial that the provocative design is perceived strange enough, but not too strange, in order to be effective [33].

In the remainder of this paper we present related work on using physiological sensors to support data collection in the wild. We then describe considerations on our lifelogging tool based on provocative design, followed by a description of our study method and results. Finally, we discuss our findings and conclude on these.

2 Related Work

In this section we outline studies that emphasize design of lifelogging tools and report on participant experiences in using these. Lifelogging denotes the collecting of data for self-monitoring and reflection on personal information [26, 27]. Lifelogging tools gather data about people's daily life using for instance wearable cameras, physiological sensors or smartphone sensors combined with pc or mobile apps to visualize the data [11, 27]. In this study we are particularly interested in studying the use of lifelogging tools based on gathering data from physiological sensors. Such sensors indicate emotional states of participants where e.g. Galvanic Skin Response (GSR) sensors measure changes in arousal [10, 18]. Emotions are relevant to consider in relation to studying behavior in the wild. This is because emotions are weaved on the basis of stimuli perceived through our senses and our following reactions. We thus use our emotions to plan our actions in order to cope with changing situations in daily life [35]. This does not only apply to intense or life-threatening situations, but also in more subtle

cases such as interacting with products as stated by Forlizzi and Battarbee [17]: *"Emotion affects how we plan to interact with products, how we actually interact with products, and the perceptions and outcomes that surround those interactions"*.

2.1 Making Sense of Data

A critical point to consider is how participants make sense of physiological data. Using e.g. heart rate data to infer the physical state of our body is commonly known by people utilizing tools related to support quantified-self purposes. Yet, such tools are developed with physical exercise purposes in mind. The use of physiological data to get insights on our emotional states is, however, more limited.

Be Open for Interpretation. Ståhl et al. created a lifelogging diary tool named the Affective Diary [37]. The Affective Diary uses a GSR sensor to measure participant's emotional arousal. The Affective Diary also collects contextual data from participant's smartphone about sent and received text messages, photos taken and people nearby (via Bluetooth scanning). Participants in the study were able to make sense of the contextual data from their phone, which they frequently referred to when explaining their diary to the researchers during the interviews [37]. The physiological data was visualized using abstract colored human shapes where e.g. a red color signified high arousal and blue low arousal. Findings revealed that some of the participants could not make sense of the abstract human shapes and color scheme. Ståhl et al. suggest that tools based on affective data should be designed to enable participants to interpret the data themselves rather than dictating what should be interpreted [37].

Provide a Condensed View. Pavel et al. Designed a lifelogging tool to support lifestyle management [31]. The article emphasize the ordering and display of data gathered from wearable sensors and a pc in a way that should be meaningful to the user. To this end the data is combined into stories about the user's day. This is done by categorizing the collected data, for instance in relation to what the user was doing, emotional states as well as physical and social contexts. Participants could also manually add data for the stories in the form of notes about events they found interesting. The stories represent a condensed view of the collected data with text and background images of where the story has taken place. Above the stories are icons that users can press to get more specific details about the data used in the story. The study showed that participants found it valuable to have a condensed view of the collected data [31]. Using the stories as a condensed alternative to the detailed information available from the data sources, helped users understand the essence of the data. This stimulated reflections about their behavior. The study also showed that it varied what sort of data the participants found relevant to include in their story. This depended on the event they experienced [31].

Similarly, the study by Kelly and Jones deals with designing a lifelogging tool to enable participants to more effectively interact with the large amounts of heterogeneous data, which are collected through wearable and mobile sensors [23]. In their study, participants wore a GSR sensor, to collect physiological data about their emotional arousal. Participants also wore a lifelog camera to collect contextual data, which was stored together with activity data from mobile phones and pc activity in a combined

lifelog. The physiological data from the GSR sensor were then used as cues to extract contextual data from the users lifelog for self-reflection. The contextual data items were categorized into minimum, medium and high GSR measurements. Results from the study show that items correlating with high GSR measurements were perceived as most usable for self-reflection. This indicates that physiological data, e.g. high GSR measurements, is useful for highlighting the most important contextual data. This in turn may be used to present a condensed view of lifelog data [23].

2.2   Improving Data Richness in Recalling Events

Arvola et al. studied the use of wearable lifelogging technology to support self-reflection [2]. Participants in that study wore a lifelogging camera, which took a photo every 30 s and an activity tracker that collected data about participant's heart rate during the day. To examine how sensor and camera data would increase richness of self-reported reflections, participants were not allowed to access data until the end of the study. They were asked to self-report at the end of each day about their experiences, which is based on free recall [2]. From studies in psychology we know that such an approach (very similar to the Day Reconstruction Method) suffers from a significant memory recall bias [12]. Therefore, at end of the study participants were told to compare their free recall notes from each day with the lifelog camera photos labeled with timestamps [2]. This made participants recall a considerable amount of extra details about their experiences. Afterwards they were also allowed to compare the notes and photos with the heart rate data, which was visualized using a graph with time stamps. This resulted in recollecting further details about their experiences. This shows that using different data types to complement each other supports user reflection and increases data richness. However, as the lifelog camera took a large number of photos each day, it was considered too time-consuming to go through all the data during the reflection process. Arvola et al. therefore suggest reducing the data volume [2]. This is in line with the condensed view proposed by Pavel et al. [31] and Kelly and Jones [23] mentioned above.

2.3   Engaging Participants

One of the aims of this study is to explore how participants engage in data collection through their appropriation and experience in using a provocative lifelogging tool. While a few lifelogging studies have touched upon how users engage in data collection, more research is needed. In the following we outline discussions from previous studies on this, but also introduce provocative design as a potential approach to further motivate participants into collecting data in the wild.

Engaging Through Activation. Participants in the Pavel et al. study on lifestyle management (mentioned above), embraced the opportunity of engaging in the data collection themselves during the day. This was done by adding notes to the stories made within the lifelogging tool. They liked that they could consciously personalize the data, which they were to use for reflection later [31]. This suggests that lifelogging tools should engage users in the data collection, yet this should not be too time

consuming as it would diminish participant motivation [28]. This is also in line with the Affective Diary study by Ståhl and colleagues, in which it was found that participants preferred to interpret data themselves rather than having a tool dictate what should be interpreted [37].

Engaging Through Provocation. Provocative design has emerged as a way of using artefacts that stand out in order to study behavior in the wild [34]. Provocative design aims at using such artefacts to challenge existing norms, hereby engaging participants in reflecting on their behavior [33, 34]. The focus of provocative design studies is on producing knowledge and not the immediate development or refinement of specific artefacts [38]. This fits well with the aim of our study, as we want to study participant behavior and experiences surrounding the use of a lifelogging tool. At the same time, this tool needs to motivate and engage participants into reflecting on their behavior.

The behavior that the design is trying to challenge is what Bardzell et al. describes as the conceptual provocation of the design [3]. By (slightly) stirring up normal routines and beliefs, provocative designs can encourage study participants to reflect upon their actions [33]. It is key that the artefact design is strange enough to fulfil its purpose so that it does not readily blend into the everyday routines [3, 33]. Yet, it should not be so provocative that participants find the artifact weird and rejects it, i.e. a slight strangeness is the key [13]. Also, it should not be fantasy but instead relatable as a plausible next step from the current available artefacts [14]. The recent studies by Bardzell et al. and Raptis et al. have shown that provocative design is efficient in making participants reflect upon their actions through an object [3, 33].

Raptis et al. recommends that the provocative designer embraces design authorship, meaning that not all design decisions have to be mapped directly to requirements or user needs [33]. Instead, design decisions can also be based on the curiosity and intuition of the designer. Rogers and Marshall similarly states that using provocative design to study phenomena in the wild involves deploying a technology, that have been primarily developed by the researchers [34].

2.4   Existing Lifelogging Tools

There is a wide range of consumer apps and devices available for lifelogging on smartphone app stores. While we do not intent to provide a comprehensive list here, we do highlight some of the most popular tools. Journaly is a lifelogging app that supports both manual and automatic functionality to add entries. In a daily entry, the app can automatically add user's photos, mobile sensor information about location, sleeping patterns, driving and walking [21]. Several entries can be added to the journal on the same day, if the user does so manually. The app uses a timeline with date/time, pictures, and weather information.

Optimized is a lifelogging app with focus on psychological state and social interaction [1]. The concept is to track information about sleep, exercise, social activities, people and how time spent on these activities correlates with the user's current mood. The functionality is mainly based on manual entries, which are visualized on a timeline or on a graph. Users manually adjusts their mood on a scale from zero to one hundred.

SenseCam developed by Microsoft has also been widely used throughout research studies, cf. [16, 29, 36]. This wearable camera takes a picture up to every 30 s in the default setting, but also includes built-in sensors, which can help in filtering this vast amount of data. SenseCam includes a light detection sensor as well as a sensor that identifies when a person is standing in front of you [19]. So far we have not seen any studies using SenseCam to automatically capture images of emotionally charged events.

3   Design of a Provocative Lifelogging Tool

This section describes our considerations in terms of creating a lifelogging tool. We sought inspiration within related research as well as existing commercial tools, yet aimed to differentiate our tool by applying a provocative design approach.

3.1   Conceptual and Functional Provocation

The conceptual provocation of our lifelogging tool relies on the philosophy of hedonism and the ideal of being present in the moment. It is about showing the world what our lives are truly about, doing what our emotions tell us to do, and not being controlled by technology to put up a façade that lives up to societal norms and expectations. We denote our tool "In the Moment" and the concept is in Fig. 1.

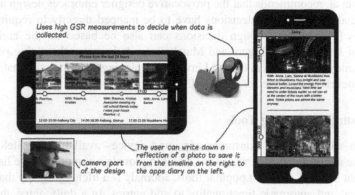

Fig. 1. Conceptual sketch of In the moment.

The conceptual provocation manifests itself through the functional provocation of the tool. Users are not in conscious control of the technology, which in our case is a wearable camera. Rather, photos are taken the moment users feel emotionally excited. Thus, In the Moment automatically takes a photo every time participants have an increase in emotional arousal. They can therefore stay in the moment with no option of controlling the technology to put up the right façade.

3.2   Inspirational Sources

The design is inspired by the Journaly app. In the Moment is designed to get participants to reflect on and write about their thoughts in a photo diary consisting of the photos taken while wearing the tool. The diary has its own timeline showing the images taken. Compared to Journaly, In the Moment takes a provocative approach for collecting data to support participant reflection. We also condense the amount of photos shown to participants in the diary. Thus, In the Moment does not show all the pictures taken during the day for participants to reflect upon. This is similar to the functionality featured within SenseCam, in which a built-in light sensor and a sensor to detect people can be used to decide when photos are taken. We used a GSR sensor instead to detect emotional excitement rather than relying on light and co-presence. At the end of the day, we selected the 10 photos taken at points in time with the highest GSR levels. This decision is based on the findings of Kelly and Jones [23]. In that study, data items such as photos or contextual information, which correlated with high intensity GSR measurements, were perceived most usable for self-reflection [23]. Pavel et al. [31] also found that a condensed view of data enabled their participants to extract the essence of the data, which in turn stimulated reflections on behavior.

3.3   Technical Implementation

A physical prototype of In the Moment was implemented using a Narrative clip lifelogging camera [30] and an E4 wristband to collect GSR data [15], see Fig. 2. We also developed a pc application to visualize the data. The PC application was preferred over e.g. a smartphone or tablet app, because the Narrative clip takes a vast number of photos, which would be too cumbersome to transfer wirelessly.

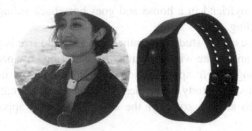

Fig. 2. Left - Narrative clip lifelogging camera, Right - Empatica E4 wristband.

The E4 wristband measures participants' GSR level four times per second, which is recorded in an accompanying app on the user's smartphone and then transferred to the E4 webserver. The PC Application accesses the E4 webserver to find the 10 most exciting emotional reactions (states of arousal). It does so by selecting the largest increases in GSR readings (spikes).

The Narrative clip camera automatically takes a photo every 20 s and adds a timestamp in a log file. Timestamps of the 10 most exciting emotional reactions obtained from the E4 wristband are compared with the timestamped photos from the

camera. The pc application then shows the photos taken in closest temporal proximity to the timestamp of each of the 10 emotional reactions. The 10 photos are ordered by the timestamps which are also visualized next to each photo. Each photo can be commented in order for researchers to gather qualitative self-reflection data.

4 Study Method

The In the moment prototype was used for an In the Wild study. This section describes the participants and procedure of the In the Wild study.

4.1 Participants

The In the Moment tool was used by three participants in the wild. One was female and two male. Participants were included on the basis of their varying occupation, family structure (kids/no-kids) and spare time interests. Participants volunteered to participate and did not receive any gifts or money for their efforts, they did, however, express interest in finding out what sort of photos the tool would visualize to them, based on their emotional reactions to situations in their everyday lives. All three were used take photos with their smartphone on a daily basis and two owned a smartwatch. The latter is relevant as the E4 wristband has a similar form factor to a smartwatch.

John (age 32) did not have any children at the time of the study, but was soon to be a father. He worked as a forklift driver and lived with his girlfriend in their house. He never misses a home match on the local football stadium. He also considered himself as gaming a lot in his spare time. Andreas (age 30) had two small children of the age 2 and 5. He was a student living with his girlfriend in a house and likes watching sport on TV. Marie (age 28) also has two small kids below 6 years old. She worked as a teacher and lived with her boyfriend in a house and goes horseback riding in her spare time. She also enjoys reading.

Given the purpose of this study, this rather small sample size is appropriate in order to build an in-depth and in the wild case study of exploring how participants engage in data collection through their appropriation and experience in using a provocative lifelogging tool. Thus, the study is not designed to be representative of a large population, but rather to sample some of the engagement and appropriation strategies employed here.

4.2 Procedure

The participants each had the tool for three consecutive days and were each interviewed on the day after their three-day period with the tool. During the interviews they went through their photos and comments from each day with the moderator and were also asked questions about their experiences with the tool and their own and others behavior while they wore the tool.

To try and make the In the Wild study more natural, the participants were told to use the tool as they saw fit. They were not given any specific tasks to do with the tool and there were no expectations to how much they would use the tool, or which

situations they would use the tool in. They were also told it was optional if they wanted to write a comment for a photo in the PC application.

Due to the automatic nature of data collection, in particular the image capture, we considered the ethical framework suggested in [24]. That framework deals specifically with ethics in relation to automated wearable cameras. In order to live up to the framework, we obtained informed written consent from our participants informing them on the nature and type of data collected during the study. We also dealt with privacy and confidentiality issues by e.g. configuring the data capture such that it was only the participants and the researchers that had access to the data. We also followed the recently introduced GDPR regulative as the study was conducted within the EU.

4.3 Data Analysis

The interviews were recorded on audio and transcribed. Transcribed data was then coded by one of the authors to review and categorize the data into themes. Given the novelty of our tool and the exploratory purpose of our study, we opted for using open coding based on the method described in [7]. Within the data, we emphasized themes related to the appropriation and experience of using our lifelogging tool.

5 Results

This section presents our findings on how participants appropriated and experienced using our In the Moment tool.

5.1 Hiding the Tool from Others

The participants approached In the Moment differently by making the tool fit into their everyday practices, particularly in order to stay within the boundaries of existing social norms.

In Public. John said he had been thinking about how other people would react, when he was wearing the tool in their vicinity. He tried to mask the tool by making it visually blend in with his other devices: *"I have thought about it in general because I knew it was there and what it did. For instance, when facing a bus driver, where I wonder if people behave differently because it looks like there is a camera pointed at them. (...) When I was using my headset, I tried to arrange the cord for the headset in a way that could make it look like it [In the Moment tool] was connected to the headset so people wouldn't notice."* This is similar to Andreas who choose a specific set of clothes to mask the camera when he wore it to school (see Fig. 3), as he did not like to have a camera pointed at him: *"I wore a sweater also, so the camera was marginally visible on my white t-shirt (...) to make it more discrete. A white camera on a black shirt is very noticeable. (...) I don't like it when people takes photos in my face"*. In other situations, Andreas decided to put the camera part of the tool completely away, and for specific events he decided he would not wear the tool at all. His reasoning was that he was afraid of people's reaction against him wearing a camera in public. He also added

that he was unsure about the legal issues for photography in certain places: *"I put the camera away, when I delivered my little girl at the daycare, so the personnel would not see it (...) I don't know, maybe they would think it was a little weird if I was wearing a camera."* and *"I had planned on wearing it [In the Moment tool] to the circus, but then my girlfriend and I talked about whether this allowed at all. (...) we were going together with my girlfriend's work colleagues, so it could be weird if I was wearing a camera".*

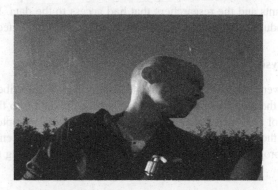

Fig. 3. Andreas tried to make the camera part of the tool less noticeable by wearing a white shirt to fit with the white camera and by zipping his jumper almost all the way up.

Marie also tried to make the camera less noticeable. While at a trip to the zoo she did this by attaching the camera to the strap on her bag near her waist. She was afraid that people would think she was monitoring them if they could see the camera: *"Fewer people look at your stomach than your face when you are at the zoo (...) The goal was to hide it. The reason is, that when a person is wearing a camera, it is to prove that another person is doing something illegal (...) For instance at the zoo it could be to document that the animals are living under poor conditions".* However, it was not only the feeling of monitoring others that was on Marie's mind. She also felt monitored herself while wearing the tool at home, even when she was by herself: *"It is nice to have a day at home for yourself but with a device like that you are not completely alone. (...) Because the photos may be seen by others I don't feel alone".*

At Work. Marie said that she chose not to wear the tool to work, because she did not want to have to explain why she was wearing a camera. Also, it was a technology that was unknown to the many people: *"At first, I planned on using it at work but then I remembered it takes photos of others, and I did not want to have to explain it. (...) Because no one knows it is possible, that the watch and camera is connected. It sounds a little flighty and I doubt that people will believe what I tell them".*

With Family. Andreas used the tool on a leisure walk with his family. He chose to wear the tool, even though there would be other people around. His reasoning is that it is okay to wear the tool in public as long as he is doing a private activity: *"We went for a walk one day while I was wearing it where I did not think about it (...) we talked to*

some people but when we go for a walk we are private. We are doing what we feel like so if people approach us it is their own choice. However, if you approach others with a camera it could be stepping on their toes ".

5.2   When Others Become Aware

As the only participant, John sometimes wore the tool without trying to disguise it. This resulted in mixed reactions from the people who noticed the camera.

Initial Skepticism. The tool made John's girlfriend feel uncomfortable, because she was afraid there would be unflattering photos of her: *"The first day I used it [In the Moment tool] we went out for dinner and were sitting opposite each other like we always do. She was afraid that it would take a lot of photos while she was stuffing her face with food ".* He also wore the tool to a family get-together without telling them that he was participating in the study: *"I couldn't help thinking, for instance yesterday, when I was at my parents' house for a barbecue if people were not themselves because they could see there was a camera. But that was only in the beginning. When I explained what it was, I don't believe people thought about it ".* Their initial questions about the tool were e.g. how the tool was recording their behavior: *"My sister-in-law dislikes having her picture taken, so when she first noticed it. she turned away until I told her it was not something that was taking pictures or video constantly ".*

Playfulness. John wore the tool while he was on a visit to his girlfriend's parents. He told them what the tool did and why he was wearing it. When he was about to leave, a family member became playful and tried to affect what the tool would photograph: *"When we were about to leave, my father in law started to talk about the tool. He tried to startle me to try and make me have a reaction. He acted out in front of the camera ".*

5.3   Excitement When Unboxing Photos

During the interviews the participants talked about the expectations they had while using the tool.

Own Expectations. John was looking forward to seeing which situations he had reacted to when he opened the application. He was expecting that the tool would photograph something that he would not have photographed himself: *"I was excited to see at the end of the day what sort of photos it had taken. I am a used to taking good photos with my phone and here I had to remember it could be anything. Something totally random. I was hoping there would be something good, like a good situation ".* However even though John was looking forward to seeing photos he would not have taken himself, he actually tried to use the tool to take photographs of specific situations, as he would normally have been able to do with a manually operated camera: *"There was a situation where my little niece was being a brat. I turned around a bit to make sure the camera was pointing in her direction to see if I had a reaction to the situation. (...) I am used to be able to photograph things that I want a photo of".*

When Marie wore the tool during the second day, she started having expectations about which situations that the tool would react to. For instance, she explained a

situation where she was stressed because she was busy and hot: *"It gets really cool when you wear it the second time, because then I could predict that something would be photographed. (…) I am doing the dishes and I start to get a stomach ache. Also, I have the sun in my face, it is very hot, and I am sweating plus my son is refusing to put his pajamas on. I am really stressed, and I just need to lie down. While this was happening, I thought to myself that there would probably be photos of this, because I am mentally on the edge. And it did also take a photo of the situations"*. Thus, it turned out that photos of these situations were among the most arousing top ten.

Expectations of Others. It was not just John who had expectations about which situations the tool had photographed. His girlfriend wanted to look through the photos with him, as she had expectations of her own: *"My girlfriend wanted to look at the photos in the application together with me. When she saw there were no photos of her she got disappointed because she expected me to have an emotional reaction while we were doing things together"*.

Want More Photos. Participants knew that the tool would only show photographs of the top 10 situations in which they had the strongest emotional reactions. Yet, John was in conflict with himself about wanting to see more photos: *"I wish there were more photos. I know it is only supposed to show the photos where you have had the strongest reactions. But I wish there would have been a bit more. Of course, then there would just be lots of photos. There should be a reason they are taken"*. Related to this, Marie specifically said she had expected to see photos about a particular situation she experienced as very enjoyable. She was surprised that there were no photos of this: *"Here from half past seven to a quarter to nine I went for a long walk. It was a lovely walk in the sun where I stopped to look at some horses playing in the field, but there were no photos of this at all. I had expected that there would be photos of this because it was a very pleasant experience"*.

5.4   Making Sense of Lifelog Data

At the end of the day, participants went through the photos in the pc application. During the interviews they talked about the process of making sense of the photos and writing comments for these.

Writing Comments. John had written comments for most of his photos the first day as illustrated in Fig. 4, but almost none the second day. Even though he mostly wrote comments for his photos on the first day, he could still recall situations on the photos from the second day, when he talked about them during the interview. He said that his reason for not writing more comments the second day was a lack of time: *"There are some of the photos from the day before where I can remember exactly, like you know it makes sense that I had a reaction (…) It was a bit late that night and I didn't know which comment I could write. I wanted to write something that was fit for the photo. Something to sum up the essence of the photo, why it could have taken the photo (…) If I had more time I am sure I would have written a comment"*. He also said that he was used to being meticulous when writing comments for photos he posted on social media, as he wanted his comments to be entertaining: *"I might be a bit damaged by social*

media. Because you have this idea that you must come up with something funny or fitting for the photo (...) Maybe it was because I knew that someone [the interviewer] would be looking at it".

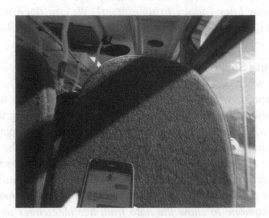

Fig. 4. Example of a photo where John commented: "arranging a dinner date with my girlfriend".

Using Timestamps. Figure 5 shows one of the photos from John's second day, for which he had not written a comment. The way he made sense of the photo was by looking at the timestamp of the photo and then describing what was happening outside of the border of the photo at the time the photo was taken: *"You can't see it but just above the top of the photo is the television and here [points to timestamp] we have been watching a football match with my favorite team. And they didn't do too well".*

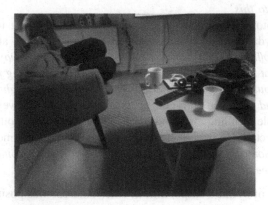

Fig. 5. Example of a photo where John also used the timestamp to explain what happened.

This is similar to Marie who also made sense of some of her photos using timestamps. Below is an example where she relates the timestamp from the photo combined with her and her boyfriend's posture at the dinner table: *"My boyfriend is sitting like this and I am sitting like this [points to photo]. We are both sitting in a relaxed position. It is 30 min later [points to timestamp]. We are done with dinner and no screaming kids. It is just relaxed. I can't remember that we were talking about anything special"*.

Using External Data Sources. Additionally, Marie also made use of a messenger log on her smartphone when describing a photo during the interview. On the photo she was working on her laptop, which could be seen in front of her. In her hand, she was holding her smartphone with the messenger app open. While going through the photos during the interview, she picked up her smartphone to show a comparison with the data from her messenger app with the photo and timestamp data from the pc application: *"I had missed my little boy all day but here I just received some photos that he is having a wonderful time which makes me very happy. (...) I know this because I can see that I received the photos one minute before and here I am forwarding them to my boyfriend [picks up her smartphone to show the data from her messenger app]. I received the photos from my mother in law 12:05 and 12:06 I forwarded these to my boyfriend"*.

5.5   Self-reflection

The participants seemed to recal their experiences and reflect on these by using the tool.

Recalling Details. There were several photos where John could be seen using his smartphone. When talking about these photos he was able to remember details of what he had used the phone for. There were for instance a photo of him on the bus writing a text message: *"I am trying to find a good comeback (...) we typically send funny gif files to each other while texting. I must have found something good since it [In the Moment] reacted to this"*.

Using the photos to recall his experiences Andreas was able to remember what happened in everyday situations that he otherwise had forgotten about: *"Here I am about to put my coffee cup and drinking bottle in the car on my way to school when I realize that I forgot my keys (...) it is funny because it is something from everyday life that you forget about again shortly after. (...) I could remember right away when I saw the photo, but I had forgotten about the episode before that"*. However, in some cases Andreas had trouble recalling a situation from a photograph and could not make sense of why it was selected. He instead hypothesized that he had an emotional reaction to internal stimuli: *"Some of the photos does not make sense and it could be because I am thinking about something that has caused the reaction"*.

Becoming Aware of What's Important in Life. Andreas was positively surprised to see, that there were several photos of situations where he is doing activities with his kids. This was because photos were taken based on his emotional reactions: *"...like my comment here were I wrote 'daddy is proud'. It is great to see that I had a physical reaction to this (...) It is situations like this that I forget about fast, but that I can see are a big part of my life"*.

When asked if there were photographs that she would not have thought about taking herself, Marie refereed to some of the photos as joyous photos: *"The joyous photos they surprised me, but it is very pleasant to see that I have reacted so strongly on the things that make me happy. That is a pleasant eyeopener."* One of the photos she refers to as a joyous photo is a situation where she is having dinner with her family: *"Here we are sitting down and there is food on the table. We are doing this thing where my little boy learns to tell us what he has experienced during the day instead of us asking him about it (...) I am happy that it photographed this because this is not a situation that I had thought about. But I can see now that it took the photo because the situation made me happy. (...) It was a positive surprise"*.

6 Discussion

In the following we highlight and discuss our findings from the perspective of using a provocative lifelogging tool to support in the wild studies. This discussion takes a participant centered view on the topic in terms of how they experienced and appropriated using our In the Moment Tool. Our participants were encouraged to use the In the Moment tool like they wanted to and as much (or little) as they saw fit for their daily lives. This differs from related in the wild studies of lifelogging tools, where participants have been asked to use the tools for the entire day [31, 37].

6.1 Breaking Social Norms

The result of our study shows, that the participants in some situations chose not to wear the tool, for instance to work, or in public places or at specific events, because they did not want to break social norms. Due to the camera and the fact of being unable to consciously control this, participants had concerns about others feeling monitored if they realized there was a camera present at all times. One of the participants said that she also felt monitored by the tool herself while she wore it at home, yet she kept using the tool. It was not so much about participants themselves feeling monitored, but more about how others would react to this. Referring to a situation where a participant wore the camera when being around other people, he thought about the behavior of others and whether or not they behaved differently because of this. When around family some of them initially behaved differently as the camera made them feel uncomfortable. On the other hand, one family member took a playful approach to appropriate the tool, e.g. by scaring the participant who wore the camera in order to force a picture being taken.

It is key that the design is strange enough to fulfil its purpose so that it does not readily blend into the everyday routines [3, 33]. Yet, it should not be so provocative that participants find the it weird and rejects it, i.e. a slight strangeness is the key [13].

This suggests that the provocation worked as intended, in particular since participants chose to wear the camera in spite of the fear of breaking social norms. Our participants were at times confronted with initial skepticism by family members or their partner while wearing the camera. None, however, experienced confrontation by strangers in public settings. This may be explained by the efforts made in making the tool blend in with the clothing, i.e. hiding the tool. This highlights the importance for

researchers to discuss with their study participants how to handle social situations while wearing data collection tools of this automatically curated nature. Such a discussion should be initiated before conducting the study, e.g. as part of the session in which consent forms are signed. We refer to the work of Kelly et al. for a further discussion and guidelines on how to deal with data gathered from automated wearable cameras [24]. Although participants chose to wear the camera in most situations, it should be noted that there were a few examples of participants leaving the tool at home. This was case when they doubted the legality of using the camera, which follows one of the recommendations suggested in [24].

6.2   Recalling Details

Generally, we found that participants were able to vividly recall details about their past experiences by using the photos with timestamps in the pc application. Participants expressed that they were able to recall being excited at the time that photos were taken, albeit with some exceptions. This is similar to Kelly and Jones' findings where data items, that correlated with intense GSR readings, were perceived as the most usable for self-reflection and self-awareness [23].

Participants also added additional data sources by themselves to help recollection. This could for instance be opening up a message service on their smartphones to view previously sent and received messages at specific points in time. This was an unin-tended advantage with our design, yet supported within previous studies. Pavel et al. for instance show that participants include the data sources they deem relevant in order to reflect on past events [31]. The study by Arvola et al. [2] also indicates that com-plementary data sources increase richness of self-reflection descriptions. This further-more supports the recommendation in [37] on designing lifelogging tools such that data is left open for interpretation without dictating how participants felt at given moments.

Thus, lifelogging tools that provide complementary cues seem to reduce the memory recall bias known from free recall settings such as the widely applied Day Reconstruction Method (DRM) [12]. We also highlight, that DRM was developed by Kahneman and colleagues [22] as a more feasible solution to the Experience Sampling Method (ESM), in which participants receive prompts multiple times per day at which point they should report self-reflection data. DRM only requires participants to report their self-reflection data at the end of the day, yet at the cost of introducing a memory bias. Given the cued recall nature supported by lifelogging tools, these seem to be a valid, and, perhaps more precise alternative, to DRM when conducting studies in the wild.

6.3   Encouraging (Unexpected) Reflections

Our participants were able to use our lifelogging tool to self-reflect on behavior in everyday life that meant something special to them, behavior which some expressed never to have thought of as explicitly before. They were able to use the tool to make broader reflections in what makes them happy, which is a direct effect of letting the camera be curated through emotional reactions. As an example, one of our participants reflected on photos of him doing activities with his kids. Since the photos were taken

on basis of emotional reactions, he expressed feeling good about having a reaction in that situation, and that he usually forget about such situations after a short time. Similarly, another participant noted that she was surprised and pleased to find a picture of her reacting strongly to a joyful moment. This indicates a highly positive effect of our conceptual and functional provocation related to not being able to consciously control when the camera takes photos. This finding is in line with one of the aims of provocative design in encouraging and motivating participants to reflect upon their daily practices [33, 34].

Further indications of how the provocative design encouraged participants is the excitement of unboxing photos at the end of the day. One participant expressed looking forward to seeing which situations he reacted to. He also found that the tool became *"cool"* to use during the second day as he was engaging himself in predicting when a photo was taken. Not only did this participant show interest in the lifelogged photos, in one case his partner wanted to look at which photos were taken. Another participant expressed the urge to unbox even more photos.

6.4   Study Limitations

Although we did not empirically compare our provocative design against existing lifelogging tools, our findings in several areas are in line with related work. We further extend previous studies by exploring the potential value of a provocative design to support data gathering in the wild. In our study such provocation led to participant reflections that they did not expect themselves as well as inducing the feeling of excitement when about to view the photos taken.

Also, instructing the participants in using the tool as they saw fit, might have contributed to a more natural behavior during the three days they used the tool. While this supports the notion of studying phenomena in the wild, this may also have resulted in participants sometimes choosing not to use the tool in specific situations. This limits the results as the tool did not collect data during an entire day.

Additionally, one participant felt that someone else was in her house, even though she was alone. This is likely because she knew that the photos would be included during the interview. This could also have affected her behavior while wearing the tool. The same could apply in relation to the self-reflection comments given for the photos, which would also be touched upon during the interviews. Commenting on photos for the purpose of a research study was also commented on by one participant. He said that he was used to thinking meticulously of something funny to write when commenting photos on social media for others to see. Being used to think hard about what to write and knowing that the comments would be read by others as part of the study influenced him in a way where he chose not to provide comments on one of the days. This would have taken too much time as he came home late from work.

In the HCI research community we also see a movement towards conducting longitudinal studies in the wild [34]. As this perspective was not included in our exploratory study it is a relevant next step to consider. Also, the study included three participants, which limits the representativeness of a large population. However, the study was not designed for this purpose but rather to sample some of the engagement

and appropriation strategies employed when introducing a provocative lifelogging tool to capture user experiences in the wild.

6.5 Future Implications

Our study indicates that lifelogging tools based on the use of physiological sensors and a wearable camera have the potential of supporting continuous data collection to study phenomena in the wild. However, given that the camera of our In the Moment tool could not be consciously controlled, participants in some cases exhibited caution in order not to break social norms. Yet, participants used the tool actively and reported reactions of being positively excited and surprised over the photos taken. This furthermore demonstrates the potential value of basing lifelogging tools on physiological sensors that continuously measure emotional states. We believe our main finding relates to demonstrate the potential value for participants to self-reflect on photos taken outside their own control. This is also supported by Boucher et al. [6], who discusses the use of cameras for cultural probe studies: *"Perhaps most importantly, probe returns are most revealing when they are spontaneous and unedited, whereas most common digital devices allow review, editing and deletion"*. This study thus provides an example of how to use an emotionally curated lifelogging tool in the wild and the value hereof. Given the novelty of our study, we believe this contributes with a starting point starting point that can inform and inspire future studies to explore the use of provocative design to motivate participants to self-reflect and report on daily experiences.

7 Conclusions

Research in the wild is receiving increasing attention as a way of studying participant experiences and behavior in natural environments. This study contributes by exploring how participants appropriate and experience wearing a provocative lifelogging tool using a wearable camera that takes photos based on participants' most intense emotional reactions. The design rationale aimed to promote unconscious curation of images, which was done in order to further motivate participant reflection.

The tool was employed by three participants in the wild, who were asked to use the tool freely as they saw fit. At the end of each day they were asked to use the lifelogging tool to view the photos while reflecting over their daily experiences.

Our findings show that participants were able to make sense of the photos presented within the tool and participants could vividly recall details about their experiences. Given the emotional curation of images participants reported that the tool enabled them to reflect on their experiences and become more aware episodes that are special to them and makes them happy in their lives, e.g. doing activities with their kids. However, the study also showed that the participants were concerned about breaking social norms, e.g. by not being able to control when photos of others were taken. They appropriated the tool by making this blend into their clothes and in some cases even chose their clothing to mask the camera. We believe our main finding is that of demonstrating how provocative design, in our case not being in conscious control of the technology, seems

to motivate participants in reflecting of their daily lives. They found it exciting to unbox the photos taken during the day to explore which situations they reacted to emotionally. Our findings have relevance for research practice as they illustrate the potential value of using physiological sensors to engage participants in self-reflection.

References

1. Apple: optimized. https://itunes.apple.com/us/app/optimized-lifelogging-quantified-self-improvement-app/id785042895?mt=8
2. Arvola, M., et al.: Lifelogging in user experience research: supporting recall and improving data richness. Des. J. **20**(sup1), S3954–S3965 (2017). https://doi.org/10.1080/14606925.2017.1352898
3. Bardzell, S., et al.: Critical design and critical theory. In: Proceedings of the Designing Interactive Systems Conference on - DIS 2012, p. 288. ACM Press, New York (2012). https://doi.org/10.1145/2317956.2318001
4. Bargas-Avila, J.A., Hornbæk, K.: Old wine in new bottles or novel challenges. In: Proceedings of CHI, pp. 2689–2698. ACM, New York (2011). https://doi.org/10.1145/1978942.1979336
5. Berry, E., et al.: The use of a wearable camera, SenseCam, as a pictorial diary to improve autobiographical memory in a patient with limbic encephalitis: a preliminary report. Neuropsychol. Rehabil. **17**(4–5), 582–601 (2007). https://doi.org/10.1080/09602010601029780
6. Boucher, A., et al.: TaskCam. In: Proceedings of the 2018 CHI Conference on Human Factors in Computing Systems, CHI 2018, pp. 1–12. ACM Press, New York (2018). https://doi.org/10.1145/3173574.3173645
7. Braun, V., Clarke, V.: Using thematic analysis in psychology. Qual. Res. Psychol. **3**(2), 77–101 (2006). https://doi.org/10.1191/1478088706qp063oa
8. Bruun, A., et al.: Asserting real-time emotions through cued-recall: is it valid? In: ACM International Conference Proceeding Series (2016). https://doi.org/10.1145/2971485.2971516
9. Bruun, A., et al.: Understanding the relationship between frustration and the severity of usability problems: what can psychophysiological data (not) tell us? In: Proceedings of the 2016 CHI Conference on Human Factors in Computing Systems, pp. 3975–3987. ACM, New York (2016). https://doi.org/10.1145/2858036.2858511
10. Bruun, A., Ahm, S.: Mind the gap! Comparing retrospective and concurrent ratings of emotion in user experience evaluation. In: Abascal, J., Barbosa, S., Fetter, M., Gross, T., Palanque, P., Winckler, M. (eds.) INTERACT 2015. LNCS, vol. 9296, pp. 237–254. Springer, Cham (2015). https://doi.org/10.1007/978-3-319-22701-6_17
11. Byrne, D., et al.: The SenseCam as a tool for task observation. In: Proceedings of the 22nd British HCI Group Annual Conference on People and Computers: Culture, Creativity, Interaction, vol. 2, pp. 19–22. British Computer Society (2008). 10.1.1.153.1040
12. Diener, E., Tay, L.: Review of the day reconstruction method (DRM). Soc. Indic. Res. **116**(1), 255–267 (2014). https://doi.org/10.1007/s11205-013-0279-x
13. Dunne, A., Raby, F.: Design Noir: The Secret Life of Electronic Objects. Springer, Berlin (2001)
14. Dunne, A., Raby, F.: Speculative Everything: Design, Fiction, and Social Dreaming. MIT Press, Cambridge (2013)

15. Empatica: Real-time physiological signals|E4 EDA/GSR sensor. https://www.empatica.com/research/e4/

16. Fleck, R., Fitzpatrick, G.: Teachers' and tutors' social reflection around SenseCam images. Int. J. Hum Comput Stud. **67**(12), 1024–1036 (2009). https://doi.org/10.1016/J.IJHCS.2009.09.004

17. Forlizzi, J., Battarbee, K.: Understanding experience in interactive systems. In: Proceedings of the DIS, pp. 261–268. ACM, New York (2004). https://doi.org/10.1145/1013115.1013152

18. Ganglbauer, E., et al.: Applying psychophysiological methods for measuring user experience: possibilities, challenges and feasibility. In: User Experience Evaluation Methods in Product Development (UXEM), Uppsala, Sweden (2009). 10.1.1.189.3410

19. Hodges, D., Berry, E., Wood, K.: SenseCam: a wearable camera which stimulates and rehabilitates autobiographical memory. Memory **19**(7), 685–696 (2011)

20. Hodges, S., et al.: SenseCam: a retrospective memory aid. In: Dourish, P., Friday, A. (eds.) UbiComp 2006. LNCS, vol. 4206, pp. 177–193. Springer, Heidelberg (2006). https://doi.org/10.1007/11853565_11

21. Journaly. https://emberify.com/journaly/

22. Kahneman, D., et al.: A survey method for characterizing daily life experience: the day reconstruction method. Science **306**(5702), 1776–1780 (2004)

23. Kelly, L., Jones, G.J.F.: An exploration of the utility of GSR in locating events from personal lifelogs for reflection, pp. 82–85 (2010)

24. Kelly, P., et al.: An ethical framework for automated, wearable cameras in health behavior research. Am. J. Prev. Med. **44**(3), 314–319 (2013). https://doi.org/10.1016/j.amepre.2012.11.006

25. Kerr, J., et al.: Using the SenseCam to improve classifications of sedentary behavior in free-living settings. Am. J. Prev. Med. **44**(3), 290–296 (2013). https://doi.org/10.1016/J.AMEPRE.2012.11.004

26. Lee, K., Hong, H.: Designing for self-tracking of emotion and experience with tangible modality. In: Proceedings of the 2017 Conference on Designing Interactive Systems, DIS 2017, pp. 465–475. ACM Press, New York (2017). https://doi.org/10.1145/3064663.3064697

27. Li, I., et al.: A stage-based model of personal informatics systems. In: Proceedings of the 28th International Conference on Human Factors in Computing Systems, CHI 2010, p. 557. ACM Press, New York (2010). https://doi.org/10.1145/1753326.1753409

28. Li, I., et al.: Using context to reveal factors that affect physical activity. ACM Trans. Comput. Interact. **19**(1), 1–21 (2012). https://doi.org/10.1145/2147783.2147790

29. Lindley, S.E., et al.: "Oh and how things just don't change, the more things stay the same": reflections on SenseCam images 18 months after capture. Int. J. Hum Comput Stud. **69**(5), 311–323 (2011). https://doi.org/10.1016/j.ijhcs.2010.12.010

30. Narrative: The world's most wearable HD video camera - narrative clip 2. http://getnarrative.com/

31. Pavel, D., et al.: Lifestyle stories: correlating user information through a story-inspired paradigm. In: Proceedings of the ICTs for Improving Patients Rehabilitation Research Techniques. IEEE (2013). https://doi.org/10.4108/icst.pervasivehealth.2013.252131

32. Radesky, J.S., et al.: Patterns of mobile device use by caregivers and children during meals in fast food restaurants. Pediatrics **133**(4), e843–e849 (2014). https://doi.org/10.1542/peds.2013-3703

33. Raptis, D., et al.: Aesthetic, functional and conceptual provocation in research through design. In: Proceedings of the 2017 Conference on Designing Interactive Systems, DIS 2017, pp. 29–41 (2017). https://doi.org/10.1145/3064663.3064739

34. Rogers, Y., Marshall, P.: Research in the wild. Synth. Lect. Hum.-Centered Inform. **10**(3), i–97 (2017). https://doi.org/10.2200/S00764ED1V01Y201703HCI037
35. Scherer, K.R.: What are emotions? And how can they be measured? Soc. Sci. Inf. **44**(4), 695–729 (2005). https://doi.org/10.1177/0539018405058216
36. Sellen, A.J., et al.: Do life-logging technologies support memory for the past? In: Proceedings of the SIGCHI Conference on Human Factors in Computing Systems, CHI 2007, p. 81. ACM Press, New York (2007). https://doi.org/10.1145/1240624.1240636
37. Ståhl, A., et al.: Experiencing the affective diary. Pers. Ubiquit. Comput. **13**(5), 365–378 (2009). https://doi.org/10.1007/s00779-008-0202-7
38. Zimmerman, J., et al.: Research through design as a method for interaction design research in HCI. In: Proceedings of the SIGCHI Conference on Human Factors in Computing Systems, CHI 2007, p. 493. ACM Press, New York (2007). https://doi.org/10.1145/1240624.1240704

34. Rogers, Y., Marshall, P.: Research in the wild. Synth. Lect. Hum.-Centered Inform. 10(3), 1–97 (2017). https://doi.org/10.2200/S00764ED1V01Y201703HCI037

35. Scherer, K.R.: What are emotions? And how can they be measured? Soc. Sci. Inf. 44(4), 695–729 (2005). https://doi.org/10.1177/0539018405058216

36. Sellen, A.J., et al.: Do life-logging technologies support memory for the past? In: Proceedings of the SIGCHI Conference on Human Factors in Computing Systems, CHI 2007, p. 81. ACM Press, New York (2007). https://doi.org/10.1145/1240624.1240636

37. Ståhl, A., et al.: Experiencing the affective diary. Pers. Ubiquit. Comput. 13(5), 365–378 (2009). https://doi.org/10.1007/s00779-008-0202-7

38. Zimmerman, J., et al.: Research through design as a method for interaction design research in HCI. In: Proceedings of the SIGCHI Conference on Human Factors in Computing Systems, CHI 2007, p. 493. ACM Press, New York (2007). https://doi.org/10.1145/1240624.1240704

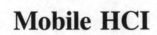

Mobile HCI

A Comparative Study of Younger and Older Adults' Interaction with a Crowdsourcing Android TV App for Detecting Errors in TEDx Video Subtitles

Kinga Skorupska(✉) ⓘ, Manuel Núñez ⓘ, Wiesław Kopeć ⓘ,
and Radosław Nielek ⓘ

Polish-Japanese Academy of Information Technology,
Warsaw, Poland
kinga.skorupska@pja.edu.pl,
http://www.pja.edu.pl

Abstract. In this paper we report the results of a pilot study comparing the older and younger adults' interaction with an Android TV application which enables users to detect errors in video subtitles. Overall, the interaction with the TV-mediated crowdsourcing system relying on language proficiency was seen as intuitive, fun and accessible, but also cognitively demanding; more so for younger adults who focused on the task of detecting errors, than for older adults who concentrated more on the meaning and edutainment aspect of the videos. We also discuss participants' motivations and preliminary recommendations for the design of TV-enabled crowdsourcing tasks and subtitle QA systems.

Keywords: Crowdsourcing · Smart TV · Android TV ·
Design evaluation · Subtitles · Older adults · Younger adults

1 Introduction and Related Works

With the increasing amount of video content it is necessary to ensure its accessibility to the deaf, the hard of hearing and international audiences through quality same language and multilingual subtitles. Therefore, crowdsourcing subtitle quality assurance (QA) models are an important research frontier, especially as subtitles are often created by volunteers, as in the case of TED and TEDx [7] or generated automatically. At the same time, there are groups who may benefit from more fun and accessible crowdsourcing projects.

For example, older adults, who comprised 19.2% of the EU-28 population in 2016 [1], benefit from all forms of volunteering, as it slows the negative effects of aging and helps combat depression [10]. Yet, there exist multiple barriers to their inclusion in typical crowdsourcing tasks, such as lower ICT skills, uncomfortable and costly setup of such solutions [16], unfamiliar interfaces and lack of

© IFIP International Federation for Information Processing 2019
Published by Springer Nature Switzerland AG 2019
D. Lamas et al. (Eds.): INTERACT 2019, LNCS 11748, pp. 455–464, 2019.
https://doi.org/10.1007/978-3-030-29387-1_25

motivation due to unclear personal benefit [4], unsocial nature of the task [18] or their perception of not being qualified [8].

Younger adults, on the other hand, who are more open to online crowdsourcing and microtasking, comprise a significant number of online video viewers, as, according to We Are Flint about 96% of people in UK and US aged 18–34 watch YouTube videos [2]. Both groups are relevant to the development of TV-enabled subtitle QA crowdsourcing tasks as potential contributors and audience.

Therefore, the key research goal was to validate a novel interface for creating no-grind crowdsourcing solutions, ones that do not rely on tedious repetition, with two relevant user groups. To do this, we deployed a Smart TV-based system based on best practices of designing for older users [6,12] with a comfortable at-home setup, large screen size, and remote relying on familiar interaction patterns [13] with engaging edutainment crowdsourcing tasks. This lowered ICT and other participation barriers and allowed us to signal some possible differences in the participants' approach, motivation, mode of use, experience and expectations. We lay ground to the discussion of the extent to which one may build a universal crowdsourcing system suited to the needs of these different groups, to tap into their potential, facilitate social inclusion and build social capital.

2   Methods

2.1   Comparative Study Design

To explore these considerations we conducted a comparative qualitative study in the course of which we compared results from a study involving older adults [17] to the results of a study with younger adults conducted in February-March 2019.

The study examined the interaction with the DreamTV application we created [17] which allows users to watch TEDx videos with volunteer-created subtitles retrieved from Amara API. Once they spot an error they can pause the video to display an overlay (Fig. 1) where they choose the error category among grammar, meaning, style and timing. These error categories were chosen based on preliminary tests and research to be more intuitive than existing models of quality assessment of subtitles by professionals [15] and to aid in improving the subtitles later within the pipeline or during post-editing.

The research protocol, which took about two hours to complete, involved individual testing at participants' homes, where an Android TV set-top box was connected to participants' TV sets, to provide the most natural use conditions, as proposed in multiple studies on Living Labs [3,9]. It consisted of the DigComp survey[1], a semi-structured interview to evaluate experience with subtitles, the explanation of the project, that is the study and its benefits, an introduction to subtitles and a subtitle error detection written exercise, an app demonstration

---

[1] A survey measuring indicators of Digital Competence based on the Digital Competence Framework [5].

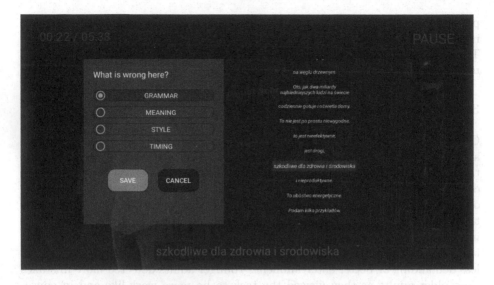

Fig. 1. The error category selection overlay in our Dream TV application

and a hands-on test, free interaction with the application and our pre-selected test videos (two in Polish, three in English) with redacted Polish subtitles.

For our study we selected five videos to represent different challenges. They were controlled for topic, length, source language (spoken), ease of comprehension and errors: saturation, category and source, either machine (using SubtitleEdit and Google Translate) or organic human or introduced by researchers based on common errors lists on TED Translators' wiki[2]. The videos selected and errors introduced allowed us to observe a variety of factors at play, in order to gather diverse insights to determine interesting areas of further inquiry.

2.2 Participants

We invited seven older adults (O1–O7) and seven younger adults (Y1–Y7) to participate in our study, in each case three female participants and four male participants. We controlled for age, occupation and ICT skills ("above basic proficiency", which is the highest level in DigComp). All participants live in Warsaw, the capital city of Poland. For older adults all owned TVs, including two Smart TVs, and had a dedicated entertainment space in their living room. There was a 20 years age span: the youngest participant was 60 years old and the oldest one was 79, mean 70.85 (SD = 6.87). For younger adults we recruited a group that would share the most relevant characteristics with our older adults, especially in terms of their housing situation and entertainment setup, which meant that in Poland they had to be between 25–35 years of age. All but one

---

[2] The TED Translators' wiki containing lists of common errors can be found at: https://translations.ted.com.

participants owned Smart TVs and had their own dedicated entertainment space in the living room. All were professionally active and none of them had children. The age span was 5 years, as the youngest participant was 28, and the oldest 33, mean 30.71 (SD = 2.28).

3   Results and Discussion

Overall, using the application was enjoyable, intuitive and easy for both younger and older participants, however there were differences in their approach to the task. While our group of younger adults saw it as an enjoyable activity one could do to improve subtitles, brag or supplement their income in a fun way, our group of older adults viewed it less as work and more an opportunity to learn something and did not expect payment for contributing. For older adults it was more interesting, as they were given access to resources they were unlikely to reach to on their own (TEDx videos) whereas younger adults agreed that they know less demanding or better entertainment. Younger adults detected more mistakes than older adults as they viewed the task to be more work-like and in consequence, demanding. Older adults seemed more lenient, especially when it came to style and punctuation, and focused more on the content of the videos, rather than correcting mistakes. There were also differences in feedback. Where older adults focused on ways to find videos that would be a better fit for them thematically, younger adults focused more on critiquing the error categories chosen and comparing the application to Netflix. This is due to the differences in experience with such services. Both groups found the interaction via the remote to be very convenient and well-suited for this activity and they learned to comfortably use the application in just one session, with older adults in general taking more time to learn and later to navigate, but with no significant other differences.

3.1   Error Detection

Reflexes. Overall, all of the older participants paused the videos one subtitle too late, and had to use the dialog list to navigate back to the subtitle where they wanted to mark the error. The same was true of all but one younger adults, as Y2 paused even before the speaker finished the sentence, indicating that they read rather than listened. This suggests that access to the full dialog list is necessary in this type of crowdsourcing for all age groups.

Number of Errors Found. In general, younger adults found more errors than older adults which may be related to their attitude towards this activity. While younger adults focused on the task of finding errors, older adults engaged with the content of the videos more and felt that they are learning new interesting things (O1–O4). This is in contrast with younger adults, except for Y4, who admitted to focus more on the content and commented that they "should watch such videos more often as they are interesting". Consequently, younger adults found many more punctuation errors, which older adults often ignored. This

may be as punctuation errors do not interfere with understanding. Older adults, who focused more on understanding the content, often chose the "meaning" category, when something was not clear to them (e.g. "it is not explained what is this photon" or "Spiderman, this is not Polish" by O2 and "kryptonite, must be a mistake" by O5, O6), suggesting the application could benefit from a built-in dictionary. Older adults' focus on meaning is in line with Radvansky's research on the effect of aging on memory and comprehension, suggesting that while lower levels of memory, which may be responsible for remembering specifics such as punctuation, deteriorate with age, the ability to form situation models on a higher level, aiding in meaning and general comprehension is less affected [14]. Moreover, different people found very different errors, depending on their interests and background (science for Y6: "the Sun vs the sun", detailed punctuation rules for Y2 with linguistic background) which shows that the effect of scale by relying more on quantity and not quality of contributions may work well here.

Error Categories. All but one of the younger participants (Y1–Y6) encountered errors in subtitles to which they wished to assign more than one error category, to remove the analysis paralysis of choosing the best fitting category ("People like me would deliberate 3 years over a single word" Y1) and likely to satisfy their need for cognitive closure [11], as many younger participants found the categories to be "fuzzy". The other participant, Y7, said that "these are short lines so if someone marks a mistake it is easy to know what it is" and proposed to remove categories, the same could be seen in O3's eagerness to just mark mistakes quickly and continue watching the videos.

Younger adults remarked that "synchronization is the most intuitive" (Y1). Other error categories requested were "punctuation" (Y6) and "subtitle division" (line breaking) (Y3) and "technical errors" such as subtitle convention errors as a separate category (Y1, Y2) and both Y7 and Y3 said that knowing subtitle conventions requires a lot of practice, and pre-teaching, for which Y3 suggested a mini-game, while older adults wished for an in-application tutorial to ensure they do not make mistakes when marking mistakes (O1, O4). One participant, Y6, also said there ought to be a way to mark recurring errors ("Here I would have to mark a lot of things, because the Sun should be written with capital letter, and it repeats a lot"), on the other hand O3 remarked "He made the same mistake, but I'll overlook it now", eager to continue watching.

Older adults (O1–O7) did not question the error categories even though they often could not decide which category to choose (O4, O5) and sometimes deliberated aloud (O3). This may be because older adults are less likely to criticize design choices in the context of technology, as they feel they lack experience in it so they are not confident enough to know they can contribute. This was also observed in the context of participatory design by Kopec et al. [8]. Also, even though some older adults had to sit closer to the screen to read (O1, O3) it was a younger adult (Y6) who voiced that they would like the interface to be bigger.

In conclusion, to ease the choice of error categories we propose to present them in the order of importance, with the top category being "meaning" -

answering the question "Is this subtitle understandable?", followed by "grammar", as it includes common punctuation mistakes, and then "style", which would have to be explained as relating to technical errors, and including also other problems. We postulate that because of conflicts of simultaneous work it is very difficult to find synchronization errors, while also looking for other types of errors ("It is difficult to catch problems with synchronization - you focus on all the other mistakes" Y3, and "I had to read" O5). This was seen in the tests with older adults, who found no synchronization errors (O1–O7), and younger adults who rarely marked them as they found it tiring to both read, and listen (Y7: "I did not listen to the guy", Y6: "difficult to focus on what the person was saying") Signalling the relationship between enjoyment, interest and errors found Y6 said: "this topic was interesting, sometimes I did not focus on finding mistakes". Both older (O1–O4, O6) and younger adults (Y3, Y4, Y6) seemed to find fewer errors the more they enjoyed the video, with Y4 saying that they were "forgetting to read". The enjoyment was also negatively correlated with the number of errors marked, with Y2 saying that "The errors were so thickly distributed, it is a very tiring video" and that "If there were fewer errors it would be more fun than work" and Y5 mentioning that "If you have to focus only on subtitles it is more like work, but if you get to mark glaring errors only it is more entertainment".

3.2 Fun or Work?

Y1 and Y5 found the application to be very fun, commenting that "you can point out someone's mistakes without arguing with that person, everyone loves that!" (Y1), adding that it is true especially when there are people around, and "How fun! I like it! I could do it all my life" (Y5). Y6 also said "it's cool, I like nitpicking". The other participants commented that it would be work if you "had to do it, like an editor in a paper" and "the movies are not long, and you can take breaks" (Y7). Similarly, Y3 mentioned that "you should be able to choose how long video you want". This aspect of controlling time was also present in older adults' feedback, as they enjoyed the ability to pause the video at will, take breaks, and O3 even said "The movies should be shorter, then I could watch anything! Just give me ten 5 min films and I can do that for an hour". Older adults overall focused on the educational aspect of the task, saying that it is good practice and one can "learn a lot" (O1–O4) from these videos. This aspect was less prominent with younger adults, who often treated the experience almost job-like as it was "mentally demanding" and felt more like "work", or that it is a bit like an "exam" (Y1) and felt judged when they did not understand a subtitle (Y3) ("I don't know what they mean by "last mile" and since it was in quotation marks it must be something that everyone knows, so now I feel stupid"). In contrast, only O4 mentioned that "It is tiring, I am not that young anymore." drawing attention to the task's cognitive load.

Table 1. Comparison of older and younger adults' motivations, rewards and wishes

	Younger adults	Older adults
Pointing out mistakes	Y1, Y2, Y5, Y6	O3
Social activity	Y1: "to do with friends"	O2: "with grandchildren"
Helping somebody	Y1: "If some friend asked me to do this for them, I would help them", Y4	
Learning new things	Our group of younger adults could watch such videos, but just watch as Y4: "they are interesting" to Y6: "focus on the content"	O1–O4, O1: "I learned a lot", O3 "I would watch movies about health, global issues, climate change or politics" but: O5 "The topics would have to be useful"
Getting paid	Y1–Y7, except for Y5: "Nobody would pay much, it's better to have bonuses, like a subscription or a small gift because earning little money is meh"	
Improving the world	Y1: "I like it, if I was convinced myself that this is making the world a bit better, then this is a convenient way to help"	
Challenging oneself cognitively	Y2 and Y3, but about other people, Y3: "blue-collar workers" and "stay at home moms" who can do it for fun and Y2: "retired people to stay active"	O3: "This task is great for old people, but only those who are mentally fit, so that they don't deteriorate"
Passion for the topic	Y3 mentioning feminists: "people who are very passionate about a topic can contribute"	
Statistics of confirmed contributions	Y4: "ranking like on Memrise", Y6: "ranking of best reviewers", Y3: "a community to care about my achievements listed on my profile". Interestingly, both Y1 and Y2 mentioned they do not need statistics	
Helping improve subtitles being used	Y3: "that there were 100 people who watched this film with improved subtitle in a month would mean something"	
Access to training	Y3, "in the community access to games that help you develop skills to contribute better"	O1: "It would be good to have a testing mode, to be able to train without consequences", O4
Addressing glaring errors	In videos they are watching with subtitles anyway (Y4, Y5)	
Reliance on linguistic experience	Y3: "I like that I don't have to learn anything to start doing it, I know the language"	O3: "There should be more subtitle testers like me, but not young people because they have little experience"

3.3   Motivation, Gamification and Rewards

While older adults' participants motivation was mostly based on the value for them, in terms usefulness, relevance to their interests and staying active, for younger adults there was almost no concern about the topic as they viewed the task to be more "work-like" and focused finding errors more than understanding and enjoying the content - likely because they have other entertainment readily available. Detailed comparison of approaches and attitudes is visible in Table 1.

3.4   Sustainability

Overall, although most of the participants found this activity to be fun, there are doubts whether they would do it in the long run without other incentives. The tests with older adults suggest that some may continue using the application as an easy foray into the world of edutainment and to stay active, except for O5 who stated "I manage, but it is not my thing - the topics would have to be useful" and O4 who expected to be bored as one has to "be focused". On the other hand, some younger adults commented "I wouldn't do it because it is time consuming, when you watch something to gain knowledge it is easier to understand the content if you are just watching" (Y6) or "it's not my type of thing, I am not a linguist and correcting errors is not my passion" (Y7). They also mentioned shortage of time (Y2, Y3) and the demanding nature of this task (Y2, Y3, Y6, Y7) as a problem. For younger adults, who have formed habits regarding their access to other forms of entertainment, it may work best as a feature integrated into their familiar experience. Both Y4 and Y5 suggested that such activity could be "integrated into a player" they "use anyway", on YouTube for Y4 ("it could be great if YouTube had something like that in their automatic subtitles, which now suck") or on VOD for Y5, who noted that "Sometimes I am tempted to mark something on VOD - there are few people who would bother to go to a film distributors' website and report errors in subtitles". Y5 concluded that "If it was easily accessible then a lot of people would do it, if they could just mark something on their remote".

4   Conclusions

As this is a pilot study with a small number of participants it is important to verify the following preliminary findings. While this task is fun for both younger and older adults, the former treat it more like work and expect payment. This group would benefit from having a similar solution integrated into their entertainment medium of choice. On the other hand, older adults are a promising target for this type of crowdsourcing, as it not only provides them with content they may otherwise miss, but also allows them to learn and stay active.

Future work ought to explore TV-mediated crowdsourcing in larger studies, and focus on the patterns of interaction with this solution, including the timing of engagement and quantitative relationship between the enjoyment of the video

and the number of subtitle errors found. It is also important to verify if this TV-mediated crowdsourcing solution can hold older adults' interest over time, and if so, what are other ways such mode of interaction can be used to allow older adults to stay active for longer, contribute to society and learn new things.

Acknowledgments. This research in part was supported by the Polish National Science Center grant 2018/29/B/HS6/02604 and the European Union's Horizon 2020 research and innovation programme under the Marie Skłodowska-Curie grant agreement No. 690962.

References

1. Population structure and ageing (2017). http://ec.europa.eu/eurostat/statistics-explained/index.php/Population_structure_and_ageing
2. Social 2018 main findings (2018). https://weareflint.co.uk/main-findings-social-media-demographics-uk-usa-2018
3. Alaoui, M., Lewkowicz, M.: A livinglab approach to involve elderly in the design of smart TV applications offering communication services. In: Ozok, A.A., Zaphiris, P. (eds.) OCSC 2013. LNCS, vol. 8029, pp. 325–334. Springer, Heidelberg (2013). https://doi.org/10.1007/978-3-642-39371-6_37
4. Brewer, R., Morris, M.R., Piper, A.M.: Why would anybody do this? Understanding older adults' motivations and challenges in crowd work. In: Proceedings of the 2016 CHI Conference on Human Factors in Computing Systems, pp. 2246–2257. ACM (2016)
5. Ferrari, A.: DIGCOMP: a framework for developing and understanding digital competence in Europe (2013)
6. Fisk, A., Czaja, S., Rogers, W., Charness, N., Sharit, J.: Designing for Older Adults: Principles and Creative Human Factors Approaches. Human Factors and Aging Series, 2nd edn. CRC Press, Boca Raton (2009)
7. de la Fuente, L.C.: Multilingual crowdsourcing motivation on global social media, case study: TED OTP. Sendebar **25**, 197–218 (2014)
8. Kopeć, W., Balcerzak, B., Nielek, R., Kowalik, G., Wierzbicki, A., Casati, F.: Older adults and hackathons: a qualitative study. Empirical Softw. Eng. **23**(4), 1895–1930 (2018). https://doi.org/10.1007/s10664-017-9565-6
9. Kopeć, W., Skorupska, K., Jaskulska, A., Abramczuk, K., Nielek, R., Wierzbicki, A.: LivingLab PJAIT: towards better urban participation of seniors. In: Proceedings of the International Conference on Web Intelligence, WI 2017, pp. 1085–1092. ACM, New York (2017). https://doi.org/10.1145/3106426.3109040
10. Lum, T.Y., Lightfoot, E.: The effects of volunteering on the physical and mental health of older people. Res. Aging **27**(1), 31–55 (2005)
11. Webster, M.D., Kruglanski, A.: Individual differences in need for cognitive closure. J. Pers. Soc. Psychol. **67**, 1049–1062 (1995). https://doi.org/10.1037/0022-3514.67.6.1049
12. Pak, R., McLaughlin, A.: Designing Displays for Older Adults. Human Factors and Aging Series. CRC Press, Boca Raton (2010)
13. Pan, Z., Miao, C., Yu, H., Leung, C., Chin, J.J.: The effects of familiarity design on the adoption of wellness games by the elderly. In: 2015 IEEE/WIC/ACM International Conference on Web Intelligence and Intelligent Agent Technology (WI-IAT), vol. 2, pp. 387–390. IEEE (2015)

K. Skorupska et al.

14. Radvansky, G.: Aging, memory, and comprehension. Curr. Dir. Psychol. Sci. **8**, 49–53 (1999). https://doi.org/10.1111/1467-8721.00012
15. Romero-Fresco, P., Pöchhacker, F.: Quality assessment in interlingual live subtitling: the NTR model. Linguistica Antverpiensia New Ser. - Themes Translation Stud. 16(0) (2018), https://lans.ua.ac.be/index.php/LANS-TTS/article/view/438
16. Sandhu, J., Damodaran, L., Ramondt, L.: ICT skills acquisition by older people: motivations for learning and barriers to progression. Int. J. Educ. Ageing **3**(1), 25–42 (2013)
17. Skorupska, K., Nunez, M., Nunez, W., Nielek, R.: Older adults and crowdsourcing: android TV app for evaluating TEDx subtitle quality. Proc. ACM Hum.-Comput. Interact. **2**(CSCW), 159:1–159:23 (2018). https://doi.org/10.1145/3274428
18. Vines, J., Blythe, M., Dunphy, P., Monk, A.: Eighty something: banking for the older old. In: Proceedings of the 25th BCS Conference on Human-Computer Interaction, pp. 64–73. British Computer Society (2011)

Effect of Ambient Light
on Mobile Interaction

Zhanna Sarsenbayeva[1]($\boxtimes$), Niels van Berkel[2], Weiwei Jiang[1],
Danula Hettiachchi[1], Vassilis Kostakos[1], and Jorge Goncalves[1]

[1] The University of Melbourne, Melbourne, Australia
{zhanna.sarsenbayeva,weiwei.jiang,danula.hettiachchi,
vassilis.kostakos,jorge.goncalves}@unimelb.edu.au
[2] University College London, London, UK
n.vanberkel@ucl.ac.uk

Abstract. In this work we investigate the effect of ambient light on
performance during mobile interaction. We evaluate three conditions of
ambient light – normal light, dimmed light, normal light while wearing
sunglasses. Our results show that wearing sunglasses and dimmed light
negatively affect reaction time, while dimmed light negatively affects
accuracy performance in target acquisition tasks. We also show that
wearing sunglasses increases memorising time in visual search tasks. Our
study contributes to the growing body of research on the effects of different situational impairments on mobile interaction.

Keywords: Mobile interaction · Situational visual impairments ·
Ambient light

1 Introduction

Smartphones have become an integral part of human daily life, and a focus
of research conducted in our community [8,9]. People find themselves using
their smartphones under various challenging contexts [23]. Factors such as cold
ambience [2,18], encumbrance [10], walking [1], and ambient noise [16] have all
been shown to hinder smartphone interaction [15] and cause situational impairments [19,24]. While the effects of a number of situational impairments on mobile
interaction have been studied and are established within the HCI research community, many situational impairments remain underexplored. In their overview
of situational impairments, Sarsenbayeva *et al.* [15] identify a research gap concerning the effects of ambient light on mobile interaction, despite the fact that it
is common to use one's smartphone in varying light conditions (*e.g.*, watching a
movie with the lights off or interacting with the device while wearing sunglasses).

Therefore, in this paper we investigate the effect of ambient light conditions
on mobile interaction. We quantify mobile interaction performance in terms of
three everyday smartphone activities – target acquisition, visual search, and
text entry – under three distinct ambient lighting conditions: (1) normal light

© IFIP International Federation for Information Processing 2019
Published by Springer Nature Switzerland AG 2019
D. Lamas et al. (Eds.): INTERACT 2019, LNCS 11748, pp. 465–475, 2019.
https://doi.org/10.1007/978-3-030-29387-1_26

condition (operationalised as recommended indoor light levels for easy to normal office work [12]), (2) dimmed light condition, and (3) normal light condition while wearing sunglasses. We limit our investigation to the effect of reduced illuminance conditions. We do not study the effect of bright light on smartphone interaction for a number of reasons. First, the existing literature has already established the adverse effect of bright light on performance in visual tasks on mobile device screens [7]. Second, we want to exclude the effect of confounding parameters, such as glare, that is caused by bright light and leads to a decrease in visual task performance on mobile phone screens [7].

Our study shows that dimmed light, as well as wearing sunglasses, negatively affects mobile interaction performance in terms of target acquisition time. We also show that tapping accuracy decreases under the dimmed light condition, while wearing sunglasses increases target memorising time. Our work contributes to the growing body of research in the HCI community on situational impairments.

2   Related Work

2.1   Situational Visual Impairments During Mobile Interaction

Tigwell *et al.* [22] identified ambient light as one of the leading causes of visual situational impairments. Ambient light has been shown to affect people's perception as well as the clarity of a smartphone's display. For example, Gong *et al.* [3] show that as ambient light intensity increases, mobile device screens become more challenging to use. This might be because increasing ambient brightness while decreasing monitor brightness reduces colour differentiation abilities, as found by Reinecke *et al.* [13]. Furthermore, it has been shown that for illuminance levels higher than 1000 lx, participants' visual task performance declines at a faster rate compared to illuminance levels lower than 1000 lx, due to screen glare [7]. Dimmed ambient light has also been shown to visually impair users; however, only limited research has investigated its effect. For example, Lee *et al.* [6] investigated the effect of ambient illuminance on performance while reading e-papers. They found that search speed and illuminance level were directly proportional: with low search speed being associated with low levels of illuminance. Liu *et al.* [7] studied the effect of ambient light on handheld display image quality. The authors found that in darker environments, participants performed better in visual tasks as compared to bright environments. These findings are in line with findings from Kim *et al.* [5] which demonstrate that perceived image quality on screens decreases in bright environments. However, both of the aforementioned studies featured a limited number of participants (3 participants in [7], 10 participants in [5]). Furthermore, both of the studies focused on the perception of image quality on mobile device screens.

3   Method

In this study, we investigate the effect of an environmental factor – ambient light – on mobile interaction. In particular, we focus on mobile interaction under

dimmed light conditions. We quantify interaction performance across three typical smartphone tasks: target acquisition, visual search, and text entry. We used the tasks developed and presented in a study by Sarsenbayeva *et al.* [16] in order to directly compare the effect of ambient light-induced situational impairments to the established effects of cold- [2,18], noise- [16], and stress-induced [14] situational impairments.

3.1   Smartphone Tasks

In this study, we used a Samsung Galaxy S7 smartphone running Android 7.0 with 1080×1920 px screen size (similar to the one used in the studies by Sarsenbayeva *et al.* [16,18]). To minimise sequence effects, participants completed the three tasks in a counterbalanced order. Furthermore, we minimised any potential learning effects by asking our participants to undergo extensive training in all three tasks prior to the start of the actual experiment. The participants completed the tasks in a standing position, interacting with the phone with the index finger of their dominant hand while holding the phone in their non-dominant hand.

Target Acquisition. In this task, participants tap circular targets (Radius = 135 px) with an indicated centre (Fig. 1A). The targets appear on a random position on the screen, one circle at a time. We asked our participants to tap the centre of the circles as precisely and quickly as possible. We measure participants' performance in terms of their reaction speed (time required to tap targets) and accuracy (offset size).

Visual Search. In this task, participants are asked to find a target icon among 24 other icons, arranged according to a 4×6 grid [4]. The participants are first shown the icon, and given as much time as required to memorise it (Fig. 1B). Then, participants must find this icon in the subsequent screen (Fig. 1C). Target icons are selected randomly from the pool, and the icons are placed at random positions on the screen to minimise any potential learning effects. We quantify participants' performance in terms of cognition (time to memorise an icon), reaction (time to find an icon), and accuracy (error rate).

Text Entry. In this task, participants are instructed to type a snippet of text shown in a text box. The texts are of two difficulties: (1) easy – consisting of only one sentence with commonly used words (Fig. 1D), and (2) difficult – consisting of several sentences with outdated words (Fig. 1E). For each round, participants are presented a randomly selected easy sentence (10 in total) and a randomly selected difficult sentence (10 in total). We measure how quick (character entry rate) and accurate (error rate) participants were in entering the text.

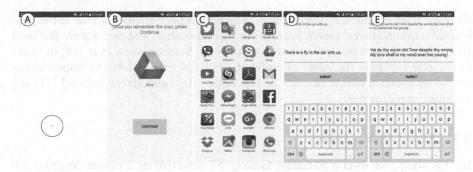

Fig. 1. Interface of the application with target acquisition task (A), visual search task (B–C), and text entry task with user's input for easy and difficult texts (D–E).

3.2 Participants

We recruited 28 participants through our university's mailing lists. Participants are between 18 and 33 ($M = 23, SD = 3.70$) years old. In total, we recruited 19 female and 9 male participants. Our participants have a diverse range of educational background (*e.g.,* Accounting, Actuarial Sciences, Biomedicine, Business, Chemistry, Food Science, Urban Planning). All participants have normal or corrected-to-normal vision (contact lenses) and are right-handed. All of our participants were used to wearing sunglasses.

3.3 Procedure

Our experiment contains three conditions: (1) normal light condition (recommended indoor light levels for easy to normal office work [12]), (2) dimmed light condition, and (3) normal light condition while wearing sunglasses. We followed the guidelines for illuminance standards in a working environment, and hence set the room's illuminance to 335 lx for the normal light condition [12]. In the dimmed light condition, the illuminance of the room was set to 20 lx, a light level which we consider a dark environment to perform most activities. Finally, for the third condition, participants were required to wear non-polarised sunglasses with category 2 lenses under the same illuminance as the normal light condition. Our choice of sunglasses is justified by its popularity of use among the general population, as a category 2 lens provides a medium level of sun glare reduction and UV protection with a visible light transmission of 18–45% [21]. We ensured that the brightness level of the smartphone was kept constant at a medium level throughout the entire experiment, and disabled brightness auto-adjustment to ensure consistency in the study setup. Furthermore, we counterbalanced the presentation order of the conditions across the participants. At the end of the experiment we conducted semi-structured interviews with each participant to understand their perceived performance during the completion of the tasks. The Human Ethics committee of our university approved this experiment.

4   Results

To investigate the effect of ambient light on performance during smartphone interaction, we conducted a one-way repeated measures ANOVA on the afore-mentioned performance-measurement variables. We describe the results of our findings per each smartphone task. We removed extreme outliers from our data (3 individual data points in total from the whole dataset).

4.1   Target Acquisition

First, we investigated the effect of ambient light on target acquisition time (milliseconds). The result of a one-way repeated measures ANOVA revealed a statistically significant effect of ambient light on target acquisition time ($F(2, 7607) = 8.20, p < 0.01$). Post-hoc comparison using the Tukey HSD test (with Bonferroni corrections) showed that there is a significant difference ($p = 0.02$) between target acquisition time under the dimmed light condition ($M = 495, SD = 110$) and the normal light condition ($M = 485, SD = 103$). Moreover, our results show that the participants took a significantly longer time tapping a target ($p < 0.01$) while wearing sunglasses ($M = 498, SD = 115$) when compared to the normal light condition. However, there was no significant difference between the dimmed light condition and wearing sunglasses ($p > 0.05$). Mean values for target acquisition time are presented in Fig. 2(a).

We then examined the effect of ambient light on touch accuracy. A one-way repeated measures ANOVA showed a statistically significant effect of ambient light on the participants' offset size ($F(2, 7607) = 7.32, p < 0.01$). Post-hoc comparison using the Tukey HSD test (with Bonferroni corrections) indicated that the offset size was significantly larger under the dimmed light condition ($M = 49.50, SD = 26.70, p = 0.02$) as compared to the normal light condition ($M = 47.70, SD = 25.80$). We also found a statistically significant difference in offset size between the dimmed light and sunglasses conditions ($M = 46.7, SD = 26.40, p < 0.01$). However, there was no significant difference between the offset size under normal light and sunglasses conditions. Mean values for offset size are presented in Fig. 2(b).

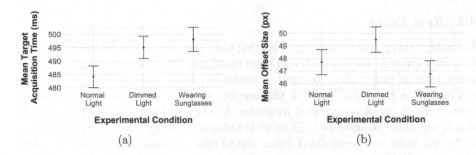

Fig. 2. Mean target acquisition time and offset size (95% CI)

We also studied the effect of ambient light on effective throughput, calculated as proposed by Soukoreff and MacKenzie [20]. A one-way repeated measures ANOVA did not reveal a significant effect of ambient light on the effective throughput during target acquisition tasks.

4.2   Visual Search

We examined the effect of ambient light on the time taken to memorise (milliseconds) and subsequently find an icon (milliseconds). The result of a one-way repeated measures ANOVA revealed a statistically significant effect of ambient light on the time taken to memorise an icon ($F(2, 2045) = 4.42, p = 0.01$). Post-hoc comparisons using the Tukey HSD test (with Bonferroni corrections) indicated that participants took significantly longer time to memorise icons in the sunglasses condition ($M = 744, SD = 271, p = 0.01$) than the dimmed light condition ($M = 703, SD = 206$). The mean values to memorise an icon are presented in Fig. 3. However, we did not find a statistically significant difference between the normal light condition and the dimmed light condition ($p > 0.05$) for the time taken to memorise an icon. We found similar results when comparing the wearing sunglasses condition to the normal light condition ($p > 0.05$).

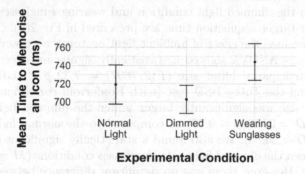

Fig. 3. Mean time to memorise an icon (95% CI)

4.3   Text Entry

In the text entry task we measured participants' performance in terms of time per character entry in milliseconds and total error rate [20]. We calculated character entry rate as time taken to input a character, while the total error rate was calculated as the ratio between the number of total errors and total entered characters. A one-way repeated measures ANOVA did not reveal a statistically significant effect of ambient light on either character entry rate or error rate ($p > 0.05$). We built two generalised linear mixed-effect models to describe the effect of ambient light on character entry rate and error rate. None of the predictors had a significant effect on text entry rate.

4.4   Qualitative Results

During the interview, our participants commented on their subjective perception of performance during the smartphone tasks. A number of participants (8 out of 28) mentioned that wearing sunglasses and dimmed light conditions affected their target acquisition time: *"A little longer when I'm wearing the sunglasses."* (P02), *"I was quicker when there was more light."* (P12), *"Longer time was required under dimmed light"* (P06). These findings are in line with our quantitative findings which show a negative effect of dimmed light and wearing sunglasses on target acquisition time.

Regarding the self-perceived accuracy during the target acquisition task, half of our participants (14 out of 28) indicated that they were more accurate under the normal light condition as compared to the dimmed light condition. *"In the dimmed light it was harder to accurately tap the center of circles"* (P04). These findings correspond to our quantitative data that shows that under the dimmed light participants were less accurate. Surprisingly, two of our participants claimed they were more accurate under the dimmed light condition, as the contrast of the screen was brighter and they could see the circle clearer: *"In the dim light I felt I was more accurate because the circles were more visible"* (P19).

When we asked the participants about their perceived performance on the time taken to memorising the icon during the visual search task, a large majority of our participants (17 out of 24) stated that the light did not affect their performance. However, these perceptive statements contradict our quantitative results, showing that participants took a significantly longer time when wearing sunglasses as compared to the dimmed light condition. Interestingly enough, one of our participants mentioned that it took them less time to memorise icons under the dimmed light condition: *"When performing in dimmed light it takes less time to memorise icons"* (P15).

Nevertheless, participants reported a negative effect of ambient light on their perceived performance in time taken to find an icon, even though our quantitative analysis does not support this observation. In total, 10 participants mentioned that they believe it took them a longer time to find an icon under the dimmed light: *"It affects me so much. I took a bit longer to find the icons in a dim light condition"* (P18); *"When the light is on, I can find the icon easier compared to when the light is dimmed"* (P13).

Regarding the text entry task, most of the participants (N = 19) claimed that the light did not have any effect on their performance. A total of 4 participants believed that they were slower to type under the dimmed light condition and when wearing sunglasses. *"It took me more time to type text under dim light"* (P20). Furthermore, 4 participants claimed to make more errors when the lights were dimmed. *"It was more difficult for me to type the text accurately with dim lighting. I was more confident in typing under normal lighting"* (P12). Nonetheless, our quantitative results did not show any significant support for these statements.

5   Discussion

5.1   Impact of Ambient Light on Mobile Interaction

Our findings show that participants took a significantly longer time to tap a target while wearing sunglasses and under the dimmed light as compared to normal light condition. However, only a minority of our participants (8 out of 28) reported the negative impact of ambient light on target acquisition time. This is an indication that dimmed light caused situational visual impairments in our participant without them noticing it. Previous work has shown that various environmental and internal factors have a different effect on target acquisition time. For example, previous research has shown that participants took a significantly longer time to tap circles under cold ambience due to stiff muscles [17,18]. However, under music (fast and slow tempo) and urban noise (indoor and outdoor) conditions [16], and when exposed to stress [14], target acquisition time was significantly shorter due to the rhythm of the music, and the anxiety caused by urban noise and stress.

Furthermore, participants were significantly less accurate in target acquisition tasks under the dimmed light condition. This was confirmed in our qualitative data as the participants mentioned that they felt the negative effect of dimmed light on their interaction. In particular, our participants acknowledged that their perceived accuracy when tapping circles in dimmed environment is worse, compared to normal ambient illumination. This may be due to the fact that as the illuminance decreases, retinal dopaminergic activation from photoreceptors drops, and, hence causes a situational visual impairment [11]. In addition, our analysis did not reveal a significant effect of wearing sunglasses on participants' tap accuracy as compared to normal light condition. This might be due to the fact that we used commonly available non-polarised sunglasses that are unlikely to cause strong visual impairments.

However, we observed a negative effect of wearing sunglasses on memorising time in visual search tasks. Moreover, we anticipate that the effect of wearing sunglasses under bright sun light might be exacerbated as the effect of glare contributes to the magnitude of the visual situational impairment. Although ambient light did not have a negative impact on our participants' visual search time, the majority of our participants claimed that it took longer time to find an icon when the light was dimmed. However, this may be the case given the simple nature of the task, as prior research has shown that low illuminance levels are associated with slower search speed [6].

Finally, our analysis did not reveal a negative effect of dimmed light or wearing sunglasses on performance during text entry tasks. This may be due to the fact that we used a limited number of text entry tasks that are not sufficient to observe the effect of ambient light on text entry performance. However, previous work has shown a significant effect on participants exposed to meaningful speech on a similar typing task (i.e. listening to someone speak in a language they understand while typing on their smartphone) [16]. This confirms that different situational factors have a different effect on typical smartphone tasks.

5.2   Accommodating Ambient Light-Induced Situational Impairments

In summary, we demonstrate the negative impact of dimmed ambient light on fundamental smartphone interaction tasks. We argue that accounting for situational visual impairments in mobile interaction is important, as the effect might accumulate as task complexity rises. Moreover, Tigwell *et al.* [22] argue that the value of reducing the effects of situational visual impairments grows as the importance of the task increases. Previous work has proposed different methods to accommodate for situational visual impairments during mobile interaction. For example, in the study by Tigwell *et al.* [23] participants suggested increasing the contrast of the screen to reduce the effect of situational visual impairments. Moreover, Reinecke *et al.* [13] suggest increasing button sizes and adjusting the background colour to reduce the adverse effect of situational visual impairments on mobile interaction. As smartphones already come equipped with an ambient light sensor, these methods can be applied once a detrimental ambient light condition is detected and the user is performing a particular task (*e.g.,* target acquisition task under the dimmed light). Given that different people have differences in their perception of contrast colours, the ambient light sensor together with adaptive techniques (*e.g.,* screen contrast, background colour) could be used to build personalised interfaces to improve the smartphone interaction experience, beyond simply adjusting the screen brightness as is the case with current devices.

5.3   Limitations

We acknowledge several limitations in this study. First, the study settings were strictly controlled. In particular, we examined only two levels of ambient illumination – normal and the dimmed light, and do not investigate the effect of bright ambient light (outdoor illuminance) on smartphone interaction performance. The reason for this exclusion is to eliminate the effect of additional external factors, such as glare and ambient noise, on smartphone interaction performance. Finally, our experiment is limited to three types of smartphone tasks. We argue that these tasks are representative of the vast majority of activities that typical users undertake while using their smartphone.

6   Conclusion

In this study, we investigate the effect of three ambient light conditions on smartphone interaction performance in target acquisition, visual search, and text entry tasks. We found that dimmed ambient light significantly impairs target acquisition. Participants took a significantly longer time to hit targets while wearing sunglasses or are under dimmed light, as compared to the normal light condition. Furthermore, participants were less accurate when tapping targets under the dimmed light condition. We also show that participants took longer to memorise icons while wearing sunglasses when completing visual search tasks. Our

findings enhance the understanding of situational visual impairments impact on mobile interaction and contribute to the growing body of research in the HCI community on situational impairments.

Acknowledgements. This work is partially funded by a Samsung GRO grant, and the ARC Discovery Project DP190102627. We also thank Silan Li for her help during data collection.

References

1. Goel, M., Findlater, L., Wobbrock, J.: WalkType: using accelerometer data to accomodate situational impairments in mobile touch screen text entry. In: Proceedings of the SIGCHI Conference on Human Factors in Computing Systems, CHI 2012, pp. 2687–2696. ACM, New York (2012). https://doi.org/10.1145/2207676.2208662
2. Goncalves, J., et al.: Tapping task performance on smartphones in cold temperature. Interact. Comput. **29**(3), 355–367 (2017). https://doi.org/10.1093/iwc/iww029
3. Gong, R., Xu, H., Wang, B., Luo, M.R.: Image quality evaluation for smart-phone displays at lighting levels of indoor and outdoor conditions. Opt. Eng. **51**(8), 084001 (2012)
4. Henze, N., Rukzio, E., Boll, S.: 100,000,000 taps: analysis and improvement of touch performance in the large. In: Proceedings of the 13th International Conference on Human Computer Interaction with Mobile Devices and Services, MobileHCI 2011, pp. 133–142. ACM, New York (2011). https://doi.org/10.1145/2037373.2037395
5. Kim, Y.J., et al.: Factors affecting the psychophysical image quality evaluation of mobile phone displays: the case of transmissive liquid-crystal displays. JOSA A **25**(9), 2215–2222 (2008)
6. Lee, D.S., Shieh, K.K., Jeng, S.C., Shen, I.H.: Effect of character size and lighting on legibility of electronic papers. Displays **29**(1), 10–17 (2008)
7. Liu, P., Zafar, F., Badano, A.: The effect of ambient illumination on handheld display image quality. J. Digit. Imaging **27**(1), 12–18 (2014)
8. Liu, Y., Goncalves, J., Ferreira, D., Hosio, S., Kostakos, V.: Identity crisis of ubicomp?: Mapping 15 years of the field's development and paradigm change. In: Proceedings of the 2014 ACM International Joint Conference on Pervasive and Ubiquitous Computing, UbiComp 2014, pp. 75–86, ACM, New York (2014). https://doi.org/10.1145/2632048.2632086
9. Liu, Y., Goncalves, J., Ferreira, D., Xiao, B., Hosio, S., Kostakos, V.: Chi 1994–2013: mapping two decades of intellectual progress through co-word analysis. In: Proceedings of the 32nd Annual ACM Conference on Human Factors in Computing Systems, CHI 2014, pp. 3553–3562. ACM, New York (2014)
10. Ng, A., Brewster, S.A., Williamson, J.H.: Investigating the effects of encumbrance on one- and two- handed interactions with mobile devices. In: Proceedings of the SIGCHI Conference on Human Factors in Computing Systems, CHI 2014, pp. 1981–1990. ACM, New York (2014). https://doi.org/10.1145/2556288.2557312
11. Norton, T.T., Siegwart Jr., J.T.: Light levels, refractive development, and myopia-a speculative review. Exp. Eye Res. **114**, 48–57 (2013)
12. Observatory TNOA: Recommended light levels (2015). https://www.noao.edu/education/QLTkit/ACTIVITY_Documents/Safety/LightLevels_outdoor+indoor.pdf

13. Reinecke, K., Flatla, D.R., Brooks, C.: Enabling designers to foresee which colors users cannot see. In: Proceedings of the 2016 CHI Conference on Human Factors in Computing Systems, pp. 2693–2704. ACM (2016)
14. Sarsenbayeva, Z., et al.: Measuring the effects of stress on mobile interaction. Proc. ACM Interact. Mob. Wear. Ubiquit. Technol. 3(1), 24:1–24:18 (2019). https://doi.org/10.1145/3314411
15. Sarsenbayeva, Z., van Berkel, N., Luo, C., Kostakos, V., Goncalves, J.: Challenges of situational impairments during interaction with mobile devices. In: Proceedings of the 29th Australian Conference on Computer-Human Interaction, pp. 477–481. ACM (2017)
16. Sarsenbayeva, Z., van Berkel, N., Velloso, E., Kostakos, V., Goncalves, J.: Effect of distinct ambient noise types on mobile interaction. Proc. ACM Interact. Mob. Wear. Ubiquit. Technol. 2(2), 82:1–82:23 (2018). https://doi.org/10.1145/3214285
17. Sarsenbayeva, Z., et al.: Sensing cold-induced situational impairments in mobile interaction using battery temperature. Proc. ACM Interact. Mob. Wear. Ubiquit. Technol. 1(3), 98:1–98:9 (2017). https://doi.org/10.1145/3130963
18. Sarsenbayeva, Z., et al.: Situational impairments to mobile interaction in cold environments. In: Proceedings of the 2016 ACM International Joint Conference on Pervasive and Ubiquitous Computing, UbiComp 2016, pp. 85–96. ACM, New York (2016). https://doi.org/10.1145/2971648.2971734
19. Sears, A., Lin, M., Jacko, J., Xiao, Y.: When computers fade: pervasive computing and situationally-induced impairments and disabilities. In: HCI International, vol. 2, pp. 1298–1302 (2003)
20. Soukoreff, R.W., MacKenzie, I.S.: Metrics for text entry research: an evaluation of MSD and KSPC, and a new unified error metric. In: Proceedings of the SIGCHI Conference on Human Factors in Computing Systems, pp. 113–120. ACM (2003)
21. Australian/New Zealand Standard: Sunglasses and fashion spectacles (2003). https://www.saiglobal.com/pdftemp/previews/osh/as/as1000/1000/1067.pdf
22. Tigwell, G.W., Flatla, D.R., Menzies, R.: It's not just the light: understanding the factors causing situational visual impairments during mobile interaction. In: Proceedings of the 10th Nordic Conference on Human-Computer Interaction, pp. 338–351. ACM (2018)
23. Tigwell, G.W., Menzies, R., Flatla, D.R.: Designing for situational visual impairments: supporting early-career designers of mobile content. In: Proceedings of the 2018 on Designing Interactive Systems Conference 2018, pp. 387–399. ACM (2018)
24. Wobbrock, J.O.: The future of mobile device research in HCI. In: CHI 2006 Workshop Proceedings: What is the Next Generation of Human-computer Interaction, pp. 131–134 (2006)

Investigating Screen Reachability
on an Articulated Dual-Display Smartphone

Mathieu Pecchioli[1], Emmanuel Dubois[1(✉)], Pourang Irani[2],
and Marcos Serrano[1]

[1] University of Toulouse III, 31062 Toulouse Cedex 9, France
{mathieu.pecchioli,emmanuel.dubois,
marcos.serrano}@irit.fr
[2] Department of Computer Science, University of Manitoba,
Winnipeg, MB, Canada
pourang.irani@cs.umanitoba.ca

Abstract. Large displays on smartphones accommodate tasks needing more screen real-estate, but at the expense of limiting the use of one-handed operations. In this paper we explore thumb reachability on an articulated dual-display smartphone. While mobile devices are featuring dual screens, no previous work has explored how each physical display's positions impact one-handed reach and interaction. We explore 32 inter-display configurations resulting from the combination of orientations of the two displays along two axes. In a preliminary study we explore how users grasp such dual-display configurations. We then conduct a study to investigate the effects of the relative position of two displays on thumb reachability. Results provide a range of dual-display configurations that are ideal for one-handed use, enabling knowledge on how apps for such emerging devices can be optimized for thumb input.

Keywords: Dual-display · Tactile reachability · Thumb input ·
One-handed input

1 Introduction

Emerging smartphones are concerned with maximizing the display real estate, leading to a variety of display sizes and blurring the limits between smartphones and tablets. While a trend towards larger displays allows for a better experience, it limits the graspability and one-handed input on such devices [10]. As recent evolution addresses this concern by introducing foldable smartphones, with dedicated apps [16], such as the Royole FlexPai, the first commercialized android-based smartphone that can bend [18]. Once folded these devices offer two displays attached by one edge, leading to two potential uses: either interacting on one display while using the other for output only, or interacting on both displays, which allows to display two complementary applications (e.g. consulting the weather forecast and the agenda to plan a hike, or a map and a list of hotels for booking the closest to a meeting). One-handed input, a common usage scenario, needs renewed consideration on such class of devices. In this paper, we study how two attached displays can be positioned and rotated along two axes to facilitate

© IFIP International Federation for Information Processing 2019
Published by Springer Nature Switzerland AG 2019
D. Lamas et al. (Eds.): INTERACT 2019, LNCS 11748, pp. 476–485, 2019.
https://doi.org/10.1007/978-3-030-29387-1_27

one-handed user input. Our principle aim is to examine what dual-display configurations facilitate one-handed screen reachability, an outcome that can benefit designers of such devices as well as for the UI of apps built for such devices.

To address our aim, we investigate the impact of the relative position of two palm-size displays when they are articulate along two junction angles (see Fig. 1). We designed and built a running prototype that allowed us to experimentally evaluate thumb reachability with 32 possible dual-display permutations (corresponding to the combinations of two display orientations and angles). Through a preliminary study we examine users grasp patterns for such dual-display configurations. We then investigate the effect of the relative position of the two displays on thumb reachability in a controlled study. We measured the size of both the comfort area (i.e. easily reachable area), as well as the useful area (i.e. reachable area through a large thumb exertion). Our results lead to the most suitable articulations and identify those offering an equal or better reachability than current smartphone-like configurations.

Our contributions are: (1) a preliminary study to investigate how users grasp dual-display configurations when articulated across two angles; (2) a study to investigate the effects of the relative position of the two displays on thumb reachability; and (3) a discussion on usage scenarios for such dual-display smartphones.

2 Related Work

Closely related to our work is that on mobile one-handed thumb reachability, multi-display devices and shape-changing devices, which we review briefly.

Studying the thumb reachable area with one-handed operation has led to models predicting the functional area for a given smartphone size, hand size and finger positions [2], even under varying device grips [3]. Solutions proposed in the literature, e.g. ThumbSpace [6], and in commercial products, e.g. the Samsung's One-Hand Mode [17] reduce the effective display size to the region reachable by the thumb. But these solutions limit the display space leading to concerns of pointing accuracy [5]. Other solutions lead to indirect input (e.g. around-the-device [4], back-of-the-device [12, 13].

Multi- and dual-display prototypes recently emerged, where the device can be physically split [7, 9, 11]. Codex [9] enabled many novel mobile scenarios, including collaborative input. However, most dual-display prototypes fold along one of the device edges [7, 11] and when opened have a form factor closer to a tablet than a smartphone. Studying the manipulation of such dual-display systems has not received much attention.

The above mentioned dual-display mobile devices led to foldable shape-changing devices, such as Paddle [15], a device concept of a highly deformable mobile device, or EXHI-bit, an expandable handheld interface [14]. These devices can dynamically change the arrangement of the displays. However, these works have mostly focused on the advantages of using a shape-changing display to extend the output interaction space, and to our knowledge none of them has explored thumb reachability on such displays. Unsurprisingly, a recent review on the grand challenges of shape-changing interface research [1], underlined the need to further explore the integration between the device form and interaction, with the goal "to realize shape-changing interfaces that

capture touch input [...] in a quality comparable to today's handheld computing devices" [1]. This goal drives our exploration of the dual-display thumb reachability, in particular for a dual-axis foldable device.

3   Dual-Display Smartphone Configurations

Our goal is to study the effect of dual-display configurations on thumb reachability. We refer to the display at the bottom, the one being gripped, as "display 1", and the display at the top as "display 2". We define a "dual-display configuration" as the relative position of displays A and B that are attached by an edge, point or joint. Given the high dimensionality of the design space for possible angle rotations with each articulated display, we explored a discrete number of static configurations (i.e. configurations where the position of the two displays cannot change). This allowed a more systematic examination of the effect of the relative angle of the two displays on thumb reachability.

3.1   Static Configurations

Three factors drive the design of the static configurations explored in this paper: (1) Orientation of the screen is portrait or landscape; (2) Alpha angle describes a vertical rotation of display 2 towards the user (see rows on Fig. 1-left); (3) Beta angle: describes a horizontal clockwise rotation of display 2 (see columns on Fig. 1-left).

For each angle type, we considered four values: 0°, 30°, 60° and 90°. We did not consider values below 0° as for Alpha it would mean tilting display 2 outside the user's view (i.e. bent backward); and for Beta it would mean tilting display 2 away from the thumb (i.e. to the left, Fig. 1-left). The configuration where Alpha and Beta are equal to 0° represents a smartphone-like shape, i.e. one flat rectangular device. The combination of these three factors (Orientation, Alpha and Beta) led to 32 dual-display configurations (2 Orientations × 4 Alpha angles × 4 Beta angles). Figure 1-left illustrates the 16 combinations of Alpha and Beta for a portrait orientation.

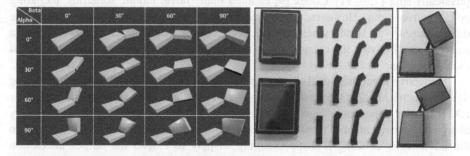

Fig. 1. Left: The 16 dual-display configurations explored for a portrait orientation (we explored the same configurations for a landscape orientation). Center: touchscreens in their 3D printed cases and the 16 connection joints used to create our 32 dual-display configurations, as on the left. Right: illustration of landscape and portrait orientations for (Alpha = 30°, Beta = 60°).

3.2   Implementation

We implemented our dual-display device using two 2.8" TFT resistive touchscreens, with a resolution of 240 × 320 pixels. Each touch screen was connected to an Arduino MKR1000. We used Arduino tactile screens to take advantage of Arduino's computing and WiFi capabilities. Once placed side-by-side, our two screens create a single screen of 144 × 58 mm (ratio = 2.5) or 116 × 77 mm (ratio = 1.5) which is close to the size of a Samsung S4, almost equivalent to ZTE AxonM and a bit smaller than the FlexPai once folded.

We then 3D designed and printed the cases for both displays and the required electronic assembly. The final 3D printed case had a size of 77 × 58 × 23 mm. For the connection joints, we 3D designed and printed 16 joints (Fig. 1-center) that could be easily interchanged.

4   Preliminary Study: Device Grasp

In a preliminary study, we investigated how users grasp our dual-display configurations. Since hand grasp affects reachability [3], we examine the set of natural grasps (used in the subsequent study), so that all participants would grasp the configurations similarly. We asked five research students to grasp the 32 dual-display configurations either holding only display 1 (Fig. 2-A), or holding the junction with the index or middle finger (Fig. 2-B, C). For each grasp, we asked them to comment whether they could reach both displays with the thumb. We took pictures of all grasps (Fig. 2).

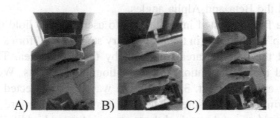

Fig. 2. Different types of device grasps obtained from participants.

Users pointed out that holding display 1 alone made touching display 2 more difficult. We observed that when grasping only display 1, it became difficult to properly hold the phone while releasing the thumb. Instead, placing one finger on the junction ensured a more secure grasp. Therefore, we chose to adopt this "junction grasp" in our subsequent study to avoid any bias due to different users employing different grasps, or the same user changing grasps during the study.

5 Study: Dual-Display Thumb Reachability

5.1 Goal, Task and Instructions

The goal of this study was to assess thumb reachability, i.e. to measure the surface reached with the thumb during one-handed interaction on our dual-display smartphone.

In order to assess the reachable surface for one-handed input on a dual screen smartphone, we emphasized three aspects: Comfort, Useful and Non-Accessible areas. The "Comfort area" of the screen requires only a small input effort (moving the joints of the thumb only). The "Useful area" requires a consequent effort (using the movement of the palm of the hand and not only the thumb articulations). The "Non-Accessible area" of the screen is inaccessible without the use of both hands.

To this end, we asked users to touch the screen with the thumb and move it inside the comfort area, and then to extend the motion to the useful area on each display. They were asked to focus on the gesture, without any time requirement.

5.2 Participants, Experimental Protocol and Collected Data

We recruited 12 participants (7 females) aged 24.3 on average (SD = 4.6), all were right-handed. Participants were recruited among students of a local university (undergraduate or PhD students). Each participant was rewarded with a 10$ Amazon gift card.

The experiment followed a $4 \times 4 \times 2$ within-participant design with Beta angle (0°, 30°, 60° and 90°), Alpha angle (0°, 30°, 60° and 90°) and Orientation (portrait or landscape mode) as factors. We counterbalanced the trials using the Orientation and randomly ordered the Beta and Alpha angles.

The procedure first consisted in explaining to users how to hold the device, using the "junction grasp", as detailed in the preliminary study. Then, for each configuration, the user explored the comfort area, followed by the useful area. The experimenter manually changed the configurations by repositioning the joints. We used the dual-display device described in Sect. 3. The device was USB-connected to the computer running the experiment. We ensured that the wires did not interfere with the manipulations of the prototype, and attached them so as not to add additional weight to it.

We recorded all the touch points of the finger on both screens. From this point cloud, we computed the reachable areas using a surface-reconstruction approach. We also asked participants to rate the comfort of each configuration on a 7-points Likert scale.

5.3 Results

We use estimation techniques with 95% BCa bootstrap confidence intervals (CI) and ratio analyses as recommended by the APA [20]. Ratio is an intra-subject measurement that expresses the effect size (pair-wise comparison) and is computed between each of the geometric means.

Surface of Comfort and Useful Areas. We report the main results for the sum of the surfaces on both screens. Indeed the average surfaces measured on display 1 and on

display 2 are very similar when considering the Comfort area (display 1: 755 mm², CI [590; 985]; display 2: 708 mm², CI[560; 881]) and the Useful area (display 1: 1306 mm², CI[1072; 1502]; display 2: 1246 mm², CI[1032; 1414]).

Interestingly, the results establish that the orientation of the screens (portrait or landscape) does not affect the size of the comfort area (landscape: 1491 mm², CI[1212; 1850]; portrait: 1437 mm², CI[1140; 1826]) or the useful area (landscape: 2550 mm², CI[2177; 2882]; portrait: 2554 mm², CI[2175; 2941]). This remains true for any given configuration. Hence, we will not differentiate the results for both orientations in the remaining analysis.

Overall, the size of the Useful area is 87% larger than the Comfort area (1464 mm², CI[1198; 1827] vs. 2552 mm², CI[2220; 2886]). The available display surface of one screen being 2596 mm², 49% of the dual-screen display is usable. This is higher than the results obtained in prior work involving a single screen: over different smartphone sizes, an average of 36.4% of the screen was reachable with the thumb without losing grip stability (see Table 3 in [13]).

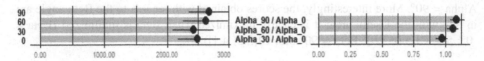

Fig. 3. Average finger reach surface in mm² (top) according to the Alpha angle (left), and surface ratio (with 95% CIs) of the Alpha angle (ratio > 1 means bigger finger reach than with Alpha = 0°).

We considered the Alpha angle, representing the relative vertical position of each screen. On average, (Fig. 3-left) configurations involving the two highest Alpha angles (60°, 90°) allow a larger useful area (2651 mm², CI[2305; 2994]) than the two smallest Alpha angles (2453 mm², CI[2127; 2807]). The intra-subject ratio analysis (see Fig. 3-right) clearly confirms this trend (ratio > 1, CI not intersecting (1): in comparison to configurations based on Alpha = 0°, the average useful area is 9% larger with Alpha = 90°, and 6% larger when Alpha = 60°. This trend also holds for the comfort area alone.

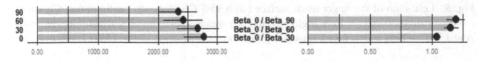

Fig. 4. Average finger reach surface in mm² (top) according to Beta angle (top), and surface ratio (with 95% CIs) of the Beta angle (ratio > 1 means smaller finger reach than with Beta = 0°).

We also considered the effect of the Beta angle, depicting the horizontal relative position between the two screens. The average size of the useful area seems to diminish

482   M. Pecchioli et al.

when Beta increases (see Fig. 4-left): in particular, this area is clearly larger with Beta = 0° (2774 mm^2, CI[2432; 3149]) than with Beta = 90° (2341 mm^2, CI[2015; 2656]). The intra-subject analysis based on the ratio strongly confirms this trend (see Fig. 4-right): the useful surface is 15% to 19% larger with Beta = 0° than with Beta = 60° or 90°, while there is no visible difference with Beta = 30°.

The four better dual-display configurations are those combining a large Alpha angle (60°, 90°) and a small Beta angle (0°, 30°). When comparing each of the 15 possible configurations to the baseline (Alpha = Beta = 0°), the intra-subject ratio confirms this outcome as the ratio range of these four configurations are among the 5 smaller ratios obtained, i.e. leading to an equivalent or larger useful area (Fig. 5-left). The resulting 4 best configurations are illustrated in portrait orientation in Fig. 5-right.

User Preference. Similarly to thumb reachability, the scores given by the participants to the different configurations was not affected by the orientation of the screens (landscape: 4.4, CI[4.1; 4.9]; portrait: 4.4, CI[4.0; 4.8]). Based on the intra-subject ratio analysis, results establish that configurations based on Alpha = 0° obtained an average score 12% (CI [4; 19]) better than for Alpha = 30°, and 16% (CI[4; 28]) better than for Alpha = 90°. More interestingly, the scores obtained with regards to the Beta angle are in line with the Useful area: it is clearly maximized when Beta is minimized (Beta = 0°: 5.4, CI[5.0; 5.9]; Beta = 90°:3.6, CI[3.3; 4.1]).

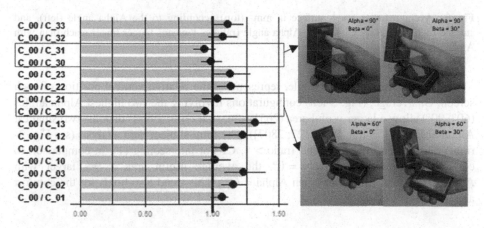

Fig. 5. Left: ratio of the finger reach surface (with 95% CIs) for each configuration Cij where i = Alpha angle/30 and j = Beta angle/30 (ratio > 1 means smaller finger reach surface than with Alpha = 0° + Beta = 0°). Right: illustrating the portrait orientation of the 4 best configurations.

Summary. This experiment revealed two surprising results: (1) the orientation of the displays (portrait or landscape) does not affect the thumb-reachable zone; and (2) the reachable zone on each display is very similar: 50% of each display can be reached during a one-handed interaction. Concerning the junction angle, we observed that the thumb-reachable surface is maximized for 4 particular configurations that combine a large vertical rotation (Alpha = 60° or 90°) and a small horizontal rotation (Beta = 0° or 30°). These configurations offer the same, or slightly higher (5%), thumb

reachability than a smartphone-like configuration (Alpha = Beta = 0°). The overall user rating on a 7 point Likert scale is 4.4 (4.9 for the 4 configurations highlighted above). Interestingly, user preference is correlated with all these results but one: users prefer the configuration without vertical rotation (Alpha = 0°).

6 Discussion

6.1 Potential Usages of Articulated Dual-Display Devices

Our results indicate that screen orientation (portrait or landscape) does not impact thumb reachability or users' preference. Therefore, the orientation can be associated to predefined modes (e.g. apps requiring text input, games, etc.). As four configurations were also identified as particularly beneficial, up to 8 modes might thus be predefined through specific articulations of the dual-display device. We also demonstrated that thumb-reachability is similar on both screens. Hence, both screens can be used equally and applications can be displayed on one or the other screen without constraints.

To identify potential usage situations for such articulated dual-display devices, we organized two brainstorming session with 10 HCI Master and PhD students. In several scenarios, participants considered display 2 as a dynamically adjustable peephole on the content or tasks displayed on Display 1: for example, in the case of map navigation, placing display 2 perpendicular to display 1 (Beta = 90°) would display the north-east of the map displayed on display 1. Alternatively, articulated dual-display devices might be used to extend the current display surface around display 1: the position of display 2 according to display 1 would correspond to a specific application. As opposed to existing around-device solutions [8] this would provide visual feedback and could be organized along the two angles considered in this experiment. Finally, participants of the brainstorming also highlighted the fact that the device might be used in different configurations according to the user task: totally folded on itself, the device is small, can be placed in a pocket and is sufficient to read a SMS. If unfolded, it can be used to read an email or browse the web.

6.2 Limitations and Future Work

First, smartphones come in multiple sizes, so future work should validate our results with different sizes of displays. Second, we will conduct a number of technical improvements to the current prototype. Tactile screens with better resolution then the ones we used are required to allow a real use of existing mobile applications. Inserting an IMU to detect in real-time the relative orientation of the two screens could also improve the encoding of the articulation. Finally, the thickness of the device, the size of the bezels, the shape of the chassis and how it sits in the hand need to be improved to correspond to more realistic settings. These improvements will allow us to further study the use of articulated dual-display devices with real applications. Another important issue is the definition of the content layout of non-horizontal display screens, in which little work has been done so far [19]. In addition, the current prototype is based on rigid, predefined joints: instead, a kneecap-like joint or an actuated joint might be used

to dynamically adjust the configuration. Finally, holding the devices was feasible but we will explore other solutions to improve grasping, placing a ring on the rear of the case.

7 Conclusion

In this paper, we explored the concept of an articulated dual-display smartphone to overcome reachability issues on large mobile screens. We designed 32 different configurations of an articulated dual-display smartphone and studied them through the analysis of the thumb-reachable surface. Participants' ratings were also positive towards such devices. Despite the limitations of the current prototype, results also establish that the thumb-reachable surface is close to 50%, which is higher than those previously found on large mobile displays. Articulated dual-display devices are therefore a promising solution to lessen the discomfort and reachability issues of the recent trend in increasing mobile display sizes, through foldable touchscreens.

References

1. Alexander, J., et al.: Grand challenges in shape-changing interface research. In Proceedings of the 2018 CHI Conference on Human Factors in Computing Systems (CHI 2018), p. 14. ACM, New York. Paper 299 (2018). https://doi.org/10.1145/3173574.3173873
2. Bergstrom-Lehtovirta, J., Oulasvirta, A.: Modeling the functional area of the thumb on mobile touchscreen surfaces. In: Proceedings of the SIGCHI Conference on Human Factors in Computing Systems (CHI 2014), pp. 1991–2000. ACM, New York (2014). https://doi.org/10.1145/2556288.2557354
3. Eardley, R., Roudaut, A., Gill, S., Thompson, S.J.: Understanding grip shifts: how form factors impact hand movements on mobile phones. In: Proceedings of the 2017 CHI Conference on Human Factors in Computing Systems (CHI 2017), pp. 4680–4691. ACM, New York, NY, USA (2017). https://doi.org/10.1145/3025453.3025835
4. Hasan, K., Kim, J., Ahlström, D., Irani, P.: Thumbs-up: 3D spatial thumb-reachable space for one-handed thumb interaction on smartphones. In: Proceedings of the 2016 Symposium on Spatial User Interaction (SUI 2016), pp. 103–106. ACM, New York (2016). https://doi.org/10.1145/2983310.2985755
5. Holz, C., Baudisch, P.: The generalized perceived input point model and how to double touch accuracy by extracting fingerprints. In: Proceedings of the SIGCHI Conference on Human Factors in Computing Systems (CHI 2010), pp. 581–590. ACM, New York (2010). https://doi.org/10.1145/1753326.1753413
6. Karlson, A.K., Bederson, B.B.: thumbspace: generalized one-handed input for touchscreen-based mobile devices. In: Baranauskas, C., Palanque, P., Abascal, J., Barbosa, S.D.J. (eds.) INTERACT 2007. LNCS, vol. 4662, pp. 324–338. Springer, Heidelberg (2007). https://doi.org/10.1007/978-3-540-74796-3_30
7. Gomes, A., Vertegaal, R.: PaperFold: evaluating shape changes for viewport transformations in foldable thin-film display devices. In Proceedings of the Ninth International Conference on Tangible, Embedded, and Embodied Interaction (TEI 2015), pp. 153–160. ACM, New York (2015). https://doi.org/10.1145/2677199.2680572

8. Hasan, K., Ahlström, D., Irani, P.: Ad-binning: leveraging around device space for storing, browsing and retrieving mobile device content. In: Proceedings of the SIGCHI Conference on Human Factors in Computing Systems (CHI 2013), pp. 899–908. ACM, New York (2013). https://doi.org/10.1145/2470654.2466115

9. Hinckley, K., Dixon, M., Sarin, R., Guimbretiere, F., Balakrishnan, R.: Codex: a dual screen tablet computer. In: Proceedings of the SIGCHI Conference on Human Factors in Computing Systems (CHI 2009), pp. 1933–1942. ACM, New York (2009). https://doi.org/10.1145/1518701.1518996

10. Kim, S., Yu, J., Lee, G.: Interaction techniques for unreachable objects on the touchscreen. In: Proceedings OzCHI 2012, pp. 295–298 (2012)

11. Khalilbeigi, M., Lissermann, R., Kleine, W., Steimle, J.: FoldMe: interacting with double-sided foldable displays. In: Spencer, S.N. (ed.) Proceedings of the Sixth International Conference on Tangible, Embedded and Embodied Interaction (TEI 2012), pp. 33–40. ACM, New York (2012). https://doi.org/10.1145/2148131.2148142

12. Le, H.V., Bader, P., Kosch, T., Henze, N.: Investigating screen shifting techniques to improve one-handed smartphone usage. In: Proceedings of the 9th Nordic Conference on Human-Computer Interaction (NordiCHI 2016), p. 10. ACM, New York (2016). https://doi.org/10.1145/2971485.2971562. Article 27

13. Le, H.V., Mayer, S., Bader, P., Henze, N.: Fingers' range and comfortable area for one-handed smartphone interaction beyond the touchscreen. In: Proceedings of the 2018 CHI Conference on Human Factors in Computing Systems (CHI 2018), p. 12. ACM, New York (2018). https://doi.org/10.1145/3173574.3173605. Paper 31

14. Ortega, M., Maisonnasse, J., Nigay, L.: EXHI-bit: a mechanical structure for prototyping EXpandable handheld interfaces. In: Proceedings of the 19th International Conference on Human-Computer Interaction with Mobile Devices and Services (MobileHCI 2017), p. 11. ACM, New York (2017). https://doi.org/10.1145/3098279.3098533. Article 4

15. Ramakers, R., Schöning, J., Luyten, K.: Paddle: highly deformable mobile devices with physical controls. In: Proceedings of the SIGCHI Conference on Human Factors in Computing Systems (CHI 2014), pp. 2569–2578. ACM, New York (2014). https://doi.org/10.1145/2556288.2557340

16. Royole FlexPai. http://www.royole.com/flexpai. Accessed Apr 2019

17. Samsung One Hand Mode. https://www.samsung.com/au/support/mobile-devices/one-hand-mode/. Accessed Apr 2019

18. Samsung foldable phone. https://www.abc.net.au/news/2018-11-08/samsung-shows-off-bendy-tablet-that-folds-down-to-phone/10478508. Accessed Apr 2019

19. Serrano, M., Roudaut, A., Irani, P.: Visual composition of graphical elements on non-rectangular displays. In: Proceedings of the 2017 CHI Conference on Human Factors in Computing Systems (CHI 2017), pp. 4405–4416. ACM, New York (2017). https://doi.org/10.1145/3025453.3025677

20. VandenBos, G.R. (ed.): Publication Manual of the American Psychological Association, 6th edn. American Psychological Association, Wahsington DC (2009)

Short Paper: Initial Recommendations for the Design of Privacy Management Tools for Smartphones

Alessandro Carelli[(✉)], Matt Sinclair, and Darren Southee

Loughborough Design School, Epinal Way, Loughborough LE11 3TU, UK
a.carelli@lboro.ac.uk

Abstract. The continuing rise in the popularity of smartphones has led to an accompanying rise in the exposure of users to privacy threats as in the case of unintended leakage of personal information from apps. To improve transparency and the ability of users to control data leakage, the design of privacy-enhancing tools aimed at reducing the burden of informed privacy-decisions should be grounded upon users' tacit needs and preferences. To this end, the present study explores users' personal perception and concerns toward privacy and their expectations. Initial recommendations include: (1) consideration of the preferences of users for preserving functionalities of their apps, informing users about both (2) the real benefits and actual possibility of using privacy management tools and (3) suspected applications' data collection behaviours in a way that matches their real concerns and values.

Keywords: Privacy · Human-centered design · Smartphones · Privacy-enhancing technology · User experience

1 Introduction

While the popularity of the smartphone continues to be a growing phenomenon worldwide [1], such devices also pose accompanying privacy threats to users, as in the case of personal information leaked by apps without users' full awareness or consent [2].

Diverse studies have pointed out how personal data leaked online represents a threat which is far more concerning than simply annoying users with invasive advertisements and potentially affecting the social life of individuals [3]. Among the potential implications for privacy there is the risk that leaked data could be used to (1) uniquely identify users without referring to their name and physical address; (2) track users across different applications and devices; (3) build a comprehensive profile on individual users which can be used to predict behaviour and make decisions affecting services such as the provision of credit or used for online political micro-targeting [3–9].

Previous studies have highlighted different causes of application privacy mismanagement such as the general unawareness of data sharing, the preference of users to trade-off privacy for the benefit of using an app, and the complexity of the system of

© IFIP International Federation for Information Processing 2019
Published by Springer Nature Switzerland AG 2019
D. Lamas et al. (Eds.): INTERACT 2019, LNCS 11748, pp. 486–496, 2019.
https://doi.org/10.1007/978-3-030-29387-1_28

permissions [10–13]. Thus, to enhance transparency and improve privacy users should be better supported through appropriate tools.

For this reason the present article is part of a broader research effort aiming at providing appropriate guidelines to design teams to help them improve the effectiveness and user experience of such tools.

2 Background

A number of contributions have addressed the potential of machine learning techniques to assist users in setting the privacy of their mobile devices through recommendations and automatic decisions [14–16]. Furthermore, [17–19] provided usability recommendations for browser extensions blocking online behavioural tracking and summarized in Table 1.

Table 1. Summary of design recommendations for browser extensions blocking online behavioural tracking from [17–19]

Guideline	Reference
Users want protections that don't break the functionality of the web pages and online service they use	[19]
The system (i.e. the online browser) should protect users automatically and be designed in a way that reduces the chance that the breakages occur	[17]
Users should be better informed about why web trackers are present, the information they are collecting and how it might be used	[18]
An indication of the privacy risks is likely to improve the meaningful of the information as well as the use of icon colour can inform users about critical situations such as when blocking may break the website's functionality. Furthermore, the information provided by the tools should be relevant and actionable for users	[18]
Setup materials which include videos and tutorials are useful to shape users' mental models and to increase the trust toward the privacy-enhancing extension	[18]

However, no previous study has focused specifically on the user experience of privacy management tools for smartphones, or offered guidelines for improving their design.

Furthermore, although user experience and Human-centred design are concepts widely accepted within the HCI community [20], understanding the experience of users with privacy and security technologies is a relatively new area of research. In this connection [20–23] indicated the importance of extending inquiry to the experiential aspects of privacy technologies, as users have values and tacit needs which may remain underrepresented if not appropriately considered.

In order to address this gap, this research has inquired into users' personal perceptions of privacy and their expectations towards a privacy management app, in order to derive recommendations for designers.

3 Study Design

3.1 Sample

The study involved an opportunity sample of nine participants recruited from the researchers' personal network and university mailing list from both Italy and UK, over a period of 18 weeks. The average age of participants was 29, in a range of ages from 23 to 34 years; eight participants had an advanced degree and one a bachelor's degree. Only one participant held a degree in computer science since priority was given to 'typical users' with no IT background and thus represented the primary focus of a PMT as understood in this article. This represents the first part of an ongoing research project investigating the users' subjective experiences while using a privacy management app.

3.2 Procedure

Participants were required to answer semi-structured questions and to think-aloud while using the interview materials. Such material included a set of interview boards aiming at helping participants elaborate their thoughts, and MyPermissions (MP), a popular privacy management app which enables smartphone users to manage the privacy settings of third party apps installed on smartphones which participants were required to install and use on their own smartphone (Fig. 1).

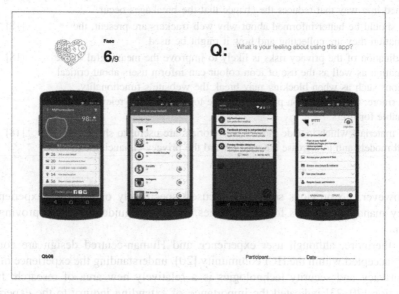

Fig. 1. A printed board used throughout the interview showing MyPermissions' screenshots.

Asking users to think-aloud while interacting with a technology or performing other tasks is a common method in usability and user experience research, as it allows researchers to probe participants' mental models, uncertainties and misconceptions

[24, 25]. During the interview participants were required to think aloud while using both the interview boards and the MP app, allowing the researcher to probe further their thoughts were appropriate.

In order to understand the personal perceptions of privacy and expectations of users towards a privacy management app, questions covered the following topics:

- 'Breaking the ice' and understand participants' attitude toward smartphone
- Comprehend participants' attitude toward app privacy
- Collect opinions about, and previous experience with, privacy management tools
- Probe participants' expectations toward MP

Such topics were grounded upon recommendations in [20] which suggests to probe user's practices, subjective meanings and the fit of privacy technologies in to user's everyday lives.

Interviews were conducted individually with each participant and lasted 100 min on average. After a break-the-ice question where participants described apps they frequently use, they were asked to reflect upon the fit of their smartphone and apps into their everyday lives by placing their smartphone in a value-based scale from 'fundamental' to 'not essential', and provide explanations. This value-based scale, which was used with the solely scope of collecting qualitative data, was informed by the survey on smartphone ownership carried out by [26] which pointed out how smartphones are being increasingly embedded in the daily lives in particular of people in the age range 18–29.

As a second task, participants were asked about their subjective perceptions of security or privacy, using their own words. This task was also intended to understand their real knowledge and perception of potential privacy threats related to smartphones and applications. The interview then moved on to asking participants about the typologies of data potentially leaked by apps, as well as the reasons, modalities and potential recipients of the data sharing.

As a third task, participants were first required to use their phone to check the permissions and privacy notes of a popular weather forecasting app and to discuss whether they were informative. Participants were then asked to express their expectations toward MP. No participants were aware of MP before entering the study, thus participants were first introduced to the app's trailer, which did not show the application's function in detail but rather metaphorically depicted the role of MP[1]. Then, participants were shown a board with screenshots of UIs of MP to better articulate their thoughts.

Finally, participants were required to install MP on their smartphone and to think aloud while freely exploring the information provided by MP on the app installed on their smartphones.

Interviews were transcribed verbatim and analysed by the author through an iterative open thematic approach aimed at identifying and organising relevant themes from the text. Before proceeding with the axial coding transcripts were firstly analysed inductively to avoid biasing the findings with the researcher's pre-assumption. The analysis of data was performed using MaxQDA, a Computer Assisted Qualitative Data

---

[1] The trailer of MyPermission app shown to participants is available at this link: https://www.youtube.com/watch?time_continue=1&v=fTiPigYxxHE.

Analysis (CAQDA) software following the guidelines suggested in [27]. Throughout the process of analysis the emerging themes and sub-themes were visualised using the dendrogram representation feature available on the CAQDA. Due to space constraints the summary of the emerging themes is available upon request.

4 Findings

Many of the findings confirmed other studies of attitudes toward mobile privacy and smartphone data leakage.

4.1 Smartphones, Privacy Information and Control Features

Participants were split regarding how fundamental their smartphone was to everyday life. As in [28], for five participants who perceived their smartphone as fundamental, such devices became an extension of the self which may lead to the experiencing of stress and anxiety when deprived of their device. As in [26], despite the divergence of opinions reported above, all participants experienced a range of conflicts concerning phone ownership which range from being exposed to undesired privacy exposition to continuous distractions.

"I feel ashamed that everything is based on the phone but I cannot escape [...] it is shamed to be based on the phone, to a machine to be happy" — P4

One participant also reported relying on their smartphone in specific situations such as while living in a foreign country, as well as simplifying their access to public services in the specific case of the UK. Such context-dependent reliance on smartphones shows how the flexibility of such devices, along with the growing number of situations in which they are used, make them deeply integrated into people's everyday lives.

As in [12, 15, 29], participants were in general not familiar, or generally did not pay particular attention to, privacy information and control points such as the Privacy policy and the list of permissions which was hidden within the settings menu.

4.2 Personal Perception and Concerns Toward Privacy

As reported in [18], all participants were generally aware and concerned about different privacy-invasive activities of their apps. Nevertheless as in [22] and [21], four participants consciously accepted the trade-off in order to keep using their relevant apps and services.

"So it's easy to close your eyes [from the] bad things they can do with your data, not necessarily bad but things that you don't want them to do with your data." — P8

However, five participants reported they were generally not entirely passive with regard to being exposed to privacy violations, and support the findings of [30] in reporting engagement in diverse, non-technical coping strategies to reduce the unintended collection of their private information. Examples of this include the denying of storing personal information for future use by digital marketplaces, and self-moderated information disclosure on social media and while using instant message apps.

Seven participants showed a strong awareness about the trade-off concerning the use of mobile apps, which is in some disagreement with [11]. Together with the general rise in the level of concern towards the sharing of personal information online [31], this discrepancy may also be accounted for by the higher level of education of the sample. Furthermore, when probed about their subjective understanding of personal information, seven participants associated personal information with traits of participants' personal identity such as personal views and opinions, political ideas as well as information on habits and daily routines.

"I would probably described it as something as intimate, that I would only want to share with certain people at certain time" — P9; Interview 1.

All participants were able to identify a wide range of personal information types that could be stored on their phones, with seven reporting having inferred these information types from indirect feedback, contextual cues and reflecting on their direct experience while using their apps. However, participants were generally unsure about which could be shared more frequently by their apps. Similarly to [31], location, photos and email address were among the personal information items that could be potentially shared more frequently by apps according to participants. Furthermore, as in [11] six participants admitted in particular of having had difficulties understanding how data could have been disclosed by their apps while the others were generally unsure.

4.3 Expectations Toward MP

As in [11, 22, 32], six participants expected MP to fulfill their interest toward the opaque data sharing mechanisms taking place inside their smartphones, as well enhancing transparency and control.

"So it would be good to now for each app [...] what they actually know about you" — P8; Interview 1.

Probed further about the features they would expect from MP, participants' answers showed misconceptions toward the scope of a privacy management app and the role of permissions. For instance, one participant mentioned deleting online footprints after a certain time and another participant described using apps without allowing permissions, which would impede the app's ability to function.

Finally, it may be tempting to interpret the desire for enhancing autonomy, freedom of choice and awareness expressed by participants as the consequence of their general understanding and frustration toward application data leakage. Indeed, they believed that data collection from apps is being voluntarily prosecuted with intended secrecy, in a way that excludes them and offers no chance to be consciously involved in the trade-offs of their privacy. Users are concerned about the asymmetry of power between themselves and the service providers, and fear that the huge amount of information taken from them may be employed to affect their decisional autonomy, as well as other unintended uses. Users therefore value the chance of enhancing their awareness of data sharing and to have more opportunities to intervene in the trade-off between privacy and functionalities underlying the use of their smartphones.

5 Discussion and Initial Recommendations

Given the growing importance of smartphones in daily life and the difficulties in tackling the related privacy issues, privacy management apps would play a crucial role in improving users' privacy.

This research was undertaken using an experiential-based inquiry which allowed researchers to understand personal perceptions of privacy and expectations toward the technology, and to ground the initial recommendations on such insights. In particular, the research allowed the revealing of participants' hidden practices, subjective meanings of privacy, and expectations toward the privacy management technology. As pointed out by [20], successful technologies are those which are able to "respond sensibly to the needs and values of users, and are not necessarily those that are the most usable" [20:83]. Considering the above insights, three main initial recommendations to enhance the transparency, reliability and user experience of such apps can be derived.

Firstly, privacy-enhancing tools should show consideration of the preferences of users for preserving functionalities of their apps. Participants showed awareness and concern toward different privacy-invasive activities concerning their apps and as in [22] consciously accepted the trade-off in order to keep using their relevant apps and services. Despite this, and as also reported in [30], they were generally not entirely passive with regard to being exposed to privacy violations, engaging in non-technical coping strategies to reduce the unintended exposition of their private information. Privacy management tools should therefore support users in finding a balance between the need for privacy the need to keep the relevant functionalities of their apps and services.

Secondly, privacy-enhancing tools should correctly inform users about the real benefits and actual possibility of using privacy management tools to enhance privacy of mobile applications. Users may not be familiar with the specific functions performed by privacy-enhancing technologies. Furthermore, as attitudes and expectations affect the users' intention to adopt a new piece of technology [33, 34], misconceptions held about the role of a privacy management tools is likely to lead to a mismatch between users' expectations, reducing their willingness to adopt the tool if these expectations are not managed.

Finally, greater effort is required from both design researchers and practitioners in order to inform users about suspected applications' data collection behaviours in a way that matches their real concerns and values. The association of personal information with traits of personal identity has interesting design implications. In particular, research suggests that the lack of cognitive and emotional understanding between users and their data suggested in [21] and [22] can be motivated by the difficulty of understanding the outcomes of the processing of such data. Indeed, as pointed out by [35], the connection between apparently innocuous data types and their use to infer more sensitive information is likely to be hard to understand by average users who do not have an extensive understanding of the matter. Thus designers must find ways to make such connection more explicit and in so doing reducing such a cognitive and emotional gap.

While the first recommendation has been partially covered in [19], who reported that users want protections that don't break the functionality of the web pages and

online services they use, the other two recommendations have not been mentioned in previous studies.

Overall, the above recommendations represent a first attempt to derive recommendations for the design of PMTs for smartphones, grounded on the analysis of subjective meanings and perceptions of privacy and technology. In so doing, this research has contributed to the growing stream of research focused on the experience of privacy and security. Furthermore, in adopting the discursive approach described in Sect. 3.2 it provided complementary insights compared to those coming from studies focused on usability as in [17–19]. The potential of such an approach is that of leveraging Human-Centred Design practices to design privacy technologies which are more adherent to the values and needs of users.

5.1 Limitations and Future Work

One limitation of the in-depth qualitative investigation reported in this article is that the small sample of relatively young and well-educated participants does not allow generalisation across a wide population of users.

However, studies enrolling a small number of participants are not uncommon in practice-based research [36–39] as they intend to provide a richer descriptive understanding of the unknown design space which can inform researchers about salient issues for future research and practices. Furthermore, the figure on smartphone ownership offered by [1], shows that in the UK people in the age groups 16–24 and 25–34 regard smartphones as the most important device for internet access, suggesting that the targeted group is indeed representative of a relevant segment of the real population.

Nonetheless, one way in which this limitation may have affected the reported findings is the general high level of awareness of data leakage reported by participants, which may be accounted for by the higher level of education of the sample. Therefore, future study may consider the involvement of a more heterogeneous sample which is representative of a wider age range groups, and different level of instructions.

Finally, as pointed out by [20], future research may also engage with groups with specific needs as it is likely that a challenging group of users can offer insights which are potentially beneficial for the wider population.

6   Conclusions

This study used both semi-structured interviews and required users to think-aloud while going through the proposed tasks to investigate users' personal perceptions and concerns towards smartphone privacy, and their expectations concerning a privacy management app. The findings were discussed in the light of those reported in the relevant literature.

To improve the design of privacy-enhancing tools for smartphones it has been recommended to (1) explore ways to support users to find the appropriate balance among privacy and functionality; (2) appropriately informing users about the real benefits and possibility of the tool and (3) further exploring the emotional and cognitive gap concerning leaked information.

To further extend the proposed set of initial recommendations, in the next step of the study design probes will be used to reveal users' experience of the privacy management app during a prolonged in-situ trial period.

References

1. Ofcom: The communications market report, 3 August 2017. https://www.ofcom.org.uk/__data/assets/pdf_file/0017/105074/cmr-2017-uk.pdf. Accessed 7 May 2018
2. Zang, J., Dummit, K., Graves, J., et al.: Who knows what about me? A survey of behind the scenes personal data sharing to third parties by mobile apps. Technology Science (2015). http://techscience.org/a/2015103001/. Accessed 28 Nov 2015
3. Book, T.R.: Privacy concerns in android advertising libraries. Thesis (2015). https://scholarship.rice.edu/handle/1911/87711. Accessed 21 Jan 2016
4. Narayanan, A., Shmatikov, V.: Myths and fallacies of 'personally identifiable information'. Commun. ACM **53**, 24–26 (2010)
5. Christl, W., Spiekermann, S.: Networks of Control (2016). http://www.facultas.at/list?isbn=9783708914732. Accessed 10 Oct 2016
6. Borgesius, F.Z.: Singling out people without knowing their names – behavioural targeting, pseudonymous data, and the new data protection regulation. SSRN Scholarly Paper ID 2733115, Social Science Research Network, Rochester, NY, 16 February 2016. https://papers.ssrn.com/abstract=2733115. Accessed 3 May 2018
7. Schiff, A.: 2015 edition: a marketer's guide to cross-device identity. AdExchanger (2015). https://adexchanger.com/data-exchanges/a-marketers-guide-to-cross-device-identity/. Accessed 31 Aug 2018
8. de Montjoye, Y.-A., Hidalgo, C.A., Verleysen, M., et al.: Unique in the crowd: the privacy bounds of human mobility. Sci. Reports **3** (2013). https://doi.org/10.1038/srep01376
9. Borgesius, F.J.Z., Möller, J., Kruikemeier, S., et al.: Online political microtargeting: promises and threats for democracy. Utrecht Law Rev. 14 (2018). https://doi.org/10.18352/ulr.420
10. Almuhimedi, H., Schaub, F., Sadeh, N., et al.: Your location has been shared 5,398 times!: a field study on mobile app privacy nudging. In: Proceedings of the 33rd Annual ACM Conference on Human Factors in Computing Systems, pp. 787–796. ACM, New York (2015)
11. Balebako, R., Jung, J., Lu, W., et al.: 'Little brothers watching you': raising awareness of data leaks on smartphones. In: Proceedings of the Ninth Symposium on Usable Privacy and Security, pp. 12:1–12:11. ACM, New York (2013)
12. Felt, A.P., Egelman, S., Wagner, D.: I've got 99 problems, but vibration ain't one: a survey of smartphone users' concerns. In: Proceedings of the Second ACM Workshop on Security and Privacy in Smartphones and Mobile Devices, pp. 33–44. ACM, New York (2012)
13. Lin, J., Amini, S., Hong, J.I., et al.: Expectation and purpose: understanding users' mental models of mobile app privacy through crowdsourcing. In: Proceedings of the 2012 ACM Conference on Ubiquitous Computing, pp. 501–510. ACM (2012)
14. Liu, B., Andersen, M.S., Schaub, F., et al.: Follow my recommendations: a personalized privacy assistant for mobile app permissions. In: Twelfth Symposium on Usable Privacy and Security (SOUPS 2016), pp. 27–41. USENIX Association, Denver (2016)
15. Tsai, L., Wijesekera, P., Reardon, J., et al.: Turtle guard: helping android users apply contextual privacy preferences. In: Thirteenth Symposium on Usable Privacy and Security (SOUPS 2017), pp. 145–162. USENIX Association, Santa Clara (2017)

16. Wijesekera, P., Baokar, A., Tsai, J.Y., et al.: The feasibility of dynamically granted permissions: aligning mobile privacy with user preferences (2017)
17. Mathur, A., Vitak, J., Narayanan, A., et al.: Characterizing the use of browser-based blocking extensions to prevent online tracking (2018). https://www.usenix.org/system/files/conference/soups2018/soups2018-mathur.pdf. Accessed 27 July 2018
18. Schaub, F., Marella, A., Kalvani, P., et al.: Watching them watching me: browser extensions impact on user privacy awareness and concern, 1 January 2016. https://doi.org/10.14722/usec.2016.23017
19. Leon, P., Ur, B., Shay, R., et al.: Why johnny can't opt out: a usability evaluation of tools to limit online behavioral advertising. In: Proceedings of the SIGCHI Conference on Human Factors in Computing Systems, pp. 589–598. ACM, New York (2012)
20. Dunphy, P., Vines, J., Coles-Kemp, L., et al.: Understanding the experience-centeredness of privacy and security technologies. In: Proceedings of the 2014 Workshop on New Security Paradigms Workshop, pp. 83–94. ACM, New York (2014)
21. Stark, L.: The emotional context of information privacy. Inf. Soc. **32**, 14–27 (2016)
22. Shklovski, I., Mainwaring, S.D., Skúladóttir, H.H., et al.: Leakiness and creepiness in app space: perceptions of privacy and mobile app use. In: Proceedings of the 32nd Annual ACM Conference on Human Factors in Computing Systems, pp. 2347–2356. ACM, New York (2014)
23. Mathiasen, N.R., Bødker, S.: Experiencing security in interaction design. In: Proceedings of the SIGCHI Conference on Human Factors in Computing Systems, pp. 2325–2334. ACM, New York (2011)
24. Nørgaard, M., Hornbæk, K.: What do usability evaluators do in practice?: An explorative study of think-aloud testing. In: Proceedings of the 6th Conference on Designing Interactive Systems, pp. 209–218. ACM, New York (2006)
25. Olmsted-Hawala, E.L., Murphy, E.D., Hawala, S., et al.: Think-aloud protocols: a comparison of three think-aloud protocols for use in testing data-dissemination web sites for usability. In: Proceedings of the SIGCHI Conference on Human Factors in Computing Systems, pp. 2381–2390. ACM, New York (2010)
26. Smith, A.: U.S. smartphone use in 2015, 1 April 2015. http://www.pewinternet.org/2015/04/01/us-smartphone-use-in-2015/. Accessed 4 Apr 2016
27. Denscombe, M.: The Good Research Guide. Open University Press, New York (2007)
28. Clayton, R.B., Leshner, G., Almond, A.: The extended iSelf: the impact of iPhone separation on cognition, emotion, and physiology. J. Comput.-Mediated Commun. **20**, 119–135 (2015)
29. Kelley, P.G., Consolvo, S., Cranor, L.F., Jung, J., Sadeh, N., Wetherall, D.: A conundrum of permissions: installing applications on an android smartphone. In: Blyth, J., Dietrich, S., Camp, L.J. (eds.) FC 2012. LNCS, vol. 7398, pp. 68–79. Springer, Heidelberg (2012). https://doi.org/10.1007/978-3-642-34638-5_6
30. Rainie, L., Madden, M.: Americans' privacy strategies post-snowden, 16 March 2015. http://www.pewinternet.org/2015/03/16/americans-privacy-strategies-post-snowden/. Accessed 18 Mar 2015
31. Rainie, L., Kiesler, S., Kang, R., et al.: Part 2: concerns about personal information online. Pew Research Center: Internet, Science & Technolgy (2013). http://www.pewinternet.org/2013/09/05/part-2-concerns-about-personal-information-online/. Accessed 27 Nov 2017
32. Jung, J., Han, S., Wetherall, D.: Short paper: enhancing mobile application permissions with runtime feedback and constraints. In: Proceedings of the Second ACM Workshop on Security and Privacy in Smartphones and Mobile Devices, pp. 45–50. ACM, New York (2012)

33. Oinas-Kukkonen, H., Harjumaa, M.: Persuasive systems design: key issues, process model, and system features. Commun. Assoc. Inf. Syst. **24** (2009). http://aisel.aisnet.org/cais/vol24/iss1/28

34. Wright, P., McCarthy, J.C.: Experience-centered design designers, users, and communities in dialogue. Morgan & Claypool, San Rafael (2010)

35. Abrams, M.: The origins of personal data and its implications for governance. SSRN Scholarly Paper ID 2510927. Social Science Research Network, Rochester, 21 March 2014. https://papers.ssrn.com/abstract=2510927. Accessed 16 Jan 2018

36. Gaver, W.W., Bowers, J., Boucher, A., et al.: The drift table: designing for ludic engagement. In: CHI 2004 Extended Abstracts on Human Factors in Computing Systems, pp. 885–900. ACM, New York (2004)

37. Hutchinson, H., Mackay, W., Westerlund, B., et al.: Technology probes: inspiring design for and with families. In: Proceedings of the SIGCHI Conference on Human Factors in Computing Systems, pp. 17–24. ACM, New York (2003)

38. Uriu, D., Odom, W.: Designing for domestic memorialization and remembrance: a field study of fenestra in Japan. In: Proceedings of the 2016 CHI Conference on Human Factors in Computing Systems, pp. 5945–5957. ACM, New York (2015)

39. Vines, J., Blythe, M., Dunphy, P., et al.: Cheque mates: participatory design of digital payments with eighty somethings. In: Proceedings of the SIGCHI Conference on Human Factors in Computing Systems, pp. 1189–1198. ACM, New York (2012)

Tilt Space: A Systematic Exploration of Mobile Tilt for Design Purpose

Chuanyi Liu(✉) ⓘ, Ningning Wu, Jiali Zhang, and Wei Su

School of Information Science and Engineering, Lanzhou University, Lanzhou, China
liuchuanyi96@hotmail.com, {wunn16,suwei}@lzu.edu.cn, jennyfocus@163.com

Abstract. Various application scenarios of a smartphone sometimes require one-handed and/or eyes-free interaction. Tilt-based interfaces have the potential to meet these requirements. Taking multiple application scenarios into account, we conducted an experiment to systematically investigate human ability in controlling tilt input of a mobile phone. Three visual feedback levels, i.e., fully visual feedback (FV), partially visual feedback (PV), and no visual feedback (NV), were investigated. Under the NV condition, the participants performed a task using an eyes-free method. The results revealed that trials were performed the fastest but were the most error-prone under the NV condition. The participants could easily distinguish 4 tilt orientation levels ($TOLs$) and 2 tilt magnitude levels ($TMLs$) or 8 $TOLs$ and 2 $TMLs$ under the NV condition with tolerance of an error rate 10% or 15%, respectively. We also found out that the participants' abilities to control tilt input were related to tilt *orientation* directions. The results have some implications for non-visual interface designs using tilt as primitive input.

Keywords: Mobile · Tilt · Design space

1 Introduction

Smartphones are essential devices for us. We use them in our work, study, and life every day. A touch screen is its basic interactive component of a smartphone. Touch screens provide us simple and intuitive interactive methods, however, coupled with some limitations, e.g., "fat finger" [31] and hand occlusion [36]. Besides these limitations, other issues can be caused by various application scenarios of smartphones. When walking on the road, we may risk a traffic accident watching the screen of a smartphone. An eyes-free interaction method is more suitable under these conditions. Sometimes, not both of one's hands are available to manipulate a mobile phone, e.g., when s/he is taking a bus or holding a bag in one hand. But one-handed thumb manipulation of a touchscreen-based mobile device is typically awkward, since one-handed thumb interaction limits the accessible area on the screen [16].

It is worth resolving these issues of a smartphone, especially for some conditions, e.g., on a bus or the road. Built-in tilt sensors provide an independent

ⓒ IFIP International Federation for Information Processing 2019
Published by Springer Nature Switzerland AG 2019
D. Lamas et al. (Eds.): INTERACT 2019, LNCS 11748, pp. 497–517, 2019.
https://doi.org/10.1007/978-3-030-29387-1_29

input channel for portable devices. Tilt gestures map 3D angles of a portable device as primitive input with interaction commands. Tilt gestures have the potential to resolve these issues, since we can feel a mobile phone's posture by our proprioception without watching the screen, and operate the mobile phone with an eyes-free method and unimanually.

It has long been interests to many researchers exploring tilt as primitive input for interfaces. Since Rekimoto [27] used the tilt of a small screen device as input, researchers have developed a variety of tilt-based interaction techniques. Early research on tilt focused on using tilt as an additional input channel for mobile devices to implement specific interactive techniques, such as menu navigation [27], scrolling [10,22], panning and zooming of maps [17,35], document and photo browsing [4,25], and text entry [23,29,38]. However, these studies mainly focused on what can be done with the tilt input channel. Few studies considered human ability on controlling mobile tilt input and the design space of tilt-based interaction, especially with an eyes-free method.

In the study, we systematically investigated human ability in controlling tilt input of a mobile phone. The major objective of our research is to determine effects of different visual feedback levels on human ability in controlling tilt input and the upper bound of the human ability, especially under the NV condition.

2   Related Work

Tilt-based interaction has long been of interests to researchers of HCI. These literature can be divided roughly into two groups: studies on general human performance of tilt control and on specific implementation examples using tilt input.

2.1   General Human Performance of Tilt Control

Teather and Mackenzie [20] proved tilt conformed to Fitts' law [7] through ISO 9241-9 [14] 2D pointing task. Later, the authors extended their work to compare position- and velocity-control for tilt-based interaction with the similar 2D pointing task [34]. They found out that position-control performed approximately 2 times faster than velocity-control and had higher pointing throughput. Wang et al. [37] also studied tilt control from viewpoint of Fitts' law; they didn't use an accelerometer for tilt input but vision-based motion tracking. Sad and Poirier [28] confirmed tilt-based scrolling and pointing tasks conformed to Fitts' law without reporting pointing throughput.

Rahman et al. [26] systematically investigated human ability of tilt control according to the human wrist movement. They found out the subjects could control comfortably at least 16 levels on the supination/pronation axis. Baglioni et al. [1] explored human control ability on tilt input with a jerk gesture. Guo and Paek [9] studied human control ability of tilt on smartwatches, and found out that *OjectPoint* performed better. Shima et al. [30] evaluated the performance of tilting operations on wrist-worn devices.

All these literature offered valuable cues for tilt-based interaction design, however, none of them had taken eyes-free method into account (to our knowledge). In our study, we explored tilt control according to different visual feedback levels, especially the eyes-free operation method was considered.

2.2 Specific Implementation Examples

Some researchers studied tilt-based text entry [5,15,23,29,38,39]. These studies typically divided letters into groups and disambiguated letter selection through device tilt. Various UI tasks, such as scrolling [2,10,22,32], document browsing [6], menu navigation [27], and display orientation switch [11], using tilt control were investigated. Pietroszek et al. [24] utilized a mobile device to perform 3D interaction on large displays. Geronimo et al. [8] also focused their study on controlling separated displays using mobile devices. They designed a tilting interaction framework for rapid developing web-based applications. Homaeian et al. [12] explored tilt input for data browsing techniques in cross-device environments, and found that tilt facilitated access to out-of-reach data. Kurosawa et al. [18] presented combination of a tilt operation and electromyography on smart watches using tilt to set the cursor's motion direction. Sun et al. [33] proposed a wrist-to-finger input approach that enabled one-handed and touch-free target selection on smart watches.

Tilt-based mobile games [3,13,21,40] have been popular for years. Typically, using tilt could not improve interaction performance in these games, but tilt interaction gave users more challenges and fun.

3   Experiment

We base our experiment on an understanding of the mobile device application contexts. Figure 1 shows the three axes of rotation of a smartphone and the tilt motion space. The built-in tilt sensor can be used to detect the pitch and roll orientations and magnitude of a mobile device by analyzing the projection of the constant gravity acceleration on the three axes. But tilt sensor does not allow the determination of the static yaw orientation [11].

However, the range of motion provides by the tilt sensor may not always be conducive to tilt control due to the ergonomic limitations of human wrists and the difficulty in obtaining visual feedback in "extreme" angles (e.g., when a device's screen is turned leftward or rightward from a horizontal posture to vertical). But under the eyes-free condition, users can control the tilt by proprioception and memory without relying on visual feedback; arms can be used besides wrists to enlarge the tilt space. In other words, the visual and ergonomic limitations are alleviated under the eyes-free condition.

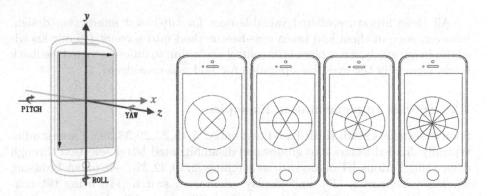

Fig. 1. The three axes of the device rotations and the three corresponding angles.

Fig. 2. The tilt space is divided into 4, 6, 8, and 12 *TOLs* (from left to right) together with 2 *TMLs*.

3.1 Apparatus

The experiment was conducted using a Huawei honor 5c smartphone with a built-in 3-axis accelerometer running Google's Android 6.0 operating system. The display resolution was 1920 × 1080 pixels. In addition, a Lenovo YT3-X50F 10.1-in. tablet with android 5.1.1 OS was used to inform the user a target under the no-visual-feedback condition.

The experimental software was developed in Java using the Android SDK. The accelerometer was used to detect tilt magnitude and tilt orientation of the smartphone, sampling at a rate of 50 samples per second.

3.2 Participants

Twelve volunteers, 10 males and 2 females, ranging in age from 22 to 32 years (Mean = 25.3, SD = 3.8), participated in the experiment. All the participants were recruited from the computer department in the local university, and they were all familiar with manipulation of smartphones and right-handed. All of them had normal or corrected to normal vision. Although none of the participants had ever used tilt to perform subtle pointing or selection tasks before, they all had prior experience with tilt-based interfaces such as gravity sensor games.

3.3 Task and Stimuli

The human control of tilt on handheld devices was decomposed into the control of tilt orientation and the control of tilt magnitude. The tilt orientation (0° to 360°) was linearly divided into four levels: 4, 6, 8, and 12 with angular intervals of 90°, 60°, 45°, and 30°, respectively. The motion space of tilt magnitude (0° to 90°) was linearly divided into three levels: 2, 3, and 4 with angular intervals of 45°, 30°, and 22.5°, respectively. A circle, standing for the tilt space, was

divided into m (the number of tilt orientation levels, $TOLs$, tilt orientation hereafter referred to as TO) × n (the number of tilt magnitude levels, $TMLs$, tilt magnitude hereafter referred to as TM) districts (e.g., $4\,TOLs \times 2\,TMLs =$ 8 districts, see Fig. 2 left). One of these districts was randomly (across trials) selected to be a target. There were three visual feedback levels (visual feedback and its level hereafter referred to as VF and VFL, respectively, see Fig. 3): fully visual (FV), partially visual (PV), and no visual (NV).

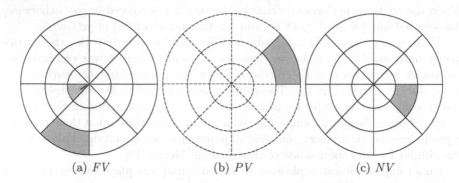

(a) FV (b) PV (c) NV

Fig. 3. Different visual feedback conditions. FV: a target district was filled in green and a district holding the pointer in gray, the blue pointer is always visible; PV (the dashed lines were not shown in the experiment): a target district was filled in green, the blue pointer disappears once tilting began; NV: districts were shown statically during a trial in the tablet PC. (Color figure online)

Under the FV and PV conditions, the cursor was displayed as a blue pointer, which was painted from the center of the device's display (i.e., the center of the circle, denoted as C). Tilt magnitude and tilt orientation were computed to the pointer's length and orientation, respectively. The tilt magnitude of device was linearly mapped to the pointer's length which varied between 0 and the maximum (the radius length of the largest circle) when a participant tilted the phone from horizontal to vertical. Under the NV condition, the pointer dimensions were calculated using the same method, but the pointer had no visual feedback (i.e., the pointer was hidden).

To confirm selection of a target, a participant manipulated tilt input to adjust the pointer's orientation and length to make it enter the target district, and kept the pointer in the district over the time threshold. The threshold was set to be one second vs. the largest selection delay, 500 ms, in [34]: the dwell time was intentionally doubled to discriminate target selection from unintentional entry and disambiguate target selection especially for NV condition. Similarly, to minimize unintentional selection and reduce selection difficulty, minute tilt magnitude variation (within 5°) was also eliminated from target selection. A non-target district was determined whether selected using the same method.

Under FV condition (Fig. 3a), visual feedback was continuous during the whole process of a trial. All the districts were painted with gray-lined borders; a

target district was filled in green, while the current district (holding the pointer) in gray. The pointer was painted in blue. When being selected, a target district was filled in red, while a non-target in yellow.

Under *PV* condition (Fig. 3b), only a target district was continuously displayed and the pointer was visible only at the beginning of a trial. Once tilting began, the pointer disappeared. A participant manipulated the hidden pointer to meet the target upon their proprioception and spatial perception and cognition. Once the pointer entered the target, the target color changed from green to gray. When the trial was performed correctly, the target was colored in red; otherwise, the selected non-target district became visible and was filled in yellow.

There was no visual feedback under *NV* condition (Fig. 3c), i.e., the participants performed trials using an eyes-free method. A target was displayed on the tablet screen using a *FV* method except the pointer, but the surface was static during a trial (Fig. 4b). The tablet was connected to the smartphone via Blue-tooth. The trial sequence in the tablet was synchronized with that in the mobile phone. The participants selected a target completely upon their proprioception, kinesthetic memory, and spatial perception and cognition. This scenario was similar to the expert mode of the Marking Menus [19].

Under any condition, a pleasure or alarm sound was played when a district was selected correctly or incorrectly, respectively.

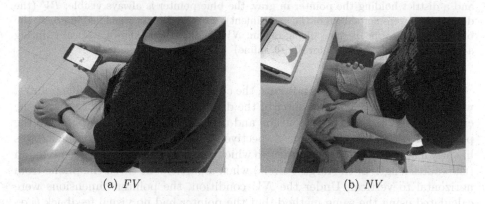

(a) *FV*   (b) *NV*

Fig. 4. A participant was performing experimental trials.

3.4 Procedure and Design

The experiment used a within-subjects full factorial design. The experimental factors and their levels were:

VF: *FV*, *PV*, *NV*.
TO: 4, 6, 8, 12.
TM: 2, 3, 4.

Before the experiment, each of the participants had been told they had the right to freely quit the experiment at any time. The participants were allowed to have a rest between any two experimental conditions, and they had been told they were not allowed to do the experiment when they felt tired. A longer rest between experimental blocks was mandatory.

After given a detailed description about the task, participants spent a few minutes in familiarizing themselves with tilt control and the three visual feedback conditions. The participants performed the experiment seated, and all of them held the device with their right hands (see Fig. 4).

In the formal experiment, the participants were required to complete three blocks of trials. A Latin square was used to counterbalance the order efforts of the three *VFLs*. For each feedback condition, the participants performed target selection beginning from *TOL4* and *TML2*. The rationale for the sequential design is that interaction performance does reduce significantly with the increase of levels of the two factors according to the previous work [26] and our observation. So the major objective of this study is not to determine whether there exists significantly different effects between these factor levels on interaction performance measures but to find out the upper bound of human ability to control tilt input according to the two experimental factors. The target appeared randomly among all the districts with 2 repetitions at the same location. The *TOLs* and the *TMLs* were always presented in ascending (smallest to largest) order for easy learning. When a wrong selection happened, a failed attempt was recorded. Not was the experiment proceeded to next trial until a trial was done correctly. Participants were allowed to try for no more than 5 times for each trial before success, otherwise, the trial was aborted. Totally, there were:

12 *participants*×
3 *blocks*×
3 *VFLs*×
(4 + 6 + 8 + 12) *TOLs*×
(2 + 3 + 4) *TMLs*×
2 repetitions
= 58320 target selection trials.

The participants were instructed to complete each trial "as quickly and accurately as possible". After performing all experimental trials, the participants were investigated for their subjective comments on the three *VFLs* with a questionnaire where they rated the usability, ease of learning, hand and eye fatigue along a Likert scale (each aspect with seven rating levels, where 1 represented the worst and 7 the best). In total, the experiment lasted approximately 3 h for each participant.

3.5 Performance Measures

The experimental measures were selection time (ST), error rate (ER, there was ONE error when participants failed at their first attempt), number of aborted trials (AT, i.e., number of trials that had failed for 5 times), and number of crossings (NC, the times of the cursor enters a target without selecting it, i.e., when dwell time in the target was less than the given time threshold). ST was defined as the time consumed from tilting the phone to selecting a target. NC was used to reveal the difficulty degrees to dwell the pointer in a target district, it was 1 in a perfect selection task. In the next section, these measures were calculated to averages per trial from the primitive experimental records.

Table 1. Statistical effects for performance measures.

Effect		ST			ER			AT			NC		
Name	df	F	p	η_p^2	F	p	η_p^2	F	p	η_p^2	F	p	η_p^2
block(b)	2,22	33	.000	.750	24.3	.000	.689	0.9	.44	.072	16.8	.000	.604
VFL(v)	2,22	119	.000	.915	197.4	.000	.947	13	.000	.541	186.3	.000	.944
TOL(o)	3,33	95.6	.000	.897	45.3	.000	.804	12.7	.000	.535	7.7	.001	.411
TML(m)	2,22	291.7	.000	.964	62.6	.000	.851	10.7	.001	.494	150.9	.000	.932
$b \times v$	4,44	2.3	.08	.170	6.9	.000	.385	0.7	.57	.064	7.8	.000	.416
$v \times o$	6,66	8.2	.000	.428	24.4	.000	.689	12.6	.000	.533	2.7	.022	.195
$v \times m$	4,44	26	.000	.702	38.9	.000	.780	107	.000	.492	78.7	.000	.877
$o \times m$	6,66	1.6	.17	.126	2.5	.03	.183	1.6	.15	.130	0.5	.79	.046
$v \times o \times m$	12,132	1.1	.41	.087	0.5	.93	.042	1.7	.07	.137	0.9	.53	.077

"×" means interaction effects.

4 Results

A 3 *blocks* × 3 *VFLs* × 4 *TOLs* × 2 *TMLs* RM-ANOVA was conducted on mean data of *ST,ER,AT,* and *NC*. Statistical reports for the four performance measures are shown in Table 1.

4.1 Selection Time

Learning effects were observed from the significant effect of *block* on *ST*. There was no significant interaction effect between *feedback* and *block*, Fig. 5 shows the similar learning effects under different visual feedback conditions.

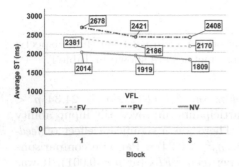

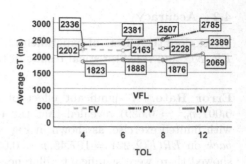

Fig. 5. Average *ST* by *blocks* and *VFLs*.

Fig. 6. Average *ST* by *TOLs* and *VFLs*.

There was a significant effect of VF ($F(2, 22) = 119.04, p < 0.001, \eta_p^2 = 0.915$) on ST. Pairwise comparisons showed significant differences between all visual feedback levels (at $p < 0.001$). The participants performed the fastest under the NV condition, but the most slowly under the PV (Fig. 5). Based on our observations, we speculate that this may because, under the FV and PV conditions, the participants tended to tilt the device from a small angle little by little to a large one and kept watching the visual feedback during a trial. But under the NV condition, the participants tended to tilt the device directly to the location they thought to be appropriate based on proprioception, kinesthetic memory, and spatial perception and cognition, since it was impossible to rely on any visual feedback.

Although the participants had more practice before the trials of the subsequent $TOLs$ (Fig. 6) and $TMLs$ (Fig. 7), tests of within-subjects contrasts revealed general ST increases with those of level numbers of the two factors. These trends indicated the significant increase of manipulation difficulty in tilt control when the number of divided districts increased, and the upper bounds of human ability to manipulate tilt input.

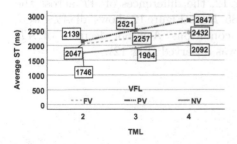

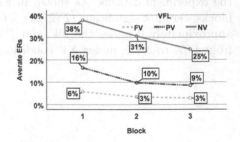

Fig. 7. Average *ST* by *TMLs* and *VFLs*.

Fig. 8. Average *ERs* by *blocks* and *VFLs*.

4.2 Accuracy

We explore the effects of experimental factors on accuracy from three aspects: *ER*, *NC*, and *AT*. Statistical results of these metrics are shown in Table 1.

Error Rate. A significant effect of *block* on *ER* ($F(2, 22) = 24.34, p < 0.001, \eta_p^2 = 0.689$) revealed that the participants improved tilt input ability with limited exercise, as shown in Fig. 8. There was a significant effect of *feedback* on $ER(F(2, 22) = 197.45, p < 0.001, \eta_p^2 = 0.947)$. Pairwise comparisons showed there were significant differences between *VFLs* (at $p < 0.001$). It was the most and least error-prone under the *NV* and the *FV* conditions, respectively. Figure 8 also reveals that there was a significant interaction effect between *block* and *VF*, and *ER* decreased the fastest under the *NV* condition. This indicated that although it was the most error-prone to perform tasks without any visual feedback, the participants improve their ability to control tilt input more quickly with an eyes-free method.

The similar variation trends and human ability upper bounds with *orientation resolution* (Fig. 9) and *magnitude* (Fig. 10) on *ST* were also observed on *ER*. We will further analyze these results in the subsequent subsections.

Number of Crossings. *NC* indicates how difficult to dwell the cursor (pointer) in a district. As shown in Table 1, the main and interaction effects (except that of $TO \times TM$ and that of $VF \times TO \times TM$) of all the experimental factors had significant impacts on *NC*. Figure 11 shows there was a significant learning effect across the three blocks ($F(2, 22) = 16.75, p < 0.001, \eta_p^2 = 0.604$) and a significant *VF* effect ($F(2, 22) = 186.32, p < 0.001, \eta_p^2 = 0.944$) on *NC*. A significant interaction effect between *block* and *feedback* is also observed in Fig. 11. *PV* possessed the largest *NC* among the three *VFLs* indicated that partially visual feedback imposed difficulty on keeping a mobile device still with a 3D angle.

Number of Aborted Trials. *AT* indicates the difficult degree to complete the experimental tasks. As shown in Fig. 12, the differences of *AT* across the blocks were not significant ($F(2, 22) = 0.85, NS$). Figure 12 shows all *AT*s were approximately 0 under the *FV* and *PV* conditions. A minor decrease of *AT*, from 4.8% to 3.5%, under *NV* condition was observed (Fig. 12).

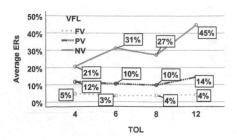

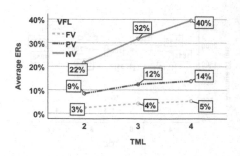

Fig. 9. Average *ERs* by *TOLs* and *VFLs*.

Fig. 10. Average *ERs* by *TMLs* and *VFLs*.

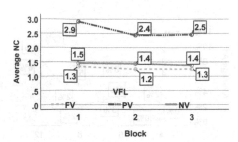

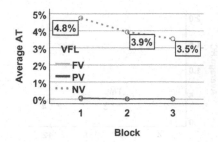

Fig. 11. Average *NC* by *blocks* and *VFLs*.

Fig. 12. Average *AT* by *blocks* and *VFLs*.

4.3   Orientation Effects Under the *NV* Condition

Generally, experimental task performance metrics of speed (according to *ST*, see Fig. 13), accuracy (according to *ERs*, see Fig. 14), difficulty to dwell in the target (according to *NC*, see Fig. 15), and difficulty to complete a selection (according to *AT*, see Fig. 16) decreased with the increase of *TOLs* and *TMLs*. But we observed an exception (from *TOL6* to *TOL8*) for *TO* from the figures. We conducted another 3 *blocks* × 4 *TOLs* × 2 *TMLs* RM-ANOVA on data under *NV* condition to get further insights. Figure 13 shows *MT* decreased minutely from *TOL6*(1888 ms) to *TOL8*(1876 ms) $(F(1,11) = 0.514, p = 0.488, \eta_p{}^2 = 0.045)$. *ERs* also decreased slightly from *TOL6*(31.3%) to *TOL8*(27.3%) $(F(1,11) = 3.28, p = 0.097, \eta_p{}^2 = 0.23)$, see Fig. 14. Similarly, there was also a slight decrease of *NC* from *TOL6*(1.42) to *TOL8*(1.4) $(F(1,11) = 0.406, p = 0.537, \eta_p{}^2 = 0.036)$, see Fig. 15. Figure 16 shows that *AT* also decreased minutely from *TOL6*(3.9%) to *TOL8*(2.8%) $(F(1,11) = 1.068, p = 0.324, \eta_p{}^2 = 0.088)$. Figure 17 illustrates the distribution of *ERs* at *TOL12* in detail: *ERs* in the device's *axial* directions were lower than in the other directions, similarly Guo and Paek [9] reported the similar results on smart watches.

508   C. Liu et al.

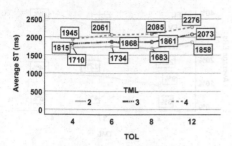

Fig. 13. Average *ST* by *TOLs* and *TMLs* under the *NV* condition.

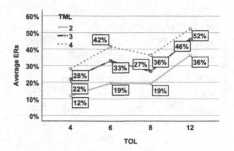

Fig. 14. Average *ERs* by *TOLs* and *TMLs* under the *NV* condition.

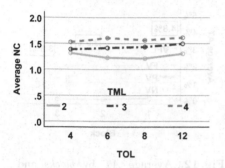

Fig. 15. Average *NC* by *TOLs* and *TMLs* under the *NV* condition.

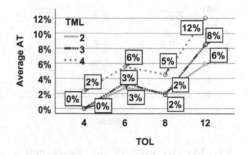

Fig. 16. Average *AT* by *TOLs* and *TMLs* under the *NV* condition.

4.4 Discernible Numbers of Orientation Resolution Levels and Magnitude Levels

The participants had to keep watching the screen during a trial under *FV* and *PV*, but *PV* was defeated by the other two *VFLs* on both speed and accuracy. This indicates that *PV* made no contribution for the experimental tasks. In the following of this subsection, we determine the participants' performance based on the data gathered when they had limited practice with tilt input, so only the data of block 3 were analyzed. A 3 *VFLs* × 4 *TOLs* × 2 *TMLs* RM-ANOVA was conducted on mean data of *ER*, *AT*, and *NC* in block 3.

The largest *NC* in *block* 3 was 1.4 and 1.6 under the *FV* (see Fig. 18) and *NV* conditions (see Fig. 19), respectively. So *NC* imposed no limitations on discernible levels of the two factors. Similarly, all the percentages of *ATs* in *block* 3 under the *FV* condition were approximately 0% (see Fig. 20), and the largest percentage of *AT* under the *NV* condition was 11% (see Fig. 21). Thus *AT* had no influences on discernible levels of the two factors, either.

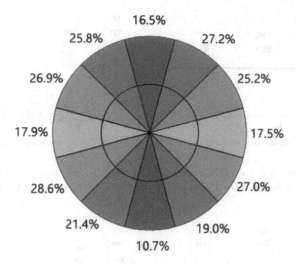

Fig. 17. Average *ERs* at *TOL12*.

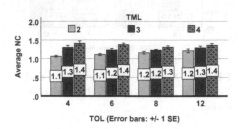

Fig. 18. Average *NC* by *TOLs* and *TMLs* in *block* 3 under the *FV* condition.

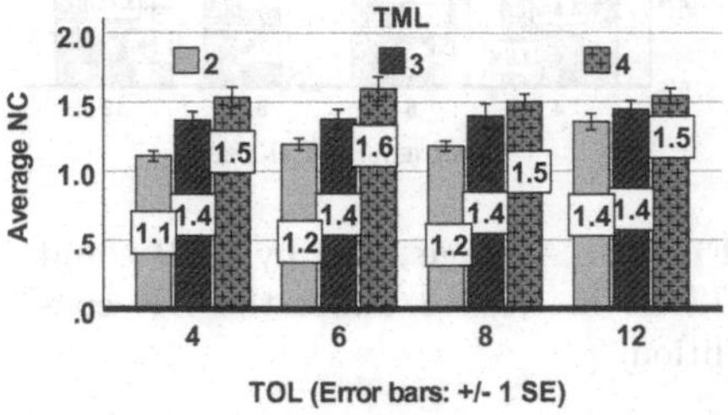

Fig. 19. Average *NC* by *TOLs* and *TMLs* in *block* 3 under the *NV* condition.

Figure 22 shows the largest *ER* in *block* 3 was 4.2% under the *FV* condition. So all the explored levels for both *TO* and *TM* are discernible, i.e., *TOLs* were 12 and *TMLs* were 4.

There was only one *ER* (8.3%) less than 10% under the *NV* condition, as shown in Fig. 23. In that case, *TOLs* and *TMLs* were 4 and 2, respectively. These two are discernible numbers for the two factors under *NV*. If we extend *ER* tolerance to 15%, the discernible numbers of *TOLs* and *TMLs* were 8 and 2, respectively.

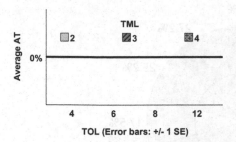

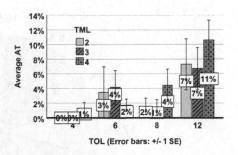

Fig. 20. Average *AT* by *TOLs* and *TMLs* in *block* 3 under the *FV* condition.

Fig. 21. Average *AT* by *TOLs* and *TMLs* in *block* 3 under the *NV* condition.

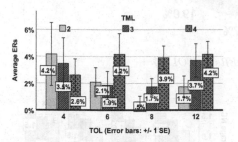

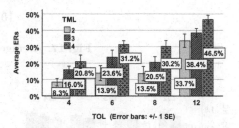

Fig. 22. Average *ERs* by *TOLs* and *TMLs* in *block* 3 under the *FV* condition.

Fig. 23. Average *ERs* by *TOLs* and *TMLs* in *block* 3 under the *NV* condition.

4.5 Subjective Feedback

The survey was to determine how the participants felt using tilt control for target acquisition and selection tasks under different *VFLs*. Participant's subjective ratings of the three levels are shown in Fig. 24. The ratings include usability, ease of learning, and hand and eye fatigue.

The participants rated *FV* the highest regarding measures of usability and ease of learning; while *NV* was rated the best for eye and hand fatigue. According to our observations, under the *FV* and the *PV* conditions, the participants tried hard to keep watching visual feedback while tilting the device, and to keep their wrists in a special posture to keep the screen in a visible range: this limited the movement of wrists and arms. While under the *NV* condition, the participants manipulated the device to perform trials with more comfortable gestures. Although the participants rated *NV* the lowest regarding usability, they believed that using a mobile with an eyes-free method is irreplaceable for some special application scenarios, e.g., while walking on the road. *NV* was rated the lowest for ease of learning, but it is conflicting with the quantitative statistical results. We speculate that, under the *NV* condition, the difficulty of

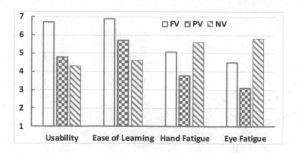

Fig. 24. Likert scale ratings by *VFLs*.

tilt manipulation made the participants think it was also difficult to obtain the ability of tilt manipulation.

Other open comments include: "Tilt to the upper right corner is very uncomfortable." Given that all the participants were right-handed, this is easy to understand the comment and consistent with the aforementioned *orientation effects*.

5   Concept Designs of Tilt-Based Interaction Using an Eyes-Free Method

Building on the experimental results and our observations, we now explore the tilt-based design space using an eyes-free method.

We often receive a phone call when walking across a crossroad, sometimes holding a bag in one hand. At that case, it is difficult to answer the call. Furthermore, we might put us in danger if we watch the mobile phone on the road. According to our experimental results, we can easily deal with the phone call with tilt input using an eyes-free method and by one hand (see Fig. 25a). Typically, we have four choices to deal with a phone call. We may first get to know the calling-number by an audio prompt message, and then determine to accept or deny the call, or send an automatic message and deny the call. The division of the tilt space with four *TOLs* and one *TML* is suitable for this case (See Fig. 25a).

Figure 25b shows the concept design of a music player supporting eyes-free interaction. Since it is easier to be controlled for "X-Y axial" orientation districts, more commands are assigned in these directions (see Fig. 25b). There are two *TOLs* in these axial directions, but only one in the diagonal. In the design, opposite functions are mirrored in one line, most functions are located alone X-Y axes. By default, the surface of the player is hidden. Users tilt a mobile phone into a certain 3D tilt district and keep its tilting posture for one second, then a function is chosen, and then the player works according to the chosen command.

In the market, there are many smart toy cars that can be manipulated by a mobile APP through Blue-tooth, see Fig. 25d. We typically manipulate a smart toy car using the GUI of an APP. But that is not the best method, since we had better keep visually tracking with the toy car when it is running on the road,

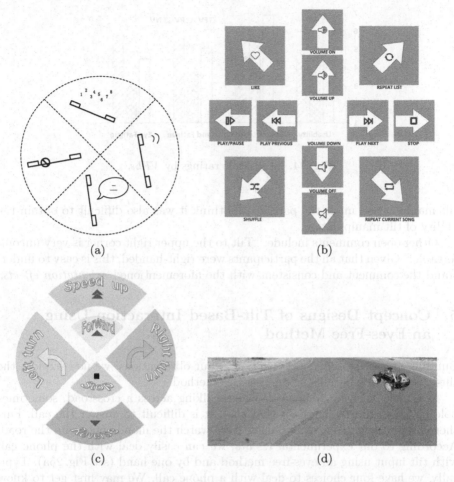

Fig. 25. Concept designs for tilt space using an eyes-free method. (a) Dealing with a phone call with tilt input. (b) Mapping between the tilt space districts and the music player commands. (c) Manipulating a toy car with tilt input. (d) A smart toy car that can be manipulated by a mobile APP through Blue-tooth.

otherwise it may run into some obstacles or even be crashed. Based on our study results, we build a pie menu that is suitable for eyes-free interaction, see Fig. 25c. We employ tilt input to make a toy car run forward by tilting a mobile phone outward (at approximately twelve o'clock) or make the toy speed up by tilting the phone further in the same direction. When we want to stop the toy, we just tilt the phone backward (at approximately six o'clock); and if we tilt back the phone further, we make the toy run reversely. We also manipulate the toy turn leftward or rightward by tilting the phone leftward or rightward, respectively. During the whole process, we keep on watching the toy car and don't need to glimpse the screen of the mobile phone.

6   Discussion

The results indicate that the participants could distinguish at least 12 *TOLs* and 4 *TMLs* under the *FV* condition. But there exist some spectra of *TM* in which the usability is not good enough, e.g., the spectrum where the *TM* is near 90°, it is difficult to keep a device in that posture and get visual feedback from the screen for our wrists and eyes, respectively. These *TM* spectra should not be used in applications or be used as mappings to some special least use commands, e.g., the command of APP exit.

For the *NV* condition, although the discernible numbers are small, *NV* had the highest speed and were the best in terms of hand and eye fatigue. *NV* is not bothered by "fat finger" [31] and hand occlusion [36], which generally exist for all direct-touch screens. And the eyes-free method can reduce some safety risks when we use a mobile phone on the road. Although *NV* has the potential to address the aforementioned issues of a mobile phone, it limits the available number of tilt input commands. *NV* is more suitable for some special interaction scenarios, where one's vision is unavailable and/or one of her/his hands is occupied and fewer interfacial commands are necessary.

The previous research [26] had probed discretizing raw angular space using linear, quadratic, and sigmoid functions to improve angular tilt control. We adopted a uniform linear discrete function for better spatial sense and cognition, especially for the *NV* condition where there is no other cues to identify a target district in a 3D tilt space.

We have found out that there are orientation effects of tilt input, especially under the *NV* condition. We speculate that these results may be caused by the bisection method. Bisection is the simplest dividing method. We can utilize n (a positive integer) times of bisection to divide something into 2^n equal parts. The numbers of 4 and 8 are both integer exponents of 2, under these dividing conditions the participants could perform trials more easily, so better performance was found at *TOL4* and *TOL8*. Especially, the impact of dividing method was magnified under the *NV* condition, since the participants had no other cues besides dividing the space upon their own sense and cognition. As for the condition of *TOL12*, the *axial* directions also conformed to the least times of bisection. The best performance in the *axial* directions may also be caused by our experience in other disciplines, e.g., the knowledge about system of rectangular coordinates from mathematics.

7   Conclusion and Future Work

In our study, a quantitative experiment was conducted to determine the effects of *visual feedback* on tilt control of a mobile phone and the upper bounds of human ability to control the tilt input under different *VFLs*. The experimental results have some indications for tilt-based interaction design. First, partially visual feedback (*PV*) performed not so well as fully visual feedback (*FV*) and no visual feedback (*NV*) in terms of both speed and accuracy. This reveals that

PV has no help for tilt input. Second, the participants could distinguish at least 12 tilt orientation levels (*TOLs*) and 4 tilt magnitude levels (*TMLs*) under the *FV* condition. Third, the participants could distinguish 4 *TOLs* and 2 *TMLs* or 8 *TOLs* and 2 *TMLs* under the *NV* condition with an error rate tolerance of 10% or 15%, respectively. Four, the ability of the participants on tilt control was related with *orientation* direction.

There exist some limitations of our work. First, the experiment was conducted when the participants were seated. But some external factors, e.g., motion status of the subjects, could influence the results. We had considered some other factors during the experiment design, but they had finally been excluded from the experiment to prevent it from becoming too complicated. Some other factors should be considered in our future work. Second, we only employed dwell time (1 s) to confirm a target selection, but different selection modes may also have impacts on the results. In the future work, we will investigate impacts of different selection modes. Third, tilt gestures have the potential to serve the blind, since the techniques support eyes-free interaction. We will explore the use of tilt for people with visual impairments. Fourth, we only utilized audio feedback under none visual feedback condition. But it is not clear whether there are some other kinds of feedback that are more suitable for eyes-free interaction. In our future work, we will explore different feedback, e.g., tactile and auditory feedback, and find out the most suitable feedback mechanism for the *NV* condition.

Acknowledgment. This work is supported by Science Foundation of Guangxi (AA17204096, AD16380076). We thank all the anonymous reviewers for their generous comments and good advice on the paper.

References

1. Baglioni, M., Lecolinet, E., Guiard, Y.: JerkTilts: using accelerometers for eight-choice selection on mobile devices. In: Proceedings of the 13th International Conference on Multimodal Interfaces, ICMI 2011, pp. 121–128. ACM Press, New York (2011). https://doi.org/10.1145/2070481.2070503
2. Bartlett, J.F.: Rock 'n' scroll is here to stay. IEEE Comput. Graph. Appl. **20**(3), 40–45 (2000). https://doi.org/10.1109/38.844371
3. Browne, K., Anand, C.: An empirical evaluation of user interfaces for a mobile video game. Entertain. Comput. **3**(1), 1–10 (2012). https://doi.org/10.1016/j.entcom.2011.06.001
4. Cho, S.J., Murray-Smith, R., Kim, Y.B.: Multi-context photo browsing on mobile devices based on tilt dynamics. In: Proceedings of the 9th International Conference on Human Computer Interaction with Mobile Devices and Services, Mobile-HCI 2007, pp. 190–197. ACM Press, New York (2007). https://doi.org/10.1145/1377999.1378006
5. Dunlop, M.D., Roper, M., Imperatore, G.: Text entry tap accuracy and exploration of tilt controlled layered interaction on Smartwatches. In: Proceedings of the 19th International Conference on Human-Computer Interaction with Mobile Devices and Services, MobileHCI 2017, pp. 23:1–23:11. ACM Press, New York (2017). https://doi.org/10.1145/3098279.3098560

6. Eslambolchilar, P., Murray-Smith, R.: Tilt-based automatic zooming and scaling in mobile devices – a state-space implementation. In: Brewster, S., Dunlop, M. (eds.) Mobile HCI 2004. LNCS, vol. 3160, pp. 120–131. Springer, Heidelberg (2004). https://doi.org/10.1007/978-3-540-28637-0_11

7. Fitts, P.M.: The information capacity of the human motor system in controlling the amplitude of movement. J. Exp. Psychol. **47**, 381–391 (1954). http://view.ncbi.nlm.nih.gov/pubmed/13174710

8. Geronimo, L.D., Canonica, A., Husmann, M., Norrie, M.C.: Continuous tilting interaction techniques on mobile devices for controlling public displays. In: Proceedings of the ACM SIGCHI Symposium on Engineering Interactive Computing Systems, EICS 2017, pp. 21–26. ACM Press, New York (2017). https://doi.org/10.1145/3102113.3102120

9. Guo, A., Paek, T.: Exploring tilt for no-touch, wrist-only interactions on smartwatches. In: Proceedings of the 18th International Conference on Human-Computer Interaction with Mobile Devices and Services, MobileHCI 2016, pp. 17–28. ACM Press, New York (2016). https://doi.org/10.1145/2935334.2935345

10. Harrison, B.L., Fishkin, K.P., Gujar, A., Mochon, C., Want, R.: Squeeze me, hold me, tilt me! An exploration of manipulative user interfaces. In: Proceedings of the SIGCHI Conference on Human Factors in Computing Systems, CHI 1998, pp. 17–24. ACM Press, New York (1998). https://doi.org/10.1145/274644.274647

11. Hinckley, K., Pierce, J., Sinclair, M., Horvitz, E.: Sensing techniques for mobile interaction. In: Proceedings of the 13th Annual ACM Symposium on User Interface Software and Technology, UIST 2000, pp. 91–100. ACM Press, New York (2000). https://doi.org/10.1145/354401.354417

12. Homaeian, L., Goyal, N., Wallace, J.R., Scott, S.D.: Group vs individual: impact of TOUCH and TILT cross-device interactions on mixed-focus collaboration. In: Mandryk, R.L., Hancock, M., Perry, M., Cox, A.L. (eds.) Proceedings of the 2018 CHI Conference on Human Factors in Computing Systems, CHI 2018, p. 73. ACM Press, New York (2018). https://doi.org/10.1145/3173574.3173647

13. Hynninen, T.: First-person shooter controls on touchscreen devices: a heuristic evaluation of three games on the iPod touch. Thesis. University of Tampere (2012)

14. ISO: ISO 9241-9 ergonomic requirements for office work with visual display terminals (VDTs) - part 9: Requirements for non-keyboard input devices (2000)

15. Jones, E., Alexander, J., Andreou, A., Irani, P., Subramanian, S.: GesText: accelerometer-based gestural text-entry systems. In: Proceedings of the 28th International Conference on Human Factors in Computing Systems, CHI 2010, pp. 2173–2182. ACM Press, New York (2010). https://doi.org/10.1145/1753326.1753655

16. Karlson, A.K., Bederson, B.B., SanGiovanni, J.: AppLens and LaunchTile: two designs for one-handed thumb use on small devices. In: Proceedings of the SIGCHI Conference on Human Factors in Computing Systems, CHI 2005, pp. 201–210. ACM Press, New York (2005). https://doi.org/10.1145/1054972.1055001

17. Kratz, S., Brodien, I., Rohs, M.: Semi-automatic zooming for mobile map navigation. In: Proceedings of the 12th International Conference on Human Computer Interaction with Mobile Devices and Services, MobileHCI 2010, pp. 63–72. ACM Press, New York (2010). https://doi.org/10.1145/1851600.1851615

18. Kurosawa, H., Sakamoto, D., Ono, T.: MyoTilt: a target selection method for smartwatches using the tilting operation and electromyography. In: Proceedings of the 20th International Conference on Human-Computer Interaction with Mobile Devices and Services, MobileHCI 2018, pp. 43:1–43:11. ACM Press, New York (2018). https://doi.org/10.1145/3229434.3229457

19. Kurtenbach, G., Buxton, W.: The limits of expert performance using hierarchic marking menus. In: Proceedings of the SIGCHI Conference on Human Factors in Computing Systems, CHI 1993, pp. 482–487. ACM Press, New York (1993). https://doi.org/10.1145/169059.169426

20. MacKenzie, I.S., Teather, R.J.: FittsTilt: the application of Fitts' law to tilt-based interaction. In: Proceedings of the 7th Nordic Conference on Human-Computer Interaction Making Sense Through Design, NordiCHI 2012, pp. 568–577. ACM Press, New York (2012). https://doi.org/10.1145/2399016.2399103

21. Medryk, S., MacKenzie, I.S.: A comparison of accelerometer and touch-based input for mobile gaming. In: Proceedings of MHCI, pp. 117.1–117.8 (2013)

22. Oakley, I., O'Modhrain, S.: Tilt to scroll: evaluating a motion based vibrotactile mobile interface. In: Proceedings of First Joint Eurohaptics Conference and Symposium on Haptic Interfaces for Virtual Environment and Teleoperator Systems, pp. 40–49. IEEE (2005). https://doi.org/10.1109/whc.2005.138

23. Partridge, K., Chatterjee, S., Sazawal, V., Borriello, G., Want, R.: TiltType: accelerometer-supported text entry for very small devices. In: Proceedings of the 15th Annual ACM Symposium on User Interface Software and Technology, UIST 2002, pp. 201–204. ACM Press, New York (2002). https://doi.org/10.1145/571985.572013

24. Pietroszek, K., Wallace, J.R., Lank, E.: Tiltcasting: 3D interaction on large displays using a mobile device. In: Proceedings of the 28th Annual ACM Symposium on User Interface Software & Technology, UIST 2015, pp. 57–62. ACM Press, New York (2015). https://doi.org/10.1145/2807442.2807471

25. Poupyrev, I., Maruyama, S., Rekimoto, J.: Ambient touch: designing tactile interfaces for handheld devices. In: Proceedings of the 15th Annual ACM Symposium on User Interface Software and Technology, UIST 2002, pp. 51–60. ACM Press, New York (2002). https://doi.org/10.1145/571985.571993

26. Rahman, M., Gustafson, S., Irani, P., Subramanian, S.: Tilt techniques: investigating the dexterity of wrist-based input. In: Proceedings of the 27th International Conference on Human Factors in Computing Systems, CHI 2009, pp. 1943–1952. ACM Press, New York (2009). https://doi.org/10.1145/1518701.1518997

27. Rekimoto, J.: Tilting operations for small screen interfaces. In: Proceedings of the 9th Annual ACM Symposium on User Interface Software and Technology, UIST 1996, pp. 167–168. ACM Press, New York (1996). https://doi.org/10.1145/237091.237115

28. Sad, H.H., Poirier, F.: Evaluation and modeling of user performance for pointing and scrolling tasks on handheld devices using tilt sensor. In: Proceedings of Second International Conferences on Advances in Computer-Human Interactions, pp. 295–300. IEEE, February 2009. https://doi.org/10.1109/achi.2009.15

29. Sazawal, V., Want, R., Borriello, G.: The unigesture approach one-handed text entry for small devices. In: Paternò, F. (ed.) Mobile HCI 2002. LNCS, vol. 2411, pp. 256–270. Springer, Heidelberg (2002). https://doi.org/10.1007/3-540-45756-9_20

30. Shima, K., Onishi, K., Takada, R., Adachi, T., Shizuki, B., Tanaka, J.: Investigating accuracy of tilting operation on wrist-worn devices with touchscreens. In: Proceedings of the 2016 CHI Conference Extended Abstracts on Human Factors in Computing Systems, CHI EA 2016, pp. 2705–2711. ACM Press, New York (2016). https://doi.org/10.1145/2851581.2892377

31. Siek, K.A., Rogers, Y., Connelly, K.H.: Fat finger worries: how older and younger users physically interact with PDAs. In: Costabile, M.F., Paternò, F. (eds.) INTER-

ACT 2005. LNCS, vol. 3585, pp. 267–280. Springer, Heidelberg (2005). https:// doi.org/10.1007/11555261_24

32. Small, D., Ishii, H.: Design of spatially aware graspable displays. In: Proceedings of CHI 1997 Extended Abstracts on Human Factors in Computing Systems, pp. 367–368. ACM, New York (1997)

33. Sun, K., Wang, Y., Yu, C., Yan, Y., Wen, H., Shi, Y.: Float: one-handed and touch-free target selection on smartwatches. In: Proceedings of the 2017 CHI Conference on Human Factors in Computing Systems, CHI 2017, pp. 692–704. ACM Press, New York (2017). https://doi.org/10.1145/3025453.3026027

34. Teather, R.J., MacKenzie, I.S.: Position vs. velocity control for tilt-based interaction. In: Proceedings of Graphics Interface Conference, pp. 51–58. ACM Press, New York (2014)

35. van Tonder, B.P., Wesson, J.L.: Improving the controllability of tilt interaction for mobile map-based applications. Int. J. Hum.-Comput. Stud. **70**(12), 920–935 (2012). https://doi.org/10.1016/j.ijhcs.2012.08.001

36. Vogel, D., Casiez, G.: Hand occlusion on a multi-touch tabletop. In: Proceedings of the 2012 ACM Annual Conference on Human Factors in Computing Systems, pp. 2307–2316. ACM, New York (2012). https://doi.org/10.1145/2208276.2208390

37. Wang, J., Zhai, S., Canny, J.: Camera phone based motion sensing: interaction techniques, applications and performance study. In: Proceedings of the 19th Annual ACM Symposium on User Interface Software and Technology, UIST 2006, pp. 101–110. ACM Press, New York (2006). https://doi.org/10.1145/1166253.1166270

38. Wigdor, D., Balakrishnan, R.: TiltText: using tilt for text input to mobile phones. In: Proceedings of UIST 2003, pp. 81–90 (2003). https://doi.org/10.1145/964696. 964705

39. Yeo, H.S., Phang, X.S., Castellucci, S.J., Kristensson, P.O., Quigley, A.: Investigating tilt-based gesture keyboard entry for single-handed text entry on large devices. In: Proceedings of the 2017 CHI Conference on Human Factors in Computing Systems, CHI 2017, pp. 4194–4202. ACM Press, New York (2017). https://doi.org/ 10.1145/3025453.3025520

40. Zaman, L., MacKenzie, I.S.: Evaluation of nano-stick, foam buttons, and other input methods for gameplay on touchscreen phones. In: Proceedings of International Conference on Multimedia and Human-Computer Interaction, MHCI, vol. 1, pp. 1–8. Citeseer (2013)

ACM 2009, LNCS, vol. 5546, pp. 207–230. Springer, Heidelberg (2009). https://doi.org/10.1007/1655301-21

32. Smith, D., Schilit, B.: Doorway[?] spatially aware graspable displays. In: Proceedings of CHI 1997 Extended Abstracts on Human Factors in Computing Systems, pp. 207–208. ACM, New York (1997).

33. Sun, K., Wang, Y., Yu, C., Yan, Y., Wen, H., Shi, Y.: Float: one-handed and touch-free target selection on smartwatches. In: Proceedings of the 2017 CHI Conference on Human Factors in Computing Systems, CHI 2017, pp. 692–704. ACM Press, New York (2017). https://doi.org/10.1145/3025453.3025607

34. Teather, R.J., MacKenzie, I.S.: Position vs. velocity control for tilt-based interaction. In: Proceedings of Graphics Interface Conference, pp. 51–58. ACM Press, New York (2014).

35. van Tonder, B.P., Wesson, J.L.: Improving the controllability of tilt interaction for mobile map-based applications. Int. J. Hum. Comput. Stud. 70(12), 920–935 (2012). https://doi.org/10.1016/j.ijhcs.2012.08.001

36. Vogel, D., Casiez, G.: Hand occlusion on a multi-touch tabletop. In: Proceedings of the 2012 ACM Annual Conference on Human Factors in Computing Systems, pp. 2307–2316. ACM, New York (2012). https://doi.org/10.1145/2208276.2208390

37. Wang, J., Zhai, S., Canny, J.: Camera phone based motion sensing: interaction techniques, applications and performance study. In: Proceedings of the 19th Annual ACM Symposium on User Interface Software and Technology, UIST 2006, pp. 101–110. ACM Press, New York (2006). https://doi.org/10.1145/1166253.1166270

38. Wigdor, D., Balakrishnan, R.: TiltText: using tilt for text input to mobile phones. In: Proceedings of UIST 2003, pp. 81–90 (2003). https://doi.org/10.1145/964696.964705

39. Yeo, H.S., Phang, X.C., Castellucci, S.J., Kristensson, P.O., Quigley, A.: Investigating tilt-based gesture keyboard entry for single-handed text entry on large devices. In: Proceedings of the 2017 CHI Conference on Human Factors in Computing Systems, CHI 2017, pp. 4194–4202. ACM, New York (2017). https://doi.org/10.1145/3025453.3025520

40. Zhang, H., MacKenzie, I.S.: Evaluation of nanoclick, foam buttons, and other input methods for game-playing touchscreen phones. In: Proceedings of International Conference on Multimedia and Human-Computer Interaction, MHCI, vol. 41, pp. 41-5. Citeseer (2013).

Personalization and Recommender Systems

"I Really Don't Know What 'Thumbs Up' Means": Algorithmic Experience in Movie Recommender Algorithms

Oscar Alvarado[1,2(✉)], Vero Vanden Abeele[1(✉)], David Geerts[2(✉)], and Katrien Verbert[1(✉)]

[1] Department of Computer Science, KU Leuven, Leuven, Belgium
{oscarluis.alvaradorodriguez, vero.vandenabeele, katrien.verbert}@kuleuven.be
[2] Mintlab, KU Leuven, Leuven, Belgium
david.geerts@kuleuven.be

Abstract. Many of our daily activities and decisions are driven by algorithms. This is particularly evident in our interactions with contemporary cultural content, where recommender algorithms deal with most of their access, production, and distribution. In this context, the Algorithmic Experience (AX) design framework emerged to guide the design of users' experiences with algorithms for social media platforms. However, thus far, a framework to design specifically for AX within the context of movie recommender algorithms was lacking. To this end, the present study combines a semiotic inspection analysis of the Netflix interface with sensitized design workshops and semi-structured interviews to explore AX requirements for movie recommender algorithms. Linking the analysis with design opportunities, we shed light on AX suited for movie recommender systems. Moreover, we extend the current AX design framework with two new design areas: algorithmic usefulness and algorithmic social practices.

Keywords: Algorithms · Movie recommendations · Algorithmic experience · Recommender systems

1 Introduction

Algorithms are involved in most of our daily activities and decisions [41], becoming publicly relevant [17], enacting power [4, 32] or governance [24, 42]. Additionally, algorithms act as cultural gatekeepers when they sort, rank, manage, distribute and produce existing music [27, 31, 34], movies or tv shows [18, 20], videos [35] and other kinds of cultural expressions. They are even seen as relevant cultural objects on their own [16], promoting the formulation of the algorithmic culture concept [38].

Unfortunately, most algorithms and their decisions possess an inscrutable nature [24], emanated from complex processes and being influenced by uses and constant changes in their inner workings or interfaces [24]. In addition, general low algorithmic awareness among users [14] may also produce negative experiences, as invisibility,

© IFIP International Federation for Information Processing 2019
Published by Springer Nature Switzerland AG 2019
D. Lamas et al. (Eds.): INTERACT 2019, LNCS 11748, pp. 521–541, 2019.
https://doi.org/10.1007/978-3-030-29387-1_30

anxiety, and inequalities [6], bias in the personalization processes [7] and possible human interventions [10].

Different researchers are trying to overcome these issues and enable more positive interactions with algorithms. For instance, Hamilton et al. [21] invite research on the design of algorithmic interfaces, balancing user needs for transparency with the advantages of automatic implementations. Diakopoulos presents a call for algorithmic accountability and propose an algorithmic transparency standard [11]. Other academics highlight the importance of a human-centered design of algorithmic systems [3, 28] or adhering to a design framework for *algorithmic experience* (AX) [1, 33] in the area of social media platforms.

Simultaneously, there are efforts to increase transparency and trust of recommender systems and, specifically, to support better user control with such recommender algorithms [2, 5, 9, 15, 26, 36, 40]. Although several researchers have presented different user interfaces to address the black-box nature of recommender systems, this research is to date still rather ad hoc [23]. A specific visualization is presented and shown to improve user trust and acceptance, but the generalizability of the results is limited. In this paper, we present a framework to support such generalizability with a framework for Algorithmic Experience (AX) of movie recommender systems.

Centering our study on the Netflix movie recommender algorithm, we applied three main methods to develop this framework. First, we analyzed the Netflix user interface to unearth the intentions of the designer towards the algorithm. Second, we performed sensitizing workshops to elicit AX requirements among Netflix users. Finally, we conducted follow-up semi-structured interviews to expand the AX requirements elicitation.

Building on the AX framework [1] for social media, we adapt the framework for movie recommender algorithms by expanding it with two new design areas: algorithmic usefulness and algorithmic social practices. This specialized framework enriches the present debate on AX and recommender algorithms, enables refined design guidelines, and promotes positive user experiences with movie recommender algorithms.

2 Background

Different academic approaches in the study of algorithms provide inspiration and insights for an AX definition of movie recommender algorithms.

2.1 Algorithms, Audiences and Cultural Content

Academics portray the relevance of algorithms in the cultural context. For instance, Striphas defines algorithmic culture as "the unfolding of human thought, conduct, organization and expression into the logic of big data and large-scale computation" [38]. Additionally, Morris states that recommender algorithms frame the interaction between cultural goods and those who encounter them [31], impacting culture management [31].

Furthermore, algorithms define cultural audiences. Gillespie argues that "trending" algorithms produce specific algorithmically identified audiences based on profiles [16], even becoming sources of cultural concern. Similarly, Prey explains how personalized media enact a sense of looking for distinct predilections of users, but "there are in fact no individuals, but only ways of seeing people as individuals" [34]. According to the author, these platforms represent individuals only by their data, defining a constantly modulated and never conclusive algorithmic identity [34]. In the end, these technologies are reducing the individual to their behavioral feedback cues on the platform [34].

Other researchers study different methods to measure algorithmic decisions on cultural products. For example, Rieder, Matamoros-Fernández, and Coromina proposed *ranking cultures* to determine the algorithm's intentions towards the cultural content [35]. They observed how YouTube's results are not only based on popularity, but also on vernaculars such as the video issue date and its own definition of novel videos.

Academics have also described the Netflix recommender algorithm and its cultural implications. Gomez-Uribe and Hunt describe the Netflix recommender engine as the key pillar [18] for its movie service. By data gathering and personalization techniques, Netflix allows the existence of niche audiences that are too small and almost impossible to exist in other impersonalized contexts [18]. They also express that personalization promotes better results from the recommender system, and increases overall engagement with the platform [18]. In a different context, Hallinan and Striphas emphasize the importance of studying the context that influences the design, development and social consequences of movie recommender algorithms [20], by analyzing results of a contest called the "Netflix Prize" proposed by the same company.

In general, these studies reflect on algorithmic culture, algorithmic effects on cultural products, audience creation, algorithms development, and how algorithms transform our current consumption and production of cultural products.

2.2 The Relevance of, and Bad Experiences with, Recommender Algorithms

Different researchers have aimed at unpacking the many algorithmic implications for users and societies. Even if this work is not specifically addressing recommender engines, it portrays various similarities with movie recommender algorithms.

Willson and Beer suggest particular attention for those algorithms in which we are delegating everyday activities, working semi-autonomously with no supervision from human counterparts [4, 41]. Additionally, Gillespie defines *public relevance algorithms* as those delimited by six provisional functions: selecting or excluding information products, inferring or anticipating information about their users, defining what is relevant or legitimating knowledge, flaunting impartiality with no human mediation, and provoking behavioral changes in users practices [17].

Research has also documented negative user experiences with recommender algorithms. Bozdag describes the layers of bias in algorithmic filtering and personalization [7]. Additionally, Bishop reports YouTubers' anxiety and inequalities with the

platform's algorithm [6]. These examples highlight the relevance of addressing AX with recommender systems.

2.3 Transparency, Human-Centered Algorithms and Algorithmic Experience

Answers to these previous challenges come from different perspectives. For example, Diakopoulos presents an *algorithmic transparency standard* for media-related algorithms based on five categories that might be considered for disclosing [11]. First, human involvement in the decisions of algorithms should be explained including the purpose of the algorithm and possible automated or human editorial goals. Second, the collected data must be described in terms of its quality, accuracy, uncertainty, timeliness, representativeness, including its definition, collection, and edition. Third, the algorithmic input data should be transparent, including its model and modeling process. Fourth, the inferences made by the algorithm must be clear, including their potential for errors. Fifth, the algorithmic presence should be clear, whether it is used at all, and if personalization is in use, promoting user awareness.

Furthermore, researchers highlight the importance of including users in algorithmic development. Baumer proposes "human-centered algorithm design" to bring together "algorithmic systems and the social interpretations thereof" [3]. Also, Lee, Kim, and Lizarondo describe a human-centered implementation of an algorithmic service [28].

Other academics turn towards the experience with these systems. Alvarado and Waern propose Algorithmic Experience (AX) as a conceptualization of "the ways in which users experience systems and interfaces that are heavily influenced by algorithmic behavior" [1]. They identify five design areas to improve AX in social media platforms [1]. First, *algorithmic profiling transparency* is described as a design opportunity to promote user perception on what the algorithm is tracking to create personalized results. Second, *algorithmic profiling management* is described as the design opportunity to manage the user's algorithmic profiling. Third, *selective algorithmic remembering* is identified as the design opportunity to allow the user to avoid future algorithmic results based on previous and no longer relevant algorithmic profiling. Fourth, *algorithmic user control* describes the design opportunity to regulate how and when the algorithm is going to produce and show its results. Finally, *algorithmic awareness* is described as the design opportunity to promote understanding of how the algorithm works and measures user behavior. Similarly, Oh et al. picture a new way on HCI research, based on Algorithmic Experience "as a new stream of research on user experience" [33] that considers constant relationships with algorithms.

2.4 Interaction Design for Recommender Systems

Extensive work has focused on designing the interaction experience with recommender systems. For example, Knijnenburg et al. present a framework to evaluate recommender systems with a user-centric approach [26]. Additionally, Jugovac and Jannach review the state of the art on user interaction with these systems [25], presenting strategies for preference elicitation and alternatives for interactive recommendations.

The "black box" nature of recommenders has also been studied with different tactics. For instance, He, Parra and Verbert survey interaction strategies in recommender systems and group them in six groups [23]: transparency, justification, controllability, diversity, cold start phase, and context. Also, Gedikli, Jannach, and Ge compare different types of explanations for recommenders algorithms [15], while Tintarev and Masthoff evaluate seven different goals for explanations in recommender systems [39, 40]: transparency, scrutability, trust, effectiveness, persuasiveness, efficiency and satisfaction.

Bakalov et al. advise five aspects to evaluate user models and personalization effects in recommender systems [2]: usefulness, ease of use and learning, satisfaction, trust, and user modeling. Also, Cramer et al. explore eight aspects to evaluate an art recommender system [9]: perceived transparency, competence, usefulness and need for explanations in the system, understanding, intent to use, acceptance, and ease of use.

In general, previous proposals bring efforts to evaluate recommender algorithms in terms of transparency and explanations after their implementation. However, there is still no framework that could provide suggestions for the human-centered design of movie recommender algorithms based on user experiences, or a specialized AX framework for movie recommender systems.

3 Methods and Results

Studying algorithmic experience (AX) with human-centered approaches constitutes a challenging endeavor, due to low algorithmic awareness among users [14]. Therefore, this study uses a mixed-method approach to understand the AX of movie recommendations in Netflix. First, we applied a self-sensitizing technique to understand the intentions of the interface designer towards the recommender algorithm interface using Semiotic Engineering [37]. Second, we held sensitizing workshops to elicit AX requirements from Netflix users. Finally, we conducted individual follow-up semi-structured interviews to explore complementary aspects of Netflix AX, based on recommender systems interface design research.

3.1   Study 1: Semiotic Inspection

The Semiotic Engineering Process (SEP) is a scientific HCI methodology derived from semiotics and communication theory [37]. It offers a method for analyzing interfaces and designers goals called the Semiotic Inspection Method (SIM) [37]. SIM recognizes interfaces as a communication process between designers and users, exposing the former's intentions behind the design. In contrast with other heuristic methods, SIM is not directed by strict usability principles and is not centered on the user's experience.

SIM consists of five stages which were applied for this paper by the main author. The first three stages allow to iteratively analyze the static, dynamic and metalinguistic signs [37] embedded in the interface of the system. While *static signs* can be interpreted at a single moment in time without temporal and causal relations, *dynamic signs* emerge only through the interaction with the interface, containing both a temporal and causal context [37]. The intrinsic relation between dynamic and static signs also

produce meanings in *metalinguistic signs* to communicate a specific message to the user [37]. The fourth stage compares all the signs collected in the previous steps, to find the designer's meta-communication message or the designer's final goal with the interface [37]. Finally, the fifth stage evaluates the system's communicability, revealing relationships and (in)consistencies between the designer goals and the interface [37].

The outcome of the method is an analysis of the communication strategy of the system and the proposed message to the user. In this paper, we applied the method to the analysis of the user interface in the Netflix recommendation system.

However, because SIM is limited in identifying absences (i.e. signs that should be present but are not) in an interface, we complemented the method by adding specific requirements for algorithms from two studies. First, we included the five categories from the *algorithmic transparency standard* [11] which serves as a design framework for accountability and transparency in media-related algorithms: explaining human involvement, describing data collection, providing limits to the algorithmic model, clarifying made inferences and promoting awareness of the algorithm. Second, we complemented this with two purposes for interactive visualizations in recommender systems proposed by He, Parra and Verbert: diversity and cold start [23]. The other four goals for interactive visualization in recommender algorithms were excluded from the analysis either because they overlapped with the categories from Diakopoulos [11], or because they were not relevant for the Netflix case.

SIM was applied using the Netflix desktop platform in English, using a 27″ screen, browsing with Mozilla Firefox explorer version 60.0.2 during June 25th and 26th, 2018.

Semiotic Inspection Results. Static signs were mostly content containers. Nowadays, static signs in web platforms are mostly wireframes or dedicated spaces with mutable contents. Also, certain areas were identified as static signs but contained dynamic contents. For example, when logging into Netflix, a prominently featured show is initially shown, as pictured in Fig. 1. This space presents a background video with other signs, such as two buttons for playing the show or adding it to the user's list, respectively.

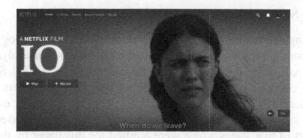

Fig. 1. Prominent featured content on Netflix's landing page.

The top area of the interface contains two features: sorting content by category and the user list with manually saved shows. Other static signs in this area are a "search icon" and the user's image (avatar). Scrolling down shows another static title "Netflix

Originals" and a horizontal list composed of different images of shows. When scrolling down, smaller horizontal lists are found, composed of images with their correspondent titles. After the lists "Trending now", "Continue Watching for [user]" and "Watch It Again", the names of these lists relate to specific reasons for why these items are proposed such as "Because you liked [content]".

Dynamic signs are mostly encountered in the constantly changing movies inside the platform every time the user logs in, usually in the recommendation lists and in the initially prominently featured show. For example, the featured show changes its title and background video according to the show or movie being promoted.

The smaller horizontal lists also change their movie background images or white titles dynamically, depending on the content category. Additionally, as shown in Fig. 2, these small images possess a dynamic feature: hovering on them presents varied texts and buttons such as a "play" button, the show's title and description, a "Match" green text next to a percentage scoring, the show's age classification, the available number of seasons for that show, the "thumbs up/down" buttons, a "+" button to add that show to the user's list, and a "down arrow". As Fig. 3 shows, a click on this "down arrow" expands the show to cover the entire screen width and provides further details about the show. Clicking on "more like this" opens a new horizontal list of recommendations containing similar shows. There is no sign or indication that explains the selection of these recommendations or the inner logic for them, except for the initial name of the show from which these recommendations are generated.

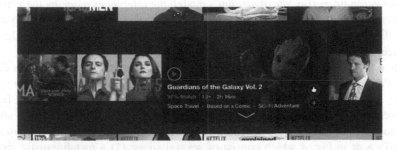

Fig. 2. Dynamic feature while hovering on a movie.

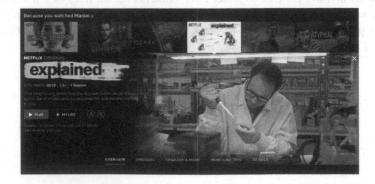

Fig. 3. The Netflix interface, dynamically expanding for details about a show.

Metalinguistic signs in the Netflix interface are mostly directed towards the voting system. There is a clear design intention in the voting system to define "thumbs up/thumbs down" icons as positive and negative feedback, respectively. Furthermore, voting seems to mean that a user has already watched that show from the perspective of the designer since all the scored shows appear later in a "Watch It Again" list. This is not confirmed by any other signs, leading to confusion because voting could also be based on past consumption outside the platform or by following peers' suggestions.

Similarly, it is not clear if there is a meta-linguistic sign in the user's list. Adding elements in this list possibly influences the recommender algorithm or it just organizes user's content, but again this is not confirmed by any sign.

The fourth phase of the method showed the general intention of the interface. After iterating and comparing static, dynamic, and metalinguistic signs, it is possible to determine the meta-communication in relation with the recommender algorithm: to promote movie watching in a fast and easy way, guided mostly by the recommendations. There is no design intention to give the user control of the recommender system besides the "thumbs up/thumbs down" buttons. Finally, the fifth phase does not picture any inconsistencies or relations with the defined meta-communication strategy.

Additionally, the complementary requirements were used to analyze Netflix's interface. When using Diakopoulos' framework for algorithmic transparency [11], no indication of possible direct human involvement on the recommendations can be found. Moreover, besides explicit signs such as recommendation lists with texts like: "Because you liked [content]", there are no signs about *the data collection process, data transformation processes, the algorithm's model, the inferences made by the system*, or any reference about the user categorization. Finally, there is no clear sign to delimit where the algorithm is presenting its results, or a space "free" from the algorithm influence.

When using the diversity and cold start goals for interactive recommenders defined by He, Parra and Verbert [23], there is no sign for diversity in the recommender system, echoing He et al.'s finding: only one surveyed recommender system included features for representing recommendation *diversity* [23]. However, Netflix's cold start solution does show signs in relation to the recommender system. In this case, the system shows an interface as in Fig. 4 which consist of several signs: (1) a metalinguistic sign that consists of "thumbs up" icons to refer to those contents being selected, (2) static signs such as texts inviting the user to select three contents he/she likes or a text explaining how this selection will help the system to find better recommendations as well as a button to proceed and a layer of pictures, and (3) a dynamic number indicating the amount of selections ("4" in Fig. 4).

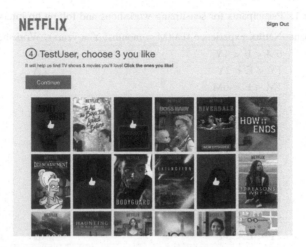

Fig. 4. The Netflix interface after registration, addressing the "cold start" phase.

3.2 Study 2: Sensitizing Workshops

This method gathers algorithmic experience (AX) requirements for the recommender algorithm in Netflix, based on the experiences of the users with the platform. Active Netflix user recruitment was done using the university departmental mailing lists and Facebook/WhatsApp groups around the city. A Netflix gift card was offered during recruitment and raffled in every workshop to encourage user participation.

Since algorithmic awareness is generally low among users [14], every workshop started with a priming tutorial about AX and algorithms in known platforms. Afterwards, participants contributed to a group discussion with their perceptions about AX of Netflix recommendations. Participants were also invited to log in with their Netflix accounts using laptops, being able to use and browse their accounts during the entire workshop. The discussion was guided by semi-structured questions derived from Alvarado and Waern groups of design opportunities for AX [1: 6], but other perspectives were also welcomed. Every workshop was recorded for further analysis.

Five different sessions were organized in total, with 15 active Netflix users between 18 and 35 years old, all undertaking at least a master's program and tech-savvy. To maintain user's anonymity, they will be referred with a number as an identifier. More information about the workshop (represented by letters from A to E) they participated in and their gender (represented by F or M) is detailed in Table 1.

530   O. Alvarado et al.

Table 1. Participants for sensitizing workshops and follow up interviews.

Participant	Netflix experience (E) (M = months; Y = years)	Workshop	Sex
P1	6M < E < 1Y	A	M
P2	1Y < E < 2Y	A	M
P3	1M < E < 6M	A	M
P4	1Y < E < 2Y	A	F
P5	3Y < E < 5Y	B	M
P6	1Y < E < 2Y	B	F
P7	3Y < E < 5Y	C	M
P8	5Y < E < 10Y	C	M
P9	1Y < E < 2Y	D	M
P10	1Y < E < 2Y	D	M
P11	5Y < E < 10Y	D	M
P12	2Y < E < 3Y	E	F
P13	1M < E < 6M	E	M
P14	5Y < E < 10Y	E	M
P15	3Y < E < 5Y	E	F

Sensitizing Workshop Results. Coding was based on the five categories from the AX framework for social media including, profiling transparency and management, algorithmic awareness and control, and selective algorithmic memory. This was complemented with new codes for results that did not fit inside the previous categories.

Algorithmic Profiling Transparency. Netflix uses a green matching score to support transparency. However, this was not properly perceived by many participants. P5, P6, P8, and P14 reported not noticing it before the workshop. Similarly, P10 did not comprehend the meaning of the matching score. In contrast, P3 and P13 noted how obvious Netflix' profiling activity is: "I can see my past in these [recommendations]".

Specific information was detailed by users for algorithmic profiling transparency. For example, P4 said she would like to know how Netflix justifies a specific match score. Likewise, P3 wanted to check past behavior to understand his recommendations.

Participants also expressed trust issues. P4 did not trust the algorithm and wondered whether popularity is a reason for recommendations. Similarly, P5 and P6 desired to understand the recommendation reasoning. Likewise, P8, P13, and P15 reported obscurity in the recommender algorithm due to the lack of explanations in the data collection.

Again, some suggestions were made in this area. For instance, P14 and P15 requested to know their preferences according to their algorithmic user profile. Moreover, P12 said that phrases like "Because you have watched this..." are approximations to explain the algorithmic profiling, but she expected more detailed information.

Algorithmic Profiling Management. This area was exemplified by P4, P6, and P10 who expressed a need to "tune up" the algorithm: "to say that you like specific actors or a genre". Furthermore, P1 desired an option to help him practice a language: an option

to delimit dubbed content characteristics for his profile. Similarly, P7, P8, P13, and P14 wanted options to avoid some contents: "I do not like it, I do not dislike it, just ignore this". Also, P7 and P9 preferred options to avoid already watched movies.

In relation to algorithmic profiling management, the profile interaction also seemed unclear to the participants. For example, P11 expressed: "You really don't know what 'thumbs up' means, or if adding content to the list changes anything". Likewise, P11 and P13 said the "thumbs up/down" options are very limited to manage their profiling. Similarly, P13 and P14 declared they did not know when to properly use the "thumbs up/down". Interestingly, P5, P6, P12, and P14 reported not using this feature.

Algorithmic Awareness. Users expressed that they were not aware of an "algorithm-free" space. For P6, the entire platform was the recommender. Likewise, P4 said it would increase her trust in the system if she knew where exactly the algorithmic influence was present inside the platform. Following AX interrelation of its design areas [1:6–8], P13 expressed that knowing where the algorithm has its influence should be part of the transparency "package" for any of these platforms.

Algorithmic User Control. P8 expressed to have an "explorative mode" and the interface did not help with it: "you cannot skip the categories they predefined for you". This encouraged "hacking" or tricks to discover new content. This was echoed by P15, who exposed that certain web sites offer category IDs to find content: "I do not understand why they do not allow you to reach all the content they have", describing a need for a space free from the algorithmic filtering. Also, P12, P13, and P15 expressed the need of "turning off" the algorithm for being able to "choose something different".

In relation, users reported that manual searching was their most common way to "bypass" the algorithm. Despite this practice, P4 described this manual search feature as limited for the user because she had to know the name of the desired show beforehand, which made her feel manipulated. "I usually want to have freedom of choice, but here it feels they want to say which way to go". A solution expressed by P6 and P15 to avoid the algorithm was an alphabetical or chronological sorting feature for the movies.

Some users expressed that there is no way to "turn off" the algorithm. P3 and P5 said that even sorting by genres showed again recommendations. P3 and P4 suggested a blank landing screen to promote content exploration and reduce the "imposed" feeling.

Other users expressed a need to avoid the algorithm only at specific moments. For instance, P11 and P12 wanted to "stop" the algorithm for precise periods of time, to "ignore" shows that were not truly what they liked and avoid them in the future.

Algorithmic user control was also expressed in the need for a way to define what the recommender algorithm should consider. This is illustrated by P3, P4, and P5 who wanted a dashboard to "turn off" certain algorithm inputs.

Similarly, P8, P9, P10, and P14 wanted to tell the system their current "watching mood" to adjust the recommendations. While P8 felt that Netflix saw him as static: "but I change constantly", P7 said the platform "pushed" him to an inert profile.

Selective Algorithmic Remembering. P3, P5, P6, P11, P13, and P15 agreed on wanting a feature to "erase" previously watched contents. Also, they desired to delete other people activities when they share their accounts to improve the recommendations.

Other Results. Other results did not fit in the current AX framework. P4 described unhelpfully how the system was "making guesses" during the *cold start phase*, offering contents that she did not know before or that would never be part of her preferences. Similarly, P3 declared that his recommendations were terribly limited during this stage.

Available content seemed also relevant for the experience. For instance, P14 felt that recommendations worked better in the US, where the platform offers more content.

It seems also that the interests of Netflix as a content producer influence the experience. P3, P13, P14, and P15 reported *impressions of dishonesty* since the system mostly offered Netflix's original content and "kept pushing those titles". Also, P6 and P11 noticed the interface tended to locate Netflix Originals with high matching scores.

Interestingly, AX seems to be affected by a common practice among users: *sharing their own accounts* with other people even though it is possible to create separate profiles in the platform. Most users like P2, P6, P11, P12, and P15 agreed that this sharing "messed up" the recommendation algorithm and its results. Similarly, users reported following peers or "real-life" recommendations rather than the recommender algorithm. P2, P6, P8, and P14 mentioned they usually do not use the recommendation engine but recommendations of friends instead. In relation, P5 and P6 desired to add a "*social perspective*" for the recommender, with features such as sending recommendations to friends or following trusted users. Also, P5, P6, P7, P10, P13, P14, and P15 agreed on using third-party recommendations and scorings such as Rotten Tomatoes, IMDB, or similar sources. For instance, P5 would like a comparison between these sources and the "Match" score in the interface.

3.3   Study 3: Follow-Up Semi-structured Interviews

We complemented the previous AX elicitation with semi-structured follow-up interviews to reinforce users' impressions about Netflix AX and to gather more results, relying on theories related to recommender systems experience.

Three theories were used for this purpose. Firstly, we used Bakalov et al.'s five aspects to evaluate user models and personalization effects in recommender systems [2]: usefulness, ease of use and learning, satisfaction, and trust. Secondly, the interviews were also inspired by three concepts from Cramer et al. [10: 473], for evaluating trust and acceptance in a content-based art recommender system: understanding of the system, acceptance of the system, and perceived need of explanations. Thirdly, Tintarev and Masthoff [40] four explanatory aims for recommenders were included for the interviews: effectiveness, persuasiveness, efficiency, and satisfaction.

Every interview was recorded for further analysis. An iterative process was implemented to code and later organize the results, described in the following section.

Follow-Up Semi-structured Interviews Results. Ten participants from all previous workshop were recruited again for the follow-up interviews, two of them female. The same participant identifiers previously used are reapplied in this section to maintain anonymity and to show their relationship with previous results.

Usefulness. Users described recommender usefulness as closely related to other key concepts such as satisfactory results, better and fast decisions, enjoying the algorithm and the system's knowledge about user preference. For instance, P3 expressed that the

algorithm knew what he wanted to watch but was not currently giving satisfactory results: "right now it prolongs the decision and makes me go somewhere else". On the other hand, when he tried to look for a show manually, he enjoyed the offering of "similar" recommendations. Similarly, the algorithm was only occasionally useful for P10: "…sometimes they surprise you, they give you happy accidents and that is a good enjoyable feeling". He expressed that the recommender did not know what he wanted to watch: "but they try to give the best guess". Likewise, P11 and P14 reported that their recommendations were arbitrary and not truly what they preferred: "It is just offering popular stuff". P11 reported spending too much time browsing around with no useful decision. Also, P15 said she did not get satisfactory results with the recommendation system and reported not noticing the matching score at all before the workshop.

Trust. This area was mostly related to Netflix' commercial interests and previous transparency results. P2 described the recommendations as "an honest guess", sometimes better than recommendations of friends. In contrast, most participants gave negative comments. For instance, P5 expressed that he did not trust or enjoy the algorithm and preferred to remove it. He did not trust the algorithm because most recommendations had a high matching score, they were not related to his preferences or the quality of the show, and because they promoted too much their own content. Similarly, P10 did not understand completely what the percentage meant, which affected his trust negatively. P11 as well preferred to know what data Netflix was collecting and to have a way to avoid recommendations to improve his trust in the system. P15, P6, and P8 agreed on not trusting the system because Netflix own contents had "more weight" in their interfaces. In a similar vein, P3 expressed that they "push" too much Netflix Originals.

Ease of Use and Learning. This category was ambiguous among users. Encouraging comments were expressed by P3 who said that his recommendations were easy to browse. Similarly, P2 said that sometimes people do not even know they are using the recommender system because of its ease of use. Likewise, P10 described the "thumbs up/down" as easy to use, but he did not know whether the user's list influenced the system. On the other hand, negative comments were voiced by P6 who described the "thumbs up/down" options as too binary to properly manage the recommender. Moreover, P15 and P13 reported the match percentage as hard to perceive. P15 also mentioned that the specific recommendations titles such as "Because you watched [show]" were hard to understand according to the inner logic for those recommendations.

User Control. P2 needed more structure in the recommendation's organization, while P15 preferred a distribution based on self-defined categories: "I'm not that committed to spend hours in the platform to improve the recommender system". Similarly, P8 desired to select between the shows' time duration and their number of seasons. Moreover, P10, P15, P6, and P8 agreed on suggesting a feature to ask the user his or her current mood and filter the recommendations based on what they felt like.

Content. P2 and P3 believed that having more content would improve the chances for satisfactory recommendations and faster decisions. Additionally, P15 and P6 said reducing the number of recommendations in the interface could speed up user decisions.

Transparency. Some contradictions were voiced the transparency of the recommender system. A positive comment was expressed by P2 when he described the system as self-explanatory with texts as "because you watched this...". On the other hand, P3, P14, P8, and P5 agreed on not having a clue on what parameters the recommender used and the weight it gave to them. Similarly, P6 and P5 preferred to know what metrics were used for the suggestions. Furthermore, P16 said that it was not helpful to know how the recommender works without being able to control it. In relation, P14 said increasing transparency would promote accountability of the recommender system and understanding on how to "guide" the algorithm for better results. Also, P13 said comprehending the match percentage would improve the ease of use and enjoyment. Also, P11 said that more transparency would rise the usefulness of the recommender and produce faster decisions.

Explanations. P3 and P13 felt they needed a feature that appears only when requested: "it needs to be there just in case I want to know the information". Likewise, P3 did not want to know how the mathematics work, but "two or three sentences" expressing a general answer. In relation, P11 desired a quantifiable explanation: for example, how many people have watched the show or how many people liked it. Finally, P15 said: "At least say something about what is the input for the algorithm".

External Sources. P15 and P6 want to include a "social" variable to the algorithm. In relation, P6 relied more on friends' inputs because the suggestions of the system were not effective. Moreover, P11, P13, and P5 suggested adding scores from Rotten Tomatoes or similar services. Additionally, P13 believed that reviews from other people could provide valuable information and increase his trust in the recommender system.

4 Algorithmic Experience for Movie Recommender Algorithms

The five groups of design opportunities for Algorithmic Experience (AX) [1] in social media, were echoed in our study case. Hence, this AX framework is also found valid for movie recommender algorithms. However, we extend the framework to include two new AX opportunities not considered before: *algorithmic social practices* and *algorithmic usefulness*, as shown in Fig. 5.

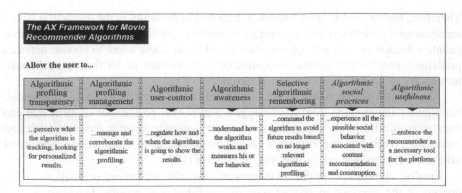

Fig. 5. Design areas for algorithmic experience in movie recommender algorithms.

This framework can also guide the requirement elicitation for other movie recommendation systems (e.g. Amazon Prime, Hulu, others). Approximations could be done outside the movie application domain (e.g. YouTube or Twitch), but they require specific studies to determine whether their streaming context possesses similar requirements.

4.1 Algorithmic Profiling Transparency

Transparency remains a relevant requirement for AX in movie recommender algorithms. This design area for AX is associated with showing clearly the profile created by the algorithm to achieve personalized recommendations. Possible improvements in this category could be defined by the algorithmic transparency standard [12]. Improvements include showing explicitly possible human involvement both in the recommendations or the user profile, explaining clearly the data collection process, model and inferences done by the algorithm. Additionally, it can be useful to explain where exactly the algorithm influence is included in the interface, both related to collecting data from the user or providing recommendations. Finally, features to check viewing history or inspect preferred user categories according to the algorithm could also improve this profiling transparency.

4.2 Algorithmic Profiling Management

During workshops and interviews, users expressed a need to manage and corroborate the preferences gathered by the recommender to promote or avoid specific types of content at specific moments. This management can be included in the user's profile [1].

A common related feature associated with the algorithmic profile management is the "cold start" phase. This phase defines the initial stage in which the recommender engine does not know enough about a user to provide effective recommendations. This concern is addressed by recommender systems designers through different strategies [23] and was also articulated during both the workshops and the SIM analysis as a new aspect that could be included in the area of *algorithmic profiling management.*

Therefore, the "cold start" phase seems to be a first opportunity in the interaction with a recommender system to offer appropriate algorithmic profiling management. Besides a simple selection of movies, opportunities could be to allow users to choose between predefined profiles for specific categories or their mixture or let them pick friends, influencers or groups with common preferences.

Algorithmic profile management is also related to negative privacy experiences. Ambiguous impressions from users suggest issues with profile management that can negatively affect the AX, depending on the user's attitude towards data collection and processing. Therefore, opportunities should be available to control/erase behavioral information when desired, in line with legislation [19].

Finally, algorithmic profile management was also discussed in relation to the options of the interface to interact with the profiling mechanisms. For example, the strategy of Netflix is delimited by the "thumbs up/down" buttons and possibly by adding movies to the user's list, features that are misunderstood and too limited according to the workshop results and the SIM analysis. Possible solutions in this area could be developing more detailed user controls for the recommendations.

4.3   Algorithmic Awareness

Algorithmic awareness requirements were also voiced during the workshops. First, there should be a clear distinction between algorithmically generated recommendations and recommendations that are simply self-promotional, an issue constantly expressed and related to Netflix's commercial interests. Second, users also reported a low understanding of the "match percentage" and the "thumbs up/down" buttons.

Third, ambiguous opinions about the platform's ease of use and learning were also articulated by the participants. These comments were mostly based upon having so many recommendations with high scores, which were found untrustworthy and negatively evaluated. Moreover, interaction with the recommender should promote algorithmic awareness. For example, implications for future recommendations using features as "Thumbs up/down" or the "User list" should be clearly stated in the interface, including when they are supposed to be used (before or after watching a show).

Understanding how the algorithm works improves algorithmic awareness, trust, and transparency and could be improved via direct explanations. Users asked for these explanations as a "second layer" option or not always directly visible.

4.4   Algorithmic User Control

Opportunities for user control were also mentioned by users. First, users need a way to communicate their current "mood" to the recommender, such as "explorative" to avoid algorithmically defined recommendations or to promote recommendations not directly related with their personal profile or preferences. Second, this explorative mode could be also related to the user's desire for an "algorithm free" space, or a way to "turn off" the recommender engine. Opportunities in this direction could be sorting the content alphabetically, by categories, by year of production, and other similar features. This functionality was described by users as an opportunity to reduce algorithm hacking or

"looking for tricks" to find alternative content in the platform. Third, users also mentioned a need to "turn off" the recommender data collection during specific periods of time or just to "stop" it so a specific movie could be avoided for future recommendations. This feature could be particularly useful when users share their account with relatives or friends and do not desire that activity to influence their own recommendations.

In relation to this area of AX, users also expressed the need to indicate faulty algorithmic recommendations with the "thumbs down" option. Also, users desired to provide explanations for the "downvoting" to detail why the recommender algorithm should avoid similar content in the future.

4.5 Selective Algorithmic Remembering

Regarding algorithmic remembering, users said they would like to make the algorithm "forget" previous specific activities to avoid related future recommendations. Again, this feature could be helpful when users share their accounts with other people to avoid future irrelevant content or just to curate their viewing history.

It may be helpful to make a distinction between algorithmic profiling management and selective algorithmic remembering. While the latter opens an opportunity to manage recommendations based on complete movie categories such as comedies, westerns, and others, the former aims to delete specific shows or movies that have been watched in the past. In this case, the user looks for a need to refine the recommendations with specific contents, rather than entire categories.

4.6 Algorithmic Usefulness

This category allows the user to embrace the recommender as a necessary tool for the platform and "enjoy using it". An initial and obvious opportunity in this area is to provide an effective recommender algorithm that could predict users' preferences as accurately as possible. Bad recommendations will affect negatively the AX. Closely related, users also expressed that the algorithm should not only recommend "guaranteed bets" or popular shows. Instead, it could take "certain calculated risks" to offer alternative/diverse contents outside of the mainstream general consumption or usual preference of the user. In this context, a recommender algorithm that only promotes own content is considered bad AX, untrustworthy, turning the feature into a "disposable" tool.

Another finding in this area was discovered during the workshops and interviews: the amount and diversity of the available content for the recommendations affects the AX. Less movies will not only create a negative experience with the recommendations but will also reduce the probabilities for appropriate algorithmically generated suggestions. In relation, when a user manually searches for a specific name of a show or movie, it seems to be a good idea to at least recommend "similar" contents when that specific content is not available in the platform, as Netflix does already.

Finally, other results were closely related with previous studies that portrayed some opportunities in this area [2, 39, 40]. For example, a positive AX in movie recommender algorithms is promoted by appropriate knowledge about the user preferences,

satisfactory results, better and faster decisions, produce enjoyment, express appropriate knowledge about the user preferences, producing enjoyment and persuading the user to choose the algorithm recommendations because of their usefulness.

4.7 Algorithmic Social Practices

This design opportunity allows the user to experience the possible social behaviors associated with content consumption, such as the recurrent habit of sharing a personal account. Even though Netflix offers many accounts in a single subscription, users continuously expressed that they share the same account with different people, which in the end negatively influences their AX. In relation, a solution supported by the users is that the algorithm should offer to "stop tracking" momentarily when a movie does not correspond to their personal preference. Moreover, users expressed a need to be able to erase previous viewing activity to "tune up" their recommendations after sharing their accounts. Another solution is to consider multiple users in front of the screen and offer a "mixed accounts" mode, providing reciprocal recommendations to improve AX.

Other design opportunities in this area were based on external recommendation sources. Users continuously mentioned the habit of following specialized platforms and friends (or "influencers") to guide their viewing preferences. Therefore, they desire to add a "social factor" to the recommender algorithm in which friends could share movie suggestions or follow trust-worthy accounts to mimic watching preferences. Furthermore, it was mentioned to add "third party" grading systems such as Rotten Tomatoes or IMDB to compare and complement their grades with the recommender matching score. Finally, users want to check other users' reviews on movies and shows.

5 Examples to Improve AX of Movie Recommender Systems

A way to improve *algorithmic profiling transparency* is generating a "profile view" showing which inputs the algorithm is currently considering for recommendations as exemplified by a previous study [30]. Likewise, a solution for *algorithmic profiling management* is proposed by an interface that offers to adjust recommendations related to current preferences and user models [2]. Solutions for the "cold start" are described by a previous study that showed significant improvements by offering groups of movies rather than single movie selection [8]. Also, this phase could use representations of movie communities, watching trends, or other "social" options [23]. Additionally, a previous study showed improvements in *user control* by letting users choose movies based on recency and popularity [22] as a way to "turn off" the algorithm. Finally, improving accuracy for *algorithmic usefulness* is not enough [29]. For instance, a significant portion of users prefers an option that allows to choose between different algorithmic strategies for movie recommendations [13].

6   Limitations

The study was performed in Belgium, inferring implications on user perceptions on their recommendations due to regionally available content. Also, the user group was dominated by males, tech-savvy and highly educated users, which could imply possible bias among the results and uncertainty of the same results among other groups.

7   Conclusion

This study explored the algorithmic experience (AX) of recommender algorithms using Netflix. It applied a mixed approach for the analysis: first, a semiotic inspection method to study the designer's intention towards the recommender system; second, a sensitized workshop to elicit AX-based requirements; and third, follow-up interviews to collect more AX requirements based in recommender systems design theories.

From the analysis, we propose a specialized AX framework for movie recommender algorithms with seven design opportunities: algorithmic profiling transparency, algorithmic management, algorithmic awareness, algorithmic user-control and selective algorithmic remembering, algorithmic usefulness and algorithmic social practices.

This new specialized AX framework for movie recommender algorithms contributes to a focused approach for designing these systems. Future research could measure if the framework already includes all the necessary aspects for a positive AX in this context and the objective implications on user experience when they are implemented.

Acknowledgements. This research has been supported by the KU Leuven Research Council (grant agreement no. C24/16/017 and RUN/16/003) and the University of Costa Rica (UCR).

References

1. Alvarado, O., Waern, A.: Towards algorithmic experience. In: Proceedings of the 2018 CHI Conference on Human Factors in Computing Systems - CHI 2018, pp. 1–9. ACM Press, Montreal (2018)
2. Bakalov, F., et al.: An approach to controlling user models and personalization effects in recommender systems. In: Proceedings of 2013 International Conference on Intelligent User Interfaces - IUI 2013, pp. 49–56 (2013)
3. Baumer, E.P.: Toward human-centered algorithm design. Big Data Soc. **4**, 1–12 (2017)
4. Beer, D.: The social power of algorithms. Inf. Commun. Soc. **20**(1), 1–13 (2017)
5. Berkovsky, S., Taib, R., Conway, D.: How to recommend ? User trust factors in movie recommender systems. In: Proceedings of the 22nd International Conference on Intelligent User Interfaces, IUI 2017, pp. 287–300 (2017)
6. Bishop, S.: Anxiety, panic and self-optimization. Converg. Int. J. Res. New Media Technol. **24**(1), 69–84 (2018)
7. Bozdag, E.: Bias in algorithmic filtering and personalization. Ethics Inf. Technol. **15**(3), 209–227 (2013)

8. Chang, S., Harper, F.M., Terveen, L.: Using groups of items to bootstrap new users in recommender systems. In: Proceedings of the 18th ACM Conference on Computer Supported Cooperative Work & Social Computing - CSCW 2015, pp. 1258–1269. ACM Press, New York (2015)

9. Cramer, H., et al.: The effects of transparency on trust in and acceptance of a content-based art recommender. User Model. User-Adapt. Interact. **18**(5), 455–496 (2008)

10. Cramer, H., Thom, J.: Not-so-autonomous, very human decisions in machine learning: questions when designing for ML the human side of machine learning. In: AAAI Spring Symposium on Designing the User Experience of Machine Learning Systems, pp. 412–414 (2017)

11. Diakopoulos, N.: Accountability in algorithmic decision making. Commun. ACM **59**(2), 56–62 (2016)

12. Diakopoulos, N., Koliska, M.: Algorithmic transparency in the news media. Digit. J. **5**(7), 809–828 (2017)

13. Ekstrand, M.D., Kluver, D., Harper, F.M., Konstan, J.A.: Letting users choose recommender algorithms. In: Proceedings of the 9th ACM Conference on Recommender Systems - RecSys 2015, pp. 11–18. ACM Press, New York (2015)

14. Eslami, M., et al.: I always assumed that I wasn't really that close to [her]. In: Proceedings of the 2015 CHI Conference on Human Factors in Computing Systems - CHI 2015, Seoul, pp. 153–162 (2015)

15. Gedikli, F., Jannach, D., Ge, M.: How should i explain? A comparison of different explanation types for recommender systems. Int. J. Hum Comput Stud. **72**(4), 367–382 (2014)

16. Gillespie, T.: #trendingistrending: when algorithms become culture. In: Algorithmic Cultures Essays Meaning, Performance New Technologies, vol. 189, pp. 52–75 (2016)

17. Gillespie, T.: The relevance of algorithms. In: Media Technologies Essays on Communication, Materiality, and Society, pp. 167–194 (2014)

18. Gomez-Uribe, C.A., Hunt, N.: The Netflix recommender system. ACM Trans. Manag. Inf. Syst. **6**(4), 1–19 (2015)

19. Goodman, B., Flaxman, S.: EU regulations on algorithmic decision-making and a "right to explanation". In: 2016 ICML Workshop on Human Interpretability in Machine Learning, WHI 2016, pp. 1–9 (2016)

20. Hallinan, B., Striphas, T.: Recommended for you: the Netflix prize and the production of algorithmic culture. New Media Soc. **18**(1), 117–137 (2016)

21. Hamilton, K., Karahalios, K., Sandvig, C., Eslami, M.: A path to understanding the effects of algorithm awareness. In: Proceedings of the Extended Abstracts of ACM Conference on Human Factors in Computing Systems - CHI EA 2014, pp. 631–642 (2014)

22. Harper, F.M., Xu, F., Kaur, H., Condiff, K., Chang, S., Terveen, L.: Putting users in control of their recommendations. In: Proceedings of the 9th ACM Conference on Recommender Systems - RecSys 2015, pp. 3–10. ACM Press, New York (2015)

23. He, C., Parra, D., Verbert, K.: Interactive recommender systems: a survey of the state of the art and future research challenges and opportunities. Expert Syst. Appl. An Int. J. **56**(C), 9–27 (2016)

24. Introna, L.D.: Algorithms, governance, and governmentality: on governing academic writing. Sci. Technol. Hum. Values **41**, 1 (2016)

25. Jugovac, M., Jannach, D.: Interacting with recommenders – overview and research directions. ACM Trans. Interact. Intell. Syst. **7**(3), 1–46 (2017)

26. Knijnenburg, B.P., Willemsen, M.C., Gantner, Z., Soncu, H., Newell, C.: Explaining the user experience of recommender systems. User Model. User-Adapt. Interact. **22**(4–5), 441–504 (2012)

27. Kulesza, T., Stumpf, S., Burnett, M., Kwan, I.: Tell me more? The effects of mental model soundness on personalizing an intelligent agent. In: Proceedings of 2012 ACM Annual Conference on Human Factors in Computing Systems - CHI 2012 (2012)

28. Lee, M.K., Kim, J.T., Lizarondo, L.: A human-centered approach to algorithmic services: considerations for fair and motivating smart community service management that allocates donations to non-profit organizations. In: Proceedings of the 2017 CHI Conference on Human Factors in Computing Systems - CHI 2017, Denver, pp. 3365–3376 (2017)

29. McNee, S.M., Riedl, J., Konstan, J.A.: Being accurate is not enough: how accuracy metrics have hurt recommender systems. In: CHI 2006 Extended Abstracts on Human Factors in Computing Systems - CHI EA 2006, pp. 1097–1101. ACM Press, New York (2006)

30. Millecamp, M., Htun, N.N., Jin, Y., Verbert, K.: Controlling spotify recommendations: effects of personal characteristics on music recommender user interfaces. In: Proceedings of the 26th Conference on User Modeling, Adaptation and Personalization - UMAP 2018, pp. 101–109 (2018)

31. Morris, J.W.: Curation by code: infomediaries and the data mining of taste. Eur. J. Cult. Stud. 18(4–5), 446–463 (2015)

32. Neyland, D., Möllers, N.: Algorithmic IF … THEN rules and the conditions and consequences of power. Inf. Commun. Soc. 20(1), 45–62 (2017)

33. Oh, C., Lee, T., Kim, Y., Park, S., Kwon, S., Suh, B.: Us vs. them: understanding artificial intelligence technophobia over the Google deepmind challenge match. In: Conference on Human Factors in Computing Systems - CHI 2017, pp. 2523–2534 (2017)

34. Prey, R.: Nothing personal: algorithmic individuation on music streaming platforms. Media Cult. Soc. 40, 1086–1100 (2017). https://doi.org/10.1177/0163443717745147

35. Rieder, B., Matamoros-Fernández, A., Coromina, Ò.: From ranking algorithms to 'ranking cultures': investigating the modulation of visibility in YouTube search results. Convergence 24(1), 50–68 (2018)

36. Sinha, R., Swearingen, K.: The role of transparency in recommender systems. In: CHI 2002 Extended Abstracts on Human Factors in Computing Systems - CHI 2002, pp. 830–831 (2002)

37. De Souza, C.S., Leitão, C.F.: Semiotic Engineering Methods for Scientific Research in HCI (2009)

38. Striphas, T.: Algorithmic culture. Eur. J. Cult. Stud. 18(4–5), 395–412 (2015)

39. Tintarev, N., Masthoff, J.: A survey of explanations in recommender systems. In: Proceedings - International Conference on Data Engineering, pp. 801–810 (2007)

40. Tintarev, N., Masthoff, J.: Evaluating the effectiveness of explanations for recommender systems: methodological issues and empirical studies on the impact of personalization. User Model. User-Adapt. Interact. 22(4–5), 399–439 (2012)

41. Willson, M.: Algorithms (and the) everyday. Inf. Commun. Soc. 20(1), 137–150 (2017)

42. Ziewitz, M.: Governing algorithms: myth, mess, and methods. Sci. Technol. Hum. Values 41(1), 3–16 (2016)

Following Wrong Suggestions: Self-blame in Human and Computer Scenarios

Andrea Beretta[1,2]([envelope]) [iD], Massimo Zancanaro[1,2] [iD],
and Bruno Lepri[2] [iD]

[1] DIPSCO, University of Trento, Rovereto, TN, Italy
andrea.beretta@unitn.it
[2] Fondazione Bruno Kessler, Trento, TN, Italy
{zancana,lepri}@fbk.com

Abstract. This paper investigates the specific experience of following a suggestion by an intelligent machine that has a wrong outcome and the emotions people feel. By adopting a typical task employed in studies on decision-making, we presented participants with two scenarios in which they follow a suggestion and have a wrong outcome by either an expert human being or an intelligent machine. We found a significant decrease in the perceived responsibility on the wrong choice when the machine offers the suggestion. At present, few studies have investigated the negative emotions that could arise from a bad outcome after following the suggestion given by an intelligent system, and how to cope with the potential distrust that could affect the long-term use of the system and the cooperation. This preliminary research has implications in the study of cooperation and decision making with intelligent machines. Further research may address how to offer the suggestion in order to better cope with user's self-blame.

Keywords: Decision-making · Intelligent systems · Negative emotions

1 Introduction

Today intelligent systems are entering into our everyday life. These systems can help people to make more effective choices by generating predictions to the user in the form of advice and suggestions. Thus, in order to improve the design of these systems a greater understanding is needed on the conditions in which people emotionally deal with suggestions provided by an intelligent machine.

In this paper, we present an initial study investigating the emotions felt by people after following a wrong suggestion provided by a supposedly intelligent machine. We have focused on four specific emotions related to non-optimal decisions: *regret, disappointment, guilt,* and *perceived responsibility.*

Our results provides evidence that users' feelings of self-blame tend to be lower when they receive a wrong suggestion by a computer and the responses have a larger variation with respect to when the suggestion is provided by a human being.

© IFIP International Federation for Information Processing 2019
Published by Springer Nature Switzerland AG 2019
D. Lamas et al. (Eds.): INTERACT 2019, LNCS 11748, pp. 542–550, 2019.
https://doi.org/10.1007/978-3-030-29387-1_31

2   Theoretical Framework

Since the envision of Artificial Intelligence, technical progress has the intent of sur-passing human performance and ability [1]. However, recently there is a growing interest in understanding the conditions for an effective cooperative relationship between human and computer agents as well as the possible biases of this cooperation.

In some recent studies, Logg [2, 3] has shown that people trust more a machine than other people when they need to make a decision in an objective context (e.g., they are looking for information). In other studies, in a subjective context (e.g., looking for book recommendations, looking for joke recommendations), people tend to rely more on other human beings [4, 5].

Machines can exceed human judgment in different ways. First, by exploiting the "wisdom of crowds", machines can surpass human accuracy in decisions even with simple algorithms (for example, averaging between the opinion of several individuals) [3, 6–8]. Second, algorithms trained with the same features used by human experts may exploit them more accurately [9]. Third, machine can automatically identify more predictive features than those commonly used by experts [10].

2.1   Emotions Related with Wrong Decisions

Regret and disappointment are *"negative, cognitively determined emotions that we may experience when a situation would have been better if: (a) we had done something different (in case of regret); or (b) the state of the world had been different (in case of disappointment)"* [11]. They are the two most important emotions related with the decision process and both of them can be defined as counterfactual [12, 13]. Early theories have been studied by economists and investigated how the feeling of antici-pated regret affects the decision process under uncertainty (e.g., [14–16]). In psycho-logical literature, the focus often is on how negative outcomes could intensify the experience of regret [17] and in how disappointment influences decision making [16, 18].

More specifically, regret is experienced when one could not obtain the expected goals, while disappointment arises when there is a goal abandonment [12]. Zeelenberg and colleagues argument that regret is related to a behavioral switch and decreases trust, whereas disappointment increases trust [19, 20]. Other studies argue that regret increases prosocial behaviors, while disappointment reduces them [19, 21, 22].

Another important aspect is how responsibility is related to these two emotions. Regret and disappointment differ from the perceived responsibility of the outcome: when a person feels more responsible for the bad outcome, regret is involved; while disappointment is involved when the person feels to not be responsible for the outcome [23, 24].

Particular attention should be paid to the difference between regret and guilt, both originated by negative outcomes related to a sense of self-responsibility. According to Zeelenberg and Breugelmans [25], regret and guilt are perceived as emotional out-comes of negative events and are related with a sense of self-agency and with the intention to change the event that happened. However, there are still not clear criteria to distinguish these two emotions while there is a general understanding that defines

regret as a broader emotion than guilt [25, 26]. For example, Berndsen and colleagues [27] distinguish guilt from regret on the basis of interpersonal and more social factors related to guilt and intrapersonal factors more related to regret.

3   A User Study on Wrong Decisions with Intelligent Machines

This study aims at investigating the emotional effects of a wrong decision taken after a suggestion by an intelligent machine with respect to when the wrong decision is taken after the suggestion from a human being. Our hypothesis is that when a suggestion is received by an intelligent machine (at least in an objective decision task), a wrong outcome may elicit less emotion directed toward the self, compared to the situation in which the suggestion is given by a human being. That is because an intelligent machine might be expected to provide more accurate suggestions [9] and the perceived agency is limited (unless the machine does have anthropomorphic features [28]).

Following a common practice in decision-making studies, we use scenarios rather than interactions with a real intelligent system in order to better control the conditions.

3.1   Hypotheses

Given the theoretical framework described above, and in particular following the results on decisions' outcomes of Logg [2, 3], we expected that a suggestion provided by an intelligent machine (in a technical and relatively complicated decision task) decreases the possibility for the user to blame the advisor and therefore should produce a lower rating on counterfactual emotions and responsibility.

Therefore, after a wrong suggestion by an intelligent machine we postulate the following hypotheses:

- *Hypothesis on regret*: the user feels less regret than after a wrong suggestion given by a human being.
- *Hypothesis on disappointment*: the user feels more disappointment than after a wrong suggestion given by a human being.
- *Hypothesis on responsibility*: the user feels less responsible for the choice and for the bad outcome than after a wrong suggestion given by a human being.
- *Hypothesis on guilt*: the user experiences less guilt than after a wrong suggestion given by a human being.

3.2   Participants

Eighty-five participants were involved through the platform Amazon Mechanical Turk. Their age ranges from 18 to 66 years old (57 males, 24 females; mean = 34 years; SD = 9.55 years). The only requirement for participation was fluency in English.

3.3 Measures

In order to measure negative and counterfactual emotions, a questionnaire was built with 13 items obtained from validated scales:

- *Responsibility (self-blame)* is assessed by two items: the first measured the responsibility on the choice done, while the second one is about having done a bad purchase (i.e., bad outcome) [29].
- *Regret* is evaluated by two items aimed to assess the regret felt on the choice done and the regret felt for having a phone that does not meet the study participant's needs [29].
- *Disappointment* is assessed by two items aimed to evaluate the disappointment felt about having done a wrong choice and the disappointment for having a phone that does not meet the study participant's needs [29].
- *Perceived Guilt* is assessed by two items aimed to assess the perceived guilt on the choice done and the perceived guilt for having a phone that does not fulfill the study participants' needs [29].

The items are all 10-point Likert scales, ranging from strongly disagree (1) to strongly agree (10). Although Giorgetta [29] used 11-point scales, we eventually decided to not to have a central point.

Two items are added to control the experience of counterfactuals measuring the affective reaction and the dissatisfaction of the participant [30]. Finally, a manipulation check to prevent random answers is included (the item simply asks to select the "totally agree" score [31]).

3.4 Procedure

The experimental design is a between-subject with two conditions: (i) when a human being provides the suggestion (condition "Human") and (ii) when an intelligent machine provides the suggestion (condition "Computer").

At the beginning of the experiment, the participant received a short introduction to the task and s/he is asked to read and accept the informed consent and a short demographic questionnaire about age, gender and self-reported English fluency.

After that, the participant is automatically assigned to one of the two conditions and asked to read the first scenario about a purchase decision. The first scenario in "Computer" condition is as follows:

> *"Imagine that you have to buy a new smartphone because yours has just stopped working. Even if you are not an expert, you go to the shop with the idea of buying XY10, because you think that is the model that best suits your preferences. Once in the shop, you enter your preferences in an **algorithm-based website** that suggests you buy smartphone WLx at the same price. Hence you decide to buy the suggested model WLx. Some time later, you realize that model XY10 would have been better for your needs, while the smartphone you have bought does not meet your expectations".*

The scenario in "Human" condition describes the same situation but it is different on the source of the advice:

*"Imagine that you have to buy a new smartphone because yours has just stopped working. Even if you are not an expert, you go to the shop with the idea of buying XY10, because you think that is the model that best suits your preferences. Once in the shop, you explain your preferences to the **clerk** who suggests you buy smartphone WLx at the same price. Hence you decide to buy the suggested model WLx. Some time later, you realize that model XY10 would have been better for your needs, while the smartphone you have bought does not meet your expectations".*

Immediately after that, the questionnaire on negative and counterfactual emotions was administered for the first time. After the questionnaire, the participant was exposed to a second situation. The second scenario was about the same choice as before after a year and asked to check how dissatisfaction emotions change for the same decisional framework. Then, the participant was presented with the questionnaire on emotions for the second time.

At the end of the task, the participant was asked to recall the source of the suggestion received as a further attentional check.

Finally, the last step was about the debriefing of the participants on the actual aims of the study.

4 Analysis

Before starting the analysis, the data has been checked for consistency. First, four participants were removed because they did not answer all the questions and another four participants were removed because they failed the consistency checks.

Then, 26 participants were removed because they showed inconsistent answers to the two control questions: "*I am sorry about what happened to me*" and "*I am satisfied about what happened to me*" in either the first or the second scenario.

Finally, 13 participants were removed because they took too long to complete the task. In order to identify these outliers, we adopted the Tukey's fences technique and we removed all the participants that took a time longer than 1.5 times the third quartile (4 min).

Eventually, 38 participants were retained for the study. The mean age was 32.5 years old (SD = 7.39) ranging from 18 to 60 years old. Fifteen were women and 36 men. The average of the male sample has the mean equal to 31.44 years old (SD = 6.57), and the female sample has mean 35.06 years old (SD = 8.78).

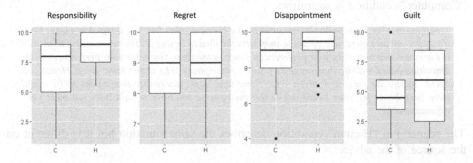

Fig. 1. The distribution of the negative and counter-factual emotions for the first scenario

The distributions of the emotions in the two conditions and in the two scenarios are shown in Fig. 1 for the first scenario and in Fig. 2, respectively.

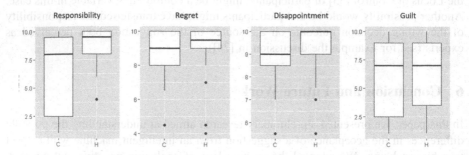

Fig. 2. The distribution of the negative and counterfactual emotions for the second scenario

For disappointment, regret and guilt there was no statistical difference in the two conditions in either scenarios. However, the responsibility on choice seems to change whether the source of suggestion was human or machine (using Kruskal-Wallis rank sum test, $p = 0.09088$ for the first scenario and $p = 0.04318$ for the second scenario). The participants showed more self-blame when the suggestion came from a human being (mean $= 6.6$ vs 8.4, sd $= 3.2$ vs 1.6 in the first scenario and mean $= 6.4$ vs 8.1, sd $= 3.6$ vs 1.7 in the second scenario). Furthermore, the variance was much higher in the computer condition with respect to the human condition in both scenarios (Fligner-Killeen test of homogeneity of variances, $p = 0.04051$ and $p = 0.00632$, respectively).

5   Discussion

The results were not what we expected since we did not find any difference in regret, disappointment and guilt. Yet, our intuition was at least partially confirmed because the effect on responsibility was rather strong. Indeed, the effect on responsibility can be related to the antecedents of regret [32].

Even if further studies need to be carried out, from a Human-Computer Interaction (HCI) point of view, the decrease of the sense of responsibility when the suggestion comes from the computer may induce risky choices and it should be counterbalanced by appropriate design solutions.

The increase of variance in the responses when the suggestion comes from the computer may suggest that there might some cofounding variable that mediate this effect. This aspect should be better explored in further studies.

The study had some limitations. First, we may note that for all emotions and in both scenarios, the values tend to be quite high. This might be due to either a bias from recruiting the participants in a crowdsourcing service (as it might be apparent from the high number of participants that we had to exclude from the analysis) or from the scenarios that may have appeared confused or unnatural. Second, the variance is quite large for all the emotions and in both scenarios. Again, this might be due to the reasons

above or it might depend by some conditions that we did not test (for example, different perceptions of the true intentions of the clerk while the computer might have look more neutral with respect to hidden intentions). Alternatively, personality traits (for example, the Locus of Control [33] of participants) might be a confounding variable in this case. Another possibility would be that participants might have transferred the responsibility of the wrong decision outcome on the source of the suggestion both perceived as experts (see for example the discussion in [24]).

6 Conclusion and Future Work

In this paper, we presented a preliminary research aimed at understanding the possible differences in the acceptance of a suggestion from an intelligent machine with respect to a human being. We adopted the specific lens of analyzing negative and counterfactual emotions when the choice is eventually wrong.

Our study, in which we manipulated the outcome for controlling the experimental condition, found that participants' feeling of self-blame is lower when they receive a wrong suggestion by a computer rather than by a human being. This may suggest that decision making with computer advice may eventually induce risky choices.

This result needs to be confirmed by other studies, in particular in view of the lack of significance for the other negative and counterfactual emotions that are well-known related with sense of responsibility. In particular, it will be important to vary the scenarios and to control for possible cofounding variables (such as personality traits or attitude toward technology).

Still, we believe that our results are interesting for a better understanding of the relation between users and intelligent machines in a decision-making process and for a better design of this type of systems.

References

1. Crandall, J.W., et al.: Cooperating with machines. Nat. Commun. 9, Article no. 233 (2018). https://doi.org/10.1038/s41467-017-02597-8
2. Logg, J.M., Minson, J.A., Moore, D.A.: Algorithmic appreciation: people prefer algorithmic to human judgment. Behav. Hum. Decis. Process. **151**, 90–103 (2019)
3. Logg, J.M., Minson, J.A., Moore, D.A.: Do people trust algorithms more than companies realize? Harvard Bus. Rev. Technol. Sect. (2018). https://hbr.org/2018/10/do-people-trust-algorithms-more-than-companies-realize
4. Yeomans, M., Shah, A., Mullainathan, S., Kleinberg, J.: Making sense of recommendations. J. Behav. Decis. Making 1–12 (2019). https://doi.org/10.1108/13287261011042903
5. Dietvorst, B.J., Simmons, J.P., Massey, C.: Algorithmic aversion; people erroneously avoid algorithms after seeing them err. J. Exp. Psychol. Gen. **144**(1), 114–126 (2015)
6. Galton, F.: Vox populi. Nature **1949**(75), 450–451 (1907)
7. Mannes, A.E., Soll, J.B., Larrick, R.P.: The wisdom of select crowds. J. Pers. Soc. Psychol. **107**(2), 276–299 (2014). https://doi.org/10.1037/a0036677

8. Surowiecki, J.: The Wisdom of Crowds: Why the Many are Smarter than the Few and How Collective Wisdom Shapes Business, Economies, Societies and Nations. Random House, New York (2004)

9. Dawes, R.M.: The robust beauty of improper linear models in decision making. Am. Psychol. **34**, 71–582 (1979). https://doi.org/10.1037/0003-066X.34.7.571

10. Khan, J., et al.: Classification and diagnostic prediction of cancers using gene expression profiling and artificial neural networks. Nat. Med. **7**, 623–679 (2001). https://doi.org/10.1038/89044

11. Giorgetta, C., Zeelenberg, M., Ferlazzo, F., D'Olimpio, F.: Cultural variation in the role of responsibility in regret and disappointment: the Italian case. J. Econ. Psychol. **33**(4), 726–737 (2012). https://doi.org/10.1016/j.joep.2012.02.003

12. Zeelenberg, M., Van Dijk, W.W., Manstead, A.S.R.: Regret and responsibility resolved? Evaluating Ordóñez and Connolly's (2000) conclusions. Organ. Behav. Hum. Decis. Process. **81**(1), 143–154 (2000). https://doi.org/10.1006/obhd.1999.2865

13. Zeelenberg, M., Van Dijk, W.W., Van Der Pligt, J., Manstead, A.S.R., van Empelen, P., Reinderman, D.: Emotional reactions to the outcomes of decisions: the role of counterfactual thought in the experience of regret and disappointment. Organ. Behav. Hum. Decis. Process. **75**(2), 117–141 (1998). https://doi.org/10.1006/obhd.1998.2784

14. Bell, D.E.: Regret in decision making under uncertainty. Oper. Res. **30**(5), 961–981 (1982). https://doi.org/10.1287/opre.30.5.961

15. Loomes, G., Sugden, R.: Regret theory: an alternative theory of rational choice under uncertainty. Econ. J. **92**(368), 805–824 (1982). https://doi.org/10.2307/2232669

16. Loomes, G., Sugden, R.: Disappointment and dynamic consistence in choice under uncertainty. Rev. Econ. Stud. **53**(2), 271–282 (1986). https://doi.org/10.2307/2297651

17. Kahneman, D., Tversky, A.: The simulation heuristic. In: Kahneman, D., Slovic, P., Tversky, A. (eds.) Judgment Under Uncertainty: Heuristics and Biases, pp. 201–208. Cambridge University Press, New York (1982)

18. Bell, D.E.: Disappointment in decision making under uncertainty. Oper. Res. **33**(1), 1–27 (1985). https://doi.org/10.1287/opre.33.1.1

19. Martinez, L.F., Zeelenberg, M.: Trust me (or not): regret and disappointment in experimental economic games. Decision **2**(2), 118–126 (2015). https://doi.org/10.1037/dec0000025

20. Zeelenberg, M., Pieters, R.: Beyond valence in customer dissatisfaction: a review and new findings on behavioral responses to regret and disappointment in failed services. J. Bus. Res. **57**(4), 445–455 (2004)

21. Martinez, L.F., Zeelenberg, M., Rijsman, J.B.: Behavioural consequences of regret and disappointment in social bargaining games. Cogn. Emot. **25**(2), 351–359 (2011). https://doi.org/10.1080/02699931.2010.485889

22. Martinez, L.F., Zeelenberg, M., Rijsman, J.B.: Regret, disappointment and the endowment effect. J. Econ. Psychol. **32**(6), 962–968 (2011). https://doi.org/10.1016/j.joep.2011.08.006

23. Frijda, N.H., Kuipers, P., ter Schure, E.: Relations among emotion, appraisal, and emotional action readiness. J. Pers. Soc. Psychol. **57**(2), 212–228 (1989)

24. Pieters, R., Zeelenberg, M.: A theory of regret regulation 1.0. J. Consum. Psychol. **17**(1), 3–18 (2007). https://doi.org/10.1207/s15327663jcp1701_6

25. Zeelenberg, M., Breugelmans, S.M.: The role of interpersonal harm in distinguishing regret from guilt. Emotion **8**(5), 589–596 (2008). https://doi.org/10.1037/a0012894

26. Landman, J.: Regret: The Persistence of the Possible. Oxford University Press, New York (1993)

27. Berndsen, M., van der Pligt, J., Doosje, B., Manstead, A.: Guilt and regret: the determining role of interpersonal and intrapersonal harm. Cogn. Emot. **18**(1), 55–70 (2004). https://doi.org/10.1080/02699930244000435

28. Waytz, A., Heafner, J., Epley, N.: The mind in the machine: anthropomorphism increases trust in an autonomous vehicle. J. Exp. Soc. Psychol. **52**, 113–117 (2014). https://doi.org/10.1016/j.jesp.2014.01.005

29. Giorgetta, C.: The Emotional Side of Decision-making: Regret and Disappointment. LAMBERT - Academic Publishing, Saarbrücken (2012)

30. Marcatto, F., Ferrante, D.: The Regret and disappointment scale: an instrument for assessing regret and disappointment in decision making. Judgment Decis. Making **3**(1), 87–99 (2008)

31. Oppenheimer, D.M., Meyvis, T., Davidenko, N.: Instructional manipulation checks: detecting satisficing to increase statistical power. J. Exp. Soc. Psychol. **45**(4), 867–872 (2009). https://doi.org/10.1016/j.jesp.2009.03.009

32. Zeelenberg, M., van Dijk, W.W., Manstead, A.S.R., vanr de Pligt, J.: On bad decisions and disconfirmed expectancies: the psychology of regret and disappointment. Cogn. Emot. **14**(4), 521–541 (2000). https://doi.org/10.1080/026999300402781

33. Ajzen, I.: Perceived behavioral control, self-efficacy, locus of control, and the theory of planned behavior. J. Appl. Soc. Psychol. **32**(4), 665–682 (2002). https://doi.org/10.1111/j.1559-1816.2002.tb00236.x

Personality Is Revealed During Weekends: Towards Data Minimisation for Smartphone Based Personality Classification

Mohammed Khwaja[1,2]([✉]) and Aleksandar Matic[1]

[1] Telefonica Alpha, Barcelona, Spain
{mohammed.khwaja,aleksandar.matic}@telefonica.com
[2] Imperial College, London, UK

Abstract. Previous literature has explored automatic personality modelling using smartphone data for its potential to personalise mobile services. Although passive modelling of personality removes the burden of completing lengthy questionnaires, the fact that such models typically require a few weeks or months of personal data can negatively impact user's engagement. In this study, we explore the feasibility of reducing the duration of data collection in the context of personality classification. We found that only one or two weekends can suffice for achieving state-of-the-art accuracy between 66% and 71% for classifying the five personality traits. These results provide lessons for practicing "data minimisation" – a key principle of privacy laws.

Keywords: Personality prediction · Smartphone sensing · Big five

1 Introduction

Personality reflects individual differences in behaviours, emotions and cognition [7]. Psychologists showed that personality traits capture stable individual characteristics that explain and predict behavioural patterns [6]. Interestingly, personality traits can also predict patterns of technology use, such as behaviours in social media [3,9], blogs [14], games [29], phone use [4,15,24] and even how users choose app permission settings [21]. Therefore, personality is considered to be relevant to a number of computing areas, among which Human Computer Interaction (HCI) can particularly benefit from understanding users' personality, by making informed decisions about their needs and preferences. Consideration of personality was shown to be highly beneficial for personalising recommender systems [8], gamification elements [12], online educational applications [13], persuasive health games [19] and other kinds of technologies. Previous work also demonstrated how personality influences adoption of new technologies [28] as well as users' satisfaction [17].

© IFIP International Federation for Information Processing 2019
Published by Springer Nature Switzerland AG 2019
D. Lamas et al. (Eds.): INTERACT 2019, LNCS 11748, pp. 551–560, 2019.
https://doi.org/10.1007/978-3-030-29387-1_32

Assessing personality typically relies on standardised questionnaires where individuals rate their typical behaviours with Likert scales. When it comes to user modelling, app designers typically avoid using this method as completing questionnaires can be cumbersome for users and can consequently drive them away from the app. For this reason, automatic prediction of personality has attracted the attention of many scholars and practitioners who relied on data collected from Twitter [3], Instagram [9], blogs [14], and smartphone use [4,15, 24]. Most of these approaches relied on collecting data from several weeks [24], months [17] and even years [15,16], in order to accurately infer personality. In practice, however, collecting such large amounts of personal data is not always trivial. Firstly, data minimisation represents a fundamental principle of privacy both in the EU (under the General Data Protection Regulation - GDPR[1]) and in the US [25], which obliges organisations to collect only minimal amount of personal data for the intended purpose. Collecting large amounts of personal data was also shown to be strongly associated with low user engagement due to privacy concerns [23]. Secondly, systems that rely on user data typically suffer from the "cold-start" problem [1] – in the case of personality prediction, requiring data collection of several weeks or months before enabling personalised services may be fatal for the user's engagement. These reasons underline the importance of understanding how to minimise data collection (or the data that is retained in the system) while at the same time reducing time needed to develop user models. This is what we explored using smartphone based personality classification.

In this study, we analysed if and to which extent the accuracy of personality inference will be affected when reducing the data collection to a few days (in contrast to weeks or months as in previous studies) and specifically to weekend days. The rationale for this study stems from the assumption that people exhibit more natural behaviours during weekends when they have more control over their time, than during working days. Zuzanek et al. [30] argued that people engage in activities of their preference more frequently during weekends than weekdays, whereas Ryan et al. [22] showed that mood is significantly better during weekends. To this end, the present study relies on 142 behavioural features extracted from two-week smartphone data collected from 166 participants to predict their Big Five personality traits. The main contributions of this paper are:

– A comparison between personality inferring machine learning models that rely on smartphone data collected during weekends versus weekdays.
– Takeaways for reducing duration of data collection (to one day, one weekend, and two weekends) for developing personality models.

2   Background

Extant literature explored personality inference approaches relying on various data from social network logs to keystroke patterns, and audio and video data.

---

[1] http://www.privacy-regulation.eu/en/article-5-principles-relating-to-processing-of-personal-data-GDPR.htm

Considering the topic of this paper, we will provide an overview of the most important literature that relied on smartphone data to detect personality traits. A comprehensive review of personality modelling using various digital cues can be found in [26].

Pioneering work in exploring phone data for personality prediction used call and message logs. Oliveira et al. [18] investigated structural characteristics of contact networks modelled through 6 months of call logs from 39 users, which resulted in promising preliminary results. Staiano et al. [24] extracted social network structures from 2 months of call logs and Bluetooth scans of 53 subjects and obtained binary classification accuracy between 65% and 80% for predicting the five traits. Chittaranjan et al. [4] and [5] used 8 months of phone data (calls, messages, Bluetooth, and applications) of 83 and 117 subjects in two trials to predict personality; F-measures for the binary classification task was between 40% and 80%. Using call logs and location data of 69 participants, Montjoye et al. [16] extracted psychology-informed indicators to predict personality between 29% and 56% better than random, relying on 12 months of data. Recent work by Monsted et al. [15] used 24 months of data from 636 university students to predict Extraversion. The authors used features from social activities extracted from calls, SMS, online networks, and physical proximity extracted from Bluetooth and GPS. Another recent research by Wang et al. [27] used mobile sensing data of 646 students from the University of Texas over 14 days to regress personality traits. This work used behavioural features like social interaction, movement, daily activity etc., from sensors including sound, activity, location and call logs to achieve Mean Average Error (MAE) between 0.39–0.61.

Past research provided a solid foundation of using smartphone data to infer personality traits, relying on datasets collected over several weeks and months to a few years. Yet, it remains unclear if data collection can be reduced in time while still achieving a comparable accuracy to the models developed using more longitudinal data. This would mitigate the cold-start problem and help service providers to enable data minimisation principles of privacy laws, while not sacrificing the quality of services. We believe that our work provides a contribution on that front.

3   Methodology

For this work, we used data from (1) smartphone sensors (microphone, light, accelerometer, pedometer, location), (2) usage logs (phone unlocks, screen on/off, battery level and charging, calls), collected using an Android app - summarised in Table 1. The data sampling was optimised for a low battery consumption which resulted in no complaints from users about the battery consumption. Phone unlock events, screen on/off, battery charging logs and calls were captured for every event. Data from the microphone, pedometer, location and light sensors was collected every 15 min, while data from the accelerometer was sampled when it was detected that a person was moving.

Table 1. Data categories

Category	Description	Num of daily features
Light	Provides the intensity of light in lux	5
Noise	Provides the level of noise in dB	15
Battery	Provides battery level, charging state	2
Accelerometer	Provides 3D acceleration during activity	12
Call	Provides duration, number and state of calls	9
Unlock	Provides screen on/off, phone lock state	9
Pedometer	Provides step count during an activity	5
Location	Provides GPS coordinates (Latitude and longitude)	13

Participants were recruited through a specialised agency from February to August 2018. They were asked to install and keep the app active for 3 weeks, which was followed by completing a set of onboarding questionnaires that included demographics (gender, age, socioeconomic status, etc.) and the 50 item Big Five personality inventory [10]. Following the GDPR, participants were presented with details about the purpose of the study and the data collected, and were enrolled in the study only upon providing their consent. They also had the flexibility to decide which sensor information they would like to be recorded, which resulted in 69% of participants providing partial data only. On successful completion, each participant received a monetary incentive of 40 EUR.

3.1 Participants

From over 1000 potential participants who were selected in this study trial, 545 participants from five countries successfully completed the study. However, due to missing sensor data the number of participants used for this analysis dropped to $N = 166$ (Spain $N = 69$, Peru $N = 25$, Colombia $N = 21$, Chile $N = 24$ and the United Kingdom $N = 27$). The gender ratio (female:male) for the eligible participants was roughly 1:2 and the age groups of the participants ranged between 18–25 ($N - 30$), 26–34 ($N = 118$) and 35–44 ($N - 18$). Within each country, the gender ratio and age range ratio was roughly the same, as well as personality distributions. Importantly, distributions of the five personality scores with and without drop-outs did not significantly differ i.e. participants who dropped-out did not differ in personality from the rest of the sample.

3.2 Feature Extraction

Using the collected data, we first extracted a set of daily features that describe typical patterns of user behaviour and contexts during a day (e.g. mean level of light and noise during the morning or evening, distance travelled per day, radius of gyration, etc.) - similar to the previous literature [26,27]. Overall, 70 daily features were created from the categories described in Table 1, and each day was tagged as a weekday or a weekend day. Table 1 also shows the number of daily features obtained from each category.

Using the tagged days, the data was then clustered into weekdays and week-end days. For each of the time periods, we also calculated the Routine Index, as defined in [2]. As participants typically finished participation during the third week of the study, we rarely collected the data from all three weeks at an individual level, and therefore we sub-sampled two weeks of data. We randomly selected four weekdays from the sub-sampled set, in order to use the same number of weekdays and weekend days when comparing the corresponding model accuracy. We aggregated the data during weekends and weekdays per participant, and extracted features by using descriptive statistics (mean and standard deviation) to describe typical behaviour during weekdays and during weekends. In this manner, we obtained 142 features for weekdays and 142 features for weekends.

3.3 Model

We approach personality inference as a machine learning classification problem. We split participants into two classes – above and below the median value of the Big Five scores (Table 2) – for each of the five traits. This approach yields two balanced classes for developing each of the five classification models, which was commonly applied in personality detection literature [4,5,24,26].

Initially, we tested several classifiers, including Support Vector Machine, Bayes Naive Classifier and Nearest Neighbour, and we chose Random Forest as it outperformed the other methods. Random Forest has already been used for classification of personality traits in [4,24] - it is a technique that typically does not require an extensive parameter tuning and feature selection. However, due to the number of features (142) in our case, feature selection brought performance improvements. We performed Recursive Feature Elimination in each step of the leave-one-out train-test method, that we used for the classifier accuracy assessment. In this way, the classifier was sequentially trained with the data from all but one user, tested with the data from the "left-out" user, and this process was repeated for all the users. As the performance metrics, we report the accuracy (Acc) of the classifier and the Cohen's Kappa (κ) value. The κ value represents the improvement over the random classification. As we used the median value to create two classes of users, random classification by assigning 1 value to all users produces Acc $\approx 50\%$ and $\kappa \approx 0$.

4 Results

4.1 Questionnaire Analysis

The Big Five personality dimensions include Extraversion, Agreeableness, Conscientiousness, Neuroticism and Openness that are obtained from the 50 item International Personality Item Pool [10]. The questionnaire asks users to rate their behaviours from 1–5 on a Likert scale, and each of the five traits is assessed through 10 questions with the aggregated score ranging from 10 to 50. The

Table 2. Statistics for the Big Five personality scores

Statistic	Extraversion	Agree.	Consc.	Neuroticism	Openness
Mean	30.01	39.50	34.17	29.34	36.81
Std. dev	7.42	5.56	5.55	7.83	5.01
Median	31.0	40.0	34.0	30.0	37.0
Max	48.0	50.0	50.0	48.0	50.0
Min	10.0	14.0	18.0	10.0	19.0

statistics of the scores for the Big Five traits are summarised in Table 2, and are comparable to past literature [24]. The scores also showed a good internal reliability, with Cronbach's alpha > 0.7 for all traits, also being in line with previous literature [11].

4.2 Personality Trait Inference

Table 3 presents the accuracy of the personality classification models - note that we removed the results with Acc $< 65\%$ or $\kappa < 0.3$ (denoted as '-' in the table). Although lower accuracy results have been reported in previous work, we set the threshold of 65% for classification accuracy as sufficient, based on [20]. For comparison with the models that rely on reduced datasets, we first developed a 'reference' model by using features computed using the full data set – 2 weeks of smartphone data collected during both weekdays and weekends. The reference model was able to accurately classify between 68% and 73% of users for Openness, Agreeableness, Extraversion, Conscientiousness and Neuroticism, in ascending order of performance, with κ ranging from 0.34–0.46. Our methodology, and moreover the results, are highly consistent with state-of-the-art work in personality classification [4,5,24].

Table 3. Results obtained from the prediction of personality traits

Model/Type of day used	Personality trait									
	Extra.		Agree.		Consc.		Neur.		Open.	
	Acc (%)	κ	Acc (%)	κ	Acc (%)	κ	Acc (%)	κ	Acc (%)	κ
Full dataset (2 weeks)	71	0.43	70	0.39	71	0.38	73	0.46	68	0.34
Weekend (2 weeks)	69	0.38	71	0.41	71	0.4	70	0.38	66	0.3
Weekday (2 weeks)	–	–	67	0.34	70	0.38	68	0.36	–	–
Weekend (1 week)	67	0.35	66	0.31	68	0.35	67	0.34	–	–
Weekday (1 week)	–	–	–	–	66	0.31	–	–	–	–
Saturday	–	–	–	–	68	0.33	67	0.34	–	–
Sunday	–	–	67	0.33	66	0.28	–	–	–	–
Random weekday	–	–	–	–	–	–	65	0.3	–	–

1. Weekend vs Weekdays Model. To compare the predictive power of weekends and weekdays, we developed two consistent classification models by using 142 features only from weekends and only from weekdays respectively. To allow for a fair comparison, we randomly selected an equal number (i.e. four) of weekdays for computing the features and repeated the classification 10 times to ensure that we covered all the combinations. We observed that the model based on behavioural features extracted during two weekends was able to classify all the five personality traits with accuracy comparable to the reference model that relied on 14 days of data – with only 1–3% difference. The reference model was built using features from both weekend and weekdays, however it appears to provide only a marginal improvement over the weekend model. The model that relied only on weekdays classified Agreeableness, Conscientiousness and Neuroticsm with 67%, 70% and 68% respectively, while not reaching the threshold of 65% in predicting Extraversion and Openness. The weekend model significantly outperformed the weekday model for Extraversion, Agreeableness and Openness (McNemar's test, $p < 0.01$).

2. One vs Two Weekends Model. To further attempt to reduce duration of smartphone data used for personality classification, we evaluated a classification model developed using the features extracted from one weekend only. The accuracy dropped in comparison to the two-weekends model and to the reference model by 2% to 6%, while not being able to detect Openness. However, the accuracy in detecting Extraversion, Agreeableness, Conscientiousness, and Neuroticism were above the threshold of 65%, despite using only one weekend (i.e. the data from two weekend days). We also compared this model with a model that uses features computed from two randomly selected weekdays and we observed statistically significant differences for prediction of all five traits - Agreeableness (McNemar's test, $p < 0.001$), Conscientiousness, Openness, Extraversion, Neuroticism (McNemar's test, $p < 0.05$). This further indicates the value that weekend behaviours bring to the personality modelling in comparison to weekdays.

3. One Day Model. Next we attempted to further reduce the dataset to one day. Given the results from one weekend data, we aimed to evaluate which of the two weekend days is more predictive of traits - Saturday or Sunday. We compare the two models by selecting a random Saturday and a random Sunday, and also a random weekday for comparison (as in the previous cases, we repeated this procedure 10 times). Interestingly, the Saturday model was able to predict Conscientiousness and Neuroticism, the Sunday model was able to predict Agreeableness, and Conscientiousness - with a moderately good accuracy above the threshold of 65%. McNemar's test indicated that the models obtained from Saturday and Sunday were significantly different for Agreeableness and Neuroticism ($p < 0.05$). A random weekday model was not capable of classifying 4 out of the 5 traits, reaching 65% only for Neuroticism. We also attempted to classify

the traits by specifically selecting a single day of the week (e.g. Monday). This produced inadequate results and are not reported here.

5 Discussion and Conclusion

Personality has been in the focus of HCI researchers for its importance in understanding user needs, preferences and satisfaction with technologies, as well as for building more personalised services. Our study provides evidence that (1) smartphone data collected during weekends has a stronger predictive power than weekday data for inferring personality traits, (2) only 2–4 days of smartphone data can be enough for achieving state-of-the-art accuracy in personality classification. We believe that this work has two main implications – takeaways for enabling data minimisation, that is one of the key principles in privacy as well as lessons for shortening the time period needed for delivering customised services based on personality.

In multiple tests (Table 3) we observed that the smartphone data collected during weekends was significantly more predictive for inferring personality traits. Interestingly, by using two weekends i.e. four weekend days, the accuracy was highly comparable with previous personality classification studies that relied on several weeks or months (in a few cases even years) of data. During weekends people typically have more control over their activities in comparison to working days, which was explored by social scientists but it is also not difficult to intuitively deduce some differences. This served as a rationale for our study in which the weekend behaviours turned out to be more informative of individuals' personality (note that the literature has not explored how personality is manifested during working versus non-working days). Our future research will explore if further improvements can be achieved by distinguishing working and non-working days at an individual level instead of weekend versus weekdays.

In practical terms, using two weekends of data does not resolve the cold-start problem as the user would still need to wait for almost two weeks until the service models his/her personality and becomes more personalised. However, our findings suggest the possibility to reduce the data retained at the service side, as a user's engagement is frequently affected by privacy concerns related to the amount of collected data. Moreover, minimising the personal data required for delivering a service is a core component in privacy guidelines. Further research in this direction can also probe the sensor modalities that are more important for personality prediction over others.

In the context of the cold-start problem, our results indicate that it is possible to detect 4 out of 5 traits with an accuracy of above 65% by using one weekend, or 3 traits by using only one weekend day. In practice, if a user did not install a service just before the weekend, it would still require several days until the modelling has been completed, yet this process significantly reduces the time needed for the personality inference.

We hope that our study will motivate further work on data minimisation approaches, not only because of privacy regulations but also to encourage applying principles of ethical computing. We also believe that our study will inspire

psychologists to delve deeper into manifestation of personality during different days of the week.

Acknowledgements. This work has been supported by the European Union's Horizon 2020 research and innovation programme, under the Marie Sklodowska-Curie grant agreement no. 722561.

References

1. Abel, F., Henze, N., Herder, E., Krause, D.: Interweaving public user profiles on the web. In: De Bra, P., Kobsa, A., Chin, D. (eds.) UMAP 2010. LNCS, vol. 6075, pp. 16–27. Springer, Heidelberg (2010). https://doi.org/10.1007/978-3-642-13470-8_4
2. Canzian, L., Musolesi, M.: Trajectories of depression: unobtrusive monitoring of depressive states by means of smartphone mobility traces analysis. In: Proceedings of the 2015 ACM international joint conference on pervasive and ubiquitous computing, pp. 1293–1304. ACM (2015)
3. Catal, C., et al.: Cross-cultural personality prediction based on twitter data. J. Softw. **12**(11), 882–892 (2017)
4. Chittaranjan, G., Blom, J., Gatica-Perez, D.: Who's who with big-five: analyzing and classifying personality traits with smartphones. In: 2011 15th Annual International Symposium on Wearable Computers (ISWC), pp. 29–36. IEEE (2011)
5. Chittaranjan, G., Blom, J., Gatica-Perez, D.: Mining large-scale smartphone data for personality studies. Pers. Ubiquit. Comput. **17**(3), 433–450 (2013)
6. Corr, P.J., Matthews, G.: The Cambridge handbook of personality psychology. Cambridge University Press Cambridge, UK (2009)
7. DeYoung, C.G., Gray, J.R.: Personality neuroscience: explaining individual differences in affect, behaviour and cognition. In: The Cambridge handbook of personality psychology, pp. 323–346 (2009)
8. Ferwerda, B., Schedl, M.: Personality-based user modeling for music recommender systems. In: Berendt, B., et al. (eds.) ECML PKDD 2016. LNCS (LNAI), vol. 9853, pp. 254–257. Springer, Cham (2016). https://doi.org/10.1007/978-3-319-46131-1_29
9. Ferwerda, B., Tkalcic, M.: You are what you post: what the content of instagram pictures tells about users' personality. In: The 23rd International on Intelligent User Interfaces (2018)
10. Goldberg, L.R., et al.: The international personality item pool and the future of public-domain personality measures. J. Res. Pers. **40**(1), 84–96 (2006)
11. Gow, A.J., Whiteman, M.C., Pattie, A., Deary, I.J.: Goldberg's 'IPIP' big-five factor markers: internal consistency and concurrent validation in Scotland. Pers. Individ. Differ. **39**(2), 317–329 (2005)
12. Jia, Y., et al.: Personality-targeted gamification: a survey study on personality traits and motivational affordances. In: Proceedings of the 2016 CHI Conference on Human Factors in Computing Systems, pp. 2001–2013. ACM (2016)
13. Lee, M.J., Ferwerda, B.: Personalizing online educational tools. In: Proceedings of the 2017 ACM Workshop on Theory-Informed User Modeling for Tailoring and Personalizing Interfaces, pp. 27–30. ACM (2017)
14. Minamikawa, A., Yokoyama, H.: Blog tells what kind of personality you have: egogram estimation from japanese weblog. In: Proceedings of the ACM 2011 Conference on Computer Supported Cooperative Work, pp. 217–220. ACM (2011)

15. Mønsted, B., Mollgaard, A., Mathiesen, J.: Phone-based metric as a predictor for basic personality traits. J. Res. Pers. **74**, 16–22 (2018)
16. de Montjoye, Y.-A., Quoidbach, J., Robic, F., Pentland, A.S.: Predicting personality using novel mobile phone-based metrics. In: Greenberg, A.M., Kennedy, W.G., Bos, N.D. (eds.) SBP 2013. LNCS, vol. 7812, pp. 48–55. Springer, Heidelberg (2013). https://doi.org/10.1007/978-3-642-37210-0_6
17. de Oliveira, R., Cherubini, M., Oliver, N.: Influence of personality on satisfaction with mobile phone services. ACM Transact. Comput. Hum. Inter. (TOCHI) **20**(2), 10 (2013)
18. de Oliveira, R., et al.: Towards a psychographic user model from mobile phone usage. In: CHI 2011 Extended Abstracts on Human Factors in Computing Systems, pp. 2191–2196. ACM (2011)
19. Orji, R., Nacke, L.E., Di Marco, C.: Towards personality-driven persuasive health games and gamified systems. In: Proceedings of the 2017 CHI Conference on Human Factors in Computing Systems, pp. 1015–1027. ACM (2017)
20. Park, S., Matic, A., Garg, K., Oliver, N.: When simpler data does not imply less information: a study of user profiling scenarios with constrained view of mobile HTTP(s) traffic. ACM Transact. Web (TWEB) **12**(2), 9 (2018)
21. Raber, F., Krueger, A.: Towards understanding the influence of personality on mobile app permission settings. In: Bernhaupt, R., Dalvi, G., Joshi, A., K. Balkrishan, D., O'Neill, J., Winckler, M. (eds.) INTERACT 2017. LNCS, vol. 10516, pp. 62–82. Springer, Cham (2017). https://doi.org/10.1007/978-3-319-68059-0_4
22. Ryan, R.M., Bernstein, J.H., Brown, K.W.: Weekends, work, and well-being: psychological need satisfactions and day of the week effects on mood, vitality, and physical symptoms. J. Soc. Clin. Psychol. **29**(1), 95–122 (2010)
23. Staddon, J., Huffaker, D., Brown, L., Sedley, A.: Are privacy concerns a turn-off?: engagement and privacy in social networks. In: Proceedings of the Eighth Symposium on Usable Privacy and Security, p. 10. ACM (2012)
24. Staiano, J., Lepri, B., Aharony, N., Pianesi, F., Sebe, N., Pentland, A.: Friends don't lie: inferring personality traits from social network structure. In: Proceedings of the 2012 ACM conference on ubiquitous computing, pp. 321–330. ACM (2012)
25. Tene, O., Polonetsky, J.: Big data for all: privacy and user control in the age of analytics. Nw. J. Tech. Intell. Prop. 11, xxvii (2012)
26. Vinciarelli, A., Mohammadi, G.: A survey of personality computing. IEEE Transact. Affect. Comput. **5**(3), 273–291 (2014)
27. Wang, W., et al.: Sensing behavioral change over time: Using within-person variability features from mobile sensing to predict personality traits. Proc. ACM Interact. Mobile Wearable Ubiquit. Technol. **2**(3), 141 (2018)
28. Xu, R., Frey, R.M., Fleisch, E., Ilic, A.: Understanding the impact of personality traits on mobile app adoption-insights from a large-scale field study. Comput. Hum. Behav. **62**, 244–256 (2016)
29. Yee, N., et al.: Introverted elves & conscientious gnomes: the expression of personality in world of warcraft. In: Proceedings of the SIGCHI Conference on Human Factors in Computing Systems pp. 753–762. ACM (2011)
30. Zuzanek, J., Smale, B.J.A.: Life-Cycle and across-the-week allocation of time to daily activities. In: Pentland, W.E., Harvey, A.S., Lawton, M.P., McColl, M.A. (eds.) Time Use Research in the Social Sciences. Springer, Boston (2002). https://doi.org/10.1007/0-306-47155-8_6

Social Influence Scale for Technology Design and Transformation

Agnis Stibe[1(⊠)] and Brian Cugelman[2,3]

[1] ESLSCA Business School Paris, Paris, France
agnis@transforms.me
[2] Statistical Cybermetrics Research Group, University of Wolverhampton,
Wolverhampton, UK
[3] AlterSpark, Toronto, ON, Canada
brian@alterspark.com

Abstract. Contrary to popular belief, social influence encompasses a much more complex area of behavioral science than the explanation offered by those who call all forms of social influence a social norm, peer pressure, or simply social proof. To help scholars and practitioners develop a deeper understanding of social influence, this study presents a measurement instrument for evaluating susceptibility to seven social influence principles, namely social learning, social comparison, social norms, social facilitation, social cooperation, social competition, and social recognition. Each principle is represented by a construct containing six theory-driven items, both positively and negatively framed. Further, the study introduces a social influence research model that describes how the seven social influence constructs are correlated and impact each other. This study extends previous scientific work on social influence by providing research tools that can be used to further study the role of social influence in designing tailored technologies for transformation.

Keywords: Social influence · Transformation · Persuasive technology · Design · Behavior change · Human-computer interaction · Socially Influencing Systems

1 Introduction

This work is emerging as an inevitable response to the ever-growing imbalance in our lives across the globe [42]. Over the decades, advanced technologies are researched designed to make our lives better [1] and businesses growing. The fundamental question still remains: with all the evolving innovations, are we gaining decent success in achieving happier societies [8] and solid organizations?

Every crucial domain of our lives continuously provides evidence of how things are getting imbalanced despite us making huge progress in building increasingly capable technological innovations, such as artificial intelligence, blockchain, augmented reality, autonomous vehicles, and drones, just to name a few. This work summarizes the state-of-the-art scientific insights and applicable research tools to transform lives and businesses globally.

© IFIP International Federation for Information Processing 2019
Published by Springer Nature Switzerland AG 2019
D. Lamas et al. (Eds.): INTERACT 2019, LNCS 11748, pp. 561–577, 2019.
https://doi.org/10.1007/978-3-030-29387-1_33

Research on designing technologies that influence people's beliefs, attitudes, and behaviors, has been steadily advancing for more than a decade after the release of the seminal book on *persuasive technology* by Fogg [18]. Scholars have been continuously expanding and providing various taxonomies, lists of influence principles, and design techniques for behavior change and transformation, e.g., Cugelman et al. [12], Harjumaa [21], Michie et al. [30], Stibe [44], and others.

Although these taxonomies are all focused on using technology to influence what people think and do, their character and qualities differ, as recently highlighted by Stibe et al. [42] in their work on *transforming wellbeing theory*. Persuasive and transforming technologies influence users' attitudes and behaviors using a variety of principles from behavioral psychology, particularly those from persuasion and social influence.

The terms *persuasion* and *social influence* are often used interchangeably when explaining how someone's behavior or attitudes are changed by the influence of other people [45]. Although both can influence people's attitudes and behaviors, earlier research suggests that persuasion and social influence operate through distinct mechanisms [22, 23], and therefore should be applied with an understanding of each distinct approach.

According to Wood [52], on the one hand *persuasion* typically relies on detailed argumentation presented to people without engaging in active social interaction. On the other hand, *social influence* is usually present and becomes possible within active and complex social settings. O'Keefe [34] has argued that persuasion mainly is built upon reasoning and argument to steer people according to a desired agenda, but social influence is commonly enabled and facilitated by the behavior and actions of surrounding people. Further, Stibe et al. [42] have explained that, in contract to traditional tactics of persuasion, social influence can serve as much stronger catalyst for achieving sustainable changes, i.e. transformation.

2   Research Questions

Social influence describes the psychological principles that exert various effects on people's attitudes and behaviors through the actual, imagined, or implied presence of other people [39]. Often, social influence is also addressed in relation to areas of minority influence in group settings, dynamic social impact theory, expectation states theory, and persuasion [11].

Social norms and social proof have been the most commonly used terms to describe influence effects. However, according to Stibe et al. [43–47], there is far more diversity and depth to social influence that what is conventionally described by these popular terms.

For these reasons, this study further investigates the multifaceted nature of social influence by addressing the following research questions:

- RQ1: *What measurement instrument can help assess and evaluate each distinct social influence principle?*
- RQ2: *How do the social influence principles relate to each other?*

To address these research questions, this study reviews relevant background literature, develops and presents a measurement instrument for studying social influence principles, tests and validates a new social influence scale though an online survey, and then introduces a social influence research model that describes how social influence principles impact each other when used simultaneously.

3 Socially Influencing Systems

Over the last years, many scholars have studied social influence in numerous persuasive and transforming technology applications. Stibe [43–45] introduced a framework for *Socially Influencing Systems* (SIS), which has been used to design and evaluate technology that improves employee engagement in bicycling to work [31, 46]. Oyibo and Vassileva [37] have used the SIS framework to investigate social predictors of competitive behavior. Orji [35] has employed it to support an exploration of the strengths and weaknesses of socially-oriented persuasive strategies.

The SIS framework has been applied to studies on design choices for health behavior change [32], persuasive strategies to encourage low-energy mobility [53], co-creation for living mobility [5], digital games for social persuasion to prevent speeding [28], and persuasive practices for home security advisory services [16]. It has also been used by Myneni and Iyengar [33] to study health promotion technology, Wais-Zechmann et al. [50] on investigating the personalized strategies, and Hamari et al. [20] for gamification.

The seven principles of social influence within the SIS framework were derived from multiple studies and theories across the social sciences, social psychology, and other disciplines. The following seven sub-sections introduce each principle, provide background, and illustrate how to apply each principle. Figure 1 provides a graphical representation of the seven principles and their dominant sub-dimensions.

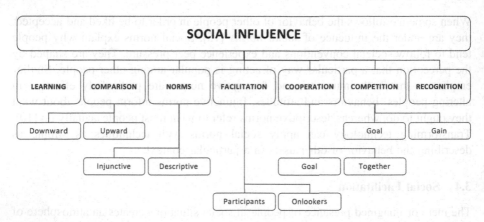

Fig. 1. Seven social influence principles with their sub-dimensions.

3.1 Social Learning

Within a social context, people learn from others by observing their behaviors [3]. This implies that the transmission of information from one individual to another happens through imitation, teaching, and spoken or written language. According to Bandura [3], *social learning* is ubiquitous and potent because it allows people to avoid the costs of individual learning. Essentially, social learning is about learning new behaviors by watching others perform them. An example includes enabling users of a transforming technology to see others are using it, when, how long, and in what way. Social learning is frequently employed by "how-to" videos that demonstrate someone performing each step in a process.

3.2 Social Comparison

When people use information about others to evaluate themselves, they engage in social comparison [17]. More precisely, social comparison is defined as the process of thinking about others in relation to oneself [51]. This process influences motivation, as people look for self-enhancement when comparing themselves with others who are worse off, or they look for self-improvement when seeking a positive example for comparison. In short, social comparison emerges as soon as an individual compares his or her behavior with others who are performing the same behavior in the same context.

An example includes a transforming technology that displays the names of active users in larger font sizes, compared to infrequent users whose names are represented in small fonts. Many gamification design patterns employ leaderboards, which force users into a social comparison ranking system, and these are often implemented without an understanding of negative social comparison, as the bottom of the leader board is a backfire design pattern called a 'loser board', a source of negative social comparison.

3.3 Social Norms

When someone follows the behavior of other people in order to be liked and accepted, they are under the influence of *social norms* [15]. Social norms explain why people tend to follow societal conventions and experience peer pressure. They are shaped by the perception that a particular way of acting is popular among other people. Studies emphasize that both injunctive and descriptive norms are particularly effective in altering peoples' behaviors and attitudes. Injunctive norms inform people about what they ought to do, whereas descriptive norms refer to what most people actually do [10]. Transforming technology can apply social norms with techniques as simple as describing the behavior of other users in a particular context.

3.4 Social Facilitation

The mere or imagined presence of people in social situations creates an atmosphere of evaluation, which enhances users' performance, speed, and accuracy of well-practiced tasks, but reduces their performance for less familiar tasks. *Social facilitation* effects occur in the presence of both passive onlookers and people who are actively engaged in

the same activity [54]. At its core, social facilitation emerges when an individual is surrounded by others who are co-performing or watching what he or she is doing. For example, a transforming technology can show users who are engaged in a common task, that other people are able to see what they are doing.

3.5 Social Cooperation

Social cooperation is an activity aimed at working together or achieving a common goal. This interpersonal factor provides important intrinsic motivation that would not be present in the absence of other people [26]. Cooperation is directed toward the same social end by at least two individuals [29]. On a social level, people cooperate when they are working together, or when they are striving to achieve common goals. With independent tasks, combining the progress of different people can encourage cooperation [26]. An example of applications in transforming technology is highlighting how much all users have achieved together.

3.6 Social Competition

Another interpersonal factor that provides important intrinsic motivation in social contexts is *social competition* [26]. People compete when they are striving to achieve the same goal that is scarce or when they seek to gain the same outcome that another person is pursuing. When independent tasks are accompanied by metrics that inform users about the performance of others, this creates a competitive environment where users can compare their performances against others [26]. For example, a transforming technology can show an ordered list of users based on their achievements, with a special place for the most successful users.

3.7 Social Recognition

People experience a positive emotional reward of *social recognition* after receiving an acknowledgement for success related to competing or cooperating with others [41]. In other words, recognition can be described as a value that individuals derive from gaining public appreciation and acknowledgement from others in front of an audience. For example, a transforming technology can provide or assign special titles (as badges of honor) in a way that is visible to all the other users.

4 Social Influence Scale

Despite growing research on the use of social influence in technology design and transformation, scholars lack suitable measurement tools, which limits their ability to conduct empirical studies on social influence. Thus, the study here addresses the first research question.

RQ1: What measurement instrument can help assess and evaluate each distinct social influence principle?

Whereas prior social influence scales have been developed to help researchers assess which social influence principles are being applied in a given technology [43–46], the social influence scale in this paper measures personal differences in susceptibility to social influence principles. This extends the method applied previously, which measured susceptibility to persuasion [24].

In developing the current scale, the authors began by pooling psychometric constructs and indicators from social influence scales previously introduced by Stibe et al. [43–46]. These prior studies were used to frame the constructs for each social influence principle and their respective measurement items.

Working within these frameworks and drawing on literature from social psychology, the authors developed survey items focused on identifying personality-based predisposition towards particular social influence principles, based on emotional, cognitive and behavioral differences between people.

Table 1 lists the seven constructs, each with six indicator items, both positively and those with a (*) being negatively framed, for measuring and assessing each construct, along with their combined factor loadings.

Table 1. The social influence scale and combined loadings.

Construct	Items	Load
Social learning	I prefer learning new things by watching others	.821
	I learn new skills by observing others	.858
	I learn new skills by watching others	.608
	To improve my skills, I learn best by observing others	.669
	I don't learn by watching others*	.857
	I don't watch others to learn new things*	.866
Social comparison	I don't compare myself to other people*	.922
	I compare myself to other people	.829
	I frequently compare how I am doing, relative to other people	.921
	I am uninterested in comparing myself against others*	.887
	I never compare myself to other people*	.796
	I assess my performance against others	.907
Social norms	I prefer to do what other people typically do	.762
	I prefer to act the way everyone else is acting	.861
	I follow behaviors that people typically do	.851
	I avoid acting in a way that is uncommon*	.714
	I don't like to do what people typically do*	.734
	I don't copy the behaviors that everyone else does*	.562
Social facilitation	When I realize people are working on something important to me, I also want to start doing it	.880
	When people are doing something that interests me, I think about doing it also	.846

(continued)

Table 1. (*continued*)

Construct	Items	Load
	When I see people doing something that inspires me, I want to do it as well	.392
	When I see people doing something I'm interested in, I feel like doing it too	.608
	When I observe people doing something important to me, it has no impact on my desire to start*	.830
	When I see people doing something relevant to me, I feel no desire to start doing it*	.853
Social cooperation	I don't like to collaborate with people*	.917
	I enjoy collaborating with people	.856
	I like to co-create with others	.697
	I like to build things with other people	.858
	I avoid invitations to collaborate with people*	.766
	I enjoy working with other people, rather than working alone	.903
Social competition	I dislike competitions*	.911
	I don't like to compete with people*	.921
	I enjoy participating in competitions	.902
	I am not a competitive person by nature*	.911
	I enjoy competing with others	.875
	I am a competitive person	.855
Social recognition	I don't like to receive acknowledgements in public*	.893
	I enjoy when my achievements are acknowledged in public	.936
	I would rather avoid being recognized in public for my achievements*	.931
	I like to be honored in public	.904
	I feel exited when I am publicly recognized for my accomplishments	.868
	I don't want my achievements to be recognized in front of others*	.803

5 Data Collection and Scale Validation

The social influence scale was developed through two stages, including three studies with exploratory factor analysis and confirmatory structural equation modelling. The first and second studies employed exploratory factor analysis to identify the factor structure. The third employed a confirmatory study to assess the scale overall goodness of fit.

In all studies, participants were recruited from Amazon's Mechanical Turk, within the United States. In each study, participants responded to statements using seven-point semantic differential scales, with the option of responding "I cannot say". Survey design followed standards for web-based surveys [14]. All questionnaires included attention and fraud detection tests, to identify insincere respondents, based on standard practice for ensuring quality samples from the Mechanical Turk [9].

5.1 Exploratory Factor Analysis

The first two studies employed exploratory factor analysis [36] for scale development, with a focus on evaluating item comprehension and validating construct validity. The first study ran in early February 2018 with 162 participants, the removal of 26 responses that were incomplete or failed our attention tests, leaving 136 responses for analysis. The second study ran in late February 2018 with 151 participants, with 16 removed for failing to pass our attention tests, leaving 135 for the analysis.

5.2 Confirmatory Structural Equation Modelling

The third study employed confirmatory structural equation modelling to assess the scale's theoretical relationships, construct validity and overall model fit. The final online questionnaire ran in March 2018 and collected feedback from 165 participants. After removing 22 responses that were incomplete or failed our attention tests, 125 responses were included in the final analysis.

Among the participants, there were 69 females (55.2%) and 56 males (44.8%). The age of the participants ranged between 21 and 82 years, with the mean age being 44 years. All of these participants marked that they understood and spoke English fluently like a native speaker. The data was analyzed with partial least squares structural equation modeling (PLS-SEM) using WarpPLS 6.0 software. This method was selected because it well suits the needs of exploratory research and is appropriate for predictive approach rather than testing an established theory [19]. Data analysis with PLS-SEM included both assessment of the reliability and validity of the measurement model and assessment of the structural model.

The measurement model includes the relationships between the constructs (Table 2) and the indicators used to measure them (Table 1). The measurement instrument for this study was developed based on the theory-driven items, which were pretested with two scholars of transforming technology and through two rounds of pilot studies involving 271 participants. Further, the properties of the developed scale were assessed in terms of item loadings, discriminant validity, and internal consistency, where item loadings and internal consistencies greater than .70 are considered acceptable (Table 2).

The constructs in the model display good internal consistency, with composite reliability scores ranging from .88 to .96. Inspection of the construct correlations and square root of the average variance extracted in Table 2 demonstrate that all constructs share more variance with their own items than with other constructs, thus providing support for internal consistency of the factor structures.

6 Social Influence Model

By better understanding how social influence principles are related to one another, researchers will be better equipped to study social influence, while practitioners will be better equipped to apply it. This section addresses the second research question.

RQ2: How do the social influence principles relate to each other?

To answer this question, the structural model of social influence (Fig. 2) originated from and was shaped upon the strongest correlations between constructs, which were observable from the measurement model (Table 2), and previous scientific literature on the SIS framework [43–46] supporting the emerging relationships.

Table 2. Latent variable coefficients and correlations.

	COOP	CMPE	NORM	RECO	CMPA	FACI	LEAR
COR	.93	.96	.89	.96	.95	.88	.91
CRA	.91	.95	.85	.95	.94	.84	.87
AVE	.70	.80	.57	.79	.77	.57	.62
VIF	1.6	1.4	1.5	1.4	1.5	1.7	1.6
COOP	**.84**						
CMPE	.32	**.90**					
NORM	.33	.16	**.75**				
RECO	.44	.41	.21	**.89**			
CMPA	.18	.38	.33	.35	**.88**		
FACI	.42	.29	.44	.30	.42	**.76**	
LEAR	.36	.01	.48	.14	.28	.48	**.79**

COR = composite reliability; CRA = Cronbach's alpha;
VIF = variance inflation factor (full collinearity);
Bolded diagonal = square root of average variance extracted (AVE);
COOP = cooperation;   CMPE = competition;   NORM = norms;
RECO = recognition;   CMPA = comparison;   FACI = facilitation;
LEAR = learning

In the analysis of the research model, a PLS mode M regression algorithm was used, in which the measurement model weights were calculated through a least squares regression, where the latent variable or construct score is the predictor and the indicators or items are the criteria [25]. As it can be observed from Fig. 2, the results of the PLS-SEM analysis provide substantial support for the structural research model. It reveals that the seven social influence features are intricately interconnected.

Social facilitation is the only independent construct having no inbound arrows in the social influence model. Social facilitation has direct arrows pointing to four other constructs, i.e. social comparison, social cooperation, social learning, and social norms. In the social influence model, social facilitation alone explains 18% of the variance in social comparison, which explains 16% of the variance in social competition, which explains 17% of the variance in social recognition. Further, social facilitation and social recognition equally contribute in explaining 30% of the variance in social cooperation. Both, social facilitation and social cooperation together are explaining 31% of the variance in social learning, where social facilitation provides a larger contribution of 21%, comparing to 10% of variance from social cooperation. social facilitation and social learning together explain 30% of the variance in social norms, but in this case, social learning turns out to be larger contributor by explaining 18% as compared to 12% coming from social facilitation.

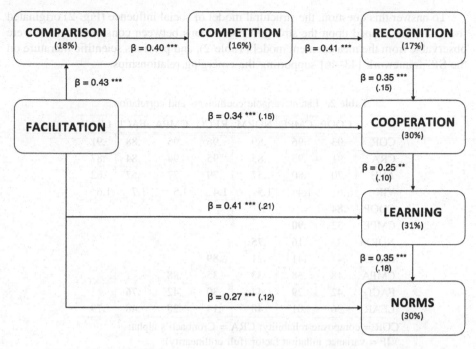

Fig. 2. The social influence model overlaid with the PLS-SEM analysis results.

The β values attached to each arrow (Fig. 2) demonstrate the strength of relationships between the constructs and the asterisks mark their statistical significance, while the R-squared contributions are presented in brackets.

Table 3. Total effects and effect sizes.

	FACI	CMPA	CMPE	RECO	COOP	LEAR
CMPA	.43*** (.18)					
CMPE	.17** (.05)	.40*** (.16)				
RECO	.07 (.02)	.17** (.06)	.41*** (.17)			
COOP	.37*** (.16)	.06 (.01)	.14* (.05)	.35*** (.15)		
LEAR	.50*** (.25)	.02 (.00)	.04 (.00)	.09 (.01)	.25** (.10)	
NORM	.45*** (.21)	.01 (.00)	.01 (.00)	.03 (.01)	.09 (.03)	.35*** (.18)

***p < .001; **p < .01; *p < .05; (f²) = Cohen's f-squared
FACI has no inbound arrows (row is blank)
NORM has no outbound arrows (column is blank)
FACI = facilitation; CMPA = comparison; CMPE = competition;
RECO = recognition; COOP = cooperation; LEAR = learning;
NORM = norms

Table 3 presents a detailed view of the social influence model, with total effects and effect sizes. Effect sizes (f^2) determine whether the effects indicated by the path coefficients are small (.02), medium (.15), or large (.35).

Additionally, the results of PLS-SEM analysis provide fit and quality indices that support the structural model [25]. Besides reporting the values of average path coefficient (APC = .357, p < .001) and average R-squared (ARS = .238, p < .001), the model demonstrates a large explanatory power (GoF = .405). Moreover, both Sympson's paradox ratio (SPR = 1.000) and the nonlinear bivariate causality direction ratio (NLBCDR = 1.000) provide evidence that the social influence model is free from Sympson's paradox instances, and the direction of causality is supported.

7 Discussion

This study has reviewed key principles in social influence and presented a scale for evaluating users' predisposition towards particular social influence principles. The study contributes empirical evidence in support of an advanced social influence scale and demonstrates its structural model. The results also advance the previous work on the SIS framework that has already demonstrated the strength and prominence of social influence principles in designing human-computer interaction and transforming technology [43–46].

This study demonstrated that the seven social influence principles influence each other at various levels. Social facilitation has the capacity to directly trigger and initiate four other principles. This can be explained by the inherent nature of social facilitation [54], as it increases motivation in the presence of other people, which is difficult to avoid in common interactive social technology. Additionally, social facilitation also exhibits a moderate but significant indirect effect on social competition through the mediation of social comparison (Table 3). Social comparison has exhibited its power to directly influence social competition [37], while indirectly affecting social recognition, through a strong and significant relationship. This reinforces earlier observations, that people experience a sense of social competition once they are able to compare their results with the performance of other people in the same context [17, 51]. Quite naturally, an increased desire to see oneself in comparison with others can explain the heightened sensitivity of individuals towards social recognition [26, 46], which arises from people competing for social recognition [26, 29, 41].

Beyond the direct relationship between social competition and social recognition [40], there is a weak but significant indirect effect of social competition on social cooperation that is mediated by social recognition (Table 3). This suggests that there can be occasions, in which social competition and social recognition actually lead to social cooperation [26, 29]. For example, as in the case one extensive bicycling study [46], where the employees of one participating company were cooperating to get their organization to a more competitive position in a ranking, which again implies a sort of recognition for the top companies. Thus, social recognition has shown capacity to drive social cooperation in such and similar contexts.

According to the social influence research model, social cooperation enables social learning, which is quite understandable, as people tend to observe others in a

collaborative setting and adjust their behavior to improve their performance [3]. Social facilitation obviously can help with this, as it provides more insights into the performance of a task, from a broader number of people [54]. Further, through social learning people usually experience normative influence or acquire awareness of new social norms [10, 15]. Again, social facilitation contributes to behavior change by providing more people to teach social norms, causing people to acquire a better understanding of what is normal among the crowd they are learning from.

The present study has developed and introduced an advanced measurement instrument or scale for assessing seven social influence principles. It has also contributed a social influence research model that reveals the strongest correlations between the principles when framed as constructs. Each construct with six validated items (Table 1) can be instrumental for further research and applied transforming design work. Nevertheless, this model should be further evaluated in settings with different combinations of the social influence principles.

In an earlier study by Stibe and Cugelman [47], the misapplication of social influence principles was the most common reason why social and behavioral change programs backfire, producing the opposite outcome, such as anti-drug programs that accidentally trigger the target to increase drug use, rather than decrease it. One explanation is widespread mistaken belief that social influence is limited to social norms or social proof. By better understanding how each social influence principle operates and typically backfires, intervention designers can reduce the risk of misapplying social influence, and instead, design higher impact transforming technologies.

8 Implications

Present knowledge on persuasive technology reveals how behavior change designs and interventions are often limited in sustaining their effects [42], thus leading mostly to *transactional* [6, 48] or *transitional* [2] rather than *transformational* [42] changes (Table 4). This work on social influence in transforming technology should ultimately empower people and organizations to succeed in their desired and more often even inevitable changes. Scholars and practitioners of human-computer interaction and behavioral computer science [38] can now benefit from novel ways to design technology that helps people not only to achieve their goals, but also to support sustaining their newly developed habits. The proposed social influence scale is extending possibilities for designers to overcome limitations of traditional change management and behavioral designs.

Majority of global problems and business challenges are byproducts of poor human decision-making and unsustainable actions [42]. Communities, societies, businesses, and organizations, basically everyone needs help with transformations [49]. Social influence has already demonstrated its nature to be one of the most persistent motivators for achieving sustainable changes [13, 46]. Thus, the developed social influence scale and research model are very instrumental for change-makers aiming at achieving sustainable effects [27], as transformation depends critically on the quality of human-computer interaction [7].

The social influence model helps user experience scholars and practitioners to better understand how their interface design features might exhibit more shades of social influence than the primary chosen principle. For example, whenever a designer would aim at implementing a social comparison principle in a mobile application, that interface will naturally provoke its users to experience a certain degree of social competition, and possibly also social recognition for best performers.

Table 4. Types of change and their characteristics [42].

	Transactional change	Transitional change	Transformational change
Definition	An occurrence producing an outcome that differs from previous preferences	A period, in which certain outcomes significantly differ from what was habitual before	A continuum having direction as well as magnitude to produce apparently irreversible shifts
Description	To carry on or conduct something to a conclusion or settlement	Relating to a period during which something is changing from one state or form into another	To change completely the appearance or character of something or someone, especially so that that thing or person is improved
Perspective	One-time decision	Durational	Paradigm shift
Time	Short-term	Defined-term	Timeless
Orientation	Cost-benefit	Goal	Identity change
Nature	Bargaining	Achievement	Directional
Metric	Decision	Milestone	Personality traits
Psychology	Economical	Motivational	Spiritual
Example	Riding a bike to a park to get free lunch	Giving up alcohol for a month	Becoming a true forgiver from now on

In the realm of interactive technologies for transformation, social influence is competing with and oftentimes demonstrating its supremacy when compared to other conceptual schools of thought, such as gamification and nudging. Due to its scientific richness and practical nature, this work on social influence is applicable in many essential life contexts, including wellbeing, health, innovation, leadership, education, mobility, social change, diversity, culture, governance, automation, emergency, sustainability, autonomy, dwelling, equality, management, marketing, commercialization, safety, energy, ecology, and economy.

9 Conclusions

This study is bridging previous scientific work on social influence to facilitate further advances in transforming technology and human-computer interaction research agendas [4]. The research results can help scholars and designers to eliminate the risks of backfiring due to misapplied behavioral psychology [47]. While many people refer to social influence as a single principle, synonymously called social proof or peer pressure, this study has demonstrated a distinct factor structure that suggests there are psychological details that matter.

The main contribution of this study is three-fold. First, it has reviewed and provided a summary of seven principles or constructs of social influence, which all have distinct characteristics and qualities. Second, it developed and introduced a tool for measuring each construct with six theory-driven items. Third, it demonstrated the interplay among constructs that can explain the potential of each constructs to influence the others.

Limitations of this study include its small sample size, its geographical location, and a few items with low but minimally acceptable factor loadings. For these reasons, the authors caution that additional research is required to further validate the instrument on a larger scale.

As interactive technologies continue to penetrate people's lives at an unprecedent pace, practitioners and researchers will increasingly find themselves making small decisions that have large impacts on individuals and society.

Without a clear understanding of what social influence is, how it works, and what causes it to backfire, the risks that designers and practitioners cause more harm than good is quite high. The authors of this paper hope that with a stronger understanding of what drives social influence among different individuals and populations, they will be empowered to design transforming technologies that lead to better lives and societal wellbeing [42].

References

1. Alluhaidan, A., Chatterjee, S., Drew, D., Stibe, A.: Sustaining health behaviors through empowerment: a deductive theoretical model of behavior change based on information and communication technology (ICT). In: Ham, J., Karapanos, E., Morita, P., Burns, C. (eds.) PERSUASIVE 2018. LNCS, vol. 10809, pp. 28–41. Springer, Cham (2018). https://doi.org/10.1007/978-3-319-78978-1_3
2. Amado, G., Ambrose, A.: The Transitional Approach to Change. Karnac Books, London (2001)
3. Bandura, A.: Social Foundations of Thought and Action: A Social Cognitive Theory. Prentice Hall, Englewood Cliffs (1986)
4. Bardzell, J., Bardzell, S., Lin, C., Lindtner, S., Toombs, A.: HCI's making agendas. Found. Trends® Hum.–Comput. Interact. 11(3), 126–200 (2017)
5. Barnes Hofmeister, T., Stibe, A.: Living mobility transitions towards bicycling. Designing practices through co-creation and socially influencing systems. Des. J. 20(Sup. 1), S3305–S3316 (2017)
6. Burke, W.W., Litwin, G.H.: A causal model of organizational performance and change. J. Manag. 18(3), 523–545 (1992)

7. Card, S.K.: The Psychology of Human-Computer Interaction. CRC Press, Boca Raton (2018)
8. Cecchinato, M.E., et al.: Designing for digital wellbeing: a research & practice agenda. In: Extended Abstracts of the 2019 CHI Conference on Human Factors in Computing Systems, p. W17. ACM (2019)
9. Chandler, J.J., Paolacci, G.: Lie for a dime: when most prescreening responses are honest but most study participants are impostors. Soc. Psychol. Pers. Sci. 8(5), 500–508 (2017)
10. Cialdini, R.B., Kallgren, C.A., Reno, R.R.: A focus theory of normative conduct: a theoretical refinement and reevaluation of the role of norms in human behavior. Adv. Exp. Soc. Psychol. 24(20), 1–243 (1991)
11. Crano, W.D., Prislin, R.: Attitudes and persuasion. Ann. Rev. Psychol. 57, 345–374 (2006)
12. Cugelman, B., Thelwall, M., Dawes, P.: Online interventions for social marketing health behavior change campaigns: a meta-analysis of psychological architectures and adherence factors. J. Med. Internet Res. 13(1), e17 (2011)
13. Damon, W.: The lifelong transformation of moral goals through social influence. In: Interactive Minds, pp. 198–220 (1996)
14. Dillman, D.A.: Mail and Internet Surveys: The Tailored Design Method. Update with New Internet, Visual, and Mixed-Mode Guide. Wiley, Hoboken (2011)
15. Deutsch, M., Gerard, H.B.: A study of normative and informational social influences upon individual judgment. J. Abnorm. Soc. Psychol. 51(3), 629 (1955)
16. Dolata, M., Comes, T., Schenk, B., Schwabe, G.: Persuasive practices: learning from home security advisory services. In: Meschtscherjakov, A., De Ruyter, B., Fuchsberger, V., Murer, M., Tscheligi, M. (eds.) PERSUASIVE 2016. LNCS, vol. 9638, pp. 176–188. Springer, Cham (2016). https://doi.org/10.1007/978-3-319-31510-2_15
17. Festinger, L.: A theory of social comparison processes. Hum. Relat. 7(2), 117–140 (1954)
18. Fogg, B.J.: Persuasive Technology: Using Computers to Change What We Think and Do. Morgan Kaufmann, San Francisco (2003)
19. Hair, J.F., Ringle, C.M., Sarstedt, M.: PLS-SEM: indeed a silver bullet. J. Mark. Theory Pract. 19(2), 139–152 (2011)
20. Hamari, J., Hassan, L., Dias, A.: Gamification, quantified-self or social networking? Matching users' goals with motivational technology. User Model. User-Adapt. Interact. 28 (1), 35–74 (2018)
21. Harjumaa, M.: On the development of persuasive systems: a framework for designing and evaluating behaviour change support systems and its applicability for e-Health, vol. 68. VTT Science (2014)
22. Haslam, S.A., McGarty, C., Turner, J.C.: Salient group memberships and persuasion: the role of social identity in the validation of beliefs (1996)
23. Hovland, C.I., Janis, I.L., Kelley, H.H.: Communication and persuasion. In: Psychological Studies of Opinion Change (1953)
24. Kaptein, M., Markopoulos, P., De Ruyter, B., Aarts, E.: Personalizing persuasive technologies: explicit and implicit personalization using persuasion profiles. Int. J. Hum Comput Stud. 77, 38–51 (2015)
25. Kock, N.: WarpPLS User Manual: Version 6.0. Script Warp Systems, Laredo (2017)
26. Malone, T.W., Lepper, M.: Making learning fun: a taxonomy of intrinsic motivations for learning. In: Snow, R.E., Farr, M.J. (eds.) Aptitude, Learning and Instruction: III. Conative and Affective Process Analyses, pp. 223–253. Erlbaum, Hillsdale (1987)
27. Maton, K.I.: Making a difference: the social ecology of social transformation. Am. J. Commun. Psychol. 28(1), 25–57 (2000)

28. Maurer, B., Gärtner, M., Wuchse, M., Meschtscherjakov, A., Tscheligi, M.: Utilizing a digital game as a mediatory artifact for social persuasion to prevent speeding. In: Meschtscherjakov, A., De Ruyter, B., Fuchsberger, V., Murer, M., Tscheligi, M. (eds.) PERSUASIVE 2016. LNCS, vol. 9638, pp. 199–210. Springer, Cham (2016). https://doi.org/10.1007/978-3-319-31510-2_17

29. May, M.A., Doob, L.W.: Cooperation and competition. Soc. Sci. Res. Council Bull. **125**, 1–15 (1937)

30. Michie, S., et al.: The behavior change technique taxonomy (v1) of 93 hierarchically clustered techniques: building an international consensus for the reporting of behavior change interventions. Ann. Behav. Med. **46**(1), 81–95 (2013)

31. Millonig, A., et al.: Gamification and social dynamics behind corporate cycling campaigns. Transp. Res. Proc. **19**, 33–39 (2016)

32. Mylonopoulou, V., Väyrynen, K., Stibe, A., Isomursu, M.: Rationale behind socially influencing design choices for health behavior change. In: Ham, J., Karapanos, E., Morita, P., Burns, C. (eds.) PERSUASIVE 2018. Lecture Notes in Computer Science, vol. 10809, pp. 147–159. Springer, Cham (2018). https://doi.org/10.1007/978-3-319-78978-1_12

33. Myneni, S., Iyengar, S.: Socially influencing technologies for health promotion: translating social media analytics into consumer-facing health solutions. In: 2016 49th Hawaii International Conference on System Sciences (HICSS), pp. 3084–3093. IEEE (2016)

34. O'Keefe, D.J.: Persuasion: Theory and Research. Sage, Newbury (1990)

35. Orji, R.: Why are persuasive strategies effective? Exploring the strengths and weaknesses of socially-oriented persuasive strategies. In: de Vries, P., Oinas-Kukkonen, H., Siemons, L., Beerlage-de Jong, N., van Gemert-Pijnen, L. (eds.) PERSUASIVE 2017. LNCS, vol. 10171, pp. 253–266. Springer, Cham (2017). https://doi.org/10.1007/978-3-319-55134-0_20

36. Osborne, J.W., Costello, A.B., Kellow, J.T.: Best practices in exploratory factor analysis. In: Best Practices in Quantitative Methods, pp. 86–99 (2008)

37. Oyibo, K., Vassileva, J.: Investigation of social predictors of competitive behavior in persuasive technology. In: de Vries, P., Oinas-Kukkonen, H., Siemons, L., Beerlage-de Jong, N., van Gemert-Pijnen, L. (eds.) PERSUASIVE 2017. LNCS, vol. 10171, pp. 279–291. Springer, Cham (2017). https://doi.org/10.1007/978-3-319-55134-0_22

38. Pedersen, T., Johansen, C., Jøsang, A.: Behavioural computer science: an agenda for combining modelling of human and system behaviours. Hum.-Centric Comput. Inf. Sci. **8**(1), 7 (2018)

39. Rashotte, L.: Social influence. In: The Blackwell Encyclopedia of Social Psychology, vol. 9, pp. 562–563 (2007)

40. Rottiers, S.: The Sociology of Social Recognition: Competition in Social Recognition Games (No. 1004) (2010)

41. Schoenau-Fog, H.: Teaching serious issues through player engagement in an interactive experiential learning scenario. Eludamos. J. Comput. Game Cult. **6**(1), 53–70 (2012)

42. Stibe, A., Röderer, K., Reisinger, M., Nyström, T.: Empowering sustainable change: emergence of Transforming Wellbeing Theory (TWT). In: Adjunct Proceedings of the 14th International Conference on Persuasive Technology (2019)

43. Stibe, A.: Socially influencing systems: persuading people to engage with publicly displayed twitter-based systems. Acta Universitatis Ouluensis (2014)

44. Stibe, A.: Towards a framework for socially influencing systems: meta-analysis of four PLS-SEM based studies. In: MacTavish, T., Basapur, S. (eds.) PERSUASIVE 2015. LNCS, vol. 9072, pp. 171–182. Springer, Cham (2015). https://doi.org/10.1007/978-3-319-20306-5_16

45. Stibe, A.: Advancing typology of computer-supported influence: moderation effects in socially influencing systems. In: MacTavish, T., Basapur, S. (eds.) PERSUASIVE 2015. LNCS, vol. 9072, pp. 251–262. Springer, Cham (2015). https://doi.org/10.1007/978-3-319-20306-5_23

46. Stibe, A., Larson, K.: Persuasive cities for sustainable wellbeing: quantified communities. In: Younas, M., Awan, I., Kryvinska, N., Strauss, C., Thanh, D. (eds.) MobiWIS 2016. LNCS, vol. 9847, pp. 271–282. Springer, Cham (2016). https://doi.org/10.1007/978-3-319-44215-0_22

47. Stibe, A., Cugelman, B.: Persuasive backfiring: when behavior change interventions trigger unintended negative outcomes. In: Meschtscherjakov, A., De Ruyter, B., Fuchsberger, V., Murer, M., Tscheligi, M. (eds.) PERSUASIVE 2016. LNCS, vol. 9638, pp. 65–77. Springer, Cham (2016). https://doi.org/10.1007/978-3-319-31510-2_6

48. Vito, G.F., Higgins, G.E., Denney, A.S.: Transactional and transformational leadership: an examination of the leadership challenge model. Policing Int. J. Police Strat. Manag. 37(4), 809–822 (2014)

49. Waddell, D., Creed, A., Cummings, T.G., Worley, C.G.: Organisational Change: Development and Transformation. Cengage AU, South Melbourne (2016)

50. Wais-Zechmann, B., Gattol, V., Neureiter, K., Orji, R., Tscheligi, M.: Persuasive technology to support chronic health conditions: investigating the optimal persuasive strategies for persons with COPD. In: Ham, J., Karapanos, E., Morita, P., Burns, C. (eds.) PERSUASIVE 2018. LNCS, vol. 10809, pp. 255–266. Springer, Cham (2018). https://doi.org/10.1007/978-3-319-78978-1_21

51. Wood, J.V.: What is social comparison and how should we study it? Pers. Soc. Psychol. Bull. 22(5), 520–537 (1996)

52. Wood, W.: Attitude change: persuasion and social influence. Ann. Rev. Psychol. 51(1), 539–570 (2000)

53. Wunsch, M., et al.: What makes you bike? Exploring persuasive strategies to encourage low-energy mobility. In: MacTavish, T., Basapur, S. (eds.) PERSUASIVE 2015. LNCS, vol. 9072, pp. 53–64. Springer, Cham (2015). https://doi.org/10.1007/978-3-319-20306-5_5

54. Zajonc, R.B.: Social facilitation. Science 149, 269–274 (1965)

Using Expert Patterns in Assisted Interactive Machine Learning: A Study in Machine Teaching

Emily Wall[1]([✉]), Soroush Ghorashi[2], and Gonzalo Ramos[2]

[1] Georgia Tech, Atlanta, GA, USA
emilywall@gatech.edu
[2] Microsoft Research, Redmond, WA, USA
{sorgh,goramos}@microsoft.com

Abstract. Machine Teaching (MT) is an emerging practice where people, without Machine Learning (ML) expertise, provide rich information beyond labels in order to create ML models. MT promises to lower the barrier of entry to creating ML models by requiring a softer set of skills from users than having ML expertise. In this paper, we explore and show how end-users without MT experience successfully build ML models using the MT process, and achieve results not far behind those of MT experts. We do this by conducting two studies. We first investigated how MT experts build models, from which we extracted expert teaching patterns. In our second study, we observed end-users without MT experience create ML models with and without guidance from expert patterns. We found that all users built models comparable to those built by MT experts. Further, we observed that users who received guidance perceived the task to require less effort and felt less mental demand than those who did not receive guidance.

Keywords: Interactive machine learning · Machine Teaching · User studies

1 Introduction

Over the past decades, the Machine Learning (ML) field has devoted its attention to the study of algorithms that extract knowledge from data. It is common to hear today about solutions where machines can make predictions with almost, or better-than, human precision. This success comes at a cost: building these ML models requires an expert model builder with knowledge of the underlying learning algorithm. Further, creating such solutions often requires large amounts of

Electronic supplementary material The online version of this chapter (https://doi.org/10.1007/978-3-030-29387-1_34) contains supplementary material, which is available to authorized users.

© IFIP International Federation for Information Processing 2019
Published by Springer Nature Switzerland AG 2019
D. Lamas et al. (Eds.): INTERACT 2019, LNCS 11748, pp. 578–599, 2019.
https://doi.org/10.1007/978-3-030-29387-1_34

pre-labeled data, which might be easy or practical to obtain for certain problems (e.g., Google Photo's image labeling), but not others (e.g., face detection in a personal photo collection).

As the ML field considers addressing an emerging set of problems, it faces the challenge of meeting a growing demand of being an accessible tool for creating models. For example, a paralegal may want to sift through and classify tens of thousands of legal documents according to a concept unique to a case; or a developer may want to create an app that classifies and filters news feeds according to the user's preferences. Instead, access to the specialists who can build ML models like the one described above is limited by their scarcity and cost.

In addition to the above challenges, there is a growing demand [16] for explainable [11] or intelligible models [35] to not only enable accountability, but also to facilitate model inspection and debugging [27]. To address some of these issues, interactive machine learning (iML) has emerged as a field at the intersection of HCI and ML that focuses on ML model-building interactive processes with a human-in-the-loop [1].

Machine Teaching (MT) [34] is an emerging perspective on iML that is complementary to the discipline of ML. It aims to address the aforementioned challenges by extending iML's notions of interactivity, and by focusing on information exchange between a human (teacher) as a non-ML expert who has rich, useful knowledge beyond labels. In particular, a *machine teacher* can be an active participant choosing elements to populate the training set, labeling them, and choosing when and how to fix prediction errors by creating semantically meaningful features influenced by what they have seen. As teachers are active protagonists in this teaching process, they can take different paths to teach a model. This is akin to the many ways there are for a programmer to implement a function. For the scope of this paper we will use the term *machine teacher* or *teacher* to denote the subject-domain expert who trains an ML model using MT's process.

While MT has not yet been widely adopted, we believe it is a promising approach to help subject-matter experts build ML models that are accessible, scalable, and intelligible. Part of its appeal is that building a model using the MT process requires from the teacher expertise about a subject-domain, and no knowledge about the details, such as type and parameters, of the underlying learning algorithm. This set-up leads to a process requiring a softer skillset than traditional ones that require ML knowledge. In this paper, we focus on exploring and showing how the MT process enables end-users (MT and ML novices) to construct ML models comparable to those built by MT experts through two studies in which participants construct binary classification models of text documents.

This work makes the following contributions. First, we conduct a qualitative study in which we characterize MT phases and expert patterns by studying how current MT experts teach. Second, we encode these patterns and practices into an MT system to guide end-users. Third, we conduct an experiment that shows (a) that given minimal prior training in ML and MT, novices are able to construct models of similar quality to those built by experts, and (b) that guiding novices

with the aforementioned expert practices helps them to approach expert teacher behavior and build models with less effort than novices without such guidance. Fourth, to our knowledge, this is the first paper that presents a study of end-users engaging in a MT process or loop, through a system that instantiates MT as stated by [34]. Finally, we discuss additional MT teaching patterns and design considerations for MT systems, as next-steps for researchers and designers to consider.

2 Background and Related Work

Interactive Machine Learning and Teaching. Our work takes place in the context of a supervised iML workflow where people build ML models by providing knowledge in an interactive loop [1,12]. In this flow, it is worth noting three main activities where people can actively express knowledge: choosing what to label (sampling), labeling, and featuring. Sampling can help the learning system see an example of something it has not seen before, and thus can learn from; labeling taps into a person's subject-domain knowledge to provide the learning system with sources of truth; and featuring enables people to identify or select the properties that can help the learning system improve its internal representation of the concept one is trying to teach. Most prior work has focused on the latter two activities in isolation, where people either (1) label while keeping features constant [13,14,17], or (2) feature while keeping labels constant [5,8,24]. Others have evaluated alternative strategies within the iML loop [4]. Only a few works have looked into systems where people provide both labels and features [3,10]; even fewer have looked into people choosing a sampling strategy to interactively build and refine the training set [7]. Our work looks at the iML loop holistically where the above three activities occur in concert, and with a deeper emphasis on human interaction. We do this within the framing of machine teaching, as defined by [34], a point of view we will expand in the next sections.

In addition to the above, the term machine teaching has been used in different contexts. Zhu et al. [38] refer to machine teaching as the inverse problem to machine learning. In this definition, the problem is about finding the optimal training set, given a particular learning algorithm and a target model. This non human-in-the loop definition addresses a different problem from the one we are trying to solve. Our focus is about facilitating the interactive extraction of knowledge from a human teacher, towards the building of a model, while not knowing details about the learning algorithm under the hood.

Democratizing ML. The promises and enthusiasm around ML fuel the desire to make it a tool that everybody can either create or use. Many efforts actively pursue and address these goals. We group these efforts to make ML accessible into two schools of thought: (1) making it easier to become an ML expert, or (2) giving end-users access to tools that hide the complexities of interacting with an ML algorithm. In the former category, places like Udacity[1] provide courses to

---

[1] https://www.udacity.com.

train individuals into ML engineers, but these solutions address a different form of democratization. We are not interested in a subject-domain expert having to go to school in order to solve an immediate problem, or one that happens rarely. Instead, we focus on changing the curricula of what an end-user needs to know to create an ML model, by abstracting the complexities of ML algorithms.

There are too many tools and experiences to enumerate that claim to lower the barrier for the general public of problem-owners to use ML solutions. Places like Amazon's Web Services ML, Microsoft's Azure ML, or Google's Cloud AI provide visual front-end solutions for the "easy" creation and deployment of ML models. Other tools hide the complexity of ML trainers in the form of end-user libraries such as Scikit-Learn [33], ml5.js[2], or turicreate[3]; or visual tools such as prodi.gy[4] or lobe.ai[5]. Some tools exist to support model-building including both data and coding capabilities [32]. Many of these tools succeed in different ways at reducing the amount of detailed ML knowledge needed in order to use them, but do not fully remove the need to be familiar with the underlying ML algorithms or theory.

Automated Machine Learning (AutoML) is a time-saving alternative designed to automate parts of the ML pipeline, including hyperparameter selection [21], feature engineering [25], and so on. Some work has begun to combine parts of this process [30,31], and while AutoML can lower the barrier to building ML models, it is still subject to the same struggles of training ML models in the traditional way. For example, automated feature engineering can come at the cost of model interpretability, since features may not be semantically meaningful. Furthermore, AutoML still requires significant labeled data, not readily available for many problems, and is hence not a catch-all solution to democratizing ML. In contrast, our efforts seek to combine the above efforts: to educate and guide subject-domain experts to be good machine teachers, and do so within a tool that hides the need to know the learner algorithm's details.

Helping Novices Use (Complex) Software. Fraser et al. [15] provide a good summary of the different strategies that can be used to help novices effectively use software. In particular, this work discusses the pros and cons of (online) tutorials, enabling expert functionality over time, and command, or task-level action suggestions. Our work is inspired by this last approach of a system providing task-level action suggestions, but applied to a different context than the aforementioned work.

Notifications are a common way to push timely information (like suggestions) to users across a wide range of applications. When designing a notification system, many factors need to be taken into consideration. Horvitz [18] presented twelve principles for mixed-initiative user interfaces that guide the ways systems balance human and machine efforts. For us, principles such as considering a user's goals and attention, minimizing cost of guesses, and maintaining working

---

[2] https://ml5js.org/.
[3] https://github.com/apple/turicreate.
[4] https://prodi.gy/.
[5] https://lobe.ai/.

memory are particularly relevant to our thinking for notifications to help novice teachers. A significant number of works also look into identifying the proper time to show notifications by building statistical and ML models of users engaged in particular task flows [19,22,23]. We choose to use notifications to guide novice teachers utilizing heuristics based on moments around specific actions teachers take, as we wanted a first approximation to a reasonable solution.

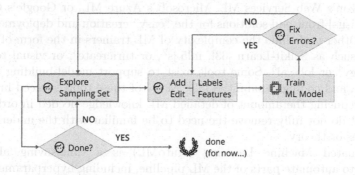

Fig. 1. Machine teaching loop. One often starts this loop by exploring the sampling set.

3   Machine Teaching

Our introduction underlines how ML's current renaissance is also accompanied by significant challenges. MT as described in [34] is an emerging discipline that has the promise to address many such challenges. As a form if iML, MT is inherently a supervised learning process that can be applied to classification and entity extraction problems for different types of data such as text, structured documents, or images. We have not consider the MT process's suitability to address regression problems, a topic that falls outside the scope of this paper. MT sits at the intersection of HCI and ML, focusing on the exchange of knowledge between a (human) teacher and a (computer or algorithm) learner. According to Simard et al.'s [34] vision, MT systems are at their core iML systems, and follow a process and philosophy of incremental iteration, stating a point-of-view about how teaching (transferring human knowledge) to a learning algorithm should be done. MT's aim is not only making the process of creating an ML model accessible and efficient for the teacher, but also producing models that are intelligible by design. MT targets domain-subject experts as its users by abstracting the complexities of the interface of the ML algorithm and its parameters.

Teachers express their domain knowledge through decisions they make while teaching. They do so in ways that hide and abstract the parameters of a learning algorithm. At a fundamental level, all teachers need to know how to do, is to *explain why they have labeled a document as a member of a certain class.* For MT to be effective, some conditions need to be met. First, having a consistent,

underlying learning algorithm guarantees that teachers will only encounter three types of errors (mislabeling errors, learner errors, and representation errors), each with a known remedy [29]. Second, a person should be able to articulate the relevant concepts that explain why an example is (or is not) a member of a class. Third, the teacher has access to a searchable and large set of unlabeled data (sampling set). As teachers use this process to build an ML model, they are participating in a teaching loop.

During this MT loop, there is no predetermined test or ground-truth set a teacher can use to assess the quality of their model. Evaluation in this case can happen by judging the number of correct predictions in a dynamically-generated set of positively predicted documents. This type of context is where MT shows the most promise, and it is not uncommon. ML services such as LUIS[6] are an example of MT in the wild where examples, labels, and features come incrementally from a subject-domain expert. The above context stands in contrast to cases where one has access to a large set of pre-labeled documents, such as images labeled through a CAPTCHA service. These later cases can be best-served with unsupervised ML methods and are not something MT aims to solve.

Figure 1 illustrates the teaching loop, and the types of teacher knowledge exchange that take place. This teacher knowledge comes in the form of choosing what example to label next; labeling an example; creating features; and detecting training errors, assessing them, and fixing them. For example, following this loop, a teacher creating a Sports news classifier from scratch (no labels or features) can (1) search for articles containing the name "Lionel Messi", (2) label them positive or negative according to their content (i.e., add to the training set), (3) (after the system retrains a new model) see if articles' labels coincide (or not) with the current model's predictions (i.e., detecting prediction errors), (4) create a feature or explanation to the system the concept of "soccer" as articles containing the word "soccer", and (5) (after the system retrains a new model) see that the training set is predicted correctly. This loop showcases how teachers can be more [1] than just a source of labels.

MATE System. We created a system, MATE (MAchine TEaching), that implements the above MT flow. This implementation of MATE supports binary classification, multi-class classification, and entity extraction for text documents. However, for the purposes of our study, we scope our description of the system and subsequent studies to binary classification of text documents, as such models often form the building blocks of more complex predictive models. The details of this implementation fall outside of the scope of this paper, hence we will only focus on its main functionality and interface. The MATE system's interface is divided into three areas. Its center area has a sampler selector (Fig. 2-2) that lets teachers decide how to get the next document to label. MATE provides six sampling or exploration strategies for teachers, described in Table 1. These strategies are a representative set of the different ways of identifying useful examples to show to the learning algorithm.

---

[6] http://luis.ai.

584   E. Wall et al.

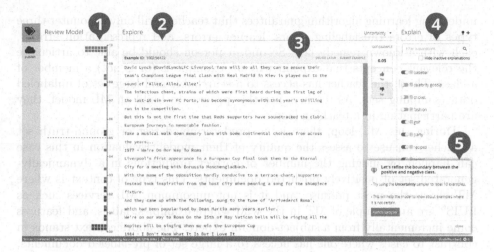

Fig. 2. MATE's main screen. (1) Model tracker. (2) Sampling interface. (3) Labeling interface. (4) Featuring interface. (5) Notifications (added after Study 1). (Color figure online)

The center area also displays documents and lets teachers *label* them as a positive (yes) or negative (no) example of the main class (Fig. 2-3). Teachers can postpone their decision by "deciding later" (i.e., to support concept evolution when the teacher is uncertain about whether a document should be positive or negative [26]). On the left side, teachers can examine and review training errors using a *model tracker*-like control [2] which displays all positive (green), negative (red), and undecided (blue) labels (Fig. 2-1) sorted vertically by prediction score. This panel lets teachers select and review previously labeled (or undecided) documents. The right side of the interface allows teachers to create or edit explanations (*features*) by defining lists of *keywords* (Fig. 2-4). When teachers see a document, the system highlights the words within that document that match keywords contained in each feature. Hovering over a highlight lets teachers see what features fire on a particular keyword or phrase.

Teaching Skills as Problem-Solving Skills. There are interesting parallels between the practice of MT and programming. For example, a predictor is a function that a person ideates (main concept), codes (sampling, labeling, and featuring), and debugs (detect and fix training errors). These similarities underline that good teachers need to have a certain mindset to problem solving, e.g., how they decompose and explain a concept using a determined language. Problem-solving skills are not something one is born with; one develops such skills over time through training and experience. Unlike programming or software engineering, MT expert patterns are yet to be codified and evaluated; i.e., there is no unique way to move through the flow defined in Fig. 1. In the next section we describe how we seek to encode these expert patterns.

Table 1. Sampling strategies supported by the MATE system.

Sampler	Description
KS: Keyword Search	Get a document containing one or more keywords
RS: Random	Get a random document
US: Uncertainty	Get a document near the decision boundary
EBS: Explanation-Based	Given a feature (explanation), get a document where it activates
PES: Possible Errors	Get a document the model is likely predicting incorrectly, when contrasted with a bag-of-words model
PPS: Predicted Positives	Get a document the model predicts as positive

4 Study 1: Modeling Expert Patterns

We aim to improve and accelerate the practice of MT by helping ML and MT novices become good machine teachers. In order to do that, we first seek to understand teaching practices among MT experts. In this qualitative study, we observe MT experts building ML models using the MATE system and analyze the rationale for their teaching decisions.

Participants. One of the challenges of this study is to encode expert behavior and decision making in an emerging area whose known expert user population is small. For our studies, we had access to a group at a research institution that developed the MT principles and has experience using them for the past four years. The ML models built by this group are used internally in a large software company. For our study, we recruited six individuals (two female) from the above pool of experts, who have more than 1 year of experience building ML models following the MT process. The average age for the participants is 37. We compensated participants with a $10 cafeteria credit and gave the incentive that the person who built the best model (according to an F-score) would receive an additional $25 Amazon gift card.

Materials. Participants used the MATE tool, described in Sect. 3, loaded with a dataset containing 90,000 documents scraped from recent news articles and blog posts from a data-aggregation service.[7] The documents belonged to sources classified as finance, health, sports, movies & TV, music, politics, travel, and undefined.

Procedure. We conducted the study in two separate one-hour long sessions. In the first session, participants used the MATE tool, which they were already

---

[7] webhose.io.

familiar with from significant prior use, to build an ML model using the MT process. Participants spent 35 min building a binary classifier for articles about movies & TV. We observed and collected screen and audio recordings, in order to avoid interrupting or altering the experts' teaching flow. After the first session, we codified the videos on a data sheet marking important moments in each participant's teaching process. This included when they changed their method of sampling and labeling the data, when they chose to review training errors, when they created or modified features, or when their process seemed to have otherwise shifted, etc.

We interviewed each participant for a second session that took place 2–3 days after the first one, to permit time for us to codify the session video and so that the expert participants could reflect on their process while their teaching experience was fresh on their minds. During this session, we used our notes from the codified videos of the first session to ask participants about their rationale for a particular teaching decision or apparent change in behavior. To assist participants with this activity, we replayed the corresponding video from the first session to jog their memory as needed.

5   Study 1: Results

Participants (expert teachers) generated an average of 69 labels (SD = 27) during their 35-minute sessions. They created an average of 76 keywords (SD = 98) across 7 features (SD = 4). The high standard deviation in keywords was due to participant S6 who searched the web for a list of 248 recent movie titles. Figure 3 summarizes experts' interactions over time, including the samplers used (colored rectangles), when they reviewed labeled documents, including errors (in red), from the model tracker (+ and − symbols), and when they created or modified features (circle symbols). In the following, we highlight the key teaching phases and expert practices we found in the study.

Machine Teaching Phases. From this study, we observed four high-level phases that experts went through during their teaching process: Cold Start phase, Boundary phase, Challenge phase, and Testing phase. These phases are non-overlapping stages of the MT process. Experts begin in the Cold Start phase, after which they iteratively cycle through the other three phases. The phases can be characterized as follows.

In the Cold Start phase (CSP), experts begin by using a Keyword Search to find and label positive examples of the classifier (S1-S5). Then, they use a Random sampling strategy to find and label diverse negative examples of the classifier (S1, S3, S6). During this phase they create features to roughly capture the positive class (S-all); they are not particularly concerned with training errors at this point. After they initialize a model with a minimum amount of positive and negative labels plus some basic features, experts transition into Boundary or Challenge phase.

The Boundary phase (BP) is characterized by a lack of clear boundary separating positive and negative labels in the training set. Experts use Uncertainty

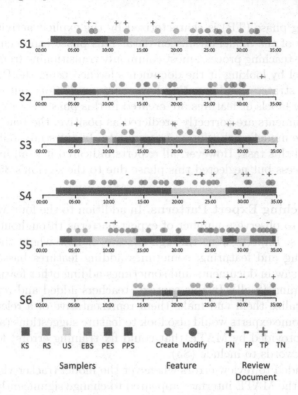

Fig. 3. The teaching actions experts went through over time, including samplers used (Table 1), creation or modification of features, and documents reviewed (false positives (FP), false negatives (FN), true positives (TP), and true negatives (TN)). (Color figure online)

sampling to find and label documents that the model does not predict confidently (S-all), i.e., documents with a prediction score around 0.5. The main goal during this phase is refining the boundary or improving the separation between the positive and negative labels. Based on the labels and features they create, experts transition from this phase to Challenge.

The Challenge phase (CP) is characterized by a training set where there is a clear boundary separating positive and negative labels. Experts use a variety of sampling strategies to (1) label diverse data and (2) attempt to challenge or 'break' the model. For example, some experts indicated they would try to frequently change sampling strategies to increase the diversity of the labeled data (S1-S3, S5), but the main task during this phase was to find documents that the model does not predict correctly (S-all). This involved particular focus on the Possible Errors (S1, S3, S5-S6) and Predicted Positives (S-all) sampling strategies (Table 1). Based on the labels and features they create, experts can transition to from this phase to Testing or back to Boundary.

The Testing phase (TP) is characterized by the explicit activity of evaluating the quality of the model on unseen data. This phase can occur periodically throughout the teaching process, most commonly transitioning from CP. Experts test their model by looking at the documents fetched using the Predicted Positives sampling strategy, and counting how many predictions out of a batch are correct; no new labels or features are created in this phase. For example, if nine out of ten documents are correctly predicted as positive, the teacher feels more confident of the model's behavior on unseen data. In our study, only one subject (S2) performed this task. However, all experts indicated it is an important part of the MT process but neglected this phase due to the session's 35-minute time constraint.

Machine Teaching Expert Patterns. In addition to the four MT phases, we were also able to observe a number of expert patterns throughout the different teaching phases. Experts went through a state of flow where they alternated between labeling and featuring; sometimes adding features based on relevant keywords they saw in documents and sometimes adding other features whenever they came to mind (S-all). In this context, teachers added and refined features to try to generalize them and make them representative of a relevant concept. Occasionally, some experts would also look to feature suggestions (a list of potential keywords provided by MATE that could fix training errors) for inspiration on relevant keywords to include (S5).

Experts tended to review errors whenever the model tracker visualization on the left side of the MATE interface appeared to change significantly (S-all), e.g., after a transition from CSP to BP. No one immediately addressed every training error that appeared. Each expert had a different threshold of the acceptable amount of errors to have, generally $< 20\%$ of labels.

To fix False Positive errors, experts would create features that explain a negative label (e.g., if the document was a White House press release and thus not about movies and television, they might create a feature to describe the concept of politics) (S-all). Conversely, to fix False Negative errors, they would create features that explain a positive label (e.g., a document talking about movie studios) (S-all).

After creating a new feature, some experts would 'test' the feature using the Explanation-Based sampling strategy (S2-S3, S5-S6). MATE showed in context the feature's keywords in the document's view and let experts assess whether the feature was working as desired. This practice happened during all phases (except Testing).

Sometimes experts faced a document that was too rare, or difficult to explain with the provided teaching language of keyword lists. Sometimes experts were just not sure how to label a document. In either of these cases they used the "decide later" option so that the document would not be used to train the model, or until they were certain how to label it.

6   Study 2: Guiding Novice Teachers

While the MT loop is something that can be straightforward for someone to learn, its effective use requires insight in terms of when and how to sample, label, and fix errors. At a different level, problem solving skills such as breaking a larger problem or concept into smaller ones are also valuable for MT. As these are not innate skills, it follows that becoming a proficient machine teacher can require practice and experience.

In Study 1, we manually extracted expert teacher patterns within the MT loop based on our observations of expert behavior. In our second study, we synthesized guiding notifications from these expert practices. In addition to observing how successfully end-users apply the MT process, we want to explore whether guiding novice machine teachers with these expert practices could help them to become better machine teachers. As a tool, MATE sits in a class of its own in terms of user prerequisites and functionality, hence we do not aim to compare it with other ML-building tools. Rather, our goal is to observe how successfully end-users apply the MT process under different guiding conditions, and see how similarly they perform compared to expert teachers. We design this guidance to help teachers by *unblocking* them in their teaching progress. We did not design or consider this type of guidance to serve as a tutoring system and hence we do not focus on retention of expert practices.

Translating Expert Practices into Notifications. Our goal of adding a notification system to MATE is to provide guidance throughout the MT process to novice teachers, including sampling, featuring, and labeling guidance. When synthesizing our observations from experts' teaching strategies into actionable guidance, we sought to characterize prescriptive actions as well as conditions for when such actions are useful. Table 2 summarizes the guiding notifications we produced from our observations.

The timing of the guidance notifications is an important factor in their effectiveness. Of the four types of interruption strategies [28], we follow a naïve mediated approach that chooses moments between tasks (a strategy supported by work like [9]), or situations of apparent inactivity. There are several such moments during a teaching session:

1. after submitting a label,
2. after closing the review of a labeled document,
3. (while reading a new document) after 30, or 60 s of inactivity[8],
4. after getting a document with the same sampler without labeling 10 times in a row,
5. after creating/editing a feature, and
6. after creating/editing features for 5 consecutive minutes.

The basic mechanics of our desired notifications work as follows: whenever an interruptible moment happens, the system chooses the proper notification

---

[8] A proxy for reading: hovering over, or scrolling a document.

Table 2. The guidance provided to participants along with heuristics for when notifications can be dispatched. We say predictions are *well-separated* when $\leq 10\%$ of prediction scores are between 0.3–0.7. We say the number of errors is *high* when $\geq 20\%$
of documents are predicted incorrectly in the model. The full text of each notification
can be found in supplemental materials.

Name	Guidance	Heuristic
CSP: Positive	Use KS to find and label 10 positive examples	At the start of the MT process
CSP: Negative	Use RS to find and label 10 negative examples	After 10 positive examples have been labeled
BP	Use US to find and label 10 examples	Predictions are not well-separated
CP	Change samplers often and find diverse documents to label	Predictions are well-separated
TP	Use PPS to see how accurately the model predicts 10 unseen documents	After every 50 labels; predictions are well-separated
Tip: Create feature	Create a feature that explains a positive label	Reviewing a false negative
Tip: Test feature	Use EBS to see if a feature captures documents in the context the teacher expects	After creating or modifying a feature, during BP or CP. Do not show during CSP
Tip: Possible errors	Use PES to find documents the model is likely predicting incorrectly	After CSP; predictions are well-separated
Tip: Review errors	Review training errors	Predictions are not well-separated; the number of errors is high
Tip: Feature suggestion	Check if the system suggests any sensible feature	The tool suggests features; number of errors is high; predictions are not well-separated
Tip: Decide later	Use "decide later" if the teacher is not sure how to label; or they cannot ideate a feature to explain a label	Reviewing a document for $\geq$ 30 s, or revisiting the same document $\geq$ 3 times
Tip: Negative feature	Create a feature to describe why a label is negative	Reviewing a false positive

to show based on the system's current state. If there is ambiguity as to which
notification to show, the system picks one at random. The chance of a notification significantly decreases if the notification has been seen (and acknowledged)
within the past 10 min.

In this study, we are inspired by [20]'s wizard-of-oz methodology and adopt
a similar strategy to both observe the significant interactions (such as hovering,
clicking on a particular UI element/area) and to emulate the system's decision about when to present suggestions. In our implementation of the guidance
functionality, we dispatch notifications through a 'Wizard of Oz' who follows
the above heuristics in a consistent way. The wizard is able to work by being
able to see a live-feed of the MATE system's screen and the teacher's actions
within, including interactions such as mouse movements and clicks. We chose
this implementation for a number of reasons: first, it let us add functionality into a complex code base quickly and with ease; second, it allowed us to
fine tune policies quickly through pilot studies; and last, it let us monitor our

heuristics while opportunistically discovering important state signals to consider in the future.

While it would be feasible to implement an automated version of this guidance system, it is not our focus and remains a topic of future work.

Participants. In this study, we recruited 24 [6] MT novices (9 female), which we screened as individuals who self reported having little or no familiarity with either ML and MT. The average age was 31. We also recruited an additional 3 MT experts (2 female). The MT experts served as a performance benchmark in our data analysis.

Materials. We randomly assigned novice participants to either the Non-Guided (NG) or the Guided (G) condition. Experts (E) performed the task under the same conditions as Non-Guided participants. In both conditions participants built models using the same 90 K article dataset from Study 1. In the Non-Guided condition, participants used MATE as described in Sect. 3. In the Guided condition, participants used a version of MATE that was modified with guidance notifications, as described above, that appeared at the bottom right of the interface (Fig. 2-5).

For both conditions, we prepared three short training videos (totaling approximately 15 min) to introduce fundamentals of ML, MT, and the MATE system, respectively. We also gave participants reading materials in the form of an MT diagram (Fig. 1) and a summary description of sampling strategies in the MATE system (Table 1). The purpose of these training materials was to provide a minimal common ground language and knowledge for all novices participating in our experiment.

Earlier work points out that despite having basic knowledge, novice ML practitioners can struggle with notions such as features, or negative concepts [1,37]. Because of this, while these off-line tutorials can help the progress from novice to expert, we still hypothesize that the addition of in-situ guidance can accelerate even further the adoption of MT expert practices.

Procedure. We divided our study into two stages. After passing an initial screening for selecting ML and MT novices, participants took part in the first stage of our study, in which we sent them our training materials. To verify that participants studied the materials, we asked them to complete an on-line quiz that tested the fundamental concepts they needed to know to use the MATE system and teach a binary classifier with it. Only participants with a score $\geq$ 80% were allowed to proceed to stage two of our study. Participants could retake the quiz as many times as necessary. We compensated participants that completed this stage with a $15 Amazon gift card.

We scheduled participants that passed the quiz to complete stage two of our study: building a binary classifier for articles about travel and tourism. Sessions took place within one week of passing the quiz. During this session we gave participants 5 min to ask questions regarding the learning materials they studied beforehand. Afterward, we gave a 2-minute interactive tour of the MATE system

and allowed them to use it for another 5 min in a sports classifier demonstration. When ready, we gave participants 45 min to build the classifier.

We did not want to test participants' memory on the details of the system or their quality as labelers. Instead, we sought to observe their teaching process. Hence, we encouraged participants to ask questions about MATE as needed (e.g., where to click to sample data, or how to label a document as "decide later"). Further, they could ask, if in doubt, if a document belonged to the travel and tourism class. We demonstrated the notifications to participants in the Guided condition, and told them that they were designed to help them build a better model. We instructed them to follow their guidance whenever possible, and that not dismissing them will give the system the impression that they did not see the notification, leading to the system 'insisting' on showing them again.

Upon completion of this second stage, we compensated participants with a $35 Amazon gift card. The novice participant in each condition who achieved the highest F1-score (described next) was awarded an additional $50 Amazon gift card.

Measuring a Model's Performance. We measured the quality of the model each participant created by computing the F1-Score over the same sampling set used during the teaching session. As participants only labeled less than 0.2% of the set, the amount of overlap is negligible, thus we consider these measures good estimates of each model's performance. While having access to these measurements will allow us to have a sense of how novices' output compares to the experts', we do not expect the overall quality of the models to be high after 45 min of teaching.

7   Study 2: Results

Non-Guided novices generated an average of 64 labels ($SD = 23$) and 70 keywords ($SD = 34$) across 12 features ($SD = 6$). Guided novices generated an average of 72 labels ($SD = 24$) and 61 keywords ($SD = 25$) across 11 features ($SD = 3$). Experts who participated as a performance baseline generated an average of 91 labels ($SD = 37$) and 131 keywords ($SD = 114$) across 11 features ($SD = 5$). One expert (E2) differed from others and focused a large portion of time creating keywords by searching the web for a list of 198 countries. The distributions of these results can be seen in Fig. 4.

Model Quality. We computed the F1-Score from the model that each participant built, as described in Sect. 6. After confirming that the sample variances were the same using Levene's test ($W = 0.0425$, $p = 0.8385$), we conducted an independent samples t-test to determine if Guided novices performed better than Non-Guided. We found $t = -0.9812$, $p = 0.3373$ and were unable to reject the null hypothesis.

While we do not see a significant difference between the groups' model quality, we see a trend by examining their distributions (Fig. 4). We observed that experts built better models, with a median F1-Score of 0.2938, followed by

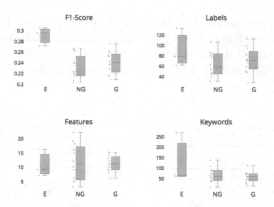

Fig. 4. Summary of models produced by participant groups Experts (E), Non-Guided (NG), and Guided (G) in Study 2, including F1-Scores in the top-left, number of labels produced in the top-right, number of features or explanations produced in the bottom-left, and number of keywords across features in the bottom-right.

Guided novices with a median F1-Score of 0.2403, and lastly by Non-Guided novices with a median F1-Score of 0.2238.

Qualitative Observations

Besides looking at the effects of guidance on the model's quality, we also wanted to see how guidance affected participants' overall user experience. After they completed the task, participants rated their experience across 5 dimensions (perceived success level, frustration, mental demand, pace, and effort) on a 7-point Likert scale. For success level, $1 =$ worst and $7 =$ best, while for the other four dimensions $1 =$ best and $7 =$ worst.

To see if there was a difference between Non-Guided and Guided novices, we conducted a Mann-Whitney U test for each of the 5 dimensions. We found the following results: success ($U = 71$, $p = 0.9762$), frustration ($U = 74.5$, $p = 0.9059$), demand ($U = 101.5$, $p = 0.0866$), pace ($U = 69$, $p = 0.8818$), and effort ($U = 81.5$, $p = 0.5824$), none of which indicate statistically significant differences.

Despite these results, we do see qualitative patterns among the distributions of ratings (Fig. 5). All conditions perceived a median success level of 4.

For three dimensions, Guided novices perceived a lower median {mental demand, rushed pace, effort level}. Guided and Non-Guided novices rated a median rush of pace of 4, compared to Expert median rating of 5. Guided novices rated a median mental demand of 3.5 compared to Non-Guided novice and Expert median ratings of 5. Similarly, Guided novices rated a median effort level of 4.5 compared to Non-Guided novice and Expert median ratings of 5. Guided novices rated a median frustration level of 3, Non-Guided novices rated a median frustration level of 2.5, and Experts rated a median frustration level of 4. While Non-Guided novices rated a lower frustration level (median 2.5) than Guided novices (median 3), both groups rated this dimension fairly low, possibly

due to the general perception that MT is an enjoyable process. For example, one participant indicated that it "feels like a game" (P20), while another indicated he "would play this all day if it were a game" (P30). When creating features to fix training errors, another participant indicated it's like a "word association game" (P24).

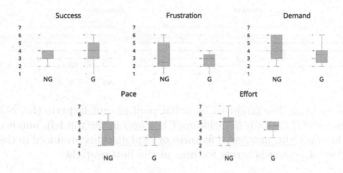

Fig. 5. Likert ratings (1–7) for Non-Guided (NG) and Guided (G) conditions in Study 2.

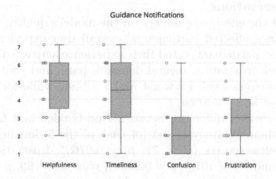

Fig. 6. Summary of Likert ratings (1–7) about the guidance notifications in Study 2, for helpfulness, timeliness, confusion, and frustration. Higher values for helpfulness and timeliness are good, while lower values for confusion and frustration are desired.

Experts tended to feel higher levels of frustration, mental demand, rushed pace, and effort level, possibly due to a common perception that with more time, they could have had a much higher quality model.

In addition to these 5 dimensions, participants in the Guided condition also rated the helpfulness, timeliness, confusion, and frustration specifically with respect to the guidance notifications (Fig. 6). Most participants expressed that the notifications were helpful (median rating of 5) and they were largely receptive to the help. For example, when presented a notification to move on to the next phase of training, one participant indicated "sure, I'll switch samplers;

thank you" (P15). Some participants indicated dissatisfaction with the timing of the notifications. One participant indicated that notifications "don't give me enough time to focus on one aspect before telling me to do something else" (P01). Despite feedback about the timing, participants overall found the notifications to be timely (median rating of 5). Similarly, participants experienced low levels of confusion (median rating of 2) and frustration (median rating of 3).

8 Discussion and Future Work

Study Limitations. The low number of expert participants in both studies was a function and challenge of the relatively small population of machine teaching expert participants. From a total of around 10 experts, 6 and 3 for Studies 1 and 2, respectively, were what was possible without having overlapping subject pools. Nonetheless, the presence of expert participants in Study 2 served only as an anecdotal baseline to put novice results in context. Furthermore, because of the relatively short duration in Study 1, experts did not fully evaluate their models. However, MATE's model tracker provided always up-to-date information regarding model performance on the training set.

Optimal Teaching Process. We started our research looking for a gold standard teaching playbook, that could lead novices on the path to teaching good models every time. More than a single playbook, we found expert patterns which we can take as current best practices. What we learned by observing experts and novices alike, is that even though the MT loop provides a sensible path to good teaching, there are still several ways to combine teaching patterns to build a good model.

For example, the Cold Start phase pattern we encouraged consisted of adding positive labels, then negative labels, and later a feature. However, these activities could have occurred in any order. In fact, we observed that many participants (e.g., P15) tended to review false positive errors, and hence created features describing "negative" concepts. Because of this, these teachers often neglected to create features describing positive examples. To address this, an alternative starting point during CSP could be to prompt users to first create a feature describing the positive concept of the classifier.

The Importance of Features. In addition, one of the fundamental observations we took from our studies, is that a model is only as good as the knowledge a teacher puts in it, regardless of the process or order of actions. In particular, the quality or generalizability of the features that teachers ideate affected the quality of their model, and thus the teaching phase one could be in. While some participants showed some understanding of the concept of overfitting (e.g., while training P08 indicated "it's probably super overfit") and the importance of precise features (e.g., P12 indicated "this is a bad word to use, I think [it's] too generic"), many participants still struggled to come up with good features. A guidance notification reminding users of the important balance between precise yet generalizable features could have been helpful.

Similarly, many novices frequently asked us about how to create negative features, or to see how positively or negative correlated an existing feature was (e.g., P04). A feature in MATE becomes negatively or positively correlated to a label depending on that feature 'firing up' on positive or negative examples. This suggests a common mental model that novices think about keywords as either positively or negatively associated with a concept. We also observed that the number of features teachers produced is negatively correlated with F1-Score $(r = -0.4700, p = 0.0205)$. This is likely caused by models overfitting the training data. These observations underscore the importance of tooling during the MT loop supporting the creation and evaluation of good features.

Model Quality. Our studies showed that the performance of models built by Guided and Non-Guided novices was not significantly different. While considerable in terms of effort for a user study, 45 min was not sufficient to teach a model of high quality, and perhaps see differences between the two guiding conditions. Even though our quantitative results do not show statistically significant differences, our study clearly highlights that with minimal on-boarding, novice machine teachers are not too far behind from experienced teachers. This reinforces the benefits of MT requiring a softer set of skills than processes that require ML or Data Science expertise. This underlines further the potential of MT as a way to democratize ML. In future research, we want to observe teaching sessions longer than 45 min where the nuanced effects of different teaching patterns might emerge.

Activities' Cadence. Our results suggest that the novices' qualitative experience benefited from guidance. We also saw how the absence of guidance affected some. For example, it was common to see Non-Guided novices spend time thinking about what to do after the model perfectly fit the training data. We also observed moments of significant focus where a Non-Guided teacher would do only one thing, such as refining features, or use a single sampler for a long time. In the absence of guidance other participants found some tasks just fun to do, and saw feature creation/refinement as a "word association game" (P24).

This is a behavior hinted at during our pilot, and our notification triggers accounted for some of these "sticky" behaviors by suggesting teachers change what they are doing. Nonetheless, we only had an opportunity to observe these behaviors in full during the study, which reinforced our view that characterizing the proper cadence of labeling, sampling and featuring activities is important future work.

Automating Guidance. Participants never realized that the system's notifications were driven by a Wizard-of-Oz. Having a consistent set of rules to follow allowed investigators to simulate this behavior, in a believable and affordable way. Part of our future efforts is to refine and automate the notification system so that it can run without a wizard's oversight. While we focused on proactive guidance in this study, future work might also compare the effectiveness of proactive guidance to reactive [36] or on-demand guidance in the context of the MT process.

9   Conclusions

In this paper we build onto the promise for Machine Teaching as a way to widen access to the use of ML by end-users and domain experts to solve problems. We look at how users without experience in the MT process apply it to create a binary classifier. Further, we look into lowering the barrier of entry to MT, by identifying and synthesizing MT expert patterns, and presenting them to novices at appropriate times during different teaching sessions. While our results on the effects of this guidance are statistically inconclusive, we see a trend that Guided novices' produce better models as well as perceive a better overall teaching experience (less effort and less mental demand) than Non-Guided novices. Chief among the results from our studies is the observation that people without special ML knowledge can successfully engage in a teaching loop to create ML classification models, and that those models are not far behind the ones created by MT experts. MT is a process that arguably requires a person's full attention, including making richer decisions than simply labeling. We believe that this apparent cost is actually low, as we observed that the proper experience and interaction loop can make it an engaging activity end-users are not only willing, but also happy, to participate in. In particular we are encouraged by feedback from users who expressed a willingness to participate in a "fun" problem-solving process. We believe there are many areas to explore in the context of MT, and we see a green field of opportunity at the intersection of HCI and ML to advance the discipline and adoption of this form of end-user ML.

References

1. Amershi, S., Cakmak, M., Knox, W.B., Kulesza, T.: Power to the people: the role of humans in interactive machine learning. AI Mag. **35**(4), 105–120 (2014)
2. Amershi, S., Chickering, M., Drucker, S.M., Lee, B., Simard, P., Suh, J.: Modeltracker: redesigning performance analysis tools for machine learning. In: Proceedings of the 33rd Annual ACM Conference on Human Factors in Computing Systems, CHI 2015, pp. 337–346. ACM, New York (2015)
3. Amershi, S., Fogarty, J., Weld, D.: Regroup: interactive machine learning for on-demand group creation in social networks. In: Proceedings of the SIGCHI Conference on Human Factors in Computing Systems, pp. 21–30. ACM (2012)
4. Bernard, J., Zeppelzauer, M., Lehmann, M., Müller, M., Sedlmair, M.: Towards user-centered active learning algorithms. In: Computer Graphics Forum, vol. 37, pp. 121–132. Wiley Online Library (2018)
5. Brooks, M., Amershi, S., Lee, B., Drucker, S.M., Kapoor, A., Simard, P.: FeatureInsight: visual support for error-driven feature ideation in text classification. In: 2015 IEEE Conference on Visual Analytics Science and Technology (VAST), pp. 105–112. IEEE (2015)
6. Caine, K.: Local standards for sample size at CHI. In: Proceedings of the 2016 CHI Conference on Human Factors in Computing Systems, pp. 981–992. ACM (2016)
7. Chen, N.C., Suh, J., Verwey, J., Ramos, G., Drucker, S., Simard, P.: AnchorViz: facilitating classifier error discovery through interactive semantic data exploration. In: 23rd International Conference on Intelligent User Interfaces, pp. 269–280. ACM (2018)

8. Cheng, J., Bernstein, M.S.: Flock: hybrid crowd-machine learning classifiers. In: Proceedings of the 18th ACM Conference on Computer Supported Cooperative Work & Social Computing, pp. 600–611. ACM (2015)

9. Cheng, J., Teevan, J., Iqbal, S.T., Bernstein, M.S.: Break it down: a comparison of macro- and microtasks. In: Proceedings of the 33rd Annual ACM Conference on Human Factors in Computing Systems, CHI 2015, pp. 4061–4064. ACM, New York (2015)

10. Das, S., Cashman, D., Chang, R., Endert, A.: BEAMES: interactive multi-model steering, selection, and inspection for regression tasks. In: Symposium on Visualization in Data Science (2018, to appear)

11. Doshi-Velez, F., et al.: Accountability of AI under the law: the role of explanation. CoRR abs/1711.01134 (2017). http://arxiv.org/abs/1711.01134

12. Dudley, J.J., Kristensson, P.O.: A review of user interface design for interactive machine learning. ACM Trans. Interact. Intell. Syst. (TiiS) **8**(2), 8 (2018)

13. Fails, J.A., Olsen, Jr., D.R.: Interactive machine learning. In: Proceedings of the 8th International Conference on Intelligent User Interfaces, IUI 2003, pp. 39–45. ACM, New York (2003)

14. Fogarty, J., Tan, D., Kapoor, A., Winder, S.: Cueflik: interactive concept learning in image search. In: Proceedings of the SIGCHI Conference on Human Factors in Computing Systems, pp. 29–38. ACM (2008)

15. Fraser, C.A., Dontcheva, M., Winnemöller, H., Ehrlich, S., Klemmer, S.: DiscoverySpace: suggesting actions in complex software. In: Proceedings of the 2016 ACM Conference on Designing Interactive Systems, DIS 2016, pp. 1221–1232. ACM, New York (2016)

16. Goodman, B., Flaxman, S.: European Union regulations on algorithmic decision-making and a "right to explanation". AI Mag. **38**(3), 50–57 (2017)

17. Hartmann, B., Abdulla, L., Mittal, M., Klemmer, S.R.: Authoring sensor-based interactions by demonstration with direct manipulation and pattern recognition. In: Proceedings of the SIGCHI Conference on Human Factors in Computing Systems, pp. 145–154. ACM (2007)

18. Horvitz, E.: Principles of mixed-initiative user interfaces. In: Proceedings of the SIGCHI Conference on Human Factors in Computing Systems, CHI 1999, pp. 159–166. ACM, New York (1999)

19. Horvitz, E., Apacible, J.: Learning and reasoning about interruption. In: Proceedings of the 5th International Conference on Multimodal Interfaces, ICMI 2003, pp. 20–27. ACM, New York (2003)

20. Hudson, S., et al.: Predicting human interruptibility with sensors: a wizard of Oz feasibility study. In: Proceedings of the SIGCHI Conference on Human Factors in Computing Systems, CHI 2003, pp. 257–264. ACM, New York (2003)

21. Hutter, F., Lücke, J., Schmidt-Thieme, L.: Beyond manual tuning of hyperparameters. KI-Künstliche Intelligenz **29**(4), 329–337 (2015)

22. Iqbal, S.T., Bailey, B.P.: Investigating the effectiveness of mental workload as a predictor of opportune moments for interruption. In: CHI 2005 Extended Abstracts on Human Factors in Computing Systems, pp. 1489–1492. ACM, New York (2005)

23. Iqbal, S.T., Bailey, B.P.: Effects of intelligent notification management on users and their tasks. In: Proceedings of the SIGCHI Conference on Human Factors in Computing Systems, CHI 2008, pp. 93–102. ACM, New York (2008)

24. Jandot, C., Simard, P., Chickering, M., Grangier, D., Suh, J.: Interactive semantic featuring for text classification. arXiv preprint arXiv:1606.07545 (2016)

25. Kanter, J.M., Veeramachaneni, K.: Deep feature synthesis: towards automating data science endeavors. In:. IEEE 2015 International Conference on Data Science and Advanced Analytics (DSAA), pp. 1–10. IEEE (2015). 36678
26. Kulesza, T., Amershi, S., Caruana, R., Fisher, D., Charles, D.: Structured labeling for facilitating concept evolution in machine learning. In: Proceedings of the SIGCHI Conference on Human Factors in Computing Systems, pp. 3075–3084. ACM (2014)
27. Kulesza, T., Burnett, M., Wong, W.K., Stumpf, S.: Principles of explanatory debugging to personalize interactive machine learning. In: Proceedings of the 20th International Conference on Intelligent User Interfaces, pp. 126–137. ACM (2015)
28. McFarlane, D.: Comparison of four primary methods for coordinating the interruption of people in human-computer interaction. Hum.-Comput. Interact. $\mathbf{17}$(1), 63–139 (2002)
29. Meek, C.: A characterization of prediction errors. CoRR abs/1611.05955 (2016). http://arxiv.org/abs/1611.05955
30. Olson, R.S., Bartley, N., Urbanowicz, R.J., Moore, J.H.: Evaluation of a tree-based pipeline optimization tool for automating data science. In: 2016 Proceedings of the Genetic and Evolutionary Computation Conference, pp. 485–492. ACM (2016)
31. Olson, R.S., Urbanowicz, R.J., Andrews, P.C., Lavender, N.A., Kidd, L.C., Moore, J.H.: Automating biomedical data science through tree-based pipeline optimization. In: Squillero, G., Burelli, P. (eds.) EvoApplications 2016. LNCS, vol. 9597, pp. 123–137. Springer, Cham (2016). https://doi.org/10.1007/978-3-319-31204-0_9
32. Patel, K., Bancroft, N., Drucker, S.M., Fogarty, J., Ko, A.J., Landay, J.: Gestalt: integrated support for implementation and analysis in machine learning. In: Proceedings of the 23nd Annual ACM Symposium on User Interface Software and Technology, pp. 37–46. ACM (2010)
33. Pedregosa, F., et al.: Scikit-learn: machine learning in Python. J. Mach. Learn. Res. $\mathbf{12}$(Oct), 2825–2830 (2011)
34. Simard, P.Y., et al.: Machine teaching: a new paradigm for building machine learning systems. arXiv preprint arXiv:1707.06742 (2017)
35. Weld, D.S., Bansal, G.: Intelligible artificial intelligence. CoRR abs/1803.04263 (2018). http://arxiv.org/abs/1803.04263
36. Xiao, J., Catrambone, R., Stasko, J.: Be quiet? Evaluating proactive and reactive user interface assistants. In: Proceedings of INTERACT, vol. 3, pp. 383–390 (2003)
37. Yang, Q., Suh, J., Chen, N.C., Ramos, G.: Grounding interactive machine learning tool design in how non-experts actually build models. ACM, June 2018
38. Zhu, X.: Machine teaching: an inverse problem to machine learning and an approach toward optimal education. In: The Twenty-Ninth AAAI Conference on Artificial Intelligence (2015)

Welcome, Computer! How Do Participants Introduce a Collaborative Application During Face-to-Face Interaction?

Mateusz Dolata[1]([⊠]), Susanne Steigler[1], Fiona Nüesch[2],
Ulrike Schock[2], Doris Agotai[2], Simon Schubiger[2], Mehmet Kilic[1],
and Gerhard Schwabe[1]

[1] University of Zurich, Zurich, Switzerland
dolata@ifi.uzh.ch
[2] University of Applied Sciences and Arts Northwestern Switzerland,
Windisch, Switzerland

Abstract. During cooperative interaction, participants introduce materials, artefacts, and other individuals into the ongoing interaction. Depending on how this introduction unfolds, the participants may embrace the new element in an easy way or not. If the new element is a collaborative application of interactive software designed to support the interaction, it may or may not improve the collaboration because of how it was introduced. Therefore, understanding and designing the initial interaction is key for unleashing the positive impact of collaborative systems. The literature has identified the fact that humans employ a specific range of behaviors when introducing an element into an ongoing interaction. Those introduction rituals are determined by whether the new element is a human or a material artefact. Introduction rituals involving interactive elements are still underexplored: How do participants introduce and initiate interaction with them? This manuscript explores the introduction behaviors emerging when an augmented-reality collaborative application is being introduced into a financial advisory service. It shows that the participants employ a wider range of introduction rituals during the introduction of this application than they do when they introduce a brochure. Notably, many of the observed behaviors resemble familiar opening rituals typically used when introducing and greeting humans. This supports the *computers-are-social-actors* argument and provides evidence that introducing a collaborative application has a social rather than a material character.

Keywords: Advisory service scenario · Mixed reality · Augmented reality · Collaborative applications · Rituals · Computers-are-social-actors

1   Introduction

When collaborating humans engage in a range of rituals, which at first glance may appear insignificant. However, those ancillary activities set the context for the interaction and require effort from participants, but are rarely acknowledged as work. Consider a group brainstorming: would you, as a participant, pay attention to the distribution of blank post-its at the beginning? Consider a lively group conversation:

© IFIP International Federation for Information Processing 2019
Published by Springer Nature Switzerland AG 2019
D. Lamas et al. (Eds.): INTERACT 2019, LNCS 11748, pp. 600–621, 2019.
https://doi.org/10.1007/978-3-030-29387-1_35

would you observe the shaking hands ritual when a person joins the setting? Trivial acts like distributing post-its or shaking hands, seem out of scope – the participants' focus is on the *actual work*. Nevertheless, ancillary activities are key: brainstorming needs post-its, or an equivalent, and greeting a person in many cultures involves a handshake.

Especially when introducing and greeting another person, humans engage in ancillary activities, which seem necessary but are unrelated to the content or topic of the conversation. Handshakes, smiles, and mutual gazing follow each other in a synchronized order and the participants execute them without explicit effort or conscious focus. However, if one does *not* engage in those acts, others might take it as an offense or antisocial behavior. In such moments, when something does not work as expected, humans notice that those ancillary activities are a crucial part of the 'real work.' If one forgets people's names when greeting them, it is as if there were not enough post-its for everyone during brainstorming. It seems that some performances, though apparently superfluous, are essential for subsequent interaction between humans.

Goffman frames those routine, socially expected and formulaic performances as interaction rituals [27]. He provides evidence that those rituals solidify the feelings of regard and respect for oneself and other participants, thus setting the stage for effective interaction [70]. By describing the extraordinary richness of interaction rituals in many situations, like introductions or greetings, Goffman draws a picture of ancillary activities as ordered and rich performances which are integral to the social interaction rather than simply accompanying it [27, 40]. He moves the ancillary activities to the center of attention and, by using ritual as metaphor, adds a touch of sacred, spiritual meaning to social interaction between individuals [40]. We follow up on Goffman's concept of an interaction ritual as distinct actions, which order an interaction and allow the participants to present themselves in a desired manner. In this article, we focus on the discrete rituals involved in introduction sequences.

Introductions do not involve only humans. Humans may introduce new material, new collaboration tools, or new software when interacting with others. However, only a handful of researchers analyze introduction rituals related to materials or technology in a face-to-face interaction. Even fewer app and technology developers evaluate their designs from this point of view. This holds true in particular for collaborative systems: studies highlight the advantages, usage patterns, and appropriation moves, but the act of introducing the application into the ongoing interaction remains obfuscated. It seems like collaborative applications were simply present during collaboration – anything else remains an ancillary activity. Consequently, we have a limited understanding of *what rituals humans employ when a collaborative application is being introduced into an ongoing face-to-face interaction*. The main objective of this study is to describe introduction rituals, i.e., singled out, routine and formulaic activities of individuals participating in a collaborative scenario, which feature the introduction of an IT-based collaborative application. Additionally, the study aims to compare the identified rituals with introduction rituals described in the literature or observed in non-IT settings to give the reader a better sense of how they are performed. In detail the study explores the relationship between rituals emerging around a collaborative application and those

involving interaction with humans, where the performances provide a way to show respect to someone. Making rituals explicit and accessible can help engineers to embrace and implement them in the design of collaborative software.

Based on the analysis of video recordings from financial advisory services, this study identifies introduction rituals that occur when the advisor introduces a collaborative application into an ongoing advisory service. Comparison to the act of introducing a common material artefact (a brochure) reveals that introducing the collaborative application makes use of a wider range of interaction rituals. Comparison to the literature on introduction suggests that when introducing computer software applications, the participants tend to employ rituals otherwise typical for human introductions and greetings. Introduction of a brochure does not exhibit such tendencies. The study employs multiple perspectives to provide a rich description of introduction rituals and identify which features of the collaborative application afford those rituals.

The study builds upon previous discourses in research and practice. It adds to the discourse on interaction with IT in collaborative settings by supporting the *computers-are-social-actors* argument: participants embrace a software application from the very beginning, from the act of introducing it, as a social actor [55, 66] and produce performances that are normally used to show respect to other humans. This complements previous research on introducing and initiating use of a computer in an institutional setting, e.g., between a doctor and a patient [60]. It also adds to the conversation analysis efforts to understand the role of materials in coordinating communication between humans [16]. It should sensitize designers to the importance of introductions and provide them with stimuli and patterns to think about how users might proceed while using their application during collaboration. In addition, practitioners such as frontline employees at banks and other institutions may benefit from a deep analysis of micro-level behaviors and better understand how those behaviors affect the client. Overall, the study provides insights that may contribute towards software design and behavioral research.

2   Related Work

This paper intends to explicate introduction rituals involving a collaborative application and to compare those rituals against the backdrop of other introduction rituals just mentioned. This section provides relevant background starting with the most traditional form of introduction rituals involving an individual, and then introduction rituals involving materials such as brochures or sheets of paper (being the most widely used collaborative resources), and finally the scarce literature covering the introduction of IT. Whereas the literature acknowledges the ritual nature of introduction between humans, material and IT-focused performances are presented as material behaviors, even though they order the sequence of an interaction and let the humans keep up appearances, thus matching the characteristics of rituals.

2.1   Introducing a Person

Conversation analysis (CA) studies established a solid basis of knowledge about how people initiate interaction with other humans [41, 63, 68]. The literature differentiates between two types of introductions: self-initiated introduction (when a person introduces oneself) and other-initiated introductions [12, 62]. Other-initiated introductions are situations in which a third person, such as a mediator, introduces a newcomer to a pre-present person or pre-existing group of people, i.e., the individuals who had interacted with the mediator before the newcomer arrived [62]. CA studies identify a range of ritualized verbal and non-verbal behaviors which accompany the introduction of a person [22, 49, 51, 52, 56, 64].

When introducing a person, humans use a range of non-verbal and verbal cues. Whereas cultural differences may occur, here we consider introductions among Europeans and Americans. Imagine a situation that might happen at a conference. Ann and Marc are enjoying a conversation during a coffee break, while Bob, a third colleague, is getting closer to them. Bob is approaching while signalizing an intention to join the conversation with gaze and movement [64]. Ann knows Bob and steps in the role of the mediator. According to CA studies, the interaction is likely to unfold as follows: Ann changes her position such that the three will form a circle [14, 41]; Marc adapts his position as well [62]. Ann makes a deictic reference to Bob (like "This is Bob") including details relevant to the context (job, position, name, etc.) [61, 63]. The deictic utterances involve specific gestures: Ann gestures toward Bob when introducing him [62]. Marc follows the indication and looks at Bob. Thereafter, Marc is likely to initiate interaction with Bob using a greeting ("Hello", "Good morning") and an adequate bodily reaction (a handshake or a short wave) [56, 62]. He might smile [22] and adapt a welcoming posture [41] – mutual gazing and palms turned open [22]. A range of verbal behaviors comes thereafter, including introduction-specific assessments ("nice to meet you"), opening-specific utterances ("how are you?"), and repetition of the name of the introduced person (Marc saying "Hi Bob"), as well as emotional semi-language ("oh", "ah", "well") [62]. The sequence takes few moments and the performances are well coordinated, even among strangers [62, 63]. Introductions have a ritual character similar to theatrical performances – all participants seem to know what to do, such that the interaction unveils smoothly [22, 29]. Furthermore, the participants behave in a respectful way and produce multiple signs of respect (positions, postures, emotional or polite utterances), which underscores the fact that rituals reinforce social order and signalize the mutual recognition between the parties [27, 40, 70]. The ritual relies not only on the mere occurrence of particular behaviors, but also on the relations between them: their sequence, mutuality, and the links between the verbal and non-verbal conduct [51, 52].

The configuration involving a mediator (Ann), a newcomer (Bob) and a pre-present participant (Marc) resemble what happens when a computer enters the stage in an advisory service. The advisor, as the one who knows the system and hosts the interaction, takes on the role of the mediator and introduces the collaborative application to the pre-present client. However, it remains unclear whether and to what extent insights about the introduction rituals related to a person can be transferred to a situation where a material, – a collaborative application or any form of interactive IT – gets introduced.

2.2 Introducing a Material Artefact

Whereas introduction among humans has been studied for decades, studies on how individuals introduce new material into an ongoing interaction arrived much later [48, 52]. Only a few articles consider the introduction and use of material artefacts in informal collaboration [53]. The primary focus lies on institutional settings ranging from academic supervision [54, 74] to performance appraisal interviews [48] to doctor-patient encounters [11] to the financial advisory services at a bank [16]. Given that paper (brochures, forms, notepads, etc.) remains the most widely spread material in institutional collaboration, most insights refer to the use of paper [16, 50, 74]. The analyses encompass the use of material in various situations as a whole and only rarely address a particular phase of interaction like beginning or closing [9, 52]. Instead, most CA studies relate the material rituals to conversational processes like turn taking or activity shifts [28, 31, 52, 54, 74]. This study takes a different path and focuses on the various verbal acts that accompany the initial use of an artefact.

Taking together the insights and observations from previous literature, one can identify some verbal and non-verbal behaviors typical for initial use of material arte-facts. Given the fact that material usage in student counselling has been extensively researched [30, 73, 74], we explore that example here. There is solid evidence that similar behaviors may occur in financial services [16] or in doctor-patient encounters [11]. Consider a situation involving Barbara, a university teacher, and a student, Mike, sitting at a table in a university office and discussing Mike's seminar thesis. Barbara has prepared by putting away documents that cluttered the table beforehand [30, 74]. While Mike explains what he has done so far, Barbara listens, first keeping a pen in her hand, and then leafing through a pile of documents to her left, while encouraging Mike to talk further [74]. She takes two pieces of paper and organizes the remaining ones back into the pile [74]; she places the two sheets of paper in the middle of the table, next to each other [74]. Mike stops talking and Barbara says: "Okay, I get it. Well, let's take this first; you can read it, right?" while pointing to one of the documents. "Then we will go through that one. Maybe I remember it" – she continues while pointing to the other document. Mike nods and responds "mhm"; they continue while looking at the doc-uments. This short scenario comprises typical behaviors that characterize the use of material in institutional collaboration [11, 16, 30, 73–75]. In particular, documents – even if central to the ongoing activity – enter the stage without explicit introduction. Instead, they are used more as an "excuse" to move to the next activity. Rituals involve ordering the documents (in the pile and on the table), as well as keeping up the ongoing interaction despite the act of introducing a material.

2.3 Introducing a Machine

The introduction of IT into an ongoing face-to-face interaction attracted researchers' attention much later. The research splits into two streams: first, studies oriented around the introduction of "traditional" desktop computer [7, 20, 59, 60, 76] and second, those

dealing with human-robot interaction [21, 25]. There is little overlap between the two streams: On the one hand, studies on the introduction of desktop computers appear in healthcare informatics [60, 76], studies of IT use in public domain [2, 45], or IT-oriented workplace studies [46]. On the other hand, studies from human-robot inter-action and from robotics attend to the initial interactions between humans and robots in the process of developing new technologies and applications [65]. Since robots are a new phenomenon, researchers are still in the process of exploring and designing the initial interactions – rituals still need to emerge. Therefore, we focus on introduction rituals involving collaborative applications using state-of-the-art interfaces.

Computers entered doctors' offices and public agencies years ago. Recall a typical interaction with a doctor (or a frontline employee, etc.). Let's call her Eve. Perhaps, Eve has a monitor standing on her desk, the display turned toward her [2, 60]. There is also a mouse and a keyboard on the table [58, 60]. Eve interacts with her conversation partner, but from time to time, she turns towards the computer; she also types things using the keyboard or uses the mouse [60, 76]. The computer remains Eve's "private" tool during the interaction; the patient/client may see some things on the screen, but they remain outside the scope of the conversation [59]. This is so until Eve turns the screen and presents an interesting artefact shown there, let's say, an X-ray image. She points to the display, says "This is your leg, you see – there is your injury from the past" and uses her pen to pinpoint a specific area in the image [2]. Eve and her conversation partner move closer to the screen and look at the picture, then at each other [60]. Eve continues talking, while the other party nods and acknowledges with "uh huh" [19]. Situations like occur millions of times every day. The desktop computer does not need an introduction: it is already there, on the table [1, 13, 57]. Nevertheless, Eve employs deictic gestures and words when using the computer for the first time as a collaborative resource. The rituals she engages in involve deictic utterances and rota-tion of the screen analogous to the introduction of a leaflet as described before.

Given the framing of computers as a collaborative resource, this behavior seems adequate. However, it contrasts with an alternative popular view on computers in social interaction: *"computers-are-social-actors"* (CASA) [55, 66]. Research following this paradigm claims and provides evidence that humans tend to treat technology like they would treat other humans, thus applying the heuristics and behavior schemata used for humans, to computers. For instance, humans may talk to their computers or assume human intelligence behind a computer's actions. During the introduction, one could expect behaviors akin to those of Marc, Ann and Bob rather than those of Barbara and Mike. But the literature on introducing computers into collaboration does not analyse the introduction sequences in terms of the CASA paradigm. The scarce evidence includes no indication that human participants treat computers in any special way.

3 Designing for Introduction Rituals

3.1 Context: Status Quo in IT-Supported Advisory Services

An advisory service is a collaborative encounter between a professional advisor and an advisee [23, 38]. The participants differ in terms of their knowledge, institutional

identity and interaction rights. The client knows about his[1] problems in the initial situation, which can be solved with the advisor's expertise on the potential solutions [39]. Advisors are in charge of distributing interaction rights and dominate the encounter in verbal [17, 32] and material [17, 74] terms. It is the advisor who distributes brochures and documents across the table and invites the advisee to contribute [43]. In the current study, we focus on mortgage advisory services of a Swiss local bank.

The Swiss real estate market depends on mortgage loans. Clients attend to advisory services if they fulfill (or they think they fulfill) the minimum requirements, e.g., 20% of house price available, or they identified a property to buy [10]. During an advisory service, the advisor first learns about the advisee's wishes and situation, then she explains the available products and makes a recommendation [38]. In a traditional mortgage advisory service, the participants first consider the chosen property, and then they assess the advisee's financial capability and eligibility for a mortgage. If those are met, the advisor describes the possible range of choices (fix-rate and flexible mortgage, with and without amortization) and prepares a composition that fits advisee's needs.

Rituals bind the various elements of an advisory service together, such that the participants, who never met before, establish a coherent encounter [8]. Many rituals relate to first impressions and the management of expectations [27]: a bank advisor dresses in a manner signaling her role [26, 36], positions documents in an orderly manner [16], manages mutual eye gaze and shows interest in advisee's spoken words and body language [42]. However, introducing a collaborative application is not an established ritual. Research shows that advisors and advisees try to embrace a new system ad-hoc and establish clumsy interaction protocols [42]. As a consequence, more and longer pauses occur than in an conventional encounter [17]. Overall, the literature suggests that initiating the use of a collaborative IT system during an advisory service yields unintended interruptions and destroys key rituals.

We propose the following interpretation of the problem: The systems presented in previous research neither fit the typical rituals of advisory services (such as advisor presenting oneself with a business card [16], advisor introducing the central topic with a drawing or leaflet [16], or advisor showing knowledge about the property to be supported with the mortgage and its location [16]), nor do they explicitly afford an alternative ritual that could accompany the introduction of the collaborative application. As a consequence, the idea of an advisory encounter embodied in routines, roles and expectations falls apart and leaves the participants in an improvisation mode.

To address this problem, we launched a project to develop a system aligned with the conventional advisors' practices. Since those practices rely on paper, pen and brochures, the designed system handles physical interaction. On the other hand, to enhance the interaction, the system allows, e.g., for dynamic adaptation of graphics, which is impossible with "normal" paper. An article, which describes the system in more detail, is under review. Herein we focus on the initial interaction with the system and thus, review only the elements used to initiate the application as a collaborative resource.

---

[1] To guarantee a balanced gender representation and readability of the manuscript, we refer to the advisee as a male (he, his, him) and the advisor as a female (she, her).

3.2   Technology: Mixed Reality for Physical Interaction

Mixed reality (MR) research has long studied integration of embodied and physical interaction with digital processing. It addresses the topic of digital and material reality in a way that allows for full use of space and body during interaction with digital content [18], thus making it possible to support specific rituals. MR embraces a set of research directions. Augmented reality (AR) studies how to overlay physical spaces with computer-generated content [3, 5]; spatial AR uses projection to put the content directly into the environment of the user [6, 15], however it requires powerful and high-fidelity overhead projectors and affordable 4 K beamers, which arrived on the market only three years ago. Organic user interfaces focus on projecting content onto non-planar spaces that users can interact with through bending, folding, and manipulating the form [33, 34]. Tangible user interfaces focus on enabling interaction, manipulation, and collaboration [69] with digital content through physical objects and space [35, 79]. Pen-and-paper user interfaces try to bridge the gap between digital interaction and paper, which remains an essential tool in many human activities [47, 71, 72]. All those areas of research share an interest in enhancing the physical world with digital content and functionalities to enable natural interaction with objects, avatars and other people [4]. The subsequent section explains how MR-inspired features were leveraged to enable introduction of the collaborative application during a mortgage advisory service.

3.3   Design: Mixed Reality for Introduction Rituals in Advisory Services

Observations and preliminary interviews with the advisors revealed that a critical point during the beginning of an advisory service is the first mention of the property. When switching from opening small talk to the core of the service, advisors often address the property in various ways [16]: an advisor demonstrates her knowledge about the specific neighborhood to give the impression of an interested and informed profes-sional; another advisor asks questions about the private motivations behind the pur-chase to better understand the client's emotions; and other advisors simply engage in a courteous discussion concerning the property to establish rapport with the client. So far, the advisors supported this part of the conversation with no material or, at most, with printouts of basic data about the house, such as an advertisement. This contributed little to the content of the conversation. Those practices inspired the design team: on the one hand, there was potential to make the conversation more informative by introducing additional information resources; on the other hand, it offered an opportunity to introduce the IT as a collaborative application before the participants move on to hard math tasks like calculating the mortgage rate and interest. Taking into account the possibilities of mixed reality, the designers proposed a *house token & map* design.

The *house token & map* builds on and extends mortgage advisory service. It envisions the following interaction: When the advisor wants to shift the conversation topic to the property, she uses a 3D model of a house made out of concrete and puts it in the middle of the table. She can zoom in or out and switch between map and satellite view. When moving the house token around the table, she moves the whole projection with it, such that the house token always marks the location of the property (based on its address). The map allows viewing of the facilities in the neighborhood, like schools,

grocery shops, or train stations to fuel the conversation about the property. The *house token & map* design sources from existing practice, but extends it and moves the focus of conversation beyond numerical and technical values (size, number of rooms, year of construction, floor covering, etc.) or purely emotional topics (motivation to buy) to the location. This design augments the conversation rituals with additional data and inspires a different outlook on the property. We developed a system that supplied the *house token & map* (Fig. 1) functionality at the beginning of service, just after small talk.

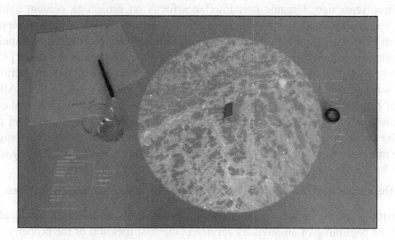

Fig. 1. Map projection with the concrete house token in the middle.

4 Methodology

4.1 Design and Implementation

LivePaper is a collaborative application for financial advisory services. It uses paper practices and augments them with projected content. The system was developed by a Swiss local bank and two universities in a joint project intended to support client-centric advisory services. It provides the means for easy generation of documentation, as well as streamlining the overall process. The whole project followed the research through design paradigm [24, 78]. Starting with practical problems, solutions were developed in a creative and iterative manner based on fieldwork, technological potentials, and models of advisory services and human interaction (e.g., theories about human introductions and greetings). Scenarios as well as clickable and functional prototypes were used to describe problems and solutions [67] and to conduct inter-mediate testing with key users, according to constructive design [44]. Scenario-based design and constructive design research have been widely used in Human-Computer Interaction (HCI) [77].

The *house token & map* design was integrated into LivePaper as one of its components. LivePaper uses a Kinect sensor to track objects on the table (sheets of paper,

tokens) as well as participants' gestures. A 4 K projector is used to project the content onto the surface of a table. Based on recognition of objects and hands, it can adjust the position of the projection, such that the content moves around together with the elements on the table. The same principle was applied to implement the *house token & map*: thanks to its form and a reflective sticker, the token could be recognized and its location tracked; the map appeared as soon as the token was placed in the projection area on the table between the advisor and the advisee; the map functionalities (zoom in, zoom out, switch view) were linked to buttons projected next to the map.

4.2   Evaluation

The developed prototype was tested in a realistic scenario to observe what kind of introduction rituals it affords. In particular, 24 non-IT and 24 LivePaper-supported service encounters were carried out within two weeks. They involved 8 professional bank advisors from the partner bank and 24 test advisees. The advisee participants were acquired through an announcement on a university platform (quota sampling). They were between 17 and 71 years old (avg. 32). There were 12 males and 12 females. Participants came from diverse professions, e.g., lawyer, therapist or architect. They received a short introduction to the setting and a realistic scenario to act upon. It included rough data about their financial status and data about two properties to be discussed with the advisor (one property per treatment). Each participant attended a LivePaper-supported and a conventional consultation. After both treatments, each advisee participated in an interview to report on their experiences and compare the two treatments. The experiment took place in two branches of the partner bank.

Overall, even though the observed advisory services were not real (the advisees were not real clients), by setting the context, scenarios and working with actual bank employees, we established a realistic situation for both clients and advisors. The advisors were neither aware of the property that the advisees received before the consultation, nor did they see the advisee beforehand. This preserves high ecological validity. In the conventional treatment, they used a calculator, notepad, and pen. In the LivePaper treatment, they employed the system designed as described above. Consequently, the task that participants needed to complete during the experiment was representative of and similar to what advisors and advisees do in actual advisory services at a bank, thus supporting the face validity. However, we acknowledge that external validity and transferability of the results beyond the scope of mortgage advisory services requires further research, as these experiments explicitly were designed to capture the complexity of mortgage advisory services.

The advisors used the *home token & map* prototype to switch between opening small talk and the core part of the encounter. Thereby they also introduced the system into an ongoing interaction: *home token & map* was the first feature of the system used during an advisory service. The advisors were trained in two iterations on how to handle the LivePaper: a half-day workshop one week before the test and a short training at the day of the session. The prototype training focused on use of LivePaper, but the advisor was free to decide when and how to introduce it to the interaction.

The primary data used for the analysis of system introduction sequences was collected through video recording. We recorded each advisory service with three

cameras: from above, from the side and facing the advisee. Consequently, we captured the conduct on the table, bodily motions, and verbal contributions of both participants, as well as the advisee's mimics. This allows for blow-by-blow study of the verbal and non-verbal conduct of how the participants introduce and accommodate the collaborative application. Observation of the conventional, non-IT treatment allows for comparison of rituals and performances between the two settings.

4.3   Data Analysis

The current study focuses on the initial interaction between human participants and LivePaper in mortgage advisory services. A set of qualitative methods is used: in-situ observation, coding of the video-recorded consultations, transcription of the interaction, and the interview analysis. For LivePaper treatment, the video-coding and the transcription focused on the 15 s surrounding the introduction of the system, i.e., putting the token in the center of the table. For conventional settings, the analysis focused on the introduction of a brochure as the first artefact of work. In both treatments, introduction occurs after the initial presentation of the concern by the advisee, thus yielding comparable episodes. The limit of 15 s was set arbitrarily, but considering time frames used in earlier studies on human introductions [41, 62].

These introduction episodes were first observed for all 48 consultations to create an ethogram of all performances. It considered body posture, face gaze direction, hand movements and gestures, semi-language ("oh", "ah"), utterances and mimics. These episodes were then encoded in the video sequences. Twenty four representative excerpts were later transcribed and annotated with multimodal data according to the Jeffersonian notation [37]. The researcher conducting the coding and multimodal transcription discussed the analysis methods and results regularly with two experienced researchers.

Apart from video analysis, interviews were used as additional source of insight. A researcher coded the 24 advisee interviews focusing on statements concerning the opening of an encounter, the first use of *house token & map*, as well as the first use of a leaflet. The coded segments were ordered according to how positive or negative they were – the results include quotes of varying sentiments. Overall, the chosen methods capture the reactions of the participants to the introduction of the collaborative application and compare it to the introduction of traditional, material artefacts.

5   Results

5.1   Introduction Sequences

The first excerpt (Table 1) shows how a female advisor introduces the system and how a male advisee reacts. We join the participants in the seventh minute of the encounter after the advisee has explained to the advisor what property he is interested in. The advisor has finished collecting the key data in her notebook (including property's

address) and puts the writing utensils away. Thereby she clearly signals an activity shift [48]. This shift is perceptible by the client, who stops looking at the property data sheet in front of him and now observes the advisor. Advisor continues by verbally referring to *"this property"* and engages in several performances to introduce and use the LivePaper for the first time in this encounter. Figure in Table 1a depicts this situation.

Table 1. Introduction of the collaborative application into an ongoing encounter according to the *home token & map* design (15 s).

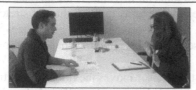

a. Indicating the end of the note-taking activity

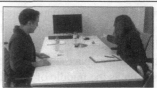

b. First approach to introduce the system

A: so yeah: this property [0.9]
A moves open palms away from the table and gazes at the table.
C remains in sitting position, his hands rest on the property data sheet he brought with him. A and C keep eye contact

A stretches her right arm far to the right, to the house token. Gaze follows her moves.
C: yeah: [1.0]
C sits upright and moves his sheets of paper away, to the left. Gaze is directed towards his sheets of paper.

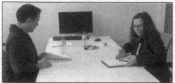

c. Interrupt and return to preparation

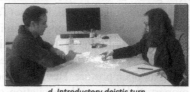

d. Introductory deictic turn

A: he:re [.]
A stops her movement and moves back to the upright sitting position. While gazing at the notepad and smiling she casts the notepad to her left, and creates a free area.
C: ˚mhm˚ [1.0]
C gazes at the pile to his left.

[...]
A: let's look at it he:re/ [0.8]
A continues to smile and places the house token with map projection on the table.
C gazes at the projection in the middle and rolls up his sleeves.

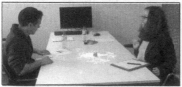

e. Making way and organizing space

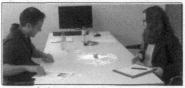

f. Showing signs of interest

A smiles and gazes at C.
C: ˚wow˚ [1.0]
C switches gaze from the middle of the table to the paper to his left and continues to pile again.
A: [laughter] [0.8]

A gazes at the house token, moves the notepad farther away to the left.
C: ah [1.2]
C smiles. Casts sheets of paper from left to right side and relaxes the arms, gazes at the projection.

First, the advisor searches for the house token and then stretches her arm to catch it. In parallel, the advisee starts preparing the space for something to come – he collects his documents, which had been distributed across two piles (Table 1b). However, the advisor stops her action suddenly and returns to her earlier position for a moment. She moves her notepad away as well. At that moment, the advisor and the advisee simultaneously engage in de-cluttering the interaction space (Table 1c). We observe the decluttering sequences before the house token arrives in the middle of the table. In all LivePaper excerpts the sequences were mostly initiated by the advisor, who starts decluttering her side of the table, and the advisee joins in. In Table 1, the advisee starts moving away pieces of paper directly after the advisor turns to the right and stretches her arm towards the house token. In any case, the advisor engages in behavior which signals something new to come and the advisees react by removing paper and other objects from the space between them.

As soon as the middle of the table is clear, the advisor moves the house token from the edge of the table to the middle and positions it between herself and the client (Table 1d). She uses a deictic expression and points to the house token or the map. The observed deictic expressions include "here", "this", "there" and "where." Often the advisors refer to the token as "this property," "your house." So does the advisor in the excerpt. The advisee reacts by engaging in several behaviors in parallel: he smiles, says "wow," gazes at the projection, moves towards the map and, as observed in this particular, case rolls up his sleeves (Table 1f). In other excerpts advisees engage in similar actions. Some advisors reorganize the interaction space even more before they proceed further with the advisee or with the system (Table 1e). The advisor alternates her gaze between the projection and the advisee. She reacts with laughter, smiling, and assuming an open posture. Having introduced the system, the advisor begins discussing the property's location. No hesitation or long explanation phases occur – the participants continue the interaction naturally. The conversation about a property's location may take from 30 s up to three minutes depending on the advisee's interest. In many cases, advisees refer to the map not only verbally, but also by pointing or even touching the surface when discussing particular elements (e.g., the way to the nearest train station). After the introduction, the advisory service continues: participants discuss the options of a mortgage credit and other important features. Finally, the advisor creates one or several offerings for the client. The overall service takes up to 45 min.

Table 2. Introduction of a leaflet into an ongoing service encounter (15 s).

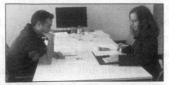

a. Indicating shift to the leaflet

```
A lifts hands and takes a leaflet out of
the folder with the left hand and holds
a pen with the right hand. She gazes at
her folder.
C gazes to the notepad of the advisor.
His head is rested on the right hand.
The left hand rests on the paper in
front of him.
```

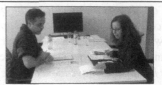

b. Deictic turn towards the leaflet

```
A: let's look at the roadmap now [2.2]
A takes out the leaflet from the folder and
starts to open it while holding a pen in the
right hand, A gazes at the leaflet and posi-
tions it at the edge of the table.
C sits up straight and moves the right hand
down. The gaze follows the leaflet.
```

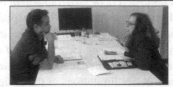

c. Interaction with the leaflet

```
A: do we have it here [1.2]
A flattens the folded leaflet with both hands. Gaze is directed towards the leaflet.
C leans forward and gazes short at the leaflet. His left hand stays calmly on his paper.
A: different options [1.0]
C: "yeah"
A moves right hand back. C and A keep eye contact. C's hands support his posture.
```

The second excerpt (Table 2) illustrates how a leaflet gets introduced in a conventional setting. One observes several introduction routines here as well. The advisor uses deictic language and gestures when putting the leaflet on the table, using a single noun to describe it ("roadmap"; Table 2b). Also, she sends out signals of an upcoming activity shift (Table 2a). However, those actions are not linked to reactions from the advisee: he does not declutter the space or spend much time gazing at the introduced artifact or say "wow" or "ah." He remains still and focused on the advisor. Even though the advisor employs some means to make the leaflet easy to read for the advisee (she flattens it, puts it in a way such that both can read it and easily point to it), the advisee's focus remains on the advisor. He keeps his hands on the table. Overall, neither the advisor nor the advisee prepares the table or make way for the common artefact to come.

5.2   Introduction Experiences

When asked about their experiences and comparison between the two settings, the advisees often explicitly refer to the introduction of the system as a special moment. An advisee remembers the opening: "*and then he places the little house and a map is shown and (…) sees everything in total – you can zoom in and out. This is an incredibly great opening. Something like this, is incredibly amazing, I was perplexed*" (K18). While many clients confirm this effect, some doubt that it has impact on the pragmatic side of

the advisory service: *"First you see the house where it is located, just this. I mean, it is really nice that I can see it already. Just «wow»! But it is not required for the business"* (K05) or *"It was pretty chic at the beginning with the house to see where it is. But the practical benefit seems limited: I know where the property is I am going to buy"* (K14). Still, when explicitly asked for their feelings, many advisees see the introduction as a relevant phase to generate positive emotions: *"The emotions were stronger with Live-Paper because we have looked at the object and where it is and how is the environment. We have zoomed out and in. During the first conventional advice, the advisor has not even asked for the street. It was really just about the purchase price and that's it. (...) That you yourself see the object again. That you are also really sure that you really want to buy the object. This is what makes you have a positive feeling"* (K15).

The advisees liked the choice to use a 3D model of a house as a token made of concrete. *"You can relate to that (...) that may be a play-house, but it attracts my attention or places me in the atmosphere or environment of this house"* (K25). However, this decision also generated problems. As an advisee explains: *"So it was great to see where is the property is - bird's eye view. What bothered me: it would be better if the property was not covered by the concrete house token. That was right in the middle of it. This means that one does not have a chance to look at the actual property on the map"* (K05). Even though the clients notice limitations of the design, they acknowledge that it positively impacted their emotional engagement in the initial interaction.

The advisees like the fact that the introduction of the system happens with an interesting topic. An advisee puts it as follows: *"The advisor was showing interest in my property (...) actually more with the LivePaper. This was so because he was really asking where it is and where it has been displayed on the map, (...) where it is exactly and what location it has, actually more with the Life Paper. The conventional service is more so serious: « I have the house and I want it and it costs so and so much » ; and then « okay, let's start to calculate»"* (K06). The observations of the frequency of advisees' positive reactions during introduction episodes confirm the overall emotional attitude of advisees towards the interaction around the house token – see Table 3.

Table 3. The frequency of specific behaviors in the introduction sequences (15 s).

Behavior	LivePaper	No IT
C smiles	11	0
C bends over the table	20	10
C declutters the table	17	0
C moves hand to the middle	4	0
C says "oh!" or "ah!"	3	0

6 Discussion

This paper's objective was to describe the rituals involved in the introduction of a collaborative application and to compare them to other typical introduction rituals. The above analysis points to key differences concerning the introduction of collaborative material artefacts and the introduction of LivePaper, which uses the *home token & map*

design. When introducing a leaflet, the advisor selects the correct leaflet from a folder, carefully positions it on the table, assuring that she and the client can read it, and verbally encourages the client to look at it and points at it with her hand. This sequence of actions resembles what earlier research described for a range of institutional situations [11, 16, 30, 73–75]. Also, the reactions of the client are not much different from what was already observed: he bends over slightly, looks at the leaflet and/or at the advisor, he shortly confirms his interest with a short "yeah." We can confirm what literature has already stated: material supports activity shift and the advisor can use it to move the focus of the client to a specific topic, as well as to push the conversation along further [28, 31, 52, 54, 74]. Perhaps because the introduction of the leaflet as the collaborative artefact is so ordinary, no participant remarks on it explicitly in the interview.

It is quite the opposite with the *house token & map*. Many interviewees refer to the house token, map or their introduction even if not asked directly. In fact, advisors and advisee behave extraordinarily when they initiate the interaction with LivePaper using the *house token & map* design. In those introduction sequences, the advisor not only produces deictic utterances and positions the token carefully on the table, but also prepares the space necessary for it, smiles, and rearranges the space again when the projection is visible on the table. She refers to the house token as a "property" and repeats some deictic reference when presenting it ("here," "it"). Even without comparison to the reference literature, one observes that the advisor puts forth additional effort during the introduction sequence. She behaves as if she was preparing the stage for an important element to enter the ongoing interaction. This goes beyond the usual rituals of introducing a material artefact [11, 16, 30, 73–75] or an artefact on a desktop computer's monitor [13, 19, 45, 46, 57–60, 76]. In particular, it is not a straightforward turn of a monitor [2] or a positioning of material [74]. The interaction with the house token is a theatrical performance and involves emotional gestures from the advisor, such as showing both palms at the beginning of the performance or repeated pointing to the token. The client's reactions confirm that the situation is unusual: he declutters the space, smiles, bends forward, and sometimes even dares to make physical contact with the application. Also, we observe some emotional semi-language ("oh!", "ah!") in addition to the more usual "yes," "mhm", and "okay." Those reactions do not resemble observations reported for the introduction of material artefacts or artefacts displayed on a desktop monitor [13, 19, 60]. Something essential is different.

We argue there is a shallow and a deeper explanation for the reported results. The shallow interpretation relies on comparison between the typical human introduction as analyzed in ethnomethodological studies [14, 41, 52, 56, 61–64]. They share a lot: participants adapt new, open positions; they are directly referring to the newcomer by explaining meaning and background; there is an intensive gazing towards the newcomer; and, finally, there are welcoming gestures, touches, and emotional semi-language expressions. It seems that the *home token & map* design affords rituals otherwise employed when introducing and greeting humans. But what makes the simple design elements (a concrete house model and a map) more *social* than the leaflet?

The *house token & map* design, in fact, implements some features that make the system and its elements easier to embrace by the participants than the leaflet (or any generic element like a piece of paper or a desktop monitor):

- The house token is *meaningful based on its form and has a clear relation to the content of the ongoing interaction.* It simply stands for the property, which the advisee is going to buy. The advisee can easily decipher the meaning of the object when the advisor moves it to the center of the table. It is similar to what happens when a human newcomer enters an ongoing interaction: the pre-present participants perceive the newcomer's intention to join based on the context and her or his apparent role. Before the newcomer enters, the pre-present participants plot a story in their minds about what the newcomer's intentions and expected behaviors are. Think of a situation when a beggar approaches someone on the bus stop with their hand stretched out – one can easily predict what to expect. This is not possible when a monitor gets turned or when a brochure enters the stage during an advisory session: those elements do not provide enough data for the advisee to craft a meaningful plot.
- The house token and the map *afford deictic, physical references.* It seems natural to the participants to point at the house as a physical object and to denote locations with "here" and "there." It resembles what happens when a newcomer joins an ongoing interaction, and someone introduces them: pointing toward someone (or something) in our physical space belongs to the standard repertoire of communication. While pointing at objects displayed on the screen or in a brochure is possible as well, it requires more precise pointing, because these things are smaller and often more numerous (screens and brochures contain multiple images). Using a pen to point to a small element seems more natural then, while pointing with a pen to a person or larger object is unusual. Due to hand-sized elements *House token & map* promotes physical reference with gestures involving hands, fingers or a pen.
- Finally, the design *affords movement in space to signalize activity shift.* And this movement is very specific: the advisor moves the house token into the center of the table from the edge. This horizontal trajectory resembles the situation when a newcomer approaches a pre-existing group of people. When someone turns a monitor around or pulls a piece of paper from a pile or a folder, the object moves along a different path and this movement is shorter. In fact, starting the house token nearer the center was not possible because it would directly turn on the map and disturb the participants' small talk. Admittedly, this technical limitation contributed to the theatrical character of the introduction sequence, but it does not explain such behaviors as decluttering the space or showing open palms. Overall, the advisor's movements marked activity shifts and signalized a new element coming to the stage.

According to this shallow interpretation of the results, the above design decisions make participants attach a social character to the introduction of the *house token & map.* This would align with the "computers-are-social-actors" paradigm: the participants conduct actions otherwise typical for ritual introduction of a human actor. They prepare a dedicated space, produce emotional semi-language or attempt physical contact in a careful and respectful manner. It seems as if the participants were following typical schemata for introducing a (small) human individual. One could claim that the results even extend the previous paradigm. Originally, the CASA paradigm claimed that users transfer human attributes to technology because modern technologies use

language as input and output, are interactive, or replace typically human roles [66]. The current results suggest that due to a hunch or intuition that an interactive technology might come to the table, users apply introduction schemata reserved for humans. This is surprising, given the fact that previous research on introducing computers has not reported similar observations [1, 13, 57]. There are two possible explanations for this difference: (1) previous studies have not topicalized the social character of the observed behavior or (2) humans treat computers like social actors only in specific circumstances. Identifying and describing those circumstances would require further research. This study suggests that the physical form and emotional value of the computer may play a role in this regard.

However, consideration of what a social ritual is and why it emerges provides a complementary, yet deeper explanation. Ritualized performances in interaction with other humans emerge not only through mindless repetition. Humans replicate rituals because, through those behaviors, they can show respect to the other party (or at least pretend to do so) [27, 40, 70]. This understanding helps interpret the results. For instance, an advisee's decluttering is a ritual response to advisor's efforts: when the advisee notices the advisor reaching for something or decluttering her side of the table, he is driven to acknowledge this by making space for what is coming. The advisee's smiles and emotional utterances show not only interest and pleasure, but also signalize acknowledgement of the advisor's efforts. Finally, advisee's bending forward or pointing towards the map do not follow only from curiosity in the content, but acknowledge the advisor's effort. Following this line of argumentation, the advisor's actions can be seen as a consequence of the physical affordances of the *house token & map* design and the reactions from the advisee as ritualized acknowledgment of the advisor's work. The collected data does not provide a conclusive answer as to which explanation is the right one. Of course, these two mechanisms (*computers-are-social-actors* and *ritualized respect signs*) are not incompatible; the observed behaviors can be driven by both of them.

7   Conclusion and Limitations

The presented insights do not come without limitations. First, we rely on data collected in a realistic, but experimental context. While this helps us to compare the encounters and identify patterns in predefined conditions, it also generates questions about external validity. Replicating this study with clients in real advisory services outside the mortgage context could produce more insight, especially because of potentially stronger emotional engagement. Second, the results rely on field observations and video material. We report on observed regularities rather than making quantitative claims about them. Measuring the occurrences of particular performances might be the next step to further support the findings. Third, the transferability of the identified design rationales still needs to be confirmed. Analyzing whether doctor-patient or teacher-student encounters exhibit similar patterns requires design and observational research.

All in all, this paper provides a genuine, focused analysis of how participants introduce and "welcome" a collaborative application. The paper makes several

contributions: It identifies atypical behaviors in introduction sequences for a collaborative application thus extending previous literature on initial interaction with computers [1, 13, 57]. It relates the observations to the implemented design decisions, thereby adding to the research on supporting advisory services [17, 42], which did not explicitly consider initial interaction or MR technology so far. Finally, it offers interpretation of the rituals in light of two social interaction theories and provides supporting evidence from realistic, controlled setting rather than from abstract experiments or anecdotes [55, 66]. It also compares those behaviors to the introduction sequences derived and consolidated from ethnomethodological research. The study highlights a crucial but neglected aspect of technology use – the "welcoming" phase, provides new perspectives on it, and offers both theoretical and practical interpretations of the observed behaviors.

References

1. Als, A.B.: The desk-top computer as a magic box: patterns of behaviour connected with the desk-top computer; GPs' and patients' perceptions. Fam. Pract. **14**, 17–23 (1997)
2. Arvola, M.: Shades of use: The dynamics of interaction design for sociable use. Linköping University. Department of Computer and Information Science, Linköping (2004)
3. Azuma, R.T.: A survey of augmented reality. Presence Teleoperators Virtual Environ. **6**, 355–385 (1997)
4. Bailenson, J.N., Blascovich, J., Beall, A.C., Loomis, J.M.: Interpersonal distance in immersive virtual environments. Pers. Soc. Psychol. Bull. **29**, 819–833 (2003)
5. Billinghurst, M., Clark, A., Lee, G.: A survey of augmented reality. Found Trends® Hum. Comput. Interact **8**, 73–272 (2015)
6. Bimber, O., Raskar, R.: Spatial Augmented Reality: Merging Real and Virtual Worlds. CRC Press, Boca Raton (2005)
7. Brassac, C., Fixmer, P., Mondada, L., Vinck, D.: Interweaving objects, gestures, and talk in context. Mind. Cult. Act. **15**, 208–233 (2008)
8. Broderick, A.J.: Role theory, role management and service performance. J. Serv. Mark. **12**, 348–361 (1998)
9. Broth, M., Mondada, L.: Walking away: the embodied achievement of activity closings in mobile interaction. J. Pragmat. **47**, 41–58 (2013)
10. Brown, M., Guin, B.: How Risky are Residential Mortgages in Switzerland? Schweizerisches Institut für Banken und Finanzen (2013)
11. Buse, C., Martin, D., Nettleton, S.: Conceptualising 'materialities of care': making visible mundane material culture in health and social care contexts. Sociol. Health Illn. **40**, 243–255 (2018)
12. Chen, F.J.: Social status and the sequencing rules of other-introductions. Work Pap. Educ. Linguist. **9**, 13–27 (1993)
13. Christopher, P., Pushpa, K., de Lusignan, S.: Getting seamless care right from the beginning-integrating computers into the human interaction. Stud. Health Technol. Inform. **155**, 196–202 (2010)
14. Ciolek, M.T., Kendon, A.: Environment and the spatial arrangement of conversational encounters. Sociol. Inq. **50**, 237–271 (1980). Ciolek - 1980 - Sociological Inquiry - Wiley Online Library
15. Cuendet, S., Bonnard, Q., Do-Lenh, S., Dillenbourg, P.: Designing augmented reality for the classroom. Comput. Educ. **68**, 557–569 (2013)

16. Dolata, M., Schwabe, G.: Paper practices in institutional talk: how financial advisors impress their clients. Comput. Support. Coop. Work CSCW **26**, 769–805 (2017)
17. Dolata, M., Schwabe, G.: Tuning in to more interactivity – learning from IT support for advisory service encounters. Com. J. Interact. Media. **16**, 23–33 (2017)
18. Dourish, P.: Where the Action is: the Foundations of Embodied Interaction. MIT Press, Cambridge (2001)
19. Dowell, A., Stubbe, M., Scott-Dowell, K., Macdonald, L., Dew, K.: Talking with the alien: interaction with computers in the GP consultation. Aust. J. Prim. Health **19**, 275–282 (2013)
20. Duke, P., Frankel, R.M., Reis, S.: How to integrate the electronic health record and patient-centered communication into the medical visit: a skills-based approach. Teach. Learn. Med. **25**, 358–365 (2013)
21. Edwards, A., Edwards, C., Westerman, D., Spence, P.R.: Initial expectations, interactions, and beyond with social robots. Comput. Hum. Behav. **90**, 308–314 (2019)
22. Firth, R.: Verbal and bodily rituals of greeting and parting. In: La Fontaine, J. (ed.) The Interpretation of Ritual: Essays in Honour of A.I. Richards, pp. 1–38. Tavistock Publications (1972)
23. Fischer, J.E., Costanza, E., Ramchurn, S.D., Colley, J., Rodden, T.: Energy advisors at work: charity work practices to support people in fuel poverty, pp. 447–458. ACM Press (2014)
24. Gaver, W.: What should we expect from research through design? In: Proceedings of Conference Human Factors in Computing Systems, pp. 937–946. ACM (2012)
25. Gehle, R., Pitsch, K., Dankert, T., Wrede, S.: How to open an interaction between robot and museum visitor?: strategies to establish a focused encounter in HRI. In: Proceedings of International Conference of Human-Robot Interaction, pp. 187–195. ACM Press, Vienna (2017)
26. Goffman, E.: The Presentation of Self in Everyday Life, 1st Anchor Books ed., [rev. and expanded]. Anchor Books, New York (1959)
27. Goffman, E.: Interaction Ritual: Essays on Face-to-face Behavior, 1st Pantheon Books ed. Pantheon Books, New York (1967)
28. Goodwin, C.: Action and embodiment within situated human interaction. J. Pragmat. **32**, 1489–1522 (2000)
29. Goody, E.: Greeting, begging, and the presentation of respect. In: Interpret Ritual Essays Honour AI Richards Lond 39–72 (1972)
30. Hazel, S., Mortensen, K.: Embodying the institution—object manipulation in developing interaction in study counselling meetings. J. Pragmat. **65**, 10–29 (2014)
31. Heidtman, D.: Zur Herstellung von Situationseröffnungen in Arbeitsgruppen. In: Situationseröffnungen: zur multimodalen Herstellung fokussierter Interaktion. Institut für Deutsche Sprache, Bibliothek (2010)
32. Heritage, J., Clayman, S.: Dimensions of institutional talk. In: Talk in Action, pp. 34–50. Wiley-Blackwell, Chichester (2010)
33. Holman, D., Vertegaal, R.: Organic user interfaces: designing computers in any way, shape, or form. Commun. ACM **51**, 48–55 (2008)
34. Holman, D., Vertegaal, R., Altosaar, M., Troje, N., Johns, D.: Paper windows: interaction techniques for digital paper. In: Proceedings of Conference Human Factors in Computing Systems, pp. 591–599. ACM (2005)
35. Ishii, H.: The tangible user interface and its evolution. Commun. ACM **51**, 32–36 (2008)
36. Jacobsen, M., Kristiansen, S.: Goffman's sociology of everyday life interaction. The Social Thought of Erving Goffman, pp. 67–84. SAGE Publication Inc., Thousand Oaks (2015)
37. Jefferson, G.: Glossary of transcript symbols with an introduction. Pragmat. New Ser. **125**, 13–34 (2004)

38. Jungermann, H.: Advice giving and taking. In: Proceedings of Hawaii International Conference System Sciences, p. 11 (1999)
39. Jungermann, H., Fischer, K.: Using expertise and experience for giving and taking advice. In: Routines Decis Mak, pp. 157–173 (2005)
40. Kemper, T.D.: Ritual: Goffman's Big Idea. In: Status, power and ritual interaction: a relational reading of Durkheim, Goffman, and Collins. Ashgate Pub, Farnham, Surrey, England ; Burlington, VT (2011)
41. Kendon, A., Ferber, A.: A description of some human greetings. In: Michael, R., Crook, J. (eds.) Comparative Ecology and Behaviour of Primates. Academic Press, Cambridge (1973)
42. Kilic, M., Dolata, M., Schwabe, G.: How IT-artifacts disturb advice giving – insights from analyzing implicit communication. In: Proceedings of Hawaii International Conference System Sciences, pp. 878–887 (2016)
43. Kilic, M., Dolata, M., Schwabe, G.: Why do you ask all those questions? Supporting client profiling in financial service encounters. In: Proceedings of Hawaii International Conference System Sciences. Waikoloa Beach, HI (2017)
44. Koskinen, I., Zimmerman, J., Binder, T., Redstrom, J., Wensveen, S.: Design research through practice: from the lab, field, and showroom. IEEE Trans. Prof. Commun. 56, 262–263 (2013)
45. Landsbergen, D.: Screen level bureaucracy: databases as public records. Gov. Inf. Q. 21, 24–50 (2004)
46. Luff, P., Heath, C., Greatbatch, D.: Tasks-in-interaction: paper and screen based documentation in collaborative activity. In: Proceedings of Conference of Computer Supported Cooperative Work, pp. 163–170. ACM, New York (1992)
47. Luff, P., Pitsch, K., Heath, C., Herdman, P., Wood, J.: Swiping paper: the second hand, mundane artifacts, gesture and collaboration. Pers. Ubiquitous Comput. 14, 287–299 (2009)
48. Mikkola, P., Lehtinen, E.: Initiating activity shifts through use of appraisal forms as material objects during performance appraisal interviews. In: Interact Objects Lang Mater Soc Act, pp. 57–78 (2014)
49. Mondada, L.: Emergent focused interactions in public places: A systematic analysis of the multimodal achievement of a common interactional space. J. Pragmat. 41, 1977–1997 (2009)
50. Mondada, L.: Video analysis and the temporality of inscriptions within social interaction: the case of architects at work. Qual. Res. 12, 304–333 (2012)
51. Mondada, L.: Greetings as a device to find out and establish the language of service encounters in multilingual settings. J. Pragmat. 126, 10–28 (2018)
52. Mondada, L., Schmitt, R.: Zur Multimodalität von Situationseröffnungen. In: Situationseröffnungen: zur multimodalen Herstellung fokussierter Interaktion. Institut für Deutsche Sprache, Bibliothek (2010)
53. Mondada, L., Svinhufvud, K.: Writing-in-interaction. lang. Dialogue 6, 1–53 (2016)
54. Mortensen, K., Hazel, S.: Moving into interaction—social practices for initiating encounters at a help desk. J. Pragmat. 62, 46–67 (2014)
55. Nass, C., Fogg, B.J., Moon, Y.: Can computers be teammates? Int. J. Hum Comput Stud. 45, 669–678 (1996)
56. Oloff, F.: Ankommen und Hinzukommen. Zur Struktur der Ankunft von Gästen. Schmitt Hg Koord Anal Zur Multimodalen Interakt Tüb Narr, pp. 171–228 (2010)
57. Patel, M.R., Vichich, J., Lang, I., Lin, J., Zheng, K.: Developing an evidence base of best practices for integrating computerized systems into the exam room: a systematic review. J. Am. Med. Inform. Assoc. 24, ocw121 (2016)

58. Pearce, C.: Chapter 1 - computers, patients, and doctors—theoretical and practical perspectives. In: Shachak, A., Borycki, E.M., Reis, S.P. (eds.) Health Professionals' Education in the Age of Clinical Information Systems, Mobile Computing and Social Networks, pp. 5–22. Academic Press, Cambridge (2017)

59. Pearce, C., Arnold, M., Phillips, C., Trumble, S., Dwan, K.: The patient and the computer in the primary care consultation. J. Am. Med. Inform. Assoc. JAMIA **18**, 138–142 (2011)

60. Pearce, C., Trumble, S., Arnold, M., Dwan, K., Phillips, C.: Computers in the new consultation: within the first minute. Fam. Pract. **25**, 202–208 (2008)

61. Pillet-Shore, D.: Making way and making sense: including newcomers in interaction. Soc. Psychol. Q. **73**, 152–175 (2010)

62. Pillet-Shore, D.: Doing introductions: the work involved in meeting someone new. Commun. Monogr. **78**, 73–95 (2011)

63. Pillet-Shore, D.: How to Begin. Res Lang Soc Interact 31 (2018)

64. Pillet-Shore, D.M.: Coming together: creating and maintaining social relationships through the openings of face-to-face interactions. Ph.D., Univ. of California, Los Angeles (2008)

65. Pitsch, K., Kuzuoka, H., Suzuki, Y., Sussenbach, L., Luff, P., Heath, C.: The first five seconds;: contingent stepwise entry into an interaction as a means to secure sustained engagement in HRI. In: Proceedings of IEEE International Symposium Robot and Human Interactive Communication, pp. 985–991. IEEE, Toyama (2009)

66. Reeves, B., Nass, C.: The media equation: how people treat computers, television, and new media like real people and places, 1. paperback ed., [reprint.]. CSLI Publication, Stanford, Calif (2003, reprint)

67. Rosson, M.B., Carroll, J.M.: Usability engineering: scenario-based development of human-computer interaction. Morgan Kaufmann Publishers Inc., San Francisco (2002)

68. Schegloff, E.A.: Sequencing in conversational openings. Am. Anthropol. **70**, 1075–1095 (1968)

69. Schneider, B., Sharma, K., Cuendet, S., Zufferey, G., Dillenbourg, P., Pea, R.D.: 3D tangibles facilitate joint visual attention in dyads. In: Proceedings of International Conference of Computer Supported Collaborative Learning, pp. 156–165 (2015)

70. Smith, G.W.H.: Erving Goffman. Routledge, Abingdon (2006)

71. Steimle, J.: Designing pen-and-paper user interfaces for interaction with documents. In: Proceedings of the 3rd International Conference on Tangible and Embedded Interaction, pp. 197–204. ACM (2009)

72. Steimle, J.: Pen-and-Paper User Interfaces. Springer, Heidelberg (2012). https://doi.org/10.1007/978-3-642-20276-6

73. Svinhufvud, K.: Nodding and note-taking. Lang. Dialogue **6**, 81–109 (2016)

74. Svinhufvud, K., Vehviläinen, S.: Papers, documents, and the opening of an academic supervision encounter. Text Talk **33**, 139–166 (2013)

75. Ten Have, P.: Talk and institution: a reconsideration of the 'asymmetry'of doctor patient interaction.' In: Talk Soc Struct Stud Ethnomethodology Conversat Anal, pp. 138–163 (1991)

76. Toerien, M.: Using electronic patient records in practice: a focused review of the evidence of risks to the clinical interaction. Seizure **22**, 601–603 (2013)

77. Zimmerman, J., Forlizzi, J.: Research through design in HCI. In: Olson, J.S., Kellogg, W.A. (eds.) Ways of Knowing in HCI, pp. 167–189. Springer, New York (2014). https://doi.org/10.1007/978-1-4939-0378-8_8

78. Zimmerman, J., Forlizzi, J., Evenson, S.: Research through design as a method for interaction design research in HCI. In: Proceedings of the SIGCHI Conference on Human Factors in Computing Systems, pp. 493–502. ACM (2007)

79. Zuckerman, O., Gal-Oz, A.: To TUI or not to TUI: evaluating performance and preference in tangible vs. graphical user interfaces. Int. J. Hum Comput Stud. **71**, 803–820 (2013)

Pointing, Touch, Gesture and Speech-Based Interaction Techniques

A Comparative Study of Pointing Techniques for Eyewear Using a Simulated Pedestrian Environment

Quentin Roy[1,2]($\boxtimes$), Camelia Zakaria[1], Simon Perrault[3], Mathieu Nancel[4], Wonjung Kim[1], Archan Misra[1], and Andy Cockburn[5]

[1] Singapore Management University, Singapore, Singapore
quentin@quentinroy.fr, ncamelliaz.2014@phdis.smu.edu.sg,
kwj1189@gmail.com, archanm@smu.edu.sg
[2] School of Computer Science, University of Waterloo, Waterloo, Canada
[3] Singapore University of Technology and Design (SUTD), Singapore, Singapore
perrault.simon@gmail.com
[4] Inria and University of Lille, UMR 9189 - CRIStAL, Lille, France
mathieu.nancel@inria.fr
[5] University of Canterbury, Christchurch, New Zealand
andrew.cockburn@canterbury.ac.nz

Abstract. Eyewear displays allow users to interact with virtual content displayed over real-world vision, in active situations like standing and walking. Pointing techniques for eyewear displays have been proposed, but their social acceptability, efficiency, and situation awareness remain to be assessed. Using a novel street-walking simulator, we conducted an empirical study of target acquisition while standing and walking under different levels of street crowdedness. We evaluated three phone-based eyewear pointing techniques: indirect touch on a touchscreen, and two in-air techniques using relative device rotations around forward and a downward axes. Direct touch on a phone, without eyewear, was used as a control condition. Results showed that indirect touch was the most efficient and socially acceptable technique, and that in-air pointing was inefficient when walking. Interestingly, the eyewear displays did not improve situation awareness compared to the control condition. We discuss implications for eyewear interaction design.

1 Introduction

Although introduced in the 1960s [54], until recently see-through head-mounted displays (eyewear) were essentially dedicated to military and research environments [35]. Recently, however, there has been substantial commercial interest in developing eyewear technologies for public use, including Microsoft Hololens or

Electronic supplementary material The online version of this chapter (https://doi.org/10.1007/978-3-030-29387-1_36) contains supplementary material, which is available to authorized users.

© IFIP International Federation for Information Processing 2019
Published by Springer Nature Switzerland AG 2019
D. Lamas et al. (Eds.): INTERACT 2019, LNCS 11748, pp. 625–646, 2019.
https://doi.org/10.1007/978-3-030-29387-1_36

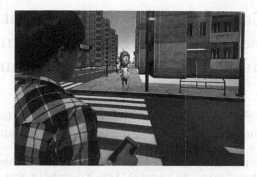

Fig. 1. Illustrating the simulator: using a phone to point on eyewear while walking. (Color figure online)

Epson Moverio. While current devices have limitations, like narrow field-of-view, hardware is quickly improving, creating new possibilities for interaction in the office and home as well as during daily activities such as commuting. Indeed, academic and industry experts have suggested that eyewear displays might underpin a foundational change for the next generation of mobile interaction [7,27,30,38].

One potentially important advantage of eyewear displays is that they enable head-up interaction, which may enhance the user's situational awareness while engaged in concurrent activities, such as walking along a busy sidewalk. Current phones, in contrast, encourage a posture in which the head is bent down rather than looking outwards at the environment, causing poor environmental focus and attention, and raising significant safety concerns [3,19,26,34,40].

Research on input methods for eyewear displays is in its infancy, especially when considering the interplay between the user's *external* urban activity and their *internal* (eyewear-driven) task. We focus on two-dimensional pointing as a basic interaction for input on eyewear displays. While other interaction modalities are being explored (for example gesture and voice), pointing remains fundamental in most vision-based human-computer interfaces. However, the design and evaluation of pointing techniques for eyewear displays poses particular challenges: their design must be properly adapted to mobility (e.g. efficient interaction while walking), and evaluations should account for environmental factors (e.g. navigating through a crowd), including impact on situation awareness and social acceptability.

As a first step in exploring the design space of eyewear pointing techniques, we examined practical solutions that can be readily adapted and implemented using today's off-the-shelf devices. We used a phone as an input device, a choice based on versatility (numerous sensors packaged in a small volume, allowing it to simulate handheld trackpads or in-air controllers for example), its ubiquitous ownership (smartglass users are likely to own and carry a phone) and its mobile pragmatics (for example bimanual techniques or bulky apparatus are impractical while walking).

We present an empirical study in which pointing techniques that have been proven useful in comparable contexts (like standing in front of an ultra-wall [39])

are adapted to phone input for eyewear displays—including variants of in-air pointing as well as using the phone as a hand-held trackpad. Direct touch on the phone, without eyewear, was used as control condition. We compare these techniques in three different environments: no simulator (while being stationary), simulated empty street and simulated busy street. Running such an experiment directly in a busy city street would put participants at risk, and is therefore ethically undesirable. Therefore, inspired by the work of Schwebel [49], we developed a street simulator that enabled us to gain insights on the use of these techniques in pedestrian environments, while keeping our participants safe and preserving internal validity. Finally, we looked at three key metrics: perceived social acceptability, performance as a function of the simulated environment, and impact on situation awareness.

Our results demonstrate that (a) the trackpad technique was the most socially acceptable, most accurate, and fastest for eyewear, and (b) the in-air techniques (which are increasingly integrated in commercial AR products) tended to perform poorly and were subjectively unacceptable. Importantly, while a key expected benefit of eyewear is that their head-up view should improve situation awareness and safety while walking [27,30,38], our results indicate that this may not be true: results indicate that situation awareness was worse when using the candidate techniques (i.e., with eyewear) than in the control condition without eyewear.

We make three specific research contributions:

1. empirical evidence of the perceived social acceptability of pointing techniques for eyewear, collected through interviews and web survey;
2. empirical evidence of the relative performance of eyewear pointing techniques in terms of speed, accuracy and ability to maintain situation awareness (for example avoid simulated pedestrian hazards);
3. demonstration of a Virtual Reality method for safely evaluating interaction techniques in a simulated pedestrian environment.

2 Background and Related Work

Two categories of previous research are briefly reviewed in the following subsections: first, general background research on pointing methods that might be adapted to eyewear displays, and second, research that focuses on interaction while engaged in other activities such as walking a busy street.

2.1 Pointing with Eyewear

Pointing to targets is an elemental component of interaction with graphically displayed content, and it is therefore important that efficient and acceptable pointing methods are developed for eyewear displays. While alternative selection methods that negate the need for pointing have been proposed—such as speech (e.g., [31]) or hand-gestures (e.g., [36])—pointing-based methods offer substantial advantages due to their familiarity and learnability ('see and point versus learn and remember' [52]).

Abundant novel or improved pointing techniques are represented in the HCI literature, and many could be adapted for eyewear. A key requirement for pedestrian pointing, however, is that the method can be operated while standing or walking. When eyewear displays are explicitly considered, the most commonly suggested pointing techniques are based on in-air pointing, in which the movement of the hand or a hand-held object is mapped to cursor movement (e.g., [9,17,22]); a similar in-air pointing method is used with the Microsoft Hololens. Another approach is to use trackpad-like interaction, with a dedicated device held in the hand [33,39], on the body [5,6,15,16,47] or the environment [14,56]. Finally, the use of eye-tracking or head-tracking is also possible [21,39].

All these pointing techniques are promising and most are valid candidates for eyewear pointing (providing the sensing mechanism can be made mobile). Research on large display interaction is also of interest as it often considers the users' need to stand or walk near the display [28,39,55]. Only a few previous works specifically investigated pointing on eyewear. The work of Jalaliniya et al. on head and eye tracking [21], or Hsieh et al. on gloves [17] are examples. However, as far as we know, none of these works comprehensively tackle social acceptability and formally investigate pointing performance under realistic urban movement, or used exotic, unrealistically bulky hardware. As a result, it is still unclear what is currently the best solution.

We focused on one-handed pointing techniques rather than bi-manual techniques because users often carry objects while walking. We used phones as input devices because they are readily available without requiring users to acquire a specialised input device; they also embed sensors that provide both touch (trackpad) and movement sensing (in-air controllers).

2.2 Interaction in Pedestrian Environments

The design of interaction techniques for use in pedestrian environments raises special challenges, including the need for the user to maintain situation awareness during interaction (to reduce safety concerns such as collisions with people or vehicles) and the need for the movements or actions required for interaction to be socially acceptable. In addition, there are also challenges for researchers in evaluating new technologies for pedestrian environments.

Situation Awareness. Several recent studies have highlighted evidence that the use of mobile phones in urban areas is elevating the risk of personal injury [3,40]. Rather than looking upwards and outwards at the environment, when interacting with a phone, the user's posture has the head bent down, causing poor environmental focus and divided attention [31,42,48]. This leads to the emergence of the "phone zombies" phenomenon: pedestrians who pay insufficient attention to their environment while looking at their phones, sometime walking into other people or traffic [3,19,34,40]. In an attempt to ease these problems, cities such as Singapore and Melbourne have started to install LED strips on pavements at pedestrian crossings [26].

Rather than altering the environment, another approach to improving situation awareness is to alter the interface [31], and to explore interaction mechanisms that are more fit for the challenges of pedestrian environments [30,31,43,57], such as eyes-free interaction [20,57] or the use of eyewear [17,30]. Researchers have argued that eyewear displays allow more seamless integration between the display of information and the surrounding environment, and as a result, improve situation awareness [27,30,38]. However, there is a lack of empirical study testing this assumption, possibly due to the risks associated with placing experimental participants in congested urban settings.

Social Acceptability. Montero et al. define social acceptability as the combination of the *user's social acceptance*, which defines how comfortable a user is in executing a particular action, as well as *spectators' social acceptance*, which refers to the impression it makes on witnesses of such action [37]. Interacting with eyewear displays need to be socially acceptable for public performance—this is especially relevant for eyewear given the current scepticism toward such devices [25]. While the social acceptability of actions may change as technologies become widespread [37], the likelihood of technology adoption is greatly improved if its interaction requirements are socially acceptable [12,45]. Several factors are known to influence the social acceptability of actions, including movement duration (the shorter the better) [8], and movement amplitude (small, discreet movements are better) [37,46].

Evaluating Interaction Techniques for Pedestrian Environments. There are well known trade-offs between lab and field studies, with lab studies facilitating internal validity at the cost of external validity, and field studies the inverse [18,24].

Beyond concerns of internal validity, there are additional and important safety concerns that complicate the potential conduct of field studies in urban pedestrian environments [49]. Consequently, researchers have examined the use of simulations to reproduce some of the realistic interaction context in safe settings. When the research focus is on the act of walking (e.g., to understand motor perturbations to interaction caused by pacing) treadmills have been used [2,4,41]. And when the research focus is on environmental artefacts, video projection [32] and virtual reality [18,23,49,50] can be used. We chose the later approach. Notably, we were inspired by the work of Schwebel et al. who used a simulated street environment to investigate child safety at road crossings [50]. Using a simulated environment not only replicates common pedestrian constraints, but also provides better control of parameters and allows us to put participants in simulated risky situations without physical risks.

3 Perceived Social Acceptability

To reiterate, social acceptability is a key issue in the design of interaction techniques for use in public settings. We structured our investigation of social accept-

ability in two parts: (1) semi-structured interviews, (2) a large-scale web survey. The goal of the study was to seek participants' perception of the social acceptability of the investigated interaction techniques. We focused on the user's social acceptance [37].

Our interview sessions were inspired by Rico and Brewster's methodology [45]: participants were asked to perform different gestures as if they were interacting with the device, and we gathered their feedback on the gestures' social acceptability (for public and private use). All interviews took place in a public setting within a local university campus.

For the web survey, participants watched online videos of the techniques, and were asked to rate their social acceptability. Videos are often used as a way to assess social acceptability [1,6,45,51]. The web survey was included to broaden participation in the study.

In our interview sessions, we examined a set of nine pointing techniques selected from previous literature (c.f. Table 1). Five of them were in-air gestures and one used a hand-held device as a trackpad. Though not the main focus of this work, we also included three body-touch techniques to learn about people's perception of less-common input methods.

After the interview sessions, we discarded the techniques with very poor rankings and kept Front Rotation, Down Rotation, Trackpad, Finger Touch and Pocket Touch for the web survey. Palm Touch was excluded because it was comparable to Trackpad. Front Rotation was slightly modified to allow movements from both the elbow and the wrist. Pocket Touch, which received polarized feedback in our interviews, was also modified so that the control area was shifted to the side of the thigh, further away from the genitals.

Table 1. Techniques included in our social acceptability study

In-air techniques	
Front Translation	Translation of the hand on a plane facing the user [39,55]
Down Translation	Translation of the hand on a plane parallel to the ground [22]
Front Rotation	Rotation of the wrist and forearm as if laser-pointing on a plane in front of the user (Fig. 2 left) [39,55]
Down Rotation	Rotation of the wrist and forearm as if laser-pointing on the ground [22]
Front Taps	in-air taps on a plane parallel to the user (back-and-forth movements of the forearm and the index finger) [9]
On-body touch techniques	
Finger Touch	The tip of the index is used as a trackpad controlled with the thumb [5]
Palm Touch	The joined area of the four long fingers is used as a trackpad controlled with the thumb [6]
Pocket Touch	The pocket area is used as a trackpad [47]
On-device touch technique	
Trackpad	A hand-held device is used as a touch surface (Fig. 2 right)

3.1   Participants and Procedure

For the interview sessions, we recruited eight participants (5 female), aged 22 to 45 years old ($M = 32.1$, $SD = 6.5$) from our students and university staff. Seven participants lived in Singapore and one in France. No compensation was offered. Each session lasted 45 min.

For each of the nine pointing techniques, we carried out the following procedure: (1) demonstrated the pointing movements for that technique and made sure its principles were understood, (2) asked the participant to perform the movements for approximately 30 s in a busy public area of our university campuses, (3) conducted a semi-structured interview focusing on their perception of the social acceptability of the techniques, at home or in the street. We finished the session by asking our participants to rank all techniques by order of social acceptability for usage in a private setting (e.g. home) and public setting (e.g. a street).

From our web survey, we gathered 56 responses (25 female, 1 preferred not to disclose) from 18 to 57 years old ($M = 27.7$, $SD = 8.2$, 7 preferred not to disclose). The web survey was advertised using our university's mailing lists. 50% of the participants were students (undergraduate and post-grads), 26% were IT Professionals and 5% in Academia and Research. They were mostly from South-East Asia ($n = 41$) and Europe ($n = 8$). The survey was divided into six parts, one dedicated to each TECHNIQUE, and a summary. In each survey part, participants were shown a short video of an actor walking in a street and demonstrating the use of the technique. Then they were asked to provide feedback on the perceived social acceptability of these techniques. Finally, they ranked techniques in order of perceived acceptability both for public and private contexts (1, most acceptable; 6, least acceptable).

3.2   Results and Discussion

During the interview sessions and in the web survey, we asked participants about their perception of the social acceptability of the techniques in private and in public. We did not observe any statistically significant effect of the participants' continent of origin on the recorded answers.

Private Use. In the interviews, Finger Touch was ranked as being the most socially acceptable technique ($M = 1.8/9$), followed by Phone Touch ($M = 3.3/9$),

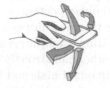

Fig. 2. Pointing techniques explored during our experiment: Front Rotation (left), Relaxed Rotation (middle) and trackpad (right).

632   Q. Roy et al.

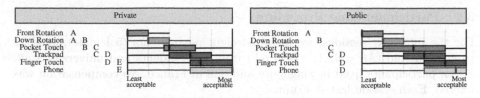

Fig. 3. Web survey: mean postulated social acceptability ranking for each technique. Levels not connected by the same letter are significantly different.

Pocket Touch and Palm Touch (both $M = 3.8/9$). Among the in-air technique, Front Taps was ranked as the least socially acceptable ($M = 4.6/9$). A Friedman test showed a significant effect of TECHNIQUE on average ranking ($\chi^2(8) = 37.3$, $p < .00001$), although Bonferroni corrected analysis showed no pairwise differences.

In general, the interview results suggested that for private use, smaller on-body or on-device actions were perceived as more socially acceptable than larger in-air movements of the device. On-body movements were perceived to be less tiring (2 interview participants) and as a result easier to use in private, and on-device actions were reported as being familiar (5). The in-air techniques were considered as "tiresome" (4) and "intrusive" (5). Our web survey results tended to confirm this trend: we found a significant main effect of TECHNIQUE on the average ranking for private use ($\chi^2(5) = 108.3$, $p < .0001$, see Fig. 3 for post-hoc comparisons).

Public Use. Results for use in public spaces reflected those for private use. Among the on-body techniques, Finger Touch was ranked as being the most socially acceptable ($M = 1.4/9$) followed by Trackpad ($M = 2.9/9$), Palm Touch ($M = 3.4/9$) and Pocket Touch ($M = 5.0/9$). Among in-air techniques Down Rotation was ranked best ($M = 4.6/9$) followed by Front Rotation ($M = 4.6/9$), Down Translation ($M = 6.5/9$), Front Taps ($M = 7.5/9$) and Front Translation ($M = 8.4/9$). A Friedman test showed a significant main effect of TECHNIQUE on average ranking ($\chi^2(8) = 43.2$, $p < .00001$).

Consistent with previous work [37,46], participants expressed concerns with high amplitude movements. In particular, five interview participants reported that Front Translation exceeded their "personal space", and got "in the way of others". Participants also expressed strong concerns on Front Taps [9] that made them appear as though they were pointing at others, explaining the large ranking difference compared to a private setting. This is potentially important, as contemporary implementations such as Microsoft Hololens use this modality as a primary means for interaction. Finally, Pocket Touch was polarizing in our interviews: half of our participants expressed little social concern, the other half strongly opposed to what they perceived as sexually suggestive (2 participants, 1 male and 1 female, even entirely refused to perform the gesture in public as per protocol).

As suggested by one of the interview participants, in the web survey videos we moved the control area for Pocket Touch further to the outside thigh region.

This improved the ranking of the technique compared to our interviews. The rest of our web survey results tend to confirm the trend observed during the interviews: we found a main effect of TECHNIQUE on the average ranking for public use ($\chi^2(5) = 119.7$, $p < .0001$, see Fig. 3.

4   Performance and Situation Awareness

We explored pointing techniques enabled by everyday devices and usable by pedestrians. We compared the three techniques presented in Fig. 2: Front Rotation, Down Rotation and Trackpad. Front Rotation requires positioning the phone flat (screen up), then pressing and holding the screen while rotating the wrist and forearm left, right, up, or down to move the cursor[1], not unlike tilt techniques [44]. Trackpad requires sliding the thumb on the screen to move the cursor. Relaxed Rotation requires holding the phone sideways while keeping the arm down in a relaxed position; the cursor is then moved by pressing and holding on screen while rotating the wrist left, right, up, or down. We designed Relaxed Rotation to require movements comparable in amplitude to Down Rotation. As a result, we believe that it should be perceived to have similar social acceptability (Down Rotation was perceived as the most socially acceptable in-air technique in the previous study). In all three techniques, target acquisition could be performed either by tapping on the screen or pressing one of the volume buttons. In practice, and due to the different grasps, the volume buttons were only used with Relaxed Rotation.

We included direct touch pointing on the phone display as a control condition, with participants instructed to hold and interact with the phone using one hand. Eyewear was disabled and removed in this condition, so participants had to look down while acquiring the targets.

Except for the control condition, all techniques made use of a mobile phone as an indirect, eyes-free controller. The controller was always manipulated with only one hand because pedestrians often need their other hand for activities such as opening doors, carrying bags, etc. In all techniques but direct touch (control), the visual feedback was exclusively displayed on the smartglasses.

Our social acceptability study included several on-body techniques that we did not include in this experiment because we wanted to focus on currently pragmatic phone-based techniques. Furthermore, our pre-tests and pilots indicated that the Down Rotation technique was excessively hard to control, so we eliminated it. In-air translation-based techniques and Front Taps were also excluded due to their poor social-acceptability findings in the previous study.

We compared the remaining techniques under three different environments: No Simulator in which participants stood while performing pointing task; Empty Street, where participants walked in an empty street simulation with no red

---

[1] Our initial design used press-and-hold for clutching: the cursor was moving by default, but users could hold the screen to freeze it and reposition themselves. However, our pre-tests quickly revealed that it was counter-intuitive.

lights or pedestrians; and Crowded Street, where participants walked in a street simulation including traffic lights and pedestrians (Fig. 1).

We formulated the following hypotheses:

H_1: Users achieve *the fastest pointing with Phone* because of their familiarity with traditional direct-touch pointing,

H_2: Users achieve *the lowest walking speed and poorest situational awareness with Phone* because they are required to look down (at the phone),

H_3: In the two street environments, users achieve *faster pointing with Trackpad than with Front Rotation and Relaxed Rotation*, because they are accustomed to trackpads and because the technique's input is arguably less sensitive to walking movements,

H_4: Users achieve *the highest walking speed and best situational awareness using Trackpad* because they are not required to look down, and Trackpad's input is arguably less sensitive to walking movements.

4.1 Street Simulation

Exploring safety or situation awareness in the wild implies putting participants at risk (e.g., within close vicinity to vehicle traffic), which is not ethically acceptable. Instead, inspired by previous works in social science [49], we rely on a street simulator to investigate the ability of users to maintain situational awareness while interacting with the eyewear device (see Fig. 1 and video figure). Participants stood in front of a wide display, and their body movements were tracked using fiducial markers. Walking on the spot caused the camera to move forward at a speed that the participant could control (treadmills, often used in previous works [2,4,41], do not allow pace control). Participants had to step sideways to avoid incoming pedestrians in the Crowded environment, and stop at red lights.

As realistic as it is, a simulation cannot be as externally valid as an in-the-wild experiment. The generalizability of our findings to real street scenarios remains for further work. Nevertheless, the method does require participants to remain aware of the situation and as a result provides actionable insights on situation awareness.

Street Elements. Several factors influence a pedestrian's walking behavior, such as street layout, illumination, and other pedestrians. Previous work in social sciences have focused on distracted behavior in road-crossings [3,49,50]. However, Oulasvirta et al. observed that the most attention-taxing situations encountered by pedestrians are when they walk in busy streets [42]. After discussion and further observations of our own behavior in the street, we included incoming pedestrians and changing traffic lights.

We used a simple street layout: a series of blocks with the same length and walkway width, not unlike some North-American cities. We designed these blocks to appear shorter (in length) than usual, to increase the number of intersections encountered by the participants.

Layout and Traffic Lights. Each street block was separated by a crosswalk and a traffic light. Traffic lights could have four different behaviors: Fixed Green, Fixed Red, Changing Green and Changing Red. Fixed Green remained green, Changing Green and Changing Red changed from one to the other when participants were 0.016 to 0.039 blocks away. Changing Green and Fixed Red switched to green after a wait time of 1 to 2.5 s. The ordering of Light behaviors were randomized, but we ensured that each behavior appeared at least once every four lights. Audio feedback of a car honk was played if participants jaywalked.

Pedestrian Behavior. Simulated pedestrians walked towards the participants at a speed randomly assigned between 2.46 and 3.78 blocks per minutes. They walked in straight lines, stopped to avoid "bumping" into participants, and respected traffic lights. Audio feedback of a pedestrian shouting "hey!" was also played if participants collided into them. In the Crowded Street condition, the street contained approximately 8 pedestrians per block (see companion video).

Steps and Position Tracking. Fiducial markers [10] were attached on the participants' ankles to track stomping motions, as well as the participant's lateral position in front of the display. Our tracking algorithm enabled us to map the participants' simulated walking speed as a function of both their stomping pace and the vertical amplitude of their steps.

Vanishing Point Adaptation. The vanishing point of the scene was kept aligned with the participant's position in front of the display when they stepped sideways, as opposed to constantly fixed at the center of the display, to further support the realism and immersiveness of the simulation (see video figure).

4.2 Participants and Apparatus

Twelve right-handed participants were recruited from Singapore Management University's students and staff (7 female) aged 20 to 30 years old. Remuneration was the equivalent of 7.4 USD. All but one reported that they had used their phone while walking in the street at least once in the two days before the experiment.

The experimental software was run on an Epson Moverio BT-300 smart-glass, a Samsung S7 Edge smart-phone and two computers (one for the simulation, one for the devices). The simulation was run on a large TV monitor (75 inches diagonal, 1.65×0.93 m) positioned 1 m from the ground. Participants stood 1 m from the display, and could move left and right in front of it.

4.3 Task

Participants were instructed to perform an ISO 9241–9 standard Fitts multi-directional pointing task as established by Soukoreff et al. [53] (see Fig. 4) using one of the four techniques (see Fig. 2). We chose a Fitts' Law task type for internal validity: controlling pointing distance and size simplifies comparison between

techniques and with previous and future work. Except for the Phone condition, the display area on the eyewear appeared to be approximately 199.2×199.2 mm one meter away from the user (720×720 px), the radius of the targets layout (see Fig. 4) was 84.7 mm (306 px) and the radius of the targets was 10.5 mm (38 px). In the Phone condition, the total pointing area was 65.4×65.4 mm ($1,376 \times 1,376$ px), the radius of the target layout was 27.9 mm (585 px) and the radius of the targets was 3.5 mm (73 px). In both cases, the ratio of the layout radius on the target radius remains constant ($\frac{306}{38} = \frac{585}{73} = 8$), yielding the same Index of Difficulty [11]. The extra space around the targets discouraged the use of edge pointing.

All three eyewear techniques (Front Rotation, Relaxed Rotation, and Trackpad) were indirect and relative. We defined transfer functions to map participant's input to cursor movements using Nancel et al.'s sigmoid function [39]:

$$G_t = G_{\min} + \frac{G_{\max} - G_{\min}}{1 + e^{-\lambda(v_t - V_{\inf})}}$$

with v_t and G_t respectively the input speed and gain at time t and λ a constant. Reporting generalizable (typically, physical) display units is complicated with smart glasses: the pixels can be perceived as if they were at any distance from the user's eyes. Furthermore, since the virtual display is displayed as a flat surface facing the user, rather than a spherical one, angular units cannot be used consistently. For simplicity and generalizability, we report distance and speeds on the display as if the display was projected one meter away from the user's eyes. The 1280×720 pixel map of the Moverio BT-300 corresponds to a 354×199 mm area one meter away, so one pixel is 0.277 mm wide[2]. We tuned its parameters separately for each technique (see Table 2).

In the No Simulator condition, participants executed the task while standing. In both street conditions, participants completed the task while navigating through the simulated street. Specifically in the Empty Street condition, participants were only required to walk on the spot. They were instructed to strive to

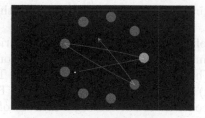

Fig. 4. Pointing task interface used during the experiment (black is transparent on the glasses). Each time a participant validates a target (currently the rightmost disk on the figure), a new one is highlighted until completion of the task. The superimposed arrow indicates the path to alternating targets following ISO 9241-9 standard procedure [53].

---

[2] Or 40 inches, 2.5 m away according to the manufacturer.

Table 2. Parameters of the gain functions

Technique	G_{min}	G_{max}	λ	V_{inf}
Trackpad	6.28 $^{mm}/_{mm}$	18.84 $^{mm}/_{mm}$	0.113 $^{s}/_{mm}$	26.46 $^{mm}/_{s}$
Front Rot.	0.48 $^{mm}/_{deg}$	2.9 $^{mm}/_{deg}$	10.47 $^{ms}/_{deg}$	143.24 $^{deg}/_{s}$
Relaxed Rot.	0.24 $^{mm}/_{deg}$	3.38 $^{mm}/_{deg}$	10.47 $^{ms}/_{deg}$	137.51 $^{deg}/_{s}$

maintain a natural walking speed. In the Crowded Street condition, they were asked to also avoid pedestrians and respect traffic rules, as in real world. If they failed to meet these rules, the simulation flashed red while the corresponding audio feedback was played (a man shooting "hey!" for pedestrians, and a car honk for the lights). We simplified this experiment by standardizing the walk to a straight path, under the hypothesis that it is reasonably similar to following a well-known path in term of cognitive load. This method was designed to simulate the most common external constraints encountered by pedestrians while enabling measures of pace, awareness, and interaction performance, as realistically as possible.

We finished the experiment with a short semi-structured interview during which participants provided subjective feedback. Before starting the experiment and as a training, participants were introduced to both conditions of the street simulator. During this training, we also asked participants to find what they thought was their usual walking speed and we recorded it for later comparison. Before each technique and under each environment, participants also had the opportunity to train themselves with the technique before starting.

4.4 Design

We used a 3 × 4 within-subjects design with the following factors and levels: ENVIRONMENT {No Simulator, Crowded Street, Empty Street} and TECHNIQUE {Front Rotation, Relaxed Rotation, Trackpad, Phone}. To ensure consistency of the simulation across all participants, we generated four predefined crowded street configurations (including pedestrian position and speed, lights, etc.).

The experiment was divided into three parts, one for each ENVIRONMENT condition. Each of these parts were divided into four blocks, each one dedicated to a technique. In accordance with ISO 9241-9 [53], each block started with the cursor centered and an initial unmeasured target selection, followed by four selections of each of the 9 targets in opposing order (see Fig. 4). ENVIRONMENT and TECHNIQUE orders were counterbalanced using a Latin Square. In the street conditions, the simulation ran uninterrupted during a block, and restarted afterwards. For all trials, we measured selection time, wrong selections (clicks outside of the target), "walking" speed, number of pedestrian collisions, and jaywalking. Participants were allowed to take breaks between each block. We recorded 12 participants × 4 techniques × 3 environments × 9 targets × 4 repetitions = 5, 184 trials. The experiment lasted one hour per participant.

4.5   Results

We ran two-way ANOVAs with two within-subjects factors (TECHNIQUE and ENVIRONMENT) on *Selection Time, Selection Error, Walking Speed,* pedestrian collisions, and jaywalking. We applied Greenhouse-Geiser sphericity correction when needed, with adjusted *p*-values and degrees of freedom. We ran pairwise t-tests with Bonferroni correction applied to the p-values of post-hoc tests.

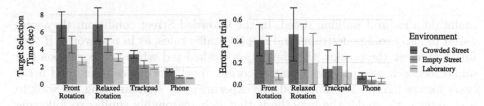

Fig. 5. Results of the experiment. Error bars show .95 confidence intervals.

Selection Time. As per ISO 9241–9 [53], Selection Time was measured as the time between two target selections (first excluded). We observed a significant main effect of TECHNIQUE on *Selection Time* ($F_{2.07,22.8} = 61.7$, $p < .0001$). Post-hoc comparisons show significant differences between all pairs (all $p < .0001$), except Relaxed Rotation × Front Rotation ("$\ll$" indicates significant differences):

$$\underset{1.06\,\text{s}}{\text{Phone}} \ll \underset{2.58\,\text{s}}{\text{Trackpad}} \ll \underset{4.69\,\text{s}}{\text{Front Rot.}} \text{,} \underset{4.8\,\text{s}}{\text{Relaxed Rot.}}$$

ENVIRONMENT also had an effect on *Selection Time* ($F_{2,22} = 42.2$, $p < .0001$). We found significant differences between all pairs (all $p < .0001$):

$$\underset{2.11\,\text{s}}{\text{No Simulator}} \ll \underset{3.04\,\text{s}}{\text{Empty Street}} \ll \underset{4.7\,\text{s}}{\text{Crowded Street}}$$

We also found a significant TECHNIQUE × ENVIRONMENT interaction ($F_{2.38,26.18} = 6.5$, $p < .01$). Figure 5-top summarizes the averaged times across conditions.

Selection Errors. We observed significant main effects of both TECHNIQUE ($F_{2.0,22.09} = 10.5$, $p < .001$) and ENVIRONMENT ($F_{2,22} = 4.4$, $p = .024$) on *Selection Errors.* Pairwise t-tests showed significant differences between all pairs of Techniques except between Relaxed Rotation and Front Rotation:

$$\underset{0.05}{\text{Phone}} \ll \underset{0.14}{\text{Trackpad}} \ll \underset{0.26}{\text{Front Rot.}} \text{,} \underset{0.33}{\text{Relaxed Rot.}}$$

We found a significant difference between the No Simulator ($M = 0.1$ errors/trial) and Crowded Street (0.22) conditions ($p < .001$). Figure 5 illustrates the results.

Walking Speed. We draw comparisons of walking speed between techniques and between the two street conditions (Empty Street and Crowded Street). We measured the time it took each participant to walk through an entire block whilst

in the simulation. We found a significant main effect of Street Environment ($F_{1,11} = 6.69$, $p < .05$), TECHNIQUE ($F_{3,33} = 17.74$, $p < .0001$), as well a ENVIRONMENT × TECHNIQUE interaction ($F_{3,33} = 6.93$, $p < .001$) on the *Walking speed*. Post-hoc comparison showed significant differences between two groups of techniques ($p < .01$, $sec/block$):

$$\underset{20.9 \quad ' \quad 21.4}{\text{Phone Trackpad}} \ll \underset{28.1 \quad ' \quad 29.1}{\text{Front Rot. Relaxed Rot.}}$$

Jaywalking and Collisions. We only considered the Crowded Street scenario when investigating jaywalking and pedestrian collisions. Note that because of the differences in selection time (Fig. 5-top), we computed the average number of jaywalkings and pedestrian-collisions per block (a block is a unit of distance in the simulator). We did not found a significant effect of TECHNIQUE on jaywalking ($p = .13$, with 0.1 jaywalk/block on average), nor on collisions ($p = .49$, 0.659 collisions/block on average).

Subjective Assessments. We asked participants to rate the techniques on a 7-level Likert-scale in term of (1) ease of use, (2) enjoyability, (3) effectiveness, (4) safety, (5) situation awareness, (6) ease to avoid pedestrians and (7) respect of traffic lights. A Friedman's test showed a significant main effect of TECHNIQUE on all questions: ease of use ($\chi^2(3) = 23.4$, $p < .0001$), enjoyability ($\chi^2(3) = 18.5$, $p < .001$), effectiveness ($\chi^2(3) = 22.2$, $p < .001$), safety ($\chi^2(3) = 14.9$, $p < .01$), situation awareness ($\chi^2(3) = 12.2$, $p < .01$), ease to avoid pedestrians ($\chi^2(3) = 11.9$, $p < .01$) and respect of traffic lights ($\chi^2(3) = 9.9$, $p = .019$). Figure 6 shows these results.

At the end of the experiment, participants also ranked the techniques from most-preferred to least-preferred, specifically in a crowded environment. Five participants ranked Trackpad best, while five others ranked it second-best. Accordingly, five participants preferred the Phone first, one participant second-best, and another one third-best. One participant ranked Phone worst. Front Rotation was ranked second by three participants, while Relaxed Rotation was consistently ranked either third-best or least-preferred. Many participants felt that the Trackpad technique poses less danger on the streets, in comparison to frequent look-ups while interacting with the phone.

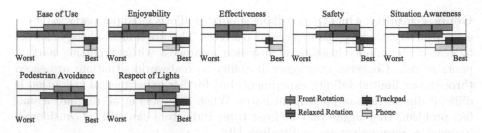

Fig. 6. Subjective Assessments of the techniques.

4.6 Ecological Validity Experiment

As an extra validation step, we ran an ecological validity experiment to challenge
our simulation-bound results in a real street situation. For safety reasons, it was
not ethically acceptable to use external participants. Four of the authors took
part in the experiment to test the four pointing techniques in the (actual) wild.
We used the same techniques and protocol, with two ENVIRONMENT conditions:
Wild and Inside, and 5 repetitions of each pointing target instead of 4 during
the controlled experiment. In the Wild condition, the authors walked along a
busy underground concourse. We measured an average 22.9 pedestrians/minute at
this location and time, with a large variance. In the Inside condition, the authors
performed the pointing tasks standing but without walking. We counterbalanced
the order of the techniques using a Latin Square, and measured both selection
times and selection errors.

Due to the small population, we only report descriptive statistics, shown
in Fig. 7. None of the four authors collided with a pedestrian. The results of
this experiment show the same trend as our main experiment. Participants were
generally faster and more accurate, which can be explained by a higher expertise
with the techniques and by a lower pedestrian density.

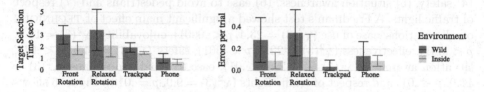

Fig. 7. Results of the ecological validity experiment. Error bars show .95 confidence
intervals.

4.7 Limitations

Techniques. Some participants reported difficulties with Relaxed Rotation due
to the width of the phone: it made it difficult to press-and-hold or click. Relaxed
Rotation may perform differently with a more ergonomically adapted in-air controller. Two participants also reported visual fatigue. Hopefully, this issue can
be resolved on future eyewear displays.

Generalizability. Our street-walking simulator allows us to put participants in
controlled situations resembling crowded streets. This novel methodology enables
to gather preliminary insights on situation awareness without putting participants at risk. Concerns over generalizability to real-world situations are eased
through our limited validity experiment, but further experimental validation is
difficult due to risks of participant harm. When Schwebel et al. run into a similar problem, they argue that at least three indicators can still be considered:
immersion, interactiveness, and realism [49].

Though not as immersive as a virtual-reality "cave", we join Schwebel et al.
in the argument that a large display area covering most of the participant's field

of view provides sufficient immersion. At least four of our participants agreed and described our simulation as "immersive".

We think interactiveness is a strength of our simulator as it included pace and position control (using feet tracking) instead of less interactive controller like a joystick, or pure absence of control as when using treadmills.

On the realism side, our participants' opinions were more divided: three reported the simulation as "unrealistic" and four stated that it was "realistic". Criticisms mostly concerned the in-place stepping mechanism, although two participants described the speed control as being "natural". This is a trade-off for the interactiveness required by our experiment. When VR treadmills are commercialized, allowing pace control, they may provide a better alternative.

Allowing participants to change direction, like walking around a corner, would allow more complex paths to be walked and add interesting factors. Similarly, half of our participants observed that real-world pedestrians typically give way when a collision is about to occur (rather than stop in front of the participant in our simulation). This behavior can easily be added, though we needed participants to actively avoid the pedestrians.

Less trivially, the stakes of colliding into a pedestrian or jaywalking remain limited compared to real-life. Keeping participants safe is of course the main point of using a simulation, but recent approaches such as force-feedback [29] could be put to use to produce physical sensations at no cost of safety.

5   Discussion

Participants were able to point faster and with fewer errors using the Phone technique. We therefore find support for H_1. Contrary to our expectations, the better performance of Phone did not come at the cost of slower walking speed or worse situation awareness. Therefore, we reject H_2 and H_4. This can be explained by a strong discrepancy in participants' prior experience between the control and candidate techniques.

Trackpad emerged as the best pointing technique for eyewear in terms of speed and error rate, in both the No Simulator and our street simulations. Therefore, we find support for H_3. Trackpad was also perceived as more socially acceptable, easier to use and more enjoyable than the in-air techniques. These results could be influenced by the smaller movements or lower cognitive burden associated with highly familiar touch interaction.

The in-air techniques, Front Rotation and Relaxed Rotation, performed worse in every condition. Performance with these techniques was also more adversely affected by street crowding than the other techniques (selection times increased dramatically in the Street conditions). Despite the higher movement amplitude and the need to keep the forearm up, Front Rotation was found easier to use than Relaxed Rotation. This might be due to the additional joint involved (wrist + elbow vs. wrist only) [13]. We observe significant differences in selection time for all environments, and increased errors in the Crowded Street compared to the No Simulator condition. The participants were also able to walk faster in Empty Street than in Crowded Street.

Interestingly, Trackpad and Phone performance were not significantly affected by the simulated Empty Street condition and were close to the No Simulator's. The two techniques did not significantly differ in term of situation awareness with our simulator. The two in-air techniques suffered substantially more from the simulator.

Though these results could only be safely obtained using a simulation, we believe they provide valuable insights sufficient to reliably recommend the use of the Trackpad for eyewear pointing by pedestrians (provided that it is implemented with an efficient transfer function[3]).

Contrarily to previous assumptions [27, 30, 31, 38] we were surprised that the use of eyewear did not improve situation awareness in our simulator; indeed, situation awareness with eyewear was worse than regular phone interaction with harder-to-use input techniques. User feedback was divided: five participants reported that it was easier to deal with divided attention using the smartglasses, while four others stated the opposite. One obvious caveat on this, however, is that people are highly familiar with current touchscreen interaction, and our participants' performance with eyewear conditions might improve with familiarization. In terms of pure input performance, as expected, Phone was superior.

6   Conclusion

This work contributed the first empirical study of eyewear pointing while mobile, taking into account environmental awareness and perceived social acceptability. In our street simulations or in a quiet building, participants were faster using a hand-held trackpad than with every investigated variant of in-air techniques. The trackpad was also perceived as the most socially acceptable technique.

Research on eyewear for pedestrians is still in its infancy. Our results indicate muted benefits regarding situation awareness. However, we remain confident that eyewear might expose situation awareness advantages, in particular for more passive tasks such as reading, and we plan to explore it as future work. Also, we would like to explore body-based techniques, like Finger- and Pocket Touch as they were deemed highly acceptable. But, there are also many other promising paths to investigate, as outlined in our related works.

We believe that our simulation-based method is promising, particularly given the ethical concerns associated with evaluation in-the-wild. While the generalizability of our simulation cannot be fully assessed, we argue it provides valuable insights on situation awareness. However, the generalizability of other aspects, such as path finding, might be easier to investigate in future work. Simulations will never be as externally valid as in-the-wild studies, but they require less resources and allows much greater control. Compared to other form of lab studies, we argue they do can provide opportune improvements of external validity.

---

[3] During initial tests, the trackpad shipped with the Epson Moverio glasses proved to be particularly cumbersome to use (in contrast with our transfer function).

Acknowledgements. This research was partially supported by Singapore Ministry of Education Academic Research Fund Tier 2 under research grant MOE2014-T2-1063, the University of Waterloo, the University of Canterbury, and INRIA.

References

1. Bailly, G., Müller, J., Rohs, M., Wigdor, D., Kratz, S.: ShoeSense: a new perspective on gestural interaction and wearable applications. In: Proceedings of the SIGCHI Conference on Human Factors in Computing Systems, pp. 1239–1248. ACM (2012). https://doi.org/10.1145/2207676.2208576
2. Barnard, L., Yi, J.S., Jacko, J.A., Sears, A.: An empirical comparison of use-in-motion evaluation scenarios for mobile computing devices. Int. J. Hum.-Comput. Stud. **62**(4), 487–520 (2005). https://doi.org/10.1016/j.ijhcs.2004.12.002
3. Basch, C.H., Ethan, D., Zybert, P., Basch, C.E.: Pedestrian behavior at five dangerous and busy Manhattan intersections. J. Commun. Health **40**(4), 789–792 (2015). https://doi.org/10.1007/s10900-015-0001-9
4. Bergstrom-Lehtovirta, J., Oulasvirta, A., Brewster, S.: The effects of walking speed on target acquisition on a touchscreen interface. In: Proceedings of the 13th International Conference on Human Computer Interaction with Mobile Devices and Services, pp. 143–146. ACM (2011). https://doi.org/10.1145/2037373.2037396
5. Chan, L., et al.: FingerPad: private and subtle interaction using fingertips. In: Proceedings of the 26th Annual ACM Symposium on User Interface Software and Technology, pp. 255–260. ACM (2013). https://doi.org/10.1145/2501988.2502016
6. Chen, K.Y., Lyons, K., White, S., Patel, S.: uTrack: 3D input using two magnetic sensors. In: Proceedings of the 26th Annual ACM Symposium on User Interface Software and Technology, pp. 237–244. ACM (2013). https://doi.org/10.1145/2501988.2502035
7. Costanza, E., Inverso, S.A., Allen, R.: Toward subtle intimate interfaces for mobile devices using an EMG controller. In: Proceedings of the SIGCHI Conference on Human Factors in Computing Systems, pp. 481–489. ACM (2005). https://doi.org/10.1145/1054972.1055039
8. Dobbelstein, D., Hock, P., Rukzio, E.: Belt: an unobtrusive touch input device for head-worn displays. In: Proceedings of the 33rd Annual ACM Conference on Human Factors in Computing Systems, pp. 2135–2138. ACM (2015). https://doi.org/10.1145/2702123.2702450
9. Ens, B., Byagowi, A., Han, T., Hincapié-Ramos, J.D., Irani, P.: Combining ring input with hand tracking for precise, natural interaction with spatial analytic interfaces. In: Proceedings of the 2016 Symposium on Spatial User Interaction, pp. 99–102. ACM (2016). https://doi.org/10.1145/2983310.2985757
10. Fiala, M.: Designing highly reliable fiducial markers. IEEE Trans. Pattern Anal. Mach. Intell. **32**(7), 1317–1324 (2010). https://doi.org/10.1109/TPAMI.2009.146
11. Fitts, P.M.: The information capacity of the human motor system in controlling the amplitude of movement. J. Exp. Psychol. **74**, 381–391 (1954). https://doi.org/10.1037/h0055392
12. Goffman, E.: The Presentation of Self in Everyday Life 1959. Doubleday, Garden City (2002)
13. Guiard, Y.: The kinematic chain as a model for human asymmetrical bimanual cooperation. In: Colley, A.M., Beech, J.R. (eds.) Cognition and Action in Skilled Behaviour, vol. 55, pp. 205–228. North-Holland, Amsterdam (1988). https://doi.org/10.1016/S0166-4115(08)60623-8. B.T.A.i.P

14. Harrison, C., Benko, H., Wilson, A.D.: OmniTouch: wearable multitouch interaction everywhere. In: Proceedings of the 24th Annual ACM Symposium on User Interface Software and Technology, pp. 441–450. ACM (2011). https://doi.org/10.1145/2047196.2047255

15. Harrison, C., Tan, D., Morris, D.: Skinput: appropriating the body as an input surface. In: Proceedings of the SIGCHI Conference on Human Factors in Computing Systems, pp. 453–462. ACM (2010). https://doi.org/10.1145/1753326.1753394

16. Holleis, P., Schmidt, A., Paasovaara, S., Puikkonen, A., Häkkilä, J.: Evaluating capacitive touch input on clothes. In: Proceedings of the 10th International Conference on Human Computer Interaction with Mobile Devices and Services, pp. 81–90. ACM (2008). https://doi.org/10.1145/1409240.1409250

17. Hsieh, Y.T., Jylhä, A., Orso, V., Gamberini, L., Jacucci, G.: Designing a willing-to-use-in-public hand gestural interaction technique for smart glasses. In: Proceedings of the 2016 CHI Conference on Human Factors in Computing Systems, pp. 4203–4215. ACM (2016). https://doi.org/10.1145/2858036.2858436

18. Hühn, A.E., Khan, V.J., Lucero, A., Ketelaar, P.: On the use of virtual environments for the evaluation of location-based applications. In: Proceedings of the SIGCHI Conference on Human Factors in Computing Systems, pp. 2569–2578. ACM (2012). https://doi.org/10.1145/2207676.2208646

19. IPSOS: Distracted Walking Study: Topline Summary Findings, pp. 1–6. American Academy of Orthopedic Surgeons (2015)

20. Jain, M., Balakrishnan, R.: User learning and performance with bezel menus. In: CHI 2012, pp. 2221–2230. ACM (2012). https://doi.org/10.1145/2207676.2208376

21. Jalaliniya, S., Mardanbeigi, D., Pederson, T., Hansen, D.W.: Head and eye movement as pointing modalities for eyewear computers. In: 2014 11th International Conference on Wearable and Implantable Body Sensor Networks Workshops, pp. 50–53, June 2014. https://doi.org/10.1109/BSN.Workshops.2014.14

22. Katsuragawa, K., Pietroszek, K., Wallace, J.R., Lank, E.: Watchpoint: freehand pointing with a smartwatch in a ubiquitous display environment. In: Proceedings of the International Working Conference on Advanced Visual Interfaces, pp. 128–135. ACM (2016). https://doi.org/10.1145/2909132.2909263

23. Kim, W., Choo, K.T.W., Lee, Y., Misra, A., Balan, R.K.: Empath-D: VR-based empathetic app design for accessibility. In: Proceedings of the 16th Annual International Conference on Mobile Systems, Applications, and Services, MobiSys 2018, pp. 123–135. ACM (2018). https://doi.org/10.1145/3210240.3210331

24. Kjeldskov, J., Skov, M.B.: Was it worth the hassle?: Ten years of mobile HCI research discussions on lab and field evaluations. In: Proceedings of the 16th International Conference on Human-Computer Interaction with Mobile Devices & #38; Services, pp. 43–52. ACM (2014). https://doi.org/10.1145/2628363.2628398

25. Koelle, M., El Ali, A., Cobus, V., Heuten, W., Boll, S.C.J.: All about acceptability?: Identifying factors for the adoption of data glasses. In: Proceedings of the 2017 CHI Conference on Human Factors in Computing Systems, pp. 295–300. ACM (2017). https://doi.org/10.1145/3025453.3025749

26. Koh, F.: Singapore trials LED lights on pavements: what other places are doing to keep smartphone zombies safe. The Straits Times (4), 789–792 (2017)

27. Lauber, F., Butz, A.: In-your-face, yet unseen?: Improving head-stabilized warnings to reduce reaction time. In: Proceedings of the SIGCHI Conference on Human Factors in Computing Systems, pp. 3201–3204. ACM (2014). https://doi.org/10.1145/2556288.2557063

28. Liu, M., Nancel, M., Vogel, D.: Gunslinger: subtle arms-down mid-air interaction. In: Proceedings of the 28th Annual ACM Symposium on User Interface Software and Technology, pp. 63–71. ACM (2015). https://doi.org/10.1145/2807442.2807489

29. Lopes, P., Baudisch, P.: Muscle-propelled force feedback: bringing force feedback to mobile devices. In: Proceedings of the SIGCHI Conference on Human Factors in Computing Systems, pp. 2577–2580. ACM (2013). https://doi.org/10.1145/2470654.2481355

30. Lucero, A., Vetek, A.: NotifEye: using interactive glasses to deal with notifications while walking in public. In: Proceedings of the 11th Conference on Advances in Computer Entertainment Technology. pp. 17:1–17:10. ACM (2014). https://doi.org/10.1145/2663806.2663824

31. Lumsden, J., Brewster, S.: A paradigm shift: alternative interaction techniques for use with mobile & wearable devices. In: Proceedings of CASCON, pp. 197–210. IBM Press (2003)

32. Lumsden, J., Kondratova, I., Durling, S.: Investigating microphone efficacy for facilitation of mobile speech-based data entry. In: Proceedings of British HCI, pp. 89–97. British Computer Society (2007)

33. McCallum, D.C., Irani, P.: ARC-pad: absolute+relative cursor positioning for large displays with a mobile touchscreen. In: Proceedings of the 22nd Annual ACM Symposium on User Interface Software and Technology, pp. 153–156. ACM (2009). https://doi.org/10.1145/1622176.1622205

34. McCullough, M.: On attention to surroundings. Interactions 19, 40–49 (2012)

35. Melzer, J.E.: Head-Mounted Displays: Designing for the User. McGraw-Hill Professional, New York (1997)

36. Mistry, P., Maes, P., Chang, L.: WUW - Wear Ur World: a wearable gestural interface. In: CHI 2009 Extended Abstracts on Human Factors in Computing Systems, pp. 4111–4116. ACM (2009). https://doi.org/10.1145/1520340.1520626

37. Montero, C.S., Alexander, J., Marshall, M.T., Subramanian, S.: Would you do that?: Understanding social acceptance of gestural interfaces. In: Proceedings of the 12th International Conference on Human Computer Interaction with Mobile Devices and Services, pp. 275–278. ACM (2010). https://doi.org/10.1145/1851600.1851647

38. Mustonen, T., Berg, M., Kaistinen, J., Kawai, T., Häkkinen, J.: Visual task performance using a monocular see-through head-mounted display (HMD) while walking (2013). https://doi.org/10.1037/a0034635

39. Nancel, M., Pietriga, E., Chapuis, O., Beaudouin-Lafon, M.: Mid-air pointing on ultra-walls. ACM Trans. Comput.-Hum. Interact. 22(5), 21:1–21:62 (2015). https://doi.org/10.1145/2766448

40. Nasar, J.L., Troyer, D.: Pedestrian injuries due to mobile phone use in public places. Accid. Anal. Prev. 57, 91–95 (2013). https://doi.org/10.1016/j.aap.2013.03.021

41. Ng, A., Williamson, J.H., Brewster, S.A.: Comparing evaluation methods for encumbrance and walking on interaction with touchscreen mobile devices. In: Proceedings of ICMI, pp. 23–32. ACM (2014). https://doi.org/10.1145/2628363.2628382

42. Oulasvirta, A., Tamminen, S., Roto, V., Kuorelahti, J.: Interaction in 4-second Bursts: the fragmented nature of attentional resources in mobile HCI. In: Proceedings of the SIGCHI Conference on Human Factors in Computing Systems, pp. 919–928. ACM (2005). https://doi.org/10.1145/1054972.1055101

43. Pirhonen, A., Brewster, S., Holguin, C.: Gestural and audio metaphors as a means of control for mobile devices. In: Proceedings of the SIGCHI Conference on Human Factors in Computing Systems, pp. 291–298. ACM (2002). https://doi.org/10.1145/503376.503428

44. Rahman, M., Gustafson, S., Irani, P., Subramanian, S.: Tilt techniques: investigating the dexterity of wrist-based input. In: Proceedings of the SIGCHI Conference on Human Factors in Computing Systems, pp. 1943–1952 (2009). https://doi.org/10.1145/1518701.1518997

45. Rico, J., Brewster, S.: Usable gestures for mobile interfaces: evaluating social acceptability. In: Proceedings of the SIGCHI Conference on Human Factors in Computing Systems, pp. 887–896. ACM (2010). https://doi.org/10.1145/1753326.1753458

46. Ronkainen, S., Häkkilä, J., Kaleva, S., Colley, A., Linjama, J.: Tap input as an embedded interaction method for mobile devices. In: Proceedings of the 1st International Conference on Tangible and Embedded Interaction, pp. 263–270. ACM (2007). https://doi.org/10.1145/1226969.1227023

47. Saponas, T.S., Harrison, C., Benko, H.: PocketTouch: through-fabric capacitive touch input. In: Proceedings of the 24th Annual ACM Symposium on User Interface Software and Technology, pp. 303–308. ACM (2011). https://doi.org/10.1145/2047196.2047235

48. Sawhney, N., Schmandt, C.: Nomadic radio: speech and audio interaction for contextual messaging in nomadic environments. ACM Trans. Comput.-Hum. Interact. 7(3), 353–383 (2000). https://doi.org/10.1145/355324.355327

49. Schwebel, D.C., Gaines, J., Severson, J.: Validation of virtual reality as a tool to understand and prevent child pedestrian injury. Accid. Anal. Prev. 40(4), 1394–1400 (2008). https://doi.org/10.1016/j.aap.2008.03.005

50. Schwebel, D.C., Stavrinos, D., Byington, K.W., Davis, T., O'Neal, E.E., de Jong, D.: Distraction and pedestrian safety: how talking on the phone, texting, and listening to music impact crossing the street. Accid. Anal. Prev. 45, 266–271 (2012). https://doi.org/10.1016/j.aap.2011.07.011

51. Serrano, M., Ens, B.M., Irani, P.P.: Exploring the use of hand-to-face input for interacting with head-worn displays. In: Proceedings of the 32nd Annual ACM Conference on Human Factors in Computing Systems, pp. 3181–3190. ACM (2014). https://doi.org/10.1145/2556288.2556984

52. Shneiderman, B.: Direct manipulation for comprehensible, predictable and controllable user interfaces. In: Proceedings of the 2nd International Conference on Intelligent User Interfaces - IUI 1997, pp. 33–39 (1997). https://doi.org/10.1145/238218.238281

53. Soukoreff, R.W., MacKenzie, S.: Towards a standard for pointing device evaluation, perspectives on 27 years of Fitts' law research in HCI. Int. J. Hum.-Comput. Stud. 61(6), 751–789 (2004). https://doi.org/10.1016/j.ijhcs.2004.09.001

54. Sutherland, I.E.: A head-mounted three dimensional display. In: Proceedings of the Fall Joint Computer Conference, Part I, 9–11 December 1968, pp. 757–764. ACM (1968). https://doi.org/10.1145/1476589.1476686

55. Vogel, D., Balakrishnan, R.: Distant freehand pointing and clicking on very large, high resolution displays. In: Proceedings of the 18th Annual ACM Symposium on User Interface Software and Technology, pp. 33–42. ACM (2005). https://doi.org/10.1145/1095034.1095041

56. Yang, X.D., Grossman, T., Wigdor, D., Fitzmaurice, G.: Magic finger: always-available input through finger instrumentation. In: Proceedings of UIST 2012, pp. 147–156. ACM (2012). https://doi.org/10.1145/2380116.2380137

57. Zhao, S., Dragicevic, P., Chignell, M., Balakrishnan, R., Baudisch, P.: EarPod: eyes-free menu selection using touch input and reactive audio feedback. In: Proceedings of CHI, pp. 1395–1404. ACM (2007). https://doi.org/10.1145/1240624.1240836

Are Split Tablet Keyboards Better? A Study of Soft Keyboard Layout and Hand Posture

Thomas Bekken Aschim[1], Julie Lidahl Gjerstad[1], Lars Vidar Lien[1], Rukaiya Tahsin[1], and Frode Eika Sandnes[1,2(✉)] (iD)

[1] Oslo Metropolitan University, P.O. Box 4 St. Olavs plass, 0130 Oslo, Norway
tbaschim@gmail.com, julielgjerstad@gmail.com,
{s326313,s326295,frodes}@oslomet.no
[2] Kristiania University College,
Prinsens Gate 7-9, Postboks 1190 Sentrum, 0107 Oslo, Norway

Abstract. Soft Qwerty keyboards are widely used on mobile devices such as tablets and smartphones. Research into physical keyboards have found split keyboards to be ergonomically better than ordinary physical keyboards. Consequently, the idea of split keyboards has also been applied to tablet soft keyboards. A controlled experiment with $n = 20$ participants was conducted to assess if split soft keyboards pose an improvement over ordinary soft keyboard on tables with both one-handed and two-handed use. The results show that the split keyboard performs worse than ordinary keyboards in terms of text entry speed, error rate and preference.

Keywords: Split keyboard · Text entry · Qwerty · Soft keyboard · Tablet

1 Introduction

Tablets offer users a convenient computing platform with visually and highly interactive access to information via large touch displays. Although direct manipulation through various browsing gestures is one of the huge benefits of touch interaction, the task of entering text is still highly prevalent for sending messages and filling in forms.

Although many innovative text entry methods have been proposed for touch displays the simple Qwerty virtual keyboard appears to be still the most popular as users already are familiar with physical Qwerty keyboards and many users have developed highly efficient touch-typing skills. On tables users typically enter text with one or two fingers if using one or two hands as touch-typing is difficult due to the lack of tactile feedback. Unlike touch-typing where the eight fingers only move up or down or to the side with one finger text entry the finger must move across the virtual keyboard from one key to another. Clearly, the large distance travelled by the finger slows down text entry and imposes more physical load on the user. The distance travelled is proportional to the size of the keyboard and using larger tablets thus takes longer time than using a smartphone with comparatively much smaller displays. Clearly, instead using two fingers with two hands to cover the left and the right side of the virtual keyboard speeds up text entry as each finger must travel much shorter distances.

© IFIP International Federation for Information Processing 2019
Published by Springer Nature Switzerland AG 2019
D. Lamas et al. (Eds.): INTERACT 2019, LNCS 11748, pp. 647–655, 2019.
https://doi.org/10.1007/978-3-030-29387-1_37

When text is input on a mobile device such as a smartphone or tablet with one hand the other hand is usually used to hold the device. When holding the device with two hands only the thumb is free for typing. The pointing range of the thumbs are therefore limited. Consequently, split keyboards have emerged where the left and right sides of the keyboard have been moved to the left and the right side closer aligned to the position where users typically will hold the tablet. One may thus expect that two-handed text entry will lead to improved text entry rates as the keys are even closer to the two fingers reducing both the physical effort and dexterity needed to input text.

This study set out to determine if this virtual keyboard configurations indeed leads to improvements in text entry performance though a controlled experiment. The rest of this paper is organized as follows. First related work on text entry is presented followed by a presentation of the methodology. Next, the results section presents the empirical findings which are analyzed in the discussions section.

2   Related Work

There is a vast body of research into text entry on touch-displays. Many of these studies evolve around letter shaped gestures [1, 2], variations on menu selection with directional gestures [3, 4] and interactive gestures [5]. Still, much research attention has also been directed at virtual or soft keyboards that are direct representations of physical keyboards. Early work on soft keyboards attempted to optimize the keyboard layouts to achieve higher text entry rates [6, 7]. However, users are usually already trained with the Qwerty layout and are therefore unlikely to adopt new keyboard layouts. Researchers have therefore attempted to optimize the keyboard layout by making small variations on the Qwerty configuration [8, 9].

Touch typing on Qwerty is a unique skill and one of few bimanual ways of operating computers. With touch typing the left and right sides of the keyboard is operated by the two hands. Several researchers have attempted to tap into users' Qwerty skills by exploiting skill transfer across hands to achieve one-handed touch typing [10] or mimic two handed Qwerty keyboard input with two joysticks [11]. The fact that touch typing is performed with two hands did lead to the idea that split keyboards, also called adjustable keyboards, would lead to improved comfort [12, 13] and there is much attention in the ergonomics literature on physical split keyboards, for example its effect on wrist posture [14, 15] and upper body posture [16].

The idea of touch typing or ten-finger typing on touch displays has also been addressed [17, 18]. However, it is a challenging problem due to the lack of tactile feedback and consequently noisy input that is hard to decode. Still, for most practical application text entry on touch devices is performed using one or two fingers. Experiments have shown that two thumb smartphone text entry is much faster than text input using just one finger or thumb [19].

Although optimized split tablet keyboards have been proposed [20], the main emphasis is on the established Qwerty layout. In a study on hand posture with tablet text entry it was found that a narrow keyboard in portrait mode yielded improved results over landscape mode [21], yet their results with 12 participants showed that the narrow Qwerty keyboard layout resulted in higher text entry rates than the split keyboard. In a study (also including 12 participants) comparing narrow, wide and tilted split tablet keyboard used in the lap, on a desk and in bed, found that the split keyboard design received the highest comfort rating when the keyboard was used in bed [22]. Note that these studies focused on measuring ergonomic aspects of the keyboard design such as wrist extensions and wrist angles. They did not explicitly focus on text entry speeds or error rates. Nor did they explore the effects of one-handed use.

3   Method

3.1   Experimental Design

A 2 × 2 within groups experimental design was chosen with hands and keyboard type as independent variables and text entry speed in words per minute (wpm) and error rate as dependent variables. The hands factor had two levels, namely one-handed interaction and two handed (bimanual) interaction. The keyboard factor had two levels, namely ordinary soft keyboard and split soft keyboard.

3.2   Participants

A total of 20 participants were recruited at the authors institution. All the participants were students of which 8 were female (40%) and 12 were male (60%). Their age ranged from 19 to 33 years of age ($M = 24.5$, $SD = 3.75$). All the participants were Norwegian speakers but having mid to high command of English (using a Likert scale from 1–5). Total of 18 participants (90%) had some or much prior experience using iPad tablets. Only 3 participants (15%) reported experience with the split iPad keyboard.

3.3   Task

A text copying task was devised where participants copied displayed phrases using the given keyboard. MacKenzie and Soukoreff's list of 500 simple English phrases was used [23] as a source of text to be copied. These phrases do not include capital letters, punctuations or other non-alphabetical characters.

3.4   Equipment

The experiment was conducted using an iPad Air with a 9.7-inch display in landscape mode. The virtual keyboard was configured for Norwegian as participants were expected to be familiar with this layout. Note that no Norwegian letters were used during the experiment. Word suggestions and autocomplete and error-correction was disabled during the tests. The text was written in the SimpleNote application. The phrases to be copied were displayed on a notebook computer in front of the participant.

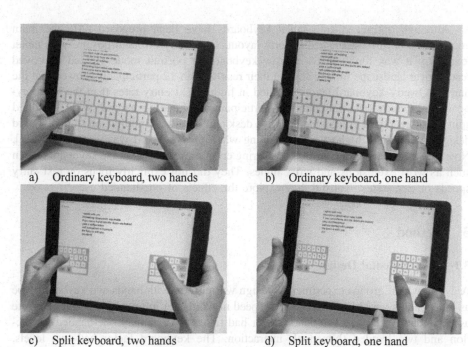

a)   Ordinary keyboard, two hands   b)   Ordinary keyboard, one hand

c)   Split keyboard, two hands   d)   Split keyboard, one hand

Fig. 1. The hand postures used in the experiment.

3.5   Procedure

Each participant was tested individually in a meeting room in the authors university to keep the conditions as constant as possible. The four conditions of experiment were balanced by varying the presentation order according to a Latin square to compensate for learning effects. The total time taken was measured using a stopwatch. The text logs and the measured time were used to calculate the text entry speed in wpm. The iPad was held in either one or two hands. In the one-handed condition the tablet was held with one hand and text input with the index finger. In the two-handed condition the tablet was held with two hands and text input with the two thumbs. The four conditions are shown in Fig. 1. The laptop with the phrases to be copied was controlled by one of the experimenters. After completing the text entry tasks, the participants were asked to complete a simple questionnaire asking demographic information and their subjective assessment of the four input modes. Each session lasted approximately 25 min.

3.6   Analysis

The number of characters input was extracted from the text logs. The number of characters input and the measured time were used to calculate the text entry speed in wpm. The error rates associated with the inputted text were computed using a custom-made script. Error rates were computed using the Levenshtein distance between the inputted and the source text. Statistical analyses were conducted using JASP version 0.9.1 [24].

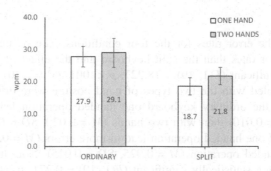

Fig. 2. Mean text entry performance in wpm. Error bars show SD.

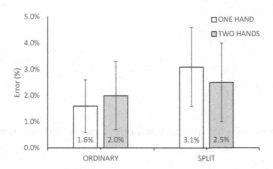

Fig. 3. Mean error rates. Error bars show SD.

4   Results

4.1   Performance

The results show that there were significant effects of both hand ($F(1, 19) = 92.164$, $p = .002$, $\omega^2 = .104$) and type of keyboard ($F(1, 19) = 217.326$, $p < .001$, $\omega^2 = .649$). Figure 2 shows that using two hands lead to higher text entry rates than using just one hand. This observation was observed for both keyboards. The results also show that the text entry rates were higher with the ordinary keyboard compared to the split keyboard. Hence, the fastest text entry rates were achieved using the ordinary keyboard with two hands ($M = 29.1$, $SD = 4.5$). This is 33.5% faster than the text entry speed achieved with the split keyboard using two hands ($M = 21.8$, $SD = 2.7$). In fact, using the ordinary keyboard with one hand ($M = 27.9$, $SD = 3.2$) is 27.9% faster than the split keyboard with two hands. The one-handed split keyboard was the slowest condition ($M = 18.74$, $SD = 2.675$). There was also a weak but significant interaction between hand and the type of keyboard ($F(1, 19) = 9.796$, $p = .006$, $\omega^2 = .025$).

4.2 Errors

Figure 3 shows the error rates for the four conditions. The ordinary soft keyboard yielded lower error rates than the split keyboard and the effect of keyboard type on error rate was significant ($F(1, 19) = 18.227$, $p < .001$, $\omega^2 = .140$). Interestingly, the error rates associated with the two types of hand posture were different for the two keyboards. With the ordinary keyboard one handed operation lead to fewer errors ($M = 0.016$, $SD = 0.010$) than with two hands ($M = 0.020$, $SD = 0.013$), while with the split keyboard one handed operation lead to more errors ($M = 0.031$, $SD = 0.015$) than with two handed operation ($M = 0.025$, $SD = 0.015$). Note that these practical differences were not statistically significant ($F(1, 19) = 0.271$, $p = .608$). No interactions between keyboard type and hand posture in terms of error rate were observed.

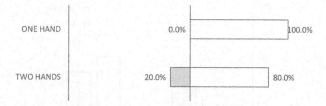

Fig. 4. Preferences for the split keyboard (grey) and the ordinary keyboard (white).

4.3 Preferences

Figure 4 shows the participants preferences for the four conditions as a diverging stacked bar chart with preferences for the split keyboard on the left and preference for the ordinary keyboard on the right. For one handed operation all the participants preferred the traditional keyboard over the split keyboard. For two handed operation 4 of the participants (20%) preferred the split keyboard. Of these four participants only one participant indicated prior experience with the split keyboard. This means that 2 of the participants with prior experience with the split keyboard still preferred the ordinary keyboard, while 3 participants who had no prior experience with the split keyboard preferred the split keyboard when using two hands.

5 Discussion

The performance results do not match the predicted outcome as the ordinary platform outperforms the split keyboard irrespective of which hand posture is adopted. Yet the findings on text entry performance agree with the previous study of two-handed split tablet keyboards [20, 21] but not in terms of preference.

To the best of our knowledge our study is the only one also including single handed operation as a condition. As expected, the text entry performance is worse with the split layout compared to the ordinary layout. This is probably due to the fact that the index finger must travel further distances between the two keyboard halves at the left and

right sides of the tablet. The participants unanimously agreed that the ordinary layout was preferable over the slit layout when operated using one hand.

It is, however, quite interesting that one-handed operation with the ordinary layout lead to a lower error rate compared to two handed input while the two-handed split keyboard lead to lower error rates than single handed operation. This phenomenon could perhaps be explained using Fitts' law which predicts the relationship between the speed, distance and target size in pointing tasks. With the split keyboard the index finger must travel further distances, possibly at higher speeds leading to missed targets, while each thumb must travel much shorter distances leading to a higher target hitting rates.

Clearly, the results obtained with split soft keyboards reported herein and in the related studies [20, 21] are negative and disagree with many of the studies of physical split keyboards [12–16]. One possible explanation for this is that the controlled studies with physical keyboards were conducted using ten finger touch typing while the controlled studies with soft keyboard where performed using hunt-and-peck for keys.

5.1 Limitations

The results are based on a single session. This session was and most participants first encounter with the split keyboard. It would have been relevant to have followed the participants over several sessions spread out in time to see if learning effects would lead to changes that would put the split layout in a more favorable light in terms of text entry speed and preference.

6 Conclusion

A controlled experiment comparing a soft split keyboard to an ordinary soft keyboard on a tablet computer in landscape mode were performed. The results show that the ordinary soft keyboard yielded better results in terms of text entry rates, error rates and participants preference compared to the soft split keyboard. Future work should conduct longitudinal studies of soft split keyboard designs to see if its theoretical benefits are reaped via prolonged use.

References

1. Castellucci, S.J., MacKenzie, I.S.: Graffiti vs. unistrokes: an empirical comparison. In: Proceedings of the SIGCHI Conference on Human Factors in Computing Systems, CHI 2008, pp. 305–308. ACM, New York (2008)
2. Wobbrock, J.O., Myers, B.A., Kembel, J.A.: EdgeWrite: a stylus-based text entry method designed for high accuracy and stability of motion. In: Proceedings of the 16th annual ACM symposium on User interface software and technology, UIST 2003, pp. 61–70. ACM, New York (2003)
3. Sandnes, F.E., Tan, T.B., Johansen, A., Sulic, E., Vesterhus, E., Iversen, E.R.: Making touch-based kiosks accessible to blind users through simple gestures. Univ. Access Inf. Soc. 11(4), 421–431 (2012)

4. Banovic, N., Yatani, K., Truong, K.N.: Escape-keyboard: a sight-free one-handed text entry method for mobile touch-screen devices. Int. J. Mob. Hum. Comput. Interact. **5**(3), 42–61 (2013)
5. Ward, D.J., Blackwell, A.F., MacKay, D.J.C.: Dasher—a data entry interface using continuous gestures and language models. In: Proceedings of the 13th annual ACM symposium on User interface software and technology, UIST 2000, pp. 129–137. ACM, New York (2000)
6. Goldberg, D., Richardson, C.: Touch-typing with a stylus. In: Proceedings of the INTERACT 1993 and CHI 1993 Conference on Human Factors in Computing Systems, CHI 1993, pp. 80–87. ACM, New York (1993)
7. MacKenzie, I.S., Zhang, S.X.: The design and evaluation of a high-performance soft keyboard. In: Proceedings of the SIGCHI conference on Human Factors in Computing Systems, CHI 1999, pp. 25–31. ACM, New York (1999)
8. Bi, X., Smith, B.A., Zhai, S.: Quasi-qwerty soft keyboard optimization. In: Proceedings of the SIGCHI Conference on Human Factors in Computing Systems, CHI 2010, pp. 283–286. ACM, New York (2010)
9. Zhai, S., Smith, B.A.: Alphabetically biased virtual keyboards are easier to use: layout does matter. In: CHI 2001 Extended Abstracts on Human Factors in Computing Systems, CHI EA 2001, pp. 321–322. ACM, New York (2001)
10. Matias, E., MacKenzie, I.S., Buxton, W.: Half-QWERTY: typing with one hand using your two-handed skills. In: Plaisant, C. (ed) Conference Companion on Human Factors in Computing Systems, CHI 1994, pp. 51–52. ACM, New York (1994)
11. Sandnes, F.E., Aubert, A.: Bimanual text entry using game controllers: relying on users' spatial familiarity with QWERTY. Interact. Comput. **19**(2), 140–150 (2007)
12. Rempel, D.: The split keyboard: an ergonomics success story. Hum. Factors **50**(3), 385–392 (2008)
13. Çaxir, A.: Acceptance of the adjustable keyboard. Ergonomics **38**(9), 1728–1744 (1995)
14. Honan, M., Serina, E., Tal, R., Rempel, D.: Wrist postures while typing on a standard and split keyboard. In: Proceedings of the Human Factors and Ergonomics Society annual meeting, vol. 39, No. 5, pp. 366–368. SAGE Publications, Los Angeles (1995)
15. Smith, M.J., et al.: Effects of a split keyboard design and wrist rest on performance, posture, and comfort. Hum. Factors **40**(2), 324–336 (1998)
16. Rempel, D., Nathan-Roberts, D., Chen, B.Y., Odell, D.: The effects of split keyboard geometry on upper body postures. Ergonomics **52**(1), 104–111 (2009)
17. Shi, W., Yu, C., Yi, X., Li, Z., Shi, Y.: TOAST: Ten-finger eyes-free typing on touchable surfaces. Proc. ACM Interact. Mob. Wearable Ubiquitous Technol. **2**(1), 33 (2018)
18. Zhu, S., Luo, T., Bi, X., Zhai, S.: Typing on an invisible keyboard. In: Proceedings of the 2018 CHI Conference on Human Factors in Computing Systems, CHI 2018, p. 439. ACM, New York (2018)
19. Azenkot, S., Zhai, S.: Touch behavior with different postures on soft smartphone keyboards. In: Proceedings of the 14th International Conference on Human-Computer Interaction with Mobile Devices and Services, MobileHCI 2012, pp. 251–260. ACM, New York (2012)
20. Trudeau, M.B., Catalano, P.J., Jindrich, D.L., Dennerlein, J.T.: Tablet keyboard configuration affects performance, discomfort and task difficulty for thumb typing in a two-handed grip. PLoS ONE **8**(6), e67525 (2013)
21. Lin, M.I.B., Hong, R.H., Chang, J.H., Ke, X.M.: Usage position and virtual keyboard design affect upper-body kinematics, discomfort, and usability during prolonged tablet typing. PLoS ONE **10**(12), e0143585 (2015)

22. Hong, J., Heo, S., Isokoski, P., Lee, G.: SplitBoard: a simple split soft keyboard for wristwatch-sized touch screens. In Proceedings of the 33rd Annual ACM Conference on Human Factors in Computing Systems, pp. 1233–1236. ACM (2015)

23. MacKenzie, I.S., Soukoreff, R.W.: Phrase sets for evaluating text entry techniques. In: CHI 2003 Extended Abstracts on Human Factors in Computing Systems, CHI EA 2003, pp. 754–755. ACM, New York (2003)

24. JASP Team: JASP (Version 0.9)[Computer software] (2018)

FittsFarm: Comparing Children's Drag-and-Drop Performance Using Finger and Stylus Input on Tablets

Brendan Cassidy[1]([⊠]), Janet C. Read[1], and I. Scott MacKenzie[2]

[1] University of Central Lancashire, Preston, UK
bcassidy1@uclan.ac.uk
[2] York University, Toronto, Canada

Abstract. We used a two-dimensional Fitts' law task to compare finger and stylus input with children when performing drag-and-drop tasks on a tablet. Twenty-eight children completed the study. Drag-and-drop performance was significantly better using a low-cost stylus compared to finger input. Throughput was 9% higher for stylus input (2.55 bps) compared to finger input (2.34 bps). Error rates were 35% percent higher for finger input (12.6%) compared to stylus input (9.3%). Error rates approximately doubled with smaller targets. There was no significant difference observed for movement time between input methods. Findings indicate schools should consider providing children with a low-cost stylus for educational activities on tablets.

Keywords: Finger input · Stylus input · Pen input · Children · Fitts' law · Tablets · Drag and drop · Touch screen

1 Introduction

The use of tablets for teaching and learning in schools is now common. In many developed countries, each child often has their own tablet during class [7]. This gives educators a wider set of options for teaching and learning activities. Many tablet devices in schools, such as the Microsoft *Surface*, can run applications traditionally designed for the desktop. It is often impractical to augment classroom tablets with mice, keyboards or trackpads due to space constraints or risk of loss or damage. And so, even for traditional desktop activities, the preferred method of interaction is often through the touch screen, using the device in tablet-mode. As a result, applications that support educational activities with reduced text input are often preferred [20]. A common method of providing input is through drag-and-drop style interaction, especially in spatial/visual-based teaching and learning activities. In this context, children have two main options when interacting with tablets: finger input or stylus input. As the cost of a stylus is low, it is interesting to know the effect finger or stylus input has when performing drag-and-drop tasks, as schools may wish to provide children with styli to use with tablets if an observable advantage is possible.

© IFIP International Federation for Information Processing 2019
Published by Springer Nature Switzerland AG 2019
D. Lamas et al. (Eds.): INTERACT 2019, LNCS 11748, pp. 656–668, 2019.
https://doi.org/10.1007/978-3-030-29387-1_38

2 Related Work

Inkpen [8] compared children's performance between mouse-based drag-and-drop tasks and point-and-click tasks. Point-and-click interaction was faster and had fewer errors. In contexts where direct selection is possible through touch, it is anticipated results would be similar to those reported in the above study.

Finger and stylus input with children has been compared in a number of studies [2,3,22,25,26]. But, to our knowledge there is no research comparing the finger and stylus when performing drag-and-drop tasks with children.

Drag-and-drop using the finger or stylus has been investigated in older adults (65+) using mobile devices [18] with an increase in accuracy observed with stylus input. As younger children have less experience holding and using a pen, more research on this user group is needed.

McKnight and Cassidy [16] investigated finger and stylus input with children in a qualitative study. Their work did not use drag-and-drop and employed now-dated resistive touch screen devices primarily designed for use with a stylus, where finger input is problematic. Perhaps unsurprisingly, a preference was found for stylus input. Since this study, the technical landscape has changed significantly. Tablets are now common in schools and are primarily designed for finger input. Tablet manufacturers do, however, sell premium pen-based accessories. Low-cost replaceable fiber-tip styli are also commonly available.

Stylus use and comfort were studied by Ren and Zhou [21], who manipulated the length and width of pens for children of different ages. They concluded that a pen-length of 7–13 cm combined with a pen tip width of 1.0–1.5 mm and a pen barrel width of 4 mm was optimal. In a more recent study, Arif and Sylla found the Wacom bamboo pen suitable for children [2].

Concerning finger interaction, Anthony et al. [1] found differences in performance with finger input when comparing children to adults. Children had more difficulty having their gestures recognized using the finger, compared to adults, and had more problems accurately acquiring on-screen targets.

Arif and Sylla [2] investigated touch and pen gestures with both adults and children (the latter were 8–11 yrs). Pen input was faster and more accurate than touch for adults, but there was no significant difference with children. One possible reason is that gesture input requires accurate input for correct recognition, and this may only develop as children get older. In addition to accuracy, there was no significant user preference reported for finger or stylus input with children.

Compared to gestural input, drag-and-drop tasks require less accuracy, and so are appropriate to evaluate with children. Due to the prolific use of tablets in schools and the potential benefits for stylus use with children engaged in learning activities, it is appropriate to revisit stylus input for tasks such as drag-and-drop.

Woodward et al. [26] found children's fingers slipped less and responded more accurately when performing pointing and gesture tasks. However, children missed more targets with finger input compared to stylus input. While limited in participant numbers (13), their work highlights the complexities in measuring pen or finger performance on tablets with children.

It would be useful for the HCI community to have robust but simplified measures of performance when considering stylus input as an alternative to touch. Once such measure is *throughput*, calculated in a testing regime known as Fitts' law.

2.1   Evaluation Using Fitts' Law and ISO 9241-9

Fitts' law [6] provides a well-established protocol for evaluating target selection operations on computing systems [11]. This is particularly true since the mid-1990s with the inclusion of Fitts' law testing in the ISO 9241-9 standard for evaluating non-keyboard input devices [9,10,23]. The most common ISO evaluation procedure uses a two-dimensional (2D) task with targets of width W arranged in a circle. Selections proceed in a sequence moving across and around the circle. See Fig. 1. Each movement covers an amplitude A, the diameter of the layout circle. The movement time (MT, in seconds) is recorded for each trial and averaged over the sequence of trials.

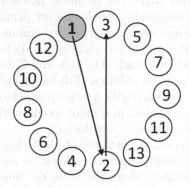

Fig. 1. Standard two-dimensional target selection task in ISO 9241-9 [9,10].

The difficulty of each trial is quantified using an index of difficulty (ID, in bits) and is calculated from A and W as

$$ID = \log_2\left(\frac{A}{W} + 1\right). \tag{1}$$

The main performance measure in ISO 9241-9 is throughput (TP, in bits/second or bps) which is calculated over a sequence of trials as the $ID{:}MT$ ratio:

$$TP = \left(\frac{ID_e}{MT}\right). \tag{2}$$

The standard specifies using the effective index of difficulty (ID_e) which includes an adjustment for accuracy to reflect the spatial variability in responses:

$$ID_e = \log_2 \left(\frac{A_e}{W_e} + 1 \right). \tag{3}$$

with

$$W_e = 4.133 \times SD_x. \tag{4}$$

The term SD_x is the standard deviation in the selection coordinates computed over a sequence of trials. For the two-dimensional task, selections are projected onto the task axis, yielding a single normalized x-coordinate for each trial. For $x = 0$, the selection was on a line orthogonal to the task axis that intersects the center of the target. x is negative for selections on the near side of the target centre and positive for selections on the far side. The factor 4.133 adjusts the target width for a nominal error rate of 4% under the assumption that the selection coordinates are normally distributed. The effective amplitude (A_e) is the actual distance traveled along the task axis. The use of A_e instead of A is only necessary if there is an overall tendency for selections to overshoot or undershoot the target (see [13] for additional details).

Throughput is a potentially valuable measure of human performance because it embeds both the speed and accuracy of participant responses. Comparisons between studies are therefore possible, with the proviso that the studies use the same method in calculating throughput. Figure 2 is an expanded formula for throughput, illustrating the presence of speed and accuracy in the calculation.

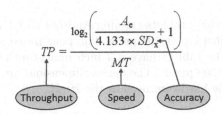

Fig. 2. Expanded formula for throughput, featuring speed ($1/MT$) and accuracy (SD_x).

Previous studies applying Fitts' law with children are scarce. One recent paper by Gottwald et al. studied the movement accuracy of 14-month-old children [19]. A study by Tsai compared the performance of children (10–14 yrs), adults, and the elderly when using a set of gestures on smartphones and concluded that the Fitts' law model held for all users [24]. They suggested that any size of device less than five inches was too small to be usable.

3   Method

Preference data are difficult to gather reliably with children, due to external factors. For example, children who are familiar with tablets, such as the Apple

Pencil or Microsoft *Surface Pen*, may indicate a preference for the device simply because it is seen as novel and "cool". As such, the focus in this paper is on children's performance between finger and stylus input, with user preference data not formally gathered. Our focus is on drag-and-drop tasks.

Fitts' law was used as the experimental procedure, with throughput, described above, as the main performance metric. Measures of speed and accuracy are also important as they often provide additional insight on the observed behaviors. Analyses are also provided on the dragging paths, the distribution of drop coordinates, and Fitts' law regression models.

3.1 Participants

Twenty-eight children aged 8 and 9 (16 male, 12 female) participated on a voluntary basis during a school visit to the university lab. Appropriate parental consent was obtained through the school in the weeks prior to the visit. This age range was selected as the children are young users whose writing and pen-holding skills are still improving. They are inside Piaget's concrete-operational stage of development, where more logical, organized communication and collaboration is observed and where more sophisticated collaborative learning exercises are possible [19].

3.2 Apparatus

Five Asus Google *Nexus 7* tablets running Android v5.1.1 were used along with five low-cost micro-fiber-tip stylus pens. The pens measured 120 mm by 9 mm with an 8 mm tip. The tablets have a 7-inch multi-touch color display with a resolution of 1920 × 1200 pixels. The device dimensions are 120 × 10 × 198 mm. Figure 3 illustrates the hardware used in the study.

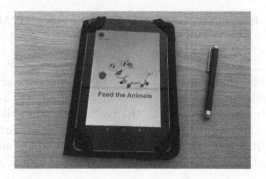

Fig. 3. Asus Google *Nexus 7* tablet and stylus.

The experiment software was an Android implementation of the ISO 2D Fitts' law software developed by MacKenzie [12] known as *FittsTaskTwo* (now

GoFitts).[1] The software was modified to support drag-and-drop interaction and to add a game-like appeal for children. To make the task "child friendly" and to keep the children engaged, the start target was an apple (i.e., food) and the end target was an animal (to be fed). The modified software is called *FittsFarm*.

The graphics changed from trial to trial, thus providing variation to maintain the children's interest. There was also a voice-over telling the children how to proceed. Apart from these changes, the adapted software contains the same features as the original ISO-conforming software, with spherical targets presented on a flat 2D-plane. Figure 4 illustrates a typical user trial with *FittsFarm*.

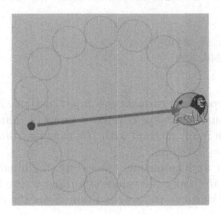

Fig. 4. *FittsFarm* user trial. The participant feeds the lion by dragging and dropping the apple. The blue arrow does not appear during use (Color figure online).

3.3   Procedure

On entering the experiment room, the children were first given a short briefing about the study. Their task was to perform an "animal feeding" activity on a tablet computer. A short training phase was conducted where the children completed two sequences of 15 "feeding" trials of a random amplitude and target width (Fig. 4). The training phase was repeated at the start of each input method (finger, stylus).

For each sequence they were asked to complete all trials once started, and to proceed at a comfortable speed and to not make many mistakes. If they missed a drag-and-drop target an audio alert sounded. At the end of each sequence, performance data appeared on the device display.

The study was divided into two blocks, one for finger input and one for stylus input. Each block had six sequences of 15 trials. Each sequence used a unique combination of movement amplitude and target width. Targets appeared in a circle to provide a full range of drag-and-drop start and end points. See Fig. 1.

---

[1] http://www.yorku.ca/mack/GoFitts/.

A trial was a single drag-and-drop interaction from a source target to a destination target. For each trial, the start point was the previous end point. This repeats clockwise around the circle until all 15 trials are complete. The start point is set at random.

Participants were organized in groups of four with each child seated separately with a facilitator assigned to oversee the study.

3.4 Design

The study was a $2 \times 3 \times 2$ within-subjects design with the following independent variables and levels:

- Input method (finger, stylus)
- Amplitude (120, 240, 480)
- Width (50, 100)

The primary independent variable was input method. Amplitude and width were included to ensure the tasks covered a range of difficulty. This results in six sequences for each input method with *ID*s ranging from $\log_2(\frac{120}{100} + 1) = 1.34$ bits to $\log_2(\frac{480}{50} + 1) = 3.41$ bits.

The target width and amplitude values are "nominal" values, not pixels. The *FittsFarm* software scales the values according to the resolution of the host device's display such that the widest condition spans the available space with a 10-pixel margin.

The participants were divided into two groups. One group was tested with the finger first; the other group was tested with the stylus first.

Aside from training, the total number of trials was 5040 (= 28 participants $\times$ 2 input methods $\times$ 3 amplitudes $\times$ 2 widths $\times$ 15 trials).

4   Results and Discussion

The results are discussion below, organized by dependent variables. Statistical analysis were performed using the *GoStats* application.[2]

4.1 Throughput

The grand mean for throughput was 2.45 bps. By input method, the means were 2.34 bps (finger) and 2.55 bps (stylus), representing a 9% performance advantage for stylus input. See Fig. 5. The effect of input method on throughput was statistically significant ($F_{1,26} = 11.11, p < .005$).

---

[2] http://www.yorku.ca/mack/GoStats/.

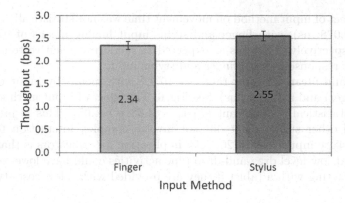

Fig. 5. Throughput (bps) by input method. Error bars show ±1 *SE*.

The finger and stylus throughput values are low compared to desktop pointing and selecting with a computer mouse or stylus, where throughputs are typically in the range of 4–5 bps [23, Table 4]. Of course, here, we are testing children and the task is drag-and-drop, not point-select. There are no throughput values in the literature for drag-and-drop tasks computed using Eq. 2.

For dragging actions there likely is a motor-control overhead in ensuring that an acquired target remains selected while moving the target from its start point to its destination. This is supported by findings elsewhere [8,14,16].

This has implications for designers of educational applications and suggests that designers should consider other types of interaction, such as select-and-tap (where an object is first selected by touch and then moved to a destination on the next touch) over a drag-and-drop approach.

A group effect was observed and was statistically significant ($F_{1,26} = 4.93, p = 0.035$), with $TP = 2.64$ bps for the finger-first group and $TP = 2.30$ bps for the stylus-first group. There was a clear advantage to beginning with finger input compared to stylus input. The most likely explanation is that the participants who used the stylus first had to learn both the experiment task and a novel input method (i.e., stylus input). This was accounted for with a training phase, but as the children are young and not as well practiced in holding a pen or stylus, a stronger learning effect for the stylus was present. It is not anticipated this would occur in older children or adults.

4.2 Movement Time and Error Rate

Since throughput is a composite measure combining speed and accuracy, the individual results for movement time and error rate are less important. They are summarized briefly below.

The effect of input method on movement time was not statistically significant ($F_{1,26} = 0.078$, ns), with finger and stylus input having means of 975 ms and 968 ms, respectively. This was as expected as modern capacitive touch screens have a fast response to both finger and stylus input.

The grand mean for error rate was 10.9% with means by input method of 12.6% (finger) and 9.3% (stylus). See Fig. 6. The effect of input method on error rate was statistically significant ($F_{1,26} = 4.33, p < .05$). This is in line with findings in other studies that did not involve complex interaction techniques such as gesture input [1,4,16,26]. The implication for educators is that children carrying out low-level drag-and-drop type activities could have lower error rates when interacting with a tablet if they are provided with a low-cost stylus.

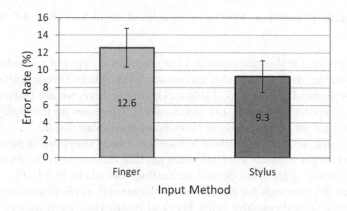

Fig. 6. Error rate (%) by input method. Error bars show ±1 *SE*.

For the large target, error rates were about 8% for both finger input and stylus input. For the small target, error rates were more than double this, at 15.2% for stylus input and 20.6% for finger input.

4.3 Dragging Paths

Drag-and-drop, whether with the finger or stylus, is an example of "direct input". This is in contrast to "indirect input" using, for example, a mouse or touchpad, where input involves maneuvering a tracking symbol, such as a cursor. It is no surprise, then, that the dragging paths were smooth overall, with reasonably direct movement of the dragged apple between targets. A typical example for the stylus is seen in Fig. 7a. In contrast, an atypical example for the finger is seen in Fig. 7b. In this case, there appears to be an element of play, as the participant's drag path proceeds around the layout circle for some of the trials.

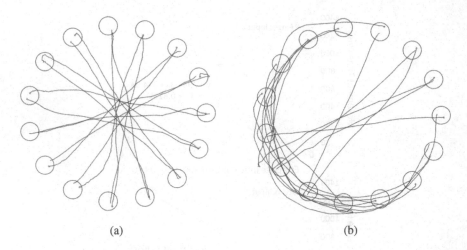

(a)   (b)

Fig. 7. Dragging paths for the stylus (top) and finger (bottom). See text for discussion.

4.4 Distribution of Drop Coordinates

An assumption when including the adjustment for accuracy, or W_e, in the calculation of throughput is that the selection coordinates are normally distributed, as noted earlier. The *FittsFarm* software logs such coordinates for all trials in a sequence. The coordinate is the location where the acquired object – the apple – was dropped. This occurs by lifting either the finger or stylus, depending on the input method. For each sequence of trials we tested the normality assumption using the Lilliefors test available in *GoStats*. Of the 720 total sequences in the experiment, the null hypothesis of normality was retained for 648, or 90%, of the sequences. Thus, the assumption of normality is generally held. The results were split evenly between the finger and stylus conditions.

4.5 Fitts' Law Models

To test for conformance to Fitts' law, we built linear regression models for each input method. As expected, both input methods follow Fitts' law with R^2 values > .9 for the *ID* models and > .8 for the ID_e models. Figure 8 provides examples for the ID_e models.

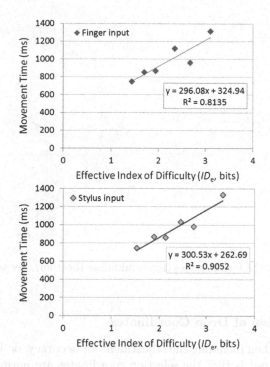

Fig. 8. Regression models for finger input and stylus input.

5 Conclusions

The reduced error rate and improved throughput indicates the stylus is both more accurate and more efficient than the finger for drag-and-drop tasks on tablet computers. As researchers who visit schools often to facilitate STEM activities, the authors have observed a greater tendency for children to collaborate when working next to each other on tablets. This is supported in the literature [5,15]. It is easier for children to perform drag-and-drop interaction using a finger or stylus on a friend's tablet than it is to take control of peripheral devices such as mouse or trackpad. This facilitates collaboration between children when working together or helping friends with their work.

One issue is that direct finger input can mark the screen and potentially discourage children from using other people's devices [17]. Stylus input is an intermediary in this context, potentially supporting more accurate, scuff-free, and efficient collaboration between children. Further work will examine the potential for stylus input in educational collaboration, but our findings indicate that stylus input is a superior choice for drag-and-drop tasks with children. The high availability and low cost means educators should consider providing styli with tablets for school-related activities.

Acknowledgments. The authors would like to thank Dominic Hodgkiss and Raid AlQaisi for their assistance in facilitating the study sessions.

References

1. Anthony, L., Brown, Q., Tate, B., Nias, J., Brewer, R., Irwin, G.: Designing smarter touch-based interfaces for educational contexts. Pers. Ubiquit. Comput. **18**(6), 1471–1483 (2014). https://doi.org/10.1007/s00779-013-0749-9
2. Arif, A.S., Sylla, C.: A comparative evaluation of touch and pen gestures for adult and child users. In: Proceedings of the 12th International Conference on Interaction Design and Children - IDC 2013, pp. 392–395. ACM, New York (2013). https://doi.org/10.1145/2485760.2485804
3. Chang, C.: Usability comparison of pen-based input for young children on mobile devices. In: IEEE International Conference on Sensor Networks, Ubiquitous, and Trustworthy Computing - SUTC 2008, pp. 531–536. IEEE, New York (2008). https://doi.org/10.1109/SUTC.2008.8
4. Chang, H.T., Tsai, T.H., Chang, Y.C., Chang, Y.M.: Touch panel usability of elderly and children. Comput. Hum. Behav. **37**, 258–269 (2014)
5. Couse, L.J., Chen, D.W.: A tablet computer for young children? Exploring its viability for early childhood education. J. Res. Technol. Educ. **43**, 75–96 (2010)
6. Fitts, P.M.: The information capacity of the human motor system in controllingthe amplitude of movement. J. Exp. Psychol. **47**, 381–391 (1954). https://doi.org/10.1037/h0055392
7. Greer, R., White, B., Zeegers, Y., Au, W., Barnes, A.: Emerging pedagogies for the use of iPads in schools. Br. J. Educ. Technol. **48**(2), 490–498 (2017)
8. Inkpen, K.M.: Drag-and-drop versus point-and-click mouse interaction styles for children. ACM Trans. Comput.-Hum. Interact. **8**, 1–33 (2001). https://doi.org/10.1145/371127.371146
9. ISO: Ergonomic requirements for office work with visual display terminals (VDTs) - part 9: Requirements for non-keyboard input devices (ISO 9241-9). Technical report, Report Number ISO/TC 159/SC4/WG3 N147, International Organisation for Standardisation (2000)
10. ISO: Evaluation methods for the design of physical input devices - ISO/TC 9241-411: 2012(e). Technical report, Report Number ISO/TS 9241-411:2102(E), International Organisation for Standardisation (2012)
11. MacKenzie, I.S.: Fitts' law as a research and design tool in human-computer interaction. Hum.-Comput. Interact. **7**, 91–139 (1992). https://doi.org/10.1207/s15327051hci0701_3
12. MacKenzie, I.S.: Human-Computer Interaction: An Empirical Research Perspective. Morgan Kaufmann, Waltham (2013)
13. MacKenzie, I.S.: Fitts' law. In: Norman, K.L., Kirakowski, J. (eds.) Handbook of Human-Computer Interaction, pp. 349–370. Wiley, Hoboken (2018). https://doi.org/10.1002/9781118976005
14. MacKenzie, I.S., Sellen, A., Buxton, W.A.S.: A comparison of input devices in elemental pointing and dragging tasks. In: Proceedings of the ACM SIGCHI Conference on Human Factors in Computing Systems - CHI 1991, pp. 161–166. ACM, New York (1991). https://doi.org/10.1145/108844.108868
15. Mann, A.M., Hinrichs, U., Read, J.C., Quigley, A.: Facilitator, functionary, friend or foe? Studying the role of iPads within learning activities across a school year. In: Proceedings of the ACM SIGCHI Conference on Human Factors in Computing Systems - CHI 2016, pp. 1833–1845. ACM, New York (2016). https://doi.org/10.1145/2858036.2858251

16. McKnight, L., Cassidy, B.: Children's interaction with mobile touch-screen devices: experiences and guidelines for design. Int. J. Mobile Hum. Comput. Interact. **2**, 1–18 (2010)
17. Morris, M.R., Huang, A., Paepcke, A., Winograd, T.: Cooperative gestures: multi-user gestural interactions for co-located groupware. In: Proceedings of the ACM SIGCHI Conference on Human Factors in Computing Systems - CHI 2006, pp. 1201–1210. ACM, New York (2006). https://doi.org/10.1145/1124772.1124952
18. Motti, L.G., Vigouroux, N., Gorce, P.: Drag-and-drop for older adults using touch-screen devices: effects of screen sizes and interaction techniques on accuracy. In: Proceedings of the 26th Conference on L'Interaction Homme-Machine - IHM 2014, pp. 139–146. ACM, New York (2014). https://doi.org/10.1145/2670444.2670460
19. Piaget, J., Inhelder, B.: Memory and Intelligence. Taylor & Francis, Milton Park (2015)
20. Pila, S., Aladé, F., Sheehan, K.J., Lauricella, A.R., Wartella, E.A.: Learning to code via tablet applications: an evaluation of Daisy the Dinosaur and Kodable as learning tools for young children. Comput. Educ. **128**, 52–62 (2019). https://doi.org/10.1016/j.compedu.2018.09.006
21. Ren, X., Zhou, X.: An investigation of the usability of the stylus pen for various age groups on personal digital assistants. Behav. Inf. Technol. **30**, 709–726 (2011)
22. Romeo, G., Edwards, S., McNamara, S., Walker, I., Ziguras, C.: Touching the screen: issues related to the use of touchscreen technology in early childhood education. Br. J. Educ. Technol. **30**, 329–339 (2003)
23. Soukoreff, R.W., MacKenzie, I.S.: Towards a standard for pointing device evaluation: perspectives on 27 years of Fitts' law research in HCI. Int. J. Hum.-Comput. Stud. **61**, 751–789 (2004). https://doi.org/10.1016/j.ijhcs.2004.09.001
24. Tsai, T.H., Tseng, K.C., Chang, Y.S.: Testing the usability of smartphonesurface gestures on different sizes of smartphones by different age groups of users. Comput. Hum. Behav. **75**, 103–116 (2017). https://doi.org/10.1016/j.ijhcs.2004.09.001
25. Vatavu, R.D., Cramariuc, G., Schipor, D.M.: Touch interaction for children aged 3 to 6 years: experimental findings and relationship to motor skills. Int. J. Hum.-Comput. Stud. **74**, 54–76 (2015)
26. Woodward, J., Shaw, A., Aloba, A., Jain, A., Ruiz, J., Anthony, L.: Tablets, table-tops, and smartphones: cross-platform comparisons of children's touchscreen interactions. In: Proceedings of the 19th ACM International Conference on Multimodal Interaction - ICMI 2017, pp. 5–14. ACM, New York (2017). https://doi.org/10.1145/3136755.3136762

Is Bigger Better? A Fitts' Law Study on the Impact of Display Size on Touch Performance

Corinna List[✉] and Michael Kipp

Augsburg University of Applied Sciences, Augsburg, Germany
{corinna.list,michael.kipp}@hs-augsburg.de

Abstract. Touch-sensitive surfaces are already a standard form of interaction. These surfaces come in many different sizes like tablets or touch
walls. However, there is little research to characterize the impact of surface size on touch performance. We conducted a Fitts' Law study of three
display sizes (13.5″ tablet, 28″ monitor, 69.5″ large monitor), comparing
various performance measures. We found that the smallest size (13.5″) is
problematic both objectively (high error rate) and subjectively (imprecise, difficult-to-use). In contrast, both the medium (28″) and the large
display (69.5″) perform equally well. However, small displays allow for
greater interaction speed compared to very large screens. Our results can
help interaction designers and automatic algorithms to optimize current
and future touch devices.

Keywords: Touchscreen surfaces · Fitts' Law · Gestural interaction

1 Introduction

Interactive surfaces can be found almost anywhere and in any size. Due to
advances in display technologies, screens are becoming both smaller and larger
than ever before. Surfaces can be as small as a watch face or as big as a shop
window. While it is clear that different sizes afford different interaction methods and approaches, it is less clear how precisely touch performance differs on
various surface sizes. We focus on surfaces with a minimal size of a tablet where
one would expect a touch movement performance that is relatively unaffected
by the boundaries of the screen.

There is little research that focuses characterizing the different sizes with
precise measurements. It has been shown that a larger display size negatively
affects the performance when using a mouse [16]: With increasing display size,
movement time increases and performance decreases. However, in another study
[5] users preferred a large display for daily work because it helped them with
multi-window or rich information tasks.

When using touch, does the above apply as well, and does performance
decrease with increased display size? One study [3] compared different screen

© IFIP International Federation for Information Processing 2019
Published by Springer Nature Switzerland AG 2019
D. Lamas et al. (Eds.): INTERACT 2019, LNCS 11748, pp. 669–678, 2019.
https://doi.org/10.1007/978-3-030-29387-1_39

sizes for performance and ergonomics using specific postures for each display (sitting with the tablet, standing in front of the public display). This makes it difficult to interpret the results. Hence, we focus on making a performance comparison with equal side conditions. For each condition (tablet, monitor, wall) the user would stand and operate on a vertical surface.

In this paper we focus on the characteristics of display sizes when using touch for basic translation movements. In a Fitts' Law [6] experiment with 16 Participants we compared three different display sizes (small 13.5", medium 28", large 69.5") regarding various performance measures such as error rate or speed. To allow comparison with other existing research, we follow Soukoreff and MacKenzie [13]: We use the Shannon formulation to calculate the Index of Difficulty (ID), we use ID values between 2 to 6. We analyzed error rate, speed, and performance. We also assessed subjective difficulty and precision for each display using questionnaires.

Our results show that a small screen (13.5") performs worst. It is not only perceived as difficult-to-use and imprecise but also has the highest error rate. Both the medium sized screen (28") and the large display (69.5") performed equally well. However, the small screen outperformed the largest screen in terms of speed.

First, we discuss various studies on the effect of display size on performance (Sect. 2). In Sect. 3, our user study is described with respect to participants, apparatus, study procedure, and measurements. Afterwards we show (Sect. 4) and discuss (Sect. 5) the results for each display and in comparison with each other. Section 6 presents our conclusion and future work.

2   Related Work

There is much research on the broader topic of touch performance. Research has looked at various touch techniques as well as side conditions like screen angle and the grip used with mobile devices. Touch techniques for translation, rotation and scaling have been investigated to understand the effect of parameters like direction and position [7,8,11,12]. Mobile devices and especially the tap gesture have been another focus of attention [9].

Nguyen and Kipp [11,12] investigated the efficiency of translation and rotation touch gestures. They compared directions and screen regions as well as the effect of the display's orientation. They found patterns of high performance, for instance that upward movements performed faster than downwards movements on a horizontal display. They also found that movement which employs a shorter kinematic chain is faster.

The efficiency of rotation as well as pinch touch gestures was investigated by Hoggan et al. [7,8]. They found that with increasing diameter the duration and failure rate increase as well. An increased distance led to increased duration and failure rate.

Although these studies investigated how different parameters of touch input affect performance, they did not include display size as a factor.

For smartphones there are a number of studies looking at the performance for different grips. Lehmann and Kipp [9] investigated the performance, precision, and errors of tapping gestures on smartphones. They showed that a two-handed use while tapping with the thumbs in landscape orientation leads to the best performance. They did not compare other display sizes.

There is also a range of studies looking at screen size as one side condition [2, 3, 5, 14, 16]. However, none of the following studies exclusively focus on size.

Wang et al. [16] investigated the impact of display size on mouse performance in a pointing task. They used four sizes: 10″, 27″, 46″, and 55″. In a Fitts' Law experiment they found that display size has no significant effect on accuracy. However, the larger the display, the larger the necessary movement time and the higher the slope and intercept.

Anslow and Wong [2] examined the effects of display angle and physical size on large touch displays in the work place for data analysis activities. The 27″ display was rated more effective than the 40″ screen. Participants claimed the 40″ screen to be too difficult for reaching and interacting effectively with all screen locations. This study focused on the comparison of only two different but relatively large screen sizes. Also, in contrast to our study, the 40″ screen was a composite screen with two displays.

In the study of Bi and Balakrishnan [5] on the other hand, a large display wall (16′ × 6′) was preferred for daily work tasks without touch. For the one week study their participants switched from their usual single or dual desktop display to a large high-resolution display wall. Participants claimed the wall to help them e.g. with multi-window tasks and rich information tasks. In this study, users that used single or dual desktop displays before starting the study, switched for one week to a wall display.

For 3D interaction, a larger screen can have a positive impact. In their cognitive comparison of 3D interaction in front of a wall (4 m × 3 m) vs. a desktop display (15″), Tyndiuk et al. [14] showed that the wall had a positive effect on performance for manipulation and naive travel tasks. Although not all users benefited to the same degree from the wall.

The first study to compare performance and ergonomics of touch surfaces was done by Bachynskyi et al. [3]. In their Fitts' Law experiment they used Motion Capture to compare pointing tasks on five different sized touch surfaces. The displays were set up in different orientations and with specific postures of the participants. They showed that tablet and laptop were poor in performance, while the larger displays (public display, tabletop) as well as the smallest display (smartphone) were high or medium in performance. Though they compared different screen sizes and their impact on performance, postures varied for the displays.

Overall, prior research has not examined the role of display size for touch interaction in a focused way. While there is some evidence that larger size negatively impacts performance [2, 16], other studies suggest that a large size is seen positive for specific applications [5, 14]. The most closely related study suggest that only the tablet/laptop size is poorer in performance than other sizes

(smaller or larger) [3]. Our study focuses on comparing screen sizes only, keeping all other factors equal (e.g. user standing for all screen sizes).

3   User Study

For this study, each task required the participants to do translation movements using touch (see Fig. 1). Participants were instructed to perform a straight dragging motion between two circles. The start area was shown with a green circle in the center labelled "START". An orange circle marked the target area. As soon as the start circle was touched, it turned grey and the outline of the target circle turned green. The position of the finger was shown with a cursor. The user was instructed to drag the cursor inside the target area. A trial was successful if the cursor was inside the target circle when lifting the finger. Success or failure were signalled by sound and visually with a coloured outline (green/red) around the target circle. Note that it is necessary to differentiate between cursor and actual finger tip position because of latency, all touch systems have a significant amount of lag [10].

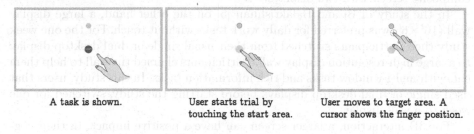

| A task is shown. | User starts trial by touching the start area. | User moves to target area. A cursor shows the finger position. |

Fig. 1. Translation movement task (Color figure online)

We tested three display sizes in our study, resulting in the following three conditions (Fig. 2):

a. condition SMALL: 13.5″ tablet (3000 × 2000 pixels)
b. condition MEDIUM: 28″ monitor (4500 × 3000 pixels)
c. condition LARGE: 69.5″ monitor (1920 × 1080 pixels)

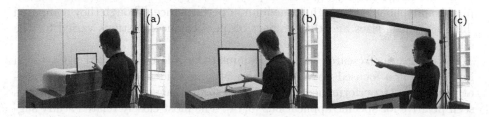

Fig. 2. Setup for conditions (a) SMALL, (b) MEDIUM, and (c) LARGE.

For an analysis in multiple directions and with different IDs, target circles were computed with three possible distances/amplitudes (17%, 23%, 30% of the display height), four directions (0°, 90°, 180°, 270°) and three different widths (see Table 1). The distances were calculated using the display height. The widths were computed based on the displays screen resolution and pixel density to create identical ID values. Each configuration was repeated three times.

Table 1. All combinations of target width (in px) and amplitude (in percentage of display height) with respective ID values for the three conditions S: SMALL display, M: MEDIUM display and L: LARGE display

Target width			Ampl.	ID	Target width			Ampl.	ID	Target width			Ampl.	ID
S	M	L			S	M	L			S	M	L		
12 px	18 px	9 px	17%	4.5	30 px	45 px	21 px	17%	3.3	60 px	90 px	42 px	17%	2.4
12 px	18 px	9 px	23%	4.9	30 px	45 px	21 px	23%	3.6	60 px	90 px	42 px	23%	2.7
12 px	18 px	9 px	30%	5.3	30 px	45 px	21 px	30%	4.0	60 px	90 px	42 px	30%	3.1

Participants: We had 16 participants in the study (5 females). The average age was 25.6 years (SD = 7.8). The average body height was 175 cm (SD = 9.9), the average arm length 71 cm (SD = 4.1). All participants were right-handed and had experience using touch displays. Most were students from Computer Science or Design.

Apparatus: The study was conducted under lab conditions. Participants received written introductions. For condition SMALL a Microsoft Surface Book (13.5″) was used, a Microsoft Surface Studio (28″) for condition MEDIUM and an Iiyama ProLite 70 (69.5″) for condition LARGE. The center of each display was positioned at the same height of 140 cm. To record the participants' interactions two cameras were set up on tripods at the sides of the main area.

Study Procedure: Each participant filled out a questionnaire for background information and was given a short briefing for the study. For each condition, the following steps were repeated: The participant performed a short training for the particular screen where each configuration was tried once per direction. After training the actual trials were conducted and measurements were taken. Then, a questionnaire was given to the participant, asking how the task was perceived in this condition regarding factors like difficulty or precision. Each participant was given the opportunity for open comments. Finally, the participant had a three-minute break to avoid fatigue.

After finishing all three conditions, the participant was given a post-test questionnaire comparing the different screen sizes. Also, the participant had the chance to revise previous answers in the questionnaires on each condition. The order of conditions was counterbalanced, i.e., it changed after each participant. For each condition, 36 configurations with three repetitions were executed. For the three conditions this resulted in $3 \times 36 \times 3 = 324$ trials per person. Therefore, with 16 participants a total of $324 \times 16 = 5,184$ trials were recorded. Each session took about 30–45 min to complete.

Measurements: Several aspects were measured in this study. In a first question-naire data such as age, gender, body height, and arm height as well as technical background and profession was collected. Further questionnaires regarding the display sizes were used to collect subjective data to measure joy, effort, fatigue, difficulty, perceived speed, and perceived precision. Based on the objective time measurements, effective throughput, and error rate were computed.

4 Results

All results were evaluated using a one-way between-subjects ANOVA and post-hoc t-tests using the Bonferroni method.

Speed: To make a fair comparison of speed across different display sizes we calculated speed in in terms of (% of display)/ms. Also, to compare different distances we normalized the paths from start to target to a unit interval of [0, 1] and looked at mean speed times along this normalized path (Fig. 3). We found significant results at the $p < .005$ level comparing the three display sizes $(F(2, 45) = 7.51)$. The post hoc comparision showed that the maximum average speed was higher for the SMALL display than for the LARGE one. The SMALL display had a maximum average speed of 0.25 $(SD = 0.051)$, while the maximum average speed for LARGE was 0.19 $(SD = 0.048)$. No significant results were found comparing the MEDIUM display $(M = 0.21, SD = 0.034)$ with the other displays.

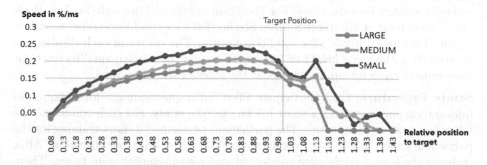

Fig. 3. Average speeds in %/ms at relative distances to the target.

Error Rate: Errors are trials where the final touch point was outside the target area. We found significant results at the $p < .01$ level $(F(2, 45) = 6.956)$. The post-hoc test indicated that the error rates of movements on the tablet $(M = 15.62\%, SD = 6.96)$ were significantly higher than on the MEDIUM monitor $(M = 7.18\%, SD = 8.09)$ or on the LARGE display $(M = 8.09\%, SD = 5.85)$ as shown in Table 2. There was no significance between MEDIUM and LARGE.

Performance: Performance was measured as Effective Throughput (TP) [13]. The Index of Difficulty (ID) was calculated using the Shannon Formulation. In

Table 2. Error rate, perceived difficulty and perceived precision. Mean and SD values.

	Small	Medium	Large
Error rate	M=15.62%, SD = 6.96	M = 7.18%, SD = 8.09	M = 8.09%, SD = 5.85
Perceived difficulty	M = 2.00, SD = 1.32	M = 1.13, SD = 0.96	M = 0.88, SD = 0.72
Perceived precision	M = 2.06, SD = 0.85	M = 3.06, SD = 0.93	M = 3.00, SD = 0.82

our study the SMALL display had TP of 4.87 (SD = 1.14). TP of the MEDIUM monitor was 5.15 (SD = 0.96), while it was 4.63 (SD = 1.33) for the LARGE display. None of the differences between the performances of the displays were significant ($F(2, 45) = 1.55$, $p = 0.223$).

Questionnaire: In our questionnaires we asked about perceived joy, effort, fatigue, difficulty, speed, and precision. Asking the same questions for each display, the subjects gave ratings on a 5-point Likert scale. The answers were mapped to values from 0 to 4. For analysis we treated these values as interval values which is common practice. No significant results could be found for joy, effort, fatigue, and speed. Regarding difficulty (see Table 2), significant results could be found at a $p < .01$ level ($F(2, 45) = 5.289$). The SMALL display (M = 2.0, D = 1.32) was perceived more difficult to use than the LARGE screen (M = 0.88, SD = 0.72). Also significant differences at a $p < .01$ were found regarding the perceived precision ($F(2, 45) = 6.67$). The SMALL screen was perceived less precise (M = 2.06, SD = 0.85) than the MEDIUM (M = 3.06, SD = 0.93) or the LARGE screen (M = 3.0, SD = 0.82) as can be seen in Table 2.

5 Discussion

Which screen size is best for which purpose? Our results give a differentiated picture.

Small Screen (tablet, notebook): Even though a small display (13.5″ tablet) has a higher average speed than a very large (69.9″) display, our results show that it is problematic objectively and subjectively. Objectively, it has the highest error rate of the three devices. Occlusion may be one reason for the high error rate. As the users move their hand to the target, both their hand and their fingertip cover the target area. As described by Vogel and Balakrishnan [15] occlusion is likely to increase errors. Subjectively, the small display is perceived both difficult to use and imprecise, which corresponds with the high error rate. This result confirms findings by Bachynskyi et al. [3] that tablets and small notebooks yield a poor performance for touch input.

Medium Screen (desktop monitor): The 27″ desktop monitor performed quite well. Regarding error rate, subjective precision, and difficulty it outperformed the smaller display (13.5″) while is not significantly slower than the small display.

Large Screen (smartboard, touch wall): While a large display was claimed to be too difficult to use in the study of Anslow and Wong [2], it performed quite well for translation movements in our study. Not the large display, but the small display was found to be difficult to use. Our findings are in accordance with studies that positively assess large screens in terms of performance [3] and for concrete applications [5,14]. However, it is significantly slower compared with the small display (13.5″). Also, it is well known that touch interactions on large displays cause fatigue [1].

Comparison: Overall a small display performs worst regarding errors, difficulty, and precision, but may be the best form factor for many applications, e.g. regarding mobility. Large displays on the other side are better in terms of display space and for the use in public scenario setups. Bachynskyi et al. [3] have shown that though the performance was poor for the tablet or the laptop, it was suitable for long-term use, while other displays like the larger public display have not been suitable for long-term use, even though their performance was high. The input method seems to influence how well a display size performs. While Wang et al. [16] found no significant difference in accuracy when using a mouse input device, there is an impact when using touch. A small display size (tablet) leads to a higher error rate and thus is less accurate. Regarding the subjective difficulty, our results differ from the research of Anslow and Wong [2]. While they showed that a larger display was perceived more difficult to use, we show that smaller displays are perceived most difficult to use, with no significant difference between medium and large displays. This contrast is even more surprising as our size difference is much larger (27″ against 69.5″) than that of Anslow/Wong (27″ against 40″). So we assume that the difference hinges on their specific scenario but we conclude that a larger display has no general disadvantages in terms of performance but certainly in terms of fatigue [1].

6   Conclusion and Future Work

We explored how display size impacts performance of touch translation movements. Three display sizes were tested: small (13.5″ tablet), medium (28″ monitor), and large (69.5″ screen). We analyzed performance, error rate, speed, and subjective values such as effort, joy, difficulty, fatigue, and precision. The smallest sized display performed worst. Though its speed was higher than for the largest display, its error rate was highest and it is perceived both imprecise and difficult-to-use. Small displays are therefore suited for scenarios that require high mobility and speed (like games). The medium and the large screens, in contrast, performed quite well. Since very large screen cause more fatigue the medium screen may be the "golden middle" for the majority of applications.

For the future, we plan to use motion capture analysis to further investigate the correlation between performance and human movement [3]. Ultimately, we want to find a model of human movement that explains various findings on display size, angle and mobile device grips and its relation to measurable performance.

References

1. Al-Megren, S., Kharrufa, A., Hook, J., Holden, A., Sutton, S., Olivier, P.: Comparing fatigue when using large horizontal and vertical multi-touch interaction displays. In: Abascal, J., Barbosa, S., Fetter, M., Gross, T., Palanque, P., Winckler, M. (eds.) INTERACT 2015. LNCS, vol. 9299, pp. 156–164. Springer, Cham (2015). https://doi.org/10.1007/978-3-319-22723-8_13
2. Anslow, C., Wong, W.: Effects of the display angle and physical size on large touch displays in the work place. In: Proceedings of the 2017 ACM International Conference on Interactive Surfaces and Spaces (ISS), pp. 318–323 (2017). https://doi.org/10.1145/3132272.3135080
3. Bachynskyi, M., et al.: Performance and ergonomics of touch surfaces. A comparative study using biomechanical simulation. In: Proceedings of the SIGCHI Conference on Human Factors in Computing Systems (CHI), pp. 1817–1826 (2015). https://doi.org/10.1145/2702123.2702607
4. Baudisch, P., et al.: Drag-and-Pop and drag-and-pick. Techniques for accessing remote screen content on touch- and pen-operated systems. In: Proceedings of Interact, pp. 57–64 (2003)
5. Bi, X., Balakrishnan, R.: Comparing usage of a large high-resolution display to single or dual desktop displays in daily work. In: Proceedings of the SIGCHI Conference on Human Factors in Computing Systems (CHI), pp. 1005–1014 (2009).https://doi.org/10.1145/1518701.1518855
6. Fitts, P.M.: The information capacity of the human motor system in controlling the amplitude of movement. J. Exp. Psychol. **47**(6), 381–391 (1954). https://doi.org/10.1037//0096-3445.121.3.262
7. Hoggan, E., et al.: Multi-touch pinch gestures: performance and ergonomics. In: Proceedings of the 2013 ACM International Conference on Interactive Tabletops and Surfaces, pp. 219–222 (2013). https://doi.org/10.1145/2512349.2512817
8. Hoggan, E., et al.: Multi-touch rotation gestures: performance and ergonomics. In: Proceedings of the SIGCHI Conference on Human Factors in Computing Systems, pp. 3047–3050 (2013). https://doi.org/10.1145/2470654.2481423
9. Lehmann, F., Kipp, M.: How to hold your phone when tapping. A comparative study of performance, precision, and errors. In: Proceedings of the ACM International Conference on Interactive Surfaces and Spaces (ISS), pp. 115–127 (2018). https://doi.org/10.1145/3279778.3279791
10. Ng, A., et al.: Designing for low-latency direct-touch input. In: Proceedings of the 25th Annual ACM Symposium on User Interface Software and Technology, pp. 453–464 (2012). https://doi.org/10.1145/2380116.2380174
11. Nguyen, Q., Kipp, M.: Orientation matters: efficiency of translation-rotation multi-touch tasks. In: Proceedings of the SIGCHI Conference on Human Factors in Computing Systems, pp. 2013–2016 (2014). https://doi.org/10.1145/2556288.2557399
12. Nguyen, Q., Kipp, M.: Where to start? Exploring the efficiency of translation movements on multitouch devices. In: Abascal, J., Barbosa, S., Fetter, M., Gross, T., Palanque, P., Winckler, M. (eds.) INTERACT 2015. LNCS, vol. 9299, pp. 173–191. Springer, Cham (2015). https://doi.org/10.1007/978-3-319-22723-8_15
13. Soukoreff, R., MacKenzie, I.: Towards a standard for pointing device evaluation, perspective on 27 years of Fitts' Law research in HCI. Int. J. Hum Comput Stud. **61**(6), 751–789 (2004). https://doi.org/10.1016/j.ijhcs.2004.09.001
14. Tyndiuk, F., et al.: Cognitive comparison of 3D interaction in front of large vs. small displays. In: Proceedings of the ACM Symposium on Virtual Reality Software

and Technology (VRST), pp. 117–123 (2005). https://doi.org/10.1145/1101616.
1101641
15. Vogel, D., Balakrishnan, R.: Occlusion-aware interfaces. In: Proceedings of the
SIGCHI Conference on Human Factors in Computing Systems, pp. 263–272 (2010).
https://doi.org/10.1145/1753326.1753365
16. Wang, Y., et al.: Exploring the effect of display size on pointing performance. In:
Proceedings of the 2013 ACM International Conference on Interactive Tabletops
and Surfaces, pp. 389–392 (2013). https://doi.org/10.1145/2512349.2514911

WeldVUI: Establishing Speech-Based Interfaces in Industrial Applications

Mirjam Augstein(✉)📵, Thomas Neumayr📵, and Sebastian Pimminger

University of Applied Sciences Upper Austria, Hagenberg, Austria
{mirjam.augstein,thomas.neumayr,sebastian.pimminger}@fh-hagenberg.at

Abstract. Voice User Interfaces (VUIs) and speech-based applications
have recently gained increasing popularity. During the past years, they
have been included in a wide range of mass-market devices (smart phones
or technology installed in common car cockpits) and are thus available
for many everyday interaction scenarios (e.g., making phone calls or
switching the lights on and off). This popularity also led to a number
of guidelines for VUI design, software libraries and devices for speech
recognition becoming available for interface designers and developers.
Although generally helpful, these resources are often broad and do not
fully satisfy the specific requirements of certain industrial applications.
First, grammar and vocabulary in such settings usually differ drastically
from everyday scenarios. Second, common software libraries and devices
are often not able to comply with the conditions in industrial environments (e.g. involving high levels of noise). This paper describes the iterative, user-centered design process for VUIs and functional speech-based
interaction prototypes for the domain of industrial welding, including
a two-stage Wizard of Oz procedure, rapid prototyping, speech recognition improvement and thorough user involvement. Our experiences
throughout this process generalize to other industrial applications and
so-called "niche applications" where grammar and vocabulary usually
have to be established from scratch. They are intended to guide other
researchers setting up a similar process for designing and prototyping
domain-specific VUIs.

Keywords: Voice user interface design · User-centered design ·
Interaction design · Speech-based interfaces · Industrial applications

1 Introduction

According to Cohen et al. [4, p. 5], a Voice User Interface (VUI) is "what a person interacts with when communicating with a spoken language application". Its
elements include prompts ("all the recordings or synthesized speech played to
the user during the dialog"), grammars (definition of "the possible things callers
can say in response to each prompt") and dialog logic (the "actions taken by the

© IFIP International Federation for Information Processing 2019
Published by Springer Nature Switzerland AG 2019
D. Lamas et al. (Eds.): INTERACT 2019, LNCS 11748, pp. 679–698, 2019.
https://doi.org/10.1007/978-3-030-29387-1_40

system", e.g., "responding to what a caller has just said or reading out information retrieved from a database"). Cohen et al. further identify the following advantages of speech systems compared with other access modes. They are *intuitive and efficient, ubiquitous, enjoyable,* and *hands-free, eyes-free.* Especially the latter is decisive in use cases or whole application domains that provoke functional impairment for the users. This is, for instance, the case during driving when the driver's hands should remain on the steering wheel and visual attention should be paid to what's happening on the road. Further, speech is generally considered to be intuitive and natural; already in 1960, John Licklider envisioned speech-based interaction as the "most natural means" of communication [17].

Nowadays, speech-based interaction has become omnipresent (e.g., in car cockpits, on smart phones and via smart speakers for home control). Most of the popular services like Amazon Alexa, Google Assistant, Apple Siri or Microsoft Cortana are cloud-based. They involve a wide spectrum of functionalities and a huge vocabulary, and many even offer a set of design guidelines. These systems often have in common that they allow for a *general, not further specified or restricted dialog about everyday things and services* (such as the weather or making phone calls). This makes them usable for a wide range of contexts and applications. Yet, it might also make them not very efficient if only a small, well-defined set of functionalities is needed. This is often the case in narrow, domain-specific scenarios such as certain industrial or other so-called "niche applications". Niche applications benefit from a VUI restricted to the most important functionalities needed in their context because (i) the respectively small vocabulary can be memorized more easily, especially if in everyday use, and (ii) they can be implemented for offline use more easily (which is often impossible for VUIs that rely on popular and high-performing cloud services). Both also enable short response times which contributes to the characteristics related to *ubiquitous use* and *efficiency* named in [4]. In contrast to VUIs for routine tasks, there are no gold standard VUI designs for most niche applications including those in the industrial domain. Thus, grammar, vocabulary and dialog structures must often be created from scratch and designed for the concrete needs of the particular target group.

This paper describes VUI design and application of speech-based interaction for industrial welding. Manual welding is a highly accurate process that requires the welder's hands to direct the welding torch or add welding rod. This leads to functional impairments during the process: neither can the hands be used for interaction with the machine (e.g., to change parameters), nor should the eyes be taken off the welding arc. There are numerous situations in which it would be beneficial regarding time and quality of the result if parameters could be changed on-the-fly, a *hands-free and eyes-free* [4] interaction method is required. The domain further involves additional restrictions: new solutions must be *low-cost, small-size, light-weight* and provide a *good User Experience (UX)* to be *integrable in the standard welding equipment* and *accepted by the market.*

We explain our methodology based on (i) a two-stage Wizard-of-Oz (WoZ) test with welders including observation, open questions and standardized

instruments (User Experience Questionnaire (UEQ) [16] and NASA TLX [9]), (ii) field tests with the resulting functional speech interaction prototypes, and (iii) systematic automated speech recognition tests and improvement. Further, we provide an overview of related work on VUI design including (industrial) niche applications and evaluation of VUIs, and an introduction to the industrial welder's work environment. The paper's main contribution lies in the detailed description of the applied methodology. It is intended as a methodological guide for other researchers who face the challenge of conceptualizing and implementing VUIs and speech-based interaction solutions for industrial and other niche applications. Although the methods themselves (such as WoZ) are not novel, we applied them for problems where there exists limited reported experience. E.g., WoZ is commonly used in early prototyping phases but, to the best of our knowledge, it has not been applied for the elicitation of grammar and vocabulary for VUIs before.

2   Related Work

Here we describe related work on the design of VUIs in general and in specific niche applications, and on the evaluation of speech-based interactive systems.

2.1   Speech-Based Interaction and VUI Design

Turunen [31] distinguishes eight layers related to speech processing categorized into three groups: *acoustic layer, articulary layer and phonemic layer* (first group), *lexical layer and syntactic layer* (second group), and *semantic layer, pragmatic layer and discourse layer* (third group). Further, Turunen (based on [29]) summarizes the first two groups as "core speech technologies" and the second and third group as "speech applications". Our work focuses on the top layers in the third group as we mainly discuss VUI design and for the implementation itself rely on existing voice recognition technology (although we also report experiences with the optimization of voice recognition). Further, Turunen identifies several properties of speech recognition systems in the following categories: (i) *vocabulary and language*, (ii) *communication style* and (iii) *usage conditions*. Our system can be described as follows, based on these categories: *vocabulary size* is *comparatively small* and uses *fixed phrases*. The *communication style* is *speaker-independent*[1] and the *speaking style* is mostly *discrete*. *Usage conditions* are *hostile* and *channel quality* might be *low*, due to the environmental conditions.

Cohen et al. [4] define five key principles for VUI design methodology that should especially help in projects with real-world constraints: (i) *end-user input* ("inform design decisions with end-user input"), (ii) *integrated business and user needs* ("find solutions that combine business goals and user goals"), (iii) *thorough early work* ("avoid expensive downstream changes by focusing on thorough work in the early definition and design stages"), (iv) *conversational design* ("move the

---

[1] This might be up to changes in a future version closer to a commercial product.

design experience close to the user experience so that the designer can experience design elements in their appropriate conversational context"), and (v) *context* ("make all design decisions with appropriate consideration of context"). These principles have been a basis for our VUI design as we thoroughly involved end users but also other stakeholders and invested a high amount of time and effort in early design phases. Further we did exhaustive usage context research (using the Contextual Design methodology [2,12]) prior to VUI design (see [1]).

An overview of specific requirements for VUIs is provided by Farinazzo et al. [8] based on [6,7]. They argue that while most requirements that are common for graphical user interfaces apply also for VUIs (e.g., usability and feedback), there are additional criteria, especially related to the *transient* attribute of voice (in contrast to graphical interfaces which are *persistent*). This is also pointed out by Schnelle and Lyardet [30] who e.g., state that "speech is one-dimensional" (while the eye is active, the ear is passive and cannot browse a set of recordings the way eyes can scan a screen of text and figures), "speech is transient" (listening is controlled by the short term memory; speech is not ideal for delivering large amounts of data), "speech is invisible" (thus it is difficult to indicate to the users what actions they may perform), and "speech is asymmetric" (people can speak faster than they type but listen more slowly than they read).

Farinazzo et al. identify three categories of requirements: (i) non-functional ones related to the *representation of the information*, (ii) requirements related to *data input*, and (iii) *technical issues*. Requirements in the first category "indicate the format that the interaction must assume in order to enable the system to deal with user inputs" and involve *consistency, feedback, support for all classes of users, minimization of the cognitive effort the user has to do in order to perform the tasks* and the *correctness, relevance and informativeness of system outputs*. Requirements in the second category include *appropriate recognition naturalness of speech and interaction, help mechanisms when the user is in difficult situations, error prevention* and *quick correction of inputs*. Finally, technical issues subsume *size of the vocabulary and the domain coverage and their effects on voice recognition, speaker dependence*, and *environmental influences such as noise*. The requirements defined by [6–8] guided our project along all phases.

Klemmer et al. [14] argue that building even simple speech-based interfaces requires technology expertise and takes considerable time and effort which is why many individuals are precluded from the design process. To allow for more rapid creation of speech interfaces, they introduce SUEDE, a prototyping tool for electronically supported WoZ. SUEDE's *design mode* enables designers to create dialogue examples including prompts and responses. The *test mode* enables testing with participants without the need for a functional speech backend. The wizard and participant are situated at different places, the wizard selects the appropriate dialogue elements and the system plays pre-recorded speech snippets to the participants according to the respective phase of a dialogue. In the *analysis mode*, SUEDE displays data collected in the test mode to the designer. The analysis interface is similar to the design interface but includes user transcripts from the test sessions and basic statistical information (e.g., the average

time it took participants to respond to prompts). In our work described in this paper, we follow a similar path of steps (see Sect. 4). We first designed our VUIs using graphs and dialogue elements. During the two WoZ phases, we tested these dialogues with real users and recorded all potentially relevant information. Next, we analyzed the data and used the findings for another iteration of VUI redesign. Our activities however exceeded the WoZ methodology as we actually implemented and tested fully functional prototypes. Yet, we fully agree with Klemmer et al. on the suitability of WoZ testing in early phases of VUI design.

2.2 Speech-Based Systems for Niche Applications

Rayner et al. [25,26] describe Clarissa, a voice-based system that enables astronauts to navigate through complex procedures using only voice input and output. They argue that "the comparative success of the Clarissa project is perhaps more than anything due to its organization" that relied on a close cooperation of developers and the NASA [26]. They further state that the original conception of the system came from the astronauts themselves. This has impacted our decision to design a VUI for professional welders based on their natural behavior. The situation of astronauts is comparable to the situation of welders as part of the astronauts' tasks are also "frequently hands-busy and eyes-busy" [26]. Initially, Clarissa had a vocabulary of less than 50 words and involved a handful commands, the last version involves about 75 commands and 260 words. Its navigation concept involves commands like "next" or "previous" and can be used to adjust audio volume with commands like "increase volume" or "quieter". Our VUI involves similar concepts for changing parameters like welding current that can be altered either by setting it to concrete values or in- or decreasing it. Clarissa focuses on a user-initiated dialog (command and response) combined with TTS feedback (repeating the values that have been set). Rayner et al. use a grammar-based architecture instead of the more popular statistical one, arguing that (i) no huge training data set was available and (ii) the system was designed for experts who would have some time to learn its coverage. They refer to Knight et al. [15] who have found grammar-based approaches to work better for this kind of users. Our situation is similar and we use a grammar-based approach, too.

Another discussion of VUIs for a specific niche application is provided by Noyes and Haas [21] who describe speech-based systems for the military domain. Military environments are "often harsh and not amendable to the use of technology per se", military personnel are "often subject to extremes of temperature and humidity". Another primary consideration is ambient noise which degrades speech recognition performance as it interferes with a user's utterances. The environmental situation in industrial welding is similar: it is extreme regarding temperature and noise (the welding arc produces volume levels above 100 dB). Noyes and Haas describe several approaches to make speech recognition more robust in high-noise contexts, e.g., microphone-based (microphone arrays, noise-cancelling microphones) and algorithmic approaches.

Pires [24] describes experiments on commanding an industrial robot using the human voice. His work is relevant for us because of the concrete application

examples which involve robotic welding. It is technically-focused and presents implementation details and concrete vocabulary used but does not describe the phase of VUI design. Our work does not tackle robotic welding but should improve efficiency, quality and UX during manual welding tasks. The welding tasks described in [24] however could also be performed manually, thus the selection of parameters is interesting. Pires points out that several parameters like welding current have to be changed during the process and explains that the VUI must allow for numerical values to be commanded by users. Due to the noisy environment negatively influencing recognition, Pires suggests enabling speech input only when necessary. This was however not applicable for us due to the more variable nature of manual tasks. We thus had to consider approaches to enhance recognition during noisy phases of welding as discussed in [21]. A parallel of our work to Pires' is the use of a grammar-based approach (also see [25,26]).

Rogowski [27] describes another industrial voice control system that facilitates voice control of robotized manufacturing cells. He notes the following requirements for industrial voice control systems: (i) *correct recognition of all words of the voice command*, (ii) *accurate recognition of numbers in commands* (as numbers are usually part of the language used in engineering), and (iii) *instant reaction to the command*. Rogowski further argues that some requirements significant in other domains are not so restrictive in industrial voice control applications, e.g.: (i) *users of such applications are usually qualified machine operators* and can be expected to *adapt themselves to some restrictions regarding voice command structure*, (ii) *they can be expected to keep some discipline in speaking* , and (iii) *the number of different actions to be performed by the machine is usually low*. These requirements and conditions apply also for our use case.

2.3 Evaluation of Speech-Based Systems

The evaluation of a VUI is a complex task that might differ from the evaluation of other interfaces. An article[2] published online by the Nielsen Norman Group e.g., points out that some classic usability criteria are severely constrained in VUIs, such as the *visibility of system status* or *supporting recognition over recall*.

Cordasco et al. [5] report the result of a lab trial evaluating vAssist, a voice-controlled care and communication service. It has been tested by 43 elderly in a WoZ setting, using several scenarios (e.g., recording and reporting users' medical data). The focus of the evaluation was on usability, learnability and intuitivity. The methodology involved interviews and questionnaires before, during and after user-system interaction, capturing qualitative and quantitative data. The Sinlge Ease Question (SEQ) [28] measured *how easy/difficult the interaction was* immediately after the respective scenario. After all scenarios, the AttrakDiff questionnaire [10] was used to assess *usability, effectiveness, efficiency, enjoyment and appeal of using*. The System Usability Scale (SUS) [3] measured *learnability* and

---

[2] https://www.nngroup.com/articles/voice-interaction-ux/.

the INTUI questionnaire [32] was used to evaluate *intuitivity*. Our procedure was similar (see Sect. 4), although we used different evaluation instruments.

A different approach to VUI evaluation is described by Farinazzo et al. [8]. They suggest an adoption of the methodology based on considerations around what is actually being evaluated (e.g., appropriate feedback) or the part of the system that is being evaluated (e.g., dialog management). These guidelines helped us to design our evaluation methodology in different phases. Farinazzo et al. also suggest usability heuristics for VUIs around several categories: *suitable feedback, user diversity and perception, minimization of memorization efforts, appropriate output sentences, output voice quality, proper recognition, natural user speech, appropriate dialog start and adequate instruction, natural dialog structure, sufficiency of interface guidance, help, error prevention* and *handling errors*. The heuristics are used for an evaluation by VUI experts. Our procedure focused on user tests but most objectives can be assigned to the same categories.

Möller [20] further discusses assessment and evaluation of speech-based interactive systems. He distinguishes between a system's performance ("assessment") and its fitness for a specific purpose by the prospective user ("evaluation"). This classification is similar to the distinction of "performance evaluation" and "adequacy evaluation" used in [11]. Möller describes both as measurement processes and discusses along his taxonomy of quality aspects for speech-based interactive systems [19]. This taxonomy describes *quality factors* (e.g., usability, communication efficiency) and *quality aspects* (the factors' composing elements, e.g., speed for the factor communication efficiency). Our VUI design process concentrated on *evaluation*, gathering user feedback on grammar and vocabulary before implementation. Further, we analyzed a small set of indicators that could be assigned to *assessment* (e.g., time needed for a task). Unlike Möller's methodology ours mainly relied on qualitative data. The reasons for this are that (i) we actually aimed at gaining insights in the users' subjective impressions, and (ii) we had restricted access to professional welders in their work environment.

3   Activities of an Industrial Welder

Generally, welding is a process to permanently join two or more metallic parts. Our work only considers the process of arc welding, where a welding power supply creates an electric arc which melts the metals at the welding point. In some applications, welders have to follow a Welding Procedure Specification (WPS), i.e., a formal document that specifies parameters and settings for welding tasks. If no WPS is provided, welders either rely on their experience or have to do a number of test runs in a trial-and-error manner to identify optimal parameter settings. Thus, some welding power supplies provide standard characteristics with predefined parameter settings. The welder then only has to apply a minimal configuration (e.g., selection of material type and thickness). Often, welders work while standing, sometimes even while kneeling or crouching. A steady hand is required to produce high-quality weld joints. Thus, welders grasp the welding torch with both hands if possible and use all available utilities for additional

stability. Further, even during the active welding process, welders need to adjust parameters like current or wire-feed speed. This may be done with a remote control integrated in the handle of the welding torch but requires a high level of experience in order to stay on the joint line and maintain a specific angle to the work surface. Often, altering parameters during the welding process is not even possible for experienced welders and the welding process needs to be interrupted. This gave rise to the need for a hands-free (and eyes-free) communication with the welding power source. The welder's work environment can generally be described as hostile (according to the definition of [31]), involving high levels of noise, extreme temperatures, electromagnetic interference, and dust and dirt.

4 VUI Design Steps

During the Contextual Design [2,12] process we followed [1], it became clear that speech would be a viable means to allow welders to manipulate parameters while still being able to use both hands for welding. Our iterative process involving two WoZ tests and analysis phases and several voice recognition improvement steps is sketched in Fig. 1 (also see Sects. 4.1 to 4.4). Our qualitative approach to user evaluation is conceptualized as a longitudinal lab experiment (with four points of data collection) that relies on observational data (audio, video and notes taken by two observers) and questionnaires answered by the participants but also quantitative data for comprehensive voice recognition tests.

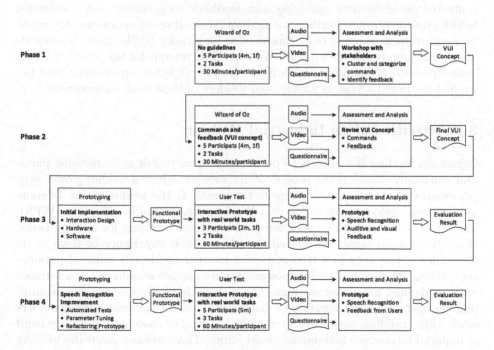

Fig. 1. Overview of the VUI design process.

4.1 Phase 1

Wizard of Oz. As we could not rely on any established VUI concepts in our specific domain, it was necessary to build the entire dialog systems from scratch. To avoid constraining the welders by assumptions, we envisioned letting users decide how they wanted to "talk" to the machines. Because of the highly performance-oriented and time-critical nature any automated speech recognition would have had to provide for in the given context, we assumed that it was not possible to use a functional prototype at this early stage (e.g., due to the many ambiguities in natural language [23]). We thus used the WoZ paradigm [13] that was successfully employed by Cordasco et al. for their early VUI prototype study [5] and e.g., also recommended by Schnelle and Lyardet [30] or Klemmer et al. [14]. However, unlike earlier approaches, we applied WoZ in a novel way in this phase: not to test a first prototype but to elicit a first version of grammar and vocabulary in the given context. We were able to recruit five[3] professional welders as participants (four male, one female, aged 24 to 45) and divided them into groups of two using a rotation approach so that each of them first acted as welder, then as wizard (with the exception of the first wizard, who acted as the last welder). The welders had to perform predefined welding tasks and were instructed to articulate their needs (e.g., certain values for parameters) solely verbally (in form of instructions for the wizard), the wizards were briefly instructed to operate the welding machine's control panel and set the requested parameters or modes. In total, we analyzed five welder-wizard groups. By not specifying vocabulary or other guidelines in beforehand, we aimed at identifying the most important and frequent keywords, parameters and commands as well as groups of coherent concepts from the analysis of the dialogs. Similarly, we did not instruct the wizards to provide any specific kind of feedback and carefully chose two representative welding tasks that require numerous adjustments of parameters. Regarding the selection of the participants we strove to recruit at least one female welder to have a greater variety of different voices although this was not relevant for the WoZ tests. It was important for later tests with functional prototypes and we aimed at involving the same participants during all phases. During the WoZ test, a movable partition wall was used to separate the welder from the wizard to prevent visual cues (e.g., gestures or facial expressions) the participants might give or receive (see Fig. 2). The tests lasted for about 30 min per group and were recorded with two cameras and four microphones, and observed by two observers. After each test, the welders answered a questionnaire consisting of open questions and two standardized instruments (NASA TLX [9] and UEQ[4] [16]). The open questions included perceived positive and negative aspects related to the voice-based interaction setting, whether the welders had to think about the commands to use, whether the voice-based interaction distracted from the welding task or whether the welder knew at any time what settings were currently active. Some of these questions were actually designed for the second

---

[3] It was not possible to recruit more welders due to restricted availability at our project partner (many of them work in international support and are not always on-site).

[4] http://www.ueq-online.org/.

WoZ test (we chose to use the same questionnaire to be able to compare the results). UEQ and NASA TLX were intended to gather participants' subjective judgments only as our small sample size does not allow to draw quantitative conclusions. After the tests, audio and video material was synchronized and transcribed. The transcript was then placed into the synchronized audio and video files as subtitles to facilitate analysis of the videos that included a wide range of different noises.

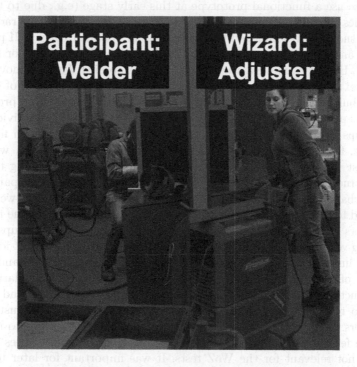

Fig. 2. Setting during WoZ phase 1.

Assessment and Analysis. We analyzed the obtained data to establish a list of the welders' most important and most frequently used concepts including the parameters that were named and changed during the test as well as the values and units thereof and responses the wizards provided as feedback. During this process, we categorized the commands and investigated how auditory feedback was obtained, resulting in a report. The report became basis for a discussion with stakeholders in a VUI design workshop where welders, welding technology specialists and engineers participated to check our assumptions made in the analysis process for plausibility. Example assumptions were that (i) welders would like to finely tune the welding current starting from an initial value which includes the need to set values both absolutely and relatively, or (ii) that only a handful of commands is sufficient to cover the most important needs during

the welding process. These assumptions could be confirmed at the workshop. To get a more complete picture, we also invited product managers and scientific researchers in the area of welding technology. We presented a first categorization of relevant commands and parameters and iteratively refined it in an interactive team process, leading to the following categories of welding scenarios:

- *Before the actual welding*: here, about 20 parameters are relevant, however only five (e.g., Job or Wire Feed Speed) are crucial for the VUI.
- *During the actual welding*: only one parameter (welding current) is needed that should, however, be fine-adjustable and configurable in several ways, e.g.: (i) set current to a certain value, (ii) continuous change (up and down) and (iii) change by a delta (up and down).
- *After the actual welding*: mostly concerning documentation, e.g., to record the quality of the result.
- *Feedback*: welders explicitly wished for confirmations of commands, clarifications in case of ambiguities or summaries of whole configuration processes.

After this step, we could answer the question *which* parameters had to be accessed and *which* ranges of values were possible, hence establishing a first version of the *vocabulary*. The next question was *how* the interactions that were formerly performed through touch screens, buttons and dials, can in future be done through speech, i.e., what the *grammar* should look like. We created an exhaustive list of sample dialogs based on our observations during the WoZ test and read the dialogs out loud to check if the envisioned commands also felt right after they were spoken, as recommended by Pearl [22]. The sample dialogs were again checked with welders to see if they made sense to them. Our observations yielded two very different approaches the welders adopted, depending on whether the welding process was currently active or not. *Before the welding process*, a *dialog-like free speech approach* was used to negotiate the necessary parameters with the wizard. As soon as the *actual welding process* was started, the interaction consisted of *short commands* regarding the necessary adjustments and short auditory responses as acknowledgements. Similarly, the vocabulary also was different for the two phases, with a much higher number of parameters relevant before the process was started. We therefore separated the use cases and created two different grammars. The third scope listed earlier (*after the actual welding*) was not further analyzed. According to the wishes of the stakeholders, the first VUI concepts were created for the German language. The VUI design also included acoustic feedback (repetition of the set value) complemented by visual feedback provided via different-color LEDs placed in the welding shield.

General Insights. Wizards often tried to *establish visual contact to the welders* (e.g., stood up to be able to look over the partition wall). This should be inhibited by test supervisors as it could enable implicit exchange of information through visual cues (e.g., mimics or gestures). The *wizards oftentimes acted "intelligently"* (e.g., one wizard asked whether the welder *really* wanted to use a certain setting, afterwards the welder corrected his command). Such intelligent behavior could be delusive for the welders as any kind of VUI that has not

been designed as intelligent assistant will not be able to provide a comparable behavior. *Feedback is of tremendous importance* which became even more clear as the wizards differed strongly in the way and intensity they provided feedback. Some repeated the parameters and values they had just set, others did not even indicate they had heard the command. In the latter case, welders asked whether the voice commands had (i) been understood and (ii) led to an adjustment of the parameters. While the participants whose wizards had provided prompt and conclusive feedback stated later that they always knew what state the system was in and felt in control of the process, those whose wizards did not provide feedback stated that they where not always aware of the parameters' values.

4.2 Phase 2

Wizard of Oz. The second WoZ phase was mainly intended to (i) confirm the vocabulary and grammar defined in the first WoZ phase and (ii) evaluate the adequateness of feedback. We planned on keeping most factors (participants, welding tasks, setup, recording equipment and questionnaires) constant to gain comparable results. One intentional change was that one fixed wizard was employed because this time his activity required a larger amount of training. He should not act intelligently and neither react to all kinds of natural language commands nor comment on the welder's instructions but strictly adhere to a predefined set of commands and reactions. Welders received an acoustic repetition of their command (i.e., the parameter and its new value) by the wizard after the parameters were set, and simple visual feedback. To make the wizard's task easier, he was provided a checklist of all relevant commands, his designated reactions and what he should do in case welders used commands that were not intended. Further, the wizard was granted a longer period of time to familiarize with his task. The welders received a quick training regarding the available commands. As the set of commands was comparatively small, all could memorize it easily. The WoZ test then involved the welding tasks already used for Phase 1 and identical questionnaires. We intended to involve the same welders that had taken part in Phase 1 but had to replace two due to a longer-term unavailability. We again had five participants (four male, one female, aged 24 to 45).

Assessment and Analysis. The second WoZ phase was intended to confirm or revise the vocabulary and grammar defined after the first phase. As we used identical questionnaires, we could compare the participants' answers after the second phase to see whether the results had changed due to restriction of grammar and vocabulary. Like for WoZ Phase 1, the results are not conclusive quantitatively due to the low number of participants. Thus, we considered the answers to NASA TLX and UEQ as weak indicators only (and do not report them in detail) while our main sources of information were the observers' notes, video and audio recordings and the participants' qualitative answers to the open questions.

General Insights. During the second WoZ test we could confirm that the *commands are easy to understand* and can be *learned and applied after a short time*

of familiarization. Further, the *acoustic feedback* provided by the wizard led to an improvement in the *participants feeling in control* over the process and *knowing the state the parameters were in*. More generally, welders stated that *voice control had no negative impact on the welding tasks* but is, to the contrary, rather supportive, especially because the process did not have to be interrupted. Further, we noted that the *restricted grammar and vocabulary* led to a *more efficient process* (the commands and reaction to them took less time compared to WoZ Phase 1) while the scope of the *vocabulary itself was sufficient*.

NASA TLX Comparison. The comparison of the answers to NASA TLX on an individual level of the three recurring participants seems to indicate that *mental demand* was increased in WoZ Phase 2. *Physical demand* tends to have decreased for two participants, although the welding tasks stayed the same. *Temporal demand* stayed on similar levels. *Performance* was estimated to be better by the participants in Phase 2. *Effort* was felt to have increased for one participant, while reduced for another. The perceived *frustration* has minimally increased for one participant but strongly decreased for another.

UEQ Comparison. The answers of the three recurring participants paint the following picture of the perceived UX in the two WoZ tests. *Attractiveness* (i.e., overall impression of the product) was slightly higher in Phase 2. *Perspicuity* (e.g., how easy it is to get familiar with a product) was notably lowered after Phase 2. The remaining categories *efficiency* (can users solve their tasks without unnecessary effort?), *dependability* (do users feel in control of the interaction?), *stimulation* (is it exciting and motivating to use the product?) and *novelty* (is the product innovative and creative?) were rated better after Phase 2.

4.3   Phase 3

Prototyping. After two WoZ iterations, we obtained a final VUI concept including vocabulary and grammar for welders for two different phases (*before* and *during the actual welding process*). Based on this approved concept, we started Phase 3 with prototyping a high-fidelity, interactive prototype. This allowed us to assess design details concerning interaction behavior, audio interface and speech recognition with our users in a real world setting. The Phase 3 prototype consisted of three main components: (i) *speech recognition*, (ii) *interaction controller*, and (iii) *welding remote controller*. The system is designed in a modular way, thus each of the components can be easily adapted and replaced independently. The *speech recognition component* can use various open source and proprietary engines. We selected the platforms considering stakeholder requirements related to *offline service*, *weight*, *price* and *size*, and requirements obtained through our user tests. Depending on the features and functionality of the speech recognition engines, we also experimented with different language and acoustic models. This includes the use of grammars and statistical language models, such as N-gram models adjusted to our vocabulary. At this stage, no adaption or retraining of the acoustic model was done. We experimented with

various prebuilt models in German (and few in English). The *speech recognition component* recognizes the spoken commands based on the vocabulary in the VUI concept and returns tokens to the *interaction controller*. The interaction controller maintains system state, controls feedback mechanisms (acoustic and visual feedback) and interfaces with the welding equipment through a *remote controller component*. Acoustic feedback is given through a TTS system with small speakers placed inside the welding shield. Multicolor LEDs provide visual feedback through ambient light. The use of a soft light is crucial to not affect the welder's vision.

User Tests. After the initial implementation and tests in our lab environment, a first user test with the functional VUI was conducted. The same measuring instruments as in the preceding WoZ phases were employed: audio and video recordings, observation and the same questionnaires. Further, we could now compare the spoken voice commands with the detected commands. As in the WoZ phases, five participants sequentially worked on the same tasks. Unfortunately, voice recognition in this phase was strongly affected by the noise level of the welding arc so that primarily in the higher current areas (with a sound pressure level of up to 110 dB resulting from a wire feed of around 8 m/min), efficient work was impossible. As the tasks involved in the user test all required the welding current to be in these areas, the experiments were canceled after three runs. Yet, important insights could be gained during this test (see below).

Assessment and Analysis. According to the observers' impression, the vocabulary and grammar could be internalized fast by all three participants (two of them already took part in a preceding WoZ test) and consequently the VUI was usable with only few errors on the participants' side. The analysis of audio and video material along with observer notes, however, confirmed our initial impression that this prototype's bad recognition rate prevented an efficient way of working although it was successfully tested in the lab before. This also led to participants using different pitches and going from screaming to whispering in order to achieve voice input in the higher current areas but to no avail. These problems were also reflected in the results of our questionnaires. To prevent a lasting frustration, it was necessary to explain that this early prototype had not been tested under realistic conditions before but it worked reasonably well in the absence of excessive environment noise, and that our next steps comprise a systematic improvement of the recognition rate. Further insights were gained regarding feedback: acoustic feedback was found to be too quiet and visual feedback was not clear enough to be easily recognized while the welding arc was active. Also, participants perceived a short delay before provision of feedback.

4.4   Phase 4

Prototyping. The prototype underwent several iterations of refactoring and improvements based on the findings of Phase 3. This included acoustic and

visual feedback and the interface to the welding machine for more robustness and faster responses during welding parameter changes. As analyzed in Phase 3, the biggest drawback of our prototype was the bad recognition rate in the loud working environment. Thus, Phase 4 mainly focused on speech recognition improvement. We set up an infrastructure for systematic, repeatable tests and automated analyses. Our experiments considered different *microphone types* (with different directional characteristic, e.g. omnidirectional, cardioid and shotgun), *noise levels* and *pre-processing of the audio signal* (normalization and filtering). Our *audio database* consisted of samples from 7 persons (4m, 3f) with 70 different commands and 3 repetitions per person. The samples were recorded with 7 microphones (in price ranges between 2€ and about 500€) in parallel, with and without welding noise, resulting in more than 17.500 recorded and transcribed audio samples. The raw samples (with a base welding background noise and further pre-processing) showed recognition rates ranging from 34.9% to 69.4% for the various microphones. By automatically adjusting the gain on some microphones, the recognition rate could be further improved. Generally, we observed that the pronunciation and dialect is important as we noted significantly higher recognition rates for our best speakers. Additionally, experiments with audio noise reduction filtering brought another improvement of 3.1% on average across all microphone types. Among others, we applied a Wiener filter [18, Ch. 6] in our noise reduction approach. It should be noted that parameterization is essential. Some filters and their parameter setting respectively, worsened the recognition rate significantly. All (even little) improvements of the recognition rates however came with considerable implementation effort and lots of additional testing. In some cases, potential improvement approaches even led to a step back and a decrease in the recognition rate, and changes had to be reverted.

User Tests. After extensive effort to improve the recognition rate in the systematic tests with recorded welding noise it was now necessary to test again under real world conditions. Therefore, the same tasks and instruments as in the previous user tests were used while focusing on (i) the correctness and timeliness of the speech detection and (ii) the participants' subjective feedback on the other. Only after a sufficient recognition rate could be achieved, is it possible to assess if the VUI concept was designed and implemented successfully.

Assessment and Analysis. Firstly, the focus of this assessment was to show whether there was a significant improvement in the recognition rate. This could be confirmed because even at the noise levels where recognition had badly failed earlier, many voice commands were now correctly recognized. Still, we could not get close to a perfect or human-like recognition when environment noise increased. Especially short commands were hard to detect and were therefore replaced by longer synonyms. Secondly, we received predominantly positive feedback by our five participants. Because only one participant had taken part in Phase 3 where the recognition had not worked sufficiently, a high *contrast effect*

could be ruled out. Nevertheless, his results are reported separately here. The participant liked the acoustic and visual feedback, although the TTS output was still too quiet for him. Thus, he was not always aware of the currently active parameters. He suggested extending the range of possible synonyms for commands and to personalize certain effects of commands. He also stated that training would help to become better at working with the VUI ("practice makes perfect"). The other participants mainly liked the short reaction times and all of them stated that the voice commands did not distract them from working. All participants also explained that there was not much thinking involved to memorize and use the commands, at least after an initial familiarization.

5 Discussion

In this section we reflect on our VUI design process, summarize our findings and discuss their implications for a broader spectrum of contexts. The paper's main contribution lies in the detailed description of our applied methodology during the process of designing VUIs, consisting of two WoZ phases and two stages of prototyping. It is important to note that we used WoZ in a rather uncommon way: not for experiments with early prototypes but for establishing first concepts for VUIs in a context-constrained domain. WoZ enabled us to elicit appropriate grammar and vocabulary for our use case which would hardly have been possible without observing potential end users' natural behavior and dialogs in their working environment. Further, it helped us in the second phase to confirm our first VUI design under realistic conditions. We strongly encourage other researchers (independent of the domain, VUIs should be designed for) to apply WoZ with real users and under realistic conditions (i.e., giving them real-world tasks and their familiar equipment). Further, it was extremely helpful not to constrain the welders' natural dialog in the first phase. Regarding the WoZ process, we observed that *visual contact* between two persons talking to each other is *very important* to them. Most participants tried to avoid the partition wall, e.g., by getting on their tiptoes. The natural visual cues that aid our face-to-face communication are usually lost in VUIs. Thus, many currently available VUIs (e.g., those integrated with Amazon Alexa[5]) use different colors or LED blinking patterns (e.g., the Amazon Echo Dot) or even more enhanced graphical user interfaces (e.g., the Amazon Echo Show). To account for this basic human need, our prototypes also use *auxiliary visual feedback*. Further, we recommend other VUI designers using WoZ to consequently prevent any visual cues to be exchanged even if this comes at high effort. Insufficient spatial separation of user and wizard might lead to unreliable results regarding the identified dialog behavior. We also highly recommend applying a two-phase WoZ process *and* involving all stakeholders before finalizing a VUI in an industrial or other niche application context. The second phase helped us to test whether the identified grammar and vocabulary also worked without further verbal information exchange. The stakeholder workshop revealed additional requirements (e.g., the need to introduce

---

[5] https://developer.amazon.com/de/alexa.

command synonyms welders don't use in their colloquial dialogs but are present in the control panels of the welding machines, for reasons of consistency).

In summary, our *experiences with WoZ* during early phases of VUI design are predominantly *positive* due to its flexibility (not being constrained by technical limitations). This was particularly important in the first WoZ phase because it would hardly have been possible to implement a functional prototype that allows for an unlimited, natural dialog around the welding domain. Prior to the WoZ tests we did experiments with popular cloud services but noted high error rates for domain-specific vocabulary (while recognition was excellent for more general dialogs). A *possible drawback of using WoZ* while establishing VUI concepts for manual welding and comparable applications lies in the *time-critical nature of the tasks*. Responding fast enough and still sticking to the predefined set of commands and responses is challenging for the wizard who has to (i) interpret the voice command solely according to a given protocol, (ii) set the parameter and (iii) give correct and timely feedback. *Thorough training of the wizard* is necessary.

Generally, the findings of our tests have shown that the niche application of *manual industrial welding can strongly benefit from the use of voice interaction*. Especially, welders pointed out (i) *the time-saving nature of voice interaction*, (ii) that they *do not have to interrupt the welding process* in case parameters need to be changed and (iii) that the *installation of this kind of new technology neither requires a major change regarding their equipment nor requires additional equipment*. The tests have also shown that although the *vocabulary needs to be sufficiently small* (to be easily memorized), *a short training period is acceptable* for the target group. In case the range of functions utilized by end users differs strongly for different usage contexts (e.g., before or during the welding process), we can recommend designing different VUIs (and related grammars etc.). This reduced the complexity of the individual VUIs and the error rate on the users' side. Yet, all related VUIs should be designed on the basis of consistent principles (e.g., related to feedback and reaction to errors). We also noted that for the welders it is of tremendous importance that the *vocabulary matches their natural usage of language in the domain* (e.g., in case there were two or more designations for the same command, they rigorously preferred the one that was closer to their colloquial term). As the related preferences might differ among persons but potentially also among languages, we chose to *introduce synonyms for parameters for which there exist different names*. This was appreciated by the welders.

Our *utilization of the two standardized instruments UEQ and Nasa TLX* suffered from the well-known *problem of longitudinal study designs* that it might be *difficult to get the same participants* for all evaluations. While this would have at least allowed us to compare the two questionnaires' results on an individual level, only three recurring participants took part in Phases 1 and 2 and only one was present during all phases. Still, in these early phases it allowed us some important insights. For example, the comparison of the two NASA TLX results shows that the perceived *mental demand* had increased for the three participants. This might be connected to the well-known challenge in VUIs that users must

memorize the set of allowed commands, and acknowledges the aforementioned infringement of Nielsen's heuristics of *visibility of system status* or *supporting recognition over recall*. Equally, the UEQ category *perspicuity* that was also rated lower after WoZ Phase 2 has a strong connection to *learnability*. All other categories of the UEQ were rated better after the second run.

Regarding implementation, we recommend early testing of functional prototypes under realistic conditions, even if first prototypes might terribly fail. Early tests allowed us to identify (i) those kinds of environmental noise where recognition rates go down drastically and (ii) the conditions where recognition is only marginally affected. Our automated test environment then allowed us to perform a great number of systematic tests. These tests enabled us to identify the best-performing settings for different conditions. If a VUI should be speaker-independent, we recommend thorough tests with different speakers who should be highly diverse regarding their timbre, volume, pronunciation and dialect. Our first tests revealed severe differences in recognition rates among different speakers of up to 25% although all of them tried to speak clearly and loudly.

6 Conclusion

VUI designers can usually resort to guidelines, gold standards or best practices (e.g., the Amazon VUI design guidelines[6]), or experiences with similar systems. Yet, we identified a lack thereof, when a VUI has to be established in a domain off well-trodden paths. Thus, we presented a four-phase approach of creating a VUI concept and functional prototype in a context-constrained application domain from scratch. By first observing the natural conversation between welders in a WoZ test during manual welding tasks, we could establish the basic vocabulary and grammar that was later discussed with domain experts and finally validated with the help of a second WoZ test. During the authoring of the sample dialogs that followed the initial observations, specific focus was placed on the requirements identified by Farinazzo et al. [8] such as *consistency* (we ensured that the same commands have the same effects in different situations), *feedback* (acoustic and visual), or the *minimization of cognitive effort* (we used a small set of commands and allowed synonyms where more than one identifier was observed in WoZ Phase 1). The analysis of data we gathered during the different phases indicates that the VUI concept we established was well usable by our participants. Phase 3 has shown the specific challenges related to voice recognition in noisy environments. However, we could reach significant and promising improvements during our extensive test and voice recognition enhancement activities in Phase 4. The prototypes have shown sufficient potential for application in real world settings in the domain of industrial welding and are currently taken one step further towards a commercial product by our industrial project partner.

Acknowledgements. The work described in this paper has been conducted within the scope of the project *Welding Interaction in Future Industry* funded through the

---

[6] https://developer.amazon.com/designing-for-voice/.

BRIDGE 1 program, managed by the Austrian Research Promotion Agency (FFG). Project partners are the University of Applied Sciences Upper Austria, LIFEtool gemeinnützige GmbH and Fronius International GmbH.

References

1. Augstein, M., Neumayr, T., Pimminger, S., Ebner, C., Altmann, J., Kurschl, W.: Contextual design in industrial settings: experiences and recommendations. In: Proceedings of the 20th International Conference on Enterprise Information Systems, Funchal, Madeira, Portugal (2018)
2. Beyer, H., Holtzblatt, K.: Contextual design. Interactions, pp. 32–42 (1999)
3. Brooke, J.: SUS - a quick and dirty usability scale. Usability Eval. Ind. **189**(194), 4–7 (1996)
4. Cohen, M., Giangola, J., Balogh, J.: Voice User Interface Design. Addison-Wesley, Boston (2004)
5. Cordasco, G., et al.: Assessing voice user interfaces: the vassist system prototype. In: Proceedings of the 5th IEEE Conference on Cognitive Infocommunications, Vietri sul Mare, Italy (2014)
6. Dybkjaer, L., Bernsen, N.O.: Usability evaluation in spoken language dialogue systems. In: Proceedings of the ACL 2001 Workshop on Evaluation Methodologies for Language and Dialogue Systems (2001)
7. Farinazzo, V., Salvador, M., De Oliveira Neto, J.S., Kawamoto, A.S.: Requirement engineering contributions to voice user interface. In: Proceedings of the First International Conference on Advances in Human-Computer Interaction. Sainte-Luce, France (2008)
8. Farinazzo, V., Salvador, M., Kawamoto, A.L., De Oliveira Neto, J.S.: An empirical approach for the evaluation of voice user interfaces. In: Matrai, R. (ed.) User Interfaces. InTech (2010)
9. Hart, S.G., Staveland, L.E.: Development of NASA-TLX (task load index): results of empirical and theoretical research. Adv. Psychol. **52**, 139–183 (1988)
10. Hassenzahl, M.: Hedonic, emotional and experiential perspectives on product quality. In: Ghaoui, C. (ed.) Encyclopedia of Human Computer Interaction. Idea Group Reference (2006)
11. Hirschman, L., Thompson, H.S.: Overview of evaluation in speech and natural language processing. In: Survey of the State of the Art in Human Language Technology. Oxford University Press, Oxford (1997)
12. Holtzblatt, K., Jones, S.: Contextual inquiry: a participatory technique for system design. In: Schuler, D., Namioka, A. (eds.) Participatory Design. Principles and Practices, vol. 9. Lawrence Erlbaum Associates, New York (1993)
13. Kelley, J.F.: An iterative design methodology for user-friendly natural language office information applications. ACM Trans. Inf. Syst. **2**(1), 26–41 (1984). https://doi.org/10.1145/357417.357420
14. Klemmer, S., et al.: Suede: a wizard of oz prototyping tool for speech user interfaces. In: Proceedings of the 13th Annual Symposium on User Interface Software and Technology, San Diego, California, USA, pp. 1–10 (2000)
15. Knight, S., Gorrell, G., Rayner, M., Milward, D., Koeling, R., Lewin, I.: Comparing grammar-based and robust approaches to speech understanding: a case study. In: Proceedings of Eurospeech 2001, Aalborg, Denmark (2001)

16. Laugwitz, B., Held, T., Schrepp, M.: Construction and evaluation of a user experience questionnaire. In: Holzinger, A. (ed.) USAB 2008. LNCS, vol. 5298, pp. 63–76. Springer, Heidelberg (2008). https://doi.org/10.1007/978-3-540-89350-9_6

17. Licklider, J.: Man-computer symbiosis. IRE Trans. Hum. Factors Electron. **HFE-1**(1), 4–11 (1960)

18. Loizou, P.C.: Speech Enhancement: Theory and Practice, 2nd edn. CRC Press Inc., Boca Raton (2013)

19. Möller, S.: A new taxonomy for the quality of telephone services based on spoken dialogue systems. In: Proceedings of the 3rd SIGdial Workshop on Discourse and Dialogue, Philadelphia, PA, USA (2002)

20. Möller, S.: Assessment and evaluation of speech-based interactive systems: from manual annotation to automatic usability evaluation. In: Chen, F., Jokinen, K. (eds.) Speech Technology. Theory and Applications. Springer, Boston (2010). https://doi.org/10.1007/978-0-387-73819-2_15

21. Noyes, J., Haas, E.: Military applications: human factors aspects of speech-based systems. In: Chen, F., Jokinen, K. (eds.) Speech Technology. Theory and Applications. Springer, Boston (2010). https://doi.org/10.1007/978-0-387-73819-2_13

22. Pearl, C.: Designing Voice User Interfaces: Principles of Conversational Experiences. O'Reilly Media Inc., Newton (2016)

23. Pieraccini, R., Suendermann, D., Dayanidhi, K., Liscombe, J.: Are we there yet? Research in commercial spoken dialog systems. In: Proceedings of the International Conference on Text, Speech and Dialogue, Pilsen, Czech Republic, pp. 3–13 (2009)

24. Pires, N.: Robot-by-voice: experiments on commanding an industrial robot using the human voice. Ind. Robot: Int. J. Robot. Res. Appl. **32**(6), 505–511 (2005)

25. Rayner, M., Hockey, B.A., Renders, J.M., Chatzichrisafis, N., Farrell, K.: Spoken language processing in the clarissa procedure browser. Nat. Lang. Eng. **1**(1), 1–28 (2005)

26. Rayner, M., Hockey, B.A., Renders, J.M., Chatzichrisafis, N., Farrell, K.: Spoken dialogue application in space: the clarissa procedure browser. In: Chen, F., Jokinen, K. (eds.) Speech Technology. Theory and Applications. Springer, Boston (2010). https://doi.org/10.1007/978-0-387-73819-2_12

27. Rogowski, A.: Industrially oriented voice control system. Robot. Comput.-Integr. Manuf. **28**(3), 303–315 (2012)

28. Sauro, J., Dumas, J.: Comparison of three one-question, post-task usability questionnaires. In: Proceedings of the 27th International Conference on Human Factors in Computing Systems, Boston, MA, USA (2009)

29. Schmandt, C.: Voice Communication with Computers: Conversational Systems. Van Nostrand Reinhold Co., New York (1994)

30. Schnelle, D., Lyardet, F.: Voice user interface design patterns. In: Proceedings of the 11th European Conference on Pattern Languages of Programs. Irrsee, Germany (2006)

31. Turunen, M.: Jaspis - A spoken dialogue architecture and its applications. Ph.D. thesis, University of Tampere, Department of Information Studies, Tampere, Finland (2004)

32. Ullrich, D., Diefenbach, S.: Intui. exploring the facets of intuitive interaction. In: Tagungsband Mensch & Computer 2010: Interaktive Kulturen, Duisburg, Germany (2010)

Social Networks and Social Media Interaction

Social Networks and Social Media
Interaction

Frameworks for Studying Social Media Interaction: A Discussion on Phenomenology and Poststructuralism

Henrik Åhman[1](✉) and Anders Hedman[2]

[1] Uppsala University, Uppsala, Sweden
henrik.ahman@im.uu.se
[2] KTH Royal Institute of Technology, Stockholm, Sweden
ahedman@kth.se

Abstract. During the past decade or so, much HCI research has, according to many researchers, become increasingly phenomenologically oriented. Some have gone so far as to argue that HCI is now in a phenomenological paradigm. But how does such a paradigmatic view work for understanding interaction in the ever growing sphere of social media? Prima facie it may look as it would work only well since social media has become increasingly richer in terms of the sheer range of phenomenologically possible user experiences provided by new and emerging interaction technologies. However, through a critical reading of three major phenomenological works in HCI, we argue that phenomenology as traditionally applied in HCI points indirectly to alternative approaches for engaging in much of contemporary social media research due to its associated semiotic and relationally oriented contents. One possible family of approaches for analyzing such content can be found, as we will argue, in poststructuralist theory. We propose an increased engagement with poststructuralist semiotics grounded in Jacques Derrida's philosophy and exemplify how this could contribute to the study of social media in the context of HCI.

Keywords: HCI theory · Social media · Phenomenology · Poststructuralism · Third paradigm

1 Introduction

Much has been said about the important role that phenomenology has had in HCI over the past 15–20 years, e.g., by Harrison et al. [1], who argue that phenomenology constitutes a new paradigm of HCI. In Harrison et al.'s view, this phenomenological paradigm is a part of a natural evolution from previous paradigms of first human factors and then cognitive science. Further to this, phenomenology as a paradigm introduces new research topics, which suggests new research methods. Harrison et al. view the phenomenological paradigm as centered around understanding and catering for emotions, embodiment, affects, feelings and fun. Although Harrison et al. do not explicitly define phenomenology it is clear what they have in mind in terms of scope: subjective experiences from a broad perspective. The evolutionary narrative told by Harrison et al. resembles that of Rogers [3], where she discusses the evolution of HCI in terms of three

© IFIP International Federation for Information Processing 2019
Published by Springer Nature Switzerland AG 2019
D. Lamas et al. (Eds.): INTERACT 2019, LNCS 11748, pp. 701–718, 2019.
https://doi.org/10.1007/978-3-030-29387-1_41

time periods, the classical, modern and contemporary. Phenomenology, according to Rogers, enters HCI in the contemporary period. The notion of phenomenology is left undefined in Rogers as well but the scope of phenomenology is essentially broad and the same as in Harrison et al. Further to this, both authors are especially concerned with and emphasize embodied user experiences. A similar account has also been suggested by Bødker even though she does not explicitly mention phenomenology [4]. All of these authors describe current HCI research as centered around subjective experiences. Given that the scope of phenomenology is subjective experiences as these authors suggest and it is true that HCI has turned paradigmatically to subjective experiences, it makes sense to think that we are in or ought to be in a phenomenological era in HCI methodologically speaking. However, while phenomenology is a strong influence in contemporary HCI and has helped develop our awareness of topics such as context [5, 6], embodiment [7–10], and user experience [11–13], the question that we want to ask in this paper is how far the paradigmatic view of phenomenology holds up in the rapidly growing field of social media research in HCI. In our view, the phenomenological paradigmatic view points, albeit indirectly through its limitations, to how a semiotic analysis might be fruitful to investigate, and we will argue for this position further in Sects. 5 and 6. We neither aim to refute the phenomenological paradigmatic view nor to prove that HCI researchers in general subscribe to it, we only use it as a starting point for exploring the potentials of using poststructuralism as approach to studying social media in HCI. By poststructuralism, we mean the philosophical tradition that sees language as a primary, constitutive structure underlying all human knowledge, which means that there is no such thing as objective knowledge or unmediated perception: "Experience is never raw, it is always cooked in a figurational code" [14]. Furthermore, poststructuralism argues that words gain their meaning from differential relations to other words, which means that meaning is relational, contingent and unstable. A more in-depth explanation of poststructuralism and its semiotic components is presented in Sect. 6.

2 Phenomenology in HCI Social Media Research

In order to get a better understanding of phenomenology and how it is being used in HCI research on social media, we decided to investigate all papers that were presented at sessions focusing on social media research during the CHI conference 2016. CHI is the most influential conference in HCI and that year CHI offered no less than eight sessions focusing explicitly on social media (Social media and location data; Front stage on social media; Social media engagement; Designing quality in social media; Mental health in technology design and social media; Politics on social media; Affording collective action in social media; Social media and health). In total, 34 papers were presented during these sessions, and we were interested in using these papers as a lens to investigate the use of phenomenology in social media research in HCI. We found that only one of the papers [15] mentioned phenomenology or any of the classical theorists in the phenomenological tradition (e.g., Husserl, Heidegger, Merleau-Ponty, or Schutz). Acknowledging that one does not have to explicitly mention these concepts or names to be performing a phenomenologically influenced

research, we engaged in a careful close-reading of the papers to try and identify more implicit, but still strong, phenomenological themes and approaches. To our surprise, we could only identify a few examples of clear phenomenological influence [15–17]. Some papers discussed topics that are often considered to be part of the phenomenological paradigm in HCI (e.g., experiences [18, 19], emotions [20, 21], and meaning [15, 22]), while others used methodological approaches that Harrison et al. [1] argue are associated with the third paradigm (e.g., ethnography [23, 24]). However, we argue that, in order to identify something as an example of phenomenologically informed research, the research needs to utilize phenomenological theories to a greater extent than merely focusing on a particular theme. Phenomenology is not the only philosophical approach that concerns people's experiences and emotions, nor is it the only approach using ethnography. Categorizing as phenomenology all research focusing on experiences or using ethnography is therefore inadequate.

We can conclude that, while individual researchers might have been influenced by phenomenology, this philosophical tradition does not currently constitute a strong analytical tool in the studies presented in the sessions focusing on social media during CHI2016. In order to see whether this was an isolated occurrence or if we could find the same tendency in papers presented at other venues than the social media sessions at CHI2016, we conducted a new search in which we included papers presented at CHI, DIS, NordiCHI, and TEI. We used the ACM Digital Library search engine and searched for articles mentioning any of the terms phenomenology, phenomenological, Heidegger, Husserl, Merleau-Ponty, and Schutz without any limitations in when the articles where written. The search resulted in 51 articles containing one or more of the search terms. However, none of these articles focused on social media. Thus, the extended search was consonant with our initial findings about the role of phenomenology in HCI social media research.

This discovery made us want to revisit the use of phenomenology in HCI to critically assess whether this theoretical tradition is suitable for research focusing on social media, or if we need other theoretical resources when we engage in such research.

3 Examples of Phenomenology in HCI

Looking at some of the most cited HCI works using phenomenology, many of them primarily draw upon three sources: Husserlian-inspired analyses of individuals' experiences of phenomena, Heideggerian-inspired analyses of being-in-the-world and its relation to social practices, and research on embodied interaction inspired by the work of Merleau-Ponty. In the following sections, we will give three examples of influential works in HCI where phenomenology has been used as theoretical framework. While these three works can obviously not be said to represent all phenomenology works in HCI since phenomenology is a broad field of inquiry with richly variated approaches, we argue that the theoretical resources they utilize demonstrate a tendency among many HCI scholars using phenomenological theory. This tendency is to emphasize phenomenology rooted in subjective experiences rather than social interaction.

3.1 Understanding Computers and Cognition: A New Foundation for Design

In 1986, Winograd and Flores published their influential book in which they used Heideggerian philosophy to critique the dominant cognitive science perspective on human-computer interaction [25]. The authors draw upon Heidegger's idea that our cognitive abilities are grounded in our being-in-the-world, i.e., there is no neutral point from which we can gain access to the world and construct an entirely sober account of an external world. In their view, Heidegger's observations render classical rationalist questions about epistemology nonsensical. For example, how can we know, in a Cartesian sense, that there is an external world? Heidegger's answer would be that we are already thrown into the world and that it is on the basis of this thrownness, our being-in-the-world, that we can come up with rationalistic accounts of the world. Winograd and Flores argue that "our ability to think and to give meaning to language is rooted in our participation in a society and a tradition". [25] This suggests that cognition is always contextual, and the authors thus want to critique the assumed dichotomy between the I (subject) and the surrounding world (object), and the consequential hope that the former will be able to construct neutral representations of the latter. However, while they acknowledge Heidegger's interest in the social character of meaning, they primarily use this to critique naïve accounts of knowledge being something neutral out there that can be captured, i.e., they are primarily interested in the way the social conditions cognition; they are not as interested in the social or relational structures as such.

The work that Heideggerian phenomenology does for Winograd and Flores in *Understanding Computers and Cognition* is to vouchsafe a critique of a rationalistic, cognitive perspective and support a new perspective on rationality based on a radical contextuality of perception and communication. They sought nothing less than a new ground for rationality that was to be as rigorous as the rationalist tradition. At the same time, they sought to understand what it means to be human. By utilizing phenomenology, Winograd and Flores proposes a general holistic perspective on computers, language and thought.

It is interesting to note that, while Winograd and Flores take on strong constructivist stands on mental life and reality, they do not discuss postmodernist or poststructuralist theories. In fact, they made clear that what they were after was not to replace rationalist approaches with more open-ended approaches to human social life such as those inspired by e.g., pragmatism or postmodernism: "We are not interested in a defense of irrationality or a mystic appeal to non-rational intuition. The rationalistic tradition is distinguished by its narrow focus on certain aspects of rationality, which (as we will show throughout the book) often leads to attitudes and activities that are not rational when viewed in a broader perspective. Our commitment is to developing a new ground for rationality—one that is as rigorous as the rationalistic tradition in its aspirations but that does not share the presuppositions behind it." [25] We believe that, had they engaged with a poststructuralist tradition, they would have come to see how they locked themselves into a certain kind of Western bias; a bias that became evident in the software The Coordinator, which they designed and which Winograd discussed in a later article [26]. The Coordinator is depicted as a system that utilizes some of the

conclusions about cognition drawn in *Understanding Computers and Cognition*. It never became a success, however. Within the then emerging field of Computer Supported Cooperative Work (CSCW) it became one of the most criticized CSCW systems ever. Most of the critique had to do with how it imposed rigid, political communicative structures on work. Some of the most famous critique came from Lucy Suchman in her 1994 article "Do Categories Have Politics" [27]. She draws upon Michel Foucault to build her argument that what came out of *Understanding Computers and Cognition* in the shape of The Coordinator was a highly politicized system. She argued that, since the system was based on a fixed set of language acts derived ultimately from rigid taxonomies of speech act theory, it had a built-in bias, which limited its scope.

This illustrates one of the limitations of Winograd and Flores' position in relation to phenomenology. While they argue that cognition is conditioned by social contexts, their account lacks a pluralistic understanding of the ideological and political dimensions of that context. According to Winograd and Flores, we should not begin by exploring the world of the user (user experiences) in the design of interaction. Instead, they want to educate people on how to act in the domain of language, and they want to do so through a rational logic that is as rigorous as the rationalistic tradition that phenomenology is often said to critique: "In their day-to-day being, people are generally not aware of what they are doing. They are simply working, speaking, etc., more or less blind to the pervasiveness of the essential dimensions of commitment. Consequently, there exists a domain for education in communicative competence: the fundamental relationships between language and successful action. People's conscious knowledge of their participation in the network of commitment can be reinforced and developed, improving their capacity to act in the domain of language." [25] What Winograd and Flores have in mind is a normative account of how language should be used in human-computer interaction. Moreover, that account effectively bottoms out in a purportedly rigid rational foundation for design built on a taxonomy of speech acts. While Winograd and Flores do discuss phenomenology, the end result of their work is normative speech act theory designed to structure work flows and enlighten users as to what they are doing and how they can use language better. As such, it is far removed from the phenomenological turn that Harrison et al. discuss, which is centered precisely on subjective experiences in a social world beyond inherently normative concerns regarding people's behavior.

3.2   Where the Action Is: The Foundations of Embodied Interaction

In 2001, Paul Dourish published his seminal book *Where the action is: The foundations of embodied interaction* [7] wherein much of his analysis concerns tangible interaction and social computing. In Dourish's view, tangible interaction and social computing are aspects of embodied interaction. Further to this, Dourish sees phenomenology as a good way of understanding and grounding embodied interaction theoretically. To do so, he explores four phenomenological thinkers (Husserl, Heidegger, Schutz, and Merleau-Ponty) and argues that there is substantial theoretical resources in the works of these thinkers that can be used for an analysis of embodied interaction. By engaging with these four thinkers, Dourish is able to explore a number of philosophical themes relevant to HCI in relation to a broad perspective on phenomenology. He covers topics

such as intersubjectivity and the social construction of meaning, the awareness that grows out of our experience of being-in-the-world, our perception of technology as phenomenon, and embodied interaction. This results in one of the more substantial explorations of phenomenology in HCI.

However, despite the fact that Dourish connects to several different phenomenologists, his analysis has a strong Heideggerian emphasis. This has consequences for his account of phenomenology and his suggestions about its potential impact for HCI, and can be said to limit his account in two ways. First, as has been pointed out by Svanaes, the book has "surprisingly little focus on the human body" [10] which might seem paradoxical, given the subtitle of the book. According to Svanaes [10], one solution to this is to engage in a deeper conversation with Merleau-Ponty's works, which is what he has tried to do in several pieces [10, 28, 29]. Second, and more important from our perspective, Dourish tends to primarily tap into individualist aspects of phenomenology, which has serious consequences for its utilization as analytical tool to approach social media use. This is evident in his discussions about social computing. As mentioned previously, Dourish argues that tangible interaction and social computing constitute embodied interaction. From this claim, one might expect to see not only a physical analysis in relation to tangible interaction, but also a social and communicative analysis in relation to social computing. However, for Dourish the notion of social computing does not refer to a general use of interactive, social systems, but is more narrowly defined as referring to "the application of sociological understanding to the design of interactive systems" [7]. By positioning social computing so closely to the domain of sociology, Dourish limits the social aspects of computing in a way that is problematic. His engagement with sociological methods may be very useful for performing certain kinds of analyses, but it leaves out the semiotic, linguistic dimensions that typically fund social media use. So, while *Where the action is* contributes with substantial material for exploring human experiences relating to being and doing, it has less to say about communication.

3.3 Interaction Design for and with the Lived Body

As previously mentioned, Dag Svanaes has, in several works [10, 28, 29], used Merleau-Ponty as inspiration for analyzing human-computer interaction, and he argues that HCI has not focused sufficiently on bodily aspects of interaction (see, e.g., his critique of Dourish's book discussed above). In his article "Interaction design for and with the lived body" [10], Svanaes delves further into phenomenology, touching upon the philosophy of Husserl and Heidegger in more depth, and how the latter can be used in the context of HCI. While Heidegger's theories are described as valuable for understanding HCI (e.g., through the well-known tool metaphors), they are also described as suffering from certain weaknesses. For example, Svanaes sees Heidegger's concept of being-in-the-world as being too general to be able to account for our experience of concrete human existence. Merleau-Ponty's emphasis on the lived body is then suggested as a key to how our concrete experience of life can be discovered and more fruitfully explored in HCI.

Svanaes describes a number of examples of how Merleau-Ponty's phenomenology can be used to shed light on interaction. He first offers a fictitious example of someone

watching and interacting with an abstract art piece in a gallery. He describes how the user's frame of reference, the phenomenal field, conditions the user's interactions and experiences, creating a directedness towards the art piece [10]. The interaction taking place and the experiences that emerge through this interaction, are described as something that occurs between the user and the art piece. One could, of course, argue that the phenomenal field cannot be sensibly de-coupled from a historical, cultural, and social context that extends the interactive network beyond the human-art relationship. However, emphasis is on how the user perceives the interaction through bodily perception, an individualist perspective on interaction.

He then continues to describe several other examples of how phenomenology can inform our understanding of embodied interaction. Most of these examples describe one individual's interaction with an artifact, e.g., a person reading and turning pages, a person scrolling text on a screen, and a physician interacting with paper medical records. Focus is on the individual's interaction with technology even though there are implicit communicative ingredients in these cases. For example, Svanaes describes how a model of design-through-enactment is used in a workshop to shed light upon the conditions for interaction in a hospital environment. In his account of the workshop, Svanaes describes how the participants interact and communicate within the frames of the defined scenario. However, there is no emphasis on the actual communication as such. What is in focus is the embodied interaction, not the communication that might occur in relation to this.

So, Svanaes' text primarily describes Merleau-Ponty's phenomenology as valuable for informing our understanding of embodied interaction in relation to an artifact, which we argue limits its use in research on communicative actions, such as what we focus on in social media research. Furthermore, even though embodied interaction has a communicative dimension in the way that physicality situates interaction in a spatial context with both human and technological interrelations, the strong focus on the physical body makes this model inadequate to use as a theoretical framework for analyzing interaction in social media.

While Svanaes' account of phenomenology, in our view, illustrates the limitations of this tradition when it comes to its potentials as theoretical framework in HCI social media research, there is, however, a vital point in Svanaes' paper that can contribute strongly to social media research. In a section called "Perception is active", Svanaes contrasts Merleau-Ponty and the cognitive tradition in HCI. He argues that the cognitive tradition represented by Card et al. [30] is primarily interested in the passive perception of sense data. In contrast, Svanaes argues that, to Merleau-Ponty, "there is no perception without action" [10]. Even though Svanaes does not mention it, this also constitutes a critique of the Cartesian tendencies of early Husserlian phenomenology. By introducing an activity perspective into what sometimes risks becoming a philosophy of passive perception, Svanaes here contributes with one component that we consider vital to research on social media use. We will return to this aspect in our section on Derridean philosophy.

4 The Individualist Character of the Phenomenological Approach in HCI

As illustrated in this overview, phenomenology has contributed substantially to the study of people's experiences of and with technology. However, in this section we will discuss some fundamental aspects of the phenomenology used in HCI that suggest that this tradition is of limited use as theoretical framework when studying social media.

Much of the phenomenology that has been used in HCI emphasizes the experience of individual people. Different as the analyses made by Winograd and Flores, Dourish, and Svanaes might be, they primarily focus on the individual human being, which, to some extent, is well motivated by the phenomenological tradition itself. Originating in Husserl's analyses of the individual's experience of an object, phenomenology is characterized by a strong emphasis on the individual. This has also been acknowledge by Dourish: "Husserl and Heidegger had developed phenomenology in different directions, but they had nonetheless both concentrated on the individual experience of the world." [7] While Dourish has a valid point, it is also important to acknowledge that, in fact, Heidegger seriously criticized Husserl for providing a philosophy that was too Cartesian in its focus on the experience of the individual. By formulating what can be called a practice-oriented or culture-oriented approach, emphasizing the cultural situatedness of knowledge and experience, Heidegger tried to present an alternative. His famous image of the carpenter whose engagement with a hammer is informed by contextual structures is an attempt to break free from the isolationist character of Husserlian phenomenology. However, this attempt to broaden the scope of phenomenology has hardly been acknowledged within HCI, where much of the work tapping into the phenomenological tradition refers to Heidegger, but in fact, uses a Husserlian phenomenology rather than a Heideggerian one. For Dourish, one possible answer to this isolationist challenge can be found in the texts of another phenomenological thinker: Alfred Schutz. Dourish continues: "The critical contribution of Alfred Schutz (1899–1959) was to extend phenomenology beyond the individual to encompass the social world." [7] To Schutz, the question of how to relate one's individual experience of the world to that of other people's experience was central. He argued that the connection of one individual's meaningful experience to that of another individual, i.e., intersubjectivity, is a result of social actions. Intersubjectivity is something we do, not something that is. This emphasis on social doing offers interesting opportunities for a domain like HCI, where there is a strong interest in engagement with socio-technological systems. Even though references to Schutz's philosophy are rare in HCI research, his thinking has influenced HCI through, e.g., the work of Garfinkel and the frequent use of ethnomethodology [31, 32].

So, would an increased engagement with Schutz's philosophy offer tools that can be used to develop a more solid theoretical, analytical approach for research on social media use? We suggest that, while Schutz's philosophy offers interesting perspectives on how people act in and create their social world, there are two reasons for looking outside of phenomenology for a theoretical framework to study social media. First, social media is characterized by a fundamentally relational logic. Whether we are studying Twitter, Instagram, Facebook, or some other platform, we encounter

configurations and reconfigurations of connections and relations. The practices of commenting, critiquing, supporting, and forwarding, illustrates that "no post is an island", to paraphrase Donne [33]. The fundamental logic of social media is to situate a communicative activity in a web of interpretations and other communicative activities. If we want to study such a relational technology and the practices within it, a theoretical framework that assumes relationality to be the *sine qua non* of the studied phenomenon should be a good starting point. The second reason is that this relational logic is rooted in semiotics. If we were to reduce social media to its core, we can say that it consists of sign-processes. Text messages, videos, images, and games are signs, and engaging with them means that we engage in semiotic processes. If we are to study these semiotic processes, it seems reasonable to suggest that a theoretical framework grounded in semiotics and/or linguistics should be able to contribute to our understanding of these technologies and practices. We acknowledge that there is an important role to play for a phenomenological research using perception as a core analytical lens in studying social media interaction. However, as will be argued below, a research that builds on semiotics as a core analytical lens will approach this field in a different way, and might reveal aspects of interaction that are not made visible through a phenomenological lens. Therefore, we suggest that an increased engagement with semiotic theories might contribute to a deeper understanding of social media interaction. While semiotics has been part of the HCI domain for a long time [5, 34–38], its utilization has often marginalized hermeneutic aspects that are core to social media engagement such as communication, negotiation of meaning, and sense-making, instead focusing on instrumental aspects of interaction: "its use is often oriented toward engineering goals, such as specifications of needs and requirements, rather than criticism, interpretation, or judgment" [36].

In the following sections, we present a poststructuralist framework for analyzing semiotic/linguistic action from a critical perspective of the general sort we have in mind for interpreting communicative actions in social media use. Our main point with presenting this framework is not to suggest that it constitutes a complete research framework, but merely to illustrate the general direction of research that we have in mind.

5 Poststructuralism in HCI

Poststructuralist/postmodernist approaches (we will refer to them both here as post-structuralist approaches), pioneered in HCI by Sherry Turkle and others, had an upswing in the analysis of virtual reality, online communities and the proto-social media of the 1990s and early 2000s [39–41]. This research was often innovative and largely radical to the point of (in some instances) being somewhat unrealistic [42]. Many authors of this early turn to poststructuralism in HCI and related fields (e.g., analysis of online communities and social life in virtual reality) sought to reveal to us entirely new digital social worlds with new rules of social interaction far beyond normal established conventions. Researchers often emphasized the linguistic foundations of social reality and suggested that digital technology could constitute a space in which humans were free to construct themselves without the limitations of the physical

body: "What I am saying is that the many manifestations of multiplicity in our culture, including the adoption of multiple on-line personae, are contributing to a general reconsideration of traditional, unitary notions of identity. On-line experiences with 'parallel lives' are part of the cultural context that supports new theorizations about multiple selves". [43]

However, after a brief period of interest, this version of poststructuralism lost popularity in HCI for a number of reasons [6, 42]. Technologically, the early post-structuralist research focused on particular text-based online worlds (e.g., MUDs), which lent themselves well to a poststructuralist text analysis. However, given the radical technological development over the past two decades, during which offline and online have become increasingly entangled, the early poststructuralists' conclusions drawn from observations made in demarcated, sub-cultural online worlds is of limited relevance. Another reason why poststructuralism lost relevance was that the initial studies focused on young, white, university students, which was a group to which many users in the MUD context belonged. Twenty years later, digital technology is being used by a much more diverse and heterogeneous demographic, and it is not obvious that the behavior of a homogeneous user group like the one Turkle studied can automatically be translated into the heterogeneous users of today.

Since this first wave of poststructuralism in HCI, other researchers have presented work influenced by poststructuralist theories. This research has contributed substantially to our understanding of topics such as gender [44, 45], identity [46], ambiguity [47, 48], and design criticism [49, 50]. Acknowledging a theoretical continuity to these initiatives, we think that an increased engagement with poststructuralism could help stimulate the development of a research approach that is more suitable for the contemporary context of social media than the first wave of poststructuralist research in HCI.

6   Returning to the Semiotic Foundations of Poststructuralism

How can we understand our interactive contemporary social media world through poststructuralist analysis? Our proposed approach begins with a return to semiotic theory. One of the most influential thinkers proposing a critical, semiotic/linguistic model of analysis is Jacques Derrida. One of the reasons why we suggest that Derrida can be used to complement the phenomenological influence in HCI, is that he has not only formulated a critique of phenomenology's individualistic focus, but also suggested how to move beyond the limitations of this tradition through a deep engagement with semiotic/linguistic philosophy.

In his book *Speech and phenomena and other essays on Husserl's theory of signs* [51], Jacques Derrida provides a number of arguments with which he criticizes Husserl's phenomenology. Derrida argues that Husserl's interpretation of meaning is based on an essentialist assumption of meaning as something present in the sign. According to Derrida, Husserl assumes that one can experience the meaning of a sign unmediated. Against this, Derrida argues that meaning is always mediated, and that therefore, there is no stable meaning of a sign. In this and other works [e.g., 21], Derrida eventually

establishes two concepts that contrast against the phenomenological tradition, and that we suggest can be used for an analysis of social media use: différance and supplement.

Différance is a term that Derrida formulated to describe how meaning emerges through a differential play between semiotic signs. The concept suggests an ambiguity in the construction of semiotic meaning. The word différance entails both a spatial dimension (differ) and a temporal dimension (defer) [51, 52]. The spatial dimension indicates that a sign receives its meaning through its difference from other signs, a thought drawing on the linguistic theories of Ferdinand de Saussure. The temporal dimension adds a chronological aspect to this differential play of signs, suggesting that a sign does not only receive meaning through its difference from other signs existing simultaneously in the linguistic structure, but also through the difference from signs that have existed before in the structure as well as signs that will appear later. This suggests that the meaning of a sign is never a stable, present quality. Instead, meaning is an emergent quality that grows out of a differential process where the sign is constantly awaiting a new meaning from future reconfigurations and repositionings within the linguistic structure. To Derrida, différance constitutes a definite end to the idea of an unmediated meaning, and he argues that meaning is always mediated through these processes of differentiation. Différance thus challenges some of the core assumptions of Husserlian phenomenology and its interpretation of the ability of individual humans to perceive phenomena in an unmediated way. Différance points to an absence that constantly haunts the assumptions of meaning and identity, thereby eroding the stability of an assumed referential character of language.

Another core concept that functions in relation to the deferring dynamic of différance is the supplement. Since, according to Derrida, meaning is temporally deferred, all signs are, in a sense, incomplete. They are in need of completion, supplementation. Derrida criticizes Rousseau's suggestion that a supplement is added on to something essential, and instead argues that the supplement in itself is a clear indication that the original is never essential [53]. That which is complete cannot be added to. Thus, the supplementary character of the sign indicates that each sign is incomplete and in need of some sort of hermeneutic action by which it can reach completion. This constitutes a forward-striving movement in Derrida's philosophy. A sign is not something that carries a particular, set meaning, but something that needs to be supplemented in order to gain meaning. This means that we as humans are engaged in a supplementary play through which we attempt to complete the incomplete and to fill an original lack. This play is, however, futile. Since each sign is a signifier of a signifier rather than a signifier of a signified, the chain of signification is a never-ending process of supplementary hermeneutic acts. Thus, the hermeneutic process of communication is motivated by the deferral nature of semiotic systems. Since meaning is not present in a sign, meaning is, in a sense, left hanging mid-air. Each sign thus functions as an invitation to perform a supplementary action. So, the idea of the supplement suggests that we are engaged in a continuous, ongoing hermeneutic process of semiotic activity. The communicative act is not a process through which a clearly defined piece of information is transferred from a writer to a reader, but a search for completion; a completion that will never succeed. To conclude, when we combine Derrida's notions of différance and supplement, all communicative actions appear, not as expressions of pre-existing meanings, but as complementary parts of differential processes through which meanings emerge. The

reason for interaction is thus not to propagate or disseminate an existing bit of information, but to complete a gap by constructing this very information as a sign that is different from other signs in the communicative chain. This attempt is, however, destined to fail, since all meaning is contingent. The communicative act can never establish semiotic closure, but only propose a temporary stability, which functions as an invitation for further supplementary acts through which this stability is once more challenged. And so the communicative process continues, without a clear beginning or a clear end.

7   Consequences for HCI

Poststructuralism can contribute to developing hitherto underdeveloped areas in HCI. Just like the influences from phenomenology have helped develop a sensibility for user experience, emotions, embodiment, and the situatedness of technology, poststructuralism can contribute to developing other perspectives that can inform our understanding of human-computer interaction. Below, we will discuss three themes that are core to poststructuralist theory and that can have interesting implications for HCI.

7.1   All Interaction Has a Semiotic Dimension

First, according to Derrida, the world in which we live is a world of signs. Whether we interact with things that we usually think of as carrying semiotic meaning (e.g., websites, social media posts, texts, icons, road signs, books etc.) or objects that we usually do not think of as semiotic (e.g., a tree, a technological artifact, or a piece of furniture), their function to us is semiotic; they function as signifiers. They carry meaning in the sense that we have socially and culturally constructed ideas of what roles they play in our lives and our society. But they also have a constructed identity in the sense that we have a notion of what they mean to us (to me as individual, to my family, to my professional role, in the ideological, religious, or political narrative to which I see myself belonging). These layers of meaning are like an onion; we can peel off layer after layer without ever finding a true core; until the object disappears. We can never reach beyond the signifier to an objective signified. This means that at a foundational level, when we engage with our surrounding world, we also engage with semiotic signs. By interacting, we position and reposition ourselves in relation to different semiotic resources. So, as we engage in this play of signs, we negotiate our own place in this web of significance, which shifts focus from the instrumental view of interaction as task-oriented and problem-solving to a view of interaction as an existential practice. An HCI analysis building on such semiotic analyses would focus on how our interaction with interactive systems constructs our lives, rather than how they function as instrumental objects or how they make us feel. In this view, interaction becomes an existential practice.

7.2   A Broadened Understanding of Context

Second, an HCI drawing on Derridean ideas would suggest that we revisit and broaden the notion of context. Human beings as well as technological artifacts are unavoidably entangled in different kinds of relations: social, personal, professional, cultural, ideological, economic, political, etc. There is no such thing as an autonomous user interacting with an artifact in an entirely demarcated way. There are always threads crisscrossing the terrain of interaction. The notion of context is, of course, a key notion in HCI, and has been so for a long time. However, context has often been treated as epiphenomenal to the user's interaction with technology [54]. Context is often understood as something that is added onto an already existing interactive intention. However, context needs to be understood not as interference, but as conditional to all interactions. When we engage in interaction, this interaction is conditioned by relational structures (as indicated previously), e.g., social, physical, temporal, cultural, ideological, economic, and political structures. Furthermore, just like Derrida's différance is a concept with both spatial and temporal aspects, so is context. In HCI, we have been rather good at identifying and analyzing certain aspects of spatial context. Looking at the place in which interaction happens has been central to HCI research since at least Lucy Suchman's work in the 1980s [54]. However, spatial context is more than physical location. Spatial context may also involve, e.g., cultural, ideological, religious, or political spaces. Dourish has made the distinction between space, which is a physical context, and place, which "refers to the way that social understandings convey an appropriate behavioral framing for an environment" [7]. While Dourish's account has merits in that it acknowledges context as something that goes beyond the physical, it still limits the understanding of context by relating it to defined groups with shared interests and experiences. According to Dourish, place is "knowledge that is shared by a particular set of people based on their common experiences over time" [7], which reduces place to a local social constellation. From a Derridean perspective, context needs to be broadened beyond social practices and shared views.

Let us imagine for example that we have heard of a YouTube clip in which a politician presents political opinions that are far from our own and that we perhaps even consider inappropriate. We want to see the clip for ourselves to learn more about the political forces that we do not like to see influencing society. We first go to the YouTube search field to search for the video. As we enter the name of the politician, we activate algorithms that will have an effect not only on our own future search results, but also on the future search results of everyone else in the sense that this politician and related messages will be placed higher on the list of search results. We might also discover how this politician, or political messages of the same kind, start appearing as ads in our social media flow or when we read the news on a newspaper website. Then we view the clip, and just by doing so (we do not even have to interact by liking the video or sharing it), we contribute to shifting the order of the YouTube ranking so that this clip is placed higher on the ranking lists. That way, we actually help making this clip more visible, which means that we contribute to disseminating political messages that we do not agree with. Let us also imagine that we are teachers, and that, some time after having viewed the clip, we want to show our students something on YouTube. As we project YouTube on to the big screen in the classroom, we find that, in the

recommended video field, the politician whose clip we watched and absolutely do not want to be associated with, appears, displaying to all the students a political message that we do not support and a potential political affiliation that is inconsistent with our personal conviction.

Thus, by viewing a simple video clip, we become agents in political and ideological processes that go far beyond our initial intention for interacting with this technology. These ideological processes and structures constitute an extended contextual condition, which a Derridean analysis would help us recognize through its emphasis on semiotic systems that are characterized by both spatial difference and temporal deferment. Furthermore, as we engage in interaction, we are also conditioned by temporal contexts. We carry with us memories of previous experiences and theoretical frames that condition the interaction. However, the temporal context is also forward-looking which relates to the supplementary dynamics of interaction. We carry with us hopes and fears about the future, and we might, for example, view the YouTube clip with the intention of understanding the future with which our children will have to struggle. The hope and fears about this future may influence both the way we experience our interaction (a poststructuralist perspective does not reject an analysis of experience, but tries to broaden it) and the way we actually perform or enact it. So, a broadened understanding of context and its conditioning role in interaction is one consequence of Derridean theory.

7.3 Conflict as a Creative Source of Identity

This brings us to the third theme: conflict as a characteristic of semiotic activity. As we have seen, according to a Derridean analysis, meaning is dependent upon difference, and the way differential meaning emerges is through an ongoing play of signs. Supplementary interaction is not based on a logic related to identity but on a differential logic. What creates meaning and identity is how we relate differentially to others. It is by positioning ourselves in relation to something else that our identity emerges. Thus, identity is not original, but is a product of processes of differentiation. This means that conflict is not necessarily a negative thing to be avoided. Instead, given that meaning occurs through differential relations, conflict is a hermeneutic condition in which meaning is established (albeit contingently) through processes of differentiation. Conflict is a necessary and creative component in negotiating meaning: without conflict no meaning. Translated into the context of social media, this indicates a different reason for the conflictual nature of much online communication than what is sometimes proposed. Instead of interpreting conflicts between humans in online environments as clashes of already formulated opinions, or as consequences of bad manners or the protecting shield of anonymity, we could interpret them as components in a larger process of constructing meaning. It would suggest that communication in social media has less to do with promoting one's own opinion than with relating differentially to the opinions of others. Through this play of positioning differentially in relation to others, meaning emerges.

Taking into consideration semiotics, context, and conflict in interaction as outlined above could help us better understand social media interaction as an arena of contemporary social reality.

8 Conclusions

Our aim in this paper has been to explore whether phenomenology is a suitable theoretical approach to use in social media research in HCI. We have argued that phenomenology as traditionally practiced in HCI lacks certain functional features relevant for analysis of social communication and that a framework based on linguistics and semiotics such as poststructuralism would be more suitable for understanding social media use. However, we want to emphasize that what we seek is not "the right" way of working with questions of social media use in HCI. We do not think there is one right approach, but we do think that there could be alternative approaches that could work better in many semiotically rich environments than what the phenomenology currently practiced in HCI can. As pointed out by our reviewers, in this paper we have neither examined work in social media nor STS research outside of the scope of core HCI research venues. To be sure there is much to be learned from these two areas of research on how to deploy semiotic analysis in relation to media. Here we offer our alternative of semiotic analysis, based on our own knowledge and understanding of HCI and poststructuralist theory. We hope that others will find it useful. Further to this, we hope that for those who do not agree with us, that such disagreement will spur much needed discussion of social media and semiotic analysis in HCI. In this light, our paper here is a call for action as much as it is a proposed solution. For our own part, we plan to further explore the role of phenomenology and poststructuralism in social media research by performing a comparative review of research papers (not limited to core HCI venues) that draw upon phenomenology and poststructuralism respectively. We want to identify the philosophical resources used in these studies, and what consequences they have for the design and outcome of the research. Through such a comparative review, we want to investigate what practical consequences the choice between phenomenological and poststructuralist approaches might have in social media research and what this could analogously mean for HCI research.

References

1. Harrison, S., Tatar, D., Sengers, P.: The three paradigms of HCI. In: Alt. Chi. Proceedings of CHI 2007. ACM Press, New York (2007)
2. Fällman, D.: The new good: exploring the potential of philosophy of technology to contribute to human-computer interaction. In: Proceedings of the SIGCHI Conference on Human Factors in Computing Systems (CHI 2011), pp. 1051–1060. ACM, New York (2011)
3. Rogers, Y.: HCI Theory: Classical, Modern, and Contemporary. Morgan & Claypool, San Rafael (2012)
4. Bødker, S.: When second wave HCI meets third wave challenges. In: Proceedings of the 4th Nordic Conference on Human-Computer Interaction (NordiCHI 2006), pp. 1–8. ACM, New York (2006)
5. O'Neill, S.: Interactive Media: The Semiotics of Embodied Interaction. Springer Science & Business Media, London (2008). https://doi.org/10.1007/978-1-84800-036-0
6. Robinson, L.: The cyberself: the self-ing project goes online, symbolic interaction in the digital age. New Media Soc. **9**, 93–110 (2007)

7. Dourish, P.: Where the Action Is: The Foundations of Embodied Interaction. MIT press, Cambridge (2004)
8. Fällman, D.: In romance with the materials of mobile interaction: a phenomenological approach to the design of mobile information technology. Umeå University, Umeå, Sweden (2003)
9. Moen, J.: Towards people based movement interaction and kinaesthetic interaction experiences. In: Proceedings of the 4th Decennial Conference on Critical Computing: Between Sense and Sensibility, pp. 121–124. ACM, New York (2005)
10. Svanaes, D.: Interaction design for and with the lived body: some implications of Merleau-Ponty's phenomenology. ACM Trans. Comput.-Hum. - Interact. (TOCHI). 20, 8 (2013)
11. Boehner, K., DePaula, R., Dourish, P., Sengers, P.: How emotion is made and measured. Int. J. Hum. Comput. Stud. 65, 275–291 (2007). https://doi.org/10.1016/j.ijhcs.2006.11.016
12. van Gennip, D., van den Hoven, E., Markopoulos, P.: The phenomenology of remembered experience: a repertoire for design. In: Proceedings of the European Conference on Cognitive Ergonomics, pp. 11:1–11:8. ACM, New York (2016)
13. Sampson, T.D.: Transitions in human–computer interaction: from data embodiment to experience capitalism. AI Soc. 34, 1–11 (2018). https://doi.org/10.1007/s00146-018-0822-z
14. Taylor, M.C.: Erring: A Postmodern A/theology. University of Chicago Press, Chicago (1987)
15. Kow, Y.M., Kou, Y., Semaan, B., Cheng, W.: Mediating the undercurrents: using social media to sustain a social movement. In: Proceedings of the SIGCHI Conference on Human Factors in Computing Systems (CHI 2016), pp. 3883–3894. ACM, New York (2016)
16. Rennick-Egglestone, S., Knowles, S., Toms, G., Bee, P., Lovell, K., Bower, P.: Health technologies "in the wild": experiences of engagement with computerised CBT. In: Proceedings of the 2016 CHI Conference on Human Factors in Computing Systems (CHI 2016), pp. 2124–2135. ACM, New York (2016)
17. Thieme, A., et al.: Challenges for designing new technology for health and wellbeing in a complex mental healthcare context. In: Proceedings of the 2016 CHI Conference on Human Factors in Computing Systems (CHI 2016), pp. 2136–2149. ACM, New York (2016)
18. Wisniewski, P., Xu, H., Rosson, M.B., Perkins, D.F., Carroll, J.M.: Dear diary: teens reflect on their weekly online risk experiences. In: Proceedings of the 2016 CHI Conference on Human Factors in Computing Systems, pp. 3919–3930. ACM, New York (2016)
19. Zhu, H., Das, S., Cao, Y., Yu, S., Kittur, A., Kraut, R.: A market in your social network: the effects of extrinsic rewards on friendsourcing and relationships. In: Proceedings of the 2016 CHI Conference on Human Factors in Computing Systems, pp. 598–609. ACM, New York (2016)
20. Ashktorab, Z., Vitak, J.: Designing cyberbullying mitigation and prevention solutions through participatory design with teenagers. In: Proceedings of the 2016 CHI Conference on Human Factors in Computing Systems, pp. 3895–3905. ACM, New York (2016)
21. Chancellor, S., Lin, Z.J., De Choudhury, M.: This post will just get taken down: characterizing removed pro-eating disorder social media content. In: Proceedings of the 2016 CHI Conference on Human Factors in Computing Systems, pp. 1157–1162. ACM, New York (2016)
22. Zhao, X., Lampe, C., Ellison, N.B.: The social media ecology: user perceptions, strategies and challenges. In: Proceedings of the 2016 CHI Conference on Human Factors in Computing Systems, pp. 89–100. ACM, New York (2016)
23. Matias, J.N.: Going dark: social factors in collective action against platform operators in the reddit blackout. In: Proceedings of the 2016 CHI Conference on Human Factors in Computing Systems, pp. 1138–1151. ACM, New York (2016)

24. Tadic, B., Rohde, M., Wulf, V., Randall, D.: ICT use by prominent activists in Republika Srpska. In: Proceedings of the 2016 CHI Conference on Human Factors in Computing Systems, pp. 3364–3377. ACM, New York (2016)
25. Winograd, T., Flores, F.: Understanding Computers and Cognition: A New Foundation for Design. Ablex Publishing, Norwood (1986)
26. Winograd, T.: A language/action perspective on the design of cooperative work. Hum.-Comput. Interact. **3**, 3–30 (1987)
27. Suchman, L.: Do categories have politics? Comput. Support. Coop. Work **2**, 177–190 (1993). https://doi.org/10.1007/bf00749015
28. Svanaes, D.: Understanding interactivity: steps to a phenomenology of human-computer interaction. Ph.D. dissertation. Norges teknisk-naturvitenskapelige universitet, Institutt for datateknikk og informasjonsvitenskap, Trondheim, Norway (2000)
29. Svanaes, D.: Context-aware technology: a phenomenological perspective. Hum.-Comput. Interact. **16**, 379–400 (2001). https://doi.org/10.1207/S15327051HCI16234_17
30. Card, S.K., Moran, T.P., Newell, A.: The Psychology of Human-Computer Interaction. Lawrence Erlbaum Associates, Hillsdale (1983)
31. Dourish, P.: Seeking a foundation for context-aware computing. Hum.-Comput. Interact. **16**, 229–241 (2001)
32. Dourish, P., Button, G.: On "technomethodology": foundational relationships between ethnomethodology and system design. Hum.-Comput. Interact. **13**, 395–432 (1998). https://doi.org/10.1207/s15327051hci1304_2
33. Donne, J.: Devotions Upon Emergent Occasions. University of Michigan Press, Ann Arbor (1959)
34. Andersen, P.B.: What semiotics can and cannot do for HCI. Knowl.-Based Syst. **14**, 419–424 (2001). https://doi.org/10.1016/S0950-7051(01)00134-4
35. Benyon, D.: The new HCI? Navigation of information space. Knowl.-Based Syst. **14**, 425–430 (2001). https://doi.org/10.1016/S0950-7051(01)00135-6
36. Blythe, M., Bardzell, J., Bardzell, S., Blackwell, A.: Critical issues in interaction design. In: Proceedings of the 22nd British HCI Group Annual Conference on People and Computers, pp. 183–184. British Computer Society (2008)
37. De Souza, C.S.: The Semiotic Engineering of Human-Computer Interaction. MIT press, Cambridge (2005)
38. Scolari, C.: The sense of the interface: applying semiotics to HCI research. Semiotica **2009**, 1–27 (2009). https://doi.org/10.1515/semi.2009.067
39. Gergen, K.J.: Technology and the self: from the essential to the sublime. In: Grodin, D., Lindlof, T.R. (eds.) Constructing the Self in a Mediated Age, pp. 127–140. SAGE Publications, Thousand Oaks (1996)
40. Turkle, S.: Constructions and reconstructions of self in virtual reality: playing in the MUDs. Mind Cult. Act. **1**, 158–167 (1994)
41. Turkle, S.: Life on the Screen: Identity in the Age of Internet. Weidenfeld & Nicholson, London (1996)
42. Katz, E., Wynn, J.E.: Hyperbole over cyberspace: self-presentation and social boundaries in internet home pages and discourse. Inf. Soc. **13**, 297–327 (1997). https://doi.org/10.1080/019722497129043
43. Turkle, S.: Computational technologies and images of the self. Soc. Res. **64**, 1093–1111 (1997)
44. Bardzell, S.: Feminist HCI: taking stock and outlining an agenda for design. In: Proceedings of CHI 2010, pp. 1301–1310. ACM, New York (2010)
45. Eklund, L.: Doing gender in cyberspace: the performance of gender by female World of Warcraft players. Convergence **17**, 323–342 (2011)

46. Bardzell, J., Bardzell, S., Zhang, G., Pace, T.: The lonely raccoon at the ball: designing for intimacy, sociability, and selfhood. In: Proceedings of CHI 2014, pp. 3943–3952. ACM, New York (2014)
47. Gaver, W.W., Beaver, J., Benford, S.: Ambiguity as a resource for design. In: Proceedings of the SIGCHI Conference on Human Factors in Computing Systems (2003)
48. Sengers, P., Gaver, B.: Staying open to interpretation: engaging multiple meanings in design and evaluation. In: Proceedings of the 6th Conference on Designing Interactive Systems, pp. 99–108. ACM, New York (2006)
49. Ferri, G., Bardzell, J., Bardzell, S., Louraine, S.: Analyzing critical designs: categories, distinctions, and canons of exemplars. In: Proceedings of the 2014 Conference on Designing Interactive Systems, pp. 355–364. ACM, New York (2014)
50. Bardzell, J., Bardzell, S.: Interaction criticism: a proposal and framework for a new discipline of HCI. In: CHI 2008 Extended Abstracts, pp. 2463–2472. ACM, New York (2008)
51. Derrida, J.: Speech and Phenomena: and Other Essays on Husserl's Theory of Signs. Northwestern University Press, Evanston (1973)
52. Derrida, J.: Margins of Philosophy. The University of Chicago Press, Chicago (1982)
53. Derrida, J.: Of Grammatology. Johns Hopkins University Press, Baltimore (1997)
54. Åhman, H.: Interaction as existential practice : an explorative study of Mark C. Taylor's philosophical project and its potential consequences for human-computer interaction (2016). http://urn.kb.se/resolve?urn=urn:nbn:se:kth:diva-191500
55. Suchman, L.A.: Plans and Situated Actions: The Problem of Human-Machine Communication. Cambridge University Press, New York (1987)

FriendGroupVR: Design Concepts Using Virtual Reality to Organize Social Network Friends

Frederic Raber[1]([✉]), Christopher Schommer[2]([✉]), and Antonio Krüger[1]

[1] DFKI Saarland Informatics Campus, Saarbrücken, Saarland, Germany
{frederic.raber,krueger}@dfki.de
[2] Saarland University, Saarbrücken, Germany
christopherschommer@gmx.de

Abstract. Creating friend lists offers social network users the ability to select a fine-grained audience for their posts, thereby reducing the amount of unwanted disclosures. However, research has shown that the user burden involved in creating and managing friend lists leads to the fact that this functionality is rarely used, despite its advantages. In this paper, we propose two design concepts using virtual reality to allow the user to create and organize her friend lists. Whereas the first "pragmatic" concept is targeted towards *usability and practicability* using a metaphor similar to card sorting, the second "playful" concept has the goal to achieve a high user experience score by offering a VR game to sort and organize the friends. In a lab study, we compared the two concepts with the Facebook interface in terms of usability, user experience and error rate (like missing friends in a group or friends placed in the wrong group). We were able to show that both designs significantly outperform the Facebook interface in both usability and user experience. The playful interface is experienced as more interesting and stimulating than its pragmatic counterpart, at the cost of an increased error rate.

1 Introduction

The perceived audience of a social network post consists only out of 27% of the actual audience [1]. This leads to a high amount of unwanted recipients of the posts information, which can be used for various attacks like stalking, identity theft, user manipulation (also known as "social engineering"), re-identification in other anonymized data sets or face re-identification [8]. The success rate for a stranger to be accepted as a facebook friend and thus be added to the post audience is surprisingly high: In a study from Gross and Acquisti, 75.000 out of 250.000 users accepted the friend invitation from an unknown person [8].

Electronic supplementary material The online version of this chapter (https://doi.org/10.1007/978-3-030-29387-1_42) contains supplementary material, which is available to authorized users.

© IFIP International Federation for Information Processing 2019
Published by Springer Nature Switzerland AG 2019
D. Lamas et al. (Eds.): INTERACT 2019, LNCS 11748, pp. 719–739, 2019.
https://doi.org/10.1007/978-3-030-29387-1_42

Social networks such as Facebook or Google+ allow their users to create custom friend lists and share content exclusively with these list. However, these tools are often not used [20]. Known causes for this behavior are the mental effort to group people [29] and usability problems, e.g. regarding the mechanics, general workflow or simply user-interface-related problems [15,16,30].

Compared to other sorting tasks, the task of social network friend grouping includes several special challenges to be solved: First, privacy preferences have shown to be highly individual in several domains like location sharing [22], mobile app permissions [24] or shopping scenarios [25] as well as the task of friend grouping [23]. Every user has her own different criteria to build groups and to categorize her friends into them, depending on her personal preferences, her personality and privacy attitude [23], and also her posting preferences, regarding post topics and intimacy of the shared information [23]. Second, there is no definite answer on the correct assignment of a friend. Some of the friends might fit into multiple groups; some might not fit in any group and will remain unassigned. This leads to the fact that for some friends, it is directly clear to which groups they should be assigned to, whereas the user needs a longer time to think about a correct assignment for other cases, as our study results will show.

Research tried to tackle this problem by creating new design concepts with an increased usability in order to reduce the mental effort to perform the friend sorting task. Some of the approaches use graph-based interfaces [7,19], where groups are represented by vertices with the corresponding friends attached as their leaves; others rely on a conventional list-based design [18] improved by an auto-grouping algorithm based on community detection [2]. Nevertheless, the usage of virtual reality to enhance the usability of social network friend sorting on the one hand, and making the task more interesting and enjoyable by enhancing the user experience on the other hand, has not been discussed in research so far to the best of our knowledge. To be more precise, we try to solve the following research questions:

1. Can we enhance the usability and user experience of the social network friend sorting using a VR environment and metaphors?
2. Do users prefer a playful or a pragmatic approach for VR sorting?
3. How do the VR designs effect the errors made during friend sorting?

For this purpose, we created two different UI designs, one focused on further increasing the usability in a virtual reality environment by adapting traditional concepts such as card sorting ("pragmatic design"), and one that is geared towards making the sorting task as fun and enjoyable as possible by packaging the task as an interactive VR game ("playful condition"). In a study comparing these to a conventional sorting interface from the Facebook social network website, we found out that we could further increase the usability with the pragmatic design. The playful condition was perceived as highly motivating and achieved a significantly higher user experience score, at the cost of an increased error rate.

2   Related Work

For the scope of our work, there are three research fields of interest that we want to discuss in this section: first, the usage of social network friend lists, strategies used and problems that arise within the current solution; second, user interface designs in other domains that enhance usability; and third, the questionnaires that are of importance for this research field and the later evaluation study.

2.1   Friend Grouping in Social Networks

A comparative user study by Kelley et al. [16] in 2011 investigated different metaphors and user strategies that arise when users start grouping friends into friend lists on the Facebook social network. Their user study included three new interfaces that have been compared to the Facebook UI: a card sorting method using printed pictures of the friends; a grid tagging approach where all friend images are printed in a grid shape on one page, so that the user can use pens of different colors representing the friend groups the friend should be assigned to; and a file explorer where the friends are represented as files that are sorted into folders using the Windows explorer. Lastly, they used the current Facebook interface as a reference interface. In a user study, they found out that there are two user strategies: the "by friend" strategy, where the groups needed for this friend are created first, and then populated by all other friends that fit inside these groups before the user proceeds to the next friend; and the "by group" strategy where all needed groups are created first, and then populated by the friends one after another. As some of their design recommendations, they advised to always keep in mind that Facebook friend grouping is not a primary task, and secondly, that the grouping changes over time. In our work, we took up these design recommendations and created a user interface that motivates the user and that packages the uninteresting sorting task as a challenging VR game, so that the task is done more frequently, especially over time.

Other studies about usage frequencies and mental effort have shown that the usability and understanding the grouping interface is not a problem for social networks like Google+ [14,29]. However, the mental effort required for finding a good assignment is very high, leading to the fact that users prefer to censor their posts rather than to use friend grouping to select the correct audience [14,29]. According to a study by Javed et al. including 200 participants, more than 50% of all Facebook users have not created any personal friend lists at all. Another 15% and 10% have created only one or two friend lists, respectively [12]. Interestingly, automatic friend groups have a small amount of overlap between them, whereas user-created friend groups have little to none: Out of all members of a friend list, 90% are not present in any other friend list for user-created friend lists compared to about 58% for automatically created lists. Usually, users never add a friend to more than two friend lists; some are not added to any friend list. On average, each self-created friend list contains about 32 members. Based on the mentioned study results, we designed our UI designs so that being able

to add friends to multiple lists should be easily possible, but is not a primary design goal of the UI.

2.2 Sorting in Virtual Reality and Other Domains

In general, the sorting task or *categorization task* described here involves several items that have to be assigned to one or multiple groups by the user, based on the individual features of each item. There are several abstraction levels of the items to be sorted that can be used for a sorting task, each with its own advantages and drawbacks [26]. The most concrete form is *object sorting*, where the user is given concrete objects to be sorted. Although this provides the most information for the user, it can contain irrelevant and distracting features as well, that may lead to a different evaluation and assignment of the object than intended. The next abstraction level is *picture sorting*, where the object is represented solely by an image of the object. Although this reduces the amount of sensory input, it is possible to trim out unimportant features from the picture, reducing the amount of irrelevant information for the user. Lastly, card sorting uses only written text on a card describing the object. While this design is most restrictive and allows limiting the information only to the sorting features that are of relevance, it can only be used for items that are known to the user, and that he can imagine from reading the description.

Apart from the level of detail, sorting techniques also differ in the group creation policy used for sorting items into groups using a desktop interface. Card sorting approaches [21] can be differentiated between "closed card sorting", where the categories are already pre-defined, and "open card sorting", where the categories are defined by the user during the sorting task. Whereas the former leads to more comparable results between subjects, the latter gives the user more degrees of freedom, which makes it more suitable for tasks with individual data, like the task of friend grouping. Finally, the UI designs for card sorting also differ in the design metaphor used to display and arrange the cards. There are several commercial applications that use a *stacked card sorting metaphor*, where the cards of the same category are arranged on top of each other. Examples are CardZort[1] or OpenSort[2]. Other designs like WebSort[3] use a more *explorer-like approach*, where the categories are displayed as a vertical list of terms that can be opened like folders in the Windows explorer. Card sorting tools have been proven to be highly efficient, but the preferred design greatly depends on the user group [5]: although researchers perferred the explorer-like approach in WebSort, most of the end-users liked the stack-based approach of OpenSort best. Studies have shown that there are no significant differences in terms of performance when comparing online and paper-based card sorting [4]. Sorting is also possible in VR, as a study on "how similar looking products influence the overall performance in a retail setting" has shown recently [11]: The participants were shown a VR

---

[1] https://cardzort.software.informer.com/.
[2] https://sourceforge.net/projects/opensort/.
[3] https://dirtarchitecture.wordpress.com/websort/.

world, where they had to sort products arriving on a conveyor belt into two different categories. Although the participants were generally succesful in the tasks, the error rate significantly increased when the similarity of the products was increased.

For the task of social network friend sorting, the abstraction level of "card sorting" might not be sufficient, as users might not remember the actual person behind a username, since users often use fake names for their online profiles. Apart from that, we cannot rule out that two or more social network friends might have similar images, leading to an increased error rate. We therefore decided on an improved "card sorting+" design, which includes a profile picture and a textual description using the username as well. The task of social network friend sorting is highly individual, which led us to the decision to use *open card sorting*, using predefined groups for convenience with the possibility to add additional groups as needed. As most of the end users opted for the "stacked card metaphor" for arranging the cards, we based our interface designs on this metaphor as well.

2.3   Measuring User Experience, Usability and Other Aspects Important for Our Work

The de-facto standard for measuring usability is the system usability scale (SUS) [3], which was introduced by John Brooke in 1986 to provide a way of "quick and dirty" quantification of a perceived usability. The SUS generates a score between 0 and 100, where a score above 68 is perceived as "good" usability. Although often used for measuring usability, the questionnaire captures only the pragmatic quality, e.g. the usability of an interface, without considering the hedonic aspects, e.g. the user experience regarding the experienced stimulation and fun when using the UI. The AttrakDiff questionnaire [10] contains questions capturing the pragmatic aspects, as well as the hedonic aspects like identity and stimulation of a user experience, and is geared especially towards comparing different interfaces to each other with regard to usability and user experience. The AttrakDiff generates three different scores that are of interest for our design experiment: The pragmatic quality (PQ) capturing the usability, similar to the SUS and two hedonic scores describing the stimulation perceived when using the interface (HQ-S) and how much subjects could identify with the UI (HQ-I). All scores range from -2.5 to 2.5, where a value above 1.0 or 2.0 is perceived as "good" or "excellent", respectively. According to the goals of our experiment capturing usability as well as user experience in a comparative study, we decided for the AttrakDiff questionnaire in our case.

Capturing the perceived workload including factors like mental or physical demand and frustration is mostly done using the NASA TLX questionnaire [9]. The questionnaire has been developed over a three-year development cycle with more than 40 lab experiments and is now cited by more than 4400 studies, denoting the widespread influence of this questionnaire [6]. The questionnaire measures the *mental demand* (e.g. cognitive load), *physical demand, temporal demand* (e.g. perceived time pressure), the perceived *effort* needed to achieve

the desired goal, as well as the perceived *frustration* and the subjects' own achieved *performance* estimated by the subject. Each single value ranges from 0 to 100 where 0 is the lowest (best) and 100 the highest (worst) workload. We included the questionnaire in our study especially to compare the mental and physical demand between the standard interface and the VR designs, and the frustration experienced with the different interfaces. Lastly, we added the motion sickness assesment questionnaire (MSAQ) to our experiment to ensure that motion sickness does not affect our UI designs in a negative way. Scores on this measure range from 11.1 for no motion sickness to 100 for highest motion sickness effects.

To conclude, research has explored several different metaphors for sorting, whereas the metaphor of card sorting has been proven to be highly effective. Related work has shown that VR creates a higher immersion compared to traditional interfaces, resulting in a feeling of being "in the game" [13,27]. VR applications can, if done well, lead to the most natural and most efficient interaction, far better than it can be achieved with traditional 2D or 3D applications [13,27]. Research has also proven that using VR for e-commerce applications like VR shopping is perceived as significantly more useful (in terms of interaction techniques), immersive and interesting by users that its two-dimensional counterparts [17,28]. These results leads us to the assumption that VR can also improve the usability and perceived fun of a friend grouping task, which we are eager to test in this paper. In our work, we build upon the idea of card sorting and transfer this metaphor into a VR design to enhance usability on the one hand, and the user experience on the other hand, to present the task of social network friend grouping as an interesting and enjoyable task that is still perceived to be easy to carry out with our designs.

3   FriendGroupVR Designs

We implemented *two* different VR design approaches to sort and organize social network friend lists, targeting different objectives: The first "pragmatic" approach is optimized towards *usability* in terms of efficiency and performance, whereas the second "playful" approach is focused on maing the sorting task as enjoyable and interesting as possible. Each world was implemented in Unity using an HTC Vive VR Kit. The setup contained a 4 m × 4 m floor equipped with an HTC Vive Lighthouse setup that allows tracking the user's movements inside the area (see Fig. 1). Each user movement was reflected in the VR world as well. In order to track hand movements, each user was given two Vive controllers, one for each hand. Grabbing gestures were realized by usage of the trigger buttons of the controllers. For our lab study, we recorded the created friend lists and the contained friend lists locally instead of applying the changes to the user's social network account.

A special problem of the friend sorting task is that the time needed for the assignment of a friend to one or multiple groups can be highly variable. For some of the friends, it is directly clear to which social circle(s) or which

friend list(s) they belong, but for others it is less clear, so that the user might need some seconds to think before he can conduct the actual assignment task. Therefore, we put a special emphasis on the possibility to interrupt the sorting task between two friends, so that the user has the possibility to think about the best assignment options in advance.

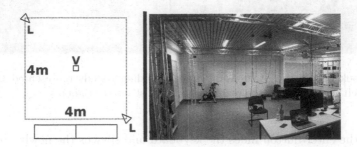

Fig. 1. VR setup in our lab using the HTC Vive. "L" denotes the positions of the lighthouse position trackers, "V" the initial position of the user wearing the HTC Vive

3.1 Pragmatic Design

According to related work, the metaphor of card sorting is one of the most efficient methodologies [5], we therefore decided to transfer the open card sorting metaphor into a VR world, leading us to an office metaphor as shown in Fig. 2. The "cards", i.e. the social network friends, are represented as picture frames ("friend frames") standing inside a bookshelf. Each friend frame consists of the friend's profile picture and forename on the front, and the fore- and surname on the back, forming a combination of a card sorting and picture sorting metaphor ("card sorting+"), as described in the related work section. Friends can be displayed with ascending tie strength (equivalent to the Facebook friend list order) or sorted by fore- or surname. As space is limited, the shelf always contains only nine friend frames at a time. To access the other frames, we placed two buttons at the left and right edge of the shelf, allowing the user to access friends that appear earlier or later in the sorted list, respectively.

According to the *stacked cards metaphor*, friend lists are represented as labeled boxes ("list box") in which the user can drag & drop friend frames using a VR controller. As a starting point, the VR world contains the five most frequently used friend lists according to related work [23], namely "family", "acquaintances", "close friends", "work" and "sport", as a box. Boxes have no physical weight in our VR world, and can therefore be placed in mid-air at any desired location. As the task of arranging friend lists is highly individual, we opted for an "open card sorting" design allowing users to create arbitrary additional friend lists. To create a new list box, we added the "box spawner" into the environment (Fig. 2): To create a list box, the user has to touch the red button with the VR controller, which opens a VR keyboard to enter the list name.

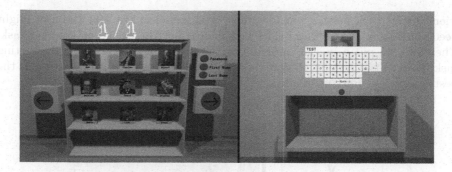

Fig. 2. Bookshelf in the pragmatic design, including friends represented by "friend frames" (left) and spawner to create new friend list boxes (right).

Pressing the enter button hides the keyboard and spawns the newly created list box, as seen in the figure.

To manage the friend lists, a user typically starts with creating and arranging the list boxes around the shelf. After that, the friend frames are traversed one after another and placed inside one or multiple list boxes that should contain the friend. As soon as a friend frame is placed inside a box, the frame is shrunk to half of its size to save space. If a friend is placed inside the wrong box or if the user decides to assign them to a different list box, he can always empty the box on the floor or grab a picture inside the box and put it into another.

3.2 Playful Design

In contrast to the former design, we concentrated on making the sorting task as joyful and interesting as possible. We therefore decided to design the approach as an interactive VR game that challenges the user, including gamification elements like high score tables, upgrades and bonus items that should motivate the user in conducting the task and competing with others. As stated in the beginning of the section, the time needed for finding an optimal assignment is very different from friend to friend. We therefore need a game design which can be interrupted or delayed at certain points in time to allow the user to take her time for the assignment decision. As related work has shown, most of the friends (about 90%) are assigned only to one friend group; we therefore decided on a game with a linear action line, where only one friend is part of the game at a time, with the possibility to manually go back to a friend again if he or she has to be added to multiple friend groups. We came up with the idea of a "can knockdown" game, where the user can assign her friend to friend lists by shooting dispatched "friend balls" to different can stacks representing the available friend lists. Using this design, the user can always wait and think about the correct assignment, before she starts the dispatch of the friend ball.

In a typical workflow, the user first creates the needed friend lists using a tool similar to the box spawner in the pragmatic design. After this task is finished,

the friend lists are represented by can stacks ("list stacks") at a distance of about five meters in front of the user. The user then starts the assignment phase, where a ball representing each social network friend is dispatched in the direction of the user one after another. The user uses a bat to redirect the friend ball to a can stack corresponding to the friend list the user has to be assigned to. As mentioned before, each friend ball is dispatched only once. If the user wants to add a friend to multiple groups, he has to press the "back" button on the control panel (see below) to display the last friend ball again and add her to another group. Depending on how many cans the user is able to hit with the friend ball, the user gains points to be added to his personal high score.

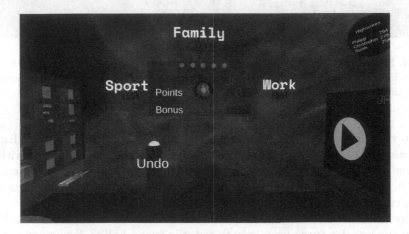

Fig. 3. Can knockdown game in the playful design.

A screenshot of the playful VR world from the user's initial position can be found in Fig. 3: The shelf on the left side of the user (Fig. 4 left) is used to create and arrange the friend lists, similar to the pragmatic design. In the shelf, friend lists are represented by a small board with the list name written on the front. Similar to the other design, the five most frequently used friend lists are already created in advance and placed at the bottom of the shelf. If the user wants to create a new friend list, he touches the button, which opens a keyboard to enter the friend list name, exactly like in the pragmatic design. To use a friend list in the can knockdown game, the user has to place a friend list board in one of containers in the shelf, which will display a can stack in the game at the respective location (e.g. if the board is placed at the container to the left of center, the corresponding can stack will also be shown to the left of center in the game). At the right hand side of the user is a control panel (Fig. 4 top right) which allows the user to switch forward or backward between the social network friends, and a button to start and pause the game at any given time, for example if more time is needed to contemplate the correct friend list assignment. Using the control panel, the user can also go back to an earlier friend and dispatch her friend ball another time to assign him to another friend list.

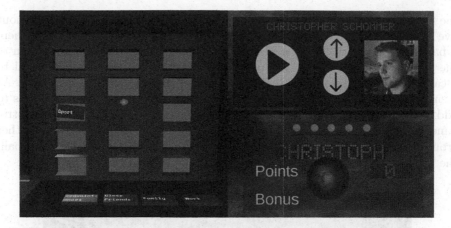

Fig. 4. Friend list management shelf (left), score and dispatch panel opposite the user, dispatching a friend ball (bottom right) and control panel to switch current friend and start/pause the game (top right) in the playful design. (Color figure online)

To the front, the user is facing a panel (Fig. 4 bottom right) which displays the name and profile picture of the next friend to be sorted, together with the current score and the remaining time for the currently collected bonus item (see below). When the game is started by pressing the "start button", the user has five seconds to think about the correct list stack that he wants to aim at. The five dots at the top of the panel represent the time in seconds that is remaining. When the last dot turns from grey to red, the friend ball is dispatched towards the user. If no can stack is hit, the same friend ball is again dispatched for another try. When the user does not want to assign the friend to any group, he can aim for the monster at the upper left of the VR world, which will then eat the friend ball, so that it is not dispatched again. If the user hits the wrong can stack, he can always undo the last assignment by hitting the "undo" buzzer directly in front of him. To further motivate the user, we integrated "bonus balls" into the game, which are dispatched in the direction of the user at randomized times. Collecting each bonus ball activates a special upgrade for a limited time, for example a score multiplier, or an increase of the friend ball size.

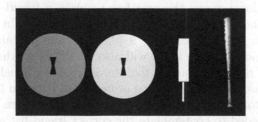

Fig. 5. Different bats available to the user with ascending difficulty from left to right.

The user has a choice of different bats (Fig. 5) with different difficulties: The easiest bat is largest and catches the ball so that the user has the possibility to aim and shoot at the desired location by pressing a button. The second easiest bat has the same size, but directly reflects the ball without catching it first. The remaining two bats have the same behavior with a smaller size, making it more difficult to hit the ball. The more difficult a bat is, the more score is rewarded for each can hit. When all friend balls have been processed, the game stops and the user's high score is displayed on the high score table in the upper right of the VR world, along with the high scores of other users, and the friend lists are stored.

4   User Study

We had the goal to find interaction designs using VR for the creation and maintenance of social network friend lists, that would be both more efficient and also more enjoyable than the current standard. In order to measure the differences from the Facebook UI, we conducted a lab study at our department, where the participants had to use both VR designs as well as a standard interface from the Facebook social network site using a desktop PC as a baseline. With each interface, the participants had to assign their 40 closest friends (according to the Facebook friend ordering) to friend groups. For each condition, we recorded usability and user experience scores using the AttrakDiff [10] questionnaire as well as an error rate (for example friends missing from a group, or friends assigned to the wrong group), as described below in more detail. To reduce training effects and to get users used to the VR environment, we implemented another vr "training" world which shows the user an overview of the 40 friends that have to be assigned in the experiment (Fig. 6). To further reduce training effects, the order of conditions was permuted for each participant so that each sequence of conditions appears equally often during the study, leading to $3! = 6$ different orders.

The procedure was the same for each participant but with a different order of conditions, as stated before. After signing a consent form and the privacy policy, the participant had to fill in a questionnaire about demographic data and previous experience using the Facebook friend grouping tool and virtual reality setups. She was then given a desktop screen to enter her Facebook login data. With the aid of the Selenium web browser automation toolkit[4], a Python script then traversed the participant's friend list and extracted the friend names and profile pictures for later use during the study. After the process was finished, the participant was given instruction in the VR hardware, and had to put on the headset for the first time. We started the training level and gave her the time to get familiar with the VR world and the controllers, and to have a first look at the friends to be sorted and to contemplate the friend lists and the assignments to be made. When the participant stated she was ready, the training world was closed, and the main experiment phase started.

---

[4] https://docs.seleniumhq.org/.

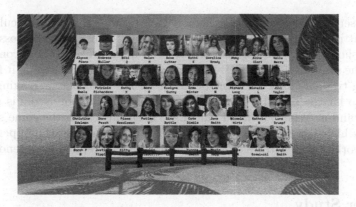

Fig. 6. Training world with 40 friends that the user is shown before the experiment starts.

In the main phase, the three interface conditions were tested one after another in a different order, as stated above. For each condition, the participant was given an introduction to the interface with all of its interaction possibilities and some time to get familiar with it and to test each functionality once. When she stated she was ready, the world was reset, and the participant had to do the friend grouping with her 40 friends until she stated she was finished. Participants were told that they should do the task seriously, as wrong assignments would be recorded. In the following, the participant had to fill in several question-naires about the current condition: the AttrakDiff questionnaire [10] measuring usability (PQ) and user experience (HQ-I, HQ-S), the NASA TLX capturing the mental and physical workload, an MSAQ questionnaire asking about motion sickness in the VR conditions as well as a custom questionnaire asking whether the interface was motivating or fun to use, and whether the participant thought it could be integrated into her daily life, on a five-point Likert scale. After a five-minute break to rest and recover, this procedure was repeated for the two other conditions. For each condition, we recorded the overall time spent on sort-ing. At the end of the study, the participant was asked which was their favorite interface, and had to traverse the friend lists created to check for errors made during the assignment. We recorded the following error measures:

- Person missing from a group (MISS)
- Person added despite not belonging to the group (TOOMUCH)
- Wrong group label (LABEL)
- Group should be split into multiple groups (SPLIT)
- Multiple groups should be merged to one group (MERGE)

5   Results

In total, we had 30 participants in the study, 18 female and 12 male. Participants were recruited at our university using postings and the university's social net-work group. As a compensation, a €25 Amazon voucher was raffled off among all

participants. The age ranged from 19 to 50 (mean $= 26.67$, SD $= 5.474$), representing a good portion of typical social network users[5]. When asked about their experiences with virtual reality, 12 people had no experience (40%) and 5 almost no experience (16.7%). 25 people answered that they had never used Facebook's grouping interface (83.3%), while 5 people had used it (16.7%). On average, the main experiment was completed within 64 min.

The experiment results can be found in Table 1. Depending on whether an F-test showed a normal distribution of the data, we performed pairwise paired T-tests or Wilcoxon signed-rank tests to compare the pragmatic quality (PQ), also known as usability; the measures from the custom questionnaire asking about experienced fun (FUN) and motivation (MOTIV) and suitability for daily use (DAILY), the NASA-TLX workload values, times needed for sorting, the error rates and the hedonic scores HQ-I and HQ-S measuring the user experience between the three conditions.

Table 1. Results for the usability and user experience scores including pragmatic quality (PQ), hedonic quality regarding stimulation (HQ-S) and identification (HQ-I) and the custom questions asking about fun (FUN) and motivation (MOTIV) to do the task and suitability for everyday usage (DAILY), as well as the Nasa TLX workload, time spent on sorting and the error rate.

Measure	M_{FB}	$M_{playful}$	$M_{pragmatic}$
PQ	−0.15	0.61	1.99
HQ-S	−1.81	2.02	1.13
HQ-I	−0.54	0.96	1.21
FUN	1.57	4.77	4.57
MOTIV	1.65	4.23	4.33
DAILY	2.10	2.87	3.77
Workload	30.61	39.42	22.86
Errors	8.50	11.93	7.60
Time(s)	418	587	512

The usability (PQ) was highest for the pragmatic interface ($M = 1.99$) and significantly better than for the playful interface ($M = 0.61, T = 4.6, p < 0.001$) which is itself significantly more usable than the Facebook standard ($M = -0.15, T = 3.1, p = 0.004$). Regarding the user experience, the user could identify significantly better with the pragmatic interface ($M = 1.20$) than with the playful interface ($M = 0.0.96, T = 2.13, p = 0.042$) which was again better than Facebook ($M = -0.53, T = 8.38, p < 0.001$), but felt most stimulated by the playful interface ($M = 2.04$) followed by the pragmatic VR design

---

[5] https://www.statista.com/statistics/274829/age-distribution-of-active-social-media-users-worldwide-by-platform/.

$(M = 1.13, Z = -4.50, p < 0.001)$ and distantly followed by the Facebook UI with a significantly lower score $(M = -1.81, T = 14.471, p < 0.001)$. The FUN was on average also highest using the playful design $(M = 4.77)$ although we could not prove the difference to be significant from the pragmatic interface $(M = 4.57, Z = 0.965, p = 0.334)$. The Facebook interface was again rated significantly worse than the pragmatic interface $(M = 1.57, T = 4.79, p < 0.001)$. The most motivating interface is the pragmatic interface $(M = 4.33)$ according to the mean values, but is again not significantly better than the playful interface $(M = 4.23, Z = 1.62, p = 0.09)$. The Facebook UI is again significantly worse than the playful UI $(M = 1.65, Z = 4.75, p < 0.001)$. The same order holds for the suitability to integrate the UI into everyday social network usage: The pragmatic interface $(M = 3.77)$ significantly outperforms the playful interface $(M = 2.87, Z = 3.24, p = 0.001)$ which is again significantly better than the current standard on Facebook $(M = 2.10, Z = 2.39, p = 0.017)$. The time in seconds needed to perform the grouping task was lowest with the Facebook interface $(M = 418)$ and significantly higher with the pragmatic $(M = 587, T = 2.722, p = 0.011)$ and playful VR designs $(M = 588, T = 2.50, p = 0.018)$. A visual analysis on the time distributions for the times needed to assign a single friend showed that the times are very different for some of the users, supporting our assumption that an interface is needed that allows users to pause the sorting task, as the time needed for an assignment can differ. Figure 7 shows the time distribution for three representative subjects of the study.

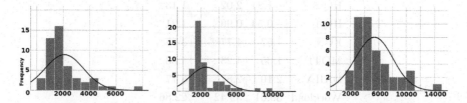

Fig. 7. Distribution of the time needed to assign a friend for three representative subjects.

The motion sickness (MSAQ) scores (ranging from $11.1 =$ best to $100 =$ worst) were very low for both VR interfaces and did not differ significantly $(M_{pragmatic} = 16.02, M_{playful} = 16.37, Z = 0.991, P = 0.322)$, attesting that motion sickness was not a noticeable problem in our UI designs. The pragmatic interface received on average the smallest error rate $(M = 7.60)$. Nevertheless, the error rate using the baseline interface is not significantly higher $(M 8.50, Z = 0.419, p = 0.675)$. The playful interface led to the highest error rates, which are significantly higher than for the standard Facebook interface $(M = 11.933, Z = 2.204, p = 0.027)$. The same holds for the workload, which is highest for the playful interface $(M = 39.42)$ and significantly lower for the Facebook UI $(M = 30.61, T = 2.79, p = 0.0009)$ and lowest for the pragmatic UI

($M = 22.85, T = 2.90, p = 0.007$). A detailed overview on the error rates and the different workload items can be found in Tables 2 and 3. We can clearly see that the main cause for the higher workload in the playful design is that the VR game was perceived as challenging, as the mental demand ($Z = 4.19, p < 0.001$), temporal demand ($T = 4.37, p < 0.001$) as well as the effort ($Z = 4.22, p < 0.001$) is significantly higher compared to the pragmatic interface. The frustration was highest using the Facebook interface, supporting our claim that friend grouping is perceived as a very frustrating and uninteresting task. Using VR, the frustration is significantly smaller for both the pragmatic ($T = 6.79, p < 0.001$) as well as the playful design ($T = 3.65, p = 0.001$). The most favored interface was the pragmatic design (73.3%) followed by the playful design (23.33%). Only one participant claimed to like the standard Facebook interface best. We observed different behaviors regarding the choice of the used bat throughout the game: 17 participants used the "sticky" bat and 9 used the "reflective" most of the time (>80% of the time), three switched between both. One used the baseball bat exclusively. However, we did not find any significant difference between these usage groups for any of our measures.

Table 2. Detailed results for the average number of errors per participants.

Measure	M_{FB}	$M_{playful}$	$M_{pragmatic}$
MISS	2.5	4.6	1.43
TOOMUCH	0.57	4.6	0.57
LABEL	0.03	0.03	0.1
SPLIT	0.23	0.27	0.17
MERGE	0.07	0.03	0.03

Table 3. Detailed results of the NASA TLX.

Measure	M_{FB}	$M_{playful}$	$M_{pragmatic}$
Mental demand	29	41.17	22.67
Physical demand	10.50	44.17	35.67
Temporal demand	39.50	47.83	25.67
Performance	30.33	34.83	20.17
Effort	26.33	42	21.50
Frustration	47.67	26.50	11.33

6   Discussion

6.1   Increased Usability Using VR

We presented two VR friend grouping interfaces, one geared towards maximizing the usability, and one towards maximizing the fun and motivation when sorting the friends. Comparing the usability scores of the interfaces, we can see that both VR interfaces were perceived as significantly more useful than the Facebook interface. The pragmatic design achieved the highest usability score of 1.99 which is very close to the theoretical maximum of 2.50 on a scale from -2.5 to 2.5, indicating that we achieved the goal of increasing the usability compared to the current standard. Interestingly, the interaction time was lowest for the Facebook interface, although it was rated with a significantly lower usability. On the other hand, the error rate was higher for the Facebook interface, leading to the assumption that the Facebook interface is fast to use on one hand, but is complicated and leads to an increased error rate on the other hand, which leads to a smaller perceived usability of this interface.

6.2   Challenging Game Design Leads to Increased Error Rates

The error rate is on average lowest for the pragmatic interface, although the difference to the standard interface is not significant. As stated earlier, we designed the playful design to be challenging for the user, including bonuses, high scores, and different levels of difficulty using different bats. This is also reflected in the perceived workload according to the NASA-TLX, where especially the mental and physical effort is higher compared to the other interfaces. Nevertheless, the frustration is low compared to the Facebook interface, indicating that the stress was perceived to be positive. However, the challenges may also lead to the increased error rate, which is also highest for the playful interface. The game may have been too challenging, or the design as a game may have led the participants to take the task less seriously and pay less attention to a correct sorting; which of these factors led to the increased error rate should be further investigated in a follow-up study.

6.3   Significantly Improved User Experience, Not only for the Playful Condition

The differences for the user experience scores are again larger than for the usability scores when comparing the VR designs with the standard interface. The playful design received a very high stimulus and FUN score, again indicating that the game was perceived as challenging, stimulating and fun to use. But the pragmatic design, which was not optimized towards user experience, also achieved a high user experience score, which was significantly higher than for the Facebook baseline. The pragmatic design was voted to be most motivating, although not significantly more so than the playful interface. One reason why it was rated to be more motivating on average might be the good combination of

an appealing and interesting user interface while still providing a high usability without trying to challenge the user. Which factors led to the higher motivation should therefore be investigated in the follow-up study.

6.4 Conclusion on the Optimal Design and Favored Interface

Taking all the aspects into account, the results indicate that VR designs are perceived as more useful on the one hand, and as more fun and motivating on the other, which gives them a clear advantage over the current mouse & keyboard interface. However, such conventional interfaces have the advantage that every computer is equipped with a mouse and keyboard; the audience that can use the Facebook interface is therefore currently significantly larger than those who own a VR kit at home to do the friend sorting with one of the two VR designs. Nevertheless, VR interfaces will gain importance in the next few years, as the number of VR users is increasing exponentially[6]. As stated in the introduction, one of the major problems of friend sorting is that the task requires a high mental demand, making it a task that is often avoided. A first approach is therefore to shape the task as an interesting and challenging game, like our playful design. However, as the results show, a playful design always has the drawback that it can lead to the task being taken less seriously or being lost in the game without paying attention to the actual task, leading to a decreased quality of the outcome of the task. Therefore, according to our results, it seems that the optimal way, and the way preferred by users, is a VR design which is targeted towards usability and that could be enhanced with some small game elements, but without losing the focus on the actual task too much. These results confirm the study findings about card sorting, which was already shown to be very efficient using a desktop interface [5], and which seems to be efficient for sorting within a VR world as well. Regarding the differences in time needed for assigning a friend to a list, our results indicate that this time indeed is very diverse, making it important to design a user interface or a VR sorting game so that it can be paused at any time, especially between the items to be sorted. Whether these assumptions can be proven to be true remains for a follow-up experiment, where we will take a closer look at the effects that led to the increased error rates in the playful condition.

6.5 Limitations and Future Work

The aim of this paper was to have a first look at how virtual reality interfaces can help in making the task of friend sorting more fun and interesting, leading to possibly higher usage rates of friend lists in social networks. We created two different designs, one trying to improve the usability of the sorting using VR metaphors, and one geared towards making it a more fun and entertaining experience. Based on different criteria like the possibility to interrupt the sorting task

---

[6] https://de.statista.com/statistik/daten/studie/426237/umfrage/prognose-zur-anzahl-der-aktiven-virtual-reality-nutzer-weltweit/.

at any given time or by using gamification elements to enhance the user experience, we came up with two different designs for our user study. Notwithstanding, plenty of other possible design ideas exist and might be suitable for this kind of task. Nevertheless, we were able to show that, with our design ideas, the user experience as well as the perceived usability could be improved. However, we would like to elaborate on other designs in the future, especially game designs that might be more prone to errors than our can knockdown game, although the increased error rate might be an effect of the gamified design, which would hold for other game types as well.

In the experiment, we used the current standard interface as a baseline to minimize side effects and to get a comparison of our designs to the current working standard. Although we were able to prove that both usability and user experience were higher using the VR design, we would like to elaborate more on the parts of the design that lead to this effect. We would especially like to discover which of the developed metaphors led to an increased rating; whether it was the representation of the friends as friend frames inside a shelf, the friend boxes or the interaction by inserting the frames inside the box. Also, the alone usage of virtual reality might already lead to some effect. In several follow-up studies we would like to find out more about which design elements have a positive effect in VR using A/B testing, and give concrete guidelines on which metaphors should be used, and which should be avoided. Finally, we would like to integrate our work into a social network, so that VR users can try the solution in their everyday social network usage. We are especially interested in acceptance and usage rates: whether the app is accepted after the first usage, or whether they fall back to using the Facebook interface after some time, and whether the usage of a VR app increases the frequency of social network friend sorting.

7   Conclusion

Neglecting privacy settings in online social networks can lead to serious harms, but privacy functionalities like friend lists are rarely used in social networks, because the mental effort for creating friend lists prior to their usage is too high, leading users to either censor their posts or to publish more information than they intended to. Related work focused on improving the usability of conventional desktop interfaces for friend sorting. In our paper, we took a first look at how friend sorting interfaces could look in virtual reality. We proposed an interface focused on usability by taking the idea of card sorting into vr, and a second interface having the goal to maximize the user experience by wrapping the sorting task in a challenging game. A comparative study with the Facebook sorting interface as a baseline has shown that both interfaces achieved their goal of improving the usability and user experience, although the error rate significantly increased within the playful design. However, which distinct factors led to the increased error rate, and which factors led to the increased user experience scores, should be further studied in future research.

Acknowledgements. This work was funded by the German Research Foundation (DFG) via the collaborative research center "Methods and Tools for Understanding and Controlling Privacy" (SFB 1223), project A7.

References

1. Bernstein, M.S., Bakshy, E., Burke, M., Karrer, B.: Quantifying the invisible audience in social networks. In: Proceedings of the SIGCHI Conference on Human Factors in Computing Systems, CHI 2013, pp. 21–30. ACM, New York (2013). https://doi.org/10.1145/2470654.2470658
2. Blondel, V.D., Guillaume, J.L., Lambiotte, R., Lefebvre, E.: Fast unfolding of communities in large networks. J. Stat. Mech: Theory Exp. **2008**(10), P10008 (2008)
3. Brooke, J.: SUS: a quick and dirty usability scale. Usability Eval. Ind. **189** (1986)
4. Bussolon, S., Russi, B., Missier, F.D.: Online card sorting: as good as the paper version. In: Proceedings of the 13th Eurpoean Conference on Cognitive Ergonomics: Trust and Control in Complex Socio-technical Systems, ECCE 2006, pp. 113–114. ACM, New York (2006). https://doi.org/10.1145/1274892.1274912
5. Chaparro, B.S., Hinkle, V.D., Riley, S.K.: The usability of computerized card sorting: a comparison of three applications by researchers and end users. J. Usability Stud. **4**(1), 31–48 (2008). http://dl.acm.org/citation.cfm?id=2835577.2835580
6. Colligan, L., Potts, H.W., Finn, C.T., Sinkin, R.A.: Cognitive workload changes for nurses transitioning from a legacy system with paper documentation to a commercial electronic health record. Int. J. Med. Inf. **84**(7), 469–476 (2015). https://doi.org/10.1016/j.ijmedinf.2015.03.003. http://www.sciencedirect.com/science/article/pii/S1386505615000635
7. De Wolf, R., Gao, B., Berendt, B., Pierson, J.: The promise of audience transparency. Exploring users' perceptions and behaviors towards visualizations of networked audiences on facebook. Telematics Inf. **32**(4), 890–908 (2015)
8. Gross, R., Acquisti, A.: Information revelation and privacy in online social networks. In: Proceedings of the 2005 ACM Workshop on Privacy in the Electronic Society, WPES 2005, pp. 71–80. ACM, New York(2005). https://doi.org/10.1145/1102199.1102214
9. Hart, S.G., Staveland, L.E.: Development of NASA-TLX (task load index): results of empirical and theoretical research. In: Hancock, P.A., Meshkati, N. (eds.) Human Mental Workload, Advances in Psychology, vol. 52, pp. 139–183. North-Holland (1988). https://doi.org/10.1016/S0166-4115(08)62386-9. http://www.sciencedirect.com/science/article/pii/S0166411508623869
10. Hassenzahl, M., Burmester, M., Koller, F.: Attrakdiff: Ein fragebogen zur messung wahrgenommener hedonischer und pragmatischer qualitaet. In: Szwillus, G., Ziegler, J. (eds.) Mensch Computer 2003: Interaktion in Bewegung. BGCACM, vol. 57, pp. 187–196. B. G. Teubner, Stuttgart (2003). https://doi.org/10.1007/978-3-322-80058-9_19
11. Hubbell, B., et al.: Understanding social and behavioral drivers and impacts of air quality sensor use. Sci. Total Environ. **621**, 886–894 (2017). https://doi.org/10.1016/j.scitotenv.2017.11.275
12. Javed, Y., Shehab, M.: How do facebookers use friendlists. In: 2012 IEEE/ACM International Conference on Advances in Social Networks Analysis and Mining (ASONAM), pp. 343–347. IEEE (2012)

13. Jerald, J.: The VR Book: Human-Centered Design for Virtual Reality. Association for Computing Machinery and Morgan & Claypool, New York (2016)
14. Kairam, S., Brzozowski, M.J., Huffaker, D., Chi, E.H.: Talking in circles: selective sharing in google+. In: Proceedings of the ACM Conference on Human Factors in Computing Systems (CHI 2012), pp. 1065–1074. New York (2012). https://doi.acm.org/10.1145/2208516.2208552
15. Karr-Wisniewski, P., Wilson, D., Richter-Lipford, H.: A new social order: mechanisms for social network site boundary regulation. In: Americas Conference on Information Systems, AMCIS (2011)
16. Kelley, P.G., Brewer, R., Mayer, Y., Cranor, L.F., Sadeh, N.: An investigation into Facebook friend grouping. In: Campos, P., Graham, N., Jorge, J., Nunes, N., Palanque, P., Winckler, M. (eds.) INTERACT 2011. LNCS, vol. 6948, pp. 216–233. Springer, Heidelberg (2011). https://doi.org/10.1007/978-3-642-23765-2_15
17. Lee, K.C., Chung, N.: Empirical analysis of consumer reaction to the virtual reality shopping mall. Comput. Hum. Behav. **24**(1), 88–104 (2008). https://doi.org/10.1016/j.chb.2007.01.018
18. Liu, Y., Mondal, M., Viswanath, B., Mondal, M., Gummadi, K.P., Mislove, A.: Simplifying friendlist management. In: Proceedings of the Twenty-First International World Wide Web Conference (WWW 2012), Lyon, France, April 2012
19. Mazzia, A., LeFevre, K., Adar, E.: The PViz comprehension tool for social network privacy settings. In: Proceedings of the Eighth Symposium on Usable Privacy and Security, SOUPS 2012, pp. 13:1–13:12. ACM, New York (2012). https://doi.org/10.1145/2335356.2335374
20. Mondal, M., Liu, Y., Viswanath, B., Gummadi, K.P., Mislove, A.: Understanding and specifying social access control lists. In: Symposium on Usable Privacy and Security (SOUPS), vol. 11 (2014)
21. Nawaz, A.: A comparison of card-sorting analysis methods. In: Proceedings of the 10th Asia Pacific Conference on Computer-Human Interaction, APCHI 2012, vol. 2, pp. 583–592. Association for Computing Machinery, USA (2012)
22. Raber, F., Krüger, A.: Deriving privacy settings for location sharing: are context factors always the best choice? In: 2018 IEEE Symposium on Privacy-Aware Computing (PAC), pp. 86–94, September 2018. https://doi.org/10.1109/PAC.2018.00015
23. Raber, F., Kosmalla, F., Krueger, A.: Fine-grained privacy setting prediction using a privacy attitude questionnaire and machine learning. In: Bernhaupt, R., Dalvi, G., Joshi, A., K. Balkrishan, D., O'Neill, J., Winckler, M. (eds.) INTERACT 2017. LNCS, vol. 10516, pp. 445–449. Springer, Cham (2017). https://doi.org/10.1007/978-3-319-68059-0_48
24. Raber, F., Krüger, A.: Towards understanding the influence of personality on mobile app permission settings. In: Bernhaupt, R., Dalvi, G., Joshi, A., K. Balkrishan, D., O'Neill, J., Winckler, M. (eds.) INTERACT 2017. LNCS, vol. 10516, pp. 62–82. Springer, Cham (2017). https://doi.org/10.1007/978-3-319-68059-0_4
25. Raber, F., Ziemann, D., Krüger, A.: The "retailio" privacy wizard: assisting users with privacy settings for intelligent retail stores. In: Weir, C., Mazurek, M. (eds.) 3rd European Workshop on Usable Security. EuroUSEC European Workshop on Usable Security (EuroUSEC-18), 23 April, London, UCL, UK. Internet Society (2018)
26. Rugg, G., McGeorge, P.: The sorting techniques: a tutorial paper on card sorts, picture sorts and item sorts. Expert Syst. **14**(2), 80–93 (1997). https://doi.org/10.1111/1468-0394.00045. https://onlinelibrary.wiley.com/doi/abs/10.1111/1468-0394.00045

27. Slater, M.: Place illusion and plausibility can lead to realistic behaviour in immersive virtual environments. Philos. Trans. R. Soc. London. Ser. B Biol. Sci. **364**, 3549–3557 (2009). https://doi.org/10.1098/rstb.2009.0138

28. Speicher, M., Hell, P., Daiber, F., Simeone, A., Krüger, A.: A virtual reality shopping experience using the apartment metaphor. In: Proceedings of the 2018 International Conference on Advanced Visual Interfaces, AVI 2018, pp. 17:1–17:9. ACM, New York (2018). https://doi.org/10.1145/3206505.3206518. http://doi.acm.org/10.1145/3206505.3206518

29. Watson, J., Besmer, A., Lipford, H.R.: +your circles: sharing behavior on Google+. In: Proceedings of the Eighth Symposium on Usable Privacy and Security, SOUPS 2012, pp. 12:1–12:9. ACM, New York (2012). https://doi.org/10.1145/2335356.2335373. http://doi.acm.org/10.1145/2335356.2335373

30. Wisniewski, P., Lipford, H., Wilson, D.: Fighting for my space: coping mechanisms for SNS boundary regulation. In: Proceedings of the SIGCHI Conference on Human Factors in Computing Systems, pp. 609–618. ACM (2012)

Investigating the Use of an Online Peer-to-Peer Car Sharing Service

Michael K. Svangren[1(✉)], Margot Brereton[2], Mikael B. Skov[1],
and Jesper Kjeldskov[1]

[1] Aalborg University, Selma Lagerlöfsvej 300, Aalborg, Denmark
{mkni,dubois,jesper}@cs.aau.dk
[2] Queensland University of Technology, Brisbane, Australia
m.brereton@qut.edu.au

Abstract. Online peer-to-peer car sharing services are increasingly being used for enabling people to share cars between them. However, our body of knowledge about peer-to-peer car sharing is still limited in terms of understanding actual use and which opportunities and challenges present for those who use them. In this paper, we investigate peer-to-peer car sharing between car-owners and car-borrowers as facilitated by the Australian car sharing service Car Next Door. We conducted a study with 6 car-owners and 10 car-borrowers. Our findings, outlined in four themes, suggest that P2P car sharing fuels different goals for both borrowers and owners. While it is complementing traditional means of transportation car sharing is also in itself a mean of mobility, for example, for recreational purposes. Further, the sharing service plays a central role in supporting the users to make it more convenient to share cars, for example, by letting borrowers find and book cars instantly reducing resources needed to borrow a car. We further discuss our findings and relate it to existing literature providing opportunities and challenges for future research and design on car sharing in HCI.

Keywords: Car sharing · Sharing economy · Mobility

1 Introduction

Car sharing services enable new and promising ways for car-owners to share their cars with drivers who do not own one [21]. At the individual level car sharing offers the car-owners an opportunity to make money on their car and car-borrowers can get a car at a cheaper price than owning one. On a societal level car sharing offer to reduce the number of privately owned cars on the road [21, 34, 43]. Car sharing, which is a part of the sharing economy, has in the recent decade become increasingly popular [1]. Observers argue that this development is largely a result of the mediation or digitalization of sharing marketplaces [4, 20, 24, 39].

In HCI research, the sharing economy has sparked an interest in recent years [12]. A number of mobility-related studies focus on applications such as sharing rides and carpooling, modes of transportation where people can ride together (e.g., [11, 33, 46]). These studies highlight important aspects such as motivational factors towards making

© IFIP International Federation for Information Processing 2019
Published by Springer Nature Switzerland AG 2019
D. Lamas et al. (Eds.): INTERACT 2019, LNCS 11748, pp. 740–759, 2019.
https://doi.org/10.1007/978-3-030-29387-1_43

people participate in the sharing economy but also challenges such as the lack of trust in fellow sharers (e.g., [12, 36, 45]). Within HCI, car sharing has received little attention. Although areas such as social sciences have provided valuable insights into the use of car sharing, such as highlighting differences between owning and sharing cars (e.g., [9, 15, 32]), we still lack HCI insights into how emerging services are actually used.

Inspired by similar studies on other sharing economy platforms such as ride-sharing and accommodation, in this paper, we extend previous work in HCI on the sharing economy with an empirical understanding of a specific type of car sharing where cars are shared between car-owners and car-borrowers (P2P car sharing). As such, we investigate how and why people share cars, in which situations they share it, how they reflect on their own mobility, and what role the sharing services have. The research presented in this paper is based on a qualitative study with 6 car-owners and 10 car-borrowers that use the Australian peer-to-peer car sharing service Car Next Door [8]. Our findings, presented in four themes, suggest that car sharing services provide opportunities for both borrowers and owners of cars. On one hand, specific characteristics of these systems provide important support to create efficiency for example by reducing time spent when booking cars. As a result, car sharing is seen as a viable option to many other means of transportation and not just for shorter trips. On the other hand, our findings also suggest challenges exist such as the feeling of alienation for borrowers and owners when face-to-face communication is reduced. This led to a decrease in trust and as a consequence, coping strategies were used such as leaving personal objects to make borrowers take better care of the cars. Finally, we discuss our findings and implications that our findings have for future HCI research and design on car sharing and how it scales up in sharing economy in general.

2 Related Work

Although the sharing economy in general has gained an increased interest in the HCI community in the last 5 years [12], there is still a lack of research on car sharing. In the following two sections, we firstly unfold sharing economy in HCI, and secondly give an overview of the literature on car sharing.

2.1 The Sharing Economy

The sharing economy (with common synonyms such as collaborative consumption [4] and peer economy [3]) that focus on access to goods rather than ownership is becoming an increasingly larger part of our daily lives with an estimated global revenue of approximately 18.6 billion dollars in 2017 [38]. Sharing economy can potentially address the problem of finite resources or shared commons also described by [22] and [5]. Although sharing is not a new concept, observers tend to agree that recent development is largely a result of the mediation of the traditional sharing marketplaces to reach a wider population [4, 24]. As the sharing economy has evolved it now includes many different markets a definition has become a matter of interpretation and is not only restricted to sharing between people. As pointed out by Huurne et al. [24],

the sharing economy today remains an umbrella term because it does not refer to a specific market but to different ones which include B2B, B2C and, P2P.

2.2   The Sharing Economy in HCI Research

An increasing amount of research in HCI involving sharing economy that focuses on the digitalization of marketplaces used for sharing. Towards this end, HCI studies focus on finding reasons for the participation in sharing like motivational factors such as sustainability concerns [30, 37], belief in the commons [11, 37], and social relationships between participants [11, 33, 46]. On the other hand, some HCI studies raise concerns and report on issues such as privacy and the lack of trust between strangers online (e.g., [10, 11, 30, 46]). Towards this end, some studies also report on challenges such as discrimination and exclusion (e.g., [10, 25, 33]).

A number of studies focus on existing applications within the sharing economy. Dillahunt and Malone [10] studied how sharing economy applications (e.g., Lyft, Airbnb, and TaskRabbit) can benefit unemployed or financially constrained people. They found a large potential in the disadvantaged communities, although digital literacy, privacy and security were seen as major concerns [10]. A number of papers investigate more specific applications in sharing economy. Towards this end, several papers exist on ride-sharing and car-pooling (e.g., [7, 11, 18, 33, 46]). Towards this end, Svangren et al. [46], provides empirical understandings of ride-sharing through GoMore and Facebook. They find that searching for and booking rides can be a complex task that involves leveraging several preferences and combining transportation options. A number of papers also exist on accommodation (e.g., [25, 26, 30, 36]). As an example, Qiu et al. [36] studied the role of how reviews impact trust in Airbnb and find that people's accommodation choices are highly subjective to information such as user reviews.

2.3   Car Sharing

Many years of HCI research have provided insightful knowledge about different aspects of the car, however surprisingly, car sharing in HCI, has received little attention. In this section, we will include literature from other areas to illustrate important findings on car sharing.

Car Sharing Overview. Car sharing refers to the concept of sharing cars between groups of people. In the literature, the term "car sharing" is often mistakenly used to describe a number of other sharing concepts [14]. However, in car sharing, it is the car itself is shared and is therefore different from other sharing schemes like ride-sharing or carpooling where it is a ride that is shared [14]. The first historical examples of car sharing describe informal and unorganized groups, typically in small communities such as between friends and family [35]. According to Shaheen et al. [43], one of the first attempts of a more organized form of car sharing was a small scale initiative started in Switzerland in 1948, by individuals that could not afford to purchase a car. Organized car sharing has evolved since then, especially since the introduction of the internet, which has sparked many different digital cars sharing services that today serves more

than 7 million users worldwide [1]. Car sharing can seem similar to other businesses like car renting, however, although similarities exist, there are differences such as car sharing typically grants access to cars independent of the time of the day (e.g., users does not rely on office hours to get the keys) [43].

Car sharing as a concept is broad and covers several types of businesses [40], for example, while peer-to-peer (P2P) businesses facilitates sharing between car-owners and car-borrowers (e.g., the company Car Next Door [8]) other businesses fall into the category of business-to-consumer (B2C) where car-borrowers are borrowing cars directly from companies (e.g., the companies GoGet [19] or Zipcar [48]). Opportunities and challenges exist for each business. The P2P business potentially allows for a much greater spatial distribution of cars which potentially is anywhere car-owners live [42]. However, because people own the cars, they must also be returned to their original location after they have been borrowed, a model usually referred to as the traditional or round-trip car sharing which does not always fit into the travel patterns of the borrowers [27]. The B2C business relies on companies managing cars, however, to do this, the cars are often confined to fixed parking spaces or hubs spread across the city. The B2C business allows for different car sharing models such as free-floating car sharing where cars can be returned to any available spot owned by the car-sharing company [16]. The free-floating model has been adopted by several car sharing companies, however, although it is considered more flexible for borrowers it presents more organization overhead for the facilitating company, such as keeping track of cars [2, 31].

Car Sharing. Much of the existing research on car sharing focus on the ways it confronts the use of the private car [28]. Investigating the viability and usage of car sharing Duncan [15] finds that sharing cars requires a conscious decision and is often planned in advance. Further, the decision to car share depends on how the fixed cost of ownership is leveraged against the variable cost of sharing and because of this shared cars are used more consciously, for example, instead of a second car for the household [43]. Studies also reveal that car sharing is only part of an ecosystem of transportation options used by sharers. Small-distance trips that are not mundane are often in favor when choosing car sharing over other options [9, 32]. Motivation towards car sharing has also drawn interest. On one hand, instrumental or practical reasons such as saving money weigh heavily on the choice to car share rather than owning a car [15, 34]. However, on the other hand, some studies show that people who car share are also focused on more intrinsic reasons such as environmental consciousness and value initiatives such as carbon offsetting [9]. Most of the studies conducted focus on B2C car sharing with fewer studies specifically focusing on P2P car sharing. However, while the B2C car sharing has potentials such as cost reduction and efficiency, P2P has other qualities. Conducting expert interviews with experts on P2P car sharing, Shaheen et al. [42] found that besides monetary and environmental motivation to engage in car sharing, providing others with mobility was seen as important to P2P sharers and face-to-face communication in P2P car sharing was seen as important to create trust amongst participants. Studies also find that P2P car sharing has the potential to support wider car accessibility over traditional car sharing [21, 41, 42] and further improve interconnectivity between other modes of transportation [41].

Research within the computing literature tends to focus on more technical aspects of car sharing. For example, suggestions to improve access control systems [13] or demand modelling [23] for free floating car sharing. However, although car sharing is represented in the computing literature, there is still a lack of HCI studies on car sharing focusing on real-world applications and use of systems which have already been investigated in a number of other contexts within sharing economy (e.g., ride sharing and accommodation).

3 Empirical Study

Although research in many areas has focused on different aspects of car sharing, there is still a lack of HCI research that studies actual applications and provide insights about actual use. Responding to this gap, we have investigated digital car sharing services through a study of people using the service Car Next Door. In this section, we first describe the context of Car Next Door. Secondly, we describe our study method consisting of a three-step approach (gathering initial experiences, conducting interviews and walk through, and participant observations). Lastly, we describe data integration and analysis.

3.1 Study Context

Extending previous work on the sharing economy, in this paper, we present a study of how people from Brisbane, Australia use the P2P sharing service Car Next Door (CND) [8], and how they experience sharing cars. CND was chosen based on their status as one of the few P2P car sharing services in Australia and at the same time have a significant number of users and rentals.

CND is represented in many of the larger cities in Australia, although still a young company with a five-year-old history. The service started in Sydney in 2013, with 20 cars and 60 borrowers. In 2014, they expanded and included Melbourne and in 2017 Brisbane. By 2018 they count over 60.000 members, 1550 cars, and 2000 trips weekly across Australia. CND offers their service through an application for desktop and on smartphone on the mobile platforms IOS and Android. CND facilitates sharing between car-owners and car-borrowers. Cars are spread across town often near the owner's addresses. CND uses a traditional car sharing model where cars need to be returned to the place where they were picked up.

In addition to rational incentives such as offering low borrowing fees and a guaranteed income for owners, CND also promotes themselves on more intrinsic values. For example, they provide a social aspect as they are facilitators of car sharing between people (P2P), and they provide a sustainable aspect as they are investing in carbon emission offsetting through reforestation projects throughout Australia. CND has made a number of choices regarding their platform and includes technological features for both car-owners and car-borrowers. For example, they make sharing more convenient by providing instant bookings that requiring less time to get a car. Every car contains a lockbox for key handover, a GPS for tracking, a toll tag for automatic toll handling, and a fuel card.

When borrowing out cars, the service does not require interaction from an owner such as accepting bookings as these are automatically accepted. Further key handover is handled via the lockbox which is usually attached to the door of the car. As an extra security measure, the owner can follow the car's location through the app, however, only if the car is returned late. For borrowers, the CND platform offers transparency regarding user ratings and vehicle type, that is, the borrowed car and its ratings will be exactly the same as the one described when they book the car. In addition to regular car borrowing, CND also offers instant borrowing of cars which makes it possible to get a car with short notice. At the pick-up time, the car can be located through the CND mobile application where the GPS module provides an exact location of the car. When the borrower picks up a car, the car keys can be acquired by entering a provided pin code from the mobile application into the lockbox without face-to-face communication. Before and after the trip, borrowers are asked to take pictures of the car using the CND mobile app to document damages made before and after borrowing the car.

3.2 Study Method

In this section, we describe our study approach consisting of three methods. Firstly, we gathered initial experiences. Secondly, we conducted interviews and walk-throughs with car-owners and finally, we observed and conducted interviews with car-borrowers.

Gathering Initial Experiences. Initially, we conducted an exploratory investigation with the purpose of creating interview guides for owners and borrowers for later interviews. The first author booked and borrowed three cars through the CND mobile app. Different makes and types of cars located in different places in Brisbane were selected. For the first booking we borrowed a small size Holden Barina located in the center of the city, the second was a mid-size Toyota Camry located in the suburbs, whereas in the last booking we borrowed a large size Mitsubishi Outlander also located in the suburbs. We borrowed the cars for different periods of time. We borrowed the first car for two hours to go grocery shopping, the second car for a day to go to the nearby mountains, and the last car for a five-day period to go on a road trip. The experiences were documented in researcher notes and images. Most of the documentation was created at the time of the booking, pick-up, and drop-off point as most interaction occurs at this time. The first author shared his knowledge and notes with the remaining authors which lead to the creation of two interview guides used for semi-structured interviews [29] with owners and borrowers. Interview guides were based on Yins [47] four question forms (*how, what, where, why*).

Owner Interviews and Recalling Bookings. We explored car sharing from an owner's perspective by conducting semi-structured interviews with 6 owners. Through cooperation with CND we had access to their user email list that contained all users in and in the near vicinity of Brisbane, Australia. We deployed a questionnaire to all owners in the area asking if they were willing to participate in interviews. For sampling purposes, the questionnaire included questions about age, gender, address, number of cars in the household, number of cars on CND, and the number of times their car(s) had been borrowed out in the last three months. The questionnaire resulted in 7 candidates that were sampled based on an even distribution between questionnaire questions.

Candidates was emailed asking to participate of which 6 participants replied and were recruited. The six owners were between 26 and 69 years of age (M = 44.3) and equally distributed between male and females. Three owners lived alone, and three lived in families consisting of three, four, and six members. Four lived in houses and two in apartments. Owners had borrowed out their car between three and thirty times in the last three months and had been members of CND between four and fourteen months. Three had an additional car and three only had one car. To get a more in-depth understanding of the booking process from the owners' perspective, before the interviews, we instructed them to write down a short description of their specific actions and thoughts when receiving a booking such as checking out borrower information, rescheduling bookings, and checking payments. The owners were then instructed to bring these descriptions with them to the interviews. If no bookings were received before the interviews, we asked them to recall the last booking that they received. Interviews lasted between 45 min and 1 h and were recorded on audio. In addition, researcher notes were also taken. This resulted in a total of 4,5 h of audio and 8 pages of researcher notes.

Borrower Interviews and Observation. We explored borrower's perspectives by conducting semi-structured interviews with 10 borrowers. With an email list supplied by CND, we recruited borrowers through a questionnaire deployed to all borrowers in and in the near vicinity of Brisbane, Australia. The questionnaire was targeted borrowers who had borrowed a car at least once. For sampling purposes, we included questions about the number of cars borrowed in the last three months, if they owned another vehicle, and how many times a month they drove a car. The questionnaire yielded 21 answers from borrowers of which we selected 10 participants based on a distribution from questionnaire questions. The recruited borrowers (five female) were between 22 and 59 years of age (M = 40), and all lived in urban areas (e.g., city centers and suburbs). They had borrowed a car between one and six times within the last three months and had been a member of the CND service between five and eighteen months. Seven borrowers lived alone, three lived with their partner or families. Six borrowers were living in houses and four in apartments.

We asked the borrowers to give a short description of their last booking. We instructed them to give a short description of actions and thoughts such as looking up car and owner information, important booking criteria and reasons for borrowing. We further asked borrowers to bring their mobile phone for the interviews so that they could show us examples of how they booked a car. Owner interviews lasted between 45 min and 1,5 h and were recorded on audio and in addition researcher notes were taken. This resulted in 10.5 h of audio recorded and 20 pages of researcher notes.

3.3 Data Integration and Analysis

A total of 15 h of audio and 28 pages of researcher notes was transcribed, anonymized and coded separately for thematic analysis [6] by two of the authors. Firstly, we familiarized ourselves with the data by reading the transcriptions several times and specifically looking for use of the sharing services. We then identified suggestions for codes (e.g., "*convenience*"). Secondly, we generated codes to interview quotes (e.g.,

the code "*mundane car sharing*" for the quote "*Often I just borrow the same car down at the corner, I know all its quirks and I know the price. Besides I'm just getting the groceries and there's a limit towards how much time I'm willing to put into it*"). Thirdly, we generated and reviewed themes using affinity diagramming, where quotes were put on a bulletin board and reorganized into themes over several iterations. As a final result of this, a set of four themes emerged.

4 Findings

We found that the car sharing service investigated in this paper (CND) was a significant contributor towards car sharing for both owners and borrowers of cars in a number of ways. In the following sections, we outline our findings in four themes describing opportunities and challenges associated using P2P car sharing. The four themes are; *Fueling Individual Motivation, Supporting Daily Mobility, Facilitating Car Sharing Purposes,* and *Socializing P2P Car Sharing Services.*

All data presented have been anonymized. We distinguish between owners (**O**) and borrowers (**B**) and refer to each participant by an index like **O1** as owner one and **B5** as borrower five. Occasionally we refer to the number of participants behind a finding, for example, (8/10) is eight out of ten borrowers and (4/6) is four out of six owners.

4.1 Fueling Individual Motivation

To some participants, rational motivation such as earning money of their assets was a motivation for car sharing, and to others. To others, ideological motivation such as reducing their carbon footprint was in focus. In the following sections, we describe the individual goals achieved through the platform for both borrowers and owners.

Utilizing Unused Assets and Environmental Awareness. For most owners (5/6) the primary motivation for car sharing was bound in rational motivation such as utilizing unused cars, while one owner's primary motivation was more intrinsic as he felt like he was helping others. All six of them had at least one car that they used rarely and many of them found that sharing this car through CND would justify their owner-ship. Although owners were annoyed with own an unused asset, the car was generally perceived as necessary because of flexible mobility needs where alternative (public) transportation means didn't always suffice. As such, several of the owners (5/6) were initially attracted to having an extra income from using CND. Some of them (3/6) had considered alternative solutions like selling their car, however the perceived extra value of owning a car along with the possibility of losing money kept them from doing selling it, for example, one owner mentioned that after having purchased a new car, altered personal living arrangements made the car less needed and used, as he argued this way:

> "*I moved here recently from Sydney. And so, because I live and work in the city my car is basically in my carport just carrying rust. And because it is quite new, I was looking at different options because I didn't want to lose money by selling it*" (**O3**)

Most owners (5/6) also articulated a strong environmental awareness and car sharing made them reflect upon their own behavior and driving needs, for example one owner that had started cycling instead of taking the car every day: *"I mean now that I don't use my car I have started to cycle again, which has made me less depressed about the world and the problems that cars impose on the environment"* (**O4**). Seven of the ten borrowers also mentioned environmental concerns was something that motivated them to car share. Further, almost all borrowers (9/10) mentioned, like some of the owners, that they felt more comfortable giving money to a company that they perceive as being facilitators of relationships amongst people, which they perceived CND to be, and not just in it for the business:

> *"It's partly price, and partly ethos. I would much rather borrow from a company that I trust is not just taking my money, and that is very good at one thing and is based on a relationship with people versus a bigger company that is a business of sharing or renting cars"* (**B4**)

Convenience and Helping Others. Mentioned by both owners and borrowers were the convenience that CND handled issues that otherwise would add complexity to car sharing (e.g., finding cars, insurance, communication, and payment). Convenience was a major motivational factor for the borrowers in relation to car sharing. All ten borrowers articulated that they could not completely live their lives without the use of cars, because alternative transportation forms such as buses or bikes could only satisfy some of their needs. Many of them (7/10) lived in the inner city with limited needs for daily car transportation. Here they had access to many public transportation options and bike lanes, and as a result, these seven borrowers did not own a car. The three remaining borrowers were living outside the inner city, however, still near their workplaces and did therefore not need a car on a daily basis. However, sometimes a car was needed for going out of the city or driving a long distances where other transportation types were insufficient. All ten borrowers found car renting using CND convenient as an easy alternative to get a car when they needed one especially because of cars being distributed across town, for example:

> *"... opposed to rental companies where you have to go to a place to pick up the car and do a lot of paperwork ... with this service, in less than 5 min, I can in most cases, find a car, book it, and pick it up"* (**B3**)

Community building was also found important for both owners and borrowers when using car sharing, and many of them felt that they, in fact, helped others from their community when either renting or renting out a car. In fact, one of the primary reasons for using a peer-to-peer car sharing service like CND was that sharing was between people rather than companies owning the cars. Owners stressed a personal feeling associated with the sentiment of helping those in need, i.e. people without a car. For example, **O2**, who were the one with the most borrowing of his car, explained that he started to car share to help others: *"I think that a lot of people is in a financial position where they can't afford a car and we are in a position where we can supply one, that just makes me feel good"* (**O2**). Complementing this perspective, five borrowers mentioned that contributing to a community and the feeling of helping other people were reasons why they sometimes maintained borrowing a car:

"In my own imagination, I felt good about the fact that I'm contributing, that's why I keep doing it, I think. I know that he or she might be an oversee student and probably have the need for her car at the weekend, but it helped me feel good about myself. I felt in that case that I was helping this person because they were going to get some of my dollars" **(B6)**

4.2 Supporting Daily Mobility

Both borrowers and owners expressed the need to use many different modes of mobility to support their daily trips and that it required some degree of flexibility in order to be able to car share. The following sections we describe the reasons for choosing car sharing and some of the requirements for being a car sharer.

Transportation Types. We found that borrowers had a number of transportation types that they mentioned as being available to them and that they had to consider actively when going on a trip. Often public transportation, biking, or walking would fulfill their commuting needs for going to work or on smaller trips. However, these transportation forms were also perceived as impractical when carrying physical items like groceries. In such situations, the borrowers would consider renting or borrowing a car. As an alternative, some participants (5/10) mentioned that they had used taxi and ridesharing services. Although these services were perceived as convenient - the car would come to them and not vice versa – the borrowers also stressed that this depended on the specific trip, for example, it wasn't very well suitable for transporting larger or more personal pieces of goods:

"It's a choice depending on the trip. Sometimes I take a taxi or an Uber if I'm in a hurry and just have to go and see my friends in town. I don't think it's very suitable if you want to go shopping or want to just move some stuff. It's really only suitable for one-way stuff. For example, I don't want to be stuck outside the store, waiting for a cab. Then it's much more convenient to get a car" **(B10)**

Public transportation and taxi services were not seen as a viable alternative for trips like freighting larger goods, driving long distances, or going doing something extraordinary. For such purpose borrowers would, therefore, prefer to rent or borrow a car. In contrast to car sharing, car renting was seen as an expensive alternative even though some participants would use it from time to time. Most borrowers agreed that car sharing in some case were more practical over rentals because of price and distribution of cars instead of having to go to an office. Alternatively, if borrowers needed to borrow a car and it was beyond walking distance some borrowers (4/10) articulated that they would combine different transportation types which also meant planning and comparing them separately on each individual service:

"Sometimes, if you really want a specific car and you need to travel a bit to get it you need to find other means of transportation to get it. One time I had to take a train and then a bus to get a car, it was quite tedious because I had to compare departure times manually on each service. That would have been easier if CND would provide me an overview of the different transportation options instead" **(B1)**

Flexible Car Ownership. Occasionally owners would need to use their own car which they all believed required a degree of flexibility. Some (3/6) would book their own car and block out times on the service well in advance, while others wouldn't block out

times unless it was absolutely necessary as they wanted to get as many bookings as possible. Most owners (5/6) had previously experienced unavailability of their own car in a situation where they actually needed to use the car. In those situations, they were forced to arrange other transportation forms. Interestingly, in relation to this, car sharing actually triggered self-reflection towards own transportation needs. Several of them (4/6) commuted to work using public transportation, a bike, or walking. Many owners said that before they began to share their car, they had often taken the car to work because it was seen as easier or as a subconscious choice than having to deal with alternative transportation. Joining CND however made them reflect on their actual needs:

"Car sharing requires a degree of flexibility, that's just embedded into it. There have been a few times where we have let the car be rented and haven't thought about it, it's not until a few days before that we think oops, we've got this on and we need two cars, but then I just use a taxi, or we can just work around it. It's good because it makes you think about your options" (**O3**)

Also sharing in the household was seen as requiring flexibility which was not always shared. Some owners (3/6) expressed that they were more interested in sharing their car than the rest of their household and were motivated by different things. Owners living with a spouse and children expressed that the other family members often didn't share their enthusiasm about car sharing The reason was that even though the rest of the household thought that sharing was a good idea, they were less interested in being flexible partly because of the requirement to find another mean of transportation if their car was unavailable: *"We have four cars and we could easily make do with only two, but my wife and I are very different in terms of sharing and flexibility. She wants a car she can access and drive all the time, whereas I am much more inclined to work it out, but CND doesn't help you with it"* (**O2**).

4.3   Facilitating Car Sharing Purposes

We found that borrowers used car sharing for many different purposes which can be categorized as ad-hoc and planned car sharing. In the following sections describe the specific purposes that car sharing is used for and how it is facilitated by CND.

Ad-Hoc Car Sharing. Borrowers typically rented cars for mundane purposes to support typical day-to-day transportation needs, e.g., grocery shopping. We saw a clear preference for getting a cheaper, and also older car, for these purposes. Such trips could often only be planned ad-hoc and were last-minute bookings. None of these borrowers exclusively used car sharing for mundane purpose, however, choosing car sharing over alternative transportation options was mostly associated with convenience and what is right for the moment: *"Now and again I find the kids want to go and do something and it's a little bit of a stretch on the bike and the city is not well set up for cycling, and there are some roads that I won't take the kids to ... it's just sometimes easier to borrow a car"* (**B6**). Ad-hoc planning and easy access to cars were important in such situations, and in case no nearby cars were available, they would often consider other transportation options or means:

"I got called into the hospital one day at 2:30 am, no public transport. I checked Uber, but there were no Ubers around, so it would be like 30 min. We had patients and I had to get there

very quickly. I checked Car Next Door and the car that I normally take was available for the couple of hours that I needed it and I booked it and within seven minutes I had a car and was on my way to work. I work with humans, they will always come first, and just having that nearby made a huge difference in my ability to provide care. I came back and dropped the car off and I just walked home. It was brilliant" (**B5**)

Interestingly, we found that borrowing cars for mundane purposes and smaller trips would often result in borrowers attempting to rent a previously rented car. Several borrowers (5/10) reported that they had borrowed the same car near to them several times to save them the time of finding a new one: *"Often I just borrow the same car down at the corner, I know all its quirks and I know the price. Besides I'm just getting the groceries and there's a limit towards how much time I'm willing to put into it"* (**B10**). We found that reasons such as it was close by, were important for choosing car sharing over other transportation options. However, also important was familiarity with the car such as its location and its condition, in particular when going for a quick or short ride. To support these trips, we found that instant bookings were appreciated and perceived as necessary by the borrowers.

Planned Car Sharing. While mundane mobility needs were prevailing, borrowers would occasionally rent cars for extraordinary or special experiences, like renting an exclusive car, going on holidays, or on weekend trips outside the city. Our interviews revealed that many of these trips were for longer periods of time which indicate more use of car sharing than borrowers using it primarily for day-to-day trips. Opposed day-to-day trips, these were often planned well ahead and borrowers would often use the car sharing service to browse cars because they liked the experience. Several borrowers (5/10) mentioned that they used car sharing as a way to achieve extraordinary driving experiences by borrowing a more exclusive car than their own or a car that could impress others. Interestingly, we found that especially transparency in the service, where borrowers could see exactly which car they would get, the associated expenses, and the location was perceived as important for choosing car sharing:

"Yeah, because on CND you always can see which car model you will get, whereas all the usual car companies will just say this or similar, so you never really know what you will get most of the time" (**B6**).

Compared to day-to-day car sharing, borrowers were willing to put more resources into getting a car for a longer trip and would accept higher prices or going further to pick it up: *"I mean realistically if someone had one of those for hire (a Smart convertible) I would probably go an hour to pick it up. And even if, I don't know, $250 a day of something"* (**B6**). Several borrowers (6/10) mentioned that they had or thought about borrowing a nicer car just for fun and for showing off for friends or family. We found no preference for car age, as this mode was mostly associated with getting experiences, which could be from an older car as well as a new one. For example, **B1** mentioned that she had arranged to borrow an older convertible with her sons and going for a trip along the coast. Experiencing cars could also be associated with easing into car ownership. We found that two of the borrowers (**B2**, **B10**) knew that they had to buy a car in the future and therefore was trying out car models to see which one they liked the most.

4.4   Socializing P2P Car Sharing Services

Both borrowers and owners expressed that they were engaged in car sharing and were considering it actively in their daily lives. For example, to borrowers, the ability to access a car instantly was important and for owners the ability to not have too much interaction to borrow out their cars were important. However, the choice from CND to reduce this overhead from users also resulted in challenges

Efficiency vs. Interacting with People. One reason for many borrowers and owners using CND was the reduced overhead of not having to think about bookings, who borrows the car, who borrowed it out, the handling of practical things as payment were mentioned as a contributor towards using a service. All participants agreed that these things were best handled through the service and many participants mentioned that the complexity of handling these issues was too much for them if they were to handle it themselves, and thus, outsourcing this complexity to the service made car sharing a viable option for them in their otherwise busy lives: *"I think the service is really important, because without that I would worry too much, for example, about who borrows my car and if he will damage it its simply too complex, with the CND I know there's insurance so there's no risk in it for me, so in a way you could say that I've outsourced that part"* **(O3).** We found that many owners believed that too much management would simply exclude some borrowers because they would worry them too much and start looking up borrowers on the internet. For example, one owner mentioned that getting to know the person who borrows their car would simply start too many thoughts and be too complex for him and he, therefore, relied on CND to take care of it:

> *"My mind is so analytical and if I had to manage every booking myself then I'm going to think about what will happen if this person crashes my car and this and that. I don't have time for that. So, in a way, I'm outsourcing the job to Car Next Door"* **(O3).**

Most borrowers (7/10) shared the same opinion as owners. Part of them wanting to keep communication to a minimum with the owner was to avoid the feeling of guilt and owner's reactions, for example if they called about car damage: *"The service is critical, I wouldn't have started with borrowing if I didn't know that CND has my back if something happened. I always call them if there is a problem. Imagine calling the owner and telling him that his car is broken. I would avoid that conversation because it's probably not going to be very pleasant"* **(B4).** Interestingly, and quite opposite, not all borrowers thought this way. To them (3/10) not having any communication between owners and borrowers was expressed as alienating and that the only connection between them was the car and as expressed as somewhat odd because usually them wanting to put a face on the one they were borrowing from and not only a profile picture from the app:

> *"In a way, I would like more interaction with the people that I'm borrowing from. I have some information about the person, I can find that the app and that is fine, but it is a little bit alienating. For example, there is this one woman that I'm borrowing from quite a lot, but I have no connection with the person except via the car, I find that a little odd because I would like to thank her personally"* **(B6)**

Cars as Personal Items. To several borrowers (8/10) a borrowed car was a personal item, important to the people owning them, and therefore they took extra good care of it compared to rentals:

> *"It's interesting you know, I never take particularly good care of rentals, but I always take extra good care of the cars that I borrow. The fact that it belongs to people makes me want to take extra good care of it I suppose"* **(B7)**

Interestingly some owners (3/6) tried to facilitate this as they believed that they needed not only to provide a car but also provide a good experience to borrowers especially due to the lack of face-to-face communication. Towards the owners had started to personalize the experience by leaving small items of personal value in the car to make borrowers feel a little more at home and to make them feel less like a stranger in someone else's car. This was seen as a less resource demanding action however still adding to the borrowing experience. For example, **O1** who often left candy and her CD collection in the car and **O5,** who often left a personal note and mints from her to the borrower in the car. Further, personalizing the car was seen as a mechanism to prevent damage:

> *"I always leave a little note and some mints in the car and just say, you know, that I hope that they enjoy our car and have a great trip or whatever. Although CND offers me some security by offering me insurance for damage, I don't want the hassle of sorting that out after it's happened. They are borrowing something that is a value to our family and if you can humanize that experience for them you might catch it before by them taking a little bit better care of your car"* (**O5**).

Borrowing a car containing a few personal items were a positive experience and that a car feels more personal if it contains the owner's items which could lead to affection towards the vehicle. For example, borrower mentioned that his son was so familiar with a particular car both because they had borrowed it several times and because it contained some personal items familiar to him that he had given it a name: *"We've borrowed the same car a couple of times, and you know what, my son gave it the name Bob, because previously we had this car named Bob, and the new one reminded him of it because we had some of the same items in the car. So, in a way, you could say it became a part of the family which also made us take better care of it"* **(B4)**.

5   Discussion

Our study highlights several interesting aspects of P2P car sharing enabled through the digital service Car Next Door. For example, individual motivation and synergies between car sharing and alternative transportation forms can be highlighted as important.

Adding to these finding, in the following sections, we discuss considerations that we hope may inform and inspire further HCI research and design on car sharing.

5.1 Beyond Individual Modes of Transportation

In itself, car sharing provided transportation for many of our participants in their everyday lives. However, there were also a plethora of situations where car sharing was not perceived as being practical, for example, travelling the inner city to go to work. Car sharing has the potential to improve interconnectivity between other modes of transportation [41] however, a clear challenge is to know how and when to combine it sequentially with other transportation in order to do so. With regards to this, we think it is important to consider car sharing as part of a larger transportation ecology used by people. Ecologies are also suggested by studies of other areas of transportation available in a larger ecology where users combine the different options to fit their needs (e.g., [9, 32, 46]). Therefore, when complementing other mobility types car sharing fits into the daily lives of users and not the other way around. We argue to study car sharing as part of an ecology further, for example by drawing on inspiration from the literature describing fundamental interactions in ecologies (e.g., [44]).

One way of designing transportation ecologies could be letting them make an informed choice from a number of transportation types (e.g., bus, train, and car sharing) and letting them know when it is opportune to choose car sharing over other types. Further, going beyond choosing one specific transportation type is the opportunity for continuous [44] transportation where users can combine different types of mobility to form a larger trip. The opportunity to not only integrate other transportation types, but also other modes of car sharing services. We must remember that car sharing, and especially the type of car sharing we investigate in this paper (round-trip P2P), only provides one of many alternatives for users. For example, although our participants had said that they didn't use any other sharing services, it wasn't an active choice and they were definitely open towards open for other types like one-way ride sharing. We argue that research and design along these lines could be beneficial for the sharing services to support mobility.

5.2 Supporting Ad-Hoc and Planned Car Sharing

Our insight provides a dimension towards P2P car sharing, that is, ad-hoc trips which can't be planned in advance and further for purposes like getting groceries or commuting to work. This is different from many studies that suggest that borrowing cars are associated with smaller trips planned in advance (e.g., [9, 15, 32]), Interestingly, this describes a new and different dimension than what the literature provides. Ironically this can seem counterintuitive, that borrowers can borrow a car from an owner with little planning ahead. We argue that finding can largely be ascribed to the choices made by CND to make their platform more effective by reducing the amount of coordination between parties involved in sharing a car. Features increasing efficiency, such as instant booking, not having to interact with an owner to get the keys, and the large distribution of cars around town, which the CND platform supports, is closely related to the purpose of getting a car ad-hoc. However, although we think that designers should consider these mechanisms if aiming to support ad-hoc P2P car sharing, we see a need for further research to understand its potential.

Another insight from our findings is that car sharing often is associated with booking a car for a short period of time (e.g., [21, 42]). However, our findings also suggest evidence for car sharing being used for longer trips, that are mostly related to experiences or recreation. Interestingly, efficiency and planning become less important for borrowers of cars for these types of purposes. Based on our findings, it seems like supporting getting a car for experience or recreation requires an amount of transparency where a borrower can browse cars and get exactly the one wanted. Further, the experience of browsing through a number of options matching many and diverse cars available through a P2P platform is equally a part of the experience which reflects in our participants' willingness to travel a further distance or pay more to get the car. Besides this seemingly unique aspect of the design of P2P car sharing over other service schemes, we argue that this also presents researchers with an opportunity to inquire such uniqueness of P2P services, one that potentially could be a challenge for other services (e.g., B2C) where a more uniform car park could be preferred.

5.3 Coping Strategies and Social Car Sharing Services

What happens to trust when face-to-face communication is removed from a service? We found that borrowers took particularly good care of the cars they borrowed, mainly because of the feeling that it was a personal item to another person. This was facilitated by some owners that placed small personal items in the car to ensure a more personal experience and thus making the borrower take better care of the car. This is interesting from a trust perspective as it seems that traditional coping strategies (e.g., insurance) is not quite enough as owners still recognizing that damages happen and wanting to avoid the whole scenario of having to deal with the insurance. Trust between people is especially important and is one of the pillars in the sharing economy [4]. Trust is especially important in car sharing, where the shared object is of high personal value to many people. Shaheen et al., amongst other mechanisms for ensuring trust in P2P car sharing and finds that face-to-face communication is perceived as increasing trust and helping borrowers not damage cars [41]. Towards this end, CND does not provide the feature of face-to-face communication and we do think that they were quite happy about this choice as it saved them time. However, this also meant that some owners employed their own coping strategy to ensure that their car would not get damaged. Alternative coping strategies towards ensuring trust that the P2P services does not provide needs further exploration as it could give inspiration for future designs.

Car sharing can be seen as a way of utilizing existing resources which might fuel motivational desires as a contrast to acquiring new resources. This also goes well in line with the idea of utilizing the commons [5, 22]. One aspect is peoples' individual goals that in our findings both revealed rational (e.g., earning an additional income) and intrinsic (helping others and socializing) motivation. Rational and intrinsic motivation has been investigated before in P2P car sharing. As such, Shaheen et al. [42] reports on borrowers and owners motivation and finds that earning money and convenience as a key motivational factor and further, although less important, helping others gain access to a vehicle. Although acknowledging this finding, interestingly, we also found that for some participants this relationship was flipped around by showing helping others as a key motivation. We think that this relationship highly reflects and can be attributed the

nature of P2P sharing which seemingly is one reason why our participants chose CND as a service along with the fact that P2P car sharing was believed to be creating relations between people and was thus seen as "less evil" than other car sharing types. Our results indicate that while some aspects of optimizing a service are valued as a mean to actually share, other more intrinsic motivational aspects such as maintaining relationships between people. The aspect of social services can be an interesting dimension for designers and researchers to explore for reaching people that thinks that social values are also important. We think that car sharing is ideal to provide a clear and lucid setting [17] for such investigations, although it might scale up in all aspects of the sharing economy.

6   Conclusions

This paper has presented a study on the use of P2P car sharing services. Through a study with 6 owners and 10 borrowers using the service Car Next Door, we identified 4 themes that describe different aspects of car sharing. Our findings reveal that P2P car sharing is convenient for many participants by allowing them to utilize unused assets and helping each other out. The service explored is used for different purposes supporting ad-hoc and planned trips which allow users to complement existing transportation options at hand. Lastly, it was seen as convenient that Car Next Door provides an efficient way to car share by allowing instant bookings and getting the keys without interacting with an owner. However, the lack of face-to-face communication was in some cases perceived as alienating along with reducing trust in the people borrowing although coping strategies were identified.

To inspire HCI future research and design of sharing services we discussed three themes to serve as an inspiration to researchers and designers of car sharing services. Firstly, we have discussed that car sharing is part of an ecology of transportation options and how this perspective can be used in the design of new services. Secondly, we discuss how ad-hoc and planned car sharing can be supported and considering the uniqueness of the P2P systems. Thirdly, we argue that P2P services are social car sharing services where alternative coping strategies are developed to handle trust when face-to-face communication lacks.

Our study has some limitations. Firstly, we have only recruited participants living in cities that were already using Car Next Door. We acknowledge that other participants could have been interesting in our study, for example, those who had deselected the service or potential users such as disadvantaged populations. Secondly, we have chosen a peer-to-peer service, however, we do acknowledge that other services exist different from the one we studied. Thirdly, car use and opinions vary depending on location, and so, carrying out a similar study in a different location, such as in another country, could yield different results. Finally, our results provide qualitative insights which are not generalizable across a wider population. As such, we acknowledge that other methods are required to provide statistical generalizability.

Acknowledgements. We would like to extend our gratitude to the employees from Car Next Door who shared their knowledge about their service and car sharing in general.

References

1. ACEA and Frost & Sullivan: Number of car sharing users worldwide from 2006 to 2025 (in millions). https://www.statista.com/statistics/415636/car-sharing-number-of-users-worldwide/. Accessed 5 Sept 2018
2. Ballús-Armet, I., Shaheen, S.A., Clonts, K., Weinzimmer, D.: Peer-to-peer carsharing. Transp. Res. Rec. J. Transp. Res. Board **2416**(1), 27–36 (2014). https://doi.org/10.3141/2416-04
3. Bellotti, V., Ambard, A., Turner, D., Gossmann, C., Demkova, K., Carroll, J.M.: A muddle of models of motivation for using peer-to-peer economy systems. In: Proceedings of the 33rd Annual ACM Conference on Human Factors in Computing Systems - CHI 2015, pp. 1085–1094 (2015). https://doi.org/10.1145/2702123.2702272
4. Botsman, R., Rogers, R.: What's Mine is Yours: How Collaborative Consumption Is Changing The Way We Live. Collaborative Consumption. Collins, London (2010)
5. Brady, G.L., Ostrom, E.: Governing the commons: the evolution of institutions for collective action. South. Econ. J. **60**(1), 249 (2006). https://doi.org/10.2307/1059950
6. Braun, V., Clarke, V.: Using thematic analysis in psychology. Qual. Res. Psychol. **3**(2), 77–101 (2006). https://doi.org/10.1191/1478088706qp063oa
7. Brereton, M., Roe, P., Foth, M., Bunker, J.M., Buys, L.: Designing participation in agile ridesharing with mobile social software. In: Proceedings of the 21st Annual Conference of the Australian Computer-Human Interaction Special Interest Group on Design: Open 24/7, OZCHI 2009, p. 257 (2009). https://doi.org/10.1145/1738826.1738868
8. CarNextDoor: Car Next Door. https://www.carnextdoor.com.au. Accessed 5 Sept 2018
9. Costain, C., Ardron, C., Habib, K.N.: Synopsis of users' behaviour of a carsharing program: a case study in Toronto. Transp. Res. Part A Policy Pract. **46**(3), 421–434 (2012). https://doi.org/10.1016/J.TRA.2011.11.005
10. Dillahunt, T.R., Malone, A.R.: The promise of the sharing economy among disadvantaged communities. In: Proceedings of the 33rd Annual ACM Conference on Human Factors in Computing Systems - CHI 2015, pp. 2285–2294 (2015). https://doi.org/10.1145/2702123.2702189
11. Dillahunt, T.R., Kameswaran, V., Li, L., Rosenblat, T.: Uncovering the values and constraints of real-time ridesharing for low-resource populations. In: Proceedings of the 2017 CHI Conference on Human Factors in Computing Systems, CHI 2017, pp. 2757–2769 (2017). https://doi.org/10.1145/3025453.3025470
12. Dillahunt, T.R., Wang, X., Wheeler, E., Cheng, H.F., Hecht, B., Zhu, H.: The sharing economy in computing: a systematic literature review. In: Proceedings of the ACM on Human-Computer Interaction Article, vol. 1, no. 26, pp. 1–26 (2017). https://doi.org/10.1145/3134673
13. Dmitrienko, A., Plappert, C.: Secure free-floating car sharing for offline cars. In: Proceedings of the Seventh ACM on Conference on Data and Application Security and Privacy - CODASPY 2017, pp. 349–360 (2017). https://doi.org/10.1145/3029806.3029807
14. Dowling, R., Kent, J.: Practice and public–private partnerships in sustainable transport governance: the case of car sharing in Sydney, Australia. Transp. Policy **40**, 58–64 (2015). https://doi.org/10.1016/J.TRANPOL.2015.02.007
15. Duncan, M.: The cost saving potential of carsharing in a US context. Transportation (AMST) **38**(2), 363–382 (2011). https://doi.org/10.1007/s11116-010-9304-y
16. Firnkorn, J., Müller, M.: What will be the environmental effects of new free-floating car-sharing systems? The case of car2go in Ulm. Ecol. Econ. **70**(8), 1519–1528 (2011). https://doi.org/10.1016/j.ecolecon.2011.03.014

17. Garfinkel, H.: Ethnomethodology's Program: Working Out Durkheim's Aphorism. Rowman & Littlefield Publishers, Lanham (2002)
18. Glöss, M., McGregor, M., Brown, B.: Designing for labour. In: Proceedings of the 2016 CHI Conference on Human Factors in Computing Systems - CHI 2016, pp. 1632–1643 (2016). https://doi.org/10.1145/2858036.2858476
19. GoGet: GoGet. https://www.goget.com.au. Accessed 13 Sept 2018
20. Gransky, L.: The Mesh - Why the Future of Business is Sharing. Portfolio Penguin, Gurgaon (2014). https://doi.org/10.1007/s13398-014-0173-7.2
21. Hampshire, R.C., Gaites, C.: Peer-to-peer carsharing. Transp. Res. Rec. J. Transp. Res. Board 2217(1), 119–126 (2011). https://doi.org/10.3141/2217-15
22. Hardin, G.: The tragedy of the commons. Science 162, 1243–1248 (1968)
23. Heinrichs, M., Krajzewicz, D., Cyganski, R., Schmidt, A.: Introduction of car sharing into existing car fleets in microscopic travel demand modelling. https://doi.org/10.1007/s00779-017-1031-3
24. ter Huurne, M., Ronteltap, A., Corten, R., Busken, V.: Antecedents of trust in the sharing economy: a systematic review. J. Consum. Behav. 16(6), 485–498 (2017). https://doi.org/10.1002/cb.1667
25. Ikkala, T., Lampinen, A.: Monetizing network hospitality: hospitality and sociability in the context of Airbnb. In: CSCW 2014, pp. 14–18 (2014). https://doi.org/10.1145/2675133.2675274
26. Jung, J., Lee, K.-P.: Curiosity or certainty? A qualitative, comparative analysis of Couchsurfing and Airbnb user behaviors. In: Proceedings of Conference on Human Factors in Computing Systems - Part F1276, pp. 1740–1747 (2017). https://doi.org/10.1145/3027063.3053162
27. Katzev, R.: Car sharing: a new approach to urban transportation problems. Anal. Soc. Issues Public Policy 3(1), 65–86 (2003). https://doi.org/10.1111/j.1530-2415.2003.00015.x
28. Kent, J.L., Dowling, R.: Puncturing automobility? Carsharing practices. J. Transp. Geogr. 32 (2013), 86–92 (2013). https://doi.org/10.1016/j.jtrangeo.2013.08.014
29. Kvale, S.: InterViews: An Introduction to Qualitative Research Interviewing, pp. 129–140. Sage, Thousand Oaks (1996). https://doi.org/10.1016/S0149-7189(97)89858-8
30. Lampinen, A., Cheshire, C.: Hosting via Airbnb: motivations and financial assurances in monetized network hospitality. In: Proceedings of the 2016 CHI Conference on Human Factors in Computing Systems, pp. 1669–1680 (2016). https://doi.org/10.1145/2858036.2858092
31. Li, Q., Liao, F., Timmermans, H.J.P., Huang, H., Zhou, J.: Incorporating free-floating car-sharing into an activity-based dynamic user equilibrium model: a demand-side model. Transp. Res. Part B Methodol. 107, 102–123 (2018). https://doi.org/10.1016/j.trb.2017.11.011
32. Martin, E., Shaheen, S.: The Impact of carsharing on public transit and non-motorized travel: an exploration of North American carsharing survey data. Energies 4(11), 2094–2114 (2011). https://doi.org/10.3390/en4112094
33. Meurer, J., Stein, M., Randall, D., Rohde, M., Wulf, V.: Social dependency and mobile autonomy. In: Proceedings of the 32nd Annual ACM Conference on Human Factors in Computing Systems, CHI 2014, pp. 1923–1932 (2014). https://doi.org/10.1145/2556288.2557300
34. Millard-Ball, A.: Car-Sharing: Where and How It Succeeds. Transportation Research Board, Washington, D.C (2005). https://doi.org/10.17226/13559
35. Ornetzeder, M., Rohracher, H.: Of solar collectors, wind power, and car sharing: comparing and understanding successful cases of grassroots innovations. Glob. Environ. Change 23(5), 856–867 (2013). https://doi.org/10.1016/j.gloenvcha.2012.12.007

36. Qiu, W., Parigi, P., Abrahao, B.: More stars or more reviews? Differential effects of reputation on trust in the sharing economy. In: CHI 2018, pp. 1–11 (2018). https://doi.org/10.1145/3173574.3173727
37. Quattrone, G., Proserpio, D., Quercia, D., Capra, L., Musolesi, M.: Who Benefits from the "Sharing" Economy of Airbnb? pp. 1385–1393 (2016). https://doi.org/10.1145/2872427.2874815
38. Juniper Research: Revenue of platform providers in the sharing economy worldwide in 2017 and 2022 (in billion U.S. dollars) (2017). https://www.statista.com/statistics/878844/global-sharing-economy-revenue-platform-providers/. Accessed 13 Sept 2018
39. Rifkin, J.: The Age of Access: The New Culture of Hypercapitalism Where All of Life Is a Paid for Experience. Penguin, New York (2000)
40. Shaheen, S.A., Cohen, A.P.: Carsharing and personal vehicle services: worldwide market developments and emerging trends. Int. J. Sustain. Transp. 7(1), 5–34 (2013). https://doi.org/10.1080/15568318.2012.660103
41. Shaheen, S.A., Mallery, M.A., Kingsley, K.J.: Personal vehicle sharing services in North America. Res. Transp. Bus. Manag. 3, 71–81 (2012). https://doi.org/10.1016/J.RTBM.2012.04.005
42. Shaheen, S.A., Martin, E., Bansal, A.: Peer-To-Peer (P2P) carsharing: understanding early markets, social dynamics, and behavioral impacts. UC Berkeley Research Reports (2018). https://doi.org/10.7922/G2FN14BD
43. Shaheen, S., Sperling, D., Wagner, C.: Carsharing in Europe and North American: Past, Present, and Future (1998). https://doi.org/10.1111/ina.12046
44. Sørensen, H., Raptis, D., Kjeldskov, J., Skov, M.B.: The 4C framework. In: Proceedings of the 2014 ACM International Joint Conference on Pervasive and Ubiquitous Computing - UbiComp 2014 Adjunct, pp. 87–97 (2014). https://doi.org/10.1145/2632048.2636089
45. Svangren, M.K., Skov, M.B., Kjeldskov, J.: The connected car: an empirical study of electric cars as mobile digital devices. In: Proceedings of the 19th International Conference on Human-Computer Interaction with Mobile Devices and Services - MobileHCI 2017, pp. 1–12 (2017). https://doi.org/10.1145/3098279.3098535
46. Svangren, M.K., Skov, M.B., Kjeldskov, J.: Passenger trip planning using ride-sharing services. In: Proceedings of the 2018 CHI Conference on Human Factors in Computing Systems, CHI 2018, pp. 1–12 (2018). https://doi.org/10.1145/3173574.3174054
47. Yin, R.K.: Case Study Research: Design and Methods, 5th edn. Sage Publications, Thousand Oaks (2014). https://doi.org/10.1080/09500790.2011.582317
48. ZipCar: ZipCar. https://www.zipcar.com/. Accessed 13 Sept 2018

You Talkin' to Me? A Practical Attention-Aware Embodied Agent

Rahul R. Divekar[1,2]([⊠]), Jeffrey O. Kephart[2], Xiangyang Mou[1], Lisha Chen[1], and Hui Su[1,2]

[1] Rensselaer Polytechnic Institute, Troy, NY, USA
{divekr,moux4,chen121}@rpi.edu
[2] IBM T.J. Watson Research Center, Yorktown Heights, NY, USA
{kephart,huisuibmres}@us.ibm.com

Abstract. Most present-day voice-based assistants require that users utter a wake-up word to signify that they are addressing the assistant. While this may be acceptable for one-shot requests such as "Turn on the lights", it becomes tiresome when one is engaged in an extended interaction with such an assistant. To support the goal of developing low-complexity, low-cost alternatives to a wake-up word, we present the results of two studies in which users engage with an assistant that infers whether it is being addressed from the user's head orientation. In the first experiment, we collected informal user feedback regarding a relatively simple application of head orientation as a substitute for a wake-up word. We discuss that feedback and how it influenced the design of a second prototype assistant designed to correct many of the issues identified in the first experiment. The most promising insight was that users were willing to adapt to the interface, leading us to hypothesize that it would be beneficial to provide visual feedback about the assistant's belief about the user's attentional state. In a second experiment conducted using the improved assistant, we collected more formal user feedback on likability and usability and used it to establish that, with high confidence, head orientation combined with visual feedback is preferable to the traditional wake-up word approach. We describe the visual feedback mechanisms and quantify their usefulness in the second experiment.

Keywords: Multimodal interaction ·
User interaction and experience · Natural language interfaces

1 Introduction

Voice-activated assistants typically require users to utter a wake-up word (such as "Hey Google" or "Alexa") to indicate that they are addressing the assistant. Most interactions with these devices consist of one or two commands (Bentley et al. 2018). The use of a wake-up word is generally acceptable for short atomic requests such as "Turn on the lights" or "Set a timer for 5 min", which require no

© IFIP International Federation for Information Processing 2019
Published by Springer Nature Switzerland AG 2019
D. Lamas et al. (Eds.): INTERACT 2019, LNCS 11748, pp. 760–780, 2019.
https://doi.org/10.1007/978-3-030-29387-1_44

deliberation or discussion. However, assistants designed to assist humans with higher-level cognitive tasks are beginning to emerge, as demonstrated by Kephart et al. (2018) and Farrell et al. (2016). While by and large these agents still process one-shot requests, those requests tend to be issued in rapid succession, and may often be interleaved with discussions with other humans. Thus, from the users' perspective, communication with the agent is part of a broader conversation that they may be having with another human, making the overall dialogue multi-round. In this case, prefacing each command or request with a wake-up word is tedious and unnatural.

For assistants that support multi-round conversations with only one human, one previously-explored solution has been for the assistant to extend its period of attentiveness for a few seconds after its most recent response. However, this is not viable when multiple people are collaborating with one another and with the agent, as it becomes difficult for the assistant to distinguish requests from conversation among human collaborators. A confused agent may interrupt such side conversations with inappropriate and unwelcome chatter, such as "I'm sorry, Dave. I'm afraid I can't do that."

We seek to develop an alternative to the wake-up word that is sufficiently accurate without being unduly complex or expensive. As a starting point, we note that an approach that has been explored by the HCI/HRI community for robotic assistants is based upon real-time eye-gaze measurements (Wang and Ji 2017). A drawback of this approach is that it requires careful calibration, and moreover distance scales appropriate for multi-user scenarios require expensive Pan-Tilt-Zoom (PTZ) cameras. Fortunately, we note that other prior work has established that head orientation can adequately substitute for eye gaze in the context of gaming (Da Silva et al. 2008) and meeting analysis (Stiefelhagen and Zhu 2002)—suggesting that it may be acceptable in our scenario as well.

This paper describes our effort to ascertain whether the relatively inexpensive approach of using real-time head pose measurements as a proxy for user attention is a suitable alternative to using a wake-up word. After a review of the relevant literature in Sect. 2, Sect. 3 describes a first experiment in which we implemented a first prototype assistant that used a simple heuristic to determine whether the user was addressing the assistant. The assistant, which was based upon a previously-developed astrophysics assistant (Kephart et al. 2018) that helps users explore data about exoplanets (planets that orbit distant stars), was represented as an avatar displayed on a large TV screen, as depicted in Fig. 1. Informal feedback from this study involving several novice users indicated that the assistant was not sufficiently usable. Results from the pilot study also provided insights into how the assistant might be improved. Section 4 first describes how we translated lessons learned from the pilot study into technical enhancements to the prototype. Then, we report results from a controlled user study that we conducted with 8 university students (none of whom had participated in the pilot study). These results establish with reasonable confidence that the second (enhanced) prototype assistant is more usable and likable than a version of the assistant that is otherwise identical except that it uses a wake-up word.

We conclude in Sect. 5 with a summary and some thoughts about possible future extensions of this work.

2   Related Work

Our contribution is multi-disciplinary and hence the related work is discussed in three parts: addressee detection, HCI of Multi-modal Conversational UI and gaze detection.

2.1   Addressee Detection

Most prior work on addressee detection and turn-taking focus on using combinations of visual, acoustical and textual features from human participants in the interaction. Efforts have been strong towards fusing these multiple modalities, identifying importance of each modality and applying machine/deep learning algorithms at different stages e.g. modality fusion, attention detection, etc. as described further.

Ravuri and Stolcke (2015) have explored addressee detection but strictly with lexical and/or speech based modality. More recently, Norouzian et al. (2019) have explored sophisticated models for addressee detection based purely on acoustical cues. Frampton et al. (2009) have combined gaze and linguistic features to identify the addressee in conversations among groups of humans that involve ambiguous references like "you".

Bakx et al. (2003) and Van Turnhout et al. (2005) have contributed to the addressee recognition problem by collecting data in a Wizard-of-Oz setting in which human subjects spoke to a human partner and a human-driven kiosk that posed as an intelligent machine. They conducted statistical analyses to relate manually annotated eye-gaze data to characteristics of the conversation and trained and evaluated a Naive Bayes classifier. They found that looking away from the machine strongly signified that the addressee was the human partner, but looking at the machine only weakly signified that the human was addressing the machine.

Baba et al. (2012) and Nakano et al. (2013) have experimented, analyzed and implemented conversations with the goal of addressee detection in human-human-agent settings. They find that the tone of voice while talking to agent is higher and a speech+head orientation signal in their SVM model has given them good results. The literature thus encourages our thoughts that head orientation is an important signal. Akhtiamov et al. (2017), Shriberg et al. (2013) have done similar work in addressee detection based on speech and textual features. Le Minh et al. (2018) have explored addressee detection using gaze in data that contained images and text using deep learning approaches. Tsai et al. (2015) have studied the effect of various multi-modal features in addressee detection in human-human-computer interaction and have concluded that voice based features are more important that visual features due to headpose being affected by situational attractors claiming that headpose, by itself, is not enough.

Akhtiamov and Palkov (2018) echo similar findings as their addressee detection accuracy is highest with acoustical+textual+visual features.

Further, in the HRI field, Katzenmaier (2004) have explored in depth how to identify the addressee in a human-human-robot conversation. As do we, they find that users may look at the agent even when they are actually addressing another human. In their parlance, people usually look at the subject to whom they are speaking except when there is another "situational attractor", which they define as "objects or situations in the environment that attract people's eye gaze when they are talking to each other". Work in this field seemed to be the theme of research in the HRI community in the early 2000's. Some examples of which are Sheikhi and Odobez (2015), Mutlu et al. (2012), Gu and Badler (2006). Their contributions have determined Visual Focus of Attention (VFOA) using eye-gaze and/or head pose, identifying the addressee based on combinations of VFOA and context using several models in an effort to make robots more humanistic.

Attention detection is closely related to turn taking in multi-party conversations. Andrist et al. (2016) have summarized the turn taking problem in HCI and further motivated this problem. Kendon (1967) have shed light on the non-verbal turn-yielding cues in human-human behavior such as body movement or gaze direction, while Gravano and Hirschberg (2009) have discussed turn-yielding cues such as speaking rate, intonation, etc. giving the research community heuristics. Bohus and Horvitz (2011) have used a kiosk scenario with a humanistic face to study and look more broadly in the turn-taking domain in a game-like context. They used hand-crafted turn-taking policies to enable their prototype and emphasize how a bad turn-taking system is a conversation breaker.

2.2 Interaction Design

Interaction mechanisms for the purpose of attention detection and turn taking have previously been explored in the HRI community. van Schendel and Cuijpers (2015) have demonstrated the positive effect of robots expressing turn-yielding cues such as stop arms, turn head, flash eyes. We encourage enthusiastic readers to see Admoni and Scassellati (2017) who have in detail reviewed the state-of-the-art in social eye-gaze in human-robot behavior and discussed its role in usability, conversation, attention and turn-taking.

Visual cues have been explored in the chatbot area and are seen deployed in commercial applications like Alexa Echo, Google Home, etc. They appear as a combination of colored and patterned flickering of lights to indicate when the bot is listening, talking, thinking, etc. The importance of visual feedback in this context has been motivated in a talk by the VP of Alexa and Echo (ZDNet 2018) and documentation for Alexa's attentional system (Amazon 2019) can be seen on their webpages. However, we have not found an academic discussion of the same.

A common focus appears to emerge from literature - improving accuracy of attention detection by fusing several conversational and visual cues. However, building a system to express and interpret all of the cues in real time is a hard problem in research and in computation. We want to build a system that is not

too expensive to deploy, sufficiently accurate and easy to use. Hence we start with just using headpose as an estimation of users' gaze which activates the agent and focus on the user experience of the conversation. In doing this we have found it relatively easy to deploy interaction mechanisms that increase the usability of a system. We show that such an interaction is still preferred over the currently established paradigm of using a wake word in non-robotic conversational UI. We can only imagine that with future advances in computer science, considering other cues will be cheaper and lead to better accuracy which will even further increase the usability of our system.

2.3 Gaze Detection

Head pose estimation is one of the most popular topics in Computer Vision area. There are two major approaches applied to this specific task: the landmark-based approach and end-to-end approach.

Typically, the landmark-based approach entails three steps: first, find faces in a RGB image; then detect the facial landmarks as features i.e. contours of eyes, nose, mouth and face; and finally predict head orientation based on the landmarks. Researchers are pushing forward the frontiers for each step. For the first step, Lin and Tsai (2012) and Ranganatha and Gowramma (2017) both have focused on face detection and face tracking problems. They have use Haar-like features such as face edges and corners to find all the faces in a frame and apply different tracking algorithms for the faces in the coming frames to increase computation efficiency. Lin and Tsai (2012) used Kanade-Lucas-Tomasi (KLT) tracking algorithm and Ranganatha and Gowramma (2017) have used a combination of Continuously Adaptive Mean Shift (CAMShift) and Kalman filter. For the second step, Wu and Ji (2017) have conducted an elaborate survey about face landmark detection, grouping algorithms into 3 major categories according to the ways the facial appearance and shape information are utilized and, compared their performances. For the third step, Dementhon and Davis (1995) have described a method of pose estimation using a base of Orthography and Scaling Approximation (POS). A POS system finds translation and rotation matrices by solving a linear system. Dementhon and Davis (1995) loops over this procedure for a better pose estimation with faster computation and implementation speed and, because of its merits it eventually becomes a part of our approach. In fact, instead of taking these three steps completely apart, researchers are also interested in integrating them together to improve efficiency and performance. A unified framework has been proposed in Wu et al. (2017) with landmark detection, head pose estimation and facial deformation analysis taken into account simultaneously. It is shown to perform more robustly in cases where occlusion becomes a major issue for face detection. It is an intermediate method between independent methods and end-to-end methods. However, it is not adopted in our approach, because occlusion isn't an issue in our scenario and therefore its complexity doesn't contribute much to accomplishing our goal.

The success of deep learning and end-to-end model in various tasks and problems in Computer Vision area are encouraging researchers to utilize it in head

pose estimation. Ahn et al. (2015) have proposed a deep neural network which took low-resolution RGB images for head pose estimation. They use regression in their architecture with the aid of GPUs. The model was able to provide continuous pose results in real time. De and Kautz (2017) have leveraged the merits of Recurrent Neural Networks, borrowing the information from preceding frames and bringing extra bonuses to applications in real-time and in video head pose estimation. To summarize, the overall advantage of an end-to-end model is that it does not rely on any explicit face features or independent face feature extractors, and hence outperforms landmark-based approaches in the cases where facial features can not be detected due to occlusion.

In addition to the effort of improving the model itself, researchers are experimenting with improvements to the model input for head pose estimation in specific scenarios. Borghi et al. (2017) and Venturelli et al. (2017) respectively have created a Generative Adversarial Network and a Convolutional Neural Network to predict head pose from depth images. Again, an end-to-end model was adopted, but instead of using RGB images, the authors took depth images as the input of the model. Its main advantage over the RGB-based approaches is that the depth sensors are not affected by the environmental illumination changes, and therefore the model can be more adaptive. However, end-to-end model is computationally intensive in nature and it runs counter to our goal of being low-cost and low-overhead.

3   Experiment 1

In this section, we begin with a technical description of our first prototype assistant. Then, we report on results and lessons learned from a pilot study of this assistant involving 10 novice users.

3.1   Technical Details

Figure 1 shows a typical setup in which one or more users sit across from a large display. The agent (embodied on the screen) uses the display as a canvas for showing requested information to the users. The existing exoplanets prototype already contained ASR and intent recognition capabilities made available on a pub-sub channel. We added to the existing prototype a head-orientation application that processed video signals from a webcam to infer the user's head orientation, plus capability that combined speech transcription with head orientation to determine whether the agent should assume that an utterance was directed to it.

Capturing voice and facial image data has implications of privacy. For voice transcription, we use a commercial module and rely on their privacy guidelines. Our scenario did not require users to mention any personally identifiable information when the microphones were on.

For face data which is much more sensitive, we used a designated machine to process it. None of this data was uploaded on to the internet. The machine

received image data from the camera attached to it, computed the headpose coordinates and only sent these coordinates to the rest of the system.

To build a low-cost, low-overhead head pose estimation system for real-time inference which, at the same time, can be adopted elsewhere easily with the smallest limitation, we decided to follow the landmark-based approach described in literature review. This is because end-to-end approaches are computationally expensive and need one or several powerful GPUs for real-time performance. Considering our indoor environment, the landmark-based approaches are already good enough to handle the cases of our interest. Enthusiastic readers are encouraged to see Zhao et al. (2018) where more details of this technique are elucidated. These calculations are performed at approximately 20 Hz and published on a head-orientation pub-sub channel.

An attention inference module subscribes to the speech transcription and head-orientation channels. It checks each head-orientation event to determine whether or not the head orientation falls within a defined Region of Interest (ROI) e.g. TV Screen in Fig. 1. If the current state is *non-attentive* and the head orientation falls within the ROI, a new *attention* window is started, which ends as soon as the head orientation falls outside the ROI or the user's face is no longer detected. The ROI can be configured as needed. Given the relatively low precision of headpose system which was traded-off for deploy-ability and preference to use markerless non-intrusive technologies, we selected the entire screen as the ROI. Results in further section will show that this worked. Similarly, a *transcription* window is started when speech is received and ends on detection of a pause. For each utterance, the overlap between the *transcription* and *attention* windows is computed and thresholded to determine whether or not the utterance was addressed to the assistant. If the transcription contains the attention word (e.g. Watson/Celia), it is assumed to be intended for the assistant regardless of head orientation.

3.2 Pilot Study

We conducted a pilot study designed to get periodic early feedback on our system's usability and the nature of any shortcomings it might exhibit. The feedback was based upon direct observation of user interactions with the system captured on video, as well as user responses to written survey questions and informal interviews conducted immediately following the each user's interaction with the system.

Demographic. A total of 10 people were recruited to interact with the system. All of our subjects had some background in technology which ranged from undergraduate/graduate university students to experienced research scientists. They all were aware of commercial conversational agents (e.g. Siri, Alexa, etc.) although some used them more infrequently than the others. The population contained native and non-native English speakers. 4 subjects who work in the same lab but had never seen this project before were also recruited as they

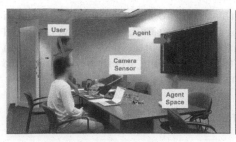 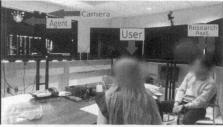

(a) Environment 1   (b) Environment 2

Fig. 1. Assistant and its environment

represent the demographic that is most acquainted with such type of a conversational agent and would give a critical assessment of the system. This group positively expressed that they would find such an attention awareness module in their demos/projects useful.

Study Details. Each subject was paired up with a partner who engaged the subject in a discussion with the AI assistant about exoplanets. Our aim in picking a specialized topic like exoplanets for conversation was so that previous experience and familiarity with the content of the conversation would not severely bias the findings. Due to inexperience with the domain, an instruction sheet encouraged the subjects to explore exoplanets and detailed the commands that the AI assistant would recognize. The task for the AI agent was to separate out the side conversation from commands given to it. The subjects mostly drove the system, except in rare circumstances. We used a combination of setups shown in Figs. 1a and b to conduct pilot testing. Both setups had the participants situated in a conference-room style seating. They both sat in chairs that faced the screen (agent space). A major difference between the two setups was location of the camera that helps determine headpose. Figure 1a used the built-in camera on a laptop to track the head orientation. This was a more fluid design and likely to be more typical of real-life meetings in which the head orientation of participants could be tracked using their own personal laptops. However, in this setup, calibration had to be done very carefully and slight changes in the laptop position would not work well. In our case, calibration would mean position of the camera, what pixels (as inferred by the headpose system) constituted as within the Region of Interest (ROI), what constituted as agent space, etc. Additionally, since the range of the camera vision is limited, subjects who were taller or shorter than the subjects for which this setup was calibrated had a tough time interacting with the system. In contrast, Fig. 1b has a web camera mounted on the display. This setup responded more reliably to variations in the physical aspects of the subjects given the field of vision of the camera.

The users were encouraged to think out loud. Their feedback was taken through a questionnaire and an informal interview. Since there existed variations

768   R. R. Divekar et al.

in each iteration of the study, we used this study to find anecdotal patterns in any difficulties that arose in the course of the interaction. A sample hypothetical interaction can be seen in Table 1. Italicized parts are utterances that the system recognizes as commands and responds to. Determining whether to respond to them or not in these cases is the challenge for the system here.

Table 1. Sample interaction (H1 = Human1, H2 = Human2, AI: AI agent)

Turn	Utterance
H1 to H2	Let's start visualizing exoplanets by just plotting them?
H1 to AI	*Show me a plot of exoplanets*
AI	Okay (display of plot)
H2 to H1	That plot doesn't tell me much. I wonder if the temperature of stars start to lower as they die down
H1 to H2	Perhaps we can ask the system to *plot temperature against age*
H1 to AI	*Plot temperature against age*
AI	Done (changed axes)
H2 to H1	Now that looks interesting. Looks like a huge cluster.
H1 to AI	*Change the x-axis to a log scale*
AI	Done (changed axes)
H2 to H1	What are we looking at here? What is that outlier dot? You can ask the system to *tell us more about that star*
H1 to AI	*Tell me more about this star*
AI	Sure (Shows a table with more details)

Feedback and Discussion. Two classes of problems emerged from the pilot study. The first arose from failures or inaccuracies in head-orientation measurements. The head-orientation system works based on facial landmarks which assumes that the full face can be seen by the camera. Head-orientation measurements failed when the system failed to detect a face, which occurred when the user turned their head beyond the angle of recognition or covered a portion of their face (e.g. while stroking their chin). It also failed when the user constantly moved their head too quickly presumably in confusion trying to get the systems attention. Moreover, mis-calibration resulting from individual differences in height or position sometimes caused inaccurate estimates of head orientation.

The second class of problem resulted from head orientation being an imperfect proxy for attention. We found that, while users looking at the display was a good first-order heuristic for determining whether an utterance was addressed to the system, there were several conditions under which intended commands were ignored, including the user reading from a page, looked away from the system trying to recollect a command or word, or looking at a human partner to seek help with completing a command. Moreover, there were situations where the system falsely interpreted an utterance as a command, such as when the user

looked at a plot on the display while discussing it with their human partner leading to a repeated and displeasing "Sorry, I can't do that" response from the agent.

A more positive finding was that users were willing to adapt their behavior to accommodate deficiencies of the assistant; for example, when the system committed transcription errors they began to enunciate commands more clearly. Baba et al. (2012) have also found that their users spoke more slowly and loudly when talking to the agent as compared to talking to their partner giving us a hint that it can possibly be attributed to humans' willingness to accommodate for the agent. This prompted us to modify the UI to provide simple visual feedback regarding the assistant's mental model of the user's attention. Our hypothesis is that given enough feedback, users would be willing to slightly adapt their behavior and that would lead to a more pleasant/usable experience. The next sections focus on that.

4   Experiment 2

In this section, we first discuss how we translated lessons learned from the pilot study of Sect. 3 into an enhanced prototype assistant. Then, we present the results of a controlled user study of 8 novice users, none of whom had participated in the pilot study, from which we establish with reasonable certainty that the second prototype is more preferable than a comparable assistant that uses wake-up words to determine whether it should respond to the user.

4.1   Technical Details

This section discusses the observations and our technical approach to incorporating them into an improved version of the agent.

Some calibration issues were addressed by placing the camera further away from the participants i.e. mounted on the TV display itself. Others were alleviated by picking the whole TV display as a region of interest instead of the logo of the AI avatar on it. This helped because a low computing cost headpose tracking system is not designed to be as precise.

It was clear from the pilot study that the assistant needed to provide the user with some sort of feedback; the question was what *sort* of feedback. Ruhland et al. (2015) have summarized many benefits of multimodal output generation by assistants. However, these generations need an animated humanoid avatars which is not our case. Animated humanoid avatars are more expensive to build/run which may be justified if the avatars want to exhibit any social intelligence e.g. facial expressions which is not our focus. We want our agent to simplify interactions with itself in group discussions. For our embodiment of AI agent, we settled upon two approaches. First, we provided feedback on the assistant's understanding of the user's head orientation. If the assistant believes the user is looking in a direction other than the display, it uses an inward-pointing orange arrow at the edge closest to the user's inferred gaze to indicate the direction in

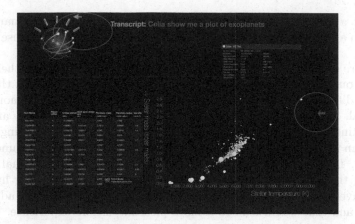

Fig. 2. Screenshot of the display showing inward pointing arrows and colored transcription (Color figure online)

which the user should move their gaze in order for the assistant to understand that the user is paying attention to it (Fig. 2). If the assistant cannot tell where the user is looking, it shows red dots in the center on all edges. When the assistant believes the user is paying attention to it, it shows green dots in the center on all four edges of the display analogous to a reciprocal gaze performed by the agent thereby letting the user know that it is listening.

Xu et al. (2016) have shown how humans were more coordinated and synchronized in their speech + gaze behavior when they successfully established mutual gaze with a robot. We think that users in our interaction paradigm will follow a similar pattern and the green dots (a proxy for system's gaze) will encourage the user to look at the system more while talking to it despite there being a "situational attractor" (Katzenmaier 2004) such as a human partner or the instruction sheet. We do not specifically aim to prove it in this paper, but use it to base our assumption that the feedback from the system makes it easy for the user to have a synchronized behaviour resulting in a usable system which is the focus.

As a second feedback element, we displayed a color-coded text transcription, such that utterances from which an actionable command was extracted while the user was looking at the display were colored green, as seen in Fig. 2. White represented "no attention", while red text represented "attention but no actionable command". This helped us eliminate unwelcome and long "Sorry I don't understand" response from the agent which takes seconds and substituted it with red text that takes just a fraction of a second and conveys the same meaning.

The effectiveness of these feedback elements is discussed through a controlled study described in the next section.

4.2   Controlled Study

Demographic. A total of 8 university students participated in the study. All of them were familiar with conversational chatbots and had interacted with them in various degrees through their phones and home devices. They had a technology background in the sense they were enrolled in STEM courses (mostly Computer Science) and were in varied levels in their formal education. We mention this as we see discussions on the effect of familiarity on the style and ease of interaction by Sciuto et al. (2018) and, by extension, perhaps the know-how of their internal working mechanism also affects it. We think that this would have minimal bias in our study because of the uniformity in the subject pool. Specifically, all subjects were at least slightly familiar with the concept of chatbots but not with a system such as ours.

Experiment Design. Each subject was paired with a research assistant who played the role of a conversation partner. A conference room style setting was used with a large display on which a camera was mounted, as seen in Fig. 1b The subjects were given a sheet listing the commands, and given an opportunity to study it for a few minutes prior to their interaction with the assistant. Once the interaction began, it consisted of interleaved conversation with the research assistant (who would explain and/or suggest specific commands) and the automated assistant, to whom the subject would issue commands.

Evaluating the quality of a conversational interface is a complicated task from the conversation intelligence perspective. Radziwill and Benton (2017) have proposed a good approach to evaluating chatbots, involving evaluation categories that include performance, humanity, affect, understanding social cues, etc. However, our goal here was not to evaluate the conversation or capability of the chatbot as a whole. Instead, we wanted to measure the usability of the headpose-based assistant, tease out the factors that contribute most greatly to its usability, and compare its usability to that of an otherwise identical assistant that requires a wake-up word.

In order to do this, we created two variants of the exoplanets assistant that were nearly identical, with the following exceptions:

1. *Condition A.* Users were required to use a wake-up word to signify that they were addressing the assistant.
2. *Condition B.* Users merely needed to look at the display to signify that they were addressing the assistant. The display included the visual feedback mechanisms (colored dots, live transcript and arrows) described in Sect. 4.1.

Each user interacted with both Condition A and Condition B. In order to reduce any bias that might result from the order in which they were exposed to these variants, half of the population were shown Condition A first while the other half were shown Condition B first. Following the interaction with each variant, we asked users questions from Table 2 and followed up with an interview.

Before the interaction began, the users were introduced to the system and were instructed about how they could interact with it. The interaction itself was moderated, such that the research assistant would help the users understand

exoplanets by working their way through the commands in the sheet and understanding the output. The subjects were encouraged to think out loud. A typical dialogue looked similar to the hypothetical dialogue in Table 1.

Results and Discussion. In this section, we detail our findings from the experiment on the second prototype assistant and evaluate its usability and likability relative to that of an assistant that is identical in every aspect except that it uses a wake-up word.

Subjects typically spent about 20–30 min in the room, including time spent on logistics and explanations. All users combined, we recorded 67.53 min of total interaction with 31.27 min of Condition A (avg 3.9 ± 1.3 min) and 36.26 min of Condition B (avg. 4.53 ± 1.1 min). The time spent was a decision of the participant and research assistant, based on the number of types of commands issued and whether the participants felt they were ready to evaluate the system or not. This statistic is noted to give the readers an idea of how long a conversation lasted and does not imply likability or usability; these issues are discussed in later sections.

Table 2 lists seven questions that were addressed to the subjects. Q1 was addressed to the subjects after they had experienced both conditions. The other

Table 2. Questions posed to users

Question number	Question	Answer format
Q1	Do you like to interact with the headpose more or without? (or similar)	Semi-structured interview
Q2	How would you rate your overall experience?	Likert Scale of *Very Unusable - Very Usable*
Q3	How easy was it to get [the bot] to know you are asking her to do something?	Likert Scale of *Very Difficult - Very Easy*
Q4	How attentive was [the bot] to you?	Likert Scale of *Very Unattentive - Very Attentive*
Q5	How helpful was it to see the transcription of what you were saying to the AI Agent?	Likert Scale of *Very Unhelpful - Very Helpful*
Q6 (Only Condition B)	How helpful was the green dot in giving you feedback about AI Agent's attentiveness?	Likert Scale of *Very Unhelpful - Very Helpful*
Q7 (Only Condition B)	How helpful were the arrows in knowing where to look to get AI Agent's attention?	Likert Scale of *Very Unusable - Very Usable*

questions were addressed to subjects after they experienced each variant (questions Q6 and Q7 pertained to Condition B only). The third column of the table describes how answers were elicited. For those questions whose answers were numbers on a Likert scale, the possible answers were integers ranging from 1 (least favorable) to 5 (most favorable). The remainder of this subsection presents a comparative analysis of the usability and likability of the interaction under Conditions A and B, based upon an analysis of the answers to the questions in Table 2.

Likability. To assess likability, we explored question Q1 by conducting a semi-structured interview with the subjects right after they had experienced both conditions and given written feedback. We categorized their answers into "Head-pose" and "Wake Word" systems when their opinion strongly swayed in one or the other direction using thematic analysis of the comments. As is evident from Fig. 3a most users preferred the headpose-based system to the one requiring the wake-up word. We ran a Fisher's exact test on the preference indicated by the users towards the wake-up word based vs. headpose based systems. We chose this test because it is applicable in situations with small sample sizes, for the purpose of examining the significance of association between two kinds of classification. We used a 2×2 matrix with rows (Headpose based system, wakeup word based system) and columns (preferred, not preferred). Our findings that the head pose system is preferred were significant at $p < 0.1$ ($p = 0.08$).

Subjects who indicated that they would like a system that understood a combination of both wakeword and headpose based attentions expressed that there might be a case where they would not be able to directly look at the agent and would rather address it verbally. They were excluded from the test as their opinion did not strongly favor one or the other. It is worth mentioning that the Condition B version was able to do so and the users were not stopped from using the wakeword in their Condition B interactions. The subjects who indicated that they liked the wakeword system expressed concerns such as what would happen if the agent accidentally thought it needed to take action and how it would be more unwelcome than not taking any action as, the equivalent of "undo" does not typically exist in chatbots.

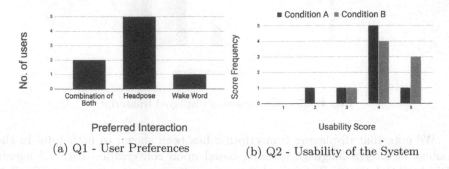

(a) Q1 - User Preferences   (b) Q2 - Usability of the System

Fig. 3. Preference and usability

Usability and Perceived Discernment. Question Q2 was aimed at assessing usability. Figure 3b shows the histogram of scores from the users on a Likert scale of Very Unusable (1) to Very Usable (5). We see that the new (Condition B) system is usable, which is our goal. On average, Condition B has better usability scores than Condition A: 4.25 ± 0.71 (Condition B) vs. 3.75 ± 0.89 (Condition A). However, applying a Wilcoxon-Mann-Whitney test to these results yields a p-value of 0.15, which is not quite enough to claim that the apparent usability advantages of the head-pose system are statistically significant.

To assess the assistant's perceived discernment—that is, the extent to which users perceived that the assistant correctly understood when it was and was not being addressed, and its attentiveness—we asked Questions Q3 and Q4 (see Table 2 for definitions and Likert scales). Likert scores for Conditions A and B were comparable in both cases: "somewhat easy" for Q3 (3.75 ± 1.04 for Condition B vs. 3.6 ± 0.74 for Condition A) and "attentive" for Q4 (4.25 ± 0.89 for Condition B vs. 4.13 ± 0.83 for Condition A). In other words, the perceived discernment of the two variants was essentially the same, and adequate.

Usability and Likability Factors. Here we analyze a variety of factors that contributed to the usability and likability of the headpose-based system.

Color-coded Transcript. For traditional HCI, users see feedback on their own input i.e. through text appearing as they type or the cursor responding as they move their mouse. Such feedback can also convey that the system is not frozen. However, standard feedback mechanisms do not exist for current voice-based systems. We believe that, for voice-based assistants in general, showing color-coded transcription would help users understand what the agent thought it heard (if anything), and thereby constitute a useful form of feedback. Figure 4, which summarizes the responses to Q5, supports such a belief in our case: the helpfulness score is 4.5 ± 0.53 for Condition B vs. 4.38 ± 0.74 for Condition A.

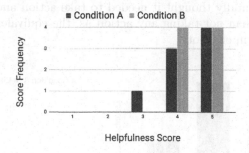

Fig. 4. Q5 - Helpfulness of displayed transcript

We note that displaying transcription has been shown to be helpful in the context of foreign language learning based upon conversation with AI agents (Divekar et al. 2018). However, their transcripts were not color-coded. To elicit whether the color-coded nature of the transcript was helpful, we asked another

question—"Did you know when your utterance was recognized as a command vs. when it was not? How?". Using thematic analysis of responses, 6 of 7 (all except for one case of illegible data) could be strongly attributed to the color-coded nature of the transcript. Thus, we see that the color-coded nature of the transcript was noticed and the meaning it carried was well understood.

Visual Attention Feedback. In the Pilot Study section (Sect. 3.2), we theorized that it would be beneficial to provide visual feedback of the agent's understanding of the user's attentional state, and as described in Sect. 4.1 we added green dots and arrows for this purpose. In order to assess the helpfulness of these two feedback mechanisms, we asked the users Q6 and Q7 after they experienced Condition B. Figure 5 shows plots of the user's ratings on question Q6 and Q7 of helpfulness on a Likert scale of 1–5. As seen, the users found the green dot Very Helpful (avg. 4.63 ± 0.52) and the arrows Helpful (avg. 3.88 ± 0.99).

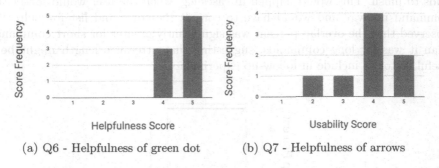

(a) Q6 - Helpfulness of green dot   (b) Q7 - Helpfulness of arrows

Fig. 5. Helpfulness of visual feedback of attention

ROI Selection. We chose headpose estimation as a cheaper, more easily deployable, and less intrusive alternative to eye gaze estimation, but of course there is a cost: it is inherently less precise. Since we were unable to reliably detect whether users were looking at the avatar or not, we chose the entire display as the Region of Interest (ROI). Anecdotally, we noticed that users coordinated their speech and gaze, and waited for the green dot when they wanted to issue commands to the system. There were some instances when the agent mistook a human-human conversation as a command and interrupted out of turn. For example, there are several graphs and other objects of interest on the display that the user might sometimes want to look at while talking to their human partner. Such instances were rare and didn't seem to affect the usability/likability. We anticipate that advances in headpose recognition systems will result in improved accuracy, enabling the ROI to be reduced in area, which may further improve the likability of headposed-based assistants beyond what we have measured here.

Natural, Learnable Interaction. To gauge where people looked while giving commands, we manually annotated videos of 7 users[1] under Condition A, as

---

[1] Video data were missing for one subject.

this was the more natural case in which the user's head pose has no impact on the system's behavior. Annotations included the times at which each utterance started and ended and the times during which the subject was looking at the display. We found that users looked at the assistant's embodiment (the display) anyway, suggesting that this is indeed a natural interaction paradigm.

To help quantify this phenomenon, the overlap between their speech command and the time during which their headpose intersected with the display is shown in Fig. 6. Table 3 shows the percentage overlap between the users' speech and their head gaze oriented towards the display, in time, when intended to issue commands to the agent. Column 1 (Overall) shows the average percent intersection of all users. Column 2 and Column 3 show the average percent intersection of users who were exposed to Condition A first and Condition B first, respectively. Column 3 and Column 4 show the average percent overlap for long commands and short commands. Long commands are those which took more than 4 seconds to finish. This would happen in cases e.g. when the user would forget the command midway and would have to consult the command list for help. We observed that the overlap percent was significantly greater for short commands than it was for long commands, suggesting that utterance length might be a useful factor to include in follow-up experiments.

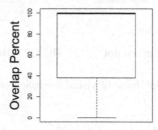

Fig. 6. Percentage overlap across users in Condition A

Table 3. Percentage of overlap between speech and head gaze (Condition A)

	Overall	Condition A first	Condition B first	Long commands	Short commands
Avg	70.06 ± 36.2	53.22 ± 38.47	76.96 ± 33.3	34.63 ± 37.16	78.57 ± 30.69
N	62	18	44	12	50

Comparing columns 2 and 3 of Table 3, it is apparent that subjects who were exposed to Condition B first (headpose based attention system) have a larger overlap percentage under Condition A (wake-up word system) than those who are first exposed to Condition A. To ascertain whether this observation was statistically significant, we applied a Wilcoxon Rank-Sum Test (which is applicable for non-normal distributions) to the data that underlie columns 2

and 3 of Table 3, finding that the overlap difference was significant with a p-value of 0.02 (thus significant at $p < 0.05$). The fact that users who first used the head pose system continued to exhibit a behavior that no longer had any impact may suggest that the behavior is readily learned, and so natural as to be almost subconscious.

5   Conclusions and Future Work

In this work, we have demonstrated that one can build a practical embodied agent that is capable of operating in environments where multiple humans are conversing with one another and interacting with the agent in an interleaved fashion. The agent is practical in the sense that (a) it does an adequate job of discerning when it is being addressed without imposing on the user the burden of using a wake-up word, and (b) it is relatively inexpensive to implement—requiring only a simple camera and headpose estimation software.

A key finding from a first informal pilot study was that head pose estimation did not work adequately by itself, but there were hints that users might adapt to some form of feedback indicating when the agent believed the user was looking at the system. Inspired by this finding, we enhanced the agent by providing such feedback in the form of dots and arrows, and ran a second experiment that allowed us to quantify its likability and usability relative to that of an alternate variant of the agent that required a wake-up word. We found that users adapted very readily (perhaps even subconsciously) to this form of feedback, thereby amplifying what would otherwise be a weaker signal. Analysis of user responses showed that the enhanced agent was both likeable and usable, and that its likability was greater than that of the wake-up word agent to a statistically significant degree. (There were indications that the usability was also greater for the headpose-based agent, but not quite at a statistically significant level).

Based upon these initial implementations and studies, we feel encouraged that head orientation can be used as a simple, low-cost basis for more natural interactions with cognitive assistants that engage in extended multi-modal dialogues with multiple people. We see multiple avenues for future efforts. In addition to pursuing improvements in the cost and accuracy of headpose estimation, it would be worthwhile to couple headpose estimation with other non-verbal clues regarding the addressee. We have identified the length of an utterance as one such factor; the Related Work section of this paper contains numerous other factors that prior authors have identified as being correlated with attention and are therefore good candidates for future study. An important question to be resolved is the tradeoff between the incremental accuracy (and concomitant likability and usability) provided by these additional factors versus their additional cost. Opening up the interaction to multiple agents who are aware of their human partners as well as the other agents is another exciting direction to pursue (for example, an early prototype of two shopkeeper agents negotiating with humans is reported by Divekar et al. 2019).

Acknowledgment. This work is supported by the Cognitive and Immersive Systems Laboratory (CISL), a collaboration between IBM Research and Rensselaer Polytechnic Institute, and also a center in IBM's AI Horizon Network. Part of this work was done while the first author was an intern at IBM T.J. Watson Research Center, Yorktown Heights, NY.

References

Admoni, H., Scassellati, B.: Social eye gaze in human-robot interaction: a review. J. Hum. Robot Interact. **6**(1), 25–63 (2017)

Ahn, B., Park, J., Kweon, I.S.: Real-time head orientation from a monocular camera using deep neural network. In: Cremers, D., Reid, I., Saito, H., Yang, M.-H. (eds.) ACCV 2014. LNCS, vol. 9005, pp. 82–96. Springer, Cham (2015). https://doi.org/10.1007/978-3-319-16811-1_6

Akhtiamov, O., Palkov, V.: Gaze, prosody and semantics: relevance of various multimodal signals to addressee detection in human-human-computer conversations. In: Karpov, A., Jokisch, O., Potapova, R. (eds.) SPECOM 2018. LNCS (LNAI), vol. 11096, pp. 1–10. Springer, Cham (2018). https://doi.org/10.1007/978-3-319-99579-3_1

Akhtiamov, O., Sidorov, M., Karpov, A.A., Minker, W.: Speech and text analysis for multimodal addressee detection in human-human-computer interaction. In: INTERSPEECH, pp. 2521–2525 (2017)

Amazon: Avs ux attention system (2019). https://developer.amazon.com/docs/alexa-voice-service/ux-design-attention.html. Accessed 24 Jan 2019

Andrist, S., Bohus, D., Mutlu, B., Schlangen, D.: Turn-taking and coordination in human-machine interaction. AI Mag. **37**(4), 5–6 (2016)

Baba, N., Huang, H.H., Nakano, Y.I.: Addressee identification for human-human-agent multiparty conversations in different proxemics. In: Proceedings of the 4th Workshop on Eye Gaze in Intelligent Human Machine Interaction, p. 6. ACM (2012)

Bakx, I., Van Turnhout, K., Terken, J.M.: Facial orientation during multi-party interaction with information kiosks. In: INTERACT (2003)

Bentley, F., Luvogt, C., Silverman, M., Wirasinghe, R., White, B., Lottrjdge, D.: Understanding the long-term use of smart speaker assistants. Proc. ACM Interact Mobile Wearable Ubiquit. Technol. **2**(3), 91 (2018)

Bohus, D., Horvitz, E.: Multiparty turn taking in situated dialog: Study, lessons, and directions. In: Proceedings of the SIGDIAL 2011 Conference, pp. 98–109. Association for Computational Linguistics (2011)

Borghi, G., Fabbri, M., Vezzani, R., Calderara, S., Cucchiara, R.: Face-from-depth for head pose estimation on depth images. arXiv preprint arXiv:1712.05277 (2017)

Perreira Da Silva, M., Courboulay, V., Prigent, A., Estraillier, P.: Real-time face tracking for attention aware adaptive games. In: Gasteratos, A., Vincze, M., Tsotsos, J.K. (eds.) ICVS 2008. LNCS, vol. 5008, pp. 99–108. Springer, Heidelberg (2008). https://doi.org/10.1007/978-3-540-79547-6_10

De, J.G.X.Y.S., Kautz, M.J.: Dynamic facial analysis: from Bayesian filtering to recurrent neural network (2017)

Dementhon, D.F., Davis, L.S.: Model-based object pose in 25 lines of code. Int. J. Comput. Vis. **15**(1–2), 123–141 (1995)

Divekar, R.R., et al.: Interaction challenges in ai equipped environments built to teach foreign languages through dialogue and task-completion. In: Proceedings of the 2018 Designing Interactive Systems Conference, DIS 2018, pp. 597–609. ACM, New York (2018). ISBN 978-1-4503-5198-0, https://doi.org/10.1145/3196709.3196717

Divekar, R.R., Mou, X., Chen, L., de Bayser, M.G., Guerra, M.A., Su, H.: Embodied conversational AI agents in a multi-modal multi-agent competitive dialogue. In: IJCAI (2019)

Farrell, R.G., et al.: Symbiotic cognitive computing. AI Mag. **37**(3), 81–93 (2016)

Frampton, M., Fernández, R., Ehlen, P., Christoudias, M., Darrell, T., Peters, S.: Who is you?: combining linguistic and gaze features to resolve second-person references in dialogue. In: Proceedings of the 12th Conference of the European Chapter of the Association for Computational Linguistics, pp. 273–281. Association for Computational Linguistics (2009)

Gravano, A., Hirschberg, J.: Turn-yielding cues in task-oriented dialogue. In: Proceedings of the SIGDIAL 2009 Conference: The 10th Annual Meeting of the Special Interest Group on Discourse and Dialogue, pp. 253–261. Association for Computational Linguistics (2009)

Gu, E., Badler, N.I.: Visual attention and eye gaze during multiparty conversations with distractions. In: Gratch, J., Young, M., Aylett, R., Ballin, D., Olivier, P. (eds.) IVA 2006. LNCS (LNAI), vol. 4133, pp. 193–204. Springer, Heidelberg (2006). https://doi.org/10.1007/11821830_16

Katzenmaier, M.: Identifying the addressee in human-human-robot interactions based on head pose and speech. Ph.D. thesis, Carnegie Mellon University, USA and University of Karlsruhe TH, Germany (2004)

Kendon, A.: Some functions of gaze-direction in social interaction. Acta Psychol. **26**, 22–63 (1967)

Kephart, J.O., Dibia, V.C., Ellis, J., Srivastava, B., Talamadupula, K., Dholakia, M.: A cognitive assistant for visualizing and analyzing exoplanets. In: Proc. AAAI 2018 (2018)

Le Minh, T., Shimizu, N., Miyazaki, T., Shinoda, K.: Deep learning based multi-modal addressee recognition in visual scenes with utterances. In: IJCAI 2018, pp. 1546–1553 (2018). https://doi.org/10.24963/ijcai.2018/214

Lin, G.S., Tsai, T.S.: A face tracking method using feature point tracking. In: 2012 International Conference on Information Security and Intelligence Control, ISIC, pp. 210–213. IEEE (2012)

Mutlu, B., Kanda, T., Forlizzi, J., Hodgins, J., Ishiguro, H.: Conversational gaze mechanisms for humanlike robots. ACM Transact. Interact. Intell. Syst. **1**(2), 1–33 (2012). https://doi.org/10.1145/2070719.2070725. ISSN 21606455, http://dl.acm.org/citation.cfm?doid=2070719.2070725

Nakano, Y.I., Baba, N., Huang, H.H., Hayashi, Y.: Implementation and evaluation of a multimodal addressee identification mechanism for multiparty conversation systems. In: Proceedings of the 15th ACM on International conference on multimodal interaction, pp. 35–42. ACM (2013)

Norouzian, A., Mazoure, B., Connolly, D., Willett, D.: Exploring attention mechanism for acoustic-based classification of speech utterances into system-directed and non-system-directed. arXiv preprint arXiv:1902.00570 (2019)

Radziwill, N.M., Benton, M.C.: Evaluating quality of chatbots and intelligent conversational agents. arXiv preprint arXiv:1704.04579 (2017)

Ranganatha, S., Gowramma, Y.: An integrated robust approach for fast face tracking in noisy real-world videos with visual constraints. In: 2017 International Conference on Advances in Computing, Communications and Informatics (ICACCI), pp. 772–776. IEEE (2017)

Ravuri, S., Stolcke, A.: Recurrent neural network and LSTM models for lexical utterance classification. In: Sixteenth Annual Conference of the International Speech Communication Association (2015)

Ruhland, K., et al.: A review of eye gaze in virtual agents, social robotics and hci: Behaviour generation, user interaction and perception. In: Computer Graphics Forum, vol. 34, pp. 299–326. Wiley (2015)

van Schendel, J.A., Cuijpers, R.H.: Turn-yielding cues in robot-human conversation. New Front. Hum. Robot Interact., p. 85 (2015). URL http://www.mahasalem.net/AISB2015/NF-HRI-2015-full_proceedings.pdf#page=86

Sciuto, A., Saini, A., Forlizzi, J., Hong, J.I.: Hey alexa, what's up?: A mixed-methods studies of in-home conversational agent usage. In: Proceedings of the 2018 on Designing Interactive Systems Conference 2018, pp. 857–868. ACM (2018)

Sheikhi, S., Odobez, J.M.: Combining dynamic head pose-gaze mapping with the robot conversational state for attention recognition in human-robot interactions. Pattern Recogn. Lett. **66**, 81–90 (2015). https://doi.org/10.1016/j.patrec.2014.10.002. ISSN 01678655

Shriberg, E., Stolcke, A., Ravuri, S.V.: Addressee detection for dialog systems using temporal and spectral dimensions of speaking style. In: INTERSPEECH, pp. 2559–2563 (2013)

Stiefelhagen, R., Zhu, J.: Head orientation and gaze direction in meetings. In: CHI 2002 Extended Abstracts on Human Factors in Computing Systems, pp. 858–859. ACM (2002)

Tsai, T., Stolcke, A., Slaney, M.: A study of multimodal addressee detection in human-human-computer interaction. IEEE Transact. Multimedia **17**(9), 1550–1561 (2015)

Van Turnhout, K., Terken, J., Bakx, I., Eggen, B.: Identifying the intended addressee in mixed human-human and human-computer interaction from non-verbal features. In: Proceedings of the 7th international conference on Multimodal interfaces, pp. 175–182. ACM (2005)

Venturelli, M., Borghi, G., Vezzani, R., Cucchiara, R.: From depth data to head pose estimation: a siamese approach. arXiv preprint arXiv:1703.03624 (2017)

Wang, K., Ji, Q.: Real time eye gaze tracking with 3D deformable eye-face model. In: Procecdings of IEEE CVPR, pp. 1003–1011 (2017)

Wu, Y., Gou, C., Ji, Q.: Simultaneous facial landmark detection, pose and deformation estimation under facial occlusion. arXiv preprint arXiv:1709.08130 (2017)

Wu, Y., Ji, Q.: Facial landmark detection: a literature survey. Int. J. Comput. Vis. **127**, 1–28 (2017)

Xu, T.L., Zhang, H., Yu, C.: See you see me: The role of eye contact in multimodal human-robot interaction. ACM Transact. Interact. Intell. Syst. (TIIS) **6**(1), 2 (2016)

ZDNet: How alexa developers are using visual elements for echo show (2018). https://www.youtube.com/watch?v=eZIouIY5p8Q

Zhao, R., Wang, K., Divekar, R., Rouhani, R., Su, H., Ji, Q.: An immersive system with multi-modal human-computer interaction. In: 13th IEEE International Conference on Automatic Face and Gesture Recognition, FG 2018, pp. 517–524 (2018)

Author Index

Printed in the United States
By Bookmasters

T0189573

Printed in the United States
By Bookmasters